Exploring Literature
FICTION·POETRY·DRAMA·CRITICISM

Edited by Lynn Altenbernd · UNIVERSITY OF ILLINOIS

THE MACMILLAN COMPANY

© Copyright, Lynn Altenbernd, 1970

PRINTED IN THE UNITED STATES OF AMERICA

All rights reserved. No part of this book may be reproduced or transmitted in any form or by any means, electronic or mechanical, including photocopying, recording or by any information storage and retrieval system, without permission in writing from the Publisher.

THE MACMILLAN COMPANY
866 THIRD AVENUE, NEW YORK, NEW YORK 10022
COLLIER-MACMILLAN CANADA, LTD., TORONTO, ONTARIO

Library of Congress catalog card number: 74-96454

First Printing

CREDITS AND ACKNOWLEDGMENTS

Copyrighted works, listed in the order of appearance, are printed in the United States, its possessions and dependencies, the Philippines, and Canada by permission of the following.

FICTION

Joseph Conrad, "Youth." By permission of J. M. Dent & Sons, Ltd., Publishers, and the Trustees of the Joseph Conrad Estate.

Luigi Pirandello, "The Captive." Reprinted from BETTER THINK TWICE ABOUT IT by Luigi Pirandello, translated by Arthur and Henri Mayne, © by Luigi Pirandello.

W. Somerset Maugham, "The Outstation." Copyright 1924 by W. Somerset Maugham, from *The Casuarina Tree* by W. Somerset Maugham. Reprinted by permission of Doubleday & Company, Inc. By permission of the Literary Executor and Wm. Heinemann.

Thomas Mann, "Disorder and Early Sorrow." Copyright 1936 and renewed 1964 by Alfred A. Knopf, Inc. Reprinted from STORIES OF THREE DECADES, by Thomas Mann, translated by H. T. Lowe-Porter, by permission of the publisher.

James Joyce, "The Dead." From DUBLINERS by James Joyce. Originally published by B. W. Huebsch, Inc., in 1916. Copyright © 1967 by the Estate of James Joyce. All rights reserved. Reprinted by permission of The Viking Press, Inc.

Franz Kafka, "A Hunger Artist." Reprinted by permission of Schocken Books Inc. from THE PENAL COLONY by Franz Kafka, Copyright © 1948 by Schocken Books Inc.

D. H. Lawrence, "The Blind Man." From THE COMPLETE SHORT STORIES OF D. H. LAWRENCE, Volume II. Copyright 1922 by Thomas B. Seltzer, Inc., renewed 1950 by Frieda Lawrence. Reprinted by permission of The Viking Press, Inc.

Katherine Mansfield, "The Doll's House." Copyright 1923 by Alfred A. Knopf, Inc. and renewed 1951 by John Middleton Murry. Reprinted from THE SHORT STORIES OF KATHERINE MANSFIELD by permission of the publisher. Permission to include the story has been granted by The Society of Authors as the literary representative of the Estate of Katherine Mansfield.

F. Scott Fitzgerald, "Babylon Revisited." "Babylon Revisited" (Copyright 1931 The Curtis Publishing Company; renewal copyright © 1959 Frances S. F. Lanahan) is reprinted with the permission of Charles Scribner's Sons from TAPS AT REVEILLE by F. Scott Fitzgerald.

William Faulkner, "Barn Burning." Copyright 1939 and renewed 1967 by Estelle Faulkner and Jill Faulkner Summers. Reprinted from COLLECTED STORIES OF WILLIAM FAULKNER by permission of Random House, Inc.

Ernest Hemingway, "In Another Country." "In Another Country" (Copyright 1927 Charles Scribner's Sons; renewal copyright 1955) is reprinted with the permission of Charles Scribner's Sons from MEN WITHOUT WOMEN by Ernest Hemingway.

Langston Hughes, "For the Sake of Argument," "That Word *Black*." Reprinted by permission of HAROLD OBER ASSOCIATES INCORPORATED. Copyright 1943, 1944, 1945, 1946, 1947, 1948, 1949, 1950 by Langston Hughes. Langston Hughes, "Jazz, Jive, and Jam." From THE BEST OF SIMPLE by Langston Hughes. © 1961 by Langston Hughes. Reprinted by permission of Hill and Wang, Inc.

Erskine Caldwell, "Daughter." From JACKPOT by Erskine Caldwell, by permission of Duell, Sloane and Pearce, affiliate of Meredith Press.

Eudora Welty, "Why I Live at the P.O." Copyright, 1941, 1969, by Eudora Welty. Reprinted from her volume A CURTAIN OF GREEN AND OTHER STORIES by permission of Harcourt, Brace & World, Inc.

Ann Petry, "Miss Muriel." Reprinted by permission of RUSSELL & VOLKENING, INC. Copyright © 1963 ANN PETRY.

James Baldwin, "Previous Condition." Reprinted from GOING TO MEET THE MAN by James Baldwin. Copyright © 1948, 1951, 1957, 1958, 1960, 1965 by James Baldwin and used by permission of the publisher, The Dial Press, Inc.

John Updike, "Flight." © Copyright 1962 by John Updike. Reprinted from PIGEON FEATHERS AND OTHER STORIES, by John Updike, by permission of Alfred A. Knopf, Inc. Originally appeared in *The New Yorker*.

POETRY

Emily Dickinson, "108: Surgeons must be very careful," "214: I taste a liquor never brewed," "337: I Know a place where Summer strives." Reprinted by permission of the publishers and the Trustees of Amherst College from Thomas H. Johnson, Editor, THE POEMS OF EMILY DICKINSON, Cambridge, Mass.: The Belknap Press of Harvard University Press, Copyright, 1951, 1955, by The President and Fellows of Harvard College. Emily Dickinson, "419: We grow accustomed to the Dark." Reprinted by permission of the publishers and the Trustees of Amherst College from Thomas H. Johnson, Editor, THE POEMS OF EMILY DICKINSON, Cambridge, Mass.: The Belknap Press of Harvard University Press, Copyright, 1951, 1955, by The President and Fellows of Harvard College. Copyright 1935 by Martha Dickinson Bianchi, © 1963 by Mary L. Hampson. From THE COMPLETE POEMS OF EMILY DICKINSON, ed. by Thomas H. Johnson, by permission of Little, Brown and Co. Emily Dickinson, "432: Do People moulder equally." Reprinted by permission of the publishers and the Trustees of Amherst College from Thomas H. Johnson, Editor, THE POEMS OF EMILY DICKINSON, Cambridge, Mass.: The Belknap Press of Harvard University Press, Copyright, 1951, 1955, by The President and Fellows of Harvard College. From BOLTS OF MELODY by Emily Dickinson, edited by Mabel Loomis Todd and Millicent Todd Bingham. Copyright, 1945 by The Trustees of Amherst College. Reprinted by permission of Harper & Row, Publishers. "510: It was not Death, for I stood up." Reprinted by permission of the publishers and the Trustees of Amherst College from Thomas H. Johnson, Editor, THE POEMS OF EMILY DICKINSON, Cambridge, Mass.: The Belknap Press of Harvard University Press, Copyright, 1951, 1955, by The President and Fellows of Harvard College. "531: We dream—it is good we are dreaming." Reprinted by permission of the publishers and the Trustees of Amherst College from Thomas H. Johnson, Editor, THE POEMS OF EMILY DICKINSON, Cambridge, Mass.: The Belknap Press of Harvard University Press, Copyright, 1951, 1955, by The President and Fellows of Harvard College. Copyright 1935 by Martha Dickinson Bianchi, © 1963 by Mary L. Hampson. From THE COMPLETE POEMS OF EMILY DICKINSON, ed. by Thomas H. Johnson, by permission of Little, Brown and Co. Emily Dickinson, "749: All but Death can be adjusted," "754: My Life had stood—a Loaded Gun," "760: Most she touched me by her muteness." Reprinted by permission of the publishers and the Trustees of Amherst College from Thomas H. Johnson, Editor, THE POEMS OF EMILY DICKINSON, Cambridge, Mass.: The Belknap Press of Harvard University Press, Copyright, 1951, 1955, by The President and Fellows of Harvard College. Copyright 1929, © 1957 by Mary L. Hampson. From THE COMPLETE POEMS OF EMILY DICKINSON, ed. by Thomas H. Johnson, by permission of Little, Brown and Co. Emily Dickinson, "764: Presentiment—is that long Shadow," "861: Split the Lark— And you'll find the Music," "875: I stepped from Plank to Plank." Reprinted by permission of the publishers and the Trustees of

Amherst College from Thomas H. Johnson, Editor, THE POEMS OF EMILY DICKINSON, Cambridge, Mass.: The Belknap Press of Harvard University Press, Copyright, 1951, 1955, by The President and Fellows of Harvard College. Emily Dickinson, "910: Experience is the Angled Road." Reprinted by permission of the publishers and the Trustees of Amherst College from Thomas H. Johnson, Editor, THE POEMS OF EMILY DICKINSON, Cambridge, Mass.: The Belknap Press of Harvard University Press, Copyright 1951, 1955, by The President and Fellows of Harvard College. Copyright 1914, 1942 by Martha Dickinson Bianchi. From THE COMPLETE POEMS OF EMILY DICKINSON, ed. by Thomas H. Johnson, by permission of Little, Brown and Co. Emily Dickinson, "1129: Tell all the Truth but tell it slant." Reprinted by permission of the publishers and the Trustees of Amherst College from Thomas H. Johnson, Editor, THE POEMS OF EMILY DICKINSON, Cambridge, Mass.: The Belknap Press of Harvard University Press, Copyright, 1951, 1955, by The President and Fellows of Harvard College. From BOLTS OF MELODY by Emily Dickinson, edited by Mabel Loomis Todd and Millicent Todd Bingham. Copyright, 1945 by The Trustees of Amherst College. Reprinted by permission of Harper & Row, Publishers. Emily Dickinson, "1142: The Props assist the House," "1484: We shall find the Cube of the Rainbow." Reprinted by permission of the publishers and the Trustees of Amherst College from Thomas H. Johnson, Editor, THE POEMS OF EMILY DICKINSON, Cambridge, Mass.: The Belknap Press of Harvard University Press, Copyright, 1951, 1955, by The President and Fellows of Harvard College.

Thomas Hardy, "Hap," "The Darkling Thrush," "The Contretemps," "The Fallow Deer at the Lonely House." Reprinted with permission of The Macmillan Company from COLLECTED POEMS by Thomas Hardy. Copyright 1925 by The Macmillan Company. From "COLLECTED POEMS" by Thomas Hardy, by permission of the Hardy Estate, Macmillan & Co. Ltd., London, and The Macmillan Company of Canada Limited.

All Gerard Manley Hopkins poems from *The Poems of Gerard Manley Hopkins,* ed. W. H. Gardner and N. H. MacKenzie, Fourth Edition (London, New York, and Toronto: Oxford University Press, 1967).

Robert Bridges, "Elegy," "London Snow." By permission of the Clarendon Press, Oxford.

A. E. Housman, "Into My Heart an Air That Kills," "With Rue My Heart Is Laden," "When I Was One-and-Twenty," "1887." From "A Shropshire Lad"—Authorised Edition—from THE COLLECTED POEMS OF A. E. HOUSMAN. Copyright 1939, 1940, © 1959 by Holt, Rinehart and Winston, Inc. Copyright © 1967, 1968 by Robert E. Symons. Reprinted by permission of Holt, Rinehart and Winston, Inc. A. E. Housman, "The Night Is Freezing Fast," "I Did Not Lose My Heart in Summer's Even." From THE COLLECTED POEMS OF A. E. HOUSMAN. Copyright 1922 by Holt, Rinehart and Winston, Inc. Copyright 1936, 1950 by Barclays Bank Ltd. Copyright © 1964 by Robert E. Symons. Reprinted by permission of Holt, Rinehart and Winston, Inc.

Permission to include the poems has been granted by The Society of Authors as the literary representative of the Estate of the late A. E. Housman, and Messrs. Jonathan Cape Ltd., publishers of A. E. Housman's *Collected Poems.*

William Butler Yeats, "The Lover Tells of the Rose in His Heart." Reprinted with permission of The Macmillan Company from COLLECTED POEMS by William Butler Yeats. Copyright 1906 by The Macmillan Company, renewed 1934 by William Butler Yeats. William Butler Yeats, "No Second Troy." Reprinted with permission of The Macmillan Company from COLLECTED POEMS by William Butler Yeats. Copyright 1912 by The Macmillan Company, renewed 1940 by Bertha Georgie Yeats. William Butler Yeats, "The Second Coming." Reprinted with permission of The Macmillan Company from COLLECTED POEMS by William Butler Yeats. Copyright 1924 by The Macmillan Company, renewed 1952 by Bertha Georgie Yeats. William Butler Yeats, "Leda and the Swan," "Sailing to Byzantium." Reprinted with permission of The Macmillan Company from COLLECTED POEMS by William Butler Yeats. Copyright 1928 by The Macmillan Company, renewed 1956 by Georgie Yeats.

By permission of Mr. M. B. Yeats and Macmillan Company of Canada.

Edwin Arlington Robinson, "The Man Against the Sky." Reprinted with permission of The Macmillan Company from COLLECTED POEMS by Edwin Arlington Robinson. Copyright 1916 by Edwin Arlington Robinson, renewed 1944 by Ruth Nivison.

Robert Frost, "Birches," "Stopping by Woods on a Snowy Evening," "The Onset," "Bereft," "Come In." From COMPLETE POEMS OF

ROBERT FROST. Copyright 1916, 1923, 1928 by Holt, Rinehart and Winston, Inc. Copyright 1942, 1944, 1951, © 1956 by Robert Frost. Copyright © 1970 by Lesley Frost Ballantine. Reprinted by permission of Holt, Rinehart and Winston, Inc.

Wallace Stevens, "The Snow Man," "A High-Toned Old Christian Woman," "The Emperor of Ice-Cream." Copyright 1923 and renewed 1951 by Wallace Stevens. Reprinted from THE COLLECTED POEMS OF WALLACE STEVENS by permission of Alfred A. Knopf, Inc. Wallace Stevens, "A Postcard from a Volcano." Copyright 1936 and renewed 1964 by Elsie Stevens and Holly Stevens Stephenson. Reprinted from THE COLLECTED POEMS OF WALLACE STEVENS by permission of Alfred A. Knopf, Inc. Wallace Stevens, "The Glass of Water." Copyright 1942 by Wallace Stevens. Reprinted from THE COLLECTED POEMS OF WALLACE STEVENS by permission of Alfred A. Knopf, Inc.

William Carlos Williams, "Tract," "Dawn," "The Poor," "Spring and All." William Carlos Williams, COLLECTED EARLIER POEMS. Copyright 1938 by William Carlos Williams. Reprinted by permission of New Directions Publishing Corporation.

T. S. Eliot, "The Love Song of J. Alfred Prufrock." From COLLECTED POEMS 1909–1962 by T. S. Eliot, copyright, 1936, by Harcourt, Brace & World, Inc.; copyright, © 1963, 1964, by T. S. Eliot. Reprinted by permission of the publisher. Reprinted by permission of Faber and Faber Ltd. from *Collected Poems 1909–1962.*

Claude McKay, "Harlem Dancer," "America," "The White City," "The Tropics in New York," "Outcast," "Flame-Heart." From SELECTED POEMS OF CLAUDE McKAY. By permission of Twayne Publishers.

E. E. Cummings, "Chanson Innocente: in Just- spring," "Sonnet: a wind has blown the rain away." Copyright, 1923, 1951 by E. E. Cummings. Reprinted from his volume, POEMS 1923–1954 by permission of Harcourt, Brace & World, Inc. E. E. Cummings, "as freedom is a breakfastfood." Copyright, 1940, by E. E. Cummings; renewed, 1968, by Marion Morehouse Cummings. Reprinted from his volume, POEMS 1923–1954 by permission of Harcourt, Brace & World, Inc.

Langston Hughes, "Dream Boogie." Reprinted by permission of HAROLD OBER ASSOCIATES INCORPORATED. Copyright 1951 by Langston Hughes. Langston Hughes, "Children's Rhymes." Copyright 1951 by Langston Hughes. Reprinted from THE PANTHER AND THE LASH, by Langston Hughes, by permission of Alfred A. Knopf, Inc. Langston Hughes, "Buddy," "Juke Box Love Song," "Wonder," "Easy Boogie," "Movies," "What? So Soon!" "Comment Against Lamp Post." Reprinted by permission of HAROLD OBER ASSOCIATES INCORPORATED. Copyright 1951 by Langston Hughes. Langston Hughes, "Motto." Copyright 1951 by Langston Hughes. Reprinted from THE PANTHER AND THE LASH, by Langston Hughes, by permission of Alfred A. Knopf, Inc. Langston Hughes, "Advice," "Green Memory," "Mellow," "Live and Let Live," "Theme for English B," "College Formal: Renaissance Casino," "Testimonial," "Passing," "Blues at Dawn," "Argument," "Likewise." Reprinted by permission of HAROLD OBER ASSOCIATES INCORPORATED. Copyright 1951 by Langston Hughes. Langston Hughes, "Harlem." Copyright 1951 by Langston Hughes. Reprinted from THE PANTHER AND THE LASH, by Langston Hughes, by permission of Alfred A. Knopf, Inc. (poem is entitled "Dream Deferred" there). Langston Hughes, "Island." Reprinted by permission of HAROLD OBER ASSOCIATES INCORPORATED. Copyright 1951 by Langston Hughes.

Countee Cullen, "Yet Do I Marvel," "For My Grandmother," "For John Keats, Apostle of Beauty," "For Paul Laurence Dunbar," "For a Lady I Know." Copyright, 1925 by Harper & Brothers. Countee Cullen, "Scottsboro, Too, Is Worth Its Song." Copyright, 1935 by Harper & Brothers, renewed, 1963 by Ida M. Cullen.

From ON THESE I STAND by Countee Cullen. Reprinted by permission of Harper & Row, Publishers.

W. H. Auden, "Song: Now the Leaves Are Falling Fast." Copyright 1937 and renewed 1965 by W. H. Auden. Reprinted from COLLECTED SHORTER POEMS 1927–1957, by W. H. Auden, by permission of Random House, Inc. W. H. Auden, "Musée des Beaux Arts." Copyright 1940 and renewed 1968 by W. H. Auden. Reprinted from COLLECTED SHORTER POEMS 1927–1957, by W. H. Auden, by permission of Random House, Inc. W. H. Auden, "The Shield of Achilles." Copyright 1952 by W. H. Auden. Reprinted from COLLECTED SHORTER POEMS 1927–1957, by W. H. Auden, by permission of Random House, Inc.

Reprinted by permission of Faber and Faber Ltd. from *Collected Shorter Poems 1927–1957.*

vii

Theodore Roethke, "Moss-Gathering," "Orchids," "The Waking," "I Knew a Woman," "In a Dark Time." "Moss-Gathering," copyright 1946 by Editorial Publications, Inc.; "Orchids," copyright 1948 by Theodore Roethke; "The Waking," copyright 1953 by Theodore Roethke; "I Knew a Woman," copyright 1954 by Theodore Roethke; and "In a Dark Time," copyright © 1960 by Beatrice Roethke as Administratrix of the Estate of Theodore Roethke. All from *The Collected Poems of Theodore Roethke*. Reprinted by permission of Doubleday & Company, Inc.

Karl Shapiro, "Nostalgia." Copyright 1942 by Karl Shapiro. Karl Shapiro, "The Leg." Copyright 1944 by Karl Shapiro. Karl Shapiro, "The Progress of Faust." Copyright 1946 by Karl Shapiro. Originally appeared in *The New Yorker*.

Reprinted from SELECTED POEMS, by Karl Shapiro, by permission of Random House, Inc.

Dylan Thomas, "Incarnate Devil," "Fern Hill," "A Refusal to Mourn the Death, by Fire, of a Child in London." Dylan Thomas, COLLECTED POEMS. Copyright 1939, 1946 by New Directions Publishing Corporation. Reprinted by permission of New Directions Publishing Corporation. By permission of J. M. Dent & Sons, Ltd., Publishers, and the Trustees for the Copyrights of the late Dylan Thomas.

Gwendolyn Brooks, "the children of the poor." From SELECTED POEMS by Gwendolyn Brooks. Copyright, 1949 by Gwendolyn Brooks Blakely. Gwendolyn Brooks, "We Real Cool." From SELECTED POEMS by Gwendolyn Brooks. Copyright © 1959 by Gwendolyn Brooks. Gwendolyn Brooks, "The Chicago Picasso." From IN THE MECCA by Gwendolyn Brooks. © 1968 by Gwendolyn Brooks Blakely. Gwendolyn Brooks, "The Wall." From IN THE MECCA by Gwendolyn Brooks. Copyright © 1967 by Gwendolyn Brooks Blakely.

Reprinted by permission of Harper & Row, Publishers.

Richard Wilbur, "Bell Speech." From THE BEAUTIFUL CHANGES AND OTHER POEMS, copyright, 1947, by Richard Wilbur. Reprinted by permission of Harcourt, Brace & World, Inc. Richard Wilbur, "After the Last Bulletins." Copyright, 1953, by The New Yorker Magazine. Reprinted from THINGS OF THIS WORLD by Richard Wilbur by permission of Harcourt, Brace & World, Inc. Richard Wilbur, "Juggler." Copyright, 1949, by The New Yorker Magazine. Reprinted from CEREMONY AND OTHER POEMS by Richard Wilbur by permission of Harcourt, Brace & World, Inc.

Alan Dugan, "The Life and Death of the Cantata System," "Winter: For an Untenable Situation." From Alan Dugan, POEMS 2. Copyright © 1963 by Yale University. Alan Dugan, "One Waking in a Northern Fall," "On a Snake," "Sailing to Jerusalem." From Alan Dugan, POEMS 3. Copyright © 1967 by Yale University.

Reprinted by permission of Yale University Press.

Sylvia Plath, "Morning Song." Copyright © 1961 by Ted Hughes. Sylvia Plath, "The Arrival of the Bee Box," "Little Fugue." Copyright © 1963 by Ted Hughes. From ARIEL by Sylvia Plath. Reprinted by permission of Harper & Row, Publishers. By permission of Olwyn Hughes.

Laurence Lieberman, "Flying Below Sea Level," "Flying on the Surface." Reprinted by permission from *The Hudson Review*, Vol. XXI, No. 3 (Autumn, 1968). Copyright © 1968 by The Hudson Review, Inc.

DRAMA

Sophocles, *Oedipus Rex*. THE OEDIPUS REX OF SOPHOCLES: An English Version by Dudley Fitts and Robert Fitzgerald, copyright, 1949, by Harcourt, Brace & World, Inc. and reprinted with their permission.

CAUTION: All rights, including professional, amateur, motion picture, recitation, lecturing, public reading, radio broadcasting, and television are strictly reserved. Inquiries on all rights should be addressed to Harcourt, Brace & World, Inc., 757 Third Avenue, New York, New York 10017.

Henrik Ibsen, *Hedda Gabler*. From *Hedda Gabler* by Henrik Ibsen, trans. Otto Reinert, published by Chandler Publishing Company, San Francisco. Copyright © 1962 by Chandler Publishing Company. Reprinted by permission.

Robert Lowell, *My Kinsman, Major Molineux*. Reprinted with the permission of Farrar, Straus & Giroux, Inc. from *The Old Glory* by Robert Lowell. Copyright © 1964, 1965 by Robert Lowell.

Lorraine Hansberry, *A Raisin in the Sun*. © Copyright as an unpublished work, 1958 by Lorraine Hansberry. © Copyright 1959 by Lorraine Hansberry. Reprinted by permission of Random House, Inc.

CAUTION: Professionals and amateurs are hereby warned that A RAISIN IN THE SUN, being fully protected under the Copyright Laws of the United States of America, the British Empire, including the Dominion of Canada, and all other countries of the Universal Copyright and Berne Conventions, is subject to royalty. All rights, including professional, amateur, motion picture, recitation, lecturing, public reading, radio and television broadcasting, and the rights of translation into foreign languages, are strictly reserved. Particular emphasis is laid on the question of readings, permission for which must be secured in writing. All inquiries should be addressed to the publisher.

CRITICISM

John Galsworthy, "Some Platitudes Concerning Drama." "Some Platitudes on Drama" is reprinted with the permission of Charles Scribner's Sons from THE INN OF TRANQUILITY by John Galsworthy. Copyright 1912 Charles Scribner's Sons; renewal copyright 1940 Ada Galsworthy. By permission of William Heinemann, Ltd., publishers of the British edition.

Virginia Woolf, "How Should One Read a Book?" From THE SECOND COMMON READER by Virginia Woolf, copyright, 1932, by Harcourt, Brace & World, Inc.; renewed, 1960, by Leonard Woolf. Reprinted by permission of the publisher. By permission of Mr. Leonard Woolf and The Hogarth Press, Ltd.

Oscar Cargill, "Toward a Pluralistic Criticism." From *Toward a Pluralistic Criticism* by Oscar Cargill. Copyright © 1965 by Southern Illinois University Press. Reprinted by permission of Southern Illinois University Press.

Arthur P. Davis, "Trends in Negro American Literature (1940–1965)." Reprinted by permission of the author, Arthur P. Davis.

Lionel Trilling, "The Meaning of a Literary Idea." From THE LIBERAL IMAGINATION by Lionel Trilling. Copyright 1949 by Lionel Trilling. Reprinted by permission of The Viking Press, Inc.

Gilbert Highet, "What Use Is Poetry?" From *A Clerk of Oxenford* by Gilbert Highet. Copyright 1954 by Gilbert Highet. Reprinted by permission of Oxford University Press, Inc.

Preface

This one-volume anthology is designed for use in introductory literature courses at the college level. The editor's intention has been to provide a generous and broadly representative selection of literature from the earliest times to the present. Thus, at least, he represents his intention to himself. What he really means, of course, is that he is offering a selection of literary materials that rather closely matches the prevailing practice in our introductory literature courses. This means that the fiction used was all written after 1800 and that American and British writers are most heavily represented. Some of the work is translated from western European languages, but Africa and the Orient are not represented. Modern writing makes its strongest showing in the fiction section, though it bulks large in the drama section as well. All of the poetry was originally written in some variety of English; we distrust (properly, I think) translated poetry and doubt the value of studying it—at least in the earliest stages of study when very close attention must be given to the nuances of the meaning of language and to its sound values. The poetry section here—and again this is true generally of anthologies of this kind—is more accurately representative than the other sections of the whole body of work sampled, but, again, the sample is limited to works in English. Representing the world's drama in any collection small enough for a moderately healthy coed to carry to class is the despair of all anthologists. The tradition is too richly various (and the individual works are too long) to permit any sensible sampling. Hence, the limitation this time is to "the Western tradition," though the playhouses of many countries and centuries are dark and silent. I have tried to represent the types of drama, though I noted with irritation and even a little surprise, when the contents had all been selected, that I had not managed to get in a pure comedy. *A Midsummer-Night's Dream* is most usefully considered a romantic comedy; it is delightful enough, I hope, to divert attention from the absence of a more formal comedy. The modest selection of essays offered is not even an attempt to sample the vast body of criticism; it is intended to give students some tools, even at the risk of a few cut fingers.

Thus, though the book is intended to be "broadly representative," is it so in the way that our introductory courses usually are. And that is no bad thing, I think. Our purpose in such courses, it seems to me, is properly to provide tools and to impart the skill to use them. These are, quite baldly, courses in How to Read; and all the other values, such as that of giving students a glimpse into the far vistas of all the world's literature, are incidental benefits. Hence, the real representativeness, the one that counts, is of literary types, modes, and strategies, so that the student can learn to understand and appreciate many different kinds of works when he goes on to his own exploration of many countries in all times.

The arrangement of materials is intended to make sense rather than to convey any master plan of the learned world. The genres are arranged in an order that many teachers find convenient for teaching. Within the genre sections the work is arranged in the order of the authors' birth dates not only in the hope that some sense of history may throw a faint, old-fashioned fragrance into the air but also in the hope that the editor, having used a headsman's axe to select your material, could relinquish all further efforts to influence the shape of your course—here, at least. There is a teacher's manual that is as officious as you please, where all the wise saws and modern instances are gathered into one convenient location.

The suggestions and encouragement of many colleagues have helped me along in this work. My specific and now long-continued debt to Mr. J. G. Case of The Macmillan Company is evident at many points. My wife has given practical help, encouragement, and forbearance that have left their mark on all these pages and days.

L. A.

Contents

FICTION

NATHANIEL HAWTHORNE · 1804–1864
   My Kinsman, Major Molineux *3*
EDGAR ALLAN POE · 1809–1849
   The Fall of the House of Usher *15*
HENRY JAMES · 1843–1916
   The Pupil *27*
JOSEPH CONRAD · 1857–1924
   Youth *54*
LUIGI PIRANDELLO · 1867–1936
   The Captive (*Translated by Arthur and Henri Mayne*) *73*
STEPHEN CRANE · 1871–1900
   The Bride Comes to Yellow Sky *84*
W. SOMERSET MAUGHAM · 1874–1965
   The Outstation *91*
THOMAS MANN · 1875–1955
   Disorder and Early Sorrow (*Translated by H. T. Low-Porter*) *110*
JAMES JOYCE · 1882–1941
   The Dead *130*
FRANZ KAFKA · 1883–1924
   A Hunger Artist (*Translated by Willa and Edwin Muir*) *155*
D. H. LAWRENCE · 1885–1930
   The Blind Man *161*
KATHERINE MANSFIELD · 1888–1923
   The Doll's House *173*
F. SCOTT FITZGERALD · 1896–1940
   Babylon Revisited *178*
WILLIAM FAULKNER · 1897–1962
   Barn Burning *191*
ERNEST HEMINGWAY · 1898–1961
   In Another Country *203*
LANGSTON HUGHES · 1902–1967
   For the Sake of Argument *207*
   That Word *Black* *210*
   Jazz, Jive, and Jam *211*
ERSKINE CALDWELL · 1903–
   Daughter *214*
EUDORA WELTY · 1909–
   Why I Live at the P.O. *217*
ANN PETRY · 1911–
   Miss Muriel *225*
JAMES BALDWIN · 1924–
   Previous Condition *252*
JOHN UPDIKE · 1932–
   Flight *261*

POETRY

ANONYMOUS
   Sumer Is Icumen In *273*
   Ubi Sunt Qui ante Nos Fuerunt? *273*
   Edward *273*
   The Brown Girl *275*
   Sir Patrick Spens *275*
   Johnny, I Hardly Knew Ye *276*
GEOFFREY CHAUCER · 1340?–1400
   To Rosemounde *278*
   The Compleint of Chaucer to His Empty Purse *278*
SIR THOMAS WYATT · 1503?–1542
   The Long Love *279*
   Divers Doth Use *279*
   They Flee from Me *280*
HENRY HOWARD, EARL OF SURREY · 1517?–1547
   Description of Spring *280*
   Love That Doth Reign *281*

SIR EDWARD DYER · 1540?–1607
   My Mind to Me a Kingdom Is *281*
GEORGE GASCOIGNE · 1542?–1577
   Gascoigne's Good-Night *282*
   from *The Steel Glass* *283*
EDMUND SPENSER · 1552–1599
   Sonnets from *Amoretti:* XV, Ye tradefull Merchants *284*/ XIX, The merry Cuckow *285*/ XXII, This holy season *285*/ XXXIV, Lyke as a ship *285*/ LXVII, Lyke as a huntsman *286*/ LXXV, One day I wrote her name *286*
SIR WALTER RALEGH · 1552?–1618
   The Nymph's Reply to the Shepherd *286*
   The Passionate Man's Pilgrimage *287*
   What Is Our Life? *288*
SIR PHILIP SIDNEY · 1554–1586
   Sonnets from *Astrophel and Stella:* I, Loving in truth *288*/ XV, You that do search *288*/ XXVIII, You that with allegory's curious frame *289*/ XXXI, With how sad steps *289*
   My True Love Hath My Heart *289*
CHRISTOPHER MARLOWE · 1564–1593
   The Passionate Shepherd to His Love *290*
WILLIAM SHAKESPEARE · 1564–1616
   Songs from the Plays: from *Love's Labour's Lost*, Spring *290*/ Winter *291*/ from *The Merchant of Venice*, Tell Me Where Is Fancy Bred *291*/ Blow, Blow, Thou Winter Wind *291*/ from *Twelfth Night*, Come Away, Death *291*/ from *Cymbeline*, Hark! Hark! the Lark *292*/ from *The Tempest*, Full Fathom Five *292*
   from *The Sonnets:* XVIII, Shall I compare thee *292*/ LXXI, No longer mourn for me *292*/ LXXIII, That time of year *293*/ CXVI, Let me not to the marriage of true minds *293*
THOMAS CAMPION · 1567–1620
   When to Her Lute Corinna Sings *294*
   There Is a Garden in Her Face *294*
BEN JONSON · 1572–1637
   Slow, Slow, Fresh Fount *294*
   Still to Be Neat *295*
   To the Memory of My Beloved, the Author Master William Shakespeare *295*
   Here She Was Wont to Go *297*
JOHN DONNE · 1572–1631
   Song: Go and catch a falling star *297*
   A Valediction: Forbidding Mourning *297*
   Holy Sonnets: VII, At the round earth's imagined corners, *298*/ X, Death, be not proud *298*/ XIV, Batter my heart, three personed God *299*
   The Ecstasy *299*
JOHN WEBSTER · 1580?–1634?
   from *The White Devil* *300*
WILLIAM BROWNE · 1591?–1643?
   On the Countess Dowager of Pembroke *300*
ROBERT HERRICK · 1591–1674
   Delight in Disorder *301*
   To the Virgins to Make Much of Time *301*
   The Night-Piece, to Julia *301*
   Upon Julia's Clothes *301*
   His Return to London *301*
GEORGE HERBERT · 1593–1633
   The Collar *302*
   To His Mother *303*
   Jordan: I *303*
   The Windows *303*
EDMUND WALLER · 1606–1687
   Song: Stay, Phoebus, stay! *304*
   Go, Lovely Rose *304*
JOHN MILTON · 1608–1674
   Lycidas *304*
   L'Allegro *309*
   Il Penseroso *311*
ANDREW MARVELL · 1621–1678
   The Mower Against Gardens *314*
   To His Coy Mistress *315*
HENRY VAUGHAN · 1622–1695
   The Bird *315*
   The Waterfall *316*
JOHN DRYDEN · 1631–1700
   Song from *Marriage à la Mode* *317*
   Prologue to *Aureng-Zebe* *318*

CONTENTS

THOMAS TRAHERNE · 1636–1674
  Insatiableness *319*
JONATHAN SWIFT · 1667–1745
  A Description of the Morning *319*
  The Day of Judgement *320*
ALEXANDER POPE · 1688–1744
  The Rape of the Lock *320*
WILLIAM BLAKE · 1757–1827
  Introduction to *Songs of Innocence* *338*
  The Lamb *338*
  The Little Black Boy *339*
  The Tyger *339*
  The Sick Rose *340*
  London *340*
WILLIAM WORDSWORTH · 1770–1850
  Lines: Composed a Few Miles Above Tintern Abbey *340*
  She Dwelt Among the Untrodden Ways *344*
  I Travelled Among Unknown Men *344*
  Three Years She Grew in Sun and Shower *344*
  My Heart Leaps Up When I Behold *345*
  Composed upon Westminster Bridge *345*
  London, 1802 *345*
  The Solitary Reaper *345*
  I Wandered Lonely As a Cloud *346*
SAMUEL TAYLOR COLERIDGE · 1772–1834
  Frost at Midnight *346*
  Kubla Khan *348*
GEORGE GORDON, LORD BYRON · 1788–1824
  She Walks in Beauty *349*
  Stanzas for Music: There be none of Beauty's daughters *350*
  Sonnet on Chillon *350*
  So We'll Go No More A-Roving *350*
PERCY BYSSHE SHELLEY · 1792–1822
  Ozymandias *351*
  Ode to the West Wind *351·*
  To Night *353*
  To———: Music, when soft voices die *354*
  To———: One word is too often profaned *354*
  Lines: When the Lamp Is Shattered *354*
JOHN KEATS · 1795–1821
  On First Looking into Chapman's Homer *355*
  On the Grasshopper and the Cricket *355*
  Lines on the Mermaid Tavern *356*
  When I Have Fears That I May Cease to Be *356*
  Bright Star! Would I Were Steadfast As Thou Art *356*
  La Belle Dame sans Merci *357*
  Ode on a Grecian Urn *357*
  Ode on Melancholy *359*
  Ode to a Nightingale *360*
  To Autumn *362*
JOHN HENRY, CARDINAL NEWMAN · 1801–1890
  The Pillar of the Cloud *363*
THOMAS LOVELL BEDDOES · 1803–1849
  Stanzas from the Ivory Gate *363*
EDGAR ALLAN POE · 1809–1849
  Romance *364*
  The City in the Sea *364*
OLIVER WENDELL HOLMES · 1809–1894
  The Chambered Nautilus *365*
EDWARD FITZGERALD · 1809–1883
  from *The Rubáiyát of Omar Khayyám of Naishápúr* *366*
ALFRED, LORD TENNYSON · 1809–1892
  The Kraken *370*
  Break, Break, Break *370*
  Ulysses *370*
  Songs from *The Princess:* Sweet and Low *372/* The Splendour Falls on Castle Walls *372/* Now Sleeps the Crimson Petal *373*
  The Eagle *373*
  De Profundis: I *374*
  Crossing the Bar *374*
ROBERT BROWNING · 1812–1889
  Meeting at Night *375*
  Parting at Morning *375*
  Home-Thoughts, from Abroad *375*
  Home-Thoughts, from the Sea *376*
  Up at a Villa—Down in the City *376*
  "Childe Roland to the Dark Tower Came" *378*

EMILY BRONTË · 1818–1848
   Remembrance *384*
   To Imagination *385*
WALT WHITMAN · 1819–1892
   There Was a Child Went Forth *385*
MATTHEW ARNOLD · 1822–1888
   from *Parting* *387*
   To Marguerite *387*
   Philomela *387*
   Requiescat *388*
   Dover Beach *388*
COVENTRY PATMORE · 1823–1896
   The Toys *389*
   Magna Est Veritas *390*
DANTE GABRIEL ROSSETTI · 1828–1882
   The Sea-Limits *390*
   Sudden Light *391*
   The Woodspurge *391*
EMILY DICKINSON · 1830–1886
   108: Surgeons must be very careful *392*
   214: I taste a liquor never brewed *392*
   337: I know a place where Summer strives *392*
   419: We grow accustomed to the Dark *392*
   432: Do People moulder equally *393*
   510: It was not Death, for I stood up *393*
   531: We dream—it is good we are dreaming *393*
   749: All but Death can be Adjusted *393*
   754: My Life had stood—a Loaded Gun *393*
   760: Most she touched me by her muteness *394*
   764: Presentiment—is that long Shadow *394*
   861: Split the Lark—and you'll find the Music *394*
   875: I stepped from Plank to Plank *394*
   910: Experience is the Angled Road *395*
   1129: Tell all the Truth but tell it slant *395*
   1142: The Props assist the House *395*
   1484: We shall find the Cube of the Rainbow *395*
WILLIAM MORRIS · 1834–1896
   The Haystack in the Floods *395*
THOMAS HARDY · 1840–1928
   Hap *397*
   The Darkling Thrush *398*
   The Contretemps *398*
   The Fallow Deer at the Lonely House *400*
GERARD MANLEY HOPKINS · 1844–1889
   God's Grandeur *400*
   The Starlight Night *400*
   Spring *401*
   The Windhover *401*
   Pied Beauty *402*
   The Candle Indoors *402*
ROBERT BRIDGES · 1844–1930
   Elegy: The wood is bare *402*
   London Snow *403*
A. E. HOUSMAN · 1859–1936
   Into My Heart an Air That Kills *404*
   With Rue My Heart Is Laden *404*
   When I Was One-and-Twenty *405*
   1887 *405*
   The Night Is Freezing Fast *405*
   I Did Not Lose My Heart in Summer's Even *406*
WILLIAM BUTLER YEATS · 1865–1939
   The Lover Tells of the Rose in His Heart *406*
   No Second Troy *406*
   The Second Coming *407*
   Leda and the Swan *407*
   Sailing to Byzantium *408*
ERNEST DOWSON · 1867–1900
   Non Sum Qualis Eram Bonae sub Regno Cynarae *409*
EDWIN ARLINGTON ROBINSON · 1869–1935
   The Man Against the Sky *409*
ROBERT FROST · 1874–1963
   Birches *416*
   Stopping by Woods on a Snowy Evening *418*
   The Onset *418*
   Bereft *419*
   Come In *419*

WALLACE STEVENS · 1879–1955
   The Snow Man *419*
   A High-Toned Old Christian Woman *420*
   The Emperor of Ice-Cream *420*
   A Postcard from the Volcano *421*
   The Glass of Water *421*
WILLIAM CARLOS WILLIAMS · 1883–1963
   Tract *422*
   Dawn *422*
   The Poor *423*
   Spring and All *423*
T. S. ELIOT · 1888–1965
   The Love Song of J. Alfred Prufrock *424*
CLAUDE MCKAY · 1890–1948
   Harlem Dancer *427*
   America *428*
   The White City *428*
   The Tropics in New York *429*
   Outcast *429*
   Flame-Heart *429*
E. E. CUMMINGS · 1894–1962
   Chanson Innocente: in Just- spring *430*
   Sonnet: a wind has blown the rain away *431*
   as freedom is a breakfastfood *431*
LANGSTON HUGHES · 1902–1967
   from *Montage of a Dream Deferred* *432*
COUNTEE CULLEN · 1903–1946
   Yet Do I Marvel *441*
   Four Epitaphs *441*
   Scottsboro, Too, Is Worth Its Song *442*
W. H. AUDEN · 1907–
   Song: Now the Leaves Are Falling Fast *443*
   Musée des Beaux Arts *443*
   The Shield of Achilles *444*
THEODORE ROETHKE · 1908–1963
   Moss-Gathering *446*
   Orchids *446*
   The Waking *446*
   I Knew a Woman *447*
   In a Dark Time *448*

KARL SHAPIRO · 1913–
   Nostalgia *448*
   The Leg *449*
   The Progress of Faust *450*
DYLAN THOMAS · 1914–1953
   Incarnate Devil *451*
   Fern Hill *452*
   A Refusal to Mourn the Death, by Fire, of a Child in London *453*
GWENDOLYN BROOKS · 1917–
   the children of the poor: 1, People who have no children *454*/ 4, First fight. Then fiddle *454*
   We Real Cool *455*
   Two Dedications: I, The Chicago Picasso *455*/ II, The Wall *456*
RICHARD WILBUR · 1921–
   Bell Speech *457*
   After the Last Bulletins *458*
   Juggler *459*
ALAN DUGAN · 1923–
   The Life and Death of the Cantata System *459*
   Winter: For an Untenable Situation *460*
   One Waking in a Northern Fall *460*
   On a Snake *461*
   Sailing to Jerusalem *461*
SYLVIA PLATH · 1932–1963
   Morning Song *462*
   The Arrival of the Bee Box *463*
   Little Fugue *464*
LAURENCE LIEBERMAN · 1935–
   Flying Below Sea Level *465*
   Flying on the Surface *466*

DRAMA

SOPHOCLES · 495?–405 B.C.
   Oedipus Rex (*An English Version by Dudley Fitts and Robert Fitzgerald*) *471*
WILLIAM SHAKESPEARE · 1564–1616
   A Midsummer-Night's Dream *500*
HENRIK IBSEN · 1828–1906
   Hedda Gabler (*Translated by Otto Reinert*) *537*
ROBERT LOWELL · 1917–
   My Kinsman, Major Molineux *583*

LORRAINE HANSBERRY · 1931–1965
   A Raisin in the Sun   598

CRITICISM

THOMAS DE QUINCEY · 1785–1859
   The Literature of Knowledge and the Literature of Power   651
JOHN GALSWORTHY · 1867–1933
   Some Platitudes Concerning Drama   655
VIRGINIA WOOLF · 1882–1941
   How Should One Read a Book?   660

OSCAR CARGILL · 1898–
   Toward a Pluralistic Criticism   667
ARTHUR P. DAVIS · 1904–
   Trends in American Negro Literature (1940–1965)   674
LIONEL TRILLING · 1905–
   The Meaning of a Literary Idea   680
GILBERT HIGHET · 1906–
   What Use Is Poetry?   692

Index of Authors and Titles   699

Fiction

NATHANIEL HAWTHORNE • 1804–1864

My Kinsman, Major Molineux

AFTER the kings of Great Britain had assumed the right of appointing the colonial governors, the measures of the latter seldom met with the ready and general approbation which had been paid to those of their predecessors, under the original charters. The people looked with most jealous scrutiny to the exercise of power which did not emanate from themselves, and they usually rewarded their rulers with slender gratitude for the compliances by which, in softening their instructions from beyond the sea, they had incurred the reprehension of those who gave them. The annals of Massachusetts Bay will inform us, that of six governors in the space of about forty years from the surrender of the old charter, under James II, two were imprisoned by a popular insurrection; a third, as Hutchinson inclines to believe, was driven from the province by the whizzing of a musket-ball; a fourth, in the opinion of the same historian, was hastened to his grave by continual bickerings with the House of Representatives; and the remaining two, as well as their successors, till the Revolution, were favored with few and brief intervals of peaceful sway. The inferior members of the court party, in times of high political excitement, led scarcely a more desirable life. These remarks may serve as a preface to the following adventures, which chanced upon a summer night, not far from a hundred years ago. The reader, in order to avoid a long and dry detail of colonial affairs, is requested to dispense with an account of the train of circumstances that had caused much temporary inflammation of the popular mind.

It was near nine o'clock of a moonlight evening, when a boat crossed the ferry with a single passenger, who had obtained his conveyance at that unusual hour by the promise of an extra fare. While he stood on the landing-place, searching in either pocket for the means of fulfilling his agreement, the ferryman lifted a lantern, by the aid of which, and the newly risen moon, he took a very accurate survey of the stranger's figure. He was a youth of barely eighteen years, evidently country-bred, and now, as it should seem, upon his first visit to town. He was clad in a coarse gray coat, well worn, but in excellent repair; his under garments were durably constructed of leather, and fitted tight to a pair of serviceable and well-shaped limbs; his stockings of blue yarn were the incontrovertible work of a mother or a sister; and on his head was a three-cornered hat, which in its better days had perhaps sheltered the graver brow of the lad's father. Under his left arm was a heavy cudgel formed of an oak sapling, and retaining a part of the hardened root; and his equipment was completed by a wallet, not so abundantly stocked as to incommode the vigorous shoulders on which it hung. Brown, curly hair, well-shaped features, and bright, cheerful eyes were nature's gifts, and worth all that art could have done for his adornment.

The youth, one of whose names was Robin, finally drew from his pocket the half of a little province bill of five shillings, which, in the depreciation in that sort of currency, did but satisfy the ferryman's demand, with the surplus of a sexangular piece of parchment, valued at three pence. He then walked forward into the town, with as light a step as if his day's journey had not already exceeded thirty miles, and with as eager an eye as if he were entering London city, instead of the little metropolis of a New England colony. Before Robin had proceeded far, however, it occurred to him that he knew not whither to direct his steps; so he paused, and looked up and down the narrow street, scrutinizing the small and mean wooden buildings that were scattered on either side.

"This low hovel cannot be my kinsman's dwelling," thought he, "nor yonder old house, where the moonlight enters at the broken casement; and truly I see none hereabouts that might be worthy of him. It would have been wise to inquire my way of the ferryman, and doubtless he would have gone with me, and earned a shilling from the Major for his pains. But the next man I meet will do as well."

He resumed his walk, and was glad to perceive that the street now became wider, and the houses more respectable in their appearance. He soon discerned a figure moving on moderately in advance, and hastened his steps to overtake it. As Robin drew nigh, he saw that the passenger was a man in years, with a full periwig of gray hair, a wide-skirted coat of dark cloth, and silk stockings rolled above his knees. He carried a long and polished cane, which he struck down perpendicularly before him at every step; and at regular intervals he uttered two successive hems, of a peculiarly solemn and sepulchral intonation. Having made these observations, Robin laid hold of the skirt of the old man's coat, just when the light from the open door and windows of a barber's shop fell upon both their figures.

"Good evening to you, honored sir," said he, making a low bow, and still retaining his hold of the skirt. "I pray you tell me whereabouts is the dwelling of my kinsman, Major Molineux."

The youth's question was uttered very loudly; and one of the barbers, whose razor was descending on a well-soaped chin, and another who was dressing a Ramillies wig, left their occupations, and came to the door. The citizen, in the mean time, turned a long-favored countenance upon Robin, and answered him in a tone of excessive anger and annoyance. His two sepulchral hems, however, broke into the very centre of his rebuke, with most singular effect, like a thought of the cold grave obtruding among wrathful passions.

"Let go my garment, fellow! I tell you, I know not the man you speak of. What! I have authority, I have—hem, hem—authority; and if this be the respect you show for your betters, your feet shall be brought acquainted with the stocks by daylight, tomorrow morning!"

Robin released the old man's skirt, and hastened away, pursued by an ill-mannered roar of laughter from the barber's shop. He was at first considerably surprised by the result of his question, but, being a shrewd youth, soon thought himself able to account for the mystery.

"This is some country representative," was his conclusion, "who has never seen the inside of my kinsman's door, and lacks the breeding to answer a stranger civilly. The man is old, or verily—I might be tempted to turn back and smite him on the nose. Ah, Robin, Robin! even the barber's boys laugh at you for choosing such a guide! You will be wiser in time, friend Robin."

He now became entangled in a succession of crooked and narrow streets, which crossed each other, and meandered at no great distance from the water-side. The smell of tar was obvious to his nostrils, the masts of vessels pierced the moonlight above the tops of the buildings, and the numerous signs, which Robin paused to read, informed him that he was near the centre of business. But the streets were empty, the shops were closed, and lights were visible only in the second stories of a few dwelling houses. At length, on the corner of a narrow lane, through which he was passing, he beheld the broad countenance of a British hero swinging before the door of an inn, whence proceeded the voices of many guests. The casement of one of the lower windows was thrown back, and a very thin curtain permitted Robin to distinguish a party at supper, round a well-furnished table. The fragrance of the good cheer steamed forth into the outer air, and the youth could not fail to recollect that the last remnant of his travelling stock of provision had yielded to his morning appetite, and that noon had found and left him dinnerless.

"Oh, that a parchment three-penny might give me a right to sit down at yonder table!" said Robin, with a sigh. "But the Major will make me welcome to the best of his victuals; so I will even step boldly in, and inquire my way to his dwelling."

He entered the tavern, and was guided by the murmur of voices and the fumes of tobacco to the public-room. It was a long and low apartment, with oaken walls, grown dark in the continual smoke, and a floor which was thickly sanded, but of no immaculate purity. A number of persons—the larger part of whom appeared to be mariners, or in some way connected with the sea—occupied the wooden benches, or leather-bottomed chairs, conversing on various matters, and occasionally lending their attention to some topic of general interest. Three or four little groups were draining as many bowls of punch, which the West India trade had long since made a familiar drink in the colony. Others, who had the appearance of men who lived by regular and laborious handicraft, preferred the insulated bliss of an unshared potation, and became more taciturn under its influence. Nearly all, in short, evinced a predilection for the Good Creature in some of its various shapes, for this is a vice to which, as Fast Day sermons of a hundred years ago will testify, we have a long hereditary claim. The only guests to whom Robin's sympathies inclined him were two or three sheepish countrymen, who were using the inn somewhat after the fashion of a Turkish caravansary; they had gotten themselves into the darkest corner of the room, and heedless of the Nicotian atmosphere, were supping on the bread of their own ovens, and the bacon cured in their own chimney-smoke. But though Robin felt a sort of brotherhood with these strangers, his eyes were attracted from them to a person who stood near the door, holding whispered conversation with a group of ill-dressed associates. His features were separately striking almost to grotesqueness, and the whole face left a deep impression on the memory. The forehead bulged out into a double prominence, with a vale between; the nose came boldly forth in an irregular curve, and its bridge was of more than a finger's breadth; the eyebrows were deep and shaggy, and the eyes glowed beneath them like fire in a cave.

While Robin deliberated of whom to inquire respecting his kinsman's dwelling, he was accosted by the innkeeper, a little man in a stained white apron, who had come to pay his professional welcome to the stranger. Being in the second generation from a French Protestant, he seemed to have inherited the courtesy of his parent nation; but no variety of circumstances was ever known to change his voice from the one shrill note in which he now addressed Robin.

"From the country, I presume, sir?" said he, with a profound bow. "Beg leave to congratulate you on your arrival, and trust you intend a long stay with us. Fine town here, sir, beautiful buildings, and much that may interest a stranger. May I hope for the honor of your commands in respect to supper?"

"The man sees a family likeness! the rogue has guessed that I am related to the Major!" thought Robin, who had hitherto experienced little superfluous civility.

All eyes were now turned on the country lad, standing at the door, in his worn three-cornered hat, gray coat, leather breeches, and blue yarn stockings, leaning on an oaken cudgel, and bearing a wallet on his back.

Robin replied to the courteous innkeeper, with such an assumption of confidence as befitted the Major's relative. "My honest friend," he said, "I shall make it a point to patronize your house on some occasion, when"—here he could not help lowering his voice—"when I may have more than a parchment threepence in my pocket. My present business," continued he, speaking with lofty confidence, "is merely to inquire my way to the dwelling of my kinsman, Major Molineux."

There was a sudden and general movement in the room, which Robin interpreted as expressing the eagerness of each individual to become his guide. But the innkeeer turned his eyes to a written paper on the wall, which he read, or seemed to read, with occasional recurrences to the young man's figure.

"What have we here?" said he, breaking his speech into little dry fragments. "'Left the house of the subscriber, bounden servant, Hezekiah Mudge,— had on, when he went away, gray coat, leather breeches, master's third-best hat. One pound currency reward to whosoever shall lodge him in any jail of the province.' Better trudge, boy; better trudge!"

Robin had begun to draw his hand towards the lighter end of the oak cudgel, but a strange hostility in every countenance induced him to relinquish his purpose of breaking the courteous innkeeper's head. As he turned to leave the room, he encountered a sneering glance from the bold-featured personage whom he had before noticed; and no sooner was he beyond the door, than he heard a general laugh, in which the innkeeper's voice might be distinguished, like the dropping of small stones into a kettle.

"Now, is it not strange," thought Robin, with his usual shrewdness,—"is it not strange that the confession of an empty pocket should outweigh the name of my kinsman, Major Molineux? Oh, if I had one of those grinning rascals in the woods, where I and my oak sapling grew up together, I would teach him that my arm is heavy though my purse be light!"

On turning the corner of the narrow lane, Robin found himself in a spacious street, with an unbroken line of lofty houses on each side, and a steepled building at the upper end, whence the ringing of a bell announced the hour of nine. The light of the moon, and the lamps from the numerous shop-windows, discovered people promenading on the pavement, and amongst them Robin hoped to recognize his hitherto inscrutable relative. The result of his former inquiries made him unwilling to hazard another, in a scene of such publicity, and he determined to walk slowly and silently up the street, thrusting his face close to that of every elderly gentleman, in search of the Major's lineaments. In his progress, Robin encountered many gay and gallant figures. Embroidered garments of showy colors, enormous periwigs, gold-laced hats, and silver-hilted swords glided past him and dazzled his optics. Travelled youths, imitators of the European fine gentlemen of the period, trod jauntily along, half dancing to the fashionable tunes which they hummed, and making poor Robin ashamed of his quiet and natural gait. At length, after many pauses to examine the gorgeous display of goods in the shop-windows, and after suffering some rebukes for the impertinence of his scrutiny into people's faces, the Major's kinsman found himself near the steepled building, still unsuccessful in his search. As yet, however, he had seen only one side of the thronged street; so Robin crossed, and continued the same sort of inquisition down the opposite pavement, with stronger hopes than the philosopher seeking an honest man, but with no better fortune. He had arrived about midway towards the lower end, from which his course began, when he overheard the approach of some one who struck down a cane on the flag-stones at every step, uttering, at regular intervals, two sepulchral hems.

"Mercy on us!" quoth Robin, recognizing the sound.

Turning a corner, which chanced to be close at his right hand, he hastened to pursue his researches in some other part of the town. His patience now was wearing low, and he seemed to feel more fatigue from his rambles since he crossed the ferry, than from his journey of several days on the other side. Hunger also pleaded loudly within him, and Robin began to balance the propriety of demanding, violently, and with lifted cudgel, the necessary guidance from the first solitary passenger whom he should meet. While a resolution to this effect was gaining strength, he entered a street of mean appearance, on either side of which a row of ill-built houses was straggling towards the harbor. The moonlight fell upon no passenger along the whole extent, but in the third domicile which Robin passed there was a half-opened door, and his keen glance detected a woman's garment within.

"My luck may be better here," said he to himself.

Accordingly, he approached the door, and beheld it shut closer as he did so; yet an open space remained, sufficing for the fair occupant to observe the stranger, without a corresponding display on her part. All that Robin could discern was a strip of scarlet petticoat, and the occasional sparkle of an eye, as if the moonbeams were trembling on some bright thing.

"Pretty mistress," for I may call her so with a good conscience, thought the shrewd youth, since I know nothing to the contrary,—"my sweet pretty mistress, will you be kind enough to tell me whereabouts I must seek the dwelling of my kinsman, Major Molineux?"

Robin's voice was plaintive and winning, and the female, seeing nothing to be shunned in the handsome country youth, thrust open the door, and came forth into the moonlight. She was a dainty little figure, with a white neck, round arms, and a slender waist, at the extremity of which her scarlet petticoat jutted out over a hoop, as if she were standing in a balloon. Moreover, her face was oval and pretty, her hair dark beneath the little cap, and her bright eyes possessed a sly freedom, which triumphed over those of Robin.

"Major Molineux dwells here," said this fair woman.

Now, her voice was the sweetest Robin had heard that night, the airy counterpart of a stream of melted silver; yet he could not help doubting whether that sweet voice spoke Gospel truth. He looked up and down the mean street, and then surveyed the house before which they stood. It was a small, dark edifice of two stories, the second of which projected over the lower floor, and the front apartment had the aspect of a shop for petty commodities.

"Now, truly, I am in luck," replied Robin, cunningly, "and so indeed is my kinsman, the Major, in having so pretty a housekeeper. But I prithee trouble him to step to the door; I will deliver him a message from his friends in the country, and then go back to my lodgings at the inn."

"Nay, the Major has been abed this hour or more," said the lady of the scarlet petticoat; "and it would be to little purpose to disturb him to-night, seeing his evening draught was of the strongest. But he is a kind-hearted man, and it would be as much as my life's worth to let a kinsman of his turn away from the door. You are the good old gentleman's very picture, and I could swear that was his rainy-weather hat. Also he has garments very much resembling those leather small-clothes. But come in, I pray, for I bid you hearty welcome in his name."

So saying, the fair and hospitable dame took our hero by the hand; and the touch was light, and the force was gentleness, and though Robin read in her eyes what he did not hear in her words, yet the slender-waisted woman in the scarlet petticoat proved stronger than the athletic country youth. She had drawn his half-willing footsteps nearly to the threshold, when the opening of a door in the neighborhood startled the Major's housekeeper, and, leaving the Major's kinsman, she vanished speedily into her own domicile. A heavy yawn preceded the appearance of a man, who, like the Moonshine of Pyramus and Thisbe, carried a lantern, needlessly aiding his sister luminary in the heavens. As he walked sleepily up the street, he turned his broad, dull face on Robin, and displayed a long staff, spiked at the end.

"Home, vagabond, home!" said the watchman, in accents that seemed to fall asleep as soon as they were uttered. "Home, or we'll set you in the stocks by peep of day!"

"This is the second hint of the kind," thought Robin. "I wish they would end my difficulties, by setting me there to-night."

Nevertheless, the youth felt an instinctive antipathy towards the guardian of midnight order, which at first prevented him from asking his usual question. But just when the man was about to vanish behind the corner, Robin resolved not to lose the opportunity, and shouted lustily after him,—

"I say, friend! will you guide me to the house of my kinsman, Major Molineux?"

The watchman made no reply, but turned the corner and was gone; yet Robin seemed to hear the sound of drowsy laughter stealing along the solitary street. At that moment, also, a pleasant titter saluted him from the open window above his head; he looked up, and caught the sparkle of a saucy eye; a round arm beckoned to him, and next he heard light footsteps descending the staircase within. But Robin, being of the household of a New England clergyman, was a good youth, as well as a shrewd one; so he resisted temptation, and fled away.

He now roamed desperately, and at random, through the town, almost ready to believe that a spell was on him, like that by which a wizard of his country had once kept three pursuers wandering, a whole winter night, within twenty paces of the cottage which they sought. The streets lay before him, strange and desolate, and the lights were extinguished in almost every house. Twice, however, little parties of men, among whom Robin distinguished individuals in outlandish attire, came hurrying along; but, though on both occasions they paused to address him, such intercourse did not at all enlighten his perplexity. They did but utter a few words in some language of which Robin knew nothing, and perceiving his inability to answer, bestowed a curse upon him in plain English and hastened away. Finally, the lad determined to knock at the door of every mansion that might appear worthy to be occupied by his kinsman, trusting that perseverance would overcome the fatality that had hitherto thwarted him. Firm in this resolve, he was passing beneath the walls of a church, which formed the corner of two streets, when, as he turned into the shade of its steeple, he encountered a bulky stranger, muffled in a cloak. The man was proceeding with the speed of earnest business, but Robin planted himself full before him, holding the oak cudgel with both hands across his body as a bar to further passage.

"Halt, honest man, and answer me a

question," said he, very resolutely. "Tell me, this instant, whereabouts is the dwelling of my kinsman, Major Molineux!"

"Keep your tongue between your teeth, fool, and let me pass!" said a deep, gruff voice, which Robin partly remembered. "Let me pass, I say, or I'll strike you to the earth!"

"No, no, neighbor!" cried Robin, flourishing his cudgel, and then thrusting its larger end close to the man's muffled face. "No, no, I'm not the fool you take me for, nor do you pass till I have an answer to my question. Whereabouts is the dwelling of my kinsman, Major Molineux?"

The stranger, instead of attempting to force his passage, stepped back into the moonlight, unmuffled his face, and stared full into that of Robin.

"Watch here an hour, and Major Molineux will pass by," said he.

Robin gazed with dismay and astonishment on the unprecedented physiognomy of the speaker. The forehead with its double prominence, the broad hooked nose, the shaggy eyebrows, and fiery eyes were those which he had noticed at the inn, but the man's complexion had undergone a singular, or, more properly, a twofold change. One side of the face blazed an intense red, while the other was black as midnight, the division line being in the broad ridge of the nose; and a mouth which seemed to extend from ear to ear was black or red, in contrast to the color of the cheek. The effect was as if two individual devils, a fiend of fire and a fiend of darkness, had united themselves to form this infernal visage. The stranger grinned in Robin's face, muffled his parti-colored features, and was out of sight in a moment.

"Strange things we travellers see!" ejaculated Robin.

He seated himself, however, upon the steps of the church-door, resolving to wait the appointed time for his kinsman. A few moments were consumed in philosophical speculations upon the species of man who had just left him; but having settled this point shrewdly, rationally, and satisfactorily, he was compelled to look elsewhere for his amusement. And first he threw his eyes along the street. It was of more respectable appearance than most of those into which he had wandered; and the moon, creating, like the imaginative power, a beautiful strangeness in familiar objects, gave something of romance to a scene that might not have possessed it in the light of day. The irregular and often quaint architecture of the houses, some of whose roofs were broken into numerous little peaks, while others ascended, steep and narrow, into a single point, and others again were square; the pure snow-white of some of their complexions, the aged darkness of others, and the thousand sparklings, reflected from bright substances in the walls of many; these matters engaged Robin's attention for a while, and then began to grow wearisome. Next he endeavored to define the forms of distant objects, starting away, with almost ghostly indistinctness, just as his eye appeared to grasp them; and finally he took a minute survey of an edifice which stood on the opposite side of the street, directly in front of the church-door, where he was stationed. It was a large, square mansion, distinguished from its neighbors by a balcony, which rested on tall pillars, and by an elaborate Gothic window, communicating therewith.

"Perhaps this is the very house I have been seeking," thought Robin.

Then he strove to speed away the time, by listening to a murmur which swept continually along the street, yet was scarcely audible, except to an unaccustomed ear like his; it was a low, dull, dreamy sound, compounded of many noises, each of which was at too great a distance to be separately heard. Robin marvelled at this snore of a sleeping town, and marvelled more whenever its continuity was broken by now and then a distant shout, apparently loud where it originated. But altogether it was a sleep-inspiring sound, and, to shake off its drowsy influence, Robin arose, and climbed a windowframe, that he might view the interior of the church. There the moonbeams came trembling in, and fell down upon the deserted pews, and extended along the quiet aisles. A fainter yet more awful radiance was hovering around the pulpit, and one solitary ray had dared to rest upon the open page of the great Bible. Had nature, in that deep hour, become a worshipper in the house which man had builded? Or was that heavenly light the visible sanctity of the place,—visible because no earthly and impure feet were within the walls? The scene made Robin's heart shiver with a sensation of loneliness stronger than he had ever felt in the remotest depths of his native woods; so he turned away and sat down again before the door. There were graves around the church, and now an uneasy thought obtruded into Robin's breast. What if the object of his search, which had been so often and so strangely thwarted, were all the time mouldering in his shroud? What if his kinsman should glide through yonder gate, and nod and smile to him in dimly passing by?

"Oh that any breathing thing were here with me!" said Robin.

Recalling his thoughts from this uncomfortable track, he sent them over forest, hill, and stream, and attempted to imagine how that evening of ambiguity and weariness had been spent by his father's household. He pictured them assembled at the door, beneath the tree, the great old tree, which had been spared for its huge twisted trunk and venerable shade, when a thousand leafy brethren fell. There, at the going down of the summer sun, it was his father's custom to perform domestic worship, that the neighbors might come and join with him like brothers of the family, and that the wayfaring man might pause to drink at that fountain, and keep his heart pure by freshening the memory of home. Robin distinguished the seat of every individual of the little audience; he saw the good man in the midst, holding the Scriptures in the golden light that fell from the western clouds; he beheld him close the book and all rise up to pray. He heard the old thanksgivings for daily mercies, the old supplications for their continuance, to which he had so often listened in weariness, but which were now among his dear remembrances. He perceived the slight inequality of his father's voice when he came to speak of the absent one; he noted how his mother turned her face to the broad and knotted trunk; how his elder brother scorned, because the beard was rough upon his upper lip, to permit his features to be moved; how the younger sister drew down a low hanging branch before her eyes; and how the little one of all, whose sports had hitherto broken the decorum of the scene, understood the prayer for her playmate, and burst into clamorous grief. Then he saw them go in at the door; and when Robin would have entered also, the latch tinkled into its place, and he was excluded from his home.

"Am I here, or there?" cried Robin, starting; for all at once, when his thoughts had become visible and audible in a dream, the long, wide, solitary street shone out before him.

He aroused himself, and endeavored to fix his attention steadily upon the large edifice which he had surveyed before. But still his mind kept vibrating between fancy and reality; by turns, the pillars of the balcony lengthened into the tall, bare stems of pines, dwindled down to human figures, settled again into their true shape and size, and then commenced a new succession of changes. For a single moment, when he deemed himself awake, he could have sworn that a visage—one which he seemed to remember, yet could not absolutely name as his kinsman's—was looking towards him from the Gothic window. A deeper sleep wrestled with and nearly overcame him, but fled at the sound of footsteps along the opposite pavement. Robin rubbed his eyes, discerned a man passing at the foot of the balcony, and addressed him in a loud, peevish, and lamentable cry.

"Hallo, friend! must I wait here all night for my kinsman, Major Molineux?"

The sleeping echoes awoke, and answered the voice; and the passenger, barely able to discern a figure sitting in the oblique shade of the steeple, traversed the street to obtain a nearer view. He was himself a gentleman in his prime, of open, intelligent, cheerful, and altogether prepossessing countenance. Perceiving a country youth, apparently homeless and without friends, he accosted him in a tone of real kindness, which had become strange to Robin's ears.

"Well, my good lad, why are you sitting here?" inquired he. "Can I be of service to you in any way?"

"I am afraid not, sir," replied Robin, despondingly; "yet I shall take it kindly, if you'll answer me a single question. I've been searching, half the night, for one Major Molineux; now, sir, is there really such a person in these parts, or am I dreaming?"

"Major Molineux! The name is not altogether strange to me," said the gentleman, smiling. "Have you any objection to telling me the nature of your business with him?"

Then Robin briefly related that his father was a clergyman, settled on a small salary, at a long distance back in the country, and that he and Major Molineux were brothers' children. The Major, having inherited riches, and acquired civil and military rank, had visited his cousin, in great pomp, a year or two before; had manifested much interest in Robin and an elder brother, and, being childless himself, had thrown out hints respecting the future establishment of one of them in life. The elder brother was destined to succeed to the farm which his father cultivated in the interval of sacred duties; it was therefore determined that Robin should profit by his kinsman's generous intentions, especially as he seemed to be rather the favorite, and was thought to possess other necessary endowments.

"For I have the name of being a shrewd youth," observed Robin, in this part of his story.

"I doubt not you deserve it," replied his new friend, good-naturedly; "but pray proceed."

"Well, sir, being nearly eighteen years old, and well grown, as you see," continued Robin, drawing himself up to his full height, "I thought it high time to begin the world. So my mother and sister put me in handsome trim, and my father gave me half the remnant of his last year's salary, and five days ago I started for this place to pay the Major a visit. But, would you believe it, sir! I crossed the ferry a little after dark, and have yet found nobody that would show me the way to his dwelling; only, an hour or two since, I was told to wait here, and Major Molineux would pass by."

"Can you describe the man who told you this?" inquired the gentleman.

"Oh, he was a very ill-favored fellow, sir," replied Robin, "with two great bumps on his forehead, a hook nose, fiery eyes; and, what struck me as the strangest, his face was of two different colors. Do you happen to know such a man, sir?"

"Not intimately," answered the stranger, "but I chanced to meet him a little time previous to your stopping me. I believe you may trust his word, and that the Major will very shortly pass through this street. In the mean time, as I have a singular curiosity to witness your meeting, I will sit down here upon the steps and bear you company."

He seated himself accordingly, and

soon engaged his companion in animated discourse. It was but of brief continuance, however, for a noise of shouting, which had long been remotely audible, drew so much nearer that Robin inquired its cause.

"What may be the meaning of this uproar?" asked he. "Truly, if your town be always as noisy, I shall find little sleep while I am an inhabitant."

"Why, indeed, friend Robin, there do appear to be three or four riotous fellows abroad to-night," replied the gentleman. "You must not expect all the stillness of your native woods here in our streets. But the watch will shortly be at the heels of these lads and"—

"Ay, and set them in the stocks by peep of day," interrupted Robin, recollecting his own encounter with the drowsy lantern-bearer. "But, dear sir, if I may trust my ears, an army of watchmen would never make head against such a multitude of rioters. There were at least a thousand voices went up to make that one shout."

"May not a man have several voices, Robin, as well as two complexions?" said his friend.

"Perhaps a man may; but Heaven forbid that a woman should!" responded the shrewd youth, thinking of the seductive tones of the Major's housekeeper.

The sounds of a trumpet in some neighboring street now became so evident and continual, that Robin's curiosity was strongly excited. In addition to the shouts, he heard frequent bursts from many instruments of discord, and a wild and confused laughter filled up the intervals. Robin rose from the steps, and looked wistfully towards a point whither people seemed to be hastening.

"Surely some prodigious merry-making is going on," exclaimed he. "I have laughed very little since I left home, sir, and should be sorry to lose an opportunity. Shall we step round the corner by that darkish house, and take our share of the fun?"

"Sit down again, sit down, good Robin," replied the gentleman, laying his hand on the skirt of the gray coat. "You forget that we must wait here for your kinsman; and there is reason to believe that he will pass by, in the course of a very few moments."

The near approach of the uproar had now disturbed the neighborhood; windows flew open on all sides; and many heads, in the attire of the pillow, and confused by sleep suddenly broken, were protruded to the gaze of whoever had leisure to observe them. Eager voices hailed each other from house to house, all demanding the explanation, which not a soul could give. Half-dressed men hurried towards the unknown commotion, stumbling as they went over the stone steps that thrust themselves into the narrow foot-walk. The shouts, the laughter, and the tuneless bray, the antipodes of music, came onwards with increasing din, till scattered individuals, and then denser bodies, began to appear round a corner at the distance of a hundred yards.

"Will you recognize your kinsman, if he passes in this crowd?" inquired the gentleman.

"Indeed, I can't warrant it, sir; but I'll take my stand here, and keep a bright lookout," answered Robin, descending to the outer edge of the pavement.

A mighty stream of people now emptied into the street, and came rolling slowly towards the church. A single horseman wheeled the corner in the midst of them, and close behind him came a band of fearful wind-instruments, sending forth a fresher discord now that no intervening buildings kept it from the ear. Then a redder light disturbed the moonbeams, and a dense multitude of torches shone along the street, concealing, by their glare, whatever object they illuminated. The single horseman, clad in a military dress, and bearing a drawn sword, rode onward as the leader, and, by his fierce and variegated countenance, appeared like war personified; the red of one cheek was an emblem of fire and sword; the blackness of the other betokened the mourning that attends them. In his train were wild figures in the Indian dress, and many fantastic shapes without a model, giving the whole march a visionary air, as if a dream had broken forth from some feverish brain, and were sweeping visibly through the midnight streets. A mass of people, inactive, except as applauding spectators, hemmed the procession in; and several women ran along the sidewalk, piercing the confusion of heavier sounds with their shrill voices of mirth or terror.

"The double-faced fellow has his eye upon me," muttered Robin, with an indefinite but an uncomfortable idea that he was himself to bear a part in the pageantry.

The leader turned himself in the saddle, and fixed his glance full upon the country youth, as the steed went slowly by. When Robin had freed his eyes from those fiery ones, the musicians were passing before him, and the torches were close at hand; but the unsteady brightness of the latter formed a veil which he could not penetrate. The rattling of wheels over the stones sometimes found its way to his ear, and confused traces of a human form appeared at intervals, and then melted into the vivid light. A moment more, and the leader thundered a command to halt: the trumpets vomited a horrid breath, and then held their peace; the shouts and laughter of the people died away, and there remained only a universal hum, allied to silence. Right before Robin's eyes was an uncovered cart. There the torches blazed the brightest, there the moon shone out like day, and there, in tar-and-feathery dignity, sat his kinsman, Major Molineux!

He was an elderly man, of large and majestic person, and strong, square features, betokening a steady soul; but steady as it was, his enemies had found means to shake it. His face was pale as death, and far more ghastly; the broad forehead was contracted in his agony, so that his eyebrows formed one grizzled line; his eyes were red and wild, and the foam hung white upon his quivering lip. His whole frame was agitated by a quick and continual tremor, which his pride strove to quell, even in those circumstances of overwhelming humiliation. But perhaps the bitterest pang of all was when his eyes met those of Robin; for he evidently knew him on the instant, as the youth stood witnessing the foul disgrace of a head grown gray in honor. They stared at each other in silence, and Robin's knees shook, and his hair bristled, with a mixture of pity and terror. Soon, however, a bewildering excitement began to seize upon his mind; the preceding adventures of the night, the unexpected appearance of the crowd, the torches, the confused din and the hush that followed, the spectre of his kinsman reviled by that great multitude,—all this, and, more than all, a perception of tremendous ridicule in the whole scene, affected him with a sort of mental inebriety. At that moment a voice of sluggish merriment saluted Robin's ears; he turned instinctively, and just behind the corner of the church stood the lantern-bearer, rubbing his eyes, and drowsily enjoying the lad's amazement. Then he heard a peal of laughter like the ringing of silvery bells; a woman twitched his arm, a saucy eye met his, and he saw the lady of the scarlet petticoat. A sharp, dry cachinnation appealed to his memory, and, standing on tiptoe in the crowd, with his white apron over his head, he beheld the courteous little innkeeper. And lastly, there sailed over the heads of the multitude a great, broad laugh, broken in the midst by two sepulchral hems; thus,

"Haw, haw, haw—hem, hem,—haw, haw, haw, haw!"

The sound proceeded from the balcony of the opposite edifice, and thither Robin turned his eyes. In front of the Gothic window stood the old citizen, wrapped in a wide gown, his gray periwig exchanged for a nightcap, which was thrust back from his forehead, and his silk stockings hanging about his legs. He supported himself on his polished cane in a fit of convulsive merriment, which manifested itself on his solemn old features like a funny inscription on a tombstone. Then Robin seemed to hear the voices of the barbers, of the guests of the inn, and of all who had made sport of him that night. The contagion was spreading among the multitude, when all at once, it seized upon Robin, and he sent forth a shout of laughter that echoed through the street,—every man shook his sides, every man emptied his lungs, but Robin's shout was the loudest there. The cloud-spirits peeped from their silvery islands, as the congregated mirth went roaring up the sky! The Man in the Moon heard the far bellow. "Oho," quoth he, "the old earth is frolicsome to-night!"

When there was a momentary calm in that tempestuous sea of sound, the leader gave the sign, the procession resumed its march. On they went, like fiends that throng in mockery around some dead potentate, mighty no more, but majestic still in his agony. On they went, in counterfeited pomp, in senseless uproar, in frenzied merriment, trampling all on an old man's heart. On swept the tumult, and left a silent street behind.

"Well, Robin, are you dreaming?" inquired the gentleman, laying his hand on the youth's shoulder.

Robin started, and withdrew his arm from the stone post to which he had instinctively clung, as the living stream rolled by him. His cheek was somewhat pale, and his eye not quite as lively as in the earlier part of the evening.

"Will you be kind enough to show me the way to the ferry?" said he, after a moment's pause.

"You have, then, adopted a new subject of inquiry?" observed his companion, with a smile.

"Why, yes, sir," replied Robin, rather dryly. "Thanks to you, and to my other friends, I have at last met my kinsman, and he will scarce desire to see my face again. I begin to grow weary of a town life, sir. Will you show me the way to the ferry?"

"No, my good friend Robin—not to-night, at least," said the gentleman. "Some few days hence, if you wish it, I will speed you on your journey. Or, if you prefer to remain with us, perhaps, as you are a shrewd youth, you may rise in the world without the help of your kinsman, Major Molineux."

EDGAR ALLAN POE • 1809–1849

The Fall of the House of Usher

*Son cœur est un luth suspendu;
Sitôt qu'on le touche il résonne.*[1]
DE BÉRANGER

DURING the whole of a dull, dark, and soundless day in the autumn of the year, when the clouds hung oppressively low in the heavens, I had been passing alone, on horseback, through a singularly dreary tract of country, and at length found myself, as the shades of the evening drew on, within view of the melancholy House of Usher. I know not how it was—but, with the first glimpse of the building, a sense of insufferable gloom pervaded my spirit. I say insufferable; for the feeling was unrelieved by any of that half-pleasurable, because poetic, sentiment with which the mind usually receives even the sternest natural images of the desolate or terrible. I looked upon the scene before me—upon the mere house, and the simple landscape features of the domain—upon the bleak walls—upon the vacant eye-like windows—upon a few rank sedges—and upon a few white trunks of decayed trees—with an utter depression of soul which I can compare to no earthly sensation more properly than to the after-dream of the reveller upon opium—the bitter lapse into everyday life—the hideous dropping off of the veil. There was an iciness, a sinking, a sickening of the heart—an unredeemed dreariness of thought which no goading of the imagination could torture into aught of the sublime. What was it—I paused to think—what was it that so unnerved me in the contemplation of the House of Usher? It was a mystery all insoluble; nor could I grapple with the shadowy fancies that crowded upon me as I pondered. I was forced to fall back upon the unsatisfactory conclusion, that while, beyond doubt, there *are* combinations of very simple natural objects which have the power of thus affecting us, still the analysis of this power lies among considerations beyond our depth. It was possible, I reflected, that a mere different arrangement of the particulars of the scene, of the details of the picture, would be sufficient to modify, or perhaps to annihilate its capacity for sorrowful impression; and, acting upon this idea, I reined my horse to the precipitous brink of a black and lurid tarn that lay in unruffled lustre by the dwelling, and gazed down—but with a shudder even more thrilling than before—upon the remodelled and inverted images of the gray sedge, and the ghastly tree-stems, and the vacant and eye-like windows.

Nevertheless, in this mansion of gloom I now proposed to myself a sojourn of some weeks. Its proprietor, Roderick Usher, had been one of my boon companions in boyhood; but many years had elapsed since our last meeting. A letter, however, had lately reached me in a distant part of the country—a letter from him—which, in its wildly importunate nature, had admitted of no other than a personal reply. The MS. gave evidence of nervous agitation. The writer spoke of acute bodily illness—of a mental disorder which oppressed him—and of an earnest desire to see me, as his best and indeed his only personal friend, with a view of attempting, by the cheerfulness of my society, some alleviation of his malady.

[1] His heart is a suspended lute; As soon as one touches it, it resounds.

15

It was the manner in which all this, and much more, was said—it was the apparent *heart* that went with his request—which allowed me no room for hesitation; and I accordingly obeyed forthwith what I still considered a very singular summons.

Although, as boys, we had been intimate associates, yet I really knew little of my friend. His reserve had been always excessive and habitual. I was aware, however, that his very ancient family had been noted, time out of mind, for a peculiar sensibility of temperament, displaying itself, through long ages, in many works of exalted art, and manifested, of late, in repeated deeds of munificent yet unobtrusive charity, as well as in a passionate devotion to the intricacies, perhaps even more than to the orthodox and easily recognizable beauties, of musical science. I had learned, too, the very remarkable fact, that the stem of the Usher race, all time-honoured as it was, had put forth, at no period, any enduring branch; in other words, that the entire family lay in the direct line of descent, and had always, with very trifling and very temporary variation, so lain. It was this deficiency, I considered, while running over in thought the perfect keeping of the character of the premises with the accredited character of the people, and while speculating upon the possible influence which the one, in the long lapse of centuries, might have exercised upon the other—it was this deficiency, perhaps, of collateral issue, and the consequent undeviating transmission, from sire to son, of the patrimony with the name, which had, at length, so identified the two as to merge the original title of the estate in the quaint and equivocal appellation of the "House of Usher"—an appellation which seemed to include, in the minds of the peasantry who used it, both the family and the family mansion.

I have said that the sole effect of my somewhat childish experiment—that of looking down within the tarn—had been to deepen the first singular impression. There can be no doubt that the consciousness of the rapid increase of my superstition—for why should I not so term it?—served mainly to accelerate the increase itself. Such, I have long known, is the paradoxical law of all sentiments having terror as a basis. And it might have been for this reason only, that, when I again uplifted my eyes to the house itself, from its image in the pool, there grew in my mind a strange fancy—a fancy so ridiculous, indeed, that I but mention it to show the vivid force of the sensations which oppressed me. I had so worked upon my imagination as really to believe that about the whole mansion and domain there hung an atmosphere peculiar to themselves and their immediate vicinity—an atmosphere which had no affinity with the air of heaven, but which had reeked up from the decayed trees, and the gray wall, and the silent tarn—a pestilent and mystic vapour, dull, sluggish, faintly discernible, and leaden-hued.

Shaking off from my spirit what *must* have been a dream, I scanned more narrowly the real aspect of the building. Its principal feature seemed to be that of an excessive antiquity. The discoloration of ages had been great. Minute fungi overspread the whole exterior, hanging in a fine tangled web-work from the eaves. Yet all this was apart from any extraordinary dilapidation. No portion of the masonry had fallen; and there appeared to be a wild inconsistency between its still perfect adaptation of parts, and the crumbling condition of the individual stones. In this there was much that reminded me of the specious totality of old woodwork which has rotted for long years in some neglected vault, with no disturbance from the breath of the external air. Beyond this indication of extensive decay, however, the fabric gave little token of instability. Perhaps the eye of a scrutinizing observer might have discovered a barely perceptible fissure, which, extending from the roof of the building in front, made its way down the wall in a zigzag direction, until it became lost in the sullen waters of the tarn.

Noticing these things, I rode over a short causeway to the house. A servant in waiting took my horse, and I entered the Gothic archway of the hall. A valet, of stealthy step, thence conducted me, in silence, through many dark and intricate passages in my progress to the *studio* of his master. Much that I encountered on the way contributed, I know not how, to heighten the vague sentiments of which I have already spoken. While the objects around me—while the carvings of the ceilings, the sombre tapestries of the walls, the ebon blackness of the floors, and the phantasmagoric armorial trophies which rattled as I strode, were but matters to which, or to such as which, I had been accustomed from my infancy—while I hesitated not to acknowledge how familiar was all this—I still wondered to find how unfamiliar were the fancies which ordinary images were stirring up. On one of the staircases, I met the physician of the family. His countenance, I thought, wore a mingled expression of low cunning and perplexity. He accosted me with trepidation and passed on. The valet now threw open a door and ushered me into the presence of his master.

The room in which I found myself was very large and lofty. The windows were long, narrow, and pointed, and at so vast a distance from the black oaken floor as to be altogether inaccessible from within. Feeble gleams of encrimsoned light made their way through the trellissed panes, and served to render sufficiently distinct the more prominent objects around; the eye, however, struggled in vain to reach the remoter angles of the chamber, or the recesses of the vaulted and fretted ceiling. Dark draperies hung upon the walls. The general furniture was profuse, comfortless, antique, and tattered. Many books and musical instruments lay scattered about, but failed to give any vitality to the scene. I felt that I breathed an atmosphere of sorrow. An air of stern, deep, and irredeemable gloom hung over and pervaded all.

Upon my entrance, Usher arose from a sofa on which he had been lying at full length, and greeted me with a vivacious warmth which had much in it, I at first thought, of an overdone cordiality—of the constrained effort of the *ennuyé*[2] man of the world. A glance, however, at his countenance convinced me of his perfect sincerity. We sat down; and for some moments, while he spoke not, I gazed upon him with a feeling of pity, half of awe. Surely, man had never before so terribly altered, in so brief a period, as had Roderick Usher! It was with difficulty that I could bring myself to admit the identity of the wan being before me with the companion of my early boyhood. Yet the character of his face had been at all times remarkable. A cadaverousness of complexion; an eye large, liquid, and luminous beyond comparison; lips somewhat thin and very pallid, but of a surpassingly beautiful curve; a nose of a delicate Hebrew model, but with a breadth of nostril unusual in similar formations; a finely moulded chin, speaking, in its want of prominence, of a want of moral energy; hair of a more than web-like softness and tenuity; these features, with an inordinate expansion above the regions of the temple, made up altogether a countenance not easily to be forgotten. And now in the mere exaggeration of the prevailing character of these features, and of the expression they were wont to convey, lay so much of change that I doubted to whom I spoke. The now ghastly pallor of the skin, and the now miraculous lustre of the eye, above all things startled and even awed me. The silken hair, too, had been suffered to grow all unheeded, and as,

[2] bored

in its wild gossamer texture, it floated rather than fell about the face. I could not, even with effort, connect its Arabesque expression with any idea of simple humanity.

In the manner of my friend I was at once struck with an incoherence—an inconsistency; and I soon found this to arise from a series of feeble and futile struggles to overcome an habitual trepidancy—an excessive nervous agitation. For something of this nature I had indeed been prepared, no less by his letter, than by reminiscences of certain boyish traits, and by conclusions deduced from his peculiar physical conformation and temperament. His action was alternately vivacious and sullen. His voice varied rapidly from a tremulous indecision (when the animal spirits seemed utterly in abeyance) to that species of energetic concision—that abrupt, weighty, unhurried, and hollow-sounding enunciation—that leaden, self-balanced, and perfectly modulated guttural utterance, which may be observed in the lost drunkard, or the irreclaimable eater of opium, during the periods of his most intense excitement.

It was thus that he spoke of the object of my visit, of his earnest desire to see me, and of the solace he expected me to afford him. He entered, at some length, into what he conceived to be the nature of his malady. It was, he said, a constitutional and a family evil, and one for which he despaired to find a remedy—a mere nervous affection, he immediately added, which would undoubtedly soon pass off. It displayed itself in a host of unnatural sensations. Some of these, as he detailed them, interested and bewildered me; although, perhaps, the terms and the general manner of their narration had their weight. He suffered much from a morbid acuteness of the senses; the most insipid food was alone endurable; he could wear only garments of certain texture; the odours of all flowers were oppressive; his eyes were tortured by even a faint light; and there were but peculiar sounds, and these from stringed instruments, which did not inspire him with horror.

To an anomalous species of terror I found him a bounden slave. "I shall perish," said he, "I *must* perish in this deplorable folly. Thus, thus, and not otherwise, shall I be lost. I dread the events of the future, not in themselves, but in their results. I shudder at the thought of any, even the most trivial, incident, which may operate upon this intolerable agitation of soul. I have, indeed, no abhorrence of danger, except in its absolute effect—in terror. In this unnerved—in this pitiable condition—I feel that the period will sooner or later arrive when I must abandon life and reason together, in some struggle with the grim phantasm, FEAR."

I learned, moreover, at intervals, and through broken and equivocal hints, another singular feature of his mental condition. He was enchained by certain superstitious impressions in regard to the dwelling which he tenanted, and whence, for many years, he had never ventured forth—in regard to an influence whose supposititious force was conveyed in terms too shadowy here to be re-stated—an influence which some peculiarities in the mere form and substance of his family mansion had, by dint of long sufferance, he said, obtained over his spirit—an effect which the *physique* of the gray walls and turrets, and of the dim tarn into which they all looked down, had, at length, brought about upon the *morale* of his existence.

He admitted, however, although with hesitation, that much of the peculiar gloom which thus afflicted him could be traced to a more natural and far more palpable origin—to the severe and long-continued illness—indeed to the evidently approaching dissolution—of a tenderly beloved sister, his sole companion for long years, his last and only relative on earth. "Her decease," he said, with a bitterness which I can never forget, "would leave him (him, the hopeless and the frail) the last of the ancient race of the Ushers." While he spoke, the lady Madeline (for so was she called) passed slowly through a remote portion of the apartment, and, without having noticed my presence, disappeared. I regarded her with an utter astonishment not unmingled with dread; and yet I found it impossible to account for such feelings. A sensation of stupor oppressed me, as my eyes followed her retreating steps. When a door, at length, closed upon her, my glance sought instinctively and eagerly the countenance of the brother—but he had buried his face in his hands, and I could only perceive that a far more than ordinary wanness had overspread the emaciated fingers through which trickled many passionate tears.

The disease of the lady Madeline had long baffled the skill of her physicians. A settled apathy, a gradual wasting away of the person, and frequent although transient affections of a partially cataleptical character were the unusual diagnosis. Hitherto she had steadily borne up against the pressure of her malady, and had not betaken herself finally to bed; but on the closing in of the evening of my arrival at the house, she succumbed (as her brother told me at night with inexpressible agitation) to the prostrating power of the destroyer; and I learned that the glimpse I had obtained of her person would thus probably be the last I should obtain—that the lady, at least while living, would be seen by me no more.

For several days ensuing, her name was unmentioned by either Usher or myself: and during this period I was busied in earnest endeavours to alleviate the melancholy of my friend. We painted and read together, or I listened, as if in a dream, to the wild improvisations of his speaking guitar. And thus, as a closer and still closer intimacy admitted me more unreservedly into the recesses of his spirit, the more bitterly did I perceive the futility of all attempt at cheering a mind from which darkness, as if an inherent positive quality, poured forth upon all objects of the moral and physical universe in one unceasing radiation of gloom.

I shall ever bear about me a memory of the many solemn hours I thus spent alone with the master of the House of Usher. Yet I should fail in any attempt to convey an idea of the exact character of the studies, or of the occupations, in which he involved me, or led me the way. An excited and highly distempered ideality threw a sulphureous lustre over all. His long improvised dirges will ring forever in my ears. Among other things, I hold painfully in mind a certain singular perversion and amplification of the wild air of the last waltz of Von Weber. From the paintings over which his elaborate fancy brooded, and which grew, touch by touch, into vaguenesses at which I shuddered the more thrillingly, because I shuddered knowing not why;—from these paintings (vivid as their images now are before me) I would in vain endeavour to educe more than a small portion which should lie within the compass of merely written words. By the utter simplicity, by the nakedness of his designs, he arrested and overawed attention. If ever mortal painted an idea, that mortal was Roderick Usher. For me at least, in the circumstances then surrounding me, there arose out of the pure abstractions which the hypochondriac contrived to throw upon his canvas, an intensity of intolerable awe, no shadow of which felt I ever yet in the contemplation of the certainly glowing yet too concrete reveries of Fuseli.

One of the phanatasmagoric conceptions of my friend, partaking not so rigidly of the spirit of abstraction, may be shadowed forth, although feebly, in words. A small picture presented the interior of an immensely long and rectangular vault or tunnel, with low walls, smooth, white, and without interruption or device. Certain accessory points of the design served well to convey the idea that this excavation lay at an exceeding depth below the surface of the earth. No outlet was observed in any portion of its vast extent, and no torch or other artificial source of light was discernible; yet a flood of intense rays rolled throughout, and bathed the whole in a ghastly and inappropriate splendour.

I have just spoken of that morbid condition of the auditory nerve which rendered all music intolerable to the sufferer, with the exception of certain effects of stringed instruments. It was, perhaps, the narrow limits to which he thus confined himself upon the guitar which gave birth, in great measure, to the fantastic character of his performances. But the fervid *facility* of his *impromptus* could not be so accounted for. They must have been, and were, in the notes, as well as in the words of his wild fantasias (for he not unfrequently accompanied himself with rhymed verbal improvisations), the result of that intense mental collectedness and concentration to which I have previously alluded as observable only in particular moments of the highest artificial excitement. The words of one of these rhapsodies I have easily remembered. I was, perhaps, the more forcibly impressed with it as he gave it, because, in the under or mystic current of its meaning, I fancied that I perceived, and for the first time, a full consciousness on the part of Usher of the tottering of his lofty reason upon her throne. The verses, which were entitled "The Haunted Palace," ran very nearly, if not accurately, thus:

I

In the greenest of our valleys,
By good angels tenanted,
Once a fair and stately palace—
Radiant palace—reared its head.
In the monarch Thought's dominion—
It stood there!
Never seraph spread a pinion
Over fabric half so fair.

II

Banners yellow, glorious, golden,
On its roof did float and flow
(This—all this—was in the olden
Time long ago)
And every gentle air that dallied,
In that sweet day,
Along the ramparts plumed and pallid,
A winged odour went away.

III

Wanderers in that happy valley
Through two luminous windows saw
Spirits moving musically
To a lute's well-tunèd law,
Round about a throne, where sitting
(Porphyrogene!)[3]
In state his glory well befitting,
The ruler of the realm was seen.

IV

And all with pearl and ruby glowing
Was the fair palace door,
Through which came flowing, flowing,
 flowing
And sparkling evermore,
A troop of Echoes whose sweet duty
Was but to sing,
In voices of surpassing beauty,
The wit and wisdom of their king.

V

But evil things, in robes of sorrow,
Assailed the monarch's high estate;
(Ah, let us mourn, for never morrow
Shall dawn upon him, desolate!)
And, round about his home, the glory
That blushed and bloomed
Is but a dim-remembered story
Of the old time entombed.

VI

And travellers now within that valley,
Through the red-litten windows see
Vast forms that move fantastically
To a discordant melody;
While, like a rapid ghastly river,
Through the pale door,
A hideous throng rush out forever,
And laugh—but smile no more.

I well remember that suggestions arising from this ballad, led us into a train

[3] born to the purple

of thought, wherein there became manifest an opinion of Usher's which I mention not so much on account of its novelty, (for other men have thought thus,) as on account of the pertinacity with which he maintained it. This opinion, in its general form, was that of the sentience of all vegetable things. But, in his disordered fancy, the idea had assumed a more daring character, and trespassed, under certain conditions, upon the kingdom of inorganization. I lack words to express the full extent, or the earnest *abandon* of his persuasion. The belief, however, was connected (as I have previously hinted) with the gray stones of the home of his forefathers. The conditions of the sentience had been here, he imagined, fulfilled in the method of collocation of these stones—in the order of their arrangement, as well as in that of the many *fungi* which overspread them, and of the decayed trees which stood around —above all, in the long undisturbed endurance of this arrangement, and in its reduplication in the still waters of the tarn. Its evidence—the evidence of the sentience—was to be seen, he said (and I here started as he spoke), in the gradual yet certain condensation of an atmosphere of their own about the waters and the walls. The result was discoverable, he added, in that silent yet importunate and terrible influence which for centuries had moulded the destinies of his family, and which made *him* what I now saw him— what he was. Such opinions need no comment, and I will make none.

Our books—the books which, for years, had formed no small portion of the mental existence of the invalid—were, as might be supposed, in strict keeping with this character of phantasm. We pored together over such works as the Ververt et Chartreuse of Gresset; the Belphegor of Machiavelli; the Heaven and Hell of Swedenborg; the Subterranean Voyage of Nicholas Klimm of Holberg; the Chiromancy of Robert Flud, of Jean D'Indaginé, and of De la Chambre; the Journey into the Blue Distance of Tieck; and the City of the Sun of Campanella. One favourite volume was a small octavo edition of the *Directorium Inquisitorum,* by the Dominican Eymeric de Gironne; and there were passages in Pomponius Mela, about the old African Satyrs and Œgipans, over which Usher would sit dreaming for hours. His chief delight, however, was found in the perusal of an exceedingly rare and curious book in quarto Gothic—the manual of a forgotten church—the *Vigiliæ Mortuorum secundum Chorum Ecclesiæ Maguntinæ.*

I could not help thinking of the wild ritual of this work, and of its probable influence upon the hypochondriac, when, one evening, having informed me abruptly that the lady Madeline was no more, he stated his intention of preserving her corpse for a fortnight, (previously to its final interment,) in one of the numerous vaults within the main walls of the building. The worldly reason, however, assigned for this singular proceeding, was one which I did not feel at liberty to dispute. The brother had been led to his resolution (so he told me) by consideration of the unusual character of the malady of the deceased, of certain obtrusive and eager inquiries on the part of her medical men, and of the remote and exposed situation of the burial-ground of the family. I will not deny that when I called to mind the sinister countenance of the person whom I met upon the staircase, on the day of my arrival at the house, I had no desire to oppose what I regarded as at best but a harmless, and by no means an unnatural, precaution.

At the request of Usher, I personally aided him in the arrangements for the temporary entombment. The body having been encoffined, we two alone bore it to its rest. The vault in which we placed it (and which had been so long unopened that our torches, half smothered in its oppressive atmosphere, gave us little opportunity for investigation) was small, damp, and entirely without means of admission for light; lying, at great depth, immediately beneath that portion of the building in which was my own sleeping apartment. It had been used, apparently, in remote feudal times, for the worst purposes of a donjon-keep, and, in later days, as a place of deposit for powder, or some other highly combustible substance, as a portion of its floor, and the whole interior of a long archway through which we reached it, were carefully sheathed with copper. The door, of massive iron, had been, also, similarly protected. Its immense weight caused an unusually sharp grating sound, as it moved upon its hinges.

Having deposited our mournful burden upon tressels within this region of horror, we partially turned aside the yet unscrewed lid of the coffin, and looked upon the face of the tenant. A striking similitude between the brother and sister now first arrested my attention; and Usher, divining, perhaps, my thoughts, murmured out some few words from which I learned that the deceased and himself had been twins, and that sympathies of a scarcely intelligible nature had always existed between them. Our glances, however, rested not long upon the dead—for we could not regard her unawed. The disease which had thus entombed the lady in the maturity of youth, had left, as usual in all maladies of a strictly cataleptical character, the mockery of a faint blush upon the bosom and the face, and that suspiciously lingering smile upon the lip which is so terrible in death. We replaced and screwed down the lid, and, having secured the door of iron, made our way, with toil, into the scarcely less gloomy apartments of the upper portion of the house.

And now, some days of bitter grief having elapsed, an observable change came over the features of the mental disorder of my friend. His ordinary manner had vanished. His ordinary occupations were neglected or forgotten. He roamed from chamber to chamber with hurried, unequal, and objectless step. The pallor of his countenance had assumed, if possible, a more ghastly hue—but the luminousness of his eye had utterly gone out. The once occasional huskiness of his tone was heard no more; and a tremulous quaver, as if of extreme terror, habitually characterized his utterance. There were times, indeed, when I thought his unceasingly agitated mind was labouring with some oppressive secret, to divulge which he struggled for the necessary courage. At times, again, I was obliged to resolve all into the mere inexplicable vagaries of madness, for I beheld him gazing upon vacancy for long hours, in an attitude of the profoundest attention, as if listening to some imaginary sound. It was no wonder that his condition terrified—that it infected me. I felt creeping upon me, by slow yet certain degrees, the wild influences of his own fantastic yet impressive superstitions.

It was, especially, upon retiring to bed late in the night of the seventh or eighth day after the placing of the lady Madeline within the donjon, that I experienced the full power of such feelings. Sleep came not near my couch—while the hours waned and waned away. I struggled to reason off the nervousness which had dominion over me. I endeavoured to believe that much, if not all of what I felt, was due to the bewildering influence of the gloomy furniture of the room—of the dark and tattered draperies, which, tortured into motion by the breath of a rising tempest, swayed fitfully to and fro upon the walls, and rustled uneasily about the decorations of the bed. But my efforts were fruitless. An irrepressible tremour gradually pervaded my frame; and, at length, there sat upon my very heart an incubus of utterly causeless alarm. Shaking this off with a gasp and a struggle, I uplifted myself upon the pillows, and, peering earnestly within the intense darkness of the chamber, hearkened—I know not why, except that an instinctive spirit prompted me—to certain low and indefinite sounds which came, through the pauses of the storm, at long intervals, I knew not whence. Overpowered by an intense sentiment of horror, unaccountable yet unendurable, I threw on my clothes with haste, (for I felt that I should sleep no more during the night,) and endeavoured to arouse myself from the pitiable condition into which I had fallen, by pacing rapidly to and fro through the apartment.

I had taken but few turns in this manner, when a light step on an adjoining staircase arrested my attention. I presently recognized it as that of Usher. In an instant afterward he rapped, with a gentle touch, at my door, and entered, bearing a lamp. His countenance was, as usual, cadaverously wan—but, moreover, there was a species of mad hilarity in his eyes —an evidently restrained *hysteria* in his whole demeanour. His air appalled me— but anything was preferable to the solitude which I had so long endured, and I even welcomed his presence as a relief.

"And you have not seen it?" he said abruptly, after having stared about him for some moments in silence—"you have not then seen it?—but, stay! you shall." Thus speaking, and having carefully shaded his lamp, he hurried to one of the casements, and threw it freely open to the storm.

The impetuous fury of the entering gust nearly lifted us from our feet. It was, indeed, a tempestuous yet sternly beautiful night, and one wildly singular in its terror and its beauty. A whirlwind had apparently collected its force in our vicinity; for there were frequent and violent alterations in the direction of the wind; and the exceeding density of the clouds (which hung so low as to press upon the turrets of the house) did not prevent our perceiving the life-like velocity with which they flew careering from all points against each other, without passing away into the distance. I say that even their exceeding density did not prevent our perceiving this—yet we had no glimpse of the moon or stars—nor was there any flashing forth of the lightning. But the under surfaces of the huge masses of agitated vapour, as well as all terrestrial objects immediately around us, were glowing in the unnatural light of a faintly luminous and distinctly visible gaseous exhalation which hung about and enshrouded the mansion.

"You must not—you shall not behold this!" said I, shuddering, to Usher, as I led him, with a gentle violence, from the window to a seat. "These appearances, which bewilder you, are merely electrical phenomena not uncommon—or it may be that they have their ghastly origin in the rank miasma of the tarn. Let us close this casement;—the air is chilling and dangerous to your frame. Here is one of your favourite romances. I will read, and you shall listen;—and so we will pass away this terrible night together."

The antique volume which I had taken up was the "Mad Trist" of Sir Launcelot Canning; but I had called it a favourite of Usher's more in sad jest than in earnest; for, in truth, there is little in its uncouth and unimaginative prolixity which could have had interest for the lofty and spiritual ideality of my friend. It was, however, the only book immediately at hand; and I indulged a vague hope that the excitement which now agitated the hypochondriac, might find relief (for the history of mental disorder is full of similar anomalies) even in the extremeness of the folly which I should read. Could I have judged, indeed, by the wild overstrained air of vivacity with which he hearkened, or apparently hearkened, to the words of the tale, I might well have congratulated myself upon the success of my design.

I had arrived at that well-known portion of the story where Ethelred, the hero of the Trist, having sought in vain for peaceable admission into the dwelling of the hermit, proceeds to make good an entrance by force. Here, it will be remembered, the words of the narrative run thus:

"And Ethelred, who was by nature of a doughty heart, and who was now mighty withal, on account of the powerfulness of the wine which he had drunken, waited no longer to hold parley with the hermit, who, in sooth, was of an obstinate and maliceful turn, but, feeling the rain upon his shoulders, and fearing the rising of the tempest, uplifted his mace outright, and, with blows, made quickly room in the plankings of the door for his gauntleted hand; and now pulling therewith sturdily, he so cracked, and ripped, and tore all asunder, that the noise of the dry and hollow-sounding wood alarumed and reverberated throughout the forest."

At the termination of this sentence I started and, for a moment, paused; for it appeared to me (although I at once concluded that my excited fancy had deceived me)—it appeared to me that, from some very remote portion of the mansion, there came, indistinctly, to my ears, what might have been, in its exact similarity of character, the echo (but a stifled and dull one certainly) of the very cracking and ripping sound which Sir Launcelot had so particularly described. It was, beyond doubt, the coincidence alone which had arrested my attention; for, amid the rattling of the sashes of the casements, and the ordinary commingled noises of the still increasing storm, the sound, in itself, had nothing, surely, which should have interested or disturbed me. I continued the story:

"But the good champion Ethelred, now entering within the door, was sore enraged and amazed to perceive no signal of the maliceful hermit; but, in the stead thereof, a dragon of a scaly and prodigious demeanour, and of a fiery tongue, which sate in guard before a palace of gold, with a floor of silver; and upon the wall there hung a shield of shining brass with this legend enwritten—

Who entereth herein, a conqueror hath bin;
Who slayeth the dragon, the shield he shall win.

And Ethelred uplifted his mace, and struck upon the head of the dragon, which fell before him, and gave up his pesty breath, with a shriek so horrid and harsh, and withal so piercing, that Ethelred had fain to close his ears with his hands against the dreadful noise of it, the like whereof was never before heard."

Here again I paused abruptly, and now with a feeling of wild amazement—for there could be no doubt whatever that, in this instance, I did actually hear (although from what direction it proceeded I found it impossible to say) a low and apparently distant, but harsh, protracted, and most unusual screaming or grating sound—the exact counterpart of what my fancy had already conjured up for the dragon's unnatural shriek as described by the romancer.

Oppressed, as I certainly was, upon the occurrence of this second and most extraordinary coincidence, by a thousand conflicting sensations, in which wonder and extreme terror were predominant, I still retained sufficient presence of mind to avoid exciting, by any observation, the sensitive nervousness of my companion. I was by no means certain that he had noticed the sounds in question; although, assuredly, a strange alteration had, during the last few minutes, taken place in his demeanour. From a position fronting my own, he had gradually brought round his chair, so as to sit with his face to the door of the chamber; and thus I could but partially perceive his features, although I saw that his lips trembled as if he were murmuring inaudibly. His head had dropped upon his breast—yet I knew that he was not asleep, from the wide and rigid opening of the eye as I caught a glance of it in profile. The motion of his body, too, was at variance with this idea—for he rocked from side to side with a gentle yet constant and uniform sway. Having rapidly taken notice of all this, I resumed the narrative of Sir Launcelot, which thus proceeded:

"And now, the champion, having escaped from the terrible fury of the dragon, bethinking himself of the brazen shield, and of the breaking up of the enchantment which was upon it, removed the carcass from out of the way before him, and approached valorously over the silver pavement of the castle to where the shield was upon the wall; which in sooth tarried not for his full coming, but fell down at his feet upon the silver floor, with a mighty great and terrible ringing sound."

No sooner had these syllables passed my lips, than—as if a shield of brass had indeed, at the moment, fallen heavily upon a floor of silver—I became aware of a distinct, hollow, metallic, and clangorous, yet apparently muffled, reverberation. Completely unnerved, I leaped to my feet; but the measured rocking movement of Usher was undisturbed. I rushed to the chair in which he sat. His eyes were bent fixedly before him, and throughout his whole countenance there reigned a stony rigidity. But, as I placed my hand upon his shoulder, there came a strong shudder over his whole person; a sickly smile quivered about his lips; and I saw that he spoke in a low, hurried, and gibbering murmur, as if unconscious of my presence. Bending closely over him, I at length drank in the hideous import of his words.

"Not hear it?—yes, I hear it, and *have* heard it. Long—long—long—many minutes, many hours, many days, have I heard it—yet I dared not—oh, pity me, miserable wretch that I am!—I dared not —I *dared* not speak! *We have put her living in the tomb!* Said I not that my senses were acute? I *now* tell you that I heard her first feeble movements in the hollow coffin. I heard them—many, many days ago—yet I dared not—I *dared not speak!* And now—to-night—Ethelred—ha! ha! —the breaking of the hermit's door, and the death-cry of the dragon, and the clangour of the shield!—say, rather, the rending of her coffin, and the grating of the iron hinges of her prison, and her struggles within the coppered archway of the vault! Oh whither shall I fly? Will she not be here anon? Is she not hurrying to upbraid me for my haste? Have I not heard her footstep on the stair? Do I not distinguish that heavy and horrible beating of her heart? MADMAN!"—here he sprang furiously to his feet, and shrieked out his syllables, as if in the effort he were giving up his soul—"MADMAN! I TELL YOU THAT SHE NOW STANDS WITHOUT THE DOOR!"

As if in the superhuman energy of his utterance there had been found the potency of a spell, the huge antique panels to which the speaker pointed threw slowly back, upon the instant, their ponderous and ebony jaws. It was the work of the rushing gust—but then without those doors there DID stand the lofty and enshrouded figure of the lady Madeline of Usher. There was blood upon her white robes, and the evidence of some bitter struggle upon every portion of her emaciated frame. For a moment she remained trembling and reeling to and fro upon the threshold, then, with a low moaning cry, fell heavily inward upon the person of her brother, and in her violent and now final death-agonies, bore him to the floor a corpse, and a victim of the terrors he had anticipated.

From that chamber, and from that mansion, I fled aghast. The storm was still abroad in all its wrath as I found myself crossing the old causeway. Suddenly there shot along the path a wild light, and I turned to see whence a gleam so unusual could have issued; for the vast house and its shadows were alone behind me. The radiance was that of the full, setting, and blood-red moon, which now shone vividly through that once barely discernible fissure, of which I have before spoken as extending from the roof of the building, in a zigzag direction, to the base. While I gazed, this fissure rapidly widened—there came a fierce breath of the whirlwind—the entire orb of the satellite burst at once upon my sight—my brain reeled as I saw the mighty walls rushing asunder—there was a long tumultuous shouting sound like the voice of a thousand waters—and the deep and dank tarn at my feet closed sullenly and silently over the fragments of the "HOUSE OF USHER."

HENRY JAMES • 1843-1916

The Pupil

I

THE poor young man hesitated and procrastinated: it cost him such an effort to broach the subject of terms, to speak of money to a person who spoke only of feelings and, as it were, of the aristocracy. Yet he was unwilling to take leave, treating his engagement as settled, without some more conventional glance in that direction than he could find an opening for in the manner of the large, affable lady who sat there drawing a pair of soiled *gants de Suède* through a fat, jewelled hand and, at once pressing and gliding, repeated over and over everything but the thing he would have liked to hear. He would have liked to hear the figure of his salary; but just as he was nervously about to sound that note the little boy came back—the little boy Mrs. Moreen had sent out of the room to fetch her fan. He came back without the fan, only with the casual observation that he couldn't find it. As he dropped this cynical confession he looked straight and hard at the candidate for the honour of taking his education in hand. This personage reflected, somewhat grimly, that the first thing he should have to teach his little charge would be to appear to address himself to his mother when he spoke to her—especially not to make her such an improper answer as that.

When Mrs. Moreen bethought herself of this pretext for getting rid of their companion, Pemberton supposed it was precisely to approach the delicate subject of his remuneration. But it had been only to say some things about her son which it was better that a boy of eleven shouldn't catch. They were extravagantly to his advantage, save when she lowered her voice to sigh, tapping her left side familiarly: "And all overclouded by *this,* you know—all at the mercy of a weakness—!" Pemberton gathered that the weakness was in the region of the heart. He had known the poor child was not robust: this was the basis on which he had been invited to treat, through an English lady, an Oxford acquaintance, then at Nice, who happened to know both his needs and those of the amiable American family looking out for something really superior in the way of a resident tutor.

The young man's impression of his prospective pupil, who had first come into the room, as if to see for himself, as soon as Pemberton was admitted, was not quite the soft solicitation the visitor had taken for granted. Morgan Moreen was, somehow, sickly without being delicate, and that he looked intelligent (it is true Pemberton wouldn't have enjoyed his being stupid), only added to the suggestion that, as with his big mouth and big ears he really couldn't be called pretty, he might be unpleasant. Pemberton was modest—he was even timid; and the chance that his small scholar might prove cleverer than himself had quite figured, to his nervousness, among the dangers of an untried experiment. He reflected, however, that these were risks one had to run when one accepted a position, as it was called, in a private family; when as yet one's University honours had, pecuniarily speaking, remained barren. At any rate, when Mrs. Moreen got up as if to intimate that, since it was understood he would enter upon his duties within the week she would let him off now, he succeeded, in spite of the presence of the

27

child, in squeezing out a phrase about the rate of payment. It was not the fault of the conscious smile which seemed a reference to the lady's expensive identity, if the allusion did not sound rather vulgar. This was exactly because she became still more gracious to reply: "Oh! I can assure you that all that will be quite regular."

Pemberton only wondered, while he took up his hat, what "all that" was to amount to—people had such different ideas. Mrs. Moreen's words, however, seemed to commit the family to a pledge definite enough to elicit from the child a strange little comment, in the shape of the mocking, foreign ejaculation, "Oh, là-là!"

Pemberton, in some confusion, glanced at him as he walked slowly to the window with his back turned, his hands in his pockets and the air in his elderly shoulders of a boy who didn't play. The young man wondered if he could teach him to play, though his mother had said it would never do and that this was why school was impossible. Mrs. Moreen exhibited no discomfiture; she only continued blandly: "Mr. Moreen will be delighted to meet your wishes. As I told you, he has been called to London for a week. As soon as he comes back you shall have it out with him."

This was so frank and friendly that the young man could only reply, laughing as his hostess laughed: "Oh! I don't imagine we shall have much of a battle."

"They'll give you anything you like," the boy remarked unexpectedly, returning from the window. "We don't mind what anything costs—we live awfully well."

"My darling, you're too quaint!" his mother exclaimed, putting out to caress him a practiced but ineffectual hand. He slipped out of it, but looked with intelligent, innocent eyes at Pemberton, who had already had time to notice that from one moment to the other his small satiric face seemed to change its time of life. At this moment it was infantine; yet it appeared also to be under the influence of curious intuitions and knowledges. Pemberton rather disliked precocity, and he was disappointed to find gleams of it in a disciple not yet in his teens. Nevertheless he divined on the spot that Morgan wouldn't prove a bore. He would prove on the contrary a kind of excitement. This idea held the young man, in spite of a certain repulsion.

"You pompous little person! We're not extravagant!" Mrs. Moreen gayly protested, making another unsuccessful attempt to draw the boy to her side. "You must know what to expect," she went on to Pemberton.

"The less you expect the better!" her companion interposed. "But we *are* people of fashion."

"Only so far as *you* make us so!" Mrs. Moreen mocked, tenderly. "Well, then, on Friday—don't tell me you're superstitious—and mind you don't fail us. Then you'll see us all. I'm so sorry the girls are out. I guess you'll like the girls. And, you know, I've another son, quite different from this one."

"He tries to imitate me," said Morgan to Pemberton.

"He tries? Why, he's twenty years old!" cried Mrs. Moreen.

"You're very witty," Pemberton remarked to the child—a proposition that his mother echoed with enthusiasm, declaring that Morgan's sallies were the delight of the house. The boy paid no heed to this; he only inquired abruptly of the visitor, who was surprised afterwards that he hadn't struck him as offensively forward: "Do you *want* very much to come?"

"Can you doubt it, after such a description of what I shall hear?" Pemberton replied. Yet he didn't want to come at all; he was coming because he had to go somewhere, thanks to the collapse of his fortune at the end of a year abroad, spent on the system of putting his tiny patrimony into a single full wave of experience. He had had his full wave, but he couldn't pay his hotel bill. Moreover, he had caught in the boy's eyes the glimpse of a far-off appeal.

"Well, I'll do the best I can for you," said Morgan; with which he turned away again. He passed out of one of the long windows; Pemberton saw him go and lean on the parapet of the terrace. He remained there while the young man took leave of his mother, who, on Pemberton's looking as if he expected a farewell from him, interposed with: "Leave him, leave him! he's so strange!" Pemberton suspected she was afraid of something he might say. "He's a genius—you'll love him," she added. "He's much the most interesting person in the family." And before he could invent some civility to oppose to this, she wound up with: "But we're all good, you know!"

"He's a genius—you'll love him!" were words that recurred to Pemberton before the Friday, suggesting, among other things that geniuses were not invariably lovable. However, it was all the better if there was an element that would make tutorship absorbing: he had perhaps taken too much for granted that it would be dreary. As he left the villa after his interview, he looked up at the balcony and saw the child leaning over it. "We shall have great larks!" he called up.

Morgan hesitated a moment: then he answered, laughing: "By the time you come back I shall have thought of something witty!"

This made Pemberton say to himself: "After all he's rather nice."

II

On the Friday he saw them all, as Mrs. Moreen had promised, for her husband had come back and the girls and the other son were at home. Mr. Moreen had a white moustache, a confiding manner and, in his buttonhole, the ribbon of a foreign order—bestowed, as Pemberton eventually learned, for services. For what services he never clearly ascertained: this was a point—one of a large number—that Mr. Moreen's manner never confided. What it emphatically did confide was that he was a man of the world. Ulick, the firstborn, was in visible training for the same profession—under the disadvantage as yet, however, of a buttonhole only feebly floral and a moustache with no pretensions to type. The girls had hair and figures and manners and small fat feet, but had never been out alone. As for Mrs. Moreen, Pemberton saw on a nearer view that her elegance was intermittent and her parts didn't always match. Her husband, as she had promised, met with enthusiasm Pemberton's ideas in regard to a salary. The young man had endeavoured to make them modest, and Mr. Moreen confided to him that *he* found them positively meagre. He further assured him that he aspired to be intimate with his children, to be their best friend, and that he was always looking out for them. That was what he went off for, to London and other places—to look out; and this vigilance was the theory of life, as well as the real occupation, of the whole family. They all looked out, for they were very frank on the subject of its being necessary. They desired it to be understood that they were earnest people, and also that their fortune, though quite adequate for earnest people, required the most careful administration. Mr. Moreen, as the parent bird, sought sustenance for the nest. Ulick found sustenance mainly at the club, where Pemberton guessed that it was usually served on green cloth. The girls used to do up their hair and their frocks themselves, and our young man felt appealed to to be glad, in regard to Morgan's education, that, though it must naturally be of the best, it didn't cost too much. After a little he *was* glad, forgetting at times his own needs in the interest inspired by the child's nature and education and the pleasure of making easy terms for him.

During the first weeks of their acquaintance Morgan had been as puzzling as a page in an unknown language—altogether different from the obvious little Anglo-Saxons who had misrepresented childhood to Pemberton. Indeed the whole mystic volume in which the boy had been bound demanded some practice in translation. Today, after a considerable interval, there is something phantasmagoric, like a prismatic reflection or a serial novel, in Pemberton's memory of the queerness of the Moreens. If it were not for a few tangible tokens—a lock of Morgan's hair, cut by his own hand, and the half-dozen letters he got from him when they were separated—the whole episode and the figures peopling it would seem too inconsequent for anything but dreamland. The queerest thing about them was their success (as it appeared to him for a while at the time), for he had never seen a family so brilliantly equipped for failure. Wasn't it success to have kept him so hatefully long? Wasn't it success to have drawn him in that first morning at *déjeuner,* the Friday he came—it was enough to *make* one superstitious—so that he utterly committed himself, and this not by calculation or a *mot d'ordre,* but by a happy instinct which made them, like a band of gipsies, work so neatly together? They amused him as much as if they had really been a band of gipsies. He was still young and had not seen much of the world—his English years had been intensely usual; therefore the reversed conventions of the Moreens (for they had their standards), struck him as topsyturvy. He had encountered nothing like them at Oxford; still less had any such note been struck to his younger American ear during the four years at Yale in which he had richly supposed himself to be reacting against Puritanism. The reaction of the Moreens, at any rate, went ever so much further. He had thought himself very clever that first day in hitting them all off in his mind with the term "cosmopolite." Later, it seemed feeble and colourless enough—confessedly, helplessly provisional.

However, when he first applied it to them he had a degree of joy—for an instructor he was still empirical—as if from the apprehension that to live with them would really be to see life. Their sociable strangeness was an intimation of that— their chatter of tongues, their gaiety and good humour, their infinite dawdling (they were always getting themselves up, but it took forever, and Pemberton had once found Mr. Moreen shaving in the drawing-room), their French, their Italian and, in the spiced fluency, their cold, tough slices of American. They lived on macaroni and coffee (they had these articles prepared in perfection), but they knew recipes for a hundred other dishes. They overflowed with music and song, were always humming and catching each other up, and had a kind of professional acquaintance with continental cities. They talked of "good places" as if they had been strolling players. They had at Nice a villa, a carriage, a piano and a banjo, and they went to official parties. They were a perfect calendar of the "days" of their friends, which Pemberton knew them, when they were indisposed, to get out of bed to go to, and which made the week larger than life when Mrs. Moreen talked of them with Paula and Amy. Their romantic initiations gave their new inmate at first an almost dazzling sense of culture. Mrs. Moreen had translated something, at some former period— an author whom it made Pemberton feel *borné* never to have heard of. They could imitate Venetian and sing Neapolitan, and when they wanted to say something very particular they communicated with each other in an ingenious dialect of their own —a sort of spoken cipher, which Pemberton at first took for Volapuk, but which he learned to understand as he would not have understood Volapuk.

"It's the family language—Ultramoreen," Morgan explained to him drolly enough; but the boy rarely condescended to use it himself, though he attempted colloquial Latin as if he had been a little prelate.

Among all the "days" with which Mrs. Moreen's memory was taxed she managed to squeeze in one of her own, which her friends sometimes forgot. But the house derived a frequented air from the number of fine people who were freely named there and from several mysterious men with foreign titles and English clothes whom Morgan called the princes and who, on sofas with the girls, talked French very loud, as if to show they were saying nothing improper. Pemberton wondered how the princes could ever propose in that tone and so publicly: he took for granted cynically that this was what was desired of them. Then he acknowledged that even for the chance of such an advantage Mrs. Moreen would never allow Paula and Amy to receive alone. These young ladies were not at all timid, but it was just the safeguards that made them so graceful. It was a houseful of Bohemians who wanted tremendously to be Philistines.

In one respect, however, certainly, they achieved no rigour—they were wonderfully amiable and ecstatic about Morgan. It was a genuine tenderness, an artless admiration, equally strong in each. They even praised his beauty, which was small, and were rather afraid of him, as if they recognised that he was of a finer clay. They called him a little angel and a little prodigy and pitied his want of health effusively. Pemberton feared at first that their extravagance would make him hate the boy, but before this happened he had become extravagant himself. Later, when he had grown rather to hate the others, it was a bribe to patience for him that they were at any rate nice about Morgan, going on tiptoe if they fancied he was showing symptoms, and even giving up somebody's "day" to procure him a pleasure. But mixed with this was the oddest wish to make him independent, as if they felt that they were not good enough for him. They passed him over to Pemberton very much as if they wished to force a constructive adoption on the obliging bachelor and shirk altogether a responsibility. They were delighted when they perceived that Morgan liked his preceptor, and could think of no higher praise for the young man. It was strange how they contrived to reconcile the appearance, and indeed the essential fact, of adoring the child with their eagerness to wash their hands of him. Did they want to get rid of him before he should find them out? Pemberton was finding them out month by month. At any rate, the boy's relations turned their backs with exaggerated delicacy, as if to escape the charge of interfering. Seeing in time how little he had in common with them (it was by *them* he first observed it—they proclaimed it with complete humility), his preceptor was moved to speculate on the mysteries of transmission, the far jumps of heredity. Where his detachment from most of the things they represented had come from was more than an observer could say—it certainly had burrowed under two or three generations.

As for Pemberton's own estimate of his pupil, it was a good while before he got the point of view, so little had he been prepared for it by the smug young barbarians to whom the tradition of tutorship, as hitherto revealed to him, had been adjusted. Morgan was scrappy and surprising, deficient in many properties supposed common to the *genus* and abounding in others that were the portion only of the supernaturally clever. One day Pemberton made a great stride: it cleared up the question to perceive that Morgan *was* supernaturally clever and that, though the formula was temporarily meagre, this would be the only assumption on which one could successfully deal with him. He had the general quality of a child for whom life had not been simplified by school, a kind of homebred sensibility which might have been bad for himself but was charming for others, and a whole range of refinement and perception—little musical vibrations as taking as picked-up airs—begotten by wandering about Europe at the tail of his migratory tribe. This might not have been an education to recommend in advance, but its results with Morgan were as palpable as a fine texture. At the same time he had in his composition a sharp spice of stoicism, doubtless the fruit of having had to begin early to bear pain, which produced the impression of pluck and made it of less consequence that he might have been thought at school rather a polyglot little beast. Pemberton indeed quickly found himself rejoicing that school was out of the question: in any million of boys it was probably good for all but one, and Morgan was that millionth. It would have made him comparative and superior —it might have made him priggish. Pemberton would try to be school himself—a bigger seminary than five hundred grazing donkeys; so that, winning no prizes, the boy would remain unconscious and irresponsible and amusing—amusing, because, though life was already intense in his childish nature, freshness still made there a strong draught for jokes. It turned out that even in the still air of Morgan's various disabilities jokes flourished greatly. He was a pale, lean, acute, undeveloped little cosmopolite, who liked intellectual gymnastics and who, also, as regards the behaviour of mankind, had noticed more things than you might suppose, but who nevertheless had his proper playroom of superstitions, where he smashed a dozen toys a day.

III

At Nice once, towards evening, as the pair sat resting in the open air after a walk, looking over the sea at the pink western lights, Morgan said suddenly to his companion: "Do you like it—you know, being with us all in this intimate way?"

"My dear fellow, why should I stay if I didn't?"

"How do I know you will stay? I'm almost sure you won't, very long."

"I hope you don't mean to dismiss me," said Pemberton.

Morgan considered a moment, looking at the sunset. "I think if I did right I ought to."

"Well, I know I'm supposed to instruct you in virtue; but in that case don't do right."

"You're very young—fortunately," Morgan went on, turning to him again.

"Oh yes, compared with you!"

"Therefore, it won't matter so much if you do lose a lot of time."

"That's the way to look at it," said Pemberton accommodatingly.

They were silent a minute; after which the boy asked: "Do you like my father and mother very much?"

"Dear me, yes. They're charming people."

Morgan received this with another silence; then, unexpectedly, familiarly, but at the same time affectionately, he remarked: "You're a jolly old humbug!"

For a particular reason the words made Pemberton change colour. The boy noticed in an instant that he had turned red, whereupon he turned red himself and the pupil and the master exchanged a longish glance in which there was a consciousness of many more things than are usually touched upon, even tacitly, in such a relation. It produced for Pemberton an embarrassment; it raised, in a shadowy form, a question (this was the first glimpse of it), which was destined to play as singular and, as he imagined, owing to the altogether peculiar conditions, an unprecedented part in his intercourse with his little companion. Later, when he found himself talking with this small boy in a way in which few small boys could ever have been talked with, he thought of that clumsy moment on the bench at Nice as the dawn of an understanding that had broadened. What had added to the clumsiness then was that he thought it his duty to declare to Morgan that he might abuse him (Pemberton) as much as he liked, but must never abuse his parents. To this Morgan had the easy reply that he hadn't dreamed of abusing them; which appeared to be true; it put Pemberton in the wrong.

"Then why am I a humbug for saying *I* think them charming?" the young man asked, conscious of a certain rashness.

"Well—they're not *your* parents."

"They love you better than anything in the world—never forget that," said Pemberton.

"Is that why you like them so much?"

"They're very kind to me," Pemberton replied, evasively.

"You *are* a humbug!" laughed Morgan, passing an arm into his tutor's. He leaned against him, looking off at the sea again and swinging his long, thin legs.

"Don't kick my shins," said Pemberton, while he reflected: "Hang it, I can't complain of them to the child!"

"There's another reason, too," Morgan went on, keeping his legs still.

"Another reason for what?"

"Besides their not being your parents."

"I don't understand you," said Pemberton.

"Well, you will before long. All right!"

Pemberton did understand, fully, before long; but he made a fight even with himself before he confessed it. He thought it the oddest thing to have a struggle with the child about. He wondered he didn't detest the child for launching him in such a struggle. But by the time it began the resource of detesting the child was closed to him. Morgan was a special case, but to know him was to accept him on his own odd terms. Pemberton had spent his aversion to special cases before arriving at knowledge. When at last he did arrive he felt that he was in an extreme predicament. Against every interest he had attached himself. They would have to meet things together. Before they went home that evening, at Nice, the boy had said, clinging to his arm:

"Well, at any rate you'll hang on to the last."

"To the last?"

"Till you're fairly beaten."

"*You* ought to be fairly beaten!" cried the young man, drawing him closer.

IV

A year after Pemberton had come to live with them Mr. and Mrs. Moreen suddenly gave up the villa at Nice. Pemberton had got used to suddenness, having seen it practiced on a considerable scale during two jerky little tours—one in Switzerland the first summer, and the other late in the winter, when they all ran down to Florence and then, at the end of ten days, liking it much less than they had intended, straggled back in mysterious depression. They had returned to Nice "for ever," as they said; but this didn't prevent them from squeezing, one rainy, muggy May night, into a second-class railway-carriage—you could never tell by which class they would travel—where Pemberton helped them to stow away a wonderful collection of bundles and bags. The explanation of this manœuvre was that they had determined to spend the summer "in some bracing place;" but in Paris they dropped into a small furnished apartment—a fourth floor in a third-rate avenue, where there was a smell on the staircase and the *portier* was hateful—and passed the next four months in blank indigence.

The better part of this baffled sojourn was for the preceptor and his pupil, who, visiting the Invalides and Notre Dame, the Conciergerie and all the museums, took a hundred remunerative rambles. They learned to know their Paris, which was useful, for they came back another year for a longer stay, the general character of which in Pemberton's memory to-day mixes pitiably and confusedly with that of the first. He sees Morgan's shabby knickerbockers—the everlasting pair that didn't match his blouse and that as he grew longer could only grow faded. He remembers the particular holes in his three or four pair of coloured stockings.

Morgan was dear to his mother, but he never was better dressed than was absolutely necessary—partly, no doubt, by his own fault, for he was as indifferent to his appearance as a German philosopher. "My dear fellow, you *are* coming to pieces," Pemberton would say to him in sceptical remonstrance; to which the child would reply, looking at him serenely up and down: "My dear fellow, so are you! I don't want to cast you in the shade." Pemberton could have no rejoinder for this—the assertion so closely represented the fact. If however the deficiencies of his own wardrobe were a chapter by themselves he didn't like his little charge to look too poor. Later he used to say: "Well, if we are poor, why, after all, shouldn't we look it?" and he consoled himself with thinking there was something rather elderly and gentlemanly in Morgan's seediness—it differed from the untidiness of the urchin who plays and spoils his things. He could trace perfectly the degrees by which, in proportion as her little son confined himself to his tutor for society, Mrs. Moreen shrewdly forbore to renew his garments. She did nothing that didn't show, neglected him because he escaped notice, and then, as he illustrated this clever policy, discouraged at home his public appearances. Her position was logical enough—those members of her family who did show had to be showy.

During this period and several others Pemberton was quite aware of how he and his comrade might strike people; wandering languidly through the Jardin des Plantes as if they had nowhere to go, sitting, on the winter days, in the galleries of the Louvre, so splendidly ironical to the homeless, as if for the advantage of the *calorifère*.[1] They joked about it sometimes: it was the sort of joke that was perfectly within the boy's compass. They figured themselves as part of the vast, vague, hand-to-mouth multitude of the enormous city and pretended they were proud of their position in it—it showed them such a lot of life and made them conscious of a sort of democratic brotherhood. If Pemberton could not feel a sympathy in destitution with his small companion (for after all Morgan's fond parents would never have let him really suffer), the boy would at least feel it with him, so it came to the same thing. He used sometimes to wonder what people would think they were—fancy they were looked askance at, as if it might be a suspected case of kidnapping. Morgan wouldn't be taken for a young patrician with a preceptor—he wasn't smart enough; though he might pass for his companion's sickly little brother. Now and then he had a five-franc piece, and except once, when they bought a couple of lovely neckties, one of which he made Pemberton accept, they laid it out scientifically in old books. It was a great day, always spent on the quays, rummaging among the dusty boxes that garnish the parapets. These were occasions that helped them to live, for their books ran low very soon after the beginning of their acquaintance. Pemberton had a good many in England, but he was obliged to

[1] heating

write to a friend and ask him kindly to get some fellow to give him something for them.

If the bracing climate was untasted that summer the young man had an idea that at the moment they were about to make a push the cup had been dashed from their lips by a movement of his own. It had been his first blow-out, as he called it, with his patrons; his first successful attempt (though there was little other success about it), to bring them to a consideration of his impossible position. As the ostensible eve of a costly journey the moment struck him as a good one to put in a signal protest—to present an ultimatum. Ridiculous as it sounded he had never yet been able to compass an uninterrupted private interview with the elder pair or with either of them singly. They were always flanked by their elder children, and poor Pemberton usually had his own little charge at his side. He was conscious of its being a house in which the surface of one's delicacy got rather smudged; nevertheless he had kept the bloom of his scruple against announcing to Mr. and Mrs. Moreen with publicity that he couldn't go on longer without a little money. He was still simple enough to suppose Ulick and Paula and Amy might not know that since his arrival he had only had a hundred and forty francs; and he was magnanimous enough to wish not to compromise their parents in their eyes. Mr. Moreen now listened to him, as he listened to every one and to everything, like a man of the world, and seemed to appeal to him— though not of course too grossly—to try and be a little more of one himself. Pemberton recognized the importance of the character from the advantage it gave Mr. Moreen. He was not even confused, whereas poor Pemberton was more so than there was any reason for. Neither was he surprised—at least any more than a gentleman had to be who freely confessed himself a little shocked, though not, strictly, at Pemberton.

"We must go into this, mustn't we, dear?" he said to his wife. He assured his young friend that the matter should have his very best attention; and he melted into space as elusively as if, at the door, he were taking an inevitable but deprecatory precedence. When, the next moment, Pemberton found himself alone with Mrs. Moreen it was to hear her say: "I see, I see," stroking the roundness of her chin and looking as if she were only hesitating between a dozen easy remedies. If they didn't make their push Mr. Moreen could at least disappear for several days. During his absence his wife took up the subject again spontaneously, but her contribution to it was merely that she had thought all the while they were getting on so beautifully. Pemberton's reply to this revelation was that unless they immediately handed him a substantial sum he would leave them for ever. He knew she would wonder how he would get away, and for a moment expected her to inquire. She didn't, for which he was almost grateful to her, so little was he in a position to tell.

"You won't, you know you won't— you're too interested," she said. "You *are* interested, you know you are, you dear, kind man!" She laughed, with almost condemnatory archness, as if it were a reproach (but she wouldn't insist), while she flirted a soiled pocket-handkerchief at him.

Pemberton's mind was fully made up to quit the house the following week. This would give him time to get an answer to a letter he had despatched to England. If he did nothing of the sort— that is, if he stayed another year and then went away only for three months— it was not merely because before the answer to his letter came (most unsatisfactory when it did arrive), Mr. Moreen generously presented him—again with all the precautions of a man of the world—three hundred francs. He was exasperated to find that Mrs. Moreen was right, that he couldn't bear to leave the child. This stood out clearer for the very reason that, the night of his desperate appeal to his patrons, he had seen fully for the first time where he was. Wasn't it another proof of the success with which those patrons practiced their arts that they had managed to avert for so long the illuminating flash? It descended upon Pemberton with a luridness which perhaps would have struck a spectator as comically excessive, after he had returned to his little servile room, which looked into a close court where a bare, dirty opposite wall took, with the sound of shrill clatter, the reflection of lighted back-windows. He had simply given himself away to a band of adventurers. The idea, the word itself, had a sort of romantic horror for him—he had always lived on such safe lines. Later it assumed a more interesting, almost a soothing, sense: it pointed a moral, and Pemberton could enjoy a moral. The Moreens were adventurers not merely because they didn't pay their debts, because they lived on society, but because their whole view of life, dim and confused and instinctive, like that of clever colour-blind animals, was speculative and rapacious and mean. Oh! they were "respectable," and that only made them more *immondes*. The young man's analysis of them put it at last very simply—they were adventurers because they were abject snobs. That was the completest account of them —it was the law of their being. Even when this truth became vivid to their ingenious inmate he remained unconscious of how much his mind had been prepared for it by the extraordinary little boy who had now become such a complication in his life. Much less could he then calculate on the information he was still to owe to the extraordinary little boy.

V

But it was during the ensuing time that the real problem came up—the problem of how far it was excusable to discuss the turpitude of parents with a child of twelve, of thirteen, of fourteen. Absolutely inexcusable and quite impossible it of course at first appeared; and indeed the question didn't press for a while after Pemberton had received his three hundred francs. They produced a sort of lull, a relief from the sharpest pressure. Pemberton frugally amended his wardrobe and even had a few francs in his pocket. He thought the Moreens looked at him as if he were almost too smart, as if they ought to take care not to spoil him. If Mr. Moreen hadn't been such a man of the world he would perhaps have said something to him about his neckties. But Mr. Moreen was always enough a man of the world to let things pass—he had certainly shown that. It was singular how Pemberton guessed that Morgan, though saying nothing about it, knew something had happened. But three hundred francs, especially when one owed money, couldn't last for ever; and when they were gone— the boy knew when they were gone— Morgan did say something. The party had returned to Nice at the beginning of the winter, but not to the charming villa. They went to an hotel, where they stayed three months, and then they went to another hotel, explaining that they had left the first because they had waited and waited and couldn't get the rooms they wanted. These apartments, the rooms they wanted, were generally very splendid; but fortunately they never *could* get them— fortunately, I mean, for Pemberton, who reflected always that if they had got them there would have been still less for educational expenses. What Morgan said at last was said suddenly, irrelevantly, when the moment came, in the middle of a lesson, and consisted of the apparently unfeeling words: "You ought to *filer,* you know—you really ought."

Pemberton stared. He had learnt enough French slang from Morgan to know that to *filer* meant to go away. "Ah, my dear fellow, don't turn me off!"

Morgan pulled a Greek lexicon toward him (he used a Greek-German), to look out a word, instead of asking it of Pemberton. "You can't go on like this, you know."

"Like what, my boy?"

"You know they don't pay you up," said Morgan, blushing and turning his leaves.

"Don't pay me?" Pemberton stared again and feigned amazement. "What on earth put that into your head?"

"It has been there a long time," the boy replied, continuing his search.

Pemberton was silent, then he went on: "I say, what are you hunting for? They pay me beautifully."

"I'm hunting for the Greek for transparent fiction," Morgan dropped.

"Find that rather for gross impertinence, and disabuse your mind. What do I want of money?"

"Oh, that's another question!"

Pemberton hesitated—he was drawn in different ways. The severely correct thing would have been to tell the boy that such a matter was none of his business and bid him go on with his lines. But they were really too intimate for that; it was not the way he was in the habit of treating him; there had been no reason it should be. On the other hand Morgan had quite lighted on the truth—he really shouldn't be able to keep it up much longer; therefore why not let him know one's real motive for forsaking him? At the same time it wasn't decent to abuse to one's pupil the family of one's pupil; it was better to misrepresent than to do that. So in reply to Morgan's last exclamation he just declared, to dismiss the subject, that he had received several payments.

"I say—I say!" the boy ejaculated, laughing.

"That's all right," Pemberton insisted. "Give me your written rendering."

Morgan pushed a copybook across the table, and his companion began to read the page, but with something running in his head that made it no sense. Looking up after a minute or two he found the child's eyes fixed on him, and he saw something strange in them. Then Morgan said: "I'm not afraid of the reality."

"I haven't yet seen the thing you *are* afraid of—I'll do you that justice!"

This came out with a jump (it was perfectly true), and evidently gave Morgan pleasure. "I've thought of it a long time," he presently resumed.

"Well, don't think of it any more."

The child appeared to comply, and they had a comfortable and even an amusing hour. They had a theory that they were very thorough, and yet they seemed always to be in the amusing part of lessons, the intervals between the tunnels, where there were waysides and views. Yet the morning was brought to a violent end by Morgan's suddenly leaning his arms on the table, burying his head in them and bursting into tears. Pemberton would have been startled at any rate; but he was doubly startled because, as it then occurred to him, it was the first time he had ever seen the boy cry. It was rather awful.

The next day, after much thought, he took a decision and, believing it to be just, immediately acted upon it. He cornered Mr. and Mrs. Moreen again and informed them that if, on the spot, they didn't pay him all they owed him, he would not only leave their house, but would tell Morgan exactly what had brought him to it.

"Oh, you *haven't* told him?" cried Mrs.

Moreen, with a pacifying hand on her well-dressed bosom.

"Without warning you? For what do you take me?"

Mr. and Mrs. Moreen looked at each other, and Pemberton could see both that they were relieved and that there was a certain alarm in their relief. "My dear fellow," Mr. Moreen demanded, "what use *can* you have, leading the quiet life we all do, for such a lot of money?" —an inquiry to which Pemberton made no answer, occupied as he was in perceiving that what passed in the mind of his patrons was something like: "Oh, then, if we've felt that the child, dear little angel, has judged us and how he regards us, and we haven't been betrayed, he must have guessed—and, in short, it's *general!*" an idea that rather stirred up Mr. and Mrs. Moreen, as Pemberton had desired that it should. At the same time, if he had thought that his threat would do something towards bringing them round, he was disappointed to find they had taken for granted (how little they appreciated his delicacy!) that he had already given them away to his pupil. There was a mystic uneasiness in their parental breasts, and that was the way they had accounted for it. None the less his threat did touch them; for if they had escaped it was only to meet a new danger. Mr. Moreen appealed to Pemberton, as usual, as a man of the world; but his wife had recourse, for the first time since the arrival of their inmate, to a fine *hauteur,* reminding him that a devoted mother, with her child, had arts that protected her against gross misrepresentation.

"I should misrepresent you grossly if I accused you of common honesty!" the young man replied; but as he closed the door behind him sharply, thinking he had not done himself much good, while Mr. Moreen lighted another cigarette, he heard Mrs. Moreen shout after him, more touchingly:

"Oh, you do, you *do,* put the knife to one's throat!"

The next morning, very early, she came to his room. He recognised her knock, but he had no hope that she brought him money; as to which he was wrong, for she had fifty francs in her hand. She squeezed forward in her dressing-gown, and he received her in his own, between his bath-tub and his bed. He had been tolerably schooled by this time to the "foreign ways" of his hosts. Mrs. Moreen was zealous, and when she was zealous she didn't care what she did; so she now sat down on his bed, his clothes being on the chairs, and, in her preoccupation, forgot, as she glanced round, to be ashamed of giving him such a nasty room. What Mrs. Moreen was zealous about on this occasion was to persuade him that in the first place she was very good-natured to bring him fifty francs, and, in the second, if he would only see it, he was really too absurd to expect to be *paid*. Wasn't he paid enough, without perpetual money—wasn't he paid by the comfortable, luxurious home that he enjoyed with them all, without a care, an anxiety, a solitary want? Wasn't he sure of his position, and wasn't that everything to a young man like him, quite unknown, with singularly little to show, the ground of whose exorbitant pretensions it was not easy to discover? Wasn't he paid, above all, by the delightful relation he had established with Morgan—quite ideal, as from master to pupil—and by the simple privilege of knowing and living with so amazingly gifted a child, than whom really—she meant literally what she said —there was no better company in Europe? Mrs. Moreen herself took to appealing to him as a man of the world; she said "Voyons, mon cher," and "My dear sir, look here now;" and urged him to be reasonable, putting it before him that it was really a chance for him. She spoke as if, according as he *should* be reasonable, he would prove himself worthy to be her son's tutor and of the extraordinary confidence they had placed in him.

After all, Pemberton reflected, it was only a difference of theory, and the theory didn't matter much. They had hitherto gone on that of remunerated, as now they would go on that of gratuitous, service; but why should they have so many words about it? Mrs. Moreen, however, continued to be convincing; sitting there with her fifty francs she talked and repeated, as women repeat, and bored and irritated him, while he leaned against the wall with his hands in the pockets of his wrapper, drawing it together round his legs and looking over the head of his visitor at the grey negations of his window. She wound up with saying: "You see I bring you a definite proposal."

"A definite proposal?"

"To make our relations regular, as it were—to put them on a comfortable footing."

"I see—it's a system," said Pemberton. "A kind of blackmail."

Mrs. Moreen bounded up, which was what the young man wanted.

"What do you mean by that?"

"You practice on one's fears—one's fears about the child if one should go away."

"And, pray, what would happen to him in that event?" demanded Mrs. Moreen, with majesty.

"Why, he'd be alone with *you*."

"And, pray, with whom *should* a child be but with those whom he loves most?"

"If you think that, why don't you dismiss me?"

"Do you pretend that he loves you more than he loves *us*?" cried Mrs. Moreen.

"I think he ought to. I make sacrifices for him. Though I've heard of those *you* make, I don't see them."

Mrs. Moreen stared a moment; then, with emotion, she grasped Pemberton's hand. "*Will* you make it—the sacrifice?"

Pemberton burst out laughing. "I'll see —I'll do what I can—I'll stay a little longer. Your calculation is just—I *do* hate intensely to give him up; I'm fond of him and he interests me deeply, in spite of the inconvenience I suffer. You know my situation perfectly; I haven't a penny in the world, and, occupied as I am with Morgan, I'm unable to earn money."

Mrs. Moreen tapped her undressed arm with her folded banknote. "Can't you write articles? Can't you translate, as *I* do?"

"I don't know about translating; it's wretchedly paid."

"I am glad to earn what I can," said Mrs. Moreen virtuously, with her head high.

"You ought to tell me who you do it for." Pemberton paused a moment, and she said nothing; so he added: "I've tried to turn off some little sketches, but the magazines won't have them—they're declined with thanks."

"You see then you're not such a phœnix —to have such pretensions," smiled his interlocutress.

"I haven't time to do things properly," Pemberton went on. Then as it came over him that he was almost abjectly good-natured to give these explanations he added: "If I stay on longer it must be on one condition—that Morgan shall know distinctly on what footing I am."

Mrs. Moreen hesitated. "Surely you don't want to show off to a child?"

"To show *you* off, do you mean?"

Again Mrs. Moreen hesitated, but this time it was to produce a still finer flower. "And *you* talk of blackmail!"

"You can easily prevent it," said Pemberton.

"And *you* talk of practicing on fears," Mrs. Moreen continued.

"Yes, there's no doubt I'm a great scoundrel."

His visitor looked at him a moment—

it was evident that she was sorely bothered. Then she thrust out her money at him. "Mr. Moreen desired me to give you this on account."

"I'm much obliged to Mr. Moreen; but we have no account."

"You won't take it?"

"That leaves me more free," said Pemberton.

"To poison my darling's mind?" groaned Mrs. Moreen.

"Oh, your darling's mind!" laughed the young man.

She fixed him a moment, and he thought she was going to break out tormentedly, pleadingly: "For God's sake, tell me what *is* in it!" But she checked this impulse—another was stronger. She pocketed the money—the crudity of the alternative was comical—and swept out of the room with the desperate concession: "You may tell him any horror you like!"

VI

A couple of days after this, during which Pemberton had delayed to profit by Mrs. Moreen's permission to tell her son any horror, the two had been for a quarter of an hour walking together in silence when the boy became sociable again with the remark: "I'll tell you how I know it; I know it through Zénobie."

"Zénobie? Who in the world is *she?*"

"A nurse I used to have—ever so many years ago. A charming woman. I liked her awfully, and she liked me."

"There's no accounting for tastes. What is it you know through her?"

"Why, what their idea is. She went away because they didn't pay her. She did like me awfully, and she stayed two years. She told me all about it—that at last she could never get her wages. As soon as they saw how much she liked me they stopped giving her anything. They thought she'd stay for nothing, out of devotion. And she did stay ever so long— as long as she could. She was only a poor girl. She used to send money to her mother. At last she couldn't afford it any longer, and she went away in a fearful rage one night—I mean of course in a rage against *them*. She cried over me tremendously, she hugged me nearly to death. She told me all about it," Morgan repeated. "She told me it was their idea. So I guessed, ever so long ago, that they had the same idea with you."

"Zénobie was very shrewd," said Pemberton. "And she made you so."

"Oh, that wasn't Zénobie; that was nature. And experience!" Morgan laughed.

"Well, Zénobie was a part of your experience."

"Certainly I was a part of hers, poor dear!" the boy exclaimed. "And I'm a part of yours."

"A very important part. But I don't see how you know that I've been treated like Zénobie."

"Do you take me for an idiot?" Morgan asked. "Haven't I been conscious of what we've been through together?"

"What we've been through?"

"Our privations—our dark days."

"Oh, our days have been bright enough."

Morgan went on in silence for a moment. Then he said: "My dear fellow, you're a hero!"

"Well, you're another!" Pemberton retorted.

"No, I'm not; but I'm not a baby. I won't stand it any longer. You must get some occupation that pays. I'm ashamed, I'm ashamed!" quavered the boy in a little passionate voice that was very touching to Pemberton.

"We ought to go off and live somewhere together," said the young man.

"I'll go like a shot if you'll take me."

"I'd get some work that would keep us both afloat," Pemberton continued.

"So would I. Why shouldn't *I* work? I ain't such a *crétin!*"

"The difficulty is that your parents

wouldn't hear of it," said Pemberton. "They would never part with you; they worship the ground you tread on. Don't you see the proof of it? They don't dislike me; they wish me no harm; they're very amiable people; but they're perfectly ready to treat me badly for your sake."

The silence in which Morgan received this graceful sophistry struck Pemberton somehow as expressive. After a moment Morgan repeated: "You *are* a hero!" Then he added: "They leave me with you altogether. You've all the responsibility. They put me off on you from morning till night. Why, then, should they object to my taking up with you completely? I'd help you."

"They're not particularly keen about my being helped, and they delight in thinking of you as *theirs*. They're tremendously proud of you."

"I'm not proud of them. But you know *that*," Morgan returned.

"Except for the little matter we speak of they're charming people," said Pemberton, not taking up the imputation of lucidity, but wondering greatly at the child's own, and especially at this fresh reminder of something he had been conscious of from the first—the strangest thing in the boy's large little composition, a temper, a sensibility, even a sort of ideal, which made him privately resent the general quality of his kinsfolk. Morgan had in secret a small loftiness which begot an element of reflection, a domestic scorn not imperceptible to his companion (though they never had any talk about it), and absolutely anomalous in a juvenile nature, especially when one noted that it had not made this nature "old-fashioned," as the word is of children—quaint or wizened or offensive. It was as if he had been a little gentleman and had paid the penalty by discovering that he was the only such person in the family. This comparison didn't make him vain; but it could make him melancholy and a trifle austere. When Pemberton guessed at these young dimnesses he saw him serious and gallant, and was partly drawn on and partly checked, as if with a scruple, by the charm of attempting to sound the little cool shallows which were quickly growing deeper. When he tried to figure to himself the morning twilight of childhood, so as to deal with it safely, he perceived that it was never fixed, never arrested, that ignorance, at the instant one touched it, was already flushing faintly into knowledge, that there was nothing that at a given moment you could say a clever child didn't know. It seemed to him that *he* both knew too much to imagine Morgan's simplicity and too little to disembroil his tangle.

The boy paid no heed to his last remark; he only went on: "I should have spoken to them about their idea, as I call it, long ago, if I hadn't been sure what they would say."

"And what would they say?"

"Just what they said about what poor Zénobie told me—that it was a horrid, dreadful story, that they paid her every penny they owed her."

"Well, perhaps they had," said Pemberton.

"Perhaps they've paid you!"

"Let us pretend they have and *n'en parlons plus*."[2]

"They accused her of lying and cheating," Morgan insisted perversely. "That's why I don't want to speak to them."

"Lest they should accuse me, too?"

To this Morgan made no answer, and his companion, looking down at him (the boy turned his eyes, which had filled, away), saw that he couldn't have trusted himself to utter.

"You're right. Don't squeeze them," Pemberton pursued. "Except for that, they *are* charming people."

"Except for *their* lying and *their* cheating?"

"I say—I say!" cried Pemberton, imi-

[2] say no more about it

tating a little tone of the lad's which was itself an imitation.

"We must be frank, at the last; we *must* come to an understanding," said Morgan, with the importance of the small boy who lets himself think he is arranging great affairs—almost playing at shipwreck or at Indians. "I know all about everything," he added.

"I daresay your father has his reasons," Pemberton observed, too vaguely, as he was aware.

"For lying and cheating?"

"For saving and managing and turning his means to the best account. He has plenty to do with his money. You're an expensive family."

"Yes, I'm very expensive," Morgan rejoined, in a manner which made his preceptor burst out laughing.

"He's saving for *you*," said Pemberton. "They think of you in everything they do."

"He might save a little——" The boy paused. Pemberton waited to hear what. Then Morgan brought out oddly: "A little reputation."

"Oh, there's plenty of that. That's all right!"

"Enough of it for the people they know, no doubt. The people they know are awful."

"Do you mean the princes? We mustn't abuse the princes."

"Why not? They haven't married Paula—they haven't married Amy. They only clean out Ulick."

"You *do* know everything!" Pemberton exclaimed.

"No, I don't, after all. I don't know what they live on, or how they live, or *why* they live! What have they got and how did they get it? Are they rich, are they poor, or have they a *modeste aisance?*[3] Why are they always chiveying about—living one year like ambassadors and the next like paupers? Who are they, any way, and what are they? I've thought

of all that—I've thought of a lot of things. They're so beastly worldly. That's what I hate most—oh, I've *seen* it! All they care about is to make an appearance and to pass for something or other. What do they want to pass for? What *do* they, Mr. Pemberton?"

"You pause for a reply," said Pemberton, treating the inquiry as a joke, yet wondering too, and greatly struck with the boy's intense, if imperfect, vision. "I haven't the least idea."

"And what good does it do? Haven't I seen the way people treat them—the 'nice' people, the ones they want to know? They'll take anything from them —they'll lie down and be trampled on. The nice ones hate that—they just sicken them. You're the only really nice person we know."

"Are you sure? They don't lie down for me!"

"Well, you shan't lie down for them. You've got to go—that's what you've got to do," said Morgan.

"And what will become of you?"

"Oh, I'm growing up. I shall get off before long. I'll see you later."

"You had better let me finish you," Pemberton urged, lending himself to the child's extraordinarily competent attitude.

Morgan stopped in their walk, looking up at him. He had to look up much less than a couple of years before—he had grown, in his loose leanness, so long and high. "Finish me?" he echoed.

"There are such a lot of jolly things we can do together yet. I want to turn you out—I want you to do me credit."

Morgan continued to look at him. "To give you credit—do you mean?"

"My dear fellow, you're too clever to live."

"That's just what I'm afraid you think. No, no; it isn't fair—I can't endure it. We'll part next week. The sooner it's over the sooner to sleep."

"If I hear anything—any other chance, I promise to go," said Pemberton.

Morgan consented to consider this.

[3] modest competence

"But you'll be honest," he demanded; "you won't pretend you haven't heard?"

"I'm much more likely to pretend I have."

"But what can you hear of, this way, stuck in a hole with us? You ought to be on the spot, to go to England—you ought to go to America."

"One would think you were *my* tutor!" said Pemberton.

Morgan walked on, and after a moment he began again: "Well, now that you know that I know and that we look at the facts and keep nothing back—it's much more comfortable, isn't it?"

"My dear boy, it's so amusing, so interesting, that it surely will be quite impossible for me to forego such hours as these."

This made Morgan stop once more. "You *do* keep something back. Oh, you're not straight—*I* am!"

"Why am I not straight?"

"Oh, you've got your idea!"

"My idea?"

"Why, that I probably sha'n't live, and that you can stick it out till I'm removed."

"You *are* too clever to live!" Pemberton repeated.

"I call it a mean idea," Morgan pursued. "But I shall punish you by the way I hang on."

"Look out or I'll poison you!" Pemberton laughed.

"I'm stronger and better every year. Haven't you noticed that there hasn't been a doctor near me since you came?"

"*I'm* your doctor," said the young man, taking his arm and drawing him on again.

Morgan proceeded, and after a few steps he gave a sigh of mingled weariness and relief. "Ah, now that we look at the facts, it's all right!"

VII

They looked at the facts a good deal after this; and one of the first consequences of their doing so was that Pemberton stuck it out, as it were, for the purpose. Morgan made the facts so vivid and so droll, and at the same time so bald and so ugly, that there was fascination in talking them over with him, just as there would have been heartlessness in leaving him alone with them. Now that they had such a number of perceptions in common it was useless for the pair to pretend that they didn't judge such people; but the very judgment, and the exchange of perceptions, created another tie. Morgan had never been so interesting as now that he himself was made plainer by the sidelight of these confidences. What came out in it most was the soreness of his characteristic pride. He had plenty of that, Pemberton felt—so much that it was perhaps well it should have had to take some early bruises. He would have liked his people to be gallant, and he had waked up too soon to the sense that they were perpetually swallowing humble-pie. His mother would consume any amount, and his father would consume even more than his mother. He had a theory that Ulick had wriggled out of an "affair" at Nice: there had once been a flurry at home, a regular panic, after which they all went to bed and took medicine, not to be accounted for on any other supposition. Morgan had a romantic imagination, fed by poetry and history, and he would have liked those who "bore his name" (as he used to say to Pemberton with the humour that made his sensitiveness manly), to have a proper spirit. But their one idea was to get in with people who didn't want them and to take snubs as if they were honourable scars. Why people didn't want them more he didn't know—that was people's own affair; after all they were not superficially repulsive—they were a hundred times cleverer than most of the dreary grandees, the "poor swells" they rushed about Europe to catch up with. "After all, they *are* amusing—they are!" Morgan used to say, with the wisdom of the ages. To which Pemberton always replied: "Amusing—the great Moreen troupe? Why, they're altogether delightful; and if it were not for the hitch that you and I (feeble performers!) make in the *ensemble,* they would carry everything before them."

What the boy couldn't get over was that this particular blight seemed, in a tradition of self-respect, so undeserved and so arbitrary. No doubt people had a right to take the line they liked; but why should *his* people have liked the line of pushing and toadying and lying and cheating? What had their forefathers— all decent folk, so far as he knew—done to them, or what had *he* done to them? Who had poisoned their blood with the fifth-rate social ideal, the fixed idea of making smart acquaintances and getting into the *monde chic,*[4] especially when it was foredoomed to failure and exposure? They showed so what they were after; that was what made the people they wanted not want *them.* And never a movement of dignity, never a throb of shame at looking each other in the face, never any independence or resentment or disgust. If his father or his brother would only knock some one down once or twice a year! Clever as they were they never guessed how they appeared. They were good-natured, yes—as good-natured as Jews at the doors of clothing-shops! But was that the model one wanted one's family to follow? Morgan had dim memories of an old grandfather, the maternal, in New York, whom he had been taken across the ocean to see, at the age of five: a gentleman with a high neckcloth and a good deal of pronunciation, who wore a dress-coat in the morning, which made one wonder what he wore in the evening, and had, or was supposed to have, "property" and something to do with the Bible Society. It couldn't have been but that *he* was a good type. Pemberton himself remembered Mrs. Clancy, a widowed sister of Mr. Moreen's, who was as irritating as a moral tale and had paid a fortnight's visit to the family at Nice shortly after he came to live with them. She was "pure and refined," as Amy said, over the banjo, and had the air of not knowing what they meant and of keeping something back. Pemberton judged that what she kept back was an approval of many of their ways; therefore it was to be supposed that she too was of a good type, and that Mr. and Mrs. Moreen and Ulick and Paula and Amy might easily have been better if they would.

But that they wouldn't was more and more perceptible from day to day. They continued to "chivey," as Morgan called it, and in due time became aware of a variety of reasons for proceeding to Venice. They mentioned a great many of them—they were always strikingly frank, and had the brightest friendly chatter, at the late foreign breakfast in especial, before the ladies had made up their faces, when they leaned their arms on the table, had something to follow the *demi-tasse,* and, in the heat of familiar discussion as to what they "really ought" to do, fell inevitably into the languages in which they could *tutoyer.*[5] Even Pemberton liked them, then; he could endure even Ulick when he heard him give his little flat voice for the "sweet sea-city." That was what made him have a sneaking kindness for them—that they were so out of the workaday world and kept him so out of it. The summer had waned when, with cries of ecstasy, they all passed out on the balcony that overhung the Grand Canal; the sunsets were splendid—the Dorringtons had arrived. The Dorringtons were the only reason they had not talked of at breakfast; but the reasons that they didn't talk of at breakfast always came out in the end. The Dorringtons, on the other hand, came out very little; or else, when they did, they stayed—as was natural—for hours, during which periods Mrs.

[4] fashionable world

[5] address each other with the familiar pronouns

Moreen and the girls sometimes called at their hotel (to see if they had returned) as many as three times running. The gondola was for the ladies; for in Venice too there were "days," which Mrs. Moreen knew in their order an hour after she arrived. She immediately took one herself, to which the Dorringtons never came, though on a certain occasion when Pemberton and his pupil were together at St. Mark's—where, taking the best walks they had ever had and haunting a hundred churches, they spent a great deal of time—they saw the old lord turn up with Mr. Moreen and Ulick, who showed him the dim basilica as if it belonged to them. Pemberton noted how much less, among its curiosities, Lord Dorrington carried himself as a man of the world; wondering too whether, for such services, his companions took a fee from him. The autumn, at any rate, waned, the Dorringtons departed, and Lord Verschoyle, the eldest son, had proposed neither for Amy nor for Paula.

One sad November day, while the wind roared round the old palace and the rain lashed the lagoon, Pemberton, for exercise and even somewhat for warmth (the Moreens were horribly frugal about fires —it was a cause of suffering to their inmate), walked up and down the big bare *sala* with his pupil. The scagliola floor was cold, the high battered casements shook in the storm, and the stately decay of the place was unrelieved by a particle of furniture. Pemberton's spirits were low, and it came over him that the fortune of the Moreens was now even lower. A blast of desolation, a prophecy of disaster and disgrace, seemed to draw through the comfortless hall. Mr. Moreen and Ulick were in the Piazza, looking out for something, strolling drearily, in mackintoshes, under the arcades; but still, in spite of mackintoshes, unmistakable men of the world. Paula and Amy were in bed—it might have been thought they were staying there to keep warm. Pemberton looked askance at the boy at his side, to see to what extent he was conscious of these portents. But Morgan, luckily for him, was now mainly conscious of growing taller and stronger and indeed of being in his fifteenth year. This fact was intensely interesting to him—it was the basis of a private theory (which, however, he had imparted to his tutor) that in a little while he should stand on his own feet. He considered that the situation would change—that, in short, he should be "finished," grown up, producible in the world of affairs and ready to prove himself of sterling ability. Sharply as he was capable, at times, of questioning his circumstances, there were happy hours when he was as superficial as a child; the proof of which was his fundamental assumption that he should presently go to Oxford, to Pemberton's college, and, aided and abetted by Pemberton, do the most wonderful things. It vexed Pemberton to see how little, in such a project, he took account of ways and means: on other matters he was so sceptical about them. Pemberton tried to imagine the Moreens at Oxford, and fortunately failed; yet unless they were to remove there as a family there would be no *modus vivendi*[6] for Morgan. How could he live without an allowance, and where was the allowance to come from? He (Pemberton) might live on Morgan; but how could Morgan live on him? What was to become of him anyhow? Somehow, the fact that he was a big boy now, with better prospects of health, made the question of his future more difficult. So long as he was frail the consideration that he inspired seemed enough of an answer to it. But at the bottom of Pemberton's heart was the recognition of his probably being strong enough to live and not strong enough to thrive. He himself, at any rate, was in a period of natural, boyish rosiness about all this, so that the

[6] way of living

beating of the tempest seemed to him only the voice of life and the challenge of fate. He had on his shabby little overcoat, with the collar up, but he was enjoying his walk.

It was interrupted at last by the appearance of his mother at the end of the *sala*. She beckoned to Morgan to come to her, and while Pemberton saw him, complacent, pass down the long vista, over the damp false marble, he wondered what was in the air. Mrs. Moreen said a word to the boy and made him go into the room she had quitted. Then, having closed the door after him, she directed her steps swiftly to Pemberton. There *was* something in the air, but his wildest flight of fancy wouldn't have suggested what it proved to be. She signified that she had made a pretext to get Morgan out of the way, and then she inquired—without hesitation—if the young man could lend her sixty francs. While, before bursting into a laugh, he stared at her with surprise, she declared that she was awfully pressed for the money; she was desperate for it—it would save her life.

"Dear lady, *c'est trop fort!*"[7] Pemberton laughed. "Where in the world do you suppose I should get sixty francs, *du train dont vous allez?*"[8]

"I thought you worked—wrote things; don't they pay you?"

"Not a penny."

"Are you such a fool as to work for nothing?"

"You ought surely to know that."

Mrs. Moreen stared an instant, then she coloured a little. Pemberton saw she had quite forgotten the terms—if "terms" they could be called—that he had ended by accepting from herself; they had burdened her memory as little as her conscience. "Oh, yes, I see what you mean—you have been very nice about that; but why go back to it so often?" She had been perfectly urbane with him ever since

the rough scene of explanation in his room, the morning he made her accept *his* "terms"—the necessity of his making his case known to Morgan. She had felt no resentment, after seeing that there was no danger of Morgan's taking the matter up with her. Indeed, attributing this immunity to the good taste of his influence with the boy, she had once said to Pemberton: "My dear fellow; it's an immense comfort you're a gentleman." She repeated this, in substance, now. "Of course you're a gentleman—that's a bother the less!" Pemberton reminded her that he had not "gone back" to anything; and she also repeated her prayer that, somewhere and somehow, he would find her sixty francs. He took the liberty of declaring that if he could find them it wouldn't be to lend them to *her*—as to which he consciously did himself injustice, knowing that if he had them he would certainly place them in her hand. He accused himself, at bottom and with some truth, of a fantastic, demoralised sympathy with her. If misery made strange bedfellows it also made strange sentiments. It was moreover a part of the demoralisation and of the general bad effect of living with such people that one had to make rough retorts, quite out of the tradition of good manners. "Morgan, Morgan, to what pass have I come for you?" he privately exclaimed, while Mrs. Moreen floated voluminously down the *sala* again, to liberate the boy; groaning, as she went, that everything was too odious.

Before the boy was liberated there came a thump at the door communicating with the staircase, followed by the apparition of a dripping youth who poked in his head. Pemberton recognised him as the bearer of a telegram and recognised the telegram as addressed to himself. Morgan came back as, after glancing at the signature (that of a friend in London), he was reading the words: "Found jolly job for you—engagement to coach opulent youth on your own terms. Come immediately." The answer, happily, was paid, and the

---

[7] It's just too much!
[8] at the rate you go along

messenger waited. Morgan, who had drawn near, waited too, and looked hard at Pemberton; and Pemberton, after a moment, having met his look, handed him the telegram. It was really by wise looks (they knew each other so well), that, while the telegraph-boy, in his waterproof cape, made a great puddle on the floor, the thing was settled between them. Pemberton wrote the answer with a pencil against the frescoed wall, and the messenger departed. When he had gone Pemberton said to Morgan:

"I'll make a tremendous charge; I'll earn a lot of money in a short time, and we'll live on it."

"Well, I hope the opulent youth will be stupid—he probably will—" Morgan parenthesised, "and keep you a long time."

"Of course, the longer he keeps me the more we shall have for our old age."

"But suppose *they* don't pay you!" Morgan awfully suggested.

"Oh, there are not two such—!" Pemberton paused, he was on the point of using an invidious term. Instead of this he said "two such chances."

Morgan flushed—the tears came to his eyes. *"Dites toujours,*[9] two such rascally crews!" Then, in a different tone, he added: "Happy opulent youth!"

"Not if he's stupid!"

"Oh, they're happier then. But you can't have everything, can you?" the boy smiled.

Pemberton held him, his hands on his shoulders. "What will become of *you,* what will you do?" He thought of Mrs. Moreen, desperate for sixty francs.

"I shall turn into a man." And then, as if he recognised all the bearings of Pemberton's allusion: "I shall get on with them better when you're not here."

"Ah, don't say that—it sounds as if I set you against them!"

"You do—the sight of you. It's all right: you know what I mean. I shall be beautiful. I'll take their affairs in hand; I'll marry my sisters."

"You'll marry yourself!" joked Pemberton; as high, rather tense pleasantry would evidently be the right, or the safest, tone for their separation.

It was, however, not purely in this strain that Morgan suddenly asked: "But I say—how will you get to your jolly job? You'll have to telegraph to the opulent youth for money to come on."

Pemberton bethought himself. "They won't like that, will they?"

"Oh, look out for them!"

Then Pemberton brought out his remedy. "I'll go to the American Consul; I'll borrow some money of him—just for the few days, on the strength of the telegram."

Morgan was hilarious. "Show him the telegram—then stay and keep the money!"

Pemberton entered into the joke enough to reply that, for Morgan, he was really capable of that; but the boy, growing more serious, and to prove that he hadn't meant what he said, not only hurried him off to the Consulate (since he was to start that evening, as he had wired to his friend), but insisted on going with him. They splashed through the tortuous perforations and over the humpbacked bridges, and they passed through the Piazza, where they saw Mr. Moreen and Ulick go into a jeweller's shop. The Consul proved accommodating (Pemberton said it wasn't the letter, but Morgan's grand air), and on their way back they went into St. Mark's for a hushed ten minutes. Later they took up and kept up the fun of it to the very end; and it seemed to Pemberton a part of that fun that Mrs. Moreen, who was very angry when he had announced to her his intention, should charge him, grotesquely and vulgarly, and in reference to the loan she had vainly endeavoured to effect, with bolting lest they should "get something out" of him. On the other hand he had to do Mr. Moreen and Ulick the justice to

---

[9] say anyhow

recognise that when, on coming in, *they* heard the cruel news, they took it like perfect men of the world.

VIII

When Pemberton got at work with the opulent youth, who was to be taken in hand for Balliol, he found himself unable to say whether he was really an idiot or it was only, on his own part, the long association with an intensely living little mind that made him seem so. From Morgan he heard half-a-dozen times: the boy wrote charming young letters, a patchwork of tongues, with indulgent postscripts in the family Volapuk and, in little squares and rounds and crannies of the text, the drollest illustrations—letters that he was divided between the impulse to show his present disciple, as a kind of wasted incentive, and the sense of something in them that was profanable by publicity. The opulent youth went up, in due course, and failed to pass; but it seemed to add to the presumption that brilliancy was not expected of him all at once that his parents, condoning the lapse, which they good-naturedly treated as little as possible as if it were Pemberton's, should have sounded the rally again, begged the young coach to keep his pupil in hand another year.

The young coach was now in a position to lend Mrs. Moreen sixty francs, and he sent her a post-office order for the amount. In return for this favour he received a frantic, scribbled line from her: "Implore you to come back instantly—Morgan dreadfully ill." They were on the rebound, once more in Paris—often as Pemberton had seen them depressed he had never seen them crushed—and communication was therefore rapid. He wrote to the boy to ascertain the state of his health, but he received no answer to his letter. Accordingly he took an abrupt leave of the opulent youth and, crossing the Channel, alighted at the small hotel, in the quarter of the Champs Elysées, of which Mrs. Moreen had given him the address. A deep if dumb dissatisfaction with this lady and her companions bore him company: they couldn't be vulgarly honest, but they could live at hotels, in velvety *entresols*,[10] amid a smell of burnt pastilles, in the most expensive city in Europe. When he had left them, in Venice, it was with an irrepressible suspicion that something was going to happen; but the only thing that had happened was that they succeeded in getting away. "How is he? where is he?" he asked of Mrs. Moreen; but before she could speak, these questions were answered by the pressure round his neck of a pair of arms, in shrunken sleeves, which were perfectly capable of an effusive young foreign squeeze.

"Dreadfully ill—I don't see it!" the young man cried. And then, to Morgan: "Why on earth didn't you relieve me? Why didn't you answer my letter?"

Mrs. Moreen declared that when she wrote he was very bad, and Pemberton learned at the same time from the boy that he had answered every letter he had received. This led to the demonstration that Pemberton's note had been intercepted. Mrs. Moreen was prepared to see the fact exposed, as Pemberton perceived, the moment he faced her, that she was prepared for a good many other things. She was prepared above all to maintain that she had acted from a sense of duty, that she was enchanted she had got him over, whatever they might say; and that it was useless of him to pretend that he didn't *know*, in all his bones, that his place at such a time was with Morgan. He had taken the boy away from them, and now he had no right to abandon him. He had created for himself the gravest responsibilities; he must at least abide by what he had done.

"Taken him away from you?" Pemberton exclaimed indignantly.

"Do it—do it, for pity's sake; that's

[10] mezzanines

just what I want. I can't stand *this*—and such scenes. They're treacherous!" These words broke from Morgan, who had intermitted his embrace, in a key which made Pemberton turn quickly to him, to see that he had suddenly seated himself, was breathing with evident difficulty and was very pale.

"*Now* do you say he's not ill—my precious pet?" shouted his mother, dropping on her knees before him with clasped hands, but touching him no more than if he had been a gilded idol. "It will pass—it's only for an instant; but don't say such dreadful things!"

"I'm all right—all right," Morgan panted to Pemberton, whom he sat looking up at with a strange smile, his hands resting on either side of the sofa.

"Now do you pretend I've been treacherous—that I've deceived?" Mrs. Moreen flashed at Pemberton as she got up.

"It isn't *he* says it, it's I!" the boy returned, apparently easier, but sinking back against the wall; while Pemberton, who had sat down beside him, taking his hand, bent over him.

"Darling child, one does what one can; there are so many things to consider," urged Mrs. Moreen. "It's his *place*—his only place. You see *you* think it is now."

"Take me away—take me away," Morgan went on, smiling to Pemberton from his white face.

"Where shall I take you, and how—oh, *how*, my boy?" the young man stammered, thinking of the rude way in which his friends in London held that, for his convenience, and without a pledge of instantaneous return, he had thrown them over; of the just resentment with which they would already have called in a successor, and of the little help as regarded finding fresh employment that resided for him in the flatness of his having failed to pass his pupil.

"Oh, we'll settle that. You used to talk about it," said Morgan. "If we can only go, all the rest's a detail."

"Talk about it as much as you like, but don't think you can attempt it. Mr. Moreen would never consent—it would be so precarious," Pemberton's hostess explained to him. Then to Morgan she explained: "It would destroy our peace, it would break our hearts. Now that he's back it will be all the same again. You'll have your life, your work and your freedom, and we'll all be happy as we used to be. You'll bloom and grow perfectly well, and we won't have any more silly experiments, will we? They're too absurd. It's Mr. Pemberton's place—every one in his place. You in yours, your papa in his, me in mine—*n'est-ce pas, chéri?*"[11] We'll all forget how foolish we've been, and we'll have lovely times."

She continued to talk and to surge vaguely about the little draped, stuffy *salon*, while Pemberton sat with the boy, whose colour gradually came back; and she mixed up her reasons, dropping that there were going to be changes, that the other children might scatter (who knew?—Paula had her ideas), and that then it might be fancied how much the poor old parent-birds would want the little nestling. Morgan looked at Pemberton, who wouldn't let him move; and Pemberton knew exactly how he felt at hearing himself called a little nestling. He admitted that he had had one or two bad days, but he protested afresh against the iniquity of his mother's having made them the ground of an appeal to poor Pemberton. Poor Pemberton could laugh now, apart from the comicality of Mrs. Moreen's producing so much philosophy for her defence (she seemed to shake it out of her agitated petticoats, which knocked over the light gilt chairs), so little did the sick boy strike him as qualified to repudiate any advantage.

He himself was in for it, at any rate. He should have Morgan on his hands again indefinitely; though indeed he saw the lad had a private theory to produce which would be intended to smooth this down.

[11] Isn't it so, my dear?

He was obliged to him for it in advance; but the suggested amendment didn't keep his heart from sinking a little, any more than it prevented him from accepting the prospect on the spot, with some confidence moreover that he would do so even better if he could have a little supper. Mrs. Moreen threw out more hints about the changes that were to be looked for, but she was such a mixture of smiles and shudders (she confessed she was very nervous), that he couldn't tell whether she were in high feather or only in hysterics. If the family were really at last going to pieces why shouldn't she recognise the necessity of pitching Morgan into some sort of lifeboat? This presumption was fostered by the fact that they were established in luxurious quarters in the capital of pleasure; that was exactly where they naturally *would* be established in view of going to pieces. Moreover didn't she mention that Mr. Moreen and the others were enjoying themselves at the opera with Mr. Granger, and wasn't *that* also precisely where one would look for them on the eve of a smash? Pemberton gathered that Mr. Granger was a rich, vacant American—a big bill with a flourishy heading and no items; so that one of Paula's "ideas" was probably that this time she had really done it, which was indeed an unprecedented blow to the general cohesion. And if the cohesion was to terminate what was to become of poor Pemberton? He felt quite enough bound up with them to figure, to his alarm, as a floating spar in case of a wreck.

It was Morgan who eventually asked if no supper had been ordered for him; sitting with him below, later, at the dim, delayed meal, in the presence of a great deal of corded green plush, a plate of ornamental biscuit and a languor marked on the part of the waiter. Mrs. Moreen had explained that they had been obliged to secure a room for the visitor out of the house; and Morgan's consolation (he offered it while Pemberton reflected on the nastiness of lukewarm sauces), proved to be, largely, that this circumstance would facilitate their escape. He talked of their escape (recurring to it often afterwards), as if they were making up a "boy's book" together. But he likewise expressed his sense that there was something in the air, that the Moreens couldn't keep it up much longer. In point of fact, as Pemberton was to see, they kept it up for five or six months. All the while, however, Morgan's contention was designed to cheer him. Mr. Moreen and Ulick, whom he had met the day after his return, accepted that return like perfect men of the world. If Paula and Amy treated it even with less formality an allowance was to be made for them, inasmuch as Mr. Granger had not come to the opera after all. He had only placed his box at their service, with a bouquet for each of the party; there was even one apiece, embittering the thought of his profusion, for Mr. Moreen and Ulick. "They're all like that," was Morgan's comment; "at the very last, just when we think we've got them fast, we're chucked!"

Morgan's comments, in these days, were more and more free; they even included a large recognition of the extraordinary tenderness with which he had been treated while Pemberton was away. Oh, yes, they couldn't do enough to be nice to him, to show him they had him on their mind and make up for his loss. That was just what made the whole thing so sad, and him so glad, after all, of Pemberton's return—he had to keep thinking of their affection less, had less sense of obligation. Pemberton laughed out at this last reason, and Morgan blushed and said: "You know what I mean." Pemberton knew perfectly what he meant; but there were a good many things it didn't make any clearer. This episode of his second sojourn in Paris stretched itself out wearily, with their resumed readings and wanderings and maunderings, their potterings on the quays, their hauntings of the museums, their occasional lingerings in the Palais Royal, when the first sharp weather came on and there was a comfort in warm emanations, before Chevet's wonderful succulent window. Morgan wanted to hear a great deal about the opulent youth—he took an immense interest in him. Some of the details of his opulence—Pemberton could spare him none of them—evidently intensified the boy's appreciation of all his friend had given up to come back to him; but in addition to the greater reciprocity established by such a renunciation he had always his little brooding theory, in which there was a frivolous gaiety too, that their long probation was drawing to a close. Morgan's conviction that the Moreens couldn't go on much longer kept pace with the unexpended impetus with which, from month to month, they did go on. Three weeks after Pemberton had rejoined them they went on to another hotel, a dingier one than the first; but Morgan rejoiced that his tutor had at least still not sacrificed the advantage of a room outside. He clung to the romantic utility of this when the day, or rather the night, should arrive for their escape.

For the first time, in this complicated connection, Pemberton felt sore and exasperated. It was, as he had said to Mrs. Moreen in Venice, *trop fort*—everything was *trop fort*.[12] He could neither really throw off his blighting burden nor find in it the benefit of a pacified conscience or of a rewarded affection. He had spent all the money that he had earned in England, and he felt that his youth was going and that he was getting nothing back for it. It was all very well for Morgan to seem to consider that he would make up to him for all inconveniences by settling himself upon him permanently—there was an irritating flaw in such a view. He saw what the boy had in his mind; the conception that as his friend had had the generosity to come back to him he must show his gratitude by giving him his life. But the poor friend didn't desire the gift —what could he do with Morgan's life? Of course at the same time that Pemberton was irritated he remembered the reason, which was very honourable to Morgan and which consisted simply of the fact that he was perpetually making one forget that he was after all only a child. If one dealt with him on a different basis one's misadventures were one's own fault. So Pemberton waited in a queer confusion of yearning and alarm for the catastrophe which was held to hang over the house of Moreen, of which he certainly at moments felt the symptoms brush his cheek and as to which he wondered much in what form it would come.

Perhaps it would take the form of dispersal—a frightened *sauve qui peut*,[13] a scuttling into selfish corners. Certainly they were less elastic than of yore; they were evidently looking for something they didn't find. The Dorringtons hadn't reappeared, the princes had scattered; wasn't that the beginning of the end? Mrs. Moreen had lost her reckoning of the famous "days"; her social calendar was blurred—it had turned its face to the wall. Pemberton suspected that the great, the cruel, discomfiture had been the extraordinary behaviour of Mr. Granger, who seemed not to know what he wanted, or, what was much worse, what *they* wanted. He kept sending flowers, as if to bestrew the path of his retreat, which was never the path of return. Flowers were all very well, but—Pemberton could complete the proposition. It was now positively conspicuous that in the long run the Moreens were a failure; so that the young man was almost grateful the run had not been short. Mr. Moreen, indeed, was still occasionally able to get away on business, and, what was more surprising, he was

---

[12] too much

[13] Everyone for himself!

also able to get back. Ulick had no club, but you could not have discovered it from his appearance, which was as much as ever that of a person looking at life from the window of such an institution; therefore Pemberton was doubly astonished at an answer he once heard him make to his mother, in the desperate tone of a man familiar with the worst privations. Her question Pemberton had not quite caught; it appeared to be an appeal for a suggestion as to whom they could get to take Amy. "Let the devil take her!" Ulick snapped; so that Pemberton could see that not only they had lost their amiability, but had ceased to believe in themselves. He could also see that if Mrs. Moreen was trying to get people to take her children she might be regarded as closing the hatches for the storm. But Morgan would be the last she would part with.

One winter afternoon—it was a Sunday—he and the boy walked far together in the Bois de Boulogne. The evening was so splendid, the cold lemon-coloured sunset so clear, the stream of carriages and pedestrians so amusing and the fascination of Paris so great, that they stayed out later than usual and became aware that they would have to hurry home to arrive in time for dinner. They hurried accordingly, arm-in-arm, good-humoured and hungry, agreeing that there was nothing like Paris after all and that after all, too, that had come and gone they were not yet sated with innocent pleasures. When they reached the hotel they found that, though scandalously late, they were in time for all the dinner they were likely to sit down to. Confusion reigned in the apartments of the Moreens (very shabby ones this time, but the best in the house), and before the interrupted service of the table (with objects displaced almost as if there had been a scuffle, and a great wine stain from an overturned bottle), Pemberton could not blink the fact that there had been a scene of proprietary mutiny. The storm had come—they were all seeking refuge. The hatches were down —Paula and Amy were invisible (they had never tried the most casual art upon Pemberton, but he felt that they had enough of an eye to him not to wish to meet him as young ladies whose frocks had been confiscated), and Ulick appeared to have jumped overboard. In a word, the host and his staff had ceased to "go on" at the pace of their guests, and the air of embarrassed detention, thanks to a pile of gaping trunks in the passage, was strangely commingled with the air of indignant withdrawal.

When Morgan took in all this—and he took it in very quickly—he blushed to the roots of his hair. He had walked, from his infancy, among difficulties and dangers, but he had never seen a public exposure. Pemberton noticed, in a second glance at him, that the tears had rushed into his eyes and that they were tears of bitter shame. He wondered for an instant, for the boy's sake, whether he might successfully pretend not to understand. Not successfully, he felt, as Mr. and Mrs. Moreen, dinnerless by their extinguished hearth, rose before him in their little dishonoured *salon,* considering apparently with much intensity what lively capital would be next on their list. They were not prostrate, but they were very pale, and Mrs. Moreen had evidently been crying. Pemberton quickly learned however that her grief was not for the loss of her dinner, much as she usually enjoyed it, but on account of a necessity much more tragic. She lost no time in laying this necessity bare, in telling him how the change had come, the bolt had fallen, and how they would all have to turn themselves about. Therefore cruel as it was to them to part with their darling she must look to him to carry a little further the influence he had so fortunately acquired with the boy—to induce his young charge to follow him into some modest retreat. They depended upon him, in a word, to take their delightful child temporarily under his protection—it would leave Mr. Moreen and herself so much more free to give the proper attention (too little, alas! had been given), to the readjustment of their affairs.

"We trust you—we feel that we can," said Mrs. Moreen, slowly rubbing her plump white hands and looking, with compunction, hard at Morgan, whose chin, not to take liberties, her husband stroked with a tentative paternal forefinger.

"Oh, yes; we feel that we can. We trust Mr. Pemberton fully, Morgan," Mr. Moreen conceded.

Pemberton wondered again if he might pretend not to understand; but the idea was painfully complicated by the immediate perception that Morgan had understood.

"Do you mean that he may take me to live with him—for ever and ever?" cried the boy. "Away, away, anywhere he likes?"

"For ever and ever? *Comme vous-y-allez!*"[14] Mr. Moreen laughed indulgently. "For as long as Mr. Pemberton may be so good."

"We've struggled, we've suffered," his wife went on; "but you've made him so your own that we've already been through the worst of the sacrifice."

Morgan had turned away from his father—he stood looking at Pemberton with a light in his face. His blush had died out, but something had come that was brighter and more vivid. He had a moment of boyish joy, scarcely mitigated by the reflection that, with this unexpected consecration of his hope—too sudden and too violent; the thing was a good deal less like a boy's book—the "escape" was left on their hands. The boyish joy was there for an instant, and Pemberton was almost frightened at the revelation of gratitude and affection that shone through his humiliation. When Morgan stammered "My dear fellow, what do you say to *that?*" he felt that he should say something enthusiastic. But he was still more frightened at something else that immediately followed and that made the lad sit down quickly on the nearest chair. He had turned very white and had raised his hand to his left side. They were all three looking at him, but Mrs. Moreen was the first to bound forward. "Ah, his darling little heart!" she broke out; and this time, on her knees before him and without respect for the idol, she caught him ardently in her arms. "You walked him too far, you hurried him too fast!" she tossed over her shoulder at Pemberton. The boy made no protest, and the next instant his mother, still holding him, sprang up with her face convulsed and with the terrified cry "Help, help! he's going, he's gone!" Pemberton saw, with equal horror, by Morgan's own stricken face, that he *was* gone. He pulled him half out of his mother's hands, and for a moment, while they held him together, they looked, in their dismay, into each other's eyes. "He couldn't stand it, with his infirmity," said Pemberton—"the shock, the whole scene, the violent emotion."

"But I thought he *wanted* to go to you!" wailed Mrs. Moreen.

"I *told* you he didn't, my dear," argued Mr. Moreen. He was trembling all over, and he was, in his way, as deeply affected as his wife. But, after the first, he took his bereavement like a man of the world.

---

[14] How you do run on!

JOSEPH CONRAD • 1857-1924

Youth

THIS could have occurred nowhere but in England, where men and sea interpenetrate, so to speak—the sea entering into the life of most men, and the men knowing something or everything about the sea, in the way of amusement, of travel, or of bread-winning.

We were sitting round a mahogany table that reflected the bottle, the claret-glasses, and our faces as we leaned on our elbows. There was a director of companies, an accountant, a lawyer, Marlow, and myself. The director had been a *Conway*[1] boy, the accountant had served four years at sea, the lawyer—a fine crusted Tory, High Churchman, the best of old fellows, the soul of honour—had been chief officer in the P. & O.[2] service in the good old days when mail-boats were square-rigged at least on two masts, and used to come down the China Sea before a fair monsoon with stun'-sails set alow and aloft. We all began life in the merchant service. Between the five of us there was the strong bond of the sea, and also the fellowship of the craft, which no amount of enthusiasm for yachting, cruising, and so on can give, since one is only the amusement of life and the other is life itself.

Marlow (at least I think that is how he spelt his name) told the story, or rather the chronicle, of a voyage:—

"Yes, I have seen a little of the Eastern seas; but what I remember best is my first voyage there. You fellows know there are those voyages that seem ordered for the illustration of life, that might stand for a symbol of existence. You fight, work, sweat, nearly kill yourself, sometimes do kill yourself, trying to accomplish something—and you can't. Not from any fault of yours. You simply can do nothing, neither great nor little—not a thing in the world—not even marry an old maid, or get a wretched 600-ton cargo of coal to its port of destination.

"It was altogether a memorable affair. It was my first voyage to the East, and my first voyage as second mate; it was also my skipper's first command. You'll admit it was time. He was sixty if a day; a little man, with a broad, not very straight back, with bowed shoulders and one leg more bandy than the other, he had that queer twisted-about appearance you see so often in men who work in the fields. He had a nut-cracker face—chin and nose trying to come together over a sunken mouth—and it was framed in iron-gray fluffy hair, that looked like a chin-strap of cotton-wool sprinkled with coal-dust. And he had blue eyes in that old face of his, which were amazingly like a boy's, with that candid expression some quite common men preserve to the end of their days by a rare internal gift of simplicity of heart and rectitude of soul. What induced him to accept me was a wonder. I had come out of a crack Australian clipper, where I had been third officer, and he seemed to have a prejudice against crack clippers as aristocratic and high-toned. He said to me, 'You know, in this ship you will have to work.' I said I had to work in every ship I had ever been in. 'Ah, but this is different, and you gentlemen out of them big ships; . . . but there! I dare say you will do. Join to-morrow.'

[1] one who has served on the frigate "Conway," a training ship for sailors
[2] Pacific and Orient Lines

"I joined to-morrow. It was twenty-two years ago; and I was just twenty. How time passes! It was one of the happiest days of my life. Fancy! Second mate for the first time—a really responsible officer! I wouldn't have thrown up my new billet for a fortune. The mate looked me over carefully. He was also an old chap, but of another stamp. He had a Roman nose, a snow-white, long beard, and his name was Mahon, but he insisted that it should be pronounced Mann. He was well connected; yet there was something wrong with his luck, and he had never got on.

"As to the captain, he had been for years in coasters, then in the Mediterranean, and last in the West Indian trade. He had never been round the Capes. He could just write a kind of sketchy hand, and didn't care for writing at all. Both were thorough good seamen of course, and between those two old chaps I felt like a small boy between two grandfathers.

"The ship also was old. Her name was the *Judea*. Queer name, isn't it? She belonged to a man Wilmer, Wilcox—some name like that; but he has been bankrupt and dead these twenty years or more, and his name don't matter. She had been laid up in Shadwell basin for ever so long. You may imagine her state. She was all rust, dust, grime—soot aloft, dirt on deck. To me it was like coming out of a palace into a ruined cottage. She was about 400 tons, had a primitive windlass, wooden latches to the doors, not a bit of brass about her, and a big square stern. There was on it, below her name in big letters, a lot of scrollwork, with the gilt off, and some sort of a coat of arms, with the motto 'Do or Die' underneath. I remember it took my fancy immensely. There was a touch of romance in it, something that made me love the old thing—something that appealed to my youth!

"We left London in ballast—sand ballast—to load a cargo of coal in a northern port for Bankok. Bankok! I thrilled. I had been six years at sea, but had only seen Melbourne and Sydney, very good places, charming places in their way—but Bankok!

"We worked out of the Thames under canvas, with a North Sea pilot on board. His name was Jermyn, and he dodged all day long about the galley drying his handkerchief before the stove. Apparently he never slept. He was a dismal man, with a perpetual tear sparkling at the end of his nose, who either had been in trouble, or was in trouble, or expected to be in trouble—couldn't be happy unless something went wrong. He mistrusted my youth, my common sense, and my seamanship, and made a point of showing it in a hundred little ways. I dare say he was right. It seems to me I knew very little then, and I know not much more now; but I cherish a hate for that Jermyn to this day.

"We were a week working up as far as Yarmouth Roads, and then we got into a gale—the famous October gale of twenty-two years ago. It was wind, lightning, sleet, snow, and a terrific sea. We were flying light, and you may imagine how bad it was when I tell you we had smashed bulwarks and a flooded deck. On the second night she shifted her ballast into the lee bow, and by that time we had been blown off somewhere on the Dogger Bank. There was nothing for it but go below with shovels and try to right her, and there we were in that vast hold, gloomy like a cavern, the tallow dips stuck and flickering on the beams, the gale howling above, the ship tossing about like mad on her side; there we all were, Jermyn, the captain, every one, hardly able to keep our feet, engaged on that gravedigger's work, and trying to toss shovelfuls of wet sand up to windward. At every tumble of the ship you could see vaguely in the dim light men falling down with a great flourish of shovels. One of the ship's boys (we had two), impressed by the weirdness of the scene, wept as if his heart would break. We could hear him blubbering somewhere in the shadows.

"On the third day the gale died out, and by and by a north-country tug picked us up. We took sixteen days in all to get from London to the Tyne! When we got into dock we had lost our turn for loading, and they hauled us off to a tier where we remained for a month. Mrs. Beard (the captain's name was Beard) came from Colchester to see the old man. She lived on board. The crew of runners had left, and there remained only the officers, one boy and the steward, a mulatto who answered to the name of Abraham. Mrs. Beard was an old woman, with a face all wrinkled and ruddy like a winter apple, and the figure of a young girl. She caught sight of me once, sewing on a button, and insisted on having my shirts to repair. This was something different from the captains' wives I had known on board crack clippers. When I brought her the shirts, she said: 'And the socks? They want mending, I am sure, and John's—Captain Beard's—things are all in order now. I would be glad of something to do.' Bless the old woman. She overhauled my outfit for me, and meantime I read for the first time *Sartor Resartus* and Burnaby's *Ride to Khiva*. I didn't understand much of the first then; but I remember I preferred the soldier to the philosopher at the time; a preference which life has only confirmed. One was a man, and the other was either more—or less. However, they are both dead and Mrs. Beard is dead, and youth, strength, genius, thoughts, achievements, simple hearts—all die. . . . No matter.

"They loaded us at last. We shipped a crew. Eight able seamen and two boys. We hauled off one evening to the buoys at the dockgates, ready to go out, and with a fair prospect of beginning the voyage next day. Mrs. Beard was to start for home by a late train. When the ship was fast we went to tea. We sat rather silent through the meal—Mahon, the old couple, and I. I finished first, and slipped away for a smoke, my cabin being in a deck-house just against the poop. It was high water, blowing fresh with a drizzle; the double dock-gates were opened, and the steam-colliers were going in and out in the darkness with their lights burning bright, a great plashing of propellers, rattling of winches, and a lot of hailing on the pier-heads. I watched the procession of head-lights gliding high and of green lights gliding low in the night, when suddenly a red gleam flashed at me, vanished, came into view again, and remained. The fore-end of a steamer loomed up close. I shouted down the cabin, 'Come up, quick!' and then heard a startled voice saying afar in the dark, 'Stop her, sir.' A bell jingled. Another voice cried warningly, 'We are going right into that barque, sir.' The answer to this was a gruff 'All right,' and the next thing was a heavy crash as the steamer struck a glancing blow with the bluff of her bow about our fore-rigging. There was a moment of confusion, yelling, and running about. Steam roared. Then somebody was heard saying, 'All clear, sir.' . . . 'Are you all right?' asked the gruff voice. I had jumped forward to see the damage, and hailed back, 'I think so.' 'Easy astern,' said the gruff voice. A bell jingled. 'What steamer is that?' screamed Mahon. By that time she was no more to us than a bulky shadow manœuvring a little way off. They shouted at us some name—a woman's name, Miranda or Melissa—or some such thing. 'This means another month in this beastly hole,' said Mahon to me, as we peered with lamps about the splintered bulwarks and broken braces. 'But where's the captain?'

"We had not heard or seen anything of him all that time. We went aft to look. A doleful voice arose hailing somewhere in the middle of the dock, *'Judea* ahoy!' . . . How the devil did he get there? . . . 'Hallo!' we shouted. 'I am adrift in our boat without oars,' he cried. A belated water-man offered his services, and Mahon struck a bargain with him for half-a-crown to tow our skipper alongside; but it was Mrs. Beard that came up the ladder first. They had been floating about the dock in that mizzly cold rain for nearly an hour. I was never so surprised in my life.

"It appears that when he heard my shout 'Come up' he understood at once what was the matter, caught up his wife, ran on deck, and across, and down into our boat, which was fast to the ladder. Not bad for a sixty-year old. Just imagine that old fellow saving heroically in his arms that old woman—the woman of his life. He set her down on a thwart, and was ready to climb back on board when the painter came adrift somehow, and away they went together. Of course in the confusion we did not hear him shouting. He looked abashed. She said cheerfully, 'I suppose it does not matter my losing the train now?' 'No, Jenny—you go below and get warm,' he growled. Then to us: 'A sailor has no business with a wife—I say. There I was, out of the ship. Well, no harm done this time. Let's go and look at what that fool of a steamer smashed.'

"It wasn't much, but it delayed us three weeks. At the end of that time, the captain being engaged with his agents, I carried Mrs. Beard's bag to the railway-station and put her all comfy into a third-class carriage. She lowered the window to say, 'You are a good young man. If you see—John—Captain Beard—without his muffler at night, just remind him from me to keep his throat well wrapped up.' 'Certainly, Mrs. Beard,' I said. 'You are a good young man; I noticed how attentive you are to John—to Captain——' The train pulled out suddenly; I took my cap off to the old woman: I never saw her again. . . . Pass the bottle.

"We went to sea next day. When we made that start for Bankok we had been already three months out of London. We had expected to be a fortnight or so—at the outside.

"It was January, and the weather was beautiful—the beautiful sunny winter weather that has more charm than in the summer-time, because it is unexpected, and crisp, and you know it won't, it can't, last long. It's like a windfall, like a godsend, like an unexpected piece of luck.

"It lasted all down the North Sea, all down Channel; and it lasted till we were three hundred miles or so to the westward of the Lizards: then the wind went round to the sou'west and began to pipe up. In two days it blew a gale. The *Judea,* hove to, wallowed on the Atlantic like an old candle-box. It blew day after day: it blew with spite, without interval, without mercy, without rest. The world was nothing but an immensity of great foaming waves rushing at us, under a sky low enough to touch with the hand and dirty like a smoked ceiling. In the stormy space surrounding us there was as much flying spray as air. Day after day and night after night there was nothing round the ship but the howl of the wind, the tumult of the sea, the noise of water pouring over her deck. There was no rest for her and no rest for us. She tossed, she pitched, she stood on her head, she sat on her tail, she rolled, she groaned, and we had to hold on while on deck and cling to our bunks when below, in a constant effort of body and worry of mind.

"One night Mahon spoke through the small window of my berth. It opened right into my bed, and I was lying there sleepless, in my boots, feeling as though I had not slept for years, and could not if I tried. He said excitedly—

" 'You got the sounding-rod in here, Marlow? I can't get the pumps to suck. By God! it's no child's play.'

"I gave him the sounding-rod and lay down again, trying to think of various things—but I thought only of the pumps. When I came on deck they were still at it, and my watch relieved at the pumps. By the light of the lantern brought on deck to examine the sounding-rod I caught a glimpse of their weary, serious faces. We pumped all the four hours. We pumped all night, all day, all the week—watch and watch. She was working herself loose, and leaked badly—not enough to drown us at once, but enough to kill us with the work at the pumps. And while we pumped the ship was going from us piecemeal: the bulwarks went, the stanchions were torn out, the ventilators smashed, the cabin-door burst in. There was not a dry spot in the ship. She was being gutted bit by bit. The long-boat changed, as if by magic, into matchwood where she stood in her gripes. I had lashed her myself, and was rather proud of my handiwork, which had withstood so long the malice of the sea. And we pumped. And there was no break in the weather. The sea was white like a sheet of foam, like a caldron of boiling milk; there was not a break in the clouds, no—not the size of a man's hand—no, not for so much as ten seconds. There was for us no sky, there were for us no stars, no sun, no universe—nothing but angry clouds and an infuriated sea. We pumped watch and watch, for dear life; and it seemed to last for months, for years, for all eternity, as though we had been dead and gone to a hell for sailors. We forgot the day of the week, the name of the month, what year it was, and whether we had ever been ashore. The sails blew away, she lay broadside on under a weather-cloth, the ocean poured over her, and we did not care. We turned those handles, and had the eyes of idiots. As soon as we had crawled on deck I used to take a round turn with a rope about the men, the pumps, and the mainmast, and we turned, we turned incessantly, with the water to our waists, to our necks, over our heads. It was all one. We had forgotten how it felt to be dry.

"And there was somewhere in me the thought: By Jove! this is the deuce of an adventure—something you read about; and it is my first voyage as second mate—and I am only twenty—and here I am lasting it out as well as any of these men, and keeping my chaps up to the mark. I was pleased. I would not have given up the experience for worlds. I had moments of exultation. Whenever the old dismantled craft pitched heavily with her counter high in the air, she seemed to me to throw up, like an appeal, like a defiance, like a cry to the clouds without mercy, the words written on her stern: '*Judea*, London. Do or Die.'

"O youth! The strength of it, the faith of it, the imagination of it! To me she was not an old rattletrap carting about the world a lot of coal for a freight—to me she was the endeavor, the test, the trial of life. I think of her with pleasure, with affection, with regret—as you would think of someone dead you have loved. I shall never forget her. . . . Pass the bottle.

"One night when tied to the mast, as I explained, we were pumping on, deafened with the wind, and without spirit enough in us to wish ourselves dead, a heavy sea crashed aboard and swept clean over us. As soon as I got my breath I shouted, as in duty bound, 'Keep on, boys!' when suddenly I felt something hard floating on deck strike the calf of my leg. I made a grab at it and missed. It was so dark we could not see each other's faces within a foot—you understand.

"After that thump the ship kept quiet for a while, and the thing, whatever it was, struck my leg again. This time I caught it—and it was a saucepan. At first, being stupid with fatigue and thinking of nothing but the pumps, I did not understand what I had in my hand. Suddenly it dawned upon me, and I shouted, 'Boys, the house on deck is gone. Leave this, and let's look for the cook.'

"There was a deck-house forward, which contained the galley, the cook's berth, and the quarters of the crew. As we had expected for days to see it swept away, the hands had been ordered to sleep in the cabin—the only safe place in the ship. The steward, Abraham, however, persisted in clinging to his berth, stupidly, like a mule—from sheer fright I believe, like an animal that won't leave a stable falling in an earthquake. So we went to look for him. It was chancing death, since once out of our lashings we were as exposed as if on a raft. But we went. The house was shattered as if a shell had exploded inside. Most of it had gone overboard—stove, men's quarters, and their property, all was gone; but two posts, holding a portion of the bulkhead to which Abraham's bunk was attached, remained as if by a miracle. We groped in the ruins and came upon this, and there he was, sitting in his bunk, surrounded by foam and wreckage, jabbering cheerfully to himself. He was out of his mind; completely and for ever mad, with this sudden shock coming upon the fag-end of his endurance. We snatched him up, lugged him aft, and pitched him head-first down the cabin companion. You understand there was no time to carry him down with infinite precautions and wait to see how he got on. Those below would pick him up at the bottom of the stairs all right. We were in a hurry to go back to the pumps. That business could not wait. A bad leak is an inhuman thing.

"One would think that the sole purpose of that fiendish gale had been to make a lunatic of that poor devil of a mulatto. It eased before morning, and next day the sky cleared, and as the sea went down the leak took up. When it came to bending a fresh set of sails the crew demanded to put back—and really there was nothing else to do. Boats gone, decks swept clean, cabin gutted, men without a stitch but what they stood in, stores spoiled, ship strained. We put her head for home, and —would you believe it? The wind came east right in our teeth. It blew fresh, it blew continuously. We had to beat up every inch of the way, but she did not leak so badly, the water keeping comparatively smooth. Two hours' pumping in every four is no joke—but it kept her afloat as far as Falmouth.

"The good people there live on casualties of the sea, and no doubt were glad to see us. A hungry crowd of shipwrights sharpened their chisels at the sight of that carcass of a ship. And, by Jove! they had pretty pickings off us before they were done. I fancy the owner was already in a tight place. There were delays. Then it was decided to take part of the cargo out and caulk her topsides. This was done, the repairs finished, cargo reshipped; a new crew came on board, and we went out—for Bankok. At the end of a week we were back again. The crew said they weren't going to Bankok—a hundred and fifty days' passage—in a something hooker that wanted pumping eight hours out of the twenty-four; and the nautical papers inserted again the little paragraph: 'Judea. Barque. Tyne to Bankok; coals; put back to Falmouth leaky and with crew refusing duty.'

"There were more delays—more tinkering. The owner came down for a day, and said she was as right as a fiddle. Poor old Captain Beard looked like the ghost of a Geordie skipper—through the worry and humiliation of it. Remember he was sixty, and it was his first command. Mahon said it was a foolish business, and would end badly. I loved the ship more than ever, and wanted awfully to get to Bankok. To Bankok! Magic name, blessed name. Mesopotamia wasn't a patch on it. Remember I was twenty, and it was my first second-mate's billet, and the East was waiting for me.

"We went out and anchored in the outer roads with a fresh crew—the third. She leaked worse than ever. It was as if those confounded shipwrights had actually made a hole in her. This time we did not even go outside. The crew simply refused to man the windlass.

"They towed us back to the inner harbour, and we became a fixture, a feature, an institution of the place. People pointed us out to visitors as 'That 'ere barque that's going to Bankok—has been here six months—put back three times.' On holidays the small boys pulling about in boats would hail, '*Judea,* ahoy!' and if a head showed above the rail shouted, 'Where you bound to?—Bankok?' and jeered. We were only three on board. The poor old skipper mooned in the cabin. Mahon undertook the cooking, and unexpectedly developed all a Frenchman's genius for preparing nice little messes. I looked languidly after the rigging. We became citizens of Falmouth. Every shopkeeper knew us. At the barber's or tobacconist's they asked familiarly, 'Do you think you will ever get to Bankok?' Meantime the owner, the underwriters, and the charterers squabbled amongst themselves in London, and our pay went on. . . . Pass the bottle.

"It was horrid. Morally it was worse than pumping for life. It seemed as though we had been forgotten by the world, belonged to nobody, would get nowhere; it seemed that, as if bewitched, we would have to live for ever and ever in that inner harbour, a derision and a byword to generations of long-shore loafers and dishonest boatmen. I obtained three months' pay and a five days' leave, and made a rush for London. It took me a day to get there and pretty well another to come back—but three months' pay went all the same. I don't know what I did with it. I went to a music-hall, I believe, lunched, dined, and supped in a swell place in Regent Street, and was back in time, with nothing but a complete set of Byron's works and a new railway rug to show for three months' work. The boat-man who pulled me off to the ship said: 'Hallo! I thought you had left the old thing. *She will never get to Bankok.*' 'That's all *you* know about it,' I said scornfully—but I didn't like that prophecy at all.

"Suddenly a man, some kind of agent to somebody, appeared with full powers. He had grog-blossoms all over his face, an indomitable energy, and was a jolly soul. We leaped into life again. A hulk came alongside, took our cargo, and then we went into dry dock to get our copper stripped. No wonder she leaked. The poor thing, strained beyond endurance by the gale, had, as if in disgust, spat out all the oakum of her lower seams. She was recaulked, new coppered, and made as tight as a bottle. We went back to the hulk and reshipped our cargo.

"Then, on a fine moonlight night, all the rats left the ship.

"We had been infested with them. They had destroyed our sails, consumed more stores than the crew, affably shared our beds and our dangers, and now, when the ship was made seaworthy, concluded to clear out. I called Mahon to enjoy the spectacle. Rat after rat appeared on our rail, took a last look over his shoulder, and leaped with a hollow thud into the empty hulk. We tried to count them, but soon lost the tale. Mahon said: 'Well, well! don't talk to me about the intelligence of rats. They ought to have left before, when we had that narrow squeak from foundering. There you have the proof how silly is the superstition about them. They leave a good ship for an old rotten hulk, where there is nothing to eat, too, the fools! . . . I don't believe they know what is safe or what is good for them, any more than you or I.'

"And after some more talk we agreed that the wisdom of rats had been grossly overrated, being in fact no greater than that of men.

"The story of the ship was known, by this, all up the Channel from Land's End to the Forelands, and we could get no crew on the south coast. They sent us one all complete from Liverpool, and we left once more—for Bankok.

"We had fair breezes, smooth water right into the tropics, and the old *Judea* lumbered along in the sunshine. When she went eight knots everything cracked aloft, and we tied our caps to our heads;

but mostly she strolled on at the rate of three miles an hour. What could you expect? She was tired—that old ship. Her youth was where mine is—where yours is—you fellows who listen to this yarn; and what friend would throw your years and your weariness in your face? We didn't grumble at her. To us aft, at least, it seemed as though we had been born in her, reared in her, had lived in her for ages, had never known any other ship. I would just as soon have abused the old village church at home for not being a cathedral.

"And for me there was also my youth to make me patient. There was all the East before me, and all life, and the thought that I had been tried in that ship and had come out pretty well. And I thought of men of old who, centuries ago, went that road in ships that sailed no better, to the land of palms, and spices, and yellow sands, and of brown nations ruled by kings more cruel than Nero the Roman, and more splendid than Solomon the Jew. The old bark lumbered on, heavy with her age and the burden of her cargo, while I lived the life of youth in ignorance and hope. She lumbered on through an interminable procession of days; and the fresh gilding flashed back at the setting sun, seemed to cry out over the darkening sea the words painted on her stern, 'Judea, London. Do or Die.'

"Then we entered the Indian Ocean and steered northerly for Java Head. The winds were light. Weeks slipped by. She crawled on, do or die, and people at home began to think of posting us as overdue.

"One Saturday evening, I being off duty, the men asked me to give them an extra bucket of water or so—for washing clothes. As I did not wish to screw on the fresh-water pump so late, I went forward whistling, and with a key in my hand to unlock the forepeak scuttle, intending to serve the water out of a spare tank we kept there.

"The smell down below was as unexpected as it was frightful. One would have thought hundreds of paraffin-lamps had been flaring and smoking in that hole for days. I was glad to get out. The man with me coughed and said, 'Funny smell, sir.' I answered negligently, 'It's good for the health they say,' and walked aft.

"The first thing I did was to put my head down the square of the midship ventilator. As I lifted the lid a visible breath, something like a thin fog, a puff of faint haze, rose from the opening. The ascending air was hot, and had a heavy, sooty, paraffiny smell. I gave one sniff, and put down the lid gently. It was no use choking myself. The cargo was on fire.

"Next day she began to smoke in earnest. You see it was to be expected, for though the coal was of a safe kind, that cargo had been so handled, so broken up with handling, that it looked more like smithy coal than anything else. Then it had been wetted—more than once. It rained all the time we were taking it back from the hulk, and now with this long passage it got heated, and there was another case of spontaneous combustion.

"The captain called us into the cabin. He had a chart spread on the table, and looked unhappy. He said, 'The coast of West Australia is near, but I mean to proceed to our destination. It is the hurricane month, too; but we will just keep her head for Bankok, and fight the fire. No more putting back anywhere, if we all get roasted. We will try first to stifle this 'ere damned combustion by want of air.'

"We tried. We battened down everything, and still she smoked. The smoke kept coming out through imperceptible crevices; it forced itself through bulkheads and covers; it oozed here and there and everywhere in slender threads, in an invisible film, in an incomprehensible manner. It made its way into the cabin, into the forecastle; it poisoned the sheltered places on the deck, it could be sniffed as high as the mainyard. It was clear that if the smoke came out the air came in. This was disheartening. This combustion refused to be stifled.

"We resolved to try water, and took the hatches off. Enormous volumes of smoke, whitish, yellowish, thick, greasy, misty, choking, ascended as high as the trucks. All hands cleared out aft. Then the poisonous cloud blew away, and we went back to work in a smoke that was no thicker now than that of an ordinary factory chimney.

"We rigged the force-pump, got the hose along, and by and by it burst. Well, it was as old as the ship—a prehistoric hose, and past repair. Then we pumped with the feeble head-pump, drew water with buckets, and in this way managed in time to pour lots of Indian Ocean into the main hatch. The bright stream flashed in sunshine, fell into a layer of white crawling smoke, and vanished on the black surface of coal. Steam ascended mingling with the smoke. We poured salt water as into a barrel without a bottom. It was our fate to pump in that ship, to pump out of her, to pump into her; and after keeping water out of her to save ourselves from being drowned, we frantically poured water into her to save ourselves from being burnt.

"And she crawled on, do or die, in the serene weather. The sky was a miracle of purity, a miracle of azure. The sea was polished, was blue, was pellucid, was sparkling like a precious stone, extending on all sides, all round to the horizon—as if the whole terrestrial globe had been one jewel, one colossal sapphire, a single gem fashioned into a planet. And on the lustre of the great calm waters the *Judea* glided imperceptibly, enveloped in languid and unclean vapours, in a lazy cloud that drifted to leeward, light and slow; a pestiferous cloud defiling the splendour of sea and sky.

"All this time of course we saw no fire. The cargo smouldered at the bottom somewhere. Once Mahon, as we were working side by side, said to me with a queer smile: 'Now, if she only would spring a tidy leak—like that time when we first left the Channel—it would put a stopper on this fire. Wouldn't it?' I remarked irrelevantly, 'Do you remember the rats?'

"We fought the fire and sailed the ship too as carefully as though nothing had been the matter. The steward cooked and attended on us. Of the other twelve men, eight worked while four rested. Everyone took his turn, captain included. There was equality, and if not exactly fraternity, then a deal of good feeling. Sometimes a man, as he dashed a bucketful of water down the hatchway, would yell out, 'Hurrah for Bankok!' and the rest laughed. But generally we were taciturn and serious—and thirsty. Oh! how thirsty! And we had to be careful with the water. Strict allowance. The ship smoked, the sun blazed. . . . Pass the bottle.

"We tried everything. We even made an attempt to dig down to the fire. No good, of course. No man could remain more than a minute below. Mahon, who went first, fainted there, and the man who went to fetch him out did likewise. We lugged them out on deck. Then I leaped down to show how easily it could be done. They had learned wisdom by that time, and contented themselves by fishing for me with a chain-hook tied to a broom-handle, I believe. I did not offer to go and fetch up my shovel, which was left down below.

"Things began to look bad. We put the long-boat into the water. The second boat was ready to swing out. We had also another, a 14-foot thing, on davits aft, where it was quite safe.

"Then, behold, the smoke suddenly decreased. We redoubled our efforts to flood the bottom of the ship. In two days there was no smoke at all. Everybody was on the broad grin. This was on a Friday. On Saturday no work, but sailing the ship of course, was done. The men washed their clothes and their faces for the first time in a fortnight, and had a special dinner given them. They spoke of spontaneous combustion with contempt, and implied *they* were the boys to put out combustions. Somehow we all felt as though we each had inherited a large fortune. But a beastly smell of burning hung about the ship. Captain Beard had hollow eyes and sunken cheeks. I had never noticed so much before how twisted and bowed he was. He and Mahon prowled soberly about hatches and ventilators, sniffing. It struck me suddenly poor Mahon was a very, very old chap. As to me, I was as pleased and proud as though I had helped to win a great naval battle. O! Youth!

"The night was fine. In the morning a homeward-bound ship passed us hull down—the first we had seen for months; but we were nearing the land at last, Java Head being about 190 miles off, and nearly due north.

"Next day it was my watch on deck from eight to twelve. At breakfast the captain observed, 'It's wonderful how that smell hangs about the cabin.' About ten, the mate being on the poop, I stepped down on the main-deck for a moment. The carpenter's bench stood abaft the mainmast: I leaned against it sucking at my pipe, and the carpenter, a young chap, came to talk to me. He remarked, 'I think we have done very well, haven't we?' and then I perceived with annoyance the fool was trying to tilt the bench. I said curtly, 'Don't, Chips,' and immediately became aware of a queer sensation, of an absurd delusion,—I seemed somehow to be in the air. I heard all round me like a pent-up breath released—as if a thousand giants simultaneously had said Phoo!—and felt a dull concussion which made my ribs ache suddenly. No doubt about it—I was in the air, and my body was describing a short parabola. But short as it was, I had the time to think several thoughts in, as far as I can remember, the following order: 'This can't be the carpenter—What is it?—Some accident—Submarine volcano?—Coals, gas!—By Jove! we are being blown up—Everybody's dead—I am falling into the afterhatch—I see fire in it.'

"The coal-dust suspended in the air of the hold had glowed dull-red at the moment of the explosion. In the twinkling of an eye, in an infinitesimal fraction of a second since the first tilt of the bench, I was sprawling full length on the cargo. I picked myself up and scrambled out. It was quick like a rebound. The deck was a wilderness of smashed timber, lying crosswise like trees in a wood after a hurricane; an immense curtain of soiled rags waved gently before me—it was the mainsail blown to strips. I thought, The masts will be toppling over directly; and to get out of the way bolted on all-fours towards the poop-ladder. The first person I saw was Mahon, with eyes like saucers, his mouth open, and the long white hair standing straight on end round his head like a silver halo. He was just about to go down when the sight of the main-deck stirring, heaving up, and changing into splinters before his eyes, petrified him on the top step. I stared at him in unbelief, and he stared at me with a queer kind of shocked curiosity. I did not know that I had no hair, no eyebrows, no eyelashes, that my young moustache was burnt off, that my face was black, one cheek laid open, my nose cut, and my chin bleeding. I had lost my cap, one of my slippers, and my shirt was torn to rags. Of all this I was not aware. I was amazed to see the ship still afloat, the poop-deck whole—and, most of all, to see anybody alive. Also the peace of the sky and the serenity of the sea were distinctly surprising. I suppose I expected to see them convulsed with horror. . . . Pass the bottle.

"There was a voice hailing the ship from somewhere—in the air, in the sky —I couldn't tell. Presently I saw the captain—and he was mad. He asked me eagerly, 'Where's the cabin-table?' and to hear such a question was a frightful shock. I had just been blown up, you understand, and vibrated with that experience,—I wasn't quite sure whether I was alive. Mahon began to stamp with both feet and yelled at him, 'Good God! don't you see the deck's blown out of her?' I found my voice, and stammered out as if conscious of some gross neglect of duty, 'I don't know where the cabin-table is.' It was like an absurd dream.

"Do you know what he wanted next? Well, he wanted to trim the yards. Very placidly, and as if lost in thought, he insisted on having the foreyard squared. 'I don't know if there's anybody alive,' said Mahon, almost tearfully. 'Surely,' he said, gently, 'there will be enough left to square the foreyard.'

"The old chap, it seems, was in his own berth winding up the chronometers, when the shock sent him spinning. Immediately it occurred to him—as he said afterwards—that the ship had struck something, and he ran out into the cabin. There, he saw, the cabin-table had vanished somewhere. The deck being blown up, it had fallen down into the lazarette of course. Where we had our breakfast that morning he saw only a great hole in the floor. This appeared to him so awfully mysterious, and impressed him so immensely, that what he saw and heard after he got on deck were mere trifles in comparison. And, mark, he noticed directly the wheel deserted and his barque off her course—and his only thought was to get that miserable, stripped, undecked, smouldering shell of a ship back again with her head pointing at her port of destination. Bankok! That's what he was after. I tell you this quiet, bowed, bandy-legged, almost deformed little man was immense in the singleness of his idea and in his placid ignorance of our agitation. He motioned us forward with a commanding gesture, and went to take the wheel himself.

"Yes; that was the first thing we did—trim the yards of that wreck! No one was killed, or even disabled, but everyone was more or less hurt. You should have seen them! Some were in rags, with black faces, like coal-heavers, like sweeps, and had bullet heads that seemed closely cropped, but were in fact singed to the skin. Others, of the watch below, awakened by being shot out from their collapsing bunks, shivered incessantly, and kept on groaning even as we went about our work. But they all worked. That crew of Liverpool hard cases had in them the right stuff. It's my experience they always have. It is the sea that gives it—the vastness, the loneliness surrounding their dark stolid souls. Ah! Well! we stumbled, we crept, we fell, we barked our shins on the wreckage, we hauled. The masts stood, but we did not know how much they might be charred down below. It was nearly calm, but a long swell ran from the west and made her roll. They might go at any moment. We looked at them with apprehension. One could not foresee which way they would fall.

"Then we retreated aft and looked about us. The deck was a tangle of planks on edge, of planks on end, of splinters, of ruined woodwork. The masts rose from that chaos like big trees above a matted undergrowth. The interstices of that mass of wreckage were full of something whitish, sluggish, stirring—of something that was like a greasy fog. The smoke of the invisible fire was coming up again, was trailing, like a poisonous thick mist in some valley choked with dead wood. Already lazy wisps were beginning to curl upwards amongst the mass of splinters. Here and there a piece of timber, stuck upright, resembled a post. Half of a fife-rail had been shot through the foresail, and the sky made a patch of glorious blue in the ignobly soiled canvas. A portion of several boards holding together had fallen across the rail, and one end protruded overboard, like a gangway leading upon nothing, like a gangway leading over the deep sea, leading to death—as if inviting us to walk the plank at once and be done with our ridiculous troubles. And still the air, the sky—a ghost, something invisible was hailing the ship.

"Someone had the sense to look over, and there was the helmsman, who had impulsively jumped overboard, anxious to come back. He yelled and swam lustily like a merman, keeping up with the ship. We threw him a rope, and presently he stood amongst us streaming with water and very crestfallen. The captain had surrendered the wheel, and apart, elbow on rail and chin in hand, gazed at the sea wistfully. We asked ourselves, What next? I thought, Now, this is something like. This is great. I wonder what will happen. O youth!

"Suddenly Mahon sighted a steamer far astern. Captain Beard said, 'We may do something with her yet.' We hoisted two flags, which said in the international language of the sea, 'On fire. Want immediate assistance.' The steamer grew bigger rapidly, and by and by spoke with two flags on her foremast, 'I am coming to your assistance.'

"In half an hour she was abreast, to windward, within hail, and rolling slightly, with her engines stopped. We lost our composure, and yelled all together with excitement, 'We've been blown up.' A man in a white helmet, on the bridge, cried, 'Yes! All right! all right!' and he nodded his head, and smiled, and made soothing motions with his hand as though at a lot of frightened children. One of the boats dropped in the water, and walked towards us upon the sea with her long oars. Four Calashes pulled a swinging stroke. This was my first sight of Malay seamen. I've known them since, but what struck me then was their unconcern: they came alongside, and even the bowman standing up and holding to our main-chains with the boat-hook did not deign to lift his head for a glance. I thought people who had been blown up deserved more attention.

"A little man, dry like a chip and agile like a monkey, clambered up. It was the mate of the steamer. He gave one look, and cried, 'O boys—you had better quit.'

"We were silent. He talked apart with the captain for a time,—seemed to argue with him. Then they went away together to the steamer.

"When our skipper came back we learned that the steamer was the *Somerville*, Captain Nash, from West Australia to Singapore *via* Batavia with mails, and that the agreement was she should tow us to Anjer or Batavia, if possible, where we could extinguish the fire by scuttling, and then proceed on our voyage—to Bankok! The old man seemed excited. 'We will do it yet,' he said to Mahon, fiercely. He shook his fist at the sky. Nobody else said a word.

"At noon the steamer began to tow. She went ahead slim and high, and what was left of the *Judea* followed at the end of seventy fathom of tow-rope,—followed her swiftly like a cloud of smoke with mast-heads protruding above. We went aloft to furl the sails. We coughed on the yards, and were careful about the bunts. Do you see the lot of us there, putting a neat furl on the sails of that ship doomed to arrive nowhere? There was not a man who didn't think that at any moment the masts would topple over. From aloft we could not see the ship for smoke, and they worked carefully, passing the gaskets with even turns. 'Harbour furl —aloft there!' cried Mahon from below.

"You understand this? I don't think one of those chaps expected to get down in the usual way. When we did I heard them saying to each other, 'Well, I thought we would come down overboard, in a lump—sticks and all—blame me if I didn't.' 'That's what I was thinking to myself,' would answer wearily another battered and bandaged scarecrow. And, mind, these were men without the drilled-in habit of obedience. To an onlooker they would be a lot of profane scallywags without a redeeming point. What made them do it—what made them obey me when I, thinking consciously how fine it was, made them drop the bunt of the foresail twice to try and do it better? What? They had no professional reputation—no examples, no praise. It wasn't a sense of duty; they all knew well enough how to shirk, and laze, and dodge—when they had a mind to it—and mostly they had. Was it the two pounds ten a-month that sent them there? They didn't think their pay half good enough. No; it was something in them, something inborn and subtle and everlasting. I don't say positively that the crew of a French or German merchantman wouldn't have done it, but I doubt whether it would have been done in the same way. There was a completeness in it, something solid like a principle, and masterful like an instinct—a disclosure of something secret—of that hidden something, that gift of good or evil that makes racial difference, that shapes the fate of nations.

"It was that night at ten that, for the first time since we had been fighting it, we saw the fire. The speed of the towing had fanned the smouldering destruction. A blue gleam appeared forward, shining below the wreck of the deck. It wavered in patches, it seemed to stir and creep like the light of a glowworm. I saw it first, and told Mahon. 'Then the game's up,' he said. 'We had better stop this towing, or she will burst out suddenly fore and aft before we can clear out.' We set up a yell; rang bells to attract their attention; they towed on. At last Mahon and I had to crawl forward and cut the rope with an axe. There was no time to cast off the lashings. Red tongues could be seen licking the wilderness of splinters under our feet as we made our way back to the poop.

"Of course they very soon found out in the steamer that the rope was gone. She gave a loud blast of her whistle, her lights were seen sweeping in a wide circle, she came up ranging close alongside, and stopped. We were all in a tight group on the poop looking at her. Every man had saved a little bundle or a bag. Suddenly a conical flame with a twisted top shot up forward and threw upon the black sea a circle of light, with the two vessels side by side and heaving gently in its centre. Captain Beard had been sitting on the gratings still and mute for hours, but now he rose slowly and advanced in front of us, to the mizzen-shrouds. Captain Nash hailed: 'Come along! Look sharp. I have mail-bags on board. I will take you and your boats to Singapore.'

"'Thank you! No!' said our skipper. 'We must see the last of the ship.'

"'I can't stand by any longer,' shouted the other. 'Mails—you know.'

"'Ay! ay! We are all right.'

"'Very well! I'll report you in Singapore. . . . Good-bye!'

"He waved his hand. Our men dropped their bundles quietly. The steamer moved ahead, and passing out of the circle of light, vanished at once from our sight, dazzled by the fire which burned fiercely. And then I knew that I would see the East first as commander of a small boat. I thought it fine; and the fidelity to the old ship was fine. We should see the last of her. Oh, the glamour of youth! Oh! the fire of it, more dazzling than the flames of the burning ship, throwing a magic light on the wide earth, leaping audaciously to the sky, presently to be quenched by time, more cruel, more pitiless, more bitter than the sea—and like the flames of the burning ship surrounded by an impenetrable night.

"The old man warned us in his gentle and inflexible way that it was part of our duty to save for the underwriters as much as we could of the ship's gear. Accordingly we went to work aft, while she blazed forward to give us plenty of light. We lugged out a lot of rubbish. What didn't we save? An old barometer fixed with an absurd quantity of screws nearly cost me my life: a sudden rush of smoke came upon me, and I just got away in time. There were various stores, bolts of canvas, coils of rope; the poop looked like a marine bazaar, and the boats were lumbered to the gunwales. One would have thought the old man wanted to take as much as he could of his first command with him. He was very, very quiet, but off his balance evidently. Would you believe it? He wanted to take a length of old stream-cable and a kedge-anchor with him in the long-boat. We said, 'Ay, ay, sir,' deferentially, and on the quiet let the things slip overboard. The heavy medicine-chest went that way, two bags of green coffee, tins of paint—fancy, paint! —a whole lot of things. Then I was ordered with two hands into the boats to make a stowage and get them ready against the time it would be proper for us to leave the ship.

"We put everything straight, stepped the long-boat's mast for our skipper, who was to take charge of her, and I was not sorry to sit down for a moment. My face felt raw, every limb ached as if broken, I was aware of all my ribs, and would have sworn to a twist in the backbone. The boats, fast astern, lay in a deep shadow, and all around I could see the circle of the sea lighted by the fire. A gigantic flame arose forward straight and clear. It flared fierce, with noises like the whirr of wings, with rumbles as of thunder. There were cracks, detonations, and from the cone of flame the sparks flew upwards, as man is born to trouble, to leaky ships, and to ships that burn.

"What bothered me was that the ship, lying broadside to the swell and to such wind as there was—a mere breath—the boats would not keep astern where they were safe, but persisted, in a pig-headed way boats have, in getting under the counter and then swinging alongside. They were knocking about dangerously and coming near the flame, while the ship rolled on them, and, of course, there was always the danger of the masts going over the side at any moment. I and my two boat-keepers kept them off as best we could, with oars and boat-hooks; but to be constantly at it became exasperating, since there was no reason why we should not leave at once. We could not see those on board, nor could we imagine what caused the delay. The boat-keepers were swearing feebly, and I had not only my share of the work but also had to keep at it two men who showed a constant inclination to lay themselves down and let things slide.

"At last I hailed, 'On deck there,' and someone looked over. 'We're ready here,' I said. The head disappeared, and very soon popped up again. 'The captain says, All right, sir, and to keep the boats well clear of the ship.'

"Half an hour passed. Suddenly there was a frightful racket, rattle, clanking of chain, hiss of water, and millions of sparks flew up into the shivering colmn of smoke that stood leaning slightly above the ship. The cat-heads had burned away, and the two red-hot anchors had gone to the bottom, tearing out after them two hundred fathom of red-hot chain. The ship trembled, the mass of flame swayed as if ready to collapse, and the fore topgallant-mast fell. It darted down like an arrow of fire, shot under, and instantly leaping up within an oar's-length of the boats, floated quietly, very black on the luminous sea. I hailed the deck again. After some time a man in an unexpectedly cheerful but also muffled tone, as though he had been trying to speak with his mouth shut, informed me, 'Coming directly, sir,' and vanished. For a long time

I heard nothing but the whirr and roar of the fire. There were also whistling sounds. The boats jumped, tugged at the painters, ran at each other playfully, knocked their sides together, or, do what we would, swung in a bunch against the ship's side. I couldn't stand it any longer, and swarming up a rope, clambered aboard over the stern.

"It was as bright as day. Coming up like this, the sheet of fire facing me was a terrifying sight, and the heat seemed hardly bearable at first. On a settee cushion dragged out of the cabin Captain Beard, his legs drawn up and one arm under his head, slept with the light playing on him. Do you know what the rest were busy about? They were sitting on deck right aft, round an open case, eating bread and cheese and drinking bottled stout.

"On the background of flames twisting in fierce tongues above their heads they seemed at home like salamanders, and looked like a band of desperate pirates. The fire sparkled in the whites of their eyes, gleamed on patches of white skin seen through the torn shirts. Each had the marks as of a battle about him—bandaged heads, tied-up arms, a strip of dirty rag round a knee—and each man had a bottle between his legs and a chunk of cheese in his hand. Mahon got up. With his handsome and disreputable head, his hooked profile, his long white beard, and with an uncorked bottle in his hand, he resembled one of those reckless sea-robbers of old making merry amidst violence and disaster. 'The last meal on board,' he explained solemnly. 'We had nothing to eat all day, and it was no use leaving all this.' He flourished the bottle and indicated the sleeping skipper. 'He said he couldn't swallow anything, so I got him to lie down,' he went on; and as I stared, 'I don't know whether you are aware, young fellow, the man had no sleep to speak of for days—and there will be dam' little sleep in the boats.' 'There will be no boats by-and-by if you fool about much longer,' I said, indignantly. I walked up to the skipper and shook him by the shoulder. At last he opened his eyes, but did not move. 'Time to leave her, sir,' I said quietly.

"He got up painfully, looked at the flames, at the sea sparkling round the ship, and black, black as ink farther away; he looked at the stars shining dim through a thin veil of smoke in a sky black, black as Erebus.

"'Youngest first,' he said.

"And the ordinary seaman, wiping his mouth with the back of his hand, got up, clambered over the taffrail, and vanished. Others followed. One, on the point of going over, stopped short to drain his bottle, and with a great swing of his arm flung it at the fire. 'Take this!' he cried.

"The skipper lingered disconsolately, and we left him to commune alone for a while with his first command. Then I went up again and brought him away at last. It was time. The ironwork on the poop was hot to the touch.

"Then the painter of the long-boat was cut, and the three boats, tied together, drifted clear of the ship. It was just sixteen hours after the explosion when we abandoned her. Mahon had charge of the second boat, and I had the smallest—the 14-foot thing. The long-boat would have taken the lot of us; but the skipper said we must save as much property as we could—for the underwriters—and so I got my first command. I had two men with me, a bag of biscuits, a few tins of meat, and a breaker of water. I was ordered to keep close to the long-boat, that in case of bad weather we might be taken into her.

"And do you know what I thought? I thought I would part company as soon as I could. I wanted to have my first command all to myself. I wasn't going to sail in a squadron if there were a chance for independent cruising. I would make land by myself. I would beat the other boats.

Youth! All youth! The silly, charming, beautiful youth.

"But we did not make a start at once. We must see the last of the ship. And so the boats drifted about that night, heaving and setting on the swell. The men dozed, waked, sighed, groaned. I looked at the burning ship.

"Between the darkness of earth and heaven she was burning fiercely upon a disc of purple sea shot by the blood-red play of gleams; upon a disc of water glittering and sinister. A high, clear flame, an immense and lonely flame, ascended from the ocean, and from its summit the black smoke poured continuously at the sky. She burned furiously; mournful and imposing like a funeral pile kindled in the night, surrounded by the sea, watched over by the stars. A magnificent death had come like a grace, like a gift, like a reward to that old ship at the end of her laborious days. The surrender of her weary ghost to the keeping of stars and sea was stirring like the sight of a glorious triumph. The masts fell just before daybreak, and for a moment there was a burst and turmoil of sparks that seemed to fill with flying fire the night patient and watchful, the vast night lying silent upon the sea. At daylight she was only a charred shell, floating still under a cloud of smoke and bearing a glowing mass of coal within.

"Then the oars were got out, and the boats forming in a line moved round her remains as if in procession—the longboat leading. As we pulled across her stern a slim dart of fire shot out viciously at us, and suddenly she went down, head first, in a great hiss of steam. The unconsumed stern was the last to sink; but the paint had gone, had cracked, had peeled off, and there were no letters, there was no word, no stubborn device that was like her soul, to flash at the rising sun her creed and her name.

"We made our way north. A breeze sprang up, and about noon all the boats came together for the last time. I had no mast or sail in mine, but I made a mast out of a spare oar and hoisted a boat-awning for a sail, with a boat-hook for a yard. She was certainly over-masted, but I had the satisfaction of knowing that with the wind aft I could beat the other two. I had to wait for them. Then we all had a look at the captain's chart, and, after a sociable meal of hard bread and water, got our last instructions. There were simple: steer north, and keep together as much as possible. 'Be careful with that jury-rig, Marlow,' said the captain; and Mahon, as I sailed proudly past his boat, wrinkled his curved nose and hailed, 'You will sail that ship of yours under water, if you don't look out, young fellow.' He was a malicious old man—and may the deep sea where he sleeps now rock him gently, rock him tenderly to the end of time!

"Before sunset a thick rain-squall passed over the two boats, which were far astern, and that was the last I saw of them for a time. Next day I sat steering my cockle-shell—my first command—with nothing but water and sky around me. I did sight in the afternoon the upper sails of a ship far away, but said nothing, and my men did not notice her. You see I was afraid she might be homeward bound, and I had no mind to turn back from the portals of the East. I was steering for Java—another blessed name—like Bankok, you know. I steered many days.

"I need not tell you what it is to be knocking about in an open boat. I remember nights and days of calm, when we pulled, we pulled, and the boat seemed to stand still, as if bewitched within the circle of the sea horizon. I remember the heat, the deluge of rain-squalls that kept us baling for dear life (but filled our water cask), and I remember sixteen hours on end with a mouth dry as a cinder and a steering-oar over the stern to keep my first command head on to a breaking sea. I did not know how good a man I was till then. I remember the drawn faces, the dejected figures of my two men, and I remember my youth and the feeling that will never come back any more—the feeling that I could last for ever, outlast the sea, the earth, and all men; the deceitful feeling that lures us on to joys, to perils, to love, to vain effort—to death; the triumphant conviction of strength, the heat of life in the handful of dust, the glow in the heart that with every year grows dim, grows cold, grows small, and expires—and expires, too soon, too soon—before life itself.

"And this is how I see the East. I have seen its secret places and have looked into its very soul; but now I see it always from a small boat, a high outline of mountains, blue and afar in the morning; like faint mist at noon; a jagged wall of purple at sunset. I have the feel of the oar in my hand, the vision of a scorching blue sea in my eyes. And I see a bay, a wide bay, smooth as glass and polished like ice, shimmering in the dark. A red light burns far off upon the gloom of the land, and the night is soft and warm. We drag at the oars with aching arms, and suddenly a puff of wind, a puff faint and tepid and laden with strange odours of blossoms, of aromatic wood, comes out of the still night—the first sigh of the East on my face. That I can never forget. It was impalpable and enslaving, like a charm, like a whispered promise of mysterious delight.

"We had been pulling this finishing spell for eleven hours. Two pulled, and he whose turn it was to rest sat at the tiller. We had made out the red light in that bay and steered for it, guessing it must mark some small coasting port. We passed two vessels, outlandish and high-sterned, sleeping at anchor, and, approaching the light, now very dim, ran the boat's nose against the end of a jutting wharf. We were blind with fatigue. My men dropped the oars and fell off the thwarts as if dead. I made fast to a pile. A current rippled softly. The scented obscurity of the shore was grouped into vast masses, a density of colossal clumps of vegetation, probably—mute and fantastic shapes. And at their foot the semicircle of a beach gleamed faintly, like an illusion. There was not a light, not a stir, not a sound. The mysterious East faced me, perfumed like a flower, silent like death, dark like a grave.

"And I sat weary beyond expression, exulting like a conqueror, sleepless and entranced as if before a profound, a fateful enigma.

"A splashing of oars, a measured dip reverberating on the level of water, intensified by the silence of the shore into loud claps, made me jump up. A boat, a European boat, was coming in. I invoked the name of the dead; I hailed: *Judea* ahoy! A thin shout answered.

"It was the captain. I had beaten the flagship by three hours, and I was glad to hear the old man's voice again, tremulous and tired. 'Is it you, Marlow?' 'Mind the end of that jetty, sir,' I cried.

"He approached cautiously, and brought up with the deep-sea lead-line which we had saved—for the underwriters. I eased my painter and fell alongside. He sat, a broken figure at the stern, wet with dew, his hands clasped in his lap. His men were asleep already. 'I had a terrible time of it,' he murmured. 'Mahon is behind—not very far.' We conversed in whispers, in low whispers, as if afraid to wake up the land. Guns, thunder, earthquakes would not have awakened the men just then.

"Looking round as we talked, I saw away at sea a bright light travelling in the night. 'There's a steamer passing the bay,' I said. She was not passing, she was entering, and she even came close and anchored. 'I wish,' said the old man, 'you would find out whether she is English. Perhaps they could give us a passage somewhere.' He seemed nervously anxious. So by dint of punching and kicking I started one of my men into a state of somnambulism, and giving him an oar, took another and pulled towards the lights of the steamer.

"There was a murmur of voices in her, metallic hollow clangs of the engine-room, footsteps on the deck. Her ports shone, round like dilated eyes. Shapes moved about, and there was a shadowy man high up on the bridge. He heard my oars.

"And then, before I could open my lips, the East spoke to me, but it was in a Western voice. A torrent of words was poured into the enigmatical, the fateful silence; outlandish, angry words, mixed with words and even whole sentences of good English, less strange but even more surprising. The voice swore and cursed violently; it riddled the solemn peace of the bay by a volley of abuse. It began by calling me Pig, and from that went crescendo into unmentionable adjectives —in English. The man up there raged aloud in two languages, and with a sincerity in his fury that almost convinced me I had, in some way, sinned against the harmony of the universe. I could hardly see him, but began to think he would work himself into a fit.

"Suddenly he ceased, and I could hear him snorting and blowing like a porpoise. I said—

" 'What steamer is this, pray?'

" 'Eh? What's this? And who are you?'

" 'Castaway crew of an English barque burnt at sea. We came here to-night. I am the second mate. The captain is in the long-boat, and wishes to know if you would give us a passage somewhere.'

" 'Oh, my goodness! I say. . . . This is the *Celestial* from Singapore on her return trip. I'll arrange with your captain in the morning, . . . and, . . . I say, . . . did you hear me just now?'

" 'I should think the whole bay heard you.'

" 'I thought you were a shore-boat. Now, look here—this infernal lazy scoundrel of a caretaker has gone to sleep again—curse him. The light is out, and I nearly ran foul of the end of this damned jetty. This is the third time he plays me this trick. Now, I ask you, can anybody stand this kind of thing? It's enough to drive a man out of his mind. I'll report him. . . . I'll get the Assistant Resident to give him the sack, by . . . ! See—there's no light. It's out, isn't it? I take you to witness the light's out. There should be a light, you know. A red light on the——'

" 'There was a light,' I said, mildly.

" 'But it's out, man! What's the use of talking like this? You can see for yourself it's out—don't you? If you had to take a valuable steamer along this God-forsaken coast you would want a light, too. I'll kick him from end to end of his miserable wharf. You'll see if I don't. I will——'

" 'So I may tell my captain you'll take us?' I broke in.

" 'Yes, I'll take you. Good-night,' he said, brusquely.

"I pulled back, made fast again to the jetty, and then went to sleep at last. I had faced the silence of the East. I had heard some of its language. But when I opened my eyes again the silence was as complete as though it had never been broken. I was lying in a flood of light, and the sky had never looked so far, so high, before. I opened my eyes and lay without moving.

"And then I saw the men of the East —they were looking at me. The whole length of the jetty was full of people. I saw brown, bronze, yellow faces, the black eyes, the glitter, the colour of an Eastern crowd. And all these beings stared without a murmur, without a sigh, without a movement. They stared down at the boats, at the sleeping men who at night had come to them from the sea. Nothing moved. The fronds of palms stood still against the sky. Not a branch stirred along the shore, and the brown roofs of hidden houses peeped through the green foliage, through the big leaves that hung shining and still like leaves forged of heavy metal. This was the East of the ancient navigators, so old, so mysterious, resplendent and sombre, living and unchanged, full of danger and promise. And these were the men. I sat up suddenly. A wave of movement passed through the crowd from end to end, passed along the heads, swayed the bodies, ran along the jetty like a ripple on the water, like a breath of wind on a field—and all was still again. I see it now—the wide sweep of the bay, the glittering sands, the wealth of green infinite and varied, the sea blue like the sea of a dream, the crowd of attentive faces, the blaze of vivid colour—the water reflecting it all, the curve of the shore, the jetty, the high-sterned outlandish craft floating still, and the three boats with the tired men from the West sleeping, unconscious of the land and the people and of the violence of sunshine. They slept thrown across the thwarts, curled on bottom-boards, in the careless attitudes of death. The head of the old skipper, leaning back in the stern of the long-boat, had fallen on his breast, and he looked as though he would never wake. Farther out old Mahon's face was upturned to the sky, with the long white beard spread out on his breast, as though he had been shot where he sat at the tiller; and a man, all in a heap in the bows of the boat, slept with both arms embracing the stem-head and with his cheek laid on the gunwale. The East looked at them without a sound.

"I have known its fascination since; I have seen the mysterious shores, the still water, the lands of brown nations, where a stealthy Nemesis lies in wait, pursues, overtakes so many of the conquering race, who are proud of their wisdom, of their knowledge, of their strength. But for me all the East is contained in that vision of my youth. It is all in that moment when I opened my young eyes on it. I came upon it from a tussle with the sea—and I was young—and I saw it looking at me. And this is all that is left of it! Only a moment; a moment of strength, of romance, of glamour—of youth! . . . A flick of sunshine upon a strange shore, the time to remember, the time for a sigh, and—good-bye!—Night—Good-bye . . . !"

He drank.

"Ah! The good old time—the good old time. Youth and the sea. Glamour and the sea! The good, strong sea, the salt, bitter sea, that could whisper to you and roar at you and knock your breath out of you."

He drank again.

"By all that's wonderful it is the sea, I believe, the sea itself—or is it youth alone? Who can tell? But you here—you all had something out of life: money, love—whatever one gets on shore—and, tell me, wasn't that the best time, that time when we were young at sea; young and had nothing, on the sea that gives nothing, except hard knocks—and sometimes a chance to feel your strength—that only—what you all regret?"

And we all nodded at him: the man of finance, the man of accounts, the man of law, we all nodded at him over the polished table that like a still sheet of brown water reflected our faces, lined, wrinkled; our faces marked by toil, by deceptions, by success, by love; our weary eyes looking still, looking always, looking anxiously for something out of life, that while it is expected is already gone—has passed unseen, in a sigh, in a flash—together with the youth, with the strength, with the romance of illusions.

LUIGI PIRANDELLO • 1867–1936

The Captive

IT looked as if old Vicé Guarnotta were walking along the road—so regularly did his body sway from side to side with the movements of the little donkey on which he sat. His legs dangled outside the stirrups and nearly dragged along the dusty highway. He was returning, as he did every day at that hour, from his holding on the edge of the plateau, almost overhanging the sea. The aged donkey, even more tired and melancholy than her master, had begun to pant from the effort of ascending the interminable road, which wound its way up the mountain in a succession of steep curves and hairpin bends. At the summit of the spur stood the ramshackle houses of the little town, huddled closely together, one above another. It was so late that the peasants had all returned home from the countryside and the road was deserted. If Guarnotta did happen to meet anyone, he always received a friendly greeting, for—God be thanked —they all thought well of him.

In the old man's eyes, the whole world was now as lonely as that highway, and his own life gray as that twilight. He glanced at the bare branches projecting over the low, cracked walls, the tall dusty cacti, and the heaps of road metal lying here and there—which someone really might have thought of spreading over the numerous holes and ruts. Everything about him was still, silent and deserted, as if, like him, oppressed by a sense of infinite boredom and futility. Even the silence seemed to have turned into dust—dust that lay so thick that he could not hear the footsteps of his donkey.

What quantities of that road dust had the old man carried home every evening! Whenever he took off his coat, his wife seized it and held it out at arm's length. To relieve her feelings, she displayed it round the room—to the chairs and the wardrobe, the bed and the coffer, exclaiming, "Just look at it! Look! Why, you could write on it with your finger!"

If only he would yield to her persuasion and not wear his black suit of broadcloth out on the farm. Hadn't she ordered three corduroy suits for him, for that very purpose—three of them? And while she raged and angrily gesticulated, Guarnotta, sitting in his shirt sleeves, often felt tempted to sink his teeth into the three stumpy fingers she brandished in front of his eyes; but, like a well-behaved dog, he confined himself to giving her a side glance of dissatisfaction and let her continue her nagging. Fifteen years before—on the death of his only son—had he not vowed that he would dress in black for the rest of his life? So, therefore . . .

"But why d'you want to wear black out in the fields? I'll put crepe bands on the sleeves of your corduroy coats. That and a black tie will be quite enough— after fifteen years!"

He let her nag. Was he not out on his holding by the sea the whole blessed day? For years past, he had never been seen in the town. Therefore, if he did not wear mourning for his son out on the countryside, where was he to wear it? Why, in God's name, didn't she think a little before opening her mouth; then she would leave him in peace. . . . Oh! so he was to wear mourning in his heart, was he? Indeed! And who said that he didn't wear it in his heart? But he wanted people to see some external sign of it. Let the

73

trees see it, and the birds of the air—since the boy, alas! was unable to see that he wore it for him. . . . Why on earth was his wife grumbling so about it? Was it because she had to shake and brush the clothes every evening? Why not let the servants do it? There were three of them to wait upon only two persons. Was it for economy's sake? Come, what nonsense! One black suit a year cost only eighty or ninety lire. She ought to realize that it wasn't right—it wasn't kind of her to go on like that. She was his second wife: the son, who had died, had been by the first one. He had no other relatives—even distant ones; therefore, on his death, all his property (and it was no small amount) would pass to her and to her nephews and nieces. She should keep quiet then, if only for decency's sake. . . . Ah well! Being the sort of woman she was, she didn't, of course, see it in that way.

So that was why he stayed out all day, alone on his land, alone with his trees and the panorama of the sea spread just below him; and, as he listened to the continuous gentle rustling of the foliage and the sad little song of the waves—which seemed to float up to him from an endless distance—his soul was constantly oppressed by a sense of the vanity of all things and the insufferable boredom of life.

He had reached a point less than half a mile from the little town and could hear the soft chimes of the Ave Maria from the chapel of the Addolorata on the top of the hill, when at a sharp bend in the road, there came a shout, "Face to the ground!"

Three men, who had lain ambushed in the shadow, sprang out upon him; he noticed that they wore masks and carried guns. One seized his ass's bridle, while the others, in the twinkling of an eye, dragged him from the saddle and threw him on the road; one man knelt on his legs and fastened his wrists together, the other meanwhile bandaging his eyes with a folded handkerchief tied tightly round his head.

He had barely time to say, "But what do you want, my lads?"—when he was forced to his feet, pushed and hustled off the road, and dragged violently down the stony hillside toward the valley.

"But, my lads. . . ."

"Silence or you're a dead man!"

He was frightened by their rough handling, but still more so by the state of terror that the three men were in—obviously on account of their deed of violence. He could hear them panting like wild beasts. They were going to do something horrible to him.

But perhaps they did not mean to kill him—at any rate not at once. If they had been paid to murder him, or were carrying out a vendetta, they would have despatched him up there on the highroad, from their ambush in the shadows. So it must be that they were carrying him off for a ransom.

"My lads. . . ."

They gripped his arms more tightly, shook him, and told him again to be silent.

"But at least loosen the bandage a little. It's very tight on my eyes. . . . I can't . . ."

"Go on! Move."

First down, then up, now straight on, then turning back; down again, then up and up and up. Where could they be taking him?

Sinister imaginings haunted his mind on that terrible, blind march over rocks and thorns, pushed and pulled along in total darkness. And then, suddenly, he saw the lights—the lights of the little town on top of the ridge—the oil lamps shining from the houses and streets—just as he had seen them round the bend a moment before he was attacked, just as he had seen them again and again on his way home from his holding at that evening hour. How strange! He saw them plainly through the tight bandage over his eyes—as clearly as before when his eyes were open. How strange.... As he stumbled on and on, savagely pulled and pushed by his captors, so that his heart filled with terror, he took the little lamps with him; and not only those soft, sad little lamps, but the whole of the mountain spur with the town on its summit—the town whose other inhabitants went safely and peacefully about their business, unconscious of his horrible adventure.

At one point he caught the sound of the hurried patter of his ass's hoofs.

Oh! So they were dragging his weary old donkey along, too! She, poor beast, could not understand. All she would notice would be the unwonted hurry and rough treatment, but she would go where she was taken, without any idea of what had happened. If only they would stop a moment and let him speak, he would tell them quietly that he was ready to pay whatever they demanded. He had not long now to live, and it really was not worth while suffering such hideous treatment just for the sake of a little money—money which brought him no satisfaction.

"My lads...."

"Silence! Go on!"

"I can't imagine it.... Why are you doing this to me? I'm ready to..."

"Silence! We'll talk later. Go on!"

They made him trudge like that for what seemed eternity. At last, overcome by weariness and sick and giddy from the tight bandage, he fainted and remained unconscious.

He recovered his senses next morning and found himself lying, utterly exhausted, in a low cavern.

A strong, musty smell seemed to emanate from the first light of dawn, which entered wanly through the winding entrance to the chalky grotto. Faint though it was, that light comforted him in his pain—the pain he felt from the rough handling he had undergone. He remembered that brutal violence as if it had been a nightmare—remembered how, when he had been unable to keep on his feet, he had been carried, first on one man's back and then on another's, dropped on the ground and dragged along, then held up by his arms and legs.

Where was he now? He listened attentively: from the stillness outside, he imagined that he was high on some lofty peak. The idea made him feel quite giddy. He was unable to move, for his hands and feet were tied, and he lay stretched on the ground like a dead animal. His limbs and head were so heavy that they seemed made of lead. He wondered whether he was wounded. Perhaps they had left him there for dead.

No. There they were, discussing something outside the cave. So his fate was not yet settled.... He considered what had happened, and found that he had no longer any thought of attempting to escape from his position of danger. He knew that he could not escape, and he had almost lost the will to do so. The disaster was accomplished—it was as if it had happened a long time ago, almost in a previous life. That life had been a miserable affair, and he had left it far, far away, down below in the valley, where they had captured him. Now he had only the silence of that high place—a void in which the past was forgotten. Even if they set him free, he no longer had the strength, perhaps not even the desire, to go down and restart the old life.

Suddenly a wave of self-pity swept over him, and he began to shudder with horror at the fate awaiting him, as he saw one of his captors crawling into the cave on all fours. The man's face was concealed by a red handkerchief with holes made in front for the eyes. Guarnotta looked quickly at his hands. They carried no weapons, only a new pencil—the kind you buy for a penny—not yet sharpened. In his other hand was a crumpled sheet of common note paper, with an envelope held in its fold.

The old man felt reassured. He smiled involuntarily. At that moment, the other two—also masked—entered the cave on their hands and knees. One of them came up to him and undid his hands, but not his feet. Then the first to enter spoke, "Now have some sense! You must write as we tell you."

Guarnotta thought he recognized the voice. Yes, of course! It was Manuzza—so called because he had one arm shorter than the other. But was it really he? A glance at the man's left arm confirmed his suspicion. He felt sure that he would recognize the other two, if they removed their masks, for he knew everyone in the town.

He replied, "Have some sense, indeed! It's you, my lads, who ought to have some sense. To whom do you want me to write? And what am I to write with? That thing?" He pointed to the pencil.

"Why not? It's a pencil, isn't it?"

"Yes, it's a pencil, all right. But you don't even understand how such things are used."

"What d'you mean?"

"Why! You must sharpen it first!"

"Sharpen it?"

"Yes, sharpen it, with a penknife, there —at the tip."

"Penknife—I haven't got one," said Manuzza, and added, "Have some sense, now—here, have some sense!" followed by a string of oaths.

"Yes, I've got sense, all right, Manuzza . . . ."

"Oh!" shouted the fellow. "So you've recognized me?"

"What else can you expect, when you hide your face and leave your left arm exposed? Take off that handkerchief and look me straight in the eyes. Why are you doing this . . . to me?"

"Stop all that chatter!" bellowed Manuzza, pulling the handkerchief from his face. "I've told you to have some sense. Either you write or I'll kill you!"

"Yes, yes! I'm ready to write," rejoined Guarnotta, "when you've sharpened the pencil. But—if you don't mind my asking—it's money you want, my lads, isn't it? How much?"

"Three thousand florins!"

"Three thousand? That's no small sum."

"You're worth that much! Let's have no nonsense about it!"

"Three thousand florins?"

"Yes, and more too! More than that!"

"Quite true. I am worth more than that, but I've not got that sum at home, in ready money. I should have to sell some houses and fields. D'you think that can be done at a day's notice and without my presence there?"

"Tell them to borrow the money!"

"Tell who?"

"Your wife and nephews!"

Guarnotta smiled bitterly and tried to raise himself up on one of his elbows. "That's just the point I wanted to explain," he answered. "My lads, you have made a great mistake. Are you counting on my wife and her nephews? If you're bent on killing me, kill me. Here I am! Kill me and no more said about it. But if it's money you're after, you can only get the money from me, on condition that you let me return home so I can raise it."

"What are you talking about? Let you go home? Do you think we're mad? You're joking!"

"Well, then . . ." began Guarnotta, with a sigh.

Manuzza snatched the sheet of writing paper angrily from his companion's hand and repeated, "Stop all that chatter, as I told you—just you write! The pencil . . . Oh God, yes! . . . it has to be sharpened. . . . How's that done?"

Guarnotta explained the way and the men exchanged glances and left the cave. As he saw them crawl out, on all fours—looking like three animals—he could not refrain from smiling once more. He reflected that they were now engaged in trying to sharpen the pencil, and that perhaps, by dint of pruning it like a branch of a tree, they would fail in their attempts. That was what might well happen, and he smiled at the idea, at the thought that, at that moment, his life depended on the absurd difficulty which those three men would be up against, in trying to carry out an operation they had never performed before. Perhaps, when they saw the pencil growing smaller and smaller they would be so annoyed that, on their next entry, they would show him that though their knives might be no good for sharpening a pencil, they were quite good for cutting his throat. . . . He had been a fool and had committed an unpardonable mistake in letting that fellow Manuzza know that he had recognized him. . . . Yes, he could hear them all talking at once—outside the cave shouting and cursing. He was sure they were passing that wretched penny pencil from one to another and that it was growing shorter and shorter under their clumsy treatment. Heaven knows what kind of knives they held in their great chalky fists. . . . There they were, crawling back in single file, having failed in their endeavor.

"The wood's rotten," said Manuzza. "That pencil's no good. As you know how to write, haven't you got a decent pencil in your pocket, properly sharpened?"

"No, I haven't, my lads," replied Guarnotta. "And anyhow it would be useless, I assure you. I would have written if you'd given me a pencil and paper. But to whom should I write? To my wife and nephews? They are her nephews, not mine—d'you understand that? You may be quite sure that none of them would have answered. They'd have pretended that they never received the threatening letter, and wash their hands of me. If you want money from them, you shouldn't have begun by falling on me. You should have made terms with them—say a thousand florins—for killing me. But they wouldn't even have paid that much. . . . I quite admit that they look forward to my death, but—you see— I'm an old man, and they expect that God will very soon grant it to them free of expense and in that way there'll be no feeling of remorse. You surely don't imagine they'd pay you a *centesimo,* one single *centesimo,* to *save* my life? You have muddled the whole business. My life is only of interest to myself; and it isn't of much interest even to me—that's the truth. Still, I admit, I don't want to die like this—it's a horrible death. And therefore, simply to escape that kind of end, I promise and swear to you, by the soul of my dear son, that, as soon as I possibly can—within two or three days—I myself will bring you the money to the place you appoint."

"Yes! After you've already reported us!"

"I swear that I will not do so. I swear that I will not breathe a word of this matter to anyone. Remember, my life is at stake!"

"It is at present, but will it be when you are free? Why, even before going home, you'll report us to the police!"

"I swear to you that I will not! You really ought to trust me. Remember that I go out every day into the country, and my life, out there, is in your hands. And have I not always been a father to you boys? God knows, you have always looked up to me and respected me. . . . Do you think that I'm anxious to expose myself to the danger of a vendetta? No, you ought to trust my word and let me return home, and you can be sure that you'll have the money."

They said no more to him, but exchanged glances and left the cave crawling away on hands and knees.

All day long he did not see them again. At first he could hear them engaged in discussion outside; after a while, no further sound reached him.

He lay there, turning over in his mind all the probabilities, and wondering what decision they would come to. One thing seemed clear to him—that he had fallen into the hands of three stupid fellows, mere amateurs, and that this was probably their first essay in crime. They had entered on it blindly, thinking solely of his money, without giving any previous consideration to their position as married men with families. Now that they realized their blunder, they did not know what to do next, and could see no way out of their difficulties. As for his oath that he would not denounce them, none of the three would trust in it, least of all Manuzza, who had been recognized. What was to happen then?

His only hope was that it would not occur to anyone of them to feel repentance for their stupid, unreasonable act, and a consequent desire to wipe out every trace of this first offence. If they decided to continue brigandage as outlaws, they might as well spare his life and set him free, without worrying about his denouncing them; but, if they repented and wanted to return to an honest livelihood, they must necessarily prevent the denunciation which they were convinced would follow on his freedom, and therefore they must murder him.

It followed from this that God might, he hoped, come to his assistance by enlightening them—by bringing them to see that it would not profit them to live an honest life. It should not be difficult to persuade them of this, seeing that they had already shown, by kidnapping him, that they were prepared to imperil their immortal souls. But he was very anxious about the disillusionment which they must have experienced when their eyes were opened to the great blunder they had committed, at the outset of a career of crime; for disillusionment is very apt to turn into repentance and into a desire to abandon a path which has begun badly. To withdraw from it, obliterating every trace of their previous steps, they might logically hold that they had no alternative but to commit a crime; for if they were willing to set him free, would they not, with equal logic, be forced to go on committing crimes? They would conclude then that it was better to commit that one crime at the outset—a deed which would remain secret, entirely untraced—than to commit any number of crimes, done openly as outlaws. At the cost of one misdeed, they could still hope to save themselves, not indeed as far as their consciences were concerned, but in the sight of men: if they were to release him—they would argue—they would be irretrievably lost.

As a result of these harassing reflections, he arrived at the conclusion that on that day or on the morrow, perhaps that very night while he slept, they would assassinate him.

He waited until it grew dark inside the cave. Then, overcome with terror at the thought of falling asleep in that silent and dreadful place, he determined to crawl outside the cave, even though his hands and feet were still tied. He moved forward with infinite difficulty, wriggling along like a worm, restraining his instinctive fears in an endeavor to make the least possible noise. What could he possibly hope for, in trying to poke his head out, like a glowworm from its hole? Nothing. But at least he would see the sky and meet his death in the open, face to face, and not have it come upon him treacherously in his sleep. That was something.

Ah! there he was, at last . . . Quietly. . . . Was that moonlight? Yes, there was the young moon, and countless stars. . . . What a splendid night! Where was he? . . . On some mountaintop—the air and the silence proved that . . . Perhaps that was Monte Caltafaraci over there, or San Benedetto. . . . Then what was that valley? Either the plain of Consolida or the valley of Clerici? Yes, and that mountain to the west must be the Carapezza. But if so, what were those twinkling lights over there, glittering like clusters of fireflies in the opal moonlight? Were they the lights of Girgenti? Why then—good God!—then he was quite near! And it had seemed as if they had made him walk so far, so far. . . .

He looked anxiously round him, as if the possibility that they might have gone off, leaving him there, aroused his fear rather than hope. Dark and motionless, squatting like a great owl on a bank of chalk, sat one of the three men, left on guard; he showed plainly in the faint, pale light of the moon. Was he asleep?

The old man tried to squirm his way out a little farther, but all at once his arms lost all their power, as he heard a voice saying quite calmly, "I'm watching you, Don Vicé. Back you go, or I shoot!"

He held his breath and lay motionless, looking out. Perhaps the man might think that he had made a mistake.

"I'm watching you."

"Let me have a breath of fresh air," he then begged. "I'm suffocated inside there. D'you mean to keep me like this? I'm dying of thirst—"

The man made a threatening gesture. "Well, you can stay there, but only on condition you don't utter a sound. I'm hungry and thirsty too, as well as you. Keep silent or I make you go back inside."

Silence . . . But at least he had the moon, reavealing all those quiet valleys and mountains . . . and the relief of the fresh air . . . and the sad glimmer of those distant lights shining from his native town.

Where had the other two gone? Had they left to this third man the task of despatching him during the night? If so, why did he not do it at once? What was he waiting for? Was he perhaps waiting for the other two to come back that night?

Again he felt tempted to speak, but restrained himself. Well, if that was what they had decided to do . . .

He looked again at the slope where the man had been squatting and saw that he had resumed his former position. Judging from his voice and accent, Guarnotta concluded that he came from Grotte, a large village among the sulphur mines. Could it possibly be Fillico, a quiet, kindly fellow, a regular beast of burden, strong as a horse? If it really was he—if that silent, hard-working man had left the straight path, it was a bad business.

He could not stand it any longer, but spoke almost automatically, not as a question, in fact without any clear intention—it seemed as if he meant the name to sound as if uttered by some one else.

"Fillico . . ." The man did not stir.

Guarnotta waited, then repeated it in the same tone, as if it were some other person talking; as he spoke, he gazed intently at his finger with which he was drawing marks on the sand.

"Fillico."

This time a shudder ran down his spine at the thought that his obstinacy in repeating that name—almost involuntarily—was likely to be paid for by a gunshot in return.

But again the man made no movement. Then Guarnotta gave a loud sigh of despair; suddenly his head was a dead weight which he could no longer support. He lay like a dying animal, with his face in the sand—the sand running into his open mouth—and, in spite of the prohibition against speaking and the threat of shooting, he began to rave—to rave interminably. He spoke of the beautiful moon—he cried a farewell to it, for it had by this time set; he spoke of the stars which God had created and placed in the distant heavens, so that the brute creation could not know that they were really countless worlds, much larger than this earth; he spoke of the earth, saying that everyone who is not a brute—a mere animal—knows that it spins like a top; it seemed to relieve his feelings to declare that at that very moment there were men on it with their heads pointing downward, and that they did not fall off into the sky for reasons which everyone ought to take the trouble to find out, unless he were the lowest of the low—a mere clod into which our Lord God has not breathed the divine spirit.

In the midst of all his wild raving, he suddenly found that he was talking astronomy, expounding it like a professor; and the man who had gradually drawn nearer to him was now sitting beside him there, close to the mouth of the cave; and it actually was as he had guessed—Fillico from Grotte; and that it so happened that Fillico had wanted to know about these matters for years—all about the zodiac, the milky way, the nebulae.... But he was not easy to convince; he did not think the explanations given were true.

It was a strange situation. It was strange, too, that though he was at the end of his strength, exhausted by despair, though he had a gun barrel pointing at him—yet he was able to devote great attention to cleaning his fingernails with a stalk of grass, taking care that it did not break or bend. He also examined his remaining teeth—only three incisors and one canine—and devoted much consideration to the problem whether his neighbor, the maker of wine jars, who had lost his wife a fortnight back, was left with three children or with four....

"Now, let's talk seriously. Just tell me, what d'you think I am? By the Madonna! D'you think I am a blade of grass—that blade of grass there, which you can pluck like this, just as if it were nothing? Feel me! By the Madonna, I'm made of flesh and blood, and I have a soul, which God gave me, just as He has given you one. Yet you mean to cut my throat while I'm asleep? No . . . don't go . . . wait here, listen to me.... What? You're not going? Oh! I see—as long as I was speaking of the stars.... Listen to what I've got to say. Cut my throat here while I'm awake —not treacherously while I'm asleep ... d'you hear? What d'you say to that? You won't answer? But why are you putting it off? What are you waiting for, I want to know? If it's money you're after, you won't get it. You can't keep me here and you don't want to let me go . . . you mean to kill me? Well, for God's sake do it and get it over!"

But he was talking to empty space. The man had gone off and was again squatting like an owl on the slope, to show him that it was quite useless to speak on that subject—he would not listen to a word.

After all, thought Guarnotta, how stupid it was to worry like that. If he had to be murdered, was it not better to be murdered during his sleep? He even decided that if he was still awake when he heard them crawl into the cave later on, he would shut his eyes and pretend to be sleeping. Not that there was any need to shut his eyes really—it would be dark and he could keep them open. All he had to do was to make no movement when they came close and were feeling for his throat, to cut it like a sheep's.

So he simply said, "Good night," and crawled away inside the cave.

They did not, however, murder him. They admitted their blunder; but were unwilling either to free him or to kill him. They would keep him there.

"What! Forever?"

For as long as God saw fit. They placed themselves in His hands. The captivity would terminate sooner or later, according as He wished to impose upon them a short or a long expiation for their fault in taking Guarnotta captive.

What was their intention then? That he should die a natural death up there? Could that be their intention? he asked.

Yes, that was it.

"But by all that is holy, can't you silly idiots see that it's not God, in the least, who is going to kill me? It's you who will be doing it, keeping me here in this cave, dying of hunger and thirst and cold, tied up like an animal, sleeping on the ground, easing myself here on the ground like an animal.

His protest was in vain: they had placed the matter in God's hands and their prisoner might as well have been talking to stones. They pointed out to him, however, that as for dying of starvation, it was not true; neither was it true that he would have to sleep on the ground. They had brought him up three bundles of straw for his bed, and, to keep off the cold, there was an old cloak padded with cotton wool, which belonged to one of them. And, moreover, there would be his daily bread and something to eat with it. They took it out of their own mouths and from the mouths of their wives and children to give it to him. It was bread which cost them much toil to procure, for one of them would have to keep guard over him, taking it in turns, while the other two went out to work. In the earthen pitcher was drinking water—and God only knew how hard it was to find water in that thirsty tract. As for his having to ease himself on the floor of his cave, he could go outside at night into the open.

When he found that he could make no impression on his stupid obduracy, he began to stamp his feet like a child. Were they brutes, then, with hearts of stone?

"Look here! Do you admit you've made a grave mistake—yes or no?"

Yes, they admitted it.

"Do you admit that you've got to pay for that mistake?"

Yes, they would pay for it by refraining from killing him, by waiting till God granted them his death and by endeavoring to alleviate, to the utmost of their power, the suffering which they had brought upon him.

"Very good. Oh, very good indeed! That's your expiation—you blockheads—for the sin you yourselves confess that you've committed? But what about me? Where do I come in? What sin did I commit? Am I, or am I not, the victim of your mistake? Why should you make me pay the penalty for the sin which you committed? Since I had nothing to do with it, why should I suffer in this way—for your fault? How can you justify that?"

No, they did not attempt any justification, but simply listened to him—their harsh-stained features impassive, their eyes dull and fixed. There was the straw—there was the overcoat . . . and there the pitcher of water . . . and the bread which they had earned with the sweat of their brows . . . and he could come outside when he had to.

They persisted in their expiation, taking it in turns to remain behind on guard over him. When keeping him company, they made him tell them about the stars and about all manner of things in town and country—what splendid harvests there were in former times when people were truly religious and how certain diseases of plants were not known in those good old days when there was more religion. They brought him an old almanac picked up somewhere, so that he could beguile his leisure by reading it, and stood around him watching, full of envy at his being able to read.

"Do tell us what it means—this printed sheet with that moon and the scales and those fish and the scorpion?"

His words stimulated their curiosity and they were gluttons for further knowledge, listening to him with childlike wonder and uttering low grunts of amazement. Little by little, he came to enjoy his talks with them. In telling of so much that was new to them, it almost seemed to be new to him too, as if something alive were stirring within him, as if his soul were awakening after long years of torpor in his former distressful existence. Once his anger had subsided, he found that a new life was beginning for him and tried to adapt himself to it. As time passed, he bowed before the inevitable. Though his surroundings were strange and devoid of interest, he was no longer under the threat of a horrible end.

By this time, he reflected, he was already dead to everyone, on his distant farm overlooking the sea and in the town whose lights he could see at night. Perhaps no one had bothered to search for him after his mysterious disappearance; even if they had searched, they would not have put much energy into the task, as there was nobody keenly interested in finding him.

Since his heart had withered long years ago, what object was there now in returning to life—to that life which he had been leading? He felt that he had no real ground for complaint at his deprivations; for if he could recover his former comfort, he would recover also the terrible depression of his former life—a life that dragged its weary way through years of intolerable boredom! There was this to be said for his captivity, that although he spent his time merely lying on the ground, he did not feel the hours drag so wearily. Day followed day on the silent mountain spur devoid of all sense and purpose, and it seemed to him as if time had ceased. In that extreme seclusion, even the consciousness of his own existence dropped away from him. He would look round at his shoulders and the chalk wall of the cave beside him, as the only things which had a real existence; or his hand, if his eyes rested on it—yes, that too was real and lived just on its own account; or it might be that rock or twig —they existed in a world of frightful isolation.

As the old man's anger at his unjust treatment died down, and he came gradually to the conclusion that what had befallen him was not such a disaster as had at first appeared, he began to perceive that it was indeed a very severe punishment that those three men had inflicted upon themselves—the task of keeping him there as a prisoner. Dead though he was to everyone else, he remained alive solely for them, and they had taken on the entire burden of his support. They could have freed themselves from that burden without the slightest difficulty, since his person no longer possessed value to anyone, since nobody took any interest in him. But, on the contrary, they continued to bear it, and carried through with resignation their self-imposed punishment. Not only did they never complain, but they even did their best to render their task still more arduous by the little attentions which they lavished on him. For, quite apart from the duty imposed by their consciences, they had, all three of them, become genuinely attached to the old man, regarding him as their own private property in which no one else had any claim. In some mysterious manner, they derived a great satisfaction from this—a satisfaction which they would miss for the rest of their lives, when the time came to lose him.

One day, Fillico brought his wife to the cave. She had her baby at her breast and was holding a little girl by the hand; the child had carried up a fine homemade cake as a gift for "granddad."

How they stared at him—the mother and daughter. He reflected that by then he must have been several months in captivity and presented a lamentable appearance—dirty, ragged, and with tufts of bushy hair on his chin and cheeks. Pleased at their visit, he received them with a friendly smile. Perhaps it was the sight of a smile on the emaciated face which so startled the good woman and her daughter.

"Don't be afraid, my darling! Come here, little one . . . that's right. See, there's a bit for you. Yes, you eat it. So Mummy made it, did she?"

"Mummy."

"That's lovely. Have you got any little brothers? . . . Three? Oh! Poor Fillico! Four children already. . . . Bring the boys up here to me. I'd like to see them. Next week, yes, that's right—only I hope there won't be any next week for me...."

The next week duly arrived: in truth God wished the three men's expiation to last a long time, for it dragged on for over two months more.

He died on a Sunday, on a splendid evening when it was still bright as day, up on the heights. Fillico had brought his children to see old granddad and Manuzza his also. He died while he was playing with the children, behaving like a boy himself, wearing a red handkerchief over his head to cloak his bushy hair. While amusing the children and laughing at his own antics, he suddenly collapsed on the ground; the men rushed forward to pick him up and found him dead.

They put the children on one side and sent them and the women down from the mountain. Kneeling around the corpse, the three men burst into floods of tears, with fervent prayers for his soul and for their own salvation. They then buried him in the cave.

The rest of their lives, if anyone happened to mention Guarnotta in their presence and speak of his mysterious disappearance, they would say. "He was a saint, that man. . . . I'm sure he was admitted straight to paradise."

—Translated by
Arthur and Henri Mayne

STEPHEN CRANE • 1871-1900

The Bride Comes to Yellow Sky

THE great Pullman was whirling onward with such dignity of motion that a glance from the window seemed simply to prove that the plains of Texas were pouring eastward. Vast flats of green grass, dull-hued spaces of mesquit and cactus, little groups of frame houses, woods of light and tender trees, all were sweeping into the east, sweeping over the horizon, a precipice.

A newly married pair had boarded this coach at San Antonio. The man's face was reddened from many days in the wind and sun, and a direct result of his new black clothes was that his brick-coloured hands were constantly performing in a most conscious fashion. From time to time he looked down respectfully at his attire. He sat with a hand on each knee, like a man waiting in a barber's shop. The glances he devoted to other passengers were furtive and shy.

The bride was not pretty, nor was she very young. She wore a dress of blue cashmere, with small reservations of velvet here and there, and with steel buttons abounding. She continually twisted her head to regard her puff sleeves, very stiff, straight, and high. They embarrassed her. It was quite apparent that she had cooked, and that she expected to cook, dutifully. The blushes caused by the careless scrutiny of some passengers as she had entered the car were strange to see upon this plain, under-class countenance, which was drawn in placid, almost emotionless lines.

They were evidently very happy. "Ever been in a parlour-car before?" he asked, smiling with delight.

"No," she answered; "I never was. It's fine, ain't it?"

"Great! And then after a while we'll go forward to the diner, and get a big lay-out. Finest meal in the world. Charge a dollar."

"Oh, do they?" cried the bride. "Charge a dollar? Why, that's too much—for us—ain't it, Jack?"

"Not this trip, anyhow," he answered bravely. "We're going to go the whole thing."

Later he explained to her about the trains. "You see, it's a thousand miles from one end of Texas to the other; and this train runs right across it, and never stops but four times." He had the pride of an owner. He pointed out to her the dazzling fittings of the coach; and in truth her eyes opened wider as she contemplated the sea-green figured velvet, the shining brass, silver, and glass, the wood that gleamed as darkly brilliant as the surface of a pool of oil. At one end a bronze figure sturdily held a support for a separated chamber, and at convenient places on the ceiling were frescos in olive and silver.

To the minds of the pair, their surroundings reflected the glory of their marriage that morning in San Antonio; this was the environment of their new estate; and the man's face in particular beamed with an elation that made him appear ridiculous to the Negro porter. This individual at times surveyed them from afar with an amused and superior grin. On other occasions he bullied them with skill in ways that did not make it exactly plain to them that they were being bullied. He subtly used all the manners of the most unconquerable kind of snobbery. He oppressed them; but of this oppression they had small knowledge, and they speedily forgot that infrequently a number of travellers covered them with stares of derisive enjoyment. Historically there was supposed to be something infinitely humorous in their situation.

"We are due in Yellow Sky at 3:42," he said, looking tenderly into her eyes.

"Oh, are we?" she said, as if she had not been aware of it. To evince surprise at her husband's statement was part of her wifely amiability. She took from a pocket a little silver watch; and as she held it before her, and stared at it with a frown of attention, the new husband's face shone.

"I bought it in San Anton' from a friend of mine," he told her gleefully.

"It's seventeen minutes past twelve," she said, looking up at him with a kind of shy and clumsy coquetry. A passenger, noting this play, grew excessively sardonic, and winked at himself in one of the numerous mirrors.

At last they went to the dining-car. Two rows of Negro waiters, in glowing white suits, surveyed their entrance with the interest, and also the equanimity, of men who had been forewarned. The pair fell to the lot of a waiter who happened to feel pleasure in steering them through their meal. He viewed them with the manner of a fatherly pilot, his countenance radiant with benevolence. The patronage, entwined with the ordinary deference, was not plain to them. And yet, as they returned to their coach, they showed in their faces a sense of escape.

To the left, miles down a long purple slope, was a little ribbon of mist where moved the keening Rio Grande. The train was approaching it at an angle, and the apex was Yellow Sky. Presently it was apparent that, as the distance from Yellow Sky grew shorter, the husband became commensurately restless. His brick-red hands were more insistent in their prominence. Occasionally he was even rather absent-minded and far-away when the bride leaned forward and addressed him.

As a matter of truth, Jack Potter was beginning to find the shadow of a deed weigh upon him like a leaden slab. He, the town marshal of Yellow Sky, a man known, liked, and feared in his corner, a prominent person, had gone to San Antonio to meet a girl he believed he loved, and there, after the usual prayers, had actually induced her to marry him, without consulting Yellow Sky for any part of the transaction. He was now bringing his bride before an innocent and unsuspecting community.

Of course people in Yellow Sky married as it pleased them, in accordance with a general custom; but such was Potter's thought of his duty to his friends, or of their idea of his duty, or of an unspoken form which does not control men in these matters, that he felt he was heinous. He had committed an extraordinary crime. Face to face with this girl in San Antonio, and spurred by his sharp impulse, he had gone headlong over all the social hedges. At San Antonio he was like a man hidden in the dark. A knife to sever any friendly duty, any form, was easy to his hand in that remote city. But the hour of Yellow Sky—the hour of daylight—was approaching.

He knew full well that his marriage was an important thing to his town. It could only be exceeded by the burning of the new hotel. His friends could not forgive him. Frequently he had reflected on the advisability of telling them by telegraph, but a new cowardice had been upon him. He feared to do it. And now the train was hurrying him toward a scene of amazement, glee, and reproach. He glanced out of the window at the line of haze swinging slowly in toward the train.

Yellow Sky had a kind of brass band, which played painfully, to the delight of the populace. He laughed without heart as he thought of it. If the citizens could dream of his prospective arrival with his bride, they would parade the band at the station and escort them, amid cheers and laughing congratulations, to his adobe home.

He resolved that he would use all the devices of speed and plainscraft in making the journey from the station to his house. Once within that safe citadel, he could issue some sort of vocal bulletin, and then not go among the citizens until they had time to wear off a little of their enthusiasm.

The bride looked anxiously at him. "What's worrying you, Jack?"

He laughed again. "I'm not worrying, girl; I'm only thinking of Yellow Sky."

She flushed in comprehension.

A sense of mutual guilt invaded their minds and developed a finer tenderness. They looked at each other with eyes softly aglow. But Potter often laughed the same nervous laugh; the flush upon the bride's face seemed quite permanent.

The traitor to the feelings of Yellow Sky narrowly watched the speeding landscape. "We're nearly there," he said.

Presently the porter came and announced the proximity of Potter's home. He held a brush in his hand, and, with all his airy superiority gone, he brushed Potter's new clothes as the latter slowly turned this way and that way. Potter fumbled out a coin and gave it to the porter, as he had seen others do. It was a heavy and muscle-bound business, as that of a man shoeing his first horse.

The porter took their bag, and as the train began to slow they moved forward to the hooded platform, and he was glad and astonished to see there was none upon it but the station-agent, who, with a slightly hurried and anxious air, was walking toward the water-tanks. When the train had halted, the porter alighted first, and placed in position a little temporary step.

"Come on, girl," said Potter, hoarsely.

As he helped her down each laughed on a false note. He took the bag from the Negro, and bade his wife cling to his arm. As they slunk rapidly away, his hang-dog glance perceived that they were unloading the two trunks, and also that the station-agent, far ahead near the baggage-car, had turned and was running toward him, making gestures. He laughed, and groaned as he laughed, when he noted the first effect of his marital bliss upon Yellow Sky. He gripped his wife's arm firmly to his side, and they fled. Behind them the porter stood, chuckling fatuously.

II

The California express on the Southern Railway was due at Yellow Sky in twenty-one minutes. There were six men at the bar of the Weary Gentleman saloon. One was a drummer who talked a great deal and rapidly; three were Texans who did not care to talk at that time; and two were Mexican sheep-herders, who did not talk as a general practice in the Weary Gentleman saloon. The barkeeper's dog lay on the board walk that crossed in front of the door. His head was on his paws, and he glanced drowsily here and there with the constant vigilance of a dog that is kicked on occasion. Across the sandy street were some vivid green grass-plots, so wonderful in appearance, amid the sands that burned near them in a blazing sun, that they caused a doubt in the mind. They exactly resembled the grass mats used to represent lawns on the stage. At the cooler end of the railway station, a man without a coat sat in a tilted chair and smoked his pipe. The fresh-cut bank of the Rio Grande circled near the town, and there could be seen beyond it a great plum-coloured plain of mesquit.

Save for the busy drummer and his companions in the saloon, Yellow Sky was dozing. The new-comer leaned gracefully upon the bar, and recited many tales with the confidence of a bard who has come upon a new field.

"—and at the moment that the old man fell downstairs with the bureau in his arms, the old woman was coming up with two scuttles of coal, and of course—"

The drummer's tale was interrupted by a young man who suddenly appeared in the open door. He cried: "Scratchy Wilson's drunk, and has turned loose with both hands." The two Mexicans at once set down their glasses and faded out of the rear entrance of the saloon.

The drummer, innocent and jocular, answered: "All right, old man. S'pose he has? Come in and have a drink, anyhow."

But the information had made such an obvious cleft in every skull in the room that the drummer was obliged to see its importance. All had become instantly solemn. "Say," said he, mystified, "what is this?" His three companions made the introductory gesture of eloquent speech; but the young man at the door forestalled them.

"It means, my friend," he answered, as he came into the saloon, "that for the next two hours this town won't be a health resort."

The barkeeper went to the door, and locked and barred it; reaching out of the window, he pulled in heavy wooden shutters, and barred them. Immediately a solemn, chapel-like gloom was upon the place. The drummer was looking from one to another.

"But say," he cried, "what is this, anyhow? You don't mean there is going to be a gun-fight?"

"Don't know whether there'll be a fight or not," answered one man, grimly; "but there'll be some shootin'—some good shootin'."

The young man who had warned them waved his hand. "Oh, there'll be a fight fast enough, if any one wants it. Anybody can get a fight out there in the street. There's a fight just waiting."

The drummer seemed to be swayed between the interest of a foreigner and a perception of personal danger.

"What did you say his name was?" he asked.

"Scratchy Wilson," they answered in chorus.

"And will he kill anybody? What are you going to do? Does this happen often? Does he rampage around like this once a week or so? Can he break in that door?"

"No; he can't break down that door," replied the barkeeper. "He's tried it three times. But when he comes you'd better lay down on the floor, stranger. He's dead sure to shoot at it, and a bullet may come through."

Thereafter the drummer kept a strict eye upon the door. The time had not yet been called for him to hug the floor, but, as a minor precaution, he sidled near to the wall. "Will he kill anybody?" he said again.

The men laughed low and scornfully at the question.

"He's out to shoot, and he's out for trouble. Don't see any good in experimentin' with him."

"But what do you do in a case like this? What do you do?"

A man responded: "Why, he and Jack Potter—"

"But," in chorus the other men interrupted, "Jack Potter's in San Anton'."

"Well, who is he? What's he got to do with it?"

"Oh, he's the town marshal. He goes out and fights Scratchy when he gets on one of these tears."

"Wow!" said the drummer, mopping his brow. "Nice job he's got."

The voices had toned away to mere whisperings. The drummer wished to ask further questions, which were born of an increasing anxiety and bewilderment; but when he attempted them, the men merely looked at him in irritation and motioned him to remain silent. A tense waiting hush was upon them. In the deep shadows of the room their eyes shone as they listened for sounds from the street. One man made three gestures at the barkeeper; and the latter, moving like a ghost, handed him a glass and a bottle. The man poured a full glass of whisky, and set down the bottle noiselessly. He gulped the whisky in a swallow, and turned again toward the door in immovable silence. The drummer saw that the barkeeper, without a sound, had taken a Winchester from beneath the bar. Later he saw this individual beckoning to him, so he tiptoed across the room.

"You better come with me back of the bar."

"No, thanks," said the drummer, perspiring; "I'd rather be where I can make a break for the back door."

Whereupon the man of bottles made a kindly but peremptory gesture. The drummer obeyed it, and, finding himself seated on a box with his head below the level of the bar, balm was laid upon his soul at sight of various zinc and copper fittings that bore a resemblance to armour-plate. The barkeeper took a seat comfortably upon an adjacent box.

"You see," he whispered, "this here Scratchy Wilson is a wonder with a gun—a perfect wonder; and when he goes on the war-trail, we hunt our holes—naturally. He's about the last one of the old gang that used to hang out along the river here. He's a terror when he's drunk. When he's sober he's all right—kind of simple—wouldn't hurt a fly—nicest fellow in town. But when he's drunk—whoo!"

There were periods of stillness. "I wish Jack Potter was back from San Anton'," said the barkeeper. "He shot Wilson up once—in the leg—and he would sail in and pull out the kinks in this thing."

Presently they heard from a distance the sound of a shot, followed by three wild yowls. It instantly removed a bond from the men in the darkened saloon. There was a shuffling of feet. They looked at each other. "Here he comes," they said.

III

A man in a maroon-coloured flannel shirt, which had been purchased for purposes of decoration, and made principally by some Jewish women on the East Side of New York, rounded a corner and walked into the middle of the main street of Yellow Sky. In either hand the man held a long, heavy, blue-black revolver. Often he yelled, and these cries rang through a semblance of a deserted village, shrilly flying over the roofs in a volume that seemed to have no relation to the ordinary vocal strength of a man. It was as if the surrounding stillness formed the arch of a tomb over him. These cries of ferocious challenge rang against walls of silence. And his boots had red tops with gilded imprints, of the kind beloved in winter by little sledding boys on the hillsides of New England.

The man's face flamed in a rage begot of whisky. His eyes, rolling, and yet keen for ambush, hunted the still doorways and windows. He walked with the creeping movement of the midnight cat. As it occurred to him, he roared menacing information. The long revolvers in his hands were as easy as straws; they were moved with an electric swiftness. The little fingers of each hand played sometimes in a musician's way. Plain from the low collar of the shirt, the cords of his neck straightened and sank, straightened and sank, as passion moved him. The only sounds were his terrible invitations. The calm adobes preserved their demeanour at the passing of this small thing in the middle of the street.

There was no offer of fight—no offer of fight. The man called to the sky. There were no attractions. He bellowed and fumed and swayed his revolvers here and everywhere.

The dog of the barkeeper of the Weary Gentleman saloon had not appreciated the advance of events. He yet lay dozing in front of his master's door. At sight of the dog, the man paused and raised his revolver humorously. At sight of the man, the dog sprang up and walked diagonally away, with a sullen head, and growling. The man yelled, and the dog broke into a gallop. As it was about to enter an alley, there was a loud noise, a whistling, and something spat the ground directly before it. The dog screamed, and, wheeling in terror, galloped headlong in a new direction. Again there was a noise, a whistling, and sand was kicked viciously before it. Fear-stricken, the dog turned and flurried like an animal in a pen. The man stood laughing, his weapons at his hips.

Ultimately the man was attracted by the closed door of the Weary Gentleman saloon. He went to it and, hammering with a revolver, demanded drink.

The door remaining imperturbable, he picked a bit of paper from the walk, and nailed it to the framework with a knife. He then turned his back contemptuously upon this popular resort and, walking to the opposite side of the street and spinning there on his heel quickly and lithely, fired at the bit of paper. He missed it by a half-inch. He swore at himself, and went away. Later he comfortably fusilladed the windows of his most intimate friend. The man was playing with this town; it was a toy for him.

But still there was no offer of fight. The name of Jack Potter, his ancient antagonist, entered his mind, and he concluded that it would be a glad thing if he should go to Potter's house, and by bombardment induce him to come out and fight. He moved in the direction of his desire, chanting Apache scalp-music.

When he arrived at it, Potter's house presented the same still front as had the other adobes. Taking up a strategic position, the man howled a challenge. But this house regarded him as might a great stone god. It gave no sign. After a decent wait, the man howled further challenges, mingling with them wonderful epithets.

Presently there came the spectacle of a man churning himself into deepest rage over the immobility of a house. He fumed at it as the winter wind attacks a prairie cabin in the North. To the distance there should have gone the sound of a tumult like the fighting of two hundred Mexicans. As necessity bade him, he paused for breath or to reload his revolvers.

IV

Potter and his bride walked sheepishly and with speed. Sometimes they laughed together shamefacedly and low.

"Next corner, dear," he said finally.

They put forth the efforts of a pair walking bowed against a strong wind. Potter was about to raise a finger to point the first appearance of the new home when, as they circled the corner, they came face to face with a man in a maroon-coloured shirt, who was feverishly pushing cartridges into a large revolver. Upon the instant the man dropped his revolver to the ground and, like lightning, whipped another from its holster. The second weapon was aimed at the bridegroom's chest.

There was a silence. Potter's mouth seemed to be merely a grave for his tongue. He exhibited an instinct to at once loosen his arm from the woman's grip, and he dropped the bag to the sand. As for the bride, her face had gone as yellow as old cloth. She was a slave to hideous rites, gazing at the apparitional snake.

The two men faced each other at a distance of three paces. He of the revolver smiled with a new and quiet ferocity.

"Tried to sneak up on me," he said. "Tried to sneak up on me!" His eyes grew more baleful. As Potter made a slight movement, the man thrust his revolver venomously forward. "No; don't you do it, Jack Potter. Don't you move a finger toward a gun just yet. Don't you move an eyelash. The time has come for me to settle with you, and I'm goin' to do it my own way, and loaf along with no interferin'. So if you don't want a gun bent on you, just mind what I tell you."

Potter looked at his enemy. "I ain't got a gun on me Scratchy," he said. "Honest, I ain't." He was stiffening and steadying, but yet somewhere at the back of his mind a vision of the Pullman floated: the sea-green figured velvet, the shining brass, silver, and glass, the wood that gleamed as darkly brilliant as the surface of a pool of oil—all the glory of the marriage, the environment of the new estate. "You know I fight when it comes to fighting, Scratchy Wilson; but I ain't got a gun on me. You'll have to do all the shootin' yourself."

His enemy's face went livid. He stepped forward, and lashed his weapon to and fro before Potter's chest. "Don't you tell me you ain't got no gun on you, you whelp. Don't tell me no lie like that. There ain't a man in Texas ever seen you without no gun. Don't take me for no kid." His eyes blazed with light, and his throat worked like a pump.

"I ain't takin' you for no kid," answered Potter. His heels had not moved an inch backward. "I'm takin' you for a damn fool. I tell you I ain't got a gun, and I ain't. If you're goin' to shoot me up, you better begin now; you'll never get a chance like this again."

So much enforced reasoning had told on Wilson's rage; he was calmer. "If you ain't got a gun, why ain't you got a gun?" he sneered. "Been to Sunday-school?"

"I ain't got a gun because I've just come from San Anton' with my wife. I'm married," said Potter. "And if I'd thought there was going to be any galoots like you prowling around when I brought my wife home, I'd had a gun, and don't you forget it."

"Married!" said Scratchy, not at all comprehending.

"Yes, married. I'm married," said Potter, distinctly.

"Married?" said Scratchy. Seemingly for the first time, he saw the drooping, drowning woman at the other man's side. "No!" he said. He was like a creature allowed a glimpse of another world. He moved a pace backward, and his arm, with the revolver, dropped to his side. "Is this the lady?" he asked.

"Yes; this is the lady," answered Potter.

There was another period of silence.

"Well," said Wilson at last, slowly, "I s'pose it's all off now."

"It's all off if you say so, Scratchy. You know I didn't make the trouble." Potter lifted his valise.

"Well, I 'low it's off, Jack," said Wilson. He was looking at the ground. "Married!" He was not a student of chivalry; it was merely that in the presence of this foreign condition he was a simple child of the earlier plains. He picked up his starboard revolver, and, placing both weapons in their holsters, he went away. His feet made funnel-shaped tracks in the heavy sand.

W. SOMERSET MAUGHAM • 1874–1965

The Outstation

THE new assistant arrived in the afternoon. When the Resident, Mr. Warburton, was told that the prahu[1] was in sight he put on his solar topee[2] and went down to the landing-stage The guard, eight little Dyak[3] soldiers, stood to attention as he passed. He noted with satisfaction that their bearing was martial, their uniforms neat and clean, and their guns shining. They were a credit to him. From the landing-stage he watched the bend of the river round which in a moment the boat would sweep. He looked very smart in his spotless ducks and white shoes. He held under his arm a gold-headed Malacca cane which had been given him by the Sultan of Perak. He awaited the newcomer with mingled feelings. There was more work in the district than one man could properly do, and during his periodical tours of the country under his charge it had been inconvenient to leave the station in the hands of a native clerk, but he had been so long the only white man there that he could not face the arrival of another without misgiving. He was accustomed to loneliness. During the war he had not seen an English face for three years; and once when he was instructed to put up an afforestation officer he was seized with panic, so that when the stranger was due to arrive, having arranged everything for his reception, he wrote a note telling him he was obliged to go up-river, and fled; he remained away till he was informed by a messenger that his guest had left.

[1] proa, a Malaysian outrigger canoe with a sail
[2] pith helmet
[3] native of Borneo

Now the prahu appeared in the broad reach. It was manned by prisoners, Dyaks under various sentences, and a couple of warders were waiting on the landing-stage to take them back to jail. They were sturdy fellows, used to the river, and they rowed with a powerful stroke. As the boat reached the side a man got out from under the attap awning and stepped on shore. The guard presented arms.

"Here we are at last. By God, I'm as cramped as the devil. I've brought you your mail."

He spoke with exuberant joviality. Mr. Warburton politely held out his hand.

"Mr. Cooper, I presume?"

"That's right. Were you expecting any one else?"

The question had a facetious intent, but the Resident did not smile.

"My name is Warburton. I'll show you your quarters. They'll bring your kit along."

He preceded Cooper along the narrow pathway and they entered a compound in which stood a small bungalow.

"I've had it made as habitable as I could, but of course no one has lived in it for a good many years."

It was built on piles. It consisted of a long living-room which opened on to a broad verandah, and behind, on each side of a passage, were two bedrooms.

"This'll do me all right," said Cooper.

"I daresay you want to have a bath and a change. I shall be very much pleased if you'll dine with me to-night. Will eight o'clock suit you?"

"Any old time will do for me."

The Resident gave a polite, but slightly disconcerted, smile and withdrew. He returned to the Fort where his own residence was. The impression which Allen Cooper had given him was not very favourable, but he was a fair man, and he knew that it was unjust to form an opinion on so brief a glimpse. Cooper seemed to be about thirty. He was a tall, thin fellow, with a sallow face in which there was not a spot of colour. It was a face all in one tone. He had a large, hooked nose and blue eyes. When, entering the bungalow, he had taken off his topee and flung it to a waiting boy, Mr. Warburton noticed that his large skull, covered with short, brown hair, contrasted somewhat oddly with a weak, small chin. He was dressed in khaki shorts and a khaki shirt; but they were shabby and soiled; and his battered topee had not been cleaned for days. Mr. Warburton reflected that the young man had spent a week on a coasting steamer and had passed the last forty-eight hours lying in the bottom of a prahu.

"We'll see what he looks like when he comes in to dinner."

He went into his room where his things were as neatly laid out as if he had an English valet, undressed, and, walking down the stairs to the bath-house, sluiced himself with cool water. The only concession he made to the climate was to wear a white dinner-jacket; but otherwise, in a boiled shirt and a high collar, silk socks and patent-leather shoes, he dressed as formally as though he were dining at his club in Pall Mall. A careful host, he went into the dining-room to see that the table was properly laid. It was gay with orchids and the silver shone brightly. The napkins were folded into elaborate shapes. Shaded candles in silver candlesticks shed a soft light. Mr. Warburton smiled his approval and returned to the sitting-room to await his guest. Presently he appeared. Cooper was wearing the khaki shorts, the khaki shirt, and the ragged jacket in which he had landed. Mr. Warburton's smile of greeting froze on his face.

"Hulloa, you're all dressed up," said Cooper. "I didn't know you were going to do that. I very nearly put on a sarong."

"It doesn't matter at all. I daresay your boys were busy."

"You needn't have bothered to dress on my account, you know."

"I didn't. I always dress for dinner."

"Even when you're alone?"

"Especially when I'm alone," replied Mr. Warburton, with a frigid stare.

He saw a twinkle of amusement in Cooper's eyes, and he flushed an angry red. Mr. Warburton was a hot-tempered man; you might have guessed that from his red face with its pugnacious features and from his red hair, now growing white; his blue eyes, cold as a rule and observing, could flush with sudden wrath; but he was a man of the world and he hoped a just one. He must do his best to get on with this fellow.

"When I lived in London I moved in circles in which it would have been just as eccentric not to dress for dinner every night as not to have a bath every morning. When I came to Borneo I saw no reason to discontinue so good a habit. For three years, during the war, I never saw a white man. I never omitted to dress on a single occasion on which I was well enough to come in to dinner. You have not been very long in this country; believe me, there is no better way to maintain the proper pride which you should have in yourself. When a white man surrenders in the slightest degree to the influences that surround him he very soon loses his self-respect, and when he loses his self-respect you may be quite sure that the natives will soon cease to respect him."

"Well, if you expect me to put on a boiled shirt and a stiff collar in this heat I'm afraid you'll be disappointed."

"When you are dining in your own bungalow you will, of course, dress as you think fit, but when you do me the pleasure of dining with me, perhaps you will come to the conclusion that it is only polite to wear the costume usual in civilized society."

Two Malay boys, in sarongs and songkoks, with smart white coats and brass buttons, came in, one bearing gin pahits, and the other a tray on which were olives and anchovies. Then they went in to dinner. Mr. Warburton flattered himself that he had the best cook, a Chinese, in Borneo, and he took great trouble to have as good food as in the difficult circumstances was possible. He exercised much ingenuity in making the best of his materials.

"Would you care to look at the menu?" he said, handing it to Cooper.

It was written in French and the dishes had resounding names. They were waited on by the two boys. In opposite corners of the room two more waved immense fans, and so gave movement to the sultry air. The fare was sumptuous and the champagne excellent.

"Do you do yourself like this every day?" said Cooper.

Mr. Warburton gave the menu a careless glance.

"I have not noticed that the dinner is any different from usual," he said. "I eat very little myself, but I make a point of having a proper dinner served to me every night. It keeps the cook in practice and it's good discipline for the boys."

The conversation proceeded with effort. Mr. Warburton was elaborately courteous, and it may be that he found a slightly malicious amusement in the embarrassment which he thereby occasioned in his companion. Cooper had not been more than a few months in Sembulu, and Mr. Warburton's enquiries about friends of his in Kuala Solor were soon exhausted.

"By the way," he said presently, "did you meet a lad called Hennerley? He's come out recently, I believe."

"Oh, yes, he's in the police. A rotten bounder."

"I should hardly have expected him to be that. His uncle is my friend Lord Barraclough. I had a letter from Lady Barraclough only the only day asking me to look out for him."

"I heard he was related to somebody or other. I suppose that's how he got the job. He's been to Eton and Oxford and he doesn't forget to let you know it."

"You surprise me," said Mr. Warburton. "All his family have been at Eton and Oxford for a couple of hundred years. I should have expected him to take it as a matter of course."

"I thought him a damned prig."

"To what school did you go?"

"I was born in Barbadoes. I was educated there."

"Oh, I see."

Mr. Warburton managed to put so much offensiveness into his brief reply that Cooper flushed. For a moment he was silent.

"I've had two or three letters from Kuala Solor," continued Mr. Warburton, "and my impression was that young Hennerley was a great success. They say he's a first-rate sportsman."

"Oh, yes, he's very popular. He's just the sort of fellow they would like in K.S. I haven't got much use for the first-rate sportsman myself. What does it amount to in the long run that a man can play golf and tennis better than other people? And who cares if he can make a break of seventy-five at billiards? They attach a damned sight too much importance to that sort of thing in England."

"Do you think so? I was under the impression that the first-rate sportsman had come out of the war certainly no worse than any one else."

"Oh, if you're going to talk of the war then I do know what I'm talking about. I was in the same regiment as Hennerley and I can tell you that the men couldn't stick him at any price."

"How do you know?"

"Because I was one of the men."

"Oh, you hadn't got a commission."

"A fat chance I had of getting a commission. I was what was called a Colonial. I hadn't been to a public school and I had no influence. I was in the ranks the whole damned time."

Cooper frowned. He seemed to have difficulty in preventing himself from breaking into violent invective. Mr. Warburton watched him, his little blue eyes narrowed, watched him and formed his opinion. Changing the conversation, he began to speak to Cooper about the work that would be required of him, and as the clock struck ten he rose.

"Well, I won't keep you any more. I daresay you're tired by your journey."

They shook hands.

"Oh, I say, look here," said Cooper, "I wonder if you can find me a boy. The boy I had before never turned up when I was starting from K.S. He took my kit on board and all that and then disappeared. I didn't know he wasn't there till we were out of the river."

"I'll ask my head-boy. I have no doubt he can find you some one."

"All right. Just tell him to send the boy along and if I like the look of him I'll take him."

There was a moon, so that no lantern was needed. Cooper walked across from the Fort to his bungalow.

"I wonder why on earth they've sent me a fellow like that?" reflected Mr. Warburton. "If that's the kind of man they're going to get out now I don't think much of it."

He strolled down his garden. The Fort was built on the top of a little hill and the garden ran down to the river's edge; on the bank was an arbour, and hither it was his habit to come after dinner to smoke a cheroot. And often from the river that flowed below him a voice was heard, the voice of some Malay too timorous to venture into the light of day, and a complaint or an accusation was softly wafted to his ears, a piece of information was whispered to him or a useful hint, which otherwise would never have come into his official ken. He threw himself heavily into a long rattan chair. Cooper! An envious, ill-bred fellow, bumptious, self-assertive and vain. But Mr. Warburton's irritation could not withstand the silent beauty of the night. The air was scented with the sweet-smelling flowers of a tree that grew at the entrance to the arbour, and the fireflies, sparkling dimly, flew with their slow and silvery flight. The moon made a pathway on the broad river for the light feet of Siva's bride, and on the further bank a row of palm trees was delicately silhouetted against the sky. Peace stole into the soul of Mr. Warburton.

He was a queer creature and he had had a singular career. At the age of twenty-one he had inherited a considerable fortune, a hundred thousand pounds, and when he left Oxford he threw himself into the gay life which in those days (now Mr. Warburton was a man of four and fifty) offered itself to the young man of good family. He had his flat in Mount Street, his private hansom, and his hunting-box in Warwickshire. He went to all the places where the fashionable congregate. He was handsome, amusing and generous. He was a figure in the society of London in the early nineties, and society then had not lost its exclusiveness nor its brilliance. The Boer War which shook it was unthought of; the Great War which destroyed it was prophesied only by the pessimists. It was no unpleasant thing to be a rich young man in those days, and Mr. Warburton's chimney-piece during the season was packed with cards for one great function after another. Mr. Warburton displayed them with complacency. For Mr. Warburton was a snob. He was not a timid snob, a little ashamed of being impressed by his betters, nor a snob who sought the intimacy of persons who had acquired celebrity in politics or notoriety in the arts, nor the snob who was dazzled by riches; he was the naked, unadulterated common snob who dearly loved a lord. He was touchy and quick-tempered, but he would much rather have been snubbed by a person of quality than flattered by a commoner. His name figured insignificantly in Burke's Peerage, and it was marvellous to watch the ingenuity he used to mention his distant relationship to the noble family he belonged to; but never a word did he say of the honest Liverpool manufacturer from whom, through his mother, a Miss Gubbins, he had come by his fortune. It was the terror of his fashionable life that at Cowes, maybe, or at Ascot, when he was with a duchess or even with a prince of the blood, one of these relatives would claim acquaintance with him.

His failing was too obvious not soon to become notorious, but its extravagance saved it from being merely despicable. The great whom he adored laughed at him, but in their hearts felt his adoration not unnatural. Poor Warburton was a dreadful snob, of course, but after all he was a good fellow. He was always ready to back a bill for an impecunious nobleman, and if you were in a tight corner you could safely count on him for a hundred pounds. He gave good dinners. He played whist badly, but never minded how much he lost if the company was select. He happened to be a gambler, an unlucky one, but he was a good loser, and it was impossible not to admire the coolness with which he lost five hundred pounds at a sitting. His passion for cards, almost as strong as his passion for titles, was the cause of his undoing. The life he led was expensive and his gambling losses were formidable. He began to plunge more heavily, first on horses, and then on the Stock Exchange. He had a certain simplicity of character and the unscrupulous found him an ingenuous prey. I do not know if he ever realized that his smart friends laughed at him behind his back, but I think he had an obscure instinct that he could not afford to appear other than careless of his money. He got into the hands of money-lenders. At the age of thirty-four he was ruined.

He was too much imbued with the spirit of his class to hesitate in the choice of his next step. When a man in his set had run through his money he went out to the colonies. No one heard Mr. Warburton repine. He made no complaint because a noble friend had advised a disastrous speculation, he pressed nobody to whom he had lent money to repay it, he paid his debts (if he had only known it, the despised blood of the Liverpool manufacturer came out in him there), sought help from no one, and, never having done a stroke of work in his life, looked for a means of livelihood. He remained cheerful, unconcerned and full of humour. He had no wish to make any one with whom he happened to be uncomfortable by the recital of his misfortune. Mr. Warburton was a snob, but he was also a gentleman.

The only favour he asked of any of the great friends in whose daily company he had lived for years was a recommendation. The able man who was at that time Sultan of Sembulu took him into his service. The night before he sailed he dined for the last time at his club.

"I hear you're going away, Warburton," the old Duke of Hereford said to him.

"Yes, I'm going to Borneo."

"Good God, what are you going there for?"

"Oh, I'm broke."

"Are you? I'm sorry. Well, let us know when you come back. I hope you have a good time."

"Oh, yes. Lots of shooting, you know."

The Duke nodded and passed on. A few hours later Mr. Warburton watched the coast of England recede into the mist, and he left behind everything which to him made life worth living.

Twenty years had passed since then.

He kept up a busy correspondence with various great ladies and his letters were amusing and chatty. He never lost his love for titled persons and paid careful attention to the announcements in The Times (which reached him six weeks after publication) of their comings and goings. He perused the column which records births, deaths, and marriages, and he was always ready with his letter of congratulations or condolence. The illustrated papers told him how people looked and on his periodical visits to England, able to take up the threads as though they had never been broken, he knew all about any new person who might have appeared on the social surface. His interest in the world of fashion was as vivid as when himself had been a figure in it. It still seemed to him the only thing that mattered.

But insensibly another interest had entered into his life. The position he found himself in flattered his vanity; he was no longer the sycophant craving the smiles of the great, he was the master whose word was law. He was gratified by the guard of Dyak soldiers who presented arms as he passed. He liked to sit in judgment on his fellow men. It pleased him to compose quarrels between rival chiefs. When the head-hunters were troublesome in the old days he set out to chastise them with a thrill of pride in his own behaviour. He was too vain not to be of dauntless courage, and a pretty story was told of his coolness in adventuring single-handed into a stockaded village and demanding the surrender of a bloodthirsty pirate. He became a skillful administrator. He was strict, just and honest.

And little by little he conceived a deep love for the Malays. He interested himself in their habits and customs. He was never tired of listening to their talk. He admired their virtues, and with a smile and a shrug of the shoulders condoned their vices.

"In my day," he would say, "I have been on intimate terms with some of the greatest gentlemen in England, but I have never known finer gentlemen than some well-born Malays whom I am proud to call my friends."

He liked their courtesy and their distinguished manners, their gentleness and their sudden passions. He knew by instinct exactly how to treat them. He had a genuine tenderness for them. But he never forgot that he was an English gentleman and he had no patience with the white men who yielded to native customs. He made no surrenders. And he did not imitate so many of the white men in taking a native woman to wife, for an intrigue of this nature, however sanctified by custom, seemed to him not only shocking but undignified. A man who had been called George by Albert Edward, Prince of Wales, could hardly be expected to have any connection with a native. And when he returned to Borneo from his visits to England it was now with something like relief. His friends, like himself, were no longer young, and there was a new generation which looked upon him as a tiresome old man. It seemed to him that the England of to-day had lost a good deal of what he had loved in the England of his youth. But Borneo remained the same. It was home to him now. He meant to remain in the service as long as was possible, and the hope in his heart was that he would die before at last he was forced to retire. He had stated in his will that wherever he died he wished his body to be brought back to Sembulu and buried among the people he loved within sound of the softly flowing river.

But these emotions he kept hidden from the eyes of men; and no one, seeing this spruce, stout, well-set-up man, with his clean-shaven strong face and his whitening hair, would have dreamed that he cherished so profound a sentiment.

He knew how the work of the station should be done, and during the next few days he kept a suspicious eye on his assistant. He saw very soon that he was painstaking and competent. The only fault he had to find with him was that he was brusque with the natives.

"The Malays are shy and very sensitive," he said to him. "I think you will find that you will get much better results if you take care always to be polite, patient and kindly."

Cooper gave a short, grating laugh.

"I was born in Barbadoes and I was in Africa in the war. I don't think there's much about niggers that I don't know."

"I know nothing," said Mr. Warburton acidly. "But we were not talking of them. We were talking of Malays."

"Aren't they niggers?"

"You are very ignorant," replied Mr. Warburton.

He said no more.

On the first Sunday after Cooper's arrival he asked him to dinner. He did everything ceremoniously, and though they had met on the previous day in the office and later, on the Fort verandah where they drank a gin and bitters together at six o'clock, he sent a polite note across to the bungalow by a boy. Cooper, however, unwillingly, came in evening dress and Mr. Warburton, though gratified that his wish was respected, noticed with disdain that the young man's clothes were badly cut and his shirt ill-fitting. But Mr. Warburton was in a good temper that evening.

"By the way," he said to him, as he shook hands, "I've talked to my head-boy about finding you some one and he recommends his nephew. I've seen him and he seems a bright and willing lad. Would you like to see him?"

"I don't mind."

"He's waiting now."

Mr. Warburton called his boy and told him to send for his nephew. In a moment a tall, slender youth of twenty appeared. He had large dark eyes and a good profile. He was very neat in his sarong, a little white coat, and a fez, without a tassel, of plum-coloured velvet. He answered to the name of Abas. Mr. Warburton looked on him with approval, and his manner insensibly softened as he spoke to him in fluent and idiomatic Malay. He was inclined to be sarcastic with white people, but with the Malays he had a happy mixture of condescension and kindliness. He stood in the place of the Sultan. He knew perfectly how to preserve his own dignity, and at the same time put a native at his ease.

"Will he do?" said Mr. Warburton, turning to Cooper.

"Yes, I daresay he's no more of a scoundrel than any of the rest of them."

Mr. Warburton informed the boy that he was engaged and dismissed him.

"You're very lucky to get a boy like that," he told Cooper. "He belongs to a very good family. They came over from Malacca nearly a hundred years ago."

"I don't much mind if the boy who cleans my shoes and brings me a drink when I want it has blue blood in his veins or not. All I ask is that he should do what I tell him and look sharp about it."

Mr. Warburton pursed his lips, but made no reply.

They went in to dinner. It was excellent, and the wine was good. Its influence presently had its effect on them and they talked not only without acrimony, but even with friendliness. Mr. Warburton liked to do himself well, and on Sunday night he made it a habit to do himself even a little better than usual. He began to think he was unfair to Cooper. Of course he was not a gentleman, but that was not his fault, and when you got to know him it might be that he would turn out a very good fellow. His faults, perhaps, were faults of manner. And he was certainly good at his work, quick, conscientious and thorough. When they reached the dessert Mr. Warburton was feeling kindly disposed towards all mankind.

"This is your first Sunday and I'm going to give you a very special glass of port.

I've only got about two dozen of it left and I keep it for special occasions."

He gave his boy instructions and presently the bottle was brought. Mr. Warburton watched the boy open it.

"I got this port from my old friend Charles Hollington. He'd had it for forty years and I've had it for a good many. He was well known to have the best cellar in England."

"Is he a wine merchant?"

"Not exactly," smiled Mr. Warburton. "I was speaking of Lord Hollington of Castle Reagh. He's one of the richest peers in England. A very old friend of mine. I was at Eton with his brother."

This was an opportunity that Mr. Warburton could never resist and he told a little anecdote of which the only point seemed to be that he knew an earl. The port was certainly very good; he drank a glass and then a second. He lost all caution. He had not talked to a white man for months. He began to tell stories. He showed himself in the company of the great. Hearing him you would have thought that at one time ministries were formed and policies decided on his suggestion whispered into the ear of a duchess or thrown over the dinner-table to be gratefully acted on by the confidential adviser of the sovereign. The old days at Ascot, Goodwood and Cowes lived again for him. Another glass of port. There were the great house-parties in Yorkshire and in Scotland to which he went every year.

"I had a man called Foreman then, the best valet I ever had, and why do you think he gave me notice? You know in the Housekeeper's Room the ladies' maids and the gentlemen's gentlemen sit according to the precedence of their masters. He told me he was sick of going to party after party at which I was the only commoner. It meant that he always had to sit at the bottom of the table and all the best bits were taken before a dish reached him. I told the story to the old Duke of Hereford and he roared. 'By God, Sir,' he said, 'if I were King of England I'd make you a viscount just to give your man a chance.' 'Take him yourself, Duke,' I said. 'He's the best valet I've ever had.' 'Well, Warburton,' he said, 'if he's good enough for you he's good enough for me. Send him along.' "

Then there was Monte Carlo where Mr. Warburton and the Grand Duke Fyodor, playing in partnership, had broken the bank one evening; and there was Marienbad. At Marienbad Mr. Warburton had played baccarat with Edward VII.

"He was only Prince of Wales then, of course. I remember him saying to me, 'George, if you draw on a five you'll lose your shirt.' He was right; I don't think he ever said a truer word in his life. He was a wonderful man. I always said he was the greatest diplomatist in Europe. But I was a young fool in those days, I hadn't the sense to take his advice. If I had, if I'd never drawn on a five, I daresay I shouldn't be here to-day."

Cooper was watching him. His blue eyes, deep in their sockets, were hard and supercilious, and on his lips was a mocking smile. He had heard a good deal about Mr. Warburton in Kuala Solor. Not a bad sort, and he ran his district like clockwork, they said, but by heaven, what a snob! They laughed at him good-naturedly, for it was impossible to dislike a man who was so generous and so kindly, and Cooper had already heard the story of the Prince of Wales and the game of baccarat. But Cooper listened without indulgence. From the beginning he had resented the Resident's manner. He was very sensitive and he writhed under Mr. Warburton's polite sarcasms. Mr. Warburton had a knack of receiving a remark of which he disapproved with a devastating silence. Cooper had lived little in England and he had a peculiar dislike of the English. He resented especially the public-school boy since he always feared that he was going to patronize him. He was so much afraid of others putting on airs with him that, in order as it were to get in first, he put on such airs as to make every one think him insufferably conceited.

"Well, at all events the war has done one good thing for us," he said at last. "It's smashed up the power of the aristocracy. The Boer War started it, and 1914 put the lid on."

"The great families of England are doomed," said Mr. Warburton with the complacent melancholy of an *émigré* who remembered the court of Louis XV. "They cannot afford any longer to live in their splendid palaces and their princely hospitality will soon be nothing but a memory."

"And a damned good job too in my opinion."

"My poor Cooper, what can you know of the glory that was Greece and the grandeur that was Rome?"

Mr. Warburton made an ample gesture. His eyes for an instant grew dreamy with a vision of the past.

"Well, believe me, we're fed up with all that rot. What we want is a business government by business men. I was born in a Crown Colony and I've lived practically all my life in the colonies. I don't give a row of pins for a lord. What's wrong with England is snobbishness. And if there's anything that gets my goat it's a snob."

A snob! Mr. Warburton's face grew purple and his eyes blazed with anger. That was a word that had pursued him all his life. The great ladies whose society he had enjoyed in his youth were not inclined to look upon his appreciation of themselves as unworthy, but even great ladies are sometimes out of temper and more than once Mr. Warburton had had the dreadful word flung in his teeth. He knew, he could not help knowing, that there were odious people who called him a snob. How unfair it was! Why, there was no vice he found so detestable as snobbishness. After all, he liked to mix with people of his own class, he was only at home in their company, and how in heaven's name could any one say that was snobbish? Birds of a feather.

"I quite agree with you," he answered. "A snob is a man who admires or despises another because he is of a higher social rank than his own. It is the most vulgar failing of our English middle class."

He saw a flicker of amusement in Cooper's eyes. Cooper put up his hand to hide the broad smile that rose to his lips, and so made it more noticeable. Mr. Warburton's hands trembled a little.

Probably Cooper never knew how greatly he had offended his chief. A sensitive man himself he was strangely insensitive to the feelings of others.

Their work forced them to see one another for a few minutes now and then during the day, and they met at six to have a drink on Mr. Warburton's verandah. This was an old-established custom of the country which Mr. Warburton would not for the world have broken. But they ate their meals separately, Cooper in his bungalow and Mr. Warburton at the Fort. After the office work was over they walked till dusk fell, but they walked apart. There were but few paths in this country, where the jungle pressed close upon the plantations of the village, and when Mr. Warburton caught sight of his assistant passing along with his loose stride, he would make a circuit in order to avoid him. Cooper, with his bad manners, his conceit in his own judgment and his intolerance, had already got on his nerves; but it was not till Cooper had been on the station for a couple of months that an incident happened which turned the Resident's dislike into bitter hatred.

Mr. Warburton was obliged to go up-country on a tour of inspection, and he left the station in Cooper's charge with more confidence, since he had definitely come to the conclusion that he was a capable fellow. The only thing he did not like was that he had no indulgence. He was honest, just and painstaking, but he had no sympathy for the natives. It bitterly amused Mr. Warburton to observe that this man, who looked upon himself as every man's equal, should look upon so many men as his own inferiors. He was hard, he had no patience with the native mind, and he was a bully. Mr. Warburton very quickly realized that the Malays disliked and feared him. He was not altogether displeased. He would not have liked it very much if his assistant had enjoyed a popularity which might rival his own. Mr. Warburton made his elaborate preparations, set out on his expedition, and in three weeks returned. Meanwhile the mail had arrived. The first thing that struck his eyes when he entered his sitting-room was a great pile of open newspapers. Cooper had met him, and they went into the room together. Mr. Warburton turned to one of the servants who had been left behind and sternly asked him what was the meaning of those open papers. Cooper hastened to explain.

"I wanted to read all about the Wolverhampton murder and so I borrowed your Times. I brought them back again. I knew you wouldn't mind."

Mr. Warburton turned to him, white with anger.

"But I do mind. I mind very much."

"I'm sorry," said Cooper, with composure. "The fact is, I simply couldn't wait till you came back."

"I wonder you didn't open my letters as well."

Cooper, unmoved, smiled at his chief's exasperation.

"Oh, that's not quite the same thing. After all, I couldn't imagine you'd mind my looking at your newspapers. There's nothing private in them."

"I very much object to any one reading my paper before me." He went up to the pile. There were nearly thirty numbers there. "I think it's extremely impertinent of you. They're all mixed up."

"We can easily put them in order," said Cooper, joining him at the table.

"Don't touch them," cried Mr. Warburton.

"I say, it's childish to make a scene about a little thing like that."

"How dare you speak to me like that?"

"Oh, go to hell," said Cooper, and he flung out of the room.

Mr. Warburton, trembling with passion, was left contemplating his papers. His greatest pleasure in life had been destroyed by those callous, brutal hands. Most people living in out-of-the-way places when the mail comes tear open impatiently their papers and taking the last ones first glance at the latest news from home. Not so Mr. Warburton. His newsagent had instructions to write on the outside of the wrapper the date of each paper he despatched and when the great bundle arrived Mr. Warburton looked at these dates and with his blue pencil numbered them. His head-boy's orders were to place one on the table every morning in the verandah with the early cup of tea, and it was Mr. Warburton's especial delight to break the wrapper as he sipped his tea, and read the morning paper. It gave him the illusion of living at home. Every Monday morning he read the Monday Times of six weeks back and so went through the week. On Sunday he read The Observer. Like his habit of dressing for dinner it was a tie to civilization. And it was his pride that no matter how exciting the news was he had never yielded to the temptation of opening a paper before its allotted time. During the war the suspense sometimes had been intolerable, and when he read one day that a push was begun he had undergone agonies of suspense which he might have saved himself by the simple expedient of opening a later paper which lay waiting for him on a shelf. It had been the severest trial to which he had ever exposed himself, but he victoriously surmounted it. And that clumsy fool had broken open those neat tight packages because he wanted to know whether some horrid woman had murdered her odious husband.

Mr. Warburton sent for his boy and told him to bring wrappers. He folded up the papers as neatly as he could, placed a wrapper round each and numbered it. But it was a melancholy task.

"I shall never forgive him," he said. "Never."

Of course his boy had been with him on his expedition; he never travelled without him, for his boy knew exactly how he liked things, and Mr. Warburton was not the kind of jungle traveller who was prepared to dispense with his comforts; but in the interval since their arrival he had been gossiping in the servants' quarters. He had learnt that Cooper had had trouble with his boys. All but the youth Abas had left him. Abas had desired to go too, but his uncle had placed him there on the instructions of the Resident, and he was afraid to leave without his uncle's permission.

"I told him he had done well, Tuan,"[4] said the boy. "But he is unhappy. He says it is not a good house and he wishes to know if he may go as the others have gone."

"No, he must stay. The tuan must have servants. Have those who went been replaced?"

"No, Tuan, no one will go."

Mr. Warburton frowned. Cooper was an insolent fool, but he had an official position and must be suitably provided with servants. It was not seemly that his house should be improperly conducted.

"Where are the boys who ran away?"

"They are in the kampong,[5] Tuan."

"Go and see them to-night and tell them that I expect them to be back at Tuan Cooper's house at dawn to-morrow."

[4] Lord
[5] village

"They say they will not go, Tuan."

"On my order?"

The boy had been with Mr. Warburton for fifteen years, and he knew every intonation of his master's voice. He was not afraid of him, they had gone through too much together, once in the jungle the Resident had saved his life and once, upset in some rapids, but for him the Resident would have been drowned; but he knew when the Resident must be obeyed without question.

"I will go to the kampong," he said.

Mr. Warburton expected that his subordinate would take the first opportunity to apologize for his rudeness, but Cooper had the ill-bred man's inability to express regret; and when they met next morning in the office he ignored the incident. Since Mr. Warburton had been away for three weeks it was necessary for them to have a somewhat prolonged interview. At the end of it Mr. Warburton dismissed him.

"I don't think there's anything else, thank you." Cooper turned to go, but Mr. Warburton stopped him. "I understand you've been having some trouble with your boys."

Cooper gave a harsh laugh.

"They tried to blackmail me. They had the damned cheek to run away, all except that incompetent fellow Abas—he knew when he was well off—but I just sat tight. They've all come to heel again."

"What do you mean by that?"

"This morning they were all back on their jobs, the Chinese cook and all. There they were, as cool as cucumbers; you would have thought they owned the place. I suppose they'd come to the conclusion that I wasn't such a fool as I looked."

"By no means. They came back on my express order."

Cooper flushed slightly.

"I should be obliged if you wouldn't interfere with my private concerns."

"They're not your private concerns. When your servants run away it makes you ridiculous. You are perfectly free to make a fool of yourself, but I cannot allow you to be made a fool of. It is unseemly that your house should not be properly staffed. As soon as I heard that your boys had left you, I had them told to be back in their place at dawn. That'll do."

Mr. Warburton nodded to signify that the interview was at an end. Cooper took no notice.

"Shall I tell you what I did? I called them and gave the whole bally lot the sack. I gave them ten minutes to get out of the compound."

Mr. Warburton shrugged his shoulders.

"What makes you think you can get others?"

"I've told my own clerk to see about it."

Mr. Warburton reflected for a moment.

"I think you behaved very foolishly. You will do well to remember in future that good masters make good servants."

"Is there anything else you want to teach me?"

"I should like to teach you manners, but it would be an arduous task, and I have not the time to waste. I will see that you get boys."

"Please don't put yourself to any trouble on my account. I'm quite capable of getting them for myself."

Mr. Warburton smiled acidly. He had an inkling that Cooper disliked him as much as he disliked Cooper, and he knew that nothing is more galling than to be forced to accept the favours of a man you detest.

"Allow me to tell you that you have no more chance of getting Malay or Chinese servants here now than you have of getting an English butler or a French chef. No one will come to you except on an order from me. Would you like me to give it?"

"No."

"As you please. Good morning."

Mr. Warburton watched the development of the situation with acrid humour. Cooper's clerk was unable to persuade Malay, Dyak or Chinese to enter the house of such a master. Abas, the boy who remained faithful to him, knew how to cook only native food, and Cooper, a coarse feeder, found his gorge rise against the everlasting rice. There was no water-carrier, and in that great heat he needed several baths a day. He cursed Abas, but Abas opposed him with sullen resistance and would not do more than he chose. It was galling to know that the lad stayed with him only because the Resident insisted. This went on for a fortnight and then, one morning, he found in his house the very servants whom he had previously dismissed. He fell into a violent rage, but he had learnt a little sense, and this time, without a word, he let them stay. He swallowed his humiliation, but the impatient contempt he had felt for Mr. Warburton's idiosyncrasies changed into a sullen hatred; the Resident with this malicious stroke had made him the laughing-stock of all the natives.

The two men now held no communication with one another. They broke the time-honoured custom of sharing, notwithstanding personal dislike, a drink at six o'clock with any white man who happened to be at the station. Each lived in his own house as though the other did not exist. Now that Cooper had fallen into the work, it was necessary for them to have little to do with one another in the office. Mr. Warburton used his orderly to send any message he had to give his assistant, and his instructions he sent by formal letter. They saw one another constantly, that was inevitable, but did not exchange half a dozen words in a week. The fact that they could not avoid catching sight of one another got on their nerves. They brooded over their antagonism and Mr. Warburton, taking his daily walk, could think of nothing but how much he detested his assistant.

And the dreadful thing was that in all probability they would remain thus, facing each other in deadly enmity, till Mr. Warburton went on leave. It might be three years. He had no reason to send in a complaint to headquarters: Cooper did his work very well, and at that time men were hard to get. True, vague complaints reached him and hints that the natives found Cooper harsh. There was certainly a feeling of dissatisfaction among them. But when Mr. Warburton looked into specific cases, all he could say was that Cooper had shown severity where mildness would not have been misplaced and had been unfeeling when himself would have been sympathetic. He had done nothing for which he could be taken to task. But Mr. Warburton watched him. Hatred will often make a man clear-sighted, and he had a suspicion that Cooper was using the natives without consideration, yet keeping within the law, because he felt that thus he could exasperate his chief. One day perhaps he would go too far. None knew better than Mr. Warburton how irritable the incessant heat could make a man and how difficult it was to keep one's self-control after a sleepless night. He smiled softly to himself. Sooner or later Cooper would deliver himself into his hand.

When at last the opportunity came Mr. Warburton laughed aloud. Cooper had charge of the prisoners; they made roads, built sheds, rowed when it was necessary to send the prahu up- or down-stream, kept the town clean and otherwise usefully employed themselves. If well-behaved they even on occasion served as house-boys. Cooper kept them hard at it. He liked to see them work. He took pleasure in devising tasks for them; and seeing quickly enough that they were being made to do useless things the prisoners worked badly. He punished them by lengthening their hours. This was contrary to the regulations, and as soon as it was brought to the attention of Mr. Warburton, without referring the matter back to his subordinate, he gave instructions that the old hours should be kept; Cooper, going out for his walk, was astounded to see the prisoners strolling back to the jail, he had given instructions that they were not to knock off till dusk. When he asked the warder in charge why they had left off work he was told that it was the Resident's bidding.

White with rage he strode to the Fort. Mr. Warburton, in his spotless white ducks and his neat topee, with a walking-stick in his hand, followed by his dogs, was on the point of starting out on his afternoon stroll. He had watched Cooper go and knew that he had taken the road by the river. Cooper jumped up the steps and went straight up to the Resident.

"I want to know what the hell you mean by countermanding my order that the prisoners were to work till six," he burst out, beside himself with fury.

Mr. Warburton opened his cold blue eyes very wide and assumed an expression of great surprise.

"Are you out of your mind? Are you so ignorant that you do not know that that is not the way to speak to your official superior?"

"Oh go to hell. The prisoners are my pidgin and you've got no right to interfere. You mind your business and I'll mind mine. I want to know what the devil you mean by making a damned fool of me. Every one in the place will know that you've countermanded my order."

Mr. Warburton kept very cool.

"You had no power to give the order you did. I countermanded it because it was harsh and tyrannical. Believe me, I have not made half such a damned fool of you as you have made of yourself."

"You disliked me from the first moment I came here. You've done everything you could to make the place impossible for me because I wouldn't lick your boots for you. You got your knife into me because I wouldn't flatter you."

Cooper, spluttering with rage, was nearing dangerous ground, and Mr. Warburton's eyes grew on a sudden colder and more piercing.

"You are wrong. I thought you were a cad, but I was perfectly satisfied with the way you did your work."

"You snob. You damned snob. You thought me a cad because I hadn't been to Eton. Oh, they told me in K.S. what to expect. Why, don't you know that you're the laughing-stock of the whole country? I could hardly help bursting into a roar of laughter when you told your celebrated story about the Prince of Wales. My God, how they shouted at the club when they told it. By God, I'd rather be the cad I am than the snob you are."

He got Mr. Warburton on the raw.

"If you don't get out of my house this minute I shall knock you down," he cried.

The other came a little closer to him and put his face in his.

"Touch me, touch me," he said. "By God, I'd like to see you hit me. Do you want me to say it again? Snob. Snob."

Cooper was three inches taller than Mr. Warburton, a strong, muscular young man. Mr. Warburton was fat and fifty-four. His clenched fist shot out. Cooper caught him by the arm and pushed him back.

"Don't be a damned fool. Remember I'm not a gentleman, I know how to use my hands."

He gave a sort of hoot, and, grinning all over his pale, sharp face, jumped down the verandah steps. Mr. Warburton, his heart in his anger pounding against his ribs, sank exhausted into a chair. His body tingled as though he had prickly heat. For one horrible moment he thought he was going to cry. But suddenly he was conscious that his head-boy was on the verandah and instinctively regained control of himself. The boy came forward and filled him a glass of whisky and soda. Without a word Mr. Warburton took it and drank it to the dregs.

"What do you want to say to me?" asked Mr. Warburton, trying to force a smile on to his strained lips.

"Tuan, the assistant tuan is a bad man. Abas wishes again to leave him."

"Let him wait a little. I shall write to Kuala Solor and ask that Tuan Cooper should go elsewhere."

"Tuan Cooper is not good with the Malays."

"Leave me."

The boy silently withdrew. Mr. Warburton was left alone with his thoughts. He saw the club at Kuala Solor, the men sitting round the table in the window in their flannels, when the night had driven them in from golf and tennis, drinking whiskies and gin pahits and laughing when they told the celebrated story of the Prince of Wales and himself at Marienbad. He was hot with shame and misery. A snob! They all thought him a snob. And he had always thought them very good fellows, he had always been gentleman enough to let it make no difference to him that they were of very second-rate position. He hated them now. But his hatred for them was nothing compared with his hatred for Cooper. And if it had come to blows Cooper could have thrashed him. Tears of mortification ran down his red, fat face. He sat there for a couple of hours smoking cigarette after cigarette, and he wished he were dead.

At last the boy came back and asked him if he would dress for dinner. Of course! He always dressed for dinner. He rose wearily from his chair and put on his stiff shirt and the high collar. He sat down at the prettily decorated table and was waited on as usual by the two boys while two others waved their great fans. Over there in the bungalow, two hundred yards away, Cooper was eating a filthy meal clad only in a sarong and a baju. His feet were bare and while he ate he probably read a detective story. After dinner Mr. Warburton sat down to write a letter. The Sultan was away, but he wrote, privately and confidentially, to his representative. Cooper did his work very well, he said, but the fact was that he couldn't get on with him. They were getting dreadfully on each other's nerves and he would look upon it as a very great favour if Cooper could be transferred to another post.

He despatched the letter next morning by special messenger. The answer came a fortnight later with the month's mail. It was a private note and ran as follows:

My dear Warburton:—

I do not want to answer your letter officially and so I am writing you a few lines myself. Of course if you insist I will put the matter up to the Sultan, but I think you would be much wiser to drop it. I know Cooper is a rough diamond, but he is capable, and he had a pretty thin time in the war, and I think he should be given every chance. I think you are a little too much inclined to attach importance to a man's social position. You must remember that times have changed. Of course it's a very good thing for a man to be a gentleman, but it's better that he should be competent and hard-working. I think if you'll exercise a little tolerance you'll get on very well with Cooper.

Yours very sincerely
Richard Temple.

The letter dropped from Mr. Warburton's hand. It was easy to read between the lines. Dick Temple, whom he had known for twenty years, Dick Temple, who came from quite a good county family, thought him a snob and for that reason had no patience with his request. Mr. Warburton felt on a sudden discouraged with life. The world of which he was a part had passed away, and the future belonged to a meaner generation. Cooper represented it and Cooper he hated with all his heart. He stretched out his hand to fill his glass and at the gesture his head-boy stepped forward.

"I didn't know you were there."

The boy picked up the official letter. Ah, that was why he was waiting.

"Does Tuan Cooper go, Tuan?"

"No."

"There will be a misfortune."

For a moment the words conveyed nothing to his lassitude. But only for a moment. He sat up in his chair and looked at the boy. He was all attention.

"What do you mean by that?"

"Tuan Cooper is not behaving rightly with Abas."

Mr. Warburton shrugged his shoulders. How should a man like Cooper know how to treat servants? Mr. Warburton knew the type: he would be grossly familiar with them at one moment and rude and inconsiderate the next.

"Let Abas go back to his family."

"Tuan Cooper holds back his wages so that he may not run away. He has paid him nothing for three months. I tell him to be patient. But he is angry, he will not listen to reason. If the tuan continues to use him ill there will be a misfortune."

"You were right to tell me."

The fool! Did he know so little of the Malays as to think he could safely injure them? It would serve him damned well right if he got a kris[6] in his back. A kris. Mr. Warburton's heart seemed on a sudden to miss a beat. He had only to let things take their course and one fine day he would be rid of Cooper. He smiled faintly as the phrase, a masterly inactivity, crossed his mind. And now his heart beat a little quicker, for he saw the man he hated lying on his face in a pathway of the jungle with a knife in his back. A fit end for the cad and the bully. Mr. Warburton sighed. It was his duty to warn him and of course he must do it. He wrote a brief and formal note to Cooper asking him to come to the Fort at once.

In ten minutes Cooper stood before him. They had not spoken to one another since the day when Mr. Warburton had

---

[6] a dagger having a sinuous blade

nearly struck him. He did not now ask him to sit down.

"Did you wish to see me?" Cooper asked.

He was untidy and none too clean. His face and hands were covered with little red blotches where mosquitoes had bitten him and he had scratched himself till the blood came. His long, thin face bore a sullen look.

"I understand that you are again having trouble with your servants. Abas, my head-boy's nephew, complains that you have held back his wages for three months. I consider it a most arbitrary proceeding. The lad wishes to leave you, and I certainly do not blame him. I must insist on your paying what is due to him."

"I don't choose that he should leave me. I am holding back his wages as a pledge of his good behaviour."

"You do not know the Malay character. The Malays are very sensitive to injury and ridicule. They are passionate and revengeful. It is my duty to warn you that if you drive this boy beyond a certain point you run a great risk."

Cooper gave a contemptuous chuckle.

"What do you think he'll do?"

"I think he'll kill you."

"Why should you mind?"

"Oh, I wouldn't," replied Mr. Warburton, with a faint laugh. "I should bear it with the utmost fortitude. But I feel the official obligation to give you a proper warning."

"Do you think I'm afraid of a damned nigger?"

"It's a matter of entire indifference to me."

"Well, let me tell you this, I know how to take care of myself; that boy Abas is a dirty, thieving rascal, and if he tries any monkey tricks on me, by God, I'll wring his bloody neck."

"That was all I wished to say to you," said Mr. Warburton. "Good evening."

Mr. Warburton gave him a little nod of dismissal. Cooper flushed, did not for a moment know what to say or do, turned on his heel and stumbled out of the room. Mr. Warburton watched him go with an icy smile on his lips. He had done his duty. But what would he have thought had he known that when Cooper got back to his bungalow, so silent and cheerless, he threw himself down on his bed and in his bitter loneliness on a sudden lost all control of himself? Painful sobs tore his chest and heavy tears rolled down his thin cheeks.

After this Mr. Warburton seldom saw Cooper, and never spoke to him. He read his Times every morning, did his work at the office, took his exercise, dressed for dinner, dined and sat by the river smoking his cheroot. If by chance he ran across Cooper he cut him dead. Each, though never for a moment unconscious of the propinquity, acted as though the other did not exist. Time did nothing to assuage their animosity. They watched one another's actions and each knew what the other did. Though Mr. Warburton had been a keen shot in his youth, with age he had acquired a distaste for killing the wild things of the jungle, but on Sundays and holidays Cooper went out with his gun: if he got something it was a triumph over Mr. Warburton; if not, Mr. Warburton shrugged his shoulders and chuckled. These counter-jumpers trying to be sportsmen! Christmas was a bad time for both of them: they ate their dinners alone, each in his own quarters, and they got deliberately drunk. They were the only white men within two hundred miles and they lived within shouting distance of each other. At the beginning of the year Cooper went down with fever, and when Mr. Warburton caught sight of him again he was surprised to see how thin he had grown. He looked ill and worn. The solitude, so much more unnatural because it was due to no necessity, was getting on his nerves. It was getting on Mr. Warburton's too, and often he could not sleep at night. He lay awake brooding. Cooper was drinking heavily and surely the breaking point was near; but in his dealings with the natives he took care to do nothing that might expose him to his chief's rebuke. They fought a grim and silent battle with one another. It was a test of endurance. The months passed, and neither gave sign of weakening. They were like men dwelling in regions of eternal night, and their souls were oppressed with the knowledge that never would the day dawn for them. It looked as though their lives would continue for ever in this dull and hideous monotony of hatred.

And when at last the inevitable happened it came upon Mr. Warburton with all the shock of the unexpected. Cooper accused the boy Abas of stealing some of his clothes, and when the boy denied the theft took him by the scruff of the neck and kicked him down the steps of the bungalow. The boy demanded his wages, and Cooper flung at his head every word of abuse he knew. If he saw him in the compound in an hour he would hand him over to the police. Next morning the boy waylaid him outside the Fort when he was walking over to his office, and again demanded his wages. Cooper struck him in the face with his clenched fist. The boy fell to the ground and got up with blood streaming from his nose.

Cooper walked on and set about his work. But he could not attend to it. The blow had calmed his irritation, and he knew that he had gone too far. He was worried. He felt ill, miserable and discouraged. In the adjoining office sat Mr. Warburton, and his impulse was to go and tell him what he had done; he made a movement in his chair, but he knew with what icy scorn he would listen to the story. He could see his patronizing smile. For a moment he had an uneasy fear of what Abas might do. Warburton had warned him all right. He sighed. What a fool he had been! But he shrugged his shoulders impatiently. He did not care;

a fat lot he had to live for. It was all Warburton's fault; if he hadn't put his back up nothing like this would have happened. Warburton had made life a hell for him from the start. The snob. But they were all like that: it was because he was a Colonial. It was a damned shame that he had never got his commission in the war; he was as good as any one else. They were a lot of dirty snobs. He was damned if he was going to knuckle under now. Of course Warburton would hear of what had happened; the old devil knew everything. He wasn't afraid. He wasn't afraid of any Malay in Borneo, and Warburton could go to blazes.

He was right in thinking that Mr. Warburton would know what had happened. His head-boy told him when he went in to tiffin.[7]

"Where is your nephew now?"

"I do not know, Tuan. He has gone."

Mr. Warburton remained silent. After luncheon as a rule he slept a little, but to-day he found himself very wide awake. His eyes involuntarily sought the bungalow where Cooper was now resting.

The idiot! Hesitation for a little was in Mr. Warburton's mind. Did the man know in what peril he was? He supposed he ought to send for him. But each time he had tried to reason with Cooper, Cooper had insulted him. Anger, furious anger welled up suddenly in Mr. Warburton's heart, so that the veins on his temple stood out and he clenched his fists. The cad had had his warning. Now let him take what was coming to him. It was no business of his and if anything happened it was not his fault. But perhaps they would wish in Kuala Solor that they had taken his advice and transferred Cooper to another station.

He was strangely restless that night. After dinner he walked up and down the verandah. When the boy went away to his quarters, Mr. Warburton asked him

[7] luncheon

whether anything had been seen of Abas.

"No, Tuan, I think maybe he has gone to the village of his mother's brother."

Mr. Warburton gave him a sharp glance, but the boy was looking down and their eyes did not meet. Mr. Warburton went down to the river and sat in his arbour. But peace was denied him. The river flowed ominously silent. It was like a great serpent gliding with sluggish movement towards the sea. And the trees of the jungle over the water were heavy with a breathless menace. No bird sang. No breeze ruffled the leaves of the cassias. All around him it seemed as though something waited.

He walked across the garden to the road. He had Cooper's bungalow in full view from there. There was a light in his sitting-room and across the road floated the sound of ragtime. Cooper was playing his gramophone. Mr. Warburton shuddered; he had never got over his instinctive dislike of that instrument. But for that he would have gone over and spoken to Cooper. He turned and went back to his own house. He read late into the night, and at last he slept. But he did not sleep very long, he had terrible dreams, and he seemed to be awakened by a cry. Of course that was a dream too, for no cry—from the bungalow for instance—could be heard in his room. He lay awake till dawn. Then he heard hurried steps and the sound of voices, his head-boy burst suddenly into the room without his fez, and Mr. Warburton's heart stood still.

"Tuan, Tuan."

Mr. Warburton jumped out of bed.

"I'll come at once."

He put on his slippers, and in his sarong and pyjama-jacket walked across his compound and into Cooper's. Cooper was lying in bed, with his mouth open, and a kris sticking in his heart. He had been killed in his sleep. Mr. Warburton started, but not because he had not expected to see just such a sight, he started because he felt in himself a sudden glow of exultation. A great burden had been lifted from his shoulders.

Cooper was quite cold, Mr. Warburton took the kris out of the wound, it had been thrust in with such force that he had to use an effort to get it out, and looked at it. He recognized it. It was a kris that a dealer had offered him some weeks before and which he knew Cooper had bought.

"Where is Abas?" he asked sternly.

"Abas is at the village of his mother's brother."

The sergeant of the native police was standing at the foot of the bed.

"Take two men and go to the village and arrest him."

Mr. Warburton did what was immediately necessary. With set face he gave orders. His words were short and peremptory. Then he went back to the Fort. He shaved and had his bath, dressed and went into the dining-room. By the side of his plate The Times in its wrapper lay waiting for him. He helped himself to some fruit. The head-boy poured out his tea while the second handed him a dish of eggs. Mr. Warburton ate with a good appetite. The head-boy waited.

"What is it?" asked Mr. Warburton.

"Tuan, Abas, my nephew, was in the house of his mother's brother all night. It can be proved. His uncle will swear that he did not leave the kampong."

Mr. Warburton turned upon him with a frown.

"Tuan Cooper was killed by Abas. You know it as well as I know. Justice must be done."

"Tuan, you would not hang him?"

Mr. Warburton hesitated an instant, and though his voice remained set and stern a change came into his eyes. It was a flicker which the Malay was quick to notice and across his own eyes flashed an answering look of understanding.

"The provocation was very great. Abas will be sentenced to a term of imprisonment." There was a pause while Mr. Warburton helped himself to marmalade. "When he has served a part of his sentence in prison I will take him into this house as a boy. You can train him in his duties. I have no doubt that in the house of Tuan Cooper he got into bad habits."

"Shall Abas give himself up, Tuan?"

"It would be wise of him."

The boy withdrew. Mr. Warburton took his Times and neatly slit the wrapper. He loved to unfold the heavy, rustling pages. The morning, so fresh and cool, was delicious and for a moment his eyes wandered out over his garden with a friendly glance. A great weight had been lifted from his mind. He turned to the columns in which were announced the births, deaths, and marriages. That was what he always looked at first. A name he knew caught his attention. Lady Ormskirk had had a son at last. By George, how pleased the old dowager must be! He would write her a note of congratulation by the next mail. Abas would make a very good house-boy. That fool Cooper!

THOMAS MANN • 1875–1955

Disorder and Early Sorrow

THE principal dish at dinner had been croquettes made of turnip greens. So there follows a trifle, concocted out of one of those dessert powders we use nowadays, that taste like almond soap. Xaver, the youthful man-servant, in his outgrown striped jacket, white woollen gloves, and yellow sandals, hands it round, and the "big folk" take this opportunity to remind their father, tactfully, that company is coming today.

The "big folk" are two, Ingrid and Bert. Ingrid is brown-eyed, eighteen, and perfectly delightful. She is on the eve of her exams, and will probably pass them, if only because she knows how to wind masters, and even headmasters, round her finger. She does not, however, mean to use her certificate once she gets it; having leanings towards the stage, on the ground of her ingratiating smile, her equally ingratiating voice, and a marked and irresistible talent for burlesque. Bert is blond and seventeen. He intends to get done with school somehow, anyhow, and fling himself into the arms of life. He will be a dancer, or a cabaret actor, possibly even a waiter—but not a waiter anywhere else save at the Cairo, the night-club, whither he has once already taken flight, at five in the morning, and been brought back crestfallen. Bert bears a strong resemblance to the youthful manservant Xaver Kleinsgutl, of about the same age as himself; not because he looks common—in features he is strikingly like his father, Professor Cornelius—but by reason of an approximation of types, due in its turn to far-reaching compromises in matters of dress and bearing generally. Both lads wear their heavy hair very long on top, with a cursory parting in the middle, and give their heads the same characteristic toss to throw it off the forehead. When one of them leaves the house, by the garden gate, bareheaded in all weathers, in a blouse rakishly girt with a leather strap, and sheers off bent well over with his head on one side; or else mounts his push-bike—Xaver makes free with his employers', of both sexes, or even, in acutely irresponsible mood, with the Professor's own—Dr. Cornelius from his bedroom window cannot, for the life of him, tell whether he is looking at his son or his servant. Both, he thinks, look like young moujiks.[1] And both are impassioned cigarette-smokers, though Bert has not the means to compete with Xaver, who smokes as many as thirty a day, of a brand named after a popular cinema star. The big folk call their father and mother the "old folk"—not behind their backs, but as a form of address and in all affection: "Hullo, old folks," they will say; though Cornelius is only forty-seven years old and his wife eight years younger. And the Professor's parents, who lead in his household the humble and hesitant life of the really old, are on the big folk's lips the "ancients." As for the "little folk," Ellie and Snapper, who take their meals upstairs with blue-faced Ann—so-called because of her prevailing facial hue—Ellie and Snapper follow their mother's example and address their father by his first name, Abel. Unutterably comic it sounds, in its pert, confiding familiarity; particularly on the lips, in the sweet accents, of five-year-old Eleanor, who is the

[1] Russian peasants

image of Frau Cornelius's baby pictures and whom the Professor loves above everything else in the world.

"Darling old thing," says Ingrid affably, laying her large but shapely hand on his, as he presides in proper middle-class style over the family table, with her on his left and the mother opposite: "Parent mine, may I ever so gently jog your memory, for you have probably forgotten: this is the afternoon we were to have our little jollification, our turkey-trot with eats to match. You haven't a thing to do but just bear up and not funk it; everything will be over by nine o'clock."

"Oh—ah!" says Cornelius, his face falling. "Good!" he goes on, and nods his head to show himself in harmony with the inevitable. "I only meant—is this really the day? Thursday, yes. How time flies! Well, what time are they coming?"

"Half past four they'll be dropping in, I should say," answers Ingrid, to whom her brother leaves the major rôle in all dealings with the father. Upstairs, while he is resting, he will hear scarcely anything, and from seven to eight he takes his walk. He can slip out by the terrace if he likes.

"Tut!" says Cornelius deprecatingly, as who should say: "You exaggerate." But Bert puts in: "It's the one evening in the week Wanja doesn't have to play. Any other night he'd have to leave by half past six, which would be painful for all concerned."

Wanja is Ivan Herzl, the celebrated young leading man at the Stadttheater. Bert and Ingrid are on intimate terms with him, they often visit him in his dressing-room and have tea. He is an artist of the modern school, who stands on the stage in strange and, to the Professor's mind, utterly affected dancing attitudes, and shrieks lamentably. To a professor of history, all highly repugnant; but Bert has entirely succumbed to Herzl's influence, blackens the lower rim of his eyelids—despite painful but fruitless scenes with the father—and with youthful carelessness of the ancestral anguish declares that not only will he take Herzl for his model if he becomes a dancer, but in case he turns out to be a waiter at the Cairo he means to walk precisely thus.

Cornelius slightly raises his brows and makes his son a little bow—indicative of the unassumingness and self-abnegation that befits his age. You could not call it a mocking bow or suggestive in any special sense. Bert may refer it to himself or equally to his so talented friend.

"Who else is coming?" next inquires the master of the house. They mention various people, names all more or less familiar, from the city, from the suburban colony, from Ingrid's school. They still have some telephoning to do, they say. They have to phone Max. This is Max Hergesell, an engineering student; Ingrid utters his name in the nasal drawl which according to her is the traditional intonation of all the Hergesells. She goes on to parody it in the most abandonedly funny and lifelike way, and the parents laugh until they nearly choke over the wretched trifle. For even in these times when something funny happens people have to laugh.

From time to time the telephone bell rings in the Professor's study, and the big folk run across, knowing it is their affair. Many people had to give up their telephones the last time the price rose, but so far the Corneliuses have been able to keep theirs, just as they have kept their villa, which was built before the war, by dint of the salary Cornelius draws as professor of history—a million marks, and more or less adequate to the chances and changes of post-war life. The house is comfortable, even elegant, though sadly in need of repairs that cannot be made for lack of materials, and at present disfigured by iron stoves with long pipes. Even so, it is still the proper setting of the upper middle class, though they themselves look odd enough in it, with their worn and turned clothing and altered way of life. The children, of course, know nothing else; to them it is normal and regular, they belong by birth to the "villa proletariat." The problem of clothing troubles them not at all. They and their like have evolved a costume to fit the time, by poverty out of taste for innovation: in summer it consists of scarcely more than a belted linen smock and sandals. The middle-class parents find things rather more difficult.

The big folk's table-napkins hang over their chair-backs, they talk with their friends over the telephone. These friends are the invited guests who have rung up to accept or decline or arrange; and the conversation is carried on in the jargon of the clan, full of slang and high spirits, of which the old folk understand hardly a word. These consult together meantime about the hospitality to be offered to the impending guests. The Professor displays a middle-class ambitiousness: he wants to serve a sweet—or something that looks like a sweet—after the Italian salad and brown-bread sandwiches. But Frau Cornelius says that would be going too far. The guests would not expect it, she is sure—and the big folk, returning once more to their trifle, agree with her.

The mother of the family is of the same general type as Ingrid, though not so tall. She is languid; the fantastic difficulties of the housekeeping have broken and worn her. She really ought to go and take a cure, but feels incapable; the floor is always swaying under her feet, and everything seems upside down. She speaks of what is uppermost in her mind: the eggs, they simply must be bought today. Six thousand marks apiece they are, and just so many are to be had on this day of the week at one single shop fifteen minutes' journey away. Whatever else they do, the big folk must go and fetch them immediately after luncheon, with Danny, their neighbour's son, who will soon be calling for them; and Xaver Kleinsgutl will don civilian garb and attend his young master and mistress. For no single household is allowed more than five eggs a week; therefore the young people will enter the shop singly, one after another, under assumed names, and thus wring twenty eggs from the shopkeeper for the Cornelius family. This enterprise is the sporting event of the week for all participants, not excepting the moujik Kleinsgutl, and most of all for Ingrid and Bert, who delight in misleading and mystifying their fellowmen and would revel in the performance even if it did not achieve one single egg. They adore impersonating fictitious characters; they love to sit in a bus and carry on long lifelike conversations in a dialect which they otherwise never speak, the most commonplace dialogue about politics and people and the price of food, while the whole bus listens open-mouthed to this incredibly ordinary prattle, though with a dark suspicion all the while that something is wrong somewhere. The conversation waxes ever more shameless, it enters into revolting detail about these people who do not exist. Ingrid can make her voice sound ever so common and twittering and shrill as she impersonates a shop-girl with an illegitimate child, said child being a son with sadistic tendencies, who lately out in the country treated a cow with such unnatural cruelty that no Christian could have borne to see it. Bert nearly explodes at her twittering, but restrains himself and displays a grisly sympathy; he and the unhappy shop-girl entering into a long, stupid, depraved, and shuddery conversation over the particular morbid cruelty involved; until an old gentleman opposite, sitting with his ticket folded between his index finger and his seal ring, can bear it no more and makes public protest against the nature of the themes these young folk are discussing with such particularity. He uses the Greek plural: "themata." Whereat Ingrid pretends to be dissolving in tears, and Bert behaves as though his wrath against the old gentleman was with difficulty being held in check and would probably burst out before long. He clenches his fists, he gnashes his teeth, he shakes from head to foot; and the unhappy old gentleman, whose intentions had been of the best, hastily leaves the bus at the next stop.

Such are the diversions of the big folk. The telephone plays a prominent part in them: they ring up any and everybody—members of government, opera singers, dignitaries of the Church—in the character of shop assistants, or perhaps as Lord or Lady Doolittle. They are only with difficulty persuaded that they have the wrong number. Once they emptied their parents' card-tray and distributed its contents among the neighbours' letter-boxes, wantonly, yet not without enough impish sense of the fitness of things to make it highly upsetting, God only knowing why certain people should have called where they did.

Xaver comes in to clear away, tossing the hair out of his eyes. Now that he has taken off his gloves you can see the yellow chain-ring on his left hand. And as the Professor finishes his watery eight-thousand-mark beer and lights a cigarette, the little folk can be heard scrambling down the stair, coming, by established custom, for their after-dinner call on Father and Mother. They storm the dining-room, after a struggle with the latch, clutched by both pairs of little hands at once; their clumsy small feet twinkle over the carpet, in red felt slippers with the socks falling down on them. With prattle and shoutings each makes for his own place: Snapper to Mother, to climb on her lap, boast of all he has eaten, and thump his fat little tum; Ellie to her Abel, so much hers because she is so very much his; because she consciously luxuriates in the deep tenderness—like all deep feeling, concealing a melancholy strain—with which he holds her small form embraced; in the love in his eyes as he kisses her little fairy hand or the sweet brow with its delicate tracery of tiny blue veins.

The little folk look like each other, with the strong undefined likeness of brother and sister. In clothing and haircut they are twins. Yet they are sharply distinguished after all, and quite on sex lines. It is a little Adam and a little Eve. Not only is Snapper the sturdier and more compact, he appears consciously to emphasize his four-year-old masculinity in speech, manner, and carriage, lifting his shoulders and letting the little arms hang down quite like a young American athlete, drawing down his mouth when he talks and seeking to give his voice a gruff and forthright ring. But all this masculinity is the result of effort rather than natively his. Born and brought up in these desolate, distracted times, he has been endowed by them with an unstable and hypersensitive nervous system and suffers greatly under life's disharmonies. He is prone to sudden anger and outbursts of bitter tears, stamping his feet at every trifle; for this reason he is his mother's special nursling and care. His round, round eyes are chestnut brown and already inclined to squint, so that he will need glasses in the near future. His little nose is long, the mouth small—the father's nose and mouth they are, more plainly than ever since the Professor shaved his pointed beard and goes smooth-faced. The pointed beard had become impossible—even professors must make some concession to the changing times.

But the little daughter sits on her father's knee, his Eleonorchen, his little Eve, so much more gracious a little being, so much sweeter-faced than her brother—and he holds his cigarette away from her while she fingers his glasses with her dainty wee hands. The lenses are divided for reading and distance, and each day they tease her curiosity afresh.

At bottom he suspects that his wife's partiality may have a firmer basis than his own: that Snapper's refractory masculinity perhaps is solider stuff than his own little girl's more explicit charm and grace. But the heart will not be commanded, that he knows; and once and for all his heart belongs to the little one, as it has since the day she came, since the first time he saw her. Almost always when he holds her in his arms he remembers that first time: remembers the sunny room in the Women's Hospital, where Ellie first saw the light, twelve years after Bert was born. He remembers how he drew near, the mother smiling the while, and cautiously put aside the canopy of the diminutive bed that stood beside the large one. There lay the little miracle among the pillows: so well formed, so encompassed, as it were, with the harmony of sweet proportions, with little hands that even then, though so much tinier, were beautiful as now; with wide-open eyes blue as the sky and brighter than the sunshine —and almost in that very second he felt himself captured and held fast. This was love at first sight, love everlasting: a feeling unknown, unhoped for, unexpected— in so far as it could be a matter of conscious awareness; it took entire possession of him, and he understood, with joyous amazement, that this was for life.

But he understood more. He knows, does Dr. Cornelius, that there is something not quite right about this feeling, so unaware, so undreamed of, so involuntary. He has a shrewd suspicion that it is not by accident it has so utterly mastered him and bound itself up with his existence; that he had—even subconsciously—been preparing for it, or, more precisely, been prepared for it. There is, in short, something in him which at a given moment was ready to issue in such a feeling; and this something, highly extraordinary to relate, is his essence and quality as a professor of history. Dr. Cornelius, however, does not actually say this, even to himself; he merely realizes it, at odd times, and smiles a private smile. He knows that history professors do not love history because it is something that comes to pass, but only because it is something that *has* come to pass; that they hate a revolution like the present one because they feel it is lawless, incoherent, irrelevant—in a word, unhistoric; that their hearts belong to the coherent, disciplined, historic past. For the temper of timelessness, the temper of eternity— thus the scholar communes with himself when he takes his walk by the river before supper—that temper broods over the past; and it is a temper much better suited to the nervous system of a history professor than are the excesses of the present. The past is immortalized; that is to say, it is dead; and death is the root of all godliness and all abiding significance. Dr. Cornelius, walking alone in the dark, has a profound insight into this truth. It is this conservative instinct of his, his sense of the eternal, that has found in his love for his little daughter a way to save itself from the wounding inflicted by the times. For father love, and a little child on its mother's breast—are not these timeless, and thus very, very holy and beautiful? Yet Cornelius, pondering there in the dark, descries something not perfectly right and good in his love. Theoretically, in the interests of science, he admits it to himself. There is something ulterior about it, in the nature of it; that something is hostility, hostility against the history of today, which is still in the making and thus not history at all, in behalf of the genuine history that has already happened—that is to say, death. Yes, passing strange though all this is, yet it is true; true in a sense, that is. His devotion to this priceless little morsel of life and new growth has something to do with death, it clings to death as against life; and that is neither right nor beautiful—in a sense. Though only the most fanatical asceticism could be capable, on no other ground than such casual scientific perception, of tearing this purest and most precious of feelings out of his heart.

He holds his darling on his lap and her slim rosy legs hang down. He raises his brows as he talks to her, tenderly, with a half-teasing note of respect, and listens enchanted to her high, sweet little voice calling him Abel. He exchanges a look with the mother, who is caressing her Snapper and reading him a gentle lecture. He must be more reasonable, he must learn self-control; today again, under the manifold exasperations of life, he has given way to rage and behaved like a howling dervish. Cornelius casts a mistrustful glance at the big folk now and then, too; he thinks it not unlikely they are not unaware of those scientific preoccupations of his evening walks. If such be the case they do not show it. They stand there leaning their arms on their chair-backs and with a benevolence not untinctured with irony look on at the parental happiness.

The children's frocks are of a heavy, brick-red stuff, embroidered in modern "arty" style. They once belonged to Ingrid and Bert and are precisely alike, save that little knickers come out beneath Snapper's smock. And both have their hair bobbed. Snapper's is a streaky blond, inclined to turn dark. It is bristly and sticky and looks for all the world like a droll, badly fitting wig. But Ellie's is chestnut brown, glossy and fine as silk, as pleasing as her whole little personality. It covers her ears—and these ears are not a pair, one of them being the right size, the other distinctly too large. Her father will sometimes uncover this little abnormality and exclaim over it as though he had never noticed it before, which both makes Ellie giggle and covers her with shame. Her eyes are now golden brown, set far apart and with sweet gleams in them—such a clear and lovely look! The brows above are blond; the nose still unformed, with thick nostrils and almost circular holes; the mouth large and expressive, with a beautifully arching and mobile upper lip. When she laughs, dimples come in her cheeks and she shows her teeth like loosely strung pearls. So far she has lost but one tooth, which her father gently twisted out with his handkerchief after it had grown very wobbling. During this small operation she had paled and trembled very much. Her cheeks have the softness proper to her years, but they are not chubby; indeed, they are rather concave, due to her facial structure, with its somewhat prominent jaw. On one, close to the soft fall of her hair, is a downy freckle.

Ellie is not too well pleased with her looks—a sign that already she troubles about such things. Sadly she thinks it is best to admit it once for all, her face is "homely"; though the rest of her, "on the other hand," is not bad at all. She loves expressions like "on the other hand"; they sound choice and grown-up to her, and she likes to string them together, one after the other: "very likely," "probably," "after all." Snapper is self-critical too, though more in the moral sphere: he suffers from remorse for his attacks of rage and considers himself a tremendous sinner. He is quite certain that heaven is not for such as he; he is sure to go to "the bad place" when he dies, and no persuasions will convince him to the contrary—as that God sees the heart and gladly makes allowances. Obstinately he shakes his head, with a comic, crooked little peruke, and vows there is no place for him in heaven. When he has a cold he is immediately quite choked with mucus; rattles and rumbles from top to toe if you even look at him; his temperature flies up at once and he simply puffs. Nursy is pessimistic on the score of his constitution: such fat-blooded children as he might get a stroke any minute. Once she even thought she saw the moment at hand: Snapper had been in one of his beserker rages, and in the ensuing fit of penitence stood himself in the corner with his back to the room. Suddenly Nursy noticed that his face had gone all blue, far bluer, even, than her own. She raised the alarm, crying out that the child's all too rich blood had at length brought him to his final hour; and Snapper, to his vast astonishment, found himself, so far from being rebuked for evil-doing, encompassed in tenderness and anxiety—until it turned out that his colour was not caused by apoplexy but by the distempering on the nursery wall, which had come off on his tear-wet face.

Nursy has come downstairs too, and stands by the door sleek-haired, owl-eyed, with her hands folded over her white apron, and a severely dignified manner born of her limited intelligence. She is very proud of the care and training she gives her nurslings and declares that they are "enveloping wonderfully." She has had seventeen suppurated teeth lately removed from her jaws and been measured for a set of symmetrical yellow ones in dark rubber gums; these now embellish her peasant face. She is obsessed with the strange conviction that these teeth of hers are the subject of general conversation, that, as it were, the sparrows on the housetops chatter of them. "Everybody knows I've had a false set put in," she will say; "there has been a great deal of foolish talk about them." She is much given to dark hints and veiled innuendo: speaks, for instance, of a certain Dr. Bleifuss, whom every child knows, and "there are even some in the house who pretend to be him." All one can do with talk like this is charitably to pass it over in silence. But she teaches the children nursery rhymes: gems like:

Puff, puff, here comes the train!
Puff, puff, toot, toot,
Away it goes again.

Or that gastronomical jingle, so suited, in its sparseness, to the times, and yet seemingly with a blitheness of its own:

Monday we begin the week,
Tuesday there's a bone to pick.
Wednesday we're half way through,
Thursday what a great to-do!
Friday we eat what fish we're able,
Saturday we dance round the table.
Sunday brings us pork and greens—
Here's a feast for kings and queens!

Also a certain four-line stanza with a romantic appeal, unutterable and unuttered:

Open the gate, open the gate
And let the carriage drive in.
Who is it in the carriage sits:
A lordly sir with golden hair.

Or, finally that ballad about golden-haired Marianne who sat on a, sat on a, sat on a stone, and combed out her, combed out her, combed out her hair; and about bloodthirsty Rudolph, who pulled out a, pulled out a, pulled out a knife—and his ensuing direful end. Ellie enunciates all these ballads charmingly, with her mobile little lips, and sings them in her sweet little voice—much better than Snapper. She does everything better than he does, and he pays her honest admiration and homage and obeys her in all things except when visited by one of his attacks. Sometimes she teaches him, instructs him upon the birds in the picture-book and tells him their proper names: "This is a chaffinch, Buddy, this is a bullfinch, this is a cowfinch." He has to repeat them after her. She gives him medical instruction too, teaches him the names of diseases, such as infammation of the lungs, infammation of the blood, infammation of the air. If he does not pay attention and cannot say the words after her, she stands him in the corner. Once she even boxed his ears, but was so ashamed that she stood herself in the corner for a long time. Yes, they are fast friends, two souls with but a single thought, and have all their adventures in common. They come home from a walk and relate as with one voice that they have seen two moollies and a teenty-weenty baby calf. They are on familiar terms with the kitchen, which consists of Xaver and the ladies Hinterhofer, two sisters once of the lower middle class who, in these evil days, are reduced to living *"au pair"*[2] as the phrase goes and officiating as cook and housemaid for their board and keep. The little ones have a feeling that Xaver and the Hinterhofers are on much the same footing with their father and mother as they are themselves. At least sometimes, when they have been scolded, they go downstairs and announce that the master and mistress are cross. But playing with the servants lacks charm compared with the joys of playing upstairs. The kitchen could never rise to the height of the games their father can invent. For instance, there is "four gentlemen taking a walk." When they play it Abel will crook his knees until he is the same height with themselves and go walking with them, hand in hand. They never get enough of this sport; they could walk round and round the dining-room a whole day on end, five gentlemen in all, counting the diminished Abel.

Then there is the thrilling cushion game. One of the children, usually Ellie, seats herself, unbeknownst to Abel, in his seat at table. Still as a mouse she awaits his coming. He draws near with his head in the air, descanting in loud, clear tones upon the surpassing comfort of his chair; and sits down on top of Ellie. "What's this, what's this?" says he. And bounces about, deaf to the smothered giggles exploding behind him. "Why have they put a cushion in my chair? And what a queer, hard, awkward-shaped cushion it is!" he goes on. "Frightfully uncomfortable to sit on!" And keeps pushing and bouncing about more and more on the astonishing cushion and clutching behind him into the rapturous giggling and squeaking, until at last he turns round, and the game ends with a magnificent climax of discovery and recognition. They might go through all this a hundred times without diminishing by an iota its power to thrill.

Today is no time for such joys. The imminent festivity disturbs the atmosphere, and besides there is work to be done, and, above all, the eggs to be got. Ellie has just time to recite "Puff, puff," and Cornelius to discover that her ears are not mates, when they are interrupted by the arrival of Danny, come to fetch Bert and Ingrid. Xaver, meantime, has exchanged his striped livery for an ordinary coat, in which he looks rather rough-and-ready, though as brisk and attractive as ever. So then Nursy and the children ascend to the upper regions, the Professor withdraws to his study to read, as always after dinner, and his wife bends her energies upon the sandwiches and salad that must be prepared. And she has another errand as well. Before the young people arrive she has to take her shopping-basket and dash into town on her bicycle, to turn into provisions a sum of money she has in hand, which she dares not keep lest it lose all value.

Cornelius reads, leaning back in his chair, with his cigar between his middle and index fingers. First he reads Macaulay on the origin of the English public debt at the end of the seventeenth century; then an article in a French periodical on the rapid increase in the Spanish debt towards the end of the sixteenth. Both these for his lecture on the morrow. He intends to compare the astonishing prosperity which accompanied the phenomenon in England with its fatal effects a hundred years earlier in Spain, and to analyse the ethical and psychological grounds of the difference in results. For

---

[2] receiving board and room, but no salary

that will give him a chance to refer back from the England of William III, which is the actual subject in hand, to the time of Philip II and the Counter-Reformation, which is his own special field. He has already written a valuable work on this period; it is much cited and got him his professorship. While his cigar burns down and gets strong, he excogitates a few pensive sentences in a key of gentle melancholy, to be delivered before his class next day: about the practically hopeless struggle carried on by the belated Philip against the whole trend of history: against the new, the kingdom-disrupting power of the Germanic ideal of freedom and individual liberty. And about the persistent, futile struggle of the aristocracy, condemned by God and rejected of man, against the forces of progress and change. He savours his sentences; keeps on polishing them while he puts back the books he has been using; then goes upstairs for the usual pause in his day's work, the hour with drawn blinds and closed eyes, which he so imperatively needs. But today, he recalls, he will rest under disturbed conditions, amid the bustle of preparations for the feast. He smiles to find his heart giving a mild flutter at the thought. Disjointed phrases on the theme of black-clad Philip and his times mingle with a confused consciousness that they will soon be dancing down below. For five minutes or so he falls asleep.

As he lies and rests he can hear the sound of the garden gate and the repeated ringing at the bell. Each time a little pang goes through him, of excitement and suspense, at the thought that the young people have begun to fill the floor below. And each time he smiles at himself again—though even his smile is slightly nervous, is tinged with the pleasurable anticipations people always feel before a party. At half past four—it is already dark—he gets up and washes at the wash-stand. The basin has been out of repair for two years. It is supposed to tip, but has broken away from its socket on one side and cannot be mended because there is nobody to mend it; neither replaced because no shop can supply another. So it has to be hung up above the vent and emptied by lifting in both hands and pouring out the water. Cornelius shakes his head over this basin, as he does several times a day—whenever, in fact, he has occasion to use it. He finishes his toilet with care, standing under the ceiling light to polish his glasses till they shine. Then he goes downstairs.

On his way to the dining-room he hears the gramophone already going, and the sound of voices. He puts on a polite, society air; at his tongue's end is the phrase he means to utter: "Pray don't let me disturb you," as he passes directly into the dining-room for his tea. "Pray don't let me disturb you"—it seems to him precisely the *mot juste;* towards the guests cordial and considerate, for himself a very bulwark.

The lower floor is lighted up, all the bulbs in the chandelier are burning save one that has burned out. Cornelius pauses on a lower step and surveys the entrance hall. It looks pleasant and cosy in the bright light, with its copy of Marées over the brick chimney-piece, its wainscoted walls—wainscoted in soft wood—and red-carpeted floor, where the guests stand in groups, chatting, each with his teacup and slice of bread-and-butter spread with anchovy paste. There is a festal haze, faint scents of hair and clothing and human breath come to him across the room, it is all characteristic and familiar and highly evocative. The door into the dressing-room is open, guests are still arriving.

A large group of people is rather bewildering at first sight. The Professor takes in only the general scene. He does not see Ingrid, who is standing just at the foot of the steps, in a dark silk frock with a pleated collar falling softly over the shoulders, and bare arms. She smiles up at him, nodding and showing her lovely teeth.

"Rested?" she asks, for his private ear. With a quite unwarranted start he recognizes her, and she presents some of her friends.

"May I introduce Herr Zuber?" she says. "And this is Fräulein Plaichinger."

Herr Zuber is insignificant. But Fräulein Plaichinger is a perfect Germania, blond and voluptuous, arrayed in floating draperies. She has a snub nose, and answers the Professor's salutation in the high, shrill pipe so many stout women have.

"Delighted to meet you," he says. "How nice of you to come! A classmate of Ingrid's, I suppose?"

And Herr Zuber is a golfing partner of Ingrid's. He is in business; he works in his uncle's brewery. Cornelius makes a few jokes about the thinness of the beer and professes to believe that Herr Zuber could easily do something about the quality if he would. "But pray don't let me disturb you," he goes on, and turns towards the dining-room.

"There comes Max," says Ingrid. "Max, you sweep, what do you mean by rolling up at this time of day?" For such is the way they talk to each other, offensively to an older ear; of social forms, of hospitable warmth, there is no faintest trace. They all call each other by their first names.

A young man comes up to them out of the dressing-room and makes his bow; he has an expanse of white shirt-front and a little black string tie. He is as pretty as a picture, dark, with rosy cheeks, clean-shaven of course, but with just a sketch of side-whisker. Not a ridiculous or flashy beauty, not like a gypsy fiddler, but just charming to look at, in a winning, well-bred way, with kind dark eyes. He even wears his dinner-jacket a little awkwardly.

"Please don't scold me, Cornelia," he says; "it's the idiotic lectures." And Ingrid presents him to her father as Herr Hergesell.

Well, and so this is Herr Hergesell. He knows his manners, does Herr Hergesell, and thanks the master of the house quite ingratiatingly for his invitation as they shake hands. "I certainly seem to have missed the bus," says he jocosely. "Of course I have lectures today up to four o'clock; I would have; and after that I had to go home to change." Then he talks about his pumps, with which he has just been struggling in the dressing-room.

"I brought them with me in a bag," he goes on. "Mustn't tramp all over the carpet in our brogues—it's not done. Well, I was ass enough not to fetch along a shoe-horn, and I find I simply can't get in! What a sell! They are the tightest I've ever had, the numbers don't tell you a thing, and all the leather today is just cast iron. It's not leather at all. My poor finger"—he confidingly displays a reddened digit and once more characterizes the whole thing as a "sell," and a putrid sell into the bargain. He really does talk just as Ingrid said he did, with a peculiar nasal drawl, not affectedly in the least, but merely because that is the way of all the Hergesells.

Dr. Cornelius says it is very careless of them not to keep a shoe-horn in the cloak-room and displays proper sympathy with the mangled finger. "But now you *really* must not let me disturb you any longer," he goes on. "*Auf wiedersehen!*" And he crosses the hall into the dining-room.

There are guests there too, drinking tea; the family table is pulled out. But the Professor goes at once to his own little upholstered corner with the electric light bulb above it—the nook where he usually drinks his tea. His wife is sitting there talking with Bert and two other young men, one of them Herzl, whom Cornelius knows and greets; the other a typical "Wandervogel" named Möller, a youth who obviously neither owns nor cares to own the correct evening dress of the middle classes (in fact, there is no such thing any more), nor to ape the manners of a gentleman (and, in fact, there is no such thing any more either). He has a wilderness of hair, horn spectacles, and a long neck, and wears golf stockings and a belted blouse. His regular occupation, the Professor learns, is banking, but he is by way of being an amateur folk-lorist and collects folk-songs from all localities and in all languages. He sings them, too, and at Ingrid's command has brought his guitar; it is hanging in the dressing-room in an oilcloth case. Herzl, the actor, is small and slight, but he has a strong growth of black beard, as you can tell by the thick coat of powder on his cheeks. His eyes are larger than life, with a deep and melancholy glow. He has put on rouge besides the powder—those dull carmine high-lights on the cheeks can be nothing but a cosmetic. "Queer," thinks the Professor. "You would think a man would be one thing or the other—not melancholic and use face paint at the same time. It's a psychological contradiction. How can a melancholy man rouge? But here we have a perfect illustration of the abnormality of the artist soul-form. It can make possible a contradiction like this—perhaps it even consists in the contradiction. All very interesting—and no reason whatever for not being polite to him. Politeness is a primitive convention—and legitimate. . . . Do take some lemon, Herr Hofschauspieler!"

Court actors and court theatres—there are no such things any more, really. But Herzl relishes the sound of the title, notwithstanding he is a revolutionary artist. This must be another contradiction inherent in his soul-form; so, at least, the Professor assumes, and he is probably right. The flattery he is guilty of is a sort of atonement for his previous hard thoughts about the rouge.

"Thank you so much—it's really too good of you, sir," says Herzl, quite embarrassed. He is so overcome that he almost stammers; only his perfect enunciation saves him. His whole bearing towards his hostess and the master of the house is exaggeratedly polite. It is almost as though he had a bad conscience in respect of his rouge; as though an inward compulsion had driven him to put it on, but now, seeing it through the Professor's eyes, he disapproves of it himself, and thinks, by an air of humility toward the whole of unrouged society, to mitigate its effect.

They drink their tea and chat: about Möller's folk-songs, about Basque folk-songs and Spanish folk-songs; from which they pass to the new production of *Don Carlos* at the Stadttheater, in which Herzl plays the title-rôle. He talks about his own rendering of the part and says he hopes his conception of the character has unity. They go on to criticize the rest of the cast, the setting, and the production as a whole; and Cornelius is struck, rather painfully, to find the conversation trending towards his own special province, back to Spain and the Counter-Reformation. He has done nothing at all to give it this turn, he is perfectly innocent, and hopes it does not look as though he had sought an occasion to play the professor. He wonders, and falls silent, feeling relieved when the little folk come up to the table. Ellie and Snapper have on their blue velvet Sunday frocks; they are permitted to partake in the festivities up to bedtime. They look shy and large-eyed as they say how-do-you-do to the strangers and, under pressure, repeat their names and ages. Herr Möller does nothing but gaze at them solemnly, but Herzl is simply ravished. He rolls his eyes up to heaven and puts his hands over his mouth; he positively blesses them. It all, no doubt, comes from his heart, but he is so addicted to theatrical methods of making an impression and getting an effect that both words and behaviour ring frightfully false. And even his enthusiasm for the little folks looks too much like part of his general craving to make up for the rouge on his cheeks.

The tea-table has meanwhile emptied of guests, and dancing is going on in the hall. The children run off, the Professor prepares to retire. "Go and enjoy yourselves," he says to Möller and Herzl, who have sprung from their chairs as he rises from his. They shake hands and he withdraws into his study, his peaceful kingdom, where he lets down the blinds, turns on the desk lamp, and sits down to his work.

It is work which can be done, if necessary, under disturbed conditions: nothing but a few letters and a few notes. Of course, Cornelius's mind wanders. Vague impressions float through it: Herr Hergesell's refractory pumps, the high pipe in that plump body of the Plaichinger female. As he writes, or leans back in his chair and stares into space, his thoughts go back to Herr Möller's collection of Basque folk-songs, to Herzl's posings and humility, to "his" Carlos and the court of Philip II. There is something strange, he thinks, about conversations. They are so ductile, they will flow of their own accord in the direction of one's dominating interest. Often and often he has seen this happen. And while he is thinking, he is listening to the sounds next door—rather subdued, he finds them. He hears only voices, no sound of footsteps. The dancers do not glide or circle round the room; they merely walk about over the carpet, which does not hamper their movements in the least. Their way of holding each other is quite different and strange, and they move to the strains of the gramophone, to the weird music of the new world. He concentrates on the music and makes out that it is a jazz-band record, with various percussion instruments and the clack and clatter of castanets, which, however, are not even faintly suggestive of Spain, but merely jazz like the rest. No, not Spain. . . . His thoughts are back at their old round.

Half an hour goes by. It occurs to him it would be no more than friendly to go and contribute a box of cigarettes to the festivities next door. Too bad to ask the young people to smoke their own—though they have probably never thought of it. He goes into the empty dining-room and takes a box from his supply in the cupboard: not the best ones, nor yet the brand he himself prefers, but a certain long, thin kind he is not averse to getting rid of—after all, they are nothing but youngsters. He takes the box into the hall, holds it up with a smile, and deposits it on the mantle-shelf. After which he gives a look round and returns to his own room.

There comes a lull in dance and music. The guests stand about the room in groups or round the table at the window or are seated in a circle by the fireplace. Even the built-in stairs, with their worn velvet carpet, are crowded with young folk as in an amphitheatre: Max Hergesell is there, leaning back with one elbow on the step above and gesticulating with his free hand as he talks to the shrill, voluptuous Plaichinger. The floor of the hall is nearly empty, save just in the centre: there, directly beneath the chandelier, the two little ones in their blue velvet frocks clutch each other in an awkward embrace and twirl silently round and round, oblivious of all else. Cornelius, as he passes, strokes their hair, with a friendly word; it does not distract them from their small solemn preoccupation. But at his own door he turns to glance round and sees young Hergesell push himself off the stair by his elbow—probably because he noticed the Professor. He comes down into the arena, takes Ellie out of her brother's arms, and dances with her himself. It looks very comic, without the music, and he crouches down just as Cornelius does when he goes walking with the four gentlemen, holding the fluttered

Ellie as though she were grown up and taking little "shimmying" steps. Everybody watches with huge enjoyment, the gramophone is put on again, dancing becomes general. The Professor stands and looks, with his hand on the door-knob. He nods and laughs; when he finally shuts himself into his study the mechanical smile still lingers on his lips.

Again he turns over pages by his desk lamp, takes notes, attends to a few simple matters. After a while he notices that the guests have forsaken the entrance hall for his wife's drawing-room, into which there is a door from his own study as well. He hears their voices and the sounds of a guitar being tuned. Herr Möller, it seems, is to sing—and does so. He twangs the strings of his instrument and sings in a powerful bass a ballad in a strange tongue, possibly Swedish. The Professor does not succeed in identifying it, though he listens attentively to the end, after which there is great applause. The sound is deadened by the portière that hangs over the dividing door. The young bank-clerk begins another song. Cornelius goes softly in.

It is half-dark in the drawing-room; the only light is from the shaded standard lamp, beneath which Möller sits, on the divan, with his legs crossed, picking his strings. His audience is grouped easily about; as there are not enough seats, some stand, and more, among them many young ladies, are simply sitting on the floor with their hands clasped round their knees or even with their legs stretched out before them. Hergesell sits thus, in his dinner jacket, next the piano, with Fräulein Plaichinger beside him. Frau Cornelius is holding both children on her lap as she sits in her easy-chair opposite the singer. Snapper, the Bœotian, begins to talk loud and clear in the middle of the song and has to be intimidated with hushings and finger-shakings. Never, never would Ellie allow herself to be guilty of such conduct. She sits there daintily erect and still on her mother's knee. The Professor tries to catch her eye and exchange a private signal with his little girl; but she does not see him. Neither does she seem to be looking at the singer. Her gaze is directed lower down.

Möller sings the "joli tambour":

Sire, mon roi, donnez-moi votre fille—

They are all enchanted. "How good!" Hergesell is heard to say, in the odd, nasally condescending Hergesell tone. The next one is a beggar ballad, to a tune composed by young Möller himself: it elicits a storm of applause:

Gypsy lassie a-goin' to the fair,
Huzza!
Gypsy laddie a-goin' to be there—
Huzza, diddlety umpty dido!

Laughter and high spirits, sheer reckless hilarity, reigns after this jovial ballad. "Frightfully good!" Hergesell comments again, as before. Follows another popular song, this time a Hungarian one; Möller sings it in its own outlandish tongue, and most effectively. The Professor applauds with ostentation. It warms his heart and does him good, this outcropping of artistic, historic, and cultural elements all amongst the shimmying. He goes up to young Möller and congratulates him, talks about the songs and their sources, and Möller promises to lend him a certain annotated book of folk songs. Cornelius is the more cordial because all the time, as fathers do, he has been comparing the parts and achievements of this young stranger with those of his own son, and being gnawed by envy and chagrin. This young Möller, he is thinking, is a capable bank-clerk (though about Möller's capacity he knows nothing whatever) and has this special gift besides, which must have taken talent and energy to cultivate. "And here is my poor Bert, who knows nothing and can do nothing and thinks of nothing except playing the clown, without even talent for that!" He tries to be just; he tells himself that, after all, Bert has innate refinement; that probably there is a good deal more to him than there is to the successful Möller; that perhaps he has even something of the poet in him, and his dancing and table-waiting are due to mere boyish folly and the distraught times. But paternal envy and pessimism win the upper hand; when Möller begins another song, Dr. Cornelius goes back to his room.

He works as before, with divided attention, at this and that, while it gets on for seven o'clock. Then he remembers a letter he may just as well write, a short letter and not very important, but letter-writing is wonderful for the way it takes up the time, and it is almost half past when he has finished. At half past eight the Italian salad will be served; so now is the prescribed moment for the Professor to go out into the wintry darkness to post his letters and take his daily quantum of fresh air and exercise. They are dancing again, and he will have to pass through the hall to get his hat and coat; but they are used to him now, he need not stop and beg them not to be disturbed. He lays away his papers, takes up the letters he has written, and goes out. But he sees his wife sitting near the door of his room and pauses a little by her easy-chair.

She is watching the dancing. Now and then the big folk or some of their guests stop to speak to her; the party is at its height, and there are more onlookers than these two: blue-faced Ann is standing at the bottom of the stairs, in all the dignity of her limitations. She is waiting for the children, who simply cannot get their fill of these unwonted festivities, and watching over Snapper, lest his all too rich blood be churned to the danger-point by too much twirling round. And not only the nursery but the kitchen takes an interest: Xaver and the two ladies Hinterhofer are standing by the pantry door looking on with relish. Fräulein Walburga, the elder of the two sunken sisters (the culinary section—she objects to being called a cook), is a whimsical, good-natured sort, brown-eyed, wearing glasses with thick circular lenses; the nose-piece is wound with a bit of rag to keep it from pressing on her nose. Fräulein Cecilia is younger, though not so precisely young either. Her bearing is as self-assertive as usual, this being her way of sustaining her dignity as a former member of the middle class. For Fräulein Cecilia feels acutely her descent into the ranks of domestic service. She positively declines to wear a cap or other badge of servitude, and her hardest trial is on the Wednesday evening when she has to serve the dinner while Xaver has his afternoon out. She hands the dishes with averted face and elevated nose—a fallen queen; and so distressing is it to behold her degradation that one evening when the little folk happened to be at table and saw her they both with one accord burst into tears. Such anguish is unknown to young Xaver. He enjoys serving and does it with an ease born of practice as well as talent, for he was once a "piccolo." But otherwise he is a thorough-paced good-for-nothing and windbag—with quite distinct traits of character of his own, as his long-suffering employers are always ready to concede, but perfectly impossible and a bag of wind for all that. One must just take him as he is, they think, and not expect figs from thistles. He is the child and product of the disrupted times, a perfect specimen of his generation, follower of the revolution, Bolshevist sympathizer. The Professor's name for him is the "minute-man," because he is always to be counted on in any sudden crisis, if only it address his sense of humour or love of novelty, and will display therein amazing readiness and resources. But he utterly lacks a sense of duty and can as little be trained to the performance of the daily round and common task as some kinds of dog can be taught to jump over a stick. It goes so plainly against the grain that criticism is disarmed. One becomes resigned. On grounds that appealed to him as unusual and amusing he would be ready to turn out of his bed at any hour of the night. But he simply cannot get up before eight in the morning, he cannot do it, he will not jump over the stick. Yet all day long the evidence of this free and untrammelled existence, the sound of his mouth-organ, his joyous whistle, or his raucous but expressive voice lifted in song, rises to the hearing of the world above-stairs; and the smoke of his cigarettes fills the pantry. While the Hinterhofer ladies work he stands and looks on. Of a morning while the Professor is breakfasting, he tears the leaf off the study calendar—but does not lift a finger to dust the room. Dr. Cornelius has often told him to leave the calendar alone, for he tends to tear off two leaves at a time and thus to add to the general confusion. But young Xaver appears to find joy in this activity, and will not be deprived of it.

Again, he is fond of children, a winning trait. He will throw himself into games with the little folk in the garden, make and mend their toys with great ingenuity, even read aloud from their books—and very droll it sounds in his thick-lipped pronunciation. With his whole soul he loves the cinema; after an evening spent there he inclines to melancholy and yearning and talking to himself. Vague hopes stir in him that some day he may make his fortune in that gay world and belong to it by rights—hopes based on his shock of hair and his physical agility and daring. He likes to climb the ash tree in the front garden, mounting branch by branch to the very top and frightening everybody to death who sees him. Once there he lights a cigarette and smokes it as he sways to and fro, keeping a look-out for a cinema director who might chance to come along and engage him.

If he changed his striped jacket for mufti, he might easily dance with the others and no one would notice the difference. For the big folk's friends are rather anomalous in their clothing: evening dress is worn by a few, but it is by no means the rule. There is quite a sprinkling of guests, both male and female, in the same general style as Möller the ballad-singer. The Professor is familiar with the circumstances of most of this young generation he is watching as he stands beside his wife's chair; he has heard them spoken of by name. They are students at the high school or at the School of Applied Art; they lead, at least the masculine portion, that precarious and scrambling existence which is purely the product of the time. There is a tall, pale, spindling youth, the son of a dentist, who lives by speculation. From all the Professor hears, he is a perfect Aladdin. He keeps a car, treats his friends to champagne suppers, and showers presents upon them on every occasion, costly little trifles in mother-of-pearl and gold. So today he has brought gifts to the young givers of the feast: for Bert a gold leadpencil, and for Ingrid a pair of ear-rings of barbaric size, great gold circlets that fortunately do not have to go through the little earlobe, but are fastened over it by means of a clip. The big folk come laughing to their parents to display these trophies; and the parents shake their heads even while they admire—Aladdin bowing over and over from afar.

The young people appear to be absorbed in their dancing—if the performance they are carrying out with so much still concentration can be called dancing. They stride across the carpet, slowly, according to some unfathomable prescript, strangely embraced; in the newest attitude, tummy advanced and shoulders high, waggling the hips. They do not get tired, because nobody could. There is no such thing as heightened colour or heaving bosoms. Two girls may dance together or two young men—it is all the same. They move to the exotic strains of the gramophone, played with the loudest needles to procure the maximum of sound: shimmies, foxtrots, one-steps, double foxes, African shimmies, Java dances, and Creole polkas, the wild musky melodies follow one another, now furious, now languishing, a monotonous Negro programme in unfamiliar rhythm, to a clacking, clashing, and strumming orchestral accompaniment.

"What is that record?" Cornelius inquires of Ingrid, as she passes him by in the arms of the pale young speculator, with reference to the piece then playing, whose alternate languors and furies he finds comparatively pleasing and showing a certain resourcefulness in detail.

Prince of Pappenheim: 'Console thee, dearest child,' " she answers, and smiles pleasantly back at him with her white teeth.

The cigarette smoke wreathes beneath the chandelier. The air is blue with a festal haze compact of sweet and thrilling ingredients that stir the blood with memories of green-sick pains and are particularly poignant to those whose youth —like the Professor's own—has been over-sensitive. . . . The little folk are still on the floor. They are allowed to stop up until eight, so great is their delight in the party. The guests have got used to their presence; in their own way, they have their place in the doings of the evening. They have separated, anyhow: Snapper revolves all alone in the middle of the carpet, in his little blue velvet smock, while Ellie is running after one of the dancing couples, trying to hold the man fast by his coat. It is Max Hergesell and Fräulein Plaichinger. They dance well, it is a pleasure to watch them. One has to admit that these mad modern dances, when the right people dance them, are not so bad after all—they have something

quite taking. Young Hergesell is a capital leader, dances according to rule, yet with individuality. So it looks. With what aplomb can he walk backwards—when space permits! And he knows how to be graceful standing still in a crowd. And his partner supports him well, being unsuspectedly lithe and buoyant, as fat people often are. They look at each other, they are talking, paying no heed to Ellie, though others are smiling to see the child's persistence. Dr. Cornelius tries to catch up his little sweetheart as she passes and draw her to him. But Ellie eludes him, almost peevishly; her dear Abel is nothing to her now. She braces her little arms against his chest and turns her face away with a persecuted look. Then escapes to follow her fancy once more.

The Professor feels an involuntary twinge. Uppermost in his heart is hatred for this party, with its power to intoxicate and estrange his darling child. His love for her—that not quite disinterested, not quite unexceptionable love of his—is easily wounded. He wears a mechanical smile, but his eyes have clouded, and he stares fixedly at a point in the carpet, between the dancers' feet.

"The children ought to go to bed," he tells his wife. But she pleads for another quarter of an hour; she has promised already, and they do love it so! He smiles again and shakes his head, stands so a moment and then goes across to the cloak-room, which is full of coats and hats and scarves and overshoes. He has trouble in rummaging out his own coat, and Max Hergesell comes out of the hall, wiping his brow.

"Going out, sir?" he asks, in Hergesellian accents, dutifully helping the older man on with his coat. "Silly business this, with my pumps," he says. "They pinch like hell. The brutes are simply too tight for me, quite apart from the bad leather. They press just here on the ball of my great toe"—he stands on one foot and holds the other in his hand—"it's simply unbearable. There's nothing for it but to take them off; my brogues will have to do the business. . . . Oh, let me help you, sir."

"Thanks," says Cornelius. "Don't trouble. Get rid of your own tormentors. . . . Oh, thanks very much!" For Hergesell has gone on one knee to snap the fasteners of his snow-boots.

Once more the Professor expresses his gratitude; he is pleased and touched by so much sincere respect and youthful readiness to serve. "Go and enjoy yourself," he counsels. "Change your shoes and make up for what you have been suffering. Nobody can dance in shoes that pinch. Good-bye, I must be off to get a breath of fresh air."

"I'm going to dance with Ellie now," calls Hergesell after him. "She'll be a first-rate dancer when she grows up, and that I'll swear to."

"Think so?" Cornelius answers, already half out. "Well, you are a connoisseur, I'm sure. Don't get curvature of the spine with stooping."

He nods again and goes. "Fine lad," he thinks as he shuts the door. "Student of engineering. Knows what he's bound for, got a good clear head, and so well set up and pleasant too." And again paternal envy rises as he compares his poor Bert's status with this young man's, which he puts in the rosiest light that his son's may look the darker. Thus he sets out on his evening walk.

He goes up the avenue, crosses the bridge, and walks along the bank on the other side as far as the next bridge but one. The air is wet and cold, with a little snow now and then. He turns up his coat-collar and slips the crook of his cane over the arm behind his back. Now and then he ventilates his lungs with a long deep breath of the night air. As usual when he walks, his mind reverts to his professional preoccupations, he thinks about his lectures and the things he means to say tomorrow about Philip's struggle against the Germanic revolution, things steeped in melancholy and penetratingly just. Above all just, he thinks. For in one's dealings with the young it behoves one to display the scientific spirit, to exhibit the principles of enlightenment—not only for purposes of mental discipline, but on the human and individual side, in order not to wound them or indirectly offend their political sensibilities; particularly in these days, when there is so much tinder in the air, opinions are so frightfully split up and chaotic, and you may so easily incur attacks from one party or the other, or even give rise to scandal, by taking sides on a point of history. "And taking sides is unhistoric anyhow," so he muses. "Only justice, only impartiality is historic." And could not, properly considered, be otherwise. . . . For justice can have nothing of youthful fire and blithe, fresh, loyal conviction. It is by nature melancholy. And, being so, has secret affinity with the lost cause and the forlorn hope rather than with the fresh and blithe and loyal—perhaps this affinity is its very essence and without it it would not exist at all! . . . "And is there then no such thing as justice?" the Professor asks himself, and ponders the question so deeply that he absently posts his letters in the next box and turns round to go home. This thought of his is unsettling and disturbing to the scientific mind—but is it not after all itself scientific, psychological, conscientious, and therefore to be accepted without prejudice, no matter how upsetting? In the midst of which musings Dr. Cornelius finds himself back at his own door.

On the outer threshold stands Xaver, and seems to be looking for him.

"Herr Professor," says Xaver, tossing back his hair, "go upstairs to Ellie straight off. She's in a bad way."

"What's the matter?" asks Cornelius in alarm. "Is she ill?"

"No-o, not to say ill," answers Xaver.

"She's just in a bad way and crying fit to bust her little heart. It's along o' that chap with the shirt-front that danced with her—Herr Hergesell. She couldn't be got to go upstairs peaceably, not at no price at all, and she's b'en crying bucketfuls."

"Nonsense," says the Professor, who has entered and is tossing off his things in the cloak-room. He says no more; opens the glass door and without a glance at the guests turns swiftly to the stairs. Takes them two at a time, crosses the upper hall and the small room leading into the nursery. Xaver follows at his heels, but stops at the nursery door.

A bright light still burns within, showing the gay frieze that runs all round the room, the large row of shelves heaped with a confusion of toys, the rocking-horse on his swaying platform, with red-varnished nostrils and raised hoofs. On the linoleum lie other toys—building blocks, railway trains, a little trumpet. The two white cribs stand not far apart, Ellie's in the window corner, Snapper's out in the room.

Snapper is asleep. He has said his prayers in loud, ringing tones, prompted by Nurse, and gone off at once into vehement, profound, and rosy slumber —from which a cannon-ball fired at close range could not rouse him. He lies with both fists flung back on the pillows on either side of the tousled head with its funny crooked little slumber-tossed wig.

A circle of females surrounds Ellie's bed: not only blue-faced Ann is there, but the Hinterhofer ladies too, talking to each other and to her. They make way as the Professor comes up and reveal the child sitting all pale among her pillows, sobbing and weeping more bitterly than he has ever seen her sob and weep in her life. Her lovely little hands lie on the coverlet in front of her, the nightgown with its narrow lace border has slipped down from her shoulder—such a thin, birdlike little shoulder—and the sweet head Cornelius loves so well, set on the neck like a flower on its stalk, her head is on one side, with the eyes rolled up to the corner between wall and ceiling above her head. For there she seems to envisage the anguish of her heart and even to nod to it—either on purpose or because her head wobbles as her body is shaken with the violence of her sobs. Her eyes rain down tears. The bow-shaped lips are parted, like a little *mater dolorosa's,* and from them issue long, low wails that in nothing resemble the unnecessary and exasperating shrieks of a naughty child, but rise from the deep extremity of her heart and wake in the Professor's own a sympathy that is well-nigh intolerable. He has never seen his darling so before. His feelings find immediate vent in an attack on the ladies Hinterhofer.

"What about the supper?" he asks sharply. "There must be a great deal to do. Is my wife being left to do it alone?"

For the acute sensibilities of the former middle class this is quite enough. The ladies withdraw in righteous indignation, and Xaver Kleingutl jeers at them as they pass out. Having been born to low life instead of achieving it, he never loses a chance to mock at their fallen state.

"Childie, childie," murmurs Cornelius, and sitting down by the crib enfolds the anguished Ellie in his arms. "What is the trouble with my darling?"

She bedews his face with her tears.

"Abel . . . Abel . . ." she stammers between sobs. "Why—isn't Max—my brother? Max ought to be—my brother!"

Alas, alas! What mischance is this? Is this what the party has wrought, with its fatal atmosphere? Cornelius glances helplessly up at blue-faced Ann standing there in all the dignity of her limitations with her hands before her on her apron. She purses up her mouth and makes a long face. "It's pretty young," she says, "for the female instincts to be showing up."

"Hold your tongue," snaps Cornelius,

in his agony. He has this much to be thankful for, that Ellie does not turn from him now; she does not push him away as she did downstairs, but clings to him in her need, while she reiterates her absurd, bewildered prayer that Max might be her brother, or with a fresh burst of desire demands to be taken downstairs so that he can dance with her again. But Max, of course, is dancing with Fräulein Plaichinger, that behemoth who is his rightful partner and has every claim upon him; whereas Ellie—never, thinks the Professor, his heart torn with the violence of his pity, never has she looked so tiny and birdlike as now, when she nestles to him shaken with sobs and all unaware of what is happening in her little soul. No, she does not know. She does not comprehend that her suffering is on account of Fräulein Plaichinger, fat, overgrown, and utterly within her rights in dancing with Max Hergesell, whereas Ellie may only do it once, by way of a joke, although she is incomparably the more charming of the two. Yet it would be quite mad to reproach young Hergesell with the state of affairs or to make fantastic demands upon him. No, Ellie's suffering is without help or healing and must be covered up. Yet just as it is without understanding, so it is also without restraint—and that is what makes it so horribly painful. Xaver and blue-faced Ann do not feel this pain, it does not affect them—either because of native callousness or because they accept it as the way of nature. But the Professor's fatherly heart is quite torn by it, and by a distressful horror of this passion, so hopeless and so absurd.

Of no avail to hold forth to poor Ellie on the subject of the perfectly good little brother she already has. She only casts a distraught and scornful glance over at the other crib, where Snapper lies vehemently slumbering, and with fresh tears calls again for Max. Of no avail either the promise of a long, long walk tomorrow, all five gentlemen, round and round the dining-room table; or a dramatic description of the thrilling cushion games they will play. No, she will listen to none of all this, nor to lying down and going to sleep. She will not sleep, she will sit bolt upright and suffer. . . . But on a sudden they stop and listen, Abel and Ellie; listen to something miraculous that is coming to pass, that is approaching by strides, two strides, to the nursery door, that now overwhelmingly appears. . . .

It is Xaver's work, not a doubt of that. He has not remained by the door where he stood to gloat over the ejection of the Hinterhofers. No, he has bestirred himself, taken a notion; likewise steps to carry it out. Downstairs he has gone, twitched Herr Hergesell's sleeve, and made a thick-lipped request. So here they both are. Xaver, having done his part, remains by the door; but Max Hergesell comes up to Ellie's crib; in his dinner-jacket, with his sketchy side-whisker and charming black eyes; obviously quite pleased with his rôle of swan knight and fairy prince, as one who should say: "See, here am I, now all losses are restored and sorrows end."

Cornelius is almost as much overcome as Ellie herself.

"Just look," he says feebly, "look who's here. This is uncommonly good of you, Herr Hergesell."

"Not a bit of it," says Hergesell. "Why shouldn't I come to say good-night to my fair partner?"

And he approaches the bars of the crib, behind which Ellie sits struck mute. She smiles blissfully through her tears. A funny, high little note that is half a sigh of relief comes from her lips, then she looks dumbly up at her swan knight with her golden-brown eyes—tear-swollen though they are, so much more beautiful than the fat Plaichinger's. She does not put up her arms. Her joy, like her grief, is without understanding; but she does not do that. The lovely little hands lie quiet on the coverlet, and Max Hergesell stands with his arms leaning over the rail as on a balcony.

"And now," he says smartly, "she need not 'sit the livelong night and weep upon her bed'!" He looks at the Professor to make sure he is receiving due credit for the quotation. "Ha ha!" he laughs, "she's beginning young. 'Console thee, dearest child!' Never mind, you're all right! Just as you are you'll be wonderful! You've only got to grow up. . . . And you'll lie down and go to sleep like a good girl, now I've come to say good-night? And not cry any more, little Lorelei?"

Ellie looks up at him, transfigured. One birdlike shoulder is bare; the Professor draws the lace-trimmed nighty over it. There comes into his mind a sentimental story he once read about a dying child who longs to see a clown he had once, with unforgettable ecstasy, beheld in a circus. And they bring the clown to the bedside marvellously arrayed, embroidered before and behind with silver butterflies; and the child dies happy. Max Hergesell is not embroidered, and Ellie, thank God, is not going to die, she has only "been in a bad way." But, after all, the effect is the same. Young Hergesell leans over the bars of the crib and rattles on, more for the father's ear than the child's, but Ellie does not know that —and the father's feelings towards him are a most singular mixture of thankfulness, embarrassment, and hatred.

"Good night, little Lorelei," says Hergesell, and gives her his hand through the bars. Her pretty, soft, white little hand is swallowed up in the grasp of his big, strong, red one. "Sleep well," he says, "and sweet dreams! But don't dream about me—God forbid! Not at your age— ha ha!" And then the fairy clown's visit is at an end. Cornelius accompanies him to the door. "No, no positively, no thanks called for, don't mention it," he largeheartedly protests; and Xaver goes downstairs with him, to help serve the Italian salad.

But Dr. Cornelius returns to Ellie, who is now lying down, with her cheek pressed into her flat little pillow.

"Well, wasn't that lovely?" he says as he smooths the covers. She nods, with one last little sob. For a quarter of an hour he sits beside her and watches while she falls asleep in her turn, beside the little brother who found the right way so much earlier than she. Her silky brown hair takes the enchanting fall it always does when she sleeps; deep, deep lie the lashes over the eyes that late so abundantly poured forth their sorrow; the angelic mouth with its bowed upper lip is peacefully relaxed and a little open. Only now and then comes a belated catch in her slow breathing.

And her small hands, like pink and white flowers, lie so quietly, one on the coverlet, the other on the pillow by her face—Dr. Cornelius, gazing, feels his heart melt with tenderness as with strong wine.

"How good," he thinks, "that she breathes in oblivion with every breath she draws! That in childhood each night is a deep, wide gulf between one day and the next. Tomorrow, beyond all doubt, young Hergesell will be a pale shadow, powerless to darken her little heart. Tomorrow, forgetful of all but present joy, she will walk with Abel and Snapper, all five gentlemen, round and round the table, will play the ever-thrilling cushion game."

Heaven be praised for that!

—Translated by H. T. Lowe-Porter

JAMES JOYCE • 1882–1941

The Dead

LILY, the caretaker's daughter, was literally run off her feet. Hardly had she brought one gentleman into the little pantry behind the office on the ground floor and helped him off with his overcoat than the wheezy hall-door bell clanged again and she had to scamper along the bare hallway to let in another guest. It was well for her she had not to attend to the ladies also. But Miss Kate and Miss Julia had thought of that and had converted the bathroom upstairs into a ladies' dressing-room. Miss Kate and Miss Julia were there, gossiping and laughing and fussing, walking after each other to the head of the stairs, peering down over the banisters and calling down to Lily to ask her who had come.

It was always a great affair, the Misses Morkan's annual dance. Everybody who knew them came to it, members of the family, old friends of the family, the members of Julia's choir, any of Kate's pupils that were grown up enough and even some of Mary Jane's pupils too. Never once had it fallen flat. For years and years it had gone off in splendid style as long as anyone could remember; ever since Kate and Julia, after the death of their brother Pat, had left the house in Stoney Batter and taken Mary Jane, their only niece, to live with them in the dark gaunt house on Usher's Island, the upper part of which they had rented from Mr Fulham, the corn-factor on the ground floor. That was a good thirty years ago if it was a day. Mary Jane, who was then a little girl in short clothes, was now the main prop of the household for she had the organ in Haddington Road. She had been through the Academy and gave a pupils' concert every year in the upper room of the Antient Concert Rooms. Many of her pupils belonged to the better-class families on the Kingstown and Dalkey line. Old as they were, her aunts also did their share. Julia, though she was quite grey, was still the leading soprano in Adam and Eve's, and Kate, being too feeble to go about much, gave music lessons to beginners on the old square piano in the back room. Lily, the caretaker's daughter, did housemaid's work for them. Though their life was modest they believed in eating well; the best of everything: diamond-bone sirloins, three-shilling tea and the best bottled stout. But Lily seldom made a mistake in the orders so that she got on well with her three mistresses. They were fussy, that was all. But the only thing they would not stand was back answers.

Of course, they had good reason to be fussy on such a night. And then it was long after ten o'clock and yet there was no sign of Gabriel and his wife. Besides they were dreadfully afraid that Freddy Malins might turn up screwed. They would not wish for worlds that any of Mary Jane's pupils should see him under the influence; and when he was like that it was sometimes very hard to manage him. Freddy Malins always came late but they wondered what could be keeping Gabriel: and that was what brought them every two minutes to the banisters to ask Lily had Gabriel or Freddy come.

—O, Mr Conroy, said Lily to Gabriel when she opened the door for him, Miss Kate and Miss Julia thought you were never coming. Good-night, Mrs Conroy.

—I'll engage they did, said Gabriel, but they forget that my wife here takes three mortal hours to dress herself.

He stood on the mat, scraping the snow from his goloshes, while Lily led his wife to the foot of the stairs and called out:

—Miss Kate, here's Mrs Conroy.

Kate and Julia come toddling down the dark stairs at once. Both of them kissed Gabriel's wife, said she must be perished alive and asked was Gabriel with her.

—Here I am as right as the mail, Aunt Kate! Go on up. I'll follow, called out Gabriel from the dark.

He continued scraping his feet vigorously while the three women went upstairs, laughing, to the ladies' dressing-room. A light fringe of snow lay like a cape on the shoulders of his overcoat and like toecaps on the toes of his goloshes; and, as the buttons of his overcoat slipped with a squeaking noise through the snow-stiffened frieze, a cold fragrant air from out-of-doors escaped from crevices and folds.

—Is it snowing again, Mr Conroy? asked Lily.

She had preceded him into the pantry to help him off with his overcoat. Gabriel smiled at the three syllables she had given his surname and glanced at her. She was a slim, growing girl, pale in complexion and with hay-coloured hair. The gas in the pantry made her look still paler. Gabriel had known her when she was a child and used to sit on the lowest step nursing a rag doll.

—Yes, Lily, he answered, and I think we're in for a night of it.

He looked up at the pantry ceiling, which was shaking with the stamping and shuffling of feet on the floor above, listened for a moment to the piano and then glanced at the girl, who was folding his overcoat carefully at the end of a shelf.

—Tell me, Lily, he said in a friendly tone, do you still go to school?

—O no, sir, she answered. I'm done schooling this year and more.

—O, then, said Gabriel gaily, I suppose we'll be going to your wedding one of these fine days with your young man, eh?

The girl glanced back at him over her shoulder and said with great bitterness:

—The men that is now is only all palaver and what they can get out of you.

Gabriel coloured as if he felt he had made a mistake and, without looking at her, kicked off his goloshes and flicked actively with his muffler at his patent-leather shoes.

He was a stout tallish young man. The high colour of his cheeks pushed upwards even to his forehead, where it scattered itself in a few formless patches of pale red; and on his hairless face there scintillated restlessly the polished lenses and the bright gilt rims of the glasses which screened his delicate and restless eyes. His glossy black hair was parted in the middle and brushed in a long curve behind his ears where it curled slightly beneath the groove left by his hat.

When he had flicked lustre into his shoes he stood up and pulled his waistcoat down more tightly on his plump body. Then he took a coin rapidly from his pocket.

—O Lily, he said, thrusting it into her hands, it's Christmas-time, isn't it? Just . . . here's a little. . . .

He walked rapidly towards the door.

—O no, sir! cried the girl, following him. Really, sir, I wouldn't take it.

—Christmas-time! Christmas-time! said Gabriel, almost trotting to the stairs and waving his hand to her in deprecation.

The girl, seeing that he had gained the stairs, called out after him:

—Well, thank you, sir.

He waited outside the drawing-room door until the waltz should finish, listening to the skirts that swept against it and to the shuffling of feet. He was still discomposed by the girl's bitter and sudden retort. It had cast a gloom over him which he tried to dispel by arranging his cuffs and the bows of his tie. Then he took from his waistcoat pocket a little paper and glanced at the headings he had made for his speech. He was undecided about the lines from Robert Browning for he feared they would be above the heads of his hearers. Some quotation that they would recognise from Shakespeare or from the Melodies would be better. The indelicate clacking of the men's heels and the shuffling of their soles reminded him that their grade of culture differed from his. He would only make himself ridiculous by quoting poetry to them which they could not understand. They would think that he was airing his superior education. He would fail with them just as he had failed with the girl in the pantry. He had taken up a wrong tone. His whole speech was a mistake from first to last, an utter failure.

Just then his aunts and his wife came out of the ladies' dressing-room. His aunts were two small plainly dressed old women. Aunt Julia was an inch or so the taller. Her hair, drawn low over the tops of her ears, was grey; and grey also, with darker shadows, was her large flaccid face. Though she was stout in build and stood erect her slow eyes and parted lips gave her the appearance of a woman who did not know where she was or where she was going. Aunt Kate was more vivacious. Her face, healthier than her sister's, was all puckers and creases, like a shrivelled red apple, and her hair, braided in the same old-fashioned way, had not lost its ripe nut colour.

They both kissed Gabriel frankly. He was their favourite nephew, the son of their dead elder sister, Ellen, who had married T. J. Conroy of the Port and Docks.

—Gretta tells me you're not going to take a cab back to Monkstown tonight, Gabriel, said Aunt Kate.

—No, said Gabriel, turning to his wife, we had quite enough of that last year, hadn't we. Don't you remember, Aunt Kate, what a cold Gretta got out of it? Cab windows rattling all the way, and the east wind blowing in after we passed Merrion. Very jolly it was. Gretta caught a dreadful cold.

Aunt Kate frowned severely and nodded her head at every word.

—Quite right, Gabriel, quite right, she said. You can't be too careful.

—But as for Gretta there, said Gabriel, she'd walk home in the snow if she were let.

Mrs Conroy laughed.

—Don't mind him, Aunt Kate, she said. He's really an awful bother, what with green shades for Tom's eyes at night and making him do the dumb-bells, and forcing Eva to eat the stirabout. The poor child! And she simply hates the sight of it! . . . O, but you'll never guess what he makes me wear now!

She broke out into a peal of laughter and glanced at her husband, whose admiring and happy eyes had been wandering from her dress to her face and hair. The two aunts laughed heartily too, for Gabriel's solicitude was a standing joke with them.

—Goloshes! said Mrs Conroy. That's the latest. Whenever it's wet underfoot I must put on my goloshes. Tonight even, he wanted me to put them on, but I wouldn't. The next thing he'll buy me will be a diving suit.

Gabriel laughed nervously and patted his tie reassuringly while Aunt Kate nearly doubled herself, so heartily did she enjoy the joke. The smile soon faded from Aunt Julia's face and her mirthless eyes were directed towards her nephew's face. After a pause she asked:

—And what are goloshes, Gabriel?

—Goloshes, Julia! exclaimed her sister. Goodness me, don't you know what goloshes are? You wear them over your . . . over your boots, Gretta, isn't it?

—Yes, said Mrs Conroy. Guttapercha things. We both have a pair now. Gabriel says everyone wears them on the continent.

—O, on the continent, murmured Aunt Julia, nodding her head slowly.

Gabriel knitted his brows and said, as if he were slightly angered:

—It's nothing very wonderful but Gretta thinks it very funny because she says the word reminds her of Christy Minstrels.

—But tell me, Gabriel, said Aunt Kate, with brisk tact. Of course, you've seen about the room. Gretta was saying . . .

—O, the room is all right, replied Gabriel. I've taken one in the Gresham.

—To be sure, said Aunt Kate, by far the best thing to do. And the children, Gretta, you're not anxious about them?

—O, for one night, said Mrs Conroy. Besides, Bessie will look after them.

—To be sure, said Aunt Kate again. What a comfort it is to have a girl like that, one you can depend on! There's that Lily, I'm sure I don't know what has come over her lately. She's not the girl she was at all.

Gabriel was about to ask his aunt some questions on this point but she broke off suddenly to gaze after her sister who had wandered down the stairs and was craning her neck over the banisters.

—Now I ask you, she said almost testily, where is Julia going? Julia! Julia! Where are you going?

Julia, who had gone half way down one flight, came back and announced blandly:

—Here's Freddy.

At the same moment a clapping of hands and a final flourish of the pianist told that the waltz had ended. The drawing-room door was opened from within and some couples came out. Aunt Kate drew Gabriel aside hurriedly and whispered into his ear:

—Slip down, Gabriel, like a good fellow and see if he's all right, and don't let him up if he's screwed. I'm sure he's screwed. I'm sure he is.

Gabriel went to the stairs and listened over the banisters. He could hear two persons talking in the pantry. Then he recognised Freddy Malins' laugh. He went down the stairs noisily.

—It's such a relief, said Aunt Kate to Mrs Conroy, that Gabriel is here. I always feel easier in my mind when he's here. . . . Julia, there's Miss Daly and Miss Power will take some refreshment. Thanks for your beautiful waltz, Miss Daly. It made lovely time.

A tall wizen-faced man, with a stiff grizzled moustache and swarthy skin, who was passing out with his partner, said:

—And may we have some refreshment, too, Miss Morkan?

—Julia, said Aunt Kate summarily, and here's Mr Browne and Miss Furlong. Take them in, Julia, with Miss Daly and Miss Power.

—I'm the man for the ladies, said Mr Browne, pursing his lips until his moustache bristled and smiling in all his wrinkles. You know, Miss Morkan, the reason they are so fond of me is—

He did not finish his sentence, but, seeing that Aunt Kate was out of earshot, at once led the three young ladies into the back room. The middle of the room was occupied by two square tables placed end to end, and on these Aunt Julia and the caretaker were straightening and smoothing a large cloth. On the sideboard were arrayed dishes and plates, and glasses and bundles of knives and forks and spoons. The top of the closed square piano served also as a sideboard for viands and sweets. At a smaller sideboard in one corner two young men were standing, drinking hop-bitters.

Mr Browne led his charges thither and invited them all, in jest, to some ladies' punch, hot, strong and sweet. As they said they never took anything strong he opened three bottles of lemonade for them. Then he asked one of the young men to move aside, and, taking hold of the decanter, filled out for himself a goodly measure of whisky. The young men eyed him respectfully while he took a trial sip.

—God help me, he said, smiling, it's the doctor's orders.

His wizened face broke into a broader

smile, and the three young ladies laughed in musical echo to his pleasantry, swaying their bodies to and fro, with nervous jerks of their shoulders. The boldest said:

—O, now, Mr Browne, I'm sure the doctor never ordered anything of the kind.

Mr Browne took another sip of his whisky and said, with sidling mimicry:

—Well, you see, I'm like the famous Mrs Cassidy, who is reported to have said: *Now, Mary Grimes, if I don't take it, make me take it, for I feel I want it.*

His hot face had leaned forward a little too confidentially and he had assumed a very low Dublin accent so that the young ladies, with one instinct, received his speech in silence. Miss Furlong, who was one of Mary Jane's pupils, asked Miss Daly what was the name of the pretty waltz she had played; and Mr Browne, seeing that he was ignored, turned promptly to the two young men who were more appreciative.

A red-faced young woman, dressed in pansy, came into the room, excitedly clapping her hands and crying:

—Quadrilles! Quadrilles!

Close on her heels came Aunt Kate, crying:

—Two gentlemen and three ladies, Mary Jane!

—O, here's Mr Bergin and Mr Kerrigan, said Mary Jane. Mr Kerrigan, will you take Miss Power? Miss Furlong, may I get you a partner, Mr Bergin. O, that'll just do now.

—Three ladies, Mary Jane, said Aunt Kate.

The two young gentlemen asked the ladies if they might have the pleasure, and Mary Jane turned to Miss Daly.

—O, Miss Daly, you're really awfully good, after playing for the last two dances, but really we're so short of ladies tonight.

—I don't mind in the least, Miss Morkan.

—But I've a nice partner for you, Mr Bartell D'Arcy, the tenor. I'll get him to sing later on. All Dublin is raving about him.

—Lovely voice, lovely voice! said Aunt Kate.

As the piano had twice begun the prelude to the first figure Mary Jane led her recruits quickly from the room. They had hardly gone when Aunt Julia wandered slowly into the room, looking behind her at something.

—What is the matter, Julia? asked Aunt Kate anxiously. Who is it?

Julia, who was carrying in a column of table-napkins, turned to her sister and said, simply, as if the question had surprised her:

—It's only Freddy, Kate, and Gabriel with him.

In fact right behind her Gabriel could be seen piloting Freddy Malins across the landing. The latter, a young man of about forty, was of Gabriel's size and build, with very round shoulders. His face was fleshy and pallid, touched with colour only at the thick hanging lobes of his ears and at the wide wings of his nose. He had coarse features, a blunt nose, a convex and receding brow, tumid and protruded lips. His heavy-lidded eyes and the disorder of his scanty hair made him look sleepy. He was laughing heartily in a high key at a story which he had been telling Gabriel on the stairs and at the same time rubbing the knuckles of his left fist backwards and forwards into his left eye.

—Good evening, Freddy, said Aunt Julia.

Freddy Malins bade the Misses Morkan good-evening in what seemed an offhand fashion by reason of the habitual catch in his voice and then, seeing that Mr Browne was grinning at him from the sideboard, crossed the room on rather shaky legs and began to repeat in an undertone the story he had just told to Gabriel.

—He's not so bad, is he? said Aunt Kate to Gabriel.

Gabriel's brows were dark but he raised them quickly and answered:

—O, no, hardly noticeable.

—Now, isn't he a terrible fellow! she said. And his poor mother made him take the pledge on New Year's Eve. But come on, Gabriel, into the drawing-room.

Before leaving the room with Gabriel she signalled to Mr Browne by frowning and shaking her forefinger in warning to and fro. Mr Browne nodded in answer and, when she had gone, said to Freddy Malins:

—Now, then, Teddy, I'm going to fill you out a good glass of lemonade just to buck you up.

Freddy Malins, who was nearing the climax of his story, waved the offer aside impatiently but Mr Browne, having first called Freddy Malins' attention to a disarray in his dress, filled out and handed him a full glass of lemonade. Freddy Malins' left hand accepted the glass mechanically, his right hand being engaged in the mechanical readjustment of his dress. Mr Browne, whose face was once more wrinkling with mirth, poured out for himself a glass of whisky while Freddy Malins exploded, before he had well reached the climax of his story, in a kink of high-pitched bronchitic laughter and, setting down his untasted and overflowing glass, began to rub the knuckles of his left fist backwards and forwards into his left eye, repeating words of his last phrase as well as his fit of laughter would allow him.

. . . . . .

Gabriel could not listen while Mary Jane was playing her Academy piece, full of runs and difficult passages, to the hushed drawing-room. He liked music but the piece she was playing had no melody for him and he doubted whether it had any melody for the other listeners, though they had begged Mary Jane to play something. Four young men, who had just come from the refreshment room to stand in the doorway at the sound of the piano, had gone away quietly in couples after a few minutes. The only persons who seemed to follow the music were Mary Jane herself, her hands racing along the key-board or lifted from it at the pauses like those of a priestess in momentary imprecation, and Aunt Kate standing at her elbow to turn the page.

Gabriel's eyes, irritated by the floor, which glittered with beeswax under the heavy chandelier, wandered to the wall above the piano. A picture of the balcony scene in *Romeo and Juliet* hung there and beside it was a picture of the two murdered princes in the Tower which Aunt Julia had worked in red, blue and brown wools when she was a girl. Probably in the school they had gone to as girls that kind of work had been taught, for one year his mother had worked for him as a birthday present a waistcoat of purple tabinet, with little foxes' heads upon it, lined with brown satin and having round mulberry buttons. It was strange that his mother had had no musical talent though Aunt Kate used to call her the brains carrier of the Morkan family. Both she and Julia had always seemed a little proud of their serious and matronly sister. Her photograph stood before the pier-glass. She held an open book on her knees and was pointing out something in it to Constantine who, dressed in a man-o'-war suit, lay at her feet. It was she who had chosen the names for her sons for she was very sensible of the dignity of family life. Thanks to her, Constantine was now senior curate in Balbriggan and, thanks to her, Gabriel himself had taken his degree in the Royal University. A shadow passed over his face as he remembered her sullen opposition to his marriage. Some slighting phrases she had used still rankled in his memory; she had once spoken of Gretta as being country cute and that was not true of

Gretta at all. It was Gretta who had nursed her during all her last long illness in their house at Monkstown.

He knew that Mary Jane must be near the end of her piece for she was playing again the opening melody with runs of scales after every bar and while he waited for the end the resentment died down in his heart. The piece ended with a trill of octaves in the treble and a final deep octave in the bass. Great applause greeted Mary Jane as, blushing and rolling up her music nervously, she escaped from the room. The most vigorous clapping came from the four young men in the doorway who had gone away to the refreshment-room at the beginning of the piece but had come back when the piano had stopped.

Lancers were arranged. Gabriel found himself partnered with Miss Ivors. She was a frank-mannered talkative young lady, with a freckled face and prominent brown eyes. She did not wear a low-cut bodice and the large brooch which was fixed in the front of her collar bore on it an Irish device.

When they had taken their places she said abruptly:

—I have a crow to pluck with you.

—With me? said Gabriel.

She nodded her head gravely.

—What is it? asked Gabriel, smiling at her solemn manner.

—Who is G. C.? answered Miss Ivors, turning her eyes upon him.

Gabriel coloured and was about to knit his brows, as if he did not understand, when she said bluntly:

—O, innocent Amy! I have found out that you write for *The Daily Express.* Now, aren't you ashamed of yourself?

—Why should I be ashamed of myself? asked Gabriel, blinking his eyes and trying to smile.

—Well, I'm ashamed of you, said Miss Ivors frankly. To say you'd write for a rag like that. I didn't think you were a West Briton.

A look of perplexity appeared on Gabriel's face. It was true that he wrote a literary column every Wednesday in *The Daily Express,* for which he was paid fifteen shillings. But that did not make him a West Briton surely. The books he received for review were almost more welcome than the paltry cheque. He loved to feel the covers and turn over the pages of newly printed books. Nearly every day when his teaching in the college was ended he used to wander down the quays to the second-hand booksellers, to Hickey's on Bachelor's Walk, to Webb's or Massey's on Aston's Quay, or to O'Clohissey's in the by-street. He did not know how to meet her charge. He wanted to say that literature was above politics. But they were friends of many years' standing and their careers had been parallel, first at the University and then as teachers: he could not risk a grandiose phrase with her. He continued blinking his eyes and trying to smile and murmured lamely that he saw nothing political in writing reviews of books.

When their turn to cross had come he was still perplexed and inattentive. Miss Ivors promptly took his hand in a warm grasp and said in a soft friendly tone:

—Of course, I was only joking. Come, we cross now.

When they were together again she spoke of the University question and Gabriel felt more at ease. A friend of hers had shown her his review of Browning's poems. That was how she had found out the secret: but she liked the review immensely. Then she said suddenly:

—O, Mr Conroy, you will come for an excursion to the Aran Isles this summer? We're going to stay there a whole month. It will be splendid out in the Atlantic. You ought to come. Mr Clancy is coming, and Mr Kilkelly and Kathleen Kearney. It would be splendid for Gretta too if she'd come. She's from Connacht, isn't she?

—Her people are, said Gabriel shortly.

—But you will come, won't you? said Miss Ivors, laying her warm hand eagerly on his arm.

—The fact is, said Gabriel, I have just arranged to go—

—Go where? asked Miss Ivors.

—Well, you know, every year I go for a cycling tour with some fellows and so—

—But where? asked Miss Ivors.

—Well, we usually go to France or Belgium or perhaps Germany, said Gabriel awkwardly.

—And why do you go to France and Belgium, said Miss Ivors, instead of visiting your own land?

—Well, said Gabriel, it's partly to keep in touch with the languages and partly for a change.

—And haven't you your own language to keep in touch with—Irish? asked Miss Ivors.

—Well, said Gabriel, if it comes to that, you know, Irish is not my language.

Their neighbours had turned to listen to the cross-examination. Gabriel glanced right and left nervously and tried to keep his good humour under the ordeal which was making a blush invade his forehead.

—And haven't you your own land to visit, continued Miss Ivors, that you know nothing of, your own people, and your own country?

—O, to tell you the truth, retorted Gabriel suddenly, I'm sick of my own country, sick of it!

—Why? asked Miss Ivors.

Gabriel did not answer for his retort had heated him.

—Why? repeated Miss Ivors.

They had to go visiting together and, as he had not answered her, Miss Ivors said warmly:

—Of course, you've no answer.

Gabriel tried to cover his agitation by taking part in the dance with great energy. He avoided her eyes for he had seen a sour expression on her face. But when they met in the long chain he was surprised to feel his hand firmly pressed. She looked at him from under her brows for a moment quizzically until he smiled. Then, just as the chain was about to start again, she stood on tiptoe and whispered into his ear:

—West Briton!

When the lancers were over Gabriel went away to a remote corner of the room where Freddy Malins' mother was sitting. She was a stout feeble old woman with white hair. Her voice had a catch in it like her son's and she stuttered slightly. She had been told that Freddy had come and that he was nearly all right. Gabriel asked her whether she had had a good crossing. She lived with her married daughter in Glasgow and came to Dublin on a visit once a year. She answered placidly that she had had a beautiful crossing and that the captain had been most attentive to her. She spoke also of the beautiful house her daughter kept in Glasgow, and of all the nice friends they had there. While her tongue rambled on Gabriel tried to banish from his mind all memory of the unpleasant incident with Miss Ivors. Of course the girl or woman, or whatever she was, was an enthusiast but there was a time for all things. Perhaps he ought not to have answered her like that. But she had no right to call him a West Briton before people, even in joke. She had tried to make him ridiculous before people, heckling him and staring at him with her rabbit's eyes.

He saw his wife making her way towards him through the waltzing couples. When she reached him she said into his ear:

—Gabriel, Aunt Kate wants to know won't you carve the goose as usual. Miss Daly will carve the ham and I'll do the pudding.

—All right, said Gabriel.

—She's sending in the younger ones first as soon as this waltz is over so that we'll have the table to ourselves.

—Were you dancing? asked Gabriel.

—Of course I was. Didn't you see me? What words had you with Molly Ivors?

—No words. Why? Did she say so?

—Something like that. I'm trying to get that Mr D'Arcy to sing. He's full of conceit, I think.

—There were no words, said Gabriel moodily, only she wanted me to go for a trip to the west of Ireland and I said I wouldn't.

His wife clasped her hands excitedly and gave a little jump.

—O, do go, Gabriel, she cried, I'd love to see Galway again.

—You can go if you like, said Gabriel coldly.

She looked at him for a moment, then turned to Mrs Malins and said:

—There's a nice husband for you, Mrs Malins.

While she was threading her way back across the room Mrs Malins, without adverting to the interruption, went on to tell Gabriel what beautiful places there were in Scotland and beautiful scenery. Her son-in-law brought them every year to the lakes and they used to go fishing. Her son-in-law was a splendid fisher. One day he caught a fish, a beautiful big big fish, and the man in the hotel boiled it for their dinner.

Gabriel hardly heard what she said. Now that supper was coming near he began to think again about his speech and about the quotation. When he saw Freddy Malins coming across the room to visit his mother Gabriel left the chair free for him and retired into the embrasure of the window. The room had already cleared and from the back room came the clatter of plates and knives. Those who still remained in the drawing-room seemed tired of dancing and were conversing quietly in little groups. Gabriel's warm trembling fingers tapped the cold pane of the window. How cool it must be outside! How pleasant it would be to walk out alone, first along by the river and then through the park! The snow would be lying on the branches of the trees and forming a bright cap on the top of the Wellington Monument. How much more pleasant it would be there than at the supper-table!

He ran over the headings of his speech: Irish hospitality, sad memories, the Three Graces, Paris, the quotation from Browning. He repeated to himself a phrase he had written in his review: *One feels that one is listening to a thought-tormented music.* Miss Ivors had praised the review. Was she sincere? Had she really any life of her own behind all her propagandism? There had never been any ill-feeling between them until that night. It unnerved him to think that she would be at the supper-table, looking up at him while he spoke with her critical quizzing eyes. Perhaps she would not be sorry to see him fail in his speech. An idea came into his mind and gave him courage. He would say, alluding to Aunt Kate and Aunt Julia: *Ladies and Gentlemen, the generation which is now on the wane among us may have had its faults but for my part I think it had certain qualities of hospitality, of humour, of humanity, which the new and very serious and hypereducated generation that is growing up around us seems to me to lack.* Very good: that was one for Miss Ivors. What did he care that his aunts were only two ignorant old women?

A murmur in the room attracted his attention. Mr Browne was advancing from the door, gallantly escorting Aunt Julia, who leaned upon his arm, smiling and hanging her head. An irregular musketry of applause escorted her also as far as the piano and then, as Mary Jane seated herself on the stool, and Aunt Julia, no longer smiling, half turned so as to pitch her voice fairly into the room, gradually ceased. Gabriel recognised the prelude. It was that of an old song of Aunt Julia's—*Arrayed for the Bridal.* Her voice, strong and clear in tone, attacked with great spirit the runs which embellish the air and though she sang very rapidly she did not miss even the smallest of the grace notes. To follow the voice, without looking at the singer's face, was to feel and share the excitement of swift and secure flight. Gabriel applauded loudly with all the others at the close of the song and loud applause was borne in from the invisible supper-table. It sounded so genuine that a little colour struggled into Aunt Julia's face as she bent to replace in the music-stand the old leather-bound songbook that had her initials on the cover. Freddy Malins, who had listened with his head perched sideways to hear her better, was still applauding when everyone else had ceased and talking animatedly to his mother who nodded her head gravely and slowly in acquiescence. At last, when he could clap no more, he stood up suddenly and hurried across the room to Aunt Julia whose hand he seized and held in both his hands, shaking it when words failed him or the catch in his voice proved too much for him.

—I was just telling my mother, he said, I never heard you sing so well, never. No, I never heard your voice so good as it is to-night. Now! Would you believe that now? That's the truth. Upon my word and honour that's the truth. I never heard your voice sound so fresh and so . . . so clear and fresh, never.

Aunt Julia smiled broadly and murmured something about compliments as she released her hand from his grasp. Mr Browne extended his open hand towards her and said to those who were near him in the manner of a showman introducing a prodigy to an audience:

—Miss Julia Morkan, my latest discovery.

He was laughing very heartily at this himself when Freddy Malins turned to him and said:

—Well, Browne, if you're serious you might make a worse discovery. All I can say is I never heard her sing half so well as long as I am coming here. And that's the honest truth.

—Neither did I, said Mr Browne. I think her voice has greatly improved.

Aunt Julia shrugged her shoulders and said with meek pride:

—Thirty years ago I hadn't a bad voice as voices go.

—I often told Julia, said Aunt Kate emphatically, that she was simply thrown away in that choir. But she never would be said by me.

She turned as if to appeal to the good sense of the others against a refractory child while Aunt Julia gazed in front of her, a vague smile of reminiscence playing on her face.

—No, continued Aunt Kate, she wouldn't be said or led by anyone, slaving there in that choir night and day, night and day. Six o'clock on Christmas morning! And all for what?

—Well, isn't it for the honour of God, Aunt Kate? asked Mary Jane, twisting round on the piano-stool and smiling.

Aunt Kate turned fiercely on her niece and said:

—I know all about the honour of God, Mary Jane, but I think it's not at all honourable for the pope to turn out the women out of the choirs that have slaved there all their lives and put little whipper-snappers of boys over their heads. I suppose it is for the good of the Church if the pope does it. But it's not just, Mary Jane, and it's not right.

She had worked herself into a passion and would have continued in defence of her sister for it was a sore subject with her but Mary Jane, seeing that all the dancers had come back, intervened pacifically:

—Now, Aunt Kate, you're giving scandal to Mr Browne who is of the other persuasion.

Aunt Kate turned to Mr Browne, who was grinning at this allusion to his religion, and said hastily:

—O, I don't question the pope's being

right. I'm only a stupid old woman and I wouldn't presume to do such a thing. But there's such a thing as common everyday politeness and gratitude. And if I were in Julia's place I'd tell that Father Healey straight up to his face . . .

—And besides, Aunt Kate, said Mary Jane, we really are all hungry and when we are hungry we are all very quarrelsome.

—And when we are thirsty we are also quarrelsome, added Mr Browne.

—So that we had better go to supper, said Mary Jane, and finish the discussion afterwards.

On the landing outside the drawing-room Gabriel found his wife and Mary Jane trying to persuade Miss Ivors to stay for supper. But Miss Ivors, who had put on her hat and was buttoning her cloak, would not stay. She did not feel in the least hungry and she had already overstayed her time.

—But only for ten minutes, Molly, said Mrs Conroy. That won't delay you.

—To take a pick itself, said Mary Jane, after all your dancing.

—I really couldn't, said Miss Ivors.

—I am afraid you didn't enjoy yourself at all, said Mary Jane hopelessly.

—Ever so much, I assure you, said Miss Ivors, but you really must let me run off now.

—But how can you get home? asked Mrs Conroy.

—O, it's only two steps up the quay.

Gabriel hesitated a moment and said:

—If you will allow me, Miss Ivors, I'll see you home if you are really obliged to go.

But Miss Ivors broke away from them.

—I won't hear of it, she cried. For goodness sake go in to your suppers and don't mind me. I'm quite well able to take care of myself.

—Well, you're the comical girl, Molly, said Mrs Conroy frankly.

—*Beannacht libh*, cried Miss Ivors, with a laugh, as she ran down the staircase.

Mary Jane gazed after her, a moody puzzled expression on her face, while Mrs. Conroy leaned over the banisters to listen for the hall-door. Gabriel asked himself was he the cause of her abrupt departure. But she did not seem to be in ill humour: she had gone away laughing. He stared blankly down the staircase.

At the moment Aunt Kate came toddling out of the supper-room, almost wringing her hands in despair.

—Where is Gabriel? she cried. Where on earth is Gabriel? There's everyone waiting in there, stage to let, and nobody to carve the goose!

—Here I am, Aunt Kate! cried Gabriel, with sudden animation, ready to carve a flock of geese, if necessary.

A fat brown goose lay at one end of the table and at the other end, on a bed of creased paper strewn with sprigs of parsley, lay a great ham, stripped of its outer skin and peppered over with crust crumbs, a neat paper frill round its shin and beside this was a round of spiced beef. Between these rival ends ran parallel lines of side-dishes: two little minsters of jelly, red and yellow; a shallow dish of blocks of blancmange and red jam, a large green leaf-shaped dish with a stalk-shaped handle, on which lay bunches of purple raisins and peeled almonds, a companion dish on which lay a solid rectangle of Smyrna figs, a dish of custard topped with grated nutmeg, a small bowl full of chocolates and sweets wrapped in gold and silver papers and a glass vase in which stood some tall celery stalks. In the centre of the table there stood, as sentries to a fruit-stand which upheld a pyramid of oranges and American apples, two squat old-fashioned decanters of cut glass, one containing port and the other dark sherry. On the closed square piano a pudding in a huge yellow dish lay in waiting and behind it were three squads of bottles of stout and ale and minerals, drawn up according to the colours of their uniforms, the first two black, with brown and red labels, the third and smallest squad white, with transverse green sashes.

Gabriel took his seat boldly at the head of the table and, having looked to the edge of the carver, plunged his fork firmly into the goose. He felt quite at ease now for he was an expert carver and liked nothing better than to find himself at the head of a well-laden table.

—Miss Furlong, what shall I send you? he asked. A wing or a slice of the breast?

—Just a small slice of the breast.

—Miss Higgins, what for you?

—O, anything at all, Mr Conroy.

While Gabriel and Miss Daly exchanged plates of goose and plates of ham and spiced beef Lily went from guest to guest with a dish of hot floury potatoes wrapped in a white napkin. This was Mary Jane's idea and she had also suggested apple sauce for the goose but Aunt Kate had said that plain roast goose without any apple sauce had always been good enough for her and she hoped she might never eat worse. Mary Jane waited on her pupils and saw that they got the best slices and Aunt Kate and Aunt Julia opened and carried across from the piano bottles of stout and ale for the gentlemen and bottles of minerals for the ladies. There was a great deal of confusion and laughter and noise, the noise of orders and counter-orders, of knives and forks, of corks and glass-stoppers. Gabriel began to carve second helpings as soon as he had finished the first round without serving himself. Everyone protested loudly so that he compromised by taking a long draught of stout for he had found the carving hot work. Mary Jane settled down quietly to her supper but Aunt Kate and Aunt Julia were still toddling round the table, walking on each other's heels, getting in each other's way and giving each other unheeded orders. Mr Browne begged of them to sit down and eat their suppers and so did Gabriel but they said there was time enough so that, at last, Freddy Malins stood up and, capturing Aunt Kate, plumped her down on her chair amid general laughter.

When everyone had been well served Gabriel said, smiling:

—Now, if anyone wants a little more of what vulgar people call stuffing let him or her speak.

A chorus of voices invited him to begin his own supper and Lily came forward with three potatoes which she had reserved for him.

—Very well, said Gabriel amiably, as he took another preparatory draught, kindly forget my existence, ladies and gentlemen, for a few minutes.

He set to his supper and took no part in the conversation with which the table covered Lily's removal of the plates. The subject of talk was the opera company which was then at the Theatre Royal. Mr Bartell D'Arcy, the tenor, a dark-complexioned young man with a smart moustache, praised very highly the leading contralto of the company but Miss Furlong thought she had a rather vulgar style of production. Freddy Malins said there was a Negro chieftain singing in the second part of the Gaiety pantomime who had one of the finest tenor voices he had ever heard.

—Have you heard him? he asked Mr Bartell D'Arcy across the table.

—No, answered Mr Bartell D'Arcy carelessly.

—Because, Freddy Malins explained, now I'd be curious to hear your opinion of him. I think he has a grand voice.

—It takes Teddy to find out the really good things, said Mr Browne familiarly to the table.

—And why couldn't he have a voice too? asked Freddy Malins sharply. Is it because he's only a black?

Nobody answered this question and

Mary Jane led the table back to the legitimate opera. One of her pupils had given her a pass for *Mignon*. Of course it was very fine, she said, but it made her think of poor Georgina Burns. Mr Browne could go back farther still, to the old Italian companies that used to come to Dublin—Tietjens, Ilma de Murzka, Campanini, the great Trebelli, Giuglini, Ravelli, Aramburo. Those were the days, he said, when there was something like singing to be heard in Dublin. He told too of how the top gallery of the old Royal used to be packed night after night, of how one night an Italian tenor had sung five encores to *Let Me Like a Soldier Fall,* introducing a high C every time, and of how the gallery boys would sometimes in their enthusiasm unyoke the horses from the carriage of some great *prima donna* and pull her themselves through the streets to her hotel. Why did they never play the grand old operas now, he asked, *Dinorah, Lucrezia Borgia?* Because they could not get the voices to sing them: that was why.

—O, well, said Mr Bartell D'Arcy, I presume there are as good singers today as there were then.

—Where are they? asked Mr Browne defiantly.

—In London, Paris, Milan, said Mr Bartell D'Arcy warmly. I suppose Caruso, for example, is quite as good, if not better than any of the men you have mentioned.

—Maybe so, said Mr Browne. But I may tell you I doubt it strongly.

—O, I'd give anything to hear Caruso sing, said Mary Jane.

—For me, said Aunt Kate, who had been picking a bone, there was only one tenor. To please me, I mean. But I suppose none of you ever heard of him.

—Who was he, Miss Morkan? asked Mr Bartell D'Arcy politely.

—His name, said Aunt Kate, was Parkinson. I heard him when he was in his prime and I think he had then the purest tenor voice that was ever put into a man's throat.

—Strange, said Mr Bartell D'Arcy. I never even heard of him.

—Yes, yes, Miss Morkan is right, said Mr Browne. I remember hearing of old Parkinson but he's too far back for me.

—A beautiful pure sweet mellow English tenor, said Aunt Kate with enthusiasm.

Gabriel having finished, the huge pudding was transferred to the table. The clatter of forks and spoons began again. Gabriel's wife served out spoonfuls of the pudding and passed the plates down the table. Midway down they were held up by Mary Jane, who replenished them with raspberry or orange jelly or with blancmange and jam. The pudding was of Aunt Julia's making and she received praises for it from all quarters. She herself said that it was not quite brown enough.

—Well, I hope, Miss Morkan, said Mr Browne, that I'm brown enough for you because, you know, I'm all brown.

All the gentlemen, except Gabriel, ate some of the pudding out of compliment to Aunt Julia. As Gabriel never ate sweets the celery had been left for him. Freddy Malins also took a stalk of celery and ate it with his pudding. He had been told that celery was a capital thing for the blood and he was just then under doctor's care. Mrs Malins, who had been silent all through the supper, said that her son was going down to Mount Melleray in a week or so. The table then spoke of Mount Melleray, how bracing the air was down there, how hospitable the monks were and how they never asked for a penny-piece from their guests.

—And do you mean to say, asked Mr Browne, incredulously, that a chap can go down there and put up there as if it were a hotel and live on the fat of the land and then come away without paying a farthing?

—O, most people give some donation

to the monastery when they leave, said Mary Jane.

—I wish we had an institution like that in our Church, said Mr Browne candidly.

He was astonished to hear that the monks never spoke, got up at two in the morning and slept in their coffins. He asked what they did it for.

—That's the rule of the order, said Aunt Kate firmly.

—Yes, but why? asked Mr Browne.

Aunt Kate repeated that it was the rule, that was all. Mr Browne still seemed not to understand. Freddy Malins explained to him, as best he could, that the monks were trying to make up for the sins committed by all the sinners in the outside world. The explanation was not very clear for Mr Browne grinned and said:

—I like that idea very much but wouldn't a comfortable spring bed do them as well as a coffin?

—The coffin, said Mary Jane, is to remind them of their last end.

As the subject had grown lugubrious it was buried in a silence of the table during which Mrs Malins could be heard saying to her neighbour in an indistinct undertone:

—They are very good men, the monks, very pious men.

The raisins and almonds and figs and apples and oranges and chocolates and sweets were now passed about the table and Aunt Julia invited all the guests to have either port or sherry. At first Mr Bartell D'Arcy refused to take either but one of his neighbours nudged him and whispered something to him upon which he allowed his glass to be filled. Gradually as the last glasses were being filled the conversation ceased. A pause followed, broken only by the noise of the wine and by unsettlings of chairs. The Misses Morkan, all three, looked down at the tablecloth. Some one coughed once or twice and then a few gentlemen patted the table gently as a signal for silence.

The silence came and Gabriel pushed back his chair and stood up.

The patting at once grew louder in encouragement and then ceased altogether. Gabriel leaned his ten trembling fingers on the tablecloth and smiled nervously at the company. Meeting a row of upturned faces he raised his eyes to the chandelier. The piano was playing a waltz tune and he could hear the skirts sweeping against the drawing-room door. People, perhaps, were standing in the snow on the quay outside, gazing up at the lighted windows and listening to the waltz music. The air was pure there. In the distance lay the park where the trees were weighted with snow. The Wellington Monument wore a gleaming cap of snow that flashed westward over the white field of Fifteen Acres.

He began:

—Ladies and Gentlemen.

—It has fallen to my lot this evening, as in years past, to perform a very pleasing task but a task for which I am afraid my poor powers as a speaker are all too inadequate.

—No, no! said Mr Browne.

—But, however that may be, I can only ask you tonight to take the will for the deed and to lend me your attention for a few moments while I endeavour to express to you in words what my feelings are on this occasion.

—Ladies and Gentlemen. It is not the first time that we have gathered together under this hospitable roof, around this hospitable board. It is not the first time that we have been the recipients—or perhaps, I had better say, the victims—of the hospitality of certain good ladies.

He made a circle in the air with his arm and paused. Every one laughed or smiled at Aunt Kate and Aunt Julia and Mary Jane who all turned crimson with pleasure. Gabriel went on more boldly:

—I feel more strongly with every recurring year that our country has no tradition which does it so much honour and which it should guard so jealously as that of its hospitality. It is a tradition that is unique as far as my experience goes (and I have visited not a few places abroad) among the modern nations. Some would say, perhaps, that with us it is rather a failing than anything to be boasted of. But granted even that, it is, to my mind, a princely failing, and one that I trust will long be cultivated among us. Of one thing, at least, I am sure. As long as this one roof shelters the good ladies aforesaid—and I wish from my heart it may do so for many and many a long year to come—the tradition of genuine warm-hearted courteous Irish hospitality, which our forefathers have handed down to us and which we in turn must hand down to our descendants, is still alive among us.

A hearty murmur of assent ran round the table. It shot through Gabriel's mind that Miss Ivors was not there and that she had gone away discourteously: and he said with confidence in himself:

—Ladies and Gentlemen.

—A new generation is growing up in our midst, a generation actuated by new ideas and new principles. It is serious and enthusiastic for these new ideas and its enthusiasm, even when it is misdirected, is, I believe, in the main sincere. But we are living in a sceptical and, if I may use the phrase, a thought-tormented age: and sometimes I fear that this new generation, educated or hypereducated as it is, will lack those qualities of humanity, of hospitality, of kindly humour which belonged to an older day. Listening tonight to the names of all those great singers of the past it seemed to me, I must confess, that we were living in a less spacious age. Those days might, without exaggeration, be called spacious days: and if they are gone beyond recall let us hope, at least, that in gatherings such as this we shall still speak of them with pride and affection, still cherish in our hearts the memory of those dead and gone great ones whose fame the world will not willingly let die."

—Hear, hear! said Mr Browne loudly.

—But yet, continued Gabriel, his voice falling into a softer inflection, there are always in gatherings such as this sadder thoughts that will recur to our minds: thoughts of the past, of youth, of changes, of absent faces that we miss here tonight. Our path through life is strewn with many such sad memories: and were we to brood upon them always we could not find the heart to go on bravely with our work among the living. We have all of us living duties and living affections which claim, and rightly claim, our strenuous endeavours.

—Therefore, I will not linger on the past. I will not let any gloomy moralising intrude upon us here tonight. Here we are gathered together for a brief moment from the bustle and rush of our everyday routine. We are met here as friends, in the spirit of good-fellowship, as colleagues, also to a certain extent, in the true spirit of *camaraderie,* and as the guests of—what shall I call them?—the Three Graces of the Dublin musical world.

The table burst into applause and laughter at this sally. Aunt Julia vainly asked each of her neighbours in turn to tell her what Gabriel had said.

—He says we are the Three Graces, Aunt Julia, said Mary Jane.

Aunt Julia did not understand but she looked up, smiling, at Gabriel, who continued in the same vein:

—Ladies and Gentlemen.

—I will not attempt to play tonight the part that Paris played on another occasion. I will not attempt to choose between them. The task would be an invidious one and one beyond my poor powers. For when I view them in turn, whether it be our chief hostess herself, whose good heart, whose too good heart, has become a byword with all who know her, or her sister, who seems to be gifted with perennial youth and whose singing must have been a surprise and a revelation to us all tonight, or, last but not least, when I consider our youngest hostess, talented, cheerful, hard-working and the best of nieces, I confess, Ladies and Gentlemen, that I do not know to which of them I should award the prize.

Gabriel glanced down at his aunts and, seeing the large smile on Aunt Julia's face and the tears which had risen to Aunt Kate's eyes, hastened to his close. He raised his glass of port gallantly, while every member of the company fingered a glass expectantly, and said loudly:

—Let us toast them all three together. Let us drink to their health, wealth, long life, happiness and prosperity and may they long continue to hold the proud and self-won position which they hold in their profession and the position of honour and affection which they hold in our hearts.

All the guests stood up, glass in hand, and turning towards the three seated ladies, sang in unison, with Mr Browne as leader:

For they are jolly gay fellows,
For they are jolly gay fellows,
For they are jolly gay fellows,
Which nobody can deny.

Aunt Kate was making frank use of her handkerchief and even Aunt Julia seemed moved. Freddy Malins beat time with his pudding-fork and the singers turned towards one another, as if in melodious conference, while they sang with emphasis:

Unless he tells a lie,
Unless he tells a lie.

Then, turning once more towards their hostesses, they sang:

For they are jolly gay fellows,
For they are jolly gay fellows,
For they are jolly gay fellows,
Which nobody can deny.

The acclamation which followed was taken up beyond the door of the supper-room by many of the other guests and renewed time after time, Freddy Malins acting as officer with his fork on high.

. . . .

The piercing morning air came into the hall where they were standing so that Aunt Kate said:

—Close the door, somebody. Mrs Malins will get her death of cold.

—Browne is out there, Aunt Kate, said Mary Jane.

—Browne is everywhere, said Aunt Kate, lowering her voice.

Mary Jane laughed at her tone.

—Really, she said archly, he is very attentive.

—He has been laid on here like the gas, said Aunt Kate in the same tone, all during the Christmas.

She laughed herself this time good-humouredly and then added quickly:

—But tell him to come in, Mary Jane, and close the door. I hope to goodness he didn't hear me.

At that moment the hall-door was opened and Mr Browne came in from the doorstep, laughing as if his heart would break. He was dressed in a long green overcoat with mock astrakhan cuffs and collar and wore on his head an oval fur cap. He pointed down the snow-covered quay from where the sound of shrill prolonged whistling was borne in.

—Teddy will have all the cabs in Dublin out, he said.

Gabriel advanced from the little pantry behind the office, struggling into his overcoat and, looking round the hall, said:

—Gretta not down yet?

—She's getting on her things, Gabriel, said Aunt Kate.

—Who's playing up there? asked Gabriel.

—Nobody. They're all gone.

—O no, Aunt Kate, said Mary Jane. Bartell D'Arcy and Miss O'Callaghan aren't gone yet.

—Someone is strumming at the piano anyhow, said Gabriel.

Mary Jane glanced at Gabriel and Mr Browne and said with a shiver:

—It makes me feel cold to look at you two gentlemen muffled up like that. I wouldn't like to face your journey home at this hour.

—I'd like nothing better this minute, said Mr Browne stoutly, than a rattling fine walk in the country or a fast drive with a good spanking goer between the shafts.

—We used to have a very good horse and trap at home, said Aunt Julia sadly.

—The never-to-be-forgotten Johnny, said Mary Jane, laughing.

Aunt Kate and Gabriel laughed too.

—Why, what was wonderful about Johnny? asked Mr Browne.

—The late lamented Patrick Morkan, our grandfather, that is, explained Gabriel, commonly known in his later years as the old gentleman, was a glue-boiler.

—O, now, Gabriel, said Aunt Kate, laughing, he had a starch mill.

—Well, glue or starch, said Gabriel, the old gentleman had a horse by the name of Johnny. And Johnny used to work in the old gentleman's mill, walking round and round in order to drive the mill. That was all very well; but now comes the tragic part about Johnny. One fine day the old gentleman thought he'd like to drive out with the quality to a military review in the park.

—The Lord have mercy on his soul, said Aunt Kate compassionately.

—Amen, said Gabriel. So the old gentleman, as I said, harnessed Johnny and put on his very best tall hat and his very best stock collar and drove out in grand style from his ancestral mansion somewhere near Back Lane, I think.

Everyone laughed, even Mrs. Malins, at Gabriel's manner and Aunt Kate said:

—O, now, Gabriel, he didn't live in Back Lane, really. Only the mill was there.

—Out from the mansion of his forefathers, continued Gabriel, he drove with Johnny. And everything went on beautifully until Johnny came in sight of King Billy's statue: and whether he fell in love with the horse King Billy sits on or whether he thought he was back again in the mill, anyhow he began to walk round the statue.

Gabriel paced in a circle round the hall in his goloshes amid the laughter of the others.

—Round and round he went, said Gabriel, and the old gentleman, who was a very pompous old gentleman, was highly indignant. *Go on, sir! What do you mean, sir? Johnny! Johnny! Most extraordinary conduct! Can't understand the horse!*

The peals of laughter which followed Gabriel's imitation of the incident was interrupted by a resounding knock at the hall-door. Mary Jane ran to open it and let in Freddy Malins. Freddy Malins, with his hat well back on his head and his shoulders humped with cold, was puffing and steaming after his exertions.

—I could only get one cab, he said.

—O, we'll find another along the quay, said Gabriel.

—Yes, said Aunt Kate. Better not keep Mrs Malins standing in the draught.

Mrs Malins was helped down the front steps by her son and Mr Browne and, after many manoeuvres, hoisted into the cab. Freddy Malins clambered in after her and spent a long time settling her on the seat, Mr Browne helping him with advice. At last she was settled comfortably and Freddy Malins invited Mr Browne into the cab. There was a good deal of confused talk, and then Mr Browne got into the cab. The cabman settled his rug over his knees, and bent down for the address. The confusion grew greater and the cabman was directed differently by Freddy Malins and Mr Browne, each of whom had his head out through a window of the cab. The difficulty was to know where to drop Mr Browne along the route and Aunt Kate,

Aunt Julia and Mary Jane helped the discussion from the doorstep with cross-directions and contradictions and abundance of laughter. As for Freddy Malins he was speechless with laughter. He popped his head in and out of the window every moment, to the great danger of his hat, and told his mother how the discussion was progressing, till at last Mr Browne shouted to the bewildered cabman above the din of everybody's laughter:

—Do you know Trinity College?

—Yes, sir, said the cabman.

—Well, drive bang up against Trinity College gates, said Mr Browne, and then we'll tell you where to go. You understand now?

—Yes, sir, said the cabman.

—Make like a bird for Trinity College.

—Right, sir, said the cabman.

The horse was whipped up and the cab rattled off along the quay amid a chorus of laughter and adieus.

Gabriel had not gone to the door with the others. He was in a dark part of the hall gazing up the staircase. A woman was standing near the top of the first flight, in the shadow also. He could not see her face but he could see the terracotta and salmon-pink panels of her skirt which the shadow made appear black and white. It was his wife. She was leaning on the banisters, listening to something. Gabriel was surprised at her stillness and strained his ear to listen also. But he could hear little save the noise of laughter and dispute on the front steps, a few chords struck on the piano and a few notes of a man's voice singing.

He stood still in the gloom of the hall, trying to catch the air that the voice was singing and gazing up at his wife. There was grace and mystery in her attitude as if she were a symbol of something. He asked himself what is a woman standing on the stairs in the shadow, listening to distant music, a symbol of. If he were a painter he would paint her in that attitude. Her blue felt hat would show off the bronze of her hair against the darkness and the dark panels of her skirt would show off the light ones. *Distant Music* he would call the picture if he were a painter.

The hall-door was closed; and Aunt Kate, Aunt Julia and Mary Jane came down the hall, still laughing.

—Well, isn't Freddy terrible? said Mary Jane. He's really terrible.

Gabriel said nothing but pointed up the stairs towards where his wife was standing. Now that the hall-door was closed the voice and the piano could be heard more clearly. Gabriel held up his hand for them to be silent. The song seemed to be in the old Irish tonality and the singer seemed uncertain both of his words and of his voice. The voice, made plaintive by distance and by the singer's hoarseness, faintly illuminated the cadence of the air with words expressing grief:

O, the rain falls on my heavy locks
And the dew wets my skin,
My babe lies cold . . .

—O, exclaimed Mary Jane. It's Bartell D'Arcy singing and he wouldn't sing all the night. O, I'll get him to sing a song before he goes.

—O do, Mary Jane, said Aunt Kate.

Mary Jane brushed past the others and ran to the staircase but before she reached it the singing stopped and the piano was closed abruptly.

—O, what a pity! she cried. Is he coming down, Gretta?

Gabriel heard his wife answer yes and saw her come down towards them. A few steps behind her were Mr Bartell D'Arcy and Miss O'Callaghan.

—O, Mr D'Arcy, cried Mary Jane, it's downright mean of you to break off like that when we were all in raptures listening to you.

—I have been at him all the evening, said Miss O'Callaghan, and Mrs Conroy too and he told us he had a dreadful cold and couldn't sing.

—O, Mr D'Arcy, said Aunt Kate, now that was a great fib to tell.

—Can't you see that I'm as hoarse as a crow? said Mr D'Arcy roughly.

He went into the pantry hastily and put on his overcoat. The others, taken aback by his rude speech, could find nothing to say. Aunt Kate wrinkled her brows and made signs to the others to drop the subject. Mr D'Arcy stood swathing his neck carefully and frowning.

—It's the weather, said Aunt Julia, after a pause.

—Yes, everybody has colds, said Aunt Kate readily, everybody.

—They say, said Mary Jane, we haven't had snow like it for thirty years; and I read this morning in the newspapers that the snow is general all over Ireland.

—I love the look of snow, said Aunt Julia sadly.

—So do I, said Miss O'Callaghan. I think Christmas is never really Christmas unless we have the snow on the ground.

—But poor Mr D'Arcy doesn't like the snow, said Aunt Kate, smiling.

Mr D'Arcy came from the pantry, fully swathed and buttoned, and in a repentant tone told them the history of his cold. Everyone gave him advice and said it was a great pity and urged him to be very careful of his throat in the night air. Gabriel watched his wife, who did not join in the conversation. She was standing right under the dusty fanlight and the flame of the gas lit up the rich bronze of her hair which he had seen her drying at the fire a few days before. She was in the same attitude and seemed unaware of the talk about her. At last she turned towards them and Gabriel saw that there was colour on her cheeks and that her eyes were shining. A sudden tide of joy went leaping out of his heart.

—Mr D'Arcy, she said, what is the name of that song you were singing?

—It's called *The Lass of Aughrim,* said Mr D'Arcy, but I couldn't remember it properly. Why? Do you know it?

—*The Lass of Aughrim,* she repeated. I couldn't think of the name.

—It's a very nice air, said Mary Jane. I'm sorry you were not in voice tonight.

—Now, Mary Jane, said Aunt Kate, don't annoy Mr D'Arcy. I won't have him annoyed.

Seeing that all were ready to start she shepherded them to the door, where good-night was said:

—Well, good-night, Aunt Kate, and thanks for the pleasant evening.

—Good-night, Gabriel. Good-night Gretta!

—Good-night, Aunt Kate, and thanks ever so much. Good-night, Aunt Julia.

—O, good-night, Gretta, I didn't see you.

—Good-night, Mr D'Arcy. Good-night, Miss O'Callaghan.

—Good-night, Miss Morkan.

—Good-night, again.

—Good-night, all. Safe home.

—Good-night. Good-night.

The morning was still dark. A dull, yellow light brooded over the houses and the river; and the sky seemed to be descending. It was slushy underfoot; and only streaks and patches of snow lay on the roofs, on the parapets of the quay and on the area railings. The lamps were still burning redly in the murky air and, across the river, the palace of the Four Courts stood out menacingly against the heavy sky.

She was walking on before him with Mr Bartell D'Arcy, her shoes in a brown parcel tucked under one arm and her hands holding her skirt up from the slush. She had no longer any grace of attitude but Gabriel's eyes were still bright with happiness. The blood went bounding along his veins; and the thoughts went rioting through his brain, proud, joyful, tender, valorous.

She was walking on before him so lightly and so erect that he longed to run after her noiselessly, catch her by the shoulders and say something foolish and affectionate into her ear. She seemed to him so frail that he longed to defend her against something and then to be alone with her. Moments of their secret life together burst like stars upon his memory. A heliotrope envelope was lying beside his breakfast-cup and he was caressing it with his hand. Birds were twittering in the ivy and the sunny web of the curtain was shimmering along the floor: he could not eat for happiness. They were standing on the crowded platform and he was placing a ticket inside the warm palm of her glove. He was standing with her in the cold, looking in through a grated window at a man making bottles in a roaring furnace. It was very cold. Her face, fragrant in the cold air, was quite close to his; and suddenly he called out to the man at the furnace:

—Is the fire hot, sir?

But the man could not hear with the noise of the furnace. It was just as well. He might have answered rudely.

A wave of yet more tender joy escaped from his heart and went coursing in warm flood along his arteries. Like the tender fire of stars moments of their life together, that no one knew of or would ever know of, broke upon and illumined his memory. He longed to recall to her those moments, to make her forget the years of their dull existence together and remember only their moments of ecstasy. For the years, he felt, had not quenched his soul or hers. Their children, his writing, her household cares had not quenched all their souls' tender fire. In one letter that he had written to her then he had said: *Why is it that words like these seem to me so dull and cold? Is it because there is no word tender enough to be your name?*

Like distant music these words that he had written years before were borne towards him from the past. He longed to be alone with her. When the others had gone away, when he and she were in their room in the hotel, then they would be alone together. He would call her softly:

—Gretta!

Perhaps she would not hear at once: she would be undressing. Then something in his voice would strike her. She would turn and look at him. . . .

At the corner of Winetavern Street they met a cab. He was glad of its rattling noise as it saved him from conversation. She was looking out of the window and seemed tired. The others spoke only a few words, pointing out some building or street. The horse galloped along wearily under the murky morning sky, dragging his old rattling box after his heels, and Gabriel was again in a cab with her, galloping to catch the boat, galloping to their honeymoon.

As the cab drove across O'Connell Bridge Miss O'Callaghan said:

—They say you never cross O'Connell Bridge without seeing a white horse.

I see a white man this time, said Gabriel.

—Where? asked Mr Bartell D'Arcy.

Gabriel pointed to the statue, on which lay patches of snow. Then he nodded familiarly to it and waved his hand.

—Good-night, Dan, he said gaily.

When the cab drew up before the hotel Gabriel jumped out and, in spite of Mr Bartell D'Arcy's protest, paid the driver. He gave the man a shilling over his fare. The man saluted and said:

—A prosperous New Year to you, sir.

—The same to you, said Gabriel cordially.

She leaned for a moment on his arm in getting out of the cab and while standing at the curbstone, bidding the others good-night. She leaned lightly on his arm, as lightly as when she had danced with him a few hours before. He had felt proud and happy then, happy that she was his, proud of her grace and wifely carriage. But now, after the kindling again of so many memories, the first touch of her body, musical and strange and perfumed, sent through him a keen pang of lust. Under cover of her silence he pressed her arm closely to his side; and, as they stood at the hotel door, he felt that they had escaped from their lives and duties, escaped from home and friends and run away together with wild and radiant hearts to a new adventure.

An old man was dozing in a great hooded chair in the hall. He lit a candle in the office and went before them to the stairs. They followed him in silence, their feet falling in soft thuds on the thickly carpeted stairs. She mounted the stairs behind the porter, her head bowed in the ascent, her frail shoulders curved as with a burden, her skirt girt tightly about her. He could have flung his arms about her hips and held her still for his arms were trembling with desire to seize her and only the stress of his nails against the palms of his hands held the wild impulse of his body in check. The porter halted on the stairs to settle his guttering candle. They halted too on the steps below him. In the silence Gabriel could hear the falling of the molten wax into the tray and the thumping of his own heart against his ribs.

The porter led them along a corridor and opened a door. Then he set his unstable candle down on a toilet-table and asked at what hour they were to be called in the morning.

—Eight, said Gabriel.

The porter pointed to the tap of the electric-light and began a muttered apology but Gabriel cut him short.

—We don't want any light. We have light enough from the street. And I say, he added, pointing to the candle, you might remove that handsome article, like a good man.

The porter took up his candle again, but slowly for he was surprised by such a novel idea. Then he mumbled good-night and went out. Gabriel shot the lock to.

A ghostly light from the street lamp lay in a long shaft from one window to the door. Gabriel threw his overcoat and hat on a couch and crossed the room towards the window. He looked down into the street in order that his emotion might calm a little. Then he turned and leaned against a chest of drawers with his back to the light. She had taken off her hat and cloak and was standing before a large swinging mirror, unhooking her waist. Gabriel paused for a few moments, watching her, and then said:

—Gretta!

She turned away from the mirror slowly and walked along the shaft of light towards him. Her face looked so serious and weary that the words would not pass Gabriel's lips. No, it was not the moment yet.

—You looked tired, he said.

—I am a little, she answered.

—You don't feel ill or weak?

—No, tired: that's all.

She went on to the window and stood there, looking out. Gabriel waited again and then, fearing that diffidence was about to conquer him, he said abruptly:

—By the way, Gretta!

—What is it?

—You know that poor fellow Malins? he said quickly.

—Yes. What about him?

—Well, poor fellow, he's a decent sort of chap after all, continued Gabriel in a false voice. He gave me back that sovereign I lent him and I didn't expect it, really. It's a pity he wouldn't keep away from that Browne, because he's not a bad fellow at heart.

He was trembling now with annoyance. Why did she seem so abstracted? He did not know how he could begin. Was she annoyed, too, about something? If she would only turn to him or come to him of her own accord! To take her as she was would be brutal. No, he must see some ardour in her eyes first. He longed to be master of her strange mood.

—When did you lend him the pound? she asked, after a pause.

Gabriel strove to restrain himself from breaking out into brutal language about the sottish Malins and his pound. He longed to cry to her from his soul, to crush her body against his, to overmaster her. But he said:

—O, at Christmas, when he opened that little Christmas-card shop in Henry Street.

He was in such a fever of rage and desire that he did not hear her come from the window. She stood before him for an instant, looking at him strangely. Then, suddenly raising herself on tiptoe and resting her hands lightly on his shoulders, she kissed him.

—You are a very generous person, Gabriel, she said.

Gabriel, trembling with delight at her sudden kiss and at the quaintness of her phrase, put his hands on her hair and began smoothing it back, scarcely touching it with his fingers. The washing had made it fine and brilliant. His heart was brimming over with happiness. Just when he was wishing for it she had come to him of her own accord. Perhaps her thoughts had been running with his. Perhaps she had felt the impetuous desire that was in him and then the yielding mood had come upon her. Now that she had fallen to him so easily he wondered why he had been so diffident.

He stood, holding her head between his hands. Then, slipping one arm swiftly about her body and drawing her towards him, he said softly:

—Gretta, dear, what are you thinking about?

She did not answer nor yield wholly to his arm. He said again, softly:

—Tell me what it is, Gretta. I think I know what is the matter. Do I know?

She did not answer at once. Then she said in an outburst of tears:

—O, I am thinking about that song, *The Lass of Aughrim.*

She broke loose from him and ran to the bed and, throwing her arms across the bed-rail, hid her face. Gabriel stood stock-still for a moment in astonishment and then followed her. As he passed in the way of the cheval-glass he caught sight of himself in full length, his broad, well-filled shirt-front, the face whose expression always puzzled him when he saw it in a mirror, and his glimmering gilt-rimmed eyeglasses. He halted a few paces from her and said:

—What about the song? Why does that make you cry?

She raised her head from her arms and dried her eyes with the back of her hand like a child. A kinder note than he had intended went into his voice.

—Why, Gretta? he asked.

—I am thinking about a person long ago who used to sing that song.

—And who was the person long ago? asked Gabriel, smiling.

—It was a person I used to know in Galway when I was living with my grandmother, she said.

The smile passed away from Gabriel's face. A dull anger began to gather again at the back of his mind and the dull fires of his lust began to glow angrily in his veins.

—Someone you were in love with? he asked ironically.

—It was a young boy I used to know, she answered, named Michael Furey. He used to sing that song, *The Lass of Aughrim.* He was very delicate.

Gabriel was silent. He did not wish her to think that he was interested in this delicate boy.

—I can see him so plainly, she said after a moment. Such eyes as he had: big, dark eyes! And such an expression in them—an expression!

—Oh, then, you were in love with him? said Gabriel.

—I used to go out walking with him, she said, when I was in Galway.

A thought flew across Gabriel's mind.

—Perhaps that was why you wanted to go to Galway with that Ivors girl? he said coldly.

She looked at him and asked in surprise:

—What for?

Her eyes made Gabriel feel awkward. He shrugged his shoulders and said:

—How do I know? To see him, perhaps.

She looked away from him along the shaft of light towards the window in silence.

—He is dead, she said at length. He died when he was only seventeen. Isn't it a terrible thing to die so young as that?

—What was he? asked Gabriel, still ironically.

—He was in the gasworks, she said.

Gabriel felt humiliated by the failure of his irony and by the evocation of this figure from the dead, a boy in the gasworks. While he had been full of memories of their secret life together, full of tenderness and joy and desire, she had been comparing him in her mind with another. A shameful consciousness of his own person assailed him. He saw himself as a ludicrous figure, acting as a pennyboy for his aunts, a nervous well-meaning sentimentalist, orating to vulgarians and idealising his own clownish lusts, the pitiable fatuous fellow he had caught a glimpse of in the mirror. Instinctively he turned his back more to the light lest she might see the shame that burned upon his forehead.

He tried to keep up his tone of cold interrogation but his voice when he spoke was humble and indifferent.

—I suppose you were in love with this Michael Furey, Gretta, he said.

—I was great with him at that time, she said.

Her voice was veiled and sad. Gabriel, feeling now how vain it would be to try to lead her whither he had purposed, caressed one of her hands and said, also sadly:

—And what did he die of so young, Gretta? Consumption, was it?

—I think he died for me, she answered.

A vague terror seized Gabriel at this answer as if, at that hour when he had hoped to triumph, some impalpable and vindictive being was coming against him, gathering forces against him in its vague world. But he shook himself free of it with an effort of reason and continued to caress her hand. He did not question her again for he felt that she would tell him of herself. Her hand was warm and moist: it did not respond to his touch but he continued to caress it just as he had caressed her first letter to him that spring morning.

—It was in the winter, she said, about the beginning of the winter when I was going to leave my grandmother's and come up here to the convent. And he was ill at the time in his lodgings in Galway and wouldn't be let out and his people in Oughterard were written to. He was in decline, they said, or something like that. I never knew rightly.

She paused for a moment and sighed.

—Poor fellow, she said. He was very fond of me and he was such a gentle boy. We used to go out together, walking, you know, Gabriel, like the way they do in the country. He was going to study singing only for his health. He had a very good voice, poor Michael Furey.

—Well; and then? asked Gabriel

—And then when it came to the time for me to leave Galway and come up to the convent he was much worse and I wouldn't be let see him so I wrote him a letter saying I was going up to Dublin and would be back in the summer and hoping he would be better then.

She paused for a moment to get her voice under control and then went on:

—Then the night before I left I was in my grandmother's house in Nuns' Island, packing up, and I heard gravel thrown up against the window. The window was so wet I couldn't see so I ran downstairs as I was and slipped out the back into the garden and there was the poor fellow at the end of the garden, shivering.

—And did you not tell him to go back? asked Gabriel.

—I implored of him to go home at once and told him he would get his death in the rain. But he said he did not want to live. I can see his eyes as well as well! He was standing at the end of the wall where there was a tree.

—And did he go home? asked Gabriel.

—Yes, he went home. And when I was only a week in the convent he died and he was buried in Oughterard where his people came from. O, the day I heard that, that he was dead!

She stopped, choking with sobs, and, overcome by emotion, flung herself face downward on the bed, sobbing in the quilt. Gabriel held her hand for a moment longer, irresolutely, and then, shy of intruding on her grief, let it fall gently and walked quietly to the window.

. . . .

She was fast asleep.

Gabriel, leaning on his elbow, looked for a few moments unresentfully on her tangled hair and half-open mouth, listening to her deep-drawn breath. So she had had that romance in her life: a man had died for her sake. It hardly pained him now to think how poor a part he, her husband, had played in her life. He watched her while she slept as though he and she had never lived together as man and wife. His curious eyes rested long upon her face and on her hair: and, as he thought of what she must have been then, in that time of her first girlish beauty, a strange friendly pity for her entered his soul. He did not like to say even to himself that her face was no longer beautiful but he knew that it was no longer the face for which Michael Furey had braved death.

Perhaps she had not told him all the story. His eyes moved to the chair over which she had thrown some of her clothes. A petticoat string dangled to the floor. One boot stood upright, its limp upper fallen down: the fellow of it lay upon its side. He wondered at his riot of emotions of an hour before. From what had it proceeded? From his aunt's supper, from his own foolish speech, from the wine and dancing, the merry-making when saying good-night in the hall, the pleasure of the walk along the river in the snow. Poor Aunt Julia! She, too, would soon be a shade with the shade of Patrick Morkan and his horse. He had caught that haggard look upon her face for a moment when she was singing *Arrayed for the Bridal*. Soon, perhaps, he would be sitting in that same drawing-room, dressed in black, his silk hat on his knees. The blinds would be drawn down and Aunt Kate would be sitting beside him, crying and blowing her nose and telling him how Julia had died. He would cast about in his mind for some words that might console her, and would find only lame and useless ones. Yes, yes: that would happen very soon.

The air of the room chilled his shoulders. He stretched himself cautiously along under the sheets and lay down beside his wife. One by one they were all becoming shades. Better pass boldly into that other world, in the full glory of some passion, than fade and wither dismally with age. He thought of how she who lay beside him had locked in her heart for so many years that image of her lover's eyes when he had told her that he did not wish to live.

Generous tears filled Gabriel's eyes. He had never felt like that himself towards any woman but he knew that such a feeling must be love. The tears gathered more thickly in his eyes and in the partial darkness he imagined he saw the form of a young man standing under a dripping tree. Other forms were near. His soul had approached that region where dwell the vast hosts of the dead. He was conscious of, but could not apprehend, their wayward and flickering existence. His own identity was fading out into a grey impalpable world: the solid world itself which these dead had one time reared and lived in was dissolving and dwindling.

A few light taps upon the pane made him turn to the window. It had begun to snow again. He watched sleepily the flakes, silver and dark, falling obliquely against the lamplight. The time had come for him to set out on his journey westward. Yes, the newspapers were right: snow was general all over Ireland. It was falling on every part of the dark central plain, on the treeless hills, falling softly upon the Bog of Allen and, farther westward, softly falling into the dark mutinous Shannon waves. It was falling, too, upon every part of the lonely churchyard on the hill where Michael Furey lay buried. It lay thickly drifted on the crooked crosses and headstones, on the spears of the little gate, on the barren thorns. His soul swooned slowly as he heard the snow falling faintly through the universe and faintly falling, like the descent of their last end, upon all the living and the dead.

FRANZ KAFKA • 1883–1924

A Hunger Artist

DURING these last decades the interest in professional fasting has markedly diminished. It used to pay very well to stage such great performances under one's own management, but today that is quite impossible. We live in a different world now. At one time the whole town took a lively interest in the hunger artist; from day to day of his fast the excitement mounted; everybody wanted to see him at least once a day; there were people who bought season tickets for the last few days and sat from morning till night in front of his small barred cage; even in the nighttime there were visiting hours, when the whole effect was heightened by torch flares; on fine days the cage was set out in the open air, and then it was the children's special treat to see the hunger artist; for their elders he was often just a joke that happened to be in fashion, but the children stood open-mouthed, holding each other's hands for greater security, marveling at him as he sat there pallid in black tights, with his ribs sticking out so prominently, not even on a seat but down among straw on the ground, sometimes giving a courteous nod, answering questions with a constrained smile, or perhaps stretching an arm through the bars so that one might feel how thin it was, and then again withdrawing deep into himself, paying no attention to anyone or anything, not even to the all-important striking of the clock that was the only piece of furniture in his cage, but merely staring into vacancy with half-shut eyes, now and then taking a sip from a tiny glass of water to moisten his lips.

Besides casual onlookers there were also relays of permanent watchers selected by the public, usually butchers, strangely enough, and it was their task to watch the hunger artist day and night, three of them at a time, in case he should have some secret recourse to nourishment. This was nothing but a formality, instituted to reassure the masses, for the initiates knew well enough that during his fast the artist would never in any circumstances, not even under forcible compulsion, swallow the smallest morsel of food; the honor of his profession forbade it. Not every watcher, of course, was capable of understanding this; there were often groups of night watchers who were very lax in carrying out their duties and deliberately huddled together in a retired corner to play cards with great absorption, obviously intending to give the hunger artist the chance of a little refreshment, which they supposed he could draw from some private hoard. Nothing annoyed the artist more than such watchers; they made him miserable; they made his fast seem unendurable; sometimes he mastered his feebleness sufficiently to sing during their watch for as long as he could keep going, to show them how unjust their suspicions were. But that was of little use; they only wondered at his cleverness in being able to fill his mouth even while singing. Much more to his taste were the watchers who sat close up to the bars, who were not content with the dim night lighting of the hall but focused him in the full glare of the electric pocket torch given them by the impresario. The harsh light did not trouble him at all. In any case he could never sleep properly, and he could always drowse a little, whatever the light, at any hour, even when the hall was thronged with noisy onlookers. He was quite happy at the prospect of spending a sleepless night with such watchers; he was ready to exchange jokes with them, to tell them stories out of his nomadic life, anything at all to keep them awake and demonstrate to them again that he had no eatables in his cage and that he was fasting as not one of them could fast. But his happiest moment was when the morning came and an enormous breakfast was brought them, at his expense, on which they flung themselves with the keen appetite of healthy men after a weary night of wakefulness. Of course there were people who argued that this breakfast was an unfair attempt to bribe the watchers, but that was going rather too far, and when they were invited to take on a night's vigil without a breakfast, merely for the sake of the cause, they made themselves scarce, although they stuck stubbornly to their suspicions.

Such suspicions, anyhow, were a necessary accompaniment to the profession of fasting. No one could possibly watch the hunger artist continuously, day and night, and so no one could produce first-hand evidence that the fast had really been rigorous and continuous; only the artist himself could know that; he was therefore bound to be the sole completely satisfied spectator of his own fast. Yet for other reasons he was never satisfied; it was not perhaps mere fasting that had brought him to such skeleton thinness that many people had regretfully to keep away from his exhibitions, because the sight of him was too much for them, perhaps it was dissatisfaction with himself that had worn him down. For he alone knew, what no other initiate knew, how easy it was to fast. It was the easiest thing in the world. He made no secret of this, yet people did not believe him; at the best they set him down as modest, most of them, however, thought he was out for publicity or else was some kind of cheat who found it easy to fast because he had discovered a way of making it easy, and then had the impudence to admit the fact, more or less. He had to put up with all that, and in the course of time had got used to it, but his inner dissatisfaction always rankled, and never yet, after any term of fasting—this must be granted to his credit—had he left the cage of his own free will. The longest period of fasting was fixed by his impresario at forty days, beyond that term he was not allowed to go, not even in great cities, and there was good reason for it, too. Experience had proved that for about forty days the interest of the public could be stimulated by a steadily increasing pressure of advertisement, but after that the town began to lose interest, sympathetic support began notably to fall off; there were of course local variations as between one town and another or one country and another, but as a general rule forty days marked the limit. So on the fortieth day the flower-bedecked cage was opened, enthusiastic spectators filled the hall, a military band played, two doctors entered the cage to measure the results of the fast, which were announced through a megaphone, and finally two young ladies appeared, blissful at having been selected for the honor, to help the hunger artist down the few steps leading to a small table on which was spread a carefully chosen invalid repast. And at this very moment the artist always turned stubborn. True, he would entrust his bony arms to the outstretched helping hands of the ladies bending over him, but stand up he would not. Why stop fasting at this particular moment, after forty days of it? He had held out for a long time, an illimitably long time; why stop now, when he was in his best fasting form, or rather, not yet quite in his best fasting form? Why should he be cheated of the fame he would get for fasting longer, for being not only the record hunger artist of all time, which presumably he was already, but for beating his own record by a performance beyond human imagination, since he felt that there were no limits to his capacity for fasting? His public pretended to admire him so much, why should it have so little patience with him; if he could endure fasting longer, why shouldn't the public endure it? Besides, he was tired, he was comfortable sitting in the straw, and now he was supposed to lift himself to his full height and go down to a meal the very thought of which gave him a nausea that only the presence of the ladies kept him from betraying, and even that with an effort. And he looked up into the eyes of the ladies who were apparently so friendly and in reality so cruel, and shook his head, which felt too heavy on its strengthless neck. But then there happened yet again what always happened. The impresario came forward, without a word—for the band made speech impossible—lifted his arms in the air above the artist, as if inviting Heaven to look down upon its creature here in the straw, this suffering martyr, which indeed he was, although in quite another sense; grasped him round the emaciated waist, with exaggerated caution, so that the frail condition he was in might be appreciated; and committed him to the care of the blenching ladies, not without secretly giving him a shaking so that his legs and body tottered and swayed. The artist now submitted completely; his head lolled on his breast as if it had landed there by chance; his body was hollowed out; his legs in a spasm of self-preservation clung close to each other at the knees, yet scraped on the ground as if it were not really solid ground, as if they were only trying to find solid ground; and the whole weight of his body, a featherweight after all, relapsed onto one of the ladies, who, looking round for help and panting a little—this post of honor was not at all what she had expected it to be—first stretched her neck as far as she could to keep her face at least free from contact with the artist, then finding this impossible, and her more fortunate companion not coming to her aid but merely holding extended on her own trembling hand the little bunch of knucklebones that was the artist's, to the great delight of the spectators burst into tears and had to be replaced by an attendant who had long been stationed in readiness. Then came the food, a little of which the impresario managed to get between the artist's lips, while he sat in a kind of half-fainting trance, to the accompaniment of cheerful patter designed to distract the public's attention from the artist's condition; after that, a toast was drunk to the public, supposedly prompted by a whisper from the artist in the impresario's ear; the band confirmed it with a mighty flourish, the spectators melted away, and no one had any cause to be dissatisfied with the proceedings, no one except the hunger artist himself, he only, as always.

So he lived for many years, with small regular intervals of recuperation, in visible glory, honored by the world, yet in spite of that troubled in spirit, and all the more troubled because no one would take his trouble seriously. What comfort could he possibly need? What more could he possibly wish for? And if some good-natured person, feeling sorry for him, tried to console him by pointing out that his melancholy was probably caused by fasting, it could happen, especially when he had been fasting for some time, that he reacted with an outburst of fury and to the general alarm began to shake the bars of his cage like a wild animal. Yet the impresario had a way of punishing these outbreaks which he rather enjoyed putting into operation. He would apologize publicly for the artist's behavior, which was only to be excused, he admitted, because of the irritability caused by fasting; a condition hardly to be understood by well-fed people; then by natural transition he went on to mention the artist's equally incomprehensible boast that he could fast for much longer than he was doing; he praised the high ambition, the good will, the great self-denial undoubtedly implicit in such a statement; and then quite simply countered it by bringing out photographs, which were also on sale to the public, showing the artist on the fortieth day of a fast lying in bed almost dead from exhaustion. This perversion of the truth, familiar to the artist though it was, always unnerved him afresh and proved too much for him. What was a consequence of the premature ending of his fast was here presented as the cause of it! To fight against this lack of understanding, against a whole world of nonunderstanding, was impossible. Time and again in good faith he stood by the bars listening to the impresario, but as soon as the photographs appeared he always let go and sank with a groan back on to his straw, and the reassured public could once more come close and gaze at him.

A few years later when the witnesses of such scenes called them to mind, they often failed to understand themselves at all. For meanwhile the aforementioned change in public interest had set in; it seemed to happen almost overnight; there may have been profound causes for it, but who was going to bother about that; at any rate the pampered hunger artist suddenly found himself deserted one fine day by the amusement seekers, who went streaming past him to other more favored attractions. For the last time the impresario hurried him over half Europe to discover whether the old interest might still survive here and there; all in vain; everywhere, as if by secret agreement, a positive revulsion from professional fasting was in evidence. Of course it could not really have sprung up so suddenly as all that, and many premonitory symptoms which had not been sufficiently remarked or suppressed during the rush and glitter of success now came retrospectively to mind, but it was now too late to take any countermeasures. Fasting would surely came into fashion again at some future date, yet that was no comfort for those living in the present. What, then, was the hunger artist to do? He had been applauded by thousands in his time and could hardly come down to showing himself in a street booth at village fairs, and as for adopting another profession, he was not only too old for that but too fanatically devoted to fasting. So he took leave of the impresario, his partner in an unparalleled career, and hired himself to a large circus; in order to spare his own feelings he avoided reading the conditions of his contract.

A large circus with its enormous traffic in replacing and recruiting men, animals and apparatus can always find a use for people at any time, even for a hunger artist, provided of course that he does not ask too much, and in this particular case anyhow it was not only the artist who was taken on but his famous and long-known name as well; indeed considering the peculiar nature of his performance, which was not impaired by advancing age, it could not be objected that here was an artist past his prime, no longer at the height of his professional skill, seeking a refuge in some quiet corner of a circus; on the contrary, the hunger artist averred that he could fast as well as ever, which was entirely credible; he even alleged that if he were allowed to fast as he liked, and this was at once promised him without more ado, he could astound the world by establishing a record never yet achieved, a statement which certainly provoked a smile among the other professionals, since it left out of account the change in public opinion, which the hunger artist in his zeal conveniently forgot.

He had not, however, actually lost his sense of the real situation and took it as a matter of course that he and his cage should be stationed, not in the middle of the ring as a main attraction, but outside, near the animal cages, on a site that was after all easily accessible. Large and gaily painted placards made a frame for the cage and announced what was to be seen inside it. When the public came thronging out in the intervals to see the animals, they could hardly avoid passing the hunger artist's cage and stopping there for a moment, perhaps they might even have stayed longer had not those pressing behind them in the narrow gangway, who did not understand why they should be held up on their way towards the excitement of the menagerie, made it impossible for anyone to stand gazing quietly for any length of time. And that was the reason why the hunger artist, who had of course been looking forward to these visiting hours as the main achievement of his life, began instead to shrink from them. At first he could hardly wait for the intervals; it was exhilarating to watch the crowds come streaming his way, until only too soon—not even the most obstinate self-deception, clung to almost consciously, could hold out against the fact—the conviction was borne in upon him that these people, most of them, to judge from their actions, again and again, without exception, were all on their way to the menagerie. And the first sight of him from the distance remained the best. For when they reached his cage he was at once deafened by the storm of shouting and abuse that arose from the two contending factions, which renewed themselves continuously, of those who wanted to stop and stare at him—he soon began to dislike them more than the others—not out of real interest but only out of obstinate self-assertiveness, and those who wanted to go straight on to the animals. When the first great rush was past, the stragglers came along, and these, whom nothing could have prevented from stopping to look at him as long as they had breath, raced past with long strides, hardly even glancing at him, in their haste to get to the menagerie in time. And all too rarely did it happen that he had a stroke of luck, when some father of a family fetched up before him with his children, pointed a finger at the hunger artist and explained at length what the phenomenon meant, telling stories of earlier years when he himself had watched similar but much more thrilling performances, and the children, still rather uncomprehending, since neither inside nor outside school had they been sufficiently prepared for this lesson—what did they care about fasting?—yet showed by the brightness of their intent eyes that new and better times might be coming. Perhaps, said the hunger artist to himself many a time, things would be a little better if his cage were set not quite so near the menagerie. That made it too easy for people to make their choice, to say nothing of what he suffered from the stench of the menagerie, the animals' restlessness by night, the carrying past of raw lumps of flesh for the beasts of prey, the roaring at feeding times, which depressed him continually. But he did not dare to lodge a complaint with the management; after all, he had the animals to thank for the troops of people who passed his cage, among whom there might always be one here and there to take an interest in him, and who could tell where they might seclude him if he called attention to his existence and thereby to the fact that, strictly speaking, he was only an impediment on the way to the menagerie.

A small impediment, to be sure, one that grew steadily less. People grew familiar with the strange idea that they could be expected, in times like these, to take an interest in a hunger artist, and with this familiarity the verdict went on against him. He might fast as much as he could, and he did so; but nothing could save him now, people passed him by. Just try to explain to anyone the art of fasting! Anyone who has no feeling for it cannot be made to understand it. The fine placards grew dirty and illegible, they were torn down; the little notice board telling the number of fast days achieved, which at first was changed carefully every day, had long stayed at the same figure, for after the first few weeks even this small task seemed pointless to the staff; and so the artist simply fasted on and on, as he had once dreamed of doing, and it was no trouble to him, just as he had always foretold; but no one counted the days, no one, not even the artist himself, knew what records he was already breaking, and his heart grew heavy. And when once in a time some leisurely passer-by stopped, made merry over the old figure on the board and spoke of swindling, that was in its way the stupidest lie ever invented by indifference and inborn malice, since it was not the hunger artist who was cheating; he was working honestly, but the world was cheating him of his reward.

Many more days went by, however, and that too came to an end. An overseer's eye fell on the cage one day and he asked the attendants why this perfectly good cage should be left standing there unused with dirty straw inside it; nobody knew, until one man, helped out by the notice board, remembered about the hunger artist. They poked into the straw with sticks and found him in it. "Are you still fasting?" asked the overseer. "When on earth do you mean to stop?" "Forgive me, everybody," whispered the hunger artist; only the overseer, who had his ear to the bars, understood him. "Of course," said the overseer, and tapped his forehead with a finger to let the attendants know what state the man was in, "we forgive you." "I always wanted you to admire my fasting," said the hunger artist. "We do admire it," said the overseer, "but why shouldn't we admire it?" "Because I have to fast, I can't help it," said the hunger artist, lifting his head a little and speaking, with his lips pursed, as if for a kiss, right into the overseer's ear, so that no syllable might be lost, "because I couldn't find the food I liked. If I had found it, believe me, I should have made no fuss and stuffed myself like you or anyone else." These were his last words, but in his dimming eyes remained the firm though no longer proud persuasion that he was still continuing to fast.

"Well, clear this out now!" said the overseer, and they buried the hunger artist, straw and all. Into the cage they put a young panther. Even the most insensitive felt it refreshing to see this wild creature leaping around the cage that had so long been dreary. The panther was all right. The food he liked was brought him without hesitation by the attendants; he seemed not even to miss his freedom; his noble body, furnished almost to the bursting point with all that it needed, seemed to carry freedom around with it too; somewhere in his jaws it seemed to lurk; and the joy of life streamed with such ardent passion from his throat that for the onlookers it was not easy to stand the shock of it. But they braced themselves, crowded round the cage, and did not want ever to move away.

—*Translated by* Willa and Edwin Muir

D. H. LAWRENCE • 1885–1930

The Blind Man

ISABEL Pervin was listening for two sounds—for the sound of wheels on the drive outside and for the noise of her husband's footsteps in the hall. Her dearest and oldest friend, a man who seemed almost indispensable to her living, would drive up in the rainy dusk of the closing November day. The trap had gone to fetch him from the station. And her husband, who had been blinded in Flanders, and who had a disfiguring mark on his brow, would be coming in from the outhouses.

He had been home for a year now. He was totally blind. Yet they had been very happy. The Grange was Maurice's own place. The back was a farmstead, and the Wernhams, who occupied the rear premises, acted as farmers. Isabel lived with her husband in the handsome rooms in front. She and he had been almost entirely alone together since he was wounded. They talked and sang and read together in a wonderful and unspeakable intimacy. Then she reviewed books for a Scottish newspaper, carrying on her old interest, and he occupied himself a good deal with the farm. Sightless, he could still discuss everything with Wernham, and he could also do a good deal of work about the place—menial work, it is true, but it gave him satisfaction. He milked the cows, carried in the pails, turned the separator, attended to the pigs and horses. Life was still very full and strangely serene for the blind man, peaceful with the almost incomprehensible peace of immediate contact in darkness. With his wife he had a whole world, rich and real and invisible.

They were newly and remotely happy. He did not even regret the loss of his sight in these times of dark, palpable joy. A certain exultance swelled his soul.

But as time wore on, sometimes the rich glamour would leave them. Sometimes, after months of this intensity, a sense of burden overcame Isabel, a weariness, a terrible *ennui,* in that silent house approached between a colonnade of tall-shafted pines. Then she felt she would go mad, for she could not bear it. And sometimes he had devastating fits of depression, which seemed to lay waste his whole being. It was worse than depression—a black misery, when his own life was a torture to him, and when his presence was unbearable to his wife. The dread went down to the roots of her soul as these black days recurred. In a kind of panic she tried to wrap herself up still further in her husband. She forced the old spontaneous cheerfulness and joy to continue. But the effort it cost her was almost too much. She knew she could not keep it up. She felt she would scream with the strain, and would give anything, anything, to escape. She longed to possess her husband utterly; it gave her inordinate joy to have him entirely to herself. And yet, when again he was gone in a black and massive misery, she could not bear him, she could not bear herself; she wished she could be snatched away off the earth altogether, anything rather than live at this cost.

Dazed, she schemed for a way out. She invited friends, she tried to give him some further connection with the outer world. But it was no good. After all their joy and suffering, after their dark, great year of blindness and solitude and unspeakable nearness, other people seemed to them both shallow, rattling, rather impertinent. Shallow prattle seemed presumptuous. He became impatient and irritated, she was wearied. And so they lapsed into their solitude again. For they preferred it.

But now, in a few weeks' time, her second baby would be born. The first had died, an infant, when her husband first went out to France. She looked with joy and relief to the coming of the second. It would be her salvation. But also she felt some anxiety. She was thirty years old, her husband was a year younger. They both wanted the child very much. Yet she could not help feeling afraid. She had her husband on her hands, a terrible joy to her, and a terrifying burden. The child would occupy her love and attention. And then, what of Maurice? What would he do? If only she could feel that he, too, would be at peace and happy when the child came! She did so want to luxuriate in a rich, physical satisfaction of maternity. But the man, what would he do? How could she provide for him, how avert those shattering black moods of his, which destroyed them both?

She sighed with fear. But at this time Bertie Reid wrote to Isabel. He was her old friend, a second or third cousin, a Scotchman, as she was a Scotchwoman. They had been brought up near to one another, and all her life he had been her friend, like a brother, but better than her own brothers. She loved him—though not in the marrying sense. There was a sort of kinship between them, an affinity. They understood one another instinctively. But Isabel would never have thought of marrying Bertie. It would have seemed like marrying in her own family.

Bertie was a barrister and a man of letters, a Scotchman of the intellectual type, quick, ironical, sentimental, and on his knees before the woman he adored but did not want to marry. Maurice Pervin was different. He came of a good old country family—the Grange was not a very great distance from Oxford. He was passionate, sensitive, perhaps over-sensitive, wincing—a big fellow with heavy limbs and a forehead that flushed painfully. For his mind was slow, as if drugged by the strong provincial blood that beat in his veins. He was very sensitive to his own mental slowness, his feelings being quick and acute. So that he was just the opposite to Bertie, whose mind was much quicker than his emotions, which were not so very fine.

From the first the two men did not like each other. Isabel felt that they *ought* to get on together. But they did not. She felt that if only each could have the clue to the other there would be such a rare understanding between them. It did not come off, however. Bertie adopted a slightly ironical attitude, very offensive to Maurice, who returned the Scotch irony with English resentment, a resentment which deepened sometimes into stupid hatred.

This was a little puzzling to Isabel. However, she accepted it in the course of things. Men were made freakish and unreasonable. Therefore, when Maurice was going out to France for the second time, she felt that, for her husband's sake, she must discontinue her friendship with Bertie. She wrote to the barrister to this effect. Bertram Reid simply replied that in this, as in all other matters, he must obey her wishes, if these were indeed her wishes.

For nearly two years nothing had passed between the two friends. Isabel rather gloried in the fact; she had no compunction. She had one great article of faith, which was, that husband and wife should be so important to one another, that the rest of the world simply did not count. She and Maurice were husband and wife. They loved one another. They would have children. Then let everybody and everything else fade into insignificance outside this connubial felicity. She professed herself quite happy and ready to receive Maurice's friends. She was happy and ready: the happy wife, the ready woman in possession. Without knowing why, the friends retired abashed, and came no more. Maurice, of course, took as much satisfaction in this connubial absorption as Isabel did.

He shared in Isabel's literary activities, she cultivated a real interest in agriculture and cattle-raising. For she, being at heart perhaps an emotional enthusiast, always cultivated the practical side of life and prided herself on her mastery of practical affairs. Thus the husband and wife had spent the five years of their married life. The last had been one of blindness and unspeakable intimacy. And now Isabel felt a great indifference coming over her, a sort of lethargy. She wanted to be allowed to bear her child in peace, to nod by the fire and drift vaguely, physically, from day to day. Maurice was like an ominous thunder-cloud. She had to keep waking up to remember him.

When a little note came from Bertie, asking if he were to put up a tombstone to their dead friendship, and speaking of the real pain he felt on account of her husband's loss of sight, she felt a pang, a fluttering agitation of re-awakening. And she read the letter to Maurice.

"Ask him to come down," he said.

"Ask Bertie to come here!" she re-echoed.

"Yes—if he wants to."

Isabel paused for a few moments.

"I know he wants to—he'd only be too glad," she replied. "But what about you, Maurice? How would you like it?"

"I should like it."

"Well—in that case—But I thought you didn't care for him—"

"Oh, I don't know. I might think differently of him now," the blind man replied. It was rather abstruse to Isabel.

"Well, dear," she said, "if you're quite sure—"

"I'm sure enough. Let him come," said Maurice.

So Bertie was coming, coming this evening, in the November rain and darkness. Isabel was agitated, racked with her old restlessness and indecision. She had always suffered from this pain of doubt, just an agonizing sense of uncertainty. It had begun to pass off, in the lethargy of maternity. Now it returned, and she resented it. She struggled as usual to maintain her calm, composed, friendly bearing, a sort of mask she wore over all her body.

A woman had lighted a tall lamp beside the table and spread the cloth. The long dining-room was dim, with its elegant but rather severe pieces of old furniture. Only the round table glowed softly under the light. It had a rich, beautiful effect. The white cloth glistened and dropped its heavy, pointed lace corners almost to the carpet, the china was old and handsome, creamy-yellow, with a blotched pattern of harsh red and deep blue, the cups large and bell-shaped, the teapot gallant. Isabel looked at it with superficial appreciation.

Her nerves were hurting her. She looked automatically again at the high, uncurtained windows. In the last dusk she could just perceive outside a huge fir-tree swaying its boughs: it was as if she thought it rather than saw it. The rain came flying on the window panes. Ah, why had she no peace? These two men, why did they tear at her? Why did they not come—why was there this suspense?

She sat in a lassitude that was really suspense and irritation. Maurice, at least, might come in—there was nothing to keep him out. She rose to her feet. Catching sight of her reflection in a mirror, she glanced at herself with a slight smile of recognition, as if she were an old friend to herself. Her face was oval and calm, her nose a little arched. Her neck made a beautiful line down to her shoulder. With hair knotted loosely behind, she had something of a warm, maternal look. Thinking this of herself, she arched her eyebrows and her rather heavy eyelids, with a little flicker of a smile, and for a moment her grey eyes looked amused and wicked, a little sardonic, out of her transfigured Madonna face.

Then, resuming her air of womanly patience—she was really fatally self-determined—she went with a little jerk towards the door. Her eyes were slightly reddened.

She passed down the wide hall and through a door at the end. Then she was in the farm premises. The scent of dairy, and of farm-kitchen, and of farm-yard and of leather almost overcame her: but particularly the scent of dairy. They had been scalding out the pans. The flagged passage in front of her was dark, puddled, and wet. Light came out from the open kitchen door. She went forward and stood in the doorway. The farm-people were at tea, seated at a little distance from her, round a long, narrow table, in the centre of which stood a white lamp. Ruddy faces, ruddy hands holding food, red mouths working, heads bent over the tea-cups: men, land-girls, boys: it was tea-time, feeding-time. Some faces caught sight of her. Mrs. Wernham, going round behind the chairs with a large black tea-pot, halting slightly in her walk, was not aware of her for a moment. Then she turned suddenly.

"Oh, is it Madam!' she exclaimed. "Come in, then, come in! We're at tea." And she dragged forward a chair.

"No, I won't come in," said Isabel. "I'm afraid I interrupt your meal."

"No—no—not likely, Madam, not likely."

"Hasn't Mr. Pervin come in, do you know?"

"I'm sure I couldn't say! Missed him, have you, Madam?"

"No, I only wanted him to come in," laughed Isabel, as if shyly.

"Wanted him, did ye? Get up, boy—get up, now—"

Mrs. Wernham knocked one of the boys on the shoulder. He began to scrape to his feet, chewing largely.

"I believe he's in top stable," said another face from the table.

"Ah! No, don't get up. I'm going myself," said Isabel.

"Don't you go out of a dirty night like this. Let the lad go. Get along wi' ye, boy," said Mrs. Wernham.

"No, no," said Isabel, with a decision that was always obeyed. "Go on with your tea, Tom. I'd like to go across to the stable, Mrs. Wernham."

"Did ever you hear tell!" exclaimed the woman.

"Isn't the trap late?" asked Isabel.

"Why, no," said Mrs. Wernham, peering into the distance at the tall, dim clock. "No, Madam—we can give it another quarter or twenty minutes yet, good —yes, every bit of a quarter."

"Ah! It seems late when darkness falls so early," said Isabel.

"It do, that it do. Bother the days, that they draw in so," answered Mrs. Wernham. "Proper miserable!"

"They are," said Isabel, withdrawing.

She pulled on her overshoes, wrapped a large tartan shawl around her, put on a man's felt hat, and ventured out along the causeways of the first yard. It was very dark. The wind was roaring in the great elms behind the outhouses. When she came to the second yard the darkness seemed deeper. She was unsure of her footing. She wished she had brought a lantern. Rain blew against her. Half she liked it, half she felt unwilling to battle.

She reached at last the just visible door of the stable. There was no sign of a light anywhere. Opening the upper half, she looked in: into a simple well of darkness. The smell of horses, and ammonia, and of warmth was startling to her, in that full night. She listened with all her ears but could hear nothing save the night, and the stirring of a horse.

"Maurice!" she called, softly and musically, though she was afraid. "Maurice—are you there?"

Nothing came from the darkness. She knew the rain and wind blew in upon the horses, the hot animal life. Feeling it wrong, she entered the stable and drew the lower half of the door shut, holding the upper part close. She did not stir, because she was aware of the presence of the dark hind-quarters of the horses, though she could not see them, and she was afraid. Something wild stirred in her heart.

She listened intensely. Then she heard a small noise in the distance—far away, it seemed—the chink of a pan, and a man's voice speaking a brief word. It would be Maurice, in the other part of the stable. She stood motionless, waiting for him to come through the partition door. The horses were so terrifyingly near to her, in the invisible.

The loud jarring of the inner door-latch made her start; the door was opened. She could hear and feel her husband entering and invisibly passing among the horses near to her, darkness as they were, actively intermingled. The rather low sound of his voice as he spoke to the horses came velvety to her nerves. How near he was, and how invisible! The darkness seemed to be in a strange swirl of violent life, just upon her. She turned giddy.

Her presence of mind made her call, quietly and musically:

"Maurice! Maurice—dea-ar!"

"Yes," he answered. "Isabel?"

She saw nothing, and the sound of his voice seemed to touch her.

"Hello!" she answered cheerfully, straining her eyes to see him. He was still busy, attending to the horses near her, but she saw only darkness. It made her almost desperate.

"Won't you come in, dear?" she said.

"Yes, I'm coming. Just half a minute. *Stand over—now!* Trap's not come, has it?"

"Not yet," said Isabel.

His voice was pleasant and ordinary, but it had a slight suggestion of the stable to her. She wished he would come away. Whilst he was so utterly invisible, she was afraid of him.

"How's the time?" he asked.

"Not yet six," she replied. She disliked to answer into the dark. Presently he came very near to her, and she retreated out of doors.

"The weather blows in here," he said, coming steadily forward, feeling for the doors. She shrank away. At last she could dimly see him.

"Bertie won't have much of a drive," he said, as he closed the doors.

"He won't indeed!" said Isabel calmly, watching the dark shape at the door.

"Give me your arm, dear," she said.

She pressed his arm close to her, as she went. But she longed to see him, to look at him. She was nervous. He walked erect, with face rather lifted, but with a curious tentative movement of his powerful muscular legs. She could feel the clever, careful, strong contact of his feet with the earth, as she balanced against him. For a moment he was a tower of darkness to her, as if he rose out of the earth.

In the house-passage he wavered and went cautiously, with a curious look of silence about him as he felt for the bench. Then he sat down heavily. He was a man with rather sloping shoulders, but with heavy limbs, powerful legs that seemed to know the earth. His head was small, usually carried high and light. As he bent down to unfasten his gaiters and boots he did not look blind. His hair was brown and crisp, his hands were large, reddish, intelligent, the veins stood out in the wrists; and his thighs and knees seemed massive. When he stood up his face and neck were surcharged with blood, the veins stood out on his temples. She did not look at his blindness.

Isabel was always glad when they had passed through the dividing door into their own regions of repose and beauty.

She was a little afraid of him, out there in the animal grossness of the back. His bearing also changed, as he smelt the familiar indefinable odour that pervaded his wife's surroundings, a delicate, refined scent, very faintly spicy. Perhaps it came from the potpourri bowls.

He stood at the foot of the stairs, arrested, listening. She watched him, and her heart sickened. He seemed to be listening to fate.

"He's not here yet," he said. "I'll go up and change."

"Maurice," she said, "you're not wishing he wouldn't come, are you?"

"I couldn't quite say," he answered. "I feel myself rather on the qui vive."

"I can see you are," she answered. And she reached up and kissed his cheek. She saw his mouth relax into a slow smile.

"What are you laughing at?" she said roguishly.

"You consoling me," he answered.

"Nay," she answered. "Why should I console you? You know we love each other—you know *how* married we are! What does anything else matter?"

"Nothing at all, my dear."

He felt for her face and touched it, smiling.

"You're all right, aren't you?" he asked anxiously.

"I'm wonderfully all right, love," she answered. "It's you I am a little troubled about, at times."

"Why me?" he said, touching her cheeks delicately with the tips of his fingers. The touch had an almost hypnotizing effect on her.

He went away upstairs. She saw him mount into the darkness, unseeing and unchanging. He did not know that the lamps on the upper corridor were unlighted. He went on into the darkness with unchanging step. She heard him in the bathroom.

Pervin moved about almost unconsciously in his familiar surroundings, dark though everything was. He seemed to know the presence of objects before he touched them. It was a pleasure to him to rock thus through a world of things, carried on the flood in a sort of blood-prescience. He did not think much or trouble much. So long as he kept his sheer immediacy of blood-contact with the substantial world he was happy, he wanted no intervention of visual consciousness. In this state there was a certain rich positivity, bordering sometimes on rapture. Life seemed to move in him like a tide lapping, lapping, and advancing, enveloping all things darkly. It was a pleasure to stretch forth the hand and meet the unseen object, clasp it, and possess it in pure contact. He did not try to remember, to visualize. He did not want to. The new way of consciousness substituted itself in him.

The rich suffusion of this state generally kept him happy, reaching its culmination in the consuming passion for his wife. But at times the flow would seem to be checked and thrown back. Then it would beat inside him like a tangled sea, and he was tortured in the shattered chaos of his own blood. He grew to dread this arrest, this throw-back, this chaos inside himself, when he seemed merely at the mercy of his own powerful and conflicting elements. How to get some measure of control or surety, this was the question. And when the question rose maddening in him, he would clench his fists as if he would *compel* the whole universe to submit to him. But it was in vain. He could not even compel himself.

Tonight, however, he was still serene, though little tremors of unreasonable exasperation ran through him. He had to handle the razor very carefully, as he shaved, for it was not at one with him, he was afraid of it. His hearing also was too much sharpened. He heard the woman lighting the lamps on the corridor, and attending to the fire in the visitor's room. And then, as he went to his room, he heard the trap arrive. Then came Isabel's voice, lifted and calling, like a bell ringing:

"Is it you, Bertie? Have you come?"

And a man's voice answered out of the wind:

"Hello, Isabel! There you are."

"Have you had a miserable drive? I'm so sorry we couldn't send a closed carriage. I can't see you at all, you know."

"I'm coming. No, I liked the drive—it was like Portshire. Well, how are you? You're looking fit as ever, as far as I can see."

"Oh, yes," said Isabel. "I'm wonderfully well. How are you? Rather thin, I think—"

"Worked to death—everybody's old cry. But I'm all right, Ciss. How's Pervin?—isn't he here?"

"Oh, yes, he's upstairs changing. Yes, he's awfully well. Take off your wet things; I'll send them to be dried."

"And how are you both, in spirits? He doesn't fret?"

"No—no, not at all. No, on the contrary, really. We've been wonderfully happy, incredibly. It's more than I can understand—so wonderful: the nearness, and the peace—"

"Ah! Well, that's awfully good news—"

They moved away. Pervin heard no more. But a childish sense of desolation had come over him, as he heard their brisk voices. He seemed shut out—like a child that is left out. He was aimless and excluded, he did not know what to do with himself. The helpless desolation came over him. He fumbled nervously as he dressed himself, in a state almost of childishness. He disliked the Scotch accent in Bertie's speech, and the slight response it found on Isabel's tongue. He disliked the slight purr of complacency in the Scottish speech. He disliked intensely the glib way in which Isabel spoke of their happiness and nearness. It made him recoil. He was fretful and beside himself like a child, he had almost a childish nostalgia to be included in the life circle. And at the same time he was a man, dark and powerful and infuriated by his own weakness. By some fatal flaw, he could not be by himself, he had to depend on the support of another. And this very dependence enraged him. He hated Bertie Reid, and at the same time he knew the hatred was nonsense, he knew it was the outcome of his own weakness.

He went downstairs. Isabel was alone in the dining-room. She watched him enter, head erect, his feet tentative. He looked so strong-blooded and healthy and, at the same time, cancelled. Cancelled—that was the word that flew across her mind. Perhaps it was his scar suggested it.

"You heard Bertie come, Maurice?" she said.

"Yes—isn't he here?"

"He's in his room. He looks very thin and worn."

"I suppose he works himself to death."

A woman came in with a tray—and after a few minutes Bertie came down. He was a little dark man, with a very big forehead, thin, wispy hair, and sad, large eyes. His expression was inordinately sad—almost funny. He had odd, short legs.

Isabel watched him hesitate under the door, and glance nervously at her husband. Pervin heard him and turned.

"Here you are, now," said Isabel. "Come, let us eat."

Bertie went across to Maurice.

"How are you, Pervin?" he said, as he advanced.

The blind man stuck his hand out into space, and Bertie took it.

"Very fit. Glad you've come," said Maurice.

Isabel glanced at them, and glanced away, as if she could not bear to see them.

"Come," she said. "Come to table. Aren't you both awfully hungry? I am tremendously."

"I'm afraid you waited for me," said Bertie, as they sat down.

Maurice had a curious monolithic way of sitting in a chair, erect and distant. Isabel's heart always beat when she caught sight of him thus.

"No," she replied to Bertie. "We're very little later than usual. We're having a sort of high tea, not dinner. Do you mind? It gives us such a nice long evening, uninterrupted."

"I like it," said Bertie.

Maurice was feeling, with curious little movements, almost like a cat kneading her bed, for his plate, his knife and fork, his napkin. He was getting the whole geography of his cover into his consciousness. He sat erect and inscrutable, remote-seeming. Bertie watched the static figure of the blind man, the delicate tactile discernment of the large, ruddy hands, and the curious mindless silence of the brow, above the scar. With difficulty he looked away, and without knowing what he did, picked up a little crystal bowl of violets from the table, and held them to his nose.

"They are sweet-scented," he said. "Where do they come from?"

"From the garden—under the windows," said Isabel.

"So late in the year—and so fragrant! Do you remember the violets under Aunt Bell's south wall?"

The two friends looked at each other and exchanged a smile, Isabel's eyes lighting up.

"Don't I?" she replied. *"Wasn't* she queer!"

"A curious old girl," laughed Bertie. "There's a streak of freakishness in the family, Isabel."

"Ah—but not in you and me, Bertie," said Isabel. "Give them to Maurice, will you?" she added, as Bertie was putting down the flowers. "Have you smelled the violets, dear? Do!—they are so scented."

Maurice held out his hand, and Bertie placed the tiny bowl against his large, warm-looking fingers. Maurice's hand closed over the thin white fingers of the barrister. Bertie carefully extricated himself. Then the two watched the blind man smelling the violets. He bent his head and seemed to be thinking. Isabel waited.

"Aren't they sweet, Maurice?" she said at last, anxiously.

"Very," he said. And he held out the bowl. Bertie took it. Both he and Isabel were a little afraid, and deeply disturbed.

The meal continued. Isabel and Bertie chatted spasmodically. The blind man was silent. He touched his food repeatedly, with quick, delicate touches of his knife-point, then cut irregular bits. He could not bear to be helped. Both Isabel and Bertie suffered: Isabel wondered why. She did not suffer when she was alone with Maurice. Bertie made her conscious of a strangeness.

After the meal the three drew their chairs to the fire, and sat down to talk. The decanters were put on a table near at hand. Isabel knocked the logs on the fire, and clouds of brilliant sparks went up the chimney. Bertie noticed a slight weariness in her bearing.

"You will be glad when your child comes now, Isabel?" he said.

She looked up to him with a quick wan smile.

"Yes, I shall be glad," she answered. "It begins to seem long. Yes, I shall be very glad. So will you, Maurice, won't you?" she added.

"Yes, I shall," replied her husband.

"We are both looking forward so much to having it," she said.

"Yes, of course," said Bertie.

He was a bachelor, three or four years older than Isabel. He lived in beautiful rooms overlooking the river, guarded by a faithful Scottish man-servant. And he had his friends among the fair sex—not lovers, friends. So long as he could avoid any danger of courtship or marriage, he adored a few good women with constant and unfailing homage, and he was chivalrously fond of quite a number. But if they seemed to encroach on him, he withdrew and detested them.

Isabel knew him very well, knew his beautiful constancy, and kindness, also his incurable weakness, which made him unable ever to enter into close contact of any sort. He was ashamed of himself because he could not marry, could not approach women physically. He wanted to do so. But he could not. At the centre of him he was afraid, helplessly and even brutally afraid. He had given up hope, had ceased to expect any more that he could escape his own weakness. Hence he was a brilliant and successful barrister, also a *littérateur* of high repute, a rich man, and a great social success. At the centre he felt himself neuter, nothing.

Isabel knew him well. She despised him even while she admired him. She looked at his sad face, his little short legs, and felt contempt of him. She looked at his dark grey eyes, with their uncanny, almost childlike, intuition, and she loved him. He understood amazingly—but she had no fear of his understanding. As a man she patronized him.

And she turned to the impassive, silent figure of her husband. He sat leaning back, with folded arms, and face a little uptilted. His knees were straight and massive. She sighed, picked up the poker, and again began to prod the fire, to rouse the clouds of soft brilliant sparks.

"Isabel tells me," Bertie began suddenly, "that you have not suffered unbearably from the loss of sight."

Maurice straightened himself to attend but kept his arms folded.

"No," he said, "not unbearably. Now and again one struggles against it, you know. But there are compensations."

"They say it is much worse to be stone deaf," said Isabel.

"I believe it is," said Bertie. "Are there compensations?" he added, to Maurice.

"Yes. You cease to bother about a great many things." Again Maurice stretched his figure, stretched the strong muscles of his back, and leaned backwards, with uplifted face.

"And that is a relief," said Bertie. "But what is there in place of the bothering? What replaces the activity?"

There was a pause. At length the blind man replied, as out of a negligent, unattentive thinking:

"Oh, I don't know. There's a good deal when you're not active."

"Is there?" said Bertie. "What, exactly? It always seems to me that when there is no thought and no action, there is nothing."

Again Maurice was slow in replying.

"There is something," he replied. "I couldn't tell you what it is."

And the talk lapsed once more, Isabel and Bertie chatting gossip and reminiscence, the blind man silent.

At length Maurice rose restlessly, a big obtrusive figure. He felt tight and hampered. He wanted to go away.

"Do you mind," he said, "if I go and speak to Wernham?"

"No—go along dear," said Isabel.

And he went out. A silence came over the two friends. At length Bertie said:

"Nevertheless, it is a great deprivation, Cissie."

"It is, Bertie. I know it is."

"Something lacking all the time," said Bertie.

"Yes, I know. And yet—and yet—Maurice is right. There is something else, something *there*, which you never knew was there, and which you can't express."

"What is there?" asked Bertie.

"I don't know—it's awfully hard to define it—but something strong and immediate. There's something strange in

Maurice's presence—indefinable—but I couldn't do without it. I agree that it seems to put one's mind to sleep. But when we're alone I miss nothing; it seems awfully rich, almost splendid, you know."

"I'm afraid I don't follow," said Bertie.

They talked desultorily. The wind blew loudly outside, rain chattered on the window-panes, making a sharp drum-sound because of the closed, mellow-golden shutters inside. The logs burned slowly, with hot, almost invisible small flames. Bertie seemed uneasy, there were dark circles round his eyes. Isabel, rich with her approaching maternity, leaned looking into the fire. Her hair curled in odd, loose strands, very pleasing to the man. But she had a curious feeling of old woe in her heart, old, timeless night-woe.

"I suppose we're all deficient somewhere," said Bertie.

"I suppose so," said Isabel wearily.

"Damned, sooner or later."

"I don't know," she said, rousing herself. "I feel quite all right, you know. The child coming seems to make me indifferent to everything, just placid. I can't feel that there's anything to trouble about, you know."

"A good thing, I should say," he replied slowly.

"Well, there it is. I suppose it's just Nature. If only I felt I needn't trouble about Maurice, I should be perfectly content—"

"But you feel you must trouble about him?"

"Well—I don't know—" She even resented this much effort.

The night passed slowly. Isabel looked at the clock. "I say," she said, "It's nearly ten o'clock. Where can Maurice be? I'm sure they're all in bed at the back. Excuse me a moment."

She went out, returning almost immediately.

"It's all shut up and in darkness," she said. "I wonder where he is. He must have gone out to the farm—"

Bertie looked at her.

"I suppose he'll come in," he said.

"I suppose so," she said. "But it's unusual for him to be out now."

"Would you like me to go out and see?"

"Well—if you wouldn't mind. I'd go, but—" She did not want to make the physical effort.

Bertie put on an old overcoat and took a lantern. He went out from the side door. He shrank from the wet and roaring night. Such weather had a nervous effect on him: too much moisture everywhere made him feel almost imbecile. Unwilling, he went through it all. A dog barked violently at him. He peered in all the buildings. At last, as he opened the upper door of a sort of intermediate barn, he heard a grinding noise, and looking in, holding up his lantern, saw Maurice, in his shirtsleeves, standing listening, holding the handle of a turnip-pulper. He had been pulping sweet roots, a pile of which lay dimly heaped in a corner behind him.

"That you, Wernham?" said Maurice, listening.

"No, it's me," said Bertie.

A large, half-wild grey cat was rubbing at Maurice's leg. The blind man stooped to rub its sides. Bertie watched the scene, then unconsciously entered and shut the door behind him. He was in a high sort of barn-place, from which, right and left, ran off the corridors in front of the stalled cattle. He watched the slow, stooping motion of the other man, as he caressed the great cat.

Maurice straightened himself.

"You come to look for me?" he said.

"Isabel was a little uneasy," said Bertie.

"I'll come in. I like messing about doing these jobs."

The cat had reared her sinister, feline length against his leg, clawing at his thigh affectionately. He lifted her claws out of his flesh.

"I hope I'm not in your way at all at the Grange here," said Bertie, rather shy and stiff.

"My way? No, not a bit. I'm glad Isabel has somebody to talk to. I'm afraid it's I who am in the way. I know I'm not very lively company. Isabel's all right, don't you think? She's not unhappy, is she?"

"I don't think so."

"What does she say?"

"She says she's very content—only a little troubled about you."

"Why me?"

"Perhaps afraid that you might brood," said Bertie, cautiously.

"She needn't be afraid of that." He continued to caress the flattened grey head of the cat with his fingers. "What I am afraid of," he resumed, "is that she'll find me a dead weight, always alone with me down here."

"I don't think you need think that," said Bertie, though this was what he feared himself.

"I don't know," said Maurice. "Sometimes I feel it isn't fair that she's saddled with me." Then he dropped his voice curiously. "I say," he asked, secretly struggling, "is my face much disfigured? Do you mind telling me?"

"There is the scar," said Bertie, wondering. "Yes, it is a disfigurement. But more pitiable than shocking."

"A pretty bad scar, though," said Maurice.

"Oh, yes."

There was a pause.

"Sometimes I feel I am horrible," said Maurice, in a low voice, talking as if to himself. And Bertie actually felt a quiver of horror.

"That's nonsense," he said.

Maurice again straightened himself, leaving the cat.

"There's no telling," he said. Then again, in an odd tone, he added: "I don't really know you, do I?"

"Probably not," said Bertie.

"Do you mind if I touch you?"

The lawyer shrank away instinctively. And yet, out of very philanthropy, he said, in a small voice: "Not at all."

But he suffered as the blind man stretched out a strong, naked hand to him. Maurice accidentally knocked off Bertie's hat.

"I thought you were taller," he said, starting. Then he laid his hand on Bertie Reid's head, closing the dome of the skull in a soft, firm grasp, gathering it, as it were; then, shifting his grasp and softly closing again, with a fine, close pressure, till he had covered the skull and the face of the smaller man, tracing the brows, and touching the full, closed eyes, touching the small nose and the nostrils, the rough, short moustache, the mouth, the rather strong chin. The hand of the blind man grasped the shoulder, the arm, the hand of the other man. He seemed to take him, in the soft, travelling grasp.

"You seem young," he said quietly, at last.

The lawyer stood almost annihilated, unable to answer.

"Your head seems tender, as if you were young," Maurice repeated. "So do your hands. Touch my eyes, will you?—touch my scar."

Now Bertie quivered with revulsion. Yet he was under the power of the blind man, as if hypnotized. He lifted his hand, and laid the fingers on the scar, on the scarred eyes. Maurice suddenly covered them with his own hand, pressed the fingers of the other man upon his disfigured eye-sockets, trembling in every fibre, and rocking slightly, slowly, from side to side. He remained thus for a minute or more, whilst Bertie stood as if in a swoon, unconscious, imprisoned.

Then suddenly Maurice removed the

hand of the other man from his brow, and stood holding it in his own.

"Oh, my God," he said, "we shall know each other now, shan't we? We shall know each other now."

Bertie could not answer. He gazed mute and terror-struck, over-come by his own weakness. He knew he could not answer. He had an unreasonable fear, lest the other man should suddenly destroy him. Whereas Maurice was actually filled with hot, poignant love, the passion of friendship. Perhaps it was this very passion of friendship which Bertie shrank from most.

"We're all right together now, aren't we?" said Maurice. "It's all right now, as long as we live, so far as we're concerned?"

"Yes," said Bertie, trying by any means to escape.

Maurice stood with head lifted, as if listening. The new delicate fulfillment of mortal friendship had come as a revelation and surprise to him, something exquisite and unhoped-for. He seemed to be listening to hear if it were real.

Then he turned for his coat.

"Come," he said, "we'll go to Isabel."

Bertie took the lantern and opened the door. The cat disappeared. The two men went in silence along the causeways. Isabel, as they came, thought their footsteps sounded strange. She looked up pathetically and anxiously for their entrance. There seemed a curious elation about Maurice. Bertie was haggard, with sunken eyes.

"What is it?" she asked.

"We've become friends," said Maurice, standing with his feet apart, like a strange colossus.

"Friends!" re-echoed Isabel. And she looked again at Bertie. He met her eyes with a furtive, haggard look; his eyes were as if glazed with misery.

"I'm so glad," she said, in sheer perplexity.

"Yes," said Maurice.

He was indeed so glad. Isabel took his hand with both hers, and held it fast.

"You'll be happier now, dear," she said.

But she was watching Bertie. She knew that he had one desire—to escape from this intimacy, this friendship, which had been thrust upon him. He could not bear it that he had been touched by the blind man, his insane reserve broken in. He was like a mollusc whose shell is broken.

KATHERINE MANSFIELD • 1888-1923

The Doll's House

WHEN dear old Mrs. Hay went back to town after staying with the Burnells she sent the children a doll's house. It was so big that the carter and Pat carried it into the courtyard, and there it stayed, propped up on two wooden boxes beside the feed-room door. No harm could come of it; it was summer. And perhaps the smell of paint would have gone off by the time it had to be taken in. For, really, the smell of paint coming from that doll's house ("Sweet of old Mrs. Hay, of course; most sweet and generous!")—but the smell of paint was quite enough to make any one seriously ill, in Aunt Beryl's opinion. Even before the sacking was taken off. And when it was. . . .

There stood the doll's house, a dark, oily, spinach green, picked out with bright yellow. Its two solid little chimneys, glued on to the roof, were painted red and white, and the door, gleaming with yellow varnish, was like a little slab of toffee. Four windows, real windows, were divided into panes by a broad streak of green. There was actually a tiny porch, too, painted yellow, with big lumps of congealed paint hanging along the edge.

But perfect, perfect little house! Who could possibly mind the smell? It was part of the joy, part of the newness.

"Open it quickly, some one!"

The hook at the side was stuck fast. Pat pried it open with his penknife, and the whole house-front swung back, and—there you were, gazing at one and the same moment into the drawing-room and dining-room, the kitchen and two bedrooms. That is the way for a house to open! Why don't all houses open like that? How much more exciting than peering through the slit of a door into a mean little hall with a hatstand and two umbrellas! That is—isn't it?—what you long to know about a house when you put your hand on the knocker. Perhaps it is the way God opens houses at dead of night when He is taking a quiet turn with an angel. . . .

"O-oh!" The Burnell children sounded as though they were in despair. It was too marvellous; it was too much for them. They had never seen anything like it in their lives. All the rooms were papered. There were pictures on the walls, painted on the paper, with gold frames complete. Red carpet covered all the floors except the kitchen; red plush chairs in the drawing-room, green in the dining-room; tables, beds with real bedclothes, a cradle, a stove, a dresser with tiny plates and one big jug. But what Kezia liked more than anything, what she liked frightfully, was the lamp. It stood in the middle of the dining-room table, an exquisite little amber lamp with a white globe. It was even filled all ready for lighting, though, of course, you couldn't light it. But there was something inside that looked like oil, and that moved when you shook it.

The father and mother dolls, who sprawled very stiff as though they had fainted in the drawing-room, and their two little children asleep upstairs, were really too big for the doll's house. They didn't look as though they belonged. But the lamp was perfect. It seemed to smile at Kezia, to say, "I live here." The lamp was real.

The Burnell children could hardly walk to school fast enough the next morning. They burned to tell everybody, to describe, to—well—to boast about their

173

doll's house before the school-bell rang.

"I'm to tell," said Isabel, "because I'm the eldest. And you two can join in after. But I'm to tell first."

There was nothing to answer. Isabel was bossy, but she was always right, and Lottie and Kezia knew too well the powers that went with being eldest. They brushed through the thick buttercups at the road edge and said nothing.

"And I'm to choose who's to come and see it first. Mother said I might."

For it had been arranged that while the doll's house stood in the courtyard they might ask the girls at school, two at a time, to come and look. Not to stay to tea, of course, or to come traipsing through the house. But just to stand quietly in the courtyard while Isabel pointed out the beauties, and Lottie and Kezia looked pleased. . . .

But hurry as they might, by the time they had reached the tarred palings of the boys' playground the bell had begun to jangle. They only just had time to whip off their hats and fall into line before the roll was called. Never mind. Isabel tried to make up for it by looking very important and mysterious and by whispering behind her hand to the girls near her, "Got something to tell you at playtime."

Playtime came and Isabel was surrounded. The girls of her class nearly fought to put their arms round her, to walk away with her, to beam flatteringly, to be her special friend. She held quite a court under the huge pine trees at the side of the playground. Nudging, giggling together, the little girls pressed up close. And the only two who stayed outside the ring were the two who were always outside, the little Kelveys. They knew better than to come anywhere near the Burnells.

For the fact was, the school the Burnell children went to was not at all the kind of place their parents would have chosen if there had been any choice. But there was none. It was the only school for miles. And the consequence was all the children in the neighborhood, the Judge's little girls, the doctor's daughters, the storekeeper's children, the milkman's, were forced to mix together. Not to speak of there being an equal number of rude, rough little boys as well. But the line had to be drawn somewhere. It was drawn at the Kelveys. Many of the children, including the Burnells, were not allowed even to speak to them. They walked past the Kelveys with their heads in the air, and as they set the fashion in all matters of behaviour, the Kelveys were shunned by everybody. Even the teacher had a special voice for them, and a special smile for the other children when Lil Kelvey came up to her desk with a bunch of dreadfully common-looking flowers.

They were the daughters of a spry, hardworking little washerwoman, who went about from house to house by the day. This was awful enough. But where was Mr. Kelvey? Nobody knew for certain. But everybody said he was in prison. So they were the daughters of a washerwoman and a gaolbird. Very nice company for other people's children! And they looked it. Why Mrs. Kelvey made them so conspicuous was hard to understand. The truth was they were dressed in "bits" given to her by the people for whom she worked. Lil, for instance, who was a stout, plain child, with big freckles, came to school in a dress made from a green art-serge tablecloth of the Burnells', with red plush sleeves from the Logans' curtains. Her hat, perched on top of her high forehead, was a grown-up woman's hat, once the property of Miss Lecky, the postmistress. It was turned up at the back and trimmed with a large scarlet quill. What a little guy she looked! It was impossible not to laugh. And her little sister, our Else, wore a long white dress, rather like a nightgown, and a pair of little boy's boots. But whatever our Else wore she would have looked strange. She was a tiny wishbone of a child, with cropped hair and enormous solemn eyes

—a little white owl. Nobody had even seen her smile; she scarcely ever spoke. She went through life holding on to Lil, with a piece of Lil's skirt screwed up in her hand. Where Lil went our Else followed. In the playground, on the road going to and from the school, there was Lil marching in front and our Else holding on behind. Only when she wanted anything, or when she was out of breath, our Else gave Lil a tug, a twitch, and Lil stopped and turned round. The Kelveys never failed to understand each other.

Now they hovered at the edge; you couldn't stop them listening. When the little girls turned round and sneered, Lil, as usual, gave her silly shamefaced smile, but our Else only looked.

And Isabel's voice, so very proud, went on telling. The carpet made a great sensation, but so did the beds with real bedclothes, and the stove with an oven door.

When she finished Kezia broke in. "You've forgotten the lamp, Isabel."

"Oh, yes," said Isabel, "and there's a teeny little lamp, all made of yellow glass, with a white globe that stands on the dining-room table. You couldn't tell it from a real one."

"The lamp's best of all," cried Kezia. She thought Isabel wasn't making half enough of the little lamp. But nobody paid any attention. Isabel was choosing the two who were to come back with them that afternoon and see it. She chose Emmie Cole and Lena Logan. But when the others knew they were all to have a chance, they couldn't be nice enough to Isabel. One by one they put their arms round Isabel's waist and walked her off. They had something to whisper to her, a secret. "Isabel's *my* friend."

Only the little Kelveys moved away forgotten; there was nothing more for them to hear.

Days passed, and as more children saw the doll's house, the fame of it spread. It became the one subject, the rage. The one question was, "Have you seen Burnells' doll's house? Oh, ain't it lovely!" "Haven't you seen it? Oh, I say!"

Even the dinner hour was given up to talking about it. The little girls sat under the pines eating their thick mutton sandwiches and big slabs of johnny cake spread with butter. While always, as near as they could get, sat the Kelveys, our Else holding on to Lil, listening too, while they chewed their jam sandwiches out of a newspaper soaked with large red blobs. . . .

"Mother," said Kezia, "can't I ask the Kelveys just once?"

"Certainly not, Kezia."

"But why not?"

"Run away, Kezia; you know quite well why not."

At last everybody had seen it except them. On that day the subject rather flagged. It was the dinner hour. The children stood together under the pine trees, and suddenly, as they looked at the Kelveys eating out of their paper, always by themselves, always listening, they wanted to be horrid to them. Emmie Cole started the whisper.

"Lil Kelvey's going to be a servant when she grows up."

"O-oh, how awful!" said Isabel Burnell, and she made eyes at Emmie.

Emmie swallowed in a very meaning way and nodded to Isabel as she'd seen her mother do on those occasions.

"It's true—it's true—it's true," she said.

Then Lena Logan's little eyes snapped. "Shall I ask her?" she whispered.

"Bet you don't," said Jessie May.

"Pooh, I'm not frightened," said Lena. Suddenly she gave a little squeal and danced in front of the other girls. "Watch! Watch me! Watch me now!" said Lena. And sliding, gliding, dragging one foot, giggling behind her hand, Lena went over to the Kelveys.

Lil looked up from her dinner. She wrapped the rest quickly away. Our Else stopped chewing. What was coming now?

"Is it true you're going to be a servant

when you grow up, Lil Kelvey?" shrilled Lena.

Dead silence. But instead of answering, Lil only gave her silly, shamefaced smile. She didn't seem to mind the question at all. What a sell for Lena! The girls began to titter.

Lena couldn't stand that. She put her hands on her hips; she shot forward. "Yah, yer father's in prison!" she hissed, spitefully.

This was such a marvellous thing to have said that the little girls rushed away in a body, deeply, deeply excited, wild with joy. Some one found a long rope, and they began skipping. And never did they skip so high, run in and out so fast or do such daring things as on that morning.

In the afternoon Pat called for the Burnell children with the buggy and they drove home. There were visitors. Isabel and Lottie, who liked visitors, went upstairs to change their pinafores. But Kezia thieved out at the back. Nobody was about; she began to swing on the big white gates of the courtyard. Presently, looking along the road, she saw two little dots. They grew bigger, they were coming towards her. Now she could see that one was in front and one close behind. Now she could see that they were the Kelveys. Kezia stopped swinging. She slipped off the gate as if she was going to run away. Then she hesitated. The Kelveys came nearer, and beside them walked their shadows, very long, stretching right across the road with their heads in the buttercups. Kezia climbed back on the gate; she had made up her mind; she swung out.

"Hullo," she said to the passing Kelveys.

They were so astounded that they stopped. Lil gave her silly smile. Our Else stared.

"You can come and see our doll's house if you want to," said Kezia, and she dragged one toe on the ground. But at that Lil turned red and shook her head quickly.

"Why not?" asked Kezia.

Lil gasped, then she said, "Your ma told our ma you wasn't to speak to us."

"Oh, well," said Kezia. She didn't know what to reply. "It doesn't matter. You can come and see our doll's house all the same. Come on. Nobody's looking."

But Lil shook her head still harder.

"Don't you want to?" asked Kezia.

Suddenly there was a twitch, a tug at Lil's skirt. She turned round. Our Else was looking at her with big, imploring eyes; she was frowning; she wanted to go. For a moment Lil looked at our Else very doubtfully. But then our Else twitched her skirt again. She started forward. Kezia led the way. Like two little stray cats they followed across the courtyard to where the doll's house stood.

"There it is," said Kezia.

There was a pause. Lil breathed loudly, almost snorted; our Else was still as a stone.

"I'll open it for you," said Kezia kindly. She undid the hook and they looked inside.

"There's the drawing-room and the dining-room, and that's the—"

"Kezia!"

Oh, what a start they gave!

"Kezia!"

It was Aunt Beryl's voice. They turned round. At the back door stood Aunt Beryl, staring as if she couldn't believe what she saw.

"How dare you ask the little Kelveys into the courtyard?" said her cold, furious voice. "You know as well as I do, you're not allowed to talk to them. Run away, children, run away at once. And don't come back again," said Aunt Beryl. And she stepped into the yard and shooed them out as if they were chickens.

"Off you go immediately!" she called, cold and proud.

They did not need telling twice. Burning with shame, shrinking together, Lil huddling along like her mother, our Else dazed, somehow they crossed the big courtyard and squeezed through the white gate.

"Wicked, disobedient little girl!" said Aunt Beryl bitterly to Kezia, and she slammed the doll's house to.

The afternoon had been awful. A letter had come from Willie Brent, a terrifying, threatening letter, saying if she did not meet him that evening in Pulman's Bush, he'd come to the front door and ask the reason why! But now that she had frightened those little rats of Kelveys and given Kezia a good scolding, her heart felt lighter. That ghastly pressure was gone. She went back to the house humming.

When the Kelveys were well out of sight of Burnells', they sat down to rest on a big red drain-pipe by the side of the road. Lil's cheeks were still burning; she took off the hat with the quill and held it on her knee. Dreamily they looked over the hay paddocks, past the creek, to the group of wattles where Logan's cows stood waiting to be milked. What were their thoughts?

Presently our Else nudged up close to her sister. But now she had forgotten the cross lady. She put out a finger and stroked her sister's quill; she smiled her rare smile.

"I seen the little lamp," she said, softly.

Then both were silent once more.

F. SCOTT FITZGERALD • 1896-1940

Babylon Revisited

"AND where's Mr. Campbell?" Charlie asked.
"Gone to Switzerland. Mr. Campbell's a pretty sick man, Mr. Wales."
"I'm sorry to hear that. And George Hardt?" Charlie inquired.
"Back in America, gone to work."
"And where is the Snow Bird?"
"He was in here last week. Anyway, his friend, Mr. Schaeffer, is in Paris."

Two familiar names from the long list of a year and a half ago. Charlie scribbled an address in his notebook and tore out the page.

"If you see Mr. Schaeffer, give him this," he said. "It's my brother-in-law's address. I haven't settled on a hotel yet."

He was not really disappointed to find Paris was so empty. But the stillness in the Ritz bar was strange and portentous. It was not an American bar any more—he felt polite in it, and not as if he owned it. It had gone back into France. He felt the stillness from the moment he got out of the taxi and saw the doorman, usually in a frenzy of activity at this hour, gossiping with a *chasseur* by the servants' entrance.

Passing through the corridor, he heard only a single, bored voice in the once-clamorous women's room. When he turned into the bar he travelled the twenty feet of green carpet with his eyes fixed straight ahead by old habit; and then, with his foot firmly on the rail, he turned and surveyed the room, encountering only a single pair of eyes that fluttered up from a newspaper in the corner. Charlie asked for the head barman, Paul, who in the latter days of the bull market had come to work in his own custom-built car—disembarking, however, with due nicety at the nearest corner. But Paul was at his country house today and Alix giving him information.

"No, no more," Charlie said. "I'm going slow these days."

Alix congratulated him: "You were going pretty strong a couple of years ago."

"I'll stick to it all right," Charlie assured him. "I've stuck to it for over a year and a half now."

"How do you find conditions in America?"

"I haven't been to America for months. I'm in business in Prague, representing a couple of concerns there. They don't know about me down there."

Alix smiled.

"Remember the night of George Hardt's bachelor dinner here?" said Charlie. "By the way, what's become of Claude Fessenden?"

Alix lowered his voice confidentially: "He's in Paris, but he doesn't come here any more. Paul doesn't allow it. He ran up a bill of thirty thousand francs, charging all his drinks and his lunches, and usually his dinner, for more than a year. And when Paul finally told him he had to pay, he gave him a bad check."

Alix shook his head sadly.

"I don't understand it, such a dandy fellow. Now he's all bloated up—" He made a plump apple of his hands.

Charlie watched a group of strident queens installing themselves in a corner.

"Nothing affects them," he thought. "Stocks rise and fall, people loaf or work, but they go on forever." The place oppressed him. He called for the dice and shook with Alix for the drink.

"Here for long, Mr. Wales?"

"I'm here for four or five days to see my little girl."

"Oh-h! You have a little girl?"

Outside, the fire-red, gas-blue, ghost-green signs shone smokily through the tranquil rain. It was late afternoon and the streets were in movement; the *bistros* gleamed. At the corner of the Boulevard des Capucines he took a taxi. The Place de la Concorde moved by in pink majesty; they crossed the logical Seine, and Charlie felt the sudden provincial quality of the Left Bank.

Charlie directed his taxi to the Avenue de l'Opéra, which was out of his way. But he wanted to see the blue hour spread over the magnificent façade, and imagine that the cab horns, playing endlessly the first few bars of *La Pluie que Lent,* were the trumpets of the Second Empire. They were closing the iron grill in front of Brentano's Bookstore, and people were already at dinner behind the trim little bourgeois hedge of Duval's. He had never eaten at a really cheap restaurant in Paris. Five-course dinner, four francs fifty, eighteen cents, wine included. For some odd reason he wished that he had.

As they rolled on to the Left Bank and he felt its sudden provincialism, he thought, "I spoiled this city for myself. I didn't realize it, but the days came along one after another, and then two years were gone, and everything was gone, and I was gone."

He was thirty-five, and good to look at. The Irish mobility of his face was sobered by a deep wrinkle between his eyes. As he rang his brother-in-law's bell in the Rue Palatine, the wrinkle deepened till it pulled down his brows; he felt a cramping sensation in his belly. From behind the maid who opened the door darted a lovely little girl of nine, who shrieked "Daddy!" and flew up, struggling like a fish, into his arms. She pulled his head around by one ear and set her cheek against his.

"My old pie," he said.

"Oh, daddy, daddy, daddy, daddy, dads, dads, dads!"

She drew him into the salon, where the family waited, a boy and girl his daughter's age, his sister-in-law and her husband. He greeted Marion with his voice pitched carefully to avoid either feigned enthusiasm or dislike, but her response was more frankly tepid, though she minimized her expression of unalterable distrust by directing her regard toward his child. The two men clasped hands in a friendly way and Lincoln Peters rested his for a moment on Charlie's shoulder.

The room was warm and comfortably American. The three children moved intimately about, playing through the yellow oblongs that led to other rooms; the cheer of six o'clock spoke in the eager smacks of the fire and the sounds of French activity in the kitchen. But Charlie did not relax; his heart sat up rigidly in his body and he drew confidence from his daughter, who from time to time came close to him, holding in her arms the doll he had brought.

"Really extremely well," he declared in answer to Lincoln's question. "There's a lot of business there that isn't moving at all, but we're doing even better than ever. In fact, damn well. I'm bringing my sister over from America next month to keep house for me. My income last year was bigger than it was when I had money. You see, the Czechs———"

His boasting was for a specific purpose; but after a moment, seeing a faint restiveness in Lincoln's eye, he changed the subject:

"Those are fine children of yours, well brought up, good manners."

"We think Honoria's a great little girl too."

Marion Peters came back from the kitchen. She was a tall woman with worried eyes, who had once possessed a fresh American loveliness. Charlie had never been sensitive to it and was always surprised when people spoke of how pretty she had been. From the first there had been an instinctive antipathy between them.

"Well, how do you find Honoria?" she asked.

"Wonderful. I was astonished how much she's grown in ten months. All the children are looking well."

"We haven't had a doctor for a year. How do you like being back in Paris?"

"It seems very funny to see so few Americans around."

"I'm delighted," Marion said vehemently. "Now at least you can go into a store without their assuming you're a millionaire. We've suffered like everybody, but on the whole it's a good deal pleasanter."

"But it was nice while it lasted," said Charlie. "We were a sort of royalty, almost infallible, with a sort of magic around us. In the bar this afternoon"—he stumbled, seeing his mistake—"there wasn't a man I knew."

She looked at him keenly. "I should think you'd have had enough of bars."

"I only stayed a minute. I take one drink every afternoon, and no more."

"Don't you want a cocktail before dinner?" Lincoln asked.

"I take only one drink every afternoon, and I've had that."

"I hope you keep to it," said Marion.

Her dislike was evident in the coldness with which she spoke, but Charlie only smiled; he had larger plans. Her very aggressiveness gave him an advantage, and he knew enough to wait. He wanted them to initiate the discussion of what they knew had brought him to Paris.

At dinner he couldn't decide whether Honoria was most like him or her mother. Fortunate if she didn't combine the traits of both that had brought them to disaster. A great wave of protectiveness went over him. He thought he knew what to do for her. He believed in character; he wanted to jump back a whole generation and trust in character again as the eternally valuable element. Everything else wore out.

He left soon after dinner, but not to go home. He was curious to see Paris by night with clearer and more judicious eyes than those of other days. He bought a *strapontin* for the Casino and watched Josephine Baker go through her chocolate arabesques.

After an hour he left and strolled toward Montmartre, up the Rue Pigalle into the Place Blanche. The rain had stopped and there were a few people in evening clothes disembarking from taxis in front of cabarets, and *cocottes* prowling singly or in pairs, and many Negroes. He passed a lighted door from which issued music, and stopped with the sense of familiarity; it was Bricktop's, where he had parted with so many hours and so much money. A few doors farther on he found another ancient rendezvous and incautiously put his head inside. Immediately an eager orchestra burst into sound, a pair of professional dancers leaped to their feet and a maître d'hôtel swooped toward him, crying, "Crowd just arriving, sir!" But he withdrew quickly.

"You have to be damn drunk," he thought.

Zelli's was closed, the bleak and sinister cheap hotels surrounding it were dark; up in the Rue Blanche there was more light and a local, colloquial French crowd. The Poet's Cave had disappeared, but the two great mouths of the Café of Heaven and the Café of Hell still yawned—even devoured, as he watched, the meager contents of a tourist bus—a German, a Japanese, and an American couple who glanced at him with frightened eyes.

So much for the effort and ingenuity of Montmartre. All the catering to vice and waste was on an utterly childish scale, and he suddenly realized the meaning of the word "dissipate"—to dissipate into thin air; to make nothing out of something. In the little hours of the night every move from place to place was an enormous human jump, an increase of paying for the privilege of slower and slower motion.

He remembered thousand-franc notes given to an orchestra for playing a single number, hundred-franc notes tossed to a doorman for calling a cab.

But it hadn't been given for nothing.

It had been given, even the most wildly squandered sum, as an offering to destiny that he might not remember the things most worth remembering, the things that now he would always remember—his child taken from his control, his wife escaped to a grave in Vermont.

In the glare of a *brasserie* a woman spoke to him. He bought her some eggs and coffee, and then, eluding her encouraging stare, gave her a twenty-franc note and took a taxi to his hotel.

II

He woke up on a fine fall day—football weather. The depression of yesterday was gone and he liked the people on the streets. At noon he sat opposite Honoria at Le Grand Vatel, the only restaurant he could think of not reminiscent of champagne dinners and long luncheons that began at two and ended in a blurred and vague twilight.

"Now, how about vegetables? Oughtn't you to have some vegetables?"

"Well, yes."

"Here's *épinards* and *chou-fleur* and carrots and *haricots*."[1]

"I'd like *chou-fleur*."

"Wouldn't you like to have two vegetables?"

"I usually have only one at lunch."

The waiter was pretending to be inordinately fond of children. *"Qu'elle est mignonne la petite? Elle parle exactement comme une française."*[2]

"How about dessert? Shall we wait and see?"

[1] spinach, cauliflower, green beans
[2] "How sweet the little one is! She talks just like a French girl."

The waiter disappeared. Honoria looked at her father expectantly.

"What are we going to do?"

"First, we're going to that toy store in the Rue Saint-Honoré and buy you anything you like. And then we're going to the vaudeville at the Empire."

She hesitated. "I like it about the vaudeville, but not the toy store."

"Why not?"

"Well, you brought me this doll." She had it with her. "And I've got lots of things. And we're not rich any more, are we?"

"We never were. But today you are to have anything you want."

"All right," she agreed resignedly.

When there had been her mother and a French nurse he had been inclined to be strict; now he extended himself, reached out for a new tolerance; he must be both parents to her and not shut any of her out of communication.

"I want to get to know you," he said gravely. "First let me introduce myself. My name is Charles J. Wales, of Prague."

"Oh, daddy!" her voice cracked with laughter.

"And who are you, please?" he persisted, and she accepted a rôle immediately: "Honoria Wales, Rue Palatine, Paris."

"Married or single?"

"No, not married. Single."

He indicated the doll. "But I see you have a child, madame."

Unwilling to disinherit it, she took it to her heart and thought quickly: "Yes, I've been married, but I'm not married now. My husband is dead."

He went on quickly, "And the child's name?"

"Simone. That's after my best friend at school."

"I'm very pleased that you're doing so well at school."

"I'm third this month," she boasted. "Elsie"—that was her cousin—"is only about eighteenth, and Richard is about at the bottom."

"You like Richard and Elsie, don't you?"

"Oh, yes. I like them all right."

Cautiously and casually he asked: "And Aunt Marion and Uncle Lincoln—which do you like best?"

"Oh, Uncle Lincoln, I guess."

He was increasingly aware of her presence. As they came in, a murmur of ". . . adorable" followed them, and now the people at the next table bent all their silences upon her, staring as if she were something no more conscious than a flower.

"Why don't I live with you?" she asked suddenly. "Because mamma's dead?"

"You must stay here and learn more French. It would have been hard for daddy to take care of you so well."

"I don't really need much taking care of any more. I do everything for myself."

Going out of the restaurant, a man and a woman unexpectedly hailed him.

"Well, the old Wales!"

"Hello there, Lorraine . . . Dunc."

Sudden ghosts out of the past: Duncan Schaeffer, a friend from college. Lorraine Quarles, a lovely, pale blonde of thirty; one of a crowd who had helped them make months into days in the lavish times of three years ago.

"My husband couldn't come this year," she said, in answer to his question. "We're poor as hell. So he gave me two hundred a month, and told me I could do my worst on that. . . . This your little girl?"

"What about coming back and sitting down?" Duncan asked.

"Can't do it." He was glad for an excuse. As always, he felt Lorraine's passionate, provocative attraction, but his own rhythm was different now.

"Well, how about dinner?" she asked.

"I'm not free. Give me your address and let me call you."

"Charlie, I believe you're sober," she said judicially. "I honestly believe he's sober, Dunc. Pinch him and see if he's sober."

Charlie indicated Honoria with his head. They both laughed.

"What's your address?" said Duncan skeptically.

He hesitated, unwilling to give the name of his hotel.

"I'm not settled yet. I'd better call you. We're going to see the vaudeville at the Empire."

"There! That's what I want to do," Lorraine said. "I want to see some clowns and acrobats and jugglers. That's just what we'll do, Dunc."

"We've got to do an errand first," said Charlie. "Perhaps we'll see you there."

"All right, you snob. . . . Good-by, beautiful little girl."

"Good-by."

Honoria bobbed politely.

Somehow, an unwelcome encounter. They liked him because he was functioning, because he was serious; they wanted to see him, because he was stronger than they were now, because they wanted to draw a certain sustenance from his strength.

At the Empire, Honoria proudly refused to sit upon her father's folded coat. She was already an individual with a code of her own, and Charlie was more and more absorbed by the desire of putting a little of himself into her before she crystallized utterly. It was hopeless to try to know her in so short a time.

Between the acts they came upon Duncan and Lorraine in the lobby where the band was playing.

"Have a drink?"

"All right, but not up at the bar. We'll take a table."

"The perfect father."

Listening abstractedly to Lorraine, Charlie watched Honoria's eyes leave their table, and he followed them wistfully about the room, wondering what they saw. He met her glance and she smiled.

"I liked that lemonade," she said.

What had she said? What had he expected? Going home in a taxi afterward, he pulled her over until her head rested against his chest.

"Darling, do you ever think about your mother?"

"Yes, sometimes," she answered vaguely.

"I don't want you to forget her. Have you got a picture of her?"

"Yes, I think so. Anyhow, Aunt Marion has. Why don't you want me to forget her?"

"She loved you very much."

"I loved her too."

They were silent for a moment.

"Daddy, I want to come and live with you," she said suddenly.

His heart leaped; he had wanted it to come like this.

"Aren't you perfectly happy?"

"Yes, but I love you better than anybody. And you love me better than anybody, don't you, now that mummy's dead?"

"Of course I do. But you won't always like me best, honey. You'll grow up and meet somebody your own age and go marry him and forget you ever had a daddy."

"Yes, that's true," she agreed tranquilly.

He didn't go in. He was coming back at nine o'clock and he wanted to keep himself fresh and new for the thing he must say then.

"When you're safe inside, just show yourself in that window."

"All right. Good-by, dads, dads, dads, dads."

He waited in the dark street until she appeared, all warm and glowing, in the window above and kissed her fingers out into the night.

III

They were waiting. Marion sat behind the coffee service in a dignified black dinner dress that just faintly suggested mourning. Lincoln was walking up and down with the animation of one who had already been talking. They were as anxious as he was to get into the question. He opened it almost immediately:

"I suppose you know what I want to see you about—why I really came to Paris."

Marion played with the black stars on her necklace and frowned.

"I'm awfully anxious to have a home," he continued. "And I'm awfully anxious to have Honoria in it. I appreciate your taking in Honoria for her mother's sake, but things have changed now"—he hesitated and then continued more forcibly—"changed radically with me, and I want to ask you to reconsider the matter. It would be silly for me to deny that about three years ago I was acting badly——"

Marion looked up at him with hard eyes.

"——But all that's over. As I told you, I haven't had more than a drink a day for over a year, and I take that drink deliberately, so that the idea of alcohol won't get too big in my imagination. You see the idea?"

"No," said Marion succinctly.

"It's a sort of stunt I set myself. It keeps the matter in proportion."

"I get you," said Lincoln. "You don't want to admit it's got any attraction for you."

"Something like that. Sometimes I forget and don't take it. But I try to take it. Anyhow, I couldn't afford to drink in my position. The people I represent are more than satisfied with what I've done, and I'm bringing my sister over from Burlington to keep house for me, and I want awfully to have Honoria too. You know that even when her mother and I weren't getting along well we never let anything that happened touch Honoria. I know she's fond of me and I know I'm able to take care of her—well, there you are. How do you feel about it?"

He knew that now he would have to take a beating. It would last an hour or two hours, and it would be difficult, but if he modulated his inevitable resentment to the chastened attitude of the reformed sinner, he might win his point in the end.

Keep your temper, he told himself. You don't want to be justified. You want Honoria.

Lincoln spoke first: "We've been talking it over ever since we got your letter last month. We're happy to have Honoria here. She's a dear little thing, and we're glad to be able to help her, but of course that isn't the question——"

Marion interrupted suddenly. "How long are you going to stay sober, Charlie?" she asked.

"Permanently, I hope."

"How can anybody count on that?"

"You know I never did drink heavily until I gave up business and came over here with nothing to do. Then Helen and I began to run around with——"

"Please leave Helen out of it. I can't bear to hear you talk about her like that."

He stared at her grimly; he had never been certain how fond of each other the sisters were in life.

"My drinking only lasted about a year and a half—from the time we came over until I—collapsed."

"It was time enough."

"It was time enough," he agreed.

"My duty is entirely to Helen," she said. "I try to think what she would have wanted me to do. Frankly, from the night you did that terrible thing you haven't really existed for me. I can't help that. She was my sister."

"Yes."

"When she was dying she asked me to look out for Honoria. If you hadn't been in a sanitarium then, it might have helped matters."

He had no answer.

"I'll never in my life be able to forget the morning when Helen knocked at my door, soaked to the skin and shivering, and said you'd locked her out."

Charlie gripped the sides of the chair. This was more difficult than he expected: he wanted to launch out into a long expostulation and explanation, but he only said: "The night I locked her out—" and she interrupted, "I don't feel up to going over that again."

After a moment's silence Lincoln said: "We're getting off the subject. You want Marion to set aside her legal guardianship and give you Honoria. I think the main point for her is whether she has confidence in you or not."

"I don't blame Marion," Charlie said slowly, "but I think she can have entire confidence in me. I had a good record up to three years ago. Of course, it's within human possibilities I may go wrong again. But if we wait much longer I'll lose Honoria's childhood and my chance for a home." He shook his head. "I'll simply lose her, don't you see?"

"Yes, I see," said Lincoln.

"Why didn't you think of all this before?" Marion asked.

"I suppose I did, from time to time, but Helen and I were getting along badly. When I consented to the guardianship, I was flat on my back in a sanitarium, and the market had cleaned me out. I knew I'd acted badly, and I thought if it would bring any peace to Helen, I'd agree to anything. But now it's different. I'm functioning, I'm behaving damn well, so far as——"

"Please don't swear at me," Marion said.

He looked at her, startled. With each remark the force of her dislike became more and more apparent. She had built up all her fear of life into one wall and faced it toward him. This trivial reproof was possibly the result of some trouble with the cook several hours before. Charlie became increasingly alarmed at leaving Honoria in this atmosphere of hostility against himself; sooner or later it would come out, in a word here, a shake of the head there, and some of that distrust would be irrevocably implanted in Honoria. But he pulled his temper down out of his face and shut it up inside him; he had won a point, for Lincoln realized the absurdity of Marion's remark, and asked her lightly since when she had objected to the word "damn."

"Another thing," Charlie said: "I'm able to give her certain advantages now. I'm going to take a French governess to Prague with me. I've got a lease on a new apartment——"

He stopped, realizing that he was blundering. They couldn't be expected to accept with equanimity the fact that his income was again twice as large as their own.

"I suppose you can give her more luxuries than we can," said Marion. "When you were throwing away money we were living along watching every ten francs. . . . I suppose you'll start doing it again."

"Oh, no," he said. "I've learned. I worked hard for ten years, you know—until I got lucky in the market, like so many people. Terribly lucky. It didn't seem any use working any more, so I quit. It won't happen again."

There was a long silence. All of them felt their nerves straining, and for the first time in a year Charlie wanted a drink. He was sure now that Lincoln Peters wanted him to have his child.

Marion shuddered suddenly; part of her saw that Charlie's feet were planted on the earth now, and her own maternal feeling recognized the naturalness of his desire; but she had lived for a long time with a prejudice—a prejudice founded on a curious disbelief in her sister's happiness, which, in the shock of one terrible night, had turned to hatred for him. It had all happened at a point in her life where the discouragement of ill health and adverse circumstances made it necessary for her to believe in tangible villainy and a tangible villain.

"I can't help what I think!" she cried out suddenly. "How much you were responsible for Helen's death, I don't know. It's something you'll have to square with your own conscience."

An electric current of agony surged through him; for a moment he was almost on his feet, an unuttered sound echoing in his throat. He hung on to himself for a moment, another moment.

"Hold on there," said Lincoln uncomfortably. "I never thought you were responsible for that."

"Helen died of heart trouble," Charlie said dully.

"Yes, heart trouble." Marion spoke as if the phrase had another meaning for her.

Then, in the flatness that followed her outburst, she saw him plainly and she knew he had somehow arrived at control over the situation. Glancing at her husband, she found no help from him, and as abruptly as if it were a matter of no importance, she threw up the sponge.

"Do what you like!" she cried, springing up from her chair. "She's your child. I'm not the person to stand in your way. I think if it were my child I'd rather see her—" She managed to check herself. "You two decide it. I can't stand this. I'm sick. I'm going to bed."

She hurried from the room; after a moment Lincoln said:

"This has been a hard day for her. You know how strongly she feels——" His voice was almost apologetic: "When a woman gets an idea in her head."

"Of course."

"It's going to be all right. I think she sees now that you—can provide for the child, and so we can't very well stand in your way or Honoria's way."

"Thank you, Lincoln."

"I'd better go along and see how she is."

"I'm going."

He was still trembling when he reached the street, but a walk down the Rue Bonaparte to the quais set him up, and as he crossed the Seine, fresh and new by the quai lamps, he felt exultant. But back in his room he couldn't sleep. The image of Helen haunted him. Helen whom he had loved so until they had senselessly begun to abuse each other's love, tear it into shreds. On that terrible

February night that Marion remembered so vividly, a slow quarrel had gone on for hours. There was a scene at the Florida, and then he attempted to take her home, and then she kissed young Webb at a table; after that there was what she had hysterically said. When he arrived home alone he turned the key in the lock in wild anger. How could he know she would arrive an hour later alone, that there would be a snowstorm in which she wandered about in slippers, too confused to find a taxi? Then the aftermath, her escaping pneumonia by a miracle, and all the attendant horror. They were "reconciled," but that was the beginning of the end, and Marion, who had seen with her own eyes and who imagined it to be one of many scenes from her sister's martyrdom, never forgot.

Going over it again brought Helen nearer, and in the white, soft light that steals upon half sleep near morning he found himself talking to her again. She said that he was perfectly right about Honoria and that she wanted Honoria to be with him. She said she was glad he was being good and doing better. She said a lot of other things—very friendly things—but she was in a swing in a white dress, and swinging faster and faster all the time, so that at the end he could not hear clearly all that she said.

IV

He woke up feeling happy. The door of the world was open again. He made plans, vistas, futures for Honoria and himself, but suddenly he grew sad, remembering all the plans he and Helen had made. She had not planned to die. The present was the thing—work to do, and some one to love. But not to love too much, for he knew the injury that a father can do to a daughter or a mother to a son by attaching them too closely; afterward, out in the world, the child would seek in the marriage partner the same blind tenderness and, failing probably to find it, turn against love and life.

It was another bright, crisp day. He called Lincoln Peters at the bank where he worked and asked if he could count on taking Honoria when he left for Prague. Lincoln agreed that there was no reason for delay. One thing—the legal guardianship. Marion wanted to retain that a while longer. She was upset by the whole matter, and it would oil things if she felt that the situation was still in her control for another year. Charlie agreed, wanting only the tangible, visible child.

Then the question of a governess. Charlie sat in a gloomy agency and talked to a cross Bernaise and to a buxom Breton peasant, neither of whom he could have endured. There were others whom he would see tomorrow.

He lunched with Lincoln Peters at Griffons, trying to keep down his exultation.

"There's nothing quite like your own child," Lincoln said. "But you understand how Marion feels too."

"She's forgotten how hard I worked for seven years there," Charlie said. "She just remembers one night."

"There's another thing," Lincoln hesitated. "While you and Helen were tearing around Europe throwing money away, we were just getting along. I didn't touch any of the prosperity because I never got ahead enough to carry anything but my insurance. I think Marion felt there was some kind of injustice in it—you not even working toward the end, and getting richer and richer."

"It went just as quick as it came," said Charlie.

"Yes, a lot of it stayed in the hands of *chasseurs* and saxophone players and maîtres d'hôtel—well, the big party's over now. I just said that to explain Marion's feeling about those crazy years. If you drop in about six o'clock tonight before Marion's too tired, we'll settle the details on the spot."

Back at his hotel, Charlie found a *pneumatique*[3] that had been redirected from the Ritz bar where Charlie had left his address for the purpose of finding a certain man.

Dear Charlie: You were so strange when we saw you the other day that I wondered if I did something to offend you. If so, I'm not conscious of it. In fact, I have thought about you too much for the last year, and it's always been in the back of my mind that I might see you if I came over here. We *did* have such good times that crazy spring, like the night you and I stole the butcher's tricycle, and the time we tried to call on the president and you had the old derby rim and the wire cane. Everybody seems so old lately, but I don't feel old a bit. Couldn't we get together some time today for old time's sake? I've got a vile hang-over for the moment, but will be feeling better this afternoon and will look for you about five in the sweet-shop at the Ritz.

Always devotedly,
Lorraine.

His first feeling was one of awe that he had actually, in his mature years, stolen a tricycle and pedalled Lorraine all over the Étoile between the small hours and dawn. In retrospect it was a nightmare. Locking out Helen didn't fit in with any other act of his life, but the tricycle incident did—it was one of many. How many weeks or months of dissipation to arrive at that condition of utter irresponsibility?

He tried to picture how Lorraine had appeared to him then—very attractive; Helen was unhappy about it, though she said nothing. Yesterday, in the restaurant, Lorraine had seemed trite, blurred, worn away. He emphatically did not want to see her, and he was glad Alix had not given away his hotel address. It was a relief to think, instead, of Honoria, to think of Sundays spent with her and of saying good morning to her and of knowing she was there in his house at night, drawing her breath in the darkness.

At five he took a taxi and bought presents for all the Peters—a piquant cloth doll, a box of Roman soldiers, flowers for Marion, big linen handkerchiefs for Lincoln.

He saw, when he arrived in the apartment, that Marion had accepted the inevitable. She greeted him now as though he were a recalcitrant member of the family, rather than a menacing outsider. Honoria had been told she was going; Charlie was glad to see that her tact made her conceal her excessive happiness. Only on his lap did she whisper her delight and the question "When?" before she slipped away with the other children.

He and Marion were alone for a minute in the room, and on an impulse he spoke out boldly:

"Family quarrels are bitter things. They don't go according to any rules. They're not like aches or wounds; they're more like splits in the skin that won't heal because there's not enough material. I wish you and I could be on better terms."

"Some things are hard to forget," she answered. "It's a question of confidence." There was no answer to this and presently she asked, "When do you propose to take her?"

"As soon as I can get a governess. I hoped the day after tomorrow."

"That's impossible. I've got to get her things in shape. Not before Saturday."

He yielded. Coming back into the room, Lincoln offered him a drink.

"I'll take my daily whisky," he said.

It was warm here, it was a home, people together by a fire. The children felt very safe and important; the mother and father were serious, watchful. They had things to do for the children more important than his visit here. A spoonful of medicine was, after all, more important than the strained relations between Marion and himself. They were not dull people, but they were very much in

---

[3] letter sent across town through a pneumatic tube

the grip of life and circumstances. He wondered if he couldn't do something to get Lincoln out of his rut at the bank.

A long peal at the door-bell; the *bonne à tout faire*[4] passed through and went down the corridor. The door opened upon another long ring, and then voices, and the three in the salon looked up expectantly; Richard moved to bring the corridor within his range of vision, and Marion rose. Then the maid came back along the corridor, closely followed by the voices, which developed under the light into Duncan Schaeffer and Lorraine Quarles.

They were gay, they were hilarious, they were roaring with laughter. For a moment Charlie was astounded; unable to understand how they had ferreted out the Peters' address.

"Ah-h-h!" Duncan wagged his finger roguishly at Charlie. "Ah-h-h!"

They both slid down another cascade of laughter. Anxious and at a loss, Charlie shook hands with them quickly and presented them to Lincoln and Marion. Marion nodded, scarcely speaking. She had drawn back a step toward the fire; her little girl stood beside her, and Marion put an arm about her shoulder.

With growing annoyance at the intrusion, Charlie waited for them to explain themselves. After some concentration Duncan said:

"We came to invite you out to dinner. Lorraine and I insist that all this shishi, cagy business 'bout your address got to stop."

Charlie came closer to them, as if to force them backward down the corridor.

"Sorry, but I can't. Tell me where you'll be and I'll phone you in half an hour."

This made no impression. Lorraine sat down suddenly on the side of a chair, and focusing her eyes on Richard, cried,

"Oh, what a nice little boy! Come here, little boy." Richard glanced at his mother, but did not move. With a perceptible shrug of her shoulders, Lorraine turned back to Charlie:

"Come and dine. Sure your cousins won' mine. See you so sel'om. Or solemn."

"I can't," said Charlie sharply. "You two have dinner and I'll phone you."

Her voice became suddenly unpleasant. "All right, we'll go. But I remember once when you hammered on my door at four A.M. I was enough of a good sport to give you a drink. Come on, Dunc."

Still in slow motion, with blurred, angry faces, with uncertain feet, they retired along the corridor.

"Good night," Charlie said.

"Good night!" responded Lorraine emphatically.

When he went back into the salon Marion had not moved, only now her son was standing in the circle of her other arm. Lincoln was still swinging Honoria back and forth like a pendulum from side to side.

"What an outrage!" Charlie broke out. "What an absolute outrage!"

Neither of them answered. Charlie dropped into an armchair, picked up his drink, set it down again and said:

"People I haven't seen for two years having the colossal nerve——"

He broke off. Marion had made the sound "Oh!" in one swift, furious breath, turned her body from him with a jerk and left the room.

Lincoln set down Honoria carefully.

"You children go in and start your soup," he said, and when they obeyed, he said to Charlie:

"Marion's not well and she can't stand shocks. That kind of people make her really physically sick."

"I didn't tell them to come here. They wormed your name out of somebody. They deliberately—"

"Well, it's too bad. It doesn't help matters. Excuse me a minute."

---

[4] maid of all work

Left alone, Charlie sat tense in his chair. In the next room he could hear the children eating, talking in monosyllables, already oblivious to the scene between their elders. He heard a murmur of conversation from a farther room and then the ticking bell of a telephone receiver picked up, and in a panic he moved to the other side of the room and out of earshot.

In a minute Lincoln came back. "Look here, Charlie. I think we'd better call off dinner for tonight. Marion's in bad shape."

"Is she angry with me?"

"Sort of," he said, almost roughly. "She's not strong and——"

"You mean she's changed her mind about Honoria?"

"She's pretty bitter right now. I don't know. You phone me at the bank tomorrow."

"I wish you'd explain to her I never dreamed these people would come here. I'm just as sore as you are."

"I couldn't explain anything to her now."

Charlie got up. He took his coat and hat and started down the corridor. Then he opened the door of the dining room and said in a strange voice, "Good night, children."

Honoria rose and ran around the table to hug him.

"Good night, sweetheart," he said vaguely, and then trying to make his voice more tender, trying to conciliate something, "Good night, dear children."

v

Charlie went directly to the Ritz bar with the furious idea of finding Lorraine and Duncan, but they were not there, and he realized that in any case there was nothing he could do. He had not touched his drink at the Peters', and now he ordered a whisky-and-soda. Paul came over to say hello.

"It's a great change," he said sadly. "We do about half the business we did. So many fellows I hear about back in the States lost everything, maybe not in the first crash, but then in the second. Your friend George Hardt lost every cent, I hear. Are you back in the States?"

"No. I'm in business in Prague."

"I heard that you lost a lot in the crash."

"I did," and he added grimly, "but I lost everything I wanted in the boom."

"Selling short?"

"Something like that."

Again the memory of those days swept over him like a nightmare—the people they had met traveling; the people who couldn't add a row of figures or speak a coherent sentence. The little man Helen had consented to dance with at the ship's party, who had insulted her ten feet from the table; the women and girls carried screaming with drink or drugs out of public places . . . the men who locked their wives out in the snow, because the snow of '29 wasn't real snow. If you didn't want it to be snow, you just paid some money.

He went to the phone and called the Peters apartment; Lincoln answered.

"I called up because this thing is on my mind. Has Marion said anything definite?"

"Marion's sick," Lincoln answered shortly. "I know this thing isn't altogether your fault, but I can't have her go to pieces about it. I'm afraid we'll have to let it slide for six months; I can't take the chance of working her up to this state again."

"I see."

"I'm sorry, Charlie."

He went back to his table. His whisky glass was empty, but he shook his head when Alix looked at it questioningly. There wasn't much he could do now except send Honoria some things; he would send her a lot of things tomorrow. He thought rather angrily that this was just money—he had given so many people money. . . .

"No, no more," he said to another waiter. "What do I owe you?"

He would come back some day; they couldn't make him pay forever. But he wanted his child, and nothing was much good now, beside that fact. He wasn't young any more, with a lot of nice thoughts and dreams to have by himself. He was absolutely sure Helen wouldn't have wanted him to be so alone.

WILLIAM FAULKNER • 1897–1962

Barn Burning

THE store in which the Justice of the Peace's court was sitting smelled of cheese. The boy, crouched on his nail keg at the back of the crowded room, knew he smelled cheese, and more: from where he sat he could see the ranked shelves close-packed with the solid, squat, dynamic shapes of tin cans whose labels his stomach read, not from the lettering which meant nothing to his mind but from the scarlet devils and the silver curve of fish—this, the cheese which he knew he smelled and the hermetic meat which his intestines believed he smelled, came in intermittent gusts momentary and brief between the other constant one, the smell and sense just a little of fear because mostly of despair and grief, the old fierce pull of blood. He could not see the table where the Justice sat and before which his father and his father's enemy (*our enemy* he thought in that despair; *ourn! mine and hisn both! He's my father!*) stood, but he could hear them, the two of them that is, because his father had said no word yet:

"But what proof have you, Mr. Harris?"

"I told you. The hog got into my corn. I caught it up and sent it back to him. He had no fence that would hold it. I told him so, warned him. The next time I put the hog in my pen. When he came to get it I gave him enough wire to patch up his pen. The next time I put the hog up and kept it. I rode down to his house and saw the wire I gave him still rolled on to the spool in his yard. I told him he could have the hog when he paid me a dollar pound fee. That evening a nigger came with the dollar and got the hog. He was a strange nigger. He said, 'He say to tell you wood and hay kin burn.' I said, 'What?' 'That whut he say to tell you,' the nigger said. 'Wood and hay kin burn.' That night my barn burned. I got the stock out but I lost the barn."

"Where is the nigger? Have you got him?"

"He was a strange nigger, I tell you. I don't know what became of him."

"But that's not proof. Don't you see that's not proof?"

"Get that boy up here. He knows." For a moment the boy thought too that the man meant his older brother until Harris said, "Not him. The little one. The boy," and, crouching, small for his age, small and wiry like his father, in patched and faded jeans even too small for him, with straight, uncombed brown hair and eyes gray and wild as storm scud, he saw the men between himself and the table part and become a lane of grim faces, at the end of which he saw the Justice, a shabby, collarless, graying man in spectacles, beckoning him. He felt no floor under his bare feet; he seemed to walk beneath the palpable weight of the grim turning faces. His father, stiff in his black Sunday coat donned not for the trial but for the moving, did not even look at him. *He aims for me to lie,* he thought, again with that frantic grief and despair. *And I will have to do hit.*

"What's your name, boy?" the Justice said.

"Colonel Sartoris Snopes," the boy whispered.

"Hey?" the Justice said. "Talk louder. Colonel Sartoris? I reckon anybody named for Colonel Sartoris in this country can't help but tell the truth, can they?" The boy said nothing. *Enemy! Enemy!* he thought; for a moment he could not even see, could not see that the Justice's face was kindly nor discern that his voice was troubled when he spoke to the man named Harris: "Do you want me to question this boy?" But he could hear, and during those subsequent long seconds while there was absolutely no sound in the crowded little room save that of quiet and intent breathing it was as if he had swung outward at the end of a grape vine, over a ravine, and at the top of the swing had been caught in a prolonged instant of mesmerized gravity, weightless in time.

"No!" Harris said violently, explosively. "Damnation! Send him out of here!" Now time, the fluid world, rushed beneath him again, the voices coming to him again through the smell of cheese and sealed meat, the fear and despair and the old grief of blood:

"This case is closed. I can't find against you, Snopes, but I can give you advice. Leave this country and don't come back to it."

His father spoke for the first time, his voice cold and harsh, level, without emphasis: "I aim to. I don't figure to stay in a country among people who . . ." he said something unprintable and vile, addressed to no one.

"That'll do," the Justice said. "Take your wagon and get out of this country before dark. Case dismissed."

His father turned, and he followed the stiff black coat, the wiry figure walking a little stiffly from where a Confederate provost's man's musket ball had taken him in the heel on a stolen horse thirty years ago, followed the two backs now, since his older brother had appeared from somewhere in the crowd, no taller than the father but thicker, chewing tobacco steadily, between the two lines of grim-faced men and out of the store and across the worn gallery and down the sagging steps and among the dogs and half-grown boys in the mild May dust, where as he passed a voice hissed:

"Barn burner!"

Again he could not see, whirling; there was a face in a red haze, moonlike, bigger than the full moon, the owner of it half again his size, he leaping in the red haze toward the face, feeling no blow, feeling no shock when his head struck the earth, scrabbling up and leaping again, feeling no blow this time either and tasting no blood, scrabbling up to see the other boy in full flight and himself already leaping into pursuit as his father's hand jerked him back, the harsh, cold voice speaking above him: "Go get in the wagon."

It stood in a grove of locusts and mulberries across the road. His two hulking sisters in their Sunday dresses and his mother and her sister in calico and sunbonnets were already in it, sitting on and among the sorry residue of the dozen and more movings which even the boy could remember—the battered stove, the broken beds and chairs, the clock inlaid with mother-of-pearl, which would not run, stopped at some fourteen minutes past two o'clock of a dead and forgotten day and time, which had been his mother's dowry. She was crying, though when she saw him she drew her sleeve across her face and began to descend from the wagon. "Get back," the father said.

"He's hurt. I got to get some water and wash his . . ."

"Get back in the wagon," his father said. He got in too, over the tail-gate. His father mounted to the seat where the older brother already sat and struck the gaunt mules two savage blows with the peeled willow, but without heat. It was not even sadistic; it was exactly that same quality which in later years would cause his descendants to overrun the engine before putting a motor car into motion, striking and reining back in the same movement. The wagon went on, the store with its quiet crowd of grimly watching men dropped behind; a curve in the road hit it. *Forever* he thought. *Maybe he's done satisfied now, now that he has . . .* stopping himself, not to say it aloud even to himself. His mother's hand touched his shoulder.

"Does hit hurt?" she said.

"Naw," he said. "Hit don't hurt. Lemme be."

"Can't you wipe some of the blood off before hit dries?"

"I'll wash to-night," he said. "Lemme be, I tell you."

The wagon went on. He did not know where they were going. None of them ever did or ever asked, because it was always somewhere, always a house of sorts waiting for them a day or two days or even three days away. Likely his father had already arranged to make a crop on another farm before he . . . Again he had to stop himself. He (the father) always did. There was something about his wolflike independence and even courage when the advantage was at least neutral which impressed strangers, as if they got from his latent ravening ferocity not so much a sense of dependability as a feeling that his ferocious conviction in the rightness of his own actions would be of advantage to all whose interest lay with his.

That night they camped in a grove of oaks and beeches where a spring ran. The nights were still cool and they had a fire against it, of a rail lifted from a nearby fence and cut into lengths—a small fire, neat, niggard almost, a shrewd fire; such fires were his father's habit and custom always, even in freezing weather. Older, the boy might have remarked this and wondered why not a big one; why should not a man who had not only seen the waste and extravagance of war, but who had in his blood an inherent voracious prodigality with material not his own, have burned everything in sight? Then he might have gone a step farther and thought that that was the reason: that niggard blaze was the living fruit of nights passed during those four years in the woods hiding from all men, blue or gray, with his strings of horses (captured horses, he called them). And older still, he might have divined the true reason: that the element of fire spoke to some deep mainspring of his father's being, as the element of steel or of powder spoke to other men, as the one weapon for the preservation of integrity, else breath were not worth the breathing, and hence to be regarded with respect and used with discretion.

But he did not think this now and he had seen those same niggard blazes all his life. He merely ate his supper beside it and was already half asleep over his iron plate when his father called him, and once more he followed the stiff back, the stiff and ruthless limp, up the slope and on to the starlit road where, turning, he could see his father against the stars but without face or depth—a shape black, flat and bloodless as though cut from tin in the iron folds of the frockcoat which had not been made for him, the voice harsh like tin and without heat like tin:

"You were fixing to tell them. You would have told him." He didn't answer. His father struck him with the flat of his hand on the side of the head, hard but without heat, exactly as he had struck the two mules at the store, exactly as he would strike either of them with any stick in order to kill a horse fly, his voice still without heat or anger: "You're getting to be a man. You got to learn. You got to learn to stick to your own blood or you ain't going to have any blood to stick to you. Do you think either of them, any man there this morning, would? Don't you know all they wanted was a chance to get at me because they knew I had them beat? Eh?" Later, twenty years later, he was to tell himself, "If I had said they wanted only truth, justice, he would have hit me again." But now he said nothing. He was not crying. He just stood there. "Answer me," his father said.

"Yes," he whispered. His father turned.

"Get on to bed. We'll be there to-morrow."

To-morrow they were there. In the early afternoon the wagon stopped before a paintless two-room house identical almost with the dozen others it had stopped before even in the boy's ten years, and again, as on the other dozen occasions, his mother and aunt got down and began to unload the wagon, although his two sisters and his father and brother had not moved.

"Likely hit ain't fitten for hawgs," one of the sisters said.

"Nevertheless, fit it will and you'll hog it and like it," his father said. "Get down out of them chairs and help your Ma unload."

The two sisters got down, big, bovine, in a flutter of cheap ribbons; one of them drew from the jumbled wagon bed a battered lantern, the other a worn broom. His father handed the reins to the older son and began to climb stiffly over the wheel. "When they get unloaded, take the team to the barn and feed them." Then he said, and at first the boy thought he was still speaking to his brother: "Come with me."

"Me?" he said.

"Yes," his father said. "You."

"Abner," his mother said. His father paused and looked back—the harsh level stare beneath the shaggy, graying, irascible brows.

"I reckon I'll have a word with the man that aims to begin to-morrow owning me body and soul for the next eight months."

They went back up the road. A week ago—or before last night, that is—he would have asked where they were going, but not now. His father had struck him before last night but never before had he paused afterward to explain why; it was as if the blow and the following calm, outrageous voice still rang, repercussed, divulging nothing to him save the terrible handicap of being young, the light weight of his few years, just heavy enough to prevent his soaring free of the world as it seemed to be ordered but not heavy enough to keep him footed solid in it, to resist it and try to change the course of its events.

Presently he could see the grove of oaks and cedars and the other flowering trees and shrubs where the house would be, though not the house yet. They walked beside a fence massed with honeysuckle and Cherokee roses and came to a gate swinging open between two brick pillars, and now, beyond a sweep of drive, he saw the house for the first time and at that instant he forgot his father and the terror and despair both, and even when he remembered his father again (who had not stopped) the terror and despair did not return. Because, for all the twelve movings, they had sojourned until now in a poor country, a land of small farms and fields and houses, and he had never seen a house like this before. *Hit's big as a courthouse* he thought quietly, with a surge of peace and joy whose reason he could not have thought into words, being too young for that: *They are safe from him. People whose lives are a part of this peace and dignity are beyond his touch, be no more to them than a buzzing wasp: capable of stinging for a little moment but that's all, the spell of this peace and dignity rendering even the barns and stable and cribs which belong to it impervious to the puny flames he might contrive* . . . this, the peace and joy, ebbing for an instant as he looked again at the stiff black back, the stiff and implacable limp of the figure which was not dwarfed by the house, for the reason that it had never looked big anywhere and which now, against the serene columned backdrop, had more than ever the impervious quality of something cut ruthlessly from tin, depthless, as though, sidewise to the sun, it would cast no shadow. Watching him, the boy remarked the absolutely undeviating course which his father held and saw the stiff foot come squarely down in a pile of fresh droppings where a horse had stood in the drive and which his father could have avoided by a simple change of stride. But it ebbed only for a moment, though he could not have thought this into words either, walking on in the spell of the house, which he could even want but without envy, without sorrow, certainly never with that ravening and jealous rage which unknown to him walked in the ironlike black coat before him. *Maybe he will feel it too. Maybe it will even change him now from what maybe he couldn't help but be.*

They crossed the portico. Now he could hear his father's stiff foot as it came down on the boards with clocklike finality, a sound out of all proportion to the displacement of the body it bore and which was not dwarfed either by the white door before it, as though it had attained to a sort of vicious and ravening minimum not to be dwarfed by anything—the flat, wide, black hat, the formal coat of broadcloth which had once been black but which had now the friction-glazed greenish cast of the bodies of old house flies, the lifted sleeve which was too large, the lifted hand like a curled claw. The door opened so promptly that the boy knew the Negro must have been watching them all the time, an old man with neat grizzled hair, in a linen jacket, who stood barring the door with his body, saying, "Wipe yo foots, white man, fo you come in here. Major ain't home nohow."

"Get out of my way, nigger," his father said, without heat too, flinging the door back and the Negro also and entering, his hat still on his head. And now the boy saw the prints of the stiff foot on the doorjamb and saw them appear on the pale rug behind the machinelike deliberation of the foot which seemed to bear (or transmit) twice the weight which the body compassed. The Negro was shouting "Miss Lula! Miss Lula!" somewhere behind them, then the boy, deluged as though by a warm wave by a suave turn of carpeted stair and a pendant glitter of chandeliers and a mute gleam of gold frames, heard the swift feet and saw her too, a lady—perhaps he had never seen her like before either—in a gray, smooth gown with lace at the throat and an apron tied at the waist and the sleeves turned back, wiping cake or biscuit dough from her hands with a towel as she came up the hall, looking not at his father at all but at the tracks on the blond rug with an expression of incredulous amazement.

"I tried," the Negro cried. "I tole him to . . ."

"Will you please go away?" she said in a shaking voice. "Major de Spain is not at home. Will you please go away?"

His father had not spoken again. He did not speak again. He did not even look at her. He just stood stiff in the center of the rug, in his hat, the shaggy iron-gray brows twitching slightly above the pebble-colored eyes as he appeared to examine the house with brief deliberation. Then with the same deliberation he turned; the boy watched him pivot on the good leg and saw the stiff foot drag round the arc of the turning, leaving a final long and fading smear. His father never looked at it, he never once looked down at the rug. The Negro held the door. It closed behind them, upon the hysteric and indistinguishable woman-wail. His father stopped at the top of the steps and scraped his boot clean on the edge of it. At the gate he stopped again. He stood for a moment, planted stiffly on the stiff foot, looking back at the house. "Pretty and white, ain't it?" he said. "That's sweat. Nigger sweat. Maybe it ain't white enough yet to suit him. Maybe he wants to mix some white sweat with it."

Two hours later the boy was chopping wood behind the house within which his mother and aunt and the two sisters (the mother and aunt, not the two girls, he knew that; even at this distance and muffled by walls the flat loud voices of the two girls emanated an incorrigible idle inertia) were setting up the stove to prepare a meal, when he heard the hooves and saw the linen-clad man on a fine sorrel mare, whom he recognized even before he saw the rolled rug in front of the Negro youth following on a fat bay carriage horse—a suffused, angry face vanishing, still at full gallop, beyond the corner of the house where his father and brother were sitting in the two tilted chairs; and a moment later, almost before he could have put the axe down, he heard the hooves again and watched the sorrel mare go back out of the yard, already galloping again. Then his father began to shout one of the sisters' names, who presently emerged backward from the kitchen door dragging the rolled rug along the ground by one end while the other sister walked behind it.

"If you ain't going to tote, go on and set up the wash pot," the first said.

"You, Sarty!" the second shouted, "Set up the wash pot!" His father appeared at the door, framed against that shabbiness, as he had been against that other bland perfection, impervious to either, the mother's anxious face at his shoulder.

"Go on," the father said. "Pick it up." The two sisters stooped, broad, lethargic; stooping, they presented an incredible expanse of pale cloth and a flutter of tawdry ribbons.

"If I thought enough of a rug to have to git hit all the way from France I wouldn't keep hit where folks coming in would have to tromp on hit," the first said. They raised the rug.

"Abner," the mother said. "Let me do it."

"You go back and git dinner," his father said. "I'll tend to this."

From the woodpile through the rest of the afternoon the boy watched them, the rug spread flat in the dust beside the bubbling wash-pot, the two sisters stooping over it with that profound and lethargic reluctance, while the father stood over them in turn, implacable and grim, driving them though never raising his voice again. He could smell the harsh homemade lye they were using; he saw his mother come to the door once and look toward them with an expression not anxious now but very like despair; he saw his father turn, and he fell to with the axe and saw from the corner of his eye his father raise from the ground a flattish fragment of field stone and examine it and return to the pot, and this time his mother actually spoke: "Abner. Abner. Please don't. Please, Abner."

Then he was done too. It was dusk; the whippoorwills had already begun. He could smell coffee from the room where they would presently eat the cold food remaining from the midafternoon meal, though when he entered the house he realized they were having coffee again probably because there was a fire on the hearth, before which the rug now lay spread over the backs of the two chairs. The tracks of his father's foot were gone. Where they had been were now long, water-cloudy scoriations resembling the sporadic course of a lilliputian mowing machine.

It still hung there while they ate the cold food and then went to bed, scattered without order or claim up and down the two rooms, his mother in one bed, where his father would later lie, the older brother in the other, himself, the aunt, and the two sisters on pallets on the floor. But his father was not in bed yet. The last thing the boy remembered was the depthless, harsh silhouette of the hat and coat bending over the rug and it seemed to him that he had not even closed his eyes when the silhouette was standing over him, the fire almost dead behind it, the stiff foot prodding him awake. "Catch up the mule," his father said.

When he returned with the mule his father was standing in the black door, the rolled rug over his shoulder. "Ain't you going to ride?" he said.

"No. Give me your foot."

He bent his knee into his father's hand, the wiry, surprising power flowed smoothly, rising, he rising with it, on to the mule's bare back (they had owned a saddle once; the boy could remember it though not when or where) and with the same effortlessness his father swung the rug up in front of him. Now in the starlight they retraced the afternoon's path, up the dusty road rife with honeysuckle, through the gate and up the black tunnel of the drive to the lightless house, where he sat on the mule and felt the rough warp of the rug drag across his thighs and vanish.

"Don't you want me to help?" he whispered. His father did not answer and now he heard again that stiff foot striking the hollow portico with that wooden and clocklike deliberation, that outrageous overstatement of the weight it carried. The rug, hunched, not flung (the boy could tell that even in the darkness) from his father's shoulder struck the angle of wall and floor with a sound unbelievably loud, thunderous, then the foot again, unhurried and enormous; a light came on in the house and the boy sat, tense, breathing steadily and quietly and just a little fast, though the foot itself did not increase its beat at all, descending the steps now; now the boy could see him.

"Don't you want to ride now?" he whispered. "We kin both ride now," the light within the house altering now, flaring up and sinking. *He's coming down the stairs now,* he thought. He had already ridden the mule up beside the horse block; presently his father was up behind him and he doubled the reins over and slashed the mule across the neck, but before the animal could begin to trot the hard, thin arm came round him, the hard, knotted hand jerking the mule back to a walk.

In the first red rays of the sun they were in the lot, putting plow gear on the mules. This time the sorrel mare was in the lot before he heard it at all, the rider collarless and even bareheaded, trembling, speaking in a shaking voice as the woman in the house had done, his father merely looking up once before stooping again to the hame he was buckling, so that the man on the mare spoke to his stooping back:

"You must realize you have ruined that rug. Wasn't there anybody here, any of your women . . ." he ceased, shaking, the boy watching him, the older brother leaning now in the stable door, chewing, blinking slowly and steadily at nothing apparently. "It cost a hundred dollars. But you never had a hundred dollars. You never will. So I'm going to charge you twenty bushels of corn against your crop. I'll add it in your contract and when you come to the commissary you can sign it. That won't keep Mrs. de Spain quiet but maybe it will teach you to wipe your feet off before you enter her house again."

Then he was gone. The boy looked at his father, who still had not spoken or even looked up again, who was now adjusting the logger-head in the hame.

"Pap," he said. His father looked at him—the inscrutable face, the shaggy brows beneath which the gray eyes glinted coldly. Suddenly the boy went toward him, fast, stopping as suddenly. "You done the best you could!" he cried. "If he wanted hit done different why didn't he wait and tell you how? He won't git no twenty bushels! He won't git none! We'll gether hit and hide hit! I kin watch . . ."

"Did you put the cutter back in the straight stock like I told you?"

"No, sir," he said.

"Then go do it."

That was Wednesday. During the rest of that week he worked steadily, at what was within his scope and some which was beyond it, with an industry that did not need to be driven nor even commanded twice; he had this from his mother, with the difference that some at least of what he did he liked to do, such as splitting wood with the half-size axe which his mother and aunt had earned, or saved money somehow, to present him with at Christmas. In company with the two older women (and on one afternoon, even one of the sisters), he built pens for the shoat and the cow which were a part of his father's contract with the landlord, and one afternoon, his father being absent, gone somewhere on one of the mules, he went to the field.

They were running a middle buster now, his brother holding the plow straight while he handled the reins, and walking beside the straining mule, the rich black soil shearing cool and damp against his bare ankles, he thought *Maybe this is the end of it. Maybe even that twenty bushels that seems hard to have to pay for just a rug will be a cheap price for him to stop forever and always from being what he used to be;* thinking, dreaming now, so that his brother had to speak sharply to him to mind the mule: *Maybe he even won't collect the twenty bushels. Maybe it will all add up and balance and vanish —corn, rug, fire; the terror and grief, the being pulled two ways like between two teams of horses—gone, done with for ever and ever.*

Then it was Saturday; he looked up from beneath the mule he was harnessing and saw his father in the black coat and hat. "Not that," his father said. "The wagon gear." And then, two hours later, sitting in the wagon bed behind his father and brother on the seat, the wagon accomplished a final curve, and he saw the weathered paintless store with its tattered tobacco and patent-medicine posters and the tethered wagons and saddle animals below the gallery. He mounted the gnawed steps behind his father and brother, and there again was the lane of quiet, watching faces for the three of them to walk through. He saw the man in spectacles sitting at the plank table and he did not need to be told this was a Justice of the Peace; he sent one glare of fierce, exultant, partisan defiance at the man in collar and cravat now, whom he had seen but twice before in his life, and that on a galloping horse, who now wore on his face an expression not of rage but of amazed unbelief which the boy could not have known was at the incredible circumstance of being sued by one of his own tenants, and came and stood against his father and cried at the Justice: "He ain't done it! He ain't burnt . . . "

"Go back to the wagon," his father said.

"Burnt?" the Justice said. "Do I understand this rug was burned too?"

"Does anybody here claim it was?" his father said. "Go back to the wagon." But he did not, he merely retreated to the rear of the room, crowded as that other had been, but not to sit down this time, instead, to stand pressing among the motionless bodies, listening to the voices:

"And you claim twenty bushels of corn is too high for the damage you did to the rug?"

"He brought the rug to me and said he wanted the tracks washed out of it. I washed the tracks out and took the rug back to him."

"But you didn't carry the rug back to him in the same condition it was in before you made the tracks on it."

His father did not answer, and now for perhaps half a minute there was no sound at all save that of breathing, the faint, steady suspiration of complete and intent listening.

"You decline to answer that, Mr. Snopes?" Again his father did not answer. "I'm going to find against you, Mr. Snopes. I'm going to find that you were responsible for the injury to Major de Spain's rug and hold you liable for it. But twenty bushels of corn seems a little high for a man in your circumstances to have to pay. Major de Spain claims it cost a hundred dollars. October corn will be worth about fifty cents. I figure that if Major de Spain can stand a ninety-five dollar loss on something he paid cash for, you can stand a five-dollar loss you haven't earned yet. I hold you in damages to Major de Spain to the amount of ten bushels of corn over and above your contract with him, to be paid to him out of your crop at gathering time. Court adjourned."

It had taken no time hardly, the morning was but half begun. He thought they would return home and perhaps back to the field, since they were late, far behind all other farmers. But instead his father passed on behind the wagon, merely indicating with his hand for the older brother to follow with it, and crossed the road toward the blacksmith shop opposite, pressing on after his father, overtaking him, speaking, whispering up at the harsh, calm face beneath the weathered hat: "He won't git no ten bushels neither. He won't git one. We'll . . ." until his father glanced for an instant down at him, the face absolutely calm, the grizzled eyebrows tangled above the cold eyes, the voice almost pleasant, almost gentle:

"You think so? Well, we'll wait till October anyway."

The matter of the wagon—the setting of a spoke or two and the tightening of the tires—did not take long either, the business of the tires accomplished by driving the wagon into the spring branch behind the shop and letting it stand there, the mules nuzzling into the water from time to time, and the boy on the seat with the idle reins, looking up the slope and through the sooty tunnel of the shed where the slow hammer rang and where his father sat on an upended cypress bolt, easily, either talking or listening, still sitting there when the boy brought the dripping wagon up out of the branch and halted it before the door.

"Take them on to the shade and hitch," his father said. He did so and returned. His father and the smith and a third man squatting on his heels inside the door were talking, about crops and animals; the boy, squatting too in the ammoniac dust and hoof-parings and scales of rust, heard his father tell a long and unhurried story out of the time before the birth of the older brother even when he had been a professional horsetrader. And then his father came up beside him where he stood before a tattered last year's circus poster on the other side of the store, gazing rapt and quiet at the scarlet horses, the incredible poisings and convolutions of tulle and tights and the painted leers of comedians, and said, "I's time to eat."

But not at home. Squatting beside his brother against the front wall, he watched his father emerge from the store and produce from a paper sack a segment of cheese and divide it carefully and deliberately into three with his pocket knife and produce crackers from the same sack. They all three squatted on the gallery and ate, slowly, without talking; then in the store again, they drank from a tin dipper tepid water smelling of the cedar bucket and of living beech trees. And still they did not go home. It was a horse lot this time, a tall rail fence upon and along which men stood and sat and out of which one by one horses were led, to be walked and trotted and then cantered back and forth along the road while the slow swapping and buying went on and the sun began to slant westward, they—the three of them—watching and listening, the older brother with his muddy eyes and his steady, inevitable tobacco, the father commenting now and then on certain of the animals, to no one in particular.

It was after sundown when they reached home. They ate supper by lamplight, then, sitting on the doorstep, the boy watched the night fully accomplished, listening to the whippoorwills and the frogs, when he heard his mother's voice: "Abner! No! No! Oh, God. Oh, God. Abner!" and he rose, whirled, and saw the altered light through the door where a candle stub now burned in a bottle neck on the table and his father, still in the hat and coat, at once formal and burlesque as though dressed carefully for some shabby and ceremonial violence, emptying the reservoir of the lamp back into the five-gallon kerosene can from which it had been filled, while the mother tugged at his arm until he shifted the lamp to the other hand and flung her back, not savagely or viciously, just hard, into the wall, her hands flung out against the wall for balance, her mouth open and in her face the same quality of hopeless despair as had been in her voice. Then his father saw him standing in the door.

"Go to the barn and get the can of oil we were oiling the wagon with," he said. The boy did not move. Then he could speak.

"What . . ." he cried. "What are you . . ."

"Go get that oil," his father said. "Go."

Then he was moving, running, outside the house, toward the stable: this the old habit, the old blood which he had not been permitted to choose for himself, which had been bequeathed him willy nilly and which had run for so long (and who knew where, battening on what of outrage and savagery and lust) before it came to him. *I could keep on,* he thought. *I could run on and on and never look back, never need to see his face again. Only I can't. I can't,* the rusted can in his hand now, the liquid sploshing in it as he ran back to the house and into it, into the sound of his mother's weeping in the next room, and handed the can to his father.

"Ain't you going to even send a nigger?" he cried. "At least you sent a nigger before!"

This time his father didn't strike him. The hand came even faster than the blow had, the same hand which had set the can on the table with almost excruciating care flashing from the can toward him too quick for him to follow it, gripping him by the back of his shirt and on to tiptoe before he had seen it quit the can, the face stooping at him in breathless and frozen ferocity, the cold, dead voice speaking over him to the older brother who leaned against the table, chewing with that steady, curious, sidewise motion of cows:

"Empty the can into the big one and go on. I'll ketch up with you."

"Better tie him up to the bedpost," the brother said.

"Do like I told you," the father said. Then the boy was moving, his bunched shirt and the hard, bony hand between his shoulder-blades, his toes just touching the floor, across the room and into the other one, past the sisters sitting with spread heavy thighs in the two chairs over the cold hearth, and to where his mother and aunt sat side by side on the bed, the aunt's arms about his mother's shoulders.

"Hold him," the father said. The aunt made a startled movement. "Not you," the father said. "Lennie. Take hold of him. I want to see you do it." His mother took him by the wrist. "You'll hold him better than that. If he gets loose don't you know what he is going to do? He will go up yonder." He jerked his head toward the road. "Maybe I'd better tie him."

"I'll hold him," his mother whispered.

"See you do then." Then his father was gone, the stiff foot heavy and measured upon the boards, ceasing at last.

Then he began to struggle. His mother caught him in both arms, he jerking and wrenching at them. He would be stronger in the end, he knew that. But he had no time to wait for it. "Lemme go!" he cried. "I don't want to have to hit you!"

"Let him go!" the aunt said. "If he don't go, before God, I am going up there myself!"

"Don't you see I can't?" his mother cried. "Sarty! Sarty! No! No! Help me, Lizzie!"

Then he was free. His aunt grasped at him but it was too late. He whirled, running, his mother stumbled forward on to her knees behind him, crying to the nearer sister: "Catch him, Net! Catch him!" But that was too late too, the sister (the sisters were twins, born at the same time, yet either of them now gave the impression of being, encompassing as much living meat and volume and weight as any other two of the family) not yet having begun to rise from the chair, her head, face, alone merely turned, presenting to him in the flying instant an astonishing expanse of young female features untroubled by any surprise even, wearing only an expression of bovine interest. Then he was out of the room, out of the house, in the mild dust of the starlit road and the heavy rifeness of honeysuckle, the pale ribbon unspooling with terrific slowness under his running feet, reaching the gate at last and turning in, running, his heart and lungs drumming, on up the drive toward the lighted house, the lighted door. He did not knock, he burst in, sobbing for breath, incapable for the moment of speech; he saw the astonished face of the Negro in the linen jacket without knowing when the Negro had appeared.

"De Spain!" he cried, panted. "Where's . . . " then he saw the white man too emerging from a white door down the hall. "Barn!" he cried. "Barn!"

"What?" the white man said. "Barn?"

"Yes!" the boy cried. "Barn!"

"Catch him!" the white man shouted.

But it was too late this time too. The Negro grasped his shirt, but the entire sleeve, rotten with washing, carried away, and he was out that door too and in the drive again, and had actually never ceased to run even while he was screaming into the white man's face.

Behind him the white man was shouting, "My horse! Fetch my horse!" and he thought for an instant of cutting across the park and climbing the fence into the road, but he did not know the park nor how high the vine-massed fence might be and he dared not risk it. So he ran on down the drive, blood and breath roaring; presently he was in the road again though he could not see it. He could not hear either: the galloping mare was almost upon him before he heard her, and even then he held his course, as if the very urgency of his wild grief and need must in a moment more find him wings, waiting until the ultimate instant to hurl himself aside and into the weed-choked roadside ditch as the horse thundered past and on, for an instant in furious silhouette against the stars, the tranquil early summer night sky which, even before the shape of the horse and rider vanished, stained abruptly and violently upward: a long, swirling roar incredible and soundless, blotting the stars, and he springing up and into the road again, running again, knowing it was too late yet still running even after he heard the shot and, an instant later, two shots, pausing now without knowing he had ceased to run, crying "Pap! Pap!", running again before he knew he had begun to run, stumbling, tripping over something and scrabbling up again without ceasing to run, looking backward over his shoulder at the glare as he got up, running on among the invisible trees, panting, sobbing, "Father! Father!"

At midnight he was sitting on the crest of a hill. He did not know it was midnight and he did not know how far he had come. But there was no glare behind him now and he sat now, his back toward what he had called home for four days anyhow, his face toward the dark woods which he would enter when breath was strong again, small, shaking steadily in the chill darkness, hugging himself into the remainder of his thin, rotten shirt, the grief and despair now no longer terror and fear but just grief and despair. *Father. My father,* he thought. "He was brave!" he cried suddenly, aloud but not loud, no more than a whisper. "He was! He was in the war! He was in Colonel Sartoris' cav'ry!" not knowing that his father had gone to that war a private in the fine old European sense, wearing no uniform, admitting the authority of and giving fidelity to no man or army or flag, going to war as Malbrouck himself did: for booty—it meant nothing and less than nothing to him if it were enemy booty or his own.

The slow constellations wheeled on. It would be dawn and then sun-up after a while and he would be hungry. But that would be to-morrow and now he was only cold, and walking would cure that. His breathing was easier now and he decided to get up and go on, and then he found that he had been asleep because he knew it was almost dawn, the night almost over. He could tell that from the whippoorwills. They were everywhere now among the dark trees below him, constant and inflectioned and ceaseless, so that, as the instant for giving over to the day birds drew nearer and nearer, there was no interval at all between them. He got up. He was a little stiff, but walking would cure that too as it would the cold, and soon there would be the sun. He went on down the hill, toward the dark woods within which the liquid silver voices of the birds called unceasing—the rapid and urgent beating of the urgent and quiring heart of the late spring night. He did not look back.

ERNEST HEMINGWAY • 1898-1961

In Another Country

IN the fall the war was always there, but we did not go to it any more. It was cold in the fall in Milan and the dark came very early. Then the electric lights came on, and it was pleasant along the streets looking in the windows. There was much game hanging outside the shops, and the snow powdered in the fur of the foxes and the wind blew their tails. The deer hung stiff and heavy and empty, and small birds blew in the wind and the wind turned their feathers. It was a cold fall and the wind came down from the mountains.

We were all at the hospital every afternoon, and there were different ways of walking across the town through the dusk to the hospital. Two of the ways were alongside canals, but they were long. Always, though, you crossed a bridge across a canal to enter the hospital. There was a choice of three bridges. On one of them a woman sold roasted chestnuts. It was warm, standing in front of her charcoal fire, and the chestnuts were warm afterward in your pocket. The hospital was very old and very beautiful, and you entered through a gate and walked across a courtyard and out a gate on the other side. There were usually funerals starting from the courtyard. Beyond the old hospital were the new brick pavilions, and there we met every afternoon and were all very polite and interested in what was the matter, and sat in the machines that were to make so much difference.

The doctor came up to the machine where I was sitting and said: "What did you like best to do before the war? Did you practice a sport?"

I said: "Yes, football."

"Good," he said. "You will be able to play football again better than ever."

My knee did not bend and the leg dropped straight from the knee to the ankle without a calf, and the machine was to bend the knee and make it move as in riding a tricycle. But it did not bend yet, and instead the machine lurched when it came to the bending part. The doctor said: "That will all pass. You are a fortunate young man. You will play football again like a champion."

In the next machine was a major who had a little hand like a baby's. He winked at me when the doctor examined his hand, which was between two leather straps that bounced up and down and flapped the stiff fingers, and said: "And will I too play football, captain-doctor?" He had been a very great fencer, and before the war the greatest fencer in Italy.

The doctor went to his office in a back room and brought a photograph which showed a hand that had been withered almost as small as the major's, before it had taken a machine course, and after was a little larger. The major held the photograph with his good hand and looked at it very carefully. "A wound?" he asked.

"An industrial accident," the doctor said.

"Very interesting, very interesting," the major said, and handed it back to the doctor.

"You have confidence?"

"No," said the major.

There were three boys who came each day who were about the same age I was. They were all three from Milan, and one of them was to be a lawyer, and one was to be a painter, and one had intended to be a soldier, and after we were finished with the machines, sometimes we walked back together to the Cafe Cova, which was next door to the Scala. We walked the short way through the communist quarter because we were four together. The people hated us because we were officers, and from a wine-shop someone would call out, *"A basso gli ufficiali!"*[1] as we passed. Another boy who walked with us sometimes and made us five wore a black silk handkerchief across his face because he had no nose then and his face was to be rebuilt. He had gone out to the front from the military academy and been wounded within an hour after he had gone into the front line for the first time. They rebuilt his face, but he came from a very old family and they could never get the nose exactly right. He went to South America and worked in a bank. But this was a long time ago, and then we did not any of us know how it was going to be afterward. We only knew then that there was always the war, but that we were not going to it any more.

We all had the same medals, except the boy with the black silk bandage across his face, and he had not been at the front long enough to get any medals. The tall boy with a very pale face who was to be a lawyer had been a lieutenant of Arditi and had three medals of the sort we each had only one of. He had lived a very long time with death and was a little detached. We were all a little detached, and there was nothing that held us together except that we met every afternoon at the hospital. Although, as we walked to the Cova through the tough part of town, walking in the dark, with light and singing coming out of the wineshops, and sometimes having to walk into the street when the men and women would crowd together on the sidewalk so that we would have had to jostle them to get by, we felt held together by there being something that had happened that they, the people who disliked us, did not understand.

We ourselves all understood the Cova, where it was rich and warm and not too brightly lighted, and noisy and smoky at certain hours, and there were always girls at the tables and the illustrated papers on a rack on the wall. The girls at the Cova were very patriotic, and I found that the most patriotic people in Italy were the café girls—and I believe they are still patriotic.

The boys at first were very polite about my medals and asked me what I had done to get them. I showed them the papers, which were written in very beautiful language and full of *fratellanza* and *abnegazione*[2] but which really said, with the adjectives removed, that I had been given the medals because I was an American. After that their manner changed a little toward me, although I was their friend against outsiders. I was a friend, but I was never really one of them after they had read the citations, because it had been different with them and they had done very different things to get their medals. I had been wounded, it was true; but we all knew that being wounded, after all, was really an accident. I was never ashamed of the ribbons, though, and sometimes, after the cocktail hour, I would imagine myself having done all the things they had done to get their medals; but walking home at night through the empty streets with the cold wind and all the shops closed, trying to keep near the street lights, I knew that I would never have done such things, and I was very much afraid to die, and often lay in bed at night by myself, afraid to die and wondering how I would be when I went back to the front again.

The three with the medals were like hunting-hawks; and I was not a hawk, although I might seem a hawk to those

---

[1] Down with the officers!

[2] brotherhood and self-denial

who had never hunted; they, the three, knew better and so we drifted apart. But I stayed good friends with the boy who had been wounded his first day at the front, because he would never know now how he would have turned out; so he could never be accepted either, and I liked him because I thought perhaps he would not have turned out to be a hawk either.

The major, who had been the great fencer, did not believe in bravery, and spent much time while we sat in the machines correcting my grammar. He had complimented me on how I spoke Italian, and we talked together very easily. One day I had said that Italian seemed such an easy language to me that I could not take a great interest in it; everything was so easy to say. "Ah, yes," the major said. "Why, then, do you not take up the use of grammar?" So we took up the use of grammar, and soon Italian was such a difficult language that I was afraid to talk to him until I had the grammar straight in my mind.

The major came very regularly to the hospital. I do not think he ever missed a day, although I am sure he did not believe in the machines. There was a time when none of us believed in the machines, and one day the major said it was all nonsense. The machines were new then and it was we who were to prove them. It was an idiotic idea, he said, "a theory, like any other." I had not learned my grammar, and he said I was a stupid, impossible disgrace, and he was a fool to have bothered with me. He was a small man and he sat straight up in his chair with his right hand thrust into the machine and looked straight ahead at the wall while the straps thumped up and down with his fingers in them.

"What will you do when the war is over if it is over?" he asked me. "Speak grammatically!"

"I will go to the States."

"Are you married?"

"No, but I hope to be."

"The more of a fool you are," he said. He seemed very angry. "A man must not marry."

"Why, Signor Maggiore?"

"Don't call me 'Signor Maggiore.'"

"Why must not a man marry?"

"He cannot marry. He cannot marry," he said angrily. "If he is to lose everything, he should not place himself in a position to lose that. He should not place himself in a position to lose. He should find things he cannot lose."

He spoke very angrily and bitterly, and looked straight ahead while he talked.

"But why should he necessarily lose it?"

"He'll lose it," the major said. He was looking at the wall. Then he looked down at the machine and jerked his little hand out from between the straps and slapped it hard against his thigh. "He'll lose it," he almost shouted. "Don't argue with me!" Then he called to the attendant who ran the machines. "Come and turn this damned thing off."

He went back into the other room for the light treatment and the massage. Then I heard him ask the doctor if he might use his telephone and he shut the door. When he came back into the room, I was sitting in another machine. He was wearing his cape and had his cap on, and he came directly toward my machine and put his arm on my shoulder.

"I am so sorry," he said, and patted me on the shoulder with his good hand. "I would not be rude. My wife has just died. You must forgive me."

"Oh—" I said, feeling sick for him. "I am *so* sorry."

He stood there biting his lower lip. "It is very difficult," he said. "I cannot resign myself."

He looked straight past me and out through the window. Then he began to cry. "I am utterly unable to resign myself," he said and choked. And then, crying, his head up looking at nothing, carrying himself straight and soldierly, with tears on both his cheeks and biting his lips, he walked past the machines and out the door.

The doctor told me that the major's wife, who was very young and whom he had not married until he was definitely invalided out of the war, had died of pneumonia. She had been sick only a few days. No one expected her to die. The major did not come to the hospital for three days. Then he came at the usual hour, wearing a black band on the sleeve of his uniform. When he came back, there were large framed photographs around the wall, of all sorts of wounds before and after they had been cured by the machines. In front of the machine the major used were three photographs of hands like his that were completely restored. I do not know where the doctor got them. I always understood we were the first to use the machines. The photographs did not make much difference to the major because he only looked out of the window.

LANGSTON HUGHES • 1902–1967

For the Sake of Argument

WHEN I came out of the house about midnight to get a bite to eat, there was Simple in one corner of Paddy's Bar arguing loudly with an aggregation of beer-drinkers as to who is the darker, Paul Robeson or Jackie Robinson. I sat down on the lunch-counter side of the bar and ordered a plate of shortribs. After a while Simple spotted me and took possession of the next stool, although he had no apparent intention of eating.

"You know Robeson is not as light as Robinson," he announced.

"To me it makes not the slightest difference what their gradations of complexion are," I said. "Furthermore, I do not comprehend how you can stand around for hours in bars and on corners just arguing about nothing. You will argue with folks about which railroad has the fastest trains, or if Bojangles could tap more taps per second than Fred Astaire. And none of it is of any importance."

"I do not see how you can sit around looking so smart all the time and saying practically nothing," countered Simple. "You are company for nobody but yourself."

"I do not like to argue," I said.

"I do! I will argue about whether or not two and two makes four just for the sake of argument."

"It has been proven so long ago that two and two make four that I do not see the sense in discussing it. If you were arguing about what to do with the Germans or how to reform the South, then I could go along with you. But I do not like to argue about things on which there is really no argument."

"I do—because my argument is that it is good for a man to argue, just argue," said Simple, walking to the door of the bar and gazing out. Suddenly he turned around. "But I could not argue if you did not argue back at me. It takes two to make an argument. A man cannot argue by his self."

"The trouble with you is that you always wish to *win* the argument," I said. "For me, just an exchange of views is sufficient. But you, you always want to win."

"Naturally, I want to win. Otherwise, why should I be arguing?"

"You are so often wrong, Jess, also loud. You cannot win an argument when you are wrong. There are two sides to every question."

"There are sometimes more than two sides," said Simple, "except to the race question. For white folks don't have but one side."

"There you go bringing up the race question," I said. "How is it two Negroes can never get together without discussing the race question?"

"Because it is not even a question," said Simple. "It is a hammer over our heads and at any time it may fall. The only way I can explain what white folks does to us is that they just don't give a damn. Why, I once knowed a white man down South who were so mean he wouldn't give a sick baby a doctor's address."

"Where and when was that?" I asked.

"When I were a boy," said Simple. "I was hired out one summer on his plantation. He used to ride all around over the plantation watching everybody work. He rid on a little old girl-horse named Betsy,

207

and Betsy were as mean as he were. In fact, he had taught Betsy how to bite Negroes in the back. 'Boy, hist that there tree out of that ditch!'

"If you did not hist fast enough to suit him—'I can't Capt'n Boss!'—he would holler, 'Boy, you better, else I'll bull-whip your hide wide open!'

"Then if you still didn't hist, he would tell that little old horse, 'Get him Betsy!' Betsy would gallop up and nip you right between the shoulder blades."

"You are lying now, I do believe," I said.

"You have never lived down South," said Simple, "so you do not know."

"I admit I am not really familiar with the South," I said, "but sometimes I think conditions are exaggerated. Certainly in recent years they are getting better."

"They've still got Jim Crow cars," said Simple. "And the last time I was down home on a trip, I went to pay a visit on the old white man my uncle used to work for. I had kinder forgot how it is down there, so I just walked up on the porch where he was setting and says, 'Howdy, Mr. Doolittle.'

"He says, 'Boy, take off your hat when you address a white man.' And that is how he greeted me. He says, 'You must have been up North so long you done forgot yourself.'

"You know that kindur hurt my feelings because he used to know me when I was a boy. But I am a man now. That is the trouble with the South. They do not want to treat a Negro like a man. It's always *boy,* no matter if you are ninety-nine years old. I know some few things is getting better, but even them is slow as molasses. Here, lemme show you a little poem I writ about that very thing last week."

Simple pulled a piece of tablet paper out of his pocket and proceeded to read. "Listen fluently:

Old Jim Crow's
Just panting and a-coughing,
But he won't take wings
And fly.

Old Jim Crow
Is laying in his coffin,
But he don't want
To die.

I have writ
His obituary,
Still and yet
He tarry."

"Not bad, old man, except that 'He tarry' is not grammatical," I said. "If you want to be literary, you ought to know grammar."

"Joyce knows grammar," said Simple. "She will fix it up for me. I just have not showed her this one yet."

"A writer should never depend on anyone else to fix things for him. You ought to fix up your own things," I said.

"There are some things in life you cannot fix all by yourself," said Simple. "For me, poetries is one. And the race problem is another. Now you take for instant, we got two colored congressmen down in Washington. But they can't even stop a filibuster. Every time them Civil Rights Bills come up, them old white Southerners filibuster them to hell and gone. Why don't them colored congressmen start a filibuster, too?"

"Probably because they cannot talk as long or as loud as the Southerners," I said. "It takes Southerners to keep a filibuster going, and there are a great many of them in the House. Neither Adam Powell nor Dawson represents the South."

"They are colored and they represent me," said Simple. "If I was down yonder in Congress representing the colored race, I would start a filibuster all my own. In fact, I would filibuster to keep them filibusters from starting a filibuster."

"If you had no help," I said, "you would just have to keep on talking day and night, week after week, because once you sat down somebody else would get the floor. So how would you hold out?"

"How would I hold out?" yelled Simple. "With the fate of my Race at stake, you ask me how would *I* hold out! Why, for my people I would talk until my tongue hung out of my mouth. I would talk until I could not talk no more! Then, I would use sign language. When I got through with that, I would get down on my knees and pray in silence. And nobody better not strike no gavel while I am communing with my Maker. While I am on my knees, I would get some sleep. When I riz up, it would be the next day, so I would start all over again. I would be the greatest one-man filibuster of all time, daddy-o! But I am running dry now. Treat me to a beer."

"I will not," I said

"O.K., then," said Simple, "you are setting there eating and drinking and here I am empty-handed. You are a hell of a buddy."

"I will lend you a dime to buy your own beer," I said, "but a treat should be an invitation, not a request."

"Just so I get the beer," said Simple. "Now, I will continue. As I were saying, there ain't but one side to this race question—the white folks' side. White folks are setting on top of the world, and I wouldn't mind setting up there myself. Just look around you. Who owns this bar? White folks. Who owns mighty near every shop and store all up and down this street? White folks. But what do I own? I'm asking you."

"As far as I know, you do not own a thing. But why don't you get a bar or a store?"

"Why don't you?"

"Let's consider the broader picture," I said.

"I asked you a question," said Simple. "Why don't *you* get a bar or a store?"

"I asked you first," I countered.

"I do not get a bar or a store for the same reason that you don't," said Simple. "I have nothing to get me one with. On Saturday I draws my wages. I pay my rent, I get out my laundry, I take Joyce to a show, I pay you back your Two Dollars, I drink a little beer. What have I got left to buy a store with?"

"Do you think Tony the Italian that owns this Paddy's Bar—with its Irish name—also two stores, and a bookie joint, had anything when he came to America twenty years ago in the steerage?"

"Columbus come before him and smoothed the way," said Simple. "Besides, if you are white, you can get credit. If you are white, you can meet somebody with money. If you are white, you can come up here to Harlem and charge double prices. If I owned a store and charged what they charge, folks would say, 'That Negro is no good.' I tell you, white folks get away with murder. They murder my soul every day and my pocketbook every night. They got me going and coming. They say, 'You can't have a good job. You're black.' Then they say, 'Pay double. You can't eat downtown. We got this grease-ball joint for you in Harlem where it's a dime more for a beef stew. Pay it or else!' A man can't else. That's the way they get ahead when they come to America. Columbus didn't start out with Jim Crow around his neck. Neither did the guy who owns this bar. Any foreigner can come here, white, and Jim Crow me, black, from the day he sets foot off the boat. Also overcharge. He *starts* on top of my head so no wonder he gets on top of the world. Maybe I ought to go to Europe and come back a foreigner."

"While you are over there, in order to change your complexion, you'd have to be born again."

"As colored as I am," said Simple, "I'd have to be born two or three times."

That Word *Black*

"THIS evening," said Simple, "I feel like talking about the word *black*."

"Nobody's stopping you, so go ahead. But what you really ought to have is a soap-box out on the corner of 126th and Lenox where the rest of the orators hang out."

"They expresses some good ideas on that corner," said Simple, "but for my ideas I do not need a crowd. Now, as I were saying, the word *black*, white folks have done used that word to mean something bad so often until now when the N.A.A.C.P. asks for civil rights for the black man, they think they must be bad. Looking back into history, I reckon it all started with a *black* cat meaning bad luck. Don't let one cross your path!

"Next, somebody got up a *black-list* on which you get if you don't vote right. Then when lodges come into being, the folks they didn't want in them got *black-balled*. If you kept a skeleton in your closet, you might get *black-mailed*. And everything bad was *black*. When it came down to the unlucky ball on the pool table, the eight-rock, they made it the *black* ball. So no wonder there ain't no equal rights for the *black* man."

"All you say is true about the odium attached to the word *black*," I said. "You've even forgotten a few. For example, during the war if you bought something under the table, illegally, they said you were trading on the *black* market. In Chicago, if you're a gangster, the *Black Hand Society* may take you for a ride. And certainly if you don't behave yourself, your family will say you're a *black* sheep. Then if your mama burns a *black* candle to change the family luck, they call it *black* magic."

"My mama never did believe in voodoo so she did not burn no black candles," said Simple.

"If she had, that would have been a *black* mark against her."

"Stop talking about my mama. What I want to know is, where do white folks get off calling everything bad *black*? If it is a dark night, they say it's *black* as hell. If you are mean and evil, they say you got a *black* heart. I would like to change all that around and say that the people who Jim Crow me have got a *white* heart. People who sell dope to children have got a *white* mark against them. And all the white gamblers who were behind the basketball fix are the *white* sheep of the sports world. God knows there was few, if any, Negroes selling stuff on the black market during the war, so why didn't they call it the *white* market? No, they got to take me and my color and turn it into everything *bad*. According to white folks, black is bad.

"Wait till my day comes! In my language, bad will be *white*. Blackmail will be *white* mail. Black cats will be good luck, and *white* cats will be bad. If a white cat crosses your path, look out! I will take the black ball for the cue ball and let the *white* ball be the unlucky eight-rock. And on my blacklist—which will be a *white* list then—I will put everybody who ever Jim Crowed me from Rankin to Hitler, Talmadge to Malan, South Carolina to South Africa.

"I am black. When I look in the mirror, I see myself, daddy-o, but I am not ashamed. God made me. He also made F.D., dark as he is. He did not make us no badder than the rest of the folks. The earth is black and all kinds of good things comes out of the earth. Everything that grows comes up out of the earth. Trees and flowers and fruit and sweet potatoes and corn and all that keeps mens alive comes right up out of the earth—good old black earth. Coal is black and it warms your house and cooks your food. The night is black, which has a moon, and a million stars, and is beautiful. Sleep is black which gives you rest, so you wake up feeling good. I am black. I feel very good this evening.

"What is wrong with black?"

Jazz, Jive, and Jam

"IT being Negro History Week," said Simple, "Joyce took me to a pay lecture to hear some Negro hysterian—"

"Historian," I corrected.

"—hysterian speak," continued Simple, "and he laid our Negro race low. He said we was misbred, misread, and misled, also losing our time good-timing. Instead of time-taking and money-making, we are jazz-shaking. Oh, he enjoyed his self at the expense of the colored race—and him black as me. He really delivered a lecture—in which, no doubt, there is some truth."

"Constructive criticism, I gather—a sort of tearing down in order to build up."

"He tore us down good," said Simple. "Joyce come out saying to me, her husband, that he had really got my number. I said, 'Baby, he did not miss you, neither.' But Joyce did not consider herself included in the bad things he said.

"She come telling me on the way home by subway, 'Jess Semple, I have been pursuing culture since my childhood. But you, when I first met you, all you did was drape yourself over some beer bar and argue with the barflies. The higher things of life do not come out of a licker trough.'

"I replied, 'But, Joyce, how come culture has got to be so dry?'

"She answers me back, 'How come your gullet has got to be so wet? You are sitting in this subway right now looking like you would like to have a beer.'

" 'Solid!' I said. 'I would. How did you guess it?'

" 'Married to you for three years, I can read your mind,' said Joyce. 'We'll buy a couple of cans to take home. I might even drink one myself.'

" 'Joyce, baby,' I said, 'in that case, let's buy three cans.'

"Joyce says, 'Remember the budget, Jess.'

"I says, 'Honey, you done busted the budget going to that lecture program which cost One Dollar a head, also we put some small change in the collection to help Negroes get ahead.'

" 'Small change?' says Joyce, 'I put a dollar.'

" 'Then our budget is busted real good,' I said, 'so we might as well dent it some more. Let's get six cans of beer.'

" 'All right,' says Joyce, 'go ahead, drink yourself to the dogs—instead of saving for that house we want to buy!'

" 'Six cans of beer would not pay for even the bottom front step,' I said. 'But they would lift my spirits this evening. That Negro high-speaking doctor done tore my spirits down. I did not know before that the colored race was so misled, misread, and misbred. According to him there is hardly a pure black man left. But I was setting in the back, so I guess he did not see me.'

" 'Had you not had to go to sleep in the big chair after dinner,' says Joyce, 'we would have been there on time and had seats up front.'

" 'I were near enough to that joker,' I said. 'Loud as he could holler, we did not need to set no closer. And he certainly were nothing to look at!'

" 'Very few educated men look like Harry Belafonte,' said Joyce.

" 'I am glad I am handsome instead of wise,' I said. But Joyce did not crack a smile. She had that lecture on her mind.

" 'Dr. Conboy is smart,' says Joyce. 'Did you hear him quoting Aristotle?'

" 'Who were Harry Stottle?' I asked.

" 'Some people are not even misread,' said Joyce. 'Aristotle was a Greek philosopher like Socrates, a great man of ancient times.'

" 'He must of been before Booker T. Washington then,' I said, 'because, to tell the truth, I has not heard of him at all. But tonight being *Negro* History Week, how come Dr. Conboy has to quote some Greek?'

" 'There were black Greeks,' said Joyce. 'Did you not hear him say that Negroes have played a part in all history, throughout all time, from Eden to now?'

" 'Do you reckon Eve was brownskin?' I requested.

" 'I do not know about Eve,' said Joyce, 'but Cleopatra was of the colored race, and the Bible says Sheba, beloved of Solomon, was black but comely.'

" 'I wonder would she come to me?' I says.

" 'Solomon also found Cleopatra comely. He was a king,' says Joyce.

" 'And I am Jesse B. Semple,' I said.

"But by that time the subway had got to our stop. At the store Joyce broke the budget again, opened up her pocket purse, and bought us six cans of beer. So it were a good evening. It ended well—except that I ain't for going to any more meetings—especially interracial meetings."

"Come now! Don't you want to improve race relations?"

"Sure," said Simple, "but in my opinion, jazz, jive, and jam would be better for race relations than all this high-flown gab, gaff, and gas the orators put out. All this talking that white folks do at meetings, and big Negroes, too, about how to get along together—just a little jam session would have everybody getting along fine without having to listen to so many speeches. Why, last month Joyce took me to a Race Relations Seminar which her club and twenty other clubs gave, and man, it lasted three days! It started on a Friday night and it were not over until Sunday afternoon. They had sessions' mammy! Joyce is a fiend for culture."

"And you sat through all that?"

"I did not set," said Simple. "I stood. I walked in and walked out. I smoked on the corner and snuck two drinks at the bar. But I had to wait for Joyce, and I thought them speeches would never get over! My wife were a delegate from her club, so she had to stay, although I think Joyce got tired her own self. But she would not admit it. Joyce said, 'Dr. Hilary Thingabod was certainly brilliant, were he not?'

"I said, 'He were not.'

"Joyce said, 'What did you want the man to say?'

"I said, 'I wish he had sung, instead of *said*. That program needed some music to keep folks awake.'

"Joyce said, 'Our forum was not intended for a musical. It was intended to see how we can work out integration.'

"I said, 'With a jazz band, they could work out integration in ten minutes. Everybody would have been dancing together like they all did at the Savoy—colored and white—or down on the East Side at them Casinos on a Friday night where jam holds forth—and we would have been integrated.'

"Joyce said, 'This was a serious seminar, aiming at facts, not fun.'

"'Baby,' I said, 'what is more facts than acts? Jazz makes people get into action, move! Didn't nobody move in that hall where you were—except to jerk their head up when they went to sleep, to keep anybody from seeing that they was nodding. Why, that chairman, Mrs. Maxwell-Reeves, almost lost her glasses off her nose, she jerked her head up so quick one time when that man you say was so brilliant were speaking!'

"'Jess Semple, that is not so!' yelled Joyce. 'Mrs. Maxwell-Reeves were just lost in thought. And if you think you saw *me* sleeping—'

"'You was too busy trying to look around and see where I was,' I said. 'Thank God, I did not have to set up there like you with the delegation. I would not be a delegate to no such gabfest for nothing on earth.'

"'I thought you was so interested in saving the race!' said Joyce. 'Next time I will not ask you to accompany me to no cultural events, Jesse B., because I can see you do not appreciate them. That were a discussion of ways and means. And you are talking about jazz bands!'

"'There's more ways than one to skin a cat,' I said. 'A jazz band like Duke's or Hamp's or Basie's sure would of helped that meeting. At least on Saturday afternoon, they could have used a little music to put some pep into the proceedings. Now, just say for instant, baby, they was to open with jazz and close with jam—and do the talking in between. Start out, for example, with "The St. Louis Blues," which is a kind of colored national anthem. That would put every human in a good humor. Then play "Why Don't You Do Right?" which could be addressed to white folks. They could pat their feet to that. Then for a third number before introducing the speaker, let some guest star like Pearl Bailey sing "There'll Be Some Changes Made"—which, as I understand it, were the theme of the meeting, anyhow—and all the Negroes could say *Amen!*

"'Joyce, I wish you would let me plan them interracial seminaries next time. After the music, let the speechmaking roll for a while—with maybe a calypso between speeches. Then, along about five o'clock, bring on the jam session, extra-special. Start serving tea to "Tea For Two," played real cool. Whilst drinking tea and dancing, the race relationers could relate, the integraters could integrate, and desegregators desegregate. Joyce, you would not have to beg for a crowd to come out and support your efforts then. Jam—and the hall would be jammed! Even I would stick around, and not be outside sneaking a smoke, or trying to figure how I can get to the bar before the resolutions are voted on. *Resolved: that we solve* the race problem! Strike up the band! Hit it, men! Aw, play that thing! "How High the Moon!" How high! Wheee-ee-e!'"

"What did Joyce say to that?" I demanded.

"Joyce just thought I was high," said Simple.

ERSKINE CALDWELL • 1903–

Daughter

AT sunrise a Negro on his way to the big house to feed the mules had taken the word to Colonel Henry Maxwell, and Colonel Henry phoned the sheriff. The sheriff had hustled Jim into town and locked him up in the jail, and then he went home and ate breakfast.

Jim walked around the empty cellroom while he was buttoning his shirt, and after that he sat down on the bunk and tied his shoelaces. Everything that morning had taken place so quickly that he had not even had time to get a drink of water. He got up and went to the water bucket near the door, but the sheriff had forgotten to put water into it.

By that time there were several men standing in the jailyard. Jim went to the window and looked out when he heard them talking. Just then another automobile drove up, and six or seven men got out. Other men were coming towards the jail from both directions of the street.

"What was the trouble out at your place this morning, Jim?" somebody said.

Jim stuck his chin between the bars and looked at the faces in the crowd. He knew everyone there.

While he was trying to figure out how everybody in town had heard about his being there, somebody else spoke to him.

"It must have been an accident, wasn't it, Jim?"

A colored boy hauling a load of cotton to the gin drove up the street. When the wagon got in front of the jail, the boy whipped up the mules with the ends of the reins and made them trot.

"I hate to see the State have a grudge against you, Jim," somebody said.

The sheriff came down the street swinging a tin dinner-pail in his hand. He pushed through the crowd, unlocked the door, and set the pail inside.

Several men came up behind the sheriff and looked over his shoulder into the jail.

"Here's your breakfast my wife fixed up for you, Jim. You'd better eat a little, Jim boy."

Jim looked at the pail, at the sheriff, at the open jail door, and he shook his head.

"I don't feel hungry," he said. "Daughter's been hungry, though—awful hungry."

The sheriff backed out the door, his hand going to the handle of his pistol. He backed out so quickly that he stepped on the toes of the men behind him.

"Now, don't you get careless, Jim boy," he said. "Just sit and calm yourself."

He shut the door and locked it. After he had gone a few steps towards the street, he stopped and looked into the chamber of his pistol to make sure it had been loaded.

The crowd outside the window pressed in closer. Some of the men rapped on the bars until Jim came and looked out. When he saw them, he stuck his chin between the iron and gripped his hands around it.

"How come it to happen, Jim?" somebody asked. "It must have been an accident, wasn't it?"

Jim's long thin face looked as if it would come through the bars. The sheriff came up to the window to see if everything was all right.

"Now, just take it easy, Jim boy," he said.

The man who had asked Jim to tell what had happened, elbowed the sheriff out of the way. The other men crowded closer.

"How come, Jim?" the man said. "Was it an accident?"

"No," Jim said, his fingers twisting about the bars. "I picked up my shotgun and done it."

The sheriff pushed towards the window again.

"Go on, Jim, and tell us what it's all about."

Jim's face squeezed between the bars until it looked as though only his ears kept his head from coming through.

"Daughter said she was hungry, and I just couldn't stand it no longer. I just couldn't stand to hear her say it."

"Don't get all excited now, Jim boy," the sheriff said, pushing forward one moment and being elbowed away the next.

"She waked up in the middle of the night again and said she was hungry. I just couldn't stand to hear her say it."

Somebody pushed all the way through the crowd until he got to the window.

"Why, Jim, you could have come and asked me for something for her to eat, and you know I'd have given you all I got in the world."

The sheriff pushed forward once more.

"That wasn't the right thing to do," Jim said. "I've been working all year and I made enough for all of us to eat."

He stopped and looked down into the faces on the other side of the bars.

"I made enough working on shares, but they came and took it all away from me. I couldn't go around begging after I'd made enough to keep us. They just came and took it all off. Then Daughter woke up again this morning saying she was hungry, and I just couldn't stand it no longer."

"You'd better go and get on the bunk now, Jim boy," the sheriff said.

"It don't seem right that the little girl ought to be shot like that," somebody said.

"Daughter said she was hungry," Jim said. "She'd been saying that for all of the past month. Daughter'd wake up in the middle of the night and say it. I just couldn't stand it no longer."

"You ought to have sent her over to my house, Jim. Me and my wife could have fed her something, somehow. It don't look right to kill a little girl like her."

"I'd made enough for all of us," Jim said. "I just couldn't stand it no longer. Daughter'd been hungry all the past month."

"Take it easy, Jim boy," the sheriff said, trying to push forward.

The crowd swayed from side to side.

"And so you just picked up the gun this morning and shot her?" somebody asked.

"When she woke up this morning saying she was hungry, I just couldn't stand it."

The crowd pushed closer. Men were coming towards the jail from all directions, and those who were then arriving pushed forward to hear what Jim had to say.

"The State has got a grudge against you now, Jim," somebody said, "but somehow it don't seem right."

"I can't help it," Jim said. "Daughter woke up again this morning that way."

The jailyard, the street, and the vacant lot on the other side were filled with men and boys. All of them were pushing forward to hear Jim. Word had spread all over town by that time that Jim Carlisle had shot and killed his eight-year-old daughter, Clara.

"Who does Jim share-crop for?" somebody asked.

"Colonel Henry Maxwell," a man in the crowd said. "Colonel Henry has had Jim out there about nine or ten years."

"Henry Maxwell didn't have no business coming and taking all the shares. He's got plenty of his own. It ain't right for Henry Maxwell to come and take Jim's, too."

The sheriff was pushing forward once more.

"The State's got a grudge against Jim now," somebody said. "Somehow it don't seem right, though."

The sheriff pushed his shoulder into the crowd of men and worked his way in closer.

A man shoved the sheriff away.

"Why did Henry Maxwell come and take your share of the crop, Jim?"

"He said I owed it to him because one of his mules died about a month ago."

The sheriff got in front of the barred window.

"You ought to go to the bunk now and rest some, Jim boy," he said. "Take off your shoes and stretch out, Jim boy."

He was elbowed out of the way.

"You didn't kill the mule, did you, Jim?"

"The mule dropped dead in the barn," Jim said. "I wasn't nowhere around. It just dropped dead."

The crowd was pushing harder. The men in front were jammed against the jail, and the men behind were trying to get within earshot. Those in the middle were squeezed against each other so tightly they could not move in any direction. Everyone was talking louder.

Jim's face pressed between the bars and his fingers gripped the iron until the knuckles were white.

The milling crowd was moving across the street to the vacant lot. Somebody was shouting. He climbed up on an automobile and began swearing at the top of his lungs.

A man in the middle of the crowd pushed his way out and went to his automobile. He got in and drove off alone.

Jim stood holding to the bars and looking through the window. The sheriff had his back to the crowd, and he was saying something to Jim. Jim did not hear what he said.

A man on his way to the gin with a load of cotton stopped to find out what the trouble was. He looked at the crowd in the vacant lot for a moment, and then he turned around and looked at Jim behind the bars. The shouting across the street was growing louder.

"What's the trouble, Jim?"

Somebody on the other side of the street came to the wagon. He put his foot on a spoke in the wagon wheel and looked up at the man on the cotton while he talked.

"Daughter woke up this morning again saying she was hungry," Jim said.

The sheriff was the only person who heard him.

The man on the load of cotton jumped to the ground, tied the reins to the wagon wheel, and pushed through the crowd to the car where all the shouting and swearing was being done. After listening for a while, he came back to the street, called a Negro who was standing with several other Negroes on the corner, and handed him the reins. The Negro drove off with the cotton towards the gin, and the man went back into the crowd.

Just then the man who had driven off alone in his car came back. He sat for a moment behind the steering wheel, and then he jumped to the ground. He opened the rear door and took out a crowbar that was as long as he was tall.

"Pry that jail door open and let Jim out," somebody said. "It ain't right for him to be in there."

The crowd in the vacant lot was moving again. The man who had been standing on top of the automobile jumped to the ground, and the men moved towards the street in the direction of the jail.

The first man to reach it jerked the six-foot crowbar out of the soft earth where it had been jabbed.

The sheriff backed off.

"Now, take it easy, Jim boy," he said.

He turned and started walking rapidly up the street towards his house.

EUDORA WELTY • 1909–

Why I Live at the P.O.

I was getting along fine with Mama, Papa-Daddy and Uncle Rondo until my sister Stella-Rondo just separated from her husband and came back home again. Mr. Whitaker! Of course I went with Mr. Whitaker first, when he first appeared here in China Grove, taking "Pose Yourself" photos, and Stella-Rondo broke us up. Told him I was one-sided. Bigger on one side than the other, which is a deliberate, calculated falsehood: I'm the same. Stella-Rondo is exactly twelve months to the day younger than I am and for that reason she's spoiled.

She's always had anything in the world she wanted and then she'd throw it away. Papa-Daddy gave her this gorgeous Add-a-Pearl necklace when she was eight years old and she threw it away playing baseball when she was nine, with only two pearls.

So as soon as she got married and moved away from home the first thing she did was separate! From Mr. Whitaker! This photographer with the popeyes she said she trusted. Came home from one of those towns up in Illinois and to our complete surprise brought this child of two.

Mama said she like to made her drop dead for a second. "Here you had this marvelous blonde child and never so much as wrote your mother a word about it," says Mama. "I'm thoroughly ashamed of you." But of course she wasn't.

Stella-Rondo just calmly takes off this *hat,* I wish you could see it. She says, "Why, Mama, Shirley-T.'s adopted, I can prove it."

"How?" says Mama, but all I says was, "H'm!" There I was over the hot stove, trying to stretch two chickens over five people and a completely unexpected child into the bargain, without one moment's notice.

"What do you mean—'H'm!'?" says Stella-Rondo, and Mama says, "I heard that, Sister."

I said that oh, I didn't mean a thing, only that whoever Shirley-T. was, she was the spit-image of Papa-Daddy if he'd cut off his beard, which of course he'd never do in the world. Papa-Daddy's Mama's papa and sulks.

Stella-Rondo got furious! She said, "Sister, I don't need to tell you you got a lot of nerve and always did have and I'll thank you to make no future reference to my adopted child whatsoever."

"Very well," I said. "Very well, very well. Of course I noticed at once she looks like Mr. Whitaker's side too. That frown. She looks like a cross between Mr. Whitaker and Papa-Daddy."

"Well, all I can say is she isn't."

"She looks exactly like Shirley Temple to me," says Mama, but Shirley-T. just ran away from her.

So the first thing Stella-Rondo did at the table was turn Papa-Daddy against me.

"Papa-Daddy," she says. He was trying to cut up his meat. "Papa-Daddy!" I was taken completely by surprise. Papa-Daddy is about a million years old and's got this long-long beard. "Papa-Daddy, Sister says she fails to understand why you don't cut off your beard."

So Papa-Daddy l-a-y-s down his knife and fork! He's real rich. Mama says he is, he says he isn't. So he says, "Have I heard correctly? You don't understand why I don't cut off my beard?"

"Why," I says, "Papa-Daddy, of course I understand, I did not say any such of a thing, the idea!"

217

He says, "Hussy!"

I says, "Papa-Daddy, you know I wouldn't any more want you to cut off your beard than the man in the moon. It was the farthest thing from my mind! Stella-Rondo sat there and made that up while she was eating breast of chicken."

But he says, "So the postmistress fails to understand why I don't cut off my beard. Which job I got you through my influence with the government. 'Bird's nest'—is that what you call it?"

Not that it isn't the next to smallest P.O. in the entire state of Mississippi.

I says, "Oh, Papa-Daddy," I says, "I didn't say any such of a thing, I never dreamed it was a bird's nest, I have always been grateful though this is the next to smallest P.O. in the state of Mississippi, and I do not enjoy being referred to as a hussy by my own grandfather."

But Stella-Rondo says, "Yes, you did say it too. Anybody in the world could of heard you, that had ears."

"Stop right there," says Mama, looking at *me*.

So I pulled my napkin straight back through the napkin ring and left the table.

As soon as I was out of the room Mama says, "Call her back, or she'll starve to death," but Papa-Daddy says, "This is the beard I started growing on the Coast when I was fifteen years old." He would of gone on till nightfall if Shirley-T. hadn't lost the Milky Way she ate in Cairo.

So Papa-Daddy says, "I am going out and lie in the hammock, and you can all sit here and remember my words: I'll never cut off my beard as long as I live, even one inch, and I don't appreciate it in you at all." Passed right by me in the hall and went straight out and got in the hammock.

It would be a holiday. It wasn't five minutes before Uncle Rondo suddenly appeared in the hall in one of Stella-Rondo's flesh-colored kimonos, all cut on the bias, like something Mr. Whitaker probably thought was gorgeous.

"Uncle Rondo!" I says. "I didn't know who that was! Where are you going?"

"Sister," he says, "get out of my way, I'm poisoned."

"If you're poisoned stay away from Papa-Daddy," I says. "Keep out of the hammock. Papa-Daddy will certainly beat you on the head if you come within forty miles of him. He thinks I deliberately said he ought to cut off his beard after he got me the P.O., and I've told him and told him and told him, and he acts like he just don't hear me. Papa-Daddy must of gone stone deaf."

"He picked a fine day to do it then," says Uncle Rondo, and before you could say "Jack Robinson" flew out in the yard.

What he'd really done, he'd drunk another bottle of that prescription. He does it every single Fourth of July as sure as shooting, and it's horribly expensive. Then he falls over in the hammock and snores. So he insisted on zigzagging right on out to the hammock, looking like a half-wit.

Papa-Daddy woke up with this horrible yell and right there without moving an inch he tried to turn Uncle Rondo against me. I heard every word he said. Oh, he told Uncle Rondo I didn't learn to read till I was eight years old and he didn't see how in the world I ever got the mail put up at the P.O., much less read it all, and he said if Uncle Rondo could only fathom the lengths he had gone to to get me that job! And he said on the other hand he thought Stella-Rondo had a brilliant mind and deserved credit for getting out of town. All the time he was just lying there swinging as pretty as you please and looping out his beard, and poor Uncle Rondo was *pleading* with him to slow down the hammock, it was making him as dizzy as a witch to watch it. But that's what Papa-Daddy likes about a hammock. So Uncle Rondo was too dizzy to get turned against me for the time being. He's Mama's only brother and is a good case of a one-track mind. Ask anybody. A certified pharmacist.

Just then I heard Stella-Rondo raising the upstairs window. While she was married she got this peculiar idea that it's cooler with the windows shut and locked. So she has to raise the window before she can make a soul hear her outdoors.

So she raises the window and says, *"Oh!"* You would have thought she was mortally wounded.

Uncle Rondo and Papa-Daddy didn't even look up, but kept right on with what they were doing. I had to laugh.

I flew up the stairs and threw the door open! I says, "What in the wide world's the matter, Stella-Rondo? You mortally wounded?"

"No," she says, "I am not mortally wounded but I wish you would do me the favor of looking out that window there and telling me what you see."

So I shade my eyes and look out the window.

"I see the front yard," I says.

"Don't you see any human beings?" she says.

"I see Uncle Rondo trying to run Papa-Daddy out of the hammock," I says. "Nothing more. Naturally, it's so suffocating-hot in the house, with all the windows shut and locked, everybody who cares to stay in their right mind will have to go out and get in the hammock before the Fourth of July is over."

"Don't you notice anything different about Uncle Rondo?" asks Stella-Rondo.

"Why, no, except he's got on some terrible-looking flesh-colored contraption I wouldn't be found dead in, is all I can see," I says.

"Never mind, you won't be found dead in it, because it happens to be part of my trousseau, and Mr. Whitaker took several dozen photographs of me in it," says Stella-Rondo. "What on earth could Uncle Rondo *mean* by wearing part of my trousseau out in the broad open daylight without saying so much as 'Kiss my foot,' *knowing* I only got home this morning after my separation and hung my negligee up on the bathroom door, just as nervous as I could be?"

"I'm sure I don't know, and what do you expect me to do about it?" I says. "Jump out the window?"

"No, I expect nothing of the kind. I simply declare that Uncle Rondo looks like a fool in it, that's all," she says. "It makes me sick to my stomach."

"Well, he looks as good as he can," I says. "As good as anybody in reason could." I stood up for Uncle Rondo, please remember. And I said to Stella-Rondo, "I think I would do well not to criticize so freely if I were you and came home with a two-year-old child I had never said a word about, and no explanation whatever about my separation."

"I asked you the instant I entered this house not to refer one more time to my adopted child, and you gave me your word of honor you would not," was all Stella-Rondo would say, and started pulling out every one of her eyebrows with some cheap Kress tweezers.

So I merely slammed the door behind me and went down and made some green-tomato pickle. Somebody had to do it. Of course Mama had turned both the niggers loose; she always said no earthly power could hold one anyway on the Fourth of July, so she wouldn't even try. It turned out that Jaypan fell in the lake and came within a very narrow limit of drowning.

So Mama trots in. Lifts up the lid and says, "H'm! Not very good for your Uncle Rondo in his precarious condition, I must say. Or poor little adopted Shirley-T. Shame on you!"

That made me tired. I says, "Well, Stella-Rondo had better thank her lucky stars it was her instead of me came trotting in with that very peculiar-looking child. Now if it had been me that trotted in from Illinois and brought a peculiar-looking child of two, I shudder to think of the reception I'd of got, much less controlled the diet of an entire family."

"But you must remember, Sister, that you were never married to Mr. Whitaker in the first place and didn't go up to Illinois to live," says Mama, shaking a spoon in my face. "If you had I would of been just as overjoyed to see you and your little adopted girl as I was to see Stella-Rondo, when you wound up with your separation and came on back home."

"You would not," I says.

"Don't contradict me, I would," says Mama.

But I said she couldn't convince me though she talked till she was blue in the face. Then I said, "Besides, you know as well as I do that that child is not adopted."

"She most certainly is adopted," says Mama, stiff as a poker.

I says, "Why, Mama, Stella-Rondo had her just as sure as anything in this world, and just too stuck up to admit it."

"Why, Sister," said Mama. "Here I thought we were going to have a pleasant Fourth of July, and you start right out not believing a word your own baby sister tells you!"

"Just like Cousin Annie Flo. Went to her grave denying the facts of life," I remind Mama.

"I told you if you ever mentioned Annie Flo's name I'd slap your face," says Mama, and slaps my face.

"All right, you wait and see," I says.

"I," says Mama, "*I* prefer to take my children's word for anything when it's humanly possible." You ought to see Mama, she weighs two hundred pounds and has real tiny feet.

Just then something perfectly horrible occurred to me.

"Mama," I says, "can that child talk?" I simply had to whisper! "Mama, I wonder if that child can be—you know—in any way? Do you realize," I says, "that she hasn't spoken one single, solitary word to a human being up to the minute? This is the way she looks," I says, and I looked like this.

Well, Mama and I just stood there and stared at each other. It was horrible!

"I remember well that Joe Whitaker frequently drank like a fish," says Mama. "I believed to my soul he drank *chemicals.*" And without another word she marches to the foot of the stairs and calls Stella-Rondo.

"Stella-Rondo? O-o-o-o-o! Stella-Rondo!"

"What?" says Stella-Rondo from upstairs. Not even the grace to get up off the bed.

"Can that child of yours talk?" asks Mama.

Stella-Rondo says, "Can she what?"

"Talk! Talk!" says Mama. "Burdy-burdyburdyburdy!"

So Stella-Rondo yells back, "Who says she can't talk?"

"Sister says so," says Mama.

"You didn't have to tell me, I know whose word of honor don't mean a thing in this house," says Stella-Rondo.

And in a minute the loudest Yankee voice I ever heard in my life yells out, "OE'm Pop-OE the Sailor-r-r-r Ma-a-an!" and then somebody jumps up and down in the upstairs hall. In another second the house would of fallen down.

"Not only talks, she can tap-dance!" calls Stella-Rondo. "Which is more than some people I won't name can do."

"Why, the little precious darling thing!" Mama says, so surprised. "Just as smart as she can be!" Starts talking baby talk right there. Then she turns on me. "Sister, you ought to be thoroughly ashamed! Run upstairs this instant and apologize to Stella-Rondo and Shirley-T.

"Apologize for what?" I says. "I merely wondered if the child was normal, that's all. Now that she's proved she is, why, I have nothing further to say."

But Mama just turned on her heel and flew out, furious. She ran right upstairs and hugged the baby. She believed it was adopted. Stella-Rondo hadn't done a thing but turn her against me from upstairs while I stood there helpless over the hot stove. So that made Mama, Papa-Daddy and the baby all on Stella-Rondo's side.

Next, Uncle Rondo.

I must say that Uncle Rondo has been marvelous to me at various times in the past and I was completely unprepared to be made to jump out of my skin, the way it turned out. Once Stella-Rondo did something perfectly horrible to him—broke a chain letter from Flanders Field —and he took the radio back he had given her and gave it to me. Stella-Rondo was furious! For six months we all had to call her Stella instead of Stella-Rondo, or she wouldn't answer. I always thought Uncle Rondo had all the brains of the entire family. Another time he sent me to Mammoth Cave, with all expenses paid.

But this would be the day he was drinking that prescription, the Fourth of July.

So at supper Stella-Rondo speaks up and says she thinks Uncle Rondo ought to try to eat a little something. So finally Uncle Rondo said he would try a little cold biscuits and ketchup, but that was all. So *she* brought it to him.

"Do you think it wise to disport with ketchup in Stella-Rondo's flesh-colored kimono?" I says. Trying to be considerate! If Stella-Rondo couldn't watch out for her trousseau, somebody had to.

"Any objections?" asks Uncle Rondo, just about to pour out all the ketchup.

"Don't mind what she says, Uncle Rondo," says Stella-Rondo. "Sister has been devoting this solid afternoon to sneering out my bedroom window at the way you look."

"What's that?" says Uncle Rondo. Uncle Rondo has got the most terrible temper in the world. Anything is liable to make him tear the house down if it comes at the wrong time.

So Stella-Rondo says, "Sister says, 'Uncle Rondo certainly does look like a fool in that pink kimono!' "

Do you remember who it was really said that?

Uncle Rondo spills out all the ketchup and jumps out of his chair and tears off the kimono and throws it down on the dirty floor and puts his foot on it. It had to be sent all the way to Jackson to the cleaners and re-pleated.

"So that's your opinion of your Uncle Rondo, is it?" he says. "I look like a fool, do I? Well, that's the last straw. A whole day in this house with nothing to do, and then to hear you come out with a remark like that behind my back!"

"I didn't say any such of a thing, Uncle Rondo," I says, "and I'm not saying who did, either. Why, I think you look all right. Just try to take care of yourself and not talk and eat at the same time," I says. "I think you better go lie down."

"Lie down my foot," says Uncle Rondo. I ought to of known by that he was fixing to do something perfectly horrible.

So he didn't do anything that night in the precarious state he was in—just played Casino with Mama and Stella-Rondo and Shirley-T. and gave Shirley-T. a nickel with a head on both sides. It tickled her nearly to death, and she called him "Papa." But at 6:30 A.M. the next morning, he threw a whole five-cent package of some unsold one-inch firecrackers from the store as hard as he could into my bedroom and they every one went off. Not one bad one in the string. Anybody else, there'd be one that wouldn't go off.

Well, I'm just terribly susceptible to noise of any kind, the doctor has always told me I was the most sensitive person he had ever seen in his whole life, and I was simply prostrated. I couldn't eat! People tell me they heard it as far as the cemetery, and old Aunt Jep Patterson, that had been holding her own so good, thought it was Judgment Day and she was going to meet her whole family. It's usually so quiet here.

And I'll tell you it didn't take me any longer than a minute to make up my mind what to do. There I was with the whole entire house on Stella-Rondo's side and turned against me. If I have anything at all I have pride.

So I just decided I'd go straight down to the P.O. There's plenty of room there in the back, I says to myself.

Well! I made no bones about letting the family catch on to what I was up to. I didn't try to conceal it.

The first thing they knew, I marched in where they were all playing Old Maid and pulled the electric oscillating fan out by the plug, and everything got real hot. Next I snatched the pillow I'd done the needlepoint on right off the davenport from behind Papa-Daddy. He went "Ugh!" I beat Stella-Rondo up the stairs and finally found my charm bracelet in her bureau drawer under a picture of Nelson Eddy.

"So that's the way the land lies," says Uncle Rondo. There he was, piecing on the ham. "Well, Sister, I'll be glad to donate my army cot if you got any place to set it up, providing you'll leave right this minute and let me get some peace." Uncle Rondo was in France.

"Thank you kindly for the cot and 'peace' is hardly the word I would select if I had to resort to firecrackers at 6:30 A.M. in a young girl's bedroom," I says back to him. "And as to where I intend to go, you seem to forget my position as postmistress of China Grove, Mississippi," I says. "I've always got the P.O."

Well, that made them all sit up and take notice.

I went out front and started digging up some four-o'clocks to plant around the P.O.

"Ah-ah-ah!" says Mama, raising the window. "Those happen to be my four-o'clocks. Everything planted in that star is mine. I've never known you to make anything grow in your life."

"Very well," I says. "But I take the fern. Even you, Mama, can't stand there and deny that I'm the one watered that fern. And I happen to know where I can send in a box top and get a packet of one thousand mixed seeds, no two the same kind, free."

"Oh, where?" Mama wants to know.

But I says, "Too late. You 'tend to your house, and I'll 'tend to mine. You hear things like that all the time if you know how to listen to the radio. Perfectly marvelous offers. Get anything you want free."

So I hope to tell you I marched in and got that radio, and they could of all bit a nail in two, especially Stella-Rondo, that it used to belong to, and she well knew she couldn't get it back, I'd sue for it like a shot. And I very politely took the sewing-machine motor I helped pay the most on to give Mama for Christmas back in 1929, and a good big calendar, with the first-aid remedies on it. The thermometer and the Hawaiian ukulele certainly were rightfully mine, and I stood on the step-ladder and got all my watermelon-rind preserves and every fruit and vegetable I'd put up, every jar. Then I began to pull the tacks out of the bluebird wall vases on the archway to the dining room.

"Who told you you could have those, Miss Priss?" says Mama, fanning as hard as she could.

"I bought 'em and I'll keep track of 'em," I says. "I'll tack 'em up one on each side the post-office window, and you can see 'em when you come to ask me for your mail, if you're so dead to see 'em."

"Not I! I'll never darken the door to

that post office again if I live to be a hundred," Mama says. "Ungrateful child! After all the money we spent on you at the Normal."

"Me either," says Stella-Rondo. "You can just let my mail lie there and *rot*, for all I care. I'll never come and relieve you of a single, solitary piece."

"I should worry," I says. "And who you think's going to sit down and write you all those big fat letters and postcards, by the way? Mr. Whitaker? Just because he was the only man ever dropped down in China Grove and you got him—unfairly—is he going to sit down and write you a lengthy correspondence after you come home giving no rhyme nor reason whatsoever for your separation and no explanation for the presence of that child? I may not have your brilliant mind, but I fail to see it."

So Mama says, "Sister, I've told you a thousand times that Stella-Rondo simply got homesick, and this child is far too big to be hers," and she says, "Now, why don't you all just sit down and play Casino?"

Then Shirley-T. sticks out her tongue at me in this perfectly horrible way. She has no more manners than the man in the moon. I told her she was going to cross her eyes like that some day and they'd stick.

"It's too late to stop me now," I says. "You should have tried that yesterday. I'm going to the P.O. and the only way you can possibly see me is to visit me there."

So Papa-Daddy says, "You'll never catch me setting foot in that post office, even if I should take a notion into my head to write a letter some place." He says, "I won't have you reachin' out of that little old window with a pair of shears and cuttin' off any beard of mine. I'm too smart for you!"

"We all are," says Stella-Rondo.

But I said, "If you're so smart, where's Mr. Whitaker?"

So then Uncle Rondo says, "I'll thank you from now on to stop reading all the orders I get on postcards and telling everybody in China Grove what you think is the matter with them," but I says, "I draw my own conclusions and will continue in the future to draw them." I says, "If people want to write their inmost secrets on penny postcards, there's nothing in the wide world you can do about it, Uncle Rondo."

"And if you think we'll ever *write* another postcard you're sadly mistaken," says Mama.

"Cutting off your nose to spite your face then," I says. "But if you're all determined to have no more to do with the U. S. mail, think of this: What will Stella-Rondo do now, if she wants to tell Mr. Whitaker to come after her?"

"Wah!" says Stella-Rondo. I knew she'd cry. She had a conniption fit right there in the kitchen.

"It will be interesting to see how long she holds out," I says. "And now—I am leaving."

"Good-bye," says Uncle Rondo.

"Oh, I declare," says Mama, "to think that a family of mine should quarrel on the Fourth of July, or the day after, over Stella-Rondo leaving old Mr. Whitaker and having the sweetest little adopted child! It looks like we'd all be glad!"

"Wah!" says Stella-Rondo, and has a fresh conniption fit.

"*He* left *her*—you mark my words," I says. "That's Mr. Whitaker. I know Mr. Whitaker. After all, I knew him first. I said from the beginning he'd up and leave her. I foretold every single thing that's happened."

"Where did he go?" asks Mama.

"Probably to the North Pole, if he knows what's good for him," I says.

But Stella-Rondo just bawled and wouldn't say another word. She flew to her room and slammed the door.

"Now look what you've gone and done, Sister," says Mama. "You go apologize."

"I haven't got time, I'm leaving," I says.

"Well, what are you waiting around for?" asks Uncle Rondo.

So I just picked up the kitchen clock and marched off, without saying "Kiss my foot" or anything, and never did tell Stella-Rondo good-bye.

There was a nigger girl going along on a little wagon right in front.

"Nigger girl," I says, "come help me haul these things down the hill, I'm going to live in the post office."

Took her nine trips in her express wagon. Uncle Rondo came out on the porch and threw her a nickel.

And that's the last I've laid eyes on any of my family or my family laid eyes on me for five solid days and nights. Stella-Rondo may be telling the most horrible tales in the world about Mr. Whitaker, but I haven't heard them. As I tell everybody, I draw my own conclusions.

But oh, I like it here. It's ideal, as I've been saying. You see, I've got everything cater-cornered, the way I like it. Hear the radio? All the war news. Radio, sewing machine, book ends, ironing board and that great big piano lamp—peace, that's what I like. Butter-bean vines planted all along the front where the strings are.

Of course, there's not much mail. My family are naturally the main people in China Grove, and if they prefer to vanish from the face of the earth, for all the mail they get or the mail they write, why, I'm not going to open my mouth. Some of the folks here in town are taking up for me and some turned against me. I know which is which. There are always people who will quit buying stamps just to get on the right side of Papa-Daddy.

But here I am, and here I'll stay. I want the world to know I'm happy.

And if Stella-Rondo should come to me this minute, on bended knees, and *attempt* to explain the incidents of her life with Mr. Whitaker, I'd simply put my fingers in both my ears and refuse to listen.

ANN PETRY • 1911–

Miss Muriel

ALMOST every day, Ruth Davis and I walk home from school together. We walk very slowly because we like to talk to each other and we don't get much chance in school or after school either. We are very much alike. We are both twelve years old and we are freshmen in high school and we never study—well, not very much, because we learn faster than the rest of the class. We laugh about the same things and we are curious about the same things. We even wear our hair in the same style—thick braids halfway down our backs. We are not alike in one respect. She is white and I am colored.

Yesterday when we reached the building that houses my father's drugstore, we sat down on the front steps—long wooden steps that go all the way across the front of the building. Ruth said, "I wish I lived here," and patted the steps though they are very splintery.

Aunt Sophronia must have heard our voices, because she came to the door and said, "I left my shoes at the shoemaker's this morning. Please go and get them for me," and she handed me a little cardboard ticket with a number on it.

"You want to come with me, Ruth?"

"I've got to go home. I'm sure my aunt will have things for me to do. Just like your aunt." She smiled at Aunt Sophronia.

I walked part way home with Ruth and then turned back and went up Petticoat Lane toward the shoemaker's shop. Mr. Bemish, the shoemaker, is a little man with gray hair. He has a glass eye. This eye is not the same color as his own eye. It is a deeper gray. If I stand too close to him I get a squeamish feeling because one eye moves in its socket and the other eye does not.

Mr. Bemish and I are friends. I am always taking shoes to his shop to be repaired. We do not own a horse and buggy and so we walk a great deal. In fact, there is a family rule that we must walk any distance under three miles. As a result, our shoes are in constant need of repair, the soles and heels have to be replaced, and we always seem to be in need of shoelaces. Quite often I snag the uppers on the bull briars in the woods and then the tears have to be stitched.

When I went to get Aunt Sophronia's shoes, Mr. Bemish was sitting near the window. It is a big window and he has a very nice view of the street. He had on his leather apron and his eyeglasses. His glasses are small and they have steel rims. He was sewing a shoe and he had a long length of waxed linen thread in his needle. He waxes the thread himself.

I handed him the ticket and he got up from his workbench to get the shoes. I saw that he had separated them from the other shoes. These are Aunt Sophronia's store shoes. They had been polished so that they shone like patent leather. They lay alone, near the front of the table where he keeps the shoes he has repaired. He leaned toward me and I moved away from him. I did not like being so close to his glass eye.

"The lady who brought these shoes in. Who is she?"

I looked at him and raised one eyebrow. It has taken me two months of constant practice in front of a mirror to master the art of lifting one eyebrow.

Mr. Bemish said, "What's the matter

with you? Didn't you hear what I said? Who was that lady who brought these shoes in?"

I moved further away from him. He didn't know it but I was imitating Dottle Smith, my favorite person in all the world. Dottle tells the most wonderful stories and he can act and recite poetry. He visits our family every summer. Anyway, I bowed to Mr. Bemish and I bowed to an imaginary group of people seated somewhere on my right and I said, "Gentlemen, be seated. Mr. Bones, who was that lady I saw you with last night?" I lowered the pitch of my voice and said, "That wasn't no lady. That was my *wife*."

"Girlie—"

"Why do you keep calling me 'girlie'? I have a name."

"I cannot remember people's names. I'm too old. I've told you that before."

"How old are you, Mr. Bemish?"

"None of your business," he said pettishly. "Who—"

"Well, I only asked in order to decide whether to agree with you that you're old enough to be forgetful. Does the past seem more real to you than the present?"

Mr. Bemish scowled his annoyance. "The town is full of children," he said. "It's the children who bring the shoes and come and get them after I've fixed them. They run the errands. All those children look just alike to me. I can't remember their names. I don't even try. I don't plan to clutter up my mind with a lot of children's names. I don't see the same children that often. So I call the boys 'boy,' and I call the girls 'girlie.' I've told you this before. What's the matter with you today?"

"It's spring and the church green is filled with robins looking for worms. Don't you sometimes wish you were a robin looking for a worm?"

He sighed. "Now tell me, who was that lady that brought these shoes in?"

"My Aunt Sophronia."

"Sophronia?" he said. "What a funny name. And she's your aunt?"

"Yes."

"Does she live with you?"

Mr. Bemish's cat mewed at the door and I let her in. She is a very handsome creature, gray, with white feet, and really lovely fur. "May-a-ling, May-a-ling," I said, patting her, "where have you been?" I always have the feeling that if I wait, if I persist, she will answer me. She is a very intelligent cat and very responsive.

"Does your aunt live with you?"

"Yes."

"Has she been living with you very long?"

"About six months, I guess. She's a druggist."

"You mean she knows about medicine?"

"Yes, just like my father. They run the store together."

Mr. Bemish thrust his hands in Aunt Sophronia's shoes and held them up, studying them. Then he made the shoes walk along the edge of the table, in a mincing kind of walk, a caricature of the way a woman walks.

"She has small feet, hasn't she?"

"No." I tried to sound like my mother when she disapproves of something.

He flushed and wrapped the shoes in newspaper, making a very neat bundle.

"Is she married?"

"Who? Aunt Sophronia? No. She's not married."

Mr. Bemish took his cookie crock off the shelf. He lives in the shop. Against one wall he has a kitchen stove, a big black iron stove with nickel fenders and a tea kettle on it, and there is a black iron sink with a pump right near the stove. He cooks his meals himself, he bakes bread, and usually there is a stew bubbling in a pot on the stove. In winter the windows of his little shop frost over, so that I cannot see in and he cannot see out. He draws his red curtains just after dusk and lights his lamps, and the windows look pink because of the frost and the red curtains and the light shining from behind them.

Sometimes he forgets to draw the curtains that separate his sleeping quarters from the rest of the shop and I can see his bed. It is a brass bed. He evidently polishes it, because it shines like gold. It has a very intricate design on the headboard and the footboard. He has a little piece of flowered carpet in front of his bed. I can see his white china pot under the bed. A dark suit and some shirts hang on hooks on the wall. There is a chest of drawers with a small mirror in a gold frame over it, and a washbowl and pitcher on a washstand. The washbowl and pitcher are white with pink rosebuds painted on them.

Mr. Bemish offered me a cookie from the big stoneware crock.

"Have a cookie, girlie."

He makes big thick molasses cookies. I ate three of them without stopping. I was hungry and did not know it. I ate the fourth cookie very slowly and I talked to Mr. Bemish as I ate it.

"I don't think my Aunt Sophronia will ever get married."

"Why not?"

"Well, I never heard of a lady druggist before and I don't know who a lady druggist would marry. Would she marry another druggist? There aren't any around here anywhere except my father and certainly she couldn't marry him. He's already married to my mother."

"She looks like a gypsy," Mr. Bemish said dreamily.

"You mean my Aunt Sophronia?"

Mr. Bemish nodded.

"She does not. She looks like my mother and my Aunt Ellen. And my father and Uncle Johno say they look like Egyptian queens."

They are not very tall and they move quickly and their skins are brown and very smooth and their eyes are big and black and they stand up very straight. They are not alike though. My mother is business-minded. She likes to buy and sell things. She is a chiropodist and a hairdresser. Life sometimes seems full of other people's hair and their toenails. She makes a hair tonic and sells it to her customers. She designs luncheon sets and banquet cloths and guest towels and sells them. Aunt Ellen and Uncle Johno provide culture. Aunt Ellen lectures at schools and colleges. She plays Bach and Beethoven on the piano and organ. She writes articles for newspapers and magazines.

I do not know very much about Aunt Sophronia. She works in the store. She fills prescriptions. She does embroidery. She reads a lot. She doesn't play the piano. She is very neat. The men who come in the store look at her out of the corner of their eyes. Even though she wears her hair skinned tight back from her forehead, and wears very plain clothes, dresses with long, tight sleeves and high necks, she still looks like—well, like an Egyptian queen. She is young but she seems very quiet and sober.

Mr. Bemish offered me another cookie. "I'll eat it on my way home to keep my strength up. Thank you very much," I said primly.

When I gave the shoes to Aunt Sophronia, I said, "Mr. Bemish thinks you look like a gypsy."

My mother frowned. "Did he tell you to repeat that?"

"No, he didn't. But I thought it was an interesting statement."

"I wish you wouldn't repeat the things you hear. It just causes trouble. Now every time I look at Mr. Bemish I'll wonder about him—"

"What will you wonder—I mean—"

She said I must go and practice my music lesson and ignored my question. I wonder how old I will be before I can ask questions of an adult and receive honest answers to the questions. My family always finds something for me to do. Are they not using their power as adults to give orders in order to evade the questions?

That evening, about five o'clock, Mr. Bemish came in the store. I was sitting on the bench in the front. It is a very old bench. The customers sit there while they wait for their prescriptions to be filled. The wood is a beautiful color. It is a deep, reddish brown.

Mr. Bemish sat down beside me on the bench. His presence irritated me. He kept moving his hand up and down the arms of the bench, up and down, in a quick, nervous movement. It is as though he thought he had an awl in his hand, and he is going in and out making holes in leather and then sewing, slipping a needle in and out, as he mends a saddle or a pair of boots.

My father looked at him over the top of his glasses and said, "Well, Bemish, what can I do for you?"

"Nothing. Nothing at all. I just stopped in to pass the time of day, to see how you all were—" His voice trailed away, softly.

He comes every evening. I find this very annoying. Quite often I have to squeeze myself onto the bench. Pritchett, the sexton of the Congregational church —stout, red-faced, smelling of whiskey— rings the bell for a service at seven o'clock and then he, too, sits in the front of the store, watching the customers as they come and go until closing time. He eyed Mr. Bemish rather doubtfully at first, but then ignored him. When the sexton and Mr. Bemish were on the bench, there was just room enough for me to squeeze in between them. I didn't especially mind the sexton, because he usually went to sleep, nodding and dozing until it was time to close the store. But Mr. Bemish doesn't sit still—and the movement of his hands is distracting.

My mother finally spoke to my father about Mr. Bemish. They were standing in the back room. "Why does Mr. Bemish sit out there in the store so much?" she asked.

"Nothin' else to do."

She shook her head. "I think he's interested in Sophronia. He keeps looking around for someone."

My father laughed out loud. "That dried-up old white man?"

The laughter of my father is a wonderful sound—if you know anything about music you know he sings tenor and you know he sings in the Italian fashion with an open throat and you begin to smile, and if he laughs long enough, you laugh too, because you can't help it.

"Bemish?" he said. And he laughed so hard that he had to lean against the doorjamb in order to keep his balance.

Every night right after supper, Mr. Bemish sits in the store rubbing the arm of the bench with that quick, jerking motion of his hand, nodding to people who come in, sometimes talking to them, but mostly just sitting.

Two weeks later I walked past his shop. He came to the door and called me. "Girlie," he said, beckoning.

"Yes, Mr. Bemish?"

"Is your aunt with the peculiar name still here—that is, in town, living with you?"

"Yes, she is, Mr. Bemish."

"Don't she ever go in the drugstore?"

"Not after five o'clock, Mr. Bemish. My father doesn't approve of ladies working at night. At night we act just like other people's families. We sit around the table in the dining room and talk, and we play checkers, and we read and we—"

"Yes, yes," he said impatiently. "But don't your aunt ever go anywhere at night?"

"I don't think so. I go to bed early."

"Do you think—" And he shook his head. "Never mind, girlie, never mind," and he sighed. "Here—I just made up a fresh batch of those big cookies you like so well."

I walked down Petticoat Lane toward the drugstore eating one of Mr. Bemish's thick molasses cookies. I wished I had taken time to tell him how cozy our downstairs parlor is in the winter. We have turkey-red curtains at the windows too, and we pull the window shades and draw the curtains, and there is a very thick rug on the floor and it is a small room, so the rug completely covers the floor. The piano is in there and an old-fashioned sofa with a carved mahogany frame and a very handsome round stove and it is warm in winter; and in the summer when the windows are open, you can look right out into the back yard and smell the flowers and feel the cool air that comes from the garden.

The next afternoon, Mr. Bemish came in the drugstore about quarter past three. It was a cold, windy afternoon. I had just come from school and there was a big mug of hot cocoa for me. Aunt Sophronia had it ready and waiting for me in the back room. It had just tasted the first spoonful; it was much too hot to gulp down, and I leaned way over and blew on it gently, and inhaled the rich, chocolatey smell of it. I heard my aunt say, "Why, Mr. Bemish, what are you doing out at this hour?"

"I thought I'd like an ice-cream soda." Mr. Bemish's voice sounded breathless, lighter in weight, and the pitch was lower than normal.

I peeked out at him. He was sitting near the fountain in one of the ice-cream parlor chairs. He looked very stiff and prim and neater than usual. He seems to have flattened his hair closer to his skull. This makes his head appear smaller. He was holding his head a little to one side. He looked like a bird but I cannot decide what bird—perhaps a chickadee. He drank the soda neatly and daintily. He kept looking at Aunt Sophronia.

He comes every day now, in the middle of the afternoon. He should have been in his shop busily repairing shoes or making boots, or making stews and cookies. Instead he is in our store, and his light-gray eye, the one good eye, travels busily over Aunt Sophronia. His ears seem to waggle when he hears her voice, and he has taken to giggling in a very silly fashion.

He always arrives about the same time. Sometimes I sit in one of the ice-cream parlor chairs and talk to him. He smells faintly of leather, and of shoe polish, and of wax, and of dead flowers. It was quite a while before I could place that other smell—dead flowers. Each day he stays a little longer than he stayed the day before.

I have noticed that my father narrows his eyes a little when he looks at Mr. Bemish. I heard him say to my mother, "I don't like it. I don't want to tell him not to come in here. But I don't like it—an old white man in here every afternoon looking at Sophronia and licking his chops—well, I just don't like it."

Aunt Sophronia took a sudden interest in the garden. In the afternoon, after school, I help her set out plants and sow seed. Our yard is filled with flowers in the summer; and we have a vegetable garden that in some ways is as beautiful as the flowers—it is so neat and precise-looking. We keep chickens so that we can have fresh eggs. And we raise a pig and have him butchered in the fall.

When the weather is bad and we cannot work in the garden, Aunt Sophronia and I clean house. I do not like to clean house but I do like to sort out the contents of other people's bureau drawers. We started setting Aunt Sophronia's bureau in order. She showed me a picture of her graduating class from Pharmacy College. She was the only girl in a class of boys. She was colored and the boys were white. I did not say anything about this difference in color and neither did she. But I did try to find out what it was like to be the only member of the female sex in a class filled with males.

"Didn't you feel funny with all those boys?"

"They were very nice boys."

"Oh, I'm sure they were. But didn't you feel funny being the only girl with so many young men?"

"No. I never let them get overly friendly and we got along very well."

I looked at the picture and then I looked at her and said, "You are beautiful."

She put the picture back in her top drawer. She keeps her treasures in there. She has a collar made of real lace, and a pair of very long white kid gloves, and a necklace made of gold nuggets from Colorado that a friend of my mother's left to Aunt Sophronia in her will. The gloves and the collar smell like our garden in August when the flowers are in full bloom and the sun is shining on them.

Sometimes I forget that Aunt Sophronia is an adult and that she belongs in the enemy camp, and I make the mistake of saying what I have been thinking.

I leaned against the bureau and looked down into the drawer, at the picture, and said, "You know, this picture reminds me of the night last summer when there was a female moth, one of those huge night moths, on the inside of the screen door, and all the male moths for miles around came and clung on the outside of the screen, making their wings flutter, and you know, they didn't make any sound but it was kind of scary. Weren't you—"

Aunt Sophronia closed the drawer with a hard push. "You get a broom and a dustpan and begin to sweep in the hall," she said.

On Saturday morning, after I finished washing the breakfast dishes and scrubbing the kitchen floor, I paid a call on Mr. Bemish. He is cleaning his house, too. He has taken down the red curtains that hung at the windows all winter, and the red curtains that hung in front of his bed, separating his sleeping quarters from the rest of his shop, and he was washing these curtains in a big tub at the side of his house. He was making a terrific splashing and the soapsuds were pale pink. He had his sleeves rolled up. His arms are very white and stringy-looking.

"Too much red for summer, girlie. I've got to get out the green summer ones."

He hung them on the line and poured the wash water out on the ground. It was pink.

"Your curtains ran, didn't they?" I looked at a little pink puddle left on top of a stone. "If you keep washing them, they'll be pink instead of red."

His own eye, the real one, moved away from me, and there was something secret, and rather sly, about his expression. He said, "I haven't seen your aunt in the store lately. Where is she?"

"She's been busy fixing the garden and cleaning the house. Everybody seems to be cleaning house."

"As soon as I get my green curtains put up, I'm going to ask your aunt to come have tea."

"Where would she have tea with you?"

"In my shop."

I shook my head. "Aunt Sophronia does not drink tea in people's bedrooms and you have only that one room for your shop and there's a bed in it and it would be just like—"

"I would like to have her look at some old jewelry that I have and I thought she might have tea."

"Mr. Bemish," I said, "do you like my Aunt Sophronia?"

"Now, girlie," he said, and he tittered. "Well, now, do you think your aunt likes me?"

"Not especially. Not any more than anybody else. I think you're too old for her and besides, well, you're white and

I don't think she would be very much interested in an old white man, do you?"

He frowned and said, "You go home. You're a very rude girl."

"You asked me what I thought, Mr. Bemish. I don't see why you get mad when I tell you what I think. You did ask me, Mr. Bemish."

I followed him inside his shop. He settled himself near the window and started to work on a man's boot. It needed a new sole and he cut the sole out of leather. I looked out the front window. There is always enough breeze to make his sign move back and forth; it makes a sighing noise. In the winter if there's a wind, the sign seems to groan because it moves back and forth quickly. There is a high-laced shoe painted on the sign. The shoe must once have been a deep, dark red, but it has weathered to a soft rose color.

Mr. Bemish is my friend and I wanted to indicate that I am still fond of him though I disapprove of his interest in Aunt Sophronia. I searched for some topic that would indicate that I enjoy talking to him.

I said, "Why don't you have a picture of a man's boot on your sign?"

"I prefer ladies' shoes. More delicate, more graceful—" He made an airy gesture with his awl and simpered.

I went home and I told Aunt Sophronia that Mr. Bemish is going to ask her to have tea with him.

"Will you go?"

"Of course not," she said impatiently.

Aunt Sophronia did not have tea with Mr. Bemish. He sees her so rarely in the store that he finally came in search of her.

It is summer now and the Wheeling Inn is open for the season. The great houses along the waterfront are occupied by their rich owners. We are all very busy. At night after the store is closed, we sit in the back yard. On those warm June nights, the fireflies come out, and there is a kind of soft summer light, composed of moonlight and starlight. The grass is thick underfoot and the air is sweet. Almost every night my mother and my father and Aunt Sophronia and I, and sometimes Aunt Ellen and Uncle Johno, sit there in the quiet and in the sweetness and in that curious soft light.

Last night when we were sitting there, Mr. Bemish came around the side of the house. There was something tentative in the way he came towards us. I had been lying on the grass and I sat up straight, wondering what they would do and what they would say.

He sidled across the lawn. He didn't speak until he was practically upon us. My mother was sitting in the hammock under the cherry tree, rocking gently back and forth, and she didn't see him until he spoke. He said, "Good evening." He sounded as though he was asking a question.

We all looked at him. I hoped that someone would say: What are you doing in our back yard, our private place, our especially private place? You are an intruder, go back to your waxed thread and your awl, go back to your house and your cat. Nobody said anything.

He stood there for a while, waiting, hesitant, and then he bowed and sat down, cross-legged, on the grass near Aunt Sophronia. She was sitting on one of the benches. And he sat so close to her that her skirt was resting on one of his trouser legs. I kept watching him. One of his hands reached toward her skirt and he gently fingered the fabric. Either she felt this or the motion attracted her attention, because she moved away from him, and gathered her skirt about her, and then stood up and said, "The air is making me sleepy. Good night."

The next afternoon I took a pair of my father's shoes to Mr. Bemish to have the heels fixed. My father wears high-laced black shoes. I left them on Mr. Bemish's work table.

"You can get them tomorrow."

I did not look right at him. I leaned over and patted May-a-ling. "She has such a lovely name, Mr. Bemish. It seems to me a name especially suited for a cat."

Mr. Bemish looked at me over the top of his little steel-rimmed glasses. "You've got a nice back yard," he said.

"I don't think you should have been in it."

"Why not?" he asked sharply. "Did anybody say that I shouldn't have been in it?"

"No. But the front part of the building, the part where the drugstore is, belongs to everybody. The back part of the building, and upstairs in the building, and the yard are ours. The yard is a private part of our lives. You don't belong in it. You're not a part of our family."

"But I'd like to be a part of your family."

"You can't get to be a part of other people's families. You have to be born into a family. The family part of our lives is just for us. Besides, you don't seem to understand that you're the wrong color, Mr. Bemish."

He didn't answer this. He got up and got his cookie crock and silently offered me a cookie.

After I returned from the shoeshop, I sat on the wooden steps that run across the front of the drugstore. I was trying to decide how I really feel about Mr. Bemish. I always sit at the far end of the steps with my back against the tight-board fence. It is a very good place from which to observe the street, the front of the store, the church green. People walk past me not noticing that I am there. Sometimes their conversations are very unusual. I can see a long way down the path that bisects the green. It is a dirt path and not too straight. The only straight paths in town are those in front of the homes of people who have gardeners.

From where I sat I could see a man approaching. He was strolling down the path that crosses the church green. This is a most unusual way for a man to walk in Wheeling in the summer. It is during the summer that the year-round residents earn their living. They mow lawns, and cut hedges, and weed gardens, and generally look after the summer people. Able-bodied men in Wheeling walked fast in summer.

This tall, broad-shouldered man was strolling down the path. He was wearing a white suit, the pants quite tight in the leg, and he had his hands in his hip pockets, and a stiff straw hat, a boater, on the back of his head.

I sat up very straight when I discovered that this was a very dark colored man. I could not imagine where he came from. He could not possibly be a butler or a waiter even if he wanted to and spent a whole lifetime in trying. He would never be able to walk properly—he would always swagger, and who ever heard of a swaggering butler or a waiter who strolled around a table?

As he came nearer, I saw that he had a beard, an untidy shaggy beard like the beard of a goat. His hair was long and shaggy and rough-looking too. Though he was tall, with wide shoulders, the thick rough hair on his head and the goat's beard made his head and face look too big, out of proportion to his body.

When he saw me, he came straight toward me. He bent over me, smiling, and I moved back away from him, pressing against the fence. His eyes alarmed me. Whenever I think about his eyes, I close mine, trying to shut his out. They are reddish brown and they look hot, and having looked into them, I cannot seem to look away. I have never seen anyone with eyes that color or with that strange quality, whatever it is. I described them as looking "hot," but that's not possible. It must be that they are the color of something that I associate with fire or heat. I do not know what it is.

"You lost?" he said.

"No. Are you?"

"Yup. All us colored folks is lost." He said this in a husky, unmusical voice, and turned away and went in the store.

I went in the store, too. If this unusual-looking man with the goat's beard got into a discussion of "all of us colored folks is lost" with my father, I wanted to hear it.

My father said, "How-de-do?" and he made it a question.

The bearded man nodded and said, "The druggist in?"

"I'm the druggist."

"This your store?"

"That's right."

"Nice place you got here. You been here long?"

My father grunted. I waited for him to make the next move in the game we called Stanley and Livingstone. All colored strangers who came into our store were Livingstones—and it was up to the members of our family to find out which lost Mr. Livingstone or which lost Mrs. Livingstone we had encountered in the wilds of the all-white town of Wheeling. When you live in a town where there aren't any other colored people, naturally you're curious when another colored person shows up.

I sat down in the front of the store and waited for my father to find out which Mr. David Livingstone he was talking to and what he was doing in our town. But my father looked at him with no expression on his face and said, "And what did you want?"

The man with the goat's beard fished in the pocket of his tight white pants. In order to do this, he thrust his leg forward a little to ease the strain on the fabric, and thus he gave the impression that he was pawing the ground. He handed my father a piece of paper.

"I got a prescription for a lotion—"

"It'll take a few minutes," my father said, and went in the back room.

The bearded man came and sat beside me.

"Do you live here in Wheeling?" I asked.

"I work at the Inn. I'm the piano player."

"You play the piano?"

"And sing. I'm the whole orchestra. I play for the dinner hour. I play for all those nice rich white folks to dance at night. I'll be here all summer."

"You will?"

"That's right. And I've never seen a deader town."

"What's your name?"

"Chink."

"Mr. Chink—"

"No," he said, and stood up. "Chink is my first name. Chink Johnson."

Mr. Johnson is a restless kind of man. He keeps moving around even when he is sitting still, moving his feet, his hands, his head. He crosses his legs, uncrosses them, clasps his hands together, unclasps them.

"Why are you having a prescription filled?"

"Hand lotion. I use it for my hands."

My father came out of the back room, wrapped up a bottle, said, "Here you are."

Chink Johnson paid him, said good-by to me, and I said, "Goodby, Chink."

"What's his name?"

"Chink Johnson. He plays the piano at the Inn."

Chink Johnson seems to me a very interesting and unusual man. To my surprise, my father did not mention our newest Mr. Livingstone to the family. He said nothing about him at all. Neither did I.

Yet he comes in the drugstore fairly often. He buys cigarettes and throat lozenges. Sometimes he drives over from the Inn in a borrowed horse and carriage.

Sometimes he walks over. My father has very little to say to him.

He doesn't linger in the store, because my father's manner is designed to discourage him from lingering or hanging around. But he does seem to be looking for something. He looks past the door of the prescription room, and on hot afternoons, the door in the very back is open and you can see our yard, with its beautiful little flower gardens, and he looks out into the yard, seems to search it. When he leaves he looks at the house, examining it. It is as though he is trying to see around a corner, see through the walls, because some sixth sense has told him that there exists on the premises something that will interest him, and if he looks hard enough, he will find it.

My mother finally caught a glimpse of him as he went out the front door. She saw what I saw—the goat's beard in silhouette, the forward thrust of his head, the thick shaggy hair—because we were standing in the prescription room looking toward the door.

"Who was that?" she asked, her voice sharp.

"That's the piano player at the Inn," my father said.

"You've never mentioned him. What is his name?"

"Jones," my father said.

I started to correct him but I was afraid to interrupt him because he started talking fast and in a very loud voice. "Lightfoot Jones," he said. "Shake Jones. Barrelhouse Jones." He started tapping on the glass case in front of him. I have never heard him do this before. He sings in the Congregational church choir. He has a pure, lyric tenor voice, and he sings all the tenor solos, the "Sanctus," "The Heavens Are Telling." You can tell from his speaking voice that he sings. He is always humming or singing or whistling. There he was with a pencil in his hand, tapping out a most peculiar rhythm on the glass of a showcase.

"Shake Jones," he repeated. "Rhythm in his feet. Rhythm in his blood. Rhythm in his feet. Rhythm in his blood. Beats out his life, beats out his lungs, beats out his liver, on a piano," and he began a different and louder rhythm with his foot. "On a pi-an-o. On a pi-an-o. On a pi—"

"Samuel, what is the matter with you? What are you talking about?"

"I'm talkin' about Tremblin' Shakefoot Jones. The piano player. The piano player who can't sit still, and comes in here lookin' around and lookin' around, prancin' and stampin' his hoofs, and sniffin' the air. Just like a stallion who smells a mare—a stallion who—"

"Samuel! How can you talk that way in front of this child?"

My father was silent.

I said, "His name is Chink Johnson."

My father roared, terrible in his anger, "His name is Duke. His name is Bubber. His name is Count, is Maharajah, is King of Lions. I don't give a good goddamn what he calls himself. I don't want him and his restless feet hangin' around. He can let his long feet slap somebody else's floor. But not mine. Not here—"

He glared at me and glared at my mother. His fury silenced us. At that moment his eyes were red-brown just like Chink Jones, no, Johnson. He is shorter, he has no beard, but he had at that moment a strong resemblance to Chink.

I added to his fury. I said, "You look just like Chink Johnson."

He said, "Ah!!! . . ." He was so angry I could not understand one word he said. I went out the front door, and across the street, and sat on the church steps and watched the world go by and listened to the faint hum it made as it went around and around.

I saw Mr. Bemish go in the drugstore. He stayed a long time. That gave me a certain pleasure because I knew he had come to eat his ice-cream soda, mouthful by mouthful, from one of our long-handled ice-cream-soda spoons, and to look at Aunt Sophronia as he nibbled at the ice cream. He looks at her out of the corners of his eyes, stealing sly little glances at her. I knew that Aunt Sophronia would not be in the store until much later and that he was wasting his time. It was my father's birthday and Aunt Sophronia was in the kitchen baking a great big cake for him.

If Mr. Bemish had known this, he might have dropped in on the birthday celebration, even though he hadn't been invited. After all, he had sidled into our back yard without being invited and our yard is completely enclosed by a tight-board fence, and there is a gate that you have to open to get in the yard, so that entering our yard is like walking into our living room. It is a very private place. Mr. Bemish is the only person that I know of who has come into our yard without being invited, and he keeps coming, too.

After Mr. Bemish left the store, I crossed the street and sat outside on the store steps. It was hot. It was very quiet. Old Lady Chimble crossed the church green carrying a black silk umbrella, and she opened it and used it as a sunshade. A boy went by on a bicycle. Frances Jackins (we called her Aunt Frank), the colored cook in the boardinghouse across the street, hurried across the street carrying something in a basket. She is always cross and usually drunk. She drinks gin. Mother says this is what has made Aunt Frank's lips look as though they were turned inside out and she says this is called a "gin lip." They are bright-red, almost like a red gash across the dark skin of her face. I want very much to ask Aunt Frank about this—how it feels, when it happened, etc.—and someday I will, but I have not as yet had a suitable opportunity. When she is drunk, she cannot give a sensible answer to a sensible question, and when she is sober, or partially sober, she is very irritable and constantly finds fault with me. She is absolutely no relation to us; it is just that my mother got in the habit of calling her "Aunt" Frank many years ago and so we all call her that. Because I am young, she tries to boss me and to order me around, and she calls me "Miss" in a very unpleasant, sarcastic way.

She is a very good cook when she is sober. But when she is drunk, she burns everything, and she is always staggering across the street and stumbling up our back steps, with bread pans filled with dough which would not rise because she has forgotten the yeast, and with burned cakes and pies and burned hams and roasts of beef. When she burns things, they are not just scorched; they are blackened and hardened until they are like charcoal.

Almost every night she scratches at our back door. I have sharper hearing than everybody else; I can hear people walking around the side of the house and no one else has heard them—anyway, I always hear her first. I open the door suddenly and very fast, and she almost falls into the kitchen and stands there swaying, and fouling our kitchen with the sweetish smell of gin and the dank and musty odor of her clothes.

She always has a dip of snuff under her upper lip and she talks around this obstruction, so that her voice is peculiar. She speaks quickly to keep the snuff in place, and sometimes she pauses and works her upper lip, obviously getting the snuff in some special spot. When she comes to the back door at night, she puts the basket of ruined food just inside the door, on the floor, and says to my mother, "Here, Mar-tha, throw this away. Throw it a-way for me. Give it to the hens. Feed it to the pig—"

She turns all two-syllable words into two separate one-syllable words. She doesn't say "Martha" all in one piece. She separates it, so that it becomes "Mar-tha"; she doesn't say "away," but "a-way." It is a very jerky kind of speech.

I am always given the job of burying the stuff in the backyard, way down in the back. I dig a hole and throw the blackened mess into it and then cover it with lime to hasten decomposition and discourage skunks and dogs.

Sometimes I hide behind the fence and yell at her on her way back across the street:

> Ole Aunt Frankie
> Black as tar
> Tried to get to heaven
> In a 'lectric car.
> Car got stalled in an underpass,
> Threw Aunt Frankie right on her ass.

Whenever I singsong this rhyme at her, she invariably tries to climb over the fence, a furious drunken old woman, threatening me with the man's umbrella that she carries. I should think she would remember from past performances that she cannot possibly reach me. But she always tries. After several futile efforts, she gives up and goes back to the boardinghouse across the street. A lot of old maids and widows live there. No gentlemen. Just ladies. They spend their spare time rocking on the front porch, and playing whist, and looking over at the drugstore. Aunt Frank spends her spare time in the kitchen of the boardinghouse, rocking and emptying bottle after bottle of gin.

But on the day of my father's birthday, she was sober; at least, she walked as though she were. She had a basket on her arm with a white napkin covering its contents. I decided she must have made something special for my father's supper. She went in the drugstore, and when she came out, she didn't have the basket. She saw me sitting on the steps but she ignored me.

Aunt Sophronia came and stood in the window. She had washed the glass globes that we keep filled with blue, red, and yellow liquid. She was wearing a dark skirt and a white blouse. Her hair was no longer skinned tight back from her forehead; it was curling around her forehead, perhaps because she had been working in the garden, bending over, and the hairpins that usually hold it so tightly in place had worked themselves loose. She didn't look real. The sun was shining in the window and it reflected the lights from the jars of colored water back on her face and her figure, and she looked golden and rose-colored and lavender and it was though there was a rainbow moving in the window.

Chink Johnson drove up in his borrowed horse and carriage. He stood and talked to me and then started to go in the store, saw Aunt Sophronia, and stood still. He took a deep breath. I could hear him. He took off the stiff straw hat that he wore way back on his head and bowed to her. She nodded, as though she really didn't want to, and turned away and acted as though she were very busy.

He grabbed my arm and actually pinched it.

"What are you doin'?" I said angrily. "What is the matter with you? Let go my arm."

"Shut up," he said impatiently, pinching harder. His fingers felt as though they were made of iron. "Who is that?"

I pried his fingers loose and rubbed my arm. "Where?"

"In the window. Who is that girl in the window?"

"That's my Aunt Sophronia."

"Your aunt? Your aunt?"

"Yes."

He went in the store. One moment he was standing beside me and the next moment he had practically leaped inside the store.

I went in too. He was leaning in the window, saying "Wouldn't you like to go for a walk with me this Sunday?" She shook her head. "Well, couldn't you go for a ride with me? I'll call for you—"

Aunt Sophronia said, "I work every day."

"Every day?" he said. "But that's not possible. Nobody works every day. I'll be back tomorrow—"

And he was gone. Aunt Sophronia looked startled. She didn't look angry, just sort of surprised.

I said, "Tomorrow and tomorrow and tomorrow—" And I thought, well, she's got two suitors now. There's this Shake Jones Livingstone, otherwise known as Chink Johnson, and there's Mr. Bemish. I do not think I would pick either one. Mr. Bemish is too old even though he is my friend. I think of Chink Johnson as my friend too, but I do not think he would make a good husband. I tried to decide why I do not approve of him as a husband for Aunt Sophronia. I think it is because Aunt Sophronia is a lady and Chink Johnson is—well—he is not a gentleman.

That night at supper we celebrated my father's birthday. At that hour nobody much came in the store. Pickett, the sexton, sat on the bench in the front and if anybody came in and wanted my father, he'd come to the back door and holler for him.

There was a white tablecloth on the big, oak dining-room table, and we used my mother's best Haviland china and the sterling-silver knives and forks with the rose pattern, and there was a pile of packages by my father's plate, and there were candles on the cake and we had ice cream for dessert. My old enemy, Aunt Frank, had delivered Parker House rolls for his birthday and had made him a milk-panful of rice pudding, because my father has always said that when he dies he hopes it will be because he drowns in a sea composed of rice pudding, that he could eat his weight in rice pudding, that he could eat rice pudding morning, noon, and night. Aunt Frank must have been sober when she made the pudding, for it was creamy and delicious and I ate two helpings of it right along with my ice cream.

I kept waiting for Aunt Sophronia to say something about Chink Johnson. He is a very unusual-looking man and we've never had a customer, colored or white, with that kind of beard. She did not mention him. Neither did I. My father has never mentioned him—at least not at the table. I wonder if my father hopes he will vanish. Perhaps they are afraid he will become a part of the family circle if they mention him.

Chink Johnson has become a part of the family circle and he used the same method that Mr. Bemish used. He just walked into the yard and into the house. I was upstairs, and I happened to look out of the window, and there was Chink Johnson walking up the street. He opened our gate, walked around the side of the house and into our back yard. I hurried to the back of the house and looked out the window and saw him open the screen door and go into the kitchen. He didn't knock on the door either, he just walked in.

For the longest time I didn't hear a sound. I listened and listened. I must have stood still for fifteen minutes. Then I heard someone playing our piano. I knew it must be Chink Johnson because this was not the kind of music anyone in our house would have been playing. I ran downstairs. My mother had been in the cellar, and she came running up out of the cellar, and my father came hurrying over from the drugstore. We all stood and looked and looked.

Chink was sitting at our piano. He had a cigarette dangling from his lower lip, and the smoke from the cigarette was like a cloud—a blue-gray, hazy kind of cloud around his face, his eyes, his beard —so that you could only catch glimpses of them through the smoke. He was playing some kind of fast, discordant-sounding music and he was slapping the floor with one of his long feet and he was slapping the keys with his long fingers.

Aunt Sophronia was leaning against the piano looking down at him. He did not use music when he played, and he never once looked at the keyboard, he just kept looking right into Aunt Sophronia's eyes. I thought my father would tell Chink to go slap somebody else's floor with his long feet, but my mother gave him one of those now-don't-say-a-word looks and he glared at Chink and went back to the drugstore.

Chink stayed a long time, he played the piano, he sang, or rather I guess you would say he talked to the music. It is a very peculiar kind of musical performance. He plays some chords, a whole series of them, and he makes peculiar changes in the chords as he plays, and then he says the words of a song—he doesn't really sing, but his voice does change in pitch to, in a sense, match the chords he is playing, and he does talk to a kind of rhythm which also matches the chords. I sat down beside him and watched what he was doing, and listened to the words he said, and though it is not exactly music as I am accustomed to hearing it, I found it very interesting. He told me that what he does with those songs is known as the "talkin' blues." Only he said *talk*in'" and he made "blues" sound like it was two separate words, not just a two-syllable word, but two distinct words.

I have been trying to play the piano the way he does but I get nothing but terrible sounds. I pretend that I am blind and keep my eyes closed all the time while I feel for chords. He must have a special gift for this because it is an extremely difficult thing that he is doing and I don't know whether I will ever be able to do it. He has a much better ear for music than I have.

Chink Johnson comes to see Aunt Sophronia almost every day. Sometimes when I look out in the back yard, Mr. Bemish is out there too. He always sits on the ground, and at his age, I should think it might give him rheumatism. He must be a very brave little man or else his love for Aunt Sophronia has given him great courage. I say this because Chink Johnson is very rude to Mr. Bemish and he stares at him with a dreadfully cruel look on his face. If I were small and slender and old like Mr. Bemish, I would not sit in the same yard with a much bigger, much younger man who obviously did not want me there.

I have thought a great deal about Mr. Bemish. I like him. He is truly a friend. But I do not think he should be interested in Aunt Sophronia—at least not in a loving kind of way. The thing that bothers me is that I honestly cannot decide whether I object to him as a suitor for her because he is white or because he is old. Sometimes I think it is for both reasons. I am fairly certain it isn't just because he's old. This bothers me. If my objections to him are because he's white (and that's what I told him, but I often say things that I know people do not want to hear and that they particularly do not want to hear from someone very much younger than they are), then I have been trained on the subject of race just as I have been "trained" to be a Christian. I know how I was trained to be a Christian—Sunday school, prayers, etc. I do not know exactly how I've been "trained" on the subject of race. Then why do I feel like this about Mr. Bemish?

Shortly after I wrote that, I stopped puzzling about Mr. Bemish because summer officially started—at least for me. It is true that school had been out for a long time, and we are wearing our summer clothes, and the yard is filled with flowers—but summer never really gets under way for me until Dottle Smith comes for his yearly visit.

Dottle and Uncle Johno went to school together. They look sort of alike. They are big men and they are so light in color they look like white men. But something in them (Dottle says that it is a "cultivated and developed and carefully nourished hatred of white men") will not permit them to pass for white. Dottle teaches English and elocution and dramatics at a school for colored people in Georgia, and he gives lectures and readings during the summer to augment his income. Uncle Johno is the chief fund-raising agent for a colored school in Louisiana.

I believe that my attitude towards Mr. Bemish stems from Dottle Smith. And Johno. They are both what my father calls race-conscious. When they travel on trains in the South, they ride in Jim Crow coaches until the conductor threatens to have them arrested unless they sit in the sections of the train reserved for whites. They are always being put out of the colored sections of waiting rooms, and warned out of the colored sections of towns, and being refused lodgings in colored rooming houses on the grounds that they would be a source of embarrassment—nobody would be able to figure out why a white man wanted to live with colored people, and they would be suspected of being spies, but of what kind or to what purpose, they have never been able to determine.

I have just reread what I have written here, and I find that I've left out the reason why I am writing so much about Dottle. Yesterday afternoon when I came back from an errand, there was a large, heavy-looking bag—leather, but it was shaped like a carpet-bag—near the bench where the customers sit when they wait for prescriptions. I recognized it immediately. I have seen that bag every summer for as far back as I can remember. I wondered if Dottle had come alone this time or if he had a friend with him. Sometimes he brings a young man with him. These young men look very much alike—they are always slender, rather shy, have big dark eyes and very smooth skin just about the color of bamboo.

I looked at Dottle's big battered old bag sitting on the floor near the bench, and I could almost see him, with his long curly hair, and I could hear him reciting poetry in his rich, buttery voice. He can quote all the great speeches from *Hamlet, Macbeth, Richard II,* and he can recite the sonnets.

I loved him. He was lively and funny and unexpected. Sometimes he would grab my braid and shout in his best Shakespearean voice, "Seize on her Furies, take her to your torments!"

I looked at Dottle's battered bag and I said to my father, "Is he alone? Or has he got one of those pretty boys with him?"

My father looked at me over the top of his glasses. "Alone."

"How come he to leave his bag here?"

"Well, the Ecckles aren't home. Ellen's gone on vacation—"

"Why does Aunt Ellen always go on vacation when Dottle comes?"

My father ignored this and went on talking. "Johno's gone to Albany collecting money for the school."

"Where is Dottle now?"

"I'm right here, sugar," and Dottle Smith opened the screen door and came in. He looked bigger than he had the summer before. He hugged me. He smelled faintly of lavender.

"You went and grew, honey," he said, and took off his hat and bowed. It was a wide-brimmed panama, and he had on a starched white shirt, and a flowing Byronic kind of black tie, and I looked at him with absolute delight. He was being a Southern "cunnel" and he was such an actor—I thought I could see lace at his wrists, hear mockingbirds sing, see a white-columned mansion, hear hoofbeats in the distance, and hear a long line of slaves, suitably clad as footmen and coachmen and butlers and housemen, murmur, Yes, massah, Yes, massah. It was all there in his voice.

"Why, in another couple years I'll be recitin' poetry to you. How's your momma? This summer I'll have to teach you how to talk. These Yankah teachers you've got all talk through their noses. They got you doin' the same thing—"

For two whole days I forgot about Chink Johnson and Mr. Bemish and Aunt Sophronia. Dottle liked to go fishing and crabbing; he liked to play whist; and he could tell the most marvelous stories and act them out.

The very next day Dottle and Uncle Johno and I went crabbing. We set out early in the morning with our nets and our fishing lines and the rotten meat we used for bait, and our lunch and thermos bottles with lemonade in them. It was a two-mile walk from where we lived to the creek where we caught crabs.

There was a bridge across the creek, an old wooden bridge. Some of the planks were missing. We stood on this bridge or sat on it and threw our lines in the water. Once in a great while a horse and wagon would drive across and set the planks to vibrating. Johno and Dottle would hop off the bridge. But I stayed on and held to the railing. The bridge trembled under my feet, and the horse and wagon would thunder across, and the driver usually waved and hollered, "I gotta go fast or we'll all fall in."

The water in the creek was so clear I could see big crabs lurking way down on the bottom; I could see little pieces of white shells and beautiful stones. We didn't talk much while we were crabbing. Sometimes I lay flat on my stomach on the bridge and looked down into the water, watching the little eddies and whirlpools that formed after I threw my line in.

Before we ate our lunch, we went wading in the creek. Johno and Dottle rolled up the legs of their pants, and their legs were so white I wondered if they were that white all over, and if they were, how they could be colored. We sat on the bank of the creek and ate our lunch. Afterwards Dottle and Johno told stories, wonderful stories in which animals talk, and there are haunted houses and ghosts and demons, and old colored preachers who believe in heaven and hell.

They always started off the same way. Dottle said to Johno, "Mr. Bones, be seated."

Though I have heard some of these stories many, many times, Dottle and Johno never tell them exactly the same. They change their gestures, they vary their facial expressions and the pitch of their voices.

Dottle almost always tells the story about the colored man who goes in a store in a small town in the South and asks for Muriel cigars. The white man who owns the store says (and here Johno becomes an outraged Southern white man), "Nigger, what's the matter with you? Don't you see that picture of that beautiful white woman on the front of this box? When you ask for them cigars, you say *Miss* Muriel cigars!"

Though Uncle Johno is a good storyteller, he is not as good, not as funny or as dramatic as Dottle. When I listen to Dottle I can see the old colored preacher who spent the night in a haunted house. I see him approaching the house, the wind blowing his coattails, and finally he takes refuge inside because of the violence of the storm. He lights a fire in the fireplace and sits down by it and rubs his hands together, warming them. As he sits there, he hears heavy footsteps coming down the stairs (and Dottle makes his hand go thump, thump, thump on the bank of the creek) and the biggest cat the old man has ever seen comes in and sits down, looks at the old preacher, looks around, and says, "Has Martin got here yet?" The old man is too startled and too nervous to answer. He hears heavy footsteps again—thump, thump, thump. And a second cat, much bigger than the first one, comes in, and sits down right next to the old preacher. Both cats stare at him, and then the second cat says to the first cat, "Has Martin got here yet?" and the first cat shakes his head. There is something so speculative in their glance that the old man gets more and more uneasy. He wonders if they are deciding to eat him. The wind howls in the chimney, puffs of smoke blow back into the room. Then another and bigger cat thumps down the stairs. Finally there are six enormous cats, three on each side of him. Each one of these cats has asked the same question of the others—"Martin got here yet?" A stair-shaking tread begins at the top of the stairs, the cats all look at each other, and the old man grabs his hat, and says to the assembled cats, "You tell Martin ah been here but ah've gone."

I clapped when Dottle finished this story. I looked around thinking how glad I am he is here and what a wonderful place this is to listen to stories. The sun is warm but there is a breeze and it blows through the long marsh grass which borders the creek. The grass moves, seems to wave. Gulls fly high overhead. The only sound is the occasional cry of a gull and the lapping of water against the piling of the bridge.

Johno tells the next story. It is about an old colored preacher and a rabbit. The old man tries to outrun an overfriendly and very talkative rabbit. The rabbit keeps increasing in size. The old man runs away from him and the rabbit catches up with him. Each time the rabbit says, "That was some run we had, wasn't it, brother?" Finally the old man runs until he feels as though his lungs are going to burst and his legs will turn to rubber, and he looks back and doesn't see the rabbit anywhere in sight. He sits down on a stone to rest and catch his breath. He has just seated himself when he discovers the rabbit sitting right beside him, smiling. The rabbit is now the same size as the preacher. The rabbit rolls his eyes and lisps, "That wath thome run we had, wathn't it?" The old man stood up, got ready to run again, and said, "Yes, that was some run we had, brother, but" —he took a deep breath—"you ain't *seen* no runnin' yet."

After they finished telling stories, we all took naps. Dottle and Johno were wearing old straw hats, wide-brimmed panamas with crooked, floppy brims. Dottle had attached a piece of mosquito netting to his, and it hung down across his shoulders. From the back he looked like a woman who was wearing a veil.

When we woke up it was late in the afternoon and time to start for home. I ran part of the way. Then I sat down by the side of the road, in the shade, and waited until they caught up with me.

Dottle said, "Sugar, what are you in such a hurry for?"

I said, laughing, "Miss Muriel, you tell Martin I been here but I've gone and that he ain't *seen* no runnin' yet."

I got home first. Chink Johnson was in the store. When Dottle and Johno arrived, I introduced Chink to my uncles, Johno and Dottle. They didn't seem much impressed with each other. Johno nodded and Dottle smiled and left. Chink watched Dottle as he went toward the back room. Dottle has a very fat bottom and he sort of sways from side to side as he walks.

Chink said, "He seems kind of ladylike. He related on your mother's side?"

"He's not related at all. He's an old friend of Uncle Johno's. They went to school together. In Atlanta, Georgia." I sounded very condescending. "Do you know where that is?"

"Yeah. Nigger, read this. Nigger, don't let sundown catch you here. Nigger, if you can't read this, run anyway. If you can't run—then vanish. Just vanish out. I know the place. I came from there."

My father was standing outside on the walk talking to Aunt Frank, so I felt at liberty to speak freely and I said, "Nigger, what are you talkin' about you want Muriel cigars. You see this picture of this beautiful red-headed white woman, nigger, you say *Miss* Muriel."

Chink stood up and he was frowning and his voice was harsh. "Little girl, don't you talk that way. I talk that way if I feel like it but don't you ever talk that way."

I felt as though I had been betrayed. One moment he was my friend and we were speaking as equals and the next moment, without warning, he is an adult who is scolding me in a loud, harsh voice. I was furious and I could feel tears welling up in my eyes. This made me angrier. I couldn't seem to control my weeping. Recently, and I do not know how it happened, whenever I am furiously angry, I begin to cry.

Chink leaned over and put his hand under my chin, lifted my face, saw the tears, and he kissed my cheek. His beard was rough and scratchy. He smelled like the pine woods, and I could see pine needles in his hair and in his beard, and I wondered if he and Aunt Sophronia had been in the woods.

"Sugar," he said gently, "I don't like that Miss Muriel story. It ought to be told the other way around. A colored man should be tellin' a white man, 'White man, you see this picture of this beautiful colored woman? *White* man, you say *Miss* Muriel!'"

He went out of the store through the back room into the yard just as though he were a member of the family. It hadn't taken him very long to reach this position. Almost every afternoon he goes for a walk with Aunt Sophronia. I watch them when they leave the store. He walks so close to her that he seems to surround her, and he has his head bent so that his face is close to hers. Once I met them strolling up Petticoat Lane, his dark face so close to hers that his goat's beard was touching her smooth brown cheek.

My mother used to watch them too, as they walked side by side on the dirt path that led to the woods—miles and miles of woods. Sometimes he must have said things that Aunt Sophronia didn't like, because she would turn her head sharply away from him.

I decided that once you got used to his beard and the peculiar color and slant of his eyes, why you could say he had an interesting face. I do not know what it is about his eyes that makes me think of heat. But I know what color they are. They are the color of petrified wood after it's been polished, it's a red brown, and that's what his eyes are like.

I like the way he plays the piano, though I do not like his voice. I cannot get my mother to talk about him. My father grunts when I mention Chink's name and scowls so ferociously that it is obvious he does not like him.

I tried to find out what Aunt Sophronia thought of him. Later in the day I found her in the store alone and I said, "Do you like Chink Johnson?"

She said, "Run along and do the supper dishes."

"But do you?"

"Don't ask personal questions," she said, and her face and neck flushed.

She must have liked him though. She not only went walking with him in the afternoon, but on Sunday mornings he went to church with her. He wore a white linen suit and that same stiff straw hat way back on his head. He brought her presents—a tall bottle of violet Eau de Cologne, a bunch of Parma violets made of silk, but they looked real. On Sundays, Aunt Sophronia wore the violets pinned at her waist and they made her look elegant, like a picture in a book.

I said, "Oh, you look beautiful."

My mother said, dryly, "Very stylish."

We all crossed the street together on Sunday mornings. They went to church. I went to Sunday school. Sunday school was out first and I waited for them to come down the church steps. Aunt Sophronia came down the church steps and he would be so close behind her that he might have been dancing with her and matching his leg movements to hers. Suddenly he was in front of her and down on the path before she was and he turned and held out his hand. Even there on the sidewalk he wasn't standing still. It is as though his feet and his hands are more closely connected to his heart, to his central nervous system, than is true of other people, so that during every waking moment he moves, tapping his foot on the floor, tapping his fingers on a railing, on somebody's arm, on a table top. I wondered if he kept moving like that when he was asleep, tapping quarter notes with his foot, playing eighth notes with his right hand, half notes with his left hand. He attacked a piano when he played, violated it—violate a piano? I thought, violate Aunt Sophronia?

He stood on the dirt path and held out his hand to Aunt Sophronia, smiling, helping her down the church steps.

"Get your prayers said, sugar?" he said to me.

"Yes. I said one for you and one for the family. Aunt Sophronia, you smell delicious. Like violets—"

"She does, doesn't she?"

We walked across the street to the drugstore, hand in hand. Chink was in the middle and he held one of my hands and one of Aunt Sophronia's. He stays for dinner on Sundays. And on Sunday nights we close the store early and we all sat in the back yard, where it is cool. Mr. Bemish joined us in the yard. At dusk the fireflies come out, and then as the darkness deepens, bats swoop around us. Aunt Sophronia says "Oooooh!" and holds on to her head, afraid one might get entangled in her hair.

Dottle took out one of his big white handkerchiefs and tied it around his head, and said in his richest, most buttery voice, " 'One of the nocturnal or crepuscular flying mammals constituting the order Chiroptera.' "

Dottle sprawled in a chair and recited poetry or told long stories about the South—stories that sometimes had so much of fear and terror and horror in them that we shivered even though the air was warm. Chink didn't spend the evening. He sat in one of the lawn chairs, tapping on the arm with his long, flexible fingers, and then left. Mr. Bemish always stays until we go in for the night. He takes no part in the conversation, but sits on the ground, huddled near Aunt Sophronia's skirts. Once when a bat swooped quite close, Aunt Sophronia clutched his arm.

Sometimes Dottle recites whole acts from *Macbeth* or *Hamlet* or all of the Song of Solomon, or sometimes he recited the loveliest of Shakespeare's sonnets. We forget the bats swooping over our heads, ignore the mosquitoes that sting our ankles and our legs, and sit mesmerized while he declaims, "Shall I compare thee to a summer's day?"

The summer is going faster and faster —perhaps because of the presence of Aunt Sophronia's suitors. I don't suppose Dottle is really a suitor, but he goes through the motions. He picks little bouquets for her—bachelor buttons and candytuft—and leaves them on the kitchen table. He always calls her "Miss Sophronia." If we are outdoors and she comes out to sit in the yard, he leaps to his feet, and bows and says, "Wait, wait. Befo' you sit on that bench, let me wipe it off," and he pulls out an enormous linen handkerchief and wipes off the bench. He is always bowing and kissing her hand.

By the middle of August it was very hot. My father had the store painted, and when the blinds were taken down, the painter found whole familes of bats clinging together in back of the blinds. Evidently they lived there. I couldn't get hold of one, although I tried. They were the most peculiar-looking creatures. They looked almost like a person who wears glasses all the time and then suddenly goes without them, and they have a kind of peering look.

Chink Johnson is always in our house or in the store or in the yard or going for walks with Aunt Sophronia. Whenever he is not violating the piano at the Inn, he is with Aunt Sophronia—

He taught her how to dance—in the back yard, without any music, just his counting and clapping his hands. His feet made no sound on our thick grass. On two different sunny afternoons, he gave her dancing lessons, and on the third afternoon, he had her dancing. She was laughing and she was lively-looking and she looked young. He persuaded her to take off her shoes and she danced in her bare feet. Fortunately, nobody knows this but me.

He took her fishing. When they came back, she was quite sunburned but her eyes were shining as though they held the reflected light from the sun shining on water.

Just in that one short summer he seemed to take on all kinds of guises—fisherman, dancer, singer, churchgoer, even delivery boy.

One morning someone knocked at the back door and there was Chink Johnson with our grocery order, saying to my Aunt Sophronia, "Here's your meat, ma'am, and your vegetables," touching his hat, bowing, unloading the crate of groceries, and then sitting down at the kitchen table as though he owned it, drinking a cup of coffee that no one had offered him, just pouring it out of the enamel pot that stays on the stove, finding cream and sugar himself, and sitting there with his legs thrust way out in front of him, and those terribly tight pants he wears looking as though they were painted on his thighs.

Sometimes when he sits in our kitchen, he laughs. His laughter is not merry. When my father laughs, the sound makes you laugh, even when you don't know what he is laughing about.

When Chink Johnson laughs, I look away from him. The sound hurts my ears. It is like the ugly squawk of some big bird that you have disturbed in the woods and it flies right into your face, pecking at your eyes.

It has been a very interesting summer.

I have begun to refer to it in the past tense because there isn't much left of a summer by the middle of August. On Thursday afternoon, Aunt Sophronia and I saw that other ladies liked Chink Johnson too.

Thursday afternoon is traditionally maids' day off and Chink Johnson drove the maids from the Inn into town, in a wagon, late in the day. He stopped in front of the store with a wagon full of girls in long skirts, giggling, leaning against him, a kind of panting excitement in that wagon, their arms around him; they whispered to him, they were seized by fits of laughter, shrieks of laughter.

They came in the store and bought hairnets and hairpins and shampoo and Vaseline and hair tonics and cough medicines and court plaster and a great many items that they did not need because it was a pleasure to be spending money, and to be free of the tyranny of the housekeepers' demands—or so my mother said —some young and attractive, some not so young, about ten of them.

Aunt Sophronia was in the store and she waited on them, studying them. Every once in a while one would go to the door, and yell, "We'll be out in a minute, Chink. Just a little while!" and wave at him and throw kisses at him.

Then they were gone, all at once, piling into the wagon, long full skirts in disarray. One of them sat in Chink's lap, laughing, looking up into his face, and saying, "Let's go in the woods. Chink, take us in the woods. I'll help drive."

Aunt Sophronia and I stood in the doorway and watched them as they drove off, going towards the pine woods. The wagon seemed to be filled with wide skirts, and ruffled petticoats, all suddenly upended because Chink said, "Giddup, there!" and hit the horse with the whip, cracked it over the horse's ears, and the horse started off as though he were a race horse.

It was late when they went past the store, going home. Sitting in the back yard, we could hear the horse racing, and the girls squealing and laughing, and Chink singing a ribald song, about "Strollin', and Strollin."

Dottle stopped right in the middle of a poem and Mr. Bemish straightened up so that he was not quite so close to Aunt Sophronia's skirts. It was like having Chink Johnson right there in the back yard with us, the rough, atonal voice, the red-brown eyes that looked hot, literally hot, as though if you touched them you would have to withdraw your fingers immediately because they would be scorched or singed or burned, the jutting beard, the restless feet and hands.

We sat absolutely still. We could hear the rattling of the wagon, the clop-clop of the horses' hoofs and above it the laughter of the girls, and dominating that sound, Chink Johnson's voice lifted in song. Even after they were so far away we could not possibly hear them, these sounds seemed to linger in the air, faint, far-off.

It was a warm night, brilliant with light from the moon. I pictured the girls as sitting on top of Chink, all around him, on his arms, in his lap, on his shoulders, and I thought the prettiest one should be perched on his head.

Dottle lit a cigar and puffed out clouds of bluish smoke and said, "I never heard the mating call of the male so clearly sounded on a summer's night." He laughed so hard that he had to get out one of his big handkerchiefs and dab at his eyes with it.

Aunt Sophronia got up from the bench so fast that she brushed against Mr. Bemish, almost knocking him over. He lost his balance and regained it only because he supported himself with one hand on the ground. She must have known that she had very nearly upset him but she went marching toward the house, her back very straight and her head up in the air, and she never once looked back.

Dottle said, "Have I offended her?"

My mother said, "It's late. It's time we went in."

Mr. Bemish must have gone home when we went in the house, but he was back in the yard so early the next morning he might just as well have spent the night. Dottle and I were standing in the kitchen, looking down the back yard. He was drinking coffee out of a mug and I was eating a piece of bread and butter. Our back yard is a pretty sight on a summer morning. It is filled with flowers, and birds are singing, and the air is very cool, and there is a special smell, a summer smell compounded of grass and dew on the grass and flowers, and the suggestion of heat to come later in the day.

We looked out the door and there was Mr. Bemish down on his knees in front of Aunt Sophronia. She was sitting on the bench and she looked horrified and she seemed to have been in the act of trying to stop him, one hand extended in a thrusting-away motion. I thought: His pants legs will be very damp because there's still dew on the grass, and how did he get here so early, and did he know that she would be sitting on the bench almost before sunup?

"Ah, girlie, girlie!" he said, on his knees in our back yard, kneeling on our thick, soft grass. "Will you marry me?"

"No!"

"Is it," he said, "because I am old?" and his voice went straight up in pitch just like a scale. "I'm not old. I'm not old. Why, I can still jump up in the air and click my heels together three times!"

And he did. He got up off his knees and he jumped up, straight up, and clicked his heels together three times, and landed on the grass, and there was just a slight thumping sound when he landed.

Aunt Sophronia said, "Mr. Bemish, Mr. Bemish. Don't do that—don't do that —go away, go home—" And she ran toward the house and he started after her and then he saw us standing in the door, watching him, and he stood still. He shouted after her, "I'll put on my best coat and my best hat and you won't know me—I'll be back—and you won't know me—"

Dottle glared at him through the screen door and said, "You old fool—you old fool—"

Mr. Bemish hurried around the side of the house, pretending that he hadn't heard him.

I did not know when Mr. Bemish would be back, wearing his best coat and his best hat, but I certainly wanted to see him and, if possible, to witness his next performance. I decided that whenever Aunt Sophronia was in the store, I'd be in the store too.

When my father went to eat his dinner at twelve-thirty, Aunt Sophronia looked after the store. There weren't many people who came in at that hour; it was the dinner hour and Aunt Sophronia sat in the prescription room, with the door open, and read the morning newspaper. There was an old wooden chair, by the window, in the prescription room. It had a faded painting across the back, a wooden seat and back and arms. It was a very comfortable chair if you sat up straight, and Aunt Sophronia sat up very straight. She could look out of the window and see the church green, see the path that went up Petticoat Lane toward the pine woods, and she commanded a view of the interior of the store.

I don't think she saw Mr. Bemish when he entered. If she had, she would have gotten out of the chair immediately to wait on him. But she was reading the newspaper, and he came in very quietly. He was wearing a cutaway coat that was too long, and a pair of striped trousers, and he was carrying a silk hat in his hand, a collapsed silk hat. He stopped inside the door and put the hat in shape and then placed it carefully on his head. He looked like a circus clown who is making fun of the ringmaster, mocking him, making his costume look silly.

Mr. Bemish went straight through the store, and stood in front of Aunt Sophronia, and he jumped straight up in the air, like a dancer, and clicked his heels together three times. The bottles on the shelves rattled and the back room was filled with a pinging sound.

"Oh, my goodness," Aunt Sophronia said, frowning. "Oh, my goodness, don't jump like that." And she stood up.

My father came in through the back door and he said, "What's going on in here? What's going on in here?"

Mr. Bemish said, "I was just showing Miss Sophronia that I can still jump up in the air and click my heels together three times before I come back down again."

My father made a noise that sounded like "Boooooh!" but wasn't quite, and Mr. Bemish retreated, talking very fast. "I had asked Miss Sophronia if she would marry me and she said no, and I thought perhaps it was because she thinks I'm too old and not stylish enough and so I got dressed up and I was showing her I could still jump—"

"Get out of here! Get out of here! Get out of here!"

My father's voice kept rising and increasing in volume, and his face looked as though he were about to burst. It seemed to darken and to swell, to get bigger.

Aunt Sophronia said, "Oh, you mustn't talk to him like that—"

My father was moving toward Mr. Bemish, and Mr. Bemish was retreating, retreating, and finally he turned and ran out of the store and ran up Petticoat Lane with his long coattails flapping about his legs.

My father said, "I shouldn't have let him hang around here all these months. I can't leave this store for five minutes that I don't find one of these no-goods hangin' around when I come back. Not one of 'em worth the powder and shot to blow 'em to hell and back. That piano player pawin' the ground and this old white man jumpin' up in the air, and that friend of Johno's, that poet or whatever he is, all he needs are some starched petticoats and a bonnet and he'd make a woman—he's practically one now—and he's tee-heein' around, and if they were all put together in one piece, it still wouldn't be a whole man." My father shook his fist in the air and glared at Aunt Sophronia.

"I guess it's all my fault—" Aunt Sophronia sounded choked-up and funny.

My father said, "No, no, no, I didn't mean that," and patted her arm. "It's all perfectly natural. It's just that we're the only colored people living in this little bit of town and there aren't any fine young colored men around, only this tramp piano player, and everytime I look at him I can hear him playing some rags and see a whole line of big-bosomed women done up in sequined dresses standin' over him, moanin' about wantin' somebody to turn their dampers down, and I can see poker games and crap games and—"

My mother came in through the back room. She said, "Samuel, why are you talking about gambling games?"

"I was trying to explain to Sophy how I feel about that piano player."

To my surprise, my mother said, "Has Sophronia asked you how you feel about Mr. Johnson?"

When my father shook his head, she said, "Then I don't think there is any reason for you to say anything about him. I need you in the garden. I want you to move one of my peonies."

I wonder what my mother would say if she knew how my father chased little Mr. Bemish out of his store. I wonder if Mr. Bemish will ever come back.

Mr. Bemish did come back. He came back the following Sunday. We were all in the store, Aunt Sophronia, and Dottle, and Chink and I.

Mr. Bemish sidled in through the door. He looked as though he expected someone to jump out at him and yell "Go home!" But he came in anyway and he sat down beside me on the bench near the front of the store.

Chink was leaning on the cigar case, talking to Aunt Sophronia, his face very close to hers. I couldn't hear what he was saying, but he seemed to be trying to persuade her to do something, go for a walk, or something, and she was obviously refusing, politely but definitely. Dottle was standing near the back of the store, watching Chink.

Aunt Frank opened the store door, and she stood in the doorway holding the screen door open. She has a cross, sharp way of speaking, very fast, and very unpleasant. She saw me and she said, "Where's Mar-tha?"

I wasn't expecting to see Aunt Frank in the store at that hour and I was so surprised that I didn't answer her.

"What's the mat-ter with you? Cat got your tongue? Didn't you hear what I said? Where's your moth-er?"

"She's over on the other side of the building, in the kitchen. She's having coffee with my father."

She scowled at Chink. "How long's that bearded man been in here talkin' to Sophy?"

Chink turned around and looked toward Aunt Frank, Aunt Sophronia started toward her, moving very fast out from behind the cigar case, saying, "Can I get something for you?"

As Aunt Frank stood there holding the door open, a whole flight of bats came in the store. I say a "flight" because I don't know what else to call a large-sized group of bats. They swooped down and up in a blind, fast flight.

Aunt Frank shrieked, "Ahhh! My hair, watch out for your hair! Ahhhhhh!" and stood up on the bench, and held her black fusty skirts close about her and then pulled them over her head. I decided she had confused mice and bats, that the technique for getting rid of mice was to stand on a chair and clutch one's skirts around one, that is, if you were a lady and pretended to be afraid of mice. I did learn that Aunt Frank was wearing carpet slippers made of dark-gray felt, black cotton stockings, and under the outside layer of skirts there seemed to be a great many layers of black petticoats.

Dottle ran into the back room and held the door tightly shut. There is a glass in the door and he could look out at the rest of us as we dodged the bats. I could see his large white face, and long hair, and I supposed he was as frightened as Aunt Frank that bats would get entangled in his hair, because he squealed, all the rich, buttery quality gone from his voice, just a high-pitched squealing.

Aunt Frank cautiously lowered the outer skirt, fumbled in a pocket, and took out a bottle, not a big bottle, but about the size of an eight-ounce cough-medicine bottle, and she took two or three swigs from it, recorked it, and then re-covered her head.

Chink grabbed a newspaper and slapped at the bats as they circled. "Gotcha. Hi-hi-gotcha—hi-hi-gotcha—hi-hi!" and he folded the newspaper and belted them as they swished past him.

Mr. Bemish stared. I decided that he'd lived with bats and spiders and mice, well, not lived with perhaps, but was so accustomed to them that he could not understand why they should cause all this noise and confusion and fear. He ignored the bats entirely and went to the rescue of his lady love. He clasped Aunt Sophronia to his bosom, covering her head with his hands and arms and he kept murmuring comforting words. "Now, now. I won't let anything hurt you. Nothing can harm you." He took a deep breath and said, quite distinctly, "I love you, my darling. I love you, love you—"

Aunt Sophronia seemed to nestle in his arms, to cuddle closer to him, to lean harder every time a bat swooped past them.

Father came through the back room— he had to wrestle Dottle out of the way before he could get through the door— and he very sensibly held the screen door open, and what with the impetus offered by Chink's folded newspaper, the bats swooped outside.

It was really very exciting while it lasted, what with all the shrieks and the swift movement of the bats. When I began to really look around, the first thing I noticed was that Aunt Sophronia was still huddled in the protective arms of Mr. Bemish. Dottle came out of the back room with his mouth pursed and his cheeks were puffed out a little and I wouldn't have been surprised if he had hissed at Mr. Bemish. He and Chink headed straight towards Mr. Bemish. They are very tall men and Mr. Bemish is short and slender, and as they converged on him, one from the rear and the other from the side, he looked smaller and older than ever.

Aunt Sophronia stepped away from Mr. Bemish. She moved toward Chink. One side of her face was red where it had been pressed hard against the wool of Mr. Bemish's coat.

All of a sudden my father's hand was resting on one of Chink's shoulders. He has large, heavy hands and his hand seemed to have descended suddenly and with great weight. He said, "You'll not start any trouble in my store."

Aunt Frank said, "Bats! Bats!" She indicated that my father was to help her down from the bench. She climbed down awkwardly, holding on to him. "Worse than bats," she said, and she made a wide all-inclusive gesture that took in Chink and Dottle and Mr. Bemish. "Where's Mar-tha?" she demanded. "She still in the kitchen?"

My father nodded. He held the door

open for Mr. Bemish, and Mr. Bemish scuttled out. Dottle and Chink went out too.

I found a dead bat on the floor and sat down on the bench at the front of the store to examine it. It had a very unpleasant smell. But it was such an interesting creature that I ignored the odor. It had rather large, pointed ears that I thought were quite charming. It had very sharp little claws. I could see why the ladies had screamed and covered their heads, because if those claws got entangled in their long hair, someone would have had to cut their hair to get a bat out of it. Aunt Frank's hair isn't long; it is like a sheep's wool, tight-curled and close to the skin or scalp. But I suppose a bat's sharp little claws and peculiar wings snarled up in that might create more of a problem than it would if caught in longer and less tightly curled hair.

The wings of the bat were webbed like the feet of ducks with a thin membrane-like tissue that was attached to the body, reaching from the front legs or arms to the back legs and attached to the sides. The body was small in comparison to the wide sweep of those curious wings. I stretched its wings out and they looked like the inside of an opened umbrella, and I couldn't help admiring them. I began to think of all the things I'd heard said about bats, "blind as a bat," and the word "batty" meaning crazy, and I tried to figure out why "batty," probably because a bat's behavior didn't make sense to a human being—its fast, erratic flight would look senseless.

Then Aunt Frank's voice sounded right in my ear, and her horrible breath was in my nose, and she smelled worse than the bat. She said, "You throw that nasty thing away. You throw that nasty thing away."

I thrust the dead bat straight at her black and wrinkled face. "Look out," I yelled. "It'll suck your blood. It's still alive. Look out!"

She jumped away, absolutely furious. "You little vixen," she said, and squealed just like a pig. Then she saw my mother standing in the door of the prescription room. "Mar-tha," she commanded, "you come here and make her throw this nasty thing away. Make her throw it away. She's settin' here playin' with a dead bat."

My mother said, "If you want to look at the bat, take it outside or take it in the back room. You can't keep a dead bat here in the drugstore."

"This can't hurt her. It's dead."

She interrupted me. "Many people are afraid of bats. It doesn't make any difference whether the bats are dead or alive—they are still afraid of them."

I went outside and sat on the front steps and waited. There was a full moon and the light from it made the street and the houses and the church look as though they had been whitewashed. I put the bat beside me on the step. I was going to wait for Aunt Frank, and when she came out of the store and started down the steps, I was going to put the dead stinking bat in one of the big pockets in her skirt —the pocket where she kept her bottle of gin. And when she got home and reached for a drink, I hoped she would discover, encounter, touch with her bony fingers, the corpse of "one of the nocturnal or crepuscular flying mammals constituting the order Chiroptera" as a token of my affection.

I must have waited there on the steps for two hours. My father began putting out the lights in the store. I stayed right there, anticipating the moment when my ancient enemy, Aunt Frank, would come stumbling around the side of the building.

And then—one moment I was sitting on the splintery front steps of the store, and the next moment I was running up Petticoat Lane, going just as fast as I could, because it had suddenly occurred to me that Chink Johnson and Dottle Smith had gone out of the drugstore right behind Mr. Bemish and they hadn't returned.

By the time I reached Mr. Bemish's shop, I was panting. I couldn't catch my breath.

Mr. Bemish's wagon was drawn up close to the side of the shop. The horse was hitched to it. Mr. Bemish was loading the headboard of his beautiful brass bed on the wagon. He was obviously moving—leaving town, at night. He walked in a peculiar fashion as though he were lame. He was panting too, and making hiccuping noises like someone who has been crying a long time, so long that no real sound comes out, just a kind of hiccuping noise due to the contractions of the throat muscles and the heaving of the chest.

As I stood there, he got the headboard on the wagon, and then he struggled with his mattress, and then the springs, and then he brought out his cobbler's bench.

Dottle and Chink stood watching him, just like two guards or two sheriffs. None of us said anything.

I finally sat down on the enormous millstone that served as Mr. Bemish's front step. I sat way off to one side where I wouldn't interfere with his comings and goings.

May-a-ling, his cat, rubbed against me and then came and sat in my lap, with her back to me, facing towards Mr. Bemish.

It didn't take him very long to empty the shop of his belongings. I couldn't help thinking that if we ever moved, it would take us days to pack all the books and the pictures and the china, and all our clothes and furniture. We all collected things. Aunt Sophronia did beautiful embroidery and she collected embroidered fabrics, and mother collected old dishes and old furniture, and my father collected old glass bottles and old mortars, and they all collected books, and then all the rooms had furniture and there were all kinds of cooking pots. No one of us would ever get all of our belongings in one wagon.

Mr. Bemish came out of the shop and walked all around the little building with that peculiar stiff-legged gait. Apparently the only item he'd overlooked was his garden bench. He had trouble getting it in the wagon, and I dumped May-a-ling on the ground and went to help him.

One of Dottle's meaty hands gripped my braid. "He can manage."

I twisted away from him. "He's just a little old man and he's my friend and I'm going to help him."

Chink said, "Leave her alone."

Dottle let go of my hair. I helped put the bench in the wagon, and then went inside the shop with him, and helped him carry out the few items that were left. Each time I went inside the shop with Mr. Bemish I asked him questions. We both whispered.

"Where are you going, Mr. Bemish?"

"Massachusetts."

"Why?"

He didn't answer. His hiccups got worse.

I waited until we'd taken down the green summer curtains and carefully folded them, and put them in the little trunk that held some of his clothes, and put his broom and his dustpan and his tall kitchen cooking stool on the wagon, before I repeated my question. His hiccups had quieted down.

"Why are you leaving, Mr. Bemish?" I whispered.

"They were going to sew me up."

"Sew you up. Did you say—sew you up?"

"Yes."

"Where?" I said, staring at him, thinking: sew up? Sew up what—eyes, nostrils, mouth, ears, rectum? "They were trying to scare you, Mr. Bemish. Nobody would sew up a person, a human being, unless it was a surgeon—after an operation—"

He shook his head. "No," he whispered. "I thought so too, but—no, they meant it—with my own waxed thread—"

"Did they—"

"Hush! Hush!"

We used his little piece of flowered carpet to wrap his washbowl and pitcher in and then put the whole bulky package it made on the wagon. We went back inside to make sure that we hadn't forgotten anything. The inside of his shop looked very small and shabby and lonely. There wasn't anything left except his stove and he obviously couldn't take that. It was a very big, handsome stove and he kept it quite shiny and clean.

"Can you keep a secret?" he whispered, standing quite close to me. He smelled old and dusty and withered like dried flowers.

I nodded.

He handed me a small velvet bag. "Hide it, girlie," he whispered. "It's some old jewelry that belonged to my mother. Give it to Miss Sophronia at Christmas from me." He patted my arm.

We went outside and he took down the sign with the lady's high-laced shoe painted on it, and put it on the wagon seat. He climbed in the wagon, picked up the reins.

"May-a-ling, May-a-ling," he called. It was the most musical sound I have ever heard used to call a cat. She answered him instantly. She mewed and jumped up on the wagon seat beside him. He clucked to the horse and they drove off.

I waited not only until they were out of sight, but until I could no longer hear the creak of the wagon wheels and the clop-clop of the horses hoofs, and then I turned and ran.

Chink said, "Wait a minute—"

Dottle said, "You don't understand—"

I stopped running just long enough to shout at them, "You both stink. You stink like dead bats. You and your goddamn Miss Muriel—"

JAMES BALDWIN • 1924–

Previous Condition

I woke up shaking, alone in my room. I was clammy cold with sweat; under me the sheet and the mattress were soaked. The sheet was gray and twisted like a rope. I breathed like I had been running.

I couldn't move for the longest while. I just lay on my back, spread-eagled, looking up at the ceiling, listening to the sounds of people getting up in other parts of the house, alarm clocks ringing and water splashing and doors opening and shutting and feet on the stairs. I could tell when people left for work: the hall doorway downstairs whined and shuffled as it opened and gave a funny kind of double slam as it closed. One thud and than a louder thud and then a little final click. While the door was open I could hear the street sounds too, horses' hoofs and delivery wagons and people in the streets and big trucks and motor cars screaming on the asphalt.

I had been dreaming. At night I dreamt and woke up in the morning trembling, but not remembering the dream, except that in the dream I had been running. I could not remember when the dream—or dreams—had started; it had been long ago. For long periods maybe, I would have no dreams at all. And then they would come back, every night, I would try not to go to bed, I would go to sleep frightened and wake up frightened and have another day to get through with the nightmare at my shoulder. Now I was back from Chicago, busted, living off my friends in a dirty furnished room downtown. The show I had been with had folded in Chicago. It hadn't been much of a part—or much of a show either, to tell the truth. I played a kind of intellectual Uncle Tom, a young college student working for his race. The playwright had wanted to prove he was a liberal, I guess. But, as I say, the show had folded and here I was, back in New York and hating it. I knew that I should be getting another job, making the rounds, pounding the pavement. But I didn't. I couldn't face it. It was summer. I seemed to be fagged out. And every day I hated myself more. Acting's a rough life, even if you're white. I'm not tall and I'm not good looking and I can't sing or dance and I'm not white; so even at the best of times I wasn't in much demand.

The room I lived in was heavy ceilinged, perfectly square, with walls the color of chipped dry blood. Jules Weissman, a Jewboy, had got the room for me. It's a room to sleep in, he said, or maybe to die in but God knows it wasn't meant to live in. Perhaps because the room was so hideous it had a fantastic array of light fixtures: one on the ceiling, one on the left wall, two on the right wall, and a lamp on the table beside my bed. My bed was in front of the window through which nothing ever blew but dust. It was a furnished room and they'd thrown enough stuff in it to furnish three rooms its size. Two easy chairs and a desk, the bed, the table, a straight-backed chair, a bookcase, a cardboard wardrobe; and my books and my suitcase, both unpacked; and my dirty clothes flung in a corner. It was the kind of room that defeated you. It had a fireplace, too, and a heavy marble mantelpiece and a great gray mirror above the mantelpiece. It was hard to see anything in the mirror very clearly—which was perhaps just as well

—and it would have been worth your life to have started a fire in the fireplace.

"Well, you won't have to stay here long," Jules told me the night I came. Jules smuggled me in, sort of, after dark, when everyone had gone to bed.

"Christ, I hope not."

"I'll be moving to a big place soon," Jules said. "You can move in with me." He turned all the lights on. "Think it'll be all right for a while?" He sounded apologetic, as though he had designed the room himself.

"Oh, sure. D'you think I'll have any trouble?"

"I don't think so. The rent's paid. She can't put you out."

I didn't say anything to that.

"Sort of stay undercover," Jules said. "You know."

"Roger," I said.

I had been living there for three days, timing it so I left after everyone else had gone, coming back late at night when everyone else was asleep. But I knew it wouldn't work. A couple of the tenants had seen me on the stairs, a woman had surprised me coming out of the john. Every morning I waited for the landlady to come banging on the door. I didn't know what would happen. It might be all right. It might not be. But the waiting was getting me.

The sweat on my body was turning cold. Downstairs a radio was tuned in to the Breakfast Symphony. They were playing Beethoven. I sat up and lit a cigarette. "Peter," I said, "don't let them scare you to death. You're a man, too." I listened to Ludwig and I watched the smoke rise to the dirty ceiling. Under Ludwig's drums and horns I listened to hear footsteps on the stairs.

I'd done a lot of traveling in my time. I'd knocked about through St. Louis, Frisco, Seattle, Detroit, New Orleans, worked at just about everything. I'd run away from my old lady when I was about sixteen. She'd never been able to handle me. You'll never be nothin' *but* a bum, she'd say. We lived in an old shack in a town in New Jersey in the nigger part of town, the kind of houses colored people live in all over the U.S. I hated my mother for living there. I hated all the people in my neighborhood. They went to church and they got drunk. They were nice to the white people. When the landlord came around they paid him and took his crap.

The first time I was ever called nigger I was seven years old. It was a little white girl with long black curls. I used to leave the front of my house and go wandering by myself through town. This little girl was playing ball alone and as I passed her the ball rolled out of her hands into the gutter.

I threw it back to her.

"Let's play catch," I said.

But she held the ball and made a face at me.

"My mother don't let me play with niggers," she told me.

I did not know what the word meant. But my skin grew warm. I stuck my tongue out at her.

"I don't care. Keep your old ball." I started down the street.

She screamed after me: "Nigger, nigger, nigger!"

I screamed back: "Your mother was a nigger!"

I asked my mother what a nigger was.

"Who called you that?"

"I heard somebody say it."

"Who?"

"Just somebody."

"Go wash your face," she said. "You dirty as sin. Your supper's on the table."

I went to the bathroom and splashed water on my face and wiped my face and hands on the towel.

"You call that clean?" my mother cried. "Come here, boy!"

She dragged me back to the bathroom and began to soap my face and neck.

"You run around dirty like you do all

the time, everybody'll call you a little nigger, you hear?" She rinsed my face and looked at my hands and dried me. "Now, go on and eat your supper."

I didn't say anything. I went to the kitchen and sat down at the table. I remember I wanted to cry. My mother sat down across from me.

"Mama," I said. She looked at me. I started to cry.

She came around to my side of the table and took me in her arms.

"Baby, don't fret. Next time somebody calls you nigger you tell them you'd rather be your color than be lowdown and nasty like some white folks is."

We formed gangs when I was older, my friends and I. We met white boys and their friends on the opposite sides of fences and we threw rocks and tin cans at each other.

I'd come home bleeding. My mother would slap me and scold me and cry.

"Boy, you wanna get killed? You wanna end up like your father?"

My father was a bum and I had never seen him. I was named for him: Peter.

I was always in trouble: truant officers, welfare workers, everybody else in town.

"You ain't never gonna be nothin' *but* a bum," my mother said.

By and by older kids I knew finished school and got jobs and got married and settled down. They were going to settle down and bring more black babies into the world and pay the same rents for the same old shacks and it would go on and on—

When I was sixteen I ran away. I left a note and told Mama not to worry, I'd come back one day and I'd be all right. But when I was twenty-two she died. I came back and put my mother in the ground. Everything was like it had been. Our house had not been painted and the porch floor sagged and there was somebody's raincoat stuffed in the broken window. Another family was moving in. Their furniture was stacked along the walls and their children were running through the house and laughing and somebody was frying pork chops in the kitchen. The oldest boy was tacking up a mirror.

Last year Ida took me driving in her big car and we passed through a couple of towns upstate. We passed some crumbling houses on the left. The clothes on the line were flying in the wind.

"Are people living there?" asked Ida.

"Just darkies," I said.

Ida passed the car ahead, banging angrily on the horn. "D'you know you're becoming paranoiac, Peter?"

"All right. All right. I know a lot of white people are starving too."

"You're damn right they are. I know a little about poverty myself."

Ida had come from the kind of family called shanty Irish. She was raised in Boston. She's a very beautiful woman who married young and married for money—so now I can afford to support attractive young men, she'd giggle. Her husband was a ballet dancer who was forever on the road. Ida suspected that he went with boys. Not that I give a damn, she said, as long as he leaves me alone. When we met last year she was thirty and I was twenty-five. We had a pretty stormy relationship but we stuck. Whenever I got to town I called her; whenever I was stranded out of town I'd let her know. We never let it get too serious. She went her way and I went mine.

In all this running around I'd learned a few things. Like a prizefighter learns to take a blow or a dancer learns to fall, I'd learned how to get by. I'd learned never to be belligerent with policemen, for instance. No matter who was right, I was certain to be wrong. What might be accepted as just good old American independence in someone else would be insufferable arrogance in me. After the first few times I realized that I had to play smart, to act out the role I was expected to play. I only had one head and it was too easy to get it broken. When I faced a policeman I acted like I didn't know a thing. I let my jaw drop and I let my eyes get big, I didn't give him any smart answers, none of the crap about my rights. I figured out what answers he wanted and I gave them to him. I never let him think he wasn't king. If it was more than routine, if I was picked up on suspicion of robbery or murder in the neighborhood, I looked as humble as I could and kept my mouth shut and prayed. I took a couple of beatings but I stayed out of prison and I stayed off chain gangs. That was also due to luck, Ida pointed out once. "Maybe it would've been better for you if you'd been a little less lucky. Worse things have happened than chain gangs. Some of them have happened to you."

There was something in her voice. "What are you talking about?" I asked.

"Don't lose your temper. I said maybe."

"You mean you think I'm a coward?"

"I didn't say that, Peter."

"But you meant that. Didn't you?"

"No. I didn't mean that. I didn't mean anything. Let's not fight."

There are times and places when a Negro can use his color like a shield. He can trade on the subterranean Anglo-Saxon guilt and get what he wants that way; or some of what he wants. He can trade on his nuisance value, his value as forbidden fruit; he can use it like a knife, he can twist it and get his vengeance that way. I knew these things long before I realized that I knew them and in the beginning I used them, not knowing what I was doing. Then when I began to see it, I felt betrayed. I felt beaten as a person. I had no honest place to stand.

That was the year before I met Ida. I'd been acting in stock companies and little theaters; sometimes fairly good parts. People were nice to me. They told me I had talent. They said it sadly, as though they were thinking, What a pity, he'll never get anywhere. I had got to the point where I resented praise and I resented pity and I wondered what people were thinking when they shook my hand. In New York I met some pretty fine people; easygoing, hard-drinking, flotsam and jetsam; and they liked me; and I wondered if I trusted them; if I was able any longer to trust anybody. Not on top, where all the world could see, but underneath where everybody lives.

Soon I would have to get up. I listened to Ludwig. He shook the little room like the footsteps of a giant marching miles away. On summer evenings (and maybe we would go this summer) Jules and Ida and I would go up to the Stadium and sit beneath the pillars on the cold stone steps. There it seemed to me the sky was far away; and I was not myself, I was high and lifted up. We never talked, the three of us. We sat and watched the blue smoke curl in the air and watched the orange tips of cigarettes. Every once in a while the boys who sold popcorn and soda pop and ice cream climbed the steep steps chattering; and Ida shifted slightly and touched her blue-black hair; and Jules scowled. I sat with my knee up, watching the lighted half-moon below, the black-coated, straining conductor, the faceless men beneath him moving together in a rhythm like the sea. There were pauses in the music for the rushing, calling, halting piano. Everything would stop except the climbing soloist; he would reach a height and everything would join him, the violins first and then the horns; and then the deep blue bass and the flute and the bitter trampling drums; beating, beating and mounting together and stopping with a clash like daybreak. When I first heard the *Messiah* I was alone; my blood bubbled like fire and wine; I cried; like an infant crying for its mother's milk; or a sinner running to meet Jesus.

Now below the music I heard footsteps on the stairs. I put out my cigarette. My heart was beating so hard I thought it would tear my chest apart. Someone knocked on the door.

I thought: Don't answer. Maybe she'll go away.

But the knocking came again, harder this time.

Just a minute, I said. I sat on the edge of the bed and put on my bathrobe. I was trembling like a fool. For Christ's sake, Peter, you've been through this before. What's the worst that can happen? You won't have a room. The world's full of rooms.

When I opened the door the landlady stood there, red-and-whitefaced and hysterical.

"Who are you? I didn't rent this room to you."

My mouth was dry. I started to say something.

"I can't have no colored people here," she said. "All my tenants are complainin'. Women afraid to come home nights."

"They ain't gotta be afraid of me," I said. I couldn't get my voice up; it rasped and rattled in my throat; and I began to be angry. I wanted to kill her. "My friend rented this room for me," I said.

"Well, I'm sorry, he didn't have no right to do that, I don't have nothin' against you, but you gotta get out."

Her glasses blinked, opaque in the light on the landing. She was frightened to death. She was afraid of me but she was more afraid of losing her tenants. Her face was mottled with rage and fear, her breath came rushed and little bits of spittle gathered at the edges of her mouth; her breath smelled bad, like rotting hamburger on a July day.

"You can't put me out," I said. "This room was rented in my name." I started to close the door, as though the matter was finished: "I live here, see, this is my room, you can't put me out."

"You get outa my house!" she screamed. "I got the right to know who's in my house! This is a white neighborhood, I don't rent to colored people. Why don't you go on uptown, like you belong?"

"I can't stand niggers," I told her. I started to close the door again but she moved and stuck her foot in the way. I wanted to kill her, I watched her stupid, wrinkled frightened white face and I wanted to take a club, a hatchet, and bring it down with all my weight, splitting her skull down the middle where she parted her iron-grey hair.

"Get out of the door," I said. "I want to get dressed."

But I knew that she had won, that I was already on my way. We stared at each other. Neither of us moved. From her came an emanation of fear and fury and something else. You maggot-eaten bitch, I thought. I said evilly, "You wanna come in and watch me?" Her face didn't change, she didn't take her foot away. My skin prickled, tiny hot needles punctured my flesh. I was aware of my body under the bathrobe; and it was as though I had done something wrong, something monstrous, years ago, which no one had forgotten and for which I would be killed.

"If you don't get out," she said, "I'll get a policeman to put you out."

I grabbed the door to keep from touching her. "All right. All right. You can have the goddamn room. Now get out and let me dress."

She turned away. I slammed the door. I heard her going down the stairs. I threw stuff into my suitcase. I tried to take as long as possible but I cut myself while shaving because I was afraid she would come back upstairs with a policeman.

Jules was making coffee when I walked in.

"Good morning, good morning! What happened to you?"

"No room at the inn," I said. "Pour a cup of coffee for the notorious son of man." I sat down and dropped my suitcase on the floor.

Jules looked at me. "Oh. Well. Coffee coming up."

He got out the coffee cups. I lit a cigarette and sat there. I couldn't think of anything to say. I knew that Jules felt bad and I wanted to tell him that it wasn't his fault.

He pushed coffee in front of me and sugar and cream.

"Cheer up, baby. The world's wide and life—life, she is very long."

"Shut up. I don't want to hear any of your bad philosophy."

"Sorry."

"I mean, let's not talk about the good, the true, and the beautiful."

"All right. But don't sit there holding onto your table manners. Scream if you want to."

"Screaming won't do any good. Besides I'm a big boy now."

I stirred my coffee. "Did you give her a fight?" Jules asked.

I shook my head. "No."

"Why the hell not?"

I shrugged; a little ashamed now. "I couldn't have won it. What the hell."

"You might have won it. You might have given her a couple of bad moments."

"Goddamit to hell, I'm sick of it. Can't I get a place to sleep without dragging it through the courts? I'm goddam tired of battling every Tom, Dick, and Harry for what everybody else takes for granted. I'm tired, man, tired! Have you ever been sick to death of something? Well, I'm sick to death. And I'm scared. I've been fighting so goddamn long I'm not a person any more. I'm not Booker T. Washington. I've got no vision of emancipating anybody. I want to emancipate myself. If this goes on much longer, they'll send me to Bellevue, I'll blow my top, I'll break somebody's head. I'm not worried about that miserable little room. I'm worried about what's happening to me, *to me*, inside. I don't walk the streets, I crawl. I've never been like this before. Now when I go to a strange place I wonder what will happen, will I be accepted, if I'm accepted, can I accept?—"

"Take it easy," Jules said.

"Jules, I'm beaten."

"I don't think you are. Drink your coffee."

"Oh," I cried, "I know you think I'm making it dramatic, that I'm paranoiac and just inventing trouble! Maybe I think so sometimes, how can I tell? You get so used to being hit you find you're always waiting for it. Oh, I know, you're Jewish, you get kicked around, too, but you can walk into a bar and nobody *knows* you're Jewish and if you go looking for a job you'll get a better job than mine! How can I say what it feels like? I don't know. I know everybody's in trouble and nothing is easy, but how can I explain to you what it feels like to be black when I don't understand it and don't want to and spend all my time trying to forget it? I don't want to hate anybody—but now maybe, I can't love anybody either—are we friends? Can we be really friends?"

"We're friends," Jules said, "don't worry about it." He scowled. "If I wasn't Jewish I'd ask you why you don't live in Harlem." I looked at him. He raised his hand and smiled—"But I'm Jewish, so I didn't ask you. Ah Peter," he said, "I can't help you—take a walk, get drunk, we're all in this together."

I stood up. "I'll be around later. I'm sorry."

"Don't be sorry. I'll leave my door open. Bunk here for awhile."

"Thanks," I said.

I felt that I was drowning; that hatred had corrupted me like cancer in the bone.

I saw Ida for dinner. We met in a restaurant in the Village, an Italian place in a gloomy cellar with candles on the tables.

It was not a busy night, for which I was grateful. When I came in there were only two other couples on the other side of the room. No one looked at me. I sat down in a corner booth and ordered a Scotch old-fashioned. Ida was late and I had three of them before she came.

She was very fine in black, a high-necked dress with a pearl choker; and her hair was combed page-boy style, falling just below her ears.

"You look real sweet, baby."

"Thank you. It took fifteen extra minutes but I hoped it would be worth it."

"It was worth it. What're you drinking?"

"Oh—what're you drinking?"

"Old-fashioneds."

She sniffed and looked at me. "How many?"

I laughed. "Three."

"Well," she said, "I suppose you had to do something." The waiter came over. We decided on one Manhattan and one lasagna and one spaghetti with clam sauce and another old-fashioned for me.

"Did you have a constructive day, sweetheart? Find a job?"

"Not today," I said. I lit her cigarette. "Metro offered me a fortune to come to the coast and do the lead in *Native Son* but I turned it down. Type casting, you know. It's so difficult to find a decent part."

"Well, if they don't come up with a decent offer soon tell them you'll go back to Selznick. *He'll* find you a part with guts—the very *idea* of offering you *Native Son!* I wouldn't stand for it."

"You ain't gotta tell me. I told them if they didn't find me a decent script in two weeks I was through, that's all."

"Now that's talking, Peter my lad."

The drinks came and we sat in silence for a minute or two. I finished half of my drink at a swallow and played with the toothpicks on the table. I felt Ida watching me.

"Peter, you're going to be awfully drunk."

"Honeychile, the first thing a southern gentleman learns is how to hold his liquor."

"That myth is older than the rock of ages. And anyway you come from Jersey."

I finished my drink and snarled at her: "That's just as good as the South."

Across the table from me I could see that she was readying herself for trouble: her mouth tightened slightly, setting her chin so that the faint cleft showed: "What happened to you today?"

I resented her concern; I resented my need. "Nothing worth talking about," I muttered, "just a mood."

And I tried to smile at her, to wipe away the bitterness.

"Now I know something's the matter. Please tell me."

It sounded trivial as hell: "You know the room Jules found for me? Well, the landlady kicked me out of it today."

"God save the American republic," Ida said. "D'you want to waste some of my husband's money? We can sue her."

"Forget it. I'll end up with lawsuits in every state in the union."

"Still, as a gesture—"

"The devil with the gesture. I'll get by."

The food came. I didn't want to eat. The first mouthful hit my belly like a gong. Ida began cutting up lasagna.

"Peter," she said, "try not to feel so badly. We're all in this together the whole world. Don't let it throw you. What can't be helped you have to learn to live with."

"That's easy for you to say," I told her.

She looked at me quickly and looked away. "I'm not pretending that it's easy to do," she said.

I didn't believe that she could really understand it; and there was nothing I could say. I sat like a child being scolded, looking down at my plate, not eating, not saying anything. I wanted her to stop talking, to stop being intelligent about it, to stop being calm and grown-up about it; good Lord, none of us has ever grown up, we never will.

"It's no better anywhere else," she was

saying. "In all of Europe there's famine and disease, in France and England they hate the Jews—nothing's going to change, baby, people are too empty-headed, too empty-hearted—it's always been like that, people always try to destroy what they don't understand—and they hate almost everything because they understand so little—"

I began to sweat in my side of the booth. I wanted to stop her voice. I wanted her to eat and be quiet and leave me alone. I looked around for the waiter so I could order another drink. But he was on the far side of the restaurant, waiting on some people who had just come in; a lot of people had come in since we had been sitting there.

"Peter," Ida said, "Peter please don't look like that."

I grinned: the painted grin of the professional clown. "Don't worry, baby, I'm all right. I know what I'm going to do. I'm gonna go back to my people where I belong and find me a nice, black nigger wench and raise me a flock of babies."

Ida had an old maternal trick; the grin tricked her into using it now. She raised her fork and rapped me with it across the knuckles. "Now, stop that. You're too old for that."

I screamed and stood up screaming and knocked the candle over: "Don't *do* that, you bitch, don't *ever* do that!"

She grabbed the candle and set it up and glared at me. Her face had turned perfectly white: "Sit down! Sit *down!*"

I fell back into my seat. My stomach felt like water. Everyone was looking at us. I turned cold, seeing what they were seeing: a black boy and a white woman, alone together. I knew it would take nothing to have them at my throat.

"I'm sorry," I muttered, "I'm sorry, I'm sorry."

The waiter was at my elbow. "Is everything all right, miss?"

"Yes, quite, thank you." She sounded like a princess dismissing a slave. I didn't look up. The shadow of the waiter moved away from me.

"Baby," Ida said, "forgive me, please forgive me."

I stared at the tablecloth. She put her hand on mine, brightness and blackness.

"Let's go," I said, "I'm terribly sorry."

She motioned for the check. When it came she handed the waiter a ten dollar bill without looking. She picked up her bag.

"Shall we go to a nightclub or a movie or something?"

"No, honey, not tonight." I looked at her. "I'm tired, I think I'll go on over to Jules's place. I'm gonna sleep on his floor for a while. Don't worry about me. I'm all right."

She looked at me steadily. She said: "I'll come see you tomorrow?"

"Yes, baby, please."

The waiter brought the change and she tipped him. We stood up; as we passed the tables (not looking at the people) the ground under me seemed falling, the doorway seemed impossibly far away. All my muscles tensed; I seemed ready to spring; I was waiting for the blow.

I put my hands in my pockets and we walked to the end of the block. The lights were green and red, the lights from the theater across the street exploded blue and yellow, off and on.

"Peter?"

"Yes?"

"I'll see you tomorrow?"

"Yeah. Come by Jules's. I'll wait for you."

"Goodnight, darling."

"Goodnight."

I started to walk away. I felt her eyes on my back. I kicked a bottle-top on the sidewalk.

God save the American republic.

I dropped into the subway and got on an uptown train, not knowing where it was going and not caring. Anonymous, islanded people surrounded me, behind newspapers, behind make-up, fat, fleshy masks and flat eyes. I watched the empty faces. (No one looked at me.) I looked at the ads, unreal women and pink-cheeked men selling cigarettes, candy, shaving cream, nightgowns, chewing gum, movies, sex; sex without organs, drier than sand and more secret than death. The train stopped. A white boy and a white girl got on. She was nice, short, svelte. Nice legs. She was hanging on his arm. He was the football type, blond, ruddy. They were dressed in summer clothes. The wind from the doors blew her print dress. She squealed, holding the dress at the knees and giggled and looked at him. He said something I didn't catch and she looked at me and the smile died. She stood so that she faced him and had her back to me. I looked back at the ads. Then I hated them. I wanted to do something to make them hurt, something that would crack the pink-cheeked mask. The white boy and I did not look at each other again. They got off at the next stop.

I wanted to keep on drinking. I got off in Harlem and went to a rundown bar on Seventh Avenue. My people, my people. Sharpies stood on the corner, waiting. Women in summer dresses pranced by on wavering heels. Click clack. Click clack. There were white mounted policemen in the streets. On every block there was another policeman on foot. I saw a black cop.

God save the American republic.

The juke box was letting loose with "Hamps' Boogie." The place was jumping, I walked over to the man.

"Rye," I said.

I was standing next to somebody's grandmother. "Hello, papa. What you puttin' down?"

"Baby, you can't pick it up," I told her. My rye came and I drank.

"Nigger," she said, "you must think you's somebody."

I didn't answer. She turned away, back to her beer, keeping time to the juke box, her face sullen and heavy and aggrieved.

I watched her out of the side of my eye. She had been good looking once, pretty even, before she hit the bottle and started crawling into too many beds. She was flabby now, flesh heaved all over in her thin dress. I wondered what she'd be like in bed; then I realized that I was a little excited by her; I laughed and set my glass down.

"The same," I said. "And a beer chaser."

The juke box was playing something else now, something brassy and commercial which I didn't like. I kept on drinking, listening to the voices of my people, watching the faces of my people. (God pity us, the terrified republic.) Now I was sorry to have angered the woman who still sat next to me, now deep in conversation with another, younger woman. I longed for some opening, some sign, something to make me a part of the life around me. But there was nothing except my color. A white outsider coming in would have seen a young Negro drinking in a Negro bar, perfectly in his element, in his place, as the saying goes. But the people here knew differently, as I did. I didn't seem to have a place.

So I kept on drinking by myself, saying to myself after each drink, Now I'll go. But I was afraid; I didn't want to sleep on Jules's floor; I didn't want to go to sleep. I kept on drinking and listening to the juke box. They were playing Ella Fitzgerald, "Cow-Cow Boogie."

"Let me buy you a drink," I said to the woman.

She looked at me, startled, suspicious, ready to blow her top.

"On the level," I said. I tried to smile. "Both of you."

"I'll take a beer," the young one said.

I was shaking like a baby. I finished my drink.

"Fine," I said. I turned to the bar.

"Baby," said the old one, "what's your story?"

The man put three beers on the counter.

"I got no story, Ma," I said.

JOHN UPDIKE • 1932–

Flight

AT the age of seventeen I was poorly dressed and funny-looking, and went around thinking about myself in the third person. "Allen Dow strode down the street and home." "Allen Dow smiled a thin sardonic smile." Consciousness of a special destiny made me both arrogant and shy. Years before, when I was eleven or twelve, just on the brink of ceasing to be a little boy, my mother and I, one Sunday afternoon—my father was busy, or asleep—hiked up to the top of Shale Hill, a child's mountain that formed one side of the valley that held our town. There the town lay under us, Olinger, perhaps a thousand homes, the best and biggest of them climbing Shale Hill toward us, and beyond them the blocks of brick houses, one- and two-family, the homes of my friends, sloping down to the pale thread of the Alton Pike, which strung together the high school, the tennis courts, the movie theatre, the town's few stores and gasoline stations, the elementary school, the Lutheran church. On the other side lay more homes, including our own, a tiny white patch placed just where the land began to rise toward the opposite mountain, Cedar Top. There were rims and rims of hills beyond Cedar Top, and looking south we could see the pike dissolving in other towns and turning out of sight amid the patches of green and brown farmland, and it seemed the entire county was lying exposed under a thin veil of haze. I was old enough to feel embarrassment at standing there alone with my mother, beside a wind-stunted spruce tree, on a long spine of shale. Suddenly she dug her fingers into the hair on my head and announced, "There we all are, and there we'll all be forever." She hesitated before the word "forever," and hesitated again before adding, "Except you, Allen. You're going to fly." A few birds were hung far out over the valley, at the level of our eyes, and in her impulsive way she had just plucked the image from them, but it felt like the clue I had been waiting all my childhood for. My most secret self had been made to respond, and I was intensely embarrassed, and irritably ducked my head out from under her melodramatic hand.

She was impulsive and romantic and inconsistent. I was never able to develop this spurt of reassurance into a steady theme between us. That she continued to treat me like an ordinary child seemed a betrayal of the vision she had made me share. I was captive to a hope she had tossed off and forgotten. My shy attempts to justify irregularities in my conduct—reading late at night or not coming back from school on time—by appealing to the image of flight were received with a startled blank look, as if I were talking nonsense. It seemed outrageously unjust. Yes, but, I wanted to say, yes, but it's *your* nonsense. And of course it was just this that made my appeal ineffective: her knowing that I had not made it mine, that I cynically intended to exploit both the privileges of being extraordinary and the pleasures of being ordinary. She feared my wish to be ordinary; once she did respond to my protest that I was learning to fly, by crying with red-faced ferocity, "You'll never learn, you'll stick and die in the dirt just like I'm doing. Why should you be better than your mother?"

She had been born ten miles to the south, on a farm she and her mother had loved. Her mother, a small fierce woman who looked more like an Arab than a German, worked in the fields with the men, and drove the wagon to market ten miles away every Friday. When still a tiny girl, my mother rode with her, and my impression of those rides is of fear—the little girl's fear of the gross and beery men who grabbed and hugged her, her fear of the wagon breaking, of the produce not selling, fear of her mother's possible humiliation and of her father's condition when at nightfall they returned. Friday was his holiday, and he drank. His drinking is impossible for me to picture; for I never knew him except as an enduring, didactic, almost Biblical old man, whose one passion was reading the newspapers and whose one hatred was of the Republican Party. There was something public about him; now that he is dead I keep seeing bits of him attached to famous politicians—his watch chain and his plump square stomach in old films of Theodore Roosevelt, his high-top shoes and the tilt of his head in a photograph of Alfalfa Bill Murry. Alfalfa Bill is turning his head to talk, and holds his hat by the crown, pinching it between two fingers and a thumb, a gentle and courtly grip that reminded me so keenly of my grandfather that I tore the picture out of *Life* and put it in a drawer.

Laboring in the soil had never been congenial to my grandfather, though with his wife's help he prospered by it. Then, in an era when success was hard to avoid, he began to invest in stocks. In 1922 he bought our large white home in the town —its fashionable section had not yet shifted to the Shale Hill side of the valley —and settled in to reap his dividends. He believed to his death that women were foolish, and the broken hearts of his two must have seemed specially so. The dignity of finance for the indignity of farming must have struck him as an eminently advantageous exchange. It strikes me that way, too, and how to reconcile my idea of those fear-ridden wagon rides with the grief that my mother insists she and her mother felt at being taken from the farm? Perhaps prolonged fear is a ground of love. Or perhaps, and likelier, the equation is long and complex, and the few factors I know—the middle-aged woman's mannish pride of land, the adolescent girl's pleasure in riding horses across the fields, their common feeling of rejection in Olinger—are enclosed in brackets and heightened by coefficients that I cannot see. Or perhaps it is not love of land but its absence that needs explaining, in my grandfather's fastidiousness and pride. He believed that as a boy he had been abused, and bore his father a grudge that my mother could never understand. Her grandfather to her was a saintly slender giant, over six feet tall when this was a prodigy, who knew the names of everything, like Adam in Eden. In his old age he was blind. When he came out of the house, the dogs rushed forward to lick his hands. When he lay dying, he requested a Gravenstein apple from the tree on the far edge of the meadow, and his son brought him a Krauser from the orchard near the house. The old man refused it, and my grandfather made a second trip, but in my mother's eyes the outrage had been committed, a savage insult insanely without provocation. What had his father done to him? The only specific complaint I ever heard my grandfather make was that when he was a boy and had to fetch water for the men in the fields, his father would tell him sarcastically, "Pick up your feet; they'll come down themselves." How incongruous! As if each generation of parents commits atrocities against their children which by God's decree remain invisible to the rest of the world.

I remember my grandmother as a little dark-eyed woman who talked seldom and who tried to feed me too much, and then as a hook-nosed profile pink against the lemon cushions of the casket. She died when I was seven. All the rest I know about her is that she was the baby of thirteen children, that while she was alive she made our yard one of the most beautiful in town, and that I am supposed to resemble her brother Pete.

My mother was precocious; she was fourteen when they moved, and for three years had been attending the county normal school. She graduated from Lake College, near Philadelphia, when she was only twenty, a tall handsome girl with a deprecatory smile, to judge from one of the curling photographs kept in a shoebox that I was always opening as a child, as if it might contain the clue to the quarrels in my house. My mother stands at the end of our brick walk, beside the elaborately trimmed end of our privet hedge—in shape a thick square column mounted by a rough ball of leaf. The ragged arc of a lilac bush in flower cuts into the right edge of the photograph, and behind my mother I can see a vacant lot where there has been a house ever since I can remember. She poses with a kind of country grace in a long fur-trimmed coat, unbuttoned to expose her beads and a short yet somehow demure flapper dress. Her hands are in her coat pockets, a beret sits on one side of her bangs, and there is a swank about her that seemed incongruous to me, examining this picture on the stained carpet of an ill-lit old house in the evening years of the thirties and in the dark of the warring forties. The costume and the girl in it look so up-to-date, so formidable. It was my grandfather's pleasure, in his prosperity, to give her a generous clothes allowance. My father, the penniless younger son of a Presbyterian minister in Passaic, had worked his way through Lake College by waiting on tables, and still speaks with mild resentment of the beautiful clothes that Lillian Baer wore. This aspect of my mother caused me some pain in high school; she was a fabric snob, and insisted on buying 'my slacks and sports shirts at the best store in Alton, and since we had little money, she bought me few, when of course what I needed was what my classmates had—a wide variety of cheap clothes.

At the time the photograph was taken, my mother wanted to go to New York. What she would have done there, or exactly what she wanted to do, I don't know; but her father forbade her. "Forbid" is a husk of a word today, but at that time, in that quaint province, in the mouth of an "indulgent father," it apparently was still viable, for the great moist weight of that forbidding continued to be felt in the house for years, and when I was a child, as one of my mother's endless harangues to my grandfather screamed toward its weeping peak, I could feel it around and above me, like a huge root encountered by an earthworm.

Perhaps in a reaction of anger my mother married my father, Victor Dow, who at least took her as far away as Wilmington, where he had made a beginning with an engineering firm. But the depression hit, my father was laid off, and the couple came to the white house in Olinger, where my grandfather sat reading the newspapers that traced his stocks' cautious decline into worthlessness. I was born. My grandmother went around as a cleaning lady, and grew things in our quarter-acre yard to sell. We kept chickens, and there was a large plot of asparagus. After she had died, in a frightened way I used to seek her in the asparagus patch. By midsummer it would be a forest of dainty green trees, some as tall as I was, and in their frothy touch a spirit seemed to speak, and in the soft thick net of their intermingling branches a promise seemed to be caught, as well as a menace. The asparagus trees were frightening; in the center of the patch, far from the house and the alley, I would fall under a spell, and become tiny, and wander among the great smooth green trunks expecting to find a little house with a smoking chimney, and in it my grandmother. She herself had believed in ghosts, which made her own ghost potent. Even now, sitting alone in my own house, a board creaks in the kitchen and I look up fearing she will come through the doorway. And at night, just before I fall asleep, her voice calls my name in a penetrating whisper, or calls, *"Pete."*

My mother went to work in an Alton department store, selling inferior fabric for $14 a week. During the daytime of my first year of life it was my father who took care of me. He has said since, flattering me as he always does, that it was having me on his hands that kept him from going insane. It may have been this that has made my affection for him so inarticulate, as if I were still a wordless infant looking up into the mothering blur of his man's face. And that same shared year helps account, perhaps, for his gentleness with me, for his willingness to praise, as if everything I do has something sad and crippled in it. He feels sorry for me; my birth coincided with the birth of a great misery, a national misery—only recently has he stopped calling me by the nickname "Young America." Around my first birthday he acquired a position teaching arithmetic and algebra in the Olinger high school, and though he was so kind and humorous he couldn't enter a classroom without creating uproarious problems of discipline, he endured it day by day and year by year, and eventually came to occupy a place in this alien town, so that I believe there are now one or two dozen ex-students, men and women nearing middle age, who carry around with them some piece of encouragement my father gave them, or remember some sentence of his that helped shape them. Certainly there are many who remember the antics with which he burlesqued his discomfort in the classroom. He kept a confiscated cap pistol in his desk, and upon getting an especially stupid answer, he would take it out and, wearing a preoccupied, regretful expression, shoot himself in the head.

My grandfather was the last to go to work, and the most degraded by it. He was hired by the borough crew, men who went around the streets shoveling stones and spreading tar. Bulky and ominous in their overalls, wreathed in steam, and associated with dramatic and portentous equipment, these men had grandeur in the eyes of a child, and it puzzled me, as I walked to and from elementary school, that my grandfather refused to wave to me or confess his presence in any way. Curiously strong for a fastidious man, he kept at it well into his seventies, when his sight failed. It was my task then to read his beloved newspapers to him as he sat in his chair by the bay window, twiddling his high-top shoes in the sunshine. I teased him, reading too fast, then maddeningly slow, skipping from column to column to create one long chaotic story; I read him the sports page, which did not interest him, and mumbled the editorials. Only the speed of his feet's twiddling betrayed vexation. When I'd stop, he would plead mildly in his rather beautiful, old-fashioned, elocutionary voice, "Now just the obituaries, Allen. Just the names to see if anyone I know is there." I imagined, as I viciously barked at him the list of names that might contain the name of a friend, that I was avenging my mother; I believed that she hated him, and for her sake I tried to hate him also. From her incessant resurrection of mysterious grievances buried far back in the confused sunless earth of the time before I was born, I had been able to deduce only that he was an evil man, who had ruined her life, that fair creature in the beret. I did not understand. She fought with him not because she wanted to fight but because *she could not bear to leave him alone.*

Sometimes, glancing up from the sheet of print where our armies swarmed in retreat like harried insects, I would catch the old man's head in the act of lifting slightly to receive the warm sunshine on his face, a dry frail face ennobled by its thick crown of combed corn-silk hair. It would dawn on me then that his sins as a father were likely no worse than any father's. But my mother's genius was to give the people closest to her mythic immensity. I was the phoenix. My father and grandmother were legendary invader-saints, she springing out of some narrow vein of Arab blood in the German race and he crossing over from the Protestant wastes of New Jersey, both of them serving and enslaving their mates with their prodigious powers of endurance and labor. For my mother felt that she and her father alike had been destroyed by marriage, been made captive by people better yet less than they. It was true, my father had loved Mom Baer, and her death made him seem more of an alien than ever. He, and her ghost, stood to one side, in the shadows but separate from the house's dark core, the inheritance of frustration and folly that had descended from my grandfather to my mother to me, and that I, with a few beats of my grown wings, was destined to reverse and redeem.

At the age of seventeen, in the fall of my senior year, I went with three girls to debate at a high school over a hundred miles away. They were, all three, bright girls, A students; they were disfigured by A's as if by acne. Yet even so it excited me to be mounting a train with them early on a Friday morning, at an hour when our schoolmates miles away were slumping into the seats of their first class. Sunshine spread broad bars of dust down the length of the half-empty car, and through the windows Pennsylvania unravelled in a long brown scroll scribbled with industry. Black pipes raced beside the tracks for miles. At rhythmic intervals one of them looped upward, like the Greek letter Ω. "Why does it do that?" I asked. "Is it sick?"

"Condensation?" Judith Potteiger suggested in her shy, transparent voice. She loved science.

"No," I said. "It's in pain. It's writhing! It's going to grab the train! Look out!" I ducked, honestly a little scared. All the girls laughed.

Judith and Catharine Miller were in my class, and expected me to be amusing; the third girl, a plump small junior named Molly Bingaman, had not known what to expect. It was her fresh audience I was playing to. She was the best dressed of us four, and the most poised; this made me suspect that she was the least bright. She had been substituted at the last moment for a sick member of the debating team; I knew her just by seeing her in the halls and in assembly. From a distance she seemed dumpy and prematurely adult. But up close she was gently fragrant, and against the weary purple cloth of the train seats her skin seemed luminous. She had beautiful skin a pencil dot would have marred, and large blue eyes equally clear. Except for a double chin, and a mouth too large and thick, she would have been perfectly pretty, in a little woman's compact and cocky way. She and I sat side by side, facing the two senior girls, who more and more took on the wan slyness of matchmakers. It was they who had forced the seating arrangements.

We debated in the afternoon, and won. Yes, the German Federal Republic *should* be freed of all Allied control. The school, a posh castle on the edge of a miserable coal city, was the site of a statewide cycle of debates that was to continue into Saturday. There was a dance Friday night in the gym. I danced with Molly mostly, though to my annoyance she got in with a set of Harrisburg boys while I conscientiously pushed Judith and Catharine around the floor. We were stiff dancers, the three of us; only Molly made me seem good, floating backward from my feet fearlessly as her cheek rumpled my moist shirt. The gym was hung with orange and black crepe paper in honor of Hallowe'en, and the pennants of all the competing schools were fastened to the walls, and a twelve-piece band pumped away blissfully on the year's sad tunes—"Heartaches," "Near You," "That's My Desire." A great cloud of balloons gathered in the steel girders was released. There was pink punch, and a local girl sang.

Judith and Catharine decided to leave before the dance was over, and I made Molly come too, though she was in a literal sweat of pleasure; her perfect skin in the oval above her neckline was flushed and glazed. I realized, with a little shock of possessiveness and pity, that she was unused to attention back home, in competition with the gorgeous Olinger ignorant.

We walked together to the house where the four of us had been boarded, a large white frame owned by an old couple and standing with lonely decency in a semi-slum. Judith and Catharine turned up the walk, but Molly and I, with a diffident decision that I believe came from her initiative, continued, "to walk around the block." We walked miles, stopping off after midnight at a trolley-car-shaped diner. I got a hamburger, and she impressed me by ordering coffee. We walked back to the house and let ourselves in with the key we had been given; but instead of going upstairs to our rooms we sat downstairs in the dark living room and talked softly for more hours.

What did we say? I talked about myself. It is hard to hear, much less remember, what we ourselves say, just as it might be hard for a movie projector, given life, to see the shadows its eye of light is casting. A transcript, could I produce it, of my monologue through the wide turning point of that night, with all its word-by-word conceit, would distort the picture: this living room miles from home, the street light piercing the chinks in the curtains and erecting on the wallpaper rods of light the size of yardsticks, our hosts and companions asleep upstairs, the incessant sigh of my voice, coffee-primed Molly on the floor beside my chair, her stockinged legs stretched out on the rug; and this odd sense in the room, a tasteless and odorless aura unfamiliar to me, as a pool of water widening.

I remember one exchange. I must have been describing the steep waves of fearing death that had come over me ever since early childhood, about one every three years, and I ended by supposing that it would take great courage to be an atheist. "But I bet you'll become one," Molly said. "Just to show yourself that you're brave enough." I felt she overestimated me, and was flattered. Within a few years, while I still remembered many of her words, I realized how touchingly gauche our assumption was that an atheist is a lonely rebel; for mobs of men are united in atheism, and oblivion—the dense lead-like sea that would occasionally sweep over me—is to them a weight as negligible as the faint pressure of their wallets in their hip pockets. This grotesque and tender mis-estimate of the world flares in my memory of our conversation like one of the innumerable matches we struck.

The room filled with smoke. Too weary to sit, I lay down on the floor beside her, and stroked her silver arm in silence, yet still was too timid to act on the wide and negative aura that I did not understand was of compliance. On the upstairs landing, as I went to turn into my room, Molly came forward with a prim look and kissed me. With clumsy force I entered the negative space that had been waiting. Her lipstick smeared in little unflattering flecks into the skin around her mouth; it was as if I had been given a face to eat, and the presence of bone—skull under skin, teeth behind lips—impeded me. We stood for a long time under the burning hall light, until my neck began to ache from bowing. My legs were trembling when we finally parted and sneaked into our rooms. In bed I thought, "Allen Dow tossed restlessly," and realized it was the first time that day I had thought of myself in the third person.

On Saturday morning, we lost our debate. I was sleepy and verbose and haughty, and some of the students in the audience began to boo whenever I opened my mouth. The principal came up on the stage and made a scolding speech, which finished me and my cause, untrammeled Germany. On the train back, Catharine and Judith arranged the seating so that they sat behind Molly and me, and spied on only the tops of our heads. For the first time, on that ride home, I felt what it was to bury a humiliation in the body of a woman. Nothing but the friction of my face against hers drowned out the echo of those boos. When we kissed, a red shadow would well under my lids and eclipse the hostile hooting faces of the debate audience, and when our lips parted, the bright inner sea would ebb, and there the faces would be again, more intense than ever. With a shudder of shame I'd hide my face on her shoulder and in the warm darkness there, while a frill of her prissy collar gently scratched my nose, I felt united with Hitler and all the villains, traitors, madmen, and failures who had managed to keep, up to the moment of capture or death, a woman with them. This had puzzled me. In high school females were proud and remote; in the newspapers they were fantastic monsters of submission. And now Molly administered reassurance to me with small motions and bodily adjustments that had about them a strange flavor of the practical.

Our parents met us at the station. I was startled at how tired my mother looked. There were deep blue dents on either side of her nose, and her hair seemed somehow dissociated from her head, as if it were a ragged, half-gray wig she had put on carelessly. She was a heavy woman and her weight, which she usually carried upright, like a kind of wealth, had slumped away from her ownership and seemed, in the sullen light of the railway platform, to weigh on the world. I asked, "How's Grandpa?" He had taken to bed several months before with pains in his chest.

"He still sings," she said rather sharply. For entertainment in his increasing blindness my grandfather had long ago begun to sing, and his shapely old voice would pour forth hymns, forgotten comic ballads, and camp-meeting songs at any hour. His memory seemed to improve the longer he lived.

My mother's irritability was more manifest in the private cavity of the car; her heavy silence oppressed me. "You look so tired, Mother," I said, trying to take the offensive.

"That's nothing to how you look," she answered. "What happened up there? You stoop like an old married man."

"Nothing happened," I lied. My cheeks were parched, as if her high steady anger had the power of giving sunburn.

"I remember that Bingaman girl's mother when we first moved to town. She was the smuggest little snip south of the pike. They're real old Olinger stock, you know. They have no use for hillbillies."

My father tried to change the subject. "Well, you won one debate, Allen, and that's more than I would have done. I don't see how you do it."

"Why, he gets it from you, Victor. I've never won a debate with you."

"He gets it from Pop Baer. If that man had gone into politics, Lillian, all the misery of his life would have been avoided."

"Dad was never a debater. He was a bully. Don't go with little women, Allen. It puts you too close to the ground.

"I'm not *going* with *any*body, Mother. Really, you're so fanciful."

"Why, when she stepped off the train from the way her chins bounced I thought she had eaten a canary. And then making my poor son, all skin and bones, carry her bag. When she walked by me I honestly was afraid she'd spit in my eye."

"I had to carry somebody's bag. I'm sure she doesn't know who you are." Though it was true I had talked a good deal about my family the night before.

My mother turned away from me. "You see, Victor—he defends her. When I was his age that girl's mother gave me a cut I'm still bleeding from, and my own son attacks me on behalf of her fat little daughter. I wonder if her mother put her up to catching him."

"Molly's a nice girl," my father interceded. "She never gave me any trouble in class like some of those smug bastards." But he was curiously listless, for so Christian a man, in pronouncing this endorsement.

I discovered that nobody wanted me to go with Molly Bingaman. My friends —for on the strength of being funny I did have some friends, classmates whose love affairs went on over my head but whom I could accompany, as clown, on communal outings—never talked with me about Molly, and when I brought her to their parties gave the impression of ignoring her, so that I stopped taking her. Teachers at school would smile an odd tight smile when they saw us leaning by her locker or hanging around in the stairways. The eleventh-grade English instructor—one of my "boosters" on the faculty, a man who was always trying to "challenge" me, to "exploit" my "potential"— took me aside and told me how stupid she was. She just couldn't grasp the logical principals of syntax. He confided her parsing mistakes to me as if they betrayed —as indeed in a way they did—an obtuseness her social manner cleverly concealed. Even the Fabers, an ultra-Republican couple who ran a luncheonette near the high school, showed malicious delight whenever Molly and I broke up, and persistently treated my attachment as being a witty piece of play, like my pretense with Mr. Faber of being a Communist. The entire town seemed ensnarled in my mother's myth, that escape was my proper fate. It was as if I were a sport that the ghostly elders of Olinger had segregated from the rest of the livestock and agreed to donate in time to the air; this fitted with the ambiguous sensation I had always had in the town, of being simultaneously flattered and rejected.

Molly's parents disapproved because in their eyes my family was virtually white trash. It was so persistently hammered into me that I was too good for Molly that I scarcely considered the proposition that, by another scale, she was too good for me. Further, Molly herself shielded me. Only once, exasperated by some tedious, condescending confession of mine, did she state that her mother didn't like me. "Why not?" I asked, genuinely surprised. I admired Mrs. Bingaman—she was beautifully preserved— and I always felt gay in her house, with its white woodwork and matching furniture and vases of iris posing before polished mirrors.

"Oh, I don't know. She thinks you're flippant."

"But that's not true. Nobody takes himself more seriously than I do."

While Molly protected me from the Bingaman side of the ugliness, I conveyed the Dow side more or less directly to her. It infuriated me that nobody allowed me to be proud of her. I kept, in effect, asking her, Why was she stupid in English? Why didn't she get along with my friends? Why did she look so dumpy and smug?—this last despite the fact that she often, especially in intimate moments, looked beautiful to me. I was especially angry with her because this affair had brought out an ignoble, hysterical, brutal aspect of my mother that I might never have had to see otherwise. I had hoped to keep things secret from her, but even if her intuition had not been relentless, my father, at school, knew everything.

Sometimes, indeed, my mother said that she didn't care if I went with Molly; it was my father who was upset. Like a frantic dog tied by one leg, she snapped in any direction, mouthing ridiculous fancies—such as that Mrs. Bingaman had sicked Molly on me just to keep me from going to college and giving the Dows something to be proud of—that would make us both suddenly start laughing. Laughter in that house that winter had a guilty sound. My grandfather was dying, and lay upstairs singing and coughing and weeping as the mood came to him, and we were too poor to hire a nurse, and too kind and cowardly to send him to a "home." It was still his house, after all. Any noise he made seemed to slash my mother's heart, and she was unable to sleep upstairs near him, and waited the nights out on the sofa downstairs. In her desperate state she would say unforgivable things to me even while the tears streamed down her face. I've never seen so many tears as I saw that winter.

Every time I saw my mother cry, it seemed I had to make Molly cry. I developed a skill at it; it came naturally to an only child who had been surrounded all his life by adults ransacking each other for the truth. Even in the heart of intimacy, half-naked each of us, I would say something to humiliate her. We never made love in the final, coital sense. My reason was a mixture of idealism and superstition; I felt that if I took her virginity she would be mine forever. I depended overmuch on a technicality; she gave herself to me anyway, and I had her anyway, and have her still, for the longer I travel in a direction I could not have taken with her, the more clearly she seems the one person who loved me without advantage. I was a homely, comically ambitious hillbilly, and I even refused to tell her I loved her, to pronounce the word "love"—an icy piece of pedantry that shocks me now that I have almost forgotten the context of confusion in which it seemed wise.

In addition to my grandfather's illness, and my mother's grief, and my waiting to hear if I had won a scholarship to the one college that seemed good enough for me, I was burdened with managing too many petty affairs of my graduating class. I was in charge of yearbook writeups, art editor of the school paper, chairman of the Class Gift Committee, director of the Senior Assembly, and teachers' workhorse. Frightened by my father's tales of nervous breakdowns he had seen, I kept listening for the sounds of my brain snapping, and the image of that gray, infinitely interconnected mass seemed to extend outward, to become my whole world, one dense organic dungeon, and I felt I had to get out; if I could just get out of this, into June, it would be blue sky, and I would be all right for life.

One Friday night in spring, after trying for over an hour to write thirty-five affectionate words for the yearbook about a null girl in the Secretarial Course I had never spoken a word to, I heard my grandfather begin coughing upstairs with a sound like dry membrane tearing, and I panicked. I called up the stairs, "Mother! I must go out."

"It's nine-thirty."

"I know, but I have to. I'm going insane."

Without waiting to hear her answer or to find a coat, I left the house and got our old car out of the garage. The weekend before, I had broken up with Molly again. All week I hadn't spoken to her, though I had seen her once in Faber's, with a boy in her class, averting her face while I, hanging by the side of the pinball machine, made wisecracks in her direction. I didn't dare go up to her door and knock so late at night; I just parked across the street and watched the lit windows of her house. Through their living-room window I could see one of Mrs. Bingaman's vases of hothouse iris standing on a white mantel, and my open car window admitted the spring air, which delicately smelled of wet ashes. Molly was probably out on a date with that moron in her class. But then the Bingaman's door opened, and her figure appeared in the rectangle of light. Her back was toward me, a coat was on her arm, and her mother seemed to be screaming. Molly closed the door and ran down off the porch and across the street and quickly got into the car, her eyes downcast in their sockets of shadow. *She came.* When I have finally forgotten everything else, her powdery fragrance, her lucid cool skin, the way her lower lip was like a curved pillow of two cloths, the dusty red outer and wet pink inner, I'll still be grieved by this about Molly, that she came to me.

After I returned her to her house—she told me not to worry, her mother enjoyed shouting—I went to the all-night diner just beyond the Olinger town line and ate three hamburgers, ordering them one at a time, and drank two glasses of milk. It was close to two o'clock when I got home, but my mother was still awake. She lay on the sofa in the dark, with the radio sitting on the floor murmuring Dixieland piped up from New Orleans by way of Philadelphia. Radio music was a steady feature of her insomniac life; not only did it help drown out the noise of her father upstairs but she seemed to enjoy it in itself. She would resist my father's pleas to come to bed by saying that the New Orleans program was not over yet. The radio was an old Philco we had always had; I had once drawn a fish on the orange disc of its celluloid dial, which looked to my child's eyes like a fishbowl.

Her loneliness caught at me; I went into the living room and sat on a chair with my back to the window. For a long time she looked at me tensely out of the darkness. "Well," she said at last, "how was little hotpants?" The vulgarity this affair had brought out in her language appalled me.

"I made her cry," I told her.

"Why do you torment the girl?"
"To please you."
"It doesn't please me."
"Well, then, stop nagging me."
"I'll stop nagging you if you'll solemnly tell me you're willing to marry her."

I said nothing to this, and after waiting she went on in a different voice, "Isn't it funny, that you should show this weakness?"

"Weakness is a funny way to put it when it's the only thing that gives me strength."

"Does it really, Allen? Well. It may be. I forget, you were born here."

Upstairs, close to our heads, my grandfather, in a voice frail but still melodious, began to sing, "There is a happy land, far, far away, where saints in glory stand, bright, bright as day." We listened; and his voice broke into coughing, a terrible rending cough growing in fury, struggling to escape, and loud with fear he called my mother's name. She didn't stir. His voice grew enormous, a bully's voice, as he repeated, "Lillian! Lillian!" and I saw my mother's shape quiver with the force coming down the stairs into her; she was like a dam; and then the power, as my grandfather fell momentarily silent, flowed toward me in the darkness, and I felt intensely angry, and hated that black mass of suffering, even while I realized, with a rapid, light calculation, that I was too weak to withstand it.

In a dry tone of certainty and dislike—how hard my heart had become!—I told her, "All right. You'll win this one, Mother; but it'll be the last one you'll win."

My pang of fright following this unprecedentedly cold insolence seemed to blot my senses; the chair ceased to be felt under me, and the walls and furniture of the room fell away—there was only the dim orange glow of the radio dial down below. In a husky voice that seemed to come across a great distance my mother said, with typical melodrama, "Goodbye, Allen."

Poetry

ANONYMOUS

Sumer Is Icumen In

Sing cuccu nu![1] Sing cuccu!
Sing cuccu! Sing cuccu nu!

Sumer is icumen in,
    Lhude[2] sing cuccu;
Groweth sed and bloweth med[3]
And springth the wde[4] nu.
    Sing cuccu!
Awe[5] bleteth after lomb,
    Lhouth[6] after calve cu;
Bulluc sterteth,[7] bucke verteth;[8]   *10*
    Murie[9] sing cuccu.
        Cuccu, cuccu,
    Wel singes thu, cuccu,
    Ne swik[10] thu naver nu.

(c. 1240)

Ubi Sunt Qui ante Nos Fuerunt?[1]

Were beth they biforen us weren,
Houndes ladden and havekes beren[2]
    And hadden feld and wode?
The riche levedies[3] in hoere bour,
That wereden gold in hoere tressour,[4]
    With hoere brightte rode?[5]

Eten and drounken, and maden hem glad;
Hoere lif was al with gamen ilad;[6]
    Men kneleden hem biforen;
They beren hem wel swithe heye;[7]   *10*
And, in a twincling of an eye,
    Hoere soules were forloren.[8]

Were is that lawing[9] and that song,
That trayling and that proude gong,[10]
    Tho havekes and tho houndes?
Al that joye is went away,
That wele is comen to 'Weylaway!'—
    To manie harde stoundes.[11]

Hoere paradis they nomen[12] here,
And nou they lien in helle ifere;[13]   *20*
    The fuir hit brennes[14] hevere.[15]
Long is ay, and long is o,
Long is wy, and long is wo;
    Thennes ne cometh they nevere.

(c. 1275)

Edward

"Why dois your brand sae drap wi bluid,
    Edward, Edward,
Why dois your brand sae drap wi bluid,
    And why sae sad gang[1] yee O?"
"O I hae killed my hauke sae guid,
    Mither, mither,
O I hae killed my hauke sae guid,
    And I had nae mair bot hee O."

---

[1] now
[2] loudly. The final *e* here and elsewhere in Middle English is pronounced as an unaccented neutral vowel (approximately *uh*), so that such words as *wde*, *calve*, and *singes* have two syllables.   [3] mead, meadow
[4] wood   [5] ewe   [6] lows   [7] leaps
[8] breaks wind   [9] merrily   [10] cease

[1] Where Are Those Who Were Before Us?
[2] led hounds and bore hawks   [3] ladies
[4] tresses   [5] complexion   [6] led
[7] very high   [8] lost   [9] laughing
[10] going   [11] hours, time   [12] took
[13] together   [14] burns   [15] ever

[1] go

"Your haukis bluid was nevir sae reid,
    Edward, Edward,
Your haukis bluid was nevir sae reid,
    My deir son I tell thee O."
"O I hae killed my reid-roan steid,
    Mither, mither,
O I hae killed my reid-roan steid,
    That erst was sae fair and frie O."

"Your steid was auld, and ye hae got mair,
    Edward, Edward,
Your steid was auld, and ye hae got mair,
    Sum other dule[2] ye drie[3] O."
"O I hae killed my fadir deir,
    Mither, mither,
O I hae killed my fadir deir,
    Alas, and wae is mee O!"

"And whatten penance wul ye drie for that,
    Edward, Edward,
And whatten penance will ye drie for that?
    My deir son, now tell me O."
"Ile set my feit in yonder boat,
    Mither, mither,
Ile set my feit in yonder boat,
    And Ile fare ovir the sea O."

"And what wul ye doe wi your towirs and your ha,[4]
    Edward, Edward?
And what wul ye doe wi your towirs and your ha,
    That were sae fair to see O?"
"Ile let thame stand tul they doun fa,
    Mither, mither,
Ile let thame stand tul they doun fa,
    For here nevir mair maun I bee O."

"And what wul ye leive to your bairns and your wife,
    Edward, Edward?
And what wul ye leive to your bairns and your wife,
    Whan ye gang ovir the sea O?"
"The warldis room, late them beg thrae life,
    Mither, mither,
The wardlis room, late them beg thrae life,
    For thame nevir mair wul I see O."

"And what wul ye leive to your ain mither deir,
    Edward, Edward?

---

[2] woe   [3] suffer   [4] hall

And what wul ye leive to your ain mither deir?
  My deir son, now tell me O."
"The curse of hell frae me sall ye beir,
  Mither, mither,
The curse of hell frae me sall ye beir,
  Sic counseils ye gave to me O."

The Brown Girl

"I am as brown as brown can be,
  And my eyes as black as sloe;
I am as brisk as brisk can be,
  And wild as forest doe.

"My love he was so high and proud,
  His fortune too so high,
He for another fair pretty maid
  Me left and passed me by.

"Me did he send a love-letter,
  He sent it from the town,   10
Saying no more he loved me,
  For that I was so brown.

"I sent his letter back again,
  Saying his love I valued not,
Whether that he would fancy me,
  Whether that he would not.

"When that six months were overpassed,
  Were gone and overpassed,
O then my lover, once so bold,
  With love was sick at last.   20

"First sent he for the doctor-man:
  'You, doctor, me must cure;
The pains that now do torture me
  I can not long endure.'

"Next did he send from out the town,
  O next did send for me;
He sent for me, the brown, brown girl
  Who once his wife should be.

"O neer a bit the doctor-man
  His sufferings could relieve;   30
O never an one but the brown, brown girl
  Who could his life reprieve."

Now you shall hear what love she had
  For this poor love-sick man,
How all one day, a summer's day,
  She walked and never ran.

When that she came to his bedside,
  Where he lay sick and weak,
O then for laughing she could not stand
  Upright upon her feet.   40

"You flouted me, you scouted me,
  And many another one;
Now the reward is come at last,
  For all that you have done."

The rings she took from off her hands,
  The rings by two and three: 50
"O take, O take these golden rings,
  By them remember me."

She had a white wand in her hand,
  She strake him on the breast:
"My faith and troth I give back to thee,
  So may thy soul have rest."

"Prithee," said he, "forget, forget,
  Prithee forget, forgive;
O grant me yet a little space,
  That I may be well and live."   60

"O never will I forget, forgive,
  So long as I have breath;
I'll dance above your green, green grave
  Where you do lie beneath."

Sir Patrick Spens

The king sits in Dumferling toune,
  Drinking the blude-red wine:
"O whar will I get guid sailor,
  To sail this schip of mine?"

Up and spak an eldern knicht,
  Sat at the kings richt kne:
"Sir Patrick Spens is the best sailor,
  That sails upon the se."

The king has written a braid letter,
  And signd it wi his hand,   10
And sent it to Sir Patrick Spens,
  Was walking on the sand.

The first line that Sir Patrick red,
  A loud lauch lauchèd[1] he;
The next line that Sir Patrick red,
  The teir blinded his ee.

"O wha is this has don this deid,
  This ill deid don to me,
To send me out this time o' the yeir,
  To sail upon the se!   20

"Mak hast, mak hast, my mirry men all
  Our guid schip sails the morne:"
"O say na sae, my master deir,
  For I feir a deadlie storme.

"Late, late yestreen I saw the new moone,
  Wi the auld moone in hir arme,
And I feir, I feir, my deir master,
  That we will cum to harme."

O our Scots nobles wer richt laith[2]
  To weet their cork-heild schoone,[3]   30
Bot lang owre[4] a' the play wer playd,
  Thair hats they swam aboone.

O lang, lang may their ladies sit,
  Wi thair fans into their hand,
Or eir they se Sir Patrick Spens
  Cum sailing to the land.

O lang, lang may the ladies stand,
  Wi thair gold kems in their hair
Waiting for thar ain deir lords,
  For they'll se thame na mair.   40

Half owre,[5] half owre to Aberdour,
  It's fiftie fadom deip,
And thair lies guid Sir Patrick Spens,
  Wi the Scots lords at his feit.

Johnny, I Hardly Knew Ye

While going the road to sweet Athy,
  Hurroo! hurroo!
While going the road to sweet Athy,
  Hurroo! hurroo!
While going the road to sweet Athy,
A stick in my hand and a drop in my eye,
A doleful damsel I heard cry:
  "Och, Johnny, I hardly knew ye!
    With drums and guns, and guns and drums,
    The enemy nearly slew ye;   10
    My darling dear, you look so queer,
    Och, Johnny, I hardly knew ye!

"Where are your eyes that looked so mild?
  Hurroo! hurroo!
Where are your eyes that looked so mild?
  Hurroo! hurroo!
Where are your eyes that looked so mild?
When my poor heart you first beguiled?

---

[1] laughed [2] loath [3] shoes [4] ere [5] over

Why did you run from me and the child?
    Och, Johnny, I hardly knew ye!
      With drums, etc.

"Where are the legs with which you run?
    Hurroo! hurroo!
Where are the legs with which you run?
    Hurroo! hurroo!
Where are the legs with which you run?
When first you went to carry a gun?
Indeed, your dancing days are done?
    Och, Johnny, I hardly knew ye!
      With drums, etc.

"It grieved my heart to see you sail,
    Hurroo! hurroo!
It grieved my heart to see you sail,
    Hurroo! hurroo!
It grieved my heart to see you sail,
Though from my heart you took leg-bail;
Like a cod you're doubled up head and tail,
    Och, Johnny, I hardly knew ye!
      With drums, etc.

"You haven't an arm and you haven't a leg,
    Hurroo! hurroo!
You haven't an arm and you haven't a leg,
    Hurroo! hurroo!
You haven't an arm and you haven't a leg,
You're an eyeless, noseless, chickenless egg;
You'll have to be put with a bowl to beg:
    Och, Johnny, I hardly knew ye!
      With drums, etc.

"I'm happy for to see you home,
    Hurroo! hurroo!
I'm happy for to see you home,
    Hurroo! hurroo!
I'm happy for to see you home,
All from the Island of Sulloon;
So low in flesh, so high in bone;
    Och, Johnny, I hardly knew ye!
      With drums, etc.

"But sad it is to see you so,
    Hurroo! hurroo!
But sad it is to see you so,
    Hurroo! hurroo!

But sad it is to see you so,
And to think of you now as an object of woe,
Your Peggy'll still keep ye on as her beau;
Och, Johnny, I hardly knew ye!
With drums and guns, and guns and drums,
The enemy nearly slew ye;
My darling dear, you look so queer,
Och, Johnny, I hardly knew ye!"

GEOFFREY CHAUCER • 1340?–1400

To Rosemounde

Madame, ye ben of alle beauté shryne
As fer as cercled is the mapemounde,[1]
For as the cristal glorious ye shyne,
And lyke ruby ben your chekes rounde.
Therwith ye ben so mery and so jocounde
That at a revel whan that I see you daunce,
It is an oynement unto my wounde,
Thogh ye to me ne do no daliaunce.[2]

For thogh I wepe of teres ful a tyne,[3]
Yet may that wo myn herte nat confounde; 10
Your seemly voys, that ye so smal outtwyne,[4]
Maketh me thoght in joye and blis habounde.
So curtaysly I go, with love bounde,
That to myself I sey, in my penaunce,
"Suffyseth[5] me to love you, Rosemounde,
Thogh ye to me ne do no daliaunce."

Nas nevere pyk[6] walwed[7] in galauntyne[8]
As I in love am walwed and ywounde,
For which ful ofte I of myself devyne
That I am trewe Tristam the secounde. 20
My love may not refreyd[9] be nor affounde;[10]

I brenne ay in an amorous plesaunce.
Do what you lyst, I wyl your thral be founde,
Thogh ye to me ne do no daliaunce.

(c. 1385)

The Compleint of Chaucer to His Empty Purse

To you, my purse, and to non other wight
Compleyne I, for ye be my lady dere!
I am so sory, now that ye be light;
For certes, but ye make hevy chere,
Me were as leef be leyd up-on my bere;
For whiche un-to your mercy thus I crye:
Beth hevy ageyn, or elles mot I dye!

Now voucheth sauf this day, or[1] hit be night,
That I of you the blisful soun may here,
Or see your colour lyk the sonne bright, 10
That of yelownesse hadde never pere.
Ye be my lyf, ye be myn hertes stere,[2]
Quene of comfort and of good companye:
Beth hevy ageyn, or elles mot I dye!

Now purs, that be to me my lyves light,
And saveour, as doun in this worlde here,

---

[1] world map [2] flirting, caressing
[3] tun, large wine cask [4] utter
[5] (it) suffices [6] pike, a fish [7] wallowed
[8] a sauce [9] cooled [10] perish
[1] ere [2] star

Out of this toune help me through your might,
Sin that ye wole nat been my tresorere;
For I am shave as ny as any frere.
But yit I pray un-to your curtesye: 20
Beth hevy ageyn, or elles mot I dye!

LENVOY DE CHAUCER

O conqueror of Brutes Albioun!
Which that by lyne[3] and free eleccioun
Ben verray king, this song to you I sende;
And ye, that mowen al our harm amende, 20
Have minde up-on my supplicacioun!

SIR THOMAS WYATT • 1503?–1542

The Long Love

The long love that in my thought doth harbour,
And in mine heart doth keep his residence,
Into my face presseth with bold pretence,
And therein campeth, spreading his banner.
She that me learneth to love and suffer,
And wills that my trust and lust's negligence
Be reined by reason, shame, and reverence,
With his hardiness taketh displeasure.
Wherewithal, unto the heart's forest he fleeth,
Leaving his enterprise with pain and cry; 10
And there him hideth, and not appeareth.
What may I do when my master feareth
But in the field with him to live and die?
For good is the life ending faithfully. *(1557)*

Divers Doth Use

Divers doth use, as I have heard and know,
(When that to change their ladies do begin),
To moan and wail, and never for to lin,[1]
Hoping thereby to pease their painful woe.
And some there be, that when it chanceth so
That women change, and hate where love hath been,
They call them false, and think with words to win
The hearts of them which otherwise doth go.
But as for me, though that by chance indeed
Change hath outworn the favor that I had, 10
I will not wail, lament, nor yet be sad,
Nor call her false that falsely did me feed;
But let it pass, and think it is of kind,[2]
That often change doth please a woman's mind. *(1557)*

---

[3] line; i.e., by hereditary right   [1] cease   [2] natural

They Flee from Me

They flee from me, that sometime did me seek,
With naked foot, stalking in my chamber:
I have seen them gentle, tame, and meek,
That now are wild, and do not remember
That sometime they put themselves in danger
To take bread at my hand; and now they range,
Busily seeking with a continual change.

Thankèd be fortune, it hath been otherwise
Twenty times better; but once, in special,
In thin array, after a pleasant guise,   10
When her loose gown from her shoulders did fall,
And she me caught in her arms long and small,
Therewithal sweetly did me kiss,
And softly said, "Dear heart, how like you this?"

It was no dream; I lay broad waking.
But all is turned, thorough my gentleness,
Into a strange fashion of forsaking;
And I have leave to go of her goodness,
And she also to use new-fangleness.
But since that I so kindely am served,   20
I would fain know what she hath deserved.   (*1557*)

HENRY HOWARD, EARL OF SURREY • 1517?–1547

Description of Spring

The soote[1] season, that bud and bloom forth brings,
With green hath clad the hill and eke the vale.
The nightingale with feathers new she sings;
The turtle to her make[2] hath told her tale.
Summer is come, for every spray now springs.
The hart hath hung his old head on the pale;
The buck in brake his winter coat he flings;
The fishes float with new repairèd scale;
The adder all her slough away she slings;
The swift swallow pursueth the flies small;   10
The busy bee her honey now she mings;[3]
Winter is worn that was the flowers' bale.
And thus I see among these pleasant things
Each care decays; and yet my sorrow springs.   (*1557*)

---

[1] sweet   [2] mate   [3] mingles; blends

Love That Doth Reign

Love, that doth reign and live within my thought,
And built his seat within my captive breast,
Clad in the arms wherein with me he fought,
Oft in my face he doth his banner rest.
But she that taught me love and suffer pain,
My doubtful hope and eke my hot desire
With shamefast look to shadow and refrain,
Her smiling grace converteth straight to ire.
And coward Love, then, to the heart apace
Taketh his flight, where he doth lurk and plain,[1]   *10*
His purpose lost, and dare not show his face.
For my lord's guilt thus faultless bide I pain,
Yet from my lord shall not my foot remove:
Sweet is the death that taketh end by love.   (*1557*)

SIR EDWARD DYER • 1540?–1607

My Mind to Me a Kingdom Is

My mind to me a kingdom is,
   Such present joys therein I find,
That it excels all other bliss
   That world affords or grows by kind.
Though much I want which most would
     have,
Yet still my mind forbids to crave.

No princely pomp, no wealthy store,
   No force to win the victory,
No wily wit to salve a sore,
   No shape to feed a loving eye;   *10*
To none of these I yield as thrall,
For why my mind doth serve for all.

I see how plenty suffers oft,
   And hasty climbers soon do fall;
I see that those which are aloft
   Mishap doth threaten most of all;
They get with toil, they keep with fear:
Such cares my mind could never bear.

Content I live, this is my stay,
   I seek no more than may suffice;   *20*
I press to bear no haughty sway;
   Look, what I lack my mind supplies.
Lo! thus I triumph like a king,
Content with that my mind doth bring.

Some have too much, yet still do crave;
   I little have, and seek no more.
They are but poor, though much they
     have,
   And I am rich with little store.
They poor, I rich; they beg, I give;
They lack, I leave; they pine, I live.   *30*

I laugh not at another's loss;
   I grudge not at another's gain;
No worldly waves my mind can toss;
   My state at one doth still remain.
I fear no foe, I fawn no friend;
I loathe not life, nor dread my end.

---

[1] complain; express grief

Some weigh their pleasure by their lust,
    Their wisdom by their rage of will;
Their treasure is their only trust,
    A cloakèd craft their store of skill: *40*
But all the pleasure that I find
Is to maintain a quiet mind.

My wealth is health and perfect ease,
    My conscience clear my choice defence;
I neither seek by bribes to please,
    Nor by deceit to breed offence.
Thus do I live; thus will I die;
Would all did so as well as I!   *(1588)*

GEORGE GASCOIGNE • 1542?–1577

Gascoigne's Good-Night

When thou hast spent the lingering day in pleasure and delight,
Or after toil and weary way, dost seek to rest at night,
Unto thy pains or pleasures past, add this one labor yet:
Ere sleep close up thine eye too fast, do not thy God forget,
But search within thy secret thoughts, what deeds did thee befall;
And if thou find amiss in aught, to God for mercy call.
Yea, though thou find nothing amiss which thou canst call to mind,
Yet evermore remember this: there is the more behind;
And think how well so ever it be that thou hast spent the day,
It came of God, and not of thee, so to direct thy way.   *10*
Thus, if thou try thy daily deeds and pleasure in this pain,
Thy life shall cleanse thy corn from weeds, and thine shall be the gain;
But if thy sinful, sluggish eye will venture for to wink,
Before thy wading will may try how far thy soul may sink,
Beware and wake; for else, thy bed, which soft and smooth is made,
May heap more harm upon thy head than blows of en'my's blade.
Thus if this pain procure thine ease, in bed as thou dost lie,
Perhaps it shall not God displease to sing thus, soberly:
"I see that sleep is lent me here to ease my weary bones,
As death at last shall eke appear, to ease my grievous groans.   *20*
My daily sports, my paunch full fed, have caused my drowsy eye,
As careless life, in quiet led, might cause my soul to die.
The stretching arms, the yawning breath, which I to bedward use,
Are patterns of the pangs of death, when life will me refuse.
And of my bed each sundry part in shadows doth resemble
The sundry shapes of death, whose dart shall make my flesh to tremble.
My bed itself is like the grave, my sheets the winding sheet,
My clothes the mold which I must have to cover me most meet;
The hungry fleas, which frisk so fresh, to worms I can compare,
Which greedily shall gnaw my flesh and leave the bones full bare.   *30*
The waking cock, that early crows to wear the night away
Puts in my mind the trump that blows before the Latter Day.
And as I rise up lustily when sluggish sleep is past,
So hope I to rise joyfully to Judgment at the last.

Thus will I wake, thus will I sleep, thus will I hope to rise.
Thus will I neither wail nor weep, but sing in godly wise;
My bones shall in this bed remain, my soul in God shall trust,
By whom I hope to rise again from death and earthly dust."   (*1573*)

from The Steel Glass

But here methinks my priests begin to frown
And say that thus they shall be overcharged,
To pray for all which seem to do amiss;
And one I hear, more saucy than the rest,
Which asketh me, When shall our prayers end?

I tell thee, priest: when shoemakers make shoes
That are well sewed, with never a stitch amiss,
And use no craft in utt'ring[1] of the same;
When tailors steal no stuff from gentlemen;
When tanners are with curriers well agreed,   *10*
And both so dress their hides that we go dry;
When cutlers leave to sell old rusty blades,
And hide no cracks with solder nor deceit;
When tinkers make no more holes than they found,
When thatchers think their wages worth their work,
When colliers put no dust into their sacks,
When maltmen make us drink no firmentie,[2]
When Davie Diker digs, and dallies not,
When smiths shoe horses as they would be shod,
When millers toll not with a golden thumb,   *20*
When bakers make not barm[3] bear price of wheat,
When brewers put no baggage in their beer,
When butchers blow not over all their flesh,
When horse-coursers beguile no friends with jades,
When weavers' weight is found in housewives' web.
(But why dwell I so long among these louts?)

When mercers make more bones to swear and lie,
When vintners mix no water with their wine,
When printers pass none errors in their books,
When hatters use to buy none old cast robes,   *30*
When goldsmiths get no gain by soldered crowns,
When upholsterers sell feathers without dust,
When pewterers infect no tin with lead,
When drapers draw no gains by giving day,
When parchmenters put in no ferret silk,
When surgeons heal all wounds without delay.
(Tush! these are toys, but yet my glass showeth all.)

---

[1] selling   [3] froth
[2] a drink made from wheat and milk

When purveyors provide not for themselves,
When takers take no bribes nor use no brags,
When customers conceal no covin[4] used,
When searchers see all corners in a ship
(And spy no pence by any sight they see),
When shrieves[5] do serve all process as they ought,
When bailiffs strain[6] none other thing, but strays,
When auditors their counters cannot change,
When proud surveyors take no parting pence,
When silver sticks not on the teller's fingers,
And when receivers pay as they receive,
When all these folk have quite forgotten fraud.

. . . .

Even then, my priests, may you make holiday
And pray no more but ordinary prayers.

And yet therein I pray you, my good priests,
Pray still for me, and for my glass of steel,
That it (nor I) do any mind offend
Because we show all colors in their kind.
And pray for me, that since my hap is such
To see men so, I may perceive myself.
Oh, worthy words to end my worthless verse—
Pray for me, priests, I pray you pray for me. *(1576)*

EDMUND SPENSER • 1552-1599

Sonnets from Amoretti

XV

Ye tradefull Merchants, that with weary toyle,
So seeke most pretious things to make your gain;
And both the Indias of their treasures spoile,
What needeth you to seeke so farre in vaine?
For loe my love doth in her selfe containe
All this worlds riches that may farre be found,
If Saphyres, loe her eies be Saphyres plaine,
If Rubies, loe hir lips be Rubies sound:
If Pearles, hir teeth be pearles both pure and round;
If Yvorie, her forehead yvory weene;[1]
If Gold, her locks are finest gold on ground;
If silver, her faire hands are silver sheene.[2]
But that which fairest is, but few behold,
Her mind adornd with vertues manifold.

---

[4] deceit   [5] sheriffs   [6] restrain, confine   [1] beautiful   [2] shining

XIX

The merry Cuckow, messenger of Spring,
His trompet shrill hath thrise already sounded:
That warnes al lovers wayt upon their king,
Who now is comming forth with girland crounèd.
With noyse whereof the quyre of Byrds resounded
Their anthemes sweet devizèd of loves prayse,
That all the woods theyr ecchoes back rebounded,
As if they knew the meaning of their layes.
But mongst them all, which did Loves honor rayse
No word was heard of her that most it ought,   *10*
But she his precept proudly disobayes,
And doth his ydle message set at nought.
Therefore O love, unlesse she turne to thee
Ere Cuckow end, let her a rebell be.

XXII

This holy season fit to fast and pray,
Men to devotion ought to be inclynd:
Therefore, I lykewise on so holy day,
For my sweet Saynt some service fit will find.
Her temple fayre is built within my mind,
In which her glorious ymage placèd is,
On which my thoughts doo day and night attend
Lyke sacred priests that never thinke amisse.
There I to her as th'author of my blisse,
Will builde an altar to appease her yre: *10*
And on the same my hart will sacrifise,
Burning in flames of pure and chast desyre:
The which vouchsafe O goddesse to accept,
Amongst thy deerest relicks to be kept.

XXXIV

Lyke as a ship that through the Ocean wyde,
By conduct of some star doth make her way,
Whenas a storme hath dimd her trusty guyde,
Out of her course doth wander far astray.
So I whose star, that wont with her bright ray,
Me to direct, with cloudes is overcast,
Doe wander now in darknesse and dismay,
Through hidden perils round about me plast.
Yet hope I well, that when this storme is past
My *Helice* the lodestar of my lyfe   *10*
Will shine again, and looke on me at last,
With lovely light to cleare my cloudy grief.
Till then I wander carefull comfortlesse,
In secret sorow and sad pensivenesse.

LXVII

Lyke as a huntsman after weary chace,
Seeing the game from him escapt away,
Sits downe to rest him in some shady place,
With panting hounds beguilèd of their pray:
So after long pursuit and vaine assay,
When I all weary had the chace forsooke,
The gentle deare returnd the selfe-same way,
Thinking to quench her thirst at the next brooke.
There she beholding me with mylder looke,
Sought not to fly, but fearelesse still did bide: 10
Till I in hand her yet halfe trembling tooke,
And with her owne goodwill hir fyrmely tyde.
Strange thing me seemd to see a beast so wyld,
So goodly wonne with her owne will beguyld.

LXXV

One day I wrote her name upon the strand,
But came the waves and washèd it away:
Agayne I wrote it with a second hand,
But came the tyde, and made my paynes his pray.
Vayne man, sayd she, that does in vaine assay,
A mortall thing so to immortalize,
For I my selve shall lyke to this decay,
And eek my name bee wypèd out lykewize.
Not so, (quod I) let baser things devize
To dy in dust, but you shall live by fame: 10
My verse your vertues rare shall eternize,
And in the hevens wryte your glorious name.
Where whenas death shall all the world subdew,
Our love shall live, and later life renew. (*1595*)

SIR WALTER RALEGH • 1552?–1618

The Nymph's Reply to the Shepherd[1]

If all the world and love were young,
And truth in every shepherd's tongue,
These pretty pleasures might me move,
To live with thee, and be thy love.

Time drives the flocks from field to fold,
When rivers rage, and rocks grow cold,
And Philomel becometh dumb,
The rest complains of cares to come.

The flowers do fade, and wanton fields,
To wayward winter reckoning yields, 10

---

[1] Ralegh's poem is a reply to Marlowe's "The Passionate Shepherd to His Love," page 290.

A honey tongue, a heart of gall,
Is fancy's spring, but sorrow's fall.

Thy gowns, thy shoes, thy beds of roses,
Thy cap, thy kirtle, and thy posies,
Soon break, soon wither, soon forgotten:
In folly ripe, in reason rotten.

Thy belt of straw and ivy buds,
Thy coral clasps and amber studs,
All these in me no means can move,
To come to thee, and be thy love.   *20*

But could youth last, and love still breed,
Had joys no date, nor age no need,
Then these delights my mind might
    move,
To live with thee and be thy love.
                                          (*1600*)

The Passionate Man's Pilgrimage

Give me my scallop-shell of quiet,
My staff of faith to walk upon,
My scrip of joy, immortal diet,
My bottle of salvation,
My gown of glory, hope's true gage,
And thus I'll take my pilgrimage.

Blood must be my body's balmer,
No other balm will there be given,
Whilst my soul like a white palmer
Travels to the land of heaven,   *10*
Over the silver mountains,
Where spring the nectar fountains;
And there I'll kiss
The bowl of bliss,
And drink my everlasting fill
On every milken hill.
My soul will be a-dry before,
But after it will thirst no more.

And by the happy blissful way
More peaceful pilgrims I shall see,   *20*
That have shook off their gowns of clay
And go apparelled fresh like me.
I'll bring them first
To slake their thirst,
And then to taste those nectar suckets,
At the clear wells
Where sweetness dwells,
Drawn up by saints in crystal buckets.

And when our bottles and all we
Are filled with immortality,   *30*
Then the holy paths we'll travel,
Strewed with rubies thick as gravel,
Ceilings of diamonds, sapphire floors,
High walls of coral and pearl bowers.

From thence to heaven's bribeless hall
Where no corrupted voices brawl,
No conscience molten into gold,
Nor forged accusers bought and sold,
No cause deferred, nor vain-spent journey,
For there Christ is the King's
    Attorney,   *40*
Who pleads for all without degrees,
And he hath angels, but no fees.

When the grand twelve million jury
Of our sins and direful fury
'Gainst our souls black verdicts give,
Christ pleads his death, and then we live.
Be thou my speaker, taintless pleader,
Unblotted lawyer, true proceeder;
Thou movest salvation even for alms,
Not with a bribèd lawyer's palms.   *50*

And this is my eternal plea
To him that made heaven, earth, and sea:
Seeing my flesh must die so soon,
And want a head to dine next noon,
Just at the stroke when my veins start and
    spread,
Set on my soul an everlasting head.
Then am I ready, like a palmer fit,
To tread those blest paths which before I
    writ.   (*1604*)

What Is Our Life?

What is our life? a play of passion;
Our mirth, the music of division;[1]
Our mothers' wombs the tiring-houses[2] be
Where we are dressed for this short comedy.
Heaven the judicious sharp spectator is,
That sits and marks still who doth act amiss;
Our graves that hide us from the searching sun
Are like drawn curtains when the play is done.
Thus march we playing to our latest[3] rest;
Only we die in earnest—that's no jest.   (*c. 1612*)

SIR PHILIP SIDNEY • 1554–1586

Sonnets from Astrophel and Stella

I

Loving in truth, and fain in verse my love to show,
That she, dear she, might take some pleasure of my pain,
Pleasure might cause her read, reading might make her know,
Knowledge might pity win, and pity grace obtain,
I sought fit words to paint the blackest face of woe;
Studying inventions fine, her wits to entertain,
Oft turning others' leaves to see if thence would flow
Some fresh and fruitful showers upon my sun-burned brain.
But words came halting forth, wanting Invention's stay;
Invention, Nature's child, fled step-dame Study's blows,
And others' feet still seemed but strangers in my way.
Thus, great with child to speak, and helpless in my throes,
Biting my truant pen, beating myself for spite,
"Fool," said my Muse to me, "look in thy heart and write."

XV

You that do search for every purling spring
Which from the ribs of old Parnassus flows,
And every flower, not sweet perhaps, which grows
Near thereabout, into your poesy wring;
You that do dictionary's method bring
Into your rhymes, running in rattling rows:
You that poor Petrarch's long deceasèd woes
With newborn sighs and denizened wit do sing:

---

[1] part singing   [2] dressing rooms   [3] last

You take wrong ways; those far-fet[1] helps be such
As do bewray[2] a want of inward touch,
And sure at length stolen goods do come to light;
But if, both for your love and skill, your name
You seek to nurse at fullest breasts of Fame,
Stella behold, and then begin to indite.

XXVIII

You that with allegory's curious frame
Of others' children changelings use to make,
With me those pains, for God's sake, do not take;
I list not dig so deep for brazen fame.
When I say Stella, I do mean the same
Princess of beauty, for whose only sake
The reins of Love I love, though never slack,
And joy therein, though nations count it shame.
I beg no subject to use eloquence,
Nor in hid ways do guide philosophy;
Look at my hands for no such quintessence;
But know that I in pure simplicity
Breathe out the flames which burn within my heart,
Love only reading unto me this art.

XXXI

With how sad steps, O Moon, thou climb'st the skies!
How silently, and with how wan a face!
What! may it be that even in heavenly place
That busy archer his sharp arrows tries?
Sure, if that long-with-love-acquainted eyes
Can judge of love, thou feel'st a lover's case;
I read it in thy looks; thy languished grace
To me, that feel the like, thy state descries.
Then, even of fellowship, O Moon, tell me,
Is constant love deemed there but want of wit?
Are beauties there as proud as here they be?
Do they above, love to be loved, and yet
Those lovers scorn whom that love doth possess?
Do they call virtue there ungratefulness? (*1591*)

My True Love Hath My Heart

My true Love hath my heart, and I have his,
By just exchange one for the other given:
I hold his dear, and mine he cannot miss;
There never was a better bargain driven.

---

[1] farfetched   [2] betrayal, reveal

His heart in me keeps me and him in one,
My heart in him his thoughts and senses guides:
He loves my heart, for once it was his own;
I cherish his because in me it bides.
His heart his wound receivèd from my sight,
My heart was wounded with his wounded heart;   10
For as from me, on him his hurt did light,
So still methought in me his hurt did smart.
Both, equal hurt, in this change sought our bliss:
My true Love hath my heart, and I have his.   *(1593)*

CHRISTOPHER MARLOWE • 1564–1593

The Passionate Shepherd to His Love

Come live with me and be my love,
And we will all the pleasures prove,
That hills and valleys, dales and fields,
And all the craggy mountains yields.

There we will sit upon the rocks,
And see the shepherds feed their flocks,
By shallow rivers to whose falls
Melodious birds sing madrigals.

And I will make thee beds of roses
With a thousand fragrant posies,   10
A cap of flowers, and a kirtle
Embroidered all with leaves of myrtle;

A gown made of the finest wool
Which from our pretty lambs we pull;
Fair lined slippers for the cold,
With buckles of the purest gold;

A belt of straw and ivy buds,
With coral clasps and amber studs:
And if these pleasures may thee move,
Come live with me and be my love.   20

The shepherds' swains shall dance and sing
For thy delight each May morning:
If these delights thy mind may move,
Then live with me and be my love.
                                                    (1600)

WILLIAM SHAKESPEARE • 1564–1616

Songs from the Plays

from LOVE'S LABOUR'S LOST

SPRING

When daisies pied and violets blue
    And lady-smocks all silver-white
And cuckoo-buds of yellow hue
    Do paint the meadows with delight,
The cuckoo then, on every tree,
Mocks married men; for thus sings he,
            Cuckoo!
Cuckoo, cuckoo! O, word of fear,
Unpleasing to a married ear!

When shepherds pipe on oaten
    straws,   10

And merry larks are ploughmen's
    clocks,
When turtles tread, and rooks, and daws,
    And maidens bleach their summer
    smocks,
The cuckoo then, on every tree,
Mocks married men; for thus sings he,
            Cuckoo!
Cuckoo, cuckoo! O, word of fear,
Unpleasing to a married ear!

WINTER

When icicles hang by the wall,
    And Dick the shepherd blows his nail,
And Tom bears logs into the hall,
    And milk comes frozen home in pail,
When blood is nipped, and ways be foul,
Then nightly sings the staring owl,
            To-whit!
To-who!—a merry note,
While greasy Joan doth keel[1] the pot.

When all aloud the wind doth blow,   *10*
    And coughing drowns the parson's saw,
And birds sit brooding in the snow,
    And Marian's nose looks red and raw,
When roasted crabs hiss in the bowl,
Then nightly sings the staring owl,
            To-whit!
To-who!—a merry note,
While greasy Joan doth keel the pot.
                                (1593)

from THE MERCHANT OF VENICE

TELL ME WHERE IS FANCY BRED

   Tell me where is fancy bred,
       Or in the heart or in the head?
   How begot, how nourishèd?
       Reply, reply.

   It is engendered in the eyes,
       With gazing fed; and fancy dies
   In the cradle where it lies.
       Let us all ring fancy's knell.
       I'll begin it. Ding, dong, bell.
Chorus. Ding, dong, bell.   *(1596)*   *10*

---
[1] stir to keep from boiling over

---

from AS YOU LIKE IT

BLOW, BLOW, THOU WINTER WIND

   Blow, blow, thou winter wind,
   Thou art not so unkind
       As man's ingratitude;
   Thy tooth is not so keen,
   Because thou art not seen,
       Although thy breath be rude.
Heigh-ho! sing, heigh-ho! unto the green
            holly:
Most friendship is feigning, most loving
            mere folly.
       Then heigh-ho! the holly!
       This life is most jolly.   *10*

   Freeze, freeze, thou bitter sky,
   That dost not bite so nigh
       As benefits forgot:
   Though thou the waters warp,
   Thy sting is not so sharp
       As friend remembered not.
Heigh-ho! sing, heigh-ho! unto the green
            holly:
Most friendship is feigning, most loving
            mere folly.
       Then heigh-ho! the holly!
       This life is most jolly.   *(1600)*   *20*

from TWELFTH NIGHT

COME AWAY, DEATH

Come away, come away, Death!
    And in sad cypress[1] let me be laid;
Fly away, fly away, breath;
    I am slain by a fair cruel maid.
My shroud of white, stuck all with yew,
            O, prepare it!
My part of death, no one so true
            Did share it.

Not a flower, not a flower sweet,
    On my black coffin let there be
            strown;   *10*
Not a friend, not a friend greet
    My poor corpse, where my bones shall
            be thrown

---
[1] cypress lawn, a filmy black fabric used for burial robes

A thousand thousand sighs to save
    Lay me, O, where
Sad true lover never find my grave,
    To weep there! *(1601)*

from CYMBELINE

HARK, HARK! THE LARK

Hark, hark! the lark at heaven's gate sings,
    And Phœbus 'gins arise,
His steeds to water at those springs
    On chaliced flowers that lies;
And winking Mary-buds begin
    To ope their golden eyes:
With every thing that pretty is,
    My lady sweet, arise!
        Arise, arise! *(1609)*

from THE TEMPEST

FULL FATHOM FIVE

Full fathom five thy father lies;
    Of his bones are coral made;
Those are pearls that were his eyes:
    Nothing of him that doth fade,
But doth suffer a sea-change
Into something rich and strange:
Sea nymphs hourly ring his knell.
        Ding-dong!
    Hark! now I hear them,
        Ding-dong, bell! *(1611)*   10

from The Sonnets

XVIII

Shall I compare thee to a summer's day?
Thou art more lovely and more temperate:
Rough winds do shake the darling buds of May,
And summer's lease hath all too short a date:
Sometime too hot the eye of heaven shines,
And often is his gold complexion dimmed;
And every fair from fair sometime declines,
By chance, or nature's changing course untrimmed;
But thy eternal summer shall not fade,
Nor lose possession of that fair thou owest,   10
Nor shall Death brag thou wander'st in his shade,
When in eternal lines to time thou growest;
So long as men can breathe, or eyes can see,
So long lives this, and this gives life to thee.

LXXI

No longer mourn for me when I am dead,
Than you shall hear the surly sullen bell
Give warning to the world that I am fled
From this vile world, with vilest worms to dwell:
Nay, if you read this line, remember not
The hand that writ it; for I love you so,
That I in your sweet thoughts would be forgot,
If thinking on me then should make you woe.

O! if, I say, you look upon this verse,
When I perhaps compounded am with clay,
Do not so much as my poor name rehearse,
But let your love even with my life decay;
Lest the wise world should look into your moan,
And mock you with me after I am gone.

LXXIII

That time of year thou mayst in me behold
When yellow leaves, or none, or few, do hang
Upon those boughs which shake against the cold,
Bare ruined choirs, where late the sweet birds sang.
In me thou see'st the twilight of such day
As after sunset fadeth in the west,
Which by and by black night doth take away,
Death's second self that seals up all in rest.
In me thou see'st the glowing of such fire,
That on the ashes of his youth doth lie,
As the death-bed, whereon it must expire
Consumed with that which it was nourished by.
This thou perceiv'st, which makes thy love more strong
To love that well, which thou must leave ere long.

CXVI

Let me not to the marriage of true minds
Admit impediments. Love is not love
Which alters when it alteration finds,
Or bends with the remover to remove:
Or, no! it is an ever-fixèd mark
That looks on tempests and is never shaken;
It is the star to every wandering bark,
Whose worth's unknown, although his height be taken.
Love's not Time's fool, though rosy lips and cheeks
Within his bending sickle's compass come;
Love alters not with his brief hours and weeks,
But bears it out even to the edge of doom.
If this be error and upon me proved,
I never writ, nor no man ever loved.   (*1609*)

THOMAS CAMPION • 1567–1620

When to Her Lute Corinna Sings

When to her lute Corinna sings,
Her voice revives the leaden strings,
And doth in highest notes appear
As any challenged echo clear;
But when she doth of mourning speak,
Ev'n with her sighs the strings do break.

And as her lute doth live or die,
Led by her passion, so must I:
For when of pleasure she doth sing,
My thoughts enjoy a sudden spring,   *10*
But if she doth of sorrow speak,
Ev'n from my heart the strings do break.
(1601)

There Is a Garden in Her Face

There is a garden in her face,
  Where roses and white lilies grow,
A heavenly paradise is that place,
  Wherein all pleasant fruits do flow.
There cherries grow, which none may buy
Till "Cherry-ripe" themselves do cry.

Those cherries fairly do enclose
  Of orient pearl a double row,
Which when her lovely laughter shows,
  They look like rosebuds filled with snow. *10*
Yet them nor peer nor prince can buy,
Till "Cherry-ripe" themselves do cry.

Her eyes like angels watch them still;
  Her brows like bended bows do stand,
Threatening with piercing frowns to kill
  All that attempt with eye or hand
Those sacred cherries to come nigh,
Till "Cherry-ripe" themselves do cry.
(1617)

BEN JONSON • 1572–1637

Slow, Slow, Fresh Fount

    Slow, slow, fresh fount, keep time with my salt tears;
      Yet slow, yet, O, faintly gentle springs:
    List to the heavy part the music bears,
      Woe weeps out her division, when she sings.
        Droop herbs, and flowers;
        Fall grief in showers;
      Our beauties are not ours:
          Oh, I could still
    (Like melting snow upon some craggy hill)
        Drop, drop, drop, drop, *10*
    Since nature's pride is, now, a withered daffodil. *(1600)*

Still to Be Neat

Still to be neat, still to be dressed,
As you were going to a feast;
Still to be powdered, still perfumed:
Lady, it is to be presumed,
Though art's hid causes are not found,
All is not sweet, all is not sound.

Give me a look, give me a face
That makes simplicity a grace;
Robes loosely flowing, hair as free:
Such sweet neglect more taketh me   10
Than all th' adulteries of art;
They strike mine eyes, but not my heart.

(1609)

To the Memory of My Beloved, the Author Master William Shakespeare

To draw no envy, Shakespeare, on thy name,
Am I thus ample to thy book and fame;
While I confess thy writings to be such
As neither man nor Muse can praise too much.
'Tis true, and all men's suffrage. But these ways
Were not the paths I meant unto thy praise;
For silliest ignorance on these may light,
Which, when it sounds at best, but echoes right;
Or blind affection, which doth ne'er advance
The truth, but gropes, and urgeth all by chance;   10
Or crafty malice might pretend this praise,
And think to ruin, where it seemed to raise.
These are, as some infamous bawd or whore
Should praise a matron. What could hurt her more?
But thou art proof against them, and indeed,
Above the ill fortune of them, or the need.
I therefore will begin. Soul of the age!
The applause, delight, the wonder of our stage!
My Shakespeare, rise! I will not lodge thee by
Chaucer, or Spenser, or bid Beaumont lie   20
A little further, to make thee a room;
Thou art a monument without a tomb,
And art alive still while thy book doth live
And we have wits to read and praise to give.
That I not mix thee so, my brain excuses,
I mean with great, but disproportioned Muses;
For if I thought my judgment were of years,
I should commit thee surely with thy peers,
And tell how far thou didst our Lyly outshine,
Or sporting Kyd, or Marlowe's mighty line.   30
And though thou hadst small Latin and less Greek,
From thence to honor thee I would not seek
For names; but call forth thundering Aeschylus,
Euripides, and Sophocles to us;

Pacuvius, Accius,[1] him of Cordova[2] dead,
To life again, to hear thy buskin tread,
And shake a stage; or, when thy socks were on,
Leave thee alone for the comparison
Of all that insolent Greece or haughty Rome
Sent forth, or since did from their ashes come.   40
Triumph, my Britain, thou hast one to show
To whom all scenes of Europe homage owe.
He was not of an age, but for all time!
And all the Muses still were in their prime,
When, like Apollo, he came forth to warm
Our ears, or like a Mercury to charm!
Nature herself was proud of his designs
And joyed to wear the dressing of his lines,
Which were so richly spun, and woven so fit,
As, since, she will vouchsafe no other wit.   50
The merry Greek, tart Aristophanes,
Neat Terence, witty Plautus, now not please,
But antiquated and deserted lie,
As they were not of Nature's family.
Yet must I not give Nature all; thy art,
My gentle Shakespeare, must enjoy a part.
For though the poet's matter Nature be,
His art doth give the fashion; and, that he
Who casts to write a living line, must sweat
(Such as thine are) and strike the second heat   60
Upon the Muses' anvil; turn the same
(And himself with it) that he thinks to frame,
Or, for the laurel, he may gain a scorn;
For a good poet's made, as well as born.
And such wert thou! Look how the father's face
Lives in his issue; even so the race
Of Shakespeare's mind and manners brightly shines
In his well-turnèd, and true-filèd lines;
In each of which he seems to shake a lance,
As brandished at the eyes of ignorance.   70
Sweet Swan of Avon! what a sight it were
To see thee in our waters yet appear,
And make those flights upon the banks of Thames,
That so did take Eliza,[3] and our James!
But stay, I see thee in the hemisphere
Advanced, and made a constellation there!
Shine forth, thou star of poets, and with rage
Or influence, chide or cheer the drooping stage,
Which, since thy flight from hence, hath mourned like night,
And despairs day, but for thy volume's light.   (*1623*)   80

---

[1] Roman poets of the second century B.C.
[2] Seneca, Roman philosopher, statesman, and tragedian of the first century
[3] Queen Elizabeth; James: King James I

Here She Was Wont to Go

Here she was wont to go, and here! and here!
Just where those daisies, pinks, and violets grow;
The world may find the spring by following her,
For other print her airy steps ne'er left;
Her treading would not bend a blade of grass!
Or shake the downy blow-ball from his stalk!
But like the soft west-wind she shot along,
And where she went the flowers took thickest root,
As she had sowed 'em with her odorous foot. *(c. 1637)*

JOHN DONNE • 1572–1631

Song

Go and catch a falling star,
   Get with child a mandrake root,
Tell me where all past years are,
   Or who cleft the devil's foot,
Teach me to hear mermaids singing,
Or to keep off envy's stinging,
      And find
      What wind
Serves to advance an honest mind.

If thou be'st born to strange sights,   10
   Things invisible to see,
Ride ten thousand days and nights,
   Till age snow white hairs on thee.
Thou, when thou return'st, wilt tell me,
All strange wonders that befell thee,
      And swear,
      No where
Lives a woman true and fair.

If thou find'st one, let me know;
   Such a pilgrimage were sweet.   20
Yet do not, I would not go,
   Though at next door we might meet:
Though she were true when you met her,
And last till you write your letter,
      Yet she
      Will be
False, ere I come, to two or three.
              (1633)

A Valediction: Forbidding Mourning

As virtuous men pass mildly away,
   And whisper to their souls, to go,
Whilst some of their sad friends do say,
   The breath goes now, and some say, no:

So let us melt, and make no noise,
   No tear-floods, nor sigh-tempests move,
T'were profanation of our joys
   To tell the laity our love.

Moving of th' earth brings harms and fears,
   Men reckon what it did and meant,   10
But trepidation of the spheres,
   Though greater far, is innocent.

Dull sublunary lovers' love
   (Whose soul is sense) cannot admit
Absence, because it doth remove
   Those things which elemented it.

But we by a love, so much refined
   That our selves know not what it is,
Inter-assurèd of the mind,
   Care less, eyes, lips, and hands to miss.   20

Our two souls therefore, which are one,
   Though I must go, endure not yet
A breach, but an expansion,
   Like gold to airy thinness beat.

If they be two, they are two so
   As stiff twin compasses are two,
Thy soul, the fixt foot, makes no show
   To move, but doth, if th' other do.

And though it in the center sit,
   Yet when the other far doth roam,   *30*
It leans, and hearkens after it,
   And grows erect, as that come home.

Such wilt thou be to me, who must
   Like th' other foot, obliquely run;
Thy firmness makes my circle just,
   And makes me end, where I begun.   (*1633*)

Holy Sonnets

VII

At the round earth's imagined corners blow
Your trumpets, angels, and arise, arise
From death, you numberless infinities
Of souls, and to your scattered bodies go,
All whom the flood did, and fire shall o'erthrow,
All whom war, dearth, age, agues, tyrannies,
Despair, law, chance, hath slain, and you whose eyes
Shall behold God, and never taste death's woe.
But let them sleep, Lord, and me mourn a space;
For, if above all these my sins abound,   *10*
'Tis late to ask abundance of Thy grace,
When we are there. Here on this lowly ground,
Teach me how to repent, for that's as good
As if Thou hadst sealed my pardon with Thy blood.

X

Death, be not proud, though some have callèd thee
Mighty and dreadful, for thou art not so,
For those whom thou think'st thou dost overthrow
Die not, poor Death, nor yet canst thou kill me.
From rest and sleep, which but thy picture be,
Much pleasure, then from thee much more must flow;
And soonest our best men with thee do go—
Rest of their bones and souls' delivery!
Thou'rt slave to fate, chance, kings and desperate men,
And dost with poison, war, and sickness dwell,   *10*
And poppy or charms can make us sleep as well,
And better than thy stroke; why swell'st thou then?
One short sleep past, we wake eternally,
And death shall be no more: Death, thou shalt die!

XIV

Batter my heart, three personed God; for you
As yet but knock, breathe, shine, and seek to mend;
That I may rise and stand, o'erthrow me and bend
Your force to break, blow, burn and make me new.
I, like an usurped town, to another due,
Labour to admit you, but oh, to no end;
Reason, your viceroy in me, me should defend,
But is captived and proves weak or untrue.
Yet dearly I love you and would be loved fain,
But am betrothed unto your enemy: *10*
Divorce me, untie or break that knot again,
Take me to you, imprison me, for I
Except you enthrall me, never shall be free,
Nor ever chaste, except you ravish me.   (*1633*)

The Ecstasy

Where, like a pillow on a bed,
   A pregnant bank swelled up, to rest
The violet's reclining head,
   Sat we two, one another's best.

Our hands were firmly cemented
   With a fast balm, which thence did spring;
Our eye-beams twisted, and did thread
   Our eyes upon one double string;

So t' entergraft our hands, as yet
   Was all the means to make us one;   *10*
And pictures in our eyes to get
   Was all our propagation.

As, 'twixt two equal armies, Fate
   Suspends uncertain victory,
Our souls (which to advance their state
   Were gone out) hung 'twixt her, and me.

And whilst our souls negotiate there,
   We like sepulchral statues lay;
All day, the same our postures were,
   And we said nothing, all the day.   *20*

If any, so by love refined,
   That he soul's language understood,
And by good love were grown all mind,
   Within convenient distance stood,

He (though he knew not which soul spake,
   Because both meant, both spake the same)
Might then a new concoction take,
   And part far purer than he came.

This ecstasy doth unperplex
   (We said) and tell us what we love;   *30*
We see by this, it was not sex;
   We see, we saw not what did move:

But as all several souls contain
   Mixture of things, they know not what,
Love, these mixed souls, doth mix again,
   And makes both one, each this and that.

A single violet transplant,
   The strength, the colour, and the size
(All which before was poor and scant)
   Redoubles still, and multiplies.   *40*

When love with one another so
    Interinanimates two souls,
That abler soul, which thence doth flow,
    Defects of loneliness controls.

We then, who are this new soul, know,
    Of what we are composed, and made,
For th' atomies of which we grow,
    Are souls, whom no change can invade.

But, O alas! so long, so far
    Our bodies why do we forbear?   50
They are ours, though not we; we are
    Th' intelligences, they the spheres.

We owe them thanks, because they thus
    Did us, to us, at first convey,
Yielded their forces, sense, to us,
    Nor are dross to us, but allay.

On man heaven's influence works not so,
    But that it first imprints the air;
For soul into the soul may flow,
    Though it to body first repair.   60

As our blood labours to beget
    Spirits, as like souls as it can,
Because such fingers need to knit
    That subtle knot, which makes us man;

So must pure lovers' souls descend
    T' affections, and to faculties,
Which sense may reach and apprehend,
    Else a great prince in prison lies.

To our bodies turn we then, that so
    Weak men on love revealed may
        look;   70
Love's mysteries in souls do grow,
    But yet the body is his book.

And if some lover, such as we,
    Have heard this dialogue of one,
Let him still mark us, he shall see
    Small change when we're to bodies
        gone. *(1633)*

JOHN WEBSTER • 1580?–1634?

from The White Devil

Call for the robin-redbreast and the wren,
Since o'er shady groves they hover,
And with leaves and flowers do cover
The friendless bodies of unburied men.
    Call unto his funeral dole
    The ant, the field-mouse, and the mole,
To rear him hillocks that shall keep him
    warm,
And, when gay tombs are robbed, sustain
    no harm;
But keep the wolf far thence, that's foe
    to men,
For with his nails he'll dig them up
    again. *(1612)*   10

WILLIAM BROWNE • 1591?–1643?

On the Countess Dowager of Pembroke

Underneath this sable hearse
Lies the subject of all verse:
Sidney's sister, Pembroke's mother.
Death, ere thou hast slain another
Fair and learn'd and good as she,
Time shall throw a dart at thee.
Marble piles let no man raise
To her name, for after-days
Some kind woman, born as she,
Reading this, like Niobe   10
Shall turn marble, and become
Both her mourner and her tomb.
        (1623)

ROBERT HERRICK • 1591–1674

Delight in Disorder

A sweet disorder in the dress
Kindles in clothes a wantonness:
A lawn about the shoulders thrown
Into a fine distraction,
An erring lace, which here and there
Enthralls the crimson stomacher,
A cuff neglectful, and thereby
Ribbands to flow confusedly,
A winning wave (deserving note)
In the tempestuous petticoat, 10
A careless shoe-string, in whose tie
I see a wild civility,
Do more bewitch me, than when art
Is too precise in every part.   (*1648*)

To the Virgins to Make Much of Time

Gather ye rose buds while ye may,
  Old Time is still a-flying:
And this same flower that smiles today,
  Tomorrow will be dying.

The glorious lamp of heaven, the Sun,
  The higher he's a-getting
The sooner will his race be run,
  And nearer he's to setting.

That age is best which is the first,
  When youth and blood are warmer; 10
But being spent, the worse, and worst
  Times, still succeed the former.

Then be not coy, but use your time;
  And while ye may, go marry:
For having lost but once your prime,
  You may for ever tarry.   (*1648*)

The Night-Piece, to Julia

Her eyes the glow-worm lend thee,
The shooting stars attend thee;
  And the elves also,
  Whose little eyes glow
Like the sparks of fire, befriend thee.

No will-o'-th'-wisp mislight thee;
Nor snake, or slow-worm bite thee:
  But on, on thy way,
  Not making a stay,
Since ghost there's none to affright thee. 10

Let not the dark thee cumber;
What though the moon does slumber:
  The stars of the night
  Will lend thee their light,
Like tapers clear without number.

Then, Julia, let me woo thee,
Thus, thus to come unto me:
  And when I shall meet
  Thy silv'ry feet,
My soul I'll pour into thee.   (*1648*) 20

Upon Julia's Clothes

Whenas in silks my Julia goes
Then, then (methinks) how sweetly flows
That liquefaction of her clothes.

Next, when I cast mine eyes and see
That brave vibration each way free;
O how that glittering taketh me!
              (*1648*)

His Return to London

From the dull confines of the drooping west
To see the day spring from the pregnant east,
Ravished in spirit, I come, nay more, I fly

To thee, blest place of my nativity!
Thus, thus with hallowed feet I touch the ground
With thousand blessings by thy fortune crowned.
O fruitful genius! that bestowest here
An everlasting plenty, year by year.
O place! O people! Manners framed to please
All nations, customs, kindreds, languages!
I am a free-born Roman, suffer then
That I amongst you live a citizen.
London my home is, though by hard fate sent
Into a long and irksome banishment;
Yet since called back, henceforward let me be,
O native country, repossessed by thee!
For rather than I'll to the west return,
I'll beg of thee first here to have mine urn.
Weak I am grown, and must in short time fall;
Give thou my sacred relics burial. (*1648*)

GEORGE HERBERT • 1593–1633

The Collar

I struck the board, and cried, No more.
    I will abroad.
  What? shall I ever sigh and pine?
My lines and life are free; free as the road,
  Loose as the wind, as large as store.
    Shall I be still in suit?
Have I no harvest but a thorn
  To let me blood, and not restore
  What I have lost with cordial fruit?
    Sure there was wine
Before my sighs did dry it: there was corn
  Before my tears did drown it.
  Is the year only lost to me?
    Have I no bays to crown it?
No flowers, no garlands gay? all blasted?
    All wasted?
Not so, my heart: but there is fruit,
    And thou hast hands.
Recover all thy sigh-blown age
On double pleasures: leave thy cold dispute
Of what is fit, and not. Forsake thy cage,
    Thy rope of sands,
Which petty thoughts have made, and made to thee
  Good cable, to enforce and draw,
    And be thy law,
While thou didst wink and wouldst not see.
    Away; take heed:
    I will abroad.
Call in thy death's head there: tie up thy fears.
    He that forbears
    To suit and serve his need,
    Deserves his load.
But as I raved and grew more fierce and wild
    At every word,
Methought I heard one calling, *Child*.
  And I replied, *My Lord*. (*1633*)

George Herbert

To His Mother

    My God, where is that ancient heat towards thee
    Wherewith whole shoals of martyrs once did burn,
    Besides their other flames? Doth poetry
    Wear Venus' livery, only serve her turn?
    Why are not sonnets made of thee, and lays
    Upon thine altar burnt? Cannot thy love
    Heighten a spirit to sound out thy praise
    As well as any she? Cannot thy dove
    Outstrip their Cupid easily in flight?
    Or, since thy ways are deep and still the same,   10
    Will not a verse run smooth that bears thy name?
    Why doth that fire, which by thy power and might
    Each breast does feel, no braver fuel choose
    Than that which one day worms may chance refuse?   (*1633*)

Jordan: I

    Who says that fictions only and false hair
    Become a verse? Is there in truth no beauty?
    Is all good structure in a winding stair?
    May no lines pass except they do their duty
    Not to a true, but painted chair?

    Is it no verse except enchanted groves
    And sudden arbors shadow coarse-spun lines?
    Must purling streams refresh a lover's loves?
    Must all be veiled, while he that reads, divines,
    Catching the sense at two removes?   10

    Shepherds are honest people; let them sing.
    Riddle who list for me, and pull for prime;
    I envy no man's nightingale or spring,
    Nor let them punish me with loss of rhyme,
    Who plainly say, *My God, my King.*   (*1633*)

The Windows

Lord, how can man preach thy eternal word?
    He is a brittle crazy glass,
Yet in thy temple thou dost him afford
    This glorious and transcendent place
    To be a window, through thy grace.

But when thou dost anneal in glass thy story,
    Making thy life to shine within
The holy preacher's, then the light and glory
    More reverend grows, and doth more win;
    Which else shows wat'rish, bleak, and thin.   10

Doctrine and life, colors and light in one,
    When they combine and mingle, bring
A strong regard and awe; but speech alone
    Doth vanish like a flaring thing,
    And in the ear, not conscience, ring.
                      (*1633*)

EDMUND WALLER • 1606–1687

Song

Stay, Phoebus, stay!
The world to which you fly so fast,
Conveying day
From us to them, can pay your haste
With no such object, nor salute your rise
With no such wonder, as De Mornay's
  eyes.

Well does this prove
The error of those antique books,
Which made you move
About the world; her charming looks   *10*
Would fix your beams, and make it ever
  day,
Did not the rolling earth snatch her
  away.   (*1645*)

Go, Lovely Rose

Go, lovely rose,
Tell her that wastes her time and me,
  That now she knows,
When I resemble her to thee,
  How sweet and fair she seems to be.

  Tell her that's young,
And shuns to have her graces spied,
  That hadst thou sprung
In deserts, where no men abide,
  Thou must have uncommended
    died.   *10*

  Small is the worth
Of beauty from the light retired;
  Bid her come forth,
Suffer herself to be desired,
  And not blush so to be admired.

  Then die, that she
The common fate of all things rare
  May read in thee;
How small a part of time they share,
  That are so wondrous sweet and fair. *20*
                                  (*1645*)

JOHN MILTON • 1608–1674

Lycidas

In this monody the author bewails a learned friend, unfortunately drowned in his passage from Chester on the Irish Seas, 1637. And by occasion foretells the ruin of our corrupted clergy, then in their height.

Yet once more, O ye laurels, and once more,
Ye myrtles brown, with ivy never sere,
I come to pluck your berries harsh and crude,
And with forced fingers rude
Shatter your leaves before the mellowing year.
Bitter constraint and sad occasion dear
Compels me to disturb your season due;
For Lycidas is dead, dead ere his prime,
Young Lycidas, and hath not left his peer.
Who would not sing for Lycidas? he knew   *10*

Himself to sing, and build the lofty rhyme.
He must not float upon his wat'ry bier
Unwept, and welter to the parching wind,
Without the meed of some melodious tear.
    Begin, then, Sisters of the Sacred Well[1]
That from beneath the seat of Jove doth spring,
Begin, and somewhat loudly sweep the string.
Hence with denial vain and coy excuse:
So may some gentle Muse
With lucky words favor my destined urn,   20
And, as he passes, turn
And bid fair peace be to my sable shroud!
For we were nursed upon the self-same hill,
Fed the same flocks, by fountain, shade, and rill;
    Together both, ere the high lawns appeared
Under the opening eyelids of the Morn,
We drove a-field, and both together heard
What time the gray-fly winds her sultry horn,
Battening our flocks with the fresh dews of night,
Oft till the star that rose at evening bright   30
Towards Heaven's descent had sloped his westering wheel.
Meanwhile the rural ditties were not mute,
Tempered to the oaten flute,
Rough Satyrs danced, and Fauns with cloven heel
From the glad sound would not be absent long;
And old Damætas[2] loved to hear our song.
    But, O the heavy change, now thou art gone,
Now thou art gone, and never must return!
Thee, Shepherd, thee the woods and desert caves,
With wild thyme and the gadding vine o'ergrown,   40
And all their echoes mourn.
The willows, and the hazel copses green,
Shall now no more be seen
Fanning their joyous leaves to thy soft lays.
As killing as the canker to the rose,
Or taint-worm to the weanling herds that graze,
Or frost to flowers, that their gay wardrobe wear
When first the white thorn blows;
Such, Lycidas, thy loss to shepherd's ear.
    Where were ye, Nymphs, when the remorseless deep   50
Closed o'er the head of your loved Lycidas?
For neither were ye playing on the steep
Where your old bards, the famous Druids, lie,
Nor yet on the shaggy top of Mona[3] high,
Nor yet where Deva[4] spreads her wizard stream.
Ay me! I fondly dream

---

[1] the muses, who dwelt at the Pierian spring
[2] conventional pastoral name for an older man
[3] island of Anglesey, off Wales
[4] river Dee

"Had ye been there" . . . for what could that have done?
What could the Muse herself that Orpheus bore,[5]
The Muse herself, for her enchanting son,
Whom universal Nature did lament, 60
When, by the rout that made the hideous roar,
His gory visage down the stream was sent,
Down the swift Hebrus to the Lesbian shore?
   Alas! what boots it with uncessant care
To tend the homely, slighted, shepherd's trade,
And strictly meditate the thankless Muse?
Were it not better done, as others use,
To sport with Amaryllis in the shade,
Or with the tangles of Neæra's[6] hair?
Fame is the spur that the clear spirit doth raise 70
(That last infirmity of noble mind)
To scorn delights and live laborious days;
But the fair guerdon when we hope to find,
And think to burst out into sudden blaze,
Comes the blind Fury with the abhorrèd shears,
And slits the thin-spun life. "But not the praise,"
Phœbus replied, and touched my trembling ears:
"Fame is no plant that grows on mortal soil,
Nor in the glistering foil.
Set off to the world, nor in broad rumor lies, 80
But lives and spreads aloft by those pure eyes
And perfect witness of all-judging Jove;
As he pronounces lastly on each deed,
Of so much fame in Heav'n expect thy meed."
   O fountain Arethuse,[7] and thou honored flood,
Smooth-sliding Mincius,[8] crowned with vocal reeds,
That strain I heard was of a higher mood:
But now my oat proceeds,
And listen to the Herald of the Sea,[9]
That came in Neptune's plea. 90
He asked the waves, and asked the felon winds,
What hard mishap hath doomed this gentle swain?
And questioned every gust of rugged wings
That blows from off each beakèd promontory:
They knew not of his story;
And sage Hippotadés[10] their answer brings,
That not a blast was from his dungeon strayed:
The air was calm, and on the level brine

[5] Calliope could not prevent a mob of Thracian women from murdering Orpheus. They threw his head into the river Hebrus, whence it floated out to the island of Lesbos in the Aegean Sea.
[6] conventional pastoral names for shepherdesses
[7] a nymph, transformed into a fountain in Sicily
[8] river in Lombardy. Like Arethuse, it represents pastoral poetry
[9] Triton, who here pleads Neptune's innocence
[10] Aeolus, god of the winds

   Sleek Panopé[11] with all her sisters played.
It was the fatal and perfidious bark,   *100*
Built in the eclipse, and rigged with curses dark,
That sunk so low that sacred head of thine.
  Next, Camus,[12] reverend sire, went footing slow,
His mantle hairy, and his bonnet sedge,
Inwrought with figures dim, and on the edge
Like to that sanguine flower inscribed with woe.
"Ah! who hath reft," quoth he, "my dearest pledge?"
Last came, and last did go,
The pilot of the Galilean lake;[13]
Two massy keys he bore of metals twain   *110*
(The golden opes, the iron shuts amain).
He shook his mitered locks, and stern bespake:—
"How well could I have spared for thee, young swain,
Enow of such, as for their bellies' sake,
Creep, and intrude, and climb into the fold!
Of other care they little reckoning make
Than how to scramble at the shearers' feast,
And shove away the worthy bidden guest.
Blind mouths! that scarce themselves know how to hold
A sheep-hook, or have learned aught else the least   *120*
That to the faithful herdsman's art belongs!
What recks it them? What need they? they are sped;
And, when they list, their lean and flashy songs
Grate on their scrannel pipes of wretched straw;
The hungry sheep look up, and are not fed,
But, swollen with wind and the rank mist they draw,
Rot inwardly, and foul contagion spread;
Besides what the grim wolf with privy paw
Daily devours apace, and nothing said;
But that two-handed engine at the door   *130*
Stands ready to smite once, and smite no more."
  Return, Alphéus;[14] the dread voice is past
That shrunk thy streams; return, Sicilian Muse,
And call the vales, and bid them hither cast
Their bells and flowerets of a thousand hues.
Ye valleys low, where the mild whispers use
Of shades, and wanton winds, and gushing brooks,
On whose fresh lap the swart star sparely looks,
Throw hither all your quaint enameled eyes,
That on the green turf suck the honied showers,   *140*
And purple all the ground with vernal flowers.
Bring the rathe primrose that forsaken dies,
The tufted crow-toe, and pale jessamine,

[11] the principal sea nymph
[12] god of the river Cam; hence Cambridge University
[13] St. Peter, to whom Christ gave the keys of Heaven; who, as the first bishop, is pictured here as wearing a miter
[14] god of a river in Arcadia, representing pastoral poetry

The white pink, and the pansy freaked with jet,
The glowing violet,
The musk-rose, and the well-attired woodbine,
With cowslips wan that hang the pensive head,
And every flower that sad embroidery wears;
Bid Amaranthus all his beauty shed,
And daffodillies fill their cups with tears,   *150*
To strew the laureate hearse where Lycid lies.
For so, to interpose a little ease,
Let our frail thoughts dally with false surmise,
Ay me! whilst thee the shores and sounding seas
Wash far away, where'er thy bones are hurled;
Whether beyond the stormy Hebrides,
Where thou, perhaps, under the whelming tide
Visit'st the bottom of the monstrous world;
Or whether thou, to our moist vows denied,
Sleep'st by the fable of Bellerus[15] old,   *160*
Where the great Vision of the guarded mount
Looks toward Namancos and Bayona's[16] hold:
Look homeward, angel, now, and melt with ruth;
And, O ye Dolphins, waft the hapless youth.
 Weep no more, woeful shepherds, weep no more,
For Lycidas, your sorrow, is not dead,
Sunk though he be beneath the watery floor:
So sinks the day-star in the ocean bed,
And yet anon repairs his drooping head,
And tricks his beams, and with new-spangled ore   *170*
Flames in the forehead of the morning sky:
So Lycidas sunk low, but mounted high,
Through the dear might of Him that walked the waves,
Where, other groves and other streams along,
With nectar pure his oozy locks he laves,
And hears the unexpressive nuptial song,
In the blest kingdoms meek of Joy and Love.
There entertain him all the Saints above,
In solemn troops, and sweet societies,
That sing, and singing in their glory move,   *180*
And wipe the tears forever from his eyes.
Now, Lycidas, the shepherds weep no more;
Henceforth thou art the Genius of the shore,
In thy large recompense, and shalt be good
To all that wander in that perilous flood.

 Thus sang the uncouth swain to the oaks and rills,
While the still Morn went out with sandals gray;
He touched the tender stops of various quills,

---

[15] a giant of fable, said to be buried at Land's End, Cornwall   [16] Spanish strongholds of Catholic power

With eager thought warbling his Doric lay:
And now the sun had stretched out all the hills,
And now was dropped into the western bay.
At last he rose, and twitched his mantle blue:
Tomorrow to fresh woods and pastures new. (*1638*)

L'Allegro

Hence, lothèd Melancholy
   Of Cerberus[1] and blackest Midnight
      born,
In Stygian[2] cave forlorn
   'Mongst horrid shapes, and shrieks,
      and sights unholy!
Find out some uncouth cell,
   Where brooding Darkness spreads his
      jealous wings,
And the night-raven sings;
   There under ebon shades, and low-
      browed rocks
As ragged as thy locks,
   In dark Cimmerian[3] desert ever
      dwell.   10

     But come, thou Goddess fair and
      free,
In heaven yclept[4] Euphrosyne,
And by men, heart-easing Mirth,
Whom lovely Venus at a birth
With two sister Graces[5] more
To ivy-crownèd Bacchus[6] bore;
Or whether (as some sager sing)
The frolic wind that breathes the
      spring,
Zephyr,[7] with Aurora[8] playing,
As he met her once a-Maying,   20
There on beds of violets blue
And fresh-blown roses washed in dew
Filled her with thee, a daughter fair,
So buxom, blithe, and debonair.
   Haste thee, Nymph, and bring
      with thee
Jest, and youthful jollity,
Quips, and cranks, and wanton wiles,
Nods, and becks, and wreathèd
      smiles,
Such as hang on Hebe's[9] cheek,
And love to live in dimple sleek;   30
Sport that wrinkled Care derides,
And Laughter holding both his sides.
Come, and trip it as you go
On the light fantastic toe;
And in thy right hand lead with thee,
The mountain-nymph, sweet
      Liberty;
And if I give thee honour due,
Mirth, admit me of thy crew,
To live with her, and live with thee,
In unreprovèd pleasures free;   40
To hear the lark begin his flight,
And singing startle the dull night
From his watch-tower in the skies,
Till the dappled dawn doth rise;
Then to come, in spite of sorrow,
And at my window bid good-morrow
Through the sweetbriar, or the vine,
Or the twisted eglantine:
While the cock with lively din,
Scatters the rear of darkness
      thin,   50
And to the stack, or the barn-door,
Stoutly struts his dames before;
Oft listening how the hounds and
      horn
Cheerly rouse the slumbering morn,
From the side of some hoar hill,
Through the high wood echoing
      shrill.

---

[1] the three-headed dog that guarded the gate of hell
[2] of the river Styx in Hades, over which Charon ferried dead souls
[3] The Cimmerians lived in eternal darkness at the outer edge of the world.   [4] called
[5] The Graces, Euphrosyne, Aglaia, and Thalia, were personifications of grace and beauty.
[6] god of wine   [7] god of the west wind
[8] the dawn   [9] cupbearer to the gods

Sometime walking not unseen,
By hedge-row elms, on hillocks green,
Right against the eastern gate,
Where the great Sun begins his state   60
Robed in flames and amber light,
The clouds in thousand liveries dight;
While the ploughman, near at hand,
Whistles o'er the furrowed land,
And the milkmaid singeth blithe,
And the mower whets his scythe,
And every shepherd tells his tale
Under the hawthorn in the dale.
    Straight mine eye hath caught new pleasures
Whilst the landscape round it measures;   70
Russet lawns, and fallows gray,
Where the nibbling flocks do stray;
Mountains, on whose barren breast
The labouring clouds do often rest;
Meadows trim with daisies pied,
Shallow brooks, and rivers wide;
Towers and battlements it sees
Bosomed high in tufted trees,
Where perhaps some beauty lies,
The cynosure of neighbouring eyes.   80
    Hard by, a cottage chimney smokes,
From betwixt two aged oaks,
Where Corydon and Thyrsis, met,
Are at their savoury dinner set
Of herbs, and other country messes,
Which the neat-handed Phillis dresses;
And then in haste her bower she leaves,
With Thestylis[10] to bind the sheaves;
Or, if the earlier season lead
To the tanned haycock in the mead.   90
    Sometimes with secure delight
The upland hamlets will invite,
When the merry bells ring round,
And the jocund rebecks[11] sound
To many a youth and many a maid,
Dancing in the chequered shade;
And young and old come forth to play
On a sun-shine holyday,
Till the live-long day-light fail:
Then to the spicy nut-brown ale,   100
With stories told of many a feat,
How Faery Mab[12] the junkets eat,
She was pinched, and pulled, she said,
And he, by friar's lantern[13] led;
Tells how the drudging goblin sweat
To earn his cream-bowl duly set,
When in one night, ere glimpse of morn,
His shadowy flail hath threshed the corn
That ten day-labourers could not end;
Then lies him down the lubber fiend,   110
And, stretched out all the chimney's length,
Basks at the fire his hairy strength;
And crop-full out of doors he flings,
Ere the first cock his matin rings.
    Thus done the tales, to bed they creep,
By whispering winds soon lulled asleep.
    Towered cities please us then,
And the busy hum of men,
Where throngs of knights and barons bold,
In weeds of peace, high triumphs hold,   120
With store of ladies, whose bright eyes
Rain influence, and judge the prize
Of wit or arms, while both contend
To win her grace, whom all commend.
There let Hymen[14] oft appear

---

[10] conventional pastoral names
[11] a small viol   [12] queen of the fairies
[13] will o' the wisp   [14] god of marriage

In saffron robe, with taper clear,
And pomp, and feast, and revelry,
With mask, and antique pageantry;
Such sights as youthful poets dream
On summer eves by haunted
    stream. *130*
Then to the well-trod stage anon,
If Jonson's learnèd sock be on,
Or sweetest Shakespeare, Fancy's
    child,
Warble his native wood-notes wild.
    And ever against eating cares,
Lap me in soft Lydian[15] airs,
Married to immortal verse
Such as the meeting soul may pierce
In notes, with many a winding bout
Of linkèd sweetness long drawn
    out, *140*
With wanton heed and giddy
    cunning,
The melting voice through mazes
    running,
Untwisting all the chains that tie
The hidden soul of harmony;
That Orpheus' self may heave his
    head
From golden slumber, on a bed
Of heaped Elysian flowers, and hear
Such strains as would have won the
    ear
Of Pluto, to have quite set free
His half-regained Eurydice.[16] *150*
    These delights, if thou canst give,
Mirth, with thee I mean to
    live. (*1645*)

Il Penseroso

Hence, vain deluding Joys,
    The brood of Folly without father
        bred!
How little you bestead
    Or fill the fixèd mind with all your toys!
Dwell in some idle brain,
    And fancies fond with gaudy shapes
        possess
As thick and numberless
    As the gay motes that people the
        sunbeams,
Or likest hovering dreams,
    The fickle pensioners of Morpheus'
        train. *10*
    But hail, thou goddess sage and holy,
    Hail, divinest Melancholy!
Whose saintly visage is too bright
To hit the sense of human sight;
And therefore to our weaker view,
O'erlaid with black, staid Wisdom's
    hue;
Black, but such as in esteem
Prince Memnon's sister[1] might
    beseem,
Or that starred Ethiop queen[2] that
    strove
To set her beauty's praise above *20*
The sea-nymphs, and their powers
    offended.
Yet thou art higher far descended:
Thee bright-haired Vesta,[3] long of
    yore,
To solitary Saturn[4] bore;
His daughter she (in Saturn's reign
Such mixture was not held a stain)
Oft in glimmering bowers and glades
He met her, and in secret shades
Of woody Ida's[5] inmost grove,
While yet there was no fear of
    Jove. *30*
    Come, pensive Nun, devout and
    pure,
Sober, steadfast, and demure,
All in a robe of darkest grain,[6]

---

[15] an effeminate or voluptuous mode in music
[16] Orpheus followed his wife, Eurydice, into Hades when she died. His music so moved Pluto, the god of the underworld, that he agreed to release Eurydice from death if Orpheus would precede her out of Hades and not look back to see if she was following. Orpheus complied until the last moment, but then looked back, only to see Eurydice snatched back into Hades.
[1] Hemera. Prince Memnon, an Ethiopian, fought in the Trojan War.
[2] Cassiopeia, proud of her beauty, was placed among the stars after her death.
[3] goddess of the hearth
[4] mythical king of Italy's golden age
[5] sacred mountain in Crete   [6] dye

Flowing with majestic train,
And sable stole of cypress[7] lawn,
Over thy decent shoulders drawn.
Come, but keep thy wonted state,
With even step, and musing gait,
And looks commercing with the skies,
Thy rapt soul sitting in thine
    eyes: 40
There, held in holy passion still,
Forget thyself to marble, till
With a sad leaden downward cast,
Thou fix them on the earth as fast.
And join with thee calm Peace, and
    Quiet,
Spare Fast, that oft with gods doth
    diet,
And hears the Muses in a ring
Aye round about Jove's altar sing.
And add to these retired Leisure
That in trim gardens takes his
    pleasure; 50
But first and chiefest, with thee bring,
Him that yon soars on golden wing
Guiding the fiery-wheelèd throne,
The cherub Contemplation;
And the mute Silence hist along,
'Less Philomel[8] will deign a song
In her sweetest saddest plight,
Smoothing the rugged brow of Night,
While Cynthia[9] checks her dragon
    yoke,
Gently o'er the accustom'd oak. 60
—Sweet bird, that shunn'st the noise
    of folly,
Most musical, most melancholy!
Thee, chauntress, oft, the woods
    among,
I woo, to hear thy even-song;
And missing thee, I walk unseen
On the dry smooth-shaven green,
To behold the wandering Moon,
Riding near her highest noon,
Like one that had been led astray
Through the heaven's wide pathless
    way 70
And oft, as if her head she bowed,
Stooping through a fleecy cloud.
    Oft, on a plat of rising ground,
I hear the far-off curfew sound,
Over some wide-watered shore,
Swinging slow with sullen roar;
Or, if the air will not permit,
Some still removèd place will fit,
Where glowing embers through the
    room
Teach light to counterfeit a
    gloom, 80
Far from all resort of mirth,
Save the cricket on the hearth,
Or the bellman's drowsy charm
To bless the doors from nightly harm:
    Or let my lamp at midnight hour,
Be seen in some high lonely tower,
Where I may oft out-watch the Bear,[10]
With thrice-great Hermes,[11] or
    unsphere[12]
The spirit of Plato, to unfold
What worlds or what vast regions
    hold 90
The immortal mind, that hath forsook
Her mansion in this fleshly nook:
And of those demons that are found
In fire, air, flood, or under ground,
Whose power hath a true consent
With planet, or with element.
Sometimes let gorgeous Tragedy
In sceptered pall come sweeping by,
Presenting Thebes,[13] or Pelops' line,
Or the tale of Troy divine; 100
Or what (though rare) of later age
Ennobled hath the buskined stage.
    But, O sad Virgin, that thy power
Might raise Musaeus[14] from his
    bower,
Or bid the soul of Orpheus sing
Such notes as, warbled to the string,
Drew iron tears down Pluto's cheek
And made Hell grant what Love did
    seek.
Or call him that left half-told

[7] a filmy black cloth   [8] the nightingale
[9] goddess of the moon, who drove a team of dragons
[10] the Big Dipper, a constellation which never sets at England's latitude
[11] Hermes Trismegistus, allegedly the author of books of secret lore
[12] recall from immortality
[13] legendary capital of Boeotia
[14] sixth-century Greek poet

The story of Cambuscan bold,   110
Of Camball, and of Algarsife,
And who had Canacè to wife
That owned the virtuous ring and glass;
And of the wondrous horse of brass,
On which the Tartar king did ride;[15]
And if aught else great bards beside,
In sage and solemn tunes have sung,
Of tourneys, and of trophies hung;
Of forests, and enchantments drear,
Where more is meant than meets the ear.   120
   Thus, Night, oft see me in thy pale career,
Till civil-suited Morn[16] appear,
Not tricked and frounced as she was wont
With the Attic Boy[17] to hunt,
But kerchiefed in a comely cloud,
While rocking winds are piping loud,
Or ushered with a shower still,
When the gust hath blown his fill,
Ending on the rustling leaves,
With minute drops from off the eaves.   130
And when the sun begins to fling
His flaring beams, me, goddess, bring
To archèd walks of twilight groves,
And shadows brown, that Sylvan[18] loves,
Of pine, or monumental oak,
Where the rude axe, with heavèd stroke,
Was never heard the nymphs to daunt,
Or fright them from their hallowed haunt.
There in close covert by some brook,
Where no profaner eye may look,   140
Hide me from day's garish eye,
While the bee with honeyed thigh,
That at her flowery work doth sing,
And the waters murmuring,
With such consort as they keep,
Entice the dewy-feathered Sleep;
And let some strange mysterious dream
Wave at his wings in airy stream
Of lively portraiture displayed,
Softly on my eyelids laid.   150
And, as I wake, sweet music breathe
Above, about, or underneath,
Sent by some Spirit to mortals good,
Or the unseen Genius of the wood.
   But let my due feet never fail
To walk the studious cloister's pale,
And love the high-embowèd roof,
With antique pillars massy proof,
And storied windows richly dight,
Casting a dim religious light.   160
There let the pealing organ blow
To the full-voiced choir below,
In service high and anthems clear,
As may with sweetness, through mine ear,
Dissolve me into ecstasies,
And bring all Heaven before mine eyes.
   And may at last my weary age
Find out the peaceful hermitage,
The hairy gown and mossy cell,
Where I may sit and rightly spell   170
Of every star that heaven doth shew,
And every herb that sips the dew;
Till old experience do attain
To something like prophetic strain.
   These pleasures, Melancholy, give,
And I with thee will choose to live.   *(1645)*

---

[15] references to Chaucer's unfinished "Squire's Tale"   [16] Aurora
[17] Cephalus, beloved of Aurora
[18] god of the woods

ANDREW MARVELL • 1621-1678

The Mower Against Gardens

Luxurious man, to bring his vice in use,
    Did after him the world seduce,
And from the fields the flowers and plants allure,
    When nature was most plain and pure.
He first enclosed within the garden's square
    A dead and standing pool of air;
And a more luscious earth for them did knead,
    Which stupefied them while it fed.
The pink grew then as double as his mind;
    The nutriment did change the kind.   *10*
With strange perfumes he did the roses taint;
    And flowers themselves were taught to paint.
The tulip, white, did for complexion seek,
    And learned to interline its cheek;
Its onion root they then so high did hold
    That one was for a meadow sold.[1]
Another world was searched, through oceans new,
    To find the marvel of Peru.[2]
And yet these rarities might be allowed
    To man, that sov'reign thing and proud,   *20*
Had he not dealt[3] between the bark and tree,
    Forbidden mixtures there to see.
No plant now knew the stock from which it came;
    He grafts upon the wild the tame,
That the uncertain and adult'rate fruit
    Might put the palate in dispute.
His green seraglio has its eunuchs too,
    Lest any tyrant him outdo;
And in the cherry he does nature vex,
    To procreate without a sex.   *30*
'Tis all enforced, the fountain and the grot,
    While the sweet fields do lie forgot,
Where willing nature does to all dispense
    A wild and fragrant innocence;
And fauns and fairies do the meadows till
    More by their presence than their skill.
Their statues, polished by some ancient hand,
    May to adorn the gardens stand;
But howsoe'er the figures do excel,
    The gods themselves with us do dwell.   (*1681*)   *40*

---

[1] a reference to tulipomania
[2] the common garden four-o'clock
[3] delivered a blow; i.e., made a cleft in which to insert a cion

To His Coy Mistress

Had we but world enough, and time,
This coyness, lady, were no crime.
We would sit down, and think which way
To walk, and pass our long love's day.
Thou by the Indian Ganges' side
Shouldst rubies find: I by the tide
Of Humber[1] would complain. I would
Love you ten years before the Flood:
And you should if you please refuse
Till the conversion of the Jews.   10
My vegetable love should grow
Vaster than empires, and more slow.
An hundred years should go to praise
Thine eyes, and on thy forehead gaze.
Two hundred to adore each breast:
But thirty thousand to the rest.
An age at least to every part,
And the last age should show your heart.
For, lady, you deserve this state;
Nor would I love at lower rate.   20
   But at my back I always hear
Time's wingèd chariot hurrying near:
And yonder all before us lie
Deserts of vast eternity.
Thy beauty shall no more be found,
Nor, in thy marble vault, shall sound
My echoing song; then worms shall try
That long preserved virginity:
And your quaint honour turn to dust;
And into ashes all my lust.   30
The grave's a fine and private place,
But none, I think, do there embrace.
   Now therefore, while the youthful hue
Sits on thy skin like morning dew,
And while thy willing soul transpires
At every pore with instant fires,
Now let us sport us while we may;
And now, like am'rous birds of prey,
Rather at once our time devour,
Than languish in his slow-chapped[2]
   pow'r.   40
Let us roll all our strength, and all
Our sweetness, up into one ball:
And tear our pleasures with rough strife,
Thorough the iron gates of life.
Thus, though we cannot make our sun
Stand still, yet we will make him
   run. *(1681)*

HENRY VAUGHAN • 1622–1695

The Bird

Hither thou com'st; the busy wind all night
Blew through thy lodging, where thy own warm wing
Thy pillow was. Many a sullen storm,
  For which course man seems much the fitter born,
     Rained on thy bed
     And harmless head.

And now as fresh and cheerful as the light,
Thy little heart in early hymns doth sing
Unto that Providence whose unseen arm
  Curbed them, and clothed thee well and warm.   10
     All things that be praise him, and had
     Their lesson taught them when first made.

---

[1] a rather commonplace English river   [2] slow-jawed

So hills and valleys into singing break,
And though poor stones have neither speech nor tongue,
While active winds and streams both run and speak,
Yet stones are deep in admiration.
Thus praise and prayer here beneath the sun
Make lesser mornings, when the great are done.

For each encloséd spirit is a star
   Enlight'ning his own little sphere,
Whose light, though fetched and borrowéd from far,
   Both mornings makes and evenings there.

But as these birds of light make a land glad,
Chirping their solemn matins on each tree,
So in the shades of night some dark fowls be,
Whose heavy notes make all that hear them sad.

   The turtle then in palm trees mourns,
     While owls and satyrs howl;
   The pleasant land to brimstone turns
     And all her streams grow foul.

Brightness and mirth, and love and faith, all fly,
Till the day-spring breaks forth again from high.   *(1650)*

The Waterfall

With what deep murmurs through time's silent stealth
Doth thy transparent, cool, and wat'ry wealth
   Here flowing fall,
   And chide, and call,
As if his liquid, loose retínue stayed
Ling'ring, and were of this steep place afraid,
   The common pass
   Where, clear as glass,
   All must descend—
   Not to an end,
But quickened by this deep and rocky grave,
Rise to a longer course more bright and brave.

   Dear stream! dear bank, where often I
   Have sat and pleased my pensive eye,
   Why, since each drop of thy quick store
   Runs thither whence it flowed before,
   Should poor souls fear a shade or night,
   Who came, sure, from a sea of light?
   Or since those drops are all sent back

So sure to thee, that none doth lack,
Why should frail flesh doubt any more
That what God takes he'll not restore?

O useful element and clear!
My sacred wash and cleanser here,
My first consigner unto those
Fountains of life where the Lamb goes!
What sublime truths and wholesome themes
Lodge in thy mystical deep streams!
Such as dull man can never find
Unless that spirit lead his mind
Which first upon thy face did move,
And hatched all with his quick'ning love.
As this loud brook's incessant fall
In streaming rings restagnates all,
Which reach by course the bank, and then
Are no more seen, just so pass men.
O my invisible estate,
My glorious liberty, still late!
Thou art the channel my soul seeks,
Not this with cataracts and creeks.   (*1650*)

JOHN DRYDEN • 1631–1700

Song *from* Marriage à la Mode

Why should a foolish marriage vow,
    Which long ago was made,
Oblige us to each other now
    When passion is decayed?
We loved, and we loved, as long as we could,
    Till our love was loved out in us both:
But our marriage is dead, when the pleasure is fled:
    'Twas pleasure first made it an oath.

If I have pleasures for a friend,
    And farther love in store,
What wrong has he whose joys did end,
    And who could give no more?
'Tis a madness that he should be jealous of me,
    Or that I should bar him of another:
For all we can gain, is to give ourselves pain,
    When neither can hinder the other.   (*1672*)

Prologue to Aureng-Zebe

Our author by experience finds it true,
'Tis much more hard to please himself, than you:
And out of no feigned modesty, this day,
Damns his laborious trifle of a play:
Not that it's worse than what before he writ,
But he has now another taste of wit;
And to confess a truth, (though out of time)
Grows weary of his long-loved mistress, rhyme.
Passion's too fierce to be in fetters bound,
And nature flies him like enchanted ground.   10
What verse can do, he has performed in this,
Which he presumes the most correct of his.
But spite of all his pride, a secret shame
Invades his breast at Shakespeare's sacred name:
Awed when he hears his god-like Romans rage,
He, in a just despair, would quit the stage.
And to an age less polished, more unskilled,
Does, with disdain, the foremost honours yield,
As with the greater dead he dares not strive,
He would not match his verse with those who live: 20
Let him retire, betwixt two ages cast,
The first of this, and hindmost of the last.
A losing gamester, let him sneak away;
He bears no ready money from the play.
The fate which governs poets thought it fit,
He should not raise his fortunes by his wit.
The clergy thrive, and the litigious bar;
Dull heroes fatten with the spoils of war;
All southern vices, heaven be praised are here;
But wit's a luxury you think too dear.   30
When you to cultivate the plant are loath,
'Tis a shrewd sign 'twas never of your growth:
And wit in northern climates will not blow,
Except, like orange trees 'tis housed from snow.
There needs no care to put a playhouse down,
'Tis the most desert place of all the town.
Wit and our neighbours, to speak proudly, are
Like monarchs, ruined with expensive war.
While, like wise English, unconcerned, you sit,
And see us play the tragedy of wit.   (*1676*)   40

THOMAS TRAHERNE • 1633–1674

Insatiableness

This busy, vast, inquiring soul
    Brooks no control,
No limits will endure,
    Nor any rest; it will all see,
Not time alone, but ev'n eternity.
    What is it? Endless sure.

'Tis mean ambition to desire
    A single world;
To many I aspire
    Though one upon another hurled;   *10*
Nor will they all, if they be all confined,
    Delight my mind.

This busy, vast, inquiring soul
    Brooks no control;
    'Tis very curious too.
Each one of all those worlds must be
Enriched with infinite variety
    And worth, or 'twill not do.

'Tis nor delight nor perfect pleasure
    To have a purse   *20*
That hath a bottom in its treasure,
Since I must thence endless expense
    disburse.
Sure there's a God, for else there's no
    delight,
One infinite. (*c. 1660*)

JONATHAN SWIFT • 1667–1745

A Description of the Morning

Now hardly here and there a hackney-coach
Appearing, showed the ruddy morn's approach.
Now Betty from her master's bed had flown,
And softly stole to discompose her own;
The slip-shod 'prentice from his master's door
Had pared the dirt, and sprinkled round the floor.
Now Moll had whirled her mop with dext'rous airs,
Prepared to scrub the entry and the stairs.
The youth with broomy stumps began to trace
The kennel-edge where wheels had worn the place.   *10*
The small-coal man was heard with cadence deep,
Till drowned in shriller notes of chimney-sweep:
Duns at his lordship's gate began to meet;
And brick-dust Moll had screamed through half the street.
The turnkey now his flock returning sees,
Duly let out a-nights to steal for fees:
The watchful bailiffs take their silent stands,
And schoolboys lag with satchels in their hands. (*1709*)

The Day of Judgement

With a whirl of thought oppressed,
I sunk from reverie to rest.
An horrid vision seized my head,
I saw the graves give up their dead!
Jove, armed with terrors, burst the skies,
And thunder roars, and lightning flies!
Amazed, confused, its fate unknown,
The world stands trembling at his throne!
While each pale sinner hung his head,
Jove, nodding, shook the heavens, and said: *10*

"Offending race of humankind,
By nature, reason, learning, blind;
You who, through frailty, stepped aside;
And you who never fell, through pride;
You who in different sects were shamed,
And come to see each other damned
(So some folks told you, but they knew
No more of Jove's designs than you);
—The world's mad business now is o'er,
And I resent these pranks no more.   *20*
—I to such blockheads set my wit!
I damn such fools!—Go, go, you're bit."

(c. 1731)

ALEXANDER POPE • 1688–1744

The Rape of the Lock

AN HEROI-COMICAL POEM

*Nolueram, Belinda, tuos violare capillos;
Sed juvat, hoc precibus me tribuisse tuis.
—Martial, Epigrams XII, 84.*[1]

CANTO I

What dire offense from am'rous causes springs,
What mighty contests rise from trivial things,
I sing—This verse to *Caryl*,[2] Muse! is due:
This, even Belinda may vouchsafe to view:
Slight is the subject, but not so the praise,
If she inspire, and he approve my lays.
  Say what strange motive, Goddess! could compel
A well-bred lord t' assault a gentle belle?
O say what stranger cause, yet unexplored,
Could make a gentle belle reject a lord?   *10*
In tasks so bold, can little men engage,
And in soft bosoms dwells such mighty rage?
  Sol through white curtains shot a tim'rous ray,
And oped those eyes that must eclipse the day:
Now lap-dogs give themselves the rousing shake,
And sleepless lovers, just at twelve, awake:

---

[1] "I did not wish, Belinda, to profane your locks, but I am delighted to yield this to your beseeching."

[2] John Caryll, a close friend, who suggested the subject of the poem to Pope

Thrice rung the bell, the slipper knocked the ground,
And the pressed watch[3] returned a silver sound.
Belinda still her downy pillow pressed,
Her guardian sylph prolonged the balmy rest: *20*
'Twas he had summoned to her silent bed
The morning-dream that hovered o'er her head;
A youth more glitt'ring than a birth-night beau,[4]
(That even in slumber caused her cheek to glow)
Seemed to her ear his winning lips to lay,
And thus in whispers said, or seemed to say.
   "Fairest of mortals, thou distinguished care
Of thousand bright inhabitants of air!
If e'er one vision touched thy infant thought,
Of all the nurse and all the priest have taught;   *30*
Of airy elves by moonlight shadows seen,
The silver token, and the circled green,
Or virgins visited by angel-powers,
With golden crowns and wreaths of heav'nly flowers;
Hear and believe! thy own importance know,
Nor bound thy narrow views to things below.
Some secret truths, from learnèd pride concealed,
To maids alone and children are revealed:
What though no credit doubting wits may give?
The fair and innocent shall still believe.   *40*
Know, then, unnumbered spirits round thee fly,
The light militia of the lower sky:
These, though unseen, are ever on the wing,
Hang o'er the box,[5] and hover round the ring.[6]
Think what an equipage thou hast in air,
And view with scorn two pages and a chair.[7]
As now your own, our beings were of old,
And once inclosed in woman's beauteous mould;
Thence, by a soft transition, we repair
From earthly vehicles to these of air.   *50*
Think not, when woman's transient breath is fled,
That all her vanities at once are dead;
Succeeding vanities she still regards,
And though she plays no more, o'erlooks the cards.
Her joy in gilded chariots, when alive,
And love of ombre,[8] after death survive.
For when the fair in all their pride expire,
To their first elements their souls retire:
The sprites of fiery termagants[9] in flame
Mount up, and take a salamander's[10] name.   *60*

---

[3] Pressing the stem makes the watch chime the hour.
[4] young man dressed in brilliant costume for a royal birthday
[5] at the theater
[6] the drive in Hyde Park
[7] sedan chair
[8] the card game that Belinda plays with the Baron in Canto III
[9] shrewish women
[10] a lizard-like creature, once believed capable of living in fire

Soft yielding minds to water glide away,
And sip, with nymphs, their elemental tea.
The graver prude sinks downward to a gnome,
In search of mischief still on earth to roam.
The light coquettes in sylphs aloft repair,
And sport and flutter in the fields of air.
  "Know further yet; whoever fair and chaste
Rejects mankind, is by some sylph embraced:
For spirits, freed from mortal laws, with ease
Assume what sexes and what shapes they please. 70
What guards the purity of melting maids,
In courtly balls, and midnight masquerades,
Safe from the treach'rous friend, the daring spark,
The glance by day, the whisper in the dark,
When kind occasion prompts their warm desires,
When music softens, and when dancing fires?
'Tis but their sylph, the wise celestials know,
Though honor is the word with men below.
  "Some nymphs there are, too conscious of their face,
For life predestined to the gnomes' embrace. 80
These swell their prospects and exalt their pride,
When offers are disdained, and love denied:
Then gay ideas crowd the vacant brain,
While peers, and dukes, and all their sweeping train,
And garters, stars, and coronets appear,
And in soft sounds, "Your Grace" salutes their ear.
'Tis these that early taint the female soul,
Instruct the eyes of young coquettes to roll,
Teach infant-cheeks a bidden blush to know,
And little hearts to flutter at a beau. 90
  "Oft, when the world imagine women stray,
The sylphs through mystic mazes guide their way,
Through all the giddy circle they pursue,
And old impertinence expel by new.
What tender maid but must a victim fall
To one man's treat, but for another's ball?
When Florio speaks what virgin could withstand,
If gentle Damon[11] did not squeeze her hand?
With varying vanities, from every part,
They shift the moving toyshop of their heart; 100
Where wigs with wigs, with sword-knots sword-knots strive,
Beaux banish beaux, and coaches coaches drive.
This erring mortals levity may call;
Oh blind to truth! the sylphs contrive it all.
  "Of these am I, who thy protection claim,
A watchful sprite, and Ariel is my name.
Late, as I ranged the crystal wilds of air,

---

[11] conventional names in pastoral poetry

In the clear mirror of thy ruling star
I saw, alas! some dread event impend,
Ere to the main this morning sun descend,   *110*
But heaven reveals not what, or how, or where:
Warned by the sylph, oh pious maid, beware!
This to disclose is all thy guardian can:
Beware of all, but most beware of man!"
    He said; when Shock,[12] who thought she slept too long,
Leaped up, and waked his mistress with his tongue.
'Twas then, Belinda, if report say true,
Thy eyes first opened on a billet-doux;
Wounds, charms, and ardors were no sooner read,
But all the vision vanished from thy head.   *120*
    And now, unveiled, the toilet stands displayed,
Each silver vase in mystic order laid.
First, robed in white, the nymph intent adores,
With head uncovered, the cosmetic powers.
A heav'nly image in the glass appears,
To that she bends, to that her eyes she rears;
Th' inferior priestess,[13] at her altar's side,
Trembling begins the sacred rites of pride.
Unnumbered treasures ope at once, and here
The various off'rings of the world appear;   *130*
From each she nicely culls with curious[14] toil,
And decks the goddess with the glitt'ring spoil.
This casket India's glowing gems unlocks,
And all Arabia breathes from yonder box.
The tortoise here and elephant unite,
Transformed to combs, the speckled, and the white.
Here files of pins extend their shining rows,
Puffs, powders, patches, bibles,[15] billet-doux.
Now awful Beauty puts on all its arms;
The fair each moment rises in her charms,   *140*
Repairs her smiles, awakens every grace,
And calls forth all the wonders of her face;
Sees by degrees a purer blush arise,
And keener lightnings quicken in her eyes.
The busy sylphs surround their darling care,
These set the head, and those divide the hair,
Some fold the sleeve, whilst others plait the gown;
And Betty's praised for labors not her own.

CANTO II

Not with more glories, in th' etherial plain,
The sun first rises o'er the purpled main,
Than issuing forth, the rival of his beams

---

[12] Belinda's lap dog
[13] Betty, Belinda's lady's maid
[14] painstaking
[15] perhaps curling papers

Launched on the bosom of the silver Thames.
Fair nymphs, and well-dressed youths around her shone,
But every eye was fixed on her alone.
On her white breast a sparkling cross she wore,
Which Jews might kiss, and infidels adore.
Her lively looks a sprightly mind disclose,
Quick as her eyes, and as unfixed as those: 10
Favors to none, to all she smiles extends;
Oft she rejects, but never once offends.
Bright as the sun, her eyes the gazers strike,
And, like the sun, they shine on all alike.
Yet graceful ease, and sweetness void of pride,
Might hide her faults, if belles had faults to hide:
If to her share some female errors fall,
Look on her face, and you'll forget 'em all.
   This nymph, to the destruction of mankind,
Nourished two locks, which graceful hung behind 20
In equal curls, and well conspired to deck
With shining ringlets the smooth iv'ry neck.
Love in these labyrinths his slaves detains,
And mighty hearts are held in slender chains.
With hairy springes we the birds betray,
Slight lines of hair surprise the finny prey,
Fair tresses man's imperial race ensnare,
And beauty draws us with a single hair.
   Th' advent'rous Baron the bright locks admired;
He saw, he wished, and to the prize aspired. 30
Resolved to win, he meditates the way,
By force to ravish, or by fraud betray;
For when success a lover's toil attends,
Few ask, if fraud or force attained his ends.
   For this, ere Phœbus rose, he had implored
Propitious heaven, and every power adored,
But chiefly Love—to Love an altar built,
Of twelve vast French romances, neatly gilt.
There lay three garters, half a pair of gloves;
And all the trophies of his former loves; 40
With tender billet-doux he lights the pyre,
And breathes three am'rous sighs to raise the fire.
Then prostrate falls, and begs with ardent eyes
Soon to obtain, and long possess the prize:
The powers gave ear, and granted half his prayer,
The rest, the winds dispersed in empty air.
   But now secure the painted vessel glides,
The sun-beams trembling on the floating tides:
While melting music steals upon the sky,
And softened sounds along the waters die; 50
Smooth flow the waves, the zephyrs gently play,
Belinda smiled, and all the world was gay.

Th' impending woe sat heavy on his breast.
All but the sylph—with careful thoughts oppressed,
He summons straight his denizens of air;
The lucid squadrons round the sails repair;
Soft o'er the shrouds aërial whispers breathe,
That seemed but zephyrs to the train beneath.
Some to the sun their insect-wings unfold,
Waft on the breeze, or sink in clouds of gold; 60
Transparent forms, too fine for mortal sight,
Their fluid bodies half dissolved in light,
Loose to the wind their airy garments flew,
Thin glitt'ring textures of the filmy dew,
Dipped in the richest tincture of the skies,
Where light disports in ever-mingling dyes,
While every beam new transient colors flings,
Colors that change whene'er they wave their wings.
Amid the circle, on the gilded mast,
Superior by the head, was Ariel placed; 70
His purple pinions opening to the sun,
He raised his azure wand, and thus begun.
    "Ye sylphs and sylphids, to your chief give ear!
Fays, fairies, genii, elves, and dæmons, hear!
Ye know the spheres and various tasks assigned
By laws eternal to th' aërial kind.
Some in the fields of purest ether play,
And bask and whiten in the blaze of day.
Some guide the course of wand'ring orbs on high,
Or roll the planets through the boundless sky. 80
Some less refined, beneath the moon's pale light
Pursue the stars that shoot athwart the night,
Or suck the mists in grosser air below,
Or dip their pinions in the painted bow,
Or brew fierce tempests on the wintry main,
Or o'er the glebe[16] distil the kindly rain.
Others on earth o'er human race preside,
Watch all their ways, and all their actions guide:
Of these the chief the care of nations own,
And guard with arms divine the British throne. 90
    "Our humbler province is to tend the fair,
Not a less pleasing, though less glorious care;
To save the powder from too rude a gale,
Nor let th' imprisoned essences exhale;
To draw fresh colors from the vernal flowers;
To steal from rainbows e'er they drop in showers
A brighter wash; to curl their waving hairs,
Assist their blushes, and inspire their airs;
Nay oft, in dreams, invention we bestow,

---

[16] cultivated land

To change a flounce, or add a furbelow.
   "This day, black omens threat the brightest fair,
That e'er deserved a watchful spirit's care;
Some dire disaster, or by force, or sleight;
But what, or where, the fates have wrapped in night.
Whether the nymph shall break Diana's law,[17]
Or some frail China jar receive a flaw;
Or stain her honor or her new brocade;
Forget her prayers, or miss a masquerade;
Or lose her heart, or necklace, at a ball;
Or whether Heaven has doomed that Shock must fall.
Haste, then, ye spirits! to your charge repair:
The flutt'ring fan be Zephyretta's care;
The drops[18] to thee, Brillante, we consign;
And, Momentilla, let the watch be thine;
Do thou, Crispissa, tend her fav'rite lock;
Ariel himself shall be the guard of Shock.
   "To fifty chosen sylphs, of special note,
We trust th' important charge, the petticoat:
Oft have we known that seven-fold fence to fail,
Though stiff with hoops, and armed with ribs of whale;
Form a strong line about the silver bound,
And guard the wide circumference around.
   "Whatever spirit, careless of his charge,
His post neglects, or leaves the fair at large,
Shall feel sharp vengeance soon o'ertake his sins,
Be stopped in vials, or transfixed with pins;
Or plunged in lakes of bitter washes lie,
Or wedged whole ages in a bodkin's eye:
Gums and pomatums shall his flight restrain,
While clogged he beats his silken wings in vain;
Or alum styptics with contracting power
Shrink his thin essence like a riveled flower:
Or, as Ixion[19] fixed, the wretch shall feel
The giddy motion of the whirling mill,
In fumes of burning chocolate shall glow,
And tremble at the sea that froths below!"
   He spoke; the spirits from the sails descend;
Some, orb in orb, around the nymph extend;
Some thrid the mazy ringlets of her hair;
Some hang upon the pendants of her ear:
With beating hearts the dire event they wait,
Anxious, and trembling for the birth of Fate.

CANTO III

   Close by those meads, forever crowned with flowers,
Where Thames with pride surveys his rising towers,

---

[17] the law of chastity
[18] pendant earrings
[19] punished by being chained to a wheel that rolled eternally through the air

There stands a structure[20] of majestic frame,
Which from the neighb'ring Hampton takes its name.
Here Britain's statesmen oft the fall foredoom
Of foreign tyrants and of nymphs at home;
Here thou, great Anna![21] whom three realms obey,
Dost sometimes counsel take—and sometimes tea.
   Hither the heroes and the nymphs resort,
To taste awhile the pleasures of a court;   *10*
In various talk th' instructive hours they past,
Who gave the ball, or paid the visit last;
One speaks the glory of the British queen,
And one describes a charming Indian screen;
A third interprets motions, looks, and eyes;
At every word a reputation dies.
Snuff, or the fan, supply each pause of chat,
With singing, laughing, ogling, and all that.
   Meanwhile, declining from the noon of day,
The sun obliquely shoots his burning ray;   *20*
The hungry judges soon the sentence sign,
And wretches hang that jury-men may dine;
The merchant from th' Exchange returns in peace,
And the long labors of the toilet cease.
Belinda now, whom thirst of fame invites,
Burns to encounter two advent'rous knights,
At ombre[22] singly to decide their doom;
And swells her breast with conquests yet to come.
Straight the three bands prepare in arms to join,
Each band the number of the sacred nine.[23]   *30*
Soon as she spreads her hand, th' aërial guard
Descend, and sit on each important card:
First Ariel perched upon a matadore,
Then each, according to the rank they bore;
For sylphs, yet mindful of their ancient race,
Are, as when women, wondrous fond of place.
   Behold, four kings in majesty revered,
With hoary whiskers and a forky beard;
And four fair queens whose hands sustain a flower,
Th' expressive emblem of their softer power;   *40*
Four knaves in garbs succinct, a trusty band,
Caps on their heads, and halberts in their hand;
And particolored troops, a shining train,
Draw forth to combat on the velvet plain.
   The skilful nymph reviews her force with care:
Let spades be trumps! she said, and trumps they were.

[20] Hampton Court, a royal palace
[21] Queen Anne, ruler of "three realms": England, Scotland, and Wales
[22] The card game is played out accurately. The three "matadores" or high cards are called "Spadillio," "Manillio," and "Basto," but the cards which carry these names vary with the trump suit. Belinda's matadores are "sable" (1. 47) because she declares spades trumps.
[23] the Muses. A player's hand consists of nine cards.

Now move to war her sable matadores,
In show like leaders of the swarthy Moors.
Spadillio first, unconquerable lord!
Led off two captive trumps, and swept the board. 50
As many more Manillio forced to yield,
And marched a victor from the verdant field.
Him Basto followed, but his fate more hard
Gained but one trump and one plebeian card.
With his broad sabre next, a chief in years,
The hoary Majesty of Spades appears,
Puts forth one manly leg, to sight revealed,
The rest, his many-colored robe concealed.
The rebel knave, who dares his prince engage,
Proves the just victim of his royal rage. 60
Even mighty Pam,[24] that kings and queens o'erthrew
And mowed down armies in the fights of loo,
Sad chance of war! now destitute of aid,
Falls undistinguished by the victor spade!
    Thus far both armies to Belinda yield;
Now to the Baron fate inclines the field.
His warlike Amazon[25] her host invades,
Th' imperial consort of the crown of spades.
The club's black tyrant first her victim died,
Spite of his haughty mien, and barb'rous pride: 70
What boots the regal circle on his head,
His giant limbs, in state unwieldy spread;
That long behind he trails his pompous robe,
And, of all monarchs, only grasps the globe?
    The Baron now his diamonds pours apace;
Th' embroidered king who shows but half his face,
And his refulgent queen, with powers combined
Of broken troops an easy conquest find.
Clubs, diamonds, hearts, in wild disorder seen,
With throngs promiscuous strow the level green. 80
Thus when dispersed a routed army runs,
Of Asia's troops, and Afric's sable sons,
With like confusion different nations fly,
Of various habit, and of various dye,
The pierced battalions disunited fall,
In heaps on heaps; one fate o'erwhelms them all.
    The knave of diamonds tries his wily arts,
And wins (oh shameful chance!) the queen of hearts.
At this, the blood the virgin's cheek forsook,
A livid paleness spreads o'er all her look; 90
She sees, and trembles at th' approaching ill,
Just in the jaws of ruin, and codille.[26]

---

[24] in loo, the highest card, the jack (knave) of clubs
[25] in Greek mythology, one of a tribe of female warriors; here, the queen of clubs
[26] failure to make one's bid

And now (as oft in some distempered state)
On one nice trick depends the general fate.
An ace of hearts steps forth: The king unseen
Lurked in her hand, and mourned his captive queen:
He springs to vengeance with an eager pace,
And falls like thunder on the prostrate ace.
The nymph exulting fills with shouts the sky;
The walls, the woods, and long canals reply. 100
   Oh thoughtless mortals! ever blind to fate,
Too soon dejected, and too soon elate.
Sudden, these honors shall be snatched away,
And cursed for ever this victorious day.
   For lo! the board with cups and spoons is crowned,
The berries crackle,[27] and the mill turns round;
On shining altars of Japan[28] they raise
The silver lamp: the fiery spirits blaze:
From silver spouts the grateful liquors glide,
While China's earth receives the smoking tide: 110
At once they gratify their scent and taste,
And frequent cups prolong the rich repast.
Straight hover round the fair her airy band;
Some, as she sipped, the fuming liquor fanned,
Some o'er her lap their careful plumes displayed,
Trembling, and conscious of the rich brocade.
Coffee (which makes the politician wise,
And see through all things with his half-shut eyes)
Sent up in vapors to the Baron's brain
New stratagems, the radiant lock to gain. 120
Ah cease, rash youth! desist ere 'tis too late,
Fear the just gods, and think of Scylla's[29] fate!
Changed to a bird, and sent to flit in air,
She dearly pays for Nisus' injured hair!
   But when to mischief mortals bend their will,
How soon they find fit instruments of ill!
Just then, Clarissa drew with tempting grace
A two-edged weapon from her shining case:
So ladies in romance assist their knight,
Present the spear, and arm him for the fight. 130
He takes the gift with rev'rence, and extends
The little engine on his fingers' ends;
This just behind Belinda's neck he spread,
As o'er the fragrant steams she bends her head.
Swift to the lock a thousand sprites repair,
A thousand wings, by turns, blow back the hair;

---

[27] Coffee is ground at the table.
[28] japanned (lacquered) tables
[29] daughter of King Nisus of Megara. She fell in love with an enemy besieging the city, and pulled out of her father's head the golden hair on which the safety of the city depended. When Nisus, metamorphosed into a sea eagle, pounced upon Scylla, she was changed into a bird.

And thrice they twitched the diamond in her ear;
Thrice she looked back, and thrice the foe drew near.
Just in that instant, anxious Ariel sought
The close recesses of the virgin's thought;   *140*
As on the nosegay in her breast reclined,
He watched th' ideas rising in her mind,
Sudden he viewed, in spite of all her art,
An earthly lover lurking at her heart.
Amazed, confused, he found his power expired,
Resigned to fate, and with a sigh retired.
   The peer now spreads the glitt'ring forfex wide,
T' inclose the lock; now joins it, to divide.
Even then, before the fatal engine closed,
A wretched sylph too fondly interposed;   *150*
Fate urged the shears, and cut the sylph in twain,
(But airy substance soon unites again)
The meeting points the sacred hair dissever
From the fair head, forever, and forever!
   Then flashed the living lightning from her eyes,
And screams of horror rend th' affrighted skies.
Not louder shrieks to pitying heaven are cast,
When husbands, or when lap-dogs breathe their last;
Or when rich China vessels fall'n from high,
In glitt'ring dust and painted fragments lie!   *160*
   "Let wreaths of triumph now my temples twine,"
(The victor cried); "the glorious prize is mine!
While fish in streams, or birds delight in air,
Or in a coach and six the British fair,
As long as *Atalantis*[30] shall be read,
Or the small pillow grace a lady's bed,
While visits shall be paid on solemn days,
When num'rous wax-lights in bright order blaze,
While nymphs take treats, or assignations give,
So long my honor, name, and praise shall live!"   *170*
What time would spare, from steel receives its date,
And monuments, like men, submit to fate!
Steel could the labor of the gods destroy,
And strike to dust th' imperial towers of Troy;
Steel could the works of mortal pride confound,
And hew triumphal arches to the ground.
What wonder then, fair nymph! thy hairs should feel,
The conq'ring force of unresisted steel?

CANTO IV

But anxious cares the pensive nymph oppressed,
And secret passions labored in her breast.

---

[30] a contemporary book filled with fashionable gossip

Not youthful kings in battle seized alive,
Not scornful virgins who their charms survive,
Not ardent lovers robbed of all their bliss,
Not ancient ladies when refused a kiss,
Not tyrants fierce that unrepenting die,
Not Cynthia[31] when her manteau's pinned awry,
E'er felt such rage, resentment, and despair,
As thou, sad virgin! for thy ravished hair.

    For, that sad moment, when the sylphs withdrew
And Ariel weeping from Belinda flew,
Umbriel, a dusky, melancholy sprite,
As ever sullied the fair face of light,
Down to the central earth, his proper scene,
Repaired to search the gloomy Cave of Spleen.[32]

    Swift on his sooty pinions flits the gnome,
And in a vapour reached the dismal dome.
No cheerful breeze this sullen region knows,
The dreaded east is all the wind that blows.
Here in a grotto, sheltered close from air,
And screened in shades from day's detested glare,
She sighs forever on her pensive bed,
Pain at her side, and Megrim[33] at her head.

    Two handmaids wait the throne: alike in place,
But diff'ring far in figure and in face.
Here stood Ill-nature like an ancient maid,
Her wrinkled form in black and white arrayed;
With store of prayers, for mornings, nights, and noons,
Her hand is filled; her bosom with lampoons.

    There Affectation, with a sickly mien,
Shows in her cheek the roses of eighteen,
Practised to lisp, and hang the head aside,
Faints into airs, and languishes with pride,
On the rich quilt sinks with becoming woe,
Wrapt in a gown, for sickness, and for show.
The fair ones feel such maladies as these,
When each new night-dress gives a new disease.

    A constant vapor o'er the palace flies;
Strange phantoms rising as the mists arise;
Dreadful, as hermit's dreams in haunted shades,
Or bright, as visions of expiring maids.
Now glaring fiends, and snakes on rolling spires,[34]
Pale specters, gaping tombs, and purple fires:
Now lakes of liquid gold, Elysian scenes,
And crystal domes, and angels in machines.

    Unnumbered throngs on every side are seen,
Of bodies changed to various forms by Spleen.

---

[31] Diana, goddess of chastity   [34] coils
[32] bad temper; malice   [33] low spirits

Here living tea-pots stand, one arm held out,
One bent; the handle this, and that the spout: 50
A pipkin[35] there, like Homer's tripod[36] walks;
Here sighs a jar, and there a goose-pie talks;
Men prove with child, as powerful fancy works,
And maids turned bottles, call aloud for corks.
    Safe past the gnome through this fantastic band,
A branch of healing spleenwort[37] in his hand.
Then thus addressed the power: "Hail, wayward Queen!
Who rule the sex to fifty from fifteen:
Parent of vapors[38] and of female wit,
Who give th' hysteric or poetic fit, 60
On various tempers act by various ways,
Make some take physic, others scribble plays;
Who cause the proud their visits to delay,
And send the godly in a pet to pray.
A nymph there is, that all thy power disdains,
And thousands more in equal mirth maintains.
But oh! if e'er thy gnome could spoil a grace,
Or raise a pimple on a beauteous face,
Like citron-waters[39] matrons' cheeks inflame,
Or change complexions at a losing game; 70
If e'er with airy horns[40] I planted heads,
Or rumpled petticoats, or tumbled beds,
Or caus'd suspicion when no soul was rude,
Or discomposed the head-dress of a prude,
Or e'er to costive lap-dog gave disease,
Which not the tears of brightest eyes could ease:
Hear me, and touch Belinda with chagrin,
That single act gives half the world the spleen."
    The goddess with a discontented air
Seems to reject him, though she grants his prayer. 80
A wondrous bag with both her hands she binds,
Like that where once Ulysses held the winds;[41]
There she collects the force of female lungs,
Sighs, sobs, and passions, and the war of tongues.
A vial next she fills with fainting fears,
Soft sorrows, melting griefs, and flowing tears.
The gnome rejoicing bears her gifts away,
Spreads his black wings, and slowly mounts to day.
    Sunk in Thalestris'[42] arms the nymph he found,
Her eyes dejected and her hair unbound. 90

[35] earthen jar
[36] three-legged stool
[37] a fern formerly believed effective in relieving spleen.
[38] affected emotional depression
[39] a liquor prepared with citrus rinds, believed good for the complexion
[40] The man whose wife is unfaithful is traditionally pictured as growng horns; "airy" here would mean imaginary.
[41] In the Odyssey, Ulysses visits Aeolus, god of winds, who gives the wanderer a bag containing all the winds that might hinder his sailing.
[42] Pope gives this supporter of Belinda the name of a queen of the war-like Amazons.

Full o'er their heads the swelling bag he rent,
And all the furies issued at the vent.
Belinda burns with more than mortal ire,
And fierce Thalestris fans the rising fire.
"Oh wretched maid!" she spread her hands, and cried,
(While Hampton's echoes, "Wretched maid!" replied)
"Was it for this you took such constant care
The bodkin, comb, and essence to prepare?
For this your locks in paper durance bound,
For this with torturing irons wreathed around?   100
For this with fillets strained your tender head,
And bravely bore the double loads of lead?
Gods! shall the ravisher display your hair,
While the fops envy, and the ladies stare!
Honor forbid! at whose unrivaled shrine
Ease, pleasure, virtue, all our sex resign.
Methinks already I your tears survey,
Already hear the horrid things they say,
Already see you a degraded toast,
And all your honor in a whisper lost!   110
How shall I, then, your helpless fame defend?
'Twill then be infamy to seem your friend!
And shall this prize, th' inestimable prize,
Exposed through crystal to the gazing eyes,
And heightened by the diamond's circling rays,
On that rapacious hand forever blaze?
Sooner shall grass in Hyde Park Circus grow,
And wits take lodgings in the sound of Bow,[43]
Sooner let earth, air, sea, to chaos fall,
Men, monkeys, lap-dogs, parrots, perish all!"   120
    She said; then raging to Sir Plume repairs,
And bids her Beau demand the precious hairs:
(Sir Plume of amber snuff-box justly vain,
And the nice conduct of a clouded cane)
With earnest eyes, and round unthinking face,
He first the snuff-box opened, then the case,
And thus broke out—"My Lord, why, what the devil?
Z—ds! damn the lock! 'fore Gad, you must be civil!
Plague on't! 'tis past a jest—nay prithee, pox!
Give her the hair"—he spoke, and rapped his box.   130
    "It grieves me much" (replied the Peer again)
"Who speaks so well should ever speak in vain.
But by this lock, this sacred lock I swear,
(Which never more shall join its parted hair;
Which never more its honors shall renew,
Clipped from the lovely head where late it grew)

---

[43] "Within sound of Bow bells"—the bells of the church of St. Mary-le-Bow—is the cockney region of London; hence lower class and unfashionable.

That while my nostrils draw the vital air,
This hand, which won it, shall for ever wear."
He spoke, and speaking, in proud triumph spread
The long-contended honours of her head.   *140*

But Umbriel, hateful gnome! forbears not so;
He breaks the vial whence the sorrows flow.
Then see! the nymph in beauteous grief appears,
Her eyes half-languishing, half-drowned in tears;
On her heaved bosom hung her drooping head,
Which, with a sigh, she raised; and thus she said.

"Forever cursed be this detested day,
Which snatched my best, my fav'rite curl away!
Happy! ah ten times happy had I been,
If Hampton Court these eyes had never seen!   *150*
Yet am not I the first mistaken maid,
By love of courts to numerous ills betrayed.
Oh had I rather unadmired remained
In some lone isle, or distant northern land;
Where the gilt chariot never marks the way,
Where none learn ombre, none e'er taste bohea![44]
There kept my charms concealed from mortal eye,
Like roses, that in deserts bloom and die.
What moved my mind with youthful lords to roam?
Oh had I stayed, and said my prayers at home!   *160*
'Twas this, the morning omens seemed to tell,
Thrice from my trembling hand the patch-box[45] fell;
The tott'ring china shook without a wind,
Nay, Poll sat mute, and Shock was most unkind!
A sylph too warned me of the threats of fate,
In mystic visions, now believed too late!
See the poor remnants of these slighted hairs!
My hands shall rend what even thy rapine spares:
These in two sable ringlets taught to break,
Once gave new beauties to the snowy neck;   *170*
The sister-lock now sits uncouth, alone,
And in its fellow's fate foresees its own;
Uncurled it hangs, the fatal shears demands,
And tempts once more, thy sacrilegious hands.
Oh hadst thou, cruel; been content to seize
Hairs less in sight, or any hairs but these!"

CANTO V

She said: the pitying audience melt in tears.
But Fate and Jove had stopped the Baron's ears.
In vain Thalestris with reproach assails,
For who can move when fair Belinda fails?

---

[44] a kind of tea

[45] a box for "beauty spots": bits of court plaster (a forerunner of adhesive tape) used to ornament the face

Not half so fixed the Trojan could remain,
While Anna begged and Dido[46] raged in vain.
   Then grave Clarissa graceful waved her fan;
Silence ensued, and thus the nymph began.
   "Say why are beauties praised and honored most,
The wise man's passion, and the vain man's toast?
Why decked with all that land and sea afford,
Why angels called, and angel-like adored?
Why round our coaches crowd the white-gloved beaux,
Why bows the side-box from its inmost rows;
How vain are all these glories, all our pains,
Unless good sense preserve what beauty gains:
That men may say, when we the front-box grace:
'Behold the first in virtue as in face!'
Oh! if to dance all night, and dress all day,
Charmed the small-pox, or chased old age away;
Who would not scorn what housewife's cares produce,
Or who would learn one earthly thing of use?
To patch, nay ogle, might become a saint,
Nor could it sure be such a sin to paint.
But since, alas! frail beauty must decay,
Curled or uncurled, since locks will turn to gray;
Since painted, or not painted, all shall fade,
And she who scorns a man, must die a maid;
What then remains but well our power to use,
And keep good-humor still whate'er we lose?
And trust me, dear! good-humor can prevail,
When airs, and flights, and screams, and scolding fail.
Beauties in vain their pretty eyes may roll;
Charms strike the sight, but merit wins the soul."
   So spoke the dame, but no applause ensued;
Belinda frowned, Thalestris called her prude.
"To arms, to arms!" the fierce virago cries,
And swift as lightning to the combat flies.
All side in parties, and begin th' attack;
Fans clap, silks rustle, and tough whalebones crack;
Heroes and heroines' shouts confus'dly rise,
And bass and treble voices strike the skies.
No common weapons in their hands are found,
Like gods they fight, nor dread a mortal wound.
   So when bold Homer makes the gods engage,
And heavenly breasts with human passions rage;
'Gainst Pallas, Mars; Latona, Hermes arms;[47]
And all Olympus rings with loud alarms:

---

[46] Aeneas was unmoved by the reproaches of his beloved, Dido, and her sister, Anna, when he proposed to leave Carthage for further wanderings.

[47] The specific identifications are less important than the comparison of the brawl to a battle of goddesses against gods.

Jove's thunder roars, heaven trembles all around,
Blue Neptune storms, the bellowing deeps resound:
Earth shakes her nodding towers, the ground gives way,
And the pale ghosts start at the flash of day!
   Triumphant Umbriel on a sconce's height
Clapped his glad wings, and sat to view the fight:
Propped on their bodkin spears, the sprites survey
The growing combat, or assist the fray.
   While through the press enraged Thalestris flies,
And scatters death around from both her eyes,
A beau and witling perished in the throng,
One died in metaphor, and one in song.
"O cruel nymph! a living death I bear,"
Cried Dapperwit, and sunk beside his chair.
A mournful glance Sir Fopling upwards cast,
"Those eyes are made so killing"—was his last.
Thus on Meander's[48] flowery margin lies
Th' expiring swan, and as he sings he dies.
   When bold Sir Plume had drawn Clarissa down,
Chloe stepped in, and killed him with a frown;
She smiled to see the doughty hero slain,
But, at her smile, the beau revived again.
   Now Jove suspends his golden scales in air,
Weighs the men's wits against the lady's hair;
The doubtful beam long nods from side to side;
At length the wits mount up, the hairs subside.
   See, fierce Belinda on the Baron flies,
With more than usual lightning in her eyes:
Nor feared the chief th' unequal fight to try,
Who sought no more than on his foe to die.
But this bold lord with manly strength endued,
She with one finger and a thumb subdued:
Just where the breath of life his nostrils drew,
A charge of snuff the wily virgin threw;
The gnomes direct, to every atom just,
The pungent grains of titillating dust.
Sudden, with starting tears each eye o'erflows,
And the high dome re-echoes to his nose.
   "Now meet thy fate," incensed Belinda cried,
And drew a deadly bodkin from her side.
(The same, his ancient personage to deck,
Her great great grandsire wore about his neck,
In three seal-rings; which after, melted down,
Formed a vast buckle for his widow's gown:
Her infant grandame's whistle next it grew,
The bells she jingled, and the whistle blew;

---

[48] a wandering river in Phrygia. According to legend the swan, normally mute, sings once just before it dies.

Then in a bodkin graced her mother's hairs,
Which long she wore, and now Belinda wears.)
      "Boast not my fall" (he cried) "insulting foe!
Thou by some other shalt be laid as low,
Nor think, to die dejects my lofty mind:
All that I dread is leaving you behind!
Rather than so, ah let me still survive,
And burn in Cupid's flames—but burn alive."
      "Restore the lock!" she cries; and all around
"Restore the lock!" the vaulted roofs rebound.
Not fierce Othello in so loud a strain
Roared for the handkerchief that caused his pain.[49]
But see how oft ambitious aims are crossed,
And chiefs contend till all the prize is lost!
The lock, obtained with guilt, and kept with pain,
In every place is sought, but sought in vain:
With such a prize no mortal must be blest,
So heaven decrees! with heaven who can contest?
      Some thought it mounted to the lunar sphere,
Since all things lost on earth are treasured there.
There heroes' wits are kept in pond'rous vases,
And beaux' in snuff-boxes and tweezer-cases.
There broken vows and death-bed alms are found,
And lovers' hearts with ends of riband bound,
The courtier's promises, and sick man's prayers,
The smiles of harlots, and the tears of heirs,
Cages for gnats, and chains to yoke a flea,
Dried butterflies, and tomes of casuistry.
      But trust the Muse—she saw it upward rise,
Though marked by none but quick, poetic eyes:
(So Rome's great founder to the heavens withdrew,
To Proculus alone confessed in view)[50]
A sudden star, it shot through liquid air,
And drew behind a radiant trail of hair.
Not Berenice's Locks[51] first rose so bright,
The heavens bespangling with disheveled light.
The sylphs behold it kindling as it flies,
And pleased pursue its progress through the skies.
      This the beau monde shall from the Mall[52] survey,
And hail with music its propitious ray.
This the blest lover shall for Venus take,
And send up vows from Rosamonda's lake.[53]

---

[49] Othello suspects that his wife, Desdemona, has given a prized handkerchief to her supposed lover and demands that she produce it. (Shakespeare, *Othello*, III, iv.)

[50] Romulus was translated to heaven in a storm cloud; he later appeared to Proculus, a Senator.

[51] A constellation (*Coma Berenicia*) is said to have been formed from the hair which Berenice, an Egyptian queen, dedicated to the gods in exchange for her husband's return from war.

[52] a fashionable walk in St. James's Park

[53] a pond in St. James's Park

This Partridge[54] soon shall view in cloudless skies,
When next he looks through Galileo's eyes,[55]
And hence th' egregious wizard shall foredoom
The fate of Louis, and the fall of Rome.   140
    Then cease, bright nymph! to mourn thy ravished hair,
Which adds new glory to the shining sphere!
Not all the tresses that fair head can boast,
Shall draw such envy as the lock you lost.
For, after all the murders of your eye,
When, after millions slain, yourself shall die:
When those fair suns shall set, as set they must,
And all those tresses shall be laid in dust,
This lock, the Muse shall consecrate to fame,
And 'midst the stars inscribe Belinda's name.   *(1712)*   150

WILLIAM BLAKE • 1757–1827

Introduction to Songs of Innocence

Piping down the valleys wild,
  Piping songs of pleasant glee,
On a cloud I saw a child,
  And he laughing said to me:

"Pipe a song about a Lamb!"
  So I piped with merry cheer.
"Piper, pipe that song again";
  So I piped: he wept to hear.

"Drop thy pipe, thy happy pipe;
  Sing thy songs of happy cheer!"   10
So I sung the same again,
  While he wept with joy to hear.

"Piper, sit thee down and write
  In a book that all may read."
So he vanished from my sight;
  And I plucked a hollow reed,

And I made a rural pen,
  And I stained the water clear,
And I wrote my happy songs
  Every child may joy to
    hear.   *(1789)*   20

The Lamb

  Little Lamb, who made thee?
    Dost thou know who made thee?
Gave thee life, and bid thee feed
By the stream and o'er the mead;
Gave thee clothing of delight,
Softest clothing, wooly, bright;
Gave thee such a tender voice,
Making all the vales rejoice?
  Little Lamb, who made thee?
    Dost thou know who made thee?   10

  Little Lamb, I'll tell thee,
    Little Lamb, I'll tell thee:
He is callèd by thy name,
For he calls himself a Lamb.
He is meek, and he is mild;
He became a little child.
I a child, and thou a lamb,
We are callèd by his name.
  Little Lamb, God bless thee!
  Little Lamb, God bless
    thee!   *(1789)*   20

---

[54] John Partridge (1644–1715), a foolish stargazer and prognosticator, who is also the butt of Swift's "Bickerstaff" joke
[55] a telescope

William Blake

The Little Black Boy

My mother bore me in the southern wild,
And I am black, but O! my soul is white;
White as an angel is the English child,
But I am black, as if bereaved of light.

My mother taught me underneath a tree,
And sitting down before the heat of day,
She took me on her lap and kissèd me,
And pointing to the east, began to say:

"Look on the rising sun: there God does live,
And gives His light, and gives His heat away;   10
And flowers and trees and beasts and men receive
Comfort in morning, joy in the noonday.

"And we are put on earth a little space,
That we may learn to bear the beams of love;
And these black bodies and this sunburnt face
Is but a cloud, and like a shady grove.

"For when our souls have learned the heat to bear,
The cloud will vanish; we shall hear His voice,
Saying: 'Come out from the grove, my love and care,
And round my golden tent like lambs rejoice.'"   20

Thus did my mother say, and kissèd me;
And thus I say to little English boy:
When I from black and he from white cloud free,
And round the tent of God like lambs we joy,

I'll shade him from the heat, till he can bear
To lean in joy upon our Father's knee;
And then I'll stand and stroke his silver hair,
And be like him, and he will then love me.   (*1789*)

The Tyger

Tyger! Tyger! burning bright
In the forests of the night,
What immortal hand or eye
Could frame thy fearful symmetry?

In what distant deeps or skies
Burnt the fire of thine eyes?
On what wings dare he aspire?
What the hand dare seize the fire?

And what shoulder, and what art,
Could twist the sinews of thy heart?   10
And when thy heart began to beat,
What dread hand? and what dread feet?

What the hammer? what the chain?
In what furnace was thy brain?
What the anvil? what dread grasp
Dare its deadly terrors clasp?

When the stars threw down their spears,
And watered heaven with their tears,
Did he smile his work to see?
Did he who made the Lamb make
    thee?   20

Tyger! Tyger! burning bright
In the forests of the night,
What immortal hand or eye,
Dare frame thy fearful
    symmetry? (*1794*)

The Sick Rose

O rose, thou art sick!
The invisible worm
That flies in the night,
In the howling storm,

Has found out thy bed
Of crimson joy,
And his dark secret love
Does thy life destroy. (*1794*)

London

I wander through each chartered street,
Near where the chartered Thames does
    flow.
And mark in every face I meet
Marks of weakness, marks of woe.

In every cry of every man,
In every infant's cry of fear,
In every voice, in every ban,
The mind-forged manacles I hear.

How the Chimney-sweeper's cry
Every black'ning church appalls;   10
And the hapless soldier's sigh
Runs in blood down palace walls.

But most through midnight streets I hear
How the youthful harlot's curse
Blasts the new-born infant's tear,
And blights with plagues the marriage
    hearse. (*1794*)

WILLIAM WORDSWORTH • 1770–1850

Lines

COMPOSED A FEW MILES ABOVE TINTERN ABBEY, ON REVISITING THE BANKS OF THE WYE DURING A TOUR, JULY 13, 1798

Five years have past; five summers, with the length
Of five long winters! and again I hear
These waters, rolling from their mountain-springs
With a soft inland murmur.—Once again
Do I behold these steep and lofty cliffs,
That on a wild secluded scene impress
Thoughts of more deep seclusion; and connect
The landscape with the quiet of the sky.
The day is come when I again repose
Here, under this dark sycamore, and view   10
These plots of cottage-ground, these orchard-tufts,
Which at this season, with their unripe fruits,
Are clad in one green hue, and lose themselves
'Mid groves and copses. Once again I see

These hedge-rows, hardly hedge-rows, little lines
Of sportive wood run wild: these pastoral farms,
Green to the very door; and wreaths of smoke
Sent up, in silence, from among the trees!
With some uncertain notice, as might seem
Of vagrant dwellers in the houseless woods,
Or of some hermit's cave, where by his fire
The hermit sits alone.
                    These beauteous forms,
Through a long absence, have not been to me
As is a landscape to a blind man's eye:
But oft, in lonely rooms, and 'mid the din
Of towns and cities, I have owed to them
In hours of weariness, sensations sweet,
Felt in the blood, and felt along the heart;
And passing even into my purer mind,
With tranquil restoration:—feelings too
Of unremembered pleasure: such, perhaps,
As have no slight or trivial influence
On that best portion of a good man's life,
His little, nameless, unremembered, acts
Of kindness and of love. Nor less, I trust,
To them I may have owed another gift,
Of aspect more sublime; that blessèd mood,
In which the burthen of the mystery,
In which the heavy and the weary weight
Of all this unintelligible world,
Is lightened:—that serene and blessèd mood,
In which the affections gently lead us on,—
Until, the breath of this corporeal frame
And even the motion of our human blood
Almost suspended, we are laid asleep
In body, and become a living soul:
While with an eye made quiet by the power
Of harmony, and the deep power of joy,
We see into the life of things.
                              If this
Be but a vain belief, yet, oh! how oft—
In darkness and amid the many shapes
Of joyless daylight; when the fretful stir
Unprofitable, and the fever of the world,
Have hung upon the beatings of my heart—
How oft, in spirit, have I turned to thee,
O sylvan Wye! thou wanderer thro' the woods,
How often has my spirit turned to thee!
    And now, with gleams of half-extinguished thought,
With many recognitions dim and faint,
And somewhat of a sad perplexity,
The picture of the mind revives again:

While here I stand, not only with the sense
Of present pleasure, but with pleasing thoughts
That in this moment there is life and food
For future years. And so I dare to hope,
Though changed, no doubt, from what I was when first
I came among these hills; when like a roe
I bounded o'er the mountains, by the sides
Of the deep rivers, and the lonely streams,
Wherever nature led: more like a man 70
Flying from something that he dreads, than one
Who sought the thing he loved. For nature then
(The coarser pleasures of my boyish days,
And their glad animal movements all gone by)
To me was all in all. I cannot paint
What then I was. The sounding cataract
Haunted me like a passion: the tall rock,
The mountain, and the deep and gloomy wood,
Their colors and their forms, were then to me
An appetite; a feeling and a love, 80
That had no need of a remoter charm,
By thought supplied, nor any interest
Unborrowed from the eye.—That time is past,
And all its aching joys are now no more,
And all its dizzy raptures. Not for this
Faint I, nor mourn nor murmur; other gifts
Have followed; for such loss, I would believe,
Abundant recompense. For I have learned
To look on nature, not as in the hour
Of thoughtless youth; but hearing oftentimes 90
The still, sad music of humanity,
Nor harsh nor grating, though of ample power
To chasten and subdue. And I have felt
A presence that disturbs me with the joy
Of elevated thoughts; a sense sublime
Of something far more deeply interfused,
Whose dwelling is the light of setting suns,
And the round ocean and the living air,
And the blue sky, and in the mind of man;
A motion and a spirit, that impels 100
All thinking things, all objects of all thought,
And rolls through all things. Therefore am I still
A lover of the meadows and the woods,
And mountains; and of all that we behold
From this green earth; of all the mighty world
Of eye, and ear,—both what they half create,
And what perceive; well pleased to recognise
In nature and the language of the sense,
The anchor of my purest thoughts, the nurse,
The guide, the guardian of my heart, and soul 110
Of all my moral being.

                    Nor perchance,
If I were not thus taught, should I the more
Suffer my genial spirits to decay:
For thou art with me here upon the banks
Of this fair river; thou my dearest friend,
My dear, dear friend; and in thy voice I catch
The language of my former heart, and read
My former pleasures in the shooting lights
Of thy wild eyes. Oh! yet a little while
May I behold in thee what I was once,   120
My dear, dear Sister! and this prayer I make,
Knowing that Nature never did betray
The heart that loved her; 't is her privilege,
Through all the years of this our life, to lead
From joy to joy: for she can so inform
The mind that is within us, so impress
With quietness and beauty and so feed
With lofty thoughts, that neither evil tongues,
Rash judgments, nor the sneers of selfish men,
Nor greetings where no kindness is, nor all   130
The dreary intercourse of daily life,
Shall e'er prevail against us, or disturb
Our cheerful faith, that all which we behold
Is full of blessings. Therefore let the moon
Shine on thee in thy solitary walk;
For all sweet sounds and harmonies; oh! then,
Thy memory be as a dwelling-place
Shall be a mansion for all lovely forms,   140
Into a sober pleasure; when thy mind
When these wild ecstasies shall be matured
To blow against thee: and, in after years,
And let the misty mountain-winds be free
If solitude, or fear, or pain, or grief,
Should be thy portion, with what healing thoughts
Of tender joy wilt thou remember me,
And these my exhortations! Nor, perchance—
If I should be where I no more can hear
Thy voice, nor catch from thy wild eyes these gleams
Of past existence—wilt thou then forget
That on the banks of this delightful stream   150
We stood together; and that I, so long
A worshipper of Nature, hither came
Unwearied in that service; rather say
With warmer love—oh! with far deeper zeal
Of holier love. Nor wilt thou then forget,
That after many wanderings, many years
Of absence, these steep woods and lofty cliffs,
And this green pastoral landscape, were to me
More dear, both for themselves and for thy sake!   (*1798*)

She Dwelt Among the Untrodden Ways

She dwelt among the untrodden ways
    Beside the springs of Dove,
A maid whom there were none to praise,
    And very few to love.

A violet by a mossy stone
    Half-hidden from the eye!
—Fair as a star, when only one
    Is shining in the sky.

She lived unknown, and few could know
    When Lucy ceased to be;   *10*
But she is in her grave, and, oh,
    The difference to me!   *(1799)*

I Travelled Among Unknown Men

I travelled among unknown men,
    In lands beyond the sea;
Nor, England! did I know till then
    What love I bore to thee.

'Tis past, that melancholy dream!
    Nor will I quit thy shore
A second time; for still I seem
    To love thee more and more.

Among thy mountains did I feel
    The joy of my desire;   *10*
And she I cherished turned her wheel
    Beside an English fire.

Thy mornings showed, thy nights
    concealed
    The bowers where Lucy played;
And thine too is the last green field
    That Lucy's eyes surveyed.   *(1799)*

Three Years She Grew in Sun and Shower

Three years she grew in sun and shower,
Then Nature said, "A lovelier flower
On earth was never sown;
This child I to myself will take;
She shall be mine, and I will make
A lady of my own.

"Myself will to my darling be
Both law and impulse: and with me
The girl, in rock and plain,
In earth and heaven, in glade and
    bower,   *10*
Shall feel an overseeing power
To kindle or restrain.

"She shall be sportive as the fawn
That wild with glee across the lawn,
Or up the mountain springs;
And hers shall be the breathing balm,
And hers the silence and the calm
Of mute insensate things.

"The floating clouds their state shall lend
To her; for her the willow bend;   *20*
Nor shall she fail to see
Even in the motions of the storm
Grace that shall mould the maiden's form
By silent sympathy.

"The stars of midnight shall be dear
To her; and she shall lean her ear
In many a secret place
Where rivulets dance their wayward
    round,
And beauty born of murmuring sound
Shall pass into her face.   *30*

"And vital feelings of delight
Shall rear her form to stately height,
Her virgin bosom swell;
Such thoughts to Lucy I will give
While she and I together live
Here in this happy dell."

Thus Nature spake—the work was
    done—
How soon my Lucy's race was run!
She died, and left to me
This heath, this calm, and quiet
    scene;   *40*
The memory of what has been,
And never more will be.   *(1799)*

My Heart Leaps Up When I Behold

My heart leaps up when I behold
    A rainbow in the sky:
So was it when my life began;
So is it now I am a man;
So be it when I shall grow old,
    Or let me die!
The Child is father of the Man;
And I could wish my days to be
Bound each to each by natural piety.
                             (*1802*)

Composed upon Westminster Bridge

SEPT. 3, 1802

Earth has not anything to show more fair:
Dull would he be of soul who could pass by
A sight so touching in its majesty:
This city now doth, like a garment, wear
The beauty of the morning; silent, bare,
Ships, towers, domes, theatres, and temples lie
Open unto the fields, and to the sky;
All bright and glittering in the smokeless air.
Never did sun more beautifully steep
In his first splendour, valley, rock, or hill;   *10*
Ne'er saw I, never felt, a calm so deep!
The river glideth at his own sweet will:
Dear God! the very houses seem asleep;
And all that mighty heart is lying still!   (*1802*)

London, 1802

Milton! thou should'st be living at this hour:
England hath need of thee: she is a fen
Of stagnant waters: altar, sword, and pen,
Fireside, the heroic wealth of hall and bower,
Have forfeited their ancient English dower
Of inward happiness. We are selfish men;
Oh! raise us up, return to us again;
And give us manners, virtue, freedom, power.
Thy soul was like a star, and dwelt apart:
Thou hadst a voice whose sound was like the sea: *10*
Pure as the naked heavens, majestic, free,
So didst thou travel on life's common way,
In cheerful godliness; and yet thy heart
The lowliest duties on herself did lay.   (*1802*)

The Solitary Reaper

Behold her, single in the field,
Yon solitary Highland Lass!
Reaping and singing by herself;
Stop here, or gently pass!
Alone she cuts and binds the grain,
And sings a melancholy strain;

O listen! for the vale profound
Is overflowing with the sound.

No nightingale did ever chaunt
More welcome notes to weary bands   *10*
Of travellers in some shady haunt,
Among Arabian sands:
A voice so thrilling ne'er was heard
In spring-time from the cuckoo-bird,
Breaking the silence of the seas
Among the farthest Hebrides.

Will no one tell me what she sings?—
Perhaps the plaintive numbers flow
For old, unhappy, far-off things,
And battles long ago: *20*
Or is it some more humble lay,
Familiar matter of to-day?
Some natural sorrow, loss, or pain,
That has been, and may be again?

Whate'er the theme, the maiden sang
As if her song could have no ending;
I saw her singing at her work,
And o'er the sickle bending;—
I listened, motionless and still;
And, as I mounted up the hill,   *30*
The music in my heart I bore,
Long after it was heard no more.

                                (*1803*)

I Wandered Lonely As a Cloud

I wandered lonely as a cloud
That floats on high o'er vales and hills,
When all at once I saw a crowd,
A host, of golden daffodils;
Beside the lake, beneath the trees,
Fluttering and dancing in the breeze.

Continuous as the stars that shine
And twinkle on the milky way,
They stretched in never-ending line
Along the margin of a bay: *10*
Ten thousand saw I at a glance,
Tossing their heads in sprightly dance.

The waves beside them danced; but they
Out-did the sparkling waves in glee:
A poet could not but be gay,
In such a jocund company:
I gazed—and gazed—but little thought
What wealth the show to me had
    brought:

For oft, when on my couch I lie,
In vacant or in pensive mood,   *20*
They flash upon that inward eye
Which is the bliss of solitude;
And then my heart with pleasure fills,
And dances with the daffodils.   (*1804*)

SAMUEL TAYLOR COLERIDGE • 1772–1834

Frost at Midnight

The frost performs its secret ministry,
Unhelped by any wind. The owlet's cry
Came loud—and hark, again! loud as before.
The inmates of my cottage, all at rest,
Have left me to that solitude, which suits
Abstruser musings: save that at my side
My cradled infant slumbers peacefully.
'Tis calm indeed! so calm, that it disturbs
And vexes meditation with its strange
And extreme silentness. Sea, hill, and wood,   *10*

This populous village! Sea, and hill, and wood,
With all the numberless goings-on of life,
Inaudible as dreams! the thin blue flame
Lies on my low-burnt fire, and quivers not;
Only that film, which fluttered on the grate,
Still flutters there, the sole unquiet thing.
Methinks, its motion in this hush of nature
Gives it dim sympathies with me who live,
Making it a companionable form,
Whose puny flaps and freaks the idling Spirit   20
By its own moods interprets, everywhere
Echo or mirror seeking of itself,
And makes a toy of Thought.

                        But O! how oft,
How oft, at school, with most believing mind,
Presageful, have I gazed upon the bars,
To watch that fluttering *stranger!* and as oft
With unclosed lids, already had I dreamt
Of my sweet birth-place, and the old church-tower,
Whose bells, the poor man's only music, rang
From morn to evening, all the hot Fair-day,   30
So sweetly, that they stirred and haunted me
With a wild pleasure, falling on mine ear
Most like articulate sounds of things to come!
So gazed I, till the soothing things, I dreamt,
Lulled me to sleep, and sleep prolonged my dreams!
And so I brooded all the following morn,
Awed by the stern preceptor's face, mine eye
Fixed with mock study on my swimming book:
Save if the door half opened, and I snatched
A hasty glance, and still my heart leaped up,   40
For still I hoped to see the *stranger's* face,
Townsman, or aunt, or sister more beloved,
My playmate when we both were clothed alike!

   Dear Babe, that sleepest cradled by my side,
Whose gentle breathings, heard in this deep calm,
Fill up the interspersèd vacancies
And momentary pauses of the thought!
My babe so beautiful! it thrills my heart
With tender gladness, thus to look at thee,
And think that thou shalt learn far other lore,   50
And in far other scenes! For I was reared
In the great city, pent 'mid cloisters dim,
And saw nought lovely but the sky and stars.
But *thou,* my babe! shalt wander like a breeze
By lakes and sandy shores, beneath the crags
Of ancient mountain, and beneath the clouds,

Which image in their bulk both lakes and shores
And mountain crags: so shalt thou see and hear
The lovely shapes and sounds intelligible
Of that eternal language, which thy God 60
Utters who from eternity doth teach
Himself in all, and all things in himself.
Great universal Teacher! he shall mold
Thy spirit, and by giving make it ask.

   Therefore all seasons shall be sweet to thee,
Whether the summer clothe the general earth
With greenness, or the redbreast sit and sing
Betwixt the tufts of snow on the bare branch
Of mossy apple-tree, while the nigh thatch
Smokes in the sun-thaw; whether the eavedrops fall 70
Heard only in the trances of the blast,
Or if the secret ministry of frost
Shall hang them up in silent icicles,
Quietly shining to the quiet Moon.   (*1798*)

Kubla Khan

In Xanadu did Kubla Khan
   A stately pleasure-dome decree:
Where Alph, the sacred river, ran
Through caverns measureless to man
   Down to a sunless sea.
So twice five miles of fertile ground
With walls and towers were girdled round:
And here were gardens bright with sinuous rills,
Where blossomed many an incense-bearing tree,
And here were forests ancient as the hills, 10
Enfolding sunny spots of greenery.

But oh! that deep romantic chasm which slanted
Down the green hill athwart a cedarn cover!
A savage place! as holy and enchanted
As e'er beneath a waning moon was haunted
By woman wailing for her demon-lover!
And from this chasm, with ceaseless turmoil seething,
As if this earth in fast thick pants were breathing,
A mighty fountain momently was forced,
Amid whose swift half-intermitted burst 20
Huge fragments vaulted like rebounding hail,
Or chaffy grain beneath the thresher's flail:
And 'mid these dancing rocks at once and ever
It flung up momently the sacred river.
Five miles meandering with a mazy motion
Through wood and dale the sacred river ran,

Then reached the caverns measureless to man,
And sank in tumult to a lifeless ocean:
And 'mid this tumult Kubla heard from far
Ancestral voices prophesying war! 30

    The shadow of the dome of pleasure
    Floated midway on the waves;
    Where was heard the mingled measure
    From the fountain and the caves.
It was a miracle of rare device,
A sunny pleasure-dome with caves of ice!

    A damsel with a dulcimer
    In a vision once I saw:
    It was an Abyssinian maid,
    And on her dulcimer she played, 40
    Singing of Mount Abora.
    Could I revive within me
    Her symphony and song,
    To such a deep delight 'twould win me,
That with music loud and long,
I would build that dome in air,
That sunny dome! those caves of ice!
And all who heard should see them there,
And all should cry, Beware! Beware!
His flashing eyes, his floating hair! 50
Weave a circle round him thrice,
And close your eyes with holy dread,
For he on honey-dew hath fed,
And drunk the milk of Paradise. *(1798)*

GEORGE GORDON, LORD BYRON • 1788–1824

She Walks in Beauty

She walks in beauty, like the night
    Of cloudless climes and starry skies;
And all that's best of dark and bright
    Meet in her aspect and her eyes:
Thus mellowed to that tender light
    Which heaven to gaudy day denies.

One shade the more, one ray the less,
    Had half impaired the nameless grace
Which waves in every raven tress,
    Or softly lightens o'er her face; 10
Where thoughts serenely sweet express,
    How pure, how dear their dwelling-
    place.

And on that cheek, and o'er that brow,
    So soft, so calm, yet eloquent,
The smiles that win, the tints that glow,
    But tell of days in goodness spent,
A mind at peace with all below,
    A heart whose love is innocent!
(1814)

Stanzas for Music

There be none of Beauty's daughters
   With a magic like thee;
And like music on the waters
   Is thy sweet voice to me:
When, as if its sound were causing
The charmèd ocean's pausing,
The waves lie still and gleaming,
And the lull'd winds seem dreaming:

And the midnight moon is weaving
   Her bright chain o'er the deep,   *10*
Whose breast is gently heaving
   As an infant's asleep:
So the spirit bows before thee,
To listen and adore thee;
With a full but soft emotion
Like the swell of Summer's ocean.

(1816)

Sonnet on Chillon

Eternal spirit of the chainless Mind!
   Brightest in dungeons, Liberty! thou art,
   For there thy habitation is the heart—
The heart which love of thee alone can bind;
And when thy sons to fetters are consigned—
   To fetters, and the damp vault's dayless gloom,
   Their country conquers with their martyrdom,
And Freedom's fame finds wings on every wind.
Chillon! thy prison is a holy place,
   And thy sad floor an altar—for 'twas trod,   *10*
Until his very steps have left a trace
   Worn, as if thy cold pavement were a sod,
By Bonnivard[1]—May none those marks efface!
   For they appeal from tyranny to God. *(1816)*

So We'll Go No More A-Roving

So we'll go no more a-roving
   So late into the night,
Though the heart be still as loving,
   And the moon be still as bright.

For the sword outwears its sheath,
   And the soul wears out the breast,
And the heart must pause to breathe,
   And Love itself have rest.

Though the night was made for loving,
   And the day returns too soon,   *10*
Yet we'll go no more a-roving
   By the light of the moon. *(1817)*

---

[1] François Bonivard [*sic*], a Swiss cleric and political leader who was imprisoned by the Duke of Savoy in the Castle of Chillon on Lake Geneva, 1532–36, and who became a symbol of resistance to tyranny in popular ballads

PERCY BYSSHE SHELLEY • 1792–1822

Ozymandias

I met a traveller from an antique land
Who said: Two vast and trunkless legs of stone
Stand in the desert . . . Near them, on the sand,
Half sunk, a shattered visage lies, whose frown,
And wrinkled lip, and sneer of cold command,
Tell that its sculptor well those passions read
Which yet survive, stamped on these lifeless things,
The hand that mocked them, and the heart that fed:
And on the pedestal these words appear:
"My name is Ozymandias, king of kings: 10
Look on my works, ye Mighty, and despair!"
Nothing beside remains. Round the decay
Of that colossal wreck, boundless and bare
The lone and level sands stretch far away.   (*1817*)

Ode to the West Wind

I

O wild West Wind, thou breath of Autumn's being,
Thou, from whose unseen presence the leaves dead
Are driven, like ghosts from an enchanter fleeing,

Yellow, and black, and pale, and hectic red,
Pestilence-stricken multitudes: O thou,
Who chariotest to their dark wintry bed

The wingèd seeds, where they lie cold and low,
Each like a corpse within its grave, until
Thine azure sister of the Spring shall blow

Her clarion o'er the dreaming earth, and fill   10
(Driving sweet buds like flocks to feed in air)
With living hues and odours plain and hill:

Wild Spirit, which art moving everywhere;
Destroyer and preserver; hear, oh, hear!

II

Thou on whose stream, mid the steep sky's commotion,
Loose clouds like earth's decaying leaves are shed,
Shook from the tangled boughs of Heaven and Ocean,

Angels of rain and lightning: there are spread
On the blue surface of thine aëry surge,
Like the bright hair uplifted from the head

Of some fierce Maenad,[1] even from the dim verge
Of the horizon to the zenith's height,
The locks of the approaching storm. Thou dirge

Of the dying year, to which this closing night
Will be the dome of a vast sepulchre,
Vaulted with all thy congregated might

Of vapours, from whose solid atmosphere
Black rain, and fire, and hail will burst: oh, hear!

III

Thou who didst waken from his summer dreams
The blue Mediterranean, where he lay,
Lulled by the coil of his crystàlline streams,

Beside a pumice isle in Baiae's bay,[2]
And saw in sleep old palaces and towers
Quivering within the wave's intenser day,

All overgrown with azure moss and flowers
So sweet, the sense faints picturing them! Thou
For whose path the Atlantic's level powers

Cleave themselves into chasms, while far below
The sea-blooms and the oozy woods which wear
The sapless foliage of the ocean, know

Thy voice, and suddenly grow gray with fear,
And tremble and despoil themselves: oh, hear!

IV

If I were a dead leaf thou mightest bear;
If I were a swift cloud to fly with thee;
A wave to pant beneath thy power, and share

The impulse of thy strength, only less free
Than thou, O uncontrollable! If even
I were as in my boyhood, and could be

---

[1] a frenetic female worshipper of Dionysis, god of wine and fertility   [2] on the west coast of Italy

The comrade of thy wanderings over Heaven,
As then, when to outstrip thy skiey speed
Scarce seemed a vision; I would ne'er have striven

As thus with thee in prayer in my sore need.
Oh, lift me as a wave, a leaf, a cloud!
I fall upon the thorns of life! I bleed!

A heavy weight of hours has chained and bowed
One too like thee: tameless, and swift, and proud.

v

Make me thy lyre, even as the forest is:
What if my leaves are falling like its own!
The tumult of thy mighty harmonies

Will take from both a deep, autumnal tone,
Sweet though in sadness. Be thou, Spirit fierce,
My spirit! Be thou me, impetuous one!

Drive my dead thoughts over the universe
Like withered leaves to quicken a new birth!
And, by the incantation of this verse,

Scatter, as from an unextinguished hearth
Ashes and sparks, my words among mankind!
Be through my lips to unawakened earth

The trumpet of a prophecy! O, Wind,
If Winter comes, can Spring be far behind?   (*1819*)

To Night

Swiftly walk over the western wave,
    Spirit of Night!
Out of the misty eastern cave,
Where, all the long and lone daylight,
Thou wovest dreams of joy and fear
Which make thee terrible and dear,—
    Swift be thy flight!

Wrap thy form in a mantle gray,
    Star-inwrought!
Blind with thine hair the eyes of Day;
Kiss her until she be wearied out:
Then wander o'er city and sea and land,
Touching all with thine opiate wand—
    Come, long-sought!

When I arose and saw the dawn,
    I sigh'd for thee;
When light rode high, and the dew was gone,
And noon lay heavy on flower and tree,
And the weary Day turn'd to his rest
Lingering like an unloved guest,
    I sigh'd for thee.

Thy brother Death came, and cried,
    'Wouldst thou me?'
Thy sweet child Sleep, the filmy-eyed,
Murmur'd like a noontide bee,
'Shall I nestle near thy side?
Wouldst thou me?'—And I replied,
    'No, not thee!'

Death will come when thou art dead,
    Soon, too soon— *30*
Sleep will come when thou art fled;
Of neither would I ask the boon
I ask of thee, belovèd Night—
Swift be thine approaching flight,
    Come soon, soon! *(1821)*

To ———

Music, when soft voices die,
Vibrates in the memory—
Odours, when sweet violets sicken,
Live within the sense they quicken.

Rose leaves, when the rose is dead,
Are heaped for the beloved's bed;
And so thy thoughts, when thou art gone,
Love itself shall slumber on. *(1821)*

To ———

One word is too often profaned
    For me to profane it,
One feeling too falsely disdain'd
    For thee to disdain it;
One hope is too like despair
    For prudence to smother,
And Pity from thee more dear
    Than that from another.

I can give not what men call love;
    But wilt thou accept not *10*
The worship the heart lifts above
    And the Heavens reject not,—
The desire of the moth for the star,
    Of the night for the morrow,
The devotion to something afar
    From the sphere of our
        sorrow? *(1821)*

Lines: When the Lamp Is Shattered

When the lamp is shattered
The light in the dust lies dead—
    When the cloud is scattered
The rainbow's glory is shed.
    When the lute is broken,
Sweet tones are remembered not;
    When the lips have spoken,
Loved accents are soon forgot.

    As music and splendour
Survive not the lamp and the lute, *10*
    The heart's echoes render
No song when the spirit is mute:—
    No song but sad dirges,
Like the wind through a ruined cell,
    Or the mournful surges
That ring the dead seaman's knell.

    When hearts have once mingled
Love first leaves the well-built nest;
    The weak one is singled
To endure what it once possessed. *20*
    O Love! who bewailest
The frailty of all things here,
    Why choose you the frailest
For your cradle, your home, and your
        bier?

    Its passions will rock thee
As the storms rock the raven on high;
    Bright season will mock thee,
Like the sun from a wintry sky.
    From thy nest every rafter
Will rot, and thine eagle home *30*
    Leave thee naked to laughter,
When leaves fall and cold winds come.
        (1822)

JOHN KEATS • 1795–1821

On First Looking into Chapman's Homer[1]

Much have I travelled in the realms of gold,
And many goodly states and kingdoms seen;
Round many western islands have I been
Which bards in fealty to Apollo[2] hold.
Oft of one wide expanse had I been told
That deep-browed Homer ruled as his demesne;[3]
Yet did I never breathe its pure serene
Till I heard Chapman speak out loud and bold:
Then felt I like some watcher of the skies
When a new planet swims into his ken; 10
Or like stout Cortez[4] when with eagle eyes
He stared at the Pacific—and all his men
Looked at each other with a wild surmise—
Silent, upon a peak in Darien. *(1816)*

On the Grasshopper and the Cricket

The poetry of earth is never dead:
When all the birds are faint with the hot sun,
And hide in cooling trees, a voice will run
From hedge to hedge about the new-mown mead;
That is the Grasshopper's—he takes the lead
In summer luxury,—he has never done
With his delights; for when tired out with fun
He rests at ease beneath some pleasant weed.
The poetry of earth is ceasing never:
On a lone winter evening, when the frost 10
Has wrought a silence, from the stove there shrills
The Cricket's song, in warmth increasing ever,
And seems to one in drowsiness half lost,
The Grasshopper's among some grassy hills. *(1816)*

---

[1] George Chapman (c. 1559–1634) published translations of *The Iliad* (1611) and *The Odyssey* (1616).
[2] god of poetry   [3] estate
[4] Hernando Cortez (1485–1547), Spanish conqueror of Mexico. Actually it was Vasco Nuñez de Balboa (1475–1517) who first sighted the Pacific from a mountain in Darien, a region in eastern Panama.

Lines on the Mermaid Tavern[1]

Souls of poets dead and gone,
What Elysium[2] have ye known,
Happy field or mossy cavern,
Choicer than the Mermaid Tavern?
Have ye tippled drink more fine
Than mine host's Canary wine?
Or are fruits of paradise
Sweeter than those dainty pies
Of venison? O generous food!
Dressed as though bold Robin
    Hood   10
Would, with his maid Marian,
Sup and bowse[3] from horn and can.

    I have heard that on a day
Mine host's sign-board flew away,
Nobody knew whither, till
An astrologer's old quill
To a sheepskin gave the story,
Said he saw you in your glory,
Underneath a new old sign
Sipping beverage divine,   20
And pledging with contented smack
The Mermaid in the Zodiac.[4]
    Souls of Poets dead and gone,
What Elysium have ye known,
Happy field or mossy cavern,
Choicer than the Mermaid
    Tavern?   (*1818*)

When I Have Fears That I May Cease to Be

When I have fears that I may cease to be
Before my pen has gleaned my teeming brain,
Before high-pilèd books, in charactery,
Hold like rich garners the full ripened grain;
When I behold, upon the night's starred face,
Huge cloudy symbols of a high romance,
And think that I may never live to trace
Their shadows, with the magic hand of chance;
And when I feel, fair creature of an hour,
That I shall never look upon thee more,   10
Never have relish in the faery power
Of unreflecting love;—then on the shore
Of the wide world I stand alone, and think
Till love and fame to nothingness do sink.   (*1818*)

Bright Star! Would I Were Steadfast As Thou Art

Bright star! would I were steadfast as thou art—
Not in lone splendour hung aloft the night
And watching, with eternal lids apart,
Like Nature's patient, sleepless Eremite,[1]
The moving waters at their priestlike task
Of pure ablution round earth's human shores,
Or grazing on the new soft fallen mask

---

[1] a favorite London gathering place of Elizabethan poets
[2] in classical mythology, the abode of the blessed either in the western regions of the earth or in the underworld
[3] carouse
[4] a ring of constellations lying along the sun's path

[1] hermit; one who keeps a vigil

Of snow upon the mountains and the moors—
   No—yet still steadfast, still unchangeable,
   Pillow'd upon my fair love's ripening breast,   10
   To feel for ever its soft fall and swell,
   Awake for ever in a sweet unrest,
   Still, still to hear her tender-taken breath,
   And so live ever—or else swoon to death.   (*1819*)

La Belle Dame sans Merci

O what can ail thee, knight-at-arms,
   Alone and palely loitering?
The sedge has wither'd from the lake,
   And no birds sing.

O what can ail thee, knight-at-arms,
   So haggard and so woe-begone?
The squirrel's granary is full,
   And the harvest's done.

I see a lily on thy brow
   With anguish moist and fever dew,   10
And on thy cheek a fading rose
   Fast withereth too.

I met a lady in the meads,
   Full beautiful—a faery's child,
Her hair was long, her foot was light,
   And her eyes were wild.

I made a garland for her head,
   And bracelets too, and fragrant zone;
She look'd at me as she did love,
   And made sweet moan.   20

I set her on my pacing steed,
   And nothing else saw all day long,
For sidelong would she bend, and sing
   A faery's song.

She found me roots of relish sweet,
   And honey wild, and manna dew,
And sure in language strange she said—
   "I love thee true."

She took me to her elfin grot,
   And there she wept, and sigh'd full sore.   30
And there I shut her wild wild eyes
   With kisses four.

And there she lullèd me asleep,
   And there I dream'd—Ah! woe betide!
The latest dream I ever dream'd
   On the cold hill side.

I saw pale kings and princes too,
   Pale warriors, death-pale were they all;
They cried—"La Belle Dame sans Merci
   Hath thee in thrall!"   40

I saw their starved lips in the gloam,
   With horrid warning gapèd wide,
And I awoke and found me here,
   On the cold hill's side.

And this is why I sojourn here,
   Alone and palely loitering,
Though the sedge is wither'd from the lake,
   And no birds sing.   (*1819*)

Ode on a Grecian Urn

   Thou still unravished bride of quietness,
      Thou foster-child of silence and slow time,
   Sylvan historian, who canst thus express
      A flowery tale more sweetly than our rhyme:

What leaf-fringed legend haunts about thy shape
   Of deities or mortals, or of both,
      In Tempe[1] or the dales of Arcady?[2]
What men or gods are these? What maidens loth?
What mad pursuit? What struggle to escape?
      What pipes and timbrels? What wild ecstasy?   *10*

Heard melodies are sweet, but those unheard
   Are sweeter; therefore, ye soft pipes, play on;
Not to the sensual ear, but, more endeared,
   Pipe to the spirit ditties of no tone:
Fair youth, beneath the trees, thou canst not leave
   Thy song, nor ever can those trees be bare;
      Bold Lover, never, never canst thou kiss,
Though winning near the goal—yet, do not grieve;
   She cannot fade, though thou hast not thy bliss,
      For ever wilt thou love, and she be fair!   *20*

Ah, happy, happy boughs! that cannot shed
   Your leaves, nor ever bid the spring adieu;
And, happy melodist, unwearièd,
   For ever piping songs for ever new;
More happy love! more happy, happy love!
   For ever warm and still to be enjoyed,
      For ever panting, and for ever young;
All breathing human passion far above,
   That leaves a heart high-sorrowful and cloyed,
      A burning forehead, and a parching tongue.   *30*

Who are these coming to the sacrifice?
   To what green altar, O mysterious priest,
Lead'st thou that heifer lowing at the skies,
   And all her silken flanks with garlands dressed?
What little town by river or sea shore,
   Or mountain-built with peaceful citadel,
      Is emptied of this folk, this pious morn?
And, little town, thy streets for evermore
   Will silent be; and not a soul to tell
      Why thou art desolate, can e'er return.   *40*

O Attic[3] shape! Fair attitude! with brede[4]
   Of marble men and maidens overwrought,
With forest branches and the trodden weed;
   Thou, silent form, dost tease us out of thought
As doth eternity: Cold Pastoral!
   When old age shall this generation waste,

---

[1] valley in Thessaly, noted for natural beauty
[2] Arcadia, a region in Peloponnesus which is usually the setting for pastoral poetry
[3] of Attica; hence, "classic"
[4] embroidery

　　　　　Thou shalt remain, in midst of other woe
　　　Than ours, a friend to man, to whom thou say'st,
　　　　　"Beauty is truth, truth beauty,"—that is all
　　　　　　Ye know on earth, and all ye need to know.　(*1819*)

Ode on Melancholy

　　　No, no, go not to Lethe,[1] neither twist
　　　　Wolf's bane,[2] tight-rooted, for its poisonous wine;
　　　Nor suffer thy pale forehead to be kissed
　　　　By nightshade, ruby grape of Prosperine;[3]
　　　Make not your rosary of yew-berries,[4]
　　　　Nor let the beetle, nor the death-moth be
　　　　　Your mournful Psyche,[5] nor the downy owl
　　　A partner in your sorrow's mysteries;
　　　　For shade to shade will come too drowsily,
　　　　　And drown the wakeful anguish of the soul.

　　　But when the melancholy fit shall fall
　　　　Sudden from heaven like a weeping cloud,
　　　That fosters the droop-headed flowers all,
　　　　And hides the green hill in an April shroud;
　　　Then glut thy sorrow on a morning rose,
　　　　Or on the rainbow of the salt sand-wave,
　　　　　Or on the wealth of globèd peonies;
　　　Or if thy mistress some rich anger shows,
　　　　Emprison her soft hand, and let her rave,
　　　　　And feed deep, deep upon her peerless eyes.

　　　She dwells with Beauty—Beauty that must die;
　　　　And Joy, whose hand is ever at his lips
　　　Bidding adieu; and aching Pleasure nigh,
　　　　Turning to poison while the bee-mouth sips:
　　　Ay, in the very temple of delight
　　　　Veiled Melancholy has her sovran shrine,
　　　　　Though seen of none save him whose strenuous
　　　　　　tongue
　　　Can burst Joy's grape against his palate fine;
　　　　His soul shall taste the sadness of her might,
　　　　　And be among her cloudy trophies hung.　(*1819*)

---

[1] river of forgetfulness in Hades
[2] like nightshade, a poisonous herb
[3] queen of the underworld
[4] yew is associated with death and funerals
[5] the soul

Ode to a Nightingale

My heart aches, and a drowsy numbness pains
    My sense, as though of hemlock[1] I had drunk,
Or emptied some dull opiate to the drains
    One minute past, and Lethe-wards[2] had sunk:
'Tis not through envy of thy happy lot,
    But being too happy in thine happiness,—
        That thou, light-wingèd Dryad[3] of the trees,
            In some melodious plot
    Of beechen green, and shadows numberless,
        Singest of summer in full-throated ease.   *10*

O, for a draught of vintage! that hath been
    Cooled a long age in the deep-delvèd earth,
Tasting of Flora[4] and the country green,
    Dance, and Provençal[5] song, and sunburnt mirth!
O for a beaker full of the warm South,
    Full of the true, the blushful Hippocrene,[6]
        With beaded bubbles winking at the brim,
            And purple-stainèd mouth;
    That I might drink, and leave the world unseen,
        And with thee fade away into the forest dim: *20*

Fade far away, dissolve, and quite forget
    What thou among the leaves hast never known,
The weariness, the fever, and the fret
    Here, where men sit and hear each other groan;
Where palsy shakes a few, sad, last gray hairs,
    Where youth grows pale, and spectre-thin, and dies;
        Where but to think is to be full of sorrow
            And leaden-eyed despairs,
    Where Beauty cannot keep her lustrous eyes,
        Or new Love pine at them beyond to-morrow.   *30*

Away! away! for I will fly to thee,
    Not charioted by Bacchus[7] and his pards,[8]
But on the viewless wings of Poesy,
    Though the dull brain perplexes and retards:
Already with thee! tender is the night,
    And haply the Queen-Moon is on her throne,
        Clustered around by all her starry Fays;[9]
            But here is no light,

---

[1] a poisonous herb administered as a liquid
[2] toward Lethe, the river of forgetfulness in Hades   [3] wood nymph
[4] goddess of flowers; hence, flowers
[5] of Provence, a province of France noted for its minstrelsy
[6] a fountain on Mt. Helicon, sacred to the Muses   [7] god of wine   [8] leopards
[9] fairies

  Save what from heaven is with the breezes blown
   Through verdurous glooms and winding mossy
    ways.

I cannot see what flowers are at my feet,
 Nor what soft incense hangs upon the boughs,
But, in embalmèd darkness, guess each sweet
 Wherewith the seasonable month endows
The grass, the thicket, and the fruit-tree wild;
 White hawthorn, and the pastoral eglantine;
  Fast fading violets covered up in leaves;
   And mid-May's eldest child,
 The coming musk-rose, full of dewy wine,
  The murmurous haunt of flies on summer eves.

Darkling I listen; and, for many a time
 I have been half in love with easeful Death,
Called him soft names in many a musèd rhyme,
 To take into the air my quiet breath;
Now more than ever seems it rich to die,
 To cease upon the midnight with no pain,
  While thou art pouring forth thy soul abroad
   In such an ecstasy!
 Still wouldst thou sing, and I have ears in vain—
  To thy high requiem become a sod.

Thou wast not born for death, immortal Bird!
 No hungry generations tread thee down;
The voice I hear this passing night was heard
 In ancient days by emperor and clown:[10]
Perhaps the self-same song that found a path
 Through the sad heart of Ruth,[11] when, sick for home,
  She stood in tears amid the alien corn;
   The same that oft-times hath
 Charmed magic casements, opening on the foam
  Of perilous seas, in faery lands forlorn.

Forlorn! the very word is like a bell
 To toll me back from thee to my sole self!
Adieu! the fancy cannot cheat so well
 As she is famed to do, deceiving elf.
Adieu! adieu! thy plaintive anthem fades
 Past the near meadows, over the still stream,
  Up the hill-side; and now 'tis buried deep
   In the next valley-glades:
 Was it a vision, or a waking dream?
  Fled is that music:—Do I wake or sleep? (*1819*)

[10] farm hand
[11] heroine of the Old Testament Book of Ruth, who went with her mother-in-law to an alien land

To Autumn

Season of mists and mellow fruitfulness,
    Close bosom-friend of the maturing sun;
Conspiring with him how to load and bless
    With fruit the vines that round the thatch-eves run;
To bend with apples the mossed cottage-trees,
    And fill all fruit with ripeness to the core;
        To swell the gourd, and plump the hazel shells
    With a sweet kernel; to set budding more,
And still more, later flowers for the bees,
Until they think warm days will never cease,   10
        For Summer has o'er-brimmed their clammy cells.

Who hath not seen thee oft amid thy store?
    Sometimes whoever seeks abroad may find
Thee sitting careless on a granary floor,
    Thy hair soft-lifted by the winnowing wind;
Or on a half-reaped furrow sound asleep,
    Drowsed with the fume of poppies, while thy hook
        Spares the next swath and all its twinèd flowers:
And sometimes like a gleaner thou dost keep
    Steady thy laden head across a brook;   20
    Or by a cider-press, with patient look,
        Thou watchest the last oozings hours by hours.

Where are the songs of Spring? Ay, where are they?
    Think not of them, thou hast thy music too,—
While barred clouds bloom the soft-dying day,
    And touch the stubble-plains with rosy hue;
Then in a wailful choir the small gnats mourn
    Among the river sallows[1] borne aloft
        Or sinking as the light wind lives or dies;
And full-grown lambs loud bleat from hilly bourn;[2]   30
    Hedge-crickets sing; and now with treble soft
    The red-breast whistles from a garden-croft;[3]
        And gathering swallows twitter in the skies.   (*1819*)

---

[1] willows   [2] field   [3] enclosed garden

JOHN HENRY, CARDINAL NEWMAN • 1801–1890

The Pillar of the Cloud

Lead, Kindly Light, amid the encircling gloom,
    Lead Thou me on!
The night is dark, and I am far from home—
    Lead Thou me on!
Keep Thou my feet; I do not ask to see
The distant scene,—one step enough for me.

I was not ever thus, nor pray'd that Thou
    Shouldst lead me on.
I loved to choose and see my path; but now
    Lead Thou me on!   10
I loved the garish day, and, spite of fears,
Pride ruled my will: remember not past years.

So long Thy power hath blest me, sure it still
    Will lead me on,
O'er moor and fen, o'er crag and torrent, till
    The night is gone;
And with the morn those angel faces smile
Which I have loved long since, and lost awhile. (*1833*)

THOMAS LOVELL BEDDOES • 1803–1849

Stanzas from the Ivory Gate[1]

The mighty thought of an old world
Fans, like a dragon's wing unfurled,
    The surface of my yearnings deep;
And solemn shadows then awake,
Like the fish-lizard in the lake,
    Troubling a planet's morning sleep.

My waking is a Titan's[2] dream,
Where a strange sun, long set, doth beam
    Through Montezuma's[3] cypress
        bough:
Through the fern wilderness forlorn   10
Glisten the giant harts' great horn,
    And serpents vast with helmèd brow.

The measureless from caverns rise
With steps of earthquake, thunderous
    cries,
    And graze upon the lofty wood;
The palmy grove, through which doth
    gleam
Such antediluvian ocean's steam,
    Haunts shadowy my domestic mood.
                  (*c. 1837*)

---

[1] In *The Odyssey* deceptive dreams come from the Gate of Ivory, true dreams from the Gate of Horn.
[2] The Titans were children of Uranus (heaven) and Gaea (earth), a race of giants who stormed heaven.
[3] Aztec ruler of Mexico at the time of the Spanish Conquest

EDGAR ALLAN POE • 1809–1849

Romance

Romance, who loves to nod and sing,
With drowsy head and folded wing,
Among the green leaves as they shake
Far down within some shadowy lake,
To me a painted paroquet
Hath been—a most familiar bird—
Taught me my alphabet to say—
To lisp my very earliest word
While in the wild wood I did lie,
A child—with a most knowing eye. *10*

Of late, eternal Condor years
So shake the very Heaven on high
With tumult as they thunder by,
I have no time for idle cares
Through gazing on the unquiet sky.
And when an hour with calmer wings
Its down upon my spirit flings—
That little time with lyre and rhyme
To while away—forbidden things!
My heart would feel to be a crime *20*
Unless it trembled with the
 strings. (*1829*)

The City in the Sea

Lo! Death has reared himself a throne
In a strange city lying alone
Far down within the dim West,
Where the good and the bad and the
 worst and the best
Have gone to their eternal rest.
There shrines and palaces and towers
(Time-eaten towers that tremble not!)
Resemble nothing that is ours.
Around, by lifting winds forgot,
Resignedly beneath the sky *10*
The melancholy waters lie.

No rays from the holy heaven come down
On the long night-time of that town;
But light from out the lurid sea
Streams up the turrets silently—
Gleams up the pinnacles far and free—
Up domes—up spires—up kingly halls—
Up fanes—up Babylon-like walls—
Up shadowy long-forgotten bowers
Of sculptured ivy and stone
 flowers— *20*
Up many and many a marvellous shrine
Whose wreathèd friezes intertwine
The viol, the violet, and the vine.
Resignedly beneath the sky
The melancholy waters lie.
So blend the turrets and shadows there
That all seem pendulous in air,
While from a proud tower in the town
Death looks gigantically down.

There open fanes and gaping graves *30*
Yawn level with the luminous waves;
But not the riches there that lie
In each idol's diamond eye—
Not the gayly-jewelled dead
Tempt the waters from their bed;
For no ripples curl, alas!
Along that wilderness of glass—
No swellings tell that winds may be
Upon some far-off happier sea—
No heavings hint that winds have
 been *40*
On seas less hideously serene.

But lo, a stir is in the air!
The wave—there is a movement there!
As if the towers had thrust aside,
In slightly sinking, the dull tide—
As if their tops had feebly given
A void within the filmy Heaven.
The waves have now a redder glow—
The hours are breathing faint and low—
And when, amid no earthly moans,
Down, down that town shall settle hence,
Hell, rising from a thousand thrones,
Shall do it reverence. (*1831*)

OLIVER WENDELL HOLMES • 1809-1894

The Chambered Nautilus

This is the ship of pearl, which, poets feign,
    Sails the unshadowed main,—
    The venturous bark that flings
On the sweet summer wind its purpled wings
In gulfs enchanted, where the Siren[2] sings.
    And coral reefs lie bare,
Where the cold sea-maids rise to sun their streaming hair.

Its webs of living gauze no more unfurl;
    Wrecked is the ship of pearl!
    And every chambered cell,
Where its dim dreaming life was wont to dwell,
As the frail tenant shaped his growing shell,
    Before thee lies revealed,—
Its irised ceiling rent, its sunless crypt unsealed!

Year after year beheld the silent toil
    That spread his lustrous coil;
    Still, as the spiral grew,
He left the past year's dwelling for the new,
Stole with soft step its shining archway through,
    Built up its idle door,
Stretched in his last-found home, and knew the old no more.

Thanks for the heavenly message brought by thee,
    Child of the wandering sea,
    Cast from her lap, forlorn!
From thy dead lips a clearer note is born
Than ever Triton[3] blew from wreathèd horn!
    While on mine ear it rings,
Through the deep caves of thought I hear a voice that sings:—

Build thee more stately mansions, O my soul,
    As the swift seasons roll!
    Leave thy low-vaulted past!
Let each new temple, nobler than the last,
Shut thee from heaven with a dome more vast,
    Till thou at length art free,
Leaving thine outgrown shell by life's unresting sea! *(1858)*

---

[1] a shellfish which develops a spiral shell in which each year's growth is divided from earlier portions by a septum
[2] sea nymph whose song enthralled passing voyagers
[3] sea god who blew his horn to calm the waves

EDWARD FITZGERALD • 1809–1883

from The Rubáiyát of Omar Khayyám of Naishápúr[1]

I–1

Awake! for Morning in the Bowl of Night
Has flung the Stone that puts the Stars to Flight:
   And Lo! the Hunter of the East has caught
The Sultán's Turret in a Noose of Light.

I–3

And, as the Cock crew, those who stood before
The Tavern shouted—"Open then the Door!
   "You know how little while we have to stay,
"And once departed, may return no more."

V–7

Come, fill the Cup, and in the fire of Spring
Your Winter garment of Repentance fling:
   The Bird of Time has but a little way
To flutter—and the Bird is on the Wing.

I–8

And look—a thousand Blossoms with the Day
Woke—and a thousand scatter'd into Clay:
   And this first Summer Month that brings the Rose
Shall take Jamshyd and Kaikobád[2] away.

V–11

With me along the strip of Herbage strown
That just divides the desert from the sown,
   Where name of Slave and Sultán is forgot—
And Peace of Mahmúd[3] on his golden Throne!

V–12

A Book of Verses underneath the Bough,
A Jug of Wine, a Loaf of Bread—and Thou
   Beside me singing in the Wilderness—
Oh, Wilderness were Paradise enow!

V–13

Some for the Glories of This World; and some
Sigh for the Prophet's[4] Paradise to come;

---

[1] FitzGerald's poem is a free rendering of a Persian original written in *rubā 'ī* (quatrains rhyming *a a x a*) by Omar the Tentmaker (died c. 1123), a mathematician, astronomer, and poet from Naishápúr, a Persian town. The editor has selected stanzas from both the first and fifth editions, as indicated by the numbering of the quatrains.
[2] first king of the Kaianian dynasty of Persia
[3] of Ghazni (971–1030), Moslem conqueror of India
[4] Mohammed's

Ah, take the Cash, and let the Credit go,
Nor heed the rumble of a distant Drum!

v–14

Look to the blowing Rose about us—"Lo
Laughing," she says, "into the world I blow,
  "At once the silken tassel of my Purse
"Tear, and its Treasure on the Garden throw."

v–15

And those who husbanded the Golden grain,
And those who flung it to the winds like Rain,
  Alike to no such aureate[5] Earth are turn'd
As, buried once, Men want dug up again.

v–16

The Worldly Hope men set their Hearts upon
Turns Ashes—or it prospers; and anon,
  Like Snow upon the Desert's dusty Face,
Lighting a little hour or two—is gone.

v–17

Think, in this batter'd Caravanserai[6]
Whose Portals are alternate Night and Day,
  How Sultán after Sultán with his Pomp
Abode his destined Hour, and went his way.

v–18

They say the Lion and the Lizard keep
The courts where Jamshyd gloried and drank deep:
  And Bahrám,[7] that great Hunter—the Wild Ass
Stamps o'er his Head, but cannot break his Sleep.

v–19

I sometimes think that never blows so red
The Rose as where some buried Caesar bled;
  That every Hyacinth the Garden wears
Dropt in her Lap from some once lovely Head.

v–20

And this reviving Herb whose tender Green
Fledges the River-Lip on which we lean—
  Ah, lean upon it lightly! for who knows
From what once lovely Lip it springs unseen!

I–47

And if the Wine you drink, the Lip you press,
End in the Nothing all Things end in—Yes—

---

[5] golden
[6] inn for the accommodation of caravans
[7] a Persian ruler who died in a swamp while hunting the wild ass

Then fancy while Thou art, Thou art but what
Thou shalt be—Nothing—thou shalt not be less.

v–43

So when that Angel of the darker Drink
At last shall find you by the river-brink,
   And, offering his Cup, invite your Soul
Forth to your Lips to quaff—you shall not shrink.

1–42

And lately, by the Tavern Door agape,
Came stealing through the Dusk an Angel Shape
   Bearing a Vessel on his Shoulder; and
He bid me taste of it; and 'twas—the Grape!

1–43

The Grape that can with Logic absolute
The Two-and-Seventy jarring Sects[8] confute:
   The subtle Alchemist that in a Trice
Life's leaden Metal into Gold transmute.

v–71

The Moving Finger writes; and, having writ,
Moves on: nor all your Piety nor Wit
   Shall lure it back to cancel half a Line,
Nor all your Tears wash out a Word of it.

v–72

And that inverted Bowl they call the Sky,
Whereunder crawling coop'd we live and die,
   Lift not your hands to *It* for help—for It
As impotently moves as you or I.

1–57

Oh Thou, who didst with Pitfall and with Gin
Beset the Road I was to wander in,
   Thou wilt not with Predestination round
Enmesh me, and impute my Fall to Sin?

1–67

Ah, with the Grape my fading Life provide,
And wash my Body whence the Life has died,
   And in a Winding-sheet of Vine-leaf wrapt,
So bury me by some sweet Garden-side.

1–68

That ev'n my buried Ashes such a Snare
Of Perfume shall fling up into the Air,

---

[8] the number of religious sects assumed to exist in the world

As not a True Believer passing by
But shall be overtaken unaware.

1–69

Indeed the Idols I have loved so long
Have done my Credit in Men's Eyes much wrong:
   Have drown'd my Honour in a shallow Cup
And sold my Reputation for a Song.

v–95

And much as Wine has play'd the Infidel,
And robb'd me of my Robe of Honour—Well,
   I wonder often what the Vintners buy
One half so precious as the stuff they sell.

v–96

Yet Ah, that Spring should vanish with the Rose!
That Youth's sweet-scented manuscript should close!
   The Nightingale that in the branches sang,
Ah whence, and whither flown again, who knows!

1–73

Ah Love! could thou and I with Fate conspire
To grasp this sorry Scheme of Things entire,
   Would not we shatter it to bits—and then
Remould it nearer to the Heart's Desire!

1–74

Ah, Moon of my Delight who know'st no wane,
The Moon of Heav'n is rising once again:
   How oft hereafter rising shall she look
Through this same Garden after me—in vain!

1–75

And when Thyself with shining Foot shall pass
Among the Guests Star-scattered on the Grass,
   And in thy joyous Errand reach the Spot
Where I made one—turn down an empty Glass!

Tamám shud[9] (*1859; 1879*)

---

[9] It is finished.

ALFRED, LORD TENNYSON • 1809–1892

The Kraken[1]

Below the thunders of the upper deep;
Far, far beneath in the abysmal sea,
His ancient, dreamless, uninvaded sleep
The Kraken sleepeth: faintest sunlights flee
About his shadowy sides: above him swell
Huge sponges of millennial growth and height;
And far away into the sickly light,
From many a wondrous grot and secret cell
Unnumber'd and enormous polypi
Winnow with giant arms the slumbering green.   10
There hath he lain for ages and will lie
Battening upon huge seaworms in his sleep,
Until the latter fire shall heat the deep;
Then once by man and angels to be seen,
In roaring he shall rise and on the surface die.   (1830)

Break, Break, Break

Break, break, break,
   On thy cold gray stones, O Sea!
And I would that my tongue could utter
   The thoughts that arise in me.

O well for the fisherman's boy,
   That he shouts with his sister at play!
O well for the sailor lad,
   That he sings in his boat on the bay!

And the stately ships go on
   To their haven under the hill;   10
But O for the touch of a vanish'd hand,
   And the sound of a voice that is still!

Break, break, break,
   At the foot of thy crags, O Sea!
But the tender grace of a day that is dead
   Will never come back to me.   (1842)

Ulysses[1]

It little profits that an idle king,
By this still hearth, among these barren crags,
Matched with an agèd wife,[2] I mete and dole
Unequal laws unto a savage race,
That hoard, and sleep, and feed, and know not me.
I cannot rest from travel; I will drink
Life to the lees. All times I have enjoyed
Greatly, have suffered greatly, both with those
That loved me, and alone; on shore, and when
Thro' scudding drifts the rainy Hyades[3]   10
Vext the dim sea. I am become a name;
For always roaming with a hungry heart
Much have I seen and known,—cities of men

---

[1] a legendary sea creature of enormous bulk

[1] Tennyson takes his theme from Dante, who, in *The Inferno*, depicts the hero of *The Odyssey* as restless and eager to continue the search for knowledge and virtue.

[2] Penelope

[3] a constellation whose rising at the same time as the sun was anciently believed to bring rain

And manners, climates, councils, governments,
Myself not least, but honored of them all,—
And drunk delight of battle with my peers,
Far on the ringing plains of windy Troy.
I am a part of all that I have met;
Yet all experience is an arch wherethro'
Gleams that untravelled world whose margin fades 20
For ever and for ever when I move.
How dull it is to pause, to make an end,
To rust unburnished, not to shine in use!
As tho' to breathe were life! Life piled on life
Were all too little, and of one to me
Little remains; but every hour is saved
From that eternal silence, something more,
A bringer of new things; and vile it were
For some three suns to store and hoard myself,
And this gray spirit yearning in desire 30
To follow knowledge like a sinking star,
Beyond the utmost bound of human thought.
    This is my son, mine own Telemachus,
To whom I leave the sceptre and the isle,[4]
Well-loved of me, discerning to fulfill
This labor, by slow prudence to make mild
A rugged people, and thro' soft degrees
Subdue them to the useful and the good.
Most blameless is he, centred in the sphere
Of common duties, decent not to fail 40
In offices of tenderness, and pay
Meet adoration to my household gods,
When I am gone. He works his work, I mine.
    There lies the port; the vessel puffs her sail;
There gloom the dark, broad seas. My mariners,
Souls that have toiled, and wrought, and thought with me,—
That ever with a frolic welcome took
The thunder and the sunshine, and opposed
Free hearts, free foreheads,—you and I are old;
Old age hath yet his honor and his toil. 50
Death closes all; but something ere the end,
Some work of noble note, may yet be done,
Not unbecoming men that strove with Gods.
The lights begin to twinkle from the rocks;
The long day wanes; the slow moon climbs; the deep
Moans round with many voices. Come, my friends.
'T is not too late to seek a newer world.
Push off, and sitting well in order smite
The sounding furrows; for my purpose holds
To sail beyond the sunset, and the baths 60

[4] Ithaca

Of all the western stars, until I die.
It may be that the gulfs will wash us down;
It may be we shall touch the Happy Isles,[5]
And see the great Achilles,[6] whom we knew.
Tho' much is taken, much abides; and tho'
We are not now that strength which in old days
Moved earth and heaven, that which we are, we are,—
One equal temper of heroic hearts,
Made weak by time and fate, but strong in will
To strive, to seek, to find, and not to yield.   (*1842*)

Songs from The Princess

SWEET AND LOW

Sweet and low, sweet and low,
   Wind of the western sea,
Low, low, breathe and blow,
   Wind of the western sea!
Over the rolling waters go,
Come from the dying moon, and blow,
   Blow him again to me;
While my little one, while my pretty one, sleeps.

Sleep and rest, sleep and rest,
   Father will come to thee soon;
Rest, rest, on mother's breast,
   Father will come to thee soon;
Father will come to his babe in the nest,
Silver sails all out of the west
   Under the silver moon:
Sleep, my little one, sleep, my pretty one, sleep.

THE SPLENDOUR FALLS ON CASTLE WALLS

The splendour falls on castle walls
   And snowy summits old in story:
The long light shakes across the lakes,
   And the wild cataract leaps in glory.
Blow, bugle, blow, set the wild echoes flying,
Blow, bugle; answer, echoes, dying, dying, dying.

O hark, O hear; how thin and clear,
   And thinner, clearer, farther going!

---

[5] the Islands of the Blessed in the western extremity of the ocean

[6] the major hero of the Trojan War, in which he was killed

O sweet and far from cliff and scar
    The horns of Elfland faintly blowing!
Blow, let us hear the purple glens replying:
Blow, bugle; answer, echoes, dying, dying, dying.

O love, they die in yon rich sky,
    They faint on hill or field or river:
Our echoes roll from soul to soul,
    And grow for ever and for ever.
Blow, bugle, blow, set the wild echoes flying,
And answer, echoes, answer, dying, dying, dying.

NOW SLEEPS THE CRIMSON PETAL

Now sleeps the crimson petal now the white;
Nor waves the cypress in the palace walk;
Nor winks the gold fin in the porphyry font.
The fire-fly wakens; waken thou with me.

    Now droops the milk-white peacock like a ghost,
And like a ghost she glimmers on to me.

    Now lies the Earth all Danaë[1] to the stars,
And all thy heart lies open unto me.

    Now slides the silent meteor on, and leaves
A shining furrow, as thy thoughts in me.

    Now folds the lily all her sweetness up,
And slips into the bosom of the lake.
So fold thyself, my dearest, thou, and slip
Into my bosom and be lost in me.   (*1850*)

The Eagle

FRAGMENT

He clasps the crag with crooked hands;
Close to the sun in lonely lands,
Ring'd with the azure world, he stands.

The wrinkled sea beneath him crawls;
He watches from his mountain walls,
And like a thunderbolt he falls.   (*1851*)

---

[1] a princess of Greek mythology who was impregnated by Zeus disguised as a golden shower

De Profundis: I

  Out of the deep, my child, out of the deep,
  Where all that was to be, in all that was,
  Whirled for a million eons through the vast
  Waste dawn of multitudinous-eddying light—
  Out of the deep, my child, out of the deep,
  Through all this changing world of changeless law,
  And every phase of ever-heightening life,
  And nine long months of antenatal gloom,
  With this last moon, this crescent—her dark orb
  Touched with earth's light—thou comest, darling boy;   *10*
  Our own; a babe in lineament and limb
  Perfect, and prophet of the perfect man;
  Whose face and form are hers and mine in one,
  Indissolubly married like our love;
  Live, and be happy in thyself, and serve
  This mortal race thy kin so well, that men
  May bless thee as we bless thee, O young life
  Breaking with laughter from the dark; and may
  The fated channel where thy motion lives
  Be prosperously shaped, and sway thy course   *20*
  Along the years of haste and random youth
  Unshattered; then full-current through full man;
  And last in kindly curves, with gentlest fall,
  By quiet fields, a slowly-dying power,
  To that last deep where we and thou are still.   (*1880*)

Crossing the Bar[1]

  Sunset and evening star,
    And one clear call for me!
  And may there be no moaning of the bar,
    When I put out to sea,

  But such a tide as moving seems asleep,
    Too full for sound and foam,
  When that which drew from out the
    boundless deep
    Turns again home.

  Twilight and evening bell,
    And after that the dark!   *10*
  And may there be no sadness of farewell,
    When I embark;

---

[1] sandbar partly enclosing a harbor

> For tho' from out our bourne[2] of Time
> and Place
> The flood may bear me far,
> I hope to see my Pilot face to face
> When I have crost the bar.   *(1889)*

ROBERT BROWNING • 1812–1889

Meeting at Night

> The grey sea and the long black land;
> And the yellow half-moon large and low;
> And the startled little waves that leap
> In fiery ringlets from their sleep,
> As I gain the cove with pushing prow,
> And quench its speed i' the slushy sand.
>
> Then a mile of warm sea-scented beach;
> Three fields to cross till a farm appears;
> A tap at the pane, the quick sharp scratch
> And blue spurt of a lighted match,   10
> And a voice less loud, thro' its joys and fears,
> Than the two hearts beating each to each!   *(1845)*

Parting at Morning

> Round the cape of a sudden came the sea,
> And the sun looked over the mountain's
>   rim:
> And straight was a path of gold for him,
> And the need of a world of men for
>   me.   *(1845)*

Home-Thoughts, from Abroad

> Oh, to be in England
> Now that April's there,
> And whoever wakes in England
> Sees, some morning, unaware,
> That the lowest boughs and the brushwood sheaf
> Round the elm-tree bole are in tiny leaf,
> While the chaffinch sings on the orchard bough
> In England—now!

---

[2] realm

And after April, when May follows,
And the whitethroat builds, and all the swallows! 10
Hark, where my blossomed pear-tree in the hedge
Leans to the field and scatters on the clover
Blossoms and dewdrops—at the bent spray's edge—
That's the wise thrush; he sings each song twice over,
Lest you should think he never could recapture
The first fine careless rapture!

And though the fields look rough with hoary dew
All will be gay when noontide wakes anew
The buttercups, the little children's dower—
Far brighter than this gaudy melon-flower. *(1845)* 20

Home-Thoughts, from the Sea

Nobly, nobly Cape Saint Vincent to the north-west died away;
Sunset ran, one glorious blood-red, reeking into Cadiz Bay;
Bluish 'mid the burning water, full in face Trafalgar lay;
In the dimmest north-east distance, dawned Gibraltar grand and grey;
"Here and here did England help me: how can I help England?"—say,
Whoso turns as I, this evening, turn to God to praise and pray,
While Jove's planet rises yonder, silent over Africa. *(1845)*

Up at a Villa—Down in the City

(AS DISTINGUISHED BY AN ITALIAN PERSON OF QUALITY)

Had I but plenty of money, money enough and to spare,
The house for me, no doubt, were a house in the city-square;
Ah, such a life, such a life, as one leads at the window there!

Something to see, by Bacchus, something to hear, at least!
There, the whole day long, one's life is a perfect feast;
While up at a villa one lives, I maintain it, no more than a beast.

Well now, look at our villa! stuck like the horn of a bull
Just on a mountain-edge as bare as the creature's skull,
Save a mere shag of a bush with hardly a leaf to pull!
—I scratch my own, sometimes, to see if the hair's turned wool. 10

But the city, oh the city—the square with the houses! Why?
They are stone-faced, white as a curd, there's something to take the eye!
Houses in four straight lines, not a single front awry;
You watch who crosses and gossips, who saunters, who hurries by;
Green blinds, as a matter of course, to draw when the sun gets high;
And the shops with fanciful signs which are painted properly.

What of a villa? Though winter be over in March by rights,
'Tis May perhaps ere the snow shall have withered well off the heights:
You've the brown ploughed land before, where the oxen steam and wheeze,
And the hills over-smoked behind by the faint gray olive-trees.

Is it better in May, I ask you? You've summer all at once;
In a day he leaps complete with a few strong April suns.
'Mid the sharp short emerald wheat, scarce risen three fingers well,
The wild tulip, at end of its tube, blows out its great red bell
Like a thin clear bubble of blood, for the children to pick and sell.

Is it ever hot in the square? There's a fountain to spout and splash!
In the shade it sings and springs; in the shine such foambows flash
On the horses with curling fish-tails, that prance and paddle and pash
Round the lady atop in her conch—fifty gazers do not abash,
Though all that she wears is some weeds round her waist in a sort of sash.

All the year long at the villa, nothing to see though you linger,
Except yon cypress that points like death's lean lifted forefinger.
Some think fireflies pretty, when they mix i' the corn and mingle,
Or thrid the stinking hemp till the stalks of it seem a-tingle.
Late August or early September, the stunning cicala is shrill,
And the bees keep their tiresome whine round the resinous firs on the hill.
Enough of the seasons,—I spare you the months of the fever and chill.

Ere you open your eyes in the city, the blessed church-bells begin:
No sooner the bells leave off than the diligence rattles in:
You get the pick of the news, and it costs you never a pin.
By and by there's the travelling doctor gives pills, lets blood, draws teeth;
Or the Pulcinello-trumpet breaks up the market beneath.
At the post-office such a scene-picture—the new play, piping hot!
And a notice how, only this morning, three liberal thieves were shot.
Above it, behold the Archbishop's most fatherly of rebukes,
And beneath, with his crown and his lion, some little new law of the Duke's!
Or a sonnet with flowery marge, to the Reverend Don So-and-so,
Who is Dante, Boccaccio, Petrarca, Saint Jerome, and Cicero,
"And moreover," (the sonnet goes rhyming,) "the skirts of Saint Paul had reached,
Having preached us those six Lent-lectures more unctuous than ever he preached."
Noon strikes,—here sweeps the procession! our Lady borne smiling and smart
With a pink gauze gown all spangles, and seven swords stuck in her heart!
Bang-whang-whang goes the drum, *tootle-te-tootle* the fife;
No keeping one's haunches still: it's the greatest pleasure in life.

But bless you, it's dear—it's dear! fowls, wine, at double the rate.
They have clapped a new tax upon salt, and what oil pays passing the gate
It's a horror to think of. And so, the villa for me, not the city!
Beggars can scarcely be choosers: but still—ah, the pity, the pity!

Look, two and two go the priests, then the monks with cowls and sandals,
And the penitents dressed in white shirts, a-holding the yellow candles; 60
One, he carries a flag up straight, and another a cross with handles,
And the Duke's guard brings up the rear, for the better prevention of scandals:
Bang-whang-whang goes the drum, *tootle-te-tootle* the fife.
Oh, a day in the city-square, there is no such pleasure in life!   (*1855*)

"Childe[1] Roland to the Dark Tower Came"

(*SEE EDGAR'S SONG IN "LEAR"*)

1

My first thought was, he lied in every word,
    That hoary cripple, with malicious eye
    Askance to watch the working of his lie
On mine, and mouth scarce able to afford
Suppression of the glee, that pursed and scored
    Its edge, at one more victim gained thereby.

2

What else should he be set for, with his staff?
    What, save to waylay with his lies, ensnare
    All travellers who might find him posted there,
And ask the road? I guessed what skull-like laugh   10
Would break, what crutch 'gin write my epitaph
    For pastime in the dusty thoroughfare,

3

If at his counsel I should turn aside
    Into that ominous tract which, all agree,
    Hides the Dark Tower. Yet acquiescingly
I did turn as he pointed: neither pride
Nor hope rekindling at the end descried,
    So much as gladness that some end might be.

4

For, what with my whole world-wide wandering,
    What with my search drawn out through years, my hope   20
    Dwindled into a ghost not fit to cope
With that obstreperous joy success would bring,
I hardly tried now to rebuke the spring
    My heart made, finding failure in its scope.

5

As when a sick man very near to death
    Seems dead indeed, and feels begin and end
    The tears and takes the farewell of each friend,

---

[1] an apprentice knight

And hears one bid the other go, draw breath
Freelier outside ("since all is o'er," he saith,
    "And the blow fallen no grieving can amend"),   *30*

6

While some discuss if near the other graves
    Be room enough for this, and when a day
    Suits best for carrying the corpse away,
With care about the banners, scarves and staves:
And still the man hears all, and only craves
    He may not shame such tender love and stay.

7

Thus, I had so long suffered in this quest,
    Heard failure prophesied so oft, been writ
    So many times among "The Band"—to wit,
The knights who to the Dark Tower's search addressed   *40*
Their steps—that just to fail as they, seemed best,
    And all the doubt was now—should I be fit?

8

So, quiet as despair, I turned from him,
    That hateful cripple, out of his highway
    Into the path he pointed. All the day
Had been a dreary one at best, and dim
Was settling to its close, yet shot one grim
    Red leer to see the plain catch its estray.

9

For mark! no sooner was I fairly found
    Pledged to the plain, after a pace or two,   *50*
    Than, pausing to throw backward a last view
O'er the safe road, 'twas gone; gray plain all round:
Nothing but plain to the horizon's bound.
    I might go on; naught else remained to do.

10

So, on I went. I think I never saw
    Such starved ignoble nature; nothing throve:
    For flowers—as well expect a cedar grove!
But cockle, spurge, according to their law
Might propagate their kind, with none to awe,
    You'd think; a burr had been a treasure trove.   *60*

11

No! penury, inertness and grimace,
    In some strange sort, were the land's portion. "See
    Or shut your eyes," said Nature peevishly,
"It nothing skills: I cannot help my case;
'Tis the Last Judgment's fire must cure this place,
    Calcine its clods and set my prisoners free."

12

If there pushed any ragged thistle stalk
    Above its mates, the head was chopped; the bents[2]
    Were jealous else. What made those holes and rents
In the dock's harsh swarth leaves, bruised as to balk
All hope of greenness? 'tis a brute must walk
    Pashing their life out, with a brute's intents.

13

As for the grass, it grew as scant as hair
    In leprosy; thin dry blades pricked the mud
    Which underneath looked kneaded up with blood.
One stiff blind horse, his every bone a-stare,
Stood stupefied, however he came there:
    Thrust out past service from the devil's stud!

14

Alive? he might be dead for aught I know,
    With that red gaunt and colloped[3] neck a-strain,
    And shut eyes underneath the rusty mane;
Seldom went such grotesqueness with such woe;
I never saw a brute I hated so;
    He must be wicked to deserve such pain.

15

I shut my eyes and turned them on my heart.
    As a man calls for wine before he fights,
    I asked one draught of earlier, happier sights,
Ere fitly I could hope to play my part.
Think first, fight afterwards—the soldier's art:
    One taste of the old time sets all to rights.

16

Not it! I fancied Cuthbert's reddening face
    Beneath its garniture of curly gold,
    Dear fellow, till I almost felt him fold
An arm in mine to fix me to the place,
That way he used. Alas, one night's disgrace!
    Out went my heart's new fire and left it cold.

17

Giles then, the soul of honor—there he stands
    Frank as ten years ago when knighted first.
    What honest man should dare (he said) he durst.
Good—but the scene shifts—faugh! what hangman hands
Pin to his breast a parchment? His own bands
    Read it. Poor traitor, spit upon and cursed!

[2] coarse grass   [3] ridged

18

Better this present than a past like that;
    Back therefore to my darkening path again!
    No sound, no sight as far as eye could strain.
Will the night send a howlet or a bat?
I asked: when something on the dismal flat
    Came to arrest my thoughts and change their train.

19

A sudden little river crossed my path
    As unexpected as a serpent comes.
    No sluggish tide congenial to the glooms;
This, as it frothed by, might have been a bath
For the fiend's glowing hoof—to see the wrath
    Of its black eddy bespate[4] with flakes and spumes.

20

So petty yet so spiteful! All along,
    Low scrubby alders kneeled down over it;
    Drenched willows flung them headlong in a fit
Of mute despair, a suicidal throng:
The river which had done them all the wrong,
    Whate'er that was, rolled by, deterred no whit.

21

Which, while I forded—good saints, how I feared
    To set my foot upon a dead man's cheek,
    Each step, or feel the spear I thrust to seek
For hollows, tangled in his hair or beard!
—It may have been a water rat I speared,
    But, ugh! it sounded like a baby's shriek.

22

Glad was I when I reached the other bank.
    Now for a better country. Vain presage!
    Who were the strugglers, what war did they wage,
Whose savage trample thus could pad the dank
Soil to a plash? Toads in a poisoned tank,
    Or wild cats in a red-hot iron cage—

23

The fight must so have seemed in that fell cirque.[5]
    What penned them there, with all the plain to choose?
    No footprint leading to that horrid mews,[6]
None out of it. Mad brewage set to work
Their brains, no doubt, like galley slaves the Turk
    Pits for his pastime, Christians against Jews.

---

[4] spattered   [5] amphitheater   [6] pen or enclosed yard

24

And more than that—a furlong on—why, there!
    What bad use was that engine for, that wheel,   140
    Or brake,[7] not wheel—that harrow fit to reel
Men's bodies out like silk? with all the air
Of Tophet's[8] tool, on earth left unaware,
    Or brought to sharpen its rusty teeth of steel.

25

Then came a bit of stubbed ground, once a wood,
    Next a marsh, it would seem, and now mere earth
    Desperate and done with; (so a fool finds mirth,
Makes a thing and then mars it, till his mood
Changes and off he goes!) within a rood[9]—
    Bog, clay and rubble, sand and stark black dearth.   150

26

Now blotches rankling, colored gay and grim,
    Now patches where some leanness of the soil's
    Broke into moss or substances like boils;
Then came some palsied oak, a cleft in him
Like a distorted mouth that splits its rim
    Gaping at death, and dies while it recoils.

27

And just as far as ever from the end!
    Naught in the distance but the evening, naught
    To point my footstep further! At the thought,
A great black bird, Apollyon's[10] bosom friend,   160
Sailed past, nor beat his wide wing dragon-penned[11]
    That brushed my cap—perchance the guide I sought.

28

For, looking up, aware I somehow grew,
    'Spite of the dusk, the plain had given place
    All round to mountains—with such name to grace
Mere ugly heights and heaps now stolen in view.
How thus they had surprised me—solve it, you!
    How to get from them was no clearer case.

29

Yet half I seemed to recognize some trick
    Of mischief happened to me, God knows when—   170
    In a bad dream perhaps. Here ended, then,
Progress this way. When, in the very nick
Of giving up, one time more, came a click
    As when a trap shuts—you're inside the den!

---

[7] a machine for removing fiber from flax stems   [8] Hell's   [9] rod: sixteen feet   [10] Satan's   [11] pinioned

30

Burningly it came on me all at once,
    This was the place! those two hills on the right,
    Crouched like two bulls locked horn in horn in fight;
While to the left, a tall scalped mountain . . . Dunce,
Dotard, a-dozing at the very nonce,
    After a life spent training for the sight!

31

What in the midst lay but the Tower itself?
    The round squat turret, blind as the fool's heart,
    Built of brown stone, without a counterpart
In the whole world. The tempest's mocking elf
Points to the shipman thus the unseen shelf
    He strikes on, only when the timbers start.

32

Not see? because of night perhaps?—why, day
    Came back again for that! before it left,
    The dying sunset kindled through a cleft:
The hills, like giants at a hunting, lay,
Chin upon hand, to see the game at bay—
    "Now stab and end the creature—to the heft!"

33

Not hear? when noise was everywhere! it tolled
    Increasing like a bell. Names in my ears
    Of all the lost adventurers my peers—
How such a one was strong, and such was bold,
And such was fortunate, yet each of old
    Lost, lost! one moment knelled the woe of years.

34

There they stood, ranged along the hillsides, met
    To view the last of me, a living frame
    For one more picture! in a sheet of flame
I saw them and I knew them all. And yet
Dauntless the slug-horn[12] to my lips I set,
    And blew. *"Childe Roland to the Dark Tower came."*   (1852)

---

[12] trumpet

EMILY BRONTË • 1818–1848

Remembrance

Cold in the earth—and the deep snow piled above thee,
Far, far removed, cold in the dreary grave!
Have I forgot, my only Love, to love thee,
Severed at last by Time's all-severing wave?

Now, when alone, do my thoughts no longer hover
Over the mountains, on that northern shore,
Resting their wings where heath and fern-leaves cover
Thy noble heart for ever, ever more?

Cold in the earth—and fifteen wild Decembers,
From those brown hills, have melted into spring: *10*
Faithful, indeed, is the spirit that remembers
After such years of change and suffering!

Sweet Love of youth, forgive, if I forget thee,
While the world's tide is bearing me along;
Other desires and other hopes beset me,
Hopes which obscure, but cannot do thee wrong!

No later light has lightened up my heaven,
No second morn has ever shone for me;
All my life's bliss from thy dear life was given,
All my life's bliss is in the grave with thee. *20*

But, when the days of golden dreams had perished,
And even Despair was powerless to destroy;
Then did I learn how existence could be cherished,
Strengthened and fed without the aid of joy.

Then did I check the tears of useless passion—
Weaned my young soul from yearning after thine;
Sternly denied its burning wish to hasten
Down to that tomb already more than mine.

And, even yet, I dare not let it languish,
Dare not indulge in memory's rapturous pain; *30*
Once drinking deep of that divinest anguish,
How could I seek the empty world again?   *(1845)*

To Imagination

When weary with the long day's care,
    And earthly change from pain to pain,
And lost, and ready to despair,
    Thy kind voice calls me back again,
Oh, my true friend! I am not lone,
While thou canst speak with such a tone!

So hopeless is the world without,
    The world within I doubly prize;
Thy world, where guile and hate and doubt
    And cold suspicion never rise;   *10*
Where thou and I and Liberty
Have undisputed sovereignty.

What matters it, that all around
    Danger and guilt and darkness lie,
If but within our bosom's bound
    We hold a bright, untroubled sky,
Warm with ten thousand mingled rays
Of suns that know no winter days?

Reason, indeed, may oft complain
    For Nature's sad reality,   *20*
And tell the suffering heart how vain
    Its cherished dreams must always be;
And Truth may rudely trample down
    The flowers of Fancy, newly-blown:

But thou art ever there, to bring
    The hovering vision back, and breathe
New glories o'er the blighted spring,
    And call a lovelier Life from Death,
And whisper, with a voice divine,
Of real worlds, as bright as thine.   *30*

I trust not to thy phantom bliss,
    Yet, still, in evening's quiet hour,
With never-failing thankfulness,
    I welcome thee, Benignant Power,
Sure solacer of human cares,
And sweeter hope, when hope despairs!   (*1846*)

WALT WHITMAN • 1819–1892

There Was a Child Went Forth

There was a child went forth every day,
And the first object he look'd upon, that object he became,
And that object became part of him for the day or a certain part of the day,
Or for many years or stretching cycles of years.

The early lilacs became part of this child,
    And grass and white and red morning-glories, and white and red clover, and the song of the phoebe-bird,
    And the Third-month lambs and the sow's pink-faint litter, and the mare's foal and the cow's calf,
    And the noisy brood of the barnyard or by the mire of the pond-side,
    And the fish suspending themselves so curiously below there, and the beautiful curious liquid,
    And the water-plants with their graceful flat heads, all became part of him.   *10*

The field-sprouts of Fourth-month and Fifth-month became part of him, 10
Winter-grain sprouts and those of the light-yellow corn, and the esculent roots of the garden,
And the apple-trees cover'd with blossoms and the fruit afterward, and wood-berries, and the commonest weeds by the road,
And the old drunkard staggering home from the outhouse of the tavern whence he had lately risen,
And the schoolmistress that pass'd on her way to the school,
And the friendly boys that pass'd, and the quarrelsome boys,
And the tidy and fresh-cheek'd girls, and the barefoot negro boy and girl,
And all the changes of city and country wherever he went.

His own parents, he that had father'd him and she that had conceiv'd him in her womb and birth'd him,
They gave this child more of themselves than that, 20
They gave him afterward every day, they became part of him.

The mother at home quietly placing the dishes on the supper-table,
The mother with mild words, clean her cap and gown, a wholesome odor falling off her person and clothes as she walks by,
The father, strong, self-sufficient, manly, mean, anger'd, unjust,
The blow, the quick loud word, the tight bargain, the crafty lure,
The family usages, the language, the company, the furniture, the yearning and swelling heart,
Affection that will not be gainsay'd, the sense of what is real, the thought if after all it should prove unreal,
The doubts of day-time and the doubts of night-time, the curious whether and how,
Whether that which appears so is so, or is it all flashes and specks?
Men and women crowding fast in the streets, if they are not flashes and specks what are they? 30
The streets themselves and the facades of houses, and goods in the windows,
Vehicles, teams, the heavy-plank'd wharves, the huge crossing at the ferries,
The village on the highland seen from afar at sunset, the river between,
Shadows, aureola and mist, the light falling on roofs and gables of white or brown two miles off,
The schooner nearby sleepily dropping down the tide, the little boat slack-tow'd astern,
The hurrying tumbling waves, quick-broken crests, slapping,
The strata of color'd clouds, the long bar of maroon-tint away solitary by itself, the spread of purity it lies motionless in,
The horizon's edge, the flying sea-crow, the fragrance of salt marsh and shore mud,
These became part of that child who went forth every day, and who now goes, and will always go forth every day. (*1855*)

MATTHEW ARNOLD • 1822-1888

from Parting

Forgive me! forgive me!
   Ah, Marguerite, fain
Would these arms reach to clasp thee!
   But see! 'tis in vain.

In the void air, towards thee,
   My stretch'd arms are cast;
But a sea rolls between us—
   Our different past!

To the lips, ah! of others
   Those lips have been prest,   10
And others, ere I was,
   Were strain'd to that breast;

Far, far from each other
   Our spirits have grown;
And what heart knows another?
   Ah! who knows his own?

Blow, ye winds! lift me with you!
   I come to the wild.
Fold closely, O Nature!
   Thine arms round thy child.   20

To thee only God granted
   A heart ever new—
To all always open,
   To all always true.

Ah! calm me, restore me;
   And dry up my tears
On thy high mountain-platforms,
   Where morn first appears;

Where the white mists, for ever,
   Are spread and upfurl'd—   30
In the stir of the forces
   Whence issued the world.   *(1852)*

To Marguerite

Yes! in the sea of life enisled,
With echoing straits between us thrown,
Dotting the shoreless watery wild,
We mortal millions live *alone*.
The islands feel the enclasping flow,
And then their endless bounds they know.

But when the moon their hollows lights,
And they are swept by balms of spring,
And in their glens, on starry nights,
The nightingales divinely sing;   10
And lovely notes, from shore to shore,
Across the sounds and channels pour—

Oh! then a longing like despair
Is to their farthest caverns sent;
For surely once, they feel, we were
Parts of a single continent!
Now round us spreads the watery plain—
Oh might our marges meet again!

Who order'd, that their longing's fire
Should be, as soon as kindled,
   cool'd?   20
Who renders vain their deep desire?—
A God, a God their severance ruled!
And bade betwixt their shores to be
The unplumb'd, salt, estranging
   sea.   *(1852)*

Philomela[1]

Hark, ah, the nightingale—
The tawny-throated!
Hark, from that moonlit cedar what a
   burst!
What triumph! hark!—what pain!
O wanderer from a Grecian shore,

---

[1] King Tereus of Thrace married Philomela, but later raped her sister, Procne, and cut out her tongue. Procne wove a tapestry ("the too clear web"—l. 21) revealing the story and sent it to Philomela. The sisters killed Tereus' son and served the flesh to the king. When Tereus discovered the crime, he pursued the sisters, so that they called upon the gods for help. Philomela was transformed into the nightingale, Procne into the swallow.

Still, after many years, in distant lands,
Still nourishing in thy bewildered brain
That wild, unquenched, deep-sunken,
   old-world pain—
Say, will it never heal?
And can this fragrant lawn   10
With its cool trees, and night,
And the sweet, tranquil Thames,
And moonshine, and the dew,
To thy racked heart and brain
Afford no balm?

Dost thou tonight behold,
Here, through the moonlight on this
   English grass,
The unfriendly palace in the Thracian
   wild?
Dost thou again peruse
With hot cheeks and seared eyes   20
The too clear web, and thy dumb sister's
   shame?
Dost thou once more assay
Thy flight, and feel come over thee,
Poor fugitive, the feathery change
Once more, and once more seem to make
   resound
With love and hate, triumph and agony,
Lone Daulis,[2] and the high Cephissian
   vale?[3]

Listen, Eugenia[4]—
How thick the bursts come crowding
   through the leaves!
Again—thou hearest?   30
Eternal passion!
Eternal pain!   (*1853*)

Requiescat

Strew on her roses, roses,
   And never a spray of yew!
In quiet she reposes;
   Ah, would that I did too!

Her mirth the world required;
   She bathed it in smiles of glee.
But her heart was tired, tired,
   And now they let her be.

Her life was turning, turning,
   In mazes of heat and sound.   10
But for peace her soul was yearning,
   And now peace laps her round.

Her cabin'd, ample spirit,
   It flutter'd and fail'd for breath.
To-night it doth inherit
   The vasty hall of death.   (*1853*)

Dover Beach

The sea is calm to-night,
The tide is full, the moon lies fair
Upon the Straits;—on the French coast, the light
Gleams, and is gone; the cliffs of England stand,
Glimmering and vast, out in the tranquil bay.
Come to the window, sweet is the night air!
Only, from the long line of spray
Where the ebb meets the moon-blanched sand,
Listen! you hear the grating roar
Of pebbles which the waves suck back, and fling,   10
At their return, up the high strand,
Begin, and cease, and then again begin,
With tremulous cadence slow, and bring
The eternal note of sadness in.

---

[2] site of the transformation
[3] valley in Phocis, home of Tereus

[4] imaginary listener

         Sophocles[1] long ago
         Heard it on the Ægean, and it brought
         Into his mind the turbid ebb and flow
         Of human misery; we
         Find also in the sound a thought,
         Hearing it by this distant northern sea.   20

         The sea of faith
         Was once, too, at the full, and round earth's shore
         Lay like the folds of a bright girdle furled;
         But now I only hear
         Its melancholy, long, withdrawing roar,
         Retreating to the breath
         Of the night-wind down the vast edges drear
         And naked shingles[2] of the world.

         Ah, love, let us be true
         To one another! for the world, which seems   30
         To lie before us like a land of dreams,
         So various, so beautiful, so new,
         Hath really neither joy, nor love, nor light,
         Nor certitude, nor peace, nor help for pain;
         And we are here as on a darkling plain
         Swept with confused alarms of struggle and flight,
         Where ignorant armies clash by night.   *(1867)*

COVENTRY PATMORE • 1823–1896

The Toys

My little Son, who look'd from thoughtful eyes
And moved and spoke in quiet grown-up wise,
Having my law the seventh time disobey'd,
I struck him, and dismiss'd
With hard words and unkiss'd,
—His Mother, who was patient, being dead.
Then, fearing lest his grief should hinder sleep,
I visited his bed,
But found him slumbering deep,
With darken'd eyelids, and their lashes yet   10
From his late sobbing wet.
And I, with moan,
Kissing away his tears, left others of my own;
For, on a table drawn beside his head,
He had put, within his reach,
A box of counters and a red-vein'd stone,
A piece of glass abraded by the beach
And six or seven shells,
A bottle with bluebells,

---

[1] Greek tragedian (c. 496–c. 405 B.C.). In *Antigone* he likens the curse of heaven to the ebb and flow of the sea.
[2] beaches covered with coarse gravel

And two French copper coins, ranged
    there with careful art,   20
To comfort his sad heart.
So when that night I pray'd
To God, I wept, and said:
Ah, when at last we lie with trancèd
    breath,
Not vexing Thee in death,
And thou rememberest of what toys
We made our joys,
How weakly understood,
Thy great commanded good,
Then, fatherly not less   30
Than I whom thou hast moulded from
    the clay,
Thou'lt leave Thy wrath, and say,
"I will be sorry for their childishness."
                          (*1877*)

Magna Est Veritas[1]

    Here, in this little Bay,
Full of tumultuous life and great repose,
    Where, twice a day,
The purposeless, glad ocean comes and
    goes,
Under high cliffs, and far from the huge
    town,
I sit me down.
For want of me the world's course will
    not fail:
When all its work is done, the lie shall
    rot;
The truth is great, and shall prevail,
When none cares whether it prevail or
    not. (*1877*)   10

DANGE GABRIEL ROSSETTI • 1828–1882

The Sea-Limits

    Consider the sea's listless chime:
        Time's self it is, made audible,—
        The murmur of the earth's own shell.
    Secret continuance sublime
        Is the sea's end: our sight may pass
        No furlong further. Since time was,
This sound hath told the lapse of time.

    No quiet, which is death's,—it hath
        The mournfulness of ancient life,
        Enduring always at dull strife.   10
    As the world's heart of rest and wrath,
        Its painful pulse is in the sands.
        Last utterly, the whole sky stands,
Grey and not known, along its path.

    Listen alone beside the sea,
        Listen alone among the woods;
        Those voices of twin solitudes
Shall have one sound alike to thee:
        Hark where the murmurs of thronged men

---
[1] The truth is great; compare l. 9.

    Surge and sink back and surge again,—   20
  Still the one voice of wave and tree.

  Gather a shell from the strown beach
   And listen at its lips: they sigh
   The same desire and mystery,
  The echo of the whole sea's speech.
   And all mankind is thus at heart
   Not anything but what thou art:
  And Earth, Sea, Man, are all in each. (*1849*)

Sudden Light

  I have been here before,
   But when or how I cannot tell:
  I know the grass beyond the door,
   The sweet keen smell,
The sighing sound, the lights around the shore.

  You have been mine before,—
   How long ago I may not know:
  But just when at that swallow's soar
   Your neck turned so,
Some veil did fall,—I knew it all of yore.   10

  Has this been thus before?
   And shall not thus time's eddying flight
  Still with our lives our loves restore
   In death's despite,
And day and night yield one delight once more? (*1854*)

The Woodspurge

  The wind flapped loose, the wind was still,
  Shaken out dead from tree and hill:
  I had walked on at the wind's will,—
  I sat now, for the wind was still.

  Between my knees my forehead was,—
  My lips, drawn in, said not Alas!
  My hair was over in the grass,
  My naked ears heard the day pass.

  My eyes, wide open, had the run
  Of some ten weeds to fix upon;   10
  Among those few, out of the sun,
  The woodspurge flowered, three cups in one.

From perfect grief there need not be
Wisdom or even memory:
One thing then learnt remains to me,—
The woodspurge has a cup of three.   (*1856*)

EMILY DICKINSON • 1830–1886

108

Surgeons must be very careful
When they take the knife!
Underneath their fine incisions
Stirs the Culprit—*Life!*   (*c. 1859*)

214

I taste a liquor never brewed—
From Tankards scooped in Pearl—
Not all the Vats upon the Rhine
Yield such an alcohol!

Inebriate of Air—am I—
And Debauchee of Dew—
Reeling—thro endless summer days—
From inns of Molten Blue—

When "Landlords" turn the drunken Bee
Out of the Foxglove's door—
When Butterflies—renounce their
   "drams"—
I shall but drink the more!

Till Seraphs swing their snowy Hats—
And Saints—to windows run—
To see the little Tippler
Leaning against the—Sun—   (*c. 1860*)

337

I know a place where Summer strives
With such a practised Frost—
She—each year—leads her Daisies back—
Recording briefly—"Lost"—

But when the South Wind stirs the Pools
And struggles in the lanes—
Her Heart misgives Her, for her Vow—
And she pours soft Refrains

Into the lap of Adamant—
And spices—and the Dew—
That stiffens quietly to Quartz—
Upon her Amber Shoe—   (*c. 1862*)

419

We grow accustomed to the Dark—
When Light is put away—
As when the Neighbor holds the Lamp
To witness her Goodbye—

A Moment—We uncertain step
For newness of the night—
Then—fit our Vision to the Dark—
And meet the Road—erect—

And so of larger—Darknesses—
Those Evenings of the Brain—
When not a Moon disclose a sign—
Or Star—come out—within—

The Bravest—grope a little—
And sometimes hit a Tree
Directly in the Forehead—
But as they learn to see—

Either the Darkness alters—
Or something in the sight
Adjusts itself to Midnight—
And Life steps almost straight.
   (*c. 1862*)

Emily Dickinson

432

Do People moulder equally,
They bury, in the Grave?
I do believe a Species
As positively live

As I, who testify it
Deny that I—am dead—
And fill my Lungs, for Witness—
From Tanks—above my Head—

I say to you, said Jesus—
That there be standing here— 10
A Sort, that shall not taste of Death—
If Jesus was sincere—

I need no further Argue—
That statement of the Lord
Is not a controvertible—
He told me, Death was dead—
(c. 1862)

510

It was not Death, for I stood up,
And all the Dead, lie down—
It was not Night, for all the Bells
Put out their Tongues, for Noon.

It was not Frost, for on my Flesh
I felt Siroccos—crawl—
Nor Fire—for just my Marble feet
Could keep a Chancel, cool—

And yet, it tasted, like them all,
The Figures I have seen 10
Set orderly, for Burial
Reminded me, of mine—

As if my life were shaven,
And fitted to a frame,
And could not breathe without a key,
And 'twas like Midnight, some—

When everything that ticked—has
   stopped—
And Space stares all around—

Or Grisly frosts—first Autumn morns,
Repeal the Beating Ground— 20

But, most, like Chaos—Stopless—cool—
Without a Chance, or Spar—
Or even a Report of Land—
To justify—Despair. (c. 1862)

531

We dream—it is good we are dreaming—
It would hurt us—were we awake—
But since it is playing—kill us,
And we are playing—shriek—

What harm? Men die—externally—
It is truth—of Blood—
But we—are dying in Drama—
And Drama—is never dead—

Cautious—We jar each other—
And either—open the eyes— 10
Lest the Phantasm—prove the Mistake—
And the livid Surprise

Cool us to Shafts of Granite—
With just an Age—and Name—
And perhaps a phrase in Egyptian—
It's prudenter—to dream— (c. 1862)

749

All but Death can be Adjusted—
Dynasties repaired—
Systems—settled in their Sockets—
Citadels—dissolved—

Wastes of Lives—resown with Colors
By Succeeding Springs—
Death—unto itself—Exception—
Is exempt from Change— (c. 1863)

754

My Life had stood—a Loaded Gun—
In Corners—till a Day
The Owner passed—identified—
And carried Me away—

And now We roam in Sovereign Woods—
And now We hunt the Doe—
And every time I speak for Him—
The Mountains straight reply—

And do I smile, such cordial light
Upon the Valley glow—   10
It is as a Vesuvian face
Had let its pleasure through—

And when at Night—Our good Day
   done—
I guard My Master's Head—
'Tis better than the Eider-Duck's
Deep Pillow—to have shared—

To foe of His—I'm deadly foe—
None stir the second time—
On whom I lay a Yellow Eye—
Or an emphatic Thumb—   20

Though I than He—may longer live
He longer must—than I
For I have but the power to kill,
Without—the power to die—   (*c. 1863*)

760

Most she touched me by her muteness—
Most she won me by the way
She presented her small figure—
Plea itself—for Charity—

Were a Crumb my whole possession—
Were there famine in the land—
Were it my resource from starving—
Could I such a plea withstand—

Not upon her knee to thank me
Sank this Beggar from the Sky—   10
But the Crumb partook—departed—
And returned On High—

I supposed—when sudden
Such a Praise began
'Twas as Space sat singing
To herself—and men—

'Twas the Winged Beggar—
Afterward I learned
To her Benefactor
Making Gratitude   (*c. 1863*)   20

764

Presentiment—is that long Shadow—on
   the Lawn—
Indicative that Suns go down—

The Notice to the startled Grass
That Darkness—is about to pass—
               (*c. 1863*)

861

Split the Lark—and you'll find the
   Music—
Bulb after Bulb, in Silver rolled—
Scantily dealt to the Summer Morning
Saved for your Ear when Lutes be old.

Loose the Flood—you shall find it
   patent—
Gush after Gush, reserved for you—
Scarlet Experiment! Sceptic Thomas!
Now, do you doubt that your Bird was
   true?   (*c. 1864*)

875

I stepped from Plank to Plank
A slow and cautious way
The Stars about my Head I felt
About my Feet the Sea.

I knew not but the next
Would be my final inch—
This gave me that precarious Gait
Some call Experience.   (*c. 1864*)

910

Experience is the Angled Road
Preferred against the Mind
By—Paradox—the Mind itself—
Presuming it to lead

Quite Opposite—How Complicate
The Discipline of Man—
Compelling Him to Choose Himself
His Preappointed Pain—   (c. 1864)

1129

Tell all the Truth but tell it slant—
Success in Circuit lies
Too bright for our infirm Delight
The Truth's superb surprise

As Lightning to the Children eased
With explanation kind
The Truth must dazzle gradually
Or every man be blind—   (c. 1868)

1142

The Props assist the House
Until the House is built
And then the Props withdraw
And adequate, erect,
The House support itself
And cease to recollect
The Auger and the Carpenter—
Just such a retrospect
Hath the perfected Life—
A past of Plank and Nail   10
And slowness—then the Scaffolds drop
Affirming it a Soul.   (c. 1863)

1484

We shall find the Cube of the Rainbow.
Of that, there is no doubt.
But the Arc of a Lover's conjecture
Eludes the finding out.   (c. 1880)

WILLIAM MORRIS • 1834–1896

The Haystack in the Floods

Had she come all the way for this,
To part at last without a kiss?
Yea, had she borne the dirt and rain
That her own eyes might see him slain
Beside the haystack in the floods?

Along the dripping leafless woods,
The stirrup touching either shoe,
She rode astride as troopers do;
With kirtle kilted to her knee,
To which the mud splash'd
    wretchedly;   10
And the wet dripp'd from every tree
Upon her head and heavy hair,
And on her eyelids broad and fair;
The tears and rain ran down her face.

By fits and starts they rode apace,
And very often was his place
Far off from her; he had to ride
Ahead, to see what might betide
When the roads cross'd; and sometimes,
    when
There rose a murmuring from his
    men,   20
Had to turn back with promises;
Ah me! she had but little ease;
And often for pure doubt and dread
She sobb'd, made giddy in the head
By the swift riding; while, for cold,
Her slender fingers scarce could hold
The wet reins; yea, and scarcely, too,
She felt the foot within her shoe,
Against the stirrup: all for this,
To part at last without a kiss   30
Beside the haystack in the floods.

For when they near'd that old soak'd hay,
They saw across the only way
That Judas, Godmar; and the three
Red running lions dismally
Grinn'd from his pennon, under which,
In one straight line along the ditch,
They counted thirty heads.
     So then,
While Robert turn'd round to his men,
She saw at once the wretched end,   40
And, stooping down, tried hard to rend
Her coif the wrong way from her head,
And hid her eyes: while Robert said:
"Nay, love, 'tis scarcely two to one,
At Poictiers[1] where we made them run
So fast—why, sweet my love, good cheer.
The Gascon frontier is so near,
Nought after this."
     But, "O," she said,
"My God! my God! I have to tread
The long way back without you;
  then   50
The court at Paris; those six men;[2]
The gratings of the Chatelet;[3]
The swift Seine on some rainy day
Like this, and people standing by,
And laughing, while my weak hands try
To recollect how strong men swim,
All this, or else a life with him,
For which I should be damned at last,
Would God that this next hour were
  past!"

He answer'd not, but cried his cry,   60
"St. George for Marny!" cheerily;
And laid his hand upon her rein.
Alas! no man of all his train
Gave back that cheery cry again;
And, while for rage his thumb beat fast
Upon his sword-hilts, some one cast
About his neck a kerchief long,
And bound him.
    Then they went along
To Godmar; who said: "Now Jehane,

Your lover's life is on the wane   70
So fast, that, if this very hour
You yield not as my paramour,
He will not see the rain leave off—
Nay, keep your tongue from gibe and
  scoff,
Sir Robert, or I slay you now."

She laid her hand upon her brow,
Then gazed upon the palm, as though
She thought her forehead bled, and—
  "No,"
She said, and turn'd her head away,
As there were nothing else to say,   80
And everything were settled: red
Grew Godmar's face from chin to head:
"Jehane, on yonder hill there stands
My castle, guarding well my lands:
What hinders me from taking you,
And doing that I list to do
To your fair wilful body, while
Your knight lies dead?"
    A wicked smile
Wrinkled her face, her lips grew thin,
A long way out she thrust her chin: 90
"You know that I should strangle you
While you were sleeping; or bite through
Your throat, by God's help—ah!" she
  said,
"Lord Jesus, pity your poor maid!
For in such wise they hem me in,
I cannot choose but sin and sin,
Whatever happens: yet I think
They could not make me eat or drink,
And so should I just reach my rest."
"Nay, if you do not my behest,   100
O Jehane! though I love you well,"
Said Godmar, "would I fail to tell
All that I know?" "Foul lies," she said.
"Eh? lies my Jehane? by God's head,
At Paris folks would deem them true!
Do you know, Jehane, they cry for you,
'Jehane the brown! Jehane the brown!
Give us Jehane to burn or drown!'—

---

[1] Poitiers (pronounced pwah′tyay), city in western France, site of a battle (1356) in the Hundred Years' War, in which the English defeated the French. The poem is not based on an actual incident.
[2] the judges who would try Jehane, presumably as a witch   [3] a prison in Paris

Eh—gag me Robert!—sweet my friend,
This were indeed a piteous end
For those long fingers, and long feet,
And long neck, and smooth shoulders sweet;
An end that few men would forget
That saw it—So, an hour yet:
Consider, Jehane, which to take
Of life or death!"
              So scarce awake,
Dismounting, did she leave that place,
And totter some yards: with her face
Turn'd upward to the sky she lay,
Her head on a wet heap of hay,
And fell asleep: and while she slept,
And did not dream, the minutes crept
Round to twelve again; but she,
Being waked at last, sigh'd quietly,
And strangely childlike came, and said:
"I will not." Straightway Godmar's head,
As though it hung on strong wires, turn'd
Most sharply round, and his face burn'd.

For Robert—both his eyes were dry,
He could not weep, but gloomily
He seem'd to watch the rain; yea, too,
His lips were firm; he tried once more
To touch her lips; she reach'd out, sore
And vain desire so tortured them,
The poor grey lips, and now the hem
Of his sleeve brush'd them.
              With a start
Up Godmar rose, thrust them apart;
From Robert's throat he loosed the bands
Of silk and mail: with empty hands
Held out, she stood and gazed, and saw,
The long bright blade without a flaw
Glide out from Godmar's sheath, his hand
In Robert's hair; she saw him bend
Back Robert's head; she saw him send
The thin steel down; the blow told well,
Right backward the knight Robert fell,
And moan'd as dogs do, being half dead,
Unwitting, as I deem: so then
Godmar turn'd grinning to his men,
Who ran, some five or six, and beat
His head to pieces at their feet.

Then Godmar turn'd again, and said:
"So, Jehane, the first fitte is read!
Take note, my lady, that your way
Lies backward to the Chatelet!"
She shook her head and gazed awhile
At her cold hands with a rueful smile,
As though this thing had made her mad.

This was the parting that they had
Beside the haystack in the floods. (*1858*)

THOMAS HARDY • 1840–1928

Hap

        If but some vengeful god would call to me
        From up the sky, and laugh: "Thou suffering thing,
        Know that thy sorrow is my ecstasy,
        That thy love's loss is my hate's profiting!"
        Then would I bear it, clench myself, and die,
        Steeled by the sense of ire unmerited;
        Half-eased in that a Powerfuller than I
        Had willed and meted me the tears I shed.

But not so. How arrives it joy lies slain,
And why unblooms the best hope ever sown?
—Crass Casualty obstructs the sun and rain,
And dicing Time for gladness casts a moan....
These purblind Doomsters had as readily strown
Blisses about my pilgrimage as pain.   (*1866*)

The Darkling Thrush

DECEMBER 31, 1900

I leant upon a coppice[1] gate
    When Frost was spectre-gray,
And Winter's dregs made desolate
    The weakening eye of day.
The tangled bine-stems[2] scored the sky
    Like strings of broken lyres,
And all mankind that haunted nigh
    Had sought their household fires.

The land's sharp features seemed to be
    The Century's corpse outleant,
His crypt the cloudy canopy,
    The wind his death-lament.
The ancient pulse of germ and birth
    Was shrunken hard and dry,
And every spirit upon earth
    Seemed fervorless as I.

At once a voice arose among
    The bleak twigs overhead
In a full-hearted evensong
    Of joy illimited;
An aged thrush, frail, gaunt, and small,
    In blast-beruffled plume,
Had chosen thus to fling his soul
    Upon the growing gloom.

So little cause for carolings
    Of such ecstatic sound
Was written on terrestrial things
    Afar or nigh around,
That I could think there trembled through
    His happy good-night air
Some blessed Hope, whereof he knew
    And I was unaware.   (*1902*)

The Contretemps

A forward rush by the lamp in the gloom,
    And we clasped, and almost kissed;
But she was not the woman whom
I had promised to meet in the thawing brume[1]
On that harbour-bridge; nor was I he of her tryst.

So loosening from me swift she said;
    "O why, why feign to be
The one I had meant!—to whom I have sped
To fly with, being so sorrily wed!"
—'Twas thus and thus that she upbraided me.

My assignation had struck upon
    Some others' like it, I found.
And her lover rose on the night anon;

---

[1] a small thicket
[2] the wire-like shoots of a climbing plant

[1] mist

And then her husband entered on
The lamplit, snowflaked, sloppiness around.

"Take her and welcome, man!" he cried:
    "I wash my hands of her.
I'll find me twice as good a bride!"
—All this to me, whom he had eyed,
Plainly, as his wife's planned deliverer.   20

And next the lover: "Little I knew,
    Madam, you had a third!
Kissing here in my very view!"
—Husband and lover then withdrew.
I let them; and I told them not they erred.

Why not? Well, there faced she and I—
    Two strangers who'd kissed, or near,
Chancewise. To see stand weeping by
A woman once embraced, will try
The tension of a man the most austere.   30

So it began; and I was young,
    She pretty, by the lamp,
As flakes came waltzing down among
The waves of her clinging hair, that hung
Heavily on her temples, dark and damp.

And there alone still stood we two;
    She one cast off for me,
Or so it seemed: while night ondrew,
Forcing a parley what should do
We twain hearts caught in one catastrophe.   40

In stranded souls a common strait
    Wakes latencies unknown,
Whose impulse may precipitate
A life-long leap. The hour was late,
And there was the Jersey boat with its funnel agroan.

"Is wary walking worth much pother?"
    It grunted, as still it stayed.
"One pairing is as good as another
Where all is venture! Take each other,
And scrap the oaths that you have aforetime made." . . .   50

—Of the four involved there walks but one
    On earth at this late day.
And what of the chapter so begun?
In that odd complex what was done?
Well; happiness comes in full to none:
Let peace lie on lulled lips: I will not say.   (*1922*)

The Fallow Deer at the Lonely House

> One without looks in to-night
>   Through the curtain-chink
> From the sheet of glistening white;
> One without looks in to-night
>   As we sit and think
>   By the fender-brink.
>
> We do not discern those eyes
>   Watching in the snow;
> Lit by lamps of rosy dyes
> We do not discern those eyes   10
>   Wondering, aglow,
>   Fourfooted, tiptoe.   (*1922*)

GERARD MANLEY HOPKINS • 1844–1889

God's Grandeur

> The world is charged with the grandeur of God.
> It will flame out, like shining from shook foil;
> It gathers to a greatness, like the ooze of oil
> Crushed. Why do men then now not reck his rod?
> Generations have trod, have trod, have trod;
> And all is seared with trade; bleared, smeared with toil;
> And wears man's smudge and shares man's smell: the soil
> Is bare now, nor can foot feel, being shod.
> And for all this, nature is never spent;
> There lives the dearest freshness deep down things;   10
> And though the last lights off the black West went
> Oh, morning, at the brown brink eastward, springs—
> Because the Holy Ghost over the bent
> World broods with warm breast and with ah! bright wings.   (*1877*)

The Starlight Night

> Look at the stars! look, look up at the skies!
> O look at all the fire-folk sitting in the air!
> The bright boroughs, the circle-citadels there!
> Down in dim woods the diamond delves! the elves'-eyes!
> The grey lawns cold where gold, where quickgold lies!
> Wind-beat whitebeam! airy abeles set on a flare!
> Flake-doves sent floating forth at a farmyard scare!—

Ah well! it is all a purchase, all is a prize.
Buy then! bid then!—What?—Prayer, patience, alms, vows.
Look, look: a May-mess, like on orchard boughs!
Look! March-bloom, like on mealed-with-yellow sallows!
These are indeed the barn; withindoors house
The shocks. This piece-bright paling shuts the spouse
Christ home, Christ and his mother and all his hallows.   *(1877)*

Spring

Nothing is so beautiful as spring—
When weeds, in wheels, shoot long and lovely and lush;
Thrush's eggs look little low heavens, and thrush
Through the echoing timber does so rinse and wring
The ear, it strikes like lightnings to hear him sing;
The glassy peartree leaves and blooms, they brush
The descending blue; that blue is all in a rush
With richness; the racing lambs too have fair their fling.
What is all this juice and all this joy?
A strain of the earth's sweet being in the beginning
In Eden garden.—Have, get, before it cloy,
Before it cloud, Christ, lord, and sour with sinning,
Innocent mind and Mayday in girl and boy,
Most, O maid's child, thy choice and worthy the winning.   *(1877)*

The Windhover

TO CHRIST OUR LORD

I caught this morning morning's minion, king-
    dom of daylight's dauphin, dapple-dawn-drawn Falcon, in his riding
      Of the rolling level underneath him steady air, and striding
High there, how he rung upon the rein of a wimpling wing
In his ectasy! then off, off forth on swing,
    As a skate's heel sweeps smooth on a bow-bend: the hurl and gliding
      Rebuffed the big wind. My heart in hiding
Stirred for a bird,—the achieve of, the mastery of the thing!

Brute beauty and valor and act, oh, air, pride, plume, here
    Buckle! AND the fire that breaks from thee then, a billion
Times told lovelier, more dangerous, O my chevalier!

    No wonder of it: sheér plód makes plow down sillion[1]
Shine, and blue-bleak embers, ah my dear,
    Fall, gall themselves, and gash gold-vermilion.   *(1877)*

---

[1] the ridge between two furrows

Pied Beauty

   Glory be to God for dappled things—
    For skies of couple-colour as a brinded[1] cow;
     For rose-moles all in stipple[2] upon trout that swim;
   Fresh-firecoal chestnut-falls;[3] finches' wings;
    Landscape plotted and pieced—fold, fallow, and plow;
     And all trades, their gear and tackle and trim.

   All things counter, original, spare, strange;
    Whatever is fickle, freckled (who knows how?)
     With swift, slow; sweet, sour; adazzle, dim;
   He fathers-forth whose beauty is past change: *10*
     Praise him. (*1877*)

The Candle Indoors

   Some candle clear burns somewhere I come by.
   I muse at how its being puts blissful back
   With yellowy moisture mild night's blear-all black,
   Or to-fro tender trambeams truckle at the eye.

   By that window what task what fingers ply,
   I plod wondering, a-wanting, just for lack
   Of answer the eagerer a-wanting Jessy or Jack
   There/ God to aggrándize, God to glorify.—

   Come you indoors, come home; your fading fire
   Mend first and vital candle in close heart's vault: *10*
   You there are master, do your own desire;

   What hinders? Are you beam-blind, yet to a fault
   In a neighbour deft-handed? are you that liar
   And, cast by conscience out, spendsavour salt? (*1879*)

ROBERT BRIDGES • 1844–1930

Elegy

   The wood is bare: a river-mist is steeping
    The trees that winter's chill of life bereaves:
   Only their stiffened boughs break silence, weeping
     Over their fallen leaves;

---

[1] streaked or spotted
[2] shading with small dots
[3] fallen chestnuts as bright as coals of fire

That lie upon the dank earth brown and rotten,
　　Miry and matted in the soaking wet:
Forgotten with the spring, that is forgotten
　　　　By them that can forget.

Yet it was here we walked when ferns were springing,
　　And through the mossy bank shot bud and blade:—
Here found in summer, when the birds were singing,
　　　　A green and pleasant shade,

'Twas here we loved in sunnier days and greener;
　　And now, in this disconsolate decay,
I come to see her where I most have seen her,
　　　　And touch the happier day.

For on this path, at every turn and corner,
　　The fancy of her figure on me falls:
Yet walks she with the slow step of a mourner,
　　　　Nor hears my voice that calls.

So through my heart there winds a track of feeling,
　　A path of memory, that is all her own:
Whereto her phantom beauty ever stealing
　　　　Haunts the sad spot alone.

About her steps the trunks are bare, the branches
　　Drip heavy tears upon her downcast head;
And bleed from unseen wounds that no sun stanches,
　　　　For the year's sun is dead.

And dead leaves wrap the fruits that summer planted:
　　And birds that love the South have taken wing.
The wanderer, loitering o'er the scene enchanted,
　　　　Weeps, and despairs of spring.　　(*1873*)

London Snow

When men were all asleep the snow came flying,
　　In large white flakes falling on the city brown,
Stealthily and perpetually settling and loosely lying,
　　Hushing the latest traffic of the drowsy town;
Deadening, muffling, stifling its murmurs failing;
　　Lazily and incessantly floating down and down:
　　　　Silently sifting and veiling road, roof and railing;
Hiding difference, making unevenness even,
Into angles and crevices softly drifting and sailing.
All night it fell, and when full inches seven
It lay in the depth of its uncompacted lightness,
The clouds blew off from a high and frosty heaven;

    And all woke earlier for the unaccustomed brightness
Of the winter dawning, the strange unheavenly glare:
The eye marvelled—marvelled at the dazzling whiteness;
    The ear hearkened to the stillness of the solemn air;
No sound of wheel rumbling nor of foot falling,
And the busy morning cries came thin and spare.
    Then boys I heard, as they went to school, calling,
They gathered up the crystal manna to freeze
Their tongues with tasting, their hands with snowballing;
    Or rioted in a drift, plunging up to the knees;
Or peering up from under the white-mossed wonder,
"O look at the trees!" they cried, "O look at the trees!"
    With lessened load a few carts creak and blunder,
Following along the white deserted way,
A country company long dispersed asunder:
    When now already the sun, in pale display
Standing by Paul's high dome, spread forth below
His sparkling beams, and awoke the stir of the day.
    For now doors open, and war is waged with the snow;
And trains of sombre men, past tale of number,
Tread long brown paths, as toward their toil they go:
    But even for them awhile no cares encumber
Their minds diverted; the daily word is unspoken,
The daily thoughts of labour and sorrow slumber
At the sight of the beauty that greets them, for the
    charm they have broken.   (*1880*)

A. E. HOUSMAN • 1859–1936

Into My Heart an Air That Kills

Into my heart an air that kills
    From yon far country blows:
What are those blue remembered hills,
    What spires, what farms are those?

That is the land of lost content,
    I see it shining plain,
The happy highways where I went
    And cannot come again.   (*c. 1890*)

With Rue My Heart Is Laden

With rue my heart is laden
    For golden friends I had,
For many a rose-lipt maiden
    And many a lightfoot lad.

By brooks too broad for leaping
    The lightfoot boys are laid;
The rose-lipt girls are sleeping
    In fields where roses fade.   (*1893*)

When I Was One-and-Twenty

When I was one-and-twenty
    I heard a wise man say,
"Give crowns and pounds and guineas
    But not your heart away;
Give pearls away and rubies
    But keep your fancy free."
But I was one-and-twenty,
    No use to talk to me.

When I was one-and-twenty
    I heard him say again,   *10*
"The heart out of the bosom
    Was never given in vain;
'Tis paid with sighs a plenty
    And sold for endless rue."
And I am two-and-twenty,
    And oh, 'tis true, 'tis true.   (*1895*)

1887

From Clee to heaven the beacon burns,
    The shires have seen it plain,
From north and south the sign returns
    And beacons burn again.

Look left, look right, the hills are bright,
    The dales are light between,
Because 'tis fifty years to-night
    That God has saved the Queen.

Now, when the flame they watch not towers
    About the soil they trod,   *10*
Lads, we'll remember friends of ours
    Who shared the work with God.

To skies that knit their heartstrings right,
    To fields that bred them brave,
The saviours come not home to-night:
    Themselves they could not save.[1]

It dawns in Asia, tombstones show
    And Shropshire names are read;
And the Nile spills his overflow
    Beside the Severn's dead.   *20*

We pledge in peace by farm and town
    The Queen they served in war,
And fire the beacons up and down
    The land they perished for.

"God save the Queen" we living sing,
    From height to height 'tis heard;
And with the rest your voices ring,
    Lads of the Fifty-third.

Oh, God will save her, fear you not:
    Be you the men you've been,   *30*
Get you the sons your fathers got,
    And God will save the Queen.   (*1896*)

The Night Is Freezing Fast

The night is freezing fast,
    To-morrow comes December;
    And winterfalls of old
Are with me from the past;
    And chiefly I remember
    How Dick would hate the cold.

Fall, winter, fall; for he,
    Prompt hand and headpiece clever,
    Has woven a winter robe,
And made of earth and sea
    His overcoat for ever,   *10*
    And wears the turning globe.
                                (*1922*)

---

[1] Cf. St. Matthew, 27: 42

I Did Not Lose My Heart in Summer's Even

> I did not lose my heart in summer's even
>   When roses to the moonrise burst apart:
> When plumes were under heel and lead was flying,
>   In blood and smoke and flame I lost my heart.
>
> I lost it to a soldier and a foeman,
>   A chap that did not kill me, but he tried;
> That took the sabre straight and took it striking,
>   And laughed and kissed his hand to me and died.   *(1936)*

WILLIAM BUTLER YEATS • 1865–1939

The Lover Tells of the Rose in His Heart

All things uncomely and broken, all things worn out and old,
The cry of a child by the roadway, the creak of a lumbering cart,
The heavy steps of the ploughman, splashing the wintry mould,
Are wronging your image that blossoms a rose in the deeps of my heart.

The wrong of unshapely things is a wrong too great to be told;
I hunger to build them anew and sit on a green knoll apart,
With the earth and the sky and the water, remade, like a casket of gold
For my dreams of your image that blossoms a rose in the deeps of my heart.
(1899)

No Second Troy

> Why should I blame her that she filled my days
> With misery, or that she would of late
> Have taught to ignorant men most violent ways,
> Or hurled the little streets upon the great,
> Had they but courage equal to desire?
> What could have made her peaceful with a mind
> That nobleness made simple as a fire,
> With beauty like a tightened bow, a kind
> That is not natural in an age like this,
> Being high and solitary and most stern?
> Why, what could she have done, being what she is?
> Was there another Troy for her to burn?   *(1910)*

The Second Coming

Turning and turning in the widening gyre[1]
The falcon cannot hear the falconer;
Things fall apart; the centre cannot hold;
Mere anarchy is loosed upon the world,
The blood-dimmed tide is loosed, and everywhere
The ceremony of innocence is drowned;
The best lack all conviction, while the worst
Are full of passionate intensity.

Surely some revelation is at hand;
Surely the Second Coming is at hand. *10*
The Second Coming! Hardly are those words out
When a vast image out of *Spiritus Mundi*[2]
Troubles my sight: somewhere in sands of the desert
A shape with lion body and the head of a man,
A gaze blank and pitiless as the sun,
Is moving its slow thighs, while all about it
Reel shadows of the indignant desert birds.
The darkness drops again; but now I know
That twenty centuries of stony sleep
Were vexed to nightmare by a rocking cradle, *20*
And what rough beast, its hour come round at last,
Slouches towards Bethlehem to be born?
(*1921*)

Leda[1] and the Swan

A sudden blow: the great wings beating still
Above the staggering girl, her thighs caressed
By the dark web, her nape caught in his bill,
He holds her helpless breast upon his breast.

How can those terrified vague fingers push
The feathered glory from her loosening thighs?
And how can body, laid in that white rush,
But feel the strange heart beating where it lies?

A shudder in the loins engenders there
The broken wall, the burning roof and tower *10*
And Agamemnon dead.
                    Being so caught up,
So mastered by the brute blood of the air,
Did she put on his knowledge with his power
Before the indifferent beak could let her drop? (*1923*)

---

[1] a centrifugal motion which Yeats associates with the conclusion of a cycle of history
[2] the soul of the world, a reservoir of the racial memory

[1] Ravished by Zeus in the form of a swan, she gave birth to Helen of Troy and to Clytemnestra, who murdered her husband Agamemnon, after his return from the Trojan War.

Sailing to Byzantium

That is no country for old men. The young
In one another's arms, birds in the trees
—Those dying generations—at their song,
The salmon-falls, the mackerel-crowded seas,
Fish, flesh, or fowl, commend all summer long
Whatever is begotten, born, and dies.
Caught in that sensual music all neglect
Monuments of unageing intellect.

An aged man is but a paltry thing,
A tattered coat upon a stick, unless   10
Soul clap its hands and sing, and louder sing
For every tatter in its mortal dress,
Nor is there singing school but studying
Monuments of its own magnificence;
And therefore I have sailed the seas and come
To the holy city of Byzantium.

O sages, standing in God's holy fire
As in the gold mosaic of a wall,
Come from the holy fire, perne in a gyre,[2]
And be the singing-masters of my soul.   20
Consume my heart away; sick with desire
And fastened to a dying animal
It knows not what it is; and gather me
Into the artifice of eternity.

Once out of nature I shall never take
My bodily form from any natural thing,
But such a form as Grecian goldsmiths make
Of hammered gold and gold enamelling
To keep a drowsy Emperor awake;
Or set upon a golden bough to sing   30
To lords and ladies of Byzantium
Of what is past, or passing, or to come.   (*1928*)

---

[1] for Yeats, a symbol of the integrity of life perfected by art, and "out of nature"—i.e., the realm of "the artifice of eternity"

[2] turn about in a helical path—a motion identified in Yeats's work with the whirling of fate

ERNEST DOWSON • 1867–1900

Non Sum Qualis Eram Bonae sub Regno Cynarae[1]

    Last night, ah, yesternight, betwixt her lips and mine
    There fell thy shadow, Cynara! thy breath was shed
    Upon my soul between the kisses and the wine;
    And I was desolate and sick of an old passion,
        Yea, I was desolate and bowed my head:
    I have been faithful to thee, Cynara! in my fashion.

    All night upon mine heart I felt her warm heart beat,
    Night-long within mine arms in love and sleep she lay;
    Surely the kisses of her bought red mouth were sweet;
    But I was desolate and sick of an old passion,   *10*
        When I awoke and found the dawn was gray:
    I have been faithful to thee, Cynara! in my fashion.

    I have forgot much, Cynara! gone with the wind,
    Flung roses, roses riotously with the throng,
    Dancing, to put thy pale, lost lilies out of mind;
    But I was desolate and sick of an old passion,
        Yea, all the time, because the dance was long:
    I have been faithful to thee, Cynara! in my fashion.

    I cried for madder music and for stronger wine,
    But when the feast is finished and the lamps expire,   *20*
    Then falls thy shadow, Cynara! the night is thine;
    And I am desolate and sick of an old passion,
        Yea, hungry for the lips of my desire:
    I have been faithful to thee, Cynara! in my fashion.   (*1896*)

EDWIN ARLINGTON ROBINSON • 1869–1935

The Man Against the Sky

    Between me and the sunset, like a dome
    Against the glory of a world on fire,
    Now burned a sudden hill,
    Bleak, round, and high, by flame-lit height made higher,
    With nothing on it for the flame to kill

---

[1] I am not what I was under the reign of the good Cynara—Horace, *Odes,* Bk. IV, Ode I, ll. 3–4.

Save one who moved and was alone up there
To loom before the chaos and the glare
As if he were the last god going home
Unto his last desire.

Dark, marvelous, and inscrutable he moved on
Till down the fiery distance he was gone,—
Like one of those eternal, remote things
That range across a man's imaginings
When a sure music fills him and he knows
What he may say thereafter to few men,—
The touch of ages having wrought
An echo and a glimpse of what he thought
A phantom or a legend until then;
For whether lighted over ways that save,
Or lured from all repose,
If he go on too far to find a grave,
Mostly alone he goes.

Even he, who stood where I had found him,
On high with fire all round him,
Who moved along the molten west,
And over the round hill's crest
That seemed half ready with him to go down,
Flame-bitten and flame-cleft,
As if there were to be no last thing left
Of a nameless unimaginable town,—
Even he who climbed and vanished may have taken
Down to the perils of a depth not known,
From death defended though by men forsaken,
The bread that every man must eat alone;
He may have walked while others hardly dared
Look on to see him stand where many fell;
And upward out of that, as out of hell,
He may have sung and striven
To mount where more of him shall yet be given,
Bereft of all retreat,
To sevenfold heat,—
As on a day when three in Dura shared
The furnace, and were spared
For glory by that king of Babylon
Who made himself so great that God, who heard,
Covered him with long feathers, like a bird.[1]

Again, he may have gone down easily,
By comfortable altitudes, and found,

---

[1] Shadrach, Meshach, and Abednego refused to worship an image of gold set up in Dura by King Nebuchadnezzar, who had them cast into a fiery furnace. They were protected by the Lord and were then released and honored. The Lord chastized Nebuchadnezzar by causing his hairs to grow like eagles' feathers. Daniel, 1–4.

As always, underneath him solid ground
Whereon to be sufficient and to stand
Possessed already of the promised land,
Far stretched and fair to see:
A good sight, verily,
And one to make the eyes of her who bore him
Shine glad with hidden tears.
Why question of his ease of who before him,
In one place or another where they left
Their names as far behind them as their bones,
And yet by dint of slaughter toil and theft,
And shrewdly sharpened stones,
Carved hard the way for his ascendency
Through deserts of lost years?
Why trouble him now who sees and hears
No more than what his innocence requires,
And therefore to no other height aspires
Than one at which he neither quails nor tires?
He may do more by seeing what he sees
Than others eager for iniquities;
He may, by seeing all things for the best,
Incite futurity to do the rest.

Or with an even likelihood,
He may have met with atrabilious eyes
The fires of time on equal terms and passed
Indifferently down, until at last
His only kind of grandeur would have been,
Apparently, in being seen.
He may have had for evil or for good
No argument; he may have had no care
For what without himself went anywhere
To failure or to glory, and least of all
For such a stale, flamboyant miracle;
He may have been the prophet of an art
Immovable to old idolatries;
He may have been a player without a part,
Annoyed that even the sun should have the skies
For such a flaming way to advertise;
He may have been a painter sick at heart
With Nature's toiling for a new surprise;
He may have been a cynic, who now, for all
Of anything divine that his effete
Negation may have tasted,
Saw truth in his own image, rather small,
Forbore to fever the ephemeral,
Found any barren height a good retreat
From any swarming street,
And in the sun saw power superbly wasted:
And when the primitive old-fashioned stars

Came out again to shine on joys and wars
More primitive, and all arrayed for doom,
He may have proved a world a sorry thing   100
In his imagining,
And life a lighted highway to the tomb.

Or, mounting with infirm unsearching tread,
His hopes to chaos led,
He may have stumbled up there from the past,
And with an aching strangeness viewed the last
Abysmal conflagration of his dreams,—
A flame where nothing seems
To burn but flame itself, by nothing fed;
And while it all went out,   110
Not even the faint anodyne of doubt
May then have eased a painful going down
From pictured heights of power and lost renown,
Revealed at length to his outlived endeavor
Remote and unapproachable forever;
And at his heart there may have gnawed
Sick memories of a dead faith foiled and flawed
And long dishonored by the living death
Assigned alike by chance
To brutes and hierophants;   120
And anguish fallen on those he loved around him
May once have dealt the last blow to confound him,
And so have left him as death leaves a child,
Who sees it all too near;
And he who knows no young way to forget
May struggle to the tomb unreconciled.
Whatever suns may rise or set
There may be nothing kinder for him here
Than shafts and agonies;
And under these   130
He may cry out and stay on horribly;
Or, seeing in death too small a thing to fear,
He may go forward like a stoic Roman
Where pangs and terrors in his pathway lie,—
Or, seizing the swift logic of a woman,
Curse God and die.[2]

Or maybe there, like many another one
Who might have stood aloft and looked ahead,
Black-drawn against wild red,
He may have built, unawed by fiery gules[3]   140
That in him no commotion stirred,

---

[2] Job's wife recommended this course to him when he was smitten with boils. Job, 16: 2.   [3] the heraldic term for red

A living reason out of molecules
Why molecules occurred,
And one for smiling when he might have sighed
Had he seen far enough,
And in the same inevitable stuff
Discovered an odd reason too for pride
In being that he must have been by laws
Infrangible and for no kind of cause.
Deterred by no confusion or surprise   *150*
He may have seen with his mechanic eyes
A world without a meaning, and had room,
Alone amid magnificence and doom,
To build himself an airy monument
That should, or fail him in his vague intent,
Outlast an accidental universe—
To call it nothing worse—
Or, by the burrowing guile
Of Time disintegrated and effaced,
Like once-remembered mighty trees go down   *160*
To ruin, of which by man may now be traced
No part sufficient even to be rotten,
And in the book of things that are forgotten
Is entered as a thing not quite worth while.
He may have been so great
That satraps would have shivered at his frown.
And all he prized alive may rule a state
No larger than a grave that holds a clown;
He may have been a master of his fate,
And of his atoms,—ready as another   *170*
In his emergence to exonerate
His father and his mother;
He may have been a captain of a host,
Self-eloquent and ripe for prodigies,
Doomed here to swell by dangerous degrees,
And then give up the ghost.
Nahum's great grasshoppers were such as these,
Sun-scattered and soon lost.[4]

Whatever the dark road he may have taken,
This man who stood on high   *180*
And faced alone the sky,
Whatever drove or lured or guided him,—
A vision answering a faith unshaken,
An easy trust assumed of easy trials,
A sick negation born of weak denials,

---

[4] Nahum predicted the fall of Nineveh, whose captains, he said, were "as the great grasshoppers, which camp in the hedges in the cold day, but when the sun ariseth they flee away." Nahum, 3.

A crazed abhorrence of an old condition,
A blind attendance on a brief ambition,—
Whatever stayed him or derided him,
His way was even as ours;
And we, with all our wounds and all our powers, 190
Must each await alone at his own height
Another darkness or another light;
And there, of our poor self dominion reft,
If inference and reason shun
Hell, Heaven, and Oblivion,
May thwarted will (perforce precarious,
But for our conservation better thus)
Have no misgiving left
Of doing yet what here we leave undone?
Or if unto the last of these we cleave, 200
Believing or protesting we believe
In such an idle and ephemeral
Florescence of the diabolical,—
If, robbed of two fond old enormities,
Our being had no onward auguries,
What then were this great love of ours to say
For launching other lives to voyage again
A little farther into time and pain,
A little faster in a futile chase
For a kingdom and a power and a Race 210
That would have still in sight
A manifest end of ashes and eternal night?
Is this the music of the toys we shake
So loud,—as if there might be no mistake
Somewhere in our indomitable will?
Are we no greater than the noise we make
Along one blind atomic pilgrimage
Whereon by crass chance billeted we go
Because our brains and bones and cartilage
Will have it so? 220
If this we say, then let us all be still
About our share in it, and live and die
More quietly thereby.

Where was he going, this man against the sky?
You know not, nor do I.
But this we know, if we know anything:
That we may laugh and fight and sing
And of our transcience here make offering
To an orient Word that will not be erased,
Or, save in incommunicable gleams 230
Too permanent for dreams,
Be found or known.
No tonic and ambitious irritant

Of increase or of want
Has made in otherwise insensate waste
Of ages overthrown
A ruthless, veiled, implacable foretaste
Of other ages that are still to be
Depleted and rewarded variously
Because a few, by fate's economy, 240
Shall seem to move the world the way it goes;
No soft evangel of equality,
Safe-cradled in a communal repose
That huddles into death and may at last
Be covered well with equatorial snows—
And all for what, the devil only knows—
Will aggregate an inkling to confirm
The credit of a sage or of a worm,
Or tell us why one man in five
Should have a care to stay alive 250
While in his heart he feels no violence
Laid on his humor and intelligence
When infant Science makes a pleasant face
And waves again that hollow toy, the Race;
No planetary trap where souls are wrought
For nothing but the sake of being caught
And sent again to nothing will attune
Itself to any key of any reason
Why man should hunger through another season
To find out why 't were better late than soon 260
To go away and let the sun and moon
And all the silly stars illuminate
A place for creeping things,
And those that root and trumpet and have wings,
And herd and ruminate,
Or dive and flash and poise in rivers and seas,
Or by their loyal tails in lofty trees
Hang screeching lewd victorious derision
Of man's immortal vision.

Shall we, because Eternity records 270
Too vast an answer for the time-born words
We spell, whereof so many are dead that once
In our capricious lexicons
Were so alive and final, hear no more
The Word itself, the living word
That none alive has ever heard
Or ever spelt,
And few have ever felt
Without the fears and old surrenderings
And terrors that began 280
When Death let fall a feather from his wings

And humbled the first man?
Because the weight of our humility,
Wherefrom we gain
A little wisdom and much pain,
Falls here too sore and there too tedious,
Are we in anguish or complacency,
Not looking far enough ahead
To see by what mad couriers we are led
Along the roads of the ridiculous, 290
To pity ourselves and laugh at faith
And while we curse life bear it?
And if we see the soul's dead end in death,
Are we to fear it?
What folly is here that has not yet a name
Unless we say outright that we are liars?
What have we seen beyond our sunset fires
That lights again the way by which we came?
Why pay we such a price, and one we give
So clamoringly, for each racked empty day 300
That leads one more last human hope away,
As quiet fiends would lead past our crazed eyes
Our children to an unseen sacrifice?
If after all that we have lived and thought,
All comes to Nought,—
If there be nothing after Now,
And we be nothing anyhow,
And we know that,—why live?
'T were sure but weaklings' vain distress
To suffer dungeons where so many doors 310
Will open on the cold eternal shores
That look sheer down
To the dark tideless floods of Nothingness
Where all who know may drown.   (*1916*)

ROBERT FROST • 1874–1963

Birches

When I see birches bend to left and right
Across the lines of straighter darker trees,
I like to think some boy's been swinging them.
But swinging doesn't bend them down to stay.
Ice-storms do that. Often you must have seen them
Loaded with ice a sunny winter morning
After a rain. They click upon themselves

As the breeze rises, and turn many-colored
As the stir cracks and crazes their enamel.
Soon the sun's warmth makes them shed crystal shells
Shattering and avalanching on the snow-crust—
Such heaps of broken glass to sweep away
You'd think the inner dome of heaven had fallen.
They are dragged to the withered bracken by the load,
And they seem not to break; though once they are bowed
So low for long, they never right themselves:
You may see their trunks arching in the woods
Years afterwards, trailing their leaves on the ground
Like girls on hands and knees that throw their hair
Before them over their heads to dry in the sun.
But I was going to say when Truth broke in
With all her matter-of-fact about the ice-storm
(Now am I free to be poetical?)
I should prefer to have some boy bend them
As he went out and in to fetch the cows—
Some boy too far from town to learn baseball,
Whose only play was what he found himself,
Summer or winter, and could play alone.
One by one he subdued his father's trees
By riding them down over and over again
Until he took the stiffness out of them,
And not one but hung limp, not one was left
For him to conquer. He learned all there was
To learn about not launching out too soon
And so not carrying the tree away
Clear to the ground. He always kept his poise
To the top branches, climbing carefully
With the same pains you use to fill a cup
Up to the brim, and even above the brim.
Then he flung outward, feet first, with a swish,
Kicking his way down through the air to the ground.
So was I once myself a swinger of birches.
And so I dream of going back to be.
It's when I'm weary of considerations,
And life is too much like a pathless wood
Where your face burns and tickles with the cobwebs
Broken across it, and one eye is weeping
From a twig's having lashed across it open.
I'd like to get away from earth awhile
And then come back to it and begin over.
May no fate willfully misunderstand me
And half grant what I wish and snatch me away
Not to return. Earth's the right place for love:
I don't know where it's likely to go better.
I'd like to go by climbing a birch tree,
And climb black branches up a snow-white trunk

Toward heaven, till the tree could bear no more,
But dipped its top and set me down again.
That would be good both going and coming back.
One could do worse than be a swinger of birches. *(1916)*

Stopping by Woods on a Snowy Evening

Whose woods these are I think I know.
His house is in the village though;
He will not see me stopping here
To watch his woods fill up with snow.

My little horse must think it queer
To stop without a farmhouse near
Between the woods and frozen lake
The darkest evening of the year.

He gives his harness bells a shake
To ask if there is some mistake.
The only other sound's the sweep
Of easy wind and downy flake.

The woods are lovely, dark and deep.
But I have promises to keep,
And miles to go before I sleep,
And miles to go before I sleep. *(1923)*

The Onset

Always the same, when on a fated night
At last the gathered snow lets down as white
As may be in dark woods, and with a song
It shall not make again all winter long
Of hissing on the yet uncovered ground,
I almost stumble looking up and round,
As one who overtaken by the end
Gives up his errand, and lets death descend
Upon him where he is, with nothing done
To evil, no important triumph won,
More than if life had never been begun.

Yet all the precedent is on my side:
I know that winter death has never tried
The earth but it has failed: the snow may heap
In long storms an undrifted four feet deep
As measured against maple, birch and oak,
It cannot check the peeper's silver croak;
And I shall see the snow all go down hill
In water of a slender April rill
That flashes tail through last year's withered brake
And dead weeds, like a disappearing snake.
Nothing will be left white but here a birch,
And there a clump of houses with a church. *(1923)*

Bereft

Where had I heard this wind before
Change like this to a deeper roar?
What would it take my standing there for,
Holding open a restive door,
Looking down hill to a frothy shore?
Summer was past and day was past.
Sombre clouds in the west were massed.
Out in the porch's sagging floor
Leaves got up in a coil and hissed,
Blindly struck at my knee and missed.   *10*
Something sinister in the tone
Told me my secret must be known:
Word I was in the house alone
Somehow must have gotten aboard,
Word I was in my life alone,
Word I had no one left but God.   *(1928)*

Come In

As I came to the edge of the woods,
Thrush music—hark!
Now if it was dusk outside,
Inside it was dark.

Too dark in the woods for a bird
By sleight of wing
To better its perch for the night,
Though it still could sing.

The last of the light of the sun
That had died in the west   *10*
Still lived for one song more
In a thrush's breast.

Far in the pillared dark
Thrush music went—
Almost like a call to come in
To the dark and lament.

But no, I was out for stars:
I would not come in.
I meant not even if asked,
And I hadn't been.   *(1942)*   *20*

WALLACE STEVENS • 1879–1955

The Snow Man

One must have a mind of winter
To regard the frost and the boughs
Of the pine-trees crusted with snow;

And have been cold a long time
To behold the junipers shagged with ice,
The spruces rough in the distant glitter

Of the January sun; and not to think
Of any misery in the sound of the wind,
In the sound of a few leaves,

Which is the sound of the land   *10*
Full of the same wind
That is blowing in the same bare place

> For the listener, who listens in the snow,
> And, nothing himself, beholds
> Nothing that is not there and the nothing that is. *(1923)*

A High-Toned Old Christian Woman

> Poetry is the supreme fiction, madame.
> Take the moral law and make a nave of it
> And from the nave build haunted heaven. Thus,
> The conscience is converted into palms,
> Like windy citherns hankering for hymns.
> We agree in principle. That's clear. But take
> The opposing law and make a peristyle,
> And from the peristyle project a masque
> Beyond the planets. Thus, our bawdiness,
> Unpurged by epitaph, indulged at last,
> Is equally converted into palms,
> Squiggling like saxophones. And palm for palm,
> Madame, we are where we began. Allow,
> Therefore, that in the planetary scene
> Your disaffected flagellants, well-stuffed,
> Smacking their muzzy bellies in parade,
> Proud of such novelties of the sublime,
> Such tink and tank and tunk-a-tunk-tunk,
> May, merely may, madame, whip from themselves
> A jovial hullabaloo among the spheres.
> This will make widows wince. But fictive things
> Wink as they will. Wink most when widows wince. *(1923)*

The Emperor of Ice-Cream

> Call the roller of big cigars,
> The muscular one, and bid him whip
> In kitchen cups concupiscent curds.
> Let the wenches dawdle in such dress
> As they are used to wear, and let the boys
> Bring flowers in last month's newspapers.
> Let be be finale of seem.
> The only emperor is the emperor of ice-cream.
>
> Take from the dresser of deal,
> Lacking the three glass knobs, that sheet
> On which she embroidered fantails once
> And spread it so as to cover her face.
> If her horny feet protrude, they come
> To show how cold she is, and dumb.
> Let the lamp affix its beam.
> The only emperor is the emperor of ice-cream. *(1923)*

A Postcard from the Volcano

Children picking up our bones
Will never know that these were once
As quick as foxes on the hill;

And that in autumn, when the grapes
Made sharp air sharper by their smell
These had a being, breathing frost;

And least will guess that with our bones
We left much more, left what still is
The look of things, left what we felt

At what we saw. The spring clouds blow
Above the shuttered mansion-house,
Beyond our gate and the windy sky

Cries out a literate despair.
We knew for long the mansion's look
And what we said of it became

A part of what it is . . . Children,
Still weaving budded aureoles,
Will speak our speech and never know,

Will say of the mansion that it seems
As if he that lived there left behind
A spirit storming in blank walls,

A dirty house in a gutted world,
A tatter of shadows peaked to white,
Smeared with the gold of the opulent sun.

(*1935*)

The Glass of Water

That the glass would melt in heat,
That the water would freeze in cold,
Shows that this object is merely a state,
One of many, between two poles. So,
In the metaphysical, there are these poles.

Here in the centre stands the glass. Light
Is the lion that comes down to drink. There
And in that state, the glass is a pool.
Ruddy are his eyes and ruddy are his claws
When light comes down to wet his frothy jaws

And in the water winding weeds move round.
And there and in another state—the refractions,
The *metaphysica,* the plastic parts of poems
Crash in the mind—But, fat Jocundus, worrying
About what stands here in the centre, not the glass,

But in the centre of our lives, this time, this day,
It is a state, this spring among the politicians
Playing cards. In a village of the indigenes,
One would have still to discover. Among the dogs
    and dung,
One would continue to contend with one's ideas. (*1942*)

WILLIAM CARLOS WILLIAMS • 1833–1963

Tract

I will teach you my townspeople
how to perform a funeral
for you have it over a troop
of artists—
unless one should scour the world—
you have the ground sense necessary.

See! the hearse leads.
I begin with a design for a hearse.
For Christ's sake not black—
nor white either—and not polished!   10
Let it be weathered—like a farm wagon—
with gilt wheels (this could be
applied fresh at small expense)
or no wheels at all:
a rough dray to drag over the ground.

Knock the glass out!
My God—glass, my townspeople!
For what purpose? Is it for the dead
to look out or for us to see
how well he is housed or to see   20
the flowers or the lack of them—
or what?
To keep the rain and snow from him?

He will have a heavier rain soon:
pebbles and dirt and what not.
Let there be no glass—
and no upholstery, phew!
and no little brass rollers
and small easy wheels on the bottom—
my townspeople what are you thinking
   of?   30

A rough plain hearse then
with gilt wheels and no top at all.
On this the coffin lies
by its own weight.

            No wreaths please—
especially no hot house flowers.
Some common memento is better,
something he prized and is known by:
his old clothes—a few books perhaps—
God knows what! You realize
how we are about these things   40
my townspeople—
something will be found—anything
even flowers if he had come to that.
So much for the hearse.

For heaven's sake though see to the
   driver!
Take off the silk hat! In fact
that's no place at all for him—
up there unceremoniously
dragging our friend out to his own
   dignity!
Bring him down—bring him down!   50
Low and inconspicuous! I'd not have him
   ride
on the wagon at all—damn him—
the undertaker's understrapper!
Let him hold the reins
and walk at the side
and inconspicuously too!

Then briefly as to yourselves:
Walk behind—as they do in France,
seventh class, or if you ride
Hell take curtains! Go with some
   show   60
of inconvenience; sit openly—
to the weather as to grief.
Or do you think you can shut grief in?
What—from us? We who have perhaps
nothing to lose? Share with us
share with us—it will be money
in your pockets.
            Go now
I think you are ready.   *(1916)*

Dawn

Ecstatic bird songs pound
the hollow vastness of the sky
with metallic clinkings—
beating color up into it

at a far edge,—beating it, beating it
with rising, triumphant ardor,—
stirring it into warmth,
quickening in it a spreading change,—
bursting wildly against it as
dividing the horizon, a heavy sun   10
lifts himself—is lifted—
bit by bit above the edge
of things,—runs free at last
out into the open—! lumbering
glorified in full release upward—
           songs cease. (*1917*)

The Poor

It's the anarchy of poverty
delights me, the old
yellow wooden house indented
among the new brick tenements

Or a cast iron balcony
with panels showing oak branches
in full leaf. It fits
the dress of the children

reflecting every stage and
custom of necessity—   10
Chimneys, roofs, fences of
wood and metal in an unfenced

age and enclosing next to
nothing at all: the old man
in a sweater and soft black
hat who sweeps the sidewalk—

his own ten feet of it—
in a wind that fitfully
turning his corner has   19
overwhelmed the entire city (*1917*)

Spring and All

      By the road to the contagious hospital
      under the surge of the blue
      mottled clouds driven from the
      northeast—a cold wind. Beyond, the
      waste of broad, muddy fields
      brown with dried weeds, standing and fallen

      patches of standing water
      the scattering of tall trees

      All along the road the reddish
      purplish, forked, upstanding, twiggy   10
      stuff of bushes and small trees
      with dead, brown leaves under them
      leafless vines—

      Lifeless in appearance, sluggish
      dazed spring approaches—

      They enter the new world naked,
      cold, uncertain of all
      save that they enter. All about them
      the cold, familiar wind—

Now the grass, tomorrow
the stiff curl of wildcarrot leaf
One by one objects are defined—
It quickens: clarity, outline of leaf

But now the stark dignity of
entrance—Still, the profound change
has come upon them: rooted, they
grip down and begin to awaken   (*1923*)

T. S. ELIOT • 1885–1965

The Love Song of J. Alfred Prufrock

> *S'io credesse che mia risposta fosse*
> *A persona che mai tornasse al mondo,*
> *Questa fiamma staria senza piu scosse.*
> *Ma perciocche giammai di questo fondo*
> *Non torno vivo alcun, s'i'odo il vero,*
> *Senza tema d'infamia ti rispondo.*[1]

Let us go then, you and I,
When the evening is spread out against the sky
Like a patient etherised upon a table;
Let us go, through certain half-deserted streets,
The muttering retreats
Of restless nights in one-night cheap hotels
And sawdust restaurants with oyster-shells:
Streets that follow like a tedious argument
Of insidious intent
To lead you to an overwhelming question . . .
Oh, do not ask, "What is it?"
Let us go and make our visit.

In the room the women come and go
Talking of Michelangelo.

The yellow fog that rubs its back upon the window-panes,
The yellow smoke that rubs its muzzle on the window-panes
Licked its tongue into the corners of the evening,
Lingered upon the pools that stand in drains,

---

[1] Dante, *Inferno,* XXVII, ll. 61–66: "If I thought that my answer were directed to anyone who could ever return to the world, this flame would quiver no longer; but because, as I hear, no one ever returns alive from this depth, I reply to you without fear of infamy."

Let fall upon its back the soot that falls from chimneys,
Slipped by the terrace, made a sudden leap,
And seeing that it was a soft October night,
Curled once about the house, and fell asleep.

And indeed there will be time
For the yellow smoke that slides along the street,
Rubbing its back upon the window-panes;
There will be time, there will be time
To prepare a face to meet the faces that you meet;
There will be time to murder and create,
And time for all the works and days of hands
That lift and drop a question on your plate;
Time for you and time for me,
And time yet for a hundred indecisions,
And for a hundred visions and revisions,
Before the taking of a toast and tea.

In the room the women come and go
Talking of Michelangelo.

And indeed there will be time
To wonder, "Do I dare?" and, "Do I dare?"
Time to turn back and descend the stair,
With a bald spot in the middle of my hair—
(They will say: "How his hair is growing thin!")
My morning coat, my collar mounting firmly to the chin,
My necktie rich and modest, but asserted by a simple pin—
(They will say: "But how his arms and legs are thin!")
Do I dare
Disturb the universe?
In a minute there is time
For decisions and revisions which a minute will reverse.

For I have known them all already, known them all:
Have known the evenings, mornings, afternoons,
I have measured out my life with coffee spoons;
I know the voices dying with a dying fall
Beneath the music from a farther room.
  So how should I presume?

And I have known the eyes already, known them all—
The eyes that fix you in a formulated phrase,
And when I am formulated, sprawling on a pin,
When I am pinned and wriggling on the wall,
Then how should I begin
To spit out all the butt-ends of my days and ways?
  And how should I presume?

And I have known the arms already, known them all—
Arms that are braceleted and white and bare
(But in the lamplight, downed with light brown hair!)
Is it perfume from a dress
That makes me so digress?
Arms that lie along a table, or wrap about a shawl.
    And should I then presume?
    And how should I begin?

. . . .

Shall I say, I have gone at dusk through narrow streets   70
And watched the smoke that rises from the pipes
Of lonely men in shirt-sleeves, leaning out of windows? . . .

I should have been a pair of ragged claws
Scuttling across the floors of silent seas.

. . . .

And the afternoon, the evening, sleeps so peacefully!
Smoothed by long fingers,
Asleep . . . tired . . . or it malingers,
Stretched on the floor, here beside you and me.
Should I, after tea and cakes and ices,
Have the strength to force the moment to its crisis?   80
But though I have wept and fasted, wept and prayed,
Though I have seen my head (grown slightly bald) brought in upon a platter,[2]
I am no prophet—and here's no great matter;
I have seen the moment of my greatness flicker,
And I have seen the eternal Footman hold my coat, and snicker,
And in short, I was afraid.

And would it have been worth it, after all,
After the cups, the marmalade, the tea,
Among the porcelain, among some talk of you and me,
Would it have been worth while,   90
To have bitten off the matter with a smile,
To have squeezed the universe into a ball
To roll it toward some overwhelming question,
To say: "I am Lazarus,[3] come from the dead,
Come back to tell you all, I shall tell you all"—
If one, settling a pillow by her head,
    Should say: "That is not what I meant at all;
    That is not it, at all."

And would it have been worth it, after all,
Would it have been worth while,   100
    After the sunsets and the dooryards and the sprinkled streets,

---

[2] John the Baptist was beheaded at the insistence of Salome, to whom his head was delivered on a platter. See Matthew 14:3–11 or Mark 6:16–28.

[3] One of the miracles of Jesus was the raising of Lazarus from the dead after he had lain in the grave four days. See John 11:1–44.

After the novels, after the teacups, after the skirts that trail along the floor—
And this, and so much more?—
It is impossible to say just what I mean!
But as if a magic lantern threw the nerves in patterns on a screen:
Would it have been worth while
If one, settling a pillow or throwing off a shawl,
And turning toward the window, should say:
   "That is not it at all,
   That is not what I meant, at all."   *110*
. . . .

No! I am not Prince Hamlet, nor was meant to be;
Am an attendant lord, one that will do
To swell a progress, start a scene or two,
Advise the prince; no doubt, an easy tool,
Deferential, glad to be of use,
Politic, cautious, and meticulous;
Full of high sentence,[4] but a bit obtuse;
At times, indeed, almost ridiculous—
Almost, at times, the Fool.

I grow old . . . I grow old . . .   *120*
I shall wear the bottoms of my trousers rolled.

Shall I part my hair behind? Do I dare to eat a peach?
I shall wear white flannel trousers, and walk upon the beach.
I have heard the mermaids singing, each to each.

I do not think that they will sing to me.

I have seen them riding seaward on the waves
Combing the white hair of the waves blown back
When the wind blows the water white and black.

We have lingered in the chambers of the sea
By sea-girls wreathed with seaweed red and brown   *130*
Till human voices wake us, and we drown.   (*1917*)

CLAUDE MCKAY • 1890–1948

Harlem Dancer

    Applauding youths laughed with young prostitutes
    And watched her perfect, half-clothed body sway;
    Her voice was like the sound of blended flutes
    Blown by black players on a picnic day.

---

[4] *sententia,* wise sayings

She sang and danced on gracefully and calm,
The light gauze hanging loose about her form;
To me she seemed a proudly-swaying palm
Grown lovelier for passing through a storm.
Upon her swarthy neck black shiny curls
Luxuriant fell; and tossing coins in praise,   *10*
The wine-flushed, bold-eyed boys, and even the girls,
Devoured her shape with eager, passionate gaze;
But looking at her falsely-smiling face,
I knew her self was not in that strange place.   (*1917*)

America

Although she feeds me bread of bitterness,
And sinks into my throat her tiger's tooth,
Stealing my breath of life, I will confess
I love this cultured hell that tests my youth!
Her vigor flows like tides into my blood,
Giving me strength erect against her hate.
Her bigness sweeps my being like a flood.
Yet as a rebel fronts a king in state,
I stand within her walls with not a shred
Of terror, malice, not a word of jeer.   *10*
Darkly I gaze into the days ahead,
And see her might and granite wonders there,
Beneath the touch of Time's unerring hand,
Like priceless treasures sinking in the sand.   (*c. 1920*)

The White City

I will not toy with it nor bend an inch.
Deep in the secret chambers of my heart
I muse my life-long hate, and without flinch
I bear it nobly as I live my part.
My being would be a skeleton, a shell,
If this dark Passion that fills my every mood,
And makes my heaven in the white world's hell,
Did not forever feed me vital blood.
I see the mighty city through a mist—
The strident trains that speed the goaded mass,   *10*
The poles and spires and towers vapor-kissed,
The fortressed port through which the great ships pass,
The tides, the wharves, the dens I contemplate,
Are sweet like wanton loves because I hate.   (*c. 1920*)

The Tropics in New York

Bananas ripe and green, and gingerroot,
    Cocoa in pods and alligator pears,
And tangerines and mangoes and grapefruit,
    Fit for the highest prize at parish fairs,

Set in the window, bringing memories
    Of fruit trees laden by low-singing rills,
And dewy dawns, and mystical blue skies
    In benediction over nunlike hills.

My eyes grew dim, and I could no more gaze;
    A wave of longing through my body swept,
And, hungry for the old, familiar ways,
    I turned aside and bowed my head and wept. *(1920)*

Outcast

For the dim regions whence my fathers came
My spirit, bondaged by the body, longs.
Words felt, but never heard, my lips would frame;
My soul would sing forgotten jungle songs.
I would go back to darkness and to peace,
But the great western world holds me in fee,
And I may never hope for full release
While to its alien gods I bend my knee.
Something in me is lost, forever lost,
Some vital thing has gone out of my heart,
And I must walk the way of life a ghost
Among the sons of earth, a thing apart.
For I was born, far from my native clime,
Under the white man's menace, out of time. *(c. 1920)*

Flame-Heart

So much have I forgotten in ten years,
    So much in ten brief years! I have forgot
What time the purple apples come to juice,
    And what month brings the shy forget-me-not.
I have forgot the special, startling season
    Of the pimiento's flowering and fruiting;
What time of year the ground doves brown the fields
    And fill the noonday with their curious fluting.
I have forgotten much, but still remember
The poinsettia's red, blood-red in warm December.

I still recall the honey-fever grass,
    But cannot recollect the high days when
We rooted them out of the ping-wing path
    To stop the mad bees in the rabbit pen.
I often try to think in what sweet month
    The languid painted ladies used to dapple
The yellow byroad mazing from the main,
    Sweet with the golden threads of the rose apple.
I have forgotten—strange—but quite remember
The poinsettia's red, blood-red in warm December.   *20*

What weeks, what months, what time of the mild year
    We cheated school to have our fling at tops?
What days our wine-thrilled bodies pulsed with joy
    Feasting upon blackberries in the copse?
Oh, some I know! I have embalmed the days,
    Even the sacred moments when we played,
All innocent of passion, uncorrupt,
    At noon and evening in the flame-heart's shade.
We were so happy, happy, I remember,
Beneath the poinsettia's red in warm December.   (*1920*)   *30*

E. E. CUMMINGS • 1894–1962

Chanson Innocente: in Just-spring

in Just-
spring   when the world is mud-
luscious the little
lame balloonman

whistles   far   and wee

and eddieandbill come
running from marbles and
piracies and it's
spring

when the world is puddle-wonderful   *10*

the queer
old balloonman whistles
far   and   wee
and bettyandisbel come dancing

from hop-scotch and jump-rope and

it's
spring
and
      the
        goat-footed   *20*

balloonMan   whistles
far
and
wee   (*1923*)

E. E. Cummings

Sonnet: a wind has blown the rain away

a wind has blown the rain away and blown
the sky away and all the leaves away,
and the trees stand. I think i too have known
autumn too long

              (and what have you to say,
wind wind wind—did you love somebody
and have you the petal of somewhere in your heart
pinched from dumb summer?
                     O crazy daddy
of death dance cruelly for us and start

the last leaf whirling in the final brain
of air!)Let us as we have seen see
doom's integration . . . . a wind has blown the rain

away and the leaves and the sky and the
trees stand:
       the trees stand. The trees,
suddenly wait against the moon's face. (*1923*)

as freedom is a breakfastfood

as freedom is a breakfastfood
or truth can live with right and wrong
or molehills are from mountains made
—long enough and just so long
will being pay the rent of seem
and genius please the talentgang
and water most encourage flame

as hatracks into peachtrees grow
or hopes dance best on bald men's hair
and every finger is a toe
and any courage is a fear
—long enough and just so long
will the impure think all things pure
and hornets wail by children stung

or as the seeing are the blind
and robins never welcome spring
nor flatfolk prove their world is round
nor dingsters die at break of dong
and common's rare and millstones float
—long enough and just so long
tomorrow will not be too late

worms are the words but joy's the voice
down shall go which and up come who
breasts will be breasts and thighs will be thighs
deeds cannot dream what dreams can do
—time is a tree(this life one leaf)
but love is the sky and i am for you
just so long and long enough   (*1940*)

LANGSTON HUGHES • 1902–1967

from Montage of a Dream Deferred

NOTE: In terms of current Afro-American popular music and the sources from which it has progressed—jazz, ragtime, swing, blues, boogie-woogie, and be-bop—this poem on contemporary Harlem, like be-bop, is marked by conflicting changes, sudden nuances, sharp and impudent interjections, broken rhythms, and passages sometimes in the manner of the jam session, sometimes the popular song, punctuated by the riffs, runs, breaks, and disc-tortions of the music of a community in transition.
                                                                                                L.H.

BOOGIE SEGUE TO BOP

DREAM BOOGIE

Good morning daddy!
Ain't you heard
The boogie-woogie rumble
Of a dream deferred?

Listen closely:
You'll hear their feet
Beating out and beating out a—

    You think
    It's a happy beat?

Listen to it closely:
Ain't you heard
something underneath
like a—

    What did I say?

Sure,
I'm happy!
Take it away!

Hey, pop!
Re-bop!
Mop

Y-e-a-h!

. . . .

CHILDREN'S RHYMES

When I was a chile we used to play,
"One—two—buckle my shoe!"
and things like that. But now, Lord,
listen at them little varmints!

    By what sends
    the white kids
    I ain't sent:
    I know I can't
    be President.

There is two thousand children
in this block, I do believe!

    What don't bug
    them white kids
    sure bugs me:
    We knows everybody
    ain't free!

Some of these young ones is cert'ly bad—
One batted a hard ball right through my window
and my gold fish et the glass.

    What's written down
    for white folks

    ain't for us a-tall:
    "Liberty and Justice—
    Huh—For All."

    Oop-pop-a-da!
    Skee! Daddle-de-do!
    Be-bop!

    Salt'peanuts!

De-dop!

. . . .

BUDDY

That kid's my buddy,
still and yet
I don't see him much.
He works downtown for Twelve a week.
Has to give his mother Ten—
she says he can have
the other Two
to pay his carfare, buy a suit,
coat, shoes,
anything he wants out of it.

JUKE BOX LOVE SONG

I could take the Harlem night
and wrap around you
Take the neon lights and make a crown,
Take the Lenox Avenue busses,
Taxis, subways,
And for your love song tone their rumble down.
Take Harlem's heartbeat,
Make a drumbeat,
Put it on a record, let it whirl,
And while we listen to it play,
Dance with you till day—
Dance with you, my sweet brown Harlem girl.

. . . .

WONDER

Early blue evening.
Lights ain't come on yet.
    Looky yonder!
They come on now!

EASY BOOGIE

Down in the bass
That steady beat
Walking walking walking
Like marching feet.

Down in the bass
That easy roll,
Rolling like I like it
In my soul.

    Riffs, smears, breaks.

Hey, Lawdy, Mama!
Do you hear what I said?

    Easy like I rock it
    In my bed!

DIG AND BE DUG

     MOVIES

   The Roosevelt, Renaissance, Gem, Alhambra:
   Harlem laughing in all the wrong places
     at the crocodile tears
     of crocodile art
     that you know
     in your heart
     is crocodile:

    (Hollywood
    laughs at me,
    black—   *10*
    so I laugh
    back.)

 · · · · · · · · · ·

    WHAT? SO SOON!

    I believe my old lady's
    pregnant again!

    Fate must have
    some kind of trickeration
    to populate the
    cullud nation!

 COMMENT AGAINST LAMP POST
    You call it fate?

 · · · · · · · · · ·

     MOTTO

    I play it cool
    and dig all jive
    That's the reason
    I stay alive.
    My motto,
    As I live and learn,
      is:
    Dig and Be Dug
    In Return.

 · · · · · · · · · ·

     ADVICE

    Folks, I'm telling you,
    birthing is hard

and dying is mean—
so get yourself
a little loving
in between.

GREEN MEMORY

A wonderful time—the War:
when money rolled in
and blood rolled out.

But blood
was far away
from here—

Money was near.

. . . .

EARLY BRIGHT

. . . .

MELLOW

Into the laps
of black celebrities
white girls fall
like pale plums from a tree
beyond a high tension wall
wired for killing
which makes it
more thrilling.

LIVE AND LET LIVE

Maybe it ain't right—
but the people of the night
   will give even
   a snake
   a break.

. . . .

VICE VERSA TO BACH

THEME FOR ENGLISH B

The instructor said,

   Go home and write
   a page tonight.
   And let that page come out of you—
   Then, it will be true.

I wonder if it's that simple?

I am twenty-two, colored, born in Winston-Salem.
I went to school there, then Durham, then here
to this college on the hill above Harlem.
I am the only colored student in my class.
The steps from the hill lead down into Harlem,
through a park, then I cross St. Nicholas,
Eighth Avenue, Seventh, and I come to the Y,
the Harlem Branch Y, where I take the elevator
up to my room, sit down, and write this page:

It's not easy to know what is true for you or me
at twenty-two, my age. But I guess I'm what
I feel and see and hear. Harlem, I hear you:
hear you, hear me—we two—you, me talk on this page.
(I hear New York, too.) Me—who?

Well, I like to eat, sleep, drink, and be in love.
I like to work, read, learn, and understand life.
I like a pipe for a Christmas present,
or records—Bessie, bop, or Bach.

I guess being colored doesn't make me not like
the same things other folks like who are other races.
So will my page be colored that I write?
Being me, it will not be white.
But it will be
a part of you, instructor.
You are white—
yet a part of me, as I am a part of you.
That's American.
Sometimes perhaps you don't want to be a part of me.
Nor do I often want to be a part of you.
But we are, that's true!
As I learn from you,
I guess you learn from me—
although you're older—and white—
and somewhat more free.

This is my page for English B.

COLLEGE FORMAL: RENAISSANCE CASINO

  Golden girl
  in a golden gown
  in a melody night
  in Harlem town
  lad tall and brown
  tall and wise
  college boy smart
  eyes in eyes

    the music wraps
    them both around   10
    in mellow magic
    of dancing sound
    till they're the heart
    of the whole big town
    gold and brown

. . . .

DREAM DEFERRED

. . . .

TESTIMONIAL

If I just had a piano
if I just had a organ,
if I just had a drum,
how I could praise my Lord!

But I don't need no piano,
    neither organ
      nor drum
for to praise my Lord!

PASSING

On sunny summer Sunday afternoons in Harlem
when the air is one interminable ball game
and grandma cannot get her gospel hymns
from the Saints of God in Christ
on account of the Dodgers on the radio,
on sunny Sunday afternoons
when the kids look all new
and far too clean to stay that way,
and Harlem has its
washed-and-ironed-and-cleaned-best out,   10
the ones who've crossed the line
to live downtown
miss you,
Harlem of the bitter dream,
since their dream has
come true.

. . . .

BLUES AT DAWN

I don't dare start thinking in the morning
I don't dare start thinking in the morning.
  If I thought thoughts in bed,
    Them thoughts would bust my head—
So I don't dare start thinking in the morning.

      I don't dare remember in the morning.
      Don't dare remember in the morning.
         If I recall the day before,
         I wouldn't get up no more—
      So I don't dare remember in the morning.   *10*

. . . .

ARGUMENT

      White is right,
      Yellow mellow,
      Black, get back!

      Do you believe that, Jack?

Sure do!

      Then you're a dope
      for which there ain't no hope.
      Black is fine!
      And, God knows,
      It's mine!   *10*

. . . .

LIKEWISE

The Jews:
    Groceries
    Suits
    Fruit
    Watches
    Diamond rings
    THE DAILY NEWS
Jews sell me things.
Yom Kippur, no!
Shops all over Harlem   *10*
close up tight that night.

Some folks blame high prices on the Jews.
(Some folks blame too much on Jews.)
But in Harlem they don't answer back,
Just maybe shrug their shoulders,
"What's the use?"

      What's the use
      In Harlem?
      What's the use?
      What's the Harlem   *20*
      use in Harlem
      what's the lick?

    Hey!
    Baba-re-bop!
    Mop.
    On a be-bop kick!

Sometimes I think
Jews must have heard
the music of a
dream deferred.   30

. . . .

LENOX AVENUE MURAL

HARLEM

What happens to a dream deferred?

    Does it dry up
    like a raisin in the sun?
    Or fester like a sore—
    And then run?
    Does it stink like rotten meat?
    Or crust and sugar over—
    like a syrupy sweet?

    Maybe it just sags
    like a heavy load.   10

    Or does it explode?

. . . .

ISLAND

    Between two rivers,
    North of the park,
    like darker rivers
    The streets are dark.

    Black and white,
    Gold and brown—
    Chocolate-custard
    Pie of a town.

    Dream within a dream
    Our dream deferred.   10

    Good morning, daddy!

    Ain't you heard?   (*1951*)

COUNTEE CULLEN • 1903–1946

Yet Do I Marvel

I doubt not God is good, well-meaning, kind,
And did He stoop to quibble could tell why
The little buried mole continues blind,
Why flesh that mirrors Him must some day die,
Make plain the reason tortured Tantalus
Is baited by the fickle fruit, declare
If merely brute caprice dooms Sisyphus[1]
To struggle up a never-ending stair.
Inscrutable His ways are, and immune
To catechism by a mind too strewn   *10*
With petty cares to slightly understand
What awful brain compels His awful hand.
Yet do I marvel at this curious thing:
To make a poet black, and bid him sing!   (*1925*)

Four Epitaphs

1 FOR MY GRANDMOTHER

This lovely flower fell to seed;
Work gently sun and rain;
She held it as her dying creed
That she would grow again.

2 FOR JOHN KEATS, APOSTLE OF BEAUTY

Not writ in water nor in mist,
Sweet lyric throat, thy name.
Thy singing lips that cold death kissed
Have seared his own with flame.

3 FOR PAUL LAURENCE DUNBAR

Born of the sorrowful of heart
Mirth was a crown upon his head;
Pride kept his twisted lips apart
In jest, to hide a heart that bled.

4 FOR A LADY I KNOW

She even thinks that up in heaven
  Her class lies late and snores,
While poor black cherubs rise at seven
  To do celestial chores.   (*1925*)

---

[1] Corrupt king of Corinth punished in Hades by having to push uphill a huge stone which rolled down again each time it reached the top (*Odyssey*, XI, 593–600)

Scottsboro,[1] Too, Is Worth Its Song
(A POEM TO AMERICAN POETS)

I said:
Now will the poets sing,—
Their cries go thundering
Like blood and tears
Into the nation's ears,
Like lightning dart
Into the nation's heart.
Against the disease and death and all things fell,
And war,
Their strophes rise and swell   10
To jar
The foe smug in his citadel.

Remembering their sharp and pretty
Tunes for Sacco and Vanzetti,[2]
I said:
Here too's a cause divinely spun
For those whose eyes are on the sun,
Here in epitome
Is all disgrace
And epic wrong,   20
Like wine to brace
The minstrel heart, and blare it into song.

Surely, I said,
Now will the poets sing.
   But they have raised no cry.
   I wonder why.   *(1935)*

---

[1] Nine Negro boys were tried in Scottsboro, Alabama, in 1931 on charges of raping two white girls. Eight of the nine were convicted. Liberals and radicals contended that racial prejudice had produced the decision. The Supreme Court ordered a retrial. One of the girls acknowledged that she had lied, but one man was sentenced to death. A second review by the Supreme Court produced another retrial resulting in four convictions and the dismissal of charges against five of the defendants.

[2] Italian-born philosophical anarchists executed in 1927 for murder in connection with a Massachusetts payroll robbery. The inconclusiveness of the evidence against them fed the suspicion that they had been persecuted for their radical views. Their cause was taken up by left and center liberals, including a number of prominent writers.

W. H. AUDEN • 1907–

Song: Now the Leaves Are Falling Fast

Now the leaves are falling fast,
Nurse's flowers will not last,
Nurses to their graves are gone,
But the prams go rolling on.

Whispering neighbours left and right
Daunt us from our true delight,
Able hands are left to freeze
Derelict on lonely knees.

Close behind us on our track,
Dead in hundreds cry Alack,
Arms raised stiffly to reprove
In false attitudes of love.

Scrawny through a plundered wood,
Trolls run scolding for their food,
Owl and nightingale are dumb,
And the angel will not come.

Clear, unscaleable, ahead
Rise the Mountains of Instead,
From whose cold cascading streams
None may drink except in dreams.   (*1936*)

Musée des Beaux Arts

About suffering they were never wrong,
The Old Masters: how well they understood
Its human position; how it takes place
While someone else is eating or opening a window or just
    walking dully along;
How, when the aged are reverently, passionately waiting
For the miraculous birth, there always must be
Children who did not specially want it to happen, skating
On a pond at the edge of the wood:
They never forgot
That even the dreadful martyrdom must run its course
Anyhow in a corner, some untidy spot
Where the dogs go on with their doggy life and the
    torturer's horse
Scratches its innocent behind on a tree.

In Brueghel's[1] *Icarus,* for instance: how everything turns away
Quite leisurely from the disaster; the ploughman may
Have heard the splash, the forsaken cry,
But for him it was not an important failure; the sun shone
As it had to on the white legs disappearing into the green
Water; and the expensive delicate ship that must have seen
Something amazing, a boy falling out of the sky,   20
Had somewhere to get to and sailed calmly on.   (*1940*)

The Shield of Achilles[1]

      She looked over his shoulder
        For vines and olive trees,
      Marble well-governed cities
        And ships upon untamed seas,
      But there on the shining metal
        His hands had put instead
      An artificial wilderness
        And a sky like lead.

A plain without a feature, bare and brown,
    No blade of grass, no sign of neighbourhood,   10
Nothing to eat and nowhere to sit down,
    Yet, congregated on its blankness, stood
    An unintelligible multitude,
A million eyes, a million boots in line,
Without expression, waiting for a sign.

Out of the air a voice without a face
    Proved by statistics that some cause was just
In tones as dry and level as the place:
    No one was cheered and nothing was discussed;
    Column by column in a cloud of dust   20
They marched away enduring a belief
Whose logic brought them, somewhere else, to grief.

      She looked over his shoulder
        For ritual pieties,
      White flower-garlanded heifers,
        Libation and sacrifice,
      But there on the shining metal
        Where the altar should have been,

---

[1] Pieter Brueghel, Flemish painter, c. 1520–1569. Icarus and his father, Dædalus, fashioned wings and attached them to their shoulders with wax. Icarus flew too close to the sun; he fell from the sky when the sun melted the wax.

[1] Compare this description of the new shield forged for Achilles by Hephaestos with that in *Iliad,* XVIII, 480–609.

> She saw by his flickering forge-light
>   Quite another scene.

Barbed wire enclosed an arbitrary spot
  Where bored officials lounged (one cracked a joke)
And sentries sweated for the day was hot:
  A crowd of ordinary decent folk
    Watched from without and neither moved nor spoke
As three pale figures were led forth and bound
To three posts driven upright in the ground.

The mass and majesty of this world, all
  That carries weight and always weighs the same
Lay in the hands of others; they were small
  And could not hope for help and no help came:
    What their foes liked to do was done, their shame
Was all the worst could wish; they lost their pride
And died as men before their bodies died.

> She looked over his shoulder
>   For athletes at their games,
> Men and women in a dance
>   Moving their sweet limbs
> Quick, quick, to music,
>   But there on the shining shield
> His hands had set no dancing-floor
>   But a weed-choked field.

A ragged urchin, aimless and alone,
  Loitered about that vacancy, a bird
Flew up to safety from his well-aimed stone:
  That girls are raped, that two boys knife a third,
    Were axioms to him, who'd never heard
Of any world where promises were kept,
Or one could weep because another wept.

> The thin-lipped armourer,
>   Hephaestos hobbled away,
> Thetis of the shining breasts
>   Cried out in dismay
> At what the god had wrought
>   To please her son, the strong
> Iron-hearted man-slaying Achilles
>   Who would not live long.   (*1955*)

THEODORE ROETHKE • 1908–1963

Moss-Gathering

To loosen with all ten fingers held wide and limber
And lift up a patch, dark-green, the kind for lining cemetery baskets,
Thick and cushiony, like an old-fashioned door-mat,
The crumbling small hollow sticks on the underside mixed with roots,
And wintergreen berries and leaves still stuck to the top,—
That was moss-gathering.
But something always went out of me when I dug loose those carpets
Of green, or plunged to my elbows in the spongy yellowish moss of the marshes:
And afterwards I always felt mean, jogging back over the logging road,
As if I had broken the natural order of things in that swampland;   10
Disturbed some rhythm, old and of vast importance,
By pulling off flesh from the living planet;
As if I had committed, against the whole scheme of life, a desecration.   (*1948*)

Orchids

        They lean over the path
        Adder-mouthed,
        Swaying close to the face,
        Coming out, soft and deceptive,
        Limp and damp, delicate as a young bird's tongue;
        Their fluttery fledgling lips
        Move slowly,
        Drawing in the warm air.

        And at night,
        The faint moon falling through whitewashed glass,   10
        The heat going down
        So their musky smell comes even stronger,
        Drifting down from their mossy cradles:
        So many devouring infants!
        Soft luminescent fingers,
        Lips neither dead nor alive,
        Loose ghostly mouths
        Breathing.   (*1948*)

The Waking

        I wake to sleep, and take my waking slow.
        I feel my fate in what I cannot fear.
        I learn by going where I have to go.

We think by feeling. What is there to know?
I hear my being dance from ear to ear.
I wake to sleep, and take my waking slow.

Of those so close beside me, which are you?
God bless the Ground! I shall walk softly there,
And learn by going where I have to go.

Light takes the Tree; but who can tell us how?
The lowly worm climbs up a winding stair;
I wake to sleep, and take my waking slow.

Great Nature has another thing to do.
To you and me; so take the lively air,
And, lovely, learn by going where to go.

This shaking keeps me steady. I should know.
What falls away is always. And is near.
I wake to sleep, and take my waking slow.
I learn by going where I have to go.   (*1953*)

I Knew a Woman

I knew a woman, lovely in her bones,
When small birds sighed, she would sigh back at them;
Ah, when she moved, she moved more ways than one:
The shapes a bright container can contain!
Of her choice virtues only gods should speak,
Or English poets who grew up on Greek
(I'd have them sing in chorus, cheek to cheek).

How well her wishes went! She stroked my chin,
She taught me Turn, and Counter-turn, and Stand;
She taught me Touch, that undulant white skin;
I nibbled meekly from her proffered hand;
She was the sickle; I, poor I, the rake,
Coming behind her for her pretty sake
(But what prodigious mowing we did make).

Love likes a gander, and adores a goose:
Her full lips pursed, the errant note to seize;
She played it quick, she played it light and loose;
My eyes, they dazzled at her flowing knees;
Her several parts could keep a pure repose,
Or one hip quiver with a mobile nose
(She moved in circles, and those circles moved).

Let seed be grass, and grass turn into hay:
I'm martyr to a motion not my own;
What's freedom for? To know eternity.
I swear she cast a shadow white as stone.
But who would count eternity in days?
These old bones live to learn her wanton ways:
(I measure time by how a body sways).   *(1954)*

In a Dark Time

In a dark time, the eye begins to see:
I meet my shadow in the deepening shade;
I hear my echo in the echoing wood,
A lord of nature weeping to a tree.
I live between the heron and the wren,
Beasts of the hill and serpents of the den.

What's madness but nobility of soul
At odds with circumstance? The day's on fire!
I know the purity of pure despair,
My shadow pinned against a sweating wall.
That place among the rocks—is it a cave
Or winding path? The edge is what I have.

A steady storm of correspondence!—
A night flowing with birds, a ragged moon,
And in broad day the midnight come again!
A man goes far to find out what he is—
Death of the self in a long tearless night,
All natural shapes blazing unnatural light.

Dark, dark my light, and darker my desire.
My soul, like some heat-maddened summer fly,
Keeps buzzing at the sill. Which I *is* I?
A fallen man, I climb out of my fear.
The mind enters itself, and God the mind,
And one is One, free in the tearing wind.

KARL SHAPIRO • 1913–

Nostalgia

My soul stands at the window of my room,
   And I ten thousand miles away;
My days are filled with Ocean's sound of doom,
   Salt and cloud and the bitter spray.
Let the wind blow, for many a man shall die.

My selfish youth, my books with gilded edge,
  Knowledge and all gaze down the street;
The potted plants upon the window ledge
  Gaze down with selfish lives and sweet.
Let the wind blow, for many a man shall die.

My night is now her day, my day her night,
  So I lie down, and so I rise;
The sun burns close, the star is losing height,
  The clock is hunted down the skies.
Let the wind blow, for many a man shall die.

Truly a pin can make the memory bleed,
  A word explode the inward mind
And turn the skulls and flowers never freed
  Into the air, no longer blind.
Let the wind blow, for many a man shall die.

Laughter and grief join hands. Always the heart
  Clumps in the breast with heavy stride;
The face grown lined and wrinkled like a chart,
  The eyes bloodshot with tears and tide.
Let the wind blow, for many a man shall die.   (1942)

The Leg

Among the iodoform, in twilight-sleep,
What have I lost? he first inquires,
Peers in the middle distance where a pain,
Ghost of a nurse, hastily moves, and day,
Her blinding presence pressing in his eyes
And now his ears. They are handling him
With rubber hands. He wants to get up.

One day beside some flowers near his nose
He will be thinking, *When will I look at it?*
And pain, still in the middle distance, will reply
At what? and he will know it's gone,
O where! and begin to tremble and cry.
He will begin to cry as a child cries
Whose puppy is mangled under a screaming wheel.

Later, as if deliberately, his fingers
Begin to explore the stump. He learns a shape
That is comfortable and tucked in like a sock.
This has a sense of humor, this can despise
The finest surgical limb, the dignity of limping,
The nonsense of wheel-chairs. Now he smiles to the wall:
The amputation becomes an acquisition.

For the leg is wondering where he is (all is not lost)
And surely he has a duty to the leg;
He in its injury, the leg is his orphan,
He must cultivate the mind of the leg,
Pray for the part that is missing, pray for peace
In the image of man, pray, pray for its safety,
And after a little it will die quietly.

The body, what is it, Father, but a sign
To love the force that grows us, to give back
What in Thy palm is senselessness and mud?
Knead, knead the substance of our understanding
That if Thou take me angrily in hand
And hurl me to the shark, I shall not die! *(1944)*

The Progress of Faust

He was born in Deutschland, as you would suspect,
And graduated in magic from Cracow
In Fifteen Five. His portraits show a brow
Heightened by science. The eye is indirect,
As of bent light upon a crooked soul,
And that he bargained with the prince of Shame
For pleasures intellectually foul
Is known by every court that lists his name.

His frequent disappearances are put down
To visits in the regions of the damned
And to the periodic deaths he shammed,
But unregenerate and in Doctor's gown,
He would turn up to lecture at the fair
And do a minor miracle for a fee.
Many a life he whispered up the stair
To teach the black art of anatomy.

He was as deaf to angels as an oak
When, in the fall of Fifteen Ninety-four,
He went to London and crashed through the floor
In mock damnation of the play-going folk.
Weekending with the scientific crowd,
He met Sir Francis Bacon and helped draft
"Colours of Good and Evil" and read aloud
An obscene sermon at which no one laughed.

He toured the Continent for a hundred years
And subsidized among the peasantry
The puppet play, his tragic history;
With a white glove he boxed the devil's ears

And with a black his own. Tired of this,
He published penny poems about his sins,
In which he placed the heavy emphasis
On the white glove which, for a penny, wins.

Some time before the hemorrhage of the Kings
Of France, he turned respectable and taught;
Quite suddenly everything that he had thought
Seemed to grow scholars' beards and angels' wings.
It was the Overthrow. On Reason's throne
He sat with the fair Phrygian on his knees
And called all universities his own,
As plausible a figure as you please.

Then back to Germany as the sages' sage
To preach comparative science to the young
Who came from every land in a great throng
And knew they heard the master of the age.
When for a secret formula he paid
The Devil another fragment of his soul,
His scholars wept, and several even prayed
That Satan would restore him to them whole.

Backwardly tolerant, Faustus was expelled
From the Third Reich in Nineteen Thirty-nine.
His exit caused the breaching of the Rhine,
Except for which the frontier might have held.
Five years unknown to enemy and friend
He hid, appearing on the sixth to pose
In an American desert at war's end
Where, at his back, a dome of atoms rose.   *(1947)*

DYLAN THOMAS • 1914–1953

Incarnate Devil

Incarnate devil in a talking snake,
The central plains of Asia in his garden,
In shaping-time the circle stung awake,
In shapes of sin forked out the bearded apple,
And God walked there who was a fiddling warden
And played down pardon from the heavens' hill.

When we were strangers to the guided seas,
A handmade moon half holy in a cloud,
The wisemen tell me that the garden gods

Twined good and evil on an eastern tree;
And when the moon rose windily it was
Black as the beast and paler than the cross.

We in our Eden knew the secret guardian
In sacred waters that no frost could harden,
And in the mighty mornings of the earth;
Hell in a horn of sulphur and the cloven myth,
All heaven in a midnight of the sun,
A serpent fiddled in the shaping-time. (*1935*)

Fern Hill

Now as I was young and easy under the apple boughs
About the lilting house and happy as the grass was green,
    The night above the dingle starry,
      Time let me hail and climb
    Golden in the heydays of his eyes,
And honoured among wagons I was prince of the apple towns
And once below a time I lordly had the trees and leaves
      Trail with daisies and barley
    Down the rivers of the windfall light.

And as I was green and carefree, famous among the barns
About the happy yard and singing as the farm was home,
    In the sun that is young once only,
      Time let me play and be
    Golden in the mercy of his means,
And green and golden I was huntsman and herdsman, the calves
Sang to my horn, the foxes on the hills barked clear and cold,
      And the sabbath rang slowly
    In the pebbles of the holy streams.

All the sun long it was running, it was lovely, the hay
Fields high as the house, the tunes from the chimneys, it was air
      And playing, lovely and watery
      And fire green as grass.
    And nightly under the simple stars
As I rode to sleep the owls were bearing the farm away,
All the moon long I heard, blessed among stables, the nightjars
      Flying with the ricks, and the horses
      Flashing into the dark.

And then to awake, and the farm, like a wanderer white
With the dew, come back, the cock on his shoulder: it was all
      Shining, it was Adam and maiden,
      The sky gathered again
    And the sun grew round that very day.

So it must have been after the birth of the simple light
In the first, spinning place, the spellbound horses walking warm
    Out of the whinnying green stable
        On to the fields of praise.

And honoured among foxes and pheasants by the gay house
Under the new made clouds and happy as the heart was long,
    In the sun born over and over,
        I ran my heedless ways,   40
    My wishes raced through the house high hay
And nothing I cared, at my sky blue trades, that time allows
In all his tuneful turning so few and such morning songs
    Before the children green and golden
        Follow him out of grace,

Nothing I cared, in the lamb white days, that time would take me
Up to the swallow thronged loft by the shadow of my hand,
    In the moon that is always rising,
        Nor that riding to sleep
    I should hear him fly with the high fields   50
And wake to the farm forever fled from the childless land.
Oh as I was young and easy in the mercy of his means,
        Time held me green and dying
    Though I sang in my chains like the sea.   *(1946)*

A Refusal to Mourn the Death, by Fire, of a Child in London

    Never until the mankind making
    Bird beast and flower
    Fathering and all humbling darkness
    Tells with silence the last light breaking
    And the still hour
    Is come of the sea tumbling in harness

    And I must enter again the round
    Zion of the water bead
    And the synagogue of the ear of corn
    Shall I let pray the shadow of a sound   10
    Or sow my salt seed
    In the least valley of sackcloth to mourn

    The majesty and burning of the child's death.
    I shall not murder
    The mankind of her going with a grave truth
    Nor blaspheme down the stations of the breath
    With any further
    Elegy of innocence and youth.

Deep with the first dead lies London's daughter,
Robed in the long friends, 20
The grains beyond age, the dark veins of her mother,
Secret by the unmourning water
Of the riding Thames.
After the first death, there is no other. (*1946*)

GWENDOLYN BROOKS • 1917–

from the children of the poor

1

People who have no children can be hard:
Attain a mail of ice and insolence:
Need not pause in the fire, and in no sense
Hesitate in the hurricane to guard.
And when wide world is bitten and bewarred
They perish purely, waving their spirits hence
Without a trace of grace or of offense
To laugh or fail, diffident, wonder-starred.
While through a throttling dark we others hear
The little lifting helplessness, the queer 10
Whimper-whine; whose unridiculous
Lost softness softly makes a trap for us.
And makes a curse. And makes a sugar of
The malocclusions, the inconditions of love.

4

First fight. Then fiddle. Ply the slipping string
With feathery sorcery; muzzle the note
With hurting love; the music that they wrote
Bewitch, bewilder. Qualify to sing
Threadwise. Devise no salt, no hempen thing
For the dear instrument to bear. Devote
The bow to silks and honey. Be remote
A while from malice and from murdering.
But first to arms, to armor. Carry hate
In front of you and harmony behind. 10
Be deaf to music and to beauty blind.
Win war. Rise bloody, maybe not too late
For having first to civilize a space
Wherein to play your violin with grace. (*1949*)

Gwendolyn Brooks

We Real Cool

        THE POOL PLAYERS.
   SEVEN AT THE GOLDEN SHOVEL.

          We real cool. We
          Left school. We

          Lurk late. We
          Strike straight. We

          Sing sin. We
          Thin gin. We

          Jazz June. We
          Die soon.   (*1960*)

Two Dedications

I THE CHICAGO PICASSO

August 15, 1967

> "*Mayor Daley tugged a white ribbon, loosing the blue percale wrap. A hearty cheer went up as the covering slipped off the big steel sculpture that looks at once like a bird and a woman.*"
> —Chicago *Sun-Times*

    (*Seiji Ozawa leads the Symphony.*
    The Mayor smiles.
    And 50,000 See.)

Does man love Art? Man visits Art, but squirms.
Art hungers. Art urges voyages—
and it is easier to stay at home,
the nice beer ready.
   In commonrooms
we belch, or sniff, or scratch.
Are raw.

But we must cook ourselves and style ourselves for Art, who
is a requiring courtesan.
We squirm.
We do not hug the Mona Lisa.
We
may touch or tolerate
an astounding fountain, or a horse-and-rider.
At most, another Lion.

Observe the tall cold of a Flower
which is as innocent and as guilty,
as meaningful and as meaningless as any
other flower in the western field.

II THE WALL

August 27, 1967

For Edward Christmas
*"The side wall of a typical slum building on the corner of 43rd and
Langley became a mural communicating black dignity. . . ."*
—*Ebony*

    A drumdrumdrum.
    Humbly we come.
South of success and east of gloss and glass are
sandals;
flowercloth;
grave hoops of wood or gold, pendant
from black ears, brown ears, reddish-brown
and ivory ears;

black boy-men.
Black
boy-men on roofs fist out "Black Power!" Val,
a little black stampede
in African
images of brass and flowerswirl,
fists out "Black Power!"—tightens pretty eyes,
leans back on mothercountry and is tract,
is treatise through her perfect and tight teeth.

Women in wool hair chant their poetry.
Phil Cohran gives us messages and music
made of developed bone and polished and honed cult.
It is the Hour of tribe and of vibration,
the day-long Hour. It is the Hour
of ringing, rouse, of ferment-festival.

On Forty-third and Langley
black furnaces resent ancient
legislatures
of ploy and scruple and practical gelatin.
They keep the fever in,
fondle the fever.

All
worship the Wall.

I mount the rattling wood. Walter
says, "She is good." Says, "She

our Sister is." In front of me
hundreds of faces, red-brown, brown, black, ivory,
yield me hot trust, their yea and their Announcement
that they are ready to rile the high-flung ground.
Behind me, Paint.
Heroes.
No child has defiled
the Heroes of this Wall this serious Appointment
this still Wing
this Scald this Flute this heavy Light this Hinge.

An emphasis is paroled.
The old decapitations are revised,
the dispossessions beakless.

And we sing.   (*1968*)

RICHARD WILBUR • 1921–

Bell Speech

    The selfsame toothless voice for death or bridal:
It has been long since men would give the time
To tell each someone's-change with a special chime,
And a toll for every year the dead walked through.
And mostly now, above this urgent idle
Town, the bells mark time, as they can do.

This bavardage of early and of late
Is what is wanted, and yet the bells beseech
By some excess that's in their stricken speech
Less meanly to be heard. Were this not so,
Why should Great Paul shake every window plate
To warn me that my pocket watch is slow?

Whether or not attended, bells will chant
With a clear dumb sound, and wide of any word
Expound our hours, clear as the waves are heard
Crashing at Mount Desert, from far at sea,
And dumbly joining, as the night's descent
Makes deltas into dark of every tree.

Great Paul, great pail of sound, still dip and draw
Dark speech from the deep and quiet steeple well,
Bring dark for doctrine, do but dim and quell

All voice in yours, while earth will give you breath.
Still gather to a language without flaw
Our loves, and all the hours of our death.   (*1947*)

After the Last Bulletins

After the last bulletins the windows darken
And the whole city founders readily and deep,
Sliding on all its pillows
To the thronged Atlantis of personal sleep,

And the wind rises. The wind rises and bowls
The day's litter of news in the alleys. Trash
Tears itself on the railings,
Soars and falls with a soft crash.

Tumbles and soars again. Unruly flights
Scamper the park, and taking a statue for dead
Strike at the positive eyes,
Batter and flap stolid head

And scratch the noble name. In empty lots
Our journals spiral in a fierce noyade
Of all we thought to think,
Or caught in corners cramp and wad

And twist our words. And some from gutters flail
Their tatters at the tired patrolman's feet,
Like all that fisted snow
That cried beside his long retreat

Damn you! damn you! to the emperor's horse's heels.
Oh none too soon through the air white and dry
Will the clear announcer's voice
Beat like a dove, and you and I

From the heart's anarch and responsible town
Return by subway-mouth to life again,
Bearing the morning papers,
And cross the park where saintlike men,

White and absorbed with stick and bag remove
The litter of the night, and footsteps rouse
With confident morning sound
The songbirds in the public boughs.

Juggler

A ball will bounce, but less and less. It's not
A light-hearted thing, resents its own resilience.
Falling is what it loves, and the earth falls
So in our hearts from brilliance,
Settles and is forgot.
It takes a skyblue juggler with five red balls

To shake our gravity up. Where, in the air
The balls roll round, wheel on his wheeling hands,
Learning the ways of lightness, alter to spheres
Grazing his finger ends,
Cling to their courses there,
Swinging a small heaven about his ears.

But a heaven is easier made of nothing at all
Than the earth regained, and still and sole within
The spin of worlds, with a gesture sure and noble
He reels that heaven in,
Landing it ball by ball,
And trades it all for a broom, a plate, a table.

Oh, on his toe the table is turning, the broom's
Balancing up on his nose, and the plate whirls
On the tip of the broom! Damn, what a show, we cry:
The boys stamp, and the girls
Shriek, and the drum booms
And all comes down, and he bows and says good-bye.

If the juggler is tired now, if the broom stands
In the dust again, if the table starts to drop
Through the daily dark again, and though the plate
Lies flat on the table top,
For him we batter our hands
Who has won for once over the world's weight.   (*1950*)

ALAN DUGAN • 1923–

The Life and Death of the Cantata System

When the Lord was a man of war and sailed out
through the sky at night with all the stars
of all the constellations as his riding lights,
those beneath his oceanic, personal ascendancy

ascended in fated systems. The massed shouts
of the chorus sailed a regular sea of violins
as Galleons of the Line!, with hulls of bassos,
decks of baritones and altos, ornate in poop
and prow in rigging up the masts of soloists
which bore aloft, in turn, soprano mainsails, 10
top-gallants of the children's chorus, and
pennants of castrati streaming on the heights!
The Great Armada sang "Invincible!" to the deep,
but when the time came for a change in craft
the Lord's storms wrecked the vessels of the Lord
and the voices poured out on the air still singing.
The Empirical English conquered in the shallows. He
withdrew his stars to favor those made by machines.   *(1963)*

Winter: For an Untenable Situation

Outside it is cold. Inside
although the fire has gone out
and all the furniture is burnt,
it is much warmer. Oh let
the white refrigerator car
of day go by in glacial thunder:
when it gets dark, and when
the branches of the tree outside
look wet because it is so dark,
oh we will burn the house itself 10
for warmth, the wet tree too,
you will burn me, I will burn you,
and when the last brick of the fireplace
has been cracked for its nut of warmth
and the last bone cracked for its coal
and the andirons themselves sucked cold,
we will move on!, remembering
the burning house, the burning tree,
the burning you, the burning me,
the ashes, the brick-dust, the bitter iron,
and the time when we were warm,
and say, "Those were the good old days."   *(1963)*

One Waking in a Northern Fall

The red curtain moving in the still room
is frightening in portent to me housed.
The heart, in its choice cage of ribs, pounds
as if the air, which was a hurricane
all up the dangerous Atlantic coast

with gross waves and accumulative clouds,
has petered out into an indoor draught
telling the officed brain, high up inside
the dead air of its hairy capitol dome
but sensitive as a bat to every draught,   *10*
that revolutionary storms are happening down there!
to move the red curtain in the still room.   (*1967*)

On a Snake

The snake on the blue
pool table of the moss
is denser than a stick
of equal girth and heavier,
for all its lightness and
slick ways, because its
muscles organized beneath
the overlapping platelets of
oiled parchment have to be
compact to make that tense   *10*
wobble of reaction that
you feel if you should pick
it up. Now that I know
the motto: DON'T TOUCH SNAKES,
and wear the diacritical marks
the two fangs make, I say,
"Man, you are smarter than it,
that muscular intelligence:
snap off its head!" The glass
snake, weighty and complex   *20*
in otherness, must think
the whole thought of the cold
when it is cold. He would
not know the drag end
of his tail from twigs
around him in the snow
when you are wiser warm,
dreaming of venom by the fire
where a cautery instrument
turns red, and healing rum   *30*
roars when the poker is dipped in.   (*1967*)

Sailing to Jerusalem

On coming up on deck Palm Sunday morning, oh
we saw the seas the dancy little tourist ship
climbed up and down all night in cabin dreams.

They came along in ridges an horizon wide!
and ran away astern to the Americas we left,
to break on headlands and be called "the surf."
After services below, the pilgrims to the east
carried their processed palm fronds up on deck
and some of them went overboard from children's hands.
So, Christ: there were the palm leaves on the water   *10*
as the first fruits of the ocean's promised land.
They promise pilgrims resurrection out at sea,
though sea-sick fasters in their bunks below
cry out for harbor, order, and stability.
This is the place for it! The sky is high
with it, the water deep, the air its union: spray!
We all walk the water just below the decks
too, helplessly dancing to the world's variety
like your Jerusalem, Byzantium, and Rome.   (*1967*)

SYLVIA PLATH • 1932–1963

Morning Song

Love set you going like a fat gold watch.
The midwife slapped your footsoles, and your bald cry
Took its place among the elements.

Our voices echo, magnifying your arrival. New statue.
In a drafty museum, your nakedness
Shadows our safety. We stand round blankly as walls.

I'm no more your mother
Than the cloud that distils a mirror to reflect its own slow
Effacement at the wind's hand.

All night your moth-breath   *10*
Flickers among the flat pink roses. I wake to listen:
A far sea moves in my ear.

One cry, and I stumble from bed, cow-heavy and floral
In my Victorian nightgown.
Your mouth opens clean as a cat's. The window square

Whitens and swallows its dull stars. And now you try
Your handful of notes;
The clear vowels rise like balloons.   (*1966*)

The Arrival of the Bee Box

I ordered this, this clean wood box
Square as a chair and almost too heavy to lift.
I would say it was the coffin of a midget
Or a square baby
Were there not such a din in it.

The box is locked, it is dangerous.
I have to live with it overnight
And I can't keep away from it.
There are no windows, so I can't see what is in there.
There is only a little grid, no exit.

I put my eye to the grid.
It is dark, dark,
With the swarmy feeling of African hands
Minute and shrunk for export,
Black on black, angrily clambering.

How can I let them out?
It is the noise that appalls me most of all,
The unintelligible syllables.
It is like a Roman mob,
Small, taken one by one, but my god, together!

I lay my ear to furious Latin.
I am not a Caesar.
I have simply ordered a box of maniacs.
They can be sent back.
They can die, I need feed them nothing, I am the owner.

I wonder how hungry they are.
I wonder if they would forget me
If I just undid the locks and stood back and turned into a tree.
There is the laburnum, its blond colonnades,
And the petticoats of the cherry.

They might ignore me immediately
In my moon suit and funeral veil.
I am no source of honey
So why should they turn on me?
Tomorrow I will be sweet God, I will set them free.

The box is only temporary.   (*1966*)

Little Fugue

The yew's black fingers wag;
Cold clouds go over.
So the deaf and dumb
Signal the blind, and are ignored.

I like black statements.
The featurelessness of that cloud, now!
White as an eye all over!
The eye of the blind pianist

At my table on the ship.
He felt for his food.
His fingers had the noses of weasels.
I couldn't stop looking.

He could hear Beethoven:
Black yew, white cloud,
The horrific complications.
Finger-traps—a tumult of keys.

Empty and silly as plates.
So the blind smile.
I envy the big noises,
The yew hedge of the Grosse Fuge.

Deafness is something else.
Such a dark funnel, my father!
I see your voice
Black and leafy, as in my childhood,

A yew hedge of orders,
Gothic and barbarous, pure German.
Dead men cry from it.
I am guilty of nothing.

The yew my Christ, then,
Is it not as tortured?
And you, during the Great War
In the California delicatessen

Lopping the sausages!
They colour my sleep,
Red, mottled, like cut necks.
There was a silence!

Great silence of another order.
I was seven, I knew nothing.

               The world occurred.
               You had one leg, and a Prussian mind.

               Now similar clouds
               Are spreading their vacuous sheets.
               Do you say nothing?
               I am lame in the memory.

               I remember a blue eye,
               A briefcase of tangerines.
               This was a man, then!
               Death opened, like a black tree, blackly.

               I survive the while,
               Arranging my morning.
               These are my fingers, this my baby.
               The clouds are a marriage dress, of that pallor.   (*1966*)

LAURENCE LIEBERMAN • 1935–

Flying Below Sea Level

After hours under water, a mask
     for face,
          air is a ceiling,
and sky a comfortable myth,
     like heaven.
          Sun, a film
of white-hot molten light,
     floats
          on the surface,
like oil. It will scald my scalp
     if I rise—
          to get my breath.
Here and there, planes of light
     intersect
          the surface, knife
the upper field, and fan out
     in shelves.
          In shallows, they strike
bottom, spilling rainbow
     all about
          the coral. There
are brains in the fish's tail
     (alert
          for messages), the fins
are nerves, each scale a fingertip...
     My cheek,
          slapped by a moulded
soft-spongy mass, half-moon
     shaped—
          gently stinging—
I dodge a gelatin-trio, running
     with the current
          faster than I can
swim away. Then, I'm surrounded
     by hordes,
          mounds bumping
each other, sliding around me—
     painless
          between my legs,
across my face. Wherever I
     look, the sea
          is milky-translucent,
separate outlines no longer
     visible.
          The water, gelling
into a vast slug-slimy pudding—
     impenetrable—
          half-carries me along

(a man-blob swallowed in viscid
    ooze), half-
        disgorging me,
by turns. I dive, down-thrust
    through a hole
        opening just under
me, swim below the flying island
    of jelly,
        and enter the under-
water cave. I hear a high-pitched
    crackling,
        like dry twigs
burning, on all sides enclosed
    by a soundless
        hush. I hang,
motionless, at the center of the cave:
    magnetized...
        I am seen
by thousands of unseen eyes!
    I shudder at a burst of color:
        at a burst of color:
a large hog-fish, bright scarlet-
    orange, appears;
        high-finned, majestic,
wide and flat, brilliant-sheened;
    seeming twice
        its size, swelled
in enclosure. No change in his wide-eyed
    enlongated
        hog-snout at sight
of me, no change in his glide-rhythm,
    he picks up
        speed as he spins,
circling the interior of the cavern;
    so nervous
        to escape me, he misses
the exits, tunnels, again and again.
    The space
        around me expands.
Light from no source filters up
    from depths
        without bottom.
I grow larger and larger. The cave
    I filled
        fills me. As I wind,
snake-easeful, back through the cave-
    mouth, I
        feel the whole sea
tilt to fill the missing space.   (*1969*)

Flying on the Surface

      Aloft on the unpunctured float
Of lungs and flipper-rubber,
    I thread the needlefish with my spear, a snorkeling
        Head-hunter: the gar leading
           With pointed nose,
      Two interlocked

      Rows of teeth, saw-edged,
That can cut a brother
    In two—the decapitated head snapping blindly
        At whatever passes before it,
           Long after the severed
      Body has fallen

      Away: needlefish javelins
Streaking after fry,
    Targets themselves for swooping birds: one gar, struck
        By a gull divebomber—instantly
           Disembowelled—
      Dies, a still live

                Minnow in its mouth. My forehead,
Submerged, konks
        The feet of a snoozing pelican, listless, drooping
            Discarded knotty branches
                Near the raft
            Of his broad bottom,

        Shading eleven small squids
Back-jetting in an undulant
        Double-V formation: a sine wave motion, ribbon-
            Winding from end to end.
                I jab at the middle
            Link: it spurts

        Three feet ahead of the chain,
But divides in two,
        Splits—no, doubles!—leaving an inky-black pseudomorph
            In its place, impaled round
                My spear-point, thinning
            To a smoke-ring. Near

        Stumpy Point, where bay-mouth
Meets open sea,
        Breakers converging from three sides at once, mixing
            And chopping their flows, reinforcing
                Or cancelling by turns—
            I slip in shallow

        Water, yellowtail on my spear.
Juggling gun-shaft
        And spear in one hand, unsheathed knife in the other,
            Unbalancing on one leg
                In two feet of water—
            I'm struck from behind

        By a six-foot wave I didn't
Hear building over me
        From the left, the wave silently purring a surf-lip
            As the crest curls down in a fist
                On foam—to pounce
            With cat's stealth: I hear

        A cracked-whip's impact before I
Recall it is my side
        And neck that echo back; taste blood in the salt
            Before I know my life-stream
                The one opened, and on
            The run—escaping

                Smoothly as into a love-sucking
Mouth; see a black fin
                Slicing the surface and circling toward me before I
                        Register the terror-sound
                                Of flippered feet
                        Wedging between coral

                Jaws to brace the mindless
Trunk they swing upon
                Absently, my legs a lever, bending against the back-
                        Wash of the wave's undertow
                                Pulling seaward to meet
                        A next hammering wave.

                Shark-meat! Half-aliveness will eat
You alive! On all fours,
                I scramble ashore. . . . Now in dreams, I sink into brainless
                        Stupor, a carcass emptied
                                Of self, a drifting
                        Deadwood, a flotsam

                Of absent flesh: my legs two
Shanks of floating
                Sea-fodder, my arm-bones crossed sticks under a death's-
                        Head skull, my eyes looking
                                Out through a death
                        Mask of face   (*1969*)

Drama

SOPHOCLES • 495?–405 B.C.

Oedipus Rex

AN ENGLISH VERSION BY DUDLEY FITTS
AND ROBERT FITZGERALD

CHARACTERS

OEDIPUS, *King of Thebes.*
A PRIEST
CREON, *brother of Iocastê.*
TEIRESIAS, *a blind seer.*
IOCASTÊ, *the Queen, wife of Oedipus.*
MESSENGER.
SHEPHERD OF LAÏOS.
SECOND MESSENGER.
CHORUS OF THEBAN ELDERS.

THE SCENE: *Before the palace of* OEDIPUS, *King of Thebes. A central door and two lateral doors open onto a platform which runs the length of the façade. On the platform, right and left, are altars; and three steps lead down into the "orchestra," or chorus-ground. At the beginning of the action these steps are crowded by suppliants who have brought branches and chaplets of olive leaves and who lie in various attitudes of despair.* OEDIPUS *enters.*

PROLOGUE

OEDIPUS. My children, generations of the living
In the line of Kadmos, nursed at his ancient hearth:
Why have you strewn yourselves before these altars
In supplication, with your boughs and garlands?
The breath of incense rises from the city
With a sound of prayer and lamentation.
                  Children,
I would not have you speak through messengers,
And therefore I have come myself to hear you—
I, Oedipus, who bear the famous name.
   (*to a* PRIEST)
You, there, since you are eldest in the company,   10
Speak for them all, tell me what preys upon you,
Whether you come in dread, or crave some blessing:
Tell me, and never doubt that I will help you
In every way I can; I should be heartless
Were I not moved to find you suppliant here.
   PRIEST. Great Oedipus, O powerful King of Thebes!
You see how all the ages of our people
Cling to your altar steps: here are boys
Who can barely stand alone, and here are priests   19
By weight of age, as I am a priest of God,
And young men chosen from those yet unmarried;
As for the others, all that multitude,
They wait with olive chaplets in the squares,
At the two shrines of Pallas, and where Apollo
Speaks in the glowing embers.
                          Your own eyes
Must tell you: Thebes is in her extremity
And can not lift her head from the surge of death.
A rust consumes the buds and fruits of the earth;
The herds are sick; children die unborn,
And labor is vain. The god of plague and pyre   30

Raids like detestable lightning through the city,
And all the house of Kadmos is laid waste,
All emptied, and all darkened: Death alone
Battens upon the misery of Thebes.

You are not one of the immortal gods, we know;
Yet we have come to you to make our prayer
As to the man of all men best in adversity
And wisest in the ways of God. You saved us
From the Sphinx, that flinty singer,[1] and the tribute
We paid to her so long; yet you were never   40
Better informed than we, nor could we teach you:
It was some god breathed in you to set us free.

Therefore, O mighty King, we turn to you:
Find us our safety, find us a remedy,
Whether by counsel of the gods or men.
A king of wisdom tested in the past
Can act in a time of troubles, and act well.
Noblest of men, restore
Life to your city! Think how all men call you
Liberator for your triumph long ago;   50
Ah, when your years of kingship are remembered,
Let them not say *We rose, but later fell*—
Keep the State from going down in the storm!
Once, years ago, with happy augury,
You brought us fortune; be the same again!

---

[1] A female monster, part lion and part woman; the Sphinx killed any Theban who could not answer her riddle: "What has four legs in the morning, two at noonday, and three at night?" When Oedipus answered the riddle, the Sphinx killed herself.

No man questions your power to rule the land:
But rule over men, not over a dead city!
Ships are only hulls, citadels are nothing,
When no life moves in the empty passageways.

OEDIPUS. Poor children! You may be sure I know   60
All that you longed for in your coming here.
I know that you are deathly sick; and yet,
Sick as you are, not one is as sick as I.
Each of you suffers in himself alone
His anguish, not another's; but my spirit
Groans for the city, for myself, for you.

I was not sleeping, you are not waking me.
No, I have been in tears for a long while
And in my restless thought walked many ways.
In all my search, I found one helpful course,   70
And that I have taken: I have sent Creon,
Son of Menoikeus, brother of the Queen,
To Delphi, Apollo's place of revelation,
To learn there, if he can,
What act or pledge of mine may save the city.
I have counted the days, and now, this very day,
I am troubled, for he has overstayed his time.
What is he doing? He has been gone too long.
Yet whenever he comes back, I should do ill   79
To scant whatever hint the god may give.

PRIEST. It is a timely promise. At this instant
They tell me Creon is here.

OEDIPUS.   O Lord Apollo!
May his news be fair as his face is radiant!

PRIEST. It could not be otherwise: he is crowned with bay,
The chaplet is thick with berries.

OEDIPUS.   We shall soon know;
He is near enough to hear us now.

(Enter CREON.)

O Prince:
Brother: son of Menoikeus:
What answer do you bring us from the god?
  CREON. It is favorable. I can tell you, great afflictions
Will turn out well, if they are taken well.
  OEDIPUS. What was the oracle? These vague words
Leave me still hanging between hope and fear.
  CREON. Is it your pleasure to hear me with all these
Gathered around us? I am prepared to speak,
But should we not go in?
  OEDIPUS.   Let them all hear it.
It is for them I suffer, more than for myself.
  CREON. Then I will tell you what I heard at Delphi.

In plain words
The god commands us to expel from the land of Thebes
An old defilement that it seems we shelter.
It is a deathly thing, beyond expiation.
We must not let it feed upon us longer.
  OEDIPUS. What defilement? How shall we rid ourselves of it?
  CREON. By exile or death, blood for blood. It was
Murder that brought the plague-wind on the city.
  OEDIPUS. Murder of whom? Surely the god has named him?
  CREON. My lord: long ago Laïos was our king,
Before you came to govern us.
  OEDIPUS.   I know;
I learned of him from others; I never saw him.
  CREON. He was murdered; and Apollo commands us now
To take revenge upon whoever killed him.
  OEDIPUS. Upon whom? Where are they? Where shall we find a clue
To solve that crime, after so many years?
  CREON. Here in this land, he said.
    If we make enquiry,
We may touch things that otherwise escape us.
  OEDIPUS. Tell me: Was Laïos murdered in his house,
Or in the fields, or in some foreign country?
  CREON. He said he planned to make a pilgrimage.
He did not come home again.
  OEDIPUS.   And was there no one,
No witness, no companion, to tell what happened?
  CREON. They were all killed but one, and he got away
So frightened that he could remember one thing only.
  OEDIPUS. What was that one thing? One may be the key
To everything, if we resolve to use it.
  CREON. He said that a band of highwaymen attacked them,
Outnumbered them, and overwhelmed the King.
  OEDIPUS. Strange, that a highwayman should be so daring—
Unless some faction here bribed him to do it.
  CREON. We thought of that. But after Laïos' death
New troubles arose and we had no avenger.
  OEDIPUS. What troubles could prevent your hunting down the killers?
  CREON. The riddling Sphinx's song
Made us deaf to all mysteries but her own.
  OEDIPUS. Then once more I must bring what is dark to light.
It is most fitting that Apollo shows,
As you do, this compunction for the dead.
You shall see how I stand by you, as I should,
To avenge the city and the city's god,
And not as though it were for some distant friend,
But for my own sake, to be rid of evil.

Whoever killed King Laïos might—who knows?—
Decide at any moment to kill me as well.
By avenging the murdered king I protect myself.

Come, then, my children: leave the altar steps,
Lift up your olive boughs!
                        One of you go
And summon the people of Kadmos to gather here.
I will do all that I can; you may tell them that.
    (*Exit a* PAGE.)
So, with the help of God,
We shall be saved—or else indeed we are lost.
   PRIEST. Let us rise, children. It was for this we came,   *150*
And now the King has promised it himself.
Phoibos has sent us an oracle; may he descend
Himself to save us and drive out the plague.
   (*Exeunt* OEDIPUS *and* CREON *into the palace by the central door. The* PRIEST *and the* SUPPLIANTS *disperse R. and L. After a short pause the* CHORUS *enters the orchestra.*)

PÁRODOS

   CHORUS.   [*strophe 1*]
What is the god singing in his profound
Delphi of gold and shadow?
What oracle for Thebes, the sunwhipped city?

Fear unjoints me, the roots of my heart tremble.

Now I remember, O Healer, your power, and wonder:
Will you send doom like a sudden cloud, or weave it
Like nightfall of the past?   *160*

Ah no: be merciful, issue of holy sound:
Dearest to our expectancy: be tender!

                                [*antistrophe 1*]
Let me pray to Athenê, the immortal daughter of Zeus,
And to Artemis her sister
Who keeps her famous throne in the market ring,
And to Apollo, bowman at the far butts of heaven—

O gods, descend! Like three streams leap against
The fires of our grief, the fires of darkness;
Be swift to bring us rest!   *169*

As in the old time from the brilliant house
Of air you stepped to save us, come again!

                                  [*strophe 2*]
Now our afflictions have no end.
Now all our stricken host lies down
And no man fights off death with his mind;

The noble plowland bears no grain,
And groaning mothers can not bear—

See, how our lives like birds take wing,
Like sparks that fly when a fire soars,
To the shore of the god of evening.

                                [*antistrophe 2*]
The plague burns on, it is pitiless,   *180*
Though pallid children laden with death
Lie unwept in the stony ways,

And old gray women by every path
Flock to the strand about the altars

There to strike their breasts and cry
Worship of Zeus in wailing prayers:
Be kind, God's golden child![2]

                                  [*strophe 3*]
There are no swords in this attack by fire,
No shields, but we are ringed with cries.

Send the besieger plunging from our homes   *190*
Into the vast sea-room of the Atlantic

---

[2] Athene

Or into the waves that foam eastward of
     Thrace—

For the day ravages what the night
     spares—

Destroy our enemy, lord of the thunder!
Let him be riven by lightning from
     heaven!

                              [antistrophe 3]
Phoibos Apollo, stretch the sun's bow-
     string,³
That golden cord, until it sing for us,
Flashing arrows in heaven!
                              Artemis, Huntress,
Race with flaring lights upon our moun-
     tains!   199

O scarlet god, O golden-banded brow,
O Theban Bacchos in a storm of
     Maenads,
     (Enter OEDIPUS, center.)
Whirl upon Death, that all the Undying
     hate!
Come with blinding cressets, come in joy!

              SCENE I

OEDIPUS. Is this your prayer? It may
     be answered. Come,
Listen to me, act as the crisis demands,
And you shall have relief from all these
     evils.
Until now I was a stranger to this tale,
As I had been a stranger to the crime.
Could I track down the murderer without
     a clue?
But now, friends,   210
As one who became a citizen after the
     murder,
I make this proclamation to all Thebans:
If any man knows by whose hands Laïos,
     son of Labdakos,
Met his death, I direct that man to tell me
     everything,
No matter what he fears for having so
     long withheld it.

Let it stand as promised that no further
     trouble
Will come to him, but he may leave the
     land in safety.

Moreover: If anyone knows the murderer
     to be foreign,
Let him not keep silent: he shall have his
     reward from me.   219
However, if he does conceal it; if any man
Fearing for his friend or for himself
     disobeys this edict,
Hear what I propose to do:

I solemnly forbid the people of this
     country,
Where power and throne are mine, ever
     to receive that man
Or speak to him, no matter who he is, or
     let him
Join in sacrifice, lustration,⁴ or in prayer.

I decree that he be driven from every
     house,
Being, as he is, corruption itself to us: the
     Delphic
Voice of Zeus has pronounced this revela-
     tion.   229
Thus I associate myself with the oracle
And take the side of the murdered king.

As for the criminal, I pray to God—
Whether it be a lurking thief, or one of a
     number—
I pray that that man's life be consumed
     in evil and wretchedness.
And as for me, this curse applies no less
If it should turn out that the culprit is my
     guest here,
Sharing my hearth.
                    You have heard the penalty.
I lay it on you now to attend to this
For my sake, for Apollo's, for the sick
Sterile city that heaven has abandoned.
Suppose the oracle had given you no
     command: 241
Should this defilement go uncleansed for
     ever?

---

³ Apollo was the patron of archery (as well as of music and medicine).

⁴ purification by means of propitiatory offerings

You should have found the murderer: your king,
A noble king, had been destroyed!
Now I,
Having the power that he held before me,
Having his bed, begetting children there
Upon his wife, as he would have, had he lived—
Their son would have been my children's brother,
If Laïos had had luck in fatherhood!
(But surely ill luck rushed upon his reign)— 250
I say I take the son's part, just as though
I were his son, to press the fight for him
And see it won! I'll find the hand that brought
Death to Labdakos' and Polydoros' child,
Heir of Kadmos' and Agenor's line.
And as for those who fail me,
May the gods deny them the fruit of the earth,
Fruit of the womb, and may they rot utterly!
Let them be wretched as we are wretched, and worse! 259

For you, for loyal Thebans, and for all
Who find my actions right, I pray the favor
Of justice, and of all the immortal gods.
  CHORAGOS. Since I am under oath, my lord, I swear
I did not do the murder, I can not name
The murderer. Might not the oracle
That has ordained the search tell where to find him?
  OEDIPUS. An honest question. But no man in the world
Can make the gods do more than the gods will.
  CHORAGOS. There is one last expedient—
  OEDIPUS. Tell me what it is.
Though it seem slight, you must not hold it back. 270
  CHORAGOS. A lord clairvoyant to the lord Apollo,
As we all know, is the skilled Teiresias.
One might learn much about this from him, Oedipus.
  OEDIPUS. I am not wasting time:
Creon spoke of this, and I have sent for him—
Twice, in fact; it is strange that he is not here.
  CHORAGOS. The other matter—that old report—seems useless.
  OEDIPUS. Tell me. I am interested in all reports.
  CHORAGOS. The King was said to have been killed by highwaymen.
  OEDIPUS. I know. But we have no witnesses to that. 280
  CHORAGOS. If the killer can feel a particle of dread,
Your curse will bring him out of hiding!
  OEDIPUS. No.
The man who dared that act will fear no curse.
(*Enter the blind seer* TEIRESIAS, *led by a* PAGE.)
  CHORAGOS. But there is one man who may detect the criminal.
This is Teiresias, this is the holy prophet
In whom, alone of all men, truth was born.
  OEDIPUS. Teiresias: seer: student of mysteries,
Of all that's taught and all that no man tells,
Secrets of Heaven and secrets of the earth:
Blind though you are, you know the city lies 290
Sick with plague; and from this plague, my lord,
We find that you alone can guard or save us.

Possibly you did not hear the messengers?
Apollo, when we sent to him,
Sent us back word that this great pestilence
Would lift, but only if we established clearly
The identity of those who murdered Laïos.

They must be killed or exiled.
                    Can you use
Birdflight or any art of divination   *299*
To purify yourself, and Thebes, and me
From this contagion? We are in your hands.
There is no fairer duty
Than that of helping others in distress.
  TEIRESIAS.   How dreadful knowledge of the truth can be
When there's no help in truth! I knew this well,
But did not act on it: else I should not have come.
  OEDIPUS.   What is troubling you? Why are your eyes so cold?
  TEIRESIAS.   Let me go home. Bear your own fate, and I'll
Bear mine. It is better so: trust what I say.
  OEDIPUS.   What you say is ungracious and unhelpful   *310*
To your native country. Do not refuse to speak.
  TEIRESIAS.   When it comes to speech, your own is neither temperate
Nor opportune. I wish to be more prudent.
  OEDIPUS.   In God's name, we all beg you—
  TEIRESIAS.   You are all ignorant.
No; I will never tell you what I know.
Now it is my misery; then, it would be yours.
  OEDIPUS.   What! You do know something, and will not tell us?
You would betray us all and wreck the State?
  TEIRESIAS.   I do not intend to torture myself, or you.
Why persist in asking? You will not persuade me.   *320*
  OEDIPUS.   What a wicked old man you are! You'd try a stone's
Patience! Out with it! Have you no feeling at all?
  TEIRESIAS.   You call me unfeeling. If you could only see
The nature of your own feelings . . .
  OEDIPUS.   Why,
Who would not feel as I do? Who could endure
Your arrogance toward the city?
  TEIRESIAS.   What does it matter!
Whether I speak or not, it is bound to come.
  OEDIPUS.   Then, if "it" is bound to come, you are bound to tell me.
  TEIRESIAS.   No, I will not go on. Rage as you please.
  OEDIPUS.   Rage? Why not!   *329*
         And I'll tell you what I think:
You planned it, you had it done, you all but
Killed him with your own hands: if you had eyes,
I'd say the crime was yours, and yours alone.
  TEIRESIAS.   So? I charge you, then,
Abide by the proclamation you have made:
From this day forth
Never speak again to these men or to me;
You yourself are the pollution of this country.
  OEDIPUS.   You dare say that! Can you possibly think you have
Some way of going free, after such insolence?   *340*
  TEIRESIAS.   I have gone free. It is the truth sustains me.
  OEDIPUS.   Who taught you shamelessness? It was not your craft.
  TEIRESIAS.   You did. You made me speak. I did not want to.
  OEDIPUS.   Speak what? Let me hear it again more clearly.
  TEIRESIAS.   Was it not clear before? Are you tempting me?
  OEDIPUS.   I did not understand it. Say it again.
  TEIRESIAS.   I say that you are the murderer whom you seek.
  OEDIPUS.   Now twice you have spat out infamy. You'll pay for it!
  TEIRESIAS.   Would you care for more? Do you wish to be really angry?
  OEDIPUS.   Say what you will. Whatever you say is worthless.   *350*

TEIRESIAS. I say that you live in hideous love with her
Who is nearest you in blood. You are blind to the evil.
OEDIPUS. It seems you can go on mouthing like this for ever.
TEIRESIAS. I can, if there is power in truth.
OEDIPUS. There is:
But not for you, not for you,
You sightless, witless, senseless, mad old man!
TEIRESIAS. You are the madman. There is no one here
Who will not curse you soon, as you curse me.
OEDIPUS. You child of endless night! You can not hurt me
Or any other man who sees the sun. *360*
TEIRESIAS. True: it is not from me your fate will come.
That lies within Apollo's competence,
As it is his concern.
OEDIPUS. Tell me:
Are you speaking for Creon, or for yourself?
TEIRESIAS. Creon is no threat. You weave your own doom.
OEDIPUS. Wealth, power, craft of statesmanship!
Kingly position, everywhere admired!
What savage envy is stored up against these,
If Creon, whom I trusted, Creon my friend, *369*
For this great office which the city once
Put in my hands unsought—if for this power
Creon desires in secret to destroy me!

He has bought this decrepit fortune-teller, this
Collector of dirty pennies, this prophet fraud—
Why, he is no more clairvoyant than I am!
Tell us:
Has your mystic mummery ever approached the truth?

When that hellcat the Sphinx was performing here,
What help were you to these people?
Her magic was not for the first man who came along: *379*
It demanded a real exorcist. Your birds—
What good were they? or the gods, for the matter of that?
But I came by,
Oedipus, the simple man, who knows nothing—
I thought it out for myself, no birds helped me!
And this is the man you think you can destroy,
That you may be close to Creon when he's king!
Well, you and your friend Creon, it seems to me,
Will suffer most. If you were not an old man,
You would have paid already for your plot.
CHORAGOS. We can not see that his words or yours *390*
Have been spoken except in anger, Oedipus,
And of anger we have no need. How can God's will
Be accomplished best? That is what most concerns us.
TEIRESIAS. You are a king. But where argument's concerned
I am your man, as much a king as you.
I am not your servant, but Apollo's.
I have no need of Creon to speak for me.

Listen to me. You mock my blindness, do you?
But I say that you, with both your eyes, are blind:
You can not see the wretchedness of your life, *400*
Nor in whose house you live, no, nor with whom.
Who are your father and mother? Can you tell me?
You do not even know the blind wrongs

That you have done them, on earth and
in the world below.
But the double lash of your parents'
curse will whip you
Out of this land some day, with only night
Upon your precious eyes.
Your cries then—where will they not be
heard?
What fastness of Kithairon[5] will not echo
them?
And that bridal-descant of yours—you'll
know it then,   *410*
The song they sang when you came here
to Thebes
And found your misguided berthing.
All this, and more, that you can not guess
at now,
Will bring you to yourself among your
children.

Be angry, then. Curse Creon. Curse my
words.
I tell you, no man that walks upon the
earth
Shall be rooted out more horribly than
you.
   OEDIPUS. Am I to bear this from
him?—Damnation
Take you! Out of this place! Out of my
sight!
   TEIRESIAS. I would not have come at
all if you had not asked me.   *420*
   OEDIPUS. Could I have told that
you'd talk nonsense, that
You'd come here to make a fool of yourself, and of me?
   TEIRESIAS. A fool? Your parents
thought me sane enough.
   OEDIPUS. My parents again!—Wait:
who were my parents?
   TEIRESIAS. This day will give you a
father, and break your heart.
   OEDIPUS. Your infantile riddles!
Your damned abracadabra!
   TEIRESIAS. You were a great man
once at solving riddles.

[5] mountain where Oedipus had been abandoned as an infant

   OEDIPUS. Mock me with that if you
like; you will find it true.
   TEIRESIAS. It was true enough. It
brought about your ruin.   *429*
   OEDIPUS. But if it saved this town?
   TEIRESIAS. (*to the* PAGE). Boy, give
me your hand.
   OEDIPUS. Yes, boy; lead him away.
                   —While you are here
We can do nothing. Go; leave us in peace.
   TEIRESIAS. I will go when I have said
what I have to say.
How can you hurt me? And I tell you
again:
The man you have been looking for all
this time,
The damned man, the murderer of Laïos,
That man is in Thebes. To your mind he
is foreign-born,
But it will soon be shown that he is a
Theban,
A revelation that will fail to please.
                                 A blind man,
Who has his eyes now; a penniless man,
who is rich now;   *441*
And he will go tapping the strange earth
with his staff.
To the children with whom he lives now
he will be
Brother and father—the very same; to her
Who bore him, son and husband—the
very same
Who came to his father's bed, wet with
his father's blood.

Enough. Go think that over.
If later you find error in what I have said,
You may say that I have no skill in
prophecy.
   (*Exit* TEIRESIAS, *led by his* PAGE.
OEDIPUS *goes into the palace.*)

ODE I

CHORUS.   [*strophe 1*]
The Delphic stone of prophecies   *450*
Remembers ancient regicide
And a still bloody hand.

That killer's hour of flight has come.
He must be stronger than riderless
Coursers of untiring wind,
For the son of Zeus armed with his father's thunder
Leaps in lightning after him;
And the Furies follow him, the sad Furies.

[antistrophe 1]

Holy Parnassos' peak of snow
Flashes and blinds that secret man,   460
That all shall hunt him down:
Though he may roam the forest shade
Like a bull gone wild from pasture
To rage through glooms of stone.
Doom comes down on him; flight will not avail him;
For the world's heart calls him desolate,
And the immortal Furies follow, for ever follow.

[strophe 2]

But now a wilder thing is heard
From the old man skilled at hearing Fate in the wingbeat of a bird.
Bewildered as a blown bird, my soul hovers and can not find   470
Foothold in this debate, or any reason or rest of mind.
But no man ever brought—none can bring
Proof of strife between Thebes' royal house,
Labdakos' line, and the son of Polybos;[6]
And never until now has any man brought word
Of Laïos' dark death staining Oedipus the King.

[antistrophe 2]

Divine Zeus and Apollo hold
Perfect intelligence alone of all tales ever told;
And well though this diviner works, he works in his own night;

[6] Oedipus

No man can judge that rough unknown or trust in second sight,   480
For wisdom changes hands among the wise.
Shall I believe my great lord criminal
At a raging word that a blind old man let fall?
I saw him, when the carrion woman faced him of old,
Prove his heroic mind! These evil words are lies.

SCENE II

CREON.   Men of Thebes:
I am told that heavy accusations
Have been brought against me by King Oedipus.
I am not the kind of man to bear this tamely.
If in these present difficulties   490
He holds me accountable for any harm to him
Through anything I have said or done—why, then,
I do not value life in this dishonor.
It is not as though this rumor touched upon
Some private indiscretion. The matter is grave.
The fact is that I am being called disloyal
To the State, to my fellow citizens, to my friends.
   CHORAGOS.   He may have spoken in anger, not from his mind.
   CREON.   But did you not hear him say I was the one   499
Who seduced the old prophet into lying?
   CHORAGOS.   The thing was said; I do not know how seriously.
   CREON.   But you were watching him! Were his eyes steady?
Did he look like a man in his right mind?
   CHORAGOS.   I do not know.
I can not judge the behavior of great men.
But here is the King himself.

(*Enter* OEDIPUS.)

OEDIPUS. So you dared come back. Why? How brazen of you to come to my house,
You murderer!
    Do you think I do not know
That you plotted to kill me, plotted to steal my throne?
Tell me, in God's name: am I coward, a fool,
That you should dream you could accomplish this?
A fool who could not see your slippery game?
A coward, not to fight back when I saw it?
You are the fool, Creon, are you not? hoping
Without support or friends to get a throne?
Thrones may be won or bought: you could do neither.

 CREON. Now listen to me. You have talked; let me talk, too.
You can not judge unless you know the facts.

 OEDIPUS. You speak well: there is one fact; but I find it hard
To learn from the deadliest enemy I have.

 CREON. That above all I must dispute with you.

 OEDIPUS. That above all I will not hear you deny.

 CREON. If you think there is anything good in being stubborn
Against all reason, then I say you are wrong.

 OEDIPUS. If you think a man can sin against his own kind
And not be punished for it, I say you are mad.

 CREON. I agree. But tell me: what have I done to you?

 OEDIPUS. You advised me to send for that wizard, did you not?

 CREON. I did. I should do it again.

 OEDIPUS. Very well. Now tell me: How long has it been since Laïos—

 CREON. What of Laïos?

 OEDIPUS. Since he vanished in that onset by the road?

 CREON. It was long ago, a long time.

 OEDIPUS. And this prophet, Was he practicing here then?

 CREON. He was; and with honor, as now.

 OEDIPUS. Did he speak of me at that time?

 CREON. He never did; At least, not when I was present.

 OEDIPUS. But . . . the enquiry? I suppose you held one?

 CREON. We did, but we learned nothing.

 OEDIPUS. Why did the prophet not speak against me then?

 CREON. I do not know; and I am the kind of man
Who holds his tongue when he has no facts to go on.

 OEDIPUS. There's one fact that you know, and you could tell it.

 CREON. What fact is that? If I know it, you shall have it.

 OEDIPUS. If he were not involved with you, he could not say
That it was I who murdered Laïos.

 CREON. If he says that, you are the one that knows it?—
But now it is my turn to question you.

 OEDIPUS. Put your questions. I am no murderer.

 CREON. First, then: You married my sister?

 OEDIPUS. I married your sister.

 CREON. And you rule the kingdom equally with her?

 OEDIPUS. Everything that she wants she has from me.

 CREON. And I am the third, equal to both of you?

 OEDIPUS. That is why I call you a bad friend.

 CREON. No. Reason it out, as I have done.
Think of this first: Would any sane man prefer

Power, with all a king's anxieties,
To that same power and the grace of sleep?
Certainly not I.
I have never longed for the king's power
    —only his rights.
Would any wise man differ from me in this?
As matters stand, I have my way in everything
With your consent, and no responsibilities.
If I were king, I should be a slave to policy. 560

How could I desire a scepter more
Than what is now mine—untroubled influence?
No, I have not gone mad; I need no honors,
Except those with the perquisites I have now.
I am welcome everywhere; every man salutes me,
And those who want your favor seek my ear,
Since I know how to manage what they ask.
Should I exchange this ease for that anxiety?
Besides, no sober mind is treasonable.
I hate anarchy 570
And never would deal with any man who likes it.

Test what I have said. Go to the priestess
At Delphi, ask if I quoted her correctly.
And as for this other thing: if I am found
Guilty of treason with Teiresias,
Then sentence me to death! You have my word
It is a sentence I should cast my vote for—
But not without evidence!
                    You do wrong
When you take good men for bad, bad men for good.
A true friend thrown aside—why, life itself 580

Is not more precious!
            In time you will know this well:
For time, and time alone, will show the just man,
Though scoundrels are discovered in a day.
  CHORAGOS. This is well said, and a prudent man would ponder it.
Judgments too quickly formed are dangerous.
  OEDIPUS. But is he not quick in his duplicity?
And shall I not be quick to parry him?
Would you have me stand still, hold my peace, and let
This man win everything, through my inaction?
  CREON. And you want—what is it, then? To banish me? 590
  OEDIPUS. No, not exile. It is your death I want,
So that all the world may see what treason means.
  CREON. You will persist, then? You will not believe me?
  OEDIPUS. How can I believe you?
  CREON.   Then you are a fool.
  OEDIPUS. To save myself?
  CREON.   In justice, think of me.
  OEDIPUS. You are evil incarnate.
  CREON.   But suppose that you are wrong?
  OEDIPUS. Still I must rule.
  CREON. But not if you rule badly.
  OEDIPUS. O city, city!
  CREON.   It is my city, too!
  CHORAGOS. Now, my lords, be still. I see the Queen,
Iocastê, coming from her palace chambers; 600
And it is time she came, for the sake of you both.
This dreadful quarrel can be resolved through her.
  (*Enter* IOCASTÊ.)
  IOCASTÊ. Poor foolish men, what wicked din is this?
With Thebes sick to death, is it not shameful

That you should rake some private
    quarrel up?
(*to* OEDIPUS.)
Come into the house.
                    —And you, Creon, go now:
Let us have no more of this tumult over
    nothing.
    CREON.   Nothing? No, sister: what
        your husband plans for me
Is one of two great evils: exile or death.
    OEDIPUS.   He is right.   609
Why, woman I have caught him squarely
Plotting against my life.
    CREON.   No! Let me die.
Accurst if ever I have wished you harm!
    IOCASTÊ.   Ah, believe it, Oedipus!
In the name of the gods, respect this oath
    of his
For my sake, for the sake of these people
    here!

    CHORAGOS.   [*strophe 1*]
Open your mind to her, my lord. Be
    ruled by her, I beg you!
    OEDIPUS.   What would you have me
        do?
    CHORAGOS.   Respect Creon's word. He
        has never spoken like a fool,
And now he has sworn an oath.
    OEDIPUS.   You know what you ask?
    CHORAGOS.   I do.
    OEDIPUS.   Speak on, then.
    CHORAGOS.   A friend so sworn should
        not be baited so,   620
In blind malice, and without final proof.
    OEDIPUS.   You are aware, I hope, that
        what you say
Means death for me, or exile at the least.

    CHORAGOS.   [*strophe 2*]
No, I swear by Helios, first in Heaven!
May I die friendless and accurst,
The worst of deaths, if ever I meant that!
    It is the withering fields
        That hurt my sick heart:
    Must we bear all these ills,   629
        And now your bad blood as well?
    OEDIPUS.   Then let him go. And let
        me die, if I must,
Or be driven by him in shame from the
    land of Thebes.
It is your unhappiness, and not his talk,
That touches me.
                As for him—
Wherever he is, I will hate him as long as
    I live.
    CREON.   Ugly in yielding, as you were
        ugly in rage!
Natures like yours chiefly torment them-
    selves.
    OEDIPUS.   Can you not go? Can you
        not leave me?
    CREON.   I can.
You do not know me; but the city knows
    me,   639
And in its eyes I am just, if not in yours.
(*Exit* CREON.)

    CHORAGOS.   [*antistrophe 1*]
Lady Iocastê, did you not ask the King
    to go to his chambers?
    IOCASTÊ.   First tell me what has hap-
        pened.
    CHORAGOS.   There was suspicion with-
        out evidence; yet it rankled
As even false charges will.
    IOCASTÊ.   On both sides?
    CHORAGOS.   On both.
    IOCASTÊ.   But what was said?
    CHORAGOS.   Oh let it rest, let it be
        done with!
Have we not suffered enough?
    OEDIPUS.   You see to what your
        decency has brought you:
You have made difficulties where my
    heart saw none.

    CHORAGOS.   [*antistrophe 2*]
Oedipus, it is not once only I have told
    you—
You must know I should count myself
    unwise   650
To the point of madness, should I now
    forsake you—
        You, under whose hand,
        In the storm of another time,
        Our dear land sailed out free.
        But now stand fast at the helm!

IOCASTÊ. In God's name, Oedipus, inform your wife as well:
Why are you so set in this hard anger?
    OEDIPUS. I will tell you, for none of these men deserves
My confidence as you do. It is Creon's work,   659
His treachery, his plotting against me.
    IOCASTÊ. Go on, if you can make this clear to me.
    OEDIPUS. He charges me with the murder of Laïos.
    IOCASTÊ. Has he some knowledge? Or does he speak from hearsay?
    OEDIPUS. He would not commit himself to such a charge,
But he has brought in that damnable soothsayer
To tell his story.
    IOCASTÊ. Set your mind at rest.
If it is a question of soothsayers, I tell you
That you will find no man whose craft gives knowledge
Of the unknowable.
              Here is my proof:

An oracle was reported to Laïos once   670
(I will not say from Phoibos himself, but from
His appointed ministers, at any rate)
That his doom would be death at the hands of his own son—
His son, born of his flesh and of mine!
Now, you remember the story: Laïos was killed
By marauding strangers where three highways meet;
But his child had not been three days in this world
Before the King had pierced the baby's ankles
And had him left to die on a lonely mountain.

Thus, Apollo never caused that child   680
To kill his father, and it was not Laïos' fate
To die at the hands of his son, as he had feared.

This is what prophets and prophecies are worth!
Have no dread of them.
                         It is God himself
Who can show us what he wills, in his own way.
    OEDIPUS. How strange a shadowy memory crossed my mind,
Just now while you were speaking; it chilled my heart.
    IOCASTÊ. What do you mean? What memory do you speak of?
    OEDIPUS. If I understand you, Laïos was killed   689
At a place where three roads meet.
    IOCASTÊ.   So it was said;
We have no later story.
    OEDIPUS.   Where did it happen?
    IOCASTÊ. Phokis, it is called: at a place where the Theban Way
Divides into the roads toward Delphi and Daulia.
    OEDIPUS. When?
    IOCASTÊ. We had the news not long before you came
And proved the right to your succession here.
    OEDIPUS. Ah, what net has God been weaving for me?
    IOCASTÊ. Oedipus! Why does this trouble you?
    OEDIPUS. Do not ask me yet.
First, tell me how Laïos looked, and tell me
How old he was.
    IOCASTÊ. He was tall, his hair just touched
With white; his form was not unlike your own.   700
    OEDIPUS. I think that I myself may be accurst
By my own ignorant edict.
    IOCASTÊ. You speak strangely.
It makes me tremble to look at you, my King.
    OEDIPUS. I am not sure that the blind man can not see.
But I should know better if you were to tell me—

IOCASTÊ. Anything—though I dread to hear you ask it.

OEDIPUS. Was the King lightly escorted, or did he ride
With a large company, as a ruler should?

IOCASTÊ. There were five men with him in all: one was a herald;
And a single chariot, which he was driving. 710

OEDIPUS. Alas, that makes it plain enough!
But who—
Who told you how it happened?

IOCASTÊ. A household servant,
The only one to escape.

OEDIPUS. And is he still
A servant of ours?

IOCASTÊ. No; for when he came back at last
And found you enthroned in the place of the dead king,
He came to me, touched my hand with his, and begged
That I would send him away to the frontier district
Where only the shepherds go—
As far away from the city as I could send him.
I granted his prayer, for although the man was a slave, 720
He had earned more than this favor at my hands.

OEDIPUS. Can he be called back quickly?

IOCASTÊ. Easily.
But why?

OEDIPUS. I have taken too much upon myself
Without enquiry; therefore I wish to consult him.

IOCASTÊ. Then he shall come.
But am I not one also
To whom you might confide these fears of yours?

OEDIPUS. That is your right; it will not be denied you,
Now least of all; for I have reached a pitch
Of wild foreboding. Is there anyone
To whom I should sooner speak? 730

Polybos of Corinth is my father.
My mother is a Dorian: Meropê.
I grew up chief among the men of Corinth
Until a strange thing happened—
Not worth my passion, it may be, but strange.

At a feast, a drunken man maundering in his cups
Cries out that I am not my father's son!

I contained myself that night, though I felt anger
And a sinking heart. The next day I visited
My father and mother, and questioned them. They stormed, 740
Calling it all the slanderous rant of a fool;
And this relieved me. Yet the suspicion
Remained always aching in my mind;
I knew there was talk; I could not rest;
And finally, saying nothing to my parents,
I went to the shrine at Delphi.

The god dismissed my question without reply;
He spoke of other things.
Some were clear,
Full of wretchedness, dreadful, unbearable:
As, that I should lie with my own mother, breed 750
Children from whom all men would turn their eyes;
And that I should be my father's murderer.

I heard all this, and fled. And from that day
Corinth to me was only in the stars
Descending in that quarter of the sky,
As I wandered farther and farther on my way
To a land where I should never see the evil

Sung by the oracle. And I came to this country
Where, so you say, King Laïos was killed.

I will tell you all that happened there, my lady. 760

There were three highways
Coming together at a place I passed;
And there a herald came towards me, and a chariot
Drawn by horses, with a man such as you describe
Seated in it. The groom leading the horses
Forced me off the road at his lord's command;
But as this charioteer lurched over towards me
I struck at him in my rage. The old man saw me
And brought his double goad down upon my head
As I came abreast.
    He was paid back, and more!
Swinging my club in this right hand I knocked him 771
Out of his car, and he rolled on the ground.
    I killed him.

I killed them all.
Now if that stranger and Laïos were—kin,
Where is a man more miserable than I?
More hated by the gods? Citizen and alien alike
Must never shelter me or speak to me—
I must be shunned by all.
    And I myself
Pronounced this malediction upon myself!
Think of it: I have touched you with these hands, 780
These hands that killed your husband. What defilement!

Am I all evil, then? It must be so,
Since I must flee from Thebes, yet never again
See my own countrymen, my own country,
For fear of joining my mother in marriage
And killing Polybos, my father.
    Ah,
If I was created so, born to this fate,
Who could deny the savagery of God?

O holy majesty of heavenly powers!
May I never see that day! Never! 790
Rather let me vanish from the race of men
Than know the abomination destined me!
 CHORAGOS. We too, my lord, have felt dismay at this.
But there is hope: you have yet to hear the shepherd.
 OEDIPUS. Indeed, I fear no other hope is left me.
 IOCASTÊ. What do you hope from him when he comes?
 OEDIPUS.   This much:
If his account of the murder tallies with yours,
Then I am cleared.
 IOCASTÊ.   What was it that I said
Of such importance?
 OEDIPUS.   Why, "marauders," you said,
Killed the King, according to this man's story. 800
If he maintains that still, if there were several,
Clearly the guilt is not mine: I was alone.
But if he says one man, singlehanded, did it,
Then the evidence all points to me.
 IOCASTÊ. You may be sure that he said there were several;
And can he call back that story now? He can not.
The whole city heard it as plainly as I.
But suppose he alters some detail of it:
He can not ever show that Laïos death
Fulfilled the oracle: for Apollo said 810
My child was doomed to kill him; and my child—

Poor baby!—it was my child that died
    first.
No. From now on, where oracles are
    concerned,
I would not waste a second thought on
    any.
OEDIPUS.   You may be right.
            But come: let someone go
For the shepherd at once. This matter
    must be settled.
IOCASTÊ.   I will send for him.
I would not wish to cross you in anything,
And surely not in this.—Let us go in.
(*Exeunt into the palace.*)

ODE II

CHORUS.   [*strophe 1*]
Let me be reverent in the ways of right,
Lowly the paths I journey on;   *821*
Let all my words and actions keep
The laws of the pure universe
From highest Heaven handed down.
For Heaven is their bright nurse,
Those generations of the realms of light;
Ah, never of mortal kind were they begot,
Nor are they slaves of memory, lost in
    sleep:
Their Father is greater than Time, and
    ages not.

                        [*antistrophe 1*]
The tyrant is a child of Pride   *830*
Who drinks from his great sickening cup
Recklessness and vanity,
Until from his high crest headlong
He plummets to the dust of hope.
That strong man is not strong.
But let no fair ambition be denied;
May God protect the wrestler for the
    State
In government, in comely policy,
Who will fear God, and on His ordinance
    wait.

                        [*strophe 2*]
Haughtiness and the high hand of disdain
Tempt and outrage God's holy law;   *841*
And any mortal who dares hold
No immortal Power in awe
Will be caught up in a net of pain:
The price for which his levity is sold.
Let each man take due earnings, then,
And keep his hands from holy things,
And from blasphemy stand apart—
Else the crackling blast of heaven
Blows on his head, and on his desperate
    heart;   *850*
Though fools will honor impious men,
In their cities no tragic poet sings.

                        [*antistrophe 2*]
Shall we lose faith in Delphi's obscurities,
We who have heard the world's core
Discredited, and the sacred wood
Of Zeus at Elis praised no more?
The deeds and the strange prophecies
Must make a pattern yet to be under-
    stood.
Zeus, if indeed you are lord of all,
Throned in light over night and day,   *860*
Mirror this in your endless mind:
Our masters call the oracle
Words on the wind, and the Delphic
    vision blind!
Their hearts no longer know Apollo,
And reverence for the gods has died
    away.

SCENE III

(*Enter* IOCASTÊ.)

IOCASTÊ.   Princes of Thebes, it has
    occurred to me
To visit the altars of the gods, bearing
These branches as a suppliant, and this
    incense.
Our King is not himself: his noble soul
Is overwrought with fantasies of dread,
Else he would consider   *871*
The new prophecies in the light of the old.
He will listen to any voice that speaks
    disaster,
And my advice goes for nothing.
(*She approaches the altar, R.*)
            To you, then, Apollo,
Lycean lord, since you are nearest, I turn
    in prayer.

Receive these offerings, and grant us deliverance
From defilement. Our hearts are heavy with fear
When we see our leader distracted, as helpless sailors
Are terrified by the confusion of their helmsman.

(*Enter* MESSENGER.)

MESSENGER. Friends, no doubt you can direct me: 880
Where shall I find the house of Oedipus,
Or, better still, where is the King himself?

CHORAGOS. It is this very place, stranger; he is inside.
This is his wife and mother of his children.

MESSENGER. I wish her happiness in a happy house,
Blest in all the fulfillment of her marriage.

IOCASTÊ. I wish as much for you: your courtesy
Deserves a like good fortune. But now, tell me:
Why have you come? What have you to say to us? 889

MESSENGER. Good news, my lady, for your house and your husband.

IOCASTÊ. What news? Who sent you here?

MESSENGER. I am from Corinth.
The news I bring ought to mean joy for you,
Though it may be you will find some grief in it.

IOCASTÊ. What is it? How can it touch us in both ways?

MESSENGER. The people of Corinth, they say,
Intend to call Oedipus to be their king.

IOCASTÊ. But old Polybus—is he not reigning still?

MESSENGER. No. Death holds him in his sepulchre.

IOCASTÊ. What are you saying? Polybos is dead?

MESSENGER. If I am not telling the truth, may I die myself. 900

IOCASTÊ (*to a* MAID-SERVANT). Go in, go quickly; tell this to your master.

O riddlers of God's will, where are you now!
This was the man whom Oedipus, long ago,
Feared so, fled so, in dread of destroying him—
But it was another fate by which he died.

(*Enter* OEDIPUS, *center*.)

OEDIPUS. Dearest Iocastê, why have you sent for me?

IOCASTÊ. Listen to what this man says, and then tell me
What has become of the solemn prophecies.

OEDIPUS. Who is this man? What is his news for me?

IOCASTÊ. He has come from Corinth to announce your father's death! 910

OEDIPUS. Is it true, stranger? Tell me in your own words.

MESSENGER. I can not say it more clearly: the King is dead.

OEDIPUS. Was it by treason? Or by an attack of illness?

MESSENGER. A little thing brings old men to their rest.

OEDIPUS. It was sickness, then?

MESSENGER. Yes, and his many years.

OEDIPUS. Ah!
Why should a man respect the Pythian hearth,[7] or
Give heed to the birds that jangle above his head?
They prophesied that I should kill Polybos,
Kill my own father; but he is dead and buried, 920
And I am here—I never touched him, never,
Unless he died of grief for my departure,
And thus, in a sense, through me. No. Polybos

[7] the Delphic Oracle

Has packed the oracles off with him underground.
They are empty words.
IOCASTÊ. Had I not told you so?
OEDIPUS. You had; it was my faint heart that betrayed me.
IOCASTÊ. From now on never think of those things again.
OEDIPUS. And yet—must I not fear my mother's bed?
IOCASTÊ. Why should anyone in this world be afraid,
Since Fate rules us and nothing can be foreseen? 930
A man should live only for the present day.

Have no more fear of sleeping with your mother:
How many men, in dreams, have lain with their mothers!
No reasonable man is troubled by such things.
OEDIPUS. That is true; only—
If only my mother were not still alive!
But she is alive. I can not help my dread.
IOCASTÊ. Yet this news of your father's death is wonderful.
OEDIPUS. Wonderful. But I fear the living woman.
MESSENGER. Tell me, who is this woman that you fear? 940
OEDIPUS. It is Meropê, man; the wife of King Polybos.
MESSENGER. Meropê? Why should you be afraid of her?
OEDIPUS. An oracle of the gods, a dreadful saying.
MESSENGER. Can you tell me about it or are you sworn to silence?
OEDIPUS. I can tell you, and I will.
Apollo said through his prophet that I was the man
Who should marry his own mother, shed his father's blood
With his own hands. And so, for all these years
I have kept clear of Corinth, and no harm has come—

Though it would have been sweet to see my parents again. 950
MESSENGER. And is this the fear that drove you out of Corinth?
OEDIPUS. Would you have me kill my father?
MESSENGER. As for that
You must be reassured by the news I gave you.
OEDIPUS. If you could reassure me, I would reward you.
MESSENGER. I had that in mind, I will confess: I thought
I could count on you when you returned to Corinth.
OEDIPUS. No: I will never go near my parents again.
MESSENGER. Ah, son, you still do not know what you are doing—
OEDIPUS. What do you mean? In the name of God tell me!
MESSENGER. —If these are your reasons for not going home. 960
OEDIPUS. I tell you, I fear the oracle may come true.
MESSENGER. And guilt may come upon you through your parents?
OEDIPUS. That is the dread that is always in my heart.
MESSENGER. Can you not see that all your fears are groundless?
OEDIPUS. How can you say that? They are my parents, surely?
MESSENGER. Polybos was not your father.
OEDIPUS. Not my father?
MESSENGER. No more your father than the man speaking to you.
OEDIPUS. But you are nothing to me!
MESSENGER. Neither was he.
OEDIPUS. Then why did he call me son?
MESSENGER. I will tell you:
Long ago he had you from my hands, as a gift. 970
OEDIPUS. Then how could he love me so, if I was not his?
MESSENGER. He had no children, and his heart turned to you.

OEDIPUS. What of you? Did you buy me? Did you find me by chance?
MESSENGER. I came upon you in the crooked pass of Kithairon.
OEDIPUS. And what were you doing there?
MESSENGER. Tending my flocks.
OEDIPUS. A wandering shepherd?
MESSENGER. But your savior, son, that day.
OEDIPUS. From what did you save me?
MESSENGER. Your ankles should tell you that.
OEDIPUS. Ah, stranger, why do you speak of that childhood pain?
MESSENGER. I cut the bonds that tied your ankles together.
OEDIPUS. I have had the mark as long as I can remember. 980
MESSENGER. That was why you were given the name you bear.[8]
OEDIPUS. God! Was it my father or my mother who did it? Tell me!
MESSENGER. I do not know. The man who gave you to me Can tell you better than I.
OEDIPUS. It was not you that found me, but another?
MESSENGER. It was another shepherd gave you to me.
OEDIPUS. Who was he? Can you tell me who he was?
MESSENGER. I think he was said to be one of Laïos' people.
OEDIPUS. You mean the Laïos who was king here years ago? 990
MESSENGER. Yes; King Laïos; and the man was one of his herdsmen.
OEDIPUS. Is he still alive? Can I see him?
MESSENGER. These men here Know best about such things.
OEDIPUS. Does anyone here Know this shepherd that he is talking about?
Have you seen him in the fields, or in the town?
If you have, tell me. It is time things were made plain.
CHORAGOS. I think the man he means is that same shepherd
You have already asked to see. Iocastê perhaps
Could tell you something.
OEDIPUS. Do you know anything
About him, Lady? Is he the man we have summoned? 1000
Is that the man this shepherd means?
IOCASTÊ. Why think of him?
Forget this herdsman. Forget it all.
This talk is a waste of time.
OEDIPUS. How can you say that,
When the clues to my true birth are in my hands?
IOCASTÊ. For God's love, let us have no more questioning!
Is your life nothing to you?
My own is pain enough for me to bear.
OEDIPUS. You need not worry. Suppose my mother a slave,
And born of slaves: no baseness can touch you.
IOCASTÊ. Listen to me, I beg you: do not do this thing! 1010
OEDIPUS. I will not listen; the truth must be made known.
IOCASTÊ. Everything that I say is for your own good!
OEDIPUS. My own good
Snaps my patience, then; I want none of it.
IOCASTÊ. You are fatally wrong! May you never learn who you are!
OEDIPUS. Go, one of you, and bring the shepherd here.
Let us leave this woman to brag of her royal name.
IOCASTÊ. Ah, miserable!
That is the only word I have for you now.
That is the only word I can ever have.
(*Exit into the palace.*)
CHORAGOS. Why has she left us, Oedipus? Why has she gone 1020

---

[8] Oedipus = swelled foot

In such a passion of sorrow? I fear this
    silence:
Something dreadful may come of it.
    OEDIPUS.   Let it come!
However base my birth, I must know
    about it.
The Queen, like a woman, is perhaps
    ashamed
To think of my low origin. But I
Am a child of Luck; I cannot be dis-
    honored.
Luck is my mother; the passing months,
    my brothers,
Have seen me rich and poor.
                                 If this is so,
How could I wish that I were someone
    else?
How could I not be glad to know my
    birth?   *1030*

ODE III

    CHORUS.   [*strophe*]
If ever the coming time were known
To my heart's pondering,
Kithairon, now by Heaven I see the
    torches
At the festival of the next full moon,
And see the dance, and hear the choir
    sing
A grace to your gentle shade:
Mountain where Oedipus was found,
O mountain guard of a noble race!
May the god who heals us lend his aid,
And let that glory come to pass   *1040*
For our king's cradling-ground.

                                  [*antistrophe*]
Of the nymphs that flower beyond the
    years,
Who bore you, royal child,
To Pan of the hills or the timberline
    Apollo,
Cold in delight where the upland clears,
Or Hermês for whom Kyllenê's heights
    are piled?
Or flushed as evening cloud,
Great Dionysos, roamer of mountains,
He—was it he who found you there,
And caught you up in his own proud
Arms from the sweet god-ravisher[9]   *1051*
Who laughed by the Muses' fountains?

SCENE IV

    OEDIPUS.   Sirs: though I do not know
        the man,
I think I see him coming, this shepherd
    we want:
He is old, like our friend here, and the
    men
Bringing him seem to be servants of my
    house.
But you can tell, if you have ever seen
    him.
    (*Enter* SHEPHERD *escorted by ser-
vants.*)
    CHORAGOS.   I know him, he was
        Laïos' man. You can trust him.
    OEDIPUS.   Tell me first, you from
        Corinth: is this the shepherd   *1059*
We were discussing?
    MESSENGER.   This is the very man.
    OEDIPUS (*to* SHEPHERD).   Come here.
        No, look at me. You must answer
Everything I ask.—You belonged to
    Laïos?
    SHEPHERD.   Yes: born his slave,
        brought up in his house.
    OEDIPUS.   Tell me: what kind of work
        did you do for him?
    SHEPHERD.   I was a shepherd of his,
        most of my life.
    OEDIPUS.   Where mainly did you go
        for pasturage?
    SHEPHERD.   Sometimes Kithairon,
        sometimes the hills near-by.
    OEDIPUS.   Do you remember ever see-
        ing this man out there?
    SHEPHERD.   What would he be doing
        there? This man?
    OEDIPUS.   This man standing here.
        Have you ever seen him before?
    SHEPHERD.   No. At least, not to my
        recollection.   *1071*

[9] nymph who may have been the mother of Oedipus

MESSENGER. And that is not strange, my lord. But I'll refresh
His memory: he must remember when we two
Spent three whole seasons together, March to September,
On Kithairon or thereabouts. He had two flocks;
I had one. Each autumn I'd drive mine home
And he would go back with his to Laïos' sheepfold.—
Is this not true, just as I have described it?
   SHEPHERD. True, yes; but it was all so long ago.
   MESSENGER. Well, then: do you remember, back in those days,   *1080*
That you gave me a baby boy to bring up as my own?
   SHEPHERD. What if I did? What are you trying to say?
   MESSENGER. King Oedipus was once that little child.
   SHEPHERD. Damn you, hold your tongue!
   OEDIPUS. No more of that!
It is your tongue needs watching, not this man's.
   SHEPHERD. My King, my Master, what is it I have done wrong?
   OEDIPUS. You have not answered his question about the boy.
   SHEPHERD. He does not know . . . He is only making trouble . . .
   OEDIPUS. Come, speak plainly, or it will go hard with you.
   SHEPHERD. In God's name, do not torture an old man!   *1090*
   OEDIPUS. Come here, one of you; bind his arms behind him.
   SHEPHERD. Unhappy king! What more do you wish to learn?
   OEDIPUS. Did you give this man the child he speaks of?
   SHEPHERD. I did.
And I would to God I had died that very day.

   OEDIPUS. You will die now unless you speak the truth.
   SHEPHERD. Yet if I speak the truth, I am worse than dead.
   OEDIPUS. Very well; since you insist upon delaying—
   SHEPHERD. No! I have told you already that I gave him the boy.
   OEDIPUS. Where did you get him? From your house? From somewhere else?
   SHEPHERD. Not from mine, no. A man gave him to me.   *1100*
   OEDIPUS. Is that man here? Do you know whose slave he was?
   SHEPHERD. For God's love, my King, do not ask me any more!
   OEDIPUS. You are a dead man if I have to ask you again.
   SHEPHERD. Then . . . Then the child was from the palace of Laïos.
   OEDIPUS. A slave child? or a child of his own line?
   SHEPHERD. Ah, I am on the brink of dreadful speech!
   OEDIPUS. And I of dreadful hearing. Yet I must hear.
   SHEPHERD. If you must be told, then . . .
They said it was Laïos' child;
But it is your wife who can tell you about that.
   OEDIPUS. My wife! Did she give it to you?
   SHEPHERD. My lord, she did.   *1110*
   OEDIPUS. Do you know why?
   SHEPHERD. I was told to get rid of it.
   OEDIPUS. An unspeakable mother!
   SHEPHERD. There had been prophecies . . .
   OEDIPUS. Tell me.
   SHEPHERD. It was said that the boy would kill his own father.
   OEDIPUS. Then why did you give him over to this old man?
   SHEPHERD. I pitied the baby, my King,

And I thought that this man would take him far away
To his own country.
　　　　　He saved him—but for what a fate!
For if you are what this man says you are,
No man living is more wretched than Oedipus.
　OEDIPUS.　Ah God!　　　　　　　　　　1120
It was true!
　　　　All the prophecies!
　　　　　　　　　　　　—Now,
O Light, may I look on you for the last time!
I, Oedipus,
Oedipus, damned in his birth, in his marriage damned,
Damned in the blood he shed with his own hand!

(*He rushes into the palace.*)

ODE IV

　CHORUS.　　　　　　　　　　[*strophe 1*]
Alas for the seed of men.

What measure shall I give these generations
That breathe on the void and are void
And exist and do not exist?

Who bears more weight of joy　　　　1130
Than mass of sunlight shifting in images,
Or who shall make his thought stay on
That down time drifts away?

Your splendor is all fallen.

O naked brow of wrath and tears,
O change of Oedipus!
I who saw your days call no man blest—
Your great days like ghósts góne.

　　　　　　　　　　　　[*antistrophe 1*]
That mind was a strong bow.
Deep, how deep you drew it then, hard archer,　　　　　　　　　　1140
At a dim fearful range,
And brought dear glory down!

You overcame the stranger—
The virgin with her hooking lion claws—
And though death sang, stood like a tower
To make pale Thebes take heart.

Fortress against our sorrow!

Divine king, giver of laws,
Majestic Oedipus!
No prince in Thebes had ever such renown,　　　　　　　　　　1150
No prince won such grace of power.

　　　　　　　　　　　　[*strophe 2*]
And now of all men ever known
Most pitiful is this man's story:
His fortunes are most changed, his state
Fallen to a low slave's
Ground under bitter fate.

O Oedipus, most royal one!
The great door that expelled you to the light
Gave at night—ah, gave night to your glory:
As to the father, to the fathering son.

All understood too late.　　　　　　1161

How could that queen whom Laïos won,
The garden that he harrowed at his height,
Be silent when that act was done?

　　　　　　　　　　　　[*antistrophe 2*]
But all eyes fail before time's eye,
All actions come to justice there.
Though never willed, though far down the deep past,
Your bed, your dread sirings,
Are brought to book at last.
Child by Laïos doomed to die,　　　　1170
Then doomed to lose that fortunate little death,
Would God you never took breath in this air
That with my wailing lips I take to cry:

For I weep the world's outcast.

Blind I was, and cannot tell why;
Asleep, for you had given ease of breath;
A fool, while the false years went by.

ÉXODOS

(*Enter, from the palace,* SECOND MESSENGER.)

SECOND MESSENGER.   Elders of Thebes, most honored in this land,
What horrors are yours to see and hear, what weight
Of sorrow to be endured, if, true to your birth,   *1180*
You venerate the line of Labdakos!
I think neither Istros nor Phasis, those great rivers,
Could purify this place of the corruption
It shelters now, or soon must bring to light—
Evil not done unconsciously, but willed.

The greatest griefs are those we cause ourselves.
   CHORAGOS.   Surely, friend, we have grief enough already;
What new sorrow do you mean?
   SECOND MESSENGER.   The Queen is dead.
   CHORAGOS.   Iocastê? Dead? But at whose hand?
   SECOND MESSENGER.   Her own.
The full horror of what happened you cannot know,   *1190*
For you did not see it; but I, who did, will tell you
As clearly as I can how she met her death.

When she had left us,
In passionate silence, passing through the court,
She ran to her apartment in the house,
Her hair clutched by the fingers of both hands.
She closed the doors behind her; then, by that bed
Where long ago the fatal son was conceived—
That son who should bring about his father's death—
We heard her call upon Laïos, dead so many years,   *1200*
And heard her wail for the double fruit of her marriage,
A husband by her husband, children by her child.
Exactly how she died I do not know:
For Oedipus burst in moaning and would not let us
Keep vigil to the end: it was by him
As he stormed about the room that our eyes were caught.
From one to another of us he went, begging a sword,
Cursing the wife who was not his wife, the mother
Whose womb had carried his own children and himself.
I do not know: it was none of us aided him,   *1210*
But surely one of the gods was in control!
For with a dreadful cry
He hurled his weight, as though wrenched out of himself,
At the twin doors: the bolts gave, and he rushed in.
And there we saw her hanging, her body swaying
From the cruel cord she had noosed about her neck.
A great sob broke from him, heartbreaking to hear,
As he loosed the rope and lowered her to the ground.

I would blot out from my mind what happened next!
For the King ripped from her gown the golden brooches   *1220*
That were her ornament, and raised them, and plunged them down
Straight into his own eyeballs, crying,
"No more,
No more shall you look on the misery about me,
The horrors of my own doing! Too long you have known

The faces of those whom I should never
    have seen,
Too long been blind to those for whom
    I was searching!
From this hour, go in darkness!" And as
    he spoke,
He struck at his eyes—not once, but
    many times;
And the blood spattered his beard,
Bursting from his ruined sockets like red
    hail.   *1230*
So from the unhappiness of two this evil
    has sprung,
A curse on the man and woman alike.
    The old
Happiness of the house of Labdakos
Was happiness enough: where is it today?
It is all wailing and ruin, disgrace, death
    —all
The misery of mankind that has a
    name—
And it is wholly and for ever theirs.
    CHORAGOS. Is he in agony still? Is
    there no rest for him?
    SECOND MESSENGER. He is calling
    for someone to lead him to the gates
So that all the children of Kadmos may
    look upon   *1240*
His father's murderer, his mother's—no,
I can not say it!
                And then he will leave Thebes,
Self-exiled, in order that the curse
Which he himself pronounced may depart
    from the house.
He is weak, and there is none to lead him,
So terrible is his suffering.
                But you will see:
Look, the doors are opening; in a moment
You will see a thing that would crush a
    heart of stone.
    (*The central door is opened;* OEDIPUS,
blinded, is led in.)
    CHORAGOS. Dreadful indeed for men
    to see.
Never have my own eyes   *1250*
Looked on a sight so full of fear.

Oedipus!
What madness came upon you, what
    daemon
Leaped on your life with heavier
Punishment than a mortal man can bear?
No: I cannot even
Look at you, poor ruined one.
And I would speak, question, ponder,
If I were able. No.
You make me shudder.   *1260*
    OEDIPUS. God.   God.
Is there a sorrow greater?
Where shall I find harbor in this world?
My voice is hurled far on a dark wind.
What has God done to me?
    CHORAGOS. Too terrible to think of,
    or to see.

    OEDIPUS.   [*strophe 1*]
O cloud of night,
Never to be turned away: night coming
    on,   *1268*
I can not tell how: night like a shroud!

My fair winds brought me here.
                    O God. Again
The pain of the spikes where I had sight,
The flooding pain
Of memory, never to be gouged out.
    CHORAGOS. This is not strange.
You suffer it all twice over, remorse in
    pain,
Pain in remorse.

    OEDIPUS.   [*antistrophe 1*]
Ah dear friend
Are you faithful even yet, you alone?
Are you still standing near me, will you
    stay here,   *1279*
Patient, to care for the blind?
                    The blind man!
Yet even blind I know who it is attends
    me,
By the voice's tone—
Though my new darkness hide the com-
    forter.
    CHORAGOS. Oh fearful act!
What god was it drove you to rake black
Night across your eyes?

OEDIPUS.   [strophe 2]
Apollo. Apollo. Dear
Children, the god was Apollo.
He brought my sick, sick fate upon me.
But the blinding hand was my own!   *1290*
How could I bear to see
When all my sight was horror everywhere?
    CHORAGOS.   Everywhere; that is true.
    OEDIPUS.   And now what is left?
Images? Love? A greeting even,
Sweet to the senses? Is there anything?
Ah, no, friends: lead me away.
Lead me away from Thebes.
                      Lead the great wreck
And hell of Oedipus, whom the gods hate.
    CHORAGOS.   Your fate is clear, you are not blind to that.   *1300*
Would God you had never found it out!

OEDIPUS.   [antistrophe 2]
Death take the man who unbound
My feet on that hillside
And delivered me from death to life! What life?
If only I had died,
This weight of monstrous doom
Could not have dragged me and my darlings down.
    CHORAGOS.   I would have wished the same.
    OEDIPUS.   Oh never to have come here
With my father's blood upon me! Never
To have been the man they call his mother's husband!   *1311*
Oh accurst! Oh child of evil,
To have entered that wretched bed—
                      the selfsame one!
More primal than sin itself, this fell to me.
    CHORAGOS.   I do not know how I can answer you.
You were better dead than alive and blind.
    OEDIPUS.   Do not counsel me any more. This punishment
That I have laid upon myself is just.
If I had eyes,   *1319*
I do not know how I could bear the sight
Of my father, when I came to the house of Death,
Or my mother: for I have sinned against them both
So vilely that I could not make my peace
By strangling my own life.
                 Or do you think my children,
Born as they were born, would be sweet to my eyes?
Ah never, never! Nor this town with its high walls,
Nor the holy images of the gods.
                           For I,
Thrice miserable!—Oedipus, noblest of all the line
Of Kadmos, have condemned myself to enjoy
These things no more, by my own malediction   *1330*
Expelling that man whom the gods declared
To be a defilement in the house of Laïos.
After exposing the rankness of my own guilt,
How could I look men frankly in the eyes?
No, I swear it,
If I could have stifled my hearing at its source,
I would have done it and made all this body
A tight cell of misery, blank to light and sound:
So I should have been safe in a dark agony
Beyond all recollection.
                      Ah Kithairon!
Why did you shelter me? When I was cast upon you,   *1341*
Why did I not die? Then I should never
Have shown the world my execrable birth.

Ah Polybos! Corinth, city that I believed
The ancient seat of my ancestors: how fair
I seemed, your child! And all the while this evil

Was cancerous within me!
                    For I am sick
In my daily life, sick in my origin.

O three roads, dark ravine, woodland and way
Where three roads met: you, drinking my father's blood,   *1350*
My own blood, spilled by my own hand: can you remember
The unspeakable things I did there, and the things
I went on from there to do?
                    O marriage, marriage!
The act that engendered me, and again the act
Performed by the son in the same bed—
                    Ah, the net
Of incest, mingling fathers, brothers, sons,
With brides, wives, mothers: the last evil
That can be known by men: no tongue can say
How evil!
     No. For the love of God, conceal me
Somewhere far from Thebes; or kill me; or hurl me   *1360*
Into the sea, away from men's eyes for ever.

Come, lead me. You need not fear to touch me.
Of all men, I alone can bear this guilt.
     (*Enter* CREON.)
  CHORAGOS. We are not the ones to decide; but Creon here
May fitly judge of what you ask. He only
Is left to protect the city in your place.
  OEDIPUS. Alas, how can I speak to him? What right have I
To beg his courtesy whom I have deeply wronged?
  CREON. I have not come to mock you, Oedipus,
Or to reproach you, either.
     (*to* ATTENDANTS)—You, standing there: *1370*
If you have lost all respect for man's dignity,
At least respect the flame of Lord Helios:
Do not allow this pollution to show itself
Openly here, an affront to the earth
And Heaven's rain and the light of day.
          No, take him
Into the house as quickly as you can.
For it is proper
That only the close kindred see his grief.
  OEDIPUS. I pray you in God's name, since your courtesy   *1379*
Ignores my dark expectation, visiting
With mercy this man of all men most execrable:
Give me what I ask—for your good, not for mine.
  CREON. And what is it that you would have me do?
  OEDIPUS. Drive me out of this country as quickly as may be
To a place where no human voice can ever greet me.
  CREON. I should have done that before now—only,
God's will had not been wholly revealed to me.
  OEDIPUS. But his command is plain: the parricide
Must be destroyed. I am that evil man.
  CREON. That is the sense of it, yes; but as things are,   *1390*
We had best discover clearly what is to be done.
  OEDIPUS. You would learn more about a man like me?
  CREON. You are ready now to listen to the god.
  OEDIPUS. I will listen. But it is to you
That I must turn for help. I beg you, hear me.

The woman in there—
Give her whatever funeral you think proper:
She is your sister.
          —But let me go, Creon!
Let me purge my father's Thebes of the pollution

Of my living here, and go out to the wild
    hills,   *1400*
To Kithairon, that has won such fame
    with me,
The tomb my mother and father ap-
    pointed for me,
And let me die there, as they willed I
    should.
And yet I know
Death will not ever come to me through
    sickness
Or in any natural way: I have been pre-
    served
For some unthinkable fate. But let that
    be.
As for my sons, you need not care for
    them.
They are men, they will find some way
    to live.
But my poor daughters, who have shared
    my table,   *1410*
Who never before have been parted from
    their father—
Take care of them, Creon; do this for me.
And will you let me touch them with my
    hands
A last time, and let us weep together?
Be kind, my lord,
Great prince, be kind!
                  Could I but touch them,
They would be mine again, as when I
    had my eyes.

(*Enter* ANTIGONÊ *and* ISMENÊ, *attended.*)

Ah, God!
Is it my dearest children I hear weeping?
Has Creon pitied me and sent my
    daughters?   *1420*
  CREON. Yes, Oedipus: I knew that
    they were dear to you
In the old days, and know you must love
    them still.
  OEDIPUS. May God bless you for this
    —and be a friendlier
Guardian to you than he has been to me!

Children, where are you?
Come quickly to my hands: they are your
    brother's—
Hands that have brought your father's
    once clear eyes
To this way of seeing—
                  Ah dearest ones,
I had neither sight nor knowledge then,
    your father
By the woman who was the source of his
    own life!   *1430*
And I weep for you—having no strength
    to see you—,
I weep for you when I think of the
    bitterness
That men will visit upon you all your
    lives.
What homes, what festivals can you at-
    tend
Without being forced to depart again in
    tears?
And when you come to marriageable age,
Where is the man, my daughters, who
    would dare
Risk the bane that lies on all my children?
Is there any evil wanting? Your father
    killed
His father; sowed the womb of her who
    bore him;   *1440*
Engendered you at the fount of his own
    existence!
That is what they will say of you.
                  Then, whom
Can you ever marry? There are no bride-
    grooms for you,
And your lives must wither away in
    sterile dreaming.
O Creon, son of Menoikeus!
You are the only father my daughters
    have,
Since we, their parents, are both of us
    gone for ever.
They are your own blood: you will not
    let them
Fall into beggary and loneliness;
You will keep them from the miseries
    that are mine!   *1450*
Take pity on them; see, they are only
    children,
Friendless except for you. Promise me
    this,

Great Prince, and give me your hand in token of it.
(CREON *clasps his right hand.*)
Children:
I could say much, if you could understand me,
But as it is, I have only this prayer for you:
Live where you can, be as happy as you can—
Happier, please God, than God has made your father!
CREON. Enough. You have wept enough. Now go within. *1459*
OEDIPUS. I must, but it is hard.
CREON. Time eases all things.
OEDIPUS. But you must promise—
CREON. Say what you desire.
OEDIPUS. Send me from Thebes!
CREON. God grant that I may!
OEDIPUS. But since God hates me . . .
CREON. No, he will grant your wish.
OEDIPUS. You promise?
CREON. I can not speak beyond my knowledge.
OEDIPUS. Then lead me in.
CREON. Come now, and leave your children.
OEDIPUS. No! Do not take them from me!
CREON. Think no longer
That you are in command here, but rather think
How, when you were, you served your own destruction.
(*Exeunt into the house all but the* CHORUS; *the* CHORAGOS *chants directly to the audience.*)
CHORAGOS. Men of Thebes: look upon Oedipus.
This is the king who solved the famous riddle *1470*
And towered up, most powerful of men.
No mortal eyes but looked on him with envy,
Yet in the end ruin swept over him.

Let every man in mankind's frailty
Consider his last day; and let none
Presume on his good fortune until he find
Life, at his death, a memory without pain.

WILLIAM SHAKESPEARE • 1564–1616

A Midsummer-Night's Dream

DRAMATIS PERSONÆ

THESEUS, *Duke of Athens.*
EGEUS, *father to Hermia.*
LYSANDER,
DEMETRIUS, } *in love with Hermia.*
PHILOSTRATE, *master of the revels to Theseus.*
QUINCE, *a carpenter.*
SNUG, *a joiner.*
BOTTOM, *a weaver.*
FLUTE, *a bellows-mender.*
SNOUT, *a tinker.*
STARVELING, *a tailor.*
HIPPOLYTA, *queen of the Amazons, betrothed to Theseus.*
HERMIA, *daughter to Egeus, in love with Lysander.*
HELENA, *in love with Demetrius.*
OBERON, *king of the fairies.*
TITANIA, *queen of the fairies.*
PUCK, *or* ROBIN GOODFELLOW.
PEASEBLOSSOM,
COBWEB,
MOTH,
MUSTARDSEED, } *fairies.*

Other Fairies attending their King and Queen.
Attendants on THESEUS and HIPPOLYTA.

SCENE: *Athens, and a wood near it.*

Act I

SCENE 1

(*Athens. The palace of* THESEUS.)
(*Enter* THESEUS, HIPPOLYTA, PHILOSTRATE, *and* ATTENDANTS.)

THESEUS. Now, fair Hippolyta, our nuptial hour
Draws on apace; four happy days bring in
Another moon: but, O, methinks, how slow
This old moon wanes! she lingers my desires
Like to a step-dame or a dowager
Long withering out a young man's revenue.
   HIPPOLYTA. Four days will quickly steep themselves in night;
Four nights will quickly dream away the time;
And then the moon, like to a silver bow
New-bent in heaven, shall behold the night   10
Of our solemnities.
   THESEUS.   Go, Philostrate,
Stir up the Athenian youth to merriments;
Awake the pert and nimble spirit of mirth:
Turn melancholy forth to funerals;
The pale companion is not for our pomp.
   (*Exit* PHILOSTRATE.)
Hippolyta, I woo'd thee with my sword,
And won thy love, doing thee injuries;
But I will wed thee in another key,
With pomp, with triumph and with revelling.
   (*Enter* EGEUS, HERMIA, LYSANDER, *and* DEMETRIUS.)
   EGEUS. Happy be Theseus, our renownèd duke!   20
   THESEUS. Thanks, good Egeus: what's the news with thee?
   EGEUS. Full of vexation come I, with complaint
Against my child, my daughter Hermia.
Stand forth, Demetrius. My noble lord,
This man hath my consent to marry her.
Stand forth, Lysander: and, my gracious duke,

William Shakespeare

This man hath bewitch'd the bosom of
my child:
Thou, thou, Lysander, thou hast given her
rhymes
And interchanged love-tokens with my
child:
Thou hast by moonlight at her window
sung   30
With feigning voice verses of feigning
love,
And stolen the impression of her fantasy
With bracelets of thy hair, rings, gawds,
conceits,
Knacks, trifles, nosegays, sweetmeats,
messengers
Of strong prevailment in unharden'd
youth:
With cunning hast thou filch'd my daughter's heart,
Turn'd her obedience, which is due to me,
To stubborn harshness: and, my gracious
duke,
Be it so she will not here before your
grace
Consent to marry with Demetrius,   40
I beg the ancient privilege of Athens,
As she is mine, I may dispose of her:
Which shall be either to this gentleman
Or to her death, according to our law
Immediately¹ provided in that case.
   THESEUS. What say you, Hermia? be
advised, fair maid;
To you your father should be as a god;
One that composed your beauties, yea,
and one
To whom you are but as a form in wax
By him imprinted and within his power
To leave the figure or disfigure it.   51
Demetrius is a worthy gentleman.
   HERMIA. So is Lysander.
   THESEUS.   In himself he is;
But in this kind, wanting your father's
voice,
The other must be held the worthier.
   HERMIA. I would my father look'd
but with my eyes.

¹ explicitly

   THESEUS. Rather your eyes must with
his judgement look.
   HERMIA. I do entreat your grace to
pardon me.
I know not by what power I am made
bold,
Nor how it may concern my modesty,   60
In such a presence here to plead my
thoughts;
But I beseech your grace that I may know
The worst that may befall me in this case,
If I refuse to wed Demetrius.
   THESEUS. Either to die the death or
to abjure
For ever the society of men.
Therefore, fair Hermia, question your
desires;
Know of your youth, examine well your
blood,
Whether, if you yield not to your father's
choice,
You can endure the livery of a nun,   70
For aye to be in shady cloister mew'd,
To live a barren sister all your life,
Chanting faint hymns to the cold fruitless
moon.
Thrice-blessèd they that master so their
blood,
To undergo such maiden pilgrimage;
But earthlier happy is the rose distill'd,
Than that which withering on the virgin
thorn
Grows, lives and dies in single blessedness.
   HERMIA. So will I grow, so live, so
die, my lord,
Ere I will yield my virgin patent up   80
Unto his lordship, whose unwishèd yoke
My soul consents not to give sovereignty.
   THESEUS. Take time to pause; and,
by the next new moon—
The sealing-day betwixt my love and me,
For everlasting bond of fellowship—
Upon that day either prepare to die
For disobedience to your father's will,
Or else to wed Demetrius, as he would;
Or on Diana's altar to protest
For aye austerity and single life.   90
   DEMETRIUS. Relent, sweet Hermia:
and, Lysander, yield

Thy crazèd[2] title to my certain right.
  LYSANDER. You have her father's love, Demetrius;
Let me have Hermia's: do you marry him.
  EGEUS. Scornful Lysander! true, he hath my love,
And what is mine my love shall render him.
And she is mine, and all my right of her
I do estate unto Demetrius.
  LYSANDER. I am, my lord, as well derived as he,
As well possess'd; my love is more than his; *100*
My fortunes every way as fairly rank'd,
If not with vantage, as Demetrius';
And, which is more than all these boasts can be,
I am beloved of beauteous Hermia:
Why should not I then prosecute my right?
Demetrius, I'll avouch it to his head,
Made love to Nedar's daughter, Helena,
And won her soul; and she, sweet lady, dotes,
Devoutly dotes, dotes in idolatry, *109*
Upon this spotted and inconstant man.
  THESEUS. I must confess that I have heard so much,
And with Demetrius thought to have spoke thereof;
But, being over-full of self-affairs,
My mind did lose it. But, Demetrius, come;
And come, Egeus; you shall go with me,
I have some private schooling for you both.
For you, fair Hermia, look you arm yourself
To fit your fancies to your father's will;
Or else the law of Athens yields you up—
Which by no means we may extenuate—
To death, or to a vow of single life. *121*
Come, my Hippolyta: what cheer, my love?
Demetrius and Egeus, go along:
I must employ you in some business
Against our nuptial and confer with you
Of something nearly that concerns yourselves.
  EGEUS. With duty and desire we follow you.
  (*Exeunt all but* LYSANDER *and* HERMIA.)
  LYSANDER. How now, my love! why is your cheek so pale?
How chance the roses there do fade so fast?
  HERMIA. Belike for want of rain, which I could well *130*
Beteem[3] them from the tempest of my eyes.
  LYSANDER. Ay me! for aught that I could ever read,
Could ever hear by tale or history,
The course of true love never did run smooth;
But, either it was different in blood,—
  HERMIA. O cross! too high to be enthrall'd to low.
  LYSANDER. Or else misgraffèd[4] in respect of years,—
  HERMIA. O spite! too old to be engaged to young.
  LYSANDER. Or else it stood upon the choice of friends,—
  HERMIA. O hell! to choose love by another's eyes. *140*
  LYSANDER. Or, if there were a sympathy in choice,
War, death, or sickness did lay siege to it,
Making it momentany[5] as a sound,
Swift as a shadow, short as any dream;
Brief as the lightning in the collied[6] night,
That, in a spleen,[7] unfolds both heaven and earth,
And ere a man hath power to say "Behold!"
The jaws of darkness do devour it up:

[2] defective
[3] allow
[4] mismatched
[5] momentary
[6] black
[7] fit of anger

So quick bright things come to confusion.
HERMIA. If then true lovers have
been ever cross'd, 150
It stands as an edict in destiny:
Then let us teach our trial patience,
Because it is a customary cross,
As due to love as thoughts and dreams
and sighs,
Wishes and tears, poor fancy's followers.
LYSANDER. A good persuasion: therefore, hear me, Hermia.
I have a widow aunt, a dowager
Of great revénue, and she hath no child:
From Athens is her house remote seven
leagues:
And she respects me as her only son. 160
There, gentle Hermia, may I marry thee;
And to that place the sharp Athenian law
Cannot pursue us. If thou lovest me then,
Steal forth thy father's house to-morrow
night;
And in the wood, a league without the
town,
Where I did meet thee once with Helena,
To do observance to a morn of May,
There will I stay for thee.
HERMIA.   My good Lysander!
I swear to thee, by Cupid's strongest bow,
By his best arrow with the golden head,
By the simplicity of Venus' doves, 171
By that which knitteth souls and prospers
loves,
And by that fire which burn'd the Carthage queen,
When the false Troyan under sail was
seen,[8]
By all the vows that ever men have broke,
In number more than ever women spoke,
In that same place thou hast appointed
me,
To-morrow truly will I meet with thee.
LYSANDER. Keep promise, love. Look,
here comes Helena.
(*Enter* HELENA.)
HERMIA. God speed fair Helena!
whither away? 180

HELENA. Call you me fair? that fair
again unsay.
Demetrius loves your fair: O happy fair!
Your eyes are lode-stars; and your
tongue's sweet air
More tuneable than lark to shepherd's
ear,
When wheat is green, when hawthorn
buds appear.
Sickness is catching: O, were favour so,
Yours would I catch, fair Hermia, ere I
go;
My ear should catch your voice, my eye
your eye,
My tongue should catch your tongue's
sweet melody.
Were the world mine, Demetrius being
bated,[9] 190
The rest I'ld give to be to you translated.
O, teach me how you look, and with what
art
You sway the motion of Demetrius' heart.
HERMIA. I frown upon him, yet he
loves me still.
HELENA. O that your frowns would
teach my smiles such skill!
HERMIA. I give him curses, yet he
gives me love.
HELENA. O that my prayers could
such affection move!
HERMIA. The more I hate, the more
he follows me.
HELENA. The more I love, the more
he hateth me.
HERMIA. His folly, Helena, is no
fault of mine. 200
HELENA. None, but your beauty:
would that fault were mine!
HERMIA. Take comfort: he no more
shall see my face;
Lysander and myself will fly this place.
Before the time I did Lysander see,
Seem'd Athens as a paradise to me:
O, then, what graces in my love do dwell,
That he hath turn'd a heaven, unto a hell!
LYSANDER. Helen, to you our minds
we will unfold:

---

[8] Dido cast herself on a funeral pyre when Aneas deserted her (*Aeneid*, IV).

[9] all but Demetrius

To-morrow night, when Phœbe[10] doth behold
Her silvery visage in the watery glass, *210*
Decking with liquid pearl the bladed grass,
A time that lovers' flights doth still conceal,
Through Athens' gates have we devised to steal.

HERMIA. And in the wood, where often you and I
Upon faint primrose beds were wont to lie,
Emptying our bosoms of their counsel sweet,
There my Lysander and myself shall meet;
And thence from Athens turn away our eyes,
To seek new friends and stranger companies.
Farewell, sweet playfellow: pray thou for us; *220*
And good luck grant thee thy Demetrius!
Keep word, Lysander: we must starve our sight
From lovers' food till morrow deep midnight.

LYSANDER. I will, my Hermia.
(*Exit* HERMIA.)
                                  Helena, adieu:
As you on him, Demetrius dote on you!
(*Exit.*)

HELENA. How happy some o'er other some can be!
Through Athens I am thought as fair as she.
But what of that: Demetrius thinks not so;
He will not know what all but he do know: *229*
And as he errs, doting on Hermia's eyes,
So I, admiring of his qualities:
Things base and vile, holding no quantity,
Love can transpose to form and dignity:
Love looks not with the eyes, but with the mind;

And therefore is wing'd Cupid painted blind:
Nor hath Love's mind of any judgement taste;
Wings and no eyes figure unheedy haste:
And therefore is Love said to be a child,
Because in choice he is so oft beguiled.
As waggish boys in game themselves forswear, *240*
So the boy Love is perjured every where:
For ere Demetrius look'd on Hermia's eyne,[11]
He hail'd down oaths that he was only mine;
And when this hail some heat from Hermia felt,
So he dissolved, and showers of oaths did melt.
I will go tell him of fair Hermia's flight:
Then to the wood will he to-morrow night
Pursue her; and for this intelligence[12]
If I have thanks, it is a dear expense:
But herein mean I to enrich my pain, *250*
To have his sight thither and back again.
(*Exit.*)

SCENE 2

(*Athens.* QUINCE'S *house.*)
(*Enter* QUINCE, SNUG, BOTTOM, FLUTE, SNOUT, *and* STARVELING.)

QUINCE. Is all our company here?

BOTTOM. You were best to call them generally, man by man, according to the scrip.

QUINCE. Here is the scroll of every man's name, which is thought fit, through all Athens, to play in our interlude before the duke and the duchess, on his wedding-day at night.

BOTTOM. First, good Peter Quince, say what the play treats on, then read the names of the actors, and so grow to a point. *10*

[10] the moon
[11] eyes
[12] news

QUINCE. Marry, our play is, The most lamentable comedy, and most cruel death of Pyramus and Thisby.

BOTTOM. A very good piece of work, I assure you, and a merry. Now, good Peter Quince, call forth your actors by the scroll. Masters, spread yourselves.

QUINCE. Answer as I call you. Nick Bottom, the weaver.

BOTTOM. Ready. Name what part I am for, and proceed. 20

QUINCE. You, Nick Bottom, are set down for Pyramus.

BOTTOM. What is Pyramus? a lover, or a tyrant?

QUINCE. A lover, that kills himself most gallant for love.

BOTTOM. That will ask some tears in the true performing of it: if I do it, let the audience look to their eyes; I will move storms, I will condole in some 29 measure. To the rest: yet my chief humour is for a tyrant: I could play Ercles rarely, or a part to tear a cat[13] in, to make all split.

> The raging rocks
> And shivering shocks
> Shall break the locks
>   Of prison gates;
> And Phibbus' car
> Shall shine from far
> And make and mar
>   The foolish Fates. 40

This was lofty! Now name the rest of the players. This is Ercles' vein, a tyrant's vein; a lover is more condoling.

QUINCE. Francis Flute, the bellows-mender.

FLUTE. Here, Peter Quince.

QUINCE. Flute, you must take Thisby on you.

FLUTE. What is Thisby? a wandering knight?

QUINCE. It is the lady that Pyramus must love.

FLUTE. Nay, faith, let not me play a woman; I have a beard coming. 50

QUINCE. That's all one: you shall play it in a mask, and you may speak as small as you will.

BOTTOM. An[14] I may hide my face, let me play Thisby too, I'll speak in a monstrous little voice, "Thisne, Thisne;" "Ah Pyramus, my lover dear! thy Thisby dear, and lady dear!"

QUINCE. No, no; you must play Pyramus: and Flute, you Thisby.

BOTTOM. Well, proceed. 59

QUINCE. Robin Starveling, the tailor.

STARVELING. Here, Peter Quince.

QUINCE. Robin Starveling, you must play Thisby's mother. Tom Snout, the tinker.

SNOUT. Here, Peter Quince.

QUINCE. You, Pyramus' father: myself, Thisby's father. Snug, the joiner; you, the lion's part: and, I hope, here is a play fitted.

SNUG. Have you the lion's part written? pray you, if it be, give it to me, for I am slow of study. 70

QUINCE. You may do it extempore, for it is nothing but roaring.

BOTTOM. Let me play the lion too: I will roar, that I will do any man's heart good to hear me; I will roar, and that I will make the duke say "Let him roar again, let him roar again."

QUINCE. An you should do it too terribly, you would fright the duchess and the ladies, that they would shriek; and that were enough to hang us all.

ALL. That would hang us, every mother's son. 80

BOTTOM. I grant you, friends, if that you should fright the ladies out of their wits, they would have no more discretion but to hang us: but I will aggravate my voice so that I will roar you as gently as any sucking dove; I will roar you as 'twere any nightingale.

QUINCE. You can play no part but

---

[13] rant

[14] if

Pyramus; for Pyramus is a sweet-faced man; a proper man, as one shall see in a summer's day; a most lovely gentleman-like man: therefore you must needs play Pyramus. *90*

BOTTOM. Well, I will undertake it. What beard were I best to play it in?

QUINCE. Why, what you will.

BOTTOM. I will discharge it in either your straw-colour beard, your orange-tawny beard, your purple-in-grain beard, or your French-crown-colour beard, your perfect yellow. *98*

QUINCE. Some of your French crowns have no hair at all, and then you will play bare-faced. But, masters, here are your parts: and I am to entreat you, request you and desire you, to con[15] them by to-morrow night; and meet me in the palace wood, a mile without the town, by moonlight; there will we rehearse, for if we meet in the city, we shall be dogged with company, and our devices known. In the meantime I will draw a bill of properties, such as our play wants. I pray you, fail me not. *110*

BOTTOM. We will meet; and there we may rehearse most obscenely and courageously. Take pains; be perfect: adieu.

QUINCE. At the duke's oak we meet.

BOTTOM. Enough; hold or cut bow-strings.

(*Exeunt.*)

Act II

SCENE 1

(*A wood near Athens.*)

(*Enter, from opposite sides, a* FAIRY, *and* PUCK.)

PUCK. How now, spirit, whither wander you?

FAIRY. Over hill, over dale,
  Thorough bush, thorough brier,
Over park, over pale,
  Thorough flood, thorough fire,
I do wander every where,
  Swifter than the moon's sphere;
And I serve the fairy queen,
  To dew her orbs upon the green.
The cowslips tall her pensioners[16] be: *10*
In their gold coats spots you see;
Those be rubies, fairy favours,
  In those freckles live their savours:
I must go seek some dewdrops here
And hang a pearl in every cowslip's ear.
Farewell, thou lob[17] of spirits; I'll be gone:
Our queen and all her elves come here anon.

PUCK. The king doth keep his revels here to-night:
Take heed the queen come not within his sight;
For Oberon is passing fell and wrath, *20*
Because that she as her attendant hath
A lovely boy, stolen from an Indian king;
She never had so sweet a changeling;
And jealous Oberon would have the child
Knight of his train, to trace the forests wild;
But she perforce withholds the lovèd boy,
Crowns him with flowers and makes him all her joy:
And now they never meet in grove or green,
By fountain clear, or spangled starlight sheen,
But they do square, that all their elves for fear *30*
Creep into acorn-cups and hide them there.

FAIRY. Either I mistake your shape and making quite,

---

[15] learn by heart
[16] body guard
[17] bumpkin

Or else you are that shrewd and knavish sprite
Call'd Robin Goodfellow: are not you he
That frights the maidens of the villagery;
Skim milk, and sometimes labour in the quern[18]
And bootless make the breathless housewife churn;
And sometime make the drink to bear no barm;[19]
Mislead night-wanderers, laughing at their harm?
Those that Hobgoblin call you and sweet Puck,   40
You do their work, and they shall have good luck:
Are not you he?
  PUCK.   Thou speak'st aright;
I am that merry wanderer of the night.
I jest to Oberon and make him smile
When I a fat and bean-fed horse beguile,
Neighing in likeness of a filly foal:
And sometime lurk I in a gossip's bowl,
In very likeness of a roasted crab,[20]
And when she drinks, against her lips I bob   49
And on her wither'd dewlap pour the ale.
The wisest aunt, telling the saddest tale,
Sometime for three-foot stool mistaketh me;
Then slip I from her bum, down topples she,
And "tailor" cries, and falls into a cough;
And then the whole quire hold their hips and laugh,
And waxen in their mirth and neeze[21] and swear
A merrier hour was never wasted there.
But, room, fairy! here comes Oberon.
  FAIRY.   And here my mistress. Would that he were gone!
  (*Enter, from one side,* OBERON, *with his train; from the other,* TITANIA, *with hers.*)

  OBERON.   Ill met by moonlight, proud Titania.   60
  TITANIA.   What, jealous Oberon! Fairies, skip hence:
I have forsworn his bed and company.
  OBERON.   Tarry, rash wanton: am not I thy lord?
  TITANIA.   Then I must be thy lady: but I know
When thou hast stolen away from fairy land,
And in the shape of Corin sat all day,
Playing on pipes of corn[22] and versing love
To amorous Phillida. Why art thou here,
Come from the farthest steppe of India?
But that, forsooth, the bouncing Amazon,
Your buskin'd[23] mistress and your warrior love,   71
To Theseus must be wedded, and you come
To give their bed joy and prosperity.
  OBERON.   How canst thou thus for shame, Titania,
Glance at my credit with Hippolyta,
Knowing I know thy love to Theseus?
Didst thou not lead him through the glimmering night
From Perigenia, whom he ravished?
And make him with fair Ægle break his faith,
With Ariadne and Antiopa?   80
  TITANIA.   These are the forgeries of jealousy:
And never, since the middle summer's spring,
Met we on hill, in dale, forest or mead,
By pavèd fountain or by rushy brook,
Or in the beachèd margent of the sea,
To dance our ringlets to the whistling wind,
But with thy brawls thou hast disturb'd our sport.
Therefore the winds, piping to us in vain,
As in revenge, have suck'd up from the sea   89

---

[18] hand mill
[19] yeast
[20] crabapple
[21] sneeze

[22] straw
[23] booted

Contagious fogs; which falling in the land
Have every pelting river made so proud
That they have overborne their continents:[24]
The ox hath therefore stretch'd his yoke in vain,
The ploughman lost his sweat, and the green corn
Hath rotted ere his youth attain'd a beard;
The fold stands empty in the drowned field,
And crows are fatted with the murrion[25] flock;
The nine men's morris[26] is fill'd up with mud,
And the quaint mazes in the wanton green
For lack of tread are undistinguishable:
The human mortals want their winter here;   *101*
No night is now with hymn or carol blest:
Therefore the moon, the governess of floods,
Pale in her anger, washes all the air,
That rheumatic diseases do abound:
And thorough this distemperature we see
The seasons alter: hoary-headed frosts
Fall in the fresh lap of the crimson rose,
And on old Hiems'[27] thin and icy crown
An odorous chaplet of sweet summer buds   *110*
Is, as in mockery, set: the spring, the summer,
The childing[28] autumn, angry winter, change
Their wonted liveries, and the mazed world,
By their increase, now knows not which is which:
And this same progeny of evils comes
From our debate, from our dissension;
We are their parents and original.[29]
   OBERON. Do you amend it then; it lies in you:
Why should Titania cross her Oberon?

[24] banks
[25] diseased
[26] playing field
[27] god of winter
[28] fruitful
[29] origin

I do but beg a little changeling boy,   *120*
To be my henchman.
   TITANIA.   Set your heart at rest:
The fairy land buys not the child of me.
His mother was a votaress of my order:
And, in the spicèd Indian air, by night,
Full often hath she gossip'd by my side,
And sat with me on Neptune's yellow sands,
Marking the embarkèd traders[30] on the flood,
When we have laugh'd to see the sails conceive
And grow big-bellied with the wanton wind;
Which she, with pretty and with swimming gait   *130*
Following,—her womb then rich with my young squire,—
Would imitate, and sail upon the land,
To fetch me trifles, and return again,
As from a voyage, rich with merchandise.
But she, being mortal, of that boy did die;
And for her sake do I rear up her boy,
And for her sake I will not part with him.
   OBERON. How long within this wood intend you stay?
   TITANIA. Perchance till after Theseus' wedding-day.   *139*
If you will patiently dance in our round
And see our moonlight revels, go with us;
If not, shun me, and I will spare your haunts.
   OBERON. Give me that boy, and I will go with thee.
   TITANIA. Not for thy fairy kingdom. Fairies, away!
We shall chide downright, if I longer stay.
   (*Exit* TITANIA *with her train.*)
   OBERON. Well, go thy way: thou shalt not from this grove
Till I torment thee for this injury.
My gentle Puck, come hither. Thou rememberest
Since once I sat upon a promontory,   *149*
And heard a mermaid on a dolphin's back
Uttering such dulcet and harmonious breath

[30] merchant ships

That the rude sea grew civil at her song
And certain stars shot madly from their spheres,
To hear the sea-maid's music.
    PUCK.   I remember.
    OBERON. That very time I saw, but thou couldst not,
Flying between the cold moon and the earth,
Cupid all arm'd: a certain aim he took
At a fair vestal[31] thronèd by the west,
And loosed his love-shaft smartly from his bow,
As it should pierce a hundred thousand hearts;   *160*
But I might see young Cupid's fiery shaft
Quench'd in the chaste beams of the watery moon,
And the imperial votaress passèd on,
In maiden meditation, fancy-free.
Yet mark'd I where the bolt of Cupid fell:
It fell upon a little western flower,
Before milk-white, now purple with love's wound,
And maidens call it love-in-idleness.
Fetch me that flower; the herb I shew'd thee once: *169*
The juice of it on sleeping eye-lids laid
Will make or man or woman madly dote
Upon the next live creature that it sees.
Fetch me this herb; and be thou here again
Ere the leviathan[32] can swim a league.
    PUCK. I'll put a girdle round about the earth
In forty minutes.
    (*Exit.*)
    OBERON.   Having once this juice,
I'll watch Titania when she is asleep,
And drop the liquor of it in her eyes.
The next thing then she waking looks upon,
Be it on lion, bear, or wolf, or bull,   *180*
On meddling monkey, or on busy ape,
She shall pursue it with the soul of love:
And ere I take this charm from off her sight,
As I can take it with another herb,
I'll make her render up her page to me.
But who comes here? I am invisible;
And I will overhear their conference.
    (*Enter* DEMETRIUS, HELENA *following him.*)
    DEMETRIUS. I love thee not, therefore pursue me not.
Where is Lysander and fair Hermia?
The one I'll slay, the other slayeth me.
Thou told'st me they were stolen unto this wood;   *191*
And here am I, and wode[33] within this wood,
Because I cannot meet my Hermia.
Hence, get thee gone, and follow me no more.
    HELENA. You draw me, you hard-hearted adamant;
But yet you draw not iron, for my heart
Is true as steel: leave you your power to draw,
And I shall have no power to follow you.
    DEMETRIUS. Do I entice you? do I speak you fair?
Or, rather, do I not in plainest truth   *200*
Tell you, I do not, nor I cannot love you?
    HELENA. And even for that do I love you the more.
I am your spaniel; and, Demetrius,
The more you beat me, I will fawn on you:
Use me but as your spaniel, spurn me, strike me,
Neglect me, lose me; only give me leave,
Unworthy as I am, to follow you.
What worser place can I beg in your love,—
And yet a place of high respect with me,—   *209*
Than to be usèd as you use your dog?
    DEMETRIUS. Tempt not too much the hatred of my spirit,
For I am sick when I do look on thee.
    HELENA. And I am sick when I look not on you.
    DEMETRIUS. You do impeach your modesty too much,

---

[31] virgin; i.e., Queen Elizabeth
[32] whale
[33] mad

To leave the city and commit yourself
Into the hands of one that loves you not;
To trust the opportunity of night
And the ill counsel of a desert place
With the rich worth of your virginity.
    HELENA. Your virtue is my privilege:[34] for that   220
It is not night when I do see your face,
Therefore I think I am not in the night;
Nor doth this wood lack worlds of company,
For you in my respect are all the world:
Then how can it be said I am alone,
When all the world is here to look on me?
    DEMETRIUS. I'll run from thee and hide me in the brakes,
And leave thee to the mercy of wild beasts.
    HELENA. The wildest hath not such a heart as you.
Run when you will, the story shall be changed: 230
Apollo flies, and Daphne holds the chase;
The dove pursues the griffin;[35] the mild hind[36]
Makes speed to catch the tiger; bootless speed,
When cowardice pursues and valour flies.
    DEMETRIUS. I will not stay thy questions; let me go:
Or, if thou follow me, do not believe
But I shall do thee mischief in the wood.
    HELENA. Ay, in the temple, in the town, the field,
You do me mischief. Fie, Demetrius!   239
Your wrongs do set a scandal on my sex:
We cannot fight for love, as men may do;
We should be woo'd and were not made to woo.
    (*Exit* DEMETRIUS.)
I'll follow thee and make a heaven of hell,
To die upon the hand I love so well.
    (*Exit.*)
    OBERON. Fare thee well, nymph: ere he do leave this grove,

Thou shalt fly him and he shall seek thy love.
    (*Re-enter* PUCK.)
Hast thou the flower there? Welcome, wanderer.
    PUCK. Ay, there it is.
    OBERON. I pray thee, give it me.
I know a bank where the wild thyme blows,
Where oxlips and the nodding violet grows,   250
Quite over-canopied with luscious woodbine,
With sweet musk-roses and with eglantine:
There sleeps Titania sometime of the night,
Lull'd in these flowers with dances and delight;
And there the snake throws her enamell'd skin,
Weed[37] wide enough to wrap a fairy in:
And with the juice of this I'll streak her eyes,
And make her full of hateful fantasies.
Take thou some of it, and seek through this grove:
A sweet Athenian lady is in love   260
With a disdainful youth: anoint his eyes;
But do it when the next thing he espies
May be the lady: thou shalt know the man
By the Athenian garments he hath on.
Effect it with some care that he may prove
More fond on her than she upon her love:
And look thou meet me ere the first cock crow.
    PUCK. Fear not, my lord, your servant shall do so.
    (*Exeunt.*)

SCENE 2

(*Another part of the wood.*)
(*Enter* TITANIA, *with her train.*)
    TITANIA. Come, now a roundel[38] and a fairy song;

---

[34] protection
[35] monster of fable—a lion with an eagle's head
[36] doe
[37] garment
[38] ring dance

Then, for the third part of a minute, hence;
Some to kill cankers in the musk-rose buds,
Some war with rere-mice[39] for their leathern wings,
To make my small elves coats, and some keep back
The clamorous owl that nightly hoots and wonders
At our quaint spirits. Sing me now asleep;
Then to your offices and let me rest.

(THE FAIRIES *sing*.)
You spotted snakes with double tongue,
   Thorny hedgehogs, be not seen;   *10*
Newts and blind-worms, do no wrong,
   Come not near our fairy queen.
Philomel,[40] with melody
Sing in our sweet lullaby;
Lulla, lulla, lullaby, lulla, lulla, lullaby:
   Never harm,
   Nor spell nor charm,
Come our lovely lady nigh;
So, good night, with lullaby.

Weaving spiders, come not here;   *20*
   Hence, you long-legg'd spinners, hence!
Beetles black, approach not near;
   Worm nor snail, do no offence.
     Philomel, with melody, &c.

A FAIRY. Hence, away! now all is well:
     One aloof stand sentinel.
(*Exeunt* FAIRIES. TITANIA *sleeps*.)
(*Enter* OBERON, *and squeezes the flower on* TITANIA'S *eyelids*.)
OBERON.   What thou seest when thou dost wake,
     Do it for thy true-love take,
     Love and languish for his sake:
     Be it ounce,[41] or cat, or bear,   *30*
Pard, or boar with bristled hair,
In thy eye that shall appear
When thou wakest, it is thy dear:
Wake when some vile thing is near.
(*Exit*.)
(*Enter* LYSANDER *and* HERMIA.)
LYSANDER. Fair love, you faint with wandering in the wood;
And to speak troth, I have forgot our way:
We'll rest us, Hermia, if you think it good,
And tarry for the comfort of the day.
HERMIA. Be it so, Lysander: find you out a bed;   *39*
For I upon this bank will rest my head.
LYSANDER. One turf shall serve as pillow for us both;
One heart, one bed, two bosoms and one troth.
HERMIA. Nay, good Lysander; for my sake, my dear,
Lie further off yet, do not lie so near.
LYSANDER. O, take the sense, sweet, of my innocence!
Love takes the meaning in love's conference.
I mean, that my heart unto yours is knit
So that but one heart we can make of it;
Two bosoms interchainèd with an oath;
So then two bosoms and a single troth.
Then by your side no bed-room me deny;
For lying so, Hermia, I do not lie.   *52*
HERMIA. Lysander riddles very prettily:
Now much beshrew[42] my manners and my pride,
If Hermia meant to say Lysander lied.
But, gentle friend, for love and courtesy
Lie further off; in human modesty,
Such separation as may well be said
Becomes a virtuous bachelor and a maid,
So far be distant; and, good night, sweet friend: *60*

[39] bats
[40] nightingale
[41] lynx

[42] condemn

Thy love ne'er alter till thy sweet life end!
  LYSANDER. Amen, amen, to that fair prayer, say I;
And then end life when I end loyalty!
Here is my bed: sleep give thee all his rest!
  HERMIA. With half that wish the wisher's eyes be press'd!
(They sleep.)
(Enter PUCK.*)*
  PUCK. Through the forest have I gone,
    But Athenian found I none,
    On whose eyes I might approve[43]
    This flower's force in stirring love.
    Night and silence.—Who is here? 70
    Weeds of Athens he doth wear:
    This is he, my master said,
    Despisèd the Athenian maid;
    And here the maiden, sleeping sound,
    On the dank and dirty ground.
    Pretty soul! she durst not lie
    Near this lack-love, this kill-courtesy.
    Churl, upon thy eyes I throw
    All the power this charm doth owe.[44]
    When thou wakest, let love forbid 80
    Sleep his seat on thy eyelid:
    So awake when I am gone;
    For I must now to Oberon.
(Exit.)
(Enter DEMETRIUS *and* HELENA, *running.)*
  HELENA. Stay, though thou kill me, sweet Demetrius.
  DEMETRIUS. I charge thee, hence, and do not haunt me thus.
  HELENA. O, wilt thou darkling[45] leave me? do not so.
  DEMETRIUS. Stay, on thy peril: I alone will go.
(Exit.)
  HELENA. O, I am out of breath in this fond[46] chase!
The more my prayer, the lesser is my grace.
Happy is Hermia, whereso'er she lies; 90
For she hath blessèd and attractive eyes.
How came her eyes so bright? Not with salt tears:
If so, my eyes are oftener wash'd than hers.
No, no, I am as ugly as a bear;
For beasts that meet me run away for fear:
Therefore no marvel though Demetrius
Do, as a monster, fly my presence thus.
What wicked and dissembling glass of mine
Made me compare with Hermia's sphery[47] eyne?
But who is here? Lysander! on the ground! 100
Dead? or asleep? I see no blood, no wound.
Lysander, if you live, good sir, awake.
  LYSANDER *(awaking)*. And run through fire I will for thy sweet sake.
Transparent Helena! Nature shows art,
That through thy bosom makes me see thy heart.
Where is Demetrius? O, how fit a word
Is that vile name to perish on my sword!
  HELENA. Do not say so, Lysander; say not so.
What though he love your Hermia? Lord, what though?
Yet Hermia still loves you: then be content. 110
  LYSANDER. Content with Hermia! No; I do repent
The tedious minutes I with her have spent.
Not Hermia but Helena I love:
Who will not change a raven for a dove?
The will of man is by his reason sway'd;

---

[43] test
[44] possess
[45] in the dark
[46] foolish
[47] starry

And reason says you are the worthier
    maid.
Things growing are not ripe until their
    season:
So I, being young, till now ripe[48] not to
    reason;
And touching now the point of human
    skill,
Reason becomes the marshal to my
    will   120
And leads me to your eyes, where I
    o'erlook[49]
Love's stories written in love's richest
    book.
  HELENA. Wherefore was I to this keen
    mockery born?
When at your hands did I deserve this
    scorn?
Is't not enough, is't not enough, young
    man,
That I did never, no, nor never can,
Deserve a sweet look from Demetrius'
    eye,
But you must flout my insufficiency?
Good troth, you do me wrong, good sooth,
    you do,   129
In such disdainful manner me to woo.
But fare you well: perforce I must confess
I thought you lord of more true gentleness.
O, that a lady, of one man refused,
Should of another therefore be abused!
  (Exit.)
  LYSANDER. She sees not Hermia. Hermia, sleep thou there:
And never mayst thou come Lysander
    near!
For as a surfeit of the sweetest things
The deepest loathing to the stomach
    brings,
Or as the heresies that men do leave
Are hated most of those they did
    deceive,   140
So thou, my surfeit and my heresy,
Of all be hated, but the most of me!

And, all my powers, address your love
    and might
To honour Helen and to be her knight!
  (Exit.)
  HERMIA (awaking). Help me, Lysander, help me! do thy best
To pluck this crawling serpent from my
    breast!
Ay me, for pity! what a dream was here!
Lysander, look how I do quake with fear:
Methought a serpent eat my heart away,
And you sat smiling at his cruel prey.[50]
Lysander! what, removed? Lysander! lord!
What, out of hearing? gone? no sound, no
    word?   152
Alack, where are you? speak, an if you
    hear;
Speak, of all loves! I swoon almost with
    fear.
No? then I well perceive you are not nigh:
Either death or you I'll find immediately.
  (Exit.)

Act III

SCENE 1

(*The wood.* TITANIA *lying asleep.*)
(*Enter* QUINCE, SNUG, BOTTOM, FLUTE, SNOUT, *and* STARVELING.)

  BOTTOM. Are we all met?
  QUINCE. Pat, pat; and here's a marvellous convenient place for our rehearsal. This green plot shall be our stage, this hawthorn-brake our tiring-house;[51] and we will do it in action as we will do it before the duke.   6
  BOTTOM. Peter Quince,—
  QUINCE. What sayest thou, bully Bottom?
  BOTTOM. There are things in this comedy of Pyramus and Thisby that will never please. First, Pyramus must draw a sword to kill himself; which the ladies cannot abide. How answer you that?   13

---

[48] ripen
[49] peruse
[50] preying
[51] dressing room

SNOUT. By'r lakin,[52] a parlous[53] fear.

STARVELING. I believe we must leave the killing out, when all is done.

BOTTOM. Not a whit: I have a device to make all well. Write me a prologue; and let the prologue seem to say, we will do no harm with our swords and that Pyramus is not killed indeed; and, for the more better assurance, tell them that I Pyramus am not Pyramus, but Bottom the weaver: this will put them out of fear.

QUINCE. Well, we will have such a prologue; and it shall be written in eight and six.[54] 25

BOTTOM. No, make it two more; let it be written in eight and eight.

SNOUT. Will not the ladies be afeard of the lion?

STARVELING. I fear it, I promise you.

BOTTOM. Masters, you ought to consider with yourselves: to bring in—God shield us!—a lion among ladies, is a most dreadful thing; for there is not a more fearful wild-fowl than your lion living; and we ought to look to't.

SNOUT. Therefore another prologue must tell he is not a lion. 36

BOTTOM. Nay, you must name his name, and half his face must be seen through the lion's neck: and he himself must speak through, saying thus, or to the same defect,—"Ladies,"—or "Fair ladies,—I would wish you,"—or "I would request you,"—or "I would entreat you, —not to fear, not to tremble: my life for yours. If you think I come hither as a lion, it were pity of my life: no, I am no such thing; I am a man as other men are"; and there indeed let him name his name, and tell them plainly he is Snug the joiner.

QUINCE. Well, it shall be so. But there is two hard things; that is, to bring the moonlight into a chamber; for, you know, Pyramus and Thisby meet by moonlight. 51

SNOUT. Doth the moon shine that night we play our play?

BOTTOM. A calendar, a calendar! look in the almanac; find out moonshine, find out moonshine.

QUINCE. Yes, it doth shine that night.

BOTTOM. Why, then may you leave a casement of the great chamber window, where we play, open, and the moon may shine in at the casement. 59

QUINCE. Ay; or else one must come in with a bush of thorns and a lanthorn, and say he comes to disfigure, or to present, the person of Moonshine. Then, there is another thing: we must have a wall in the great chamber; for Pyramus and Thisby, says the story, did talk through the chink of a wall.

SNOUT. You can never bring in a wall. What say you, Bottom? 68

BOTTOM. Some man or other must present Wall: and let him have some plaster, or some loam, or some rough-cast about him, to signify wall; and let him hold his fingers thus, and through that cranny shall Pyramus and Thisby whisper.

QUINCE. If that may be, then all is well. Come, sit down, every mother's son, and rehearse your parts. Pyramus, you begin: when you have spoken your speech, enter into that brake: and so every one according to his cue.

(*Enter* PUCK *behind.*)

PUCK. What hempen home-spuns
    have we swaggering here, 79
So near the cradle of the fairy queen?
What, a play toward![55] I'll be an auditor;
An actor too perhaps, if I see cause.

QUINCE. Speak, Pyramus. Thisby,
    stand forth.

BOTTOM. Thisby, the flowers of
    odious savours sweet,—

QUINCE. Odorous, odorous.

BOTTOM. —— odours savours sweet: So hath thy breath, my dearest Thisby dear.

---

[52] by our Ladykin
[53] perilous
[54] in alternate tetrameter and trimeter lines; i.e., ballad meter

[55] in preparation

But hark a voice! stay thou but here awhile,
And by and by I will to thee appear.
(*Exit.*)
PUCK. A stranger Pyramus than e'er played here. 90
(*Exit.*)
FLUTE. Must I speak now?
QUINCE. Ay, marry, must you; for you must understand he goes but to see a noise that he heard, and is to come again.
FLUTE. Most radiant Pyramus, most lily-white of hue,
Of colour like the red rose on triumphant brier,
Most brisky juvenal and eke most lovely Jew,
As true as truest horse that yet would never tire
I'll meet thee, Pyramus, at Ninny's tomb.
QUINCE. "Ninus' tomb," man: 100 why, you must not speak that yet; that you answer to Pyramus: you speak all your part at once, cues and all. Pyramus enter: your cue is past; it is, "never tire."
FLUTE. O,—As true as truest horse, that yet would never tire.
(*Re-enter* PUCK, *and* BOTTOM *with an ass's head.*)
BOTTOM. If I were fair, Thisby, I were only thine.
QUINCE. O monstrous! O strange! we are haunted. Pray, masters! fly, masters! Help!
(*Exeunt* QUINCE, SNUG, FLUTE, SNOUT, *and* STARVELING.)
PUCK. I'll follow you, I'll lead you about a round,
Through bog, through bush, through brake, through brier: 110
Sometime a horse I'll be, sometime a hound,
A hog, a headless bear, sometime a fire;
And neigh, and bark, and grunt, and roar, and burn,
Like horse, hound, hog, bear, fire, at every turn.
(*Exit.*)
BOTTOM. Why do they run away? this is a knavery of them to make me afeard.
(*Re-enter* SNOUT.)
SNOUT. O Bottom, thou art changed! what do I see on thee?
BOTTOM. What do you see? you see an ass-head of your own, do you?
(*Exit* SNOUT.)
(*Re-enter* QUINCE.)
QUINCE. Bless thee, Bottom! bless thee! thou art translated. 122
(*Exit.*)
BOTTOM. I see their knavery: this is to make an ass of me; to fright me, if they could. But I will not stir from this place, do what they can: I will walk up and down here, and I will sing, that they shall hear I am not afraid.
(*Sings.*)
The ousel cock so black of hue,
  With orange-tawny bill, 129
The throstle with his note so true,
  The wren with little quill,—
TITANIA (*awaking*). What angel wakes me from my flowery bed?
BOTTOM (*sings*).
The finch, the sparrow and the lark,
  The plain-song cuckoo gray,
Whose note full many a man doth mark,
  And dares not answer nay;—
for, indeed, who would set his wit to so foolish a bird? who would give a bird the lie, though he cry "cuckoo" never so?
TITANIA. I pray thee, gentle mortal, sing again: 140
Mine ear is much enamour'd of thy note;
So is mine eye enthrallèd to thy shape;
And thy fair virtue's force perforce doth move me
On the first view to say, to swear, I love thee.
BOTTOM. Methinks, mistress, you should have little reason for that: and yet, to say the truth, reason and love keep little company together now-a-days; the more the pity that some honest neigh-

bours will not make them friends. Nay, I can gleek[56] upon occasion. *150*

TITANIA. Thou art as wise as thou art beautiful.

BOTTOM. Not so, neither: but if I had wit enough to get out of this wood, I have enough to serve mine own turn.

TITANIA. Out of this wood do not desire to go:
Thou shalt remain here, whether thou wilt or no.
I am a spirit of no common rate:
The summer still doth tend upon my state;
And I do love thee: therefore, go with me;
I'll give thee fairies to attend on thee, *160*
And they shall fetch thee jewels from the deep,
And sing while thou on pressèd flowers dost sleep:
And I will purge thy mortal grossness so
That thou shalt like an airy spirit go.
Peaseblossom! Cobweb! Moth! and Mustardseed!

(*Enter* PEASEBLOSSOM, COBWEB, MOTH, *and* MUSTARDSEED.)

PEASEBLOSSOM.   Ready.
COBWEB.   And I.
MOTH.   And I.
MUSTARDSEED.   And I.
ALL.   Where shall we go?

TITANIA. Be kind and courteous to this gentleman;
Hop in his walks and gambol in his eyes;
Feed him with apricocks and dewberries,
With purple grapes, green figs, and mulberries; *170*
The honey-bags steal from the humble-bees,
And for night-tapers crop their waxen thighs
And light them at the fiery glow-worm's eyes,
To have my love to bed and to arise;   *150*
And pluck the wings from painted butterflies
To fan the moonbeams from his sleeping eyes:
Nod to him, elves, and do him courtesies.

PEASEBLOSSOM.   Hail, mortal!
COBWEB.   Hail!
MOTH.   Hail!   *180*
MUSTARDSEED.   Hail!

BOTTOM. I cry your worships mercy, heartily:
I beseech your worship's name.

COBWEB. Cobweb.

BOTTOM. I shall desire you of more acquaintance, good Master Cobweb: if I cut my finger, I shall make bold with you.[57] Your name, honest gentleman?

PEASEBLOSSOM. Peaseblossom. *189*

BOTTOM. I pray you, commend me to Mistress Squash, your mother, and to Master Peascod, your father. Good Master Peaseblossom, I shall desire you of more acquaintance too. Your name, I beseech you, sir?

MUSTARDSEED. Mustardseed.

BOTTOM. Good Master Mustardseed, I know your patience well: that same cowardly, giant-like ox-beef hath devoured many a gentleman of your house: I promise you your kindred hath made my eyes water ere now. I desire your more acquaintance, good Master Mustardseed. *201*

TITANIA. Come, wait upon him; lead him to my bower.
The moon methinks looks with a watery eye;
And when she weeps, weeps every little flower,
Lamenting some enforcèd[58] chastity.
Tie up my love's tongue, bring him silently.

(*Exeunt.*)

---

[56] scoff

[57] Cobweb was used to stanch the flow of blood in a small cut.
[58] violated

SCENE 2

(*Another part of the wood.*)
(*Enter* OBERON.)

OBERON. I wonder if Titania be awaked;
Then, what it was that next came in her eye,
Which she must dote on in extremity.
  (*Enter* PUCK.)
Here comes my messenger.
                    How now, mad spirit!
What night-rule now about this haunted grove?
  PUCK. My mistress with a monster is in love.
Near to her close and consecrated bower,
While she was in her dull and sleeping hour,
A crew of patches, rude mechanicals,
That work for bread upon Athenian stalls,[59]   *10*
Were met together to rehearse a play
Intended for great Theseus' nuptial-day.
The shallowest thick-skin of that barren sort,
Who Pyramus presented, in their sport
Forsook his scene and enter'd in a brake:
When I did him at this advantage take,
An ass's nole[60] I fixèd on his head:
Anon his Thisbe must be answerèd,
And forth my mimic comes. When they him spy,
As wild geese that the creeping fowler eye,   *20*
Or russet-pated choughs,[61] many in sort,
Rising and cawing at the gun's report,
Sever themselves and madly sweep the sky,
So, at his sight, away his fellows fly;
And, at our stamp, here o'er and o'er one falls;
He murder cries and help from Athens calls.
Their sense thus weak, lost with their fears thus strong,
Made senseless things begin to do them wrong;
For briers and thorns at their apparel snatch;
Some sleeves, some hats, from yielders all things catch.   *30*
I led them on in this distracted fear,
And left sweet Pyramus translated there:
When in that moment, so it came to pass,
Titania waked and straightway loved an ass.
  OBERON. This falls out better than I could devise.
But hast thou yet latch'd[62] the Athenian's eyes
With the love-juice, as I did bid thee do?
  PUCK. I took him sleeping,—that is finish'd too,—
And the Athenian woman by his side;
That, when he waked, of force she must be eyed.   *40*
  (*Enter* HERMIA *and* DEMETRIUS.)
  OBERON. Stand close: this is the same Athenian.
  PUCK. This is the woman, but not this the man.
  DEMETRIUS. O, why rebuke you him that loves you so?
Lay breath so bitter on your bitter foe.
  HERMIA. Now I but chide; but I should use thee worse,
For thou, I fear, hast given me cause to curse.
If thou hast slain Lysander in his sleep,
Being o'er shoes in blood, plunge in the deep,
And kill me too.
The sun was not so true unto the day   *50*
As he to me: would he have stolen away
From sleeping Hermia? I'll believe as soon
The whole earth may be bored and that the moon

---

[59] market stalls
[60] head
[61] grackles

[62] enchanted

May through the centre creep and so displease
Her brother's noontide with the Antipodes.
It cannot be but thou hast murder'd him;
So should a murderer look, so dead, so grim.

   DEMETRIUS. So should the murder'd look, and so should I,
Pierced through the heart with your stern cruelty:
Yet you, the murderer, look as bright, as clear,   60
As yonder Venus in her glimmering sphere.

   HERMIA. What's this to my Lysander? where is he?
Ah, good Demetrius, wilt thou give him me?

   DEMETRIUS. I had rather give his carcass to my hounds.

   HERMIA. Out, dog! out, cur! thou drivest me past the bounds
Of maiden's patience. Hast thou slain him, then?
Henceforth be never number'd among men!
O, once tell true, tell true, even for my sake!
Durst thou have look'd upon him being awake,
And hast thou kill'd him sleeping? O brave touch[63]   70
Could not a worm,[64] an adder, do so much?
An adder did it; for with doubler tongue
Than thine, thou serpent, never adder stung.

   DEMETRIUS. You spend your passion on a misprised mood:
I am not guilty of Lysander's blood;
Nor is he dead, for aught that I can tell.

   HERMIA. I pray thee, tell me then that he is well.

   DEMETRIUS. An if I could, what should I get therefore?

   HERMIA. A privilege never to see me more.   79
And from thy hated presence part I so:
See me no more, whether he be dead or no.
(*Exit.*)

   DEMETRIUS. There is no following her in this fierce vein:
Here therefore for a while I will remain.
So sorrow's heaviness doth heavier grow
For debt that bankrupt sleep doth sorrow owe;
Which now in some slight measure it will pay,
If for his tender here I make some stay.
(*Lies down and sleeps.*)

   OBERON. What hast thou done? thou hast mistaken quite
And laid the love-juice on some true-love's sight.
Of thy misprision[65] must perforce ensue
Some true love turn'd and not a false turn'd true.   91

   PUCK. Then fate o'er-rules, that, one man holding troth,
A million fail, confounding oath on oath.

   OBERON. About the wood go swifter than the wind,
And Helena of Athens look thou find:
All fancy-sick she is and pale of cheer,[66]
With sighs of love, that costs the fresh blood dear:
By some illusion see thou bring her here:
I'll charm his eyes against[67] she do appear.

   PUCK. I go, I go; look how I go,
Swifter than arrow from the Tartar's bow.   101
(*Exit.*)

   OBERON.   Flower of this purple dye,
      Hit with Cupid's archery,
      Sink in apple of his eye.
      When his love he doth espy,
      Let her shine as gloriously
      As the Venus of the sky.
      When thou wakest, if she be by,

---

[63] deed
[64] snake
[65] error
[66] countenance
[67] before

          Beg of her for remedy.
(*Re-enter* PUCK.)
PUCK.   Captain of our fairy band,
          Helena is here at hand;
          And the youth, mistook by me,   *112*
          Pleading for a lover's fee.
          Shall we their fond pageant see?
          Lord, what fools these mortals be!
OBERON. Stand aside: the noise they make
          Will cause Demetrius to awake.
PUCK.   Then will two at once woo one;
          That must needs be sport alone;
          And those things do best please me   *120*
          That befall preposterously.
(*Enter* LYSANDER *and* HELENA.)
LYSANDER. Why should you think that I should woo in scorn?
Scorn and derision never come in tears:
Look, when I vow, I weep; and vows so born,
In their nativity all truth appears.
How can these things in me seem scorn to you,
Bearing the badge of faith, to prove them true?
HELENA. You do advance your cunning more and more.
When truth kills truth, O devilish-holy fray!
These vows are Hermia's: will you give her o'er?   *130*
Weigh oath with oath, and you will nothing weigh:
Your vows to her and me, put in two scales,
Will even weigh, and both as light as tales.
LYSANDER. I had no judgement when to her I swore.
HELENA. Nor none, in my mind, now you give her o'er.
LYSANDER. Demetrius loves her, and he loves not you.
DEMETRIUS (*awaking*). O Helen, goddess, nymph, perfect, divine!
To what, my love, shall I compare thine eyne?
Crystal is muddy. O, how ripe in show
Thy lips, those kissing cherries, tempting grow!   *140*
That pure congealèd white, high Taurus'[68] snow,
Fann'd with the eastern wind, turns to a crow
When thou hold'st up thy hand: O, let me kiss
This princess of pure white, this seal of bliss!
HELENA. O spite! O hell! I see you all are bent
To set against me for your merriment:
If you were civil and knew courtesy,
You would not do me thus much injury.
Can you not hate me, as I know you do,
But you must join in souls to mock me too?   *150*
If you were men, as men you are in show,
You would not use a gentle lady so;
To vow, and swear, and superpraise my parts,
When I am sure you hate me with your hearts.
You both are rivals, and love Hermia;
And now both rivals, to mock Helena:
A trim exploit, a manly enterprise,
To conjure tears up in a poor maid's eyes
With your derision! none of noble sort
Would so offend a virgin and extort[69]   *160*
A poor soul's patience, all to make you sport.
LYSANDER. You are unkind, Demetrius; be not so;
For you love Hermia; this you know I know:
And here, with all good will, with all my heart,

[68] Turkish mountain range
[69] torment

In Hermia's love I yield you up my part;
And yours of Helena to me bequeath,
Whom I do love and will do till my death.
  HELENA. Never did mockers waste more idle breath.
  DEMETRIUS. Lysander, keep thy Hermia; I will none: *169*
If e'er I loved her, all that love is gone.
My heart to her but as guest-wise sojourn'd,
And now to Helen is it home return'd,
There to remain.
  LYSANDER.   Helen, it is not so.
  DEMETRIUS. Disparage not the faith thou dost not know,
Lest, to thy peril, thou aby[70] it dear.
Look, where thy love comes; yonder is thy dear.
  (*Re-enter* HERMIA.)
  HERMIA. Dark night, that from the eye his function takes,
The ear more quick of apprehension makes;
Wherein it doth impair the seeing sense,
It pays the hearing double recompense.
Thou art not by mine eye, Lysander, found;   *181*
Mine ear, I thank it, brought me to thy sound
But why unkindly didst thou leave me so?
  LYSANDER. Why should he stay, whom love doth press to go?
  HERMIA. What love could press Lysander from my side?
  LYSANDER. Lysander's love, that would not let him bide,
Fair Helena, who more engilds the night
Than all yon fiery oes[71] and eyes of light.
Why seek'st thou me? could not this make thee know,
The hate I bear thee made me leave thee so?   *190*
  HERMIA. You speak not as you think: it cannot be.
  HELENA. Lo, she is one of this confederacy!
Now I perceive they have conjoin'd all three
To fashion this false sport, in spite of me.
Injurious Hermia! most ungrateful maid!
Have you conspired, have you with these contrived
To bait me with this foul derision?
Is all the counsel that we two have shared,
The sisters' vows, the hours that we have spent,
When we have chid the hasty-footed time
For parting us,—O, is it all forgot?   *201*
All school-days' friendship, childhood innocence?
We, Hermia, like two artificial[72] gods,
Have with our needles created both one flower,
Both on one sampler, sitting on one cushion,
Both warbling of one song, both in one key,
As if our hands, our sides, voices and minds,
Had been incorporate. So we grew together,
Like to a double cherry, seeming parted,
But yet an union in partition;   *210*
Two lovely berries moulded on one stem;
So, with two seeming bodies, but one heart;
Two of the first, like coats in heraldry,
Due but to one and crownèd with one crest.
And will you rent our ancient love asunder.
To join with men in scorning your poor friend?
It is not friendly, 'tis not maidenly:
Our sex, as well as I, may chide you for it,
Though I alone do feel the injury.
  HERMIA. I am amazèd at your passionate words.   *220*
I scorn you not: it seems that you scorn me.
  HELENA. Have you not set Lysander, as in scorn,

---

[70] answer for
[71] rings
[72] skillful in the arts

To follow me and praise my eyes and
    face?
And made your other love, Demetrius,
Who even but now did spurn me with his
    foot,
To call me goddess, nymph, divine and
    rare.
Precious, celestial? Wherefore speaks he
    this
To her he hates? and wherefore doth
    Lysander
Deny your love, so rich within his soul,
And tender me, forsooth, affection,   230
But by your setting on, by your consent?
What though I be not so in grace as you,
So hung upon with love, so fortunate,
But miserable most, to love unloved?
This you should pity rather than despise.
  HERMIA. I understand not what you
    mean by this.
  HELENA. Ay, do, persévér, counter-
    feit sad looks,
Make mouths upon me when I turn my
    back;
Wink each at other; hold the sweet jest
    up:
This sport, well carried, shall be chron-
    icled.   240
If you have any pity, grace, or manners,
You would not make me such an argu-
    ment.
But fare ye well: 'tis partly my own fault;
Which death or absence soon shall
    remedy.
  LYSANDER. Stay, gentle Helena; hear
    my excuse:
My love, my life, my soul, fair Helena!
  HELENA. O excellent!
  HERMIA. Sweet, do not scorn her so.
  DEMETRIUS. If she cannot entreat, I
    can compel.
  LYSANDER. Thou canst compel no
    more than she entreat:
Thy threats have no more strength than
    her weak prayers.   250
Helen, I love thee; by my life, I do:
I swear by that which I will lose for thee,
To prove him false that says I love thee
    not.
  DEMETRIUS. I say I love thee more
    than he can do.
  LYSANDER. If thou say so, withdraw,
    and prove it too.
  DEMETRIUS. Quick, come!
  HERMIA.   Lysander, whereto tends
    all this?
  LYSANDER. Away, you Ethiope!
  DEMETRIUS.   No, no; he'll . . .
Seem to break loose: take on as you
    would follow,
But yet come not: you are a tame man,
    go!
  LYSANDER. Hang off, thou cat, thou
    burr! vile thing, let loose,   260
Or I will shake thee from me like a
    serpent!
  HERMIA. Why are you grown so
    rude? what change is this?
Sweet love,—
  LYSANDER.   Thy love! out, tawny
    Tartar, out!
Out, loathèd medicine! hated potion,
    hence!
  HERMIA. Do you not jest?
  HELENA. Yes, sooth; and so do you.
  LYSANDER. Demetrius, I will keep my
    word with thee.
  DEMETRIUS. I would I had your
    bond, for I perceive
A weak bond holds you: I'll not trust
    your word.
  LYSANDER. What, should I hurt her,
    strike her, kill her dead?   269
Although I hate her, I'll not harm her
    so.
  HERMIA. What, can you do me
    greater harm than hate?
Hate me! wherefore? O me! what news,
    my love!
Am not I Hermia? are not you Lysander?
I am as fair now as I was erewhile.
Since night you loved me; yet since night
    you left me:
Why, then you left me—O, the gods for-
    bid!—
In earnest, shall I say?
  LYSANDER.   Ay, by my life;
And never did desire to see thee more.

Therefore be out of hope, of question, of doubt;
Be certain, nothing truer; 'tis no jest 280
That I do hate thee and love Helena.
    HERMIA. O me! you juggler! you canker-blossom!
You thief of love! what, have you come by night
And stolen my love's heart from him?
    HELENA.   Fine, i' faith!
Have you no modesty, no maiden shame,
No touch of bashfulness? What, will you tear
Impatient answers from my gentle tongue?
Fie, fie! you counterfeit, you puppet, you!
    HERMIA. Puppet? why so? ay, that way goes the game.
Now I perceive that she hath made compare 290
Between our statures; she hath urged her height;
And with her personage, her tall personage,
Her height, forsooth, she hath prevail'd with him.
And are you grown so high in his esteem,
Because I am so dwarfish and so low?
How low am I, thou painted maypole? speak;
How low am I? I am not yet so low
But that my nails can reach unto thine eyes.
    HELENA. I pray you, though you mock me, gentlemen, 299
Let her not hurt me: I was never curst;
I have no gift at all in shrewishness;
I am a right maid for my cowardice:[73]
Let her not strike me. You perhaps may think,
Because she is something lower than myself,
That I can match her.
    HERMIA.   Lower! hark, again.
    HELENA. Good Hermia, do not be so bitter with me.
I evermore did love you, Hermia,

---

[73] My timidity shows me to be truly feminine.

Did ever keep your counsels, never wrong'd you;
Save that, in love unto Demetrius, 309
I told him of your stealth unto this wood.
He follow'd you; for love I follow'd him;
But he hath chid me hence and threaten'd me
To strike me, spurn me, nay, to kill me too:
And now, so you will let me quiet go,
To Athens will I bear my folly back
And follow you no further: let me go:
You see how simple and how fond I am.
    HERMIA. Why, get you gone: who is't that hinders you?
    HELENA. A foolish heart, that I leave here behind.
    HERMIA. What, with Lysander?
    HELENA.   With Demetrius.
    LYSANDER. Be not afraid; she shall not harm thee, Helena. 321
    DEMETRIUS. No, sir, she shall not, though you take her part.
    HELENA. O, when she's angry, she is keen and shrewd!
She was a vixen when she went to school;
And though she be but little, she is fierce.
    HERMIA. "Little" again! nothing but "low" and "little"!
Why will you suffer her to flout me thus?
Let me come to her.
    LYSANDER.   Get you gone, you dwarf;
You minimus, of hindering knot-grass made; 329
You bead, you acorn.
    DEMETRIUS.   You are too officious
In her behalf that scorns your services.
Let her alone: speak not of Helena;
Take not her part; for, if thou dost intend
Never so little show of love to her,
Thou shalt aby it.
    LYSANDER.   Now she holds me not;
Now follow, if thou darest, to try whose right,
Of thine or mine, is most in Helena.
    DEMETRIUS. Follow! nay, I'll go with thee, cheek by jole.

(Exeunt LYSANDER *and* DEMETRIUS.*)*
HERMIA.   You, mistress, all this coil is 'long of you:[74]   *339*
Nay, go not back.
HELENA.   I will not trust you, I,
Nor longer stay in your curst company.
Your hands than mine are quicker for a fray,
My legs are longer though, to run away.
(Exit.)
HERMIA.   I am amazed, and know not what to say.
(Exit.)
OBERON.   This is thy negligence: still thou mistakest,
Or else committ'st thy knaveries wilfully.
PUCK.   Believe me, king of shadows, I mistook.
Did you not tell me I should know the man
By the Athenian garments he had on?
And so far blameless proves my enterprise,   *350*
That I have 'nointed an Athenian's eyes;
And so far am I glad it so did sort[75]
As this their jangling I esteem a sport.
OBERON.   Thou see'st these lovers seek a place to fight:
Hie therefore, Robin, overcast the night;
The starry welkin cover thou anon
With drooping fog as black as Acheron,[76]
And lead these testy rivals so astray
As one come not within another's way.
Like to Lysander sometime frame thy tongue,   *360*
Then stir Demetrius up with bitter wrong;
And sometime rail thou like Demetrius;
And from each other look thou lead them thus,
Till o'er their brows death-counterfeiting sleep
With leaden legs and batty wings doth creep:
Then crush this herb into Lysander's eye;
Whose liquor hath this virtuous[77] property,
To take from thence all error with his might,
And make his eyeballs roll with wonted sight.   *369*
When they next wake, all this derision
Shall seem a dream and fruitless vision,
And back to Athens shall the lovers wend,
With league whose date till death shall never end.
Whiles I in this affair do thee employ,
I'll to my queen and beg her Indian boy:
And then I will her charmèd eye release
From monster's view, and all things shall be peace.
PUCK.   My fairy lord, this must be done with haste,
For night's swift dragons cut the clouds full fast,   *379*
And yonder shines Aurora's harbinger;[78]
At whose approach, ghosts, wandering here and there,
Troop home to churchyards: damnèd spirits all,
That in crossways and floods have burial,
Already to their wormy beds are gone;
For fear lest day should look their shames upon,
They wilfully themselves exile from light
And must for aye consort with black-brow'd night.
OBERON.   But we are spirits of another sort:
I with the morning's[79] love have oft made sport,   *389*
And, like a forester, the groves may tread,
Even till the eastern gate, all fiery-red,
Opening on Neptune with fair blessèd beams,
Turns into yellow gold his salt green streams.
But, notwithstanding, haste; make no delay:

---

[74] You are responsible for all this uproar.
[75] happen
[76] a river in Hades
[77] powerful
[78] the morning star, herald of the dawn
[79] Aurora's

We may effect this business yet ere day.
(*Exit.*)
PUCK. Up and down, up and down,
I will lead them up and down:
I am fear'd in field and town:
Goblin, lead them up and down.
Here comes one. 400
(*Re-enter* LYSANDER.)
LYSANDER. Where art thou, proud Demetrius? Speak thou now.
PUCK. Here, villain; drawn and ready. Where art thou?
LYSANDER. I will be with thee straight.
PUCK. Follow me, then, To plainer[80] ground.
(*Exit* LYSANDER, *as following the voice.*)
(*Re-enter* DEMETRIUS.)
DEMETRIUS. Lysander! speak again:
Thou runaway, thou coward, art thou fled?
Speak! In some bush? Where dost thou hide thy head?
PUCK. Thou coward, art thou bragging to the stars,
Telling the bushes that thou look'st for wars,
And wilt not come? Come, recreant;[81] come, thou child,
I'll whip thee with a rod: he is defiled
That draws a sword on thee. 411
DEMETRIUS. Yea, art thou there?
PUCK. Follow my voice: we'll try no manhood here.
(*Exeunt.*)
(*Re-enter* LYSANDER.)
LYSANDER. He goes before me and still dares me on:
When I come where he calls, then he is gone.
The villain is much lighter-heel'd than I:
I follow'd fast, but faster he did fly;
That fallen am I in dark uneven way,
And here will rest me. (*Lies down.*)
Come, thou gentle day!

For if but once thou show me thy grey light, 419
I'll find Demetrius and revenge this spite.
(*Sleeps.*)
(*Re-enter* PUCK *and* DEMETRIUS.)
PUCK. Ho, ho, ho! Coward, why comest thou not?
DEMETRIUS. Abide me, if thou darest; for well I wot[82]
Thou runn'st before me, shifting every place,
And darest not stand, nor look me in the face.
Where art thou now?
PUCK. Come hither: I am here.
DEMETRIUS. Nay, then, thou mock'st me. Thou shalt buy this dear,
If ever I thy face by daylight see:
Now, go thy way. Faintness constraineth me
To measure out my length on this cold bed. 429
By day's approach look to be visited.
(*Lies down and sleeps.*)
(*Re-enter* HELENA.)
HELENA. O weary night, O long and tedious night,
Abate thy hours! Shine comforts from the east,
That I may back to Athens by daylight,
From these that my poor company detest:
And sleep, that sometimes shuts up sorrow's eye,
Steal me awhile from mine own company.
(*Lies down and sleeps.*)
PUCK. Yet but three? Come one more;
Two of both kinds makes up four.
Here she comes, curst[83] and sad:
Cupid is a knavish lad, 440
Thus to make poor females mad.

---

[80] flatter
[81] coward

[82] know
[83] shrewish

(*Re-enter* HERMIA.)

HERMIA. Never so weary, never so in woe,
Bedabbled with the dew and torn with briers,
I can no further crawl, no further go;
My legs can keep no pace with my desires.
Here will I rest me till the break of day.
Heavens shield Lysander, if they mean a fray!
(*Lies down and sleeps.*)

PUCK. On the ground
  Sleep sound:
I'll apply   450
  To your eye,
Gentle lover, remedy.
(*Squeezing the juice on* LYSANDER'S *eyes.*)
        When thou wakest,
        Thou takest
        True delight
        In the sight
Of thy former lady's eye:
And the country proverb known,
That every man should take his own,   459
In your waking shall be shown:
  Jack shall have Jill;
  Nought shall go ill;
The man shall have his mare again, and all shall be well.
(*Exit.*)

Act IV

SCENE 1

(*The same.* LYSANDER, DEMETRIUS, HELENA, *and* HERMIA *lying asleep.*)
(*Enter* TITANIA *and* BOTTOM; PEASEBLOSSOM, COBWEB, MOTH, MUSTARDSEED, *and other* FAIRIES *attending;* OBERON *behind unseen.*)

TITANIA. Come, sit thee down upon this flowery bed,
While I thy amiable cheeks do coy,[84]
And stick musk-roses in thy sleek smooth head,
And kiss thy fair large ears, my gentle joy.

BOTTOM. Where's Peaseblossom?

PEASEBLOSSOM. Ready.

BOTTOM. Scratch my head, Peaseblossom. Where's Mounsieur Cobweb?

COBWEB. Ready.   9

BOTTOM. Mounsieur Cobweb, good mounsieur, get you your weapons in your hand, and kill me a red-hipped humble-bee on the top of a thistle; and, good mounsieur, bring me the honey-bag. Do not fret yourself too much in the action, mounsieur; and, good mounsieur, have a care the honey-bag break not; I would be loath to have you overflown with a honey-bag, signior. Where's Mounsieur Mustardseed?

MUSTARDSEED. Ready.   19

BOTTOM. Give me your neaf,[85] Mounsieur Mustardseed. Pray you, leave your courtesy, good mounsieur.

MUSTARDSEED. What's your will?

BOTTOM. Nothing, good mounsieur, but to help Cavalery Cobweb to scratch. I must to the barber's, mounsieur; for methinks I am marvellous hairy about the face; and I am such a tender ass, if my hair do but tickle me, I must scratch.

TITANIA. What, wilt thou hear some music, my sweet love?   30

BOTTOM. I have a reasonable good ear in music. Let's have the tongs and the bones.

TITANIA. Or say, sweet love, what thou desirest to eat.

BOTTOM. Truly, a peck of provender: I could munch your good dry oats. Methinks I have a great desire to a bottle[86] of hay: good hay, sweet hay, hath no fellow.

TITANIA. I have a venturous fairy that shall seek

---

[84] caress

[85] fist
[86] bundle

The squirrel's hoard, and fetch thee new nuts.

BOTTOM. I had rather have a handful or two of dried peas. But, I pray you, let none of your people stir me: I have an exposition of sleep come upon me. 42

TITANIA. Sleep thou, and I will wind thee in my arms.
Fairies, be gone, and be all ways away.
(*Exeunt* FAIRIES.)
So doth the woodbine the sweet honey-suckle
Gentle entwist; the female ivy so
Enrings the barky fingers of the elm.
O, how I love thee! how I dote on thee!
(*They sleep.*)
(*Enter* PUCK.)

OBERON (*advancing*). Welcome, good Robin. See'st thou this sweet sight?
Her dotage now I do begin to pity: 50
For, meeting her of late behind the wood,
Seeking sweet favours for this hateful fool,
I did upbraid her and fall out with her;
For she his hairy temples then had rounded
With coronet of fresh and fragrant flowers;
And that same dew, which sometime on the buds
Was wont to swell like round and orient[87] pearls,
Stood now within the pretty flowerets' eyes
Like tears that did their own disgrace bewail. 59
When I had at my pleasure taunted her
And she in mild terms begg'd my patience,
I then did ask of her her changeling child;
Which straight she gave me, and her fairy sent
To bear him to my bower in fairy land.
And now I have the boy, I will undo
This hateful imperfection of her eyes:
And, gentle Puck, take this transformèd scalp
From off the head of this Athenian swain;
That, he awaking when the other do,
May all to Athens back again repair 70
And think no more of this night's accidents
But as the fierce vexation of a dream.
But first I will release the fairy queen.
  Be as thou wast wont to be;
  See as thou wast wont to see:
  Dian's bud[88] o'er Cupid's flower
  Hath such force and blessèd power.
Now, my Titania; wake you, my sweet queen.

TITANIA. My Oberon! what visions have I seen! 79
Methought I was enamour'd of an ass.

OBERON. There lies your love.

TITANIA. How came these thing to pass?
O, how mine eyes do loathe his visage now!

OBERON. Silence awhile. Robin, take off this head.
Titania, music call; and strike more dead
Than common sleep of all these five the sense.

TITANIA. Music, ho! music, such as charmeth sleep![89]
(*Music, still.*)

PUCK. Now, when thou wakest, with thine own fool's eyes peep.

OBERON. Sound, music! Come, my queen, take hands with me,
And rock the ground whereon these sleepers be. 90
Now thou and I are new in amity
And will to-morrow midnight solemnly
Dance in Duke Theseus' house triumphantly
And bless it to all fair prosperity:
There shall the pair of faithful lovers be
Wedded, with Theseus, all in jollity.

PUCK. Fairy king, attend, and mark:
  I do hear the morning lark.

---

[87] lustrous
[88] a plant whose juices supposedly protect virtue
[89] uninterrupted

OBERON. Then, my queen, in silence sad,[90] 99
Trip we after night's shade:
We the globe can compass soon,
Swifter than the wandering moon.
TITANIA. Come, my lord, and in our flight
Tell me how it came this night
That I sleeping here was found
With these mortals on the ground.
(*Exeunt.*)
(*Horns winded within.*)
(*Enter* THESEUS, HIPPOLYTA, EGEUS, *and train.*)
THESEUS. Go, one of you, find out the forester;
For now our observation[91] is perform'd;
And since we have the vaward[92] of the day,
My love shall hear the music of my hounds. 110
Uncouple in the western valley; let them go:
Dispatch, I say, and find the forester.
(*Exit an* ATTENDANT.)
We will, fair queen, up to the mountain's top
And mark the musical confusion
Of hounds and echo in conjunction.
HIPPOLYTA. I was with Hercules and Cadmus once,
When in a wood of Crete they bay'd the bear
With hounds of Sparta: never did I hear
Such gallant chiding; for, besides the groves,
The skies, the fountains, every region near 120
Seem'd all one mutual cry: I never heard
So musical a discord, such sweet thunder.

THESEUS. My hounds are bred out of the Spartan kind,
So flew'd,[93] so sanded,[94] and their heads are hung
With ears that sweep away the morning dew;
Crook-knee'd, and dew-lapp'd like Thessalian bulls;
Slow in pursuit, but match'd in mouth[95] like bells,
Each under each. A cry more tuneable
Was never holla'd to, nor cheer'd with horn,
In Crete, in Sparta, nor in Thessaly: 130
Judge when you hear. But, soft; what nymphs are these?
EGEUS. My lord, this is my daughter here asleep;
And this, Lysander; this Demetrius is;
This Helena, old Nedar's Helena:
I wonder of their being here together.
THESEUS. No doubt they rose up early to observe
The rite of May, and, hearing our intent,
Came here in grace of our solemnity.
But speak, Egeus; is not this the day
That Hermia should give answer of her choice? 140
EGEUS. It is, my lord.
THESEUS. Go, bid the huntsmen wake them with their horns. (*Horns and shout within.* LYSANDER, DEMETRIUS, HELENA, *and* HERMIA *wake and start up.*)
Good morrow, friends. Saint Valentine is past:
Begin these wood-birds but to couple now?
LYSANDER. Pardon, my lord.
THESEUS. I pray you all, stand up.
I know you two are rival enemies:
How comes this gentle concord in the world,
That hatred is so far from jealousy,
To sleep by hate, and fear no enmity?

---

[90] sober
[91] May Day ceremony
[92] vanguard
[93] with low-hanging chaps
[94] sandy in color
[95] voice

LYSANDER. My lord, I shall reply amazedly, 150
Half sleep, half waking: but as yet, I swear,
I cannot truly say how I came here;
But, as I think,—for truly would I speak,
And now I do bethink me, so it is,—
I came with Hermia hither: our intent
Was to be gone from Athens, where[96] we might,
Without the peril of the Athenian law.
   EGEUS. Enough, enough, my lord; you have enough:
I beg the law, the law, upon his head.
They would have stolen away, they would, Demetrius, 160
Thereby to have defeated you and me,
You or your wife and me of my consent,
Of my consent that she should be your wife.
   DEMETRIUS. My lord, fair Helen told me of their stealth,
Of this their purpose hither to this wood;
And I in fury hither follow'd them,
Fair Helena in fancy following me.
But, my good lord, I wot not by what power,—
But by some power it is,—my love to Hermia, 169
Melted as the snow, seems to me now
As the remembrance of an idle gawd
Which in my childhood I did dote upon;
And all the faith, the virtue of my heart,
The object and the pleasure of mine eye,
Is only Helena. To her, my lord,
Was I betroth'd ere I saw Hermia:
But, like in sickness, did I loathe this food;
But, as in health, come to my natural taste,
Now I do wish it, love it, long for it,
And will for evermore be true to it. 180
   THESEUS. Fair lovers, you are fortunately met:
Of this discourse we more will hear anon.
Egeus, I will overbear your will;
For in the temple, by and by, with us
These couples shall eternally be knit:
And, for the morning now is something worn,
Our purposed hunting shall be set aside.
Away with us to Athens; three and three,
We'll hold a feast in great solemnity.
Come, Hippolyta. 190
(*Exeunt* THESEUS, HIPPOLYTA, EGEUS, *and train.*)
   DEMETRIUS. These things seem small and undistinguishable,
Like far-off mountains turned into clouds.
   HERMIA. Methinks I see these things with parted[97] eye,
When every thing seems double.
   HELENA. So methinks:
And I have found Demetrius like a jewel,
Mine own, and not mine own.
   DEMETRIUS. Are you sure
That we are awake? It seems to me
That yet we sleep, we dream. Do not you think
The duke was here, and bid us follow him?
   HERMIA. Yea; and my father
   HELENA. And Hippolyta 200
   LYSANDER. And he did bid us follow to the temple.
   DEMETRIUS. Why, then, we are awake: let's follow him;
And by the way let us recount our dreams.
(*Exeunt.*)
   BOTTOM (*awaking*). When my cue comes, call me, and I will answer: my next is, "Most fair Pyramus." Heigh-ho! Peter Quince! Flute, the bellows-mender! Snout, the tinker! Starveling! God's my life, stolen hence, and left me asleep! I have had a most rare vision. I have 210 had a dream, past the wit of man to say what dream it was: man is but an ass, if he go about to expound this dream. Methought I was—there is no man can tell what. Methought I was,—and methought I had,—but man is but a patched fool, if he will offer to say what methought I had. The eye of man hath not heard, the

---

[96] wherever   [97] unfocussed

ear of man hath not seen, man's hand is not able to taste, his tongue to con- ceive nor his heart to report, what my dream was. I will get Peter Quince to write a ballad of this dream: it shall be called Bottom's Dream, because it hath no bottom; and I will sing it in the latter end of a play, before the duke: peradventure, to make it the more gracious, I shall sing it at her death. 220

(*Exit.*)

SCENE 2

(*Athens.* QUINCE'S *house.*)
(*Enter* QUINCE, FLUTE, SNOUT, *and* STARVELING.)

QUINCE. Have you sent to Bottom's house? is he come home yet?

STARVELING. He cannot be heard of. Out of doubt he is transported.

FLUTE. If he come not, then the play is marred: it goes not forward, doth it?

QUINCE. It is not possible: you have not a man in all Athens able to discharge Pyramus but he.

FLUTE. No, he hath simply the best wit of any handicraft man in Athens. 10

QUINCE. Yea, and the best person too; and he is a very paramour for a sweet voice.

FLUTE. You must say 'paragon:' a paramour is, God bless us, a thing of naught.98

(*Enter* SNUG.)

SNUG. Masters, the duke is coming from the temple, and there is two or three lords and ladies more married: if our sport had gone forward, we had all been made men.

FLUTE. O sweet bully Bottom! Thus hath he lost sixpence a day during his life; he could not have 'scaped sixpence a day: an the duke had not given him sixpence a day for playing Pyramus, I'll be hanged; he would have deserved it: sixpence a day in Pyramus, or nothing. 20

98 naughty; i.e., wicked

(*Enter* BOTTOM.)

BOTTOM. Where are these lads? where are these hearts?

QUINCE. Bottom! O most courageous day! O most happy hour!

BOTTOM. Masters, I am to discourse wonders: but ask me not what; for if I tell you, I am no true Athenian. I will tell you every thing, right as it fell out. 33

QUINCE. Let us hear, sweet Bottom.

BOTTOM. Not a word of me. All that I will tell you is, that the duke hath dined. Get your apparel together, good strings to your beards, new ribbons to your pumps; meet presently at the palace; every man look o'er his part; for the short and the long is, our play is preferred. In any case, let Thisby have clean linen; and let not him that plays the lion pare his nails, for they shall hang out for the lion's claws. And, most dear actors, eat no onions nor garlic, for we are to utter sweet breath; and I do not doubt but to hear them say, it is a sweet comedy. No more words: away! go, away! 40

(*Exeunt.*)

Act V

SCENE 1

(*Athens. The palace of* THESEUS.)
(*Enter* THESEUS, HIPPOLYTA, PHILOSTRATE, LORDS, *and* ATTENDANTS.)

HIPPOLYTA. 'Tis strange, my Theseus, that these lovers speak of.

THESEUS. More strange than true: I never may believe
These antique fables, nor these fairy toys.
Lovers and madmen have such seething brains,
Such shaping fantasies, that apprehend
More than cool reason ever comprehends.
The lunatic, the lover and the poet
Are of imagination all compact:
One sees more devils than vast hell can hold,
That is, the madman: the lover, all as frantic, 10

Sees Helen's beauty in a brow of Egypt:[99]
The poet's eye, in a fine frenzy rolling,
Doth glance from heaven to earth, from earth to heaven;
And as imagination bodies forth
The forms of things unknown, the poet's pen
Turns them to shapes and gives to airy nothing
A local habitation and a name.
Such tricks hath strong imagination,
That, if it would but apprehend some joy,
It comprehends some bringer of that joy;
Or in the night, imagining some fear,   *21*
How easy is a bush supposed a bear!
  HIPPOLYTA. But all the story of the night told over,
And all their minds transfigured so together,
More witnesseth than fancy's images
And grows to something of great constancy;
But, howsoever, strange and admirable.
  THESEUS. Here come the lovers, full of joy and mirth.
  (*Enter* LYSANDER, DEMETRIUS, HERMIA, *and* HELENA.)
Joy, gentle friends! joy and fresh days of love
Accompany your hearts!
  LYSANDER.   More than to us   *30*
Wait in your royal walks, your board, your bed!
  THESEUS. Come now; what masques, what dances shall we have,
To wear away this long age of three hours
Between our after-supper and bed-time?
Where is our usual manager of mirth?
What revels are in hand? Is there no play,
To ease the anguish of a torturing hour?
Call Philostrate.
  PHILOSTRATE. Here, mighty Theseus.
  THESEUS. Say, what abridgement have you for this evening?
What masque? what music? How shall we beguile   *40*
The lazy time, if not with some delight?
  PHILOSTRATE. There is a brief how many sports are ripe:
Make choice of which your highness will see first. (*Giving a paper.*)
  THESEUS (*reads*). "The battle with the Centaurs, to be sung
By an Athenian eunuch to the harp."
We'll none of that: that have I told my love,
In glory of my kinsman Hercules.
(*Reads.*) "The riot of the tipsy Bacchanals,
Tearing the Thracian singer in their rage."
That is an old device; and it was play'd
When I from Thebes came last a conqueror.   *51*
(*Reads.*) "The thrice three Muses mourning for the death
Of Learning, late deceased in beggary."
That is some satire, keen and critical,
Not sorting with[100] a nuptial ceremony.
(*Reads.*) "A tedious brief scene of young Pyramus
And his love Thisby; very tragical mirth."
Merry and tragical! tedious and brief!
That is, hot ice and wondrous strange snow.
How shall we find the concord of this discord?   *60*
  PHILOSTRATE. A play there is, my lord, some ten words long,
Which is as brief as I have known a play;
But by ten words, my lord, it is too long,
Which makes it tedious; for in all the play
There is not one word apt, one player fitted:
And tragical, my noble lord, it is;
For Pyramus therein doth kill himself.
Which, when I saw rehearsed, I must confess,
Made mine eyes water; but more merry tears   *69*
The passion of loud laughter never shed.
  THESEUS. What are they that do play it?

---

[99] sees the fair Helen's beauty in a swarthy gypsy's face

[100] inappropriate for

PHILOSTRATE.   Hard-handed men that work in Athens here,
Which never labour'd in their minds till now,
And now have toil'd their unbreathed[101] memories
With this same play, against your nuptial.
  THESEUS.   And we will hear it.
  PHILOSTRATE.   No, my noble lord;
It is not for you: I have heard it over,
And it is nothing, nothing in the world;
Unless you can find sport in their intents,
Extremely stretch'd and conn'd with cruel pain,   *80*
To do you service.
  THESEUS.   I will hear that play;
For never anything can be amiss,
When simpleness and duty tender it.
Go, bring them in: and take your places, ladies.
  (*Exit* PHILOSTRATE.)
  HIPPOLYTA.   I love not to see wretchedness o'ercharged
And duty in his service perishing.
  THESEUS.   Why, gentle sweet, you shall see no such thing.
  HIPPOLYTA.   He says they can do nothing in this kind.
  THESEUS.   The kinder we, to give them thanks for nothing.
Our sport shall be to take what they mistake: *90*
And what poor duty cannot do, noble respect
Takes it in might, not merit.
Where I have come, great clerks[102] have purposed
To greet me with premeditated welcomes;
Where I have seen them shiver and look pale,
Make periods in the midst of sentences,
Throttle their practised accent in their fears
And in conclusion dumbly have broke off,
Not paying me a welcome. Trust me, sweet,   *99*
Out of this silence yet I pick'd a welcome;
And in the modesty of fearful duty
I read as much as from the rattling tongue
Of saucy and audacious eloquence.
Love, therefore, and tongue-tied simplicity
In least speak most, to my capacity.
  (*Re-enter* PHILOSTRATE.)
  PHILOSTRATE.   So please your grace, the Prologue is address'd.
  THESEUS.   Let him approach.
  (*Flourish of trumpets.*)
  (*Enter* QUINCE *for the* PROLOGUE.)
  PROLOGUE.   If we offend, it is with our good will
That you should think, we come not to offend,
But with good will. To show our simple skill,   *110*
That is the true beginning of our end.
Consider then we come but in despite.
We do not come as minding to content you,
Our true intent is. All for your delight
We are not here. That you should here repent you,
The actors are at hand and by their show
You shall know all that you are like to know.
  THESEUS.   This fellow doth not stand upon points.   *118*
  LYSANDER.   He hath rid his prologue like a rough colt; he knows not the stop. A good moral, my lord: it is not enough to speak, but to speak true.
  HIPPOLYTA.   Indeed he hath played on his prologue like a child on a recorder; a sound, but not in government.[103]
  THESEUS.   His speech was like a tangled chain; nothing impaired, but all disordered. Who is next?
  (*Enter* PYRAMUS *and* THISBY, WALL, MOONSHINE, *and* LION.)
  PROLOGUE.   Gentles, perchance you wonder at this show;
But wonder on, till truth make all things plain.   *129*

[101] unexercised
[102] educated men
[103] under control

This man is Pyramus, if you would know;
   This beauteous lady Thisby is certain.
This man, with lime and rough-cast, doth present
   Wall, that vile Wall which did these lovers sunder;
And through Wall's chink, poor souls, they are content
   To whisper. At the which let no man wonder.
This man, with lanthorn, dog, and bush of thorn,
   Presenteth Moonshine; for, if you will know,
By moonshine did these lovers think no scorn
   To meet at Ninus' tomb, there, there to woo.
This grisly beast, which Lion hight[104] by name,   140
The trusty Thisby, coming first by night,
Did scare away, or rather did affright;
And, as she fled, her mantle she did[105] fall,
   Which Lion vile with bloody mouth did stain.
Anon comes Pyramus, sweet youth and tall,
   And finds his trusty Thisby's mantle slain:
Whereat, with blade, with bloody blameful blade,
   He bravely broach'd his boiling bloody breast;
And Thisby, tarrying in mulberry shade,
   His dagger drew, and died. For all the rest,   150
Let Lion, Moonshine, Wall, and lovers twain
At large discourse, while here they do remain.

(*Exeunt* PROLOGUE, PYRAMUS, THISBY, LION, *and* MOONSHINE.)

THESEUS. I wonder if the lion be to speak.

DEMETRIUS. No wonder, my lord: one lion may, when many asses do.

WALL. In this same interlude it doth befall
That I, one Snout by name, present a wall;
And such a wall, as I would have you think,
That had in it a crannied hole or chink,
Through which the lovers, Pyramus and Thisby,   160
Did whisper often very secretly.
This loam, this rough-cast and this stone doth show
That I am that same wall; the truth is so:
And this the cranny is, right and sinister,[106]
Through which the fearful lovers are to whisper.

THESEUS. Would you desire lime and hair to speak better?

DEMETRIUS. It is the wittiest partition that ever I heard discourse, my lord.

(*Re-enter* PYRAMUS.)

THESEUS. Pyramus draws near the wall: silence!   170

PYRAMUS. O grim-look'd night! O night with hue so black!
O night, which ever art when day is not!
O night, O night! alack, alack, alack,
I fear my Thisby's promise is forgot!
And thou, O wall, O sweet, O lovely wall,
   That stand'st between her father's ground and mine!
Thou wall, O wall, O sweet and lovely wall,
   Show me thy chink, to blink through with mine eyne! (*Wall holds up his fingers.*)
Thanks, courteous wall: Jove shield thee well for this!   179
But what see I? No Thisby do I see.
O wicked wall, through whom I see no bliss!
Cursed be thy stones for thus deceiving me!

THESEUS. The wall, methinks, being sensible, should curse again.

PYRAMUS. No, in truth, sir, he should not. "Deceiving me" is Thisby's cue: she

---

[104] is called
[105] let
[106] left

is to enter now, and I am to spy her through the wall. You shall see, it will fall pat as I told you. Yonder she comes.
(*Re-enter* THISBY.)
THISBY. O wall, full often hast thou heard my moans,   *190*
For parting my fair Pyramus and me!
My cherry lips have often kiss'd thy stones,
Thy stones with lime and hair knit up in thee.
PYRAMUS. I see a voice: now will I to the chink,
To spy an I can hear my Thisby's face. Thisby!
THISBY. My love thou art, my love I think.
PYRAMUS. Think what thou wilt, I am thy lover's grace;
And, like Limander,[107] am I trusty still.
THISBY. And I like Helen,[108] till the Fates me kill.   *200*
PYRAMUS. Not Shafalus[109] to Procrus[110] was so true.
THISBY. As Shafalus to Procrus, I to you.
PYRAMUS. O, kiss me through the hole of this vile wall!
THISBY. I kiss the wall's hole, not your lips at all.
PYRAMUS. Wilt thou at Ninny's tomb meet me straightway?
THISBY. 'Tide life, 'tide death, I come without delay.
(*Exeunt* PYRAMUS *and* THISBY.)
WALL. Thus have I, Wall, my part discharged so;
And, being done, thus Wall away doth go.
(*Exit.*)
THESEUS. Now is the mural down between the two neighbours.
DEMETRIUS. No remedy, my lord, when walls are so wilful to hear without warning.   *212*
HIPPOLYTA. This is the silliest stuff that ever I heard.

THESEUS. The best in this kind are but shadows; and the worst are no worse, if imagination amend them.
HIPPOLYTA. It must be your imagination then, and not theirs.
THESEUS. If we imagine no worse of them than they of themselves, they may pass for excellent men. Here come two noble beasts in, a man and a lion.   *221*
(*Re-enter* LION *and* MOONSHINE.)
LION. You, ladies, you, whose gentle hearts do fear
The smallest monstrous mouse that creeps on floor,
May now perchance both quake and tremble here,
When lion rough in wildest rage doth roar
Then know that I, one Snug the joiner, am
A lion-fell,[111] nor else no lion's dam;
For, if I should as lion come in strife
Into this place, 'twere pity on my life.
THESEUS. A very gentle beast, and of a good conscience.   *231*
DEMETRIUS. The very best at a beast, my lord, that e'er I saw.
LYSANDER. This lion is a very fox for his valour.
THESEUS. True; and a goose for his discretion.
DEMETRIUS. Not so, my lord; for his valour cannot carry his discretion; and the fox carries the goose.
THESEUS. His discretion, I am sure, cannot carry his valour; for the goose carries not the fox. It is well: leave it to his discretion, and let us listen to the moon.   *242*
MOONSHINE. This lanthorn doth the hornèd moon present;—
DEMETRIUS. He should have worn the horns on his head.
THESEUS. He is no crescent, and his horns are invisible within the circumference.
MOONSHINE. This lanthorn doth the hornèd moon present;
Myself the man i' the moon do seem to be.

[107] Leander
[108] Hero
[109] Cephalus
[110] Procris

[111] the hide of a lion

THESEUS. This is the greatest error of all the rest: the man should be put into the lanthorn. How is it else the man i' the moon? 252

DEMETRIUS. He dares not come there for the candle; for, you see, it is already in snuff.

HIPPOLYTA. I am aweary of this moon: would he would change!

THESEUS. It appears, by his small light of discretion, that he is in the wane; but yet, in courtesy, in all reason, we must stay the time.

LYSANDER. Proceed, Moon. 260

MOONSHINE. All that I have to say, is, to tell you that the lanthorn is the moon; I, the man in the moon; this thorn-bush, my thorn-bush; and this dog, my dog.

DEMETRIUS. Why, all these should be in the lanthorn; for all these are in the moon. But, silence! here comes Thisby.

(*Re-enter* THISBY.)

THISBY. This is old Ninny's tomb. Where is my love?

LION (*roaring*). Oh——

(THISBY *runs off.*)

DEMETRIUS. Well roared, Lion. 270

THESEUS. Well run, Thisby.

HIPPOLYTA. Well shone, Moon. Truly, the moon shines with a good grace.

(*The* LION *shakes* THISBY'S *mantle, and exit.*)

THESEUS. Well moused, Lion.

LYSANDER. And so the lion vanished.

DEMETRIUS. And then came Pyramus.

(*Re-enter* PYRAMUS.)

PYRAMUS. Sweet Moon, I thank thee for thy sunny beams;
I thank thee, Moon, for shining now so bright;
For, by thy gracious, golden, glittering gleams, 279
I trust to take of truest Thisby sight.
But stay, O spite!
But mark, poor knight,
What dreadful dole is here!
Eyes, do you see?
How can it be?

O dainty duck! O dear!
Thy mantle good,
What, stain'd with blood!
Approach, ye Furies fell!
O Fates, come, come, 290
Cut thread and thrum;
Quail, crush, conclude, and quell!

THESEUS. This passion, and the death of a dear friend, would go near to make a man look sad.

HIPPOLYTA. Beshrew my heart, but I pity the man.

PYRAMUS. O wherefore, Nature, didst thou lions frame?
Since lion vile hath here deflower'd my dear:
Which is—no, no—which was the fairest dame
That lived, that loved, that liked, that look'd with cheer.
Come, tears, confound; 300
Out, sword, and wound
The pap of Pyramus;
Ay, that left pap,
Where heart doth hop:

(*Stabs himself.*)

Thus die I, thus, thus, thus.
Now am I dead,
Now am I fled;
My soul is in the sky:
Tongue, lose thy light;
Moon, take thy flight: 310

(*Exit* MOONSHINE.)

Now die, die, die, die, die.

(*Dies.*)

DEMETRIUS. No die, but an ace, for him; for he is but one.

LYSANDER. Less than an ace, man; for he is dead; he is nothing.

THESEUS. With the help of a surgeon he might yet recover, and prove an ass.

HIPPOLYTA. How chance Moonshine is gone before Thisby comes back and finds her lover?

THESEUS. She will find him by starlight. Here she comes; and her passion ends the play. 321

(*Re-enter* THISBY.)

HIPPOLYTA. Methinks she should not

use a long one for such a Pyramus: I hope she will be brief.

DEMETRIUS. A mote will turn the balance, which Pyramus, which Thisby, is the better; he for a man, God warrant us; she for a woman, God bless us.

LYSANDER. She hath spied him already with those sweet eyes.

DEMETRIUS. And thus she means, videlicet:— 330

THISBY. Asleep, my love?
   What, dead, my dove?
    O Pyramus, arise!
     Speak, speak. Quite dumb?
     Dead, dead? A tomb
Must cover thy sweet eyes.
   These lily lips,
   This cherry nose,
These yellow cowslip cheeks,
   Are gone, are gone: 340
   Lovers, make moan:
His eyes were green as leeks.
   O Sisters Three,
   Come, come to me,
With hands as pale as milk;
   Lay them in gore,
   Since you have shore
With shears his thread of silk.
   Tongue, not a word:
   Come, trusty sword; 350
Come, blade, my breast imbrue:[112]
(*Stabs herself.*)
   And, farewell, friends;
   Thus Thisby ends:
   Adieu, adieu, adieu. (*Dies.*)

THESEUS. Moonshine and Lion are left to bury the dead.

DEMETRIUS. Ay, and Wall too.

BOTTOM (*starting up*). No, I assure you; the wall is down that parted their fathers. Will it please you to see the epilogue, or to hear a Bergomask dance between two of our company? 360

THESEUS. No epilogue, I pray you; for your play needs no excuse. Never excuse; for when the players are all dead, there need none to be blamed. Marry, if he that writ it had played Pyramus and hanged himself in Thisby's garter, it would have been a fine tragedy: and so it is, truly; and very notably discharged. But, come, your Bergomask; let your epilogue alone. (*A dance.*)
The iron tongue of midnight hath told
   twelve: 370
Lovers, to bed; 'tis almost fairy time.
I fear we shall out-sleep the coming morn
As much as we this night have over-
   watch'd.
This palpable-gross play hath well be-
   guiled
The heavy gait of night. Sweet friends,
   to bed.
A fortnight hold we this solemnity,
In nightly revels and new jollity.
(*Exeunt.*)
(*Enter* PUCK.)

PUCK. Now the hungry lion roars,
   And the wolf behowls the moon;
Whilst the heavy ploughman snores, 380
   All with weary task fordone.
Now the wasted brands do glow,
   Whilst the screech-owl, screeching
     loud,
Puts the wretch that lies in woe
   In remembrance of a shroud.
Now it is the time of night
   That the graves all gaping wide,
Every one lets forth his sprite,
   In the church-way paths to glide:
And we fairies, that do run 390
   By the triple Hecate's[113] team,
From the presence of the sun,
   Following darkness like a dream,
Now are frolic: not a mouse
Shall disturb this hallow'd house:
I am sent with broom before,
To sweep the dust behind the door.
(*Enter* OBERON *and* TITANIA *with their train.*)

OBERON. Through the house give
   glimmering light,
   By the dead and drowsy fire:
   Every elf and fairy sprite 400
     Hop as light as bird from brier;

---

[112] soak with blood

[113] Hecate in her heavenly, earthly, and hellish aspects

And this ditty, after me,
Sing, and dance it trippingly.

TITANIA. First, rehearse your song by rote,
To each word a warbling note:
Hand in hand, with fairy grace,
Will we sing, and bless this place.

(*Song and dance.*)

OBERON. Now, until the break of day,
Through this house each fairy stray.
To the best bride-bed will we,   *410*
Which by us shall blessèd be;
And the issue there create
Ever shall be fortunate.
So shall all the couples three
Ever true in loving be;
And the blots of Nature's hand
Shall not in their issue stand;
Never mole, hare lip, nor scar,
Nor mark prodigious,[114] such as are
Despisèd in nativity,   *420*
Shall upon their children be.
With this field-dew consecrate,
Every fairy take his gait;
And each several chamber bless,
Through this palace, with sweet peace;
And the owner of it blest
Ever shall in safety rest.
Trip away; make no stay;
Meet me all by break of day.   *429*

(*Exeunt* OBERON, TITANIA, *and train.*)

PUCK. If we shadows have offended,
Think but this, and all is mended,
That you have but slumber'd here
While these visions did appear.
And this weak and idle theme,
No more yielding but a dream,
Gentles, do not reprehend:
If you pardon, we will mend:
And, as I am an honest Puck,
If we have unearnèd luck   *439*
Now to 'scape the serpent's tongue,[115]
We will make amends ere long;
Else the Puck a liar call:
So, good night unto you all.
Give me your hands, if we be friends,
And Robin shall restore amends.

(*Exit.*)

[114] unnatural

[115] hissing

HENRIK IBSEN • 1828–1906

Hedda Gabler

TRANSLATED BY OTTO REINERT

CAST OF CHARACTERS

JØRGEN TESMAN, *University Research Fellow in the History of Civilization.*
HEDDA, *his wife.*
MISS JULIANE TESMAN, *his aunt.*
MRS. ELVSTED.
JUDGE BRACK.
EILERT LØVBORG.
BERTE, *the Tesman's maid.*

SCENE: *The Tesman's villa in a fashionable residential section of the town.*

Act One

(*A spacious, handsome, tastefully furnished room. Dark décor. In the rear, a wide doorway with open portieres. Beyond is a smaller room, furnished in the same style as the front room. A door, right, leads to the front hall. Left, French doors, with portieres drawn aside, through which can be seen a part of a roofed verandah and trees with autumn foliage. Front center, an oval table covered with a cloth. Chairs around it. Front right, a wide, dark, porcelain stove, a high-backed easy chair, a footstool with a pillow, and two ottomans. In the corner far right, a sofa and a small, round table. Front left, a sofa, set out from the wall. Far left, beyond the French doors, an upright piano. On both sides of the doorway, rear center, whatnots with knickknacks. Against the rear wall of the inner room, a sofa, and in front of it a table and two chairs. Above the sofa, a portrait of a handsome, elderly man in general's uniform. Over the table hangs a lamp with milky, white glass. There are several bouquets of flowers, in vases and glasses, in various places in the front room. Others are lying on the tables. Thick carpets on the floors of both rooms. The morning sun is shining through the French doors.*

MISS JULIANE TESMAN, *with hat and parasol, enters right, followed by* BERTE, *who carries a bouquet of flowers wrapped in paper.* MISS TESMAN *is a nice-looking woman of 65, of pleasant mien, neatly but not expensively dressed in a gray suit.* BERTE *is a middle-aged servant girl, of rather plain and countrified appearance.*)

MISS TESMAN (*stops inside the door, listens, says in a low voice*). On my word—I don't think they are even up yet!

BERTE (*also softly*). That's what I told you, miss. When you think how late the steamer got in last night. And afterwards—! Goodness!—all the stuff she wanted unpacked before she turned in.

MISS TESMAN. Well—just let them sleep. But fresh morning air—*that* we can give them when they come in here. (*Goes and opens the French doors wide.*)

BERTE (*by the table, lost, still holding the flowers*). Please, miss—I just don't see a bit of space anywhere! I think I'd better put these over here. (*Puts the flowers down on the piano.*)

MISS TESMAN. Well, well, my dear Berte. So you've got yourself a new mistress now. The good Lord knows it was hard for me to let you go.

BERTE (*near tears*). What about me, then, miss! What shall *I* say? I who have served you and Miss Rina all these blessed years.

MISS TESMAN. We shall just have to make the best of it, Berte. There's nothing else to do. Jørgen can't do without you, you know. He just can't. You've looked after him ever since he was a little boy.

BERTE. Yes, but miss—I'm ever so worried about leaving Miss Rina. The poor dear lying there all helpless. With that new girl and all! She'll never learn how to make things nice and comfortable for an invalid.

MISS TESMAN. Oh yes, you'll see, I'll teach her. And of course, you know, I'll do most of it myself. So don't you worry yourself about my poor sister, Berte.

BERTE. Yes, but there's another thing, too, miss. I'm scared I won't be able to suit young Mrs. Tesman.

MISS TESMAN. Oh, well. Good heavens. So there is a thing or two—Right at first—

BERTE. For I believe she's ever so particular.

MISS TESMAN. Can you wonder? General Gabler's daughter? Just think of the kind of life she was used to when the General was alive. Do you remember when she rode by with her father? That long black riding habit she wore? And the feather in her hat?

BERTE. Oh, I remember, all right. But I'll be blessed if I ever thought she and the young master would make a pair of it.

MISS TESMAN. Nor did I. By the way, while I think of it, Berte. Jørgen has a new title now. From now on you must refer to him as "the Doctor."

BERTE. Yes, the young mistress said something about that, too, last night. Soon as they were inside the door. Then it's really so, miss?

MISS TESMAN. It certainly is. Just think, Berte—they have made him a doctor abroad. During the trip, you know. I hadn't heard a thing about it till last night on the pier.

BERTE. Well, I daresay he could be anything he put his mind to, *he* could—smart as *he* is. But I must say I'd never thought he'd turn to doctoring people, too.

MISS TESMAN. Oh, that's not the kind of doctor he is. (*Nods significantly.*) And as far as that is concerned, there is no telling but pretty soon you may have to call him something grander yet.

BERTE. You don't say! What might that be, miss?

MISS TESMAN (*smiles*). Wouldn't you like to know! (*Moved.*) Ah yes, indeed—! If only dear Jochum could see from his grave what has become of his little boy! (*Looking around.*) But look, Berte—what's this for? Why have you taken off all the slip covers?

BERTE. She told me to. Said she can't stand slip covers on chairs.

MISS TESMAN. Do you think they mean to make this their everyday living room, then?

BERTE. It sure sounded that way. Mrs. Tesman did, I mean. For he—the doctor—he didn't say anything.

(JØRGEN TESMAN *enters from the right side of the inner room. He is humming to himself. He carries an open, empty suitcase. He is of medium height, youthful-looking thirty-three years old, somewhat stoutish. Round, open, cheerful face. Blond hair and beard. He wears glasses and is dressed in a comfortable, rather casual suit.*)

MISS TESMAN. Good morning, good morning, Jørgen!

TESMAN (*in the doorway*). Auntie! Dearest Aunt Julle! (*Comes forward and shakes her hand.*) All the way out here—as early as this! Hm?

MISS TESMAN. Well—I just had to drop in for a moment. To see how you are getting along, you know.

TESMAN. Even though you haven't had a good night's sleep.

MISS TESMAN. Oh, that doesn't matter at all.

TESMAN. But you did get home from the pier all right, I hope. Hm?

MISS TESMAN. Oh yes, certainly I

did, thank you. The Judge was kind enough to see me all the way to my door.

TESMAN. We were so sorry we couldn't give you a ride in our carriage. But you saw for yourself—all the boxes Hedda had.

MISS TESMAN. Yes, she certainly brought quite a collection.

BERTE (*to* TESMAN). Should I go and ask Mrs. Tesman if there's anything I can help her with?

TESMAN. No, thank you, Berte—you'd better not. She said she'll ring if she wants you.

BERTE (*going right*). Well, all right.

TESMAN. But, look—you might take this suitcase with you.

BERTE (*takes it*). I'll put it in the attic.

(*Exits right.*)

TESMAN. Just think, Auntie—that whole suitcase was brimful of copies of old documents. You wouldn't believe me if I told you all the things I have collected from libraries and archives all over. Quaint old items nobody has known anything about.

MISS TESMAN. Well, no, Jørgen. I'm sure you haven't wasted your time on your honeymoon.

TESMAN. No, I think I may say I have not. But take your hat off, Auntie—for goodness' sake. Here! Let me untie the ribbon for you. Hm?

MISS TESMAN (*while he does so*). Ah, God forgive me, if this isn't just as if you were still at home with us!

TESMAN (*inspecting the hat*). My, what a fine-looking hat you've got yourself!

MISS TESMAN. I bought it for Hedda's sake.

TESMAN. For Hedda's sake? Hm?

MISS TESMAN. So she won't need to feel ashamed of me if we ever go out together.

TESMAN (*patting her cheek*). If you don't think of everything, Auntie! (*Puts the hat down on a chair by the table.*) And now—over here to the sofa—we'll just sit and chat for a while till Hedda comes.

(*They seat themselves. She places her parasol in the corner by the sofa.*)

MISS TESMAN (*takes both his hands in hers and gazes at him*). What a blessing it is to have you back again, Jørgen, big as life! You—Jochum's little boy!

TESMAN. For me, too, Aunt Julle. To see you again. For you have been both father and mother to me.

MISS TESMAN. Ah, yes—don't you think I know you'll always keep a spot in your heart for these two old aunts of yours!

TESMAN. So Aunt Rina isn't any better, hm?

MISS TESMAN. Oh no. We mustn't look for improvement in her case, poor dear. She is lying there just as she has been all these years. Just the same, may the good Lord keep her for me a long time yet! For else I just wouldn't know what to do with myself, Jørgen. Especially now, when I don't have you to look after any more.

TESMAN (*pats her back*). There, there, now!

MISS TESMAN (*changing tone*). And to think that you are a married man, Jørgen! And that you were the one to walk off with Hedda Gabler. The lovely Hedda Gabler. Just think! As many admirers as she had!

TESMAN (*hums a little, smiles contentedly*). Yes, I daresay I have quite a few good friends here in town who'd gladly be in my shoes, hm?

MISS TESMAN. And such a lovely, long honeymoon you had! More than five—almost six months!

TESMAN. Well, you know—for me it has been a kind of study tour as well. All the collections I had to go through. And the books I had to read!

MISS TESMAN. Yes, I suppose. (*More confidentially, her voice lowered a little.*) But listen, Jørgen—haven't you got something—something special to tell me?

TESMAN. About the trip?

MISS TESMAN. Yes.

TESMAN. No—I don't know of anything besides what I wrote in my letters. They gave me a doctor's degree down there—but I told you that last night; I'm sure I did.

MISS TESMAN. Well, yes, that sort of thing—What I mean is—don't you have certain—certain—expectations?

TESMAN. Expectations?

MISS TESMAN. Ah for goodness' sake, Jørgen! I am your old Auntie, after all!

TESMAN. Certainly I have expectations.

MISS TESMAN. Well!!

TESMAN. I fully expect to be made a professor one of these days.

MISS TESMAN. Professor—oh yes—

TESMAN. I may even say I am quite certain of it. But dear Aunt Julle—you know this just as well as I do!

MISS TESMAN (*laughing a little*). Of course I do. You're quite right. (*Changing topic.*) But we were talking about the trip. It must have cost a great deal of money—hm, Jørgen?

TESMAN. Well, now; you know that large stipend went quite a long way.

MISS TESMAN. I just don't see how you made it do for both of you, though.

TESMAN. No, I suppose that's not so easy to understand, hm?

MISS TESMAN. Particularly with a lady along. For I have always heard that is ever so much more expensive.

TESMAN. Well, yes, naturally. That *is* rather more expensive. But Hedda had to have this trip, Auntie! She really had to. Nothing less would do.

MISS TESMAN. No, I daresay. For a wedding journey is quite the thing these days. But now tell me—have you had a chance to look around here yet?

TESMAN. I certainly have. I have been up and about ever since dawn.

MISS TESMAN. And what do you think of it all?

TESMAN. Delightful! Perfectly delightful! The only thing is I don't see what we are going to do with the two empty rooms between the second sitting room in there and Hedda's bedroom.

MISS TESMAN (*with a chuckle*). Oh my dear Jørgen—you may find them useful enough—when the time comes!

TESMAN. Of course, you're right, Auntie! As my library expands, hm?

MISS TESMAN. Quite so, my dear boy. It was your library I was thinking of.

TESMAN. But I'm really most happy on Hedda's behalf. For you know, before we were engaged she used to say she wouldn't care to live anywhere but in Secretary Falk's house.

MISS TESMAN. Yes, just think—wasn't that a lucky coincidence, that it was up for sale right after you had left?

TESMAN. Yes, Aunt Julle. We've certainly been lucky. Hm?

MISS TESMAN. But it will be expensive, my dear Jørgen. Terribly expensive—all this.

TESMAN (*looks at her, a bit crestfallen*). Yes, I daresay it will, Auntie.

MISS TESMAN. Heavens, yes!

TESMAN. How much, do you think? Roughly. Hm?

MISS TESMAN. No, I couldn't possibly say till all the bills arrive.

TESMAN. Well, anyway, Judge Brack managed to get very reasonable terms for us. He said so himself in a letter to Hedda.

MISS TESMAN. Yes, and I won't have you uneasy on that account, Jørgen. Besides, I have given security for the furniture and the carpets.

TESMAN. Security? You? But dear Aunt Julle—what kind of security could you give?

MISS TESMAN. The annuity.

TESMAN (*jumps up*). What! Your and Aunt Rina's annuity?

MISS TESMAN. Yes. I didn't know what else to do, you see.

TESMAN (*standing before her*). But are you clear out of your mind, Auntie! That annuity—that's all the two of you have to live on!

MISS TESMAN. Oh well, there's nothing to get so excited about, I'm sure. It's all just a matter of form, you know. That's what the Judge said, too. For he was kind enough to arrange the whole thing for me. Just a matter of form—those were his words.

TESMAN. That's all very well. Still—

MISS TESMAN. For now you'll have your own salary, you know. And, goodness—what if we do have a few expenses—Help out a bit right at first—? That would only be a joy for us—

TESMAN. Oh, Auntie! When will you ever stop making sacrifices for my sake!

MISS TESMAN (*gets up, puts her hands on his shoulders*). But what other happiness do I have in this world than being able to smooth your way a little, my own dear boy? You, who haven't had either father or mother to lean on? And now the goal is in sight, Jørgen. Things may have looked black at times. But heaven be praised: you're on top now!

TESMAN. Yes, it's really quite remarkable the way things have worked out.

MISS TESMAN. Yes—and those who were against you—who tried to block your way—now they are tasting defeat. They are down, Jørgen! He, the most dangerous of them all, his fall was the greatest! He made his bed, and now he is lying in it—poor, lost wretch that he is!

TESMAN. Have you had any news about Eilert? Since I went away, I mean?

MISS TESMAN. Just that he is supposed to have published a new book.

TESMAN. What! Eilert Løvborg? Recently? Hm?

MISS TESMAN. That's what they say. But I wonder if there can be much to it. What do you think? Ah—but when *your* new book comes, that will be something quite different, Jørgen! What is it going to be about?

TESMAN. It will deal with the domestic industries of Brabant during the Middle Ages.

MISS TESMAN. Just think—being able to write about something like that!

TESMAN. But as far as that is concerned, it may be quite some time before it is ready. I have all these collections to put in order first, you see.

MISS TESMAN. Yes, collecting and putting things in order—you certainly know how to do that. In that you are your father's son.

TESMAN. Well, I must say I am looking forward to getting started. Particularly now, that I've got my own delightful home to work in.

MISS TESMAN. And most of all now that you have the one your heart desired, dear Jørgen.

TESMAN (*embracing her*). Oh yes, yes, Aunt Julle! Hedda—she is the most wonderful part of it all! (*Looks toward the doorway.*) There—I think she is coming now, hm?

(HEDDA *enters from the left side of the inner room. She is twenty-nine years old. Both features and figure are noble and elegant. Pale, ivory complexion. Steel-gray eyes, expressive of cold, clear calm. Beautiful brown hair, though not particularly ample. She is dressed in a tasteful, rather loose-fitting morning costume.*)

MISS TESMAN (*going toward her*). Good morning, my dear Hedda! A very happy morning to you!

HEDDA (*giving her hand*). Good morning, dear Miss Tesman! So early a call? That is most kind.

MISS TESMAN (*seems slightly embarrassed*). And—has the little lady of the house slept well the first night in her new home?

HEDDA. Passably, thank you.

TESMAN (*laughs*). Passably! You are a good one, Hedda! You were sleeping like a log when I got up.

HEDDA. Fortunately. And then, of course, Miss Tesman, it always takes time to get used to new surroundings. That has to come gradually. (*Looks left.*)

Oh dear. The maid has left the verandah doors wide open. There's a veritable flood of sunlight in here.

MISS TESMAN (*toward the doors*). Well, then, we'll just close them.

HEDDA. No, no, not that. Tesman, dear, please pull the curtains. That will give a softer light.

TESMAN (*over by the French doors*). Yes, dear. There, now! Now you have both shade and fresh air, Hedda.

HEDDA. We certainly can use some air in here. Such loads of flowers—But, Miss Tesman, please—won't you be seated?

MISS TESMAN. No thanks. I just wanted to see if everything was all right—and so it is, thank goodness. I had better get back to Rina. I know she is waiting for me, poor thing.

TESMAN. Be sure to give her my love, Auntie. And tell her I'll be around to see her later today.

MISS TESMAN. I'll certainly do that! —Oh my! I almost forgot! (*Searches the pocket of her dress.*) I have something for you, Jørgen. Here.

TESMAN. What's that, Auntie? Hm?

MISS TESMAN (*pulls out a flat parcel wrapped in newspaper and gives it to him*). Here you are, dear.

TESMAN (*opens the parcel*). Well, well, well! So you took care of them for me, Aunt Julle! Hedda! Now, isn't that sweet, hm?

HEDDA (*by the whatnot, right*). If you'd tell me what it is—

TESMAN. My old slippers! *You* know!

HEDDA. Oh really? I remember you often talked about them on the trip.

TESMAN. Yes, for I missed them so. (*Walks over to her.*) Here—now you can see what they're like, Hedda.

HEDDA (*crosses toward stove*). Thanks. I don't know that I really care.

TESMAN (*following*). Just think— Aunt Rina embroidered these slippers for me. Ill as she was. You can't imagine how many memories they hold for me!

HEDDA (*by the table*). Hardly for me.

MISS TESMAN. That's true, you know, Jørgen.

TESMAN. Yes, but—I just thought that now that she's one of the family—

HEDDA (*interrupting*). I don't think we'll get on with that maid, Tesman.

MISS TESMAN. Not get on with Berte?

TESMAN. Whatever makes you say that, dear? Hm?

HEDDA (*points*). Look—she has left her old hat on the chair over there.

TESMAN (*appalled, drops the slippers*). But Hedda—!

HEDDA. What if somebody were to come and see it!

TESMAN. No, no, Hedda—that's Aunt Julle's hat!

HEDDA. Oh?

MISS TESMAN (*picking up the hat*). Yes, indeed it is. And it isn't old either, my dear young lady.

HEDDA. I really didn't look that closely—

MISS TESMAN (*tying the ribbons*). I want you to know that this is the first time I have it on my head. On my word it is!

TESMAN. And very handsome it is, too. Really a splendid-looking hat!

MISS TESMAN. Oh, I don't know that it is anything so special, Jørgen. (*Looks around.*) My parasol—? Ah, here it is. (*Picks it up.*) For that is mine, too. (*Mutters.*) Not Berte's.

TESMAN. New hat and new parasol! What do you think of that, Hedda!

HEDDA. Very nice indeed.

TESMAN. Yes, don't you think so? Hm? But, Auntie, take a good look at Hedda before you leave. See how pretty and blooming she looks.

MISS TESMAN. Dear me, Jørgen; that's nothing new. Hedda has been lovely all her days.

(*She nods and walks right.*)

TESMAN (*following*). Yes, but have you noticed how full-figured and healthy she looks after the trip? How she has filled out?

HEDDA (*crossing*). Oh—stop it!

MISS TESMAN (*halts, turns around*). Filled out?

TESMAN. Yes, Aunt Julle. You can't see it so well now when she wears that dress. But I, who have the opportunity—

HEDDA (*by the French doors, impatiently*). Oh, you have no opportunity at all!

TESMAN. It must be the mountain air in Tyrol.

HEDDA (*curtly interrupting*). I am just as I was when I left.

TESMAN. Yes, so you say. I just don't think you're right. What do you think, Auntie?

MISS TESMAN (*has folded her hands, gazes at* HEDDA). Lovely—lovely—lovely! that is what Hedda is. (*Goes over to her, inclines her head forward with both her hands, and kisses her hair.*) God bless and keep Hedda Tesman. For Jørgen's sake.

HEDDA (*gently freeing herself*). There, *there,* Now let me go.

MISS TESMAN (*in quiet emotion*). Every single day I'll be over and see you two.

TESMAN. Yes, please do, Auntie. Hm?

MISS TESMAN. Goodbye, goodbye! (*She leaves through door, right.* TESMAN *sees her out. The door remains ajar.* TESMAN *is heard repeating his greetings for* AUNT RINA *and his thanks for the slippers. In the meantime,* HEDDA *paces up and down, raises her arms, clenching her fists, as in quiet rage. Opens the curtains by the French doors and stands looking out. In a few moments,* TESMAN *re-enters and closes the door behind him.*)

TESMAN (*picking up the slippers*). What are you looking at, Hedda?

HEDDA (*once again calm and controlled*). Just the leaves. They are so yellow. And so withered.

TESMAN (*wrapping the slippers in their paper, putting the parcel down on the table*). Well, you know—we're in September now.

HEDDA (*again restless*). Yes—just think. We are already in—September.

TESMAN. Don't you think Aunt Julle acted strange, Hedda? Almost solemn. I wonder why. Hm?

HEDDA. I hardly know her, you see. Isn't she often like that?

TESMAN. Not the way she was today.

HEDDA (*turning away from the French doors*). Do you think she minded that business with the hat?

TESMAN. Oh, I don't think so. Not much. Perhaps a little bit right at the moment—

HEDDA. Well, I'm sorry, but I must say it strikes me as very odd—putting her hat down here in the living room. One just doesn't do that.

TESMAN. Well, you may be sure Aunt Julle won't ever do it again.

HEDDA. Anyway, I'll make it up to her, somehow.

TESMAN. Oh yes, Hedda; if only you would!

HEDDA. When you go over there today, why don't you ask her over for tonight?

TESMAN. I'll certainly do that. And then there is one other thing you could do that she'd appreciate ever so much.

HEDDA. What?

TESMAN. If you could just bring yourself to call her Auntie. For my sake, Hedda, hm?

HEDDA. No, Tesman, no. You really mustn't ask me to do that. I have already told you I won't. I'll try to call her Aunt Juliane. That will have to do.

TESMAN. All right, if you say so. I just thought that now that you're in the family—

HEDDA. Hmmm—I don't know about that—

(*She walks toward the doorway.*)

TESMAN (*after a brief pause*). Anything the matter, Hedda? Hm?

HEDDA. I'm just looking at my old piano. It doesn't quite go with the other furniture in here.

TESMAN. As soon as I get my first pay check we'll have it traded in.

HEDDA. No—I don't want to do that. I want to keep it. But let's put it in this inner room and get another one for out here. Whenever it's convenient, I mean.

TESMAN (*a little taken back*). Well—yes—we could do that—

HEDDA (*picks up the bouquet from the piano*). These flowers weren't here last night.

TESMAN. I suppose Aunt Julle brought them for you.

HEDDA (*looking at the flowers*). There's a card here. (*Takes it out and reads.*) "Will be back later." Can you guess who it's from?

TESMAN. No. Who? Hm?

HEDDA. Thea Elvsted.

TESMAN. No, really? Mrs. Elvsted! Miss Rysing that was.

HEDDA. That's right. The one with that irritating head of hair she used to show off with. An old flame of yours, I understand.

TESMAN (*laughs*). Well, now—that didn't last long! Anyway, that was before I knew you, Hedda. Just think—her being in town.

HEDDA. Strange, that she'd call on us. I have hardly seen her since we went to school together.

TESMAN. As far as that goes, I haven't seen her either for—God knows how long. I don't see how she can stand living in that out-of-the-way place. Hm?

HEDDA (*suddenly struck by a thought*). Listen, Tesman—isn't it some place near there that he lives—what's his name—Eilert Løvborg?

TESMAN. Yes, that's right. He is up there, too.

(BERTE *enters right.*)

BERTE. Ma'am, she's here again, that lady who brought those flowers a while back. (*Pointing.*) The flowers you're holding in your hand, ma'am.

HEDDA. Ah, she is? Well, show her in, please.

(BERTE *opens the door for* MRS. ELVSTED *and exits.* MRS. ELVSTED *is of slight build, with a pretty, soft face. Her eyes are light blue, large, round, rather prominent, of a timid and querying expression. Her hair is strikingly light in color, almost whitish, and unusually rich and wavy. She is a couple of years younger than* HEDDA. *She is dressed in a dark visiting dress, tasteful, but not quite in the most recent fashion.*)

HEDDA (*walks toward her. Friendly*). Good morning, my dear Mrs. Elvsted. How very nice to see you again.

MRS. ELVSTED (*nervous, trying not to show it*). Well, yes, it is quite some time since we met.

TESMAN (*shaking hands*). And we, too. Hm?

HEDDA. Thank you for your lovely flowers—

MRS. ELVSTED. Please, don't—I would have come here yesterday afternoon. But I was told you were still traveling—

TESMAN. You've just arrived in town, hm?

MRS. ELVSTED. I got here yesterday, at noon. Oh, I was quite desperate when I learned you weren't home.

HEDDA. Desperate? But why?

TESMAN. But my dear Mrs. Rysing —I mean Mrs. Elvsted—

HEDDA. There is nothing wrong, I hope?

MRS. ELVSTED. Yes there is. And I don't know a single soul other than you that I can turn to here.

HEDDA (*putting the flowers down on the table*). Come—let's sit down here on the sofa.

MRS. ELVSTED. Oh, I'm in no mood to sit!

HEDDA. Of course you are. Come on. (*She pulls* MRS. ELVSTED *over to the sofa and sits down next to her.*)

TESMAN. Well, now, Mrs.—? Exactly what—?

HEDDA. Has something—special happened at home?

MRS. ELVSTED. Well, yes—and no.

Oh, but I am so afraid you are going to misunderstand!

HEDDA. In that case, it seems to me you ought to tell us exactly what has happened, Mrs. Elvsted.

TESMAN. After all, that's why you are here. Hm?

MRS. ELVSTED. Yes, yes, of course. Well, then, maybe you already know—Eilert Løvborg is in town.

HEDDA. Is Løvborg—!

TESMAN. No! You don't say! Just think, Hedda—Løvborg's back!

HEDDA. All right. I can hear.

MRS. ELVSTED. He has been here a week already. Imagine—a whole week! In this dangerous place. Alone! With all that bad company around.

HEDDA. But my dear Mrs. Elvsted—why is he a concern of yours?

MRS. ELVSTED (*with an apprehensive look at her, says quickly*). He tutored the children.

HEDDA. Your children?

MRS. ELVSTED. My husband's. I don't have any.

HEDDA. In other words, your stepchildren.

MRS. ELVSTED. Yes.

TESMAN (*with some hesitation*). But was he—I don't quite know how to put this—was he sufficiently—regular—in his way of life to be thus employed? Hm?

MRS. ELVSTED. For the last two years, there hasn't been a thing to object to in his conduct.

TESMAN. No, really? Just think, Hedda!

HEDDA. I hear.

MRS. ELVSTED. Not the least little bit, I assure you! Not in any respect. And yet—knowing he's here—in the big city —And with all that money, too! I'm scared to death!

TESMAN. But in that case, why didn't he remain with you and your husband? Hm?

MRS. ELVSTED. After his book came out, he was too restless to stay.

TESMAN. Ah yes, that's right. Aunt Julle said he has published a new book.

MRS. ELVSTED. Yes, a big new book, about the course of civilization in general. It came out about two weeks ago. And since it has had such big sales and been discussed so much and made such a big splash—

TESMAN. It has, has it? I suppose this is something he has had lying around from better days?

MRS. ELVSTED. You mean from earlier?

TESMAN. Yes.

MRS. ELVSTED. No; it's all been written since he came to stay with us. During this last year.

TESMAN. Well, now! That's very good news, Hedda! Just think!

MRS. ELVSTED. Yes, if it only would last!

HEDDA. Have you seen him since you came to town?

MRS. ELVSTED. No, not yet. I had a great deal of trouble finding his address. But this morning I finally tracked him down.

HEDDA. (*looks searchingly at her*). Isn't it rather odd that your husband—hm—

MRS. ELVSTED (*with a nervous start*). My husband! What about him?

HEDDA. That he sends you to town on such an errand? That he doesn't go and look after his friend himself?

MRS. ELVSTED. Oh, no, no—my husband doesn't have time for things like that. Besides, I have some—some shopping to do, anyway.

HEDDA (*with a slight smile*). Well, in that case, of course—

MRS. ELVSTED (*getting up, restlessly*) And now I beg of you, Mr. Tesman—won't you please receive Eilert Løvborg nicely if he calls on you? And I am sure he will. After all—Such good friends as you two used to be. And then you both do the same kind of work—the same studies, as far as I know.

TESMAN. We used to, at any rate.

MRS. ELVSTED. Yes. And that's why I implore you to please, please, try to keep an eye on him—you too. You'll do that, Mr. Tesman, won't you? Promise?

TESMAN. With the greatest pleasure, Mrs. Rysing.

HEDDA. Elvsted.

TESMAN. I'll gladly do as much for Eilert as I possibly can. You may certainly count on that.

MRS. ELVSTED. Oh, how good and kind you are! (*Clasps his hands.*) Thank you, thank you, thank you! (*Nervously.*) You see, my husband is so very fond of him.

HEDDA. (*getting up*). You ought to write him a note, Tesman. Maybe he won't come without an invitation.

TESMAN. Yes, I suppose that would be the right thing to do, Hedda. Hm?

HEDDA. The sooner the better. Right away *I* think.

MRS. ELVSTED (*pleadingly*). If only you would!

TESMAN. I'll write this minute. Do you have his address, Mrs.—Mrs. Elvsted?

MRS. ELVSTED. Yes. (*Pulls a slip of paper from her bag and gives it to him.*) Here it is.

TESMAN. Very good. Well, then, if you'll excuse me—(*Looks around.*) By the way—the slippers? Ah, here we are. (*Leaving with the parcel.*)

HEDDA. Be sure you write a nice, warm, friendly letter, Tesman. And a long one, too.

TESMAN. Certainly, certainly.

MRS. ELVSTED. But not a word that it is I who—!

TESMAN. No, that goes without saying, I should think. Hm? (*Goes out right through inner room.*)

HEDDA (*goes over to* MRS. ELVSTED, *smiles, says in a low voice*). There! We've just killed two birds with one stone.

MRS. ELVSTED. What do you mean?

HEDDA. Didn't you see I wanted him out of the room?

MRS. ELVSTED. Yes, to write that letter—

HEDDA. And to speak to you alone.

MRS. ELVSTED (*flustered*). About the same thing?

HEDDA. Exactly.

MRS. ELVSTED (*anxious*). But there *is* nothing more, Mrs. Tesman! Really, there isn't!

HEDDA. Oh yes, there is. There is considerably more. I can see that much. Over here—We are going to have a real, nice, confidential talk, you and I. (*She forces* MRS. ELVSTED *down in the easy chair and seats herself on one of the ottomans.*)

MRS. ELVSTED (*worried, looks at her watch*). But my dear Mrs. Tesman—I had really thought I would be on my way now.

HEDDA. Oh, I am sure there is no rush. Now, then. Tell me about yourself. How are things at home?

MRS. ELVSTED. That is just what I don't want to talk about.

HEDDA. But to me—! After all, we are old schoolmates.

MRS. ELVSTED. But you were a year ahead of me. And I used to be so scared of you!

HEDDA. Scared of me?

MRS. ELVSTED. Terribly. For when we met on the stairs, you always ruffled my hair.

HEDDA. Did I really?

MRS. ELVSTED. Yes. And once you said you were going to burn it off.

HEDDA. Oh, but you know—I wasn't serious!

MRS. ELVSTED. No, but I was such a silly, then. Anyway. Afterwards we drifted far apart. Our circles are so very different, you know.

HEDDA. All the more reason for getting close again. Listen. In school we called each other by our first names.

MRS. ELVSTED. Oh I'm sure you're wrong—

HEDDA. I'm sure I'm not! I remember

it quite clearly. And now we want to be open with one another, just the way we used to. (*Moves the ottoman closer.*) There now! (*Kisses her cheek.*) You call me Hedda.

MRS. ELVSTED (*seizes her hands*). Oh, you are so good and kind! I'm not used to that.

HEDDA. There, there! And I'll call you my dear Thora, just as in the old days.

MRS. ELVSTED. My name is Thea.

HEDDA. So it is. Of course. I meant Thea. (*Looks at her with compassion.*) So you're not much used to goodness and kindness, Thea? Not in your own home?

MRS. ELVSTED. If I even had a home! But I don't. I never have had one.

HEDDA (*looks at her for a moment*). I thought there might be something like this.

MRS. ELVSTED (*helplessly, looking straight ahead*). Yes—yes—yes—

HEDDA. I am not sure if I quite remember—Didn't you first come to your husband as his housekeeper?

MRS. ELVSTED. I was really hired as governess. But his wife—his first wife—was ailing already then and was practically bedridden. So I had to take charge of the household as well.

HEDDA. But in the end you became his wife.

MRS. ELVSTED (*dully*). So I did.

HEDDA. Let's see. How long ago is that?

MRS. ELVSTED. Since my marriage?

HEDDA. Yes.

MRS. ELVSTED. About five years.

HEDDA. Right. It must be that long.

MRS. ELVSTED. Oh, those five years! Or mostly the last two or three! Oh, Mrs. Tesman—if you could just imagine!

HEDDA (*slaps her hand lightly*). Mrs. Tesman? Shame on you!

MRS. ELVSTED. Oh yes, all right; I'll try. Yes—if you could just—conceive—understand—

HEDDA (*casually*). And Eilert Løvborg has been living near you for some three years or so, hasn't he?

MRS. ELVSTED (*looks at her uncertainly*). Eilert Løvborg? Yes—he has.

HEDDA. Did you know him before? Here in town?

MRS. ELVSTED. Hardly at all. That is, of course I did in a way. I mean, I knew *of* him.

HEDDA. But up there—You saw a great deal of him; did you?

MRS. ELVSTED. Yes, he came over to us every day. He was supposed to tutor the children, you see. For I just couldn't do it all by myself.

HEDDA. Of course not. And your husband—? I suppose he travels quite a bit.

MRS. ELVSTED. Well, yes, Mrs. Tes—Hedda—as a public magistrate, you know, he very often has to travel all over his district.

HEDDA (*leaning against the armrest on the easy chair*). Thea—poor, sweet Thea—now you have to tell me everything—just as it is.

MRS. ELVSTED. You'd better ask me, then.

HEDDA. How *is* your husband, Thea? I mean—you know—*really?* To be with. What kind of person is he? Is he good to you?

MRS. ELVSTED (*evasively*). I believe he thinks he does everything for the best.

HEDDA. But isn't he altogether too old for you? He is more than twenty years older, isn't he?

MRS. ELVSTED (*with irritation*). Yes, there is that, too. But there isn't just one thing. Every single little thing about him repels me! We don't have a thought in common, he and I. Not a thing in the world!

HEDDA. But isn't he fond of you all the same? I mean in his own way?

MRS. ELVSTED. I don't know. I think I am just useful to him. And I don't use much money. I am inexpensive.

HEDDA. That is foolish of you.

MRS. ELVSTED (*shakes her head*).

Can't be changed. Not with him. I don't think he cares for anybody much except himself. Perhaps the children a little.

HEDDA. And Eilert Løvborg, Thea.

MRS. ELVSTED (*looks at her*). Eilert Løvborg? What makes you think that?

HEDDA. Well, it seems to me that when he sends you all the way to town to look after him—(*with an almost imperceptible smile*). Besides, you said so yourself. To Tesman.

MRS. ELVSTED (*with a nervous twitch*). Did I? I suppose I did. (*With a muted outburst.*) No! I might as well tell you now as later. For it's bound to come out, anyway.

HEDDA. But my dear Thea—?

MRS. ELVSTED. All right. My husband doesn't know I've gone!

HEDDA. What! He doesn't know?

MRS. ELVSTED. He wasn't even home. He's away again. Oh, I just couldn't take it any longer, Hedda! It had become utterly impossible. All alone as I was.

HEDDA. So what did you do?

MRS. ELVSTED. I packed some of my things. Just the most necessary. Without telling anybody. And left.

HEDDA. Just like that?

MRS. ELVSTED. Yes. And took the next train to town.

HEDDA. But dearest Thea—how did you dare to do a thing like that!

MRS. ELVSTED (*rises, walks*). What else could I do?

HEDDA. But what do you think your husband will say when you go back?

MRS. ELVSTED (*by the table; looks at her*). Go back to him?

HEDDA. Yes!

MRS. ELVSTED. I'll never go back.

HEDDA (*rises, approaches her slowly*). So you have really, seriously—left everything?

MRS. ELVSTED. Yes. It seemed to me there was nothing else I could do.

HEDDA. And quite openly, too.

MRS. ELVSTED. You can't keep a thing like that secret, anyway.

HEDDA. But what do you think people will say, Thea?

MRS. ELVSTED. In God's name, let them say whatever they like. (*Sits down on the sofa, dully, tired.*) For I have only done what I had to do.

HEDDA (*after a brief silence*). And what do you plan to do with yourself? What sort of work will you do?

MRS. ELVSTED. I don't know yet. I only know I have to live where Eilert Løvborg is. If I am to live at all.

HEDDA (*moves a chair from the table closer to* MRS. ELVSTED, *sits down, strokes her hands*). Thea—tell me. How did this—this friendship between you and Eilert Løvborg—how did it begin?

MRS. ELVSTED. Oh, it grew little by little. I got some sort of power over him.

HEDDA. Oh?

MRS. ELVSTED. He dropped his old ways. Not because I asked him to. I never dared to do that. But I think he must have noticed how I felt about that kind of life. So he changed.

HEDDA (*quickly suppresses a cynical smile*). So you have—rehabilitated him, as they say. Haven't you, Thea?

MRS. ELVSTED. At least, that's what *he* says. On the other hand, he has turned me into a real human being. Taught me to think—and understand—all sorts of things.

HEDDA. Maybe he tutored you, too?

MRS. ELVSTED. No, not tutored exactly. But he talked to me. About so many, many things. And then came that lovely, lovely time when I could share his work with him. He let me help him!

HEDDA. He did?

MRS. ELVSTED. Yes! Whatever he wrote, he wanted us to be together about it.

HEDDA. Just like two good comrades.

MRS. ELVSTED (*with animation*). Comrades!—that's it! Imagine, Hedda—that's just what he called it, too. Oh, I really ought to feel so happy. But I can't. For you see, I don't know if it will last.

HEDDA. You don't trust him any more than that?

MRS. ELVSTED (*heavily*). The shadow of a woman stands between Eilert Løvborg and me.

HEDDA (*tensely, looks at her*). Who?

MRS. ELVSTED. I don't know. Somebody or other from—his past. I don't think he has ever really forgotten her.

HEDDA. What has he told you about it?

MRS. ELVSTED. He has mentioned it only once—just casually.

HEDDA. And what did he say?

MRS. ELVSTED. He said that when they parted she was going to kill him with a gun.

HEDDA (*cold, controlled*). Oh, nonsense. People don't do that sort of thing here.

MRS. ELVSTED. No, I know. And that is why I think it must be that red-headed singer he used to—

HEDDA. Yes, I suppose so.

MRS. ELVSTED. For I remember people said she carried a loaded gun.

HEDDA. Well, then I'm sure it's she.

MRS. ELVSTED (*wringing her hands*). Yes, but just think, Hedda—now I hear that she—that singer—that she's here in town again, too! Oh, I'm just desperate—!

HEDDA (*with a glance toward the inner room*). Shhh; Here's Tesman. (*Rises and whispers.*) Not a word about all this to anybody, Thea!

MRS. ELVSTED (*jumps up*). No, no. For God's sake—!

(TESMAN, *carrying a letter, enters from the right side of the inner room.*)

TESMAN. There, now—here's the missive, all ready to go!

HEDDA. Good. But I believe Mrs. Elvsted wants to be on her way. Wait a moment. I'll see you to the garden gate.

TESMAN. Say, Hedda—do you think Berte could take care of this?

HEDDA (*takes the letter*). I'll tell her. (BERTE *enter right.*)

BERTE. Judge Brack is here and wants to know if you're receiving.

HEDDA. Yes, ask the Judge please to come in. And—here—drop this in a mailbox, will you?

BERTE (*takes the letter*). Yes, ma'am. (*She opens the door for* JUDGE BRACK *and exits. The* JUDGE *is forty-five years of age. Rather thickset, but well-built and with brisk, athletic movements. Roundish face, aristocratic profile. His hair is short, still almost completely black, very neatly dressed. Lively, sparkling eyes. Thick eyebrows and mustache with cut-off points. He is dressed in an elegant suit, a trifle youthful for his age. He wears pince-nez glasses, attached to a string, and lets them drop from time to time.*)

JUDGE BRACK (*hat in hand, salutes*). May one pay one's respects as early as this?

HEDDA. One certainly may.

TESMAN (*shaking his hand*). You are always welcome. (*Introducing.*) Judge Brack—Miss Rysing—

HEDDA (*groans*).

BRACK (*bowing*). Delighted!

HEDDA (*looks at him, laughs*). How nice it is to see you in daylight, Judge!

BRACK. You find me changed, perhaps?

HEDDA. A bit younger, I think.

BRACK. Much obliged.

TESMAN. But what do you think of Hedda? Hm? Did you ever see her in such bloom? She positively—

HEDDA. Will you please leave me out of this? You had better thank the Judge for all the trouble he has taken.

BRACK. Oh, nonsense. It's been a pleasure.

HEDDA. Yes, you are indeed a faithful soul. But my friend here is dying to be off. Don't leave, Judge. I'll be back in a minute.

(*Mutual goodbyes.* MRS. ELVSTED *and* HEDDA *exit, right.*)

BRACK. Well, now—your wife—is she tolerably satisfied?

TESMAN. Yes, indeed, and we really can't thank you enough. That is, I understand there will have to be some slight changes made here and there. And there are still a few things—just a few trifles—we'll have to get.

BRACK. Oh? Really?

TESMAN. But we certainly don't want to bother you with that. Hedda said she's going to take care of it herself. But do sit down, hm?

BRACK. Thanks. Maybe just for a moment—(*sits down by the table*). There's one thing I'd like to talk to you about, my dear Tesman.

TESMAN. Oh? Ah, I see. (*Sits down.*) I suppose it's the serious part of the festivities that's beginning now. Hm?

BRACK. Oh—there's no great rush as far as the money is concerned. Though I must say I wish we could have established ourselves a trifle more economically.

TESMAN. Out of the question, my dear fellow! Remember, it's all for Hedda! You, who know her so well—! After all, I couldn't put her up like any little middle-class housewife—

BRACK. No, I suppose—That's just it.

TESMAN. Besides—fortunately—it can't be long now before I receive my appointment.

BRACK. Well, you know—things like that have a way of hanging fire.

TESMAN. Perhaps you have heard something? Something definite? Hm?

BRACK. No, nothing certain—(*interrupting himself*). But that reminds me. I have some news for you.

TESMAN. Oh?

BRACK. Your old friend Eilert Løvborg is back in town.

TESMAN. I know that already.

BRACK. So? Who told you?

TESMAN. The lady who just left.

BRACK. I see. What did you say her name was again? I didn't quite catch—

TESMAN. Mrs. Elvsted.

BRACK. Ah yes—the Commissioner's wife. Yes, it's up in her part of the country that Løvborg has been staying, too.

TESMAN. And just think. I am so glad to hear it. He is quite respectable again.

BRACK. Yes, so they say.

TESMAN. And he has published a new book, hm?

BRACK. Oh yes.

TESMAN. Which is making quite a stir.

BRACK. Quite an unusual stir.

TESMAN. Just think! Isn't that just wonderful! He—with his remarkable gifts. And I was so sure he'd gone under for good.

BRACK. That seems to have been the general opinion.

TESMAN. What I don't understand, though, is what he is going to do with himself. What sort of living can he make? Hm?

(*During the last remark* HEDDA *reenters, right.*)

HEDDA (*to* BRACK, *with a scornful little laugh*). Tesman is forever worrying about how people are going to make a living.

TESMAN. Well, you see, we are talking about poor Eilert Løvborg, Hedda.

HEDDA (*with a quick look at him*). You are? (*Sits down in the easy chair by the stove and asks casually,*) What is the matter with him?

TESMAN. Well, you see, I believe he's run through his inheritance a long time ago. And I don't suppose he can write a new book every year. Hm? So I really must ask how he is going to make out.

BRACK. Maybe I could help you answer that.

TESMAN. Yes?

BRACK. Remember, he has relatives with considerable influence.

TESMAN. Ah—unfortunately, those relatives have washed their hands of him long ago.

BRACK. Just the same, they used to call him the hope of the family.

TESMAN. Yes, before! But he has ruined all that.

HEDDA. Who knows? (*With a little smile.*) I hear the Elvsteds have rehabilitated him.

BRACK. And then this book—

TESMAN. Well, I certainly hope they will help him to find something or other. I just wrote him a letter. Hedda, dear, I asked him to come out here tonight.

BRACK. Oh dear, I am sorry. Don't you remember—you're supposed to come to my little stag dinner tonight? You accepted last night on the pier, you know.

HEDDA. Had you forgotten, Tesman?

TESMAN. So I had.

BRACK. Oh well. I'm sure he won't come, so it doesn't really make any difference.

TESMAN. Why is that? Hm?

BRACK (*gets up somewhat hesitantly, rests his hands on the back of the chair*). Dear Tesman—and you, too, Mrs. Tesman—I cannot in good conscience let you remain in ignorance of something, which—which—

TESMAN. Something to do with Eilert?

BRACK. With both you and him.

TESMAN. But my dear Judge, do speak!

BRACK. You must be prepared to find that your appointment will not come through as soon as you hope and expect.

TESMAN (*jumps up, nervously*). Something's happened? Hm?

BRACK. It may conceivably be made contingent upon the result of a competition.

TESMAN. Competition! Just think, Hedda!

HEDDA (*leaning farther back in her chair*). Ah—I see, I see—!

TESMAN. But with whom? Don't tell me with—?

BRACK. Precisely. With Eilert Løvborg.

TESMAN (*claps his hands together*). No, no! This can't be! It is unthinkable! Quite impossible! Hm?

BRACK. All the same, that's the way it may turn out.

TESMAN. No, but Judge, this would amount to the most incredible callousness toward me! (*Waving his arms.*) For just think—I'm a married man! We married on the strength of these prospects, Hedda and I. Got ourselves deep in debt. Borrowed money from Aunt Julle, too. After all, I had practically been promised the post, you know. Hm?

BRACK. Well, well. I daresay you'll get it in the end. If only after a competition.

HEDDA (*motionless in her chair*). Just think, Tesman. It will be like a kind of contest.

TESMAN. But dearest Hedda, how can you be so unconcerned!

HEDDA (*still without moving*). I'm not at all unconcerned. I'm dying to see who wins.

BRACK. In any case, Mrs. Tesman, I'm glad you know the situation for what it is. I mean—before you proceed to make the little additional purchases I understand you threaten us with.

HEDDA. This makes no difference as far as that is concerned.

BRACK. Really? Well, in that case, of course—Goodbye! (*to* TESMAN) I'll pick you up on my afternoon walk.

TESMAN. What? Oh yes, yes, of course. I'm sorry; I'm just all confused.

HEDDA (*without getting up, gives her hand*). Goodbye, Judge. Come back soon.

BRACK. Thanks. Goodbye, goodbye.

TESMAN (*sees him to the door*). Goodbye, my dear Judge. You really must excuse me—

(JUDGE BRACK *exits, right.*)

TESMAN (*pacing the floor*). Oh, Hedda, Hedda! One should never venture into fairyland. Hm?

HEDDA (*looks at him, smiles*). Do *you* do that?

TESMAN. Well, yes—it can't be denied—it was most venturesome of me to rush into marriage and set up a home on the strength of mere prospects.

HEDDA. Well, maybe you're right.

TESMAN. Anyway—we do have our own nice, comfortable home, now. Just think, Hedda—the very home both of us dreamed about. Set our hearts on, I may almost say. Hm?

HEDDA (*rises, slowly, tired*). The agreement was that we were to maintain a certain position—entertain—

TESMAN. Don't I know it! Dearest Hedda—I have been so looking forward to seeing you as hostess in a select circle! Hm? Well, well, well! In the meantime, we'll just have to be content with one another. See Aunt Julle once in a while. Nothing more. And you were meant for such a different kind of life, altogether!

HEDDA. I suppose a footman is completely out of the question.

TESMAN. I'm afraid so. Under the circumstances, you see—we couldn't possibly—

HEDDA. And as for getting my own riding horse—

TESMAN (*aghast*). Riding horse!

HEDDA. I suppose I mustn't even think of that.

TESMAN. Good heavens, no! That goes without saying, I hope!

HEDDA (*walking*). Well—at least I have one thing to amuse myself with in the meantime.

TESMAN (*overjoyed*). Oh thank goodness for that! And what *is* that, Hedda, hm?

HEDDA (*in the doorway, looks at him with suppressed scorn*). My guns—Jørgen!

TESMAN (*in fear*). Your guns!

HEDDA (*with cold eyes*). General Gabler's guns.

(*She exits left, through the inner room.*)

TESMAN (*runs to the doorway, calls after her*). But Hedda! Good gracious! Hedda, dear! Please don't touch those dangerous things! For my sake, Hedda! Hm?

Act Two

(*The same room at the* TESMANS'. *The piano has been moved out and replaced by an elegant little writing desk. A small table has been placed near the sofa, left. Most of the flowers have been removed.* MRS. ELVSTED'S *bouquet is on the big table front center. Afternoon.*

HEDDA, *dressed to receive callers, is alone. She is standing near the open French doors loading a revolver. Its mate is lying in an open case on the desk.*)

HEDDA (*looking down into the garden, calls*). Hello there, Judge! Welcome back!

JUDGE BRACK (*off-stage*). Thanks, Mrs. Tesman!

HEDDA (*raises the gun, sights*). Now I am going to shoot you, Judge Brack!

BRACK (*calls off-stage*). No—no—no! Don't point the gun at me like that!

HEDDA. That's what you get for sneaking in the back door! (*Fires.*)

BRACK (*closer*). Are you out of your mind—!

HEDDA. Oh dear—did I hit you?

BRACK (*still off-stage*). Stop that nonsense!

HEDDA. Come on in, then.

(JUDGE BRACK, *dressed for dinner, enters left. He carries a light overcoat over his arm.*)

BRACK. Dammit! Do you still fool around with that thing? What are you shooting at, anyway?

HEDDA. Oh—just firing off into blue air.

BRACK (*gently but firmly taking the gun away from her*). With your permission, Mrs. Tesman. (*Looks at it.*) Ah yes, I remember this gun very well. (*Looks around.*) Where is the case? Ah, here we are. (*Puts the gun in the case and closes it.*) That's enough of that silliness for today.

HEDDA. But in the name of heaven, what do you expect me to do with myself?

BRACK. No callers?

HEDDA (*closing the French doors*). Not a soul. All my close friends are still out of town, it seems.

BRACK. And Tesman is out, too, perhaps?

HEDDA (*by the desk, puts the gun case in a drawer*). Yes. He took off for the aunts' right after lunch. He didn't expect you so early.

BRACK. I should have thought of that. That was stupid of me.

HEDDA (*turns her head, looks at him*). Why stupid?

BRACK. I would have come a little—sooner.

HEDDA (*crossing*). If you had, you wouldn't have found anybody home. For I have been in my room ever since lunch, changing my clothes.

BRACK. And isn't there the tiniest little opening in the door for negotiations?

HEDDA. You forgot to provide one.

BRACK. Another stupidity.

HEDDA. So we'll have to stay in here. And wait. For I don't think Tesman will be back for some time.

BRACK. By all means. I'll be very patient.

(HEDDA *sits on the sofa in the corner*. BRACK *puts his overcoat over the back of the nearest chair and sits down, keeping his hat in his hand. Brief silence. They look at one another*.)

HEDDA. Well?

BRACK (*in the same tone*). Well?

HEDDA. I said it first.

BRACK (*leans forward a little*). All right. Let's have a nice little chat, Mrs. Tesman.

HEDDA (*leans back*). Don't you think it's an eternity since last time we talked? I don't count last night and this morning. That was nothing.

BRACK. You mean—just the two of us?

HEDDA. Something like that.

BRACK. There hasn't been a day I haven't wished you were back again.

HEDDA. My feelings, exactly.

BRACK. Yours? Really, Mrs. Tesman? And I have been assuming you were having such a wonderful time.

HEDDA. I'd say!

BRACK. All Tesman's letters said so.

HEDDA. Oh yes, he! He's happy just poking through old collections of books. And copying old parchments—or whatever they are.

BRACK (*with a touch of malice*). Well, that's his calling, you know. Partly, anyway.

HEDDA. Yes, so it is. And in that case I suppose—But I! Oh, Judge! You've no idea how bored I've been.

BRACK (*with sympathy*). Really? You're serious?

HEDDA. Surely you can understand that? For a whole half year never to see anyone who knows even a little bit about our circle? And talks our language?

BRACK. Yes, I think I would find that trying, too.

HEDDA. And then the most unbearable thing of all—

BRACK. Well?

HEDDA. —everlastingly to be in the company of the same person—

BRACK (*nods in agreement*). Both early and late—yes. I can imagine—at all possible times—

HEDDA. I said everlastingly.

BRACK. All right. Still, it seems to me that with as excellent a person as our Tesman, it ought to be possible—

HEDDA. My dear Judge—Tesman is a specialist.

BRACK. Granted.

HEDDA. And specialists are not at all entertaining travel companions. Not in the long run, at any rate.

BRACK. Not even—the specialist—one happens to love?

HEDDA. Bah! That nauseating word!

BRACK (*puzzled*). Really, now, Mrs. Tesman—?

HEDDA (*half laughing, half annoyed*). You ought to try it some time! Listening to talk about the history of civilization, early and late—

BRACK. Everlastingly—

HEDDA. All right. And then this business about the domestic industry in the

Middle Ages—! That's the ghastliest part of it all!

BRACK (*looking searchingly at her*). But in that case—tell me—how I am to explain—?

HEDDA. That Jørgen Tesman and I made a pair of it, you mean?

BRACK. If you want to put it that way—yes.

HEDDA. Come now. Do you really find that so strange?

BRACK. Both yes and no—Mrs. Tesman.

HEDDA. I had danced myself tired, my dear Judge. My season was over—(*gives a slight start*). No, no—I don't really mean that. Won't think it, either!

BRACK. Nor do you have the slightest reason to, I am sure.

HEDDA. Oh—as far as reason is concerned—(*looks at him as if trying to read his mind*). And, after all, Jørgen Tesman must be said to be a most proper young man in all respects.

BRACK. Both proper and substantial. Most certainly.

HEDDA. And one can't say there is anything exactly comical about him. Do you think there is?

BRACK. Comical? No—o. I wouldn't say that—

HEDDA. All right, then. And he is a most assiduous collector. Nobody can deny that. I think it is perfectly possible he may go quite far, after all.

BRACK (*looks at her rather uncertainly*). I assumed that you, like everybody else, were convinced that he will in time become an exceptionally eminent man?

HEDDA (*with a weary expression*). Yes, I was. And then, you see—there he was, wanting so desperately to be allowed to provide for me—I don't know why I shouldn't have accepted?

BRACK. No, certainly. From that point of view—

HEDDA. For you know, Judge, that was considerably more than my other admirers were willing to do.

BRACK (*laughs*). Well! Of course I can't answer for all the others. But as far as I am concerned, I have always had a certain degree of—respect for the bonds of matrimony. You know—as a general proposition, Mrs. Tesman.

HEDDA (*lightly*). Well, I never really counted very heavily on *you*—

BRACK. All I want is a nice, confidential circle, in which I can be of service, both in deed and in counsel. Be allowed to come and go like a true and trusted friend—

HEDDA. You mean, of the master of the house—?

BRACK (*with a slight bow*). To be perfectly frank—rather of the mistress. But by all means—the master, too, of course. Do you know, that kind of—shall I say, triangular?—relationship can really be a great comfort to all parties involved.

HEDDA. Yes, many were the times I missed a second travel companion. To be twosome in the compartment—brrr!

BRACK. Fortunately, the wedding trip is over.

HEDDA (*shakes her head*). There's a long journey ahead. I've just arrived at a station on the way.

BRACK. Well, at the station one gets out and moves around a bit, Mrs. Tesman.

HEDDA. I never get out.

BRACK. Really?

HEDDA. No. For there's always someone around, who—

BRACK (*laughs*). —looks at one's legs; is that it?

HEDDA. Exactly.

BRACK. Oh well, really, now—

HEDDA (*with a silencing gesture*). I won't have it! Rather stay in my seat—once I'm seated. Twosome and all.

BRACK. But what if a third party were to join the couple?

HEDDA. Well, now—*that* would be something altogether different!

BRACK. A proven, understanding friend—

HEDDA. —entertaining in all sorts of lively ways—

BRACK. —and not at all a specialist!

HEDDA (*with audible breath*). Yes, that would indeed be a comfort.

BRACK (*hearing the front door open, looking at her*). The triangle is complete.

HEDDA (*half aloud*). And the train goes on.

(TESMAN, *in gray walking suit and soft hat, enters, right. He carries a pile of paperbound books under his arm. Others are stuffed in his pockets.*)

TESMAN (*walks up to the table in front of the corner sofa*). Puuhh—! Quite some load to carry, all this—and in this heat, too. (*Puts the books down.*) I am postively perspiring, Hedda. Well, well. So you're here already, my dear Judge. Hm? And Berte didn't tell me.

BRACK (*rises*). I came through the garden.

HEDDA. What are all those books?

TESMAN (*leafing through some of them*). Just some new publications in my special field.

HEDDA. Special field, hm?

BRACK. Ah yes—professional publications, Mrs. Tesman. (*He and* HEDDA *exchange knowing smiles.*)

HEDDA. Do you still need more books?

TESMAN. Yes, my dear. There is no such thing as having too many books in one's special field. One has to keep up with what is being written and published, you know.

HEDDA. I suppose.

TESMAN (*searching among the books*). And look. Here is Eilert Løvborg's new book, too. (*Offers it to her.*) Want to take a look at it, Hedda? Hm?

HEDDA. No—thanks just the same. Or perhaps later.

TESMAN. I glanced at it on my way home.

BRACK. And what do you think of it? As a specialist yourself?

TESMAN. It is remarkable for its sobriety. He never wrote like that before. (*Gathers up all the books.*) I just want to take these into my study. I am so much looking forward to cutting them open! And then I'll change. (*to* BRACK) I assume there's no rush to be off, is there?

BRACK. Not at all. We have plenty of time.

TESMAN. In that case, I think I'll indulge myself a little. (*On his way out with the books he halts in the doorway and turns.*) That's right, Hedda—Aunt Julle won't be out to see you tonight, after all.

HEDDA. No? Is it that business with the hat, do you think?

TESMAN. Oh, no—not at all. How can you believe a thing like that about Aunt Julle! Just think! No, it's Aunt Rina. She's feeling very poorly.

HEDDA. Isn't she always?

TESMAN. Yes, but it's especially bad today, poor thing.

HEDDA. Well, in that case I suppose she ought to stay home. I shall have to put up with it; that's all.

TESMAN. And you have no idea how perfectly delighted Aunt Julle was, even so. Because of how splendid you look after the trip, Hedda!

HEDDA (*half aloud, rising*). Oh, these everlasting aunts!

TESMAN. Hm?

HEDDA (*walks over to the French doors*). Nothing.

TESMAN. No? All right. Well, excuse me.

(*Exits right, through inner room.*)

BRACK. What is this about a hat?

HEDDA. Oh, something with Miss Tesman this morning. She had put her hat down on the chair over there. (*Looks at him, smiles.*) So I pretended to think it was the maid's.

BRACK (*shakes his head*). But my dear Mrs. Tesman—how could you do a thing like that! And to that excellent old lady, too!

HEDDA (*nervously pacing the floor*). Well, you see—something just takes hold of me at times. And then I can't help myself—(*throws herself down in the easy chair near the stove*). Oh I can't explain it even to myself.

BRACK (*behind her chair*). You aren't really happy—that's the trouble.

HEDDA (*staring into space*). I don't know any reason why I should be. Do you?

BRACK. Well, yes—partly because you've got the home you've always wanted.

HEDDA (*looks up at him and laughs*). So you too believe that story about my great desire?

BRACK. You mean, there is nothing to it?

HEDDA. Well, yes; there is *something* to it.

BRACK. Well?

HEDDA. There is this much to it, that last summer I used Tesman to see me home from evening parties.

BRACK. Unfortunately—my route was in quite a different direction.

HEDDA. True. You walked other roads last summer.

BRACK (*laughs*). Shame on you, Mrs. Tesman! So, all right—you and Tesman—?

HEDDA. One evening we passed by here. And Tesman, poor thing, was practically turning himself into knots trying to find something to talk about. So I felt sorry for all that erudition—

BRACK (*with a doubting smile*). You did? Hm—

HEDDA. I really did. So, just to help him out of his misery, I happened to say that I'd like to live in this house.

BRACK. Just that?

HEDDA. That was all—*that* evening.

BRACK. But afterwards—?

HEDDA. Yes, my frivolity had consequences, Judge.

BRACK. Unfortunately—that's often the way with frivolities. It happens to all of us, Mrs. Tesman.

HEDDA. Thanks! So in our common enthusiasm for Mr. Secretary Falk's villa Tesman and I found each other, you see! The result was engagement and wedding and honeymoon abroad and all the rest of it. Well, yes, my dear Judge—I've made my bed—I almost said.

BRACK. But this is priceless! And you didn't really care for the house at all?

HEDDA. Certainly not.

BRACK. Not even now? After all, we've set up quite a comfortable home for you here, haven't we?

HEDDA. Oh—it seems to me I smell lavender and rose sachets in all the rooms. But maybe that's a smell Aunt Julle brought with her.

BRACK (*laughs*). My guess is rather the late lamented Secretary's wife.

HEDDA. It smells of mortality, whoever it is. Like corsages—the next day. (*Clasps her hands behind her neck, leans back, looks at him.*) Judge, you have no idea how dreadfully bored I'll be—out here.

BRACK. But don't you think life may hold some task for you, too, Mrs. Tesman?

HEDDA. A task? With any kind of appeal?

BRACK. Preferably that, of course.

HEDDA. Heaven knows what kind of task that might be. There are times when I wonder if—(*interrupts herself*). No; I'm sure that wouldn't work, either.

BRACK. Who knows? Tell me.

HEDDA. It has occurred to me that maybe I could get Tesman to enter politics.

BRACK (*laughs*). Tesman! No, really—I must confess that—politics doesn't strike me as being exactly Tesman's line.

HEDDA. I agree. But suppose I were to prevail on him, all the same?

BRACK. What satisfaction could you possibly find in that? If he can't succeed—why do you want him even to try?

HEDDA. Because I am bored, I tell you! (*After a brief pause.*) So you think it's quite out of the question that Tesman could ever become prime minister?

BRACK. Well, you see, Mrs. Tesman

—to do that he'd first of all have to be a fairly wealthy man.

HEDDA (*getting up, impatiently*). Yes! There we are! These shabby circumstances I've married into! (*Crosses the floor.*) That's what makes life so mean. So outright ludicrous! For that's what it is, you know.

BRACK. Personally I believe something else is to blame.

HEDDA. What?

BRACK. You've never been through anything that's really stirred you.

HEDDA. Something serious, you mean?

BRACK. If you like. But maybe it's coming now.

HEDDA (*with a toss of her head*). You are thinking of that silly old professorship! That's Tesman's business. I refuse to give it a thought.

BRACK. As you wish. But now—to put it in the grand style—now when a solemn challenge of responsibility will be posed? Demands made on you? (*Smiles.*) New demands, Mrs. Tesman.

HEDDA (*angry*). Quiet! You'll never see anything of the kind.

BRACK (*cautiously*). We'll talk about this a year from now—on the outside.

HEDDA (*curtly*). I'm not made for that sort of thing, Judge! No demands for me!

BRACK. But surely you, like most women, are made for a duty, which—

HEDDA (*over by the French doors*). Oh, do be quiet! Often it seems to me there's only one thing in the world that I am made for.

BRACK (*coming close*). And may I ask what that is?

HEDDA (*looking out*). To be bored to death. Now you know. (*Turns, looks toward the inner room, laughs.*) Just as I thought. Here comes the professor.

BRACK (*warningly, in a low voice*). Steady, now, Mrs. Tesman!

(TESMAN, *dressed for a party, carrying his hat and gloves, enters from the right side of the inner room.*)

TESMAN. Hedda, any word yet from Eilert Løvborg that he isn't coming, hm?

HEDDA. No.

TESMAN. In that case, I wouldn't be a bit surprised if we have him here in a few minutes.

BRACK. You really think he'll come?

TESMAN. I am almost certain he will. For I'm sure it's only idle gossip what you told me this morning.

BRACK. Oh?

TESMAN. Anyway, that's what Aunt Julle said. She doesn't for a moment believe he'll stand in my way. Just think!

BRACK. I'm very glad to hear that.

TESMAN (*puts his hat and his gloves down on a chair, right*). But you must let me wait for him as long as possible.

BRACK. By all means. We have plenty of time. Nobody will arrive at my place before seven—seven-thirty, or so.

TESMAN. And in the meantime we can keep Hedda company. Take our time. Hm?

HEDDA (*carrying* BRACK'S *hat and coat over to the sofa in the corner*). And if worst comes to worst, Mr. Løvborg can stay here with me.

BRACK (*trying to take the things away from her*). Let me, Mrs. Tesman—What do you mean—"if worst comes to worst?"

HEDDA. If he doesn't want to go with you and Tesman.

TESMAN (*looks dubiously at her*). But, dearest Hedda—do you think that will quite do? He staying here with you? Hm? Remember, Aunt Julle won't be here.

HEDDA. No, but Mrs. Elvsted will. The three of us will have a cup of tea together.

TESMAN. Oh yes; *that* will be perfectly all right!

BRACK (*with a smile*). And perhaps the wiser course of action for him.

HEDDA. What do you mean?

BRACK. Begging your pardon, Mrs. Tesman—you've often enough looked askance at my little stag dinners. It's been your opinion that only men of the firmest principles ought to attend.

HEDDA. I should think Mr. Løvborg is firm-principled enough now. A reformed sinner—

(BERTE *appears in door, right.*)

BERTE. Ma'am—there's a gentleman here who asks if—

HEDDA. Show him in, please.

TESMAN (*softly*). I'm sure it's he! Just think!

(EILERT LØVBORG *enters, right. He is slim, gaunt. Of* TESMAN'S *age, but he looks older and somewhat dissipated. Brown hair and beard. Pale, longish face, reddish spots on the cheekbones. Dressed for visiting in elegant, black, brand-new suit. He carries a silk hat and dark gloves in his hand. He remains near the door, makes a quick bow. He appears a little embarrassed.*)

TESMAN (*goes over to him, shakes his hand*). My dear Eilert—at last we meet again!

EILERT LØVBORG (*subdued voice*). Thanks for your note, Jørgen! (*Approaching* HEDDA.) Am I allowed to shake your hand, too, Mrs. Tesman?

HEDDA (*accepting his proffered hand*). I am very glad to see you, Mr. Løvborg. (*With a gesture.*) I don't know if you two gentlemen—

LØVBORG (*with a slight bow*). Judge Brack, I believe.

BRACK (*also bowing lightly*). Certainly. Some years ago—

TESMAN (*to* LØVBORG, *both hands on his shoulders*). And now I want you to feel quite at home here, Eilert! Isn't that right, Hedda? For you plan to stay here in town, I understand. Hm?

LØVBORG. Yes, I do.

TESMAN. Perfectly reasonable. Listen —I just got hold of your new book, but I haven't had a chance to read it yet.

LØVBORG. You may save yourself the trouble.

TESMAN. Why do you say that?

LØVBORG. There's not much to it.

TESMAN. Just think—you saying that!

BRACK. Nevertheless, people seem to have very good things to say about it.

LØVBORG. That's exactly why I wrote it—so everybody would like it.

BRACK. Very wise of you.

TESMAN. Yes, but Eilert—!

LØVBORG. For I am trying to rebuild my position. Start all over again.

TESMAN (*with some embarrassment*). Yes, I suppose you are, aren't you? Hm?

LØVBORG (*smiles, puts his hat down, pulls a parcel out of his pocket*). When this appears—Jørgen Tesman—this you must read. For this is the real thing. This is me.

TESMAN. Oh really? And what is it?

LØVBORG. The continuation.

TESMAN. Continuation? Of what?

LØVBORG. Of this book.

TESMAN. Of the new book?

LØVBORG. Of course.

TESMAN. But Eilert—you've carried the story all the way up to the present!

LØVBORG. So I have. And this is about the future.

TESMAN. The future! But, heavens— we don't know a thing about the future!

LØVBORG. No, we don't. But there are a couple of things to be said about it all the same. (*Unwraps the parcel.*) Here, let me show you—

TESMAN. But that's not your handwriting.

LØVBORG. I have dictated it. (*Leafs through portions of the manuscript.*) It's in two parts. The first is about the forces that will shape the civilization of the future. And the second (*riffling through more pages*)—about the course that future civilization will take.

TESMAN. How remarkable! It would never occur to me to write anything like that.

HEDDA (*over by the French doors, her fingers drumming the pane*). Hmm— No—

LØVBORG (*replacing the manuscript in

its wrappings and putting it down on the table). I brought it along, for I thought maybe I'd read parts of it aloud to you this evening.

TESMAN. That's very good of you, Eilert. But this evening—? (*Looks at* BRACK.) I'm not quite sure how to arrange that—

LØVBORG. Some other time, then. There's no hurry.

BRACK. You see, Mr. Løvborg, there's a little get-together over at my house tonight. Mainly for Tesman, you know—

LØVBORG (*looking for his hat*). In that case, I certainly won't—

BRACK. No, listen. Won't you do me the pleasure to join us?

LØVBORG (*firmly*). No, I won't. But thanks all the same.

BRACK. Oh come on! Why don't you do that? We'll be a small, select circle. And I think I can promise you a fairly lively evening, as Hed—as Mrs. Tesman would say.

LØVBORG. I don't doubt that. Nevertheless—

BRACK. And you may bring your manuscript along and read aloud to Tesman over at my house. I have plenty of room.

TESMAN. Just think, Eilert! Wouldn't that be nice, hm?

HEDDA (*intervening*). But can't you see that Mr. Løvborg doesn't want to? I'm sure he would rather stay here and have supper with me.

LØVBORG (*looks at her*). With you, Mrs. Tesman?

HEDDA. And with Mrs. Elvsted.

LØVBORG. Ah—! (*Casually.*) I ran into her at noon today.

HEDDA. Oh? Well, she'll be here tonight. So you see your presence is really required, Mr. Løvborg. Otherwise she won't have anybody to see her home.

LØVBORG. True. All right, then, Mrs. Tesman—I'll stay, thank you.

HEDDA. Good. I'll just tell the maid.

(*She rings for* BERTE *over by the door, right.*)

(BERTE *appears just off-stage.* HEDDA *talks with her in a low voice, points toward the inner room.* BERTE *nods and exits.*)

TESMAN (*while* HEDDA *and* BERTE *are talking, to* LØVBORG). Tell me, Eilert—is it this new subject—about the future—is that what you plan to lecture on?

LØVBORG. Yes.

TESMAN. For the bookseller told me you have announced a lecture series for this fall.

LØVBORG. Yes, I have. I hope you won't mind too much.

TESMAN. Of course not! But—

LØVBORG. For of course I realized it is rather awkward for you.

TESMAN (*unhappily*). Oh well—I certainly can't expect—that just for my sake—

LØVBORG. But I will wait till you receive your appointment.

TESMAN. Wait? But—but—but—you mean you aren't going to compete with me? Hm?

LØVBORG. No. Just triumph over you. In people's opinion.

TESMAN. Oh, for goodness' sake! Then Aunt Julle was right, after all! I knew it all the time. Hedda! Do you hear that! Just think—Eilert Løvborg isn't going to stand in our way after all.

HEDDA (*tersely*). Our? I have nothing to do with this. (*She walks into the inner room, where* BERTE *is bringing in a tray with decanters and glasses.* HEDDA *nods her approval and comes forward again.*)

TESMAN (*during the foregoing business*). How about that, Judge? What do you say to this? Hm?

BRACK. I say that moral victory and all that—hm—may be glorious enough and beautiful enough—

TESMAN. Oh, I agree. All the same—

HEDDA (*looks at* TESMAN *with a cold*

smile). You look as if the lightning had hit you.

TESMAN. Well, I am—pretty much —I really believe—

BRACK. After all, Mrs. Tesman, that was quite a thunderstorm that just passed over.

HEDDA (*points to the inner room*). How about a glass of cold punch, gentlemen?

BRACK (*looks at his watch*). A stirrup cup. Not a bad idea.

TESMAN. Splendid, Hedda. Perfectly splendid. In such a light-hearted mood as I am now—

HEDDA. Please. You, too, Mr. Løvborg.

LØVBORG (*with a gesture of refusal*). No, thanks. Really. Nothing for me.

BRACK. Good heavens, man! Cold punch isn't poison, you know!

LØVBORG. Perhaps not for everybody.

HEDDA. I'll keep Mr. Løvborg company in the meantime.

TESMAN. All right, Hedda. You do that.

(*He and* BRACK *go into the inner room, sit down, drink punch, smoke cigarettes, and engage in lively conversation during the next scene.* EILERT LØVBORG *remains standing near the stove.* HEDDA *walks over to the desk.*)

HEDDA (*her voice a little louder than usual*). I'll show you some pictures, if you like. You see—Tesman and I, we took a trip through Tyrol on our way back.

(*She brings an album over to the table by the sofa. She sits down in the far corner of the sofa.* LØVBORG *approaches, stops, looks at her. He takes a chair and sits down at her left, his back toward the inner room.*)

HEDDA (*opens the album*). Do you see these mountains, Mr. Løvborg? They are the Ortler group. Tesman has written their name below. Here it is: "The Ortler group near Meran."

LØVBORG (*has looked steadily at her all this time. Says slowly*). Hedda—Gabler!

HEDDA (*with a quick glance sideways*). Not that! Shhh!

LØVBORG (*again*). Hedda Gabler!

HEDDA (*looking at the album*). Yes, that used to be my name. When—when we two knew each other.

LØVBORG. And so from now on—for the whole rest of my life—I must get used to never again saying Hedda Gabler.

HEDDA (*still occupied with the album*). Yes, you must. And you might as well start right now. The sooner the better, I think.

LØVBORG (*with indignation*). Hedda Gabler married? And married to—Jørgen Tesman!

HEDDA. Yes—that's the way it goes.

LØVBORG. Oh, Hedda, Hedda—how could you throw yourself away like that!

HEDDA (*with a fierce glance at him*). What's this? I won't have any of that!

LØVBORG. What do you mean?

(TESMAN *enters from the inner room.*)

HEDDA (*hears him coming and remarks casually*). And this here, Mr. Løvborg, this is from somewhere in the Ampezzo valley. Just look at those peaks over there. (*With a kindly look at* TESMAN.) What did you say those peaks were called, dear?

TESMAN. Let me see. Oh, they—they are the Dolomites.

HEDDA. Right, Those are the Dolomites, Mr. Løvborg.

TESMAN. Hedda, I thought I'd just ask you if you don't want me to bring you some punch, after all? For you, anyway? Hm?

HEDDA. Well, yes; thanks. And a couple of cookies, maybe.

TESMAN. No cigarettes?

HEDDA. No.

TESMAN. All right.

(*He returns to the inner room, then turns right.* BRACK *is in there, keeping an eye on* HEDDA *and* LØVBORG *from time to time.*)

LØVBORG (*still in a low voice*). Answer me, Hedda. How could you do a thing like that?

HEDDA (*apparently engrossed in the album*). If you keep on using my first name I won't talk to you.

LØVBORG. Not even when we're alone?

HEDDA. No. You may think it, but you must not say it.

LØVBORG. I see. It offends your love for—Jørgen Tesman.

HEDDA (*glances at him, smiles*). Love? That's a good one!

LØVBORG. Not love, then.

HEDDA. But no infidelities, either! I won't have it.

LØVBORG. Hedda—answer me just this one thing—

HEDDA. Shhh!

(TESMAN *enters with a tray from the inner room.*)

TESMAN. Here! Here are the goodies. (*Puts the tray down.*)

HEDDA. Why don't you get Berte to do it?

TESMAN (*pouring punch*). Because I think it's so much fun waiting on you, Hedda.

HEDDA. But you've filled both glasses. And Mr. Løvborg didn't want any—

TESMAN. I know, but Mrs. Elvsted will soon be here, won't she?

HEDDA. That's right. So she will.

TESMAN. Had you forgotten about her? Hm?

HEDDA. We've been so busy looking at this. (*Shows him a picture.*) Remember this little village?

TESMAN. That's the one just below the Brenner Pass, isn't it? We spent the night there—

HEDDA. —and ran into that lively crowd of summer guests.

TESMAN. Right! Just think—if we only could have had you with us, Eilert! Oh well.

(*Returns to the inner room, sits down, and resumes his conversation with* BRACK.)

LØVBORG. Just tell me this, Hedda—

HEDDA. What?

LØVBORG. Wasn't there love in your feelings for me, either? Not a touch—not a shimmer of love? Wasn't there?

HEDDA. I wonder. To me, we seemed to be simply two good comrades. Two close friends. (*smiles*) You, particularly, were very frank.

LØVBORG. You wanted it that way.

HEDDA. And yet—when I think back upon it now, there was something beautiful, something thrilling, something brave, I think, about the secret frankness—that comradeship that not a single soul so much as suspected.

LØVBORG. Yes, wasn't there, Hedda? Wasn't there? When I called on your father in the afternoons—And the General sat by the window with his newspapers—his back turned—

HEDDA. And we two in the sofa in the corner—

LØVBORG. —always with the same illustrated magazine—

HEDDA. —for want of an album, yes—

LØVBORG. Yes, Hedda—and then when I confessed to you—! Told you all about myself, things the others didn't know. Sat and told you about all my orgies by day and night. Dissipation day in and day out! Oh, Hedda—what sort of power in you was it that forced me to tell you things like that?

HEDDA. You think there was some power in me?

LØVBORG. How else can I explain it? And all those veiled questions you asked—

HEDDA. —which you understood so perfectly well—

LØVBORG. That you could ask such questions as that! With such complete frankness!

HEDDA. *Veiled,* if you please.

LØVBORG. But frankly all the same. All about—that!

HEDDA. And to think that you answered, Mr. Løvborg!

LØVBORG. Yes, that's just what I can't understand—now, afterwards. But tell me, Hedda; wasn't love at the bottom of our whole relationship? Didn't you feel some kind of urge to—purify me—when I came to you in confession? Wasn't that it?

HEDDA. No, not quite.

LØVBORG. Then what made you do it?

HEDDA. Do you find it so very strange that a young girl—when she can do so, without anyone knowing—

LØVBORG. Yes—?

HEDDA. —that she wants to take a peek into a world which—

LØVBORG. —which—?

HEDDA. —she is not supposed to know anything about?

LØVBORG. So that was it!

HEDDA. That, too. That, too—I think—

LØVBORG. Companionship in the lust for life. But why couldn't *that* at least have continued?

HEDDA. That was your own fault.

LØVBORG. You were the one who broke off.

HEDDA. Yes, when reality threatened to enter our relationship. Shame on you, Eilert Løvborg! How could you want to do a thing like that to your frank and trusting comrade!

LØVBORG (*clenching his hands*). Oh, why didn't you do it! Why didn't you shoot me down, as you said you would!

HEDDA. Because I'm scared of scandal.

LØVBORG. Yes, Hedda. You are really a coward.

HEDDA. A terrible coward. (*Changing her tone.*) But that was your good luck, wasn't it? And now the Elvsteds have healed your broken heart very nicely.

LØVBORG. I know what Thea has told you.

HEDDA. Perhaps you have told her about us?

LØVBORG. Not a word. She is too stupid to understand.

HEDDA. Stupid?

LØVBORG. In things like that.

HEDDA. And I'm a coward. (*Leans forward, without looking in his eyes, whispers.*) But now *I* am going to confess something to *you*.

LØVBORG (*tense*). What?

HEDDA. That I didn't dare to shoot—

LØVBORG. Yes—?

HEDDA. —that was not the worst of my cowardice that night.

LØVBORG (*looks at her a moment, understands, whispers passionately*). Oh, Hedda! Hedda Gabler! Now I begin to see what was behind the companionship! You and I! So it *was* your lust for life—!

HEDDA (*in a low voice, with an angry glance*). Take care! Don't you believe that!

(*Darkness is falling. The door, right, is opened, and* BERTE *enters.*)

HEDDA (*closing the album, calls out, smiling*). At last! So there you are, dearest Thea! Come in!

(MRS. ELVSTED *enters. She is dressed for a party.* BERTE *exits, closing the door behind her.*)

HEDDA (*in the sofa, reaching out for* MRS. ELVSTED). Sweetest Thea, you have no idea how I've waited for you.

(*In passing,* MRS. ELVSTED *exchanges quick greetings with* TESMAN *and* BRACK *in the inner room. She walks up to the table and shakes* HEDDA's *hand*. EILERT LØVBORG *rises. He and* MRS. ELVSTED *greet one another with a silent nod.*)

MRS. ELVSTED. Maybe I ought to go in and say hello to your husband?

HEDDA. No, never mind that. Let them be. They're soon leaving, anyway.

MRS. ELVSTED. Leaving?

HEDDA. They're off to a spree.

MRS. ELVSTED (*quickly, to* LØVBORG). Not you?

LØVBORG. No.
HEDDA. Mr. Løvborg stays here with us.
MRS. ELVSTED (*pulls up a chair, is about to sit down next to* LØVBORG). Oh, how wonderful it is to be here!
HEDDA. Oh no, little Thea. Not that. Not there. Over here by me, please. I want to be in the middle.
MRS. ELVSTED. Just as you like. (*She walks in front of the table and seats herself on the sofa, on* HEDDA'*s right.* LØVBERG *sits down again on his chair.*)
LØVBORG (*after a brief pause, to* HEDDA). Isn't she lovely to look at?
HEDDA (*gently stroking her hair*). Just to look at?
LØVBORG. Yes. For you see— she and I—we are real comrades. We have absolute faith in one another. And we can talk together in full freedom.
HEDDA. Unveiled, Mr. Løvborg?
LØVBORG. Well—
MRS. ELVSTED (*in a low voice, clinging to* HEDDA). Oh, I am so happy, Hedda! For just think—he says I have inspired him, too!
HEDDA (*looks at her with a smile*). No, really! He says that?
LØVBORG. And she has such courage, Mrs. Tesman! Such courage of action.
MRS. ELVSTED. Oh, my God—courage—! I!
LØVBORG. Infinite courage—when it concerns the comrade.
HEDDA. Yes, courage—if one only had that.
LØVBORG. What then?
HEDDA. Then maybe life would be tolerable, after all. (*Changing her tone.*) But now, dearest Thea, you want a glass of nice, cold punch.
MRS. ELVSTED. No, thanks. I never drink things like that.
HEDDA. Then what about you, Mr. Løvborg?
LØVBORG. Thanks. Nothing for me, either.

MRS. ELVSTED. No, nothing for him, either.
HEDDA (*looks firmly at him*). If I say so?
LØVBORG. Makes no difference.
HEDDA (*laughs*). Poor me! So I have no power over you at all. Is that it?
LØVBORG. Not in that respect.
HEDDA. Seriously, though; I really think you should. For your own sake.
MRS. ELVSTED. No, but Hedda—!
LØVBORG. Why so?
HEDDA. Or rather for people's sake.
LØVBORG. Oh?
HEDDA. For else they might think you don't really trust yourself—That you lack self-confidence—
MRS. ELVSTED (*softly*). Don't, Hedda!
LØVBORG. People may think whatever they like for all I care—for the time being.
MRS. ELVSTED (*happy*). Exactly!
HEDDA. I could easily tell from watching Judge Brack just now.
LØVBORG. Tell what?
HEDDA. He smiled so contemptuously when you didn't dare to join them in there.
LØVBORG. Didn't I dare to! It's just that I'd much rather stay here and talk with you!
MRS. ELVSTED. But that's only natural, Hedda.
HEDDA. The Judge had no way of knowing that. And I also noticed he smiled and looked at Tesman when you didn't dare to go to his silly old party.
LØVBORG. Didn't dare! Are you saying I didn't dare?
HEDDA. *I* am not. But that's how Judge Brack understood it.
LØVBORG. Let him.
HEDDA. So you're not going?
LØVBORG. I'm staying here with you and Thea.
MRS. ELVSTED. Of course, he is, Hedda!

HEDDA (*smiles, nods approvingly*). That's what I call firm foundations. Principled forever; that's the way a man ought to be! (*Turning to* MRS. ELVSTED, *stroking her cheek.*) What did I tell you this morning—when you came here, quite beside yourself—?

LØVBORG (*puzzled*). Beside herself?

MRS. ELVSTED (*in terror*). Hedda—Hedda—don't!

HEDDA. Now do you see? There was no need at all for that mortal fear of yours—(*interrupting herself*). There, now! Now we can all three relax and enjoy ourselves.

LØVBORG (*startled*). What's all this, Mrs. Tesman?

MRS. ELVSTED. Oh, God, Hedda—what are you saying? What are you doing?

HEDDA. Please be quiet. That horrible Judge is looking at you.

LØVBORG. In mortal fear? So that's it. For my sake.

MRS. ELVSTED (*softly, wailing*). Oh, Hedda—if you only knew how utterly miserable you have made me!

LØVBORG (*stares at her for a moment. His face is distorted*). So that was the comrade's happy confidence in me!

MRS. ELVSTED. Oh, my dearest friend—listen to me first—!

LØVBORG (*picks up one of the glasses of punch, raises it, says hoarsely*). Here's to you, Thea! (*Empties the glass, puts it down, picks up the other one.*)

MRS. ELVSTED (*softly*). Hedda, Hedda—why did you want to do this?

HEDDA. Want to! I! Are you mad?

LØVBORG. And here's to you, too, Mrs. Tesman! Thanks for telling me the truth. Long live the truth! (*He drains the glass and is about to fill it again.*)

HEDDA (*restrains him*). That's enough for now. Remember you are going to a party.

MRS. ELVSTED. No, no, no!

HEDDA. Shhh! They are looking at you.

LØVBORG (*puts his glass down*). Listen, Thea—tell me the truth—

MRS. ELVSTED. I will, I will!

LØVBORG. Did your husband know you were coming after me?

MRS. ELVSTED (*wringing her hands*). Oh, Hedda—do you hear what he's asking?

LØVBORG. Did the two of you agree that you were to come here and look after me? Maybe it was his idea, even? Did he send you? Ah, I know what it was—he missed me in the office, didn't he? Or was it at the card table?

MRS. ELVSTED (*softly, in agony*). Oh, Løvborg, Løvborg!

LØVBORG (*grabs a glass and is about to fill it*). Here's to the old Commissioner, too!

HEDDA (*stops him*). No more now. You're supposed to read aloud for Tesman tonight—remember?

LØVBORG (*calm again, puts the glass down*). This was silly of me, Thea. I'm sorry. To take it this way. Please, don't be angry with me. You'll see—both you and all those others—that even if I have been down—! With your help, Thea—dear comrade.

MRS. ELVSTED (*beaming*). Oh, thank God—!

(*In the meantime,* BRACK *has looked at his watch. He and* TESMAN *get up and come forward.*)

BRACK (*picking up his coat and hat*). Well, Mrs. Tesman; our time is up.

HEDDA. I suppose it is.

LØVBORG (*rising*). Mine, too, Judge.

MRS. ELVSTED (*softly, pleadingly*). Oh, Løvborg—don't do it!

HEDDA (*pinches her arm*). They can hear you!

MRS. ELVSTED (*with a soft exclamation*). Ouch!

LØVBORG (*to* BRACK). You were good enough to ask me—

BRACK. So you're coming, after all?

LØVBORG. If I may.

BRACK. I'm delighted.

LØVBORG (*picks up his manuscript and says to* TESMAN). For there are a couple of things here I'd like to show you before I send it off.

TESMAN. Just think! Isn't that nice! But—dearest Hedda—? In that case, how are you going to get Mrs. Elvsted home? Hm?

HEDDA. We'll manage somehow.

LØVBORG (*looking at the two women*). Mrs. Elvsted? I'll be back to pick her up, of course. (*Coming closer.*) About ten o'clock, Mrs. Tesman? Is that convenient?

HEDDA. Certainly. That will be fine.

TESMAN. Then everything is nice and settled. But don't expect me that early, Hedda.

HEDDA. You just stay as long as—as long as you want, dear.

MRS. ELVSTED (*in secret fear*). I'll be waiting for you here, then, Mr. Løvborg.

LØVBORG (*hat in hand*). Of course, Mrs. Elvsted.

BRACK. All aboard the pleasure train, gentlemen! I hope we'll have a lively evening—as a certain fair lady would say.

HEDDA. Ah—if only the fair lady could be present. Invisible.

BRACK. Why invisible?

HEDDA. To listen to some of your unadulterated liveliness, Judge.

BRACK (*laughs*). I shouldn't advise the fair lady to do that!

TESMAN (*also laughing*). You're a good one, Hedda! Just think!

BRACK. Well—good night, ladies!

LØVBORG (*with a bow*). Till about ten, then.

(BRACK, LØVBORG, *and* TESMAN *go out, right. At the same time* BERTE *enters from the inner room with a lighted lamp, which she places on the table, front center. She goes out the same way.*)

MRS. ELVSTED (*has risen and paces restlessly up and down*). Hedda, Hedda—how do you think all this will end?

HEDDA. At ten o'clock he'll be here. I see him already. With vine leaves in his hair. Flushed and confident.

MRS. ELVSTED. I only hope you're right.

HEDDA. For then, you see, he'll have mastered himself. And be a free man for all the days of his life.

MRS. ELVSTED. Dear God—how I hope you are right! That he comes back like that.

HEDDA. That is the way he will come. Not any other way. (*Rises and goes closer to* MRS. ELVSTED.) *You* may doubt as long as you like. I believe in him. And now we'll see—

MRS. ELVSTED. There is something behind all this, Hedda. Some hidden purpose.

HEDDA. Yes, there is! For once in my life I want to have power over a human destiny.

MRS. ELVSTED. But don't you already?

HEDDA. I don't and I never have.

MRS. ELVSTED. But your husband—?

HEDDA. You think that's worth the trouble? Oh, if you knew how poor I am! And you got to be so rich! (*Embraces her passionately.*) I think I'll have to burn your hair off, after all!

MRS. ELVSTED. Let me go! Let me go! You scare me, Hedda!

BERTE (*in the doorway*). Supper is served, ma'am.

HEDDA. Good. We're coming.

MRS. ELVSTED. No, no, no! I'd rather go home by myself! Right now!

HEDDA. Nonsense! You'll have your cup of tea first, you little silly. And then—at ten o'clock—Eilert Løvborg comes —with vine leaves in his hair! (*She almost pulls* MRS. ELVSTED *toward the doorway.*)

Act Three

(*The same room at the* TESMAN'S. *The doorway and the French windows both have their portieres closed. The lamp,* turned half down, is still on the table. The stove is open. Some dying embers can be seen.

MRS. ELVSTED, *wrapped in a big shawl, is in the easy chair near the stove, her feet on a footstool.* HEDDA, *also dressed, is lying on the sofa, covered by a blanket.*)

MRS. ELVSTED (*after a while suddenly sits up, listens anxiously; then she wearily sinks back in her chair, whimpers softly*). Oh my God, my God—not yet!

(BERTE *enters cautiously, right, carrying a letter.*)

MRS. ELVSTED (*turns and whispers tensely*). Well—has anybody been here?

BERTE (*in a low voice*). Yes. Just now there was a girl with this letter.

MRS. ELVSTED (*quickly, reaches for it*). A letter! Give it to me!

BERTE. No, ma'am. It's for the Doctor.

MRS. ELVSTED. I see.

BERTE. Miss Tesman's maid brought it. I'll leave it here on the table.

MRS. ELVSTED. All right.

BERTE (*puts the letter down*). I'd better put out the lamp. It just reeks.

MRS. ELVSTED. Yes, do that. It must be daylight soon, anyway.

BERTE (*putting out the lamp*). It's light already, ma'am.

MRS. ELVSTED. Light already! And still not back!

BERTE. No, so help us. Not that I didn't expect as much—

MRS. ELVSTED. You did?

BERTE. Yes, when I saw a certain character was back in town. Taking off with them. We sure heard enough about him in the old days!

MRS. ELVSTED. Not so loud. You are waking up Mrs. Tesman.

BERTE (*looks toward the sofa, sighs*). God forbid—! Let her sleep, poor thing. Do you want me to get the fire going again?

MRS. ELVSTED. Not on my account, thank you.

BERTE. All right; I won't then. (*Exits quietly, right.*)

HEDDA. (*awakened by the closing door*). What's that?

MRS. ELVSTED. Just the maid.

HEDDA (*looks around*). Why in here—? Oh, I remember! (*Sits up, rubs her eyes, stretches.*) What time is it, Thea?

MRS. ELVSTED (*looks at her watch*). Past seven.

HEDDA. When did Tesman get home?

MRS. ELVSTED. He didn't.

HEDDA. Not home yet!

MRS. ELVSTED (*getting up*). Nobody's come.

HEDDA. And we who waited till four!

MRS. ELVSTED (*wringing her hands*). And *how* we waited!

HEDDA (*her hand covering a yawn*). We—ll. We could have saved ourselves that trouble.

MRS. ELVSTED. Did you get any sleep at all?

HEDDA. Yes, I slept pretty well, I think. Didn't you?

MRS. ELVSTED. Not a wink. I just couldn't, Hedda! It was just impossible.

HEDDA (*rises, walks over to her*). Well, now! There's nothing to worry about, for heaven's sake. I know exactly what's happened.

MRS. ELVSTED. Then tell me please. Where do you think they are?

HEDDA. Well, first of all, I'm sure they were terribly late leaving the Judge's—

MRS. ELVSTED. Dear yes. I'm sure you're right. Still—

HEDDA. —and so Tesman didn't want to wake us up in the middle of the night. (*Laughs.*) Maybe he didn't want us to see him, either—after a party like that.

MRS. ELVSTED. But where do you think he has gone?

HEDDA. To the aunts', of course. His old room is still there, all ready for him.

MRS. ELVSTED. No, he can't be there. Just a few minutes ago there came a letter for him from Miss Tesman. It's over there.

HEDDA. Oh? (*Looks at the envelope.*) So it is—Auntie Julle herself. In that case, I suppose he's still at Brack's. And there's Eilert Løvborg, too—reading aloud, with vine leaves in his hair.

MRS. ELVSTED. Oh Hedda—you're only saying things you don't believe yourself.

HEDDA. My, what a little imbecile you really are, Thea!

MRS. ELVSTED. Yes, I suppose I am.

HEDDA. And you look dead tired, too.

MRS. ELVSTED. I *am* dead tired.

HEDDA. Why don't you do as I say. Go into my room and lie down.

MRS. ELVSTED. No, no—I wouldn't be able to go to sleep, anyway.

HEDDA. Of course, you would.

MRS. ELVSTED. And your husband is bound to be home any minute now. And I have to know right away.

HEDDA. I'll let you know as soon as he gets here.

MRS. ELVSTED. You promise me that, Hedda?

HEDDA. I do. You just go to sleep.

MRS. ELVSTED. Thanks. At least I'll try. (*Exits through inner room.*)

(HEDDA *goes to the French doors, opens the portieres. The room is now in full daylight. She picks up a little hand mirror from the desk, looks at herself, smooths her hair. Walks over to door, rings the bell for the maid.* BERTE *presently appears.*)

BERTE. You want something, ma'am?

HEDDA. Yes. You'll have to start the fire again. I'm cold.

BERTE. Yes, ma'am! I'll get it warm in no time. (*Rakes the embers together and puts in another piece of wood. Then she suddenly listens.*) There's the doorbell, ma'am.

HEDDA. All right. See who it is. I'll take care of the stove myself.

BERTE. You'll have a nice blaze going in a minute. (*Exits right.*)

(HEDDA *kneels on the footstool and puts in more pieces of wood. Presently* TESMAN *enters, right. He looks tired and somber. He tiptoes toward the doorway and is about to disappear between the portieres.*)

HEDDA. (*by the stove, without looking up*). Good morning.

TESMAN (*turning*). Hedda! (*Comes closer.*) For heaven's sake—you up already! Hm?

HEDDA. Yes, I got up very early this morning.

TESMAN. And I was so sure you'd still be sound asleep! Just think!

HEDDA. Not so loud. Mrs. Elvsted is asleep in my room.

TESMAN. Mrs. Elvsted stayed here all night?

HEDDA. Yes. Nobody came for her, you know.

TESMAN. No, I suppose—

HEDDA (*closes the stove, rises*). Well, did you have a good time at the Judge's?

TESMAN. Were you worried about me? Hm?

HEDDA. I'd never dream of worrying about you. I asked if you had a good time.

TESMAN. Yes, indeed. Nice for a change, anyway. But I think I liked it best early in the evening. For then Eilert read to me. Just think—we were more than an hour early! And Brack, of course, had things to see to. So Eilert read.

HEDDA (*sits down at the right side of the table*). So? Tell me all about it.

TESMAN (*sits down on an ottoman near the stove*). Oh Hedda, you'll never believe what a book that will be! It must be just the most remarkable thing ever written! Just think!

HEDDA. Yes, but I don't really care about that—

TESMAN. I must tell you, Hedda—I have a confession to make. As he was reading—something ugly came over me—

HEDDA. Ugly?

TESMAN. I sat there envying Eilert

for being able to write like that! Just think, Hedda!

HEDDA. All right. I'm thinking!

TESMAN. And yet, with all his gifts—he's incorrigible, after all.

HEDDA. I suppose you mean he has more courage for life than the rest of you?

TESMAN. No, no—I don't mean that. I mean that he's incapable of exercising moderation in his pleasures.

HEDDA. What happened—in the end?

TESMAN. Well—*I* would call it a bacchanal, Hedda.

HEDDA. Did he have vine leaves in his hair?

TESMAN. Vine leaves? No, I didn't notice any vine leaves. But he gave a long, muddled speech in honor of the woman who had inspired him in his work. Those were his words.

HEDDA. Did he say her name?

TESMAN. No, he didn't. But I'm sure it must be Mrs. Elvsted. You just wait and see if I'm not right!

HEDDA. And where did you and he part company?

TESMAN. On the way back to town. We left—the last of us did—at the same time. And Brack came along, too, to get some fresh air. Then we decided we'd better see Eilert home. You see, he had had altogether too much to drink!

HEDDA. I can imagine.

TESMAN. But then the strangest thing of all happened, Hedda! Or maybe I should say the saddest. I'm almost ashamed—on Eilert's behalf—even talking about it.

HEDDA. Well—?

TESMAN. You see, on the way back I happened to be behind the others a little. Just for a minute or two—you know—

HEDDA. All right, all right—!

TESMAN. And when I hurried to catch up with them, can you guess what I found by the roadside? Hm?

HEDDA. How can I possibly—?

TESMAN. You musn't tell this to a living soul, Hedda! Do you hear! Promise me that, for Eilert's sake. (*Pulls a parcel out of his coat pocket.*) Just think—I found this!

HEDDA. Isn't that what he had with him here yesterday?

TESMAN. Yes! It's his whole, precious, irreplaceable manuscript! And he had dropped it—just like that! Without even noticing! Just think, Hedda! Isn't that awfully sad?

HEDDA. But why didn't you give it back to him?

TESMAN. In the condition he was in! Dear—I just didn't dare to.

HEDDA. And you didn't tell any of the others that you had found it, either?

TESMAN. Of course not. I didn't want to, for Eilert's sake—don't you see?

HEDDA. So nobody knows that you have Eilert Løvborg's papers?

TESMAN. Nobody. And nobody must know, either.

HEDDA. And what did you and he talk about afterwards?

TESMAN. I didn't have a chance to talk to him at all after that. For when we came into town, he and a couple of the others simply vanished. Just think!

HEDDA. Oh? I expect they took him home.

TESMAN. I suppose that must be it. And Brack took off on his own, too.

HEDDA. And what have you been doing with yourself since then?

TESMAN. Well, you see, I and some of the others went home with one of the younger fellows and had a cup of early morning coffee. Or night coffee maybe, rather. Hm? And now, after I've rested a bit and poor Eilert's had some sleep, I'll take this back to him.

HEDDA (*reaches for the parcel*). No—don't do that! Not right away, I mean. Let me look at it first.

TESMAN. Dearest Hedda—honestly, I just don't dare to.

HEDDA. Don't you dare to?

TESMAN. No, for I'm sure you realize how utterly desperate he'll be when he wakes up and finds that the manuscript is gone. For he hasn't got a copy, you know. He said so himself.

HEDDA (*looks searchingly at him*). But can't a thing like that be written over again?

TESMAN. Hardly. I really don't think so. For, you see—the inspiration—

HEDDA. Yes, I daresay that's the main thing. (*Casually.*) By the way, here's a letter for you.

TESMAN. Imagine!

HEDDA (*gives it to him*). It came early this morning.

TESMAN. It's from Aunt Julle, Hedda! I wonder what it can be. (*Puts the manuscript down on the other ottoman, opens the letter, skims the content, jumps up.*) Oh Hedda! She says here that poor Aunt Rina is dying!

HEDDA. You know we had to expect that.

TESMAN. And if I want to see her again I had better hurry. I'll rush over right away.

HEDDA. (*suppressing a smile*). You'll rush?

TESMAN. Dearest Hedda of mine—if only you could bring yourself to come along! Hm?

HEDDA (*rises, weary, with an air of refusal*). No, no. You mustn't ask me that. I don't want to look at death and disease. I want to be free from all that's ugly.

TESMAN. Well, all right—(*rushing around*). My hat? My coat? Oh—out here in the hall. I just hope I won't be too late, Hedda. Hm?

HEDDA. Oh I'm sure that if you rush—

(BERTE *appears in the door, right.*)

BERTE. Judge Brack is here and wants to know if he may see you.

TESMAN. At this hour! No, no. I can't possibly see him now!

HEDDA. But I can. (*To* BERTE.) Tell the Judge please to come in.

(BERTE *exits.*)

HEDDA (*with a quick whisper*). Tesman! The package! (*She grabs it from the ottoman.*)

TESMAN. Yes! Give it to me!

HEDDA. No, no. I'll hide it for you till later.

(*She walks over to the desk and sticks the parcel among the books on the shelf. In his hurry* TESMAN *is having difficulties getting his gloves on.* JUDGE BRACK *enters right.*)

HEDDA (*nods to him*). If *you* aren't an early bird—

BRACK. Yes, don't you think so? (*To* TESMAN.) You're going out, too?

TESMAN. Yes, I must go and see the aunts. Just think, the invalid—she's dying!

BRACK. Oh, I'm terribly sorry! In that case, don't let me keep you. At such a moment—

TESMAN. Yes, I really must run. Goodbye, goodbye! (*Hurries out, right.*)

HEDDA (*approaching* BRACK). It appears that things were quite lively last night over at your house.

BRACK. Indeed, Mrs. Tesman—I didn't get to bed at all.

HEDDA. You didn't either?

BRACK. As you see. But tell me—what has Tesman told you about the night's adventures?

HEDDA. Just some tiresome story about having coffee with somebody someplace—

BRACK. I believe I know all about that coffee. Eilert Løvborg wasn't one of them, was he?

HEDDA. No, they had taken him home first.

BRACK. Tesman, too?

HEDDA. No. Some of the others, he said.

BRACK (*smiles*). Jørgen Tesman is really an ingenuous soul, you know.

HEDDA. He certainly is. But why do you say that? Is there something more to do this?

BRACK. Yes, there is.

HEDDA. Well! In that case, why don't

we make ourselves comfortable, Judge. You'll tell your story better, too.

(*She sits down at the left side of the table,* BRACK *near her at the adjacent side.*)

HEDDA. All right?

BRACK. For reasons of my own I wanted to keep track of my guests' movements last night. Or, rather—some of my guests.

HEDDA. Eilert Løvborg was one of them, perhaps?

BRACK. As a matter of fact—he was.

HEDDA. Now you are really making me curious.

BRACK. Do you know where he and a couple of the others spent the rest of the night, Mrs. Tesman?

HEDDA. No—tell me. If it is at all tellable.

BRACK. Oh, certainly it can be told. They turned up at an exceptionally gay early morning gathering.

HEDDA. Of the lively kind?

BRACK. The very liveliest.

HEDDA. A little more about this, Judge.

BRACK. Løvborg had been invited beforehand. I knew all about that. But he had declined. He is a reformed character, you know.

HEDDA. As of his stay with the Elvsteds—yes. But he went after all?

BRACK. Well, yes, you see, Mrs. Tesman—unfortunately, the spirit moved him over at my house last evening.

HEDDA. Yes, I understand he became inspired.

BRACK. Quite violently inspired. And that, I gather, must have changed his mind. You know, we men don't always have as much integrity as we ought to have.

HEDDA. Oh I'm sure you're an exception, Judge Brack. But about Løvborg—?

BRACK. To make a long story short—he ended up at Miss Diana's establishment.

HEDDA. Miss Diana's?

BRACK. She was the hostess at this gathering—a select circle of intimate friends, male and female.

HEDDA. Is she a redhead, by any chance?

BRACK. That's correct.

HEDDA. And a singer—of sorts?

BRACK. Yes—that, too. And a mighty huntress—of men, Mrs. Tesman. You seem to have heard of her. Eilert Løvborg used to be one of her most devoted protectors in his more affluent days.

HEDDA. And how did it all end?

BRACK. Not in a very friendly fashion, apparently. It seems that after the tenderest reception Miss Diana resorted to brute force—

HEDDA. Against Løvborg?

BRACK. Yes. He accused her or her woman friends of having stolen something of his. Said his wallet was gone. And other things, too. In brief, he's supposed to have started a pretty wicked row.

HEDDA. With what results?

BRACK. Nothing less than a general free-for-all—men and women both. Fortunately, the police stepped in—

HEDDA. The police—!

BRACK. Yes. I'm afraid this will be an expensive escapade for Eilert Løvborg, crazy fool that he is.

HEDDA. Well!

BRACK. It appears that he made quite violent objection—struck an officer in the ear and tore his coat. So they had to take him along.

HEDDA. How do you know all this?

BRACK. From the police.

HEDDA (*staring straight ahead*). So that's how it was. No vine leaves in his hair.

BRACK. Vine leaves, Mrs. Tesman?

HEDDA (*changing her tone*). But tell me, Judge Brack—why did you keep such a close watch on Eilert Løvborg?

BRACK. Well—for one thing, it is obviously of some concern to me if he testifies that he came straight from my party.

HEDDA. So you think there will be an investigation?

BRACK. Naturally. But I suppose that doesn't really matter too much. However, as a friend of the house I considered it my duty to give you and Tesman a full account of his night-time exploits.

HEDDA. Yes, but why?

BRACK. Because I very strongly suspect that he intends to use you as a kind of screen.

HEDDA. Really! Why do you think that?

BRACK. Oh, come now, Mrs. Tesman! We can use our eyes, can't we? This Mrs. Elvsted—she isn't leaving town right away, you know.

HEDDA. Well, even if there should be something going on between those two, I'd think there would be plenty of other places they could meet.

BRACK. But no home. After last night, every respectable house will once again close its doors to Eilert Løvborg.

HEDDA. And so should mine, you mean?

BRACK. Yes. I admit I would find it more than embarrassing if the gentleman were to become a daily guest here, Mrs. Tesman. If he, as an outsider—a highly dispensable outsider—if he were to intrude himself—

HEDDA. —into the triangle?

BRACK. Precisely. It would amount to homelessness for me.

HEDDA (*smiling*). Sole cock-o'-the-walk—so, that's your goal, is it, Judge?

BRACK (*nods slowly, lowers his voice*). Yes. That is my goal. And for that I will fight with every means at my disposal.

HEDDA. (*her smile fading*). You're really a dangerous person, you know—when you come right down to it.

BRACK. You think so?

HEDDA. Yes. I am beginning to think so now. And I must say I am exceedingly glad you don't have any kind of hold on me.

BRACK (*with a noncommittal laugh*). Well, well, Mrs. Tesman! Maybe there is something to what you are saying, at that. Who knows what I might do if I did.

HEDDA. Really, now, Judge Brack! Are you threatening me?

BRACK (*rising*).—Nonsense! For the triangle, you see— is best maintained on a voluntary basis.

HEDDA. My sentiments, exactly.

BRACK. Well, I have said what I came to say. And now I should get back to town. Goodbye, Mrs. Tesman! (*Walks toward the French doors.*)

HEDDA (*rises*). You're going through the garden?

BRACK. Yes. For me that's a short cut.

HEDDA. Yes, and then it's a back way.

BRACK. Quite true. I have nothing against back ways. There are times when they are most intriguing.

HEDDA. You mean when real ammunition is used?

BRACK (*already in the door, laughs back at her*). Oh good heavens! I don't suppose one shoots one's tame roosters!

HEDDA (*laughs also*). No—not if one has only one—!

(*They nod to each other, both still laughing. He leaves. She closes the door behind him. For a few moments she remains by the door, quite serious now, looking into the garden. Then she walks over to the doorway and opens the portieres wide enough to look into the inner room. Walks to the desk, pulls* LØVBORG'S *manuscript from the bookshelf and is about to read in it when* BERTE'S *voice, very loud, is heard from the hall, right.* HEDDA *turns around, listens. She hurriedly puts the manuscript into the drawer of the desk and puts the key down on its top.* EILERT LØVBORG, *wearing his coat and with his hat in his hand, flings open the door, right. He looks somewhat confused and excited.*)

LØVBORG (*turned toward the invisible* BERTE *in the hall*). And I say I must!

You can't stop me! (*He closes the door, turns, sees* HEDDA, *immediately controls himself, greets her*)

HEDDA (*by the desk*). Well, well, Mr. Løvborg—aren't you a trifle late coming for Thea?

LØVBORG. Or a trifle early for calling on you. I apologize.

HEDDA. How do you know she is still here?

LØVBORG. The people she is staying with told me she's been gone all night.

HEDDA (*walks over to the table*). Did they seem—strange—when they told you that?

LØVBORG (*puzzled*). Strange?

HEDDA. I mean, did they seem to find it a little—unusual?

LØVBORG (*suddenly understands*). Ah, I see what you mean! Of course! I'm dragging her down with me. But as a matter of fact, I didn't notice anything. I suppose Tesman isn't up yet?

HEDDA. I—I don't think so—

LØVBORG. When did he get home?

HEDDA. Very late.

LØVBORG. Did he tell you anything?

HEDDA. Yes, he said you'd all had quite a time over at Brack's.

LØVBORG. Just that?

HEDDA. I think so. But I was so awfully sleepy—

(MRS. ELVSTED *enters through portieres in the rear.*)

MRS. ELVSTED (*toward him*). Oh, Løvborg! At last!

LØVBORG. Yes, at last. And too late.

MRS. ELVSTED (*in fear*). What is too late?

LØVBORG. Everything is too late now. It's all over with me.

MRS. ELVSTED. Oh no, no! Don't say things like that!

LØVBORG. You'll say the same yourself when you hear—

MRS. ELVSTED. I don't want to hear—!

HEDDA. Maybe you'd rather talk with her alone? I'll leave.

LØVBORG. No, stay—you, too. I beg you to.

MRS. ELVSTED. But I don't want to listen, do you hear?

LØVBORG. It isn't last night I want to talk about.

MRS. ELVSTED. What about then?

LØVBORG. We'll have to part, Thea.

MRS. ELVSTED. Part!

HEDDA (*involuntarily*). I knew it!

LØVBORG. For I don't need you any more.

MRS. ELVSTED. And you can stand there and tell me a thing like that! Don't need me! Why can't I help you the way I did before? Aren't we going to keep on working together?

LØVBORG. I don't intend to work any more.

MRS. ELVSTED (*giving up*). What am I going to do with my life, then?

LØVBORG. You'll have to try to live your life as if you'd never known me.

MRS. ELVSTED. But I can't do that!

LØVBORG. Try, Thea. Go back home.

MRS. ELVSTED (*agitated*). Never again! Where you are I want to be! And you can't chase me away just like that. I want to stay right here! Be with you when the book appears.

HEDDA (*in a tense whisper*). Ah—yes—the book!

LØVBORG (*looks at her*). My book—and Thea's. For that's what it is.

MRS. ELVSTED. That's what I feel, too. And that's why I have the right to be with you when it comes out. I want to see all the honor and all the fame you'll get. And the joy—I want to share the joy, too.

LØVBORG. Thea, our book is never going to come out.

HEDDA. Ah!

MRS. ELVSTED. It won't!

LØVBORG. *Can't* ever appear.

MRS. ELVSTED (*with fearful suspicion*). Løvborg, what have you done with the manuscript?

HEDDA (*watching him tensely*). Yes—what about the manuscript?

MRS. ELVSTED. Where is it?

LØVBORG. Oh Thea—please, don't ask me about that!

MRS. ELVSTED. Yes, yes—I want to be told! I have the right to know—right now!

LØVBORG. All right. I've torn it to pieces.

MRS. ELVSTED (*screams*). Oh, no! No!

HEDDA (*involuntarily*). But that's not—!

LØVBORG (*looks at her*). Not true, you think?

HEDDA (*composing herself*). Well, of course, if you say so. You should know. It just sounds so—so unbelievable.

LØVBORG. All the same, it's true.

MRS. ELVSTED (*hands clenched*). Oh God—oh God, Hedda. He has torn his own work to pieces!

LØVBORG. I have torn my whole life to pieces, so why not my life's work as well?

MRS. ELVSTED. And that's what you did last night?

LØVBORG. Yes, I tell you! In a thousand pieces. And scattered them in the fjord. Far out—where the water is clean and salty. Let them drift there, with wind and current. Then they'll sink. Deep, deep down. Like me, Thea.

MRS. ELVSTED. Do you know, Løvborg—this thing you've done to the book—all the rest of my life I'll think of it as killing a little child.

LØVBORG. You are right. It is like murdering a child.

MRS. ELVSTED. But then, how could you? For the child was mine, too!

HEDDA (*almost soundlessly*). The child—

MRS. ELVSTED (*with a deep sigh*). So it's all over. I'll go now, Hedda.

HEDDA. But you aren't leaving town?

MRS. ELVSTED. Oh, I don't know myself what I'll do. There's only darkness before me.

(*Exits, right.*)

HEDDA (*waits for a moment*). Aren't you going to see her home, Mr. Løvborg?

LØVBORG. I? Through the streets? Letting people see her with me?

HEDDA. Of course, I don't know what else may have happened last night. But is it really so absolutely irreparable—?

LØVBORG. Last night is not the end of it. That I know. And yet, I don't really care for that kind of life any more. Not again. She has broken all the courage for life and all the defiance that was in me.

HEDDA (*staring ahead*). So that sweet little goose has had her hand in a human destiny. (*looks at him*) But that you could be so heartless, even so!

LØVBORG. Don't tell me I was heartless!

HEDDA. To ruin everything that's given her soul and mind meaning for such a long, long time! You don't call that heartless!

LØVBORG. Hedda—to you I can tell the truth.

HEDDA. The truth?

LØVBORG. But first promise me—give me your word you'll never let Thea know what I'm going to tell you now.

HEDDA. You have it.

LØVBORG. All right. It isn't true what I just told her.

HEDDA. About the manuscript?

LØVBORG. Yes. I have not torn it up. Not thrown it in the sea, either.

HEDDA. But then—where is it?

LØVBORG. I've destroyed it just the same. Really, I have, Hedda!

HEDDA. I don't understand.

LØVBORG. Thea said that what I had done seemed to her like murdering a child.

HEDDA. Yes—she did.

LØVBORG. But killing a child, that's not the worst thing a father can do to it.

HEDDA. No?

LØVBORG. No. And the worst is what I don't want Thea to know.

HEDDA. What *is* the worst?

LØVBORG. Hedda—suppose a man, say, early in the morning, after a stupid, drunken night—suppose he comes home to his child's mother and says: Listen, I've been in such and such a place. I've been here—and I've been there. And I had our child with me. In all those places. And the child is lost. Gone. Vanished! I'll be damned if I know where it is. Who's got hold of it—

HEDDA. Yes—but when all is said and done—it is only a book, you know.

LØVBORG. Thea's pure soul was in that book.

HEDDA. I realize that.

LØVBORG. Then you surely also realize that she and I can have no future together.

HEDDA. Where do you go from here?

LØVBORG. Nowhere. Just finished everything off. The sooner the better.

HEDDA (*a step closer*). Listen—Eilert Løvborg—Couldn't you make sure it's done beautifully?

LØVBORG. Beautifully? (*Smiles.*) With vine leaves in the hair, as you used to say.

HEDDA. Oh no. I don't believe in vine leaves any more. But still beautifully! For once. Goodbye. Go now. And don't come back.

LØVBORG. Goodbye, Mrs. Tesman. Give my regards to Jørgen Tesman. (*He is about to leave.*)

HEDDA. Wait! I want to give you something—a remembrance. (*Goes to the desk, opens the drawer, takes out the gun case. Returns to* LØVBORG *with one of the revolvers.*)

LØVBORG. The gun? That's the remembrance?

HEDDA (*nods slowly*). Do you recognize it? It was pointed at you once.

LØVBORG. You should have used it then.

HEDDA. Take it! *You* use it.

LØVBORG (*pockets the gun*). Thanks!

HEDDA. And beautifully, Eilert Løvborg! That's all I ask!

LØVBORG. Goodbye, Hedda Gabler. (*Exits, right.*)

(HEDDA *listens by the door for a moment. Then she crosses to the desk, takes out the manuscript, glances inside the cover, pulls some of the pages halfway out and looks at them. Carries the whole manuscript over to the chair by the stove. She sits down with the parcel in her lap. After a moment she opens the stove and then the manuscript.*)

HEDDA (*throws a bundle of sheets into the fire, whispers*). Now I'm burning your child, Thea. You—curlyhead! (*Throws more sheets in.*) Your and Eilert Løvborg's child. (*Throws all the rest of the manuscript into the stove.*) I am burning—I am burning your child.

Act Four

(*The same rooms at the* TESMANS'. *Evening. The front room is dark. The inner room is lighted by the ceiling lamp over the table. Portieres cover the French doors.*

HEDDA, *in black, is walking up and down in the dark of the front room. She goes into the inner room, turning left in the doorway. She is heard playing a few bars on the piano. She reappears and comes forward again.* BERTE *enters from the right side of the inner room. She carries a lighted lamp, which she puts down on the table in front of the corner sofa. Her eyes show signs of weeping; she wears black ribbons on her uniform. She exits quietly, right.* HEDDA *goes over to the French windows, looks between the portieres into the dark. Presently* MISS TESMAN, *in mourning, with hat and veil, enters, right.* HEDDA *walks over to meet her, gives her her hand.*)

MISS TESMAN. Yes, my dearest Hedda—here you see me in my garb of grief.

For now at last my poor sister has fought her fight to the end.

HEDDA. I already know—as you see. Tesman sent word.

MISS TESMAN. Yes, he promised he'd do that. But I thought that to you, Hedda—here in the house of life—I really ought to bring the tidings of death myself.

HEDDA. That is very kind of you.

MISS TESMAN. Ah, but Rina shouldn't have died just now. There should be no mourning in Hedda's house at this time.

HEDDA (*changing the topic*). I understand she had a very quiet end.

MISS TESMAN. Oh so beautiful, so peaceful! She left us so quietly! And then the unspeakable happiness of seeing Jørgen one more time! To say goodbye to him to her heart's content! Isn't he back yet?

HEDDA. No. He wrote I mustn't expect him back very soon. But do sit down.

MISS TESMAN. No—no, thanks, my dear, blessed Hedda. Not that I wouldn't like to. But I don't have much time. I must go back and prepare her as best I can. I want her to look right pretty when she goes into her grave.

HEDDA. Is there anything I can help you with?

MISS TESMAN. I won't have you as much as think of it! That's not for Hedda Tesman to lend a hand to. Or lend thoughts to, either. Not now, of all times!

HEDDA. Oh—thoughts! We can't always control our thoughts—

MISS TESMAN (*still preoccupied*). Ah yes—such is life. At home we're making a shroud for Rina. And here, too, there'll be sewing to do soon, I expect. But of quite different kind, thank God!

(TESMAN *enters, right*.)

HEDDA. So finally you're back!

TESMAN. You here, Aunt Julle? With Hedda? Just think!

MISS TESMAN. I am just about to leave, Jørgen dear. Well—did you do all the things you promised me you'd do?

TESMAN. No, I'm afraid I forgot half of them, Auntie. I'd better run in again tomorrow. I'm all confused today. I can't seem to keep my thoughts together.

MISS TESMAN. But dearest Jørgen—you mustn't take it this way!

TESMAN. Oh, I mustn't? How do you mean?

MISS TESMAN. You ought to be joyful in the midst of your sorrow. Glad for what's happened. The way I am.

TESMAN. Oh yes, of course. You're thinking of Aunt Rina.

HEDDA. You're going to feel lonely now, Miss Tesman.

MISS TESMAN. The first few days, yes. But I hope that won't last long. Dear Rina's little parlor won't be empty for long, if I can help it!

TESMAN. Oh? And who do you want to move in there, hm?

MISS TESMAN. Ah—it's not very hard to find some poor soul who needs nursing and comfort.

HEDDA. And you really want to take on such a burden all over again?

MISS TESMAN. Heavens! God forgive you, child—burden? It has not been a burden to me.

HEDDA. Still—a stranger, who—

MISS TESMAN. Oh, it's easy to make friends with sick people. And I sorely need something to live for, I, too. Well, the Lord be praised, maybe soon there'll be a thing or two an old aunt can turn her hand to here.

HEDDA. Please, don't let our affairs worry you—

TESMAN. Yes, just think—how lovely it would be for the three of us, if only—

HEDDA. If only—?

TESMAN (*uneasy*). Oh, nothing. I daresay it will all work out. Let's hope it will, hm?

MISS TESMAN. Well, well. I can see that you two have something to talk about. (*With a smile.*) And perhaps Hedda has something to tell *you*, Jørgen!

Goodbye! I'm going home to Rina, now. (*Turns around in the door.*) Dear, dear—how strange to think—! Now Rina is both with me and with Jochum!

TESMAN. Yes, just think, Aunt Julle! Hm?

(MISS TESMAN *exits, right.*)

HEDDA (*coldly scrutinizing* TESMAN). I wouldn't be at all surprised if you are not more affected by this death than she is.

TESMAN. Oh, it isn't just Aunt Rina's death, Hedda. It's Eilert I worry about.

HEDDA (*quickly*). Any news about him?

TESMAN. I went over to his room this afternoon to tell him the manuscript is safe.

HEDDA. Well? And didn't you see him?

TESMAN. No. He wasn't home. But I ran into Mrs. Elvsted and she told me he'd been here early this morning.

HEDDA. Yes, right after you'd left.

TESMAN. And he said he'd torn up the manuscript? Did he really say that?

HEDDA. Yes. So he claimed.

TESMAN. But dear God—in that case he really must have been out of his mind! So I assume you didn't give it to him either, hm, Hedda?

HEDDA. No. He didn't get it.

TESMAN. But you told him we had it, of course?

HEDDA. No. (*Quickly.*) Did you tell Mrs. Elvsted?

TESMAN. No, I didn't want to. But you ought to have told him, Hedda. Just think—what if he does something rash—something to hurt himself! Give me the manuscript, Hedda! I want to rush down to him with it right this minute. Where is it?

HEDDA (*cold, motionless, one arm resting on the chair*). I haven't got it any more.

TESMAN. You haven't got it! What do you mean by that?

HEDDA. I burned it—the whole thing.

TESMAN (*jumps up*). Burned it! Burned Eilert's book!

HEDDA. Don't shout. The maid might hear you.

TESMAN. Burned it? But good God—no, no, no!—This can't be—!

HEDDA. It is, all the same.

TESMAN. But do you realize what you've done, Hedda? It's illegal! Willful destruction of lost property! You just ask Judge Brack! He'll tell you!

HEDDA. You'd better not talk about this to anyone—the Judge or anybody else.

TESMAN. But how could you do a thing like that! I never heard anything like it! What came over you? What can possibly have been going on in your head? Answer me! Hm?

HEDDA (*suppresses an almost imperceptible smile*). I did it for your sake, Jørgen.

TESMAN. For my sake!

HEDDA. When you came back this morning and told me he had read aloud to you—

TESMAN. Yes, yes! What then?

HEDDA. You confessed you were jealous of him for having written such a book.

TESMAN. But good gracious—! I didn't mean it as seriously as all that!

HEDDA. All the same. I couldn't stand the thought that somebody else was to overshadow you.

TESMAN (*in an outburst of mingled doubt and joy*). Hedda—oh Hedda! Is it true what you're saying! But—but—but—I never knew you loved me like that! Just think!

HEDDA. In that case, I might as well tell you—that—just at this time—(*breaks off, vehemently*). No, no! You can ask Aunt Julle. She'll tell you.

TESMAN. I almost think I know what you mean, Hedda! (*Claps his hands.*) For goodness sake! Can that really be so! Hm?

HEDDA. Don't shout so! The maid can hear you.

TESMAN (*laughing with exuberant joy*). The maid! Well, if you don't take the prize, Hedda! The maid—but that's Berte! I'm going to tell Berte myself this very minute!

HEDDA (*her hands clenched in despair*). Oh I'll die—I'll die, in all this!

TESMAN. In what, Hedda? Hm?

HEDDA (*cold and composed*). In all this—ludicrousness, Jørgen.

TESMAN. Ludicrous? That I'm so happy? Still—maybe I oughtn't to tell Berte, after all.

HEDDA. Oh, go ahead. What difference does it make.

TESMAN. No, not yet. But on my word—Aunt Julle must be told. And that you've started to call me "Jørgen," too! Just think! She'll be ever so happy—Aunt Julle will!

HEDDA. Even when you tell her that I have burned Eilert Løvborg's papers?

TESMAN. No, oh no! That's true! That about the manuscript—nobody must know about that. But to think that you'd burn for me, Hedda—I certainly want to tell *that* to Aunt Julle! I wonder now—is that sort of thing usual with young wives, hm?

HEDDA. Why don't you ask Aunt Julle about that, too.

TESMAN. I shall—I certainly shall, when I get the chance. (*Looks uneasy and disturbed again.*) But the manuscript! Good God—I don't dare to think what this is going to do to poor Eilert!

(MRS. ELVSTED, *dressed as on her first visit, wearing hat and coat, enters, right.*)

MRS. ELVSTED (*gives a hurried greeting, is obviously upset*). Oh Hedda, you must forgive me for coming here again!

HEDDA. What has happened, Thea?

TESMAN. Something to do with Eilert Løvborg again? Hm?

MRS. ELVSTED. Yes, yes—I'm so terribly afraid something's happened to him.

HEDDA (*seizing her arm*). Ah—you think so?

TESMAN. Oh dear—why do you think that, Mrs. Elvsted?

MRS. ELVSTED. I heard them talking about him in the boarding house, just as I came in. And people are saying the most incredible things about him today.

TESMAN. Yes, imagine! I heard that, too! And I can testify that he went straight home to bed! Just think!

HEDDA. And what did they say in the boarding house?

MRS. ELVSTED. Oh, I didn't find out anything. Either they didn't know any details or—They all became silent when they saw me. And I didn't dare to ask.

TESMAN (*pacing the floor uneasily*). We'll just have to hope—to hope that you heard wrong, Mrs. Elvsted!

MRS. ELVSTED. No, no. I'm sure it was he they were talking about. And somebody said something about the hospital or—

TESMAN. The hospital—!

HEDDA. Surely, that can't be so!

MRS. ELVSTED. I got so terribly frightened! So I went up to his room and asked for him there.

HEDDA. Could you bring yourself to do that, Thea?

MRS. ELVSTED. What else could I do? For I felt I just couldn't stand the uncertainty any longer.

TESMAN. But I suppose you didn't find him in, either, did you? Hm?

MRS. ELVSTED. No. And the people there didn't know anything about him. He hadn't been home since yesterday afternoon, they said.

TESMAN. Yesterday! Just think! How could they say that!

MRS. ELVSTED. I don't know what else *to* think—something bad must have happened to him!

TESMAN. Hedda, dear—? What if I were to walk down town and ask for him at several places—?

HEDDA. No, no—don't you go and get mixed up in all this.

(JUDGE BRACK, *hat in hand, enters through the door, right, which* BERTE *opens and closes for him. He looks serious and greets the others in silence.*)

TESMAN. So here you are, Judge, hm?

BRACK. Yes. I had to see you this evening.

TESMAN. I can see you have got Aunt Julle's message.

BRACK. That, too—yes.

TESMAN. Isn't it sad, though?

BRACK. Well, my dear Tesman—that depends on how you look at it.

TESMAN (*looks at him uncertainly*). Has something else happened?

BRACK. Yes.

HEDDA (*tense*). Something sad, Judge Brack?

BRACK. That, too, depends on how you look at it, Mrs. Tesman.

MRS. ELVSTED (*bursting out*). Oh, I'm sure it has something to do with Eilert Løvborg!

BRACK (*looks at her for a moment*). Why do you think that, Mrs. Elvsted? Maybe you already know something—?

MRS. ELVSTED (*confused*). No, no; not at all. It's just—

TESMAN. For heaven's sake, Brack, out with it!

BRACK (*shrugging his shoulders*). Well—unfortunately, Eilert Løvborg's in the hospital. Dying.

MRS. ELVSTED (*screams*). Oh God, oh God!

TESMAN. In the hospital! And dying!

HEDDA (*without thinking*). So soon—!

MRS. ELVSTED (*wailing*). And we didn't even part as friends, Hedda!

HEDDA (*whispers*). Thea, Thea—for heaven's sake—!

MRS. ELVSTED (*paying no attention to her*). I want to see him! I want to see him alive!

BRACK. Won't do you any good. Mrs. Elvsted. Nobody can see him.

MRS. ELVSTED. Then tell me what's happened to him! What?

TESMAN. For, surely, he hasn't himself—!

HEDDA. I'm sure he has.

TESMAN. Hedda! How can you—!

BRACK (*observing her all this time*). I am sorry to say that your guess is absolutely correct, Mrs. Tesman.

MRS. ELVSTED. Oh, how awful!

TESMAN. Did it himself! Just think!

HEDDA. Shot himself!

BRACK. Right again, Mrs. Tesman.

MRS. ELVSTED (*trying to pull herself together*). When did this happen, Judge?

BRACK. This afternoon. Between three and four.

TESMAN. But dear me—where can he have done a thing like that? Hm?

BRACK (*a little uncertain*). Where? Well—I suppose in his room. I don't really know—

MRS. ELVSTED. No, it can't have been there. For I was up there sometime between six and seven.

BRACK. Well, then, some other place. I really can't say. All I know is that he was found. He had shot himself—in the chest.

MRS. ELVSTED. Oh, how horrible to think! That he was to end like that!

HEDDA (*to* BRACK). In the chest?

BRACK. Yes—as I just told you.

HEDDA. Not the temple?

BRACK. In the chest, Mrs. Tesman.

HEDDA. Well, well—the chest is a good place, too.

BRACK. How is that, Mrs. Tesman?

HEDDA (*turning him aside*). Oh—nothing.

TESMAN. And you say the wound is fatal? Hm?

BRACK. No doubt about it—absolutely fatal. He's probably dead already.

MRS. ELVSTED. Yes, yes! I feel you're right! It's over! It's all over! Oh, Hedda!

TESMAN. But tell me—how do *you* know all this?

BRACK (*tersely*). A man on the force told me. One I had some business with.

HEDDA (*loudly*). At last a deed!

TESMAN (*appalled*). Oh dear—what are you saying, Hedda!

HEDDA. I am saying there is beauty in this.

BRACK. Well, now—Mrs. Tesman—

TESMAN. Beauty—! Just think!

MRS. ELVSTED. Oh, Hedda—how can you talk about beauty in a thing like this!

HEDDA. Eilert Løvborg has settled this account with himself. He has had the courage to do—what had to be done.

MRS. ELVSTED. But you mustn't believe it happened that way! He did it when he was not himself!

TESMAN. In despair! That's how!

HEDDA. He did not. I am certain of that.

MRS. ELVSTED. Yes he did! He was not himself! That's the way he tore up the book, too!

BRACK (*puzzled*). The book? You mean the manuscript? Has he torn it up?

MRS. ELVSTED. Yes, last night.

TESMAN (*whispers*). Oh, Hedda—we'll never get clear of all this!

BRACK. That is strange.

TESMAN (*walking the floor*). To think that this was to be the end of Eilert! Not to leave behind him anything that would have preserved his name—

MRS. ELVSTED. Oh, if only it could be put together again!

TESMAN. Yes, if only it could. I don't know what I wouldn't give—

MRS. ELVSTED. Maybe it can, Mr. Tesman.

TESMAN. What do you mean?

MRS. ELVSTED (*searching her dress pocket*). Look. I have kept these little slips he dictated from.

HEDDA (*a step closer*). Ah—!

TESMAN. You've kept them, Mrs. Elvsted? Hm?

MRS. ELVSTED. Yes. Here they are. I took them with me when I left. And I've had them in my pocket ever since—

TESMAN. Please, let me see—

MRS. ELVSTED (*gives him a pile of small paper slips*). But it's in such a mess. Without any kind of system or order—!

TESMAN. But just think if we could make sense out of them, all the same! Perhaps if we helped each other—

MRS. ELVSTED. Oh yes! Let's try, anyway!

TESMAN. It will work! It *has* to work! I'll stake my whole life on this!

HEDDA. You, Jørgen? Your life?

TESMAN. Yes, or at any rate all the time I can set aside. My own collections can wait. Hedda, you understand—don't you? Hm? This is something I owe Eilert's memory.

HEDDA. Maybe so.

TESMAN. And now, my dear Mrs. Elvsted, we want to get to work. Good heavens, there's no point brooding over what's happened. Hm? We'll just have to acquire sufficient peace of mind to—

MRS. ELVSTED. All right, Mr. Tesman. I'll try to do my best.

TESMAN. Very well, then. Come over here. Let's look at these slips right away. Where can we sit? Here? No, it's better in the other room. If you'll excuse us, Judge! Come along, Mrs. Elvsted.

MRS. ELVSTED. Oh dear God—if only it were possible—!

(TESMAN *and* MRS. ELVSTED *go into the inner room. She takes off her hat and coat. Both sit down at the table under the hanging lamp and absorb themselves in eager study of the slips.* HEDDA *walks over toward the stove and sits down in the easy chair. After a while,* BRACK *walks over to her.*)

HEDDA (*in a low voice*). Ah, Judge—what a liberation there is in this thing with Eilert Løvborg!

BRACK. Liberation, Mrs. Tesman? Well, yes, for him perhaps one may say there was liberation of a kind—

HEDDA. I mean for me. There is liberation in knowing that there is such a thing in the world as an act of free courage. Something which becomes beautiful by its very nature.

BRACK (*smiles*). Well—dear Mrs. Tesman—

HEDDA. Oh I know what you're going to say! For you see—you really are a kind of specialist, too!

BRACK (*looks at her fixedly*). Eilert Løvborg has meant more to you than perhaps you're willing to admit, even to yourself. Or am I wrong?

HEDDA. I won't answer such questions. All I know is that Eilert Løvborg had the courage to live his own life. And then now—this—magnificence! The beauty of it! Having the strength and the will to get up and leave life's feast—so early—

BRACK. Believe me, Mrs. Tesman, this pains me, but I see it is necessary that I destroy a pretty illusion—

HEDDA. An illusion?

BRACK. Which could not have been maintained very long, anyway.

HEDDA. And what is that?

BRACK. He didn't shoot himself—of his own free will.

HEDDA. Not of his own—!

BRACK. No. To tell the truth, the circumstances of Eilert Løvborg's death aren't exactly what I said they were.

HEDDA (*tense*). You've held something back? What?

BRACK. For the sake of poor Mrs. Elvsted I used a few euphemisms.

HEDDA. What?

BRACK. First—he is already dead.

HEDDA. In the hospital.

BRACK. Yes. And without regaining consciousness.

HEDDA. What else haven't you told?

BRACK. The fact that it did not happen in his room.

HEDDA. Well, does that really make much difference?

BRACK. Some. You see—Eilert Løvborg was found shot in Miss Diana's bedroom.

HEDDA (*is about to jump up, but sinks back*). That's impossible, Judge Brack! He can't have been there again today!

BRACK. He was there this afternoon. He came to claim something he said they had taken from him. Spoke some gibberish about a lost child—

HEDDA. So that's why—!

BRACK. I thought maybe he meant his manuscript. But now I hear he has destroyed that himself. So I suppose it must have been something else.

HEDDA. I suppose. So it was there—so they found him there?

BRACK. Yes. With a fired gun in his pocket. Mortally wounded.

HEDDA. Yes—in the chest.

BRACK. No—in the guts.

HEDDA (*looks at him with an expression of disgust*). That, too! What is this curse that turns everything I touch into something ludicrous and low!

BRACK. There is something else, Mrs. Tesman. Something I'd call—nasty.

HEDDA. And what is that?

BRACK. The gun they found—

HEDDA (*breathless*). What about it?

BRACK. He must have stolen it.

HEDDA (*jumps up*). Stolen! That's not true! He didn't!

BRACK. Anything else is impossible. He *must* have stolen it.—Shhh!

(TESMAN *and* MRS. ELVSTED *have risen from the table and come forward into the front room.*)

TESMAN (*with papers in both hands*). D'you know, Hedda—you can hardly see in there with that lamp! Just think!

HEDDA. I am thinking.

TESMAN. I wonder if you'd let us use your desk, hm?

HEDDA. Certainly, if you like. (*Adds quickly.*) Wait a minute, though! Let me clear it off a bit first.

TESMAN. Ah, there's no need for that, Hedda. There's plenty of room.

HEDDA. No, no. I want to straighten it up. Carry all this in here. I'll put it on top of the piano for the time being.

(*She has pulled an object, covered by note paper, out of the bookcase. She puts several other sheets of paper on top of it and carries the whole pile into the left part of the inner room.* TESMAN *puts the papers down on the desk and moves the lamp from the corner table over to the desk. He and* MRS. ELVSTED *sit down and resume their work.* HEDDA *returns.*)

HEDDA (*behind* MRS. ELVSTED'S *chair, softly ruffling her hair*). Well, little Thea—how is Eilert Løvborg's memorial coming along?

MRS. ELVSTED (*looks up at her, discouraged*). Oh God—I'm sure it's going to be terribly hard to make anything out of all this.

TESMAN. But we have to. We just don't have a choice. And putting other people's papers in order—that's just the thing for me.

(HEDDA *walks over to the stove and sits down on one of the ottomans.* BRACK *stands over her, leaning on the easy chair.*)

HEDDA (*whispers*). What were you saying about the gun?

BRACK (*also softly*). That he must have stolen it.

HEDDA. Why, necessarily?

BRACK. Because any other explanation ought to be out of the question, Mrs. Tesman.

HEDDA. Oh?

BRACK (*looks at her for a moment*). Eilert Løvborg was here this morning, of course. Isn't that so?

HEDDA. Yes.

BRACK. Were you alone with him?

HEDDA. Yes, for a while.

BRACK. You didn't leave the room while he was here?

HEDDA. No.

BRACK. Think. Not at all? Not even for a moment?

HEDDA. Well—maybe just for a moment—out in the hall.

BRACK. And where was the gun case?

HEDDA. Down in the—

BRACK. Mrs. Tesman?

HEDDA. On the desk.

BRACK. Have you looked to see if both guns are still there?

HEDDA. No.

BRACK. You needn't bother. I saw the gun they found on Løvborg, and I knew it immediately. From yesterday—and from earlier occasions, too.

HEDDA. Perhaps you have it?

BRACK. No, the police do.

HEDDA. What are the police going to do with it?

BRACK. Try to find the owner.

HEDDA. Do you think they will?

BRACK (*leans over her, whispers*). No, Hedda Gabler—not as long as I keep quiet.

HEDDA (*with a hunted look*). And if you don't?

BRACK (*shrugs his shoulders*). Of course, there's always the chance that the gun was stolen.

HEDDA (*firmly*). Rather die!

BRACK (*smiles*). People *say* things like that. They don't *do* them.

HEDDA (*without answering*). And if the gun was not stolen—and if they find the owner—then what happens?

BRACK. Well, Hedda—then comes the scandal!

HEDDA. The scandal!

BRACK. Yes—the scandal. That you are so afraid of. You will of course be required to testify. Both you and Miss Diana. Obviously, she'll have to explain how the whole thing happened. Whether it was accident or homicide. Did he try to pull the gun out of his pocket to threaten her? And did it fire accidentally? Or did she grab the gun away from him, shoot him, and put it back in his pocket? She might just possibly have done that. She's a pretty tough girl—Miss Diana.

HEDDA. But this whole disgusting affair has nothing to do with me.

BRACK. Quite so. But you'll have to answer the question: Why did you give Eilert Løvborg the gun? And what inferences will be drawn from the fact that you did?

HEDDA (*lowers her head*). That's true. I hadn't thought of that.

BRACK. Well—luckily, there's nothing to worry about as long as I don't say anything.

HEDDA (*looks up at him*). So then I'm in your power, Judge. From now on you can do anything you like with me.

BRACK (*in an even softer whisper*). Dearest Hedda—believe me, I'll not misuse my position.

HEDDA. In your power, all the same. Dependent on your will. Servant to your demands. Not free. Not free! (*Rises suddenly.*) No—I can't stand that thought! Never!

BRACK (*looks at her, half mockingly*). Most people submit to the inevitable.

HEDDA (*returning his glance*). Perhaps. (*Walks over to the desk. Suppresses a smile and mimics* TESMAN'S *way of speaking.*) Well? Do you think you can do it, Jørgen? Hm?

TESMAN. Lord knows, Hedda. Anyway, I can already see it will take months.

HEDDA (*still mimicking*). Just think! (*Runs her hands lightly through* MRS. ELVSTED'S *hair.*) Doesn't this seem strange to you, Thea? Sitting here with Tesman —just the way you used to with Eilert Løvborg?

MRS. ELVSTED. Oh dear—if only I could inspire your husband, too!

HEDDA. Oh, I'm sure that will come —in time.

TESMAN. Well, yes—do you know, Hedda? I really think I begin to feel something of the kind. But why don't you go and talk to the Judge again.

HEDDA. Isn't there anything you two can use me for?

TESMAN. No, not a thing, dear. (*Turns around.*) From now on, you must be good enough to keep Hedda company, my dear Judge!

BRACK (*glancing at* HEDDA). I'll be only too delighted.

HEDDA. Thank you. I'm tired tonight. I think I'll go and lie down for a while on the sofa in there.

TESMAN. Yes, you do that, dear; why don't you? Hm?

(HEDDA *goes into the inner room, closes the portieres behind her. Brief pause. Suddenly, she is heard playing a frenzied dance tune on the piano.*)

MRS. ELVSTED (*jumps up*). Oh God! What's that!

TESMAN (*running to the doorway*). But dearest Hedda—you mustn't play dance music tonight, for goodness' sake! Think of Aunt Rina! And Eilert, too!

HEDDA (*peeks in from between the portieres*). And Aunt Julle. And everybody. I'll be quiet.

(*She pulls the portiers shut again.*)

TESMAN (*back at the desk*). I don't think it's good for her to see us at such a melancholy task. I'll tell you what, Mrs. Elvsted. You move in with Aunt Julle, and then I'll come over in the evenings. Then we can sit and work over there. Hm?

MRS. ELVSTED. Maybe that would be better—

HEDDA (*from the inner room*). I hear every word you're saying, Tesman. And how am I going to spend my evenings?

TESMAN (*busy with the papers*). Oh, I'm sure Judge Brack will be good enough to come out and see you, anyway.

BRACK (*in the easy chair, calls out gaily*). Every single night, as far as I'm concerned, Mrs. Tesman! I'm sure we're going to have a lovely time, you and I!

HEDDA (*loud and clear*). Yes, don't you think that would be nice, Judge Brack? You—sole cock-o'-the-walk—

(*A shot is heard from the inner room.* TESMAN, MRS. ELVSTED, *and* JUDGE BRACK *all jump up.*)

TESMAN. There she is, fooling with those guns again.

(*He pulls the portieres apart and runs inside.* MRS. ELVSTED *also.* HEDDA, *lifeless, is lying on the sofa. Cries and confusion.* BERTE, *flustered, enters, right.*)

TESMAN (*shouts to* BRACK). She's shot herself! In the temple! Just think!

BRACK (*half stunned in the easy chair*). But, merciful God—! People don't *do* things like that!

ROBERT LOWELL • 1917–

My Kinsman, Major Molineux

CAST OF CHARACTERS

ROBIN.
BOY (*his brother*).
FERRYMAN.
FIRST SOLDIER.
FIRST BARBER.
TAVERN KEEPER.
CLERGYMAN.
PROSTITUTE.
MAN WITH MASK.
MAN IN PERIWIG.
SECOND BARBER.
FIRST MAN.
SECOND SOLDIER.
SECOND MAN.
WOMAN.
WATCHMAN.
MAJOR MOLINEUX.
CITIZENS OF BOSTON.

THE SCENE

(*Boston, just before the American Revolution.*

To the left of the stage, ROBIN, *a young man barely eighteen, in a coarse grey coat, well-worn but carefully repaired, leather breeches, blue yarn stockings, and a worn three-cornered hat. He carries a heavy oak-sapling cudgel and has a wallet slung over his shoulder. Beside him, his brother, a* BOY *of ten or twelve, dressed in the same respectable but somewhat rustic manner. On the far left of the stage, the triangular prow of a dory; beside it, a huge* FERRYMAN *holding an upright oar. He has a white curling beard. His dress, although eighteenth century, half suggests that he is Charon. Lined across the stage and in the style of a primitive New England sampler, are dimly seen five miniature houses: a barber shop, a tavern, a white church, a shabby brick house with a glass bay window, and a pillared mansion, an official's house, on its cornice the golden lion and unicorn of England. The houses are miniature, but their doors are man-size. Only* ROBIN, *his* BROTHER, *and the* FERRYMAN *are lit up.*)

ROBIN.
Here's my last crown, your double price
for ferrying us across the marsh
at this ungodly hour.
FERRYMAN.
 A crown!
Do you want me to lose my soul?
Do you see King George's face?
judging us on this silver coin?
I have no price.
ROBIN.
 You asked for double.
FERRYMAN.
I'll take the crown for your return trip.
(*Takes the coin*)
No one returns.
ROBIN.
 No one?
FERRYMAN.
 No one.
Legs go round in circles here.
This is the city of the dead.
ROBIN.
What's that?
FERRYMAN.
 I said this city's Boston,
No one begs here. Are you deaf?
(*The little houses on stage light up, then dim out.*)
ROBIN.
(*To the* FERRYMAN.)
Show me my kinsman's mansion. You
must know him—Major Molineux,
the most important man in town.

FERRYMAN.
The name's familiar... Molineux...
Wasn't he mixed up with the French?
He's never at home now. If you'll wait
here, you'll meet him on his rounds.
All our important people drift
sooner or later to my ferry landing,
and stand here begging for the moon.
You'll see your cousin. You're well-placed.
ROBIN.
I know it. My kinsman's a big man here.
He told me he would make my fortune;
I'll be a partner in his firm,
either here or in London.
FERRYMAN.
Settle
for London, that's your city, Boy.
Majors are still sterling silver across
the waters. All the English-born
suddenly seem in love with London.
Your cousin's house here is up for sale.
ROBIN.
He cares for England. *Rule Britannia,*
that's the tune he taught me. I'm
surprised he's leaving.
FERRYMAN.
He's surprised!
He seemed to belong here once. He wished
to teach us *Rule Britannia,* but
we couldn't get it through our heads.
He gave us this to keep us singing.
(*The* FERRYMAN *holds up a boiled lobster.*)
ROBIN.
You're joking, it's a lobster.
FERRYMAN.
No.
Look, it's horny, boiled and red,
It is the Major's spitting image.
(*On the other side of the stage,* TWO BRITISH REDCOATS *are seen marching slowly in step with shouldered muskets.* Rule Britannia *played faintly.*)
FERRYMAN.
(*Pointing to* SOLDIERS.)
Here are the Major's chicken lobsters.
ROBIN.
Our soldiers!

FERRYMAN.
We call them lobsterbacks.
They are the Major's privates. Wherever
they are gathered together, he is present.
You'll feel his grip behind their claws.
What are you going to do now:
run home to Deerfield, take a ship
for England, Boy, or chase the soldiers?
ROBIN.
Why, I'm staying here. I like
soldiers. They make me feel at home.
They kept the Frenchmen out of Deerfield.
They'll tell me where my kinsman lives.
FERRYMAN.
The French are finished. The British
are the only Frenchmen left.
Didn't you say your cousin's name
was Molineux?
ROBIN.
He's Norman Irish.
Why are you leaving?
FERRYMAN.
Money. The soldiers
make me pay them for the pleasure
of shuttling them across the marsh.
Run, Boy, and catch those soldiers' scarlet
coat-tails, while they're still around.
(*The* FERRYMAN *goes off pushing his boat.*)
(ROBIN *and the* BOY *advance towards the* SOLDIERS.)
ROBIN.
I need your help, Sirs.
FIRST SOLDIER.
(*Smiling.*)
We are here
for service, that's our unpleasant duty.
ROBIN.
I liked the way
the soldiers smiled. I wonder how
anyone could distrust a soldier.
BOY.
We've lost our guide.
ROBIN.
We'll find another.
BOY.
Why did that boatman gnash his teeth
at Cousin Major?

ROBIN.
> He was cold.
That's how big city people talk.
Let's walk. We're here to see the city.

(*As* ROBIN *and the* BOY *start moving, the miniature houses light up one by one and then go dark. A* BARBER *comes out of the barber shop; he holds a razor, and a bowl of suds. A* TAVERN KEEPER *enters holding a newspaper.*)

BARBER.
(*Cutting away the suds with his razor.*)
That's how we shave a wig.

TAVERN KEEPER.
> You mean
a Tory.

BARBER.
> Shave them to the bone!

TAVERN KEEPER.
(*Pointing to newspaper.*)
Here's the last picture of King George;
He's passed another tax on tea.

BARBER.
Health to the King, health to the King!
Here's rum to drown him in the tea!
(*Drenches the newspaper with his mug.*)
(*A* CLERGYMAN, *white-wigged, all in black, comes out of the church.*)

CLERGYMAN.
What an ungodly hour! The city's
boiling. All's rum and revolution.
We have an everlasting city,
but here in this unsteady brightness,
nothing's clear, unless the Lord
enlightens us and show the winner!

(*A* PROSTITUTE *comes out of the bay-window house. She wears a red skirt and a low, full-bosomed white blouse.*)

PROSTITUTE.
Here in the shadow of the church,
I save whatever God despises—
Whig or Tory, saint or sinner,
I'm their refuge from the church.

(*The pillared mansion lights up. A* MAN *comes out in a blue coat and white trousers like General Washington's. He wears a grayish mask covered with pocks. His forehead juts out and divides in a double bulge. His nose is a yellow eagle's beak. His eyes flash like fire in a cave. He looks at himself in a mirror.*)

MAN WITH MASK.
My mind's on fire. This fire will burn
the pocks and paleness from my face.
Freedom has given me this palace.
I'll go and mingle with the mob.

(*Now the houses are dark.* ROBIN *rubs his eyes in a daze, stares into the darkness, then turns to his brother.*)

BOY.
Who are these people, Brother Robin?
We're in the dark and far from Deerfield.

ROBIN.
We're in the city, little brother.
Things will go smoother when we find
our kinsman, Major Molineux.

BOY.
Our kinsman isn't like these people.
He is a loyal gentleman.

ROBIN.
We'll see. He swore he'd make my for-
> tune,
and teach you Latin.

BOY.
> I want something.

ROBIN.
Let's see the city.

BOY.
> I want a flintlock.

(*A* MAN *enters from the right. He wears a full gray periwig, a wide-skirted coat of dark cloth and silk stockings rolled up above the knees. He carries a polished cane which he digs angrily into the ground at every step.* "Hem, hem," *he says in a sepulchral voice as he walks over to the barber shop. The* TWO BARBERS *appear,* ONE *with a razor, the* OTHER *with a bowl of suds.*)

MAN IN PERIWIG.
Hem! Hem!

ROBIN.
> Good evening, honored sir.
Help us. We come from out of town.

MAN IN PERIWIG.
A good face and a better shoulder!
Hem, hem! I see you're not from Boston.
We need good stock in Boston. You're
> lucky!

meeting me here was providential.
I'm on the side of youth. Hem, hem!
I'll be your guiding lamp in Boston.
Where do you come from?
>   ROBIN.
>>   Deerfield.
>   MAN IN PERIWIG.
>>   Deerfield!
Our bulwark from the savages!
Our martyred village! He's from Deerfield,
Barber. We can use his muscle.
>   BARBER.
You can feel it.
>   MAN IN PERIWIG.
>>   (*Seeing the* BOY.)
>>   Look, a child!
>   BARBER.
Shall I shave him?
>   MAN IN PERIWIG.
>>   Yes, shave him.
Shave him and teach him to beat a drum.
>   BOY.
I want a flintlock.
>   MAN IN PERIWIG.
>>   A gun! You scare me!
Come on Apollo, we must march.
We'll put that shoulder to the wheel.
Come, I'll be your host in Boston.
>   ROBIN.
I have connections here, a kinsman ...
>   MAN IN PERIWIG.
Of course you have connections here.
They will latch on to you like fleas.
This is your town! Boy! With that leg
You will find kinsmen on the moon.
>   ROBIN.
My kinsman's Major Molineux.
>   MAN IN PERIWIG.
Your kinsman's Major Molineux!
Let go my coat cuff, Fellow. I have
authority, authority!
Hem! Hem! Respect your betters. Your leg
will be acquainted with the stocks
by peep of day! You fellows help me!
Barber, this man's molesting me!
>   FIRST BARBER.
>>   (*Closing in.*)
Don't hit His Honor, Boy!
>   SECOND BARBER.
>>   His Honor
is a lover of mankind!
>   BOY.
Brain him with your cudgel, Robin!
>   ROBIN.
Come, Brother, we will see the city;
they're too many of them and one has a razor.
>   (ROBIN *and the* BOY *back off. Barber shop goes dark.*)
>   BOY.
Who was that fellow, Brother Robin?
>   ROBIN.
He is some snotty, county clerk,
chipping and chirping at his betters.
He isn't worth the Major's spit.
>   BOY.
You should have brained him with your stick.
>   ROBIN.
Let's go, now. We must see the city
and try to find our kinsman's house.
I am beginning to think he's out
of town. Look, these men will help us.
>   (*The tavern lights up. A sign with King George III's head hangs in front. There's a poster nailed to the door. The* MAN WITH THE MASK *strolls over and sits in the chair.*)
>   CROWD.
Health to the rattlesnake. A health
to Colonel Greenough! He's our man!
>   MAN WITH MASK.
A shine, men, you must shine my shoes
so bright King George will see his face
flash like a guinea on the toe.
>   CROWD.
Health to the rattlesnake!
>   TAVERN KEEPER.
>>   (*Turning to* ROBIN.)
>>   You boys
are from the country, I presume.
I envy you, you're seeing Boston
for the first time. Fine town, there's lots
to hold you, English monuments,
docks, houses, and a fleet of tea-ships
begging for buyers. I trust you'll stay;
nobody ever leaves this city.

ROBIN.
We come from Deerfield.
TAVERN KEEPER.
Then you'll stay;
no Indians scalp us in our beds;
our only scalper is this man here.
(*General laughter.*)
ROBIN.
Our massacre was eighty years
ago. We're not frontiersmen now,
we've other things to talk about.
BARBER.
He has other things to talk about.
This boy's a gentlemen. He is
no redskin in a coonskin cap.
ROBIN.
I'm on our village council. I've
read Plutarch.
TAVERN KEEPER.
You are an ancient Roman.
You'll find you like our commonwealth.
I crave the honor of your custom.
I've whiskey, gin and rum and beer,
and a spruce beer for your brother.
BOY.
I want a real beer.
BARBER.
Give them beer.
(*Shouting.*)
TAVERN KEEPER.
Two real beers for the Deerfield boys,
they have the fighting Deerfield spirit.
ROBIN.
I'm sure you'll trust me for your money.
I have connections here in Boston,
my kinsman's Major Molineux.
I spent our money on this journey.
MAN.
His kinsman's Major Molineux;
sometimes a boy is short of money!
(*Laughter*)
MAN.
(*Bringing out a silver Liberty Bowl*)
I've something stronger than beer.
Here is the Bowl of Liberty.
The Major dropped this lobster in
the bowl. It spikes the drink.
(MAN *puts down his mug and lifts a lobster out of bowl.*)
(*Cheers*)

ROBIN.
I know
the lobster is a British soldier.
MAN.
Yes, there they are.
(*The* TWO REDCOATS *march on stage as before. Silence. The* MAN WITH THE MASK *starts writing on a bench. The* SOLDIERS *saunter over to him.*)
FIRST SOLDIER.
What are you writing, Colonel Greenough?
MAN WITH MASK.
My will.
FIRST SOLDIER.
Things aren't that desperate.
MAN WITH MASK.
I'm adding up my taxes, Redcoat.
Just counting up the figures kills me.
My bankers say I'm burning money.
I can't afford your bed and board
and livery, Soldiers. We'll have to part.
SECOND SOLDIER.
I've had enough. We ought to throw
them all in jail.
FIRST SOLDIER.
Go easy.
ROBIN.
(*Walking shyly up to* SOLDIERS)
Sir,
I need your guidance, I'm looking for
my kinsman, Major Molineux.
FIRST SOLDIER.
Watch your words!
SECOND SOLDIER.
Damn your insolence!
FIRST SOLDIER.
We'll haul you to the Major's court.
(*Shots and screams off stage.* SOLDIERS *leave on the run.*)
MAN.
(*Pointing to* ROBIN)
He's one of us.
SECOND MAN.
He is a spy.
CROWD.
Both boys are spies or Tories.
TAVERN KEEPER.
(*Drawing* ROBIN *over to the poster*)

Look,
do you see this poster? It says,
"Indentured servant, Jonah Mudge:
ran from his master's house, blue vest,
oak cudgel, leather pants, small brother,
and his master's third best hat.
Pound sterling's offered any man
who nabs and lodges him in jail."
Trudge off, Young Man, you'd better trudge!
CROWD.
Trudge, Jonah Mudge, you'd better trudge!
BOY.
They're drunk. You'd better hit them, Robin.
ROBIN.
They'd only break my stick and brains.
BOY.
For God's sake stand and be a man!
ROBIN.
No, they're too many, little brother.
Come, I feel like walking.
We haven't seen the city yet.
(*Lights go off.* ROBIN *and* BOY *stand alone.*)
BOY.
We haven't seen our kinsman, Robin.
I can't see anything.
ROBIN.
You'd think
the Major's name would stand us for
a beer. It's a funny thing, Brother, naming
our kinsman, Major Molineux,
sets all these people screaming murder.
Even the soldiers.
(*The house with the bay-window lights up. A woman's red skirt and bare shoulders are clearly visible through the window. She is singing.*)
WOMAN.
Soldiers, sailors.
Whig and Tories, saints and sinners,
I'm your refuge from despair.
ROBIN.
(*Knocks*)
Sweet, pretty mistress, help me. I
am tired and lost. I'm looking for
my kinsman, Major Molineux.
You have bright eyes.
WOMAN.
I know your kinsman.
Everybody is my kinsman here.
ROBIN.
Yes, I am sure. You have kind eyes.
My kinsman is a blood relation.
WOMAN.
You're my blood relation too then.
What a fine back and leg you have!
You're made right.
ROBIN.
Oh, I will be made
when I find my kinsman. You
must know him, he's a man of some
importance in your city, Lady.
WOMAN.
The Major dwells here.
ROBIN.
You're thinking of some other major,
Lady; mine is something more
important than a major, he's
a sort of royal governor,
and a man of fortune. Molineux
tea ships sail from here to China.
He has a gilded carriage, twenty
serving men, two flags of England
flying from his lawn. You could hide
your little house behind a sofa
in his drawing-room.
WOMAN.
I know,
your kinsman is a man of parts,
that's why he likes to camp here.
Sometimes his greatness wearies him.
These days even kings draw in their horns,
and mingle with the common people.
Listen, you'll hear him snoring by
the roof.
ROBIN.
I hear a hollow sound.
My kinsman must be happy here.
I envy him this hideaway.
WOMAN.
You mean to say you envy him
the mistress of his house. Don't worry,
a kinsman of the Major's is
my kinsman. I knew you right away.
You have your kinsman's leg and shoulders.
He wears an old three-cornered hat

and leather small-clothes here in the rain.
Why, you *are* the good old gentleman,
only you're young! What is this cloth?
You've good material on your leg.
   (*The* WOMAN *feels the cloth of* ROBIN'S *trousers.*)
ROBIN.
It's deerskin. I'm from Deerfield, Lady.
WOMAN.
You must be starved. I'll make you happy.
ROBIN.
I'll wait here on your doorstep, Lady.
Run up and tell the Major that
his Deerfield cousins are in town.
WOMAN.
The Major'd kill me, if I woke him.
You see, he spilled a little too much
rum in his tea.
ROBIN.
I'll leave a note then. I must go,
my little brother needs some sleep.
   (WOMAN *takes* ROBIN'S *hat and twirls it on her finger.*)
What are you doing with my hat?
WOMAN.
I'm showing you our Boston rites
of hospitality. The Major
would kill me, if I turned you out
on such a night. I even have
a downstairs bedroom for your brother.
I find a playroom comes in handy.
BOY.
I want to go with Robin.
WOMAN.
         Oh, dear,
children keep getting me in trouble.
We have a law.
   (*A bell is heard off stage.*)
Mother of God!
   (*The* WOMAN *ducks into her house.*)
   (*Her light goes out.*)
BOY.
Why did the lady slam her door?
ROBIN.
The bell reminded her of something.
She has to catch up on her sleep.
BOY.
Has the Major left his mansion?
Is he really sleeping here?

ROBIN.
How can I tell? Everyone
answers us in riddles.
BOY.
         She said,
the Major dwells here.
ROBIN.
         That's her city
way of being friendly, Brother.
BOY.
Robin, the Major could afford
to buy the lady better clothes.
She was almost naked.
ROBIN.
         She
was dressed unwisely.
BOY.
         Isn't Eve
almost naked in our Bible?
ROBIN.
Don't ask so many questions, brother.
I wish I knew the naked truth.
   (*A* WATCHMAN *enters, dishevelled and yawning. He holds a lantern with a bell tied to it and a spiked staff.*)
WATCHMAN.
Stop, we don't allow this sort
of talk about the Bible here.
ROBIN.
You are mistaken, Sir. I said
I wished I knew the naked truth.
WATCHMAN.
You're in New England. Here we fine
mothers for bearing naked children.
You're leading this child into perdition.
We have a fine for that. What's in
your wallet, Boy?
ROBIN.
Nothing.
WATCHMAN.
         Nothing! You've been inside then!
ROBIN.
Watchman, I'm looking for my kinsman.
WATCHMAN.
And you thought you'd find him in this house
Doing his martial drill.
ROBIN.
         You know him!
My kinsman's Major Molineux.

I see you know him, he will pay you
if you will lead us to his house.
    WATCHMAN.
    (*Singing*)
        Your aunt's the lord high Sheriff,
        your uncle is King George;
        if you can't pay the tariff,
        the house will let you charge.
    ROBIN.
I asked for Major Molineux.
    WATCHMAN.
Keep asking! We are cleaning house.
The Major's lost a lot of money
lately, buying bad real estate.
He can't afford his country cousins.
Move, you filthy, sucking hayseed!
or I'll spike you with my stick!
    BOY.
Why don't you hit him, brother?
    WATCHMAN.
        I'll have
you in the stocks by daybreak, Boy.
    ROBIN.
We'll go, Sir. I'm your countryman
learning the customs of the city.
    WATCHMAN.
    (*Goes off singing*)
        Baggy buttocks, baggy buttocks,
        The Queen of England's willing
        To serve you for a shilling
        And stick you in the stocks.
    ROBIN.
        We're learning
how to live. The man was drunk.
    BOY.
Our Deerfield watchmen only drink
at Communion. Something's wrong,
these people need new blood.
    ROBIN.
        Perhaps
they'll get it. Here's a clergyman,
he'll tell us where to find our kinsman.
    (*The* CLERGYMAN *comes across the stage. He is awkwardly holding a large English flag on a staff.*)
    ROBIN.
Help me, I beg you, Reverend Sir,
I'm from Deerfield, I'm looking for
my kinsman, Major Molineux.
No one will tell me where he lives.
    CLERGYMAN.
I have just left the Major's house.
He is my patron and example.
A good man—it's a pity though
he's so outspoken; other good men
misunderstand the Major's meaning.
He just handed me this British
flag to put above my pulpit—
a bit outspoken!
    ROBIN.
        Our country's flag, Sir!
    CLERGYMAN.
Yes, a bit outspoken. Come
I'll lead you to your kinsman's house.
    (*The* MAN WITH THE MASK *strides hurriedly across the stage, and unrolls a rattlesnake flag, which he hands to the* CLERGYMAN, *who has difficulty in managing the two flags.*)
    MAN WITH MASK.
I have a present for you, Parson:
our Rattlesnake. "Don't tread on me!"
it says. I knew you'd want to have one.
Hang it up somewhere in church;
there's nothing like the Rattlesnake
for raising our declining faith.
    CLERGYMAN.
I thank you, Sir.
    MAN WITH MASK.
        You'd better hurry.
Think of the man who had no garment
for the wedding. Things are moving.
    (MAN WITH MASK *hurries off stage.*)
    CLERGYMAN.
    (*To himself*)
God help us, if we lose!
    (*Turns to go*)
    ROBIN.
Sir, you're leaving! You promised me
you'd lead me to my kinsman's house.
Please, let me help you with the flags.
    CLERGYMAN.
I'll see you later. I have to hurry.
I have a sick parishioner,
a whole sick parish! I have a notion
one of these flags will cure us. Which?
Everyone's so emphatic here.
If you should meet your kinsman, tell him

I'm praying for him in my church.
(CLERGYMAN *goes out.*)
(*A loud "hem, hem" is heard. The* MAN IN THE PERIWIG *comes jauntily forward followed by the* TWO BARBERS. *He goes to the house with the bay-window and raps with his cane. The light inside the house goes on. A rattlesnake flag has been nailed to the door. No one sees* ROBIN *and the* BOY.)
FIRST BARBER.
Look, Your Honor, Mrs. Clark
has taken on the Rattlesnake.
MAN IN PERIWIG.
Good, this pricks my fainting courage.
"Don't tread on me!" That's rather odd
for Mrs. Clark.
FIRST BARBER.
    Come on, Your Honor.
SECOND BARBER.
There's always a first time.
FIRST BARBER.
    Then a second.
MAN IN PERIWIG.
Thank God, I've but one life to give
my country.
Lay on, Macduff! I owe this to
my reputation, boys.
FIRST BARBER.
    He owes
his reputation to the boys.
SECOND BARBER.
Between the devil and the deep
blue sea, Your Honor!
FIRST BARBER.
    His Honor likes
the sea. Everyone loves a sailor.
MAN IN PERIWIG.
Hurry! I'm in torture! Open!
I have authority hem, hem!
(MAN *in* PERIWIG *knocks loudly. The* WOMAN *stands in doorway.*)
WOMAN.
(*Singing*)
    Where is my boy in leather pants,
    who gives a woman what she wants?
MAN IN PERIWIG.
    Woman, I have a royal Crown
    your countryman gave the ferryman
    a-standing on the strand;
    but money goes from hand to hand:
    the crown is on the town,
    the money's mine, I want to dine.
    Whatever we do is our affair,
    the breath of freedom's in the air.
FIRST BARBER.
The lady's ballast's in the air.
SECOND BARBER.
Two ten pound tea chests. The lady needs
a little uplift from the clergy.
MAN IN PERIWIG.
I'm breaking on the foamy breakers!
Help! help!
I wish my lady had a firm,
hard-chested figure like a mast,
but what has love to do with fact?
A lover loves his nemesis;
the patriotic act.
(*The* MAN IN THE PERIWIG *gives the lady the crown and passes in. The lights go out.*)
BARBER.
Once to every man and nation
comes the time a gentleman
wants to clear his reputation.
TAVERN KEEPER.
Once to every man and nation
comes the time a man's a man.
BARBER.
His Honor's perished on the blast.
(*The* BARBER *saunters off along with* TAVERN KEEPER. *The* BOY *turns to* ROBIN, *who is lost in thought.*)
ROBIN.
    I think the Major
has left. By watching I have learned
to read the signs. The Rattlesnake
means Major Molineux is out.
A British flag means he's at home.
BOY.
You talk in riddles like the town.
ROBIN.
Say what you mean; mean what you say:
that's how we used to talk in Deerfield.
It's not so simple here in the city.
(*The pillared mansion lights up.* ROBIN *and the* BOY *approach it. The Lion and Unicorn of England are gone. Instead, a*

large Rattlesnake flag is showing.)
Brother, we've reached our destination.
This is our kinsman's house. I know it
from the steel engraving that
he gave us when he came to Deerfield.
Our journey's over. Here's our mansion.
BOY.
Robin, it has a Rattlesnake.
ROBIN.
That means the Major's not at home.
(*The* MAN WITH THE MASK *comes out of the mansion. Half his face is now fiery red, the other half is still mottled.*)
MAN WITH MASK.
I am the man on horseback.
ROBIN.
No,
you're walking, Sir.
MAN WITH MASK.
I am a king.
ROBIN.
The king's in England. You must be sick.
Have you seen your face? Half's red,
the other half is pocked and mottled.
MAN WITH MASK.
Oh I'm as healthy as the times.
I am an image of this city.
Do you see this colored handkerchief?
(MAN WITH MASK *draws out a small British flag.*)
ROBIN.
Our British flag, Sir.
MAN WITH MASK.
Yes, it doesn't
help my illness any more,
when I try to cool my burning brow,
or blow my nose on it.
ROBIN.
I know
a man who used to own this house.
Let's see if he's still here. Perhaps,
my friend can help to heal your sickness.
MAN WITH MASK.
My face will be entirely red soon;
then I'll be well. Who is your friend?
ROBIN.
A kinsman, Major Molineux.
MAN WITH MASK.
I have a fellow feeling for him.
The Major used to own this house:
now it's mine. I'm taking over,
I've just signed the final deed.
Do you see my nameplate on the gate?
ROBIN.
The Rattlesnake?
MAN WITH MASK.
The Rattlesnake.
ROBIN.
If I pick up the Rattlesnake,
will it help me find my kinsman?
I think he needs my help. We are
his last relations in the world.
MAN WITH MASK.
The last shall be the first, my Boy.
ROBIN.
What do you mean? You talk like Christ.
MAN WITH MASK.
The first shall be the last, my Boy.
The Major has a heavy hand;
we have been beaten to the ground.
ROBIN.
My kinsman has an open hand.
MAN WITH MASK.
Ridden like horses, fleeced like sheep,
worked like cattle, clothed and fed
like hounds and hogs!
ROBIN.
I want to find him.
MAN WITH MASK.
Whipping-posts, gibbets, bastinadoes
and the rack! I must be moving.
ROBIN.
Wait, I'll take up the Rattlesnake.
Please, help me find my kinsman.
(ROBIN *takes hold of the* MAN WITH THE MASK'S *shoulder. The* MAN *steps back and draws his sword.*)
MAN WITH MASK.
Move!
You've torn my cloak. You'd better keep
a civil tongue in your teeth.
I have a mission.
(ROBIN *raises his cudgel. He and the* MAN WITH THE MASK *stand a moment facing each other.*)
BOY.
Brain him, Robin.
Mangle the bastard's bloody face.

He doesn't like our kinsman, Robin.
ROBIN.
I only asked for information.
MAN WITH MASK.
For information! Information
is my trade. I was a lawyer
before I learned the pleasures of
the military life. The Major
was my first teacher. Now I know you!
I met you at the tavern. You
were short of cash then. Take this crown:
drink to the Major, then a health
to Greenough, and the Rattlesnake.
To Greenough!
ROBIN.
    You're a fighter.
MAN WITH MASK.
I hate wars, wars leave us where
they find us, don't they, boy.
Let's talk about my health.
ROBIN.
    Where can
I find my kinsman?
MAN WITH MASK.
    He owned this house.
Men used to find him here all day,
before the storms disturbed his judgment,
He's out now ranging through the town,
looking for new accommodations.
Wait here. You'll meet him on his walk.
    (*Strides off singing*)
    The king is in his counting house;
    we're counting up his money.
BOY.
Why was that fellow's face half red now?
He's changing color.
ROBIN.
    I don't know.
He is someone out of "Revelations"—
Hell revolting on its jailers.
    (*The church lights up a little.* ROBIN *walks over to it, and looks in the window.*)
Our church is empty, brother. Moonbeams
are trembling on the snow-pure pews,
the altar's drowned in radiant fog,
a single restless ray has crept
across the open Bible.
    (*Turns to a gravestone by the church*)
I'm lonely.
What's this? A gravestone? A grave?
Whose grave?
I think the Major must have died:
everything tells me he is gone
and nothing is forever.
    (*Turns back to the church*)
    Brother,
the moon's the only worshipper!
    (*The* CLERGYMAN *comes out of the church. He lays a white clay pipe on the steps and holds up a little colored celluloid whirligig.*)
CLERGYMAN.
The wind has died.
ROBIN.
    What are you doing?
CLERGYMAN.
I'm playing with this whirligig,
and waiting to see which way the wind
will veer. It's quite amusing, Son,
trying to guess the whims of the wind.
I am waiting for a sign.
A strange thing for a modern churchman.
ROBIN.
My father says the Church is a rock.
CLERGYMAN.
Yes, yes, a rock is blind. That's why
I've shut my eyes.
ROBIN.
I see my father. He's the Deerfield
minister, and Church of England.
You remind me of my father.
CLERGYMAN.
Be careful, son. Call no man father:
that's what we tell the Roman clergy;
sometimes I think we go too far,
they get their people out for Mass.
ROBIN.
Father, When I shut
my eyes, I dream I'm back in Deerfield.
The people sit in rows below
the old oak; a horseman stops to water
his horse and to refresh his soul.
I hear my father holding forth
thanksgiving, hope and all the mercies—
CLERGYMAN.
    Those village
pastors! Once they used to preach

as if the world were everlasting;
each Sunday was longer than a summer!
That's gone now. We have competition:
taverns, papers, politics
and trade. It takes a wolfhound now
to catch a flock!
    ROBIN.
        Why are you waiting
for the wind?
    CLERGYMAN.
       (*Taking up two little flags*)
        Do you see
these two flags? One's the Union Jack,
the other is the Rattlesnake.
The wind will tell me which to fly.
    ROBIN.
I'm thinking of the absent one.
My kinsman, Major Molineux
is absent. The storms have hurt his house
lately. No one will help me find him.
    CLERGYMAN.
Perhaps the wind will blow him back.
    ROBIN.
I met a strange man, Colonel Greenough;
Half of his face was red, and half
was pocked. He said, "Wait here, and you
will meet your kinsman on his walk."
    CLERGYMAN.
You'd better wait here then. That red
and pocked man tends to speak the truth.
    ROBIN.
Why was his face two-colors, Father?
    CLERGYMAN.
He is an image of the city.
If his whole face turns red as blood,
We'll have to fly the Rattlesnake.
    ROBIN.
Say more about my kinsman, Father.
You said he was your friend and patron.
    CLERGYMAN.
Poor Molineux! he served the clergy
somewhat better than this city.
He had a special pew, you know.
He used to set a grand example.
    ROBIN.
He used to! You speak as if he were dead!
    CLERGYMAN.
Men blamed me, but I liked to watch
his red coat blazing like the sunset
at Sunday morning service here.
He was an easy-going fellow,
a lover of life, no Puritan.
He had invention, used to send
two six foot Privates here to help
with the collection. Yes, I had
to like him. He had flaws, of course.
    ROBIN.
A red coat blazing like the sunrise,
that's how the Major was in Deerfield;
the gold lion of England shone
on his gilded carriage. He had a little
white scar like a question mark
on his right cheek. He got it killing
Frenchmen. He seemed to hold the world
like a gold ball in the palm of his hand.
Ours for the asking! All! We are
his last relations in the world!
    CLERGYMAN.
No one will dispute your claim.
    ROBIN.
The Major said he was the King's
intelligence in Massachusetts.
    CLERGYMAN.
No one will dispute your claim.
What shall we do with people? They
get worse and worse, but God improves.
God was green in Moses' time;
little by little though, he blossomed.
First came the prophets, then our Lord,
and then the Church.
    ROBIN.
        The Church?
    CLERGYMAN.
                The Church
gets more enlightened every day.
We've learned to disregard the Law
and look at persons. Who is my neighbor?
Anyone human is my neighbor. Sometimes my neighbor is a man from Sodom.
    (*Great noise of shouting.* ALL FORMER CHARACTERS, *except the* MAN WITH THE MASK, *parade across the stage.* MOST OF THEM *wave Rattlesnake flags.*)
    ROBIN.
Father, I see two clergymen,
they're waving flags.
    CLERGYMAN.
        I see my sign.

(*Snaps the whirligig with his thumb*)
Look, the wind has risen! Wherever
the spirit calls me, I must follow.
CROWD.
Hurrah for the Republic!
Down with Major Molineux!
(*The* PEOPLE *sing a verse of Yankee Doodle, and draw* COLONEL GREENOUGH *on stage in a red, white and blue cart. He stands up and draws his sword. One can see that his face is now entirely red.*)
MAN WITH MASK.
The die is cast! I say, the die is cast.
ROBIN.
   Look at the Colonel,
his whole face is red as blood!
MAN WITH MASK.
Major Molineux is coming.
CLERGYMAN.
Are you sure we're strong enough?
MAN WITH MASK.
Every British soldier in Boston
is killed or captured.
CROWD.
   Don't tread on me!
Don't tread one me! Don't tread on me!
ROBIN.
What can I do to help my kinsman?
CLERGYMAN.
Swap your flag and save your soul.
ROBIN.
I want to save my kinsman, Father.
CLERGYMAN.
No, no, Son, do as I do. Here, hold
this flag a moment, while I speak.
(*The* CLERGYMAN *hands* ROBIN *his Rattlesnake flag, tosses away the whirligig, breaks his clay pipe, then takes a chair and stands on it while he addresses the* CROWD *with both hands raised. Throughout the crowd scene,* ROBIN *stands unconsciously holding the flag and suffering.*)
How long, how long now, Men of Boston!
You've faced the furious tyrant's trident,
you've borne the blandishments of
      Sodom.
The Day of Judgment is at hand,
now we'll strip the scarlet whore,
King George shall swim in scarlet blood,
Now Nebuchadnezzar shall eat grass
   and die.
How long! How long! O Men of Boston,
behave like men, if you are men!
(*The* PEOPLE *cheer and take the* CLERGYMAN *on their shoulders.*)
You've drawn the sword, Boys, throw
away the scabbard!
(*The* CLERGYMAN *draws a sword and throws down the scabbard. Many of the* PEOPLE, *including the* PROSTITUTE, *draw swords and throw the scabbards rattling across the stage. They draw* MAJOR MOLINEUX *on stage in a red coat. He is partly tarred and feathered; one cheek is bleeding; his red British uniform is torn; he shakes with terror.*)
ROBIN.
Oh my kinsman, my dear kinsman,
they have wounded you!
MAN WITH MASK.
Throw the boy from Deerfield out,
he has no garment for our wedding.
CLERGYMAN.
No, let him stay, he is just a boy.
(ROBIN, *unthinking, holds the flag in front of him, while his eyes are fixed in horror and pity on the figure of the Major. The* BOY, *unconsciously, too, mingles among the* CROWD *without thinking. Someone asks him to give some dirt to throw at the* MAJOR *and he unthinkingly picks up some from a basket, and hands it to the* TAVERN KEEPER, *who throws it at the* MAJOR.)
ROBIN.
(*With a loud cry, but unconsciously waving the flag in his grief*)
Oh my poor kinsman, you are hurt!
CROWD.
Don't tread on me! Don't tread on me!
(*The* MAJOR *slowly staggers to his feet. Slowly he stretches out his right arm and points to* ROBIN.)
MAJOR MOLINEUX.
Et tu, Brute!
TAVERN KEEPER.
The Major wants to teach us Latin.

(*The* CROWD *laughs, and* ROBIN, *once more without thinking, laughs too, very loudly.*)
(TAVERN KEEPER *goes up to the* MAJOR *and hands him a Rattlesnake flag.*)
You're out of step, Sir. Here's your flag.
(*The* MAJOR *lurches a few steps from the cart, grinds the Rattlesnake underfoot, then turns and addresses the crowd.*)
MAJOR MOLINEUX.
Long live King George! Long live King George!
I'll sing until you cut my tongue out!
CROWD.
Throw the Major in the river,
in the river, in the river!
(*With a grating sound, the* FERRYMAN *appears at the side of the stage, pushing the prow of his dory. The* MAJOR *staggers towards the* FERRYMAN.)
MAJOR MOLINEUX.
[*To* FERRYMAN]
Help me in my trouble. Let
me cross the river to my King!
(*The* FERRYMAN *stiffens.* THE MAN WITH THE MASK *throws him a silver crown.*)
MAN WITH MASK.
Ferryman, here's a silver crown,
take him or leave him, we don't care.
FERRYMAN.
(*Still more threatening*)
The crown's no longer currency.
(*The* FERRYMAN *kicks the crown into the water.*)
MAJOR MOLINEUX.
Boatman, you rowed me here in state;
save me, now that I'm fallen!
FERRYMAN.
There's no returning on my boat.
MAJOR MOLINEUX.
(*Stretching out his hands and grappling the* FERRYMAN.)
Save me in the name of God!
(*The* FERRYMAN *pushes the* MAJOR *off and hits him on the head with his oar. The* MAJOR *screams, and lies still.*)

FERRYMAN.
He's crossed the river into his kingdom;
all tyrants must die as this man died.
(*One by one, the* PRINCIPAL CHARACTERS *come up and look at the* MAJOR.)
CLERGYMAN.
He's dead. He had no time to pray.
I wish he'd called me. O Lord, remember
his past kindness to the Church;
all tyrants must die as this man died.
MAN IN PERIWIG.
(*Taking the* MAJOR'S *empty scabbard.*)
I have the Major's sword of office;
hem, hem, I have authority.
FIRST BARBER.
His Honor has the hollow scabbard.
MAN IN PERIWIG.
They build men right in England. Take
him all in all, he was a man;
all tyrants must die as this man died.
TAVERN KEEPER.
(*Holding a poster.*)
Look, this poster says the town
of Boston offers a thousand guineas
to anyone who kills the Major.
I'll take his wallet for the cause.
All tyrants must die as this man died.
PROSTITUTE.
(*Taking the* MAJOR'S *hat.*)
I'll need this hat to hide my head.
They build men right in England. Take
him all in all, he was a man;
all tyrants must die as this man died.
MAN WITH MASK.
(*Plunging his sword in the* MAJOR.)
Sic semper tyrannis!
FERRYMAN.
  His fare is paid now;
the Major's free to cross the river.
(*The* FERRYMAN *loads* MAJOR MOLINEUX'S *body on his boat, and pushes off.*)
CLERGYMAN.
(*Coming up to* MAN WITH MASK)
  Your hand! I want
to shake your hand, Sir. A great day!
MAN WITH MASK.
Great and terrible! There's nothing
I can do about it now.

(*Turns to* ROBIN.)
Here, boy, here's the Major's sword;
perhaps, you'll want a souvenir.
　(CROWD *starts to leave.* ROBIN *and* BOY *alone.*)
　BOY.
The Major's gone. We'll have to go
back home. There's no one here to help us.
　ROBIN.
Yes, Major Molineux is dead.
　(*Starts sadly towards the river.*)
　CROWD.
Long live the Republic! Long live the
Republic!
　BOY.
Look, Robin, I have found a flintlock.
　(ROBIN *looks wistfully at the* CROWD, *now almost entirely gone. He pauses and then answers in a daze.*)
　ROBIN.
A flintlock?
　BOY.
Well, that's all I came to Boston for, I
　　guess.
Let's go, I see the ferryman.
　ROBIN.
　(*Still inattentive.*)
I'm going.
　(ROBIN *takes his brother's hand and turns firmly towards the city.*)
　BOY.
We are returning to the city!
　(ALL THE PEOPLE *are gone now, the lights start to go out. A red sun shows on the river.*)
　ROBIN.
Yes, brother, we are staying here.
Look, the lights are going out,
the red sun's moving on the river.
Where will it take us to? . . . It's strange
to be here on our own—and free.
　BOY.
　(*Sighting along his flintlock*)
Major Molineux is dead.
　ROBIN.
Yes, Major Molineux is dead.

　　　　(*Curtain.*)

LORRAINE HANSBERRY • 1931-1965

A Raisin in the Sun

CAST OF CHARACTERS
(*In order of appearance*)

RUTH YOUNGER.
TRAVIS YOUNGER.
WALTER LEE YOUNGER (*Brother*).
BENEATHA YOUNGER
LENA YOUNGER (*Mama*).
JOSEPH ASAGAI.
GEORGE MURCHISON.
KARL LINDNER
BOBO.
MOVING MEN.

SCENE: The action of the play is set in Chicago's Southside, sometime between World War II and the present.

Act One
Scene 1. Friday morning.
Scene 2. The following morning.

Act Two
Scene 1. Later, the same day.
Scene 2. Friday night, a few weeks later.
Scene 3. Moving day, one week later.

Act Three
An hour later.

Act One

SCENE ONE

The YOUNGER *living room would be a comfortable and well-ordered room if it were not for a number of indestructible contradictions to this state of being. Its furnishings are typical and undistinguished and their primary feature now is that they have clearly had to accommodate the living of too many people for too many years—and they are tired. Still, we can see that at some time, a time probably no longer remembered by the family (except perhaps for* MAMA) *the furnishings of this room were actually selected with care and love and even hope—and brought to this apartment and arranged with taste and pride.*

That was a long time ago. Now the once loved pattern of the couch upholstery has to fight to show itself from under acres of crocheted doilies and couch covers which have themselves finally come to be more important than the upholstery. And here a table or a chair has been moved to disguise the worn places in the carpet; but the carpet has fought back by showing its weariness, with depressing uniformity, elsewhere on its surface.

Weariness has, in fact, won in this room. Everything has been polished, washed, sat on, used, scrubbed too often. All pretenses but living itself have long since vanished from the very atmosphere of this room.

Moreover, a section of this room, for it is not really a room unto itself, though the landlord's lease would make it seem so, slopes backward to provide a small kitchen area, where the family prepares the meals that are eaten in the living room proper, which must also serve as dining room. The single window that has been provided for these "two" rooms is located in this kitchen area. The sole natural light the family may enjoy in the course of a day is only that which fights its way through this little window.

At left, a door leads to a bedroom which is shared by MAMA *and her daughter,* BENEATHA. *At right, opposite, is a second room (which in the beginning of the life of this apartment was probably*

Lorraine Hansberry

a breakfast room) which serves as a bedroom for WALTER *and his wife,* RUTH.

Time: Sometime between World War II and the present.

Place: Chicago's Southside.

At Rise: It is morning dark in the living room. TRAVIS *is asleep on the make-down bed at center. An alarm clock sounds from within the bedroom at right, and presently* RUTH *enters from that room and closes the door behind her. She crosses sleepily toward the window. As she passes her sleeping son she reaches down and shakes him a little. At the window she raises the shade and a dusky Southside morning light comes in feebly. She fills a pot with water and puts it on to boil. She calls to the boy, between yawns, in a slightly muffled voice.*

RUTH *is about thirty. We can see that she was a pretty girl, even exceptionally so, but now it is apparent that life has been little that she expected, and disappointment has already begun to hang in her face. In a few years, before thirty-five even, she will be known among her people as a "settled woman."*

She crosses to her son and gives him a good, final, rousing shake.)

RUTH. Come on now, boy, it's seven thirty! (*Her son sits up at last, in a stupor of sleepiness.*) I say hurry up, Travis! You ain't the only person in the world got to use a bathroom! (*The child, a sturdy, handsome little boy of ten or eleven, drags himself out of the bed and almost blindly takes his towels and "today's clothes" from the drawers and a closet and goes out to the bathroom, which is in an outside hall and which is shared by another family or families on the same floor.* RUTH *crosses to the bedroom door at right and opens it and calls in to her husband.*) Walter Lee! . . . It's after seven thirty! Lemme see you do some waking up in there now! (*She waits.*) You better get up from there, man! It's after seven thirty I tell you.

(*She waits again*) All right, you just go ahead and lay there and next thing you know Travis be finished and Mr. Johnson'll be in there and you'll be fussing and cussing round here like a mad man! And be late too! (*She waits, at the end of patience.*) Walter Lee—it's time for you to get up!

(*She waits another second and then starts to go into the bedroom, but is apparently satisfied that her husband has begun to get up. She stops, pulls the door to, and returns to the kitchen area. She wipes her face with a moist cloth and runs her fingers through her sleep-disheveled hair in a vain effort and ties an apron around her housecoat. The bedroom door at right opens and her husband stands in the doorway in his pajamas, which are rumpled and mismated. He is a lean, intense young man in his middle thirties, inclined to quick nervous movements and erratic speech habits— and always in his voice there is a quality of indictment.*)

WALTER. Is he out yet?

RUTH. What do you mean *out*? He ain't hardly got in there good yet.

WALTER (*wandering in, still more oriented to sleep than to a new day*). Well, what was you doing all that yelling for if I can't even get in there yet? (*stopping and thinking*) Check coming today?

RUTH. They *said* Saturday and this is just Friday and I hopes to God you ain't going to get up here first thing this morning and start talking to me 'bout no money—'cause I 'bout don't want to hear it.

WALTER. Something the matter with you this morning?

RUTH. No—I'm just sleepy as the devil. What kind eggs you want?

WALTER. Not scrambled. (RUTH *starts to scramble eggs.*) Paper come? (RUTH *points impatiently to the rolled up* Tribune *on the table, and he gets it and spreads it out and vaguely reads the front page.*) Set off another bomb yesterday.

RUTH (*maximum indifference*). Did they?

WALTER (*looking up*). What's the matter with you?

RUTH. Ain't nothing the matter with me. And don't keep asking me that this morning.

WALTER. Ain't nobody bothering you. (*Reading the news of the day absently again.*) Say Colonel McCormick is sick.

RUTH (*affecting tea-party interest.*) Is he now? Poor thing.

WALTER (*sighing and looking at his watch*). Oh, me. (*He waits.*) Now what is that boy doing in that bathroom all this time? He just going to have to start getting up earlier. I can't be being late to work on account of him fooling around in there.

RUTH (*turning on him*). Oh, no he ain't going to be getting up no earlier no such thing! It ain't his fault that he can't get to bed no earlier nights 'cause he got a bunch of crazy good-for-nothing clowns sitting up running their mouths in what is supposed to be his bedroom after ten o'clock at night . . .

WALTER. That's what you mad about, ain't it? The things I want to talk about with my friends just couldn't be important in your mind, could they?

(*He rises and finds a cigarette in her handbag on the table and crosses to the little window and looks out, smoking and deeply enjoying this first one.*)

RUTH (*almost matter of factly, a complaint too automatic to deserve emphasis*). Why you always got to smoke before you eat in the morning?

WALTER (*at the window*). Just look at 'em down there . . . Running and racing to work . . . (*He turns and faces his wife and watches her a moment at the stove, and then, suddenly,*) You look young this morning, baby.

RUTH (*indifferently*). Yeah?

WALTER. Just for a second—stirring them eggs. It's gone now—just for a second it was—you looked real young again. (*Then, drily,*) It's gone now—you look like yourself again.

RUTH. Man, if you don't shut up and leave me alone.

WALTER (*looking out to the street again*). First thing a man ought to learn in life is not to make love to no colored woman first thing in the morning. You all some evil people at eight o'clock in the morning.

(TRAVIS *appears in the hall doorway, almost fully dressed and quite wide awake now, his towels and pajamas across his shoulders. He opens the door and signals for his father to make the bathroom in a hurry.*)

TRAVIS (*watching the bathroom*). Daddy, come on! (WALTER *gets his bathroom utensils and flies out to the bathroom.*)

RUTH. Sit down and have your breakfast, Travis.

TRAVIS. Mama, this is Friday. (*Gleefully.*) Check coming tomorrow, huh?

RUTH. You get your mind off money and eat your breakfast.

TRAVIS (*eating*). This is the morning we supposed to bring the fifty cents to school.

RUTH. Well, I ain't got no fifty cents this morning.

TRAVIS. Teacher say we have to.

RUTH. I don't care what teacher say. I ain't got it. Eat your breakfast, Travis.

TRAVIS. I *am* eating.

RUTH. Hush up now and just eat!

(*The boy gives her an exasperated look for her lack of understanding, and eats grudgingly.*)

TRAVIS. You think Grandma would have it?

RUTH. No! And I want you to stop asking your grandmother for money, you hear me?

TRAVIS (*outraged*). Gaaaleee! I don't ask her, she just gimme it sometimes!

RUTH. Travis Willard Younger—I got too much on me this morning to be—

TRAVIS. Maybe Daddy—
RUTH. *Travis!*
(*The boy hushes abruptly. They are both quiet and tense for several seconds.*)
TRAVIS (*presently*). Could I maybe go carry some groceries in front of the supermarket for a little while after school then?
RUTH. Just hush, I said. (*Travis jabs his spoon into his cereal bowl viciously, and rests his head in anger upon his fists.*) If you through eating, you can get over there and make up your bed.
(*The boy obeys stiffly and crosses the room, almost mechanically, to the bed and more or less carefully folds the covering. He carries the bedding into his mother's room and returns with his books and cap.*)
TRAVIS (*sulking and standing apart from her unnaturally*). I'm gone.
RUTH (*looking up from the stove to inspect him automatically*). Come here. (*He crosses to her and she studies his head.*) If you don't take this comb and fix this here head, you better! (TRAVIS *puts down his books with a great sigh of oppression, and crosses to the mirror. His mother mutters under her breath about his "slubbornness."*) 'Bout to march out of here with that head looking just like chickens slept in it! I just don't know where you get your stubborn ways . . . And get your jacket, too. Looks chilly out this morning.
TRAVIS (*with conspicuously brushed hair and jacket*). I'm gone.
RUTH. Get carfare and milk money —(*waving one finger*)—and not a single penny for no caps, you hear me?
TRAVIS (*with sullen politeness*). Yes'm.
(*He turns in outrage to leave. His mother watches after him as in his frustration he approaches the door almost comically. When she speaks to him, her voice has become a very gentle tease.*)
RUTH (*mocking; as she thinks he would say it*). Oh, Mama makes me so mad sometimes, I don't know what to do! (*She waits and continues to his back as he stands stock-still in front of the door.*) I wouldn't kiss that woman good-bye for nothing in this world this morning! (*The boy finally turns around and rolls his eyes at her, knowing the mood has changed and he is vindicated; he does not, however, move toward her yet.*) Not for nothing in this world! (*She finally laughs aloud at him and holds out her arms to him and we see that it is a way between them, very old and practiced. He crosses to her and allows her to embrace him warmly but keeps his face fixed with masculine rigidity. She holds him back from her presently and looks at him and runs her fingers over the features of his face. With utter gentleness—*) Now— whose little old angry man are you?
TRAVIS (*The masculinity and gruffness start to fade at last*). Aw gaalee— Mama . . .
RUTH (*mimicking*). Aw—gaaaaal-leeeee, Mama! (*She pushes him, with rough playfulness and finality, toward the door.*) Get on out of here or you going to be late.
TRAVIS (*in the face of love, new aggressiveness*). Mama, could I *please* go carry groceries?
RUTH. Honey, it's starting to get so cold evenings.
WALTER (*coming in from the bathroom and drawing a make-believe gun from a make-believe holster and shooting at his son*). What is it he wants to do?
RUTH. Go carry groceries after school at the supermarket.
WALTER. Well, let him go . . .
TRAVIS (*quickly, to the ally*). I have to—she won't gimme the fifty cents . . .
WALTER (*to his wife only*). Why not?
RUTH (*simply, and with flavor*). 'Cause we don't have it.
WALTER (*to* RUTH *only*). What you tell the boy things like that for? (*Reaching down into his pants with a rather important gesture.*) Here, son—

(*He hands the boy the coin, but his eyes are directed to his wife's.* TRAVIS *takes the money happily.*)

TRAVIS. Thanks, Daddy.

(*He starts out.* RUTH *watches both of them with murder in her eyes.* WALTER *stands and stares back at her with defiance, and suddenly reaches into his pocket again on an afterthought.*)

WALTER (*without even looking at his son, still staring hard at his wife*). In fact, here's another fifty cents . . . Buy yourself some fruit today—or take a taxicab to school or something!

TRAVIS. Whoopee—

(*He leaps up and clasps his father around the middle with his legs, and they face each other in mutual appreciation; slowly* WALTER LEE *peeks around the boy to catch the violent rays from his wife's eyes and draws his head back as if shot.*)

WALTER. You better get down now—and get to school, man.

TRAVIS (*at the door*). O.K. Goodbye.

(*He exits.*)

WALTER (*after him, pointing with pride*). That's *my* boy. (*She looks at him in disgust and turns back to her work.*) You know what I was thinking 'bout in the bathroom this morning?

RUTH. No.

WALTER. How come you always try to be so pleasant!

RUTH. What is there to be pleasant 'bout!

WALTER. You want to know what I was thinking 'bout in the bathroom or not!

RUTH. I know what you thinking 'bout.

WALTER (*ignoring he*r). 'Bout what me and Willy Harris was talking about last night.

RUTH (*immediately—a refrain*). Willy Harris is a good-for-nothing loud mouth.

WALTER. Anybody who talks to me has got to be a good-for-nothing loud mouth, ain't he? And what you know about who is just a good-for-nothing loud mouth? Charlie Atkins was just a "good-for-nothing loud mouth" too, wasn't he! When he wanted me to go in the dry-cleaning business with him. And now—he's grossing a hundred thousand a year. A hundred thousand dollars a year! You still call *him* a loud mouth!

RUTH (*bitterly*). Oh, Walter Lee . . .

(*She folds her head on her arms over the table.*)

WALTER (*rising and coming to her and standing over her*). You tired, ain't you? Tired of everything. Me, the boy, the way we live—this beat-up hole—everything. Ain't you? (*She doesn't look up, doesn't answer.*) So tired—moaning and groaning all the time, but you wouldn't do nothing to help, would you? You couldn't be on my side that long for nothing, could you?

RUTH. Walter, please leave me alone.

WALTER. A man needs for a woman to back him up . . .

RUTH. Walter—

WALTER. Mama would listen to you. You know she listen to you more than she do me and Bennie. She think more of you. All you have to do is just sit down with her when you drinking your coffee one morning and talking 'bout things like you do and—(*He sits down beside her and demonstrates graphically what he thinks her methods and tone should be.*) —you just sip your coffee, see, and say easy like that you been thinking 'bout that deal Walter Lee is so interested in, 'bout the store and all, and sip some more coffee, like what you saying ain't really that important to you—And the next thing you know, she be listening good and asking you questions and when I come home—I can tell her the details. This ain't no fly-by-night proposition, baby. I mean we figured it out, me and Willy and Bobo.

RUTH (*with a frown*). Bobo?

WALTER. Yeah. You see, this little liquor store we got in mind cost seventy-five thousand and we figured the initial investment on the place be 'bout thirty thousand, see. That be ten thousand each. Course, there's a couple of hundred you got to pay so's you don't spend your life just waiting for them clowns to let your license get approved—

RUTH. You mean graft?

WALTER (*frowning impatiently*). Don't call it that. See there, that just goes to show you what women understand about the world. Baby, don't *nothing* happen for you in this world 'less you pay *somebody* off!

RUTH. Walter, leave me alone! (*She raises her head and stares at him vigorously—then says, more quietly,*) Eat your eggs, they gonna be cold.

WALTER (*straightening up from her and looking off*). That's it. There you are. Man say to his woman: I got me a dream. His woman say: Eat your eggs. (*Sadly, but gaining in power.*) Man say: I got to take hold of this here world, baby! And a woman will say: Eat your eggs and go to work. (*Passionately now.*) Man say: I got to change my life, I'm choking to death, baby! And his woman say—(*in utter anguish as he brings his fists down on his thighs*)—Your eggs is getting cold!

RUTH (*softly*). Walter, that ain't none of our money.

WALTER (*not listening at all or even looking at her*). This morning, I was lookin' in the mirror and thinking about it . . . I'm thirty-five years old; I been married eleven years and I got a boy who sleeps in the living room—(*very, very quietly*)—and all I got to give him is stories about how rich white people live . . .

RUTH. Eat your eggs, Walter.

WALTER. *Damn my eggs . . . damn all the eggs that ever was!*

RUTH. Then go to work.

WALTER (*looking up at her*). See— I'm trying to talk to you 'bout myself— (*shaking his head with the repetition*)— and all you can say is eat them eggs and go to work.

RUTH (*wearily*). Honey, you never say nothing new. I listen to you every day, every night and every morning, and you never say nothing new. (*Shrugging.*) So you would rather *be* Mr. Arnold than be his chauffeur. So—I would *rather* be living in Buckingham Palace.

WALTER. That is just what is wrong with the colored woman in this world . . . Don't understand about building their men up and making 'em feel like they somebody. Like they can do something.

RUTH (*drily, but to hurt*). There *are* colored men who do things.

WALTER. No thanks to the colored woman.

RUTH. Well, being a colored woman, I guess I can't help myself none.

(*She rises and gets the ironing board and sets it up and attacks a huge pile of rough-dried clothes, sprinkling them in preparation for the ironing and then rolling them into tight fat balls.*)

WALTER (*mumbling*). We one group of men tied to a race of women with small minds.

(*His sister* BENEATHA *enters. She is about twenty, as slim and intense as her brother. She is not as pretty as her sister-in-law, but her lean, almost intellectual face has a handsomeness of its own. She wears a bright-red flannel nightie, and her thick hair stands wildly about her head. Her speech is a mixture of many things; it is different from the rest of the family's insofar as education has permeated her sense of English—and perhaps the Midwest rather than the South has finally— at last—won out in her inflection; but not altogether, because over all of it is a soft slurring and transformed use of vowels which is the decided influence of the Southside. She passes through the room without looking at either* RUTH *or* WALTER *and goes to the outside door and looks, a little blindly, out to the bathroom. She sees that it has been lost to the Johnsons. She closes the door with a sleepy vengeance and crosses to the table and sits down a little defeated.*)

BENEATHA. I am going to start timing those people.

WALTER. You should get up earlier.

BENEATHA (*her face in her hands. She is still fighting the urge to go back to bed*). Really—would you suggest dawn? Where's the paper?

WALTER (*pushing the paper across the table to her as he studies her almost clinically, as though he has never seen her before*). You a horrible-looking chick at this hour.

BENEATHA (*drily*). Good morning, everybody.

WALTER (*senselessly*). How is school coming?

BENEATHA (*in the same spirit*). Lovely. Lovely. And you know, biology is the greatest. (*Looking up at him.*) I dissected something that looked just like you yesterday.

WALTER. I just wondered if you've made up your mind and everything.

BENEATHA (*gaining in sharpness and impatience*). And what did I answer yesterday morning—and the day before that?

RUTH (*from the ironing board, like someone disinterested and old*). Don't be so nasty, Bennie.

BENEATHA (*still to her brother*). And the day before that and the day before that!

WALTER (*defensively*). I'm interested in you. Something wrong with that? Ain't many girls who decide—

WALTER and BENEATHA (*in unison*). —"to be a doctor."

(*Silence.*)

WALTER. Have we figured out yet just exactly how much medical school is going to cost?

RUTH. Walter Lee, why don't you leave that girl alone and get out of here to work?

BENEATHA (*exits to the bathroom and bangs on the door*). Come on out of there, please!

(*She comes back into the room.*)

WALTER (*looking at his sister intently*). You know the check is coming tomorrow.

BENEATHA (*turning on him with a sharpness all her own*). That money belongs to Mama, Walter, and it's for her to decide how she wants to use it. I don't care if she wants to buy a house or a rocket ship or just nail it up somewhere and look at it. It's hers. Not ours—*hers.*

WALTER (*bitterly*). Now ain't that fine! You just got your mother's interest at heart, ain't you, girl? You such a nice girl—but if Mama got that money she can always take a few thousand and help you through school too—can't she?

BENEATHA. I have never asked anyone around here to do anything for me!

WALTER. No! And the line between asking and just accepting when the time comes is big and wide—ain't it!

BENEATHA (*with fury*). What do you want from me, Brother—that I quit school or just drop dead, which!

WALTER. I don't want nothing but for you to stop acting holy 'round here. Me and Ruth done made some sacrifices for you—why can't you do something for the family?

RUTH. Walter, don't be dragging me in it.

WALTER. You are in it—Don't you get up and go work in somebody's kitchen for the last three years to help put clothes on her back?

RUTH. Oh, Walter—that's not fair . . .

WALTER. It ain't that nobody expects you to get on your knees and say thank you, Brother; thank you, Ruth; thank you, Mama—and thank you, Travis, for wearing the same pair of shoes for two semesters—

BENEATHA (*dropping to her knees*). Well—I *do*—all right?—thank everybody . . . and forgive me for ever wanting to be anything at all . . . forgive me, forgive me!

RUTH. Please stop it! Your mama'll hear you.

WALTER. Who the hell told you you had to be a doctor? If you so crazy 'bout messing 'round with sick people—then go be a nurse like other women—or just get married and be quiet . . .

BENEATHA. Well—you finally got it said . . . It took you three years but you finally got it said. Walter, give up; leave me alone—it's Mama's money.

WALTER. *He was my father, too!*

BENEATHA. So what? He was mine, too—and Travis' grandfather—but the insurance money belongs to Mama. Picking on me is not going to make her give it to you to invest in any liquor stores—(*underbreath, dropping into a chair*)—and I for one say, God bless Mama for that!

WALTER (*to* RUTH). See—did you hear? Did you hear!

RUTH. Honey, please go to work.

WALTER. Nobody in this house is ever going to understand me.

BENEATHA. Because you're a nut.

WALTER. Who's a nut?

BENEATHA. You—you are a nut. Thee is mad, boy.

WALTER (*looking at his wife and his sister from the door, very sadly*). The world's most backward race of people, and that's a fact.

BENEATHA (*turning slowly in her chair*). And then there are all those prophets who would lead us out of the wilderness—(WALTER *slams out of the house.*)—into the swamps!

RUTH. Bennie, why you always gotta be pickin' on your brother? Can't you be a little sweeter sometimes? (*Door opens.* WALTER *walks in.*)

WALTER (*to* RUTH). I need some money for carfare.

RUTH (*looks at him, then warms; teasing, but tenderly*). Fifty cents? (*She goes to her bag and gets money.*) Here, take a taxi.

(WALTER *exits.* MAMA *enters. She is a woman in her early sixties, full-bodied and strong. She is one of those women of a certain grace and beauty who wear it so unobtrusively that it takes a while to notice. Her dark-brown face is surrounded by the total whiteness of her hair, and, being a woman who has adjusted to many things in life and overcome many more, her face is full of strength. She has, we can see, wit and faith of a kind that keep her eyes lit and full of interest and expectancy. She is, in a word, a beautiful woman. Her bearing is perhaps most like the noble bearing of the women of the Hereros of Southwest Africa—rather as if she imagines that as she walks she still bears a basket or a vessel upon her head. Her speech, on the other hand, is as careless as her carriage is precise—she is inclined to slur everything—but her voice is perhaps not so much quiet as simply soft.*)

MAMA. Who that 'round here slamming doors at this hour?

(*She crosses through the room, goes to the window, opens it, and brings in a feeble little plant growing doggedly in a small pot on the window sill. She feels the dirt and puts it back out.*)

RUTH. That was Walter Lee. He and Bennie was at it again.

MAMA. My children and they tempers. Lord, if this little old plant don't get more sun than it's been getting it ain't never going to see spring again. (*She turns from the window.*) What's the matter with you this morning, Ruth? You looks right peaked. You aiming to iron all them things? Leave some for me. I'll get to 'em this afternoon. Bennie honey, it's too drafty for you to be sitting 'round half dressed. Where's your robe?

BENEATHA. In the cleaners.

MAMA. Well, go get mine and put it on.

BENEATHA. I'm not cold, Mama, honest.

MAMA. I know—but you so thin . . .

BENEATHA (*irritably*). Mama, I'm not cold.

MAMA (*seeing the make-down bed as*

TRAVIS *has left it*). Lord have mercy, look at that poor bed. Bless his heart—he tries, don't he?
(*She moves to the bed* TRAVIS *has sloppily made up.*)

RUTH. No—he don't half try at all 'cause he knows you going to come along behind him and fix everything. That's just how come he don't know how to do nothing right now—you done spoiled that boy so.

MAMA. Well—he's a little boy. Ain't supposed to know 'bout housekeeping. My baby, that's what he is. What you fix for his breakfast this morning?

RUTH (*angrily*). I feed my son, Lena!

MAMA. I ain't meddling—(*under breath; busy-bodyish*). I just noticed all last week he had cold cereal, and when it starts getting this chilly in the fall a child ought to have some hot grits or something when he goes out in the cold—

RUTH (*furious*). I gave him hot oats —is that all right!

MAMA. I ain't meddling. (*Pause.*) Put a lot of nice butter on it? (RUTH *shoots her an angry look and does not reply.*) He likes lots of butter.

RUTH (*exasperated*). Lena—

MAMA (*to* BENEATHA. MAMA *is inclined to wander conversationally sometimes*). What was you and your brother fussing 'bout this morning?

BENEATHA. It's not important, Mama.
(*She gets up and goes to look out at the bathroom, which is apparently free, and she picks up her towels and rushes out.*)

MAMA. What was they fighting about?

RUTH. Now you know as well as I do.

MAMA (*Shaking her head*). Brother still worrying hisself sick about that money?

RUTH. You know he is.

MAMA. You had breakfast?

RUTH. Some coffee.

MAMA. Girl, you better start eating and looking after yourself better. You almost thin as Travis.

RUTH. Lena—

MAMA. Un-hunh?

RUTH. What are you going to do with it?

MAMA. Now don't you start, child. It's too early in the morning to be talking about money. It ain't Christian.

RUTH. It's just that he got his heart set on that store—

MAMA. You mean that liquor store that Willy Harris want him to invest in?

RUTH. Yes—

MAMA. We ain't no business people, Ruth. We just plain working folks.

RUTH. Ain't nobody business people till they go into business. Walter Lee say colored people ain't never going to start getting ahead till they start gambling on some different kinds of things in the world —investments and things.

MAMA. What done got into you, girl? Walter Lee done finally sold you on investing.

RUTH. No. Mama, something is happening between Walter and me. I don't know what it is—but he needs something —something I can't give him any more. He needs this chance, Lena.

MAMA (*frowning deeply*). But liquor, honey—

RUTH. Well—like Walter say—I spec people going to always be drinking themselves some liquor.

MAMA. Well—whether they drinks it or not ain't none of my business. But whether I go into business selling it to 'em *is*, and I don't want that on my ledger this late in life. (*Stopping suddenly and studying her daughter-in-law.*) Ruth Younger, what's the matter with you today? You look like you could fall over right there.

RUTH. I'm tired.

MAMA. Then you better stay home from work today.

RUTH. I can't stay home. She'd be calling up the agency and screaming at them, "My girl didn't come in today— send me somebody! My girl didn't come in!" Oh, she just have a fit . . .

MAMA. Well, let her have it. I'll just call her up and say you got the flu—

RUTH (*laughing*). Why the flu?

MAMA. 'Cause it sounds respectable to 'em. Something white people get, too. They know 'bout the flu. Otherwise they think you been cut up or something when you tell 'em you sick.

RUTH. I got to go in. We need the money.

MAMA. Somebody would of thought my children done all but starved to death the way they talk about money here late. Child, we got a great big old check coming tomorrow.

RUTH (*sincerely, but also self-righteously*). Now that's your money. It ain't got nothing to do with me. We all feel like that—Walter and Bennie and me—even Travis.

MAMA (*thoughtfully, and suddenly very far away*). Ten thousand dollars—

RUTH. Sure is wonderful.

MAMA. Ten thousand dollars.

RUTH. You know what you should do, Miss Lena? You should take yourself a trip somewhere. To Europe or South America or someplace—

MAMA (*throwing up her hands at the thought*). Oh, child!

RUTH. I'm serious. Just pack up and leave! Go on away and enjoy yourself some. Forget about the family and have yourself a ball for once in your life—

MAMA (*drily*). You sound like I'm just about ready to die. Who'd go with me? What I look like wandering 'round Europe by myself?

RUTH. Shoot—these here rich white women do it all the time. They don't think nothing of packing up they suitcases and piling on one of them big steamships and—swoosh!—they gone, child.

MAMA. Something always told me I wasn't no rich white woman.

RUTH. Well—what are you going to do with it then?

MAMA. I ain't rightly decided. (*Thinking. She speaks now with emphasis.*) Some of it got to be put away for Beneatha and her schoolin'—and ain't nothing going to touch that part of it. Nothing. (*She waits several seconds, trying to make up her mind about something, and looks at* RUTH *a little tentatively before going on.*) Been thinking that we maybe could meet the notes on a little old two-story somewhere, with a yard where Travis could play in the summertime, if we use part of the insurance for a down payment and everybody kind of pitch in. I could maybe take on a little day work again, few days a week—

RUTH (*studying her mother-in-law furtively and concentrating on her ironing, anxious to encourage without seeming to*). Well, Lord knows, we've put enough rent into this here rat trap to pay for four houses by now . . .

MAMA (*looking up at the words "rat trap" and then looking around and leaning back and sighing—in a suddenly reflective mood—*). "Rat trap"—yes, that's all it is. (*smiling*) I remember just as well the day me and Big Walter moved in here. Hadn't been married but two weeks and wasn't planning on living here no more than a year. (*She shakes her head at the dissolved dream.*) We was going to set away, little by little, don't you know, and buy a little place out in Morgan Park. We had even picked out the house. (*Chuckling a little.*) Looks right dumpy today. But Lord, child, you should know all the dreams I had 'bout buying that house and fixing it up and making me a little garden in the back—(*She waits and stops smiling.*) And didn't none of it happen.

(*Dropping her hands in a futile gesture.*)

RUTH (*keeps her head down, ironing*). Yes, life can be a barrel of disappointments, sometimes.

MAMA. Honey, Big Walter would come in here some nights back then and slump down on that couch there and just look at the rug, and look at me and look at the rug and then back at me—and I'd know he was down then . . . really down. (*After a second very long and thoughtful pause; she is seeing back to times that only she can see.*) And then, Lord, when I lost that baby—little Claude—I almost thought I was going to lose Big Walter too. Oh, that man grieved hisself! He was one man to love his children.

RUTH. Ain't nothin' can tear at you like losin' your baby.

MAMA. I guess that's how come that man finally worked hisself to death like he done. Like he was fighting his own war with this here world that took his baby from him.

RUTH. He sure was a fine man, all right. I always liked Mr. Younger.

MAMA. Crazy 'bout his children! God knows there was plenty wrong with Walter Younger—hard-headed, mean, kind of wild with women—plenty wrong with him. But he sure loved his children. Always wanted them to have something—be something. That's where Brother gets all these notions, I reckon. Big Walter used to say, he'd get right wet in the eyes sometimes, lean his head back with the water standing in his eyes and say, "Seem like God didn't see fit to give the black man nothing but dreams—but He did give us children to make them dreams seem worth while." (*She smiles.*) He could talk like that, don't you know.

RUTH. Yes, he sure could. He was a good man, Mr. Younger.

MAMA. Yes, a fine man—just couldn't never catch up with his dreams, that's all.

(BENEATHA *comes in, brushing her hair and looking up to the ceiling where the sound of a vacuum cleaner has started up.*)

BENEATHA. What could be so dirty on that woman's rugs that she has to vacuum them every single day?

RUTH. I wish certain young women 'round here who I could name would take inspiration about certain rugs in a certain apartment I could also mention.

BENEATHA (*shrugging*). How much cleaning can a house need, for Christ's sakes.

MAMA (*not liking the Lord's name used thus*). Bennie!

RUTH. Just listen to her—just listen!

BENEATHA. Oh, God!

MAMA. If you use the Lord's name just one more time—

BENEATHA (*a bit of a whine*). Oh, Mama—

RUTH. Fresh—just fresh as salt, this girl!

BENEATHA (*drily*). Well—if the salt loses its savor—

MAMA. Now that will do. I just ain't going to have you 'round here reciting the scriptures in vain—you hear me?

BENEATHA. How did I manage to get on everybody's wrong side by just walking into a room?

RUTH. If you weren't so fresh—

BENEATHA. Ruth, I'm twenty years old.

MAMA. What time you be home from school today?

BENEATHA. Kind of late. (*With enthusiasm.*) Madeline is going to start my guitar lessons today.

(MAMA *and* RUTH *look up with the same expression.*)

MAMA. Your *what* kind of lessons?

BENEATHA. Guitar.

RUTH. Oh, Father!

MAMA. How come you done taken it in your mind to learn to play the guitar?

BENEATHA. I just want to, that's all.

MAMA (*smiling*). Lord, child, don't you know what to do with yourself? How long it going to be before you get tired of this now—like you got tired of that little play-acting group you joined last year? (*Looking at Ruth.*) And what was it the year before that?

RUTH. The horseback-riding club for which she bought that fifty-five-dollar riding habit that's been hanging in the closet ever since!

MAMA (*to* BENEATHA). Why you got to flit so from one thing to another, baby?

BENEATHA (*sharply*). I just want to learn to play the guitar. Is there anything wrong with that?

MAMA. Ain't nobody trying to stop you. I just wonders sometimes why you has to flit so from one thing to another all the time. You ain't never done nothing with all that camera equipment you brought home—

BENEATHA. I don't flit! I—I experiment with different forms of expression—

RUTH. Like riding a horse?

BENEATHA. —People have to express themselves one way or another.

MAMA. What is it you want to express?

BENEATHA (*angrily*). Me! (MAMA *and* RUTH *look at each other and burst into raucous laughter.*) Don't worry—I don't expect you to understand.

MAMA (*to change the subject*). Who you going out with tomorrow night?

BENEATHA (*with displeasure*). George Murchison again.

MAMA (*pleased*). Oh—you getting a little sweet on him?

RUTH. You ask me, this child ain't sweet on nobody but herself—(*under breath*). Express herself!

(*They laugh.*)

BENEATHA. Oh—I like George all right, Mama. I mean I like him enough to go out with him and stuff, but—

RUTH (*for devilment*). What does *and stuff* mean?

BENEATHA. Mind your own business.

MAMA. Stop picking at her now, Ruth. (*A thoughtful pause, and then a suspicious sudden look at her daughter as she turns in her chair for emphasis.*) What *does* it mean?

BENEATHA (*wearily*). Oh, I just mean I couldn't ever really be serious about George. He's—he's so shallow.

RUTH. Shallow—what do you mean he's shallow? He's *rich!*

MAMA. Hush, Ruth.

BENEATHA. I know he's rich. He knows he's rich, too.

RUTH. Well—what other qualities a man got to have to satisfy you, little girl?

BENEATHA. You wouldn't even begin to understand. Anybody who married Walter could not possibly understand.

MAMA (*outraged*). What kind of way is that to talk about your brother?

BENEATHA. Brother is a flip—let's face it.

MAMA (*to* RUTH, *helplessly*). What's a flip?

RUTH (*glad to add kindling*). She's saying he's crazy.

BENEATHA. Not crazy. Brother isn't really crazy yet—he—he's an elaborate neurotic.

MAMA. Hush your mouth!

BENEATHA. As for George. Well. George looks good—he's got a beautiful car and he takes me to nice places and, as my sister-in-law says, he is probably the richest boy I will ever get to know and I even like him sometimes—but if the Youngers are sitting around waiting to see if their little Bennie is going to tie up the family with the Murchisons, they are wasting their time.

RUTH. You mean you wouldn't marry George Murchison if he asked you someday? That pretty, rich thing? Honey, I knew you was odd—

BENEATHA. No I would not marry him if all I felt for him was what I feel now. Besides, George's family wouldn't really like it.

MAMA. Why not?

BENEATHA. Oh, Mama—The Murchisons are honest-to-God-real-*live*-rich colored people, and the only people in the world who are more snobbish than rich white people are rich colored people. I thought everybody knew that. I've met Mrs. Murchison. She's a scene!

MAMA. You must not dislike people 'cause they well off, honey.

BENEATHA. Why not? It makes just as much sense as disliking people 'cause they are poor, and lots of people do that.

RUTH (*a wisdom-of-the-ages manner.*

To MAMA). Well, she'll get over some of this—

BENEATHA. Get over it? What are you talking about, Ruth? Listen, I'm going to be a doctor. I'm not worried about who I'm going to marry yet—if I ever get married.

MAMA *and* RUTH. *If!*

MAMA. Now, Bennie—

BENEATHA. Oh, I probably will . . . but first I'm going to be a doctor, and George, for one, still thinks that's pretty funny. I couldn't be bothered with that. I am going to be a doctor and everybody around here better understand that!

MAMA (*kindly*). 'Course you going to be a doctor, honey, God willing.

BENEATHA (*drily*). God hasn't got a thing to do with it.

MAMA. Beneatha—that just wasn't necessary.

BENEATHA. Well—neither is God. I get sick of hearing about God.

MAMA. Beneatha!

BENEATHA. I mean it! I'm just tired of hearing about God all the time. What has He got to do with anything? Does he pay tuition?

MAMA. You 'bout to get your fresh little jaw slapped!

RUTH. That's just what she needs, all right!

BENEATHA. Why? Why can't I say what I want to around here, like everybody else?

MAMA. It don't sound nice for a young girl to say things like that—you wasn't brought up that way. Me and your father went to trouble to get you and Brother to church every Sunday.

BENEATHA. Mama, you don't understand. It's all a matter of ideas, and God is just one idea I don't accept. It's not important. I am not going out and be immoral or commit crimes because I don't believe in God. I don't even think about it. It's just that I get tired of Him getting credit for all the things the human race achieves through its own stubborn effort. There simply is no blasted God—there is only man and it is he who makes miracles!

(MAMA *absorbs this speech, studies her daughter and rises slowly and crosses to* BENEATHA *and slaps her powerfully across the face. After, there is only silence and the daughter drops her eyes from her mother's face, and* MAMA *is very tall before her.*)

MAMA. Now—you say after me, in my mother's house there is still God. (*There is a long pause and* BENEATHA *stares at the floor wordlessly.* MAMA *repeats the phrase with precision and cool emotion.*) In my mother's house there is still God.

BENEATHA. In my mother's house there is still God.

(*A long pause.*)

MAMA (*walking away from* BENEATHA, *too disturbed for triumphant posture. Stopping and turning back to her daughter*). There are some ideas we ain't going to have in this house. Not long as I am at the head of this family.

BENEATHA. Yes, ma'am.

(MAMA *walks out of the room.*)

RUTH (*almost gently, with profound understanding*). You think you a woman, Bennie—but you still a little girl. What you did was childish—so you got treated like a child.

BENEATHA. I see. (*Quietly.*) I also see that everybody thinks it's all right for Mama to be a tyrant. But all the tyranny in the world will never put a God in the heavens!

(*She picks up her books and goes out.*)

RUTH (*goes to* MAMA'S *door*). She said she was sorry.

MAMA (*coming out, going to her plant*). They frightens me, Ruth. My children.

RUTH. You got good children, Lena. They just a little off sometimes—but they're good.

MAMA. No—there's something come down between me and them that don't let us understand each other and I don't know what it is. One done almost lost his mind thinking 'bout money all the time and the other done commence to talk about things I can't seem to understand in no form or fashion. What is it that's changing, Ruth?

RUTH (*soothingly, older than her years*). Now . . . you taking it all too seriously. You just got strong-willed children and it takes a strong woman like you to keep 'em in hand.

MAMA (*looking at her plant and sprinkling a little water on it*). They spirited all right, my children. Got to admit they got spirit—Bennie and Walter. Like this little old plant that ain't never had enough sunshine or nothing—and look at it . . .

(*She has her back to* RUTH, *who has had to stop ironing and lean against something and put the back of her hand to her forehead.*)

RUTH (*trying to keep* MAMA *from noticing*). You . . . sure . . . loves that little old thing, don't you? . . .

MAMA. Well, I always wanted me a garden like I used to see sometimes at the back of the houses down home. This plant is close as I ever got to having one. (*She looks out of the window as she replaces the plant.*) Lord, ain't nothing as dreary as the view from this window on a dreary day, is there? Why ain't you singing this morning, Ruth? Sing that "No Ways Tired." That song always lifts me up so— (*She turns at last to see that* RUTH *has slipped quietly into a chair, in a state of semiconsciousness.*) Ruth! Ruth honey—what's the matter with you . . . Ruth!

(*Curtain.*)

SCENE TWO

(*It is the following morning; a Saturday morning, and house cleaning is in progress at the* YOUNGERS. *Furniture has been shoved hither and yon and* MAMA *is giving the kitchen-area walls a washing down.* BENEATHA, *in dungarees, with a handkerchief tied around her face, is spraying insecticide into the cracks in the walls. As they work, the radio is on and a Southside disk-jockey program is inappropriately filling the house with a rather exotic saxophone blues.* TRAVIS, *the sole idle one, is leaning on his arms, looking out of the window.*)

TRAVIS. Grandmama, that stuff Bennie is using smells awful. Can I go downstairs, please?

MAMA. Did you get all them chores done already? I ain't seen you doing much.

TRAVIS. Yes'm—finished early. Where did Mama go this morning?

MAMA (*looking at* BENEATHA). She had to go on a little errand.

TRAVIS. Where?

MAMA. To tend to her business.

TRAVIS. Can I go outside then?

MAMA. Oh, I guess so. You better stay right in front of the house, though . . . and keep a good lookout for the postman.

TRAVIS. Yes'm. (*He starts out and decides to give his* AUNT BENEATHA *a good swat on the legs as he passes her.*) Leave them poor little old cockroaches alone, they ain't bothering you none.

(*He runs as she swings the spray gun at him both viciously and playfully.* WALTER *enters from the bedroom and goes to the phone.*)

MAMA. Look out there, girl, before you be spilling some of that stuff on that child!

TRAVIS (*teasing*). That's right—look out now!

(*He exits.*)

BENEATHA (*drily*). I can't imagine that it would hurt him—it has never hurt the roaches.

MAMA. Well, little boys' hides ain't as tough as Southside roaches.

WALTER (*into phone*). Hello—Let me talk to Willy Harris.

MAMA. You better get over there behind the bureau. I seen one marching out of there like Napoleon yesterday.

WALTER. Hello, Willy? It ain't come yet. It'll be here in a few minutes. Did the lawyer give you the papers?

BENEATHA. There's really only one way to get rid of them, Mama—

MAMA. How?

BENEATHA. Set fire to this building.

WALTER. Good. Good. I'll be right over.

BENEATHA. Where did Ruth go, Walter?

WALTER. I don't know.

(*He exits abruptly.*)

BENEATHA. Mama, where did Ruth go?

MAMA (*looking at her with meaning*). To the doctor, I think.

BENEATHA. The doctor? What's the matter? (*They exchange glances.*) You don't think—

MAMA (*with her sense of drama*). Now I ain't saying what I think. But I ain't never been wrong 'bout a woman neither.

(*The phone rings.*)

BENEATHA (*at the phone*). Hay-lo . . . (*pause, and a moment of recognition*). Well—when did you get back! . . . And how was it? . . . Of course I've missed you—in my way . . . This morning? No . . . house cleaning and all that and Mama hates it if I let people come over when the house is like this . . . You *have*? Well, that's different . . . What is it—Oh, what the hell, come on over . . . Right, see you then.

(*She hangs up.*)

MAMA (*who has listened vigorously, as is her habit*). Who is that you inviting over here with this house looking like this? You ain't got the pride you was born with!

BENEATHA. Asagai doesn't care how houses look, Mama—he's an intellectual.

MAMA. *Who?*

BENEATHA. Asagai—Joseph Asagai. He's an African boy I met on campus. He's been studying in Canada all summer.

MAMA. What's his name?

BENEATHA. Asagai, Joseph. Ah-sah-guy . . . He's from Nigeria.

MAMA. Oh, that's the little country that was founded by slaves way back . . .

BENEATHA. No, Mama—that's Liberia.

MAMA. I don't think I never met no African before.

BENEATHA. Well, do me a favor and don't ask him a whole lot of ignorant questions about Africans. I mean, do they wear clothes and all that—

MAMA. Well, now, I guess if you think we so ignorant 'round here maybe you shouldn't bring your friends here––

BENEATHA. It's just that people ask such crazy things. All anyone seems to know about when it comes to Africa is Tarzan—

MAMA (*indignantly*). Why should I know anything about Africa?

BENEATHA. Why do you give money at church for the missionary work?

MAMA. Well, that's to help save people.

BENEATHA. You mean save them from *heathenism*—

MAMA (*innocently*). Yes.

BENEATHA. I'm afraid they need more salvation from the British and the French.

(RUTH *comes in forlornly and pulls off her coat with dejection. They both turn to look at her.*)

RUTH (*dispiritedly*). Well, I guess from all the happy faces—everybody knows.

BENEATHA. You pregnant?

MAMA. Lord have mercy, I sure hope it's a little old girl. Travis ought to have a sister.

(BENEATHA *and* RUTH *give her a hopeless look for this grandmotherly enthusiasm.*)

BENEATHA. How far along are you?

RUTH. Two months.
BENEATHA. Did you mean to? I mean did you plan it or was it an accident?
MAMA. What do you know about planning or not planning?
BENEATHA. Oh, Mama.
RUTH (*wearily*). She's twenty years old, Lena.
BENEATHA. Did you plan it, Ruth?
RUTH. Mind your own business.
BENEATHA. It is my business—where is he going to live, on the *roof*? (*There is silence following the remark as the three women react to the sense of it.*) Gee—I didn't mean that, Ruth, honest. Gee, I don't feel like that at all. I—I think it is wonderful.
RUTH (*dully*). Wonderful.
BENEATHA. Yes—really.
MAMA (*looking at* RUTH, *worried*). Doctor say everything going to be all right?
RUTH (*far away*). Yes—she says everything is going to be fine . . .
MAMA (*immediately suspicious*). "She"—What doctor you went to?
(RUTH *folds over, near hysteria.*)
MAMA (*worriedly hovering over* RUTH). Ruth honey—what's the matter with you—you sick?
(RUTH *has her fists clenched on her thighs and is fighting hard to suppress a scream that seems to be rising in her.*)
BENEATHA. What's the matter with her, Mama?
MAMA (*working her fingers in* RUTH'S *shoulder to relax her*). She be all right. Women gets right depressed sometimes when they get her way. (*Speaking softly, expertly, rapidly.*) Now you just relax. That's right . . . just lean back, don't think 'bout nothing at all . . . nothing at all—
RUTH. I'm all right . . .
(*The glassy-eyed look melts and then she collapses into a fit of heavy sobbing. The bell rings.*)

BENEATHA. Oh, my God—that must be Asagai.
MAMA (*To* RUTH). Come on now, honey. You need to lie down and rest awhile . . . then have some nice hot food.
(*They exit,* RUTH'S *weight on her mother-in-law.* BENEATHA, *herself profoundly disturbed, opens the door to admit a rather dramatic-looking young man with a large package.*)
ASAGAI. Hello, Alaiyo—
BENEATHA (*holding the door open and regarding him with pleasure*). Hello . . . (*Long pause*) Well—come in. And please excuse everything. My mother was very upset about my letting anyone come here with the place like this.
ASAGAI (*coming into the room*). You look disturbed too . . . Is something wrong?
BENEATHA (*still at the door, absently*). Yes . . . we've all got acute ghetto-itus. (*She smiles and comes toward him, finding a cigarette and sitting.*) So—sit down! How was Canada?
ASAGAI (*a sophisticate*). Canadian.
BENEATHA (*looking at him*). I'm very glad you are back.
ASAGAI (*looking back at her in turn*). Are you really?
BENEATHA. Yes—very.
ASAGAI. Why—you were quite glad when I went away. What happened?
BENEATHA. You went away.
ASAGAI. Ahhhhhhhh.
BENEATHA. Before—you wanted to be so serious before there was time.
ASAGAI. How much time must there be before one knows what one feels?
BENEATHA (*stalling this particular conversation. Her hands pressed together, in a deliberately childish gesture*). What did you bring me?
ASAGAI (*handing her the package*). Open it and see.
BENEATHA (*eagerly opening the package and drawing out some records and the colorful robes of a Nigerian woman*).

Oh, Asagai! . . . You got them for me! . . . How beautiful! . . . and the records, too! (*She lifts out the robes and runs to the mirror with them and holds the drapery up in front of herself.*)

ASAGAI (*coming to her at the mirror*). I shall have to teach you how to drape it properly. (*He flings the material about her for the moment and stands back to look at her.*) Ah—Oh-pay-gay-day, oh-ghah-mu-shay. (*A Yoruba exclamation for admiration.*) You wear it well . . . very well . . . mutilated hair and all.

BENEATHA (*turning suddenly*). My hair—what's wrong with my hair?

ASAGAI (*shrugging*). Were you born with it like that?

BENEATHA (*reaching up to touch it*). No . . . of course not.

(*She looks back to the mirror, disturbed.*)

ASAGAI (*smiling*). How then?

BENEATHA. You know perfectly well how . . . as crinkly as yours . . . that's how.

ASAGAI. And it is ugly to you that way?

BENEATHA (*quickly*). Oh, no—not ugly . . . (*More slowly, apologetically.*) But it's so hard to manage when it's, well —raw.

ASAGAI. And so to accommodate that—you mutilate it every week?

BENEATHA. It's not mutilation!

ASAGAI (*laughing aloud at her seriousness*). Oh . . . please! I am only teasing you because you are so very serious about these things. (*He stands back from her and folds his arms across his chest as he watches her pulling at her hair and frowning in the mirror.*) Do you remember the first time you met me at school? . . . (*He laughs.*) You came up to me and you said—and I thought you were the most serious little thing I had ever seen—you said: (*He imitates her.*) "Mr. Asagai—I want very much to talk with you. About Africa. You see, Mr. Asagai, I am looking for my *identity!*"

(*He laughs.*)

BENEATHA (*turning to him, not laughing*). Yes—

(*Her face is quizzical, profoundly disturbed.*)

ASAGAI (*still teasing and reaching out and taking her face in his hands and turning her profile to him*). Well . . . it is true that this is not so much a profile of a Hollywood queen as perhaps a queen of the Nile—(*a mock dismissal of the importance of the question*). But what does it matter? Assimilationism is so popular in your country.

BENEATHA (*wheeling, passionately, sharply*). I am not an assimilationist!

ASAGAI (*The protest hangs in the room for a moment and* ASAGAI *studies her, his laughter fading*). Such a serious one. (*There is a pause.*) So—you like the robes? You must take excellent care of them—they are from my sister's personal wardrobe.

BENEATHA (*with incredulity*). You— you sent all the way home—for me?

ASAGAI (*with charm*). For you—I would do much more . . . Well, that is what I came for. I must go.

BENEATHA. Will you call me Monday?

ASAGAI. Yes . . . We have a great deal to talk about. I mean about identity and time and all that.

BENEATHA. Time?

ASAGAI. Yes. About how much time one needs to know what one feels.

BENEATHA. You never understood that there is more than one kind of feeling which can exist between a man and a woman—or, at least, there should be.

ASAGAI (*shaking his head negatively but gently*). No. Between a man and a woman there need be only one kind of feeling. I have that for you . . . Now even . . . right this moment . . .

BENEATHA. I know—and by itself— it won't do. I can find that anywhere.

ASAGAI. For a woman it should be enough.

BENEATHA. I know—because that's what it says in all the novels that men write. But it isn't. Go ahead and laugh—but I'm not interested in being someone's little episode in America or—(*with feminine vengeance*)—one of them! (ASAGAI *has burst into laughter again.*) That's funny as hell, huh!

ASAGAI. It's just that every American girl I have known has said that to me. White—black—in this you are all the same. And the same speech, too!

BENEATHA (*angrily*). Yuk, yuk, yuk!

ASAGAI. It's how you can be sure that the world's most liberated women are not liberated at all. You all talk about it too much!

(MAMA *enters and is immediately all social charm because of the presence of a guest.*)

BENEATHA. Oh—Mama—this is Mr. Asagai.

MAMA. How do you do?

ASAGAI (*total politeness to an elder*). How do you do, Mrs. Younger. Please forgive me for coming at such an outrageous hour on a Saturday.

MAMA. Well, you are quite welcome. I just hope you understand that our house don't always look like this. (*Chatterish.*) You must come again. I would love to hear all about—(*not sure of the name*)—your country. I think it's so sad the way our American Negroes don't know nothing about Africa 'cept Tarzan and all that. And all that money they pour into these churches when they ought to be helping you people over there drive out them French and Englishmen done taken away your land.

(*The mother flashes a slightly superior look at her daughter upon completion of the recitation.*)

ASAGAI (*taken aback by this sudden and acutely unrelated expression of sympathy*). Yes . . . yes . . .

MAMA (*smiling at him suddenly and relaxing and looking him over*). How many miles is it from here to where you come from?

ASAGAI. Many thousands.

MAMA (*looking at him as she would* WALTER). I bet you don't half look after yourself, being away from your mama either. I spec you better come 'round here from time to time and get yourself some decent home-cooked meals . . .

ASAGAI (*moved*). Thank you. Thank you very much. (*They are all quiet, then—*) Well . . . I must go. I will call you Monday, Alaiyo.

MAMA. What's that he call you?

ASAGAI. Oh—"Alaiyo." I hope you don't mind. It is what you would call a nickname, I think. It is a Yoruba word. I am a Yoruba.

MAMA (*looking at* BENEATHA). I—I thought he was from—

ASAGAI (*understanding*). Nigeria is my country. Yoruba is my tribal origin—

BENEATHA. You didn't tell us what Alaiyo means . . . for all I know, you might be calling me Little Idiot or something . . .

ASAGAI. Well . . . let me see . . . I do not know how just to explain it . . . The sense of a thing can be so different when it changes languages.

BENEATHA. You're evading.

ASAGAI. No—really it is difficult . . . (*Thinking.*) It means . . . it means One for Whom Bread—Food—Is Not Enough. (*He looks at her.*) Is that all right?

BENEATHA (*understanding, softly*). Thank you.

MAMA (*looking from one to the other and not understanding any of it*). Well . . . that's nice . . . You must come see us again—Mr.—

ASAGAI. Ah-sah-guy . . .

MAMA. Yes . . . Do come again.

ASAGAI. Good-bye.

(*He exits.*)

MAMA (*after him*). Lord, that's a pretty thing just went out here! (*Insinuatingly, to her daughter.*) Yes, I guess I see why we done commence to get so interested in Africa 'round here. Missionaries my aunt Jenny!

(*She exits.*)

BENEATHA. Oh, Mama! . . .

(*She picks up the Nigerian dress and holds it up to her in front of the mirror again. She sets the headdress on haphazardly and then notices her hair again and clutches at it and then replaces the headdress and frowns at herself. Then she starts to wriggle in front of the mirror as she thinks a Nigerian woman might.* TRAVIS *enters and regards her.*)

TRAVIS. You cracking up?

BENEATHA. Shut up.

(*She pulls the headdress off and looks at herself in the mirror and clutches at her hair again and squinches her eyes as if trying to imagine something. Then, suddenly, she gets her raincoat and kerchief and hurriedly prepares for going out.*)

MAMA (*coming back into the room*). She's resting now. Travis, baby, run next door and ask Miss Johnson to please let me have a little kitchen cleanser. This here can is empty as Jacob's kettle.

TRAVIS. I just came in.

MAMA. Do as you told. (*He exits and she looks at her daughter.*) Where you going?

BENEATHA (*halting at the door*). To become a queen of the Nile!

(*She exits in a breathless blaze of glory.* RUTH *appears in the bedroom doorway.*)

MAMA. Who told you to get up?

RUTH. Ain't nothing wrong with me to be lying in no bed for. Where did Bennie go?

MAMA (*drumming her fingers*). Far as I could make out—to Egypt. (RUTH *just looks at her.*) What time is it getting to?

RUTH. Ten twenty. And the mailman going to ring that bell this morning just like he done every morning for the last umpteen years.

(TRAVIS *comes in with the cleanser can.*)

TRAVIS. She say to tell you that she don't have much.

MAMA (*angrily*). Lord, some people I could name sure is tight-fisted! (*Directing her grandson.*) Mark two cans of cleanser down on the list there. If she that hard up for kitchen cleanser, I sure don't want to forget to get her none!

RUTH. Lena—maybe the woman is just short on cleanser—

MAMA (*not listening*). —Much baking powder as she done borrowed from me all these years, she could of done gone into the baking business!

(*The bell sounds suddenly and sharply and all three are stunned—serious and silent—mid-speech. In spite of all the other conversations and distractions of the morning, this is what they have been waiting for, even* TRAVIS, *who looks helplessly from his mother to his grandmother.* RUTH *is the first to come to life again.*)

RUTH (*to* TRAVIS). Get down them steps, boy!

(TRAVIS *snaps to life and flies out to get the mail.*)

MAMA (*her eyes wide, her hand to her breast*). You mean it done really come?

RUTH (*excited*). Oh, Miss Lena!

MAMA (*collecting herself*). Well . . . I don't know what we all so excited about 'round here for. We known it was coming for months.

RUTH. That's a whole lot different from having it come and being able to hold it in your hands . . . a piece of paper worth ten thousand dollars . . . (TRAVIS *bursts back into the room. He holds the envelope high above his head, like a little dancer, his face is radiant and he is breathless. He moves to his grandmother with sudden slow ceremony and puts the envelope into her hands. She accepts it, and then merely holds it and looks at it.*) Come on! Open it . . . Lord have mercy, I wish Walter Lee was here!

TRAVIS. Open it, Grandmama!

MAMA (*staring at it*). Now you all be quiet. It's just a check.

RUTH. Open it . . .

MAMA (*still staring at it*). Now don't act silly . . . We ain't never been no people to act silly 'bout no money—

RUTH (*swiftly*). We ain't never had none before—*open it!*

(MAMA *finally makes a good strong tear and pulls out the thin blue slice of paper and inspects it closely. The boy and his mother study it raptly over* MAMA'S *shoulders.*)

MAMA. Travis! (*She is counting off with doubt.*) Is that the right number of zeros.

TRAVIS. Yes'm . . . ten thousand dollars. Gaalee, Grandmama, you rich.

MAMA (*She holds the check away from her, still looking at it. Slowly her face sobers into a mask of unhappiness*). Ten thousand dollars. (*She hands it to* RUTH.) Put it away somewhere, Ruth. (*She does not look at* RUTH; *her eyes seem to be seeing something somewhere very far off.*) Ten thousand dollars they give you. Ten thousand dollars.

TRAVIS (*to his mother, sincerely*). What's the matter with Grandmama—don't she want to be rich?

RUTH (*distractedly*). You go on out and play now, baby. (TRAVIS *exits.* MAMA *starts wiping dishes absently, humming intently to herself.* RUTH *turns to her, with kind exasperation.*) You've gone and got yourself upset.

MAMA (*not looking at her*). I spec if it wasn't for you all . . . I would just put that money away or give it to the church or something.

RUTH. Now what kind of talk is that. Mr. Younger would just be plain mad if he could hear you talking foolish like that.

MAMA (*stopping and staring off*). Yes . . . he sure would. (*Sighing.*) We got enough to do with that money, all right. (*She halts then, and turns and looks at her daughter-in-law hard;* RUTH *avoids her eyes and* MAMA *wipes her hands with finality and starts to speak firmly to* RUTH.) Where did you go today, girl?

RUTH. To the doctor.

MAMA (*impatiently*). Now, Ruth . . . you know better than that. Old Doctor Jones is strange enough in his way but there ain't nothing 'bout him make somebody slip and call him "she"—like you done this morning.

RUTH. Well, that's what happened—my tongue slipped.

MAMA. You went to see that woman, didn't you?

RUTH (*defensively, giving herself away*). What woman you talking about?

MAMA (*angrily*). That woman who—

(WALTER *enters in great excitement.*)

WALTER. Did it come?

MAMA (*quietly*). Can't you give people a Christian greeting before you start asking about money?

WALTER (*to* RUTH). Did it come? (RUTH *unfolds the check and lays it quietly before him, watching him intently with thoughts of her own.* WALTER *sits down and grasps it close and counts off the zeros.*) Ten thousand dollars— (*He turns suddenly, frantically to his mother and draws some papers out of his breast pocket.*) Mama—look. Old Willy Harris put everything on paper—

MAMA. Son—I think you ought to talk to your wife . . . I'll go on out and leave you alone if you want—

WALTER. I can talk to her later—Mama, look—

MAMA. Son—

WALTER. WILL SOMEBODY PLEASE LISTEN TO ME TODAY!

MAMA (*quietly*). I don't 'low no yellin' in this house, Walter Lee, and you know it—(WALTER *stares at them in frustration and starts to speak several times.*) And there ain't going to be no investing in no liquor stores. I don't aim to have to speak on that again.

(*A long pause.*)

WALTER. Oh—so you don't aim to have to speak on that again? So *you* have decided . . . (*Crumpling his papers.*) Well, *you* tell that to my boy tonight when you put him to sleep on the living-room couch ... (*Turning to* MAMA *and speaking directly to her.*) Yeah—and tell it to my wife, Mama, tomorrow when she has to go out of here to look after somebody else's kids. And tell it to *me,* Mama, every time we need a new pair of curtains and I have to watch *you* go out and work in somebody's kitchen. Yeah, you tell me then!

(WALTER *starts out.*)

RUTH. Where you going?

WALTER. I'm going out!

RUTH. Where?

WALTER. Just out of this house somewhere—

RUTH (*getting her coat*). I'll come too.

WALTER. I don't want you to come!

RUTH. I got something to talk to you about, Walter.

WALTER. That's too bad.

MAMA (*still quietly*). Walter Lee— (*She waits and he finally turns and looks at her.*) Sit down.

WALTER. I'm a grown man, Mama.

MAMA. Ain't nobody said you wasn't grown. But you still in my house and my presence. And as long as you are—you'll talk to your wife civil. Now sit down.

RUTH (*suddenly*). Oh, let him go on out and drink himself to death! He makes me sick to my stomach! (*She flings her coat against him.*)

WALTER (*violently*). And you turn mine too, baby! (RUTH *goes into their bedroom and slams the door behind her.*) That was my greatest mistake—

MAMA (*still quietly*). Walter, what is the matter with you?

WALTER. Matter with me? Ain't nothing the matter with *me!*

MAMA. Yes there is. Something eating you up like a crazy man. Something more than me not giving you this money. The past few years I been watching it happen to you. You get all nervous acting and kind of wild in the eyes— (WALTER *jumps up impatiently at her words.*) I said sit there now, I'm talking to you!

WALTER. Mama—I don't need no nagging at me today.

MAMA. Seem like you getting to a place where you always tied up in some kind of knot about something. But if anybody ask you 'bout it you just yell at 'em and bust out the house and go out and drink somewheres. Walter Lee, people can't live with that. Ruth's a good, patient girl in her way—but you getting to be too much. Boy, don't make the mistake of driving that girl away from you.

WALTER. Why—what she do for me?

MAMA. She loves you.

WALTER. Mama—I'm going out. I want to go off somewhere and be by myself for a while.

MAMA. I'm sorry 'bout your liquor store, son. It just wasn't the thing for us to do. That's what I want to tell you about—

WALTER. I got to go out, Mama— (*He rises.*)

MAMA. It's dangerous, son.

WALTER. What's dangerous?

MAMA. When a man goes outside his home to look for peace.

WALTER (*beseechingly*). Then why can't there never be no peace in this house then?

MAMA. You done found it in some other house?

WALTER. No—there ain't no woman! Why do women always think there's a woman somewhere when a man gets restless. (*Coming to her.*) Mama—Mama—I want so many things ...

MAMA. Yes, son—

WALTER. I want so many things that they are driving me kind of crazy. ... Mama—look at me.

MAMA. I'm looking at you. You a good-looking boy. You got a job, a nice wife, a fine boy and—

WALTER. A job. (*Looks at her.*)

Mama, a job? I open and close car doors all day long. I drive a man around in his limousine and I say, "Yes, sir; no, sir; very good, sir; shall I take the Drive, sir?" Mama, that ain't no kind of job . . . that ain't nothing at all. (*Very quietly.*) Mama, I don't know if I can make you understand.

MAMA. Understand what, baby?

WALTER (*quietly*). Sometimes it's like I can see the future stretched out in front of me—just plain as day. The future, Mama. Hanging over there at the edge of my days. Just waiting for me— a big, looming blank space—full of *nothing*. Just waiting for *me*. (*Pause.*) Mama—sometimes when I'm downtown and I pass them cool, quiet-looking restaurants where them white boys are sitting back and talking 'bout things . . . sitting there turning deals worth millions of dollars . . . sometimes I see guys don't look much older than me—

MAMA. Son—how come you talk so much 'bout money?

WALTER (*with immense passion*). Because it is life, Mama!

MAMA (*quietly*). Oh—(*very quietly*). So now it's life. Money is life. Once upon a time freedom used to be life—now it's money. I guess the world really do change . . .

WALTER. No—it was always money, Mama. We just didn't know about it.

MAMA. No . . . something has changed. (*She looks at him.*) You something new, boy. In my time we was worried about not being lynched and getting to the North if we could and how to stay alive and still have a pinch of dignity too . . . Now here come you and Beneatha— talking 'bout things we ain't never even thought about hardly, me and your daddy. You ain't satisfied or proud of nothing we done. I mean that you had a home; that we kept you out of trouble till you was grown; that you don't have to ride to work on the back of nobody's streetcar— You my children—but how different we done become.

WALTER. You just don't understand, Mama, you just don't understand.

MAMA. Son—do you know your wife is expecting another baby? (WALTER *stands, stunned, and absorbs what his mother has said.*) That's what she wanted to talk to you about. (WALTER *sinks down into a chair.*) This ain't for me to be telling—but you ought to know. (*She waits.*) I think Ruth is thinking 'bout getting rid of that child.

WALTER (*slowly understanding*). No— no—Ruth wouldn't do that.

MAMA. When the world gets ugly enough—a woman will do anything for her family. *The part that's already living.*

WALTER. You don't know Ruth, Mama, if you think she would do that.

(RUTH *opens the bedroom door and stands there a little limp.*)

RUTH (*beaten*). Yes I would too, Walter. (*Pause.*) I gave her a five-dollar down payment.

(*There is a total silence as the man stares at his wife and the mother stares at her son.*)

MAMA (*presently*). Well—(*tightly*). Well—son, I'm waiting to hear you say something . . . I'm waiting to hear how you be your father's son. Be the man he was . . . (*Pause.*) Your wife say she going to destroy your child. And I'm waiting to hear you talk like him and say we a people who give children life, not who destroys them—(*She rises.*) I'm waiting to see you stand up and look like your daddy and say we done give up one baby to poverty and that we ain't going to give up nary another one . . . I'm waiting.

WALTER. Ruth—

MAMA. If you a son of mine, tell her! (WALTER *turns, looks at her and can say nothing. She continues, bitterly.*) You . . . you are a disgrace to your father's memory. Somebody get me my hat.

(*Curtain.*)

Act Two

SCENE ONE

(*Time: Later the same day.*
At rise: RUTH *is ironing again. She has the radio going. Presently* BENEATHA'S *bedroom door opens and* RUTH'S *mouth falls and she puts down the iron in fascination.*)

RUTH. What have we got on tonight!
BENEATHA (*emerging grandly from the doorway so that we can see her thoroughly robed in the costume Asagai brought*). You are looking at what a well-dressed Nigerian woman wears— (*She parades for* RUTH, *her hair completely hidden by the headdress; she is coquettishly fanning herself with an ornate oriental fan, mistakenly more like Butterfly than any Nigerian that ever was.*) Isn't it beautiful? (*She promenades to the radio and, with an arrogant flourish, turn off the good loud blues that is playing.*) Enough of this assimilationist junk! (RUTH *follows her with her eyes as she goes to the phonograph and puts on a record and turns and waits ceremoniously for the music to come up. Then, with a shout—*) OCOMOGOSIAY!
(RUTH *jumps. The music comes up, a lovely Nigerian melody.* BENEATHA *listens, enraptured, her eyes far away—"back to the past." She begins to dance.* RUTH *is dumbfounded.*)
RUTH. What kind of dance is that?
BENEATHA. A folk dance.
RUTH (*Pearl Bailey*). What kind of folks do that, honey?
BENEATHA. It's from Nigeria. It's a dance of welcome.
RUTH. Who you welcoming?
BENEATHA. The men back to the village.
RUTH. Where they been?
BENEATHA. How should I know—out hunting or something. Anyway, they are coming back now . . .
RUTH. Well, that's good.
BENEATHA. (*With the record*).
Alundi, alundi
Alundi alunya
Jop pu a jeepua
Ang gu sooooooooooo

Ai yai yae . . .
Ayehaye—alundi . . .

(WALTER *comes in during this performance; he has obviously been drinking. He leans against the door heavily and watches his sister, at first with distaste. Then his eyes look off—"back to the past"—as he lifts both his fists to the roof, screaming.*)
WALTER. YEAH . . . AND ETHIOPIA STRETCH FORTH HER HANDS AGAIN! . . .
RUTH (*drily, looking at him*). Yes—and Africa sure is claiming her own tonight. (*She gives them both up and starts ironing again.*)
WALTER (*all in a drunken, dramatic shout*). Shut up! . . . I'm digging them drums . . . them drums move me! . . . (*He makes his weaving way to his wife's face and leans close to her.*) In my heart of hearts—(*He thumps his chest.*)—I am much warrior!
RUTH (*without even looking up*). In your heart of hearts you are much drunkard.
WALTER (*coming away from her and starting to wander around the room, shouting*). Me and Jomo . . . (*Intently, in his sister's face. She has stopped dancing to watch him in this unknown mood.*) That's my man, Kenyatta. (*Shouting and thumping his chest.*) FLAMING SPEAR! HOT DAMN! (*He is suddenly in possession of an imaginary spear and actively spearing enemies all over the room.*) OCOMOGOSIAY . . . THE LION IS WAKING . . . OWIMIWEH! (*He pulls his shirt open and leaps up on a table and gestures with his spear. The bell rings.* RUTH *goes to answer.*)

BENEATHA (*to encourage* WALTER, *thoroughly caught up with this side of him*). OCOMOGOSIAY, FLAMING SPEAR!

WALTER (*on the table, very far gone, his eyes pure glass sheets. He sees what we cannot, that he is a leader of his people, a great chief, a descendant of Chaka, and that the hour to march has come*). Listen, my black brothers—

BENEATHA. OCOMOGOSIAY!

WALTER. —Do you hear the waters rushing against the shores of the coastlands—

BENEATHA. OCOMOGOSIAY!

WALTER. —Do you hear the screeching of the cocks in yonder hills beyond where the chiefs meet in council for the coming of the mighty war—

BENEATHA. OCOMOGOSIAY!

WALTER. —Do you hear the beating of the wings of the birds flying low over the mountains and the low places of our land—

(RUTH *opens the door.* GEORGE MURCHISON *enters.*)

BENEATHA. OCOMOGOSIAY!

WALTER. —Do you hear the singing of the women, singing the war songs of our fathers to the babies in the great houses . . . singing the sweet war songs? OH, DO YOU HEAR, MY BLACK BROTHERS!

BENEATHA (*completely gone*). We hear you, Flaming Spear—

WALTER. Telling us to prepare for the greatness of the time— (*To George,*) Black Brother!

(*He extends his hand for the fraternal clasp.*)

GEORGE. Black Brother, hell!

RUTH (*having had enough, and embarrassed for the family*). Beneatha, you got company—what's the matter with you? Walter Lee Younger, get down off that table and stop acting like a fool . . .

(WALTER *comes down off the table suddenly and makes a quick exit to the bathroom.*)

RUTH. He's had a little to drink . . . I don't know what her excuse is.

GEORGE (*to* BENEATHA). Look honey, we're going to the theatre—we're not going to be *in* it . . . so go change, huh?

RUTH. You expect this boy to go out with you looking like that?

BENEATHA (*looking at* GEORGE). That's up to George. If he's ashamed of his heritage—

GEORGE. Oh, don't be so proud of yourself, Bennie—just because you look eccentric.

BENEATHA. How can something that's natural be eccentric?

GEORGE. That's what being eccentric means—being natural. Get dressed.

BENEATHA. I don't like that, George.

RUTH. Why must you and your brother make an argument out of everything people say?

BENEATHA. Because I hate assimilationist Negroes!

RUTH. Will somebody please tell me what assimila-whoever means!

GEORGE. Oh, it's just a college girl's way of calling people Uncle Toms—but that isn't what it means at all.

RUTH. Well, what does it mean?

BENEATHA (*cutting* GEORGE *off and staring at him as she replies to* RUTH). It means someone who is willing to give up his own culture and submerge himself completely in the dominant, and in this case, *oppressive* culture!

GEORGE. Oh, dear, dear, dear! Here we go! A lecture on the African past! On our Great West African Heritage! In one second we will hear all about the great Ashanti empires; the great Songhay civilizations; and the great sculpture of Bénin —and then some poetry in the Bantu— and the whole monologue will end with the word *heritage!* (*Nastily.*) Let's face it, baby, your heritage is nothing but a bunch of raggedy-assed spirituals and some grass huts!

BENEATHA. *Grass huts!* (RUTH *crosses to her and forcibly pushes her toward the bedroom.*) See there . . . you are standing there in your splendid ignorance talking about people who were the first to smelt iron on the face of the earth! (RUTH *is pushing her through the door.*) The Ashanti were performing surgical operations when the English— (RUTH *pulls the door to, with* BENEATHA *on the other side, and smiles graciously at* GEORGE. BENEATHA *opens the door and shouts the end of the sentence defiantly at* GEORGE.)—were still tatooing themselves with blue dragons . . . (*She goes back inside.*)

RUTH. Have a seat, George. (*They both sit.* RUTH *folds her hands rather primly on her lap, determined to demonstrate the civilization of the family.*) Warm, ain't it? I mean for September. (*Pause.*) Just like they always say about Chicago weather: If it's too hot or cold for you, just wait a minute and it'll change. (*She smiles happily at this cliché of clichés.*) Everybody say it's got to do with them bombs and things they keep setting off. (*Pause.*) Would you like a nice cold beer?

GEORGE. No, thank you. I don't care for beer. (*He looks at his watch.*) I hope she hurries up.

RUTH. What time is the show?

GEORGE. It's an eight-thirty curtain. That's just Chicago though. In New York standard curtain time is eight forty.

(*He is rather proud of this knowledge.*)

RUTH (*properly appreciating it*). You get to New York a lot?

GEORGE (*offhand*). Few times a year.

RUTH. Oh—that's nice. I've never been to New York.

(WALTER *enters. We feel he has relieved himself, but the edge of unreality is still with him.*)

WALTER. New York ain't got nothing Chicago ain't. Just a bunch of hustling people all squeezed up together—being "Eastern."

(*He turns his face into a screw of displeasure.*)

GEORGE. Oh—you've been?

WALTER. *Plenty* of times.

RUTH (*shocked at the lie*). Walter Lee Younger!

WALTER (*staring her down*). Plenty! (*Pause.*) What we got to drink in this house? Why don't you offer this man some refreshment. (*To* GEORGE,) They don't know how to entertain people in this house, man.

GEORGE. Thank you—I don't really care for anything.

WALTER (*feeling his head; sobriety coming*). Where's Mama?

RUTH. She ain't come back yet.

WALTER (*looking* MURCHISON *over from head to toe, scrutinizing his carefully casual tweed sports jacket over cashmere V-neck sweater over soft eyelet shirt and tie, and soft slacks, finished off with white buckskin shoes*). Why all you college boys wear them fairyish-looking white shoes?

RUTH. Walter Lee!

(GEORGE MURCHISON *ignores the remark.*)

WALTER (*to* RUTH). Well, they look crazy as hell—white shoes, cold as it is.

RUTH (*crushed*). You have to excuse him—

WALTER. No he don't! Excuse me for what? What you always excusing me for! I'll excuse myself when I needs to be excused! (*A pause.*) They look as funny as them black knee socks Beneatha wears out of here all the time.

RUTH. It's the college *style,* Walter.

WALTER. Style hell. She looks like she got burnt legs or something!

RUTH. Oh, Walter—

WALTER (*an irritable mimic*). Oh, Walter! Oh, Walter! (*to* MURCHISON) How's your old man making out? I understand you all going to buy that big hotel on the Drive? (*He finds a beer in the refrigerator, wanders over to* MURCHISON, *sipping and wiping his lips with the back of his hand, and straddling a chair backwards to talk to the other man.*) Shrewd move. Your old man is all right, man. (*Tapping his head and half winking for emphasis.*) I mean he knows how to operate. I mean he thinks *big*, you know what I mean, I mean for a *home*, you know? But I think he's kind of running out of ideas now. I'd like to talk to him. Listen, man, I got some plans that could turn this city upside down. I mean I think like he does. *Big.* Invest big, gamble big, hell, lose *big* if you have to, you know what I mean. It's hard to find a man on this whole Southside who understands my kind of thinking—you dig? (*He scrutinizes* MURCHISON *again, drinks his beer, squints his eyes and leans in close, confidential, man to man.*) Me and you ought to sit down and talk sometimes, man. Man, I got me some ideas . . .

MURCHISON (*with boredom*). Yeah—sometimes we'll have to do that, Walter.

WALTER (*understanding the indifference, and offended*). Yeah—well, when you get the time, man. I know you a busy little boy.

RUTH. Walter, please—

WALTER (*bitterly, hurt*). I know ain't nothing in this world as busy as you colored college boys with your fraternity pins and white shoes . . .

RUTH (*covering her face with humiliation*). Oh, Walter Lee—

WALTER. I see you all all the time—with the books tucked under your arms—going to your (*British A—a mimic*) "clahsses." And for what! What the hell you learning over there? Filling up your heads—(*counting off on his fingers*)—with the sociology and the psychology—but they teaching you how to be a man? How to take over and run the world? They teaching you how to run a rubber plantation or a steel mill? Naw—just to talk proper and read books and wear white shoes . . .

GEORGE (*looking at him with distaste, a little above it all*). You're all wacked up with bitterness, man.

WALTER (*intently, almost quietly, between the teeth, glaring at the boy*). And you—ain't you bitter, man? Ain't you just about had it? Don't you see no stars gleaming that you can't reach out and grab? You happy?—You contented son-of-a-bitch—you happy? You got it made? Bitter? Man, I'm a volcano. Bitter? Here I am a giant—surrounded by ants! Ants who can't even understand what it is the giant is talking about.

RUTH (*passionately and suddenly*). Oh, Walter—ain't you with nobody!

WALTER (*violently*). No! 'Cause ain't nobody with me! Not even my own mother!

RUTH. Walter, that's a terrible thing to say!

(BENEATHA *enters, dressed for the evening in a cocktail dress and earrings.*)

GEORGE. Well—hey, you look great.

BENEATHA. Let's go, George. See you all later.

RUTH. Have a nice time.

GEORGE. Thanks. Good night. (*To* WALTER, *sarcastically,*) Good night, Prometheus.

(BENEATHA *and* GEORGE *exit.*)

WALTER (*to* RUTH). Who is Prometheus?

RUTH. I don't know. Don't worry about it.

WALTER (*in fury, pointing after* GEORGE). See there—they get to a point where they can't insult you man to man—they got to go talk about something ain't nobody never heard of!

RUTH. How do you know it was an insult? (*To humor him,*) Maybe Prometheus is a nice fellow.

WALTER. Prometheus! I bet there

ain't even no such thing! I bet that simple-minded clown—

RUTH. Walter—

(*She stops what she is doing and looks at him.*)

WALTER (*yelling*). Don't start!

RUTH. Start what?

WALTER. Your nagging! Where was I? Who was I with? How much money did I spend?

RUTH (*plaintively*). Walter Lee— why don't we just try to talk about it . . .

WALTER (*not listening*). I been out talking with people who understand me. People who care about the things I got on my mind.

RUTH (*wearily*). I guess that means people like Willy Harris.

WALTER. Yes, people like Willy Harris.

RUTH (*with a sudden flash of impatience*). Why don't you all hurry up and go into the banking business and stop talking about it!

WALTER. Why? You want to know why? 'Cause we all tied up in a race of people that don't know how to do nothing but moan, pray and have babies!

(*The line is too bitter even for him and he looks at her and sits down.*)

RUTH. Oh, Walter . . . (*Softly.*) Honey, why can't you stop fighting me?

WALTER (*without thinking*). Who's fighting you? Who even cares about you?

(*This line begins the retardation of his mood.*)

RUTH. Well—(*She waits a long time, and then with resignation starts to put away her things.*) I guess I might as well go on to bed . . . (*More or less to herself,*) I don't know where we lost it . . . but we have . . . (*Then, to him,*) I—I'm sorry about this new baby, Walter. I guess maybe I better go on and do what I started . . . I guess I just didn't realize how bad things was with us . . . I guess I just didn't really realize— (*She starts out to the bedroom and stops.*) You want some hot milk?

WALTER. Hot milk?

RUTH. Yes—hot milk.

WALTER. Why hot milk?

RUTH. 'Cause after all that liquor you come home with you ought to have something hot in your stomach.

WALTER. I don't want no milk.

RUTH. You want some coffee then?

WALTER. No, I don't want no coffee. I don't want nothing hot to drink. (*Almost plaintively.*) Why you always trying to give me something to eat?

RUTH (*standing and looking at him helplessly*). What else can I give you, Walter Lee Younger?

(*She stands and looks at him and presently turns to go out again. He lifts his head and watches her going away from him in a new mood which began to emerge when he asked her "Who cares about you?"*)

WALTER. It's been rough, ain't it, baby? (*She hears and stops but does not turn around and he continues to her back.*) I guess between two people there ain't never as much understood as folks generally thinks there is. I mean like between me and you—(*She turns to face him.*) How we gets to the place where we scared to talk softness to each other. (*He waits, thinking hard himself.*) Why you think it got to be like that? (*He is thoughtful, almost as a child would be.*) Ruth, what is it gets into people ought to be close?

RUTH. I don't know, honey. I think about it a lot.

WALTER. On account of you and me, you mean? The way things are with us. The way something done come down between us.

RUTH. There ain't so much between us, Walter . . . Not when you come to me and try to talk to me. Try to be with me . . . a little even.

WALTER (*total honesty*). Sometimes . . . sometimes . . . I don't even know how to try.

RUTH. Walter—

WALTER. Yes?

RUTH (*coming to him, gently and with misgiving, but coming to him*). Honey . . . life don't have to be like this. I mean sometimes people can do things so that things are better . . . You remember how we used to talk when Travis was born . . . about the way we were going to live . . . the kind of house . . . (*She is stroking his head.*) Well, it's all starting to slip away from us . . .

(MAMA *enters, and* WALTER *jumps up and shouts at her.*)

WALTER. Mama, where have you been?

MAMA. My—them steps is longer than they used to be. Whew! (*She sits down and ignores him.*) How you feeling this evening, Ruth?

(RUTH *shrugs, disturbed some at having been prematurely interrupted and watching her husband knowingly.*)

WALTER. Mama, where have you been all day?

MAMA (*still ignoring him and leaning on the table and changing to more comfortable shoes*). Where's Travis?

RUTH. I let him go out earlier and he ain't come back yet. Boy, is he going to get it!

WALTER. Mama!

MAMA (*as if she has heard him for the first time*). Yes, son?

WALTER. Where did you go this afternoon?

MAMA. I went downtown to tend to some business that I had to tend to.

WALTER. What kind of business?

MAMA. You know better than to question me like a child, Brother.

WALTER (*rising and bending over the table*). Where were you, Mama? (*Bringing his fists down and shouting.*) Mama, you didn't go do something with that insurance money, something crazy?

(*The front door opens slowly, interrupting him, and* TRAVIS *peeks his head in, less than hopefully.*)

TRAVIS (*to his mother*). Mama, I—

RUTH. "Mama I" nothing! You're going to get it, boy! Get on in that bedroom and get yourself ready!

TRAVIS. But I—

MAMA. Why don't you all never let the child explain himself.

RUTH. Keep out of it now, Lena.

(MAMA *clamps her lips together, and* RUTH *advances toward her son menacingly.*)

RUTH. A thousand times I have told you not to go off like that—

MAMA (*holding out her arms to her grandson*). Well—at least let me tell him something. I want him to be the first one to hear . . . Come here, Travis. (*The boy obeys, gladly.*) Travis—(*She takes him by the shoulder and looks into his face.*)—you know that money we got in the mail this morning?

TRAVIS. Yes'm—

MAMA. Well—what you think your grandmama gone and done with that money?

TRAVIS. I don't know, Grandmama.

MAMA (*putting her finger on his nose for emphasis*). She went out and she bought you a house! (*The explosion comes from* WALTER *at the end of the revelation and he jumps up and turns away from all of them in a fury.* MAMA *continues, to* TRAVIS.) You glad about the house? It's going to be yours when you get to be a man.

TRAVIS. Yeah—I always wanted to live in a house.

MAMA. All right, gimme some sugar then—(TRAVIS *puts his arms around her neck as she watches her son over the boy's shoulder. Then, to* TRAVIS, *after the embrace.*) Now when you say your prayers tonight, you thank God and your grandfather—'cause it was him who give you the house—in his way.

RUTH (*taking the boy from* MAMA *and pushing him toward the bedroom*). Now you get out of here and get ready for your beating.

TRAVIS. Aw, Mama—

RUTH. Get on in there— (*Closing the door behind him and turning radiantly to her mother-in-law,*) So you went and did it!

MAMA (*quietly, looking at her son with pain*). Yes, I did.

RUTH (*raising both arms classically*). Praise God! (*Looks at* WALTER *a moment, who says nothing. She crosses rapidly to her husband.*) Please, honey—let me be glad . . . you be glad too. (*She has laid her hands on his shoulders, but he shakes himself free of her roughly, without turning to face her.*) Oh, Walter . . . a home . . . a home. (*She comes back to* MAMA.) Well—where is it? How big is it? How much it going to cost?

MAMA. Well—

RUTH. When we moving?

MAMA (*smiling at her*). First of the month.

RUTH (*throwing back her head with jubilance*). Praise God!

MAMA (*tentatively, still looking at her son's back turned against her and* RUTH). It's—it's a nice house too . . . (*She cannot help speaking directly to him. An imploring quality in her voice, her manner, makes her almost like a girl now.*) Three bedrooms—nice big one for you and Ruth. . . . Me and Beneatha still have to share our room, but Travis have one of his own—and (*with difficulty*) I figure if the—new baby—is a boy, we could get one of them double-decker outfits . . . And there's a yard with a little patch of dirt where I could maybe get to grow me a few flowers . . . And a nice big basement . . .

RUTH. Walter honey, be glad—

MAMA (*still to his back, fingering things on the table*). 'Course I don't want to make it sound fancier than it is . . . It's just a plain little old house—but it's made good and solid—and it will be *ours*. Walter Lee—it makes a difference in a man when he can walk on floors that belong to *him* . . .

RUTH. Where is it?

MAMA (*frightened at this telling*). Well—well—it's out there in Clybourne Park—

(RUTH's *radiance fades abruptly, and* WALTER *finally turns slowly to face his mother with incredulity and hostility.*)

RUTH. Where?

MAMA (*matter-of-factly*). Four o six Clybourne Street, Clybourne Park.

RUTH. Clybourne Park? Mama, there ain't no colored people living in Clybourne Park.

MAMA (*almost idiotically*). Well, I guess there's going to be some now.

WALTER (*bitterly*). So that's the peace and comfort you went out and bought for us today!

MAMA (*raising her eyes to meet his finally*). Son—I just tried to find the nicest place for the least amount of money for my family.

RUTH (*trying to recover from the shock*). Well—well—'course I ain't one never been 'fraid of no crackers, mind you—but—well, wasn't there no other houses nowhere?

MAMA. Them houses they put up for colored in them areas way out all seem to cost twice as much as other houses. I did the best I could.

RUTH (*struck senseless with the news, in its various degrees of goodness and trouble, she sits a moment, her fists propping her chin in thought, and then she starts to rise, bringing her fists down with vigor, the radiance spreading from cheek to cheek again*). Well—well!—All I can say is—if this is my time in life— my time—to say good-bye—(*And she builds with momentum as she starts to circle the room with an exuberant, almost tearfully happy release.*)—to these God-damned cracking walls!—(*She pounds the walls.*)—and these marching roaches!— (*She wipes at an imaginary army of marching roaches.*)—and this cramped little closet which ain't now or never was no kitchen! . . . then I say it loud and good, *Hallelujah! and goodbye misery*

Lorraine Hansberry

... I don't never want to see your ugly face again! (*She laughs joyously, having practically destroyed the apartment, and flings her arms up and lets them come down happily, slowly, reflectively, over her abdomen, aware for the first time perhaps that the life therein pulses with happiness and not despair.*) Lena?

MAMA (*moved, watching her happiness*). Yes, honey?

RUTH (*looking off*). Is there—is there a whole lot of sunlight?

MAMA (*understanding*). Yes, child, there's a whole lot of sunlight.

(*Long pause.*)

RUTH (*collecting herself and going to the door of the room* TRAVIS *is in*). Well —I guess I better see 'bout Travis. (*to* MAMA) Lord, I sure don't feel like whipping nobody today!

(*She exits.*)

MAMA (*The mother and son are left alone now and the mother waits a long time, considering deeply, before she speaks*). Son—you—you understand what I done, don't you? (WALTER *is silent and sullen.*) I—I just seen my family falling apart today . . . just falling to pieces in front of my eyes . . . We couldn't of gone on like we was today. We was going backwards 'stead of forwards—talking 'bout killing babies and wishing each other was dead . . . When it gets like that in life—you just got to do something different, push on out and do something bigger . . . (*She waits.*) I wish you say something, son . . . I wish you'd say how deep inside you you think I done the right thing—

WALTER (*crossing slowly to his bedroom door and finally turning there and speaking measuredly*). What you need me to say you done right for? *You* the head of this family. You run our lives like you want to. It was your money and you did what you wanted with it. So what you need for me to say it was all right for? (*Bitterly, to hurt her as deeply as he knows is possible,*) So you butchered up a dream of mine—you—who always talking 'bout your children's dreams . . .

MAMA. Walter Lee—

(*He just closes the door behind him.* MAMA *sits alone, thinking heavily.*)

(*Curtain.*)

SCENE TWO

(*Time: Friday night. A few weeks later.*

At rise: Packing crates mark the intention of the family to move. BENEATHA *and* GEORGE *come in, presumably from an evening out again.*)

GEORGE. O.K. . . . O.K., whatever you say . . . (*They both sit on the couch. He tries to kiss her. She moves away.*) Look, we've had a nice evening; let's not spoil it, huh? . . .

(*He again turns her head and tries to nuzzle in and she turns away from him, not with distaste but with momentary lack of interest; in a mood to pursue what they were talking about.*)

BENEATHA. I'm *trying* to talk to you.

GEORGE. We always talk.

BENEATHA. Yes—and I love to talk.

GEORGE (*exasperated; rising*). I know it and I don't mind it sometimes . . . I want you to cut it out, see—The moody stuff, I mean. I don't like it. You're a nice-looking girl . . . all over. That's all you need, honey, forget the atmosphere. Guys aren't going to go for the atmosphere—they're going to go for what they see. Be glad for that. Drop the Garbo routine. It doesn't go with you. As for myself, I want a nice—(*groping*)— simple (*thoughtfully*)—sophisticated girl . . . not a poet—O.K.?

(*She rebuffs him again and he starts to leave.*)

BENEATHA. Why are you angry?

GEORGE. Because this is stupid! I don't go out with you to discuss the nature of "quiet desperation" or to hear all about your thoughts—because the world will go on thinking what it thinks regardless—

BENEATHA. Then why read books? Why go to school?

GEORGE (*with artificial patience, counting on his fingers*). It's simple. You read books—to learn facts—to get grades—to pass the course—to get a degree. That's all—it has nothing to do with thoughts.

(*A long pause.*)

BENEATHA. I see. (*A longer pause as she looks at him.*) Good night, George.

(GEORGE *looks at her a little oddly, and starts to exit. He meets* MAMA *coming in.*)

GEORGE. Oh—hello, Mrs. Younger.

MAMA. Hello, George, how you feeling?

GEORGE. Fine—fine, how are you?

MAMA. Oh, a little tired. You know them steps can get you after a day's work. You all have a nice time tonight?

GEORGE. Yes—a fine time. Well, good night.

MAMA. Good night. (*He exits.* MAMA *closes the door behind her.*) Hello, honey. What you sitting like that for?

BENEATHA. I'm just sitting.

MAMA. Didn't you have a nice time?

BENEATHA. No.

MAMA. No? What's the matter?

BENEATHA. Mama, George is a fool—honest. (*She rises.*)

MAMA (*hustling around unloading the packages she has entered with. She stops*). Is he, baby?

BENEATHA. Yes.

(BENEATHA *makes up* TRAVIS' *bed as she talks.*)

MAMA. You sure?

BENEATHA. Yes.

MAMA. Well—I guess you better not waste your time with no fools.

(BENEATHA *looks up at her mother, watching her put groceries in the refrigerator. Finally she gathers up her things and starts into the bedroom. At the door she stops and looks back at her mother.*)

BENEATHA. Mama—

MAMA. Yes, baby—

BENEATHA. Thank you.

MAMA. For what?

BENEATHA. For understanding me this time.

(*She exits quickly and the mother stands, smiling a little, looking at the place where* BENEATHA *just stood.* RUTH *enters.*)

RUTH. Now don't you fool with any of this stuff, Lena—

MAMA. Oh, I just thought I'd sort a few things out.

(*The phone rings.* RUTH *answers.*)

RUTH (*at the phone*). Hello—Just a minute. (*Goes to door.*) Walter, it's Mrs. Arnold. (*Waits. Goes back to the phone. Tense.*) Hello. Yes, this is his wife speaking . . . He's lying down now. Yes . . . well, he'll be in tomorrow. He's been very sick. Yes—I know we should have called, but we were so sure he'd be able to come in today. Yes—yes, I'm very sorry. Yes . . . Thank you very much. (*She hangs up.* WALTER *is standing in the doorway of the bedroom behind her.*) That was Mrs. Arnold.

WALTER (*indifferently*). Was it?

RUTH. She said if you don't come in tomorrow that they are getting a new man . . .

WALTER. Ain't that sad—ain't that crying sad.

RUTH. She said Mr. Arnold has had to take a cab for three days . . . Walter, you ain't been to work for three days! (*This is a revelation to her.*) Where you been, Walter Lee Younger? (WALTER *looks at her and starts to laugh.*) You're going to lose your job.

WALTER. That's right . . .

RUTH. Oh, Walter, and with your mother working like a dog every day—

WALTER. That's sad too—Everything is sad.

MAMA. What you been doing for these three days, son?

WALTER. Mama—you don't know all the things a man what got leisure can find to do in this city . . . What's this—Friday night? Well—Wednesday I borrowed Willy Harris' car and I went for a drive . . . just me and myself and I drove and drove . . . Way out . . . way past South Chicago, and I parked the car and I sat and looked at the steel mills all day long. I just sat in the car and looked at them big black chimneys for hours. Then I drove back and I went to the Green Hat. (*Pause.*) And Thursday—Thursday I borrowed the car again and I got in it and I pointed it the other way and I drove the other way—for hours—way, way up to Wisconsin, and I looked at the farms. I just drove and looked at the farms. Then I drove back and I went to the Green Hat. (*Pause.*) And today—today I didn't get the car. Today I just walked. All over the Southside. And I looked at the Negroes and they looked at me and finally I just sat down on the curb at Thirty-ninth and South Parkway and I just sat there and watched the Negroes go by. And then I went to the Green Hat. You all sad? You all depressed? And you know where I am going right now—

(RUTH *goes out quietly.*)

MAMA. Oh, Big Walter, is this the harvest of our days?

WALTER. You know what I like about the Green Hat? (*He turns the radio on and a steamy, deep blues pours into the room.*) I like this little cat they got there who blows a sax . . . He blows. He talks to me. He ain't but 'bout five feet tall and he's got a conked head and his eyes is always closed and he's all music—

MAMA (*rising and getting some papers out of her handbag*). Walter—

WALTER. And there's this other guy who plays the piano . . . and they got a sound. I mean they can work on some music . . . They got the best little combo in the world in the Green Hat . . . You can just sit there and drink and listen to them three men play and you realize that don't nothing matter worth a damn, but just being there—

MAMA. I've helped do it to you, haven't I, son? Walter, I been wrong.

WALTER. Naw—you ain't never been wrong about nothing, Mama.

MAMA. Listen to me, now. I say I been wrong, son. That I been doing to you what the rest of the world been doing to you. (*She stops and he looks up slowly at her and she meets his eyes pleadingly.*) Walter—what you ain't never understood is that I ain't got nothing, don't own nothing, ain't never really wanted nothing that wasn't for you. There ain't nothing as precious to me . . . There ain't nothing worth holding on to, money, dreams, nothing else—if it means—if it means it's going to destroy my boy. (*She puts her papers in front of him and he watches her without speaking or moving.*) I paid the man thirty-five hundred dollars down on the house. That leaves sixty-five hundred dollars. Monday morning I want you to take this money and take three thousand dollars and put it in a savings account for Beneatha's medical schooling. The rest you put in a checking account—with your name on it. And from now on any penny that come out of it or that go in it is for you to look after. For you to decide. (*She drops her hands a little helplessly.*) It ain't much, but it's all I got in the world and I'm putting it in your hands. I'm telling you to be the head of this family from now on like you supposed to be.

WALTER (*stares at the money*). You trust me like that, Mama?

MAMA. I ain't never stop trusting you. Like I ain't never stop loving you.

(*She goes out, and* WALTER *sits looking at the money on the table as the music continues in its idiom, pulsing in the room. Finally, in a decisive gesture, he gets up, and, in mingled joy and desperation, picks up the money. At the same moment,* TRAVIS *enters for bed.*)

TRAVIS. What's the matter, Daddy? You drunk?

WALTER (*sweetly, more sweetly than we have ever known him*). No, Daddy ain't drunk. Daddy ain't going to never be drunk again. . . .

TRAVIS. Well, good night, Daddy.

(*The* FATHER *has come from behind*

the couch and leans over, embracing his son.)

WALTER. Son, I feel like talking to you tonight.

TRAVIS. About what?

WALTER. Oh, about a lot of things. About you and what kind of man you going to be when you grow up. . . . Son —son, what do you want to be when you grow up?

TRAVIS. A bus driver.

WALTER (*laughing a little*). A what? Man, that ain't nothing to want to be!

TRAVIS. Why not?

WALTER. 'Cause, man—it ain't big enough—you know what I mean.

TRAVIS. I don't know then. I can't make up my mind. Sometimes Mama asks me that too. And sometimes when I tell you I just want to be like you—she says she don't want me to be like that and sometimes she says she does. . . .

WALTER (*gathering him up in his arms*). You know what, Travis? In seven years you going to be seventeen years old. And things is going to be very different with us in seven years, Travis. . . . One day when you are seventeen I'll come home—home from my office downtown somewhere—

TRAVIS. You don't work in no office, Daddy.

WALTER. No—but after tonight. After what your daddy gonna do tonight, there's going to be offices—a whole lot of offices. . . .

TRAVIS. What you gonna do tonight, Daddy?

WALTER. You wouldn't understand yet, son, but your daddy's gonna make a transaction . . . a business transaction that's going to change our lives. . . . That's how come one day when you 'bout seventeen years old I'll come home and I'll be pretty tired, you know what I mean, after a day of conferences and secretaries getting things wrong the way they do . . . 'cause an executive's life is hell, man— (*The more he talks the farther away he gets.*) And I'll pull the car up on the driveway . . . just a plain black Chrysler, I think, with white walls—no—black tires. More elegant. Rich people don't have to be flashy . . . though I'll have to get something a little sportier for Ruth—maybe a Cadillac convertible to do her shopping in. . . . And I'll come up the steps to the house and the gardener will be clipping away at the hedges and he'll say, "Good evening, Mr. Younger." And I'll say, "Hello, Jefferson, how are you this evening?" And I'll go inside and Ruth will come downstairs and meet me at the door and we'll kiss each other and she'll take my arm and we'll go up to your room to see you sitting on the floor with the catalogues of all the great schools in America around you. . . . All the great schools in the world! And—and I'll say, all right son—it's your seventeenth birthday, what is it you've decided? . . . Just tell me where you want to go to school and you'll go. Just tell me, what it is you want to be—and you'll *be* it. . . . Whatever you want to be—Yessir! (*He holds his arms open for* TRAVIS.) You just name it, son . . . (TRAVIS *leaps into them.*) and I hand you the world!

(WALTER's *voice has risen in pitch and hysterical promise and on the last line he lifts* TRAVIS *high.*)

(*Blackout.*)

SCENE THREE

(*Time: Saturday, moving day, one week later.*

Before the curtain rises, RUTH'S *voice, a strident, dramatic church alto, cuts through the silence.*

It is, in the darkness, a triumphant surge, a penetrating statement of expectation: "Oh, Lord, I don't feel no ways tired! Children, oh, glory hallelujah!"

As the curtain rises we see that RUTH *is alone in the living room, finishing up the family's packing. It is moving day. She is nailing crates and tying cartons.* BENEATHA *enters, carrying a guitar case, and watches her exuberant sister-in-law.*)

RUTH. Hey!

BENEATHA (*putting away the case*). Hi.

RUTH (*pointing at a package*). Honey—look in that package there and see what I found on sale this morning at the South Center. (RUTH *gets up and moves to the package and draws out some curtains.*) Lookahere—hand-turned hems!

BENEATHA. How do you know the window size out there?

RUTH (*who hadn't thought of that*). Oh—Well, they bound to fit something in the whole house. Anyhow, they was too good a bargain to pass up. (RUTH *slaps her head, suddenly remembering something.*) Oh, Bennie—I meant to put a special note on that carton over there. That's your mama's good china and she wants 'em to be very careful with it.

BENEATHA. I'll do it.

(BENEATHA *finds a piece of paper and starts to draw large letters on it.*)

RUTH. You know what I'm going to do soon as I get in that new house?

BENEATHA. What?

RUTH. Honey—I'm going to run me a tub of water up to here . . . (*with her fingers practically up to her nostrils.*) And I'm going to get in it—and I am going to sit . . . and sit . . . and sit in that hot water and the first person who knocks to tell *me* to hurry up and come out—

BENEATHA. Gets shot at sunrise.

RUTH (*laughing happily*). You said it, sister! (*Noticing how large* BENEATHA *is absent-mindedly making the note.*) Honey, they ain't going to read that from no airplane.

BENEATHA (*laughing herself*). I guess I always think things have more emphasis if they are big, somehow.

RUTH (*looking up at her and smiling*). You and your brother seem to have that as a philosophy of life. Lord, that man—done changed so 'round here. You know—you know what we did last night? Me and Walter Lee?

BENEATHA. What?

RUTH (*smiling to herself*). We went to the movies. (*Looking at* BENEATHA *to see if she understands.*) We went to the movies. You know the last time me and Walter went to the movies together?

BENEATHA. No.

RUTH. Me neither. That's how long it been. (*Smiling again.*) But we went last night. The picture wasn't much good, but that didn't seem to matter. We went—and we held hands.

BENEATHA. Oh, Lord!

RUTH. We held hands—and you know what?

BENEATHA. What?

RUTH. When we come out of the show it was late and dark and all the stores and things was closed up . . . and it was kind of chilly and there wasn't many people on the streets . . . and we was still holding hands, me and Walter.

BENEATHA. You're killing me.

(WALTER *enters with a large package. His happiness is deep in him; he cannot keep still with his new-found exuberance. He is singing and wiggling and snapping his fingers. He puts his package in a corner and puts a phonograph record, which he has brought in with him, on the record player. As the music comes up he dances over to* RUTH *and tries to get her to dance with him. She gives in at last to his raunchiness and in a fit of giggling allows herself to be drawn into his mood and together they deliberately burlesque an old social dance of their youth.*)

BENEATHA (*regarding them a long time as they dance, then drawing in her breath for a deeply exaggerated comment which she does not particularly mean*). Talk about—olddddddddddd-fashioneddddddd—Negroes!

WALTER (*stopping momentarily*). What kind of Negroes?

(*He says this in fun. He is not angry with her today, nor with anyone. He starts to dance with his wife again.*)

BENEATHA. Old-fashioned.

WALTER (*as he dances with* RUTH). You know, when these *New Negroes* have their convention—(*pointing at his sister*)

—that is going to be the chairman of the Committee on Unending Agitation. (*He goes on dancing, then stops.*) Race, race, race! . . . Girl, I do believe you are the first person in the history of the entire human race to successfully brainwash yourself. (BENEATHA *breaks up and he goes on dancing. He stops again, enjoying his tease.*) Damn, even the N double A C P takes a holiday sometimes! (BENEATHA *and* RUTH *laugh. He dances with* RUTH *some more and starts to laugh and stops and pantomimes someone over an operating table.*) I can just see that chick someday looking down at some poor cat on an operating table before she starts to slice him, saying . . . (*pulling his sleeves back maliciously,*) "By the way, what are your views on civil rights down there? . . ."

(*He laughs at her again and starts to dance happily. The bell sounds.*)

BENEATHA. Sticks and stones may break my bones but . . . words will never hurt me!

(BENEATHA *goes to the door and opens it as* WALTER *and* RUTH *go on with the clowning.* BENEATHA *is somewhat surprised to see a quiet-looking middle-aged white man in a business suit holding his hat and a briefcase in his hand and consulting a small piece of paper.*)

MAN. Uh—how do you do, miss. I am looking for a Mrs.—(*He looks at the slip of paper.*) Mrs. Lena Younger?

BENEATHA (*smoothing her hair with slight embarrassment*). Oh—yes, that's my mother. Excuse me (*She closes the door and turns to quiet the other two.*) Ruth! Brother! Somebody's here. (*Then she opens the door. The man casts a curious quick glance at all of them.*) Uh—come in please.

MAN (*coming in*). Thank you.

BENEATHA. My mother isn't here just now. Is it business?

MAN. Yes . . . well, of a sort.

WALTER (*freely, the Man of the House*). Have a seat. I'm Mrs. Younger's son. I look after most of her business matters.

(RUTH *and* BENEATHA *exchange amused glances.*)

MAN (*regarding* WALTER, *and sitting*). Well—My name is Karl Lindner . . .

WALTER (*stretching out his hand*). Walter Younger. This is my wife—(RUTH *nods politely.*)—and my sister.

LINDNER. How do you do.

WALTER (*amiably, as he sits himself easily on a chair, leaning with interest forward on his knees and looking expectantly into the newcomer's face*). What can we do for you, Mr. Lindner!

LINDNER (*some minor shuffling of the hat and briefcase on his knees*). Well—I am a representative of the Clybourne Park Improvement Association—

WALTER (*pointing*). Why don't you sit your things on the floor?

LINDNER. Oh—yes. Thank you. (*He slides the briefcase and hat under the chair.*) And as I was saying—I am from the Clybourne Park Improvement Association and we have had it brought to our attention at the last meeting that you people—or at least your mother—has bought a piece of residential property at —(*He digs for the slip of paper again.*) —four o six Clybourne Street . . .

WALTER. That's right. Care for something to drink? Ruth, get Mr. Lindner a beer.

LINDNER (*upset for some reason*). Oh—no, really. I mean thank you very much, but no thank you.

RUTH (*innocently*). Some coffee?

LINDNER. Thank you, nothing at all.

(BENEATHA *is watching the man carefully.*)

LINDNER. Well, I don't know how much you folks know about our organization. (*He is a gentle man; thoughtful and somewhat labored in his manner.*) It is one of these community organizations set up to look after—oh, you know, things like block upkeep and special projects and we also have what we call our New Neighbors Orientation Committee . . .

BENEATHA (*Drily*). Yes—and what do they do?

LINDNER (*turning a little to her and then returning the main force to* WALTER). Well—it's what you might call a sort of welcoming committee, I guess. I mean they, we, I'm the chairman of the committee—go around and see the new people who move into the neighborhood and sort of give them the lowdown on the way we do things out in Clybourne Park.

BENEATHA (*with appreciation of the two meanings, which escape* RUTH *and* WALTER). Un-huh.

LINDNER. And we also have the category of what the association calls—(*He looks elsewhere.*)—uh—special community problems . . .

BENEATHA. Yes—and what are some of those?

WALTER. Girl, let the man talk.

LINDNER (*with understated relief*). Thank you. I would sort of like to explain this thing in my own way. I mean I want to explain to you in a certain way.

WALTER. Go ahead.

LINDNER. Yes. Well. I'm going to try to get right to the point. I'm sure we'll all appreciate that in the long run.

BENEATHA. Yes.

WALTER. Be still now!

LINDNER. Well—

RUTH (*still innocently*). Would you like another chair—you don't look comfortable.

LINDNER. (*more frustrated than annoyed*). No, thank you very much. Please. Well—to get right to the point I—(*A great breath, and he is off at last.*) I am sure you people must be aware of some of the incidents which have happened in various parts of the city when colored people have moved into certain areas—(BENEATHA *exhales heavily and starts tossing a piece of fruit up and down in the air.*) Well—because we have what I think is going to be a unique type of organization in American community life—not only do we deplore that kind of thing—but we are trying to do something about it. (BENEATHA *stops tossing and turns with a new and quizzical interest to the man.*) We feel—(*gaining confidence in his mission because of the interest in the faces of the people he is talking to*)—we feel that most of the trouble in this world, when you come right down to it—(*He hits his knee for emphasis.*)—most of the trouble exists because people just don't sit down and talk to each other.

RUTH (*nodding as she might in church, pleased with the remark*). You can say that again, mister.

LINDNER (*more encouraged by such affirmation*). That we don't try hard enough in this world to understand the other fellow's problem. The other guy's point of view.

RUTH. Now that's right.

(BENEATHA *and* WALTER *merely watch and listen with genuine interest.*)

LINDNER. Yes—that's the way we feel out in Clybourne Park. And that's why I was elected to come here this afternoon and talk to you people. Friendly like, you know, the way people should talk to each other and see if we couldn't find some way to work this thing out. As I say, the whole business is a matter of *caring* about the other fellow. Anybody can see that you are a nice family of folks, hard working and honest I'm sure. (BENEATHA *frowns slightly, quizzically, her head tilted regarding him.*) Today everybody knows what it means to be on the outside of *something*. And of course, there is always somebody who is out to take the advantage of people who don't always understand.

WALTER. What do you mean?

LINDNER. Well—you see our community is made up of people who've worked hard as the dickens for years to build up that little community. They're not rich and fancy people; just hard-working, honest people who don't really have much but those little homes and a dream of the kind of community they want to raise their children in. Now, I don't say we are perfect and there is a lot wrong in some of the things they want. But you've got to admit that a man, right or wrong, has the right to want to have the neighborhood he lives in a certain kind of way. And at the moment the overwhelming majority of our people out there feel that people get along better, take more of a common interest in the life of the community, when they share a common background. I want you to believe me when I tell you that race prejudice simply doesn't enter into it. It is a matter of the people of Clybourne Park believing, rightly or wrongly, as I say, that for the happiness of all concerned that our Negro families are happier when they live in their *own* communities.

BENEATHA (*with a grand and bitter gesture*). This, friends, is the Welcoming Committee!

WALTER (*dumfounded, looking at* LINDNER). Is this what you came marching all the way over here to tell us?

LINDNER. Well, now we've been having a fine conversation. I hope you'll hear me all the way through.

WALTER (*tightly*). Go ahead, man.

LINDNER. You see—in the face of all the things I have said, we are prepared to make your family a very generous offer . . .

BENEATHA. Thirty pieces and not a coin less!

WALTER. Yeah?

LINDNER (*putting on his glasses and drawing a form out of the briefcase*). Our association is prepared, through the collective effort of our people, to buy the house from you at a financial gain to your family.

RUTH. Lord have mercy, ain't this the living gall!

WALTER. All right, you through?

LINDNER. Well, I want to give you the exact terms of the financial arrangement—

WALTER. We don't want to hear no exact terms of no arrangements. I want to know if you got any more to tell us 'bout getting together?

LINDNER (*taking off his glasses*). Well—I don't suppose that you feel . . .

WALTER. Never mind how I feel—you got any more to say 'bout how people ought to sit down and talk to each other? . . . Get out of my house, man.

(*He turns his back and walks to the door.*)

LINDNER (*looking around at the hostile faces and reaching and assembling his hat and briefcase*). Well—I don't understand why you people are reacting this way. What do you think you are going to gain by moving into a neighborhood where you just aren't wanted and where some elements—well—people can get awful worked up when they feel that their whole way of life and everything they've ever worked for is threatened.

WALTER. Get out.

LINDNER (*at the door, holding a small card*). Well—I'm sorry it went like this.

WALTER. Get out.

LINDNER (*almost sadly regarding* WALTER). You just can't force people to change their hearts, son.

(*He turns and put his card on a table and exits.* WALTER *pushes the door to with stinging hatred, and stands looking at it.* RUTH *just sits and* BENEATHA *just stands. They say nothing.* MAMA *and* TRAVIS *enter.*)

MAMA. Well—this all the packing got done since I left out of here this morning. I testify before God that my children got all the energy of the dead. What time the moving men due?

BENEATHA. Four o'clock. You had a caller, Mama.

(*She is smiling, teasingly.*)

MAMA. Sure enough—who?

BENEATHA (*her arms folded saucily*). The Welcoming Committee.

(WALTER *and* RUTH *giggle*.)

MAMA (*innocently*). Who?

BENEATHA. The Welcoming Committee. They said they're sure going to be glad to see you when you get there.

WALTER (*devilishly*). Yeah, they said they can't hardly wait to see your face.

(*Laughter.*)

MAMA (*sensing their facetiousness*). What's the matter with you all?

WALTER. Ain't nothing the matter with us. We just telling you 'bout the gentleman who came to see you this afternoon. From the Clybourne Park Improvement Association.

MAMA. What he want?

RUTH (*in the same mood as* BENEATHA *and* WALTER). To welcome you, honey.

WALTER. He said they can't hardly wait. He said the one thing they don't have, that they just *dying* to have out there is a fine family of colored people! (*To* RUTH *and* BENEATHA,) Ain't that right!

RUTH *and* BENEATHA (*mockingly*). Yeah! He left his card in case—

(*They indicate the card, and* MAMA *picks it up and throws it on the floor—understanding and looking off as she draws her chair up to the table on which she has put her plant and some sticks and some cord.*)

MAMA. Father, give us strength. (*Knowingly—and without fun.*) Did he threaten us?

BENEATHA. Oh—Mama—they don't do it like that any more. He talked Brotherhood. He said everybody ought to learn how to sit down and hate each other with good Christian fellowship.

(*She and* WALTER *shake hands to ridicule the remark.*)

MAMA (*sadly*). Lord, protect us . . .

RUTH. You should hear the money those folks raised to buy the house from us. All we paid and then some.

BENEATHA. What they think we going to do—eat 'em?

RUTH. No, honey, marry 'em.

MAMA (*shaking her head*). Lord, Lord, Lord . . .

RUTH. Well—that's the way the crackers crumble. Joke.

BENEATHA (*laughingly noticing what her mother is doing*). Mama, what are you doing?

MAMA. Fixing my plant so it won't get hurt none on the way . . .

BENEATHA. Mama, you going to take *that* to the new house?

MAMA. Un-huh—

BENEATHA. That raggedy-looking old thing?

MAMA (*stopping and looking at her*). It expresses *me*.

RUTH (*with delight, to* BENEATHA). So there, Miss Thing!

(WALTER *comes to* MAMA *suddenly and bends down behind her and squeezes her in his arms with all his strength. She is overwhelmed by the suddenness of it and, though delighted, her manner is like that of* RUTH *with* TRAVIS.)

MAMA. Look out now, boy! You make me mess up my thing here!

WALTER (*His face lit, he slips down on his knees beside her, his arms still about her.*). Mama . . . you know what it means to climb up in the chariot?

MAMA (*gruffly, very happy*). Get on away from me now . . .

RUTH (*near the gift-wrapped package, trying to catch* WALTER'S *eye*). Psst—

WALTER. What the old song say, Mama . . .

RUTH. Walter—Now?

(*She is pointing at the package.*)

WALTER (*speaking the lines, sweetly, playfully, in his mother's face*).

I got wings . . . you got wings . . .
All God's Children got wings . . .

MAMA. Boy—get out of my face and do some work . . .

WALTER.

When I get to heaven gonna put on
my wings,
Gonna fly all over God's heaven . . .

BENEATHA (*teasingly, from across the*

room). Everybody talking 'bout heaven ain't going there!

WALTER (*to* RUTH, *who is carrying the box across to them*). I don't know, you think we ought to give her that . . . Seems to me she ain't been very appreciative around here.

MAMA (*eying the box, which is obviously a gift*). What is that?

WALTER (*taking it from* RUTH *and putting it on the table in front of* MAMA). Well—what you all think? Should we give it to her?

RUTH. Oh—she was pretty good today.

MAMA. I'll good you—

(*She turns her eyes to the box again.*)

BENEATHA. Open it, Mama.

(*She stands up, looks at it, turns and looks at all of them, and then presses her hands together and does not open the package.*)

WALTER (*sweetly*). Open it, Mama. It's for you. (MAMA *looks in his eyes. It is the first present in her life without its being Christmas. Slowly she opens her package and lifts out, one by one, a brand-new sparkling set of gardening tools.* WALTER *continues, prodding.*) Ruth made up the note—read it . . .

MAMA (*picking up the card and adjusting her glasses*). "To our own Mrs. Miniver—Love from Brother, Ruth and Beneatha." Ain't that lovely . . .

TRAVIS (*tugging at his father's sleeve*). Daddy, can I give her mine now?

WALTER. All right, son. (TRAVIS *flies to get his gift.*) Travis didn't want to go in with the rest of us, Mama. He got his own. (*Somewhat amused.*) We don't know what it is . . .

TRAVIS (*racing back in the room with a large hatbox and putting it in front of his grandmother*). Here!

MAMA. Lord have mercy, baby. You done gone and bought your grandmother a hat?

TRAVIS (*very proud*). Open it!

(*She does and lifts out an elaborate, but very elaborate, wide gardening hat, and all the adults break up at the sight of it.*)

RUTH. Travis, honey, what is that?

TRAVIS (*who thinks it is beautiful and appropriate*). It's a gardening hat! Like the ladies always have on in the magazines when they work in their gardens.

BENEATHA (*giggling fiercely*). Travis —we were trying to make Mama Mrs. Miniver—not Scarlett O'Hara!

MAMA (*indignantly*). What's the matter with you all! This here is a beautiful hat! (*absurdly*) I always wanted me one just like it!

(*She pops it on her head to prove it to her grandson, and the hat is ludicrous and considerably oversized.*)

RUTH. Hot dog! Go, Mama!

WALTER (*doubled over with laughter*). I'm sorry, Mama—but you look like you ready to go out and chop you some cotton sure enough!

(*They all laugh except* MAMA, *out of deference to* TRAVIS' *feelings.*)

MAMA (*gathering the boy up to her*). Bless your heart—this is the prettiest hat I ever owned—(WALTER, RUTH *and* BENEATHA *chime in—noisily, festively and insincerely congratulating* TRAVIS *on his gift.*) What are we all standing around here for? We ain't finished packin' yet. Bennie, you ain't packed one book.

(*The bell rings.*)

BENEATHA. That couldn't be the movers . . . it's not hardly two good yet—

(BENEATHA *goes into her room.* MAMA *starts for door.*)

WALTER (*turning, stiffening*). Wait —wait—I'll get it.

(*He stands and looks at the door.*)

MAMA. You expecting company, son?

WALTER (*just looking at the door*). Yeah—yeah . . .

(MAMA *looks at* RUTH, *and they exchange innocent and unfrightened glances.*)

MAMA (*not understanding*). Well, let them in, son.

BENEATHA (*from her room*). We need some more string.

MAMA. Travis—you run to the hardware and get me some string cord.

(MAMA *goes out and* WALTER *turns and looks at* RUTH. TRAVIS *goes to a dish for money*.)

RUTH. Why don't you answer the door, man?

WALTER (*suddenly bounding across the floor to her*). 'Cause sometimes it hard to let the future begin! (*stooping down in her face*)

    I got wings! You got wings!
    All God's children got wings! . . . . .

(*He crosses to the door and throws it open. Standing there is a very slight little man in a not too prosperous business suit and with haunted frightened eyes and a hat pulled down tightly, brim up, around his forehead.* TRAVIS *passes between the men and exits.* WALTER *leans deep in the man's face, still in his jubilance.*)

    When I get to heaven gonna put on
        my wings,
    Gonna fly all over God's heaven . . .

(*The little man just stares at him.*)

    Heaven—

(*Suddenly he stops and looks past the little man into the empty hallway.*) Where's Willy, man?

BOBO. He ain't with me.

WALTER (*not disturbed*). Oh—come on in. You know my wife.

BOBO (*dumbly, taking off his hat*). Yes—h'you, Miss Ruth.

RUTH (*quietly, a mood apart from her husband already, seeing* BOBO). Hello, Bobo.

WALTER. You right on time today . . . Right on time. That's the way! (*He slaps* BOBO *on his back.*) Sit down . . . lemme hear.

(RUTH *stands stiffly and quietly in back of them, as though somehow she senses death, her eyes fixed on her husband.*)

BOBO (*his frightened eyes on the floor, his hat in his hands*). Could I please get a drink of water, before I tell you about it, Walter Lee?

(WALTER *does not take his eyes off the man.* RUTH *goes blindly to the tap and gets a glass of water and brings it to* BOBO.)

WALTER. There ain't nothing wrong, is there?

BOBO. Lemme tell you—

WALTER. Man—didn't nothing go wrong?

BOBO. Lemme tell you—Walter Lee. (*Looking at* RUTH *and talking to her more than to* WALTER.) You know how it was. I got to tell you how it was. I mean first I got to tell you how it was all the way . . . I mean about the money I put in, Walter Lee . . .

WALTER (*with taut agitation now*). What about the money you put in?

BOBO. Well—it wasn't much as we told you—me and Willy—(*He stops.*) I'm sorry, Walter. I got a bad feeling about it. I got a real bad feeling about it . . .

WALTER. Man, what you telling me about all this for? . . . Tell me what happened in Springfield . . .

BOBO. Springfield.

RUTH (*like a dead woman*). What was supposed to happen in Springfield?

BOBO (*to her*). This deal that me and Walter went into with Willy—Me and Willy was going to go down to Springfield and spread some money 'round so's we wouldn't have to wait so long for the liquor license . . . That's what we were going to do. Everybody said that was the way you had to do, you understand, Miss Ruth?

WALTER. Man—what happened down there?

BOBO (*a pitiful man, near tears*). I'm trying to tell you, Walter.

WALTER (*screaming at him suddenly*). THEN TELL ME, GODDAMMIT . . . WHAT'S THE MATTER WITH YOU?

BOBO. Man . . . I didn't go to no Springfield, yesterday.

WALTER (*halted, life hanging in the moment*). Why not?

BOBO (*the long way, the hard way to tell*). 'Cause I didn't have no reasons to . . .

WALTER. Man, what are you talking about!

BOBO. I'm talking about the fact that when I got to the train station yesterday morning—eight o'clock like we planned . . . Man—*Willy didn't never show up.*

WALTER. Why . . . where was he . . . where is he?

BOBO. That's what I'm trying to tell you . . . I don't know . . . I waited six hours . . . I called his house . . . and I waited . . . six hours . . . I waited in that train station six hours . . . (*Breaking into tears.*) That was all the extra money I had in the world . . . (*Looking up at* WALTER *with the tears running down his face.*) Man, Willy is gone.

WALTER. Gone, what you mean Willy is gone? Gone where? You mean he went by himself. You mean he went off to Springfield by himself—to take care of getting the license—(*turns and looks anxiously at* RUTH.) You mean maybe he didn't want too many people in on the business down there? (*Looks to* RUTH *again, as before.*) You know Willy got his own ways. (*Looks back to* BOBO.) Maybe you was late yesterday and he just went on down there without you. Maybe— maybe—he's been callin' you at home tryin' to tell you what happened or something. Maybe—maybe—he just got sick. He's somewhere—he's got to be somewhere. We just got to find him—me and you got to find him. (*Grabs* BOBO *senselessly by the collar and starts to shake him.*) We got to!

BOBO (*in sudden angry, frightened agony*). What's the matter with you, Walter! *When a cat take off with your money he don't leave you no maps!*

WALTER (*turning madly, as though he is looking for* WILLY *in the very room*). Willy! . . . Willy . . . don't do it . . . Please don't do it . . . Man, not with that money . . . Man, please, not with that money . . . Oh, God . . . Don't let it be true . . . (*He is wandering around, crying out for* WILLY *and looking for him or perhaps for help from God.*) Man . . . I trusted you . . . Man, I put my life in your hands . . . (*He starts to crumple down on the floor as* RUTH *just covers her face in horror.* MAMA *opens the door and comes into the room, with* BENEATHA *behind her.*) Man . . . (*He starts to pound the floor with his fists, sobbing wildly.*) That money is made out of my father's flesh . . .

BOBO (*standing over him helplessly*). I'm sorry, Walter . . . (*Only* WALTER'S *sobs reply.* BOBO *puts on his hat.*) I had my life staked on this deal, too . . .

(*He exits.*)

MAMA (*to* WALTER). Son—(*She goes to him, bends down to him, talks to his bent head.*) Son . . . Is it gone? Son, I gave you sixty-five hundred dollars. Is it gone? All of it? Beneatha's money, too?

WALTER (*lifting his head slowly*). Mama . . . I never . . . went to the bank at all . . .

MAMA (*not wanting to believe him*). You mean . . . your sister's school money . . . you used that too . . . Walter? . . .

WALTER. Yessss! . . . All of it . . . It's all gone . . .

(*There is total silence.* RUTH *stands with her face covered with her hands;* BENEATHA *leans forlornly against a wall, fingering a piece of red ribbon from the mother's gift.* MAMA *stops and looks at her son without recognition and then, quite without thinking about it, starts to beat him senselessly in the face.* BENEATHA *goes to them and stops it.*)

BENEATHA. Mama!

(MAMA *stops and looks at both of her children and rises slowly and wanders vaguely, aimlessly away from them.*)

MAMA. I seen . . . him . . . night after night . . . come in . . . and look at that rug . . . and then look at me . . . the red showing in his eyes . . . the veins moving in his head . . . I seen him grow thin and old before he was forty . . . working and working and working like somebody's old horse . . . killing himself . . . and you—you give it all away in a day . . .

BENEATHA. Mama—

MAMA. Oh, God . . . (*She looks up to Him.*) Look down here—and show me the strength.

BENEATHA. Mama—

MAMA (*folding over*). Strength . . .

BENEATHA (*plaintively*). Mama . . .

MAMA. Strength!

(*Curtain.*)

Act Three

(*An hour later.*

At curtain, there is a sullen light of gloom in the living room, gray light not unlike that which began the first scene of Act One. At left we can see WALTER *within his room, alone with himself. He is stretched out on the bed, his shirt out and open, his arms under his head. He does not smoke, he does not cry out, he merely lies there, looking up at the ceiling, much as if he were alone in the world.*

In the living room BENEATHA *sits at the table, still surrounded by the now almost ominous packing crates. She sits looking off. We feel that this is a mood struck perhaps an hour before, and it lingers now, full of the empty sound of profound disappointment. We see on a line from her brother's bedroom the sameness of their attitudes. Presently the bell rings and* BENEATHA *rises without ambition or interest in answering. It is* ASAGAI, *smiling broadly, striding into the room with energy and happy expectation and conversation.*)

ASAGAI. I came over . . . I had some free time. I thought I might help with the packing. Ah, I like the look of packing crates! A household in preparation for a journey! It depresses some people . . . but for me . . . it is another feeling. Something full of the flow of life, do you understand? Movement, progress . . . It makes me think of Africa.

BENEATHA. Africa!

ASAGAI. What kind of a mood is this? Have I told you how deeply you move me?

BENEATHA. He gave away the money, Asagai . . .

ASAGAI. Who gave away what money?

BENEATHA. The insurance money. My brother gave it away.

ASAGAI. Gave it away?

BENEATHA. He made an investment! With a man even Travis wouldn't have trusted.

ASAGAI. And it's gone?

BENEATHA. Gone!

ASAGAI. I'm very sorry . . . And you, now?

BENEATHA. Me? . . . Me? . . . Me I'm nothing . . . Me. When I was very small . . . we used to take our sleds out in the wintertime and the only hills we had were the ice-covered stone steps of some houses down the street. And we used to fill them in with snow and make them smooth and slide down them all day . . . and it was very dangerous you know . . . far too steep . . . and sure enough one day a kid named Rufus came down too fast and hit the sidewalk . . . and we saw his face just split open right there in front of us . . . And I remember standing there looking at his bloody open face thinking that was the end of Rufus. But the ambulance came and they took him to the hospital and they fixed the broken bones and they sewed it all up . . . and the next time I saw Rufus he just had a little line down the middle of his face . . . I never got over that . . .

(WALTER *sits up, listening on the bed. Throughout this scene it is important that we feel his reaction at all times, that he visibly respond to the words of his sister and* ASAGAI.)

ASAGAI. What?

BENEATHA. That that was what one person could do for another, fix him up

—sew up the problem, make him all right again. That was the most marvelous thing in the world . . . I wanted to do that. I always thought it was the one concrete thing in the world that a human being could do. Fix up the sick, you know—and make them whole again. This was truly being God . . .

ASAGAI. You wanted to be God?

BENEATHA. No—I wanted to cure. It used to be so important to me. I wanted to cure. It used to matter. I used to care. I mean about people and how their bodies hurt . . .

ASAGAI. And you've stopped caring?

BENEATHA. Yes—I think so.

ASAGAI. Why?

(WALTER *rises, goes to the door of his room and is about to open it, then stops and stands listening, leaning on the door jamb.*)

BENEATHA. Because it doesn't seem deep enough, close enough to what ails mankind—I mean this thing of sewing up bodies or administering drugs. Don't you understand? It was a child's reaction to the world. I thought that doctors had the secret to all the hurts. . . . That's the way a child sees things—or an idealist.

ASAGAI. Children see things very well sometimes—and idealists even better.

BENEATHA. I know that's what you think. Because you are still where I left off—you still care. This is what you see for the world, for Africa. You with the dreams of the future will patch up all Africa—you are going to cure the Great Sore of colonialism with Independence—

ASAGAI. Yes!

BENEATHA. Yes—and you think that one word is the penicillin of the human spirit: "Independence!" But then what?

ASAGAI. That will be the problem for another time. First we must get there.

BENEATHA. And where does it end?

ASAGAI. End? Who even spoke of an end? To life? To living?

BENEATHA. An end to misery!

ASAGAI (*smiling*). You sound like a French intellectual.

BENEATHA. No! I sound like a human being who just had her future taken right out of her hands! While I was sleeping in my bed in there, things were happening in this world that directly concerned me—and nobody asked me, consulted me—they just went out and did things—and changed my life. Don't you see there isn't any real progress, Asagai, there is only one large circle that we march in, around and around, each of us with our own little picture—in front of us—our own little mirage that we think is the future.

ASAGAI. That is the mistake.

BENEATHA. What?

ASAGAI. What you just said—about the circle. It isn't a circle—it is simply a long line—as in geometry, you know, one that reaches into infinity. And because we cannot see the end—we also cannot see how it changes. And it is very odd but those who see the changes are called "idealists"—and those who cannot, or refuse to think, they are the "realists." It is very strange, and amusing too, I think.

BENEATHA. You—you are almost religious.

ASAGAI. Yes . . . I think I have the religion of doing what is necessary in the world—and of worshipping man—because he is so marvelous, you see.

BENEATHA. Man is foul! And the human race deserves its misery!

ASAGAI. You see: *you* have become the religious one in the old sense. Already, and after such a small defeat, you are worshipping despair.

BENEATHA. From now on, I worship the truth—and the truth is that people are puny, small and selfish. . . .

ASAGAI. Truth? Why is it that you despairing ones always think that only you have the truth? I never thought to see *you* like that. You! Your brother made a stupid, childish mistake—and you are grateful to him. So that now you can give up the ailing human race on account of it. You talk about what good is struggle; what good is anything? Where are we all going? And why are we bothering?

BENEATHA. *And you cannot answer it!* All your talk and dreams about Africa and Independence. Independence and then what? What about all the crooks and petty thieves and just plain idiots who will come into power to steal and plunder the same as before—only now they will be black and do it in the name of the new Independence—You cannot answer that.

ASAGAI (*shouting over her*). *I live the answer!* (*Pause.*) In my village at home it is the exceptional man who can even read a newspaper . . . or who ever *sees* a book at all. I will go home and much of what I will have to say will seem strange to the people of my village . . . But I will teach and work and things will happen, slowly and swiftly. At times it will seem that nothing changes at all . . . and then again . . . the sudden dramatic events which make history leap into the future. And then quiet again. Retrogression even. Guns, murder, revolution. And I even will have moments when I wonder if the quiet was not better than all that death and hatred. But I will look about my village at the illiteracy and disease and ignorance and I will not wonder long. And perhaps . . . perhaps I will be a great man . . . I mean perhaps I will hold on to the substance of truth and find my way always with the right course . . . and perhaps for it I will be butchered in my bed some night by the servants of empire . . .

BENEATHA. The martyr!

ASAGAI. . . . or perhaps I shall live to be a very old man, respected and esteemed in my new nation . . . And perhaps I shall hold office and this is what I'm trying to tell you, Alaiyo; perhaps the things I believe now for my country will be wrong and outmoded, and I will not understand and do terrible things to have things my way or merely to keep my power. Don't you see that there will be young men and women, not British soldiers then, but my own black countrymen . . . to step out of the shadows some evening and slit my then useless throat? Don't you see they have always been there . . . that they always will be. And that such a thing as my own death will be an advance? They who might kill me even . . . actually replenish me!

BENEATHA. Oh, Asagai, I know all that.

ASAGAI. Good! Then stop moaning and groaning and tell me what you plan to do.

BENEATHA. Do?

ASAGAI. I have a bit of a suggestion.

BENEATHA. What?

ASAGAI (*rather quietly for him*). That when it is all over—that you come home with me—

BENEATHA (*slapping herself on the forehead with exasperation born of misunderstanding*). Oh—Asagai—at this moment you decide to be romantic!

ASAGAI (*quickly understanding the misunderstanding*). My dear, young creature of the New World—I do not mean across the city—I mean across the ocean; home—to Africa.

BENEATHA (*slowly understanding and turning to him with murmured amazement*). To—to Nigeria?

ASAGAI. Yes! . . . (*Smiling and lifting his arms playfully.*) Three hundred years later the African Prince rose up out of the seas and swept the maiden back across the middle passage over which her ancestors had come—

BENEATHA (*unable to play*). Nigeria?

ASAGAI. Nigeria. Home. (*Coming to her with genuine romantic flippancy.*) I will show you our mountains and our stars; and give you cool drinks from gourds and teach you the old songs and the ways of our people—and, in time, we will pretend that—(*very softly*)—you have only been away for a day—

(*She turns her back to him, thinking. He swings her around and takes her full in his arms in a long embrace which proceeds to passion.*)

BENEATHA (*pulling away*). You're getting me all mixed up—

ASAGAI. Why?

BENEATHA. Too many things—too many things have happened today. I must sit down and think. I don't know what I feel about anything right this minute.

(*She promptly sits down and props her chin on her fist.*)

ASAGAI (*charmed*). All right, I shall leave you. No—don't get up. (*Touching her, gently, sweetly.*) Just sit awhile and think . . . Never be afraid to sit awhile and think. (*He goes to door and looks at her.*) How often I have looked at you and said, "Ah—so this is what the New World hath finally wrought . . ."

(*He exits.* BENEATHA *sits on alone. Presently* WALTER *enters from his room and starts to rummage through things, feverishly looking for something. She looks up and turns in her seat.*)

BENEATHA (*hissingly*). Yes—just look at what the New World hath wrought! . . . Just look! (*She gestures with bitter disgust.*) There he is! *Monsieur le petit bourgeois noir*—himself! There he is —Symbol of a Rising Class! Entrepreneur! Titan of the system! (WALTER *ignores her completely and continues frantically and destructively looking for something and hurling things to floor and tearing things out of their place in his search.* BENEATHA *ignores the eccentricity of his actions and goes on with the monologue of insult.*) Did you dream of yachts on Lake Michigan, Brother? Did you see yourself on that Great Day sitting down at the Conference Table, surrounded by all the mighty bald-headed men in America? All halted, waiting, breathless, waiting for your pronouncements on industry? Waiting for you— Chairman of the Board? (WALTER *finds what he is looking for—a small piece of white paper—and pushes it in his pocket and puts on his coat and rushes out without ever having looked at her. She shouts after him.*) I look at you and I see the final triumph of stupidity in the world!

(*The door slams and she returns to just sitting again.* RUTH *comes quickly out of* MAMA'S *room.*)

RUTH. Who was that?

BENEATHA. Your husband.

RUTH. Where did he go?

BENEATHA. Who knows—maybe he has an appointment at U.S. Steel.

RUTH (*anxiously, with frightened eyes*). You didn't say nothing bad to him, did you?

BENEATHA. Bad? Say anything bad to him? No—I told him he was a sweet boy and full of dreams and everything is strictly peachy keen, as the ofay kids say!

(MAMA *enters from her bedroom. She is lost, vague, trying to catch hold, to make some sense of her former command of the world, but it still eludes her. A sense of waste overwhelms her gait; a measure of apology rides on her shoulders. She goes to her plant, which has remained on the table, looks at it, picks it up and takes it to the window sill and sets it outside, and she stands and looks at it a long moment. Then she closes the window, straightens her body with effort and turns around to her children.*)

MAMA. Well—ain't it a mess in here, though? (*A false cheerfulness, a beginning of something.*) I guess we all better stop moping around and get some work done. All this unpacking and everything we got to do. (RUTH *raises her head slowly in response to the sense of the line; and* BENEATHA *in similar manner turns very slowly to look at her mother.*) One of you all better call the moving people and tell 'em not to come.

RUTH. Tell 'em not to come?

MAMA. Of course, baby. Ain't no need in 'em coming all the way here and having to go back. They charges for that too. (*She sits down, fingers to her brow, thinking.*) Lord, ever since I was a little girl, I always remembers people saying, "Lena—Lena Eggleston, you aims too high all the time. You needs to slow down and see life a little more like it is. Just slow down some." That's what they always used to say down home—"Lord, that Lena Eggleston is a high-minded thing. She'll get her due one day!"

RUTH. No, Lena . . .

MAMA. Me and Big Walter just didn't never learn right.

RUTH. Lena, no! We gotta go. Bennie—tell her . . . (*She rises and crosses to* BENEATHA *with her arms outstretched.* BENEATHA *doesn't respon*d.) Tell her we can still move . . . the notes ain't but a hundred and twenty-five a month. We got four grown people in this house— we can work . . .

MAMA (*to herself*). Just aimed too high all the time—

RUTH (*turning and going to* MAMA *fast—the words pouring out with urgency and desperation*). Lena—I'll work . . . I'll work twenty hours a day in all the kitchens in Chicago . . . I'll strap my baby on my back if I have to and scrub all the floors in America and wash all the sheets in America if I have to—but we got to move . . . We got to get out of here . . .

(MAMA *reaches out absently and pats* RUTH'S *hand.*)

MAMA. No—I sees things differently now. Been thinking 'bout some of the things we could do to fix this place up some. I seen a second-hand bureau over on Maxwell Street just the other day that could fit right there. (*She points to where the new furniture might go.* RUTH *wanders away from her.*) Would need some new handles on it and then a little varnish and then it look like something brand-new. And—we can put up them new curtains in the kitchen . . . Why this place be looking fine. Cheer us all up so that we forget trouble ever came . . . (*To* RUTH,) And you could get some nice screens to put up in your room round the baby's bassinet . . . (*She looks at both of them, pleadingly.*) Sometimes you just got to know when to give up some things . . . and hold on to what you got.

(WALTER *enters from the outside, looking spent and leaning against the door, his coat hanging from him.*)

MAMA. Where you been, son?

WALTER (*breathing hard*). Made a call.

MAMA. To who, son?

WALTER. To The Man.

MAMA. What man, baby?

WALTER. The Man, Mama. Don't you know who The Man is?

RUTH. Walter Lee?

WALTER. *The Man.* Like the guys in the streets say—The Man. Captain Boss —Mistuh Charley . . . Old Captain Please Mr. Bossman . . .

BENEATHA (*suddenly*). Lindner!

WALTER. That's right! That's good. I told him to come right over.

BENEATHA (*fiercely, understanding*). For what? What do you want to see him for!

WALTER (*looking at his sister*). We going to do business with him.

MAMA. What you talking 'bout son?

WALTER. Talking 'bout life, Mama. You all always telling me to see life like it is. Well—I laid in there on my back today . . . and I figured it out. Life just like it is. Who gets and who don't get. (*He sits down with his coat on and laughs.*) Mama, you know it's all divided up. Life is. Sure enough. Between the takers and the "tooken." (*He laughs.*) I've figured it out finally. (*He looks around at them.*) Yeah. Some of us always getting "tooken." (*He laughs.*) People like Willy Harris, they don't never get "tooken." And you know why the rest of us do? 'Cause we all mixed up. Mixed up bad. We get to looking 'round for the right and the wrong; and we worry about it and cry about it and stay up nights trying to figure out 'bout the wrong and the right of things all the time . . . And all the time, man, them takers is out there operating, just taking and taking. Willy Harris? Shoot—Willy Harris don't even count. He don't even count in the big scheme of things. But I'll say one thing for old Willy Harris . . . he's taught me something. He's taught me to keep my eye on what counts in this world. Yeah—(*Shouting out a little.*) Thanks, Willy!

RUTH. What did you call that man for, Walter Lee?

WALTER. Called him to tell him to come on over to the show. Gonna put on a show for the man. Just what he wants to see. You see, Mama, the man came here today and he told us that them people out there where you want us to move—well they so upset they willing to pay us not to move out there. (*He laughs again.*) And—and oh, Mama—you would of been proud of the way me and Ruth and Bennie acted. We told him to get out . . . Lord have mercy! We told the man to get out. Oh, we was some proud folks this afternoon, yeah. (*He lights a cigarette.*) We were still full of that old-time stuff . . .

RUTH (*coming toward him slowly*). You talking 'bout taking them people's money to keep us from moving in that house?

WALTER. I ain't just talking 'bout it, baby—I'm telling you that's what's going to happen.

BENEATHA. Oh, God! Where is the bottom! Where is the real honest-to-God bottom so he can't go any farther!

WALTER. See—that's the old stuff. You and that boy that was here today. You all want everybody to carry a flag and a spear and sing some marching songs, huh? You wanna spend your life looking into things and trying to find the right and the wrong part, huh? Yeah. You know what's going to happen to that boy someday—he'll find himself sitting in a dungeon, locked in forever—and the takers will have the key! Forget it, baby! There ain't no causes—there ain't noth-ing but taking in this world, and he who takes most is smartest—and it don't make a damn bit of difference *how*.

MAMA. You making something inside me cry, son. Some awful pain inside me.

WALTER. Don't cry, Mama. Understand. That white man is going to walk in that door able to write checks for more money than we ever had. It's important to him and I'm going to help him . . . I'm going to put on the show, Mama.

MAMA. Son—I come from five generations of people who was slaves and sharecroppers—but ain't nobody in my family never let nobody pay 'em no money that was a way of telling us we wasn't fit to walk the earth. We ain't never been that poor. (*Raising her eyes and looking at him.*) We ain't never been that dead inside.

BENEATHA. Well—we are dead now. All the talk about dreams and sunlight that goes on in this house. All dead.

WALTER. What's the matter with you all! I didn't make this world! It was give to me this way! Hell, yes, I want me some yachts someday! Yes, I want to hang some real pearls 'round my wife's neck. Ain't she supposed to wear no pearls? Somebody tell me—tell me, who decides which women is suppose to wear pearls in this world. I tell you I am a *man*—and I think my wife should wear some pearls in this world!

(*This last line hangs a good while and* WALTER *begins to move about the room. The word "Man" has penetrated his consciousness; he mumbles it to himself repeatedly between strange agitated pauses as he moves about.*)

MAMA. Baby, how you going to feel on the inside?

WALTER. Fine! . . . Going to feel fine . . . a man . . .

MAMA. You won't have nothing left then, Walter Lee.

WALTER (*coming to her*). I'm going to feel fine, Mama. I'm going to look that son-of-a-bitch in the eyes and say—

(*He falters.*)—and say, "All right, Mr. Lindner—(*He falters even more.*)—that's your neighborhood out there. You got the right to keep it like you want. You got the right to have it like you want. Just write the check and—the house is yours." And, and I am going to say— (*His voice almost breaks.*) And you— you people just put the money in my hand and you won't have to live next to this bunch of stinking niggers! . . . (*He straightens up and moves away from his mother, walking around the room.*) Maybe—maybe I'll just get down on my black knees . . . (*He does so;* RUTH *and* BENNIE *and* MAMA *watch him in frozen horror.*) Captain, Mistuh, Bossman. (*He starts crying.*) A-hee-hee-hee! (*Wringing his hands in profoundly anguished imitation.*) Yasssssuh! Great White Father, just gi' ussen de money, fo' God's sake, and we's ain't gwine come out deh and dirty up yo' white folks neighborhood . . .

(*He breaks down completely, then gets up and goes into the bedroom.*)

BENEATHA.   That is not a man. That is nothing but a toothless rat.

MAMA.   Yes—death done come in this here house. (*She is nodding, slowly, reflectively.*) Done come walking in my house. On the lips of my children. You what supposed to be my beginning again. You—what supposed to be my harvest. (*To* BENEATHA,) You—you mourning your brother?

BENEATHA.   He's no brother of mine.

MAMA.   What you say?

BENEATHA.   I said that that individual in that room is no brother of mine.

MAMA.   That's what I thought you said. You feeling like you better than he is today? (BENEATHA *does not answer.*) Yes? What you tell him a minute ago? That he wasn't a man? Yes? You give him up for me? You done wrote his epitaph too—like the rest of the world? Well, who give you the privilege?

BENEATHA.   Be on my side for once! You saw what he just did, Mama! You saw him—down on his knees. Wasn't it you who taught me—to despise any man who would do that. Do what he's going to do.

MAMA.   Yes—I taught you that. Me and your daddy. But I thought I taught you something else too . . . I thought I taught you to love him.

BENEATHA.   Love him? There is nothing left to love.

MAMA.   There is always something left to love. And if you ain't learned that, you ain't learned nothing. (*Looking at her.*) Have you cried for that boy today? I don't mean for yourself and for the family 'cause we lost the money. I mean for him; what he been through and what it done to him. Child, when do you think is the time to love somebody the most; when they done good and made things easy for everybody? Well then, you ain't through learning—because that ain't the time at all. It's when he's at his lowest and can't believe in hisself 'cause the world done whipped him so. When you starts measuring somebody, measure him right, child, measure him right. Make sure you done taken into account what hills and valleys he come through before he got to wherever he is.

(TRAVIS *bursts into the room at the end of the speech, leaving the door open.*)

TRAVIS.   Grandmama—the moving men are downstairs! The truck just pulled up.

MAMA (*turning and looking at him*). Are they, baby? They downstairs?

(*She sighs and sits.* LINDNER *appears in the doorway. He peers in and knocks lightly, to gain attention, and comes in. All turn to look at him.*)

LINDNER (*hat and briefcase in hand*). Uh—hello . . .

(RUTH *crosses mechanically to the bedroom door and opens it and lets it swing open freely and slowly as the lights come up on* WALTER *within, still in his coat, sitting at the far corner of the room. He looks up and out through the room to* LINDNER.)

RUTH. He's here.

(*A long minute passes and* WALTER *slowly gets up.*)

LINDNER (*coming to the table with efficiency, putting his briefcase on the table and starting to unfold papers and unscrew fountain pens.*) Well, I certainly was glad to hear from you people. (WALTER *has begun the trek out of the room, slowly and awkwardly, rather like a small boy, passing the back of his sleeve across his mouth from time to time.*) Life can really be so much simpler than people let it be most of the time. Well—with whom do I negotiate? You, Mrs. Younger, or your son here? (MAMA *sits with her hands folded on her lap and her eyes closed as* WALTER *advances.* TRAVIS *goes close to* LINDNER *and looks at the papers curiously.*) Just some official papers, sonny.

RUTH. Travis, you go downstairs.

MAMA (*opening her eyes and looking into* WALTER'S). No. Travis, you stay right here. And you make him understand what you doing, Walter Lee. You teach him good. Like Willy Harris taught you. You show where our five generations done come to. Go ahead, son—

WALTER (*looks down into his boy's eyes.* TRAVIS *grins at him merrily and* WALTER *draws him beside him with his arm lightly around his shoulder*). Well, Mr. Lindner. (BENEATHA *turns away.*) We called you—(*There is a profound, simple groping quality in his speech.*)—because, well, me and my family (*He looks around and shifts from one foot to the other.*) Well—we are very plain people . . .

LINDNER. Yes—

WALTER. I mean—I have worked as a chauffeur most of my life—and my wife here, she does domestic work in people's kitchens. So does my mother. I mean—we are plain people . . .

LINDNER. Yes, Mr. Younger—

WALTER (*really like a small boy, looking down at his shoes and then up at the man*). And—uh—well, my father, well, he was a laborer most of his life.

LINDNER (*absolutely confused*). Uh, yes—

WALTER (*looking down at his toes once again*). My father almost beat a man to death once because this man called him a bad name or something, you know what I mean?

LINDNER. No, I'm agraid I don't.

WALTER (*finally straightening up*). Well, what I mean is that we come from people who had a lot of pride. I mean—we are very proud people. And that's my sister over there and she's going to be a doctor—and we are very proud—

LINDNER. Well—I am sure that is very nice, but—

WALTER (*starting to cry and facing the man eye to eye*). What I am telling you is that we called you over here to tell you that we are very proud and that this is—this is my son, who makes the sixth generation of our family in this country, and that we have all thought about your offer and we have decided to move into our house because my father—my father—he earned it. (MAMA *has her eyes closed and is rocking back and forth as though she were in church, with her head nodding the amen yes.*) We don't want to make no trouble for nobody or fight no causes—but we will try to be good neighbors. That's all we got to say. (*He looks the man absolutely in the eyes.*) We don't want your money.

(*He turns and walks away from the man.*)

LINDNER (*looking around at all of them*). I take it then that you have decided to occupy.

BENEATHA. That's what the man said.

LINDNER (*to* MAMA *in her reverie*). Then I would like to appeal to you, Mrs. Younger. You are older and wiser and understand things better I am sure . . .

MAMA (*rising*). I am afraid you

don't understand. My son said we was going to move and there ain't nothing left for me to say. (*Shaking her head with double meaning.*) You know how these young folks is nowadays, mister. Can't do a thing with 'em. Good-bye.

LINDNER (*folding up his materials*). Well—if you are that final about it . . . There is nothing left for me to say. (*He finishes. He is almost ignored by the family, who are concentrating on* WALTER LEE. *At the door* LINDNER *halts and looks around.*) I sure hope you people know what you're doing.

(*He shakes his head and exits.*)

RUTH (*looking around and coming to life*). Well, for God's sake—if the moving men are here—LET'S GET THE HELL OUT OF HERE!

MAMA (*into action*). Ain't it the truth! Look at all this here mess. Ruth, put Travis' good jacket on him . . . Walter Lee, fix your tie and tuck your shirt in, you look just like somebody's hoodlum. Lord have mercy, where is my plant? (*She flies to get it amid the general bustling of the family, who are deliberately trying to ignore the nobility of the past moment.*) You all start on down . . . Travis child, don't go empty-handed . . . Ruth, where did I put that box with my skillets in it? I want to be in charge of it myself . . . I'm going to make us the biggest dinner we ever ate tonight . . . Beneatha, what's the matter with them stockings? Pull them things up, girl . . .

(*The family starts to file out as two moving men appear and begin to carry out the heavier pieces of furniture, bumping into the family as they move about.*)

BENEATHA. Mama, Asagai—asked me to marry him today and go to Africa—

MAMA (*in the middle of her getting-ready activity*). He did? You ain't old enough to marry nobody— (*Seeing the moving men lifting one of her chairs precariously.*) Darling, that ain't no bale of cotton, please handle it so we can sit in it again. I had that chair twenty-five years . . .

(*The movers sigh with exasperation and go on with their work.*)

BENEATHA (*girlishly and unreasonably trying to pursue the conversation*). To go to Africa, Mama—be a doctor in Africa . . .

MAMA (*distracted*). Yes, baby—

WALTER. Africa! What he want you to go to Africa for?

BENEATHA. To practice there . . .

WALTER. Girl, if you don't get all them silly ideas out your head! You better marry yourself a man with some loot . . .

BENEATHA (*angrily, precisely as in the first scene of the play*). What have you got to do with who I marry!

WALTER. Plenty. Now I think George Murchison—

(*He and* BENEATHA *go out yelling at each other vigorously;* BENEATHA *is heard saying that she would not marry* GEORGE MURCHISON *if he were Adam and she were Eve, etc. The anger is loud and real till their voices diminish.* RUTH *stands at the door and turns to* MAMA *and smiles knowingly.*)

MAMA (*fixing her hat at last*). Yeah—they something, all right, my children . . .

RUTH. Yeah—they're something. Let's go, Lena.

MAMA (*stalling, starting to look around at the house*). Yes— I'm coming. Ruth—

RUTH. Yes?

MAMA (*quietly, woman to woman*). He finally come into his manhood today, didn't he? Kind of like a rainbow after the rain . . .

RUTH (*biting her lip lest her own pride explode in front of* MAMA). Yes, Lena.

(WALTER'S *voice calls for them raucously.*)

MAMA (*waving* RUTH *out vaguely*). All right, honey—go on down. I be down directly.

(RUTH *hesitates, then exits.* MAMA *stands, at last alone in the living room, her plant on the table before her as the lights start to come down. She looks around at all the walls and ceilings and suddenly, despite herself, while the children call below, a great heaving thing rises in her and she puts her finger to her mouth, takes a final desperate look, pulls her coat about her, pats her hat and goes out. The lights dim down. The door opens and she comes back in, grabs her plant, and goes out for the last time.*)

(*Curtain.*)

Criticism

THOMAS de QUINCEY • 1785-1859

The Literature of Knowledge and the Literature of Power

WHAT is it that we mean by *literature*? Popularly, and amongst the thoughtless, it is held to include everything that is printed in a book. Little logic is required to disturb *that* definition; the most thoughtless person is easily made aware that in the idea of *literature* one essential element is—some relation to a general and common interest of man, so that what applies only to a local—or professional—or merely personal interest, even though presenting itself in the shape of a book, will not belong to literature. So far the definition is easily narrowed; and it is as easily expanded. For not only is much that takes a station in books not literature; but inversely, much that really *is* literature never reaches a station in books. The weekly sermons of Christendom, that vast pulpit literature which acts so extensively upon the popular mind—to warn, to uphold, to renew, to comfort, to alarm, does not attain the sanctuary of libraries in the ten thousandth part of its extent. The drama again, as, for instance, the finest of Shakspere's plays in England, and all leading Athenian plays in the noontide of the Attic stage, operated as a literature on the public mind, and were (according to the strictest letter of that term) *published* through the audiences that witnessed[1] their representation some time before they were published as things to be read; and they were published in this scenical mode of publication with much more effect than they could have had as books, during ages of costly copying or of costly printing.

Books, therefore, do not suggest an idea co-extensive and interchangeable with the idea of literature; since much literature, scenic, forensic, or didactic, (as from lecturers and public orators,) may never come into books; and much that *does* come into books, may connect itself with no literary interest. But a far more important correction, applicable to the common vague idea of literature, is to be sought—not so much in a better definition of literature, as in a sharper distinction of the two functions which it fulfills. In that great social organ, which collectively we call literature, there may be distinguished two separate offices that may blend and often *do* so, but capable severally of a severe insulation, and naturally fitted for reciprocal repulsion. There is first the literature of *knowledge,* and secondly, the literature of *power.* The function of the first is—to *teach;* the function of the second is—to *move:* the first is a rudder, the second an oar or a sail. The first speaks to the *mere* discursive understanding; the second speaks ultimately it may happen to the higher understanding or reason, but always *through* affections of pleasure and sympathy. Remotely, it may travel towards an object seated in what Lord Bacon calls *dry* light; but proximately it does and must operate, else it ceases to be a literature of *power,* on and through that

[1] Charles I, for example, when Prince of Wales, and many others in his father's court, gained their known familiarity with Shakspere—not through the original quartos, so slenderly diffused, nor through the first folio of 1623, but through the court representations of his chief dramas at Whitehall.

humid light which clothes itself in the mists and glittering *iris* of human passions, desires, and genial emotions. Men have so little reflected on the higher functions of literature, as to find it a paradox if one should describe it as a mean or subordinate purpose of books to give information. But this is a paradox only in the sense which makes it honourable to be paradoxical. Whenever we talk in ordinary language of seeking information or gaining knowledge, we understand the words as connected with something of absolute novelty. But it is the grandeur of all truth which *can* occupy a very high place in human interests, that it is never absolutely novel to the meanest of minds: it exists eternally by way of germ or latent principle in the lowest as in the highest, needing to be developed but never to be planted. To be capable of transplantation is the immediate criterion of a truth that ranges on a lower scale. Besides which, there is a rarer thing than truth, namely, *power* or deep sympathy with truth. What is the effect, for instance, upon society—of children? By the pity, by the tenderness, and by the peculiar modes of admiration, which connect themselves with the helplessness, with the innocence, and with the simplicity of children, not only are the primal affections strengthened and continually renewed, but the qualities which are dearest in the sight of heaven—the frailty for instance, which appeals to forbearance, the innocence which symbolizes the heavenly, and the simplicity which is most alien from the worldly, are kept up in perpetual remembrance, and their ideals are continually refreshed. A purpose of the same nature is answered by the higher literature, viz. the literature of power. What do you learn from Paradise Lost? Nothing at all. What do you learn from a cookery-book? Something new, something that you did not know before, in every paragraph. But would you therefore put the wretched cookery-book on a higher level of estimation than the divine poem? What you owe to Milton is not any knowledge, of which a million separate items are still but a million of advancing steps on the same earthly level; what you owe—is *power,* that is, exercise and expansion to your own latent capacity of sympathy with the infinite, where every pulse and each separate influx is a step upwards—a step ascending as upon a Jacob's ladder from earth to mysterious altitudes above the earth. *All* the steps of knowledge, from first to last, carry you farther on the same plane, but could never raise you one foot above your ancient level of earth: whereas, the very *first* step in power is a flight—is an ascending into another element where earth is forgotten.

Were it not that human sensibilities are ventilated and continually called out into exercise by the great phenomena of infancy, or of real life as it moves through chance and change, or of literature as it recombines these elements in the mimicries of poetry, romance, &c., it is certain that, like any animal power or muscular energy falling into disuse, all such sensibilities would gradually droop and dwindle. It is in relation to these great *moral* capacities of man that the literature of power, as contradistinguished from that of knowledge, lives and has its field of action. It is concerned with what is highest in man: for the Scriptures themselves never condescend to deal by suggestion or co-operation, with the mere discursive understanding: when speaking of man in his intellectual capacity, the Scriptures speak not of the understanding, but of *"the understanding heart,"*—making the heart, *i. e.,* the great *intuitive* (or non-discursive) organ, to be the interchangeable formula for man in his highest state of capacity for the infinite. Tragedy, romance, fairy-tale, or epopee, all alike restore to man's mind the ideals of justice, of hope, of truth, of mercy, of retribution, which else, (left to the support of daily life in its realities,) would languish for want of sufficient illustration. What is meant for instance by *poetic justice?*— It does not mean a justice that differs by its object from the ordinary justice of human jurisprudence; for then it must be confessedly a very bad kind of justice; but it means a justice that differs from common forensic justice by the degree in which it *attains* its object, a justice that is more omnipotent over its own ends, as dealing—not with the refractory elements of earthly life—but with elements of its own creation, and with materials flexible to its own purest preconceptions. It is certain that, were it not for the literature of power, these ideals would often remain amongst us as mere arid notional forms; whereas, by the creative forces of man put forth in literature, they gain a vernal life of restoration, and germinate into vital activities. The commonest novel, by moving in alliance with human fears and hopes, with human instincts of wrong and right, sustains and quickens those affections. Calling them into action, it rescues them from torpor. And hence the pre-eminency over all authors that merely *teach*, of the meanest that *moves;* or that teaches, if at all, indirectly *by* moving. The very highest work that has ever existed in the literature of knowledge, is but a *provisional* work: a book upon trial and sufferance, and *quamdiu bene se gesserit.*[1a] Let its teaching be even partially revised, let it be but expanded, nay, even let its teaching be but placed in a better order, and instantly it is superseded. Whereas the feeblest works in the literature of power, surviving at all, survive as finished and unalterable amongst men. For instance, the *Principia* of Sir Isaac Newton was a book *militant* on earth from the first. In all stages of its progress it would have to fight for its existence: 1*st*, as regards absolute truth; 2*dly*, when that combat is over, as regards its form or mode of presenting the truth. And as soon as a La Place, or anybody else, builds higher upon the foundations laid by this book, effectually he throws it out of the sunshine into decay and darkness; by weapons won from this book he superannuates and destroys this book, so that soon the name of Newton remains, as a mere *nominis umbra,*[1b] but his book, as a living power, has transmigrated into other forms. Now, on the contrary, the Iliad, the Prometheus of Æschylus—the Othello or King Lear,—the Hamlet or Macbeth, —and the Paradise Lost, are not militant but triumphant for ever as long as the languages exist in which they speak or can be taught to speak. They never *can* transmigrate into new incarnations. To reproduce *these* in new forms, or variations, even if in some things they should be improved, would be to plagiarize. A good steam-engine is properly superseded by a better. But one lovely pastoral valley is not superseded by another, nor a statue of Praxiteles by a statue of Michael Angelo. These things are not separated by imparity, but by disparity. They are not thought of as unequal under the same standard, but as differing in *kind,* and as equal under a different standard. Human works of immortal beauty and works of nature in one respect stand on the same footing: they never absolutely repeat each other: never approach so near as not to differ; and they differ not as better and worse, or simply by more and less: they differ by undecipherable and incommunicable differences, that cannot be caught by mimicries, nor be reflected in the mirror of copies, nor become ponderable in the scales of vulgar comparison.

Applying these principles to Pope, as a representative of fine literature in general, we would wish to remark the claim which he has, or which any equal writer has, to the attention and jealous winnowing of those critics in particular who watch over public morals. Clergymen, and all

---

[1a] so long as it behaves. [Ed. note]

[1b] shadow of a name. [Ed. note]

the organs of public criticism put in motion by clergymen, are more especially concerned in the just appreciation of such writers, if the two canons are remembered, which we have endeavoured to illustrate, viz., that all works in this class, as opposed to those in the literature of knowledge, 1*st,* work by far deeper agencies; and 2*dly,* are more permanent; in the strictest sense they are κτημata ἐς ἀει [possessions forever]: and what evil they do, or what good they do, is commensurate with the national language, sometimes long after the nation has departed. At this hour, 500 years since their creation, the tales of Chaucer,[2] never equalled on this earth for tenderness, and for life of picturesqueness, are read familiarly by many in the charming language of their natal day, and by others in the modernizations of Dryden, of Pope, and Wordsworth. At this hour, 1800 years since their creation, the Pagan tales of Ovid, never equalled on this earth for the gaiety of their movement and the capricious graces of their narrative, are read by all Christendom. This man's people and their monuments are dust: but *he* is alive: he has survived them, as he told us that he had it in his commission to do, by a thousand years; "and *shall* a thousand more."

All the literature of knowledge builds only ground-nests, that are swept away by floods, or confounded by the plough; but the literature of power builds nests in aerial altitudes of temples sacred from violation, or of forests inaccessible to fraud. *This* is a great prerogative of the *power* literature: and it is a greater which lies in the mode of its influence. The *knowledge* literature, like the fashion of this world, passeth away. An Encyclopædia is its abstract; and, in this respect, it may be taken for its speaking symbol —that, before one generation has passed, an Encyclopædia is superannuated; for it speaks through the dead memory and unimpassioned understanding, which have not the *rest* of higher faculties, but are continually enlarging and varying their phylacteries. But all literature, properly so called—literature κατ' ἐξοχην [i.e., great literature], for the very same reason that it is so much more durable than the literature of knowledge, is (and by the very same proportion it is) more intense and electrically searching in its impressions. The directions in which the tragedy of this planet has trained our human feelings to play, and the combinations into which the poetry of this planet has thrown our human passions of love and hatred, of admiration and contempt, exercises a power bad or good over human life, that cannot be contemplated when seen stretching through many generations, without a sentiment allied to awe.[3] And of this let every one be assured—that he owes to the impassioned books which he has read, many a thousand more of emotions than he can consciously trace back to them. Dim by their origination, these emotions yet arise in him, and mould him through life like the forgotten incidents of childhood.

[2] The Canterbury Tales were not made public until 1380 or thereabouts: but the composition must have cost 30 or more years; not to mention that the work had probably been finished for some years before it was divulged.

[3] The reason why the broad distinctions between the two literatures of power and knowledge so little fix the attention, lies in the fact, that a vast proportion of books—history, biography, travels, miscellaneous essays, &c., lying in a middle zone, confound these distinctions by interblending them. All that we call "amusement" or "entertainment," is a diluted form of the power belonging to passion, and also a mixed form; and where threads of direct *instruction* intermingle in the texture with these threads of *power,* this absorption of the duality into one representative *nuance* neutralises the separate perception of either. Fused into a *tertium quid,* or neutral state, they disappear to the popular eye as the repelling forces, which in fact they are.

JOHN GALSWORTHY • 1867-1933

Some Platitudes Concerning Drama

A drama must be shaped so as to have a spire of meaning. Every grouping of life and character has its inherent moral; and the business of the dramatist is so to pose the group as to bring the moral poignantly to the light of day. Such is the moral that exhales from plays like *Lear, Hamlet,* and *Macbeth*. But such is not the moral to be found in the great bulk of contemporary Drama. The moral of the average play is now, and probably has always been, the triumph at all costs of a supposed immediate ethical good over a supposed immediate ethical evil.

The vice of drawing these distorted morals has permeated the Drama to its spine; discoloured its art, humanity, and significance; infected its creators, actors, audience, critics; too often turned it from a picture into a caricature. A Drama which lives under the shadow of the distorted moral forgets how to be free, fair, and fine—forgets so completely that it often prides itself on having forgotten.

Now, in writing plays, there are, in this matter of the moral, three coures open to the serious dramatist. The first is: To definitely set before the public that which it wishes to have set before it, the views and codes of life by which the public lives and in which it believes. This way is the most common, successful, and popular. It makes the dramatist's position sure, and not too obviously authoritative.

The second course is: To definitely set before the public those views and codes of life by which the dramatist himself lives, those theories in which he himself believes, the more effectively if they are the opposite of what the public wishes to have placed before it, presenting them so that the audience may swallow them like powder in a spoonful of jam.

There is a third course: To set before the public no cut-and-dried codes, but the phenomena of life and character, selected and combined, *but not distorted,* by the dramatist's outlook, set down without fear, favour, or prejudice, leaving the public to draw such poor moral as nature may afford. This third method requires a certain detachment; it requires a sympathy with, a love of, and a curiosity as to, things for their own sake; it requires a far view, together with patient industry, for no immediately practical result.

It was once said of Shakespeare that he had never done any good to any one, and never would. This, unfortunately, could not, in the sense in which the word "good" was then meant, be said of most modern dramatists. In truth, the good that Shakespeare did to humanity was of a remote, and, shall we say, eternal nature; something of the good that men get from having the sky and sea to look at. And this partly because he was, in his greater plays at all events, free from the habit of drawing a distorted moral. Now, the playwright who supplies to the public the facts of life distorted by the moral which it expects, does so that he may do the public what he considers an immediate good, by fortifying its prejudices; and the dramatist who supplies to the public facts distorted by his own advanced morality, does so because he considers that he will at once benefit the public by substituting for its worn-out ethics, his own. In both cases the advantage the dramatist hopes to confer on the public is immediate and practical.

But matters change, and morals change; men remain—and to set men, and the facts about them, down faithfully, so that they draw for us the moral of their natural actions, may also possibly be of benefit to the community. It is, at all events, harder than to set men and facts down, as they ought, or ought not to be. This, however, is not to say that a dramatist should, or indeed can, keep himself and his temperamental philosophy out of his work. As a man lives and thinks, so will he write. But it is certain, that to the making of good drama, as to the practice of every other art, there must be brought an almost passionate love of discipline, a white-heat of self-respect, a desire to make the truest, fairest, best thing in one's power; and that to these must be added an eye that does not flinch. Such qualities alone will bring to a drama the selfless character which soaks it with inevitability.

The word "pessimist" is frequently applied to the few dramatists who have been content to work in this way. It has been applied, among others, to Euripides, to Shakespeare, to Ibsen; it will be applied to many in the future. Nothing, however, is more dubious than the way in which these two words "pessimist" and "optimist" are used; for the optimist appears to be he who cannot hear the world as it is, and is forced by his nature to picture it as it ought to be, and the pessimist one who cannot only bear the world as it is, but loves it well enough to draw it faithfully. The true lover of the human race is surely he who can put up with it in all its forms, in vice as well as in virtue, in defeat no less than in victory; the true seer he who sees not only joy but sorrow, the true painter of human life one who blinks nothing. It may be that he is also, incidentally, its true benefactor.

In the whole range of the social fabric there are only two impartial persons, the scientist and the artist, and under the latter heading such dramatists as desire to write not only for to-day, but for to-morrow, must strive to come.

But dramatists being as they are made —past remedy—it is perhaps more profitable to examine the various points at which their qualities and defects are shown.

The plot! A good plot is that sure edifice which slowly rises out of the interplay of circumstance on temperament, and temperament on circumstance, within the enclosing atmosphere of an idea. A human being is the best plot there is; it may be impossible to see why he is a good plot, because the idea within which he was brought forth cannot be fully grasped; but it is plain that *he is a good plot*. He is organic. And so it must be with a good play. Reason alone produces no good plots; they come by original sin, sure conception, and instinctive afterpower of selecting what benefits the germ. A bad plot, on the other hand, is simply a row of stakes, with a character impaled on each—characters who would have liked to live, but came to untimely grief; who started bravely, but fell on these stakes, placed beforehand in a row, and were transfixed one by one, while their ghosts stride on, squeaking and gibbering, through the play. Whether these stakes are made of facts or of ideas, according to the nature of the dramatist who planted them, their effect on the unfortunate characters is the same; the creatures were begotten to be staked, and staked they are! The demand for a good plot, not unfrequently heard, commonly signifies: "Tickle my sensations by stuffing the play with arbitrary adventures, so that I need not be troubled to take the characters seriously. Set the persons of the play to action, regardless of time, sequence, atmosphere, and probability!"

Now, true dramatic action is what characters do, at once contrary, as it were, to expectation, and yet because they have already done other things. No dramatist should let his audience know what is coming; but neither should he suffer his characters to act without making his audience feel that those actions are in harmony with temperament, and arise from previous known actions, together with the temperaments and previous known actions of the other characters in the play. The dramatist who hangs his characters to his plot, instead of hanging his plot to his characters, is guilty of cardinal sin.

The dialogue! Good dialogue again is character, marshalled so as continually to stimulate interest or excitement. The reason good dialogue is seldom found in plays is merely that it is hard to write, for it requires not only a knowledge of what interests or excites, but such a feeling for character as brings misery to the dramatist's heart when his creations speak as they should not speak—ashes to his mouth when they say things for the sake of saying them—disgust when they are "smart."

The art of writing true dramatic dialogue is an austere art, denying itself all license, grudging every sentence devoted to the mere machinery of the play, suppressing all jokes and epigrams severed from character, relying for fun and pathos on the fun and tears of life. From start to finish good dialogue is handmade, like good lace; clear, of fine texture, furthering with each thread the harmony and strength of a design to which all must be subordinated.

But good dialogue is also spiritual action. In so far as the dramatist divorces his dialogue from spiritual action—that is to say, from progress of events, or toward events which are significant of character—he is stultifying τὸ δράμα (the thing done); he may make pleasing disquisitions, he is not making drama. And in so far as he twists character to suit his moral or his plot, he is neglecting a first principle, that truth to Nature which alone invests art with hand-made quality.

The dramatist's license, in fact, ends with his design. In conception alone he is free. He may take what character or group of characters he chooses, see them with what eyes, knit them with what idea, within the limits of his temperament; but once taken, seen, and knitted, he is bound to treat them like a gentleman, with the tenderest consideration of their mainsprings. Take care of character; action and dialogue will take care of themselves! The true dramatist gives full rein to his temperament in the scope and nature of his subject; having once selected subject and characters, he is just, gentle, restrained, neither gratifying his lust for praise at the expense of his offspring, nor using them as puppets to flout his audience. Being himself the nature that brought them forth, he guides them in the course predestined at their conception. So only have they a chance of defying Time, which is always lying in wait to destroy the false, topical, or fashionable, all—in a word—that is not based on the permanent elements of human nature. The perfect dramatist rounds up his characters and facts within the ring-fence of a dominant idea which fulfills the craving of his spirit; having got them there, he suffers them to live their own lives.

Plot, action, character, dialogue! But there is yet another subject for a platitude. Flavour! An impalpable quality, less easily captured than the scent of a flower, the peculiar and most essential attribute of any work of art! It is the thin, poignant spirit which hovers up out of a play, and is as much its differentiating essence as is caffeine of coffee. Flavour, in fine, is the spirit of the dramatist projected into his work in a state of volatility, so that no one can exactly lay hands on it, here, there, or anywhere. This distinctive essence of a play, marking its brand, is the one thing at which the dramatist cannot work, for it is outside his consciousness. A man may have many moods, he has but one spirit; and this spirit he communicates in some subtle, unconscious way to all his work. It waxes and wanes with the currents of his vitality, but no more alters than a chestnut changes into an oak.

For, in truth, dramas are very like unto trees, springing from seedlings, shaping themselves inevitably in accordance with the laws fast hidden within themselves, drinking sustenance from the earth and air, and in conflict with the natural forces round them. So they slowly come to full growth, until warped, stunted, or risen to fair and gracious height, they stand open to all the winds. And the trees that spring from each dramatist are of different race; he is the spirit of his own sacred grove, into which no stray tree can by any chance enter.

One more platitude. It is not unfashionable to pit one form of drama against another—holding up the naturalistic to the disadvantage of the epic; the epic to the belittlement of the fantastic; the fantastic to the detriment of the naturalistic. Little purpose is thus served. The essential meaning, truth, beauty, and irony of things may be revealed under all these forms. Vision over life and human nature can be as keen and just, the revelation as true, inspiring, delight-giving, and thought-provoking, whatever fashion be employed—it is simply a question of doing it well enough to uncover the kernel of the nut. Whether the violet came from Russia, from Parma, or from England, matters little. Close by the Greek temples at Pæstum there are violets that seem redder, and sweeter, than any ever seen—as though they have sprung up out of the footprints of some old pagan goddess; but under the April sun, in a Devonshire lane, the little blue scentless violets capture every bit as much of the spring. And so it is with drama—no matter what its form—it need only be the "real thing," need only have caught some of the precious fluids, revelation, or delight, and imprisoned them within a chalice to which we may put our lips and continually drink.

And yet, starting from this last platitude, one may perhaps be suffered to speculate as to the particular forms that our renascent drama is likely to assume. For our drama is renascent, and nothing will stop its growth. It is not renascent because this or that man is writing, but because of a new spirit. A spirit that is no doubt in part the gradual outcome of the impact on our homegrown art, of Russian, French, and Scandinavian influences, but which in the main rises from an awakened humanity in the conscience of our time.

What, then, are to be the main channels down which the renascent English drama will float in the coming years? It is more than possible that these main channels will come to be two in number and situated far apart.

The one will be the broad and clearcut channel of naturalism, down which will course a drama poignantly shaped, and inspired with high intention, but faithful to the seething and multiple life around us, drama such as some are inclined to term photographic, deceived by a seeming simplicity into forgetfulness of the old proverb, *"Ars est celare artem,"*[1] and oblivious of the fact that, to be vital, to grip, such drama is in every respect as dependent on imagination, construction, selection, and elimination—the main laws of artistry—as ever was the romantic or rhapsodic play. The question of naturalistic technique will bear, indeed, much more study than has yet been given to it. The aim of the dramatist employing it is obviously to create such an illusion of actual life passing on the stage as to com-

---

[1] Art is to conceal art; i.e., true art disguises artifice.

pel the spectator to pass through an experience of his own, to think, and talk, and move with the people he sees thinking, talking, and moving in front of him. A false phrase, a single word out of tune or time, will destroy that illusion and spoil the surface as surely as a stone heaved into a still pool shatters the image seen there. But this is only the beginning of the reason why the naturalistic is the most exacting and difficult of all techniques. It is easy enough to *reproduce* the exact conversation and movements of persons in a room; it is desperately hard to *produce* the perfectly natural conversation and movements of those persons, when each natural phrase spoken and each natural movement made has not only to contribute toward the growth and perfection of a drama's soul, but also to be a revelation, phrase by phrase, movement by movement, of essential traits of character. To put it another way, naturalistic art, when alive, indeed to be alive at all, is simply the art of manipulating a procession of most delicate symbols. Its service is the swaying and focussing of men's feelings and thoughts in the various departments of human life. It will be like a steady lamp, held up from time to time, in whose light things will be seen for a space clearly and in due proportion, freed from the mists of prejudice and partisanship.

And the other of these two main channels will, I think, be a twisting and delicious stream, which will bear on its breast new barques of poetry, shaped, it may be, like prose, but a prose incarnating through its fantasy and symbolism all the deeper aspirations, yearning, doubts, and mysterious stirrings of the human spirit; a poetic prose-drama, emotionalising us by its diversity and purity of form and invention, and whose province will be to disclose the elemental soul of man and the forces of Nature, not perhaps as the old tragedies disclosed them, not necessarily in the epic mood, but always with beauty and in the spirit of discovery.

Such will, I think, be the two vital forms of our drama in the coming generation. And between these two forms there must be no crude unions; they are too far apart, the cross is too violent. For, where there is a seeming blend of lyricism and naturalism, it will on examination be found, I think, to exist only in plays whose subjects or settings—as in Synge's "Playboy of the Western World," or in Mr. Masefield's "Nan"—are so removed from our ken that we cannot really tell, and therefore do not care, whether an absolute illusion is maintained. The poetry which may and should exist in naturalistic drama, can only be that of perfect rightness of proportion, rhythm, shape—the poetry, in fact, that lies in all vital things. It is the ill-mating of forms that has killed a thousand plays. We want no more bastard drama; no more attempts to dress out the simple dignity of everyday life in the peacock's feathers of false lyricism; no more straw-stuffed heroes or heroines; no more rabbits and goldfish from the conjurer's pockets, nor any limelight. Let us have starlight, moonlight, sunlight, and the light of our own self-respects.

VIRGINIA WOOLF • 1882–1941

How Should One Read a Book?

IN the first place, I want to emphasize the note of interrogation at the end of my title. Even if I could answer the question for myself, the answer would apply only to me and not to you. The only advice, indeed, that one person can give another about reading is to take no advice, to follow your own instincts, to use your own reason, to come to your own conclusions. If this is agreed between us, then I feel at liberty to put forward a few ideas and suggestions because you will not allow them to fetter that independence which is the most important quality that a reader can possess. After all, what laws can be laid down about books? The battle of Waterloo was certainly fought on a certain day; but is *Hamlet* a better play than *Lear?* Nobody can say. Each must decide that question for himself. To admit authorities, however heavily furred and gowned, into our libraries and let them tell us how to read, what to read, what value to place upon what we read, is to destroy the spirit of freedom which is the breath of those sanctuaries. Everywhere else we may be found by laws and conventions—there we have none.

But to enjoy freedom, if the platitude is pardonable, we have of course to control ourselves. We must not squander our powers, helplessly and ignorantly, squirting half the house in order to water a single rose-bush; we must train them, exactly and powerfully, here on the very spot. This, it may be, is one of the first difficulties that faces us in a library. What is "the very spot"? There may well seem to be nothing but a conglomeration and huddle of confusion. Poems and novels, histories and memoirs, dictionaries and blue-books; books written in all languages by men and women of all tempers, races, and ages jostle each other on the shelf. And outside the donkey brays, the women gossip at the pump, the colts gallop across the fields. Where are we to begin? How are we to bring order into this multitudinous chaos and so get the deepest and widest pleasure from what we read?

It is simple enough to say that since books have classes—fiction, biography, poetry—we should separate them and take from each what it is right that each should give us. Yet few people ask from books what books can give us. Most commonly we come to books with blurred and divided minds, asking of fiction that it shall be true, of poetry that it shall be false, of biography that it shall be flattering, of history that it shall enforce our own prejudices. If we could banish all such preconceptions when we read, that would be an admirable beginning. Do not dictate to your author; try to become him. Be his fellow-worker and accomplice. If you hang back, and reserve and criticize at first, you are preventing yourself from getting the fullest possible value from what you read. But if you open your mind as widely as possible, then signs and hints of almost imperceptible fineness, from the twist and turn of the first sentences, will bring you into the presence of a human being unlike any other. Steep yourself in this, acquaint yourself with this, and soon you will find that your author is giving you, or attempting to give you, something far more definite. The thirty-two chapters of a novel—if we consider how to read a novel first—are an attempt to make something as formed and controlled as a building: but words are more impalpable than bricks; reading is a longer and more complicated process than seeing. Perhaps the quickest way to understand the elements of what a novelist is doing is not to read, but to write; to make your own experiment with the dangers and difficulties of words. Recall, then, some event that has left a distinct impression on you—how at the corner of the street, perhaps you passed two people talking. A tree shook; an electric light danced; the tone of the talk was comic, but also tragic; a whole vision, an entire conception, seemed contained in that moment.

But when you attempt to reconstruct it in words, you will find that it breaks into a thousand conflicting impressions. Some must be subdued; others emphasized; in the process you will lose, probably, all grasp upon the emotion itself. Then turn from your blurred and littered pages to the opening pages of some great novelist—Defoe, Jane Austen, Hardy. Now you will be better able to appreciate their mastery. It is not merely that we are in the presence of a different person—Defoe, Jane Austen, or Thomas Hardy—but that we are living in a different world. Here, in *Robinson Crusoe,* we are trudging a plain high road; one thing happens after another; the fact and the order of the fact is enough. But if the open air and adventure mean everything to Defoe they mean nothing to Jane Austen. Hers is the drawing-room, and people talking, and by the many mirrors of their talk revealing their characters. And if, when we have accustomed ourselves to the drawing-room and its reflections, we turn to Hardy, we are once more spun round. The moors are round us and the stars are above our heads. The other side of the mind is now exposed—the dark side that comes uppermost in solitude, not the light side that shows in company. Our relations are not towards people, but towards Nature and destiny. Yet different as these worlds are, each is consistent with itself: The maker of each is careful to observe the laws of his own perspective, and however great a strain they may put upon us they will never confuse us, as lesser writers so frequently do, by introducing two different kinds of reality into the same book. Thus to go from one great novelist to another—from Jane Austen to Hardy, from Peacock to Trollope, from Scott to Meredith—is to be wrenched and uprooted; to be thrown this way and then that. To read a novel is a difficult and complex art. You must be capable not only of great fineness of perception, but of great boldness of imagination if you are going to make use of all that the novelist—the great artist—gives you.

But a glance at the heterogeneous company on the shelf will show you that writers are very seldom "great artists"; far more often a book makes no claim to be a work of art at all. These biographies and autobiographies, for example, lives of great men, of men long dead and forgotten, that stand cheek by jowl with the novels and poems, are we to refuse to read them because they are not "art"? Or shall we read them, but read them in a different way, with a different aim? Shall we read them in the first place to satisfy that curiosity which possesses us sometimes when in the evening we linger in front of a house where the lights are lit and the blinds not yet drawn, and each floor of the house shows us a different section of human life in being? Then we are consumed with curiosity about the lives of these people—the servants gossiping, the gentlemen dining, the girl dressing for a party, the old woman at the window with her knitting. Who are they, what are they, what are their names, their occupations, their thoughts, and adventures?

Biographies and memoirs answer such questions, light up innumerable such houses; they show us people going about their daily affairs, toiling, failing, succeeding, eating, hating, loving, until they die. And sometimes as we watch, the house fades and the iron railings vanish and we are out at sea; we are hunting, sailing, fighting; we are among savages and soldiers; we are taking part in great campaigns. Or if we like to stay here in England, in London, still the scene changes; the street narrows; the house becomes small, cramped, diamond-paned, and malodorous. We see a poet, Donne, driven from such a house because the walls were so thin that when the children cried their voices cut through them. We can follow him, through the paths that lie in the pages of books, to Twickenham; to Lady Bedford's Park, a famous meeting-ground for nobles and poets; and then turn our steps to Wilton, the great house under the downs, and hear Sidney read the *Arcadia* to his sister; and ramble among the very marshes and see the very herons that figure in that famous romance; and then again travel north with that other Lady Pembroke, Anne Clifford, to her wild moors, or plunge into the city and control our merriment at the sight of Gabriel Harvey in his black velvet suit arguing about poetry with Spenser. Nothing is more fascinating than to grope and stumble in the alternate darkness and splendour of Elizabethan London. But there is no staying there. The Temples and the Swifts, the Harleys and the St. Johns beckon us on; hour upon hour can be spent disentangling their quarrels and deciphering their characters; and when we tire of them we can stroll on, past a lady in black wearing diamonds, to Samuel Johnson and Goldsmith and Garrick; or cross the channel, if we like, and meet Voltaire and Diderot, Madame du Deffand; and so back to England and Twickenham—how certain places repeat themselves and certain names!—where Lady Bedford had her Park once and Pope lived later, to Walpole's home at Strawberry Hill. But Walpole introduces us to such a swarm of new acquaintances, there are so many houses to visit and bells to ring that we may well hesitate for a moment, on the Miss Berrys' doorstep, for example, when behold, up comes Thackeray; he is the friend of the woman whom Walpole loved; so that merely by going from friend to friend, from garden to garden, from house to house, we have passed from one end of English literature to another and wake to find ourselves here again in the present, if we can so differentiate this moment from all that have gone before. This, then, is one of the ways in which we can read these lives and letters; we can make them light up the many windows of the past; we can watch the famous dead in their familiar habits and fancy sometimes that we are very close and can surprise their secrets, and sometimes we may pull out a play or a poem that they have written and see whether it reads differently in the presence of the author. But this again rouses other questions. How far, we must ask ourselves, is a book influenced by its writer's life—how far is it safe to let the man interpret the writer? How far shall we resist or give way to the sympathies and antipathies that the man himself rouses in us—so sensitive are words, so receptive of the character of the author? These are questions that press upon us when we read lives and letters, and we must answer them for ourselves, for nothing can be more fatal than to be guided by the preferences of others in a matter so personal.

But also we can read such books with another aim, not to throw light on literature, not to become familiar with famous people, but to refresh and exercise our own creative powers. Is there not an open window on the right hand of the bookcase? How delightful to stop reading and look out! How stimulating the scene is, in its unconsciousness, its irrelevance, its perpetual movement—the colts galloping round the field, the woman filling her pail at the well, the donkey throwing back his head and emitting his long, acrid moan. The greater part of any library is nothing but the record of such fleeting moments in the lives of men, women, and donkeys. Every literature, as it grows old, has its rubbish-heap, its record of vanished moments and forgotten lives told in faltering and feeble accents that have perished. But if you give yourself up to the delight of rubbish-reading you will be surprised, indeed you will be overcome, by the relics of human life that have been cast out to moulder. It may be one letter—but what a vision it gives! It may be a few sentences—but what vistas they suggest! Sometimes a whole story will come together with such beautiful humour and pathos and completeness that it seems as if a great novelist had been at work, yet it is only an old actor, Tate Wilkinson, remembering the strange story of Captain Jones; it is only a young subaltern serving under Arthur Wellesley and falling in love with a pretty girl at Lisbon; it is only Maria Allen letting fall her sewing in the empty drawing-room and sighing how she wishes she had taken Dr. Burney's good advice and had never eloped with her Rishy. None of this has any value; it is negligible in the extreme; yet how absorbing it is now and again to go through the rubbish-heaps and find rings and scissors and broken noses buried in the huge past and try to piece them together while the colt gallops round the field, the woman fills her pail at the well, and the donkey brays.

But we tire of rubbish-reading in the long run. We tire of searching for what is needed to complete the half-truth which is all that the Wilkinsons, the Bunburys, and the Maria Allens are able to offer us. They had not the artist's power of mastering and eliminating; they could not tell the whole truth even about their own lives; they have disfigured the story that might have been so shapely. Facts are all that they can offer us, and facts are a very inferior form of fiction. Thus the desire grows upon us to have done with half-statements and approximations; to cease from searching out the minute shades of human character, to enjoy the greater abstractness, the purer truth of fiction. Thus we create the mood, intense and generalised, unaware of detail, but stressed by some regular, recurrent beat, whose natural expression is poetry; and that is the time to read poetry when we are almost able to write it.

> Western wind, when wilt thou blow?
> The small rain down can rain.
> Christ, if my love were in my arms,
> And I in my bed again!

The impact of poetry is so hard and direct that for the moment there is no other sensation except that of the poem itself. What profound depths we visit then—how sudden and complete is our immersion! There is nothing here to catch hold of; nothing to stay us in our flight. The illusion of fiction is gradual; its effects are prepared; but who when they read these four lines stops to ask who wrote them, or conjures up the thought of Donne's house or Sidney's secretary; or enmeshes them in the intricacy of the past and the succession of generations? The poet is always our contemporary. Our being for the moment is centred and constricted, as in any violent shock of personal emotion. Afterwards, it is true, the sensation begins to spread in wider rings through our minds; remoter senses are reached; these begin to sound and to comment and we are aware of echoes and reflections. The intensity of poetry covers an immense range of emotion. We have only to compare the force and directness of

> I shall fall like a tree, and find my grave,
>   Only remembering that I grieve,

with the wavering modulation of

> Minutes are numbered by the fall of sands,
> As by an hour glass; the span of time

Doth waste us to our graves, and we look
    on it;
An age of pleasure, revelled out, comes
    home
At last, and ends in sorrow; but the life,
Weary of riot, numbers every sand,
Wailing in sighs, until the last drop down,
So to conclude calamity in rest,

or place the meditative calm of

> whether we be young or old,
> Our destiny, our being's heart and home,
> Is with infinitude, and only there;
> With hope it is, hope that can never die,
> Effort, and expectation, and desire,
> And something evermore about to be,

beside the complete and inexhaustible loveliness of

> The moving Moon went up the sky,
> And no where did abide:
> Softly she was going up,
> And a star or two beside—

or the splendid fantasy of

> And the woodland haunter
> Shall not cease to saunter
>   When, far down some glade,
> Of the great world's burning,
> One soft flame upturning
> Seems, to his discerning,
>   Crocus in the shade.

to bethink us of the varied art of the poet; his power to make us at once actors and spectators; his power to run his hand into character as if it were a glove, and be Falstaff or Lear; his power to condense, to widen, to state, once and for ever.

"We have only to compare"—with those words the cat is out of the bag, and the true complexity of reading is admitted. The first process, to receive impressions with the utmost understanding, is only half the process of reading; it must be completed, if we are to get the whole pleasure from a book, by another. We must pass judgment upon these multitudinous impressions; we must make of these fleeting shapes one that is hard and lasting. But not directly. Wait for the dust of reading to settle; for the conflict and the questioning to die down; walk, talk, pull the dead petals from a rose, or fall asleep. Then suddenly without our willing it, for it is thus that Nature undertakes these transitions, the book will return, but differently. It will float to the top of the mind as a whole. And the book as a whole is different from the book received currently in separate phrases. Details now fit themselves into their places. We see the shape from start to finish; it is a barn, a pig-sty, or a cathedral. Now then we can compare book with book as we compare building with building. But this act of comparison means that our attitude has changed; we are no longer the friends of the writer, but his judges; and just as we cannot be too sympathetic as friends, so as judges we cannot be too severe. Are they not criminals, books that have wasted our time and sympathy; are they not the most insidious enemies of society, corrupters, defilers, the writers of false books, faked books, books that fill the air with decay and disease? Let us then be severe in our judgments; let us compare each book with the greatest of its kind. There they hang in the mind the shapes of the books we have read solidified by the judgments we have passed on them—*Robinson Crusoe, Emma, The Return of the Native*. Compare the novels with these—even the latest and least of novels has a right to be judged with the best. And so with poetry—when the intoxication of rhythm has died down and the splendour of words has faded a visionary shape will return to us and this must be compared with *Lear*, with *Phèdre*, with *The Prelude;* or if not with these, with whatever is the best or seems to us to be the best in its own kind. And we may be sure that the newness of new poetry and fiction is its most superficial quality and that we have only to alter slightly, not to recast, the standards by which we have judged the old.

It would be foolish, then, to pretend that the second part of reading, to judge, to compare, is as simple as the first—to open the mind wide to the fast flocking of innumerable impressions. To continue reading without the book before you, to hold one shadow-shape against another, to have read widely enough and with enough understanding to make such comparisons alive and illuminating—that is difficult; it is still more difficult to press further and to say, "Not only is the book of this sort, but it is of this value; here it fails; here it succeeds; this is bad; that is good." To carry out this part of a reader's duty needs such imagination, insight, and learning that it is hard to conceive any one mind sufficiently endowed; impossible for the most self-confident to find more than the seeds of such powers in himself. Would it not be wiser, then, to remit this part of reading and to allow the critics, the gowned and furred authorities of the library, to decide the question of the book's absolute value for us? Yet how impossible! We may stress the value of sympathy; we may try to sink our own identity as we read. But we know that we cannot sympathise wholly or immerse ourselves wholly; there is always a demon in us who whispers, "I hate, I love," and we cannot silence him. Indeed, it is precisely because we hate and we love that our relation with the poets and novelists is so intimate that we find the presence of another person intolerable. And even if the results are abhorrent and our judgments are wrong, still our taste, the nerve of sensation that sends shocks through us, is our chief illuminant; we learn through feeling; we cannot suppress our own idiosyncrasy without impoverishing it. But as time goes on perhaps we can train our taste; perhaps we can make it submit to some control. When it has fed greedily and lavishly upon books of all sorts—poetry, fiction, history, biography—and has stopped reading and looked for long spaces upon the variety, the incongruity of the living world, we shall find that it is changing a little; it is not so greedy, it is more reflective. It will begin to bring us not merely judgments on particular books, but it will tell us that there is a quality common to certain books. Listen, it will say, what shall we call *this*? And it will read us perhaps *Lear* and then perhaps the *Agamemnon* in order to bring out that common quality. Thus, with our taste to guide us, we shall venture beyond the particular book in search of qualities that group books together; we shall give them names and thus frame a rule that brings order into our perceptions. We shall gain a further and a rarer pleasure from that discrimination. But as a rule only lives when it is perpetually broken by contact with the books themselves—nothing is easier and more stultifying than to make rules which exist out of touch with facts, in a vacuum—now at last, in order to steady ourselves in this difficult attempt, it may be well to turn to the very rare writers who are able to enlighten us upon literature as an art. Coleridge and Dryden and Johnson, in their considered criticism, the poets and novelists themselves in their unconsidered sayings, are often surprisingly relevant; they light up and solidify the vague ideas that have been tumbling in the misty depths of our minds. But they are only able to help us if we come to them laden with questions and suggestions won honestly in the course of our own reading. They can do nothing for us if we herd ourselves under their authority and lie down like sheep in the shade of a hedge. We can only understand their ruling when it comes in conflict with our own and vanquishes it.

If this is so, if to read a book as it should be read calls for the rarest qualities of imagination, insight, and judgment, you may perhaps conclude that literature is a very complex art and that it is unlikely that we shall be able, even after a lifetime of reading, to make any valuable contribution to its criticism. We must remain readers; we shall not put on the further glory that belongs to those rare beings who are also critics. But still we have our responsibilities as readers and even our importance. The standards we raise and the judgments we pass steal into the air and become part of the atmosphere which writers breathe as they work. An influence is created which tells upon them even if it never finds its way into print. And that influence, if it were well instructed, vigorous and individual and sincere, might be of great value now when criticism is necessarily in abeyance; when books pass in review like the procession of animals in a shooting gallery, and the critic has only one second in which to load and aim and shoot and may well be pardoned if he mistakes rabbits for tigers, eagles for barndoor fowls, or misses altogether and wastes his shot upon some peaceful cow grazing in a further field. If behind the erratic gunfire of the press the author felt that there was another kind of criticism, the opinion of people reading for the love of reading, slowly and unprofessionally, and judging with great sympathy and yet with great severity, might this not improve the quality of his work? And if by our means books were to become stronger, richer, and more varied, that would be an end worth reaching.

Yet who reads to bring about an end however desirable? Are there not some pursuits that we practise because they are good in themselves, and some pleasures that are final? And is not this among them? I have sometimes dreamt, at least, that when the Day of Judgment dawns and the great conquerors and lawyers and statesmen come to receive their rewards —their crowns, their laurels, their names carved indelibly upon imperishable marble—the Almighty will turn to Peter and will say, not without a certain envy when He sees us coming with our books under our arms, "Look, these need no reward. We have nothing to give them here. They have loved reading."

OSCAR CARGILL • 1898–

Toward a Pluralistic Criticism

THE function of the critic and scholar is to make the past functional, for unless it can be used, it is deader than death itself. The only alternative is to adopt the view of Antoine Roquetin, Jean-Paul Sartre's non-hero, that the past has no existence, a thesis which does more than alienate him from bourgeoise society—it negates all continuity, all history, all culture and renders scholarship and criticism impotent. Such an assault on animal wisdom, however, compels definition, or at least description. What is the past? Where does it begin and where does it end? Psychologists and philosophers enforce the presentness of the past by telling us that by the time our very inadequate perceptive apparatus reports an event it is already historic, and the very notion of the present is a conventional fiction. The past is time, or what we live in. The slippery present is that which has too much concerned the existentialists, certainly emotionally; but a paradoxical love of books shows how easy it would be to accept time or continuity. To emend Descartes, from whom they really take their being, "I think, therefore I exist *in time.*" With any sense of the all-enveloping past one cannot be a complete disaffiliate.

In literature, ostensibly, the great generation of the twenties exhibited the fullest sort of consciousness of continuity: *Remembrance of Things Past, Ulysses, The Waste Land, Look Homeward, Angel,* all seemed to be documents in support of the affirmation of the ever-presence of the past. Such, doubtless, their authors intended them to be, but was that saliently their effect? Loneliness and alienation are themes in each of them; analogues, parallels, symbols, and metaphors from the past in each one of them are lost in the dubious hero's swamping, dismal present. Did not they prepare the way for Camus, Sartre, Ionesco, and Duerrenmatt? Did not much that transpired in intellectual circles, in education, prepare the way? Reverence for the past was undermined in the academies in the twenties and thirties. Ancient history and Latin disappeared from the lower schools; today, anything resembling the orderly presentation of English and American literature in the colleges is following after. Much is said of the virtue of studying only masterpieces, but when the *Iliad* jostles *The Divine Comedy,* and the latter, *King Lear,* all sense of time is lost, and these masterpieces become companion works to *Crime and Punishment* and *Death in Venice,* if not to *Catcher in the Rye* and *Herzog.* In the ingenious presentations of instructors who confine themselves to the work itself, that is, the work in a modern translation, these masterpieces take on a contemporaneity scarcely achieved by the latest novel. Virgil in *The Divine Comedy,* like Ulysses before him, becomes a father image and Achilles, sulking in his tent, is a symbol of onanism. But alas, when so old-fashioned a person as I makes what he thinks is an illuminating comparison between *The Rime of the Ancient Mariner* and *The Waste Land,* he is met by blank stares—only four persons in the class have read Coleridge's poem. It has been relegated, possibly, to a deeper past than the *Iliad.* Thus the most valuable element in time, the sense of continuity, the sense of having a tradition, is lost for the young.

667

Our appropriation of the master works of the West seems to have more in common with the indiscriminate accumulations of the newspaper millionaire, William Randolph Hearst, than with the slow and painful assimilations of Bernard Berenson. We rape from frame and setting to adorn our own tales or to trigger a specious erudition. Unlike Hearst, however, we are very cautious not to carry away too much. This caution came from the vice of the previous age, when American literary scholarship reached a peak in the work of E. K. Rand, George Lyman Kittredge, Carleton Brown, W. W. Lawrence, Edwin Greenlaw, and others. The enormous erudition of these scholars, their supersaturation with the past, staggered and baffled younger minds until they made a liberating discovery—in the interest of frame and setting, in the interest of biography, their teachers were neglecting the work of art itself or burying it under mounds of "useless knowledge" from which it never could be excavated. The sensitive and intuitive John Livingston Lowes, author of *Convention and Revolt in Poetry,* undertook to correct the balance in *The Road to Xanadu,* but he was much too late. As early as 1920 T. S. Eliot was proclaiming that the essential critical function is "elucidation," not of the artist but of the work of art. The revolt against the *impedimenta* of scholarship went so far that it actually detached the artist from his creation. "Never trust the artist, trust the tale," declared D. H. Lawrence. The most iconoclastic position reached in this revolt is that of Marcel Proust in *Contre Sainte-Beuve,* in which Proust ridiculed all attempts to document the life of an author, asserting that quite a different ego produces the work of art from the ego which inhabits the common walks of life. A similar extremism severed the work of art from the "past" of its creation. "To appreciate a work of art," wrote Clive Bell, "we need bring with us nothing from life, no knowledge of its ideas and affairs, no familiarity with its emotions." Of the masterpiece, A. C. Bradley declared, "Its nature is not to be a part, nor a copy of the real world . . . , but a world in itself, independent, complete, autonomous."

Having separated the masterpiece from its creator and from its place in time, the new critic concentrated with great intensity upon elucidating the text itself. He found, we may infer from Cleanth Brooks, that he had to address an audience which could not read, since neglect of the masterpiece for facts about it and its author had caused the faculty of apprehension to atrophy. With John Crowe Ransom, Allen Tate, Robert Penn Warren, R. P. Blackmur, and others, Mr. Brooks set out to remedy this defect. That the method which they championed, *explication de texte,* had long been employed at the high school level in France, in the *lycée,* is no condemnation of it: very elementary beginnings had to be made. Whether "dry-as-dust" scholarship was responsible for general illiteracy or (as I think) neglect of composition (which forces attention on the text) in the lower schools is immaterial, *Americans could not read.* Even the errors made by some of the explicators only substantiate the fact. Regardless of whether or not the methods of the new critics provided a richer appreciation, it must be granted that they accomplished a major miracle—they taught some few Americans to read.

One of the announced aims of the new critic was not to interpose his own personality between the reader and the work itself. He saw that this was the equivalent, if not worse, of allowing the workaday ego of the author to interpose. The critic would deny his own ego, his hunger for recognition, for the ideal end of perfectly interpreting the text before him. Granted the human condition, however, he was utterly incapable of achieving this end.

Yet it is important that we note its unearthly character, its metaphysical nature. Only a writer completely cut off from the world, only a perpetual dweller among masterpieces, only an academic—such as all new critics became—could utter such nonsense and, at least partially, believe it. For only the universities provided the proper pasturage for this kind of gamboling and, lest weeds and underbrush get in, the new critics in the main concentrated on the classics of the literature of the past, erecting stiles against current literature. F. R. Leavis, the Cambridge don who founded a magazine to scrutinize texts and kept it going for twenty years, illustrated the impossibility of a depersonalized criticism operating upon a depersonalized literature—he created a school of *obita dictarists* who ever looked anxiously to him for the Word. In the main, the new critics found that the first principles they had drawn up were narrow and stultifying and, without announcing it, they one after another abandoned them. It has been said that Cleanth Brooks is the only remaining new critic, the only one tenaciously attached to the text. The others have adopted a variety of methods: they have specialized in aesthetic structure, sociological background, morals, psychology, and myths—each, however, a champion of his own special method.

Meanwhile, although crowded into the more stony part of the pasture, and scarcely visible over the high fences, research scholars in the universities had continued to exist. Indeed, in the very years when the new criticism rocked the academies, research scholarship recorded some of its most remarkable achievements. Almost anyone can enumerate a few examples of literary scholarship that seem to be more perdurable than anything produced by the whole corps of new critics: the editing of the *Diaries* of Samuel Johnson by Edward L. McAdam, Jr., and of Thackeray's *Letters* by Gordon Ray, *The Young Shelley* by Kenneth Cameron, and the study of the mind of Walt Whitman by Gay Allen. What in the new criticism can compare with Perry Miller's investigations of Puritan culture, Thomas H. Johnson's detective work in determining the text and order of Emily Dickinson's poetry, Jay Leyda's *The Melville Log,* the editions of the letters of Pope, Keats, Coleridge, and George Eliot by George Sherburn, Hyder Rollins, Earl Griggs, and Gordon Haight, respectively, and the astonishing critical life of James Joyce by Richard Ellmann? From their labors the scholars occasionally turned aside to expose gleefully the limitations of a new criticism that depended largely on impressionism, intuition, clairvoyance, and extrasensory perception. Douglas Bush had most sport at this and delighted his colleagues. Who can forget his definition of the new criticism as "an advanced course in remedial reading"? When John Crowe Ransom wondered over Shakespeare's use of the phrase "dusty death," calling it "an odd but winning detail," Bush reminded him that the same odd but winning detail is in the Bible and *The Book of Common Prayer,* with which Shakespeare was doubtless familiar. Lillian Hornstein deflated some of the pretentiousness of Caroline Spurgeon's *Shakespeare's Imagery,* an offshoot of the new criticism, in much the same way.

Though the scholars scored heavily off the critics, they themselves found the new criticism properly admonitory. Scholars wish today to be taken also for critics, and with justice they may so be regarded, for they at last have learned to emphasize the creations of the artist above his sources, background, and life, while retaining illumination from the latter. The critics, on the other hand, because they have confined their work to classics and have found the newest classics ever receding into the past, are coming more and more to respect biography and history and to take simple excursions into them. Because of their academic associations some of them undeniably have discovered it pleasing to be regarded as scholarly if not as scholars. Their choice of specialized methods applied to the all-inclusive past propels them further along the way so that harmonizing of interests seems imminent. My present concern, however, is not to scrutinize this process but to consider the values in individual programs that might prove useful in a synthesis.

Quite aware that he must work in defiance of criticism's ukàse against biography, Leon Edel has become the champion of the "art of literary biography," an art which should involve a complete critical knowledge of the works of the author. Unlike the biographer of Chaucer or Shakespeare, the modern literary biographer is all but overwhelmed by his materials. "How different," Mr. Edel remarks enviously, "is the task of the critic, especially the 'new critic'! His table, in contrast to the biographer's, is uncluttered. No birth certificates, no deeds, no letters, no diaries, no excess literary baggage: only the works, to be read and re-read, pondered and analysed. . . . The literary geographer, however, must at every moment of his task be a critic. His is an act of continual and unceasing criticism." All of us who have read the first three volumes of Edel's unfinished life of Henry James realize how much he has done to restore biography to an acceptable literary standard for both criticism and scholarship, despite the fact that Henry James himself had taken many steps to defeat him, declaring at twenty-nine, before he had written his first novel, "artists, as time goes on will be likely to take alarm, empty their tabledrawers and level the approaches to their privacy. The critics, psychologists and gossip mongers may then glean amid the stubble." The life of Henry James is no pinwheel accomplishment, like Strachey's *Eminent Victorians* or Thomas Beer's *Stephen Crane,* but a substantial and enduring literary work.

Freudian literary criticism, a generic term for all types of analysis dealing with the creative psyche, has been one of the easiest methods for the former new critics to resort to, for it contains no inherent compulsion to abandon the text. Freud himself, equipped with a considerable knowledge of literature and a keen sensibility, provided models for this kind of criticism. In *The Interpretation of Dreams,* for example, he suggested that Hamlet's unconscious guilt arising from his own Oedipal desires inhibited Hamlet from avenging his father. "Hamlet is able to do anything but take vengeance upon the man who did away with his father and has taken his father's place with his mother—the man who shows him in realization the repressed desires of his own childhood. The loathing which should have driven him to revenge is thus repressed by conscientious scruples which tell him that he himself is no better than the murderer whom he is required to punish." Capricious and unorthodox, D. H. Lawrence employs his own version of the method with such startling skill at times that Edmund Wilson has declared *Studies in Classic American Literature* to be "one of the few first-rate books to have been written on the subject." Here is Lawrence's interpretation of the close of *The Scarlet Letter:* "Right to the end Dimmesdale must have his saintly triumphs. He must preach his Election Sermon, and win his last saintly applause. At the same time he has an almost imbecile, epileptic impulse to defile the religious reality he exists in. In Dimmesdale at this time lies the whole clue to Dostoevsky."

It is no response to the Freudian critic to say that an author's intention was something other than the critic's interpretation, for the Freudian critic may know the author's motivation better than the author himself; indeed, once literature is confined to the couch, the Freudian speaks with an authority no other critic can assume. Yet a suspicion lingers that Mr. Leslie Fiedler is not always right when he assumes that every pure maiden in American fiction is but a cover for the author's animosity toward all women, and with difficulty we repress the cry, "Physician, heal thyself." Leon Edel properly cautions the Freudian to examine his grounds of attraction to, or repulsion from, an author as a basis for determining his critical stances, and this appears to be the area of real vulnerability for the Freudian. If I may tease my truly distinguished colleague, I might observe that he has sometimes appeared to feel that he might have made a better brother, in a situation of sibling rivalry, to Henry James than did William. It is a curious fact that both Henry and his biographer have philosopher brothers. That the subconscious mind of an artist is the reservoir of his invention is generally conceded. The "infamous insurance scheme" which constitutes the plot of *The Wings of the Dove* I find exists in a French novel that James had read thirty-five years earlier and possibly had forgotten. Who can say, however, that a process of gestation was not going on in his subconscious mind?

Plot parallels suggest not merely an immediate borrowing from a literary predecessor but the possibility of a remote prototype or common ancestor for similar works. This idea is basic to Sir James Frazer's great work, *The Golden Bough,* in which this Scottish anthropologist traced numerous myths back to their prehistoric and ritualistic beginnings. Carl Jung's theory that the subconscious of man is a storehouse of racial, as well as personal, history reinforced the importance of myth in creative life, and T. S. Eliot's confession that Miss Jessie Weston's *From Ritual to Romance* had influenced the creation of *The Waste Land* pointed out to the new critics a path for exploration when they found *explication de texte* too narrow a ground. Although certain British critics—F. M. Cornford, Jane Harrison, Gilbert Murray, and Andrew Lang—had dealt previously with the ritualistic background of Greek myths, it is Maud Bodkin in *Archetypal Patterns in Modern Poetry* who introduces the methods of Frazer and Jung into the study of modern literature and provides models for others to follow. Hamlet, the prime anatomical target for critical surgery in the last three hundred years, is astonishingly carved and served by Miss Bodkin. Probing the wound opened by Freud and enlarged by Ernest Jones, she accepts Hamlet as the victim of an Oedipal situation, but both Claudius and the elder Hamlet are components of the "father image," thus setting up a conflict, or "inner tension," which can only be relieved by the death of the tragic hero. The hero develops toward himself an ambivalent attitude resulting in an ego desiring self-assertion and an ego craving surrender to a greater power than itself, "the community consciousness." Thus the death of Hamlet becomes a submission or sacrifice to the tribe, like the ritual sacrifice of a king or sacred animal for the renewal of the life of the tribe. This is the significance of Hamlet's final charge to Horatio to "draw thy breath in pain,/To tell my story." Now, I find this ingenious and even fascinating, but I wonder if it is criticism. If all the great literature of the world can be reduced to a few mythological rites or archetypal patterns, do not the distinctions between works, as Professor Meyer H. Abrams contends, become less and less, and vanish? Archetypal criticism, even though it satisfies Mr. Eliot's criterion of elucidation, moves steadily away from works of art (the area of criticism) to folk superstitions (the area of the anthropologist and folklorist).

Yet if tribal rites, which symbolize elemental social processes, can be shown as buried in the racial subconscious and related in even the vaguest way to the creative psyche, why does not this fact validate the use the writer makes of his economic and social background as a means of evaluating him? Surely as much of the creative act is conscious as unconscious. Surely modern society has as many rituals of which the artist is aware as tribal rites of which he is unconscious but by which he is influenced. Mr. Eliot did not get his contempt for the Jew, the Irish, and the Cockney out of Miss Weston's book, but out of his experience, out of his connection with Lloyd's bank, his reaction to the Irish rebellion, his acquaintance with London pubs, and out of the vulgar stereotypes of his society. How is one to elucidate or scrutinize Steinbeck's *The Grapes of Wrath* with no reference to the Dust Bowl, the tractoring out of the Okies, or the labor practices of the farmer's association of California? Yet it was fully as much against sociological criticism as biographical criticism that the new criticism rebelled. Such books as Edmund Wilson's *To the Finland Station* or Granville Hicks's *The Great Tradition* seem, in retrospect, more in the nature of political tracts than works of criticism. They were, however, phenomena of the depression, and Wilson and Hicks, as well as Lionel Trilling, employing the social background of writers whom they examine, without a political *parti pris,* seem to me as able critics as America possesses. Irving Howe and Norman Podhoretz, also, with this approach, have on occasion written analyses of high merit. The lesson learned is that, while a writer's social views affect his judgment and may properly be remarked and weighed, we must ever—and without ambivalence—keep his work as an artist to the fore.

Mere elucidation must have appeared in this discussion increasingly inadequate as a definition of the function of criticism. While sticking to his contention that "poetry is not the inculcation of morals, or the direction of politics," Eliot admitted, in his Preface to the second edition of *The Sacred Wood,* that poetry did have "something to do with morals, and with religion, and even with politics," though he could not say what. Less hesitant than he, a group of writers, of whom Mr. Ivor Winters is the best known, have emphasized a moral approach to literature. In an essay called "Robert Frost, or the Spiritual Drifter as Poet" Winters declares, as a result of examining four carefully selected poems, to which "The Road Not Taken" is the key, that Frost has neither "the intelligence or energy to become a major poet." The substance of the poem is very familiar: facing the choice of divergent roads in a wood, Frost chose the least traveled one and declares his choice has "made all the difference." Winters concedes that the poet has described a comprehensible predicament—"his poem is good as far as it goes, [but] . . . it does not go far enough, it is incomplete, and it puts on the reader a burden of critical intelligence which ought to be borne by the poet." This is a just stricture, so far as this particular poem is concerned, and more or less just in regard to the companion pieces. But the selective process through which Winters condemns Frost has been somehow characteristic of moral criticism: the human limitation, whatever it is, looms larger than the general conduct of the man. Frost is no spiritual drifter in "The Black Cottage," "New Hampshire," "To a Thinker," or dozens of other poems. If "poetry is the record of the best and happiest moments," as Shelley thought, "of the best and happiest minds," it is essentially ethical, for who can imagine a superior mind finding delight in the discomfort of others? Since literature ceased providing, in the early years of our century, examples of superior conduct, as in Tom Tulliver, Henry Esmond, Captain McWhirr, and Max Gottlieb, and confined itself to the lot of the underprivileged and the outcast, its motivation has been empathy. Empathy by its very nature is ethical—it assumes redemptive power in a situation. The business of the critic is then, so far as it is ethical, to determine the quality of the empathy. Is it bathetic? Is it directed toward worthless objects? Does the author lower himself or degrade society to raise his object? So many of the answers lie in psychology and sociology that a critic, giving appreciative attention, needs to be very sure of his training before he does so; nevertheless, this is an area for fair employment of his sensibilities, and at the moment his emphasis in criticism is most needed and rarest.

The chief defect, however, of an approach to literature through only one method is the presumption that, if pursued with the utmost efficiency, it should extract all the values of a work of art. Yet if art in any sense mirrors life, it mirrors a complexity unyielding to a monist approach. I cannot go so far as Mr. Eliot and assert a poem means whatever it means to a reader, for this might reduce it to having no meaning at all, but I am willing to concede to a masterpiece many powers of ever renewing the delight it gives. Ours is a pluralistic universe, to borrow a phrase from William James, a universe without stability, its order ever threatened by disorder, a universe of contingency and change. In so far as the work of art mirrors that universe it must partake somewhat of its pluralism, even of its transiency. "Values are as unstable as the forms of clouds," John Dewey tells us. "Cultivated taste alone is capable of prolonged appreciation of the same object; and it is capable of it because it has been trained to a discriminating procedure which constantly uncovers in the object new meanings to be perceived and enjoyed." Forgotten and recovered meanings are also capable of producing delight. The instability of the very language in which a poem is written is at once a defect and a virtue: original meanings decay but the language takes on new meanings conveying new pleasures. Yet as compared with life itself, it has a relative kind of transient fixity, a retarded instability of meaning. These are the qualities that attract the reader away from the uncertainty of life to art. It is the relative "permanence" of art that solicits continuous attention fully as much as its other values. The obligation of the critic is to approach the work of art with every faculty, with every technique, with every method he can command, for he must know not only what the poem probably meant to its creator but also what it probably means to several different kinds of readers in his own generation if he is to communicate his appreciation and delight to them. In a word, he must have the keenest sense of time to deal with the pluralistic values of any given work of art; he must himself be a pluralist, athletically able to keep receding values in view, willing to embrace new values as they come on, in order to dispense in acceptable language an appreciation appropriate to the sensibilities of the youngest of his generation as the purest form of judgment. His role, if properly understood, is neither that of ambassador of the old nor ambassador of the new, for each is a partisan, but of liaison officer between the two. It is the role of both scholar and critic.

ARTHUR P. DAVIS • 1904–

Trends in Negro American Literature (1940–1965)

THE course of Negro American literature has been highlighted by a series of social and political crises over the Negro's position in America. The Abolition Movement, the Civil War, Reconstruction, and the riot-lynching periods both before and after World War I have all radically influenced Negro writing. Each crisis has brought in new themes, new motivations, new character-types, new viewpoints; and as each crisis has passed, the Negro writer has tended to drop most of the special attitudes which the crisis produced and to move toward the so-called mainstream of American literature.

Between, roughly, 1940 and 1965, two new crises occurred: the Integration Movement (which was climaxed by the 1954 Supreme Court Decision) and the Civil Rights Revolution (which is still with us and which began to take on its present day characteristics around 1960). Each of these movements has affected Negro writing. Twenty-five years is obviously a short time in which to show literary changes resulting from *one* movement, to say nothing of two, but we live in stirring and fast-moving times. For example, within a single decade a supposedly well-established program of non-violence and passive resistance has given way to a new and militant nationalist movement that makes the work of Martin Luther King seem almost gradualistic. Riots have taken the place of "marches," and the objectives of Negroes have shifted from integration to goals entirely alien to anything the black middle class envisioned. These changes have been incredibly swift and phenomenal, but Negro literature during the period in question has reflected them to a greater extent than is commonly realized.

Let us examine the Integration Movement first. Forces of integration had been at work long before 1954, but it is convenient to date the movement from that year. And, of course, the official stamp given it by the Supreme Court accelerated the social changes already in progress. After 1954 the ferment of integration seemed to go to work immediately—not only in the public schools, but in the armed forces, in Southern state universities, and in several other areas as well. A few institutions and localities and segments of the nation naturally held out, and are still holding out, but even the harshest critics of American democracy had to admit that substantial progress towards integration had been made, that the nation had committed itself officially and spiritually to that ideal. And though the commitment was largely theoretical or at best token, it changed the racial climate of America.

This change of climate, however, inadvertently dealt the Negro writer of the fifties a crushing blow. Up to that decade, our literature had been predominantly a protest literature. Ironical though it may seem, we had capitalized on oppression (in a literary sense, of course). Although one may deplore and condemn the cause, there is great creative motivation in a movement which brings all members of a group together and cements them in a common bond. And that is just what segregation did for the Negro especially during the twenties and thirties when full segregation was not only practiced in the South but tacitly condoned by the whole nation. As long as there was this common enemy, we had a common purpose and a strong urge to transform into artistic terms our deep-rooted feelings of bitterness and scorn. When the enemy capitulated, he shattered our most fruitful literary tradition. The possibility of imminent integration tended to destroy during the fifties the protest element in Negro writing.

And one must always keep in mind the paradox involved. We did not have actual integration anywhere. There was surface and token integration in many areas, but the everyday pattern of life for the overwhelming majority was unchanged. But we did have—and this is of the utmost importance—the spiritual commitment and climate out of which full integration could develop. The Negro literary artist recognized and acknowledged that climate; he accepted it in good faith; and he resolved to work with it at all costs. In the meantime, he had to live between two worlds, and that for any artist is a disturbing experience. For the Negro writers of the fifties, especially those in their middle years, it became almost a tragic experience because it meant giving up a tradition in which they had done their apprentice and journeyman work, giving it up when they were prepared to make use of that tradition as master craftsmen.

Another disturbing factor which must be considered here is that this change of climate came about rather suddenly. Perhaps it would be more exact to say that the full awareness came suddenly because there were signs of its approach all during the forties, and Negro writers from time to time showed that they recognized these signs. But the full awareness did not come until the fifties, and it came with some degree of abruptness. For example, all through World War II, all through the forties, most Negro writers were still grinding out protest and problem novels, many of them influenced by *Native Son* (1940). The list of these works is impressive: Attaway's *Blood on the Forge* (1941), Offord's *The White Face* (1943), Himes' *If He Hollers* (1945), Petry's *The Street* (1945), Kaye's *Taffy* (1950), and there were others—practically all of them naturalistic novels with the same message of protest against America's treatment of its black minority.

The poets wrote in a similar view. Walker's *For My People* (1942), Hughes' *Freedom's Plow* (1943), Brooks' *A Street in Bronzeville* (1945), and Dodson's *Powerful Long Ladder* (1946) all had strong protest elements; all dealt in part with the Negro's fight against segregation and discrimination at home and in the armed services.

Noting the dates of these works—both fiction and poetry—one realizes that, roughly speaking, up to 1950 the protest tradition was in full bloom, and that most of our best writers were still using it. Then came this awareness of a radical change in the nation's climate and with it the realization that the old protest themes had to be abandoned. The new climate tended to *date* the problem works of the forties as definitely as time had dated the New Negro "lynching-passing" literature of the twenties and thirties. In other words, protest writing had become the first casualty of the new racial climate.

Faced with the loss of his oldest and most cherished tradition, the Negro writer was forced to seek fresh ways to use his material. First of all, he attempted to find new themes within the racial framework. Retaining the Negro character and background, he shifted his emphasis from the protest aspect of Negro living and placed it on the problems and conflicts within the group itself. For example, Chester Himes pursuing this course in *Third Generation,* explores school life in the Deep South. His main conflict in this work is not concerned with interracial protest but with discord within a Negro family caused by color differences and other problems. The whole racial tone of this novel is quite different from that of *If He Hollers,* a typical protest work. One came out in 1945, the other in 1953. The two books are a good index to the changes which took place in the years separating them.

In like manner, Owen Dodson and Gwendolyn Brooks in their novels, *Boy at the Window* (1951) and *Maud Martha* (1953), respectively, show this tendency to find new themes within the racial framework. Both publications are "little novels," giving intimate and subtle vignettes of middle class living. Their main stress is on life within the group, not on conflict with outside forces. Taking a different approach, William Demby in *Beetlecreek* (1950), completely reversed the protest pattern by showing the black man's inhumanity to his white brother. In *The Outsider* (1953), Richard Wright took an even more subtle approach. He used a Negro main character, but by adroitly and persistently minimizing that character's racial importance, he succeeded in divorcing him from any real association with the traditional protest alignment. And Langston Hughes in *Sweet Flypaper of Life* (1955), though using all Negro characters, does not touch on the matter of inter-racial protest. All of these authors, it seems to me, show their awareness of the new climate by either playing down or avoiding entirely the traditional protest approach.

Another group of writers (and there is some overlapping here) showed their awareness by avoiding the Negro character. Among them are William Gardner Smith (*Anger at Innocence*), Ann Petry (*Country Place*), Richard Wright (*Savage Holiday*), and Willard Motley (*Knock on Any Door*). None of these works has Negro main characters. With the exception of *Knock on Any Door*, each was a "second" novel, following a work written in the forties which had Negro characters and background, and which was written in the protest vein. In each case, the first work was popular, and yet each of these novelists elected to avoid the theme which gave him his initial success.

So far I have spoken only of the novelists, but Negro poets also sensed the change of climate in America and reacted to it. Incidentally, several of our outstanding protest poets of the thirties and forties simply dropped out of the picture as poets. I cannot say, of course, that the new climate alone silenced them, but I do feel that it was a contributing cause. It is hard for a mature writer to slough off a tradition in which he has worked during all of his formative years. Acquiring a new approach in any field of art is a very serious and trying experience. One must also remember that the protest tradition was no mere surface fad with the Negro writer. It was part of his self-respect, part of his philosophy of life, part of his inner being. It was almost a religious experience with those of us who came up through the dark days of the twenties and thirties. When a tradition so deeply ingrained is abandoned, it tends to leave a spiritual numbness—a kind of void not easily filled with new interests or motivations. Several of our ablest poets —and novelists too, for that matter— did not try to fill that void.

A few of the poets, however, met the challenge of the new climate, among them the late M. B. Tolson and Gwendolyn Brooks. A comparison of the early and later works of these poets will show a tendency in the later works either to avoid protest themes entirely or to approach them more subtly and obliquely. Compare, for example, Tolson's *Rendezvous with America* (1944) with *A Libretto for the Republic of Liberia* (1953). The thumping rhythms of the protest verse in the former work gave way in the latter to a new technique, one that was influenced largely by Hart Crane. With this new work, Tolson successfully turned his back on the tradition in which he came to maturity. Concerning the work, Allen Tate felt that: "For the first time . . . a Negro poet has assimilated completely the full poetic language of his time and, by implication, the language of the Anglo-American poetic tradition." Two works of Gwendolyn Brooks also show a change in attitude. There is far more racial protest in *A Street in Bronzeville* (1945) than in her Pulitzer Prize-winning *Annie Allen* (1949). Moreover, the few pieces in the latter work which concern the "problem" are different in approach and technique from those in her first work.

Summing up then, I believe we can say that the Integration Movement influenced Negro writing in the following ways: it forced the black creative artist to play down his most cherished tradition; it sent him in search of new themes; it made him abandon, at least on occasion, the Negro character and background; and it possibly helped to silence a few of the older writers then living. But before the Integration Movement could come to full fruition, it was cut off by the Civil Rights Revolution, particularly the black nationalist elements in the revolution. I speak here, of course, of the literary tendencies of both movements. The main thrust, the principal tenets of black nationalism, in their very essence, negate the paramount aim of the integrationist writer which is to lose himself in the American literary mainstream.

During the 1925 New Negro Renaissance, there was an embryonic black nationalist movement, founded and led by Marcus Garvey. Though short-lived and abortive, it, nevertheless, influenced to some degree the works of Hughes, Cullen, McKay, and other New Negro poets. But Garveyism never achieved the popularity or possessed the civil and "spiritual" strength that the present day black nationalist program has. The influence of this movement goes far beyond the obvious and sensational evidences of it seen in the press or on the T.V. For better or worse, the ideas of black nationalism have influenced the thinking of far more Negroes than one would expect, and this influence has brought to recent Negro writing new themes and a new attitude on the part of the black author.

Perhaps the most important of these new attitudes is the repudiation of American middle class culture and all of the things—the good, on occasion, along with the bad—for which that culture stands. This repudiation may take various forms, and it appears in the poetry (that of LeRoi Jones, for example) as well as in the novels. One form of this attack concerns the Negro woman. She is accused of "emasculating" her husbands and lovers by insisting that they conform to middle class standards. This theme is found in Chester Himes' *Third Generation* (also in other recent works by him), and there is a strain of it in Kelley's *A Drop of Patience* (1965). In Fair's *Hog Butcher* (1966), the author not only attacks the Negro middle class in his story, but in the "Prologue to Part II," he steps into the work, after the manner of Fielding, and delivers a scathing lecture on the subject. The most striking statement of the repudiation of America's white middle class comes from Baldwin's "Letter to My Nephew" in *The Fire Next Time* (1963): "There is no reason for you to try to become like white people and there is no basis whatever for their impertinent assumption that *they* must accept *you*. The really terrible thing, old buddy, is that *you* must accept *them*. And I mean that very seriously. You must accept them and accept them with love. For these innocent people have no other hope."

The influence of the Black Revolt is also seen in the revival of the moribund protest theme in Negro writing. In some cases, the protest novel has returned practically unchanged in the matter of technique and point of view. Frank London Brown's *Trumbull Park* (1958) and Richard Wright's *The Long Dream* (1958) are very similar in spirit to the protest works of the forties. It is curious to note that Wright, after taking a sort of vacation from the protest tradition in *The Outsider* and *Savage Holiday,* comes back to it in *The Long Dream.* Though he deals with discrimination in the Army and though he moves his scene finally from America to Australia, Killens in *And Then We Heard the Thunder* (1963) is still using the old protest tradition. (This, of course, is no reflection on the quality of the novel.) And William Gardner Smith is doing the same thing although in *Stone Face* (1963) he deals primarily with French prejudice against Algerians. There are, however, two recent works in this neo-protest tradition which show freshness and originality. One of them is Kelley's *A Different Drummer* (1962). Making use of fantasy, symbol, and other modern devices and techniques, Kelley gives us not only a new, bitter, and effective type of protest novel, but also a new type of Negro character as well. Ronald Fair's *Many Thousands Gone* (1966) is equally as fresh in its approach and equally as effective. Through a morbidly exaggerated description of life in a mythical Southern locality, Fair tells us symbolically many things about the race situation in America today. He calls his work "An American Fable."

From the twenties on down to the present, the jazz musician has been popular with black writers, but he has never before received the kind and the amount of attention now given him. In these days of black nationalism and "negritude," the jazz musician has acquired a new significance. He has become for many Negro writers a symbol of the spontaneous creative impulse of the race; he represents black "original genius," something that is not indebted in any way to middle class culture. As depicted in recent works, the Negro jazz musician is often crude, sexy, uninhibited, uneducated, yet wise with a folk wisdom far superior to that which comes from schools and books. We find variants of this character in John A. Williams' *Night Song* (1961), in Kelley's *A Drop of Patience* (1965), and though the character is not fully developed, in Rufus in Baldwin's *Another Country.* On occasion these characters are based on the actual lives of famous jazz musicians.

Black Revolt literature takes an interesting and by no means simple attitude towards whites—an attitude which ranges from pity and contempt to the kind of sadistic love-hatred found in *Another Country.* In several of these novels, the black man-white woman love affair is portrayed. We find this not only in Baldwin's work, but also in *A Drop of Patience,* in *And Then We Heard the Thunder,* and in *Night Song* (a very complex analysis of guilt-laden frustration on the part of the man). LeRoi Jones' *The Dutchman,* whatever else it may be saying, also comments on this theme. To see the new type of white woman and the new role she is playing in these affairs, one should compare a novel like Himes' *If He Hollers* with, let us say, *Night Song.* It is ironic that the white woman should figure as largely as she does in the literature of the Black Revolt.

A minor theme of Black Revolt literature deals with the Negro slum boy, usually depicted as the victim of our indifferent middle class society. Three excellent and intriguing studies of the ghetto kid are found in the following works: Kennedy's *The Pecking Order* (1953), Mayfield's *The Long Night* (1958), and Fair's *Hog Butcher* (1966). In delineating the "culturally deprived" boy, the authors naturally give a lot of space and attention to police brutality, relief, bad housing for Negroes, corrupt and prejudiced city officials, and all of the other evils that the present day militant protest groups attack.

Summing up again—these, then, are the trends I find in the literature of the Black Revolt: a repudiation of American middle class values; a revival of interest in protest writing; the glorification of the black jazz musician; a "mixed" attitude towards whites, particularly white women; and a tendency to depict through the ghetto kid the evils of the inner city. In the works of the period which I have read, I have found two or three highly competent productions but none of the caliber and scope of *Invisible Man,* the finest fruit of the Integration Movement. Perhaps it is far too soon to expect that kind of synthesis.

What about the future? Where will these tendencies lead? When America grants full equality to the Negro (as it will), several of these current attitudes and themes will be dropped. The Negro American writer will do then what he has always done after each crisis in the past —continue on his trek to the mainstream of American literature.

LIONEL TRILLING • 1905–

The Meaning of a Literary Idea

...Though no great minist'ring reason sorts
Out the dark mysteries of human souls
To clear conceiving: yet there ever rolls
A vast idea before me, and I glean
Therefrom my liberty . . .
                    Keats: "Sleep and Poetry"

I. The question of the relation which should properly obtain between what we call creative literature and what we call ideas is a matter of insistent importance for modern criticism. It did not always make difficulties for the critic, and that it now makes so many is a fact which tells us much about our present relation to literature.

Ever since men began to think about poetry, they have conceived that there is a difference between the poet and the philosopher, a difference in method and in intention and in result. These differences I have no wish to deny. But a solidly established difference inevitably draws the fire of our question; it tempts us to inquire whether it is really essential or whether it is quite so settled and extreme as at first it seems. To this temptation I yield perhaps too easily, and very possibly as the result of an impercipience on my part— it may be that I see the difference with insufficient sharpness because I do not have a proper notion either of the matter of poetry or of the matter of philosophy. But whatever the reason, when I consider the respective products of the poetic and of the philosophic mind, although I see that they are by no means the same and although I can conceive that different processes, even different mental faculties, were at work to make them and to make them different, I cannot resist the impulse to put stress on their similarity and on their easy assimilation to each other.

Let me suggest some of the ways in which literature, by its very nature, is involved with ideas. I can be quite brief because what I say will not be new to you.

The most elementary thing to observe is that literature is of its nature involved with ideas because it deals with man in society, which is to say that it deals with formulations, valuations, and decisions, some of them implicit, others explicit. Every sentient organism *acts* on the principle that pleasure is to be preferred to pain, but man is the sole creature who formulates or exemplifies this as an idea and causes it to lead to other ideas. His consciousness of self abstracts this principle of action from his behavior and makes it the beginning of a process of intellection or a matter for tears and laughter. And this is but one of the innumerable assumptions or ideas that are the very stuff of literature.

This is self-evident and no one ever thinks of denying it. All that is ever denied is that literature is within its proper function in bringing these ideas to explicit consciousness, or ever gains by doing so. Thus, one of the matters of assumption in any society is the worth of men as compared with the worth of women; upon just such an assumption, more or less settled, much of the action of the *Oresteia* is based, and we don't in the least question the propriety of this —or not until it becomes the subject of open debate between Apollo and Athene, who, on the basis of an elaborate biological speculation, try to decide which is the less culpable, to kill your father or to kill your mother. At this point we, in our modern way, feel that in permitting the debate Aeschylus has made a great and rather silly mistake, that he has for the moment ceased to be *literary*. Yet what drama does not consist of the opposition of formulable ideas, what drama, indeed, is not likely to break into the explicit exposition and debate of these ideas?

This, as I say, is elementary. And scarcely less elementary is the observation that whenever we put two emotions into juxtaposition we have what we can properly call an idea. When Keats brings together, as he so often does, his emotions about love and his emotions about death, we have a very powerful idea and the source of consequent ideas. The force of such an idea depends upon the force of the two emotions which are brought to confront each other, and also, of course, upon the way the confrontation is contrived.

Then it can be said that the very form of a literary work, considered apart from its content, so far as that is possible, is in itself an idea. Whether we deal with syllogisms or poems, we deal with dialectic—with, that is, a developing series of statements. Or if the word "statements" seems to pre-judge the question so far as literature is concerned, let us say merely that we deal with a developing series— the important word is "developing." We judge the value of the development by judging the interest of its several stages and the propriety and the relevance of their connection among themselves. We make the judgment in terms of the implied purpose of the developing series.

Dialectic, in this sense, is just another word for form, and has for its purpose, in philosophy or in art, the leading of the mind to some conclusion. Greek drama, for example, is an arrangement of moral and emotional elements in such a way as to conduct the mind—"inevitably," as we like to say—to a certain affective condition. This condition is a quality of personal being which may be judged by the action it can be thought ultimately to lead to.

We take Aristotle to be a better critic of the drama than Plato because we perceive that Aristotle understood and Plato did not understand that the form of the drama was of itself an idea which controlled and brought to a particular issue the subordinate ideas it contained. The form of the drama *is* its idea, and its idea *is* its form. And form in those arts which we call abstract is no less an idea than is form in the representational arts. Governments nowadays are very simple and accurate in their perception of this— much more simple and accurate than are academic critics and aestheticians—and they are as quick to deal with the arts of "pure" form as they are to deal with ideas stated in discourse: it is as if totalitarian governments kept in mind what the rest of us tend to forget, that "idea" in one of its early significations exactly means form and was so used by many philosophers.

It is helpful to have this meaning before us when we come to consider that particular connection between literature and ideas which presents us with the greatest difficulty, the connection that involves highly elaborated ideas, or ideas as we have them in highly elaborated systems such as philosophy, or theology, or science. The modern feeling about this relationship is defined by two texts, both provided by T. S. Eliot. In his essay on Shakespeare Mr. Eliot says, "I can see no reason for believing that either Dante or Shakespeare did any thinking on his own. The people who think that Shakespeare thought are always people who are not engaged in writing poetry, but who are engaged in thinking, and we all like to think that great men were like ourselves." And in his essay on Henry James Mr. Eliot makes the well-known remark that James had a mind so fine that no idea could violate it.

In both statements, as I believe, Mr. Eliot permits his impulse to spirited phrase to run away with him, yielding too much to what he conceives to be the didactic necessities of the moment, for he has it in mind to offer resistance to the nineteenth-century way of looking at poetry as a heuristic medium, as a communication of knowledge. This is a view which is well exemplified in a sentence of Carlyle's: "If called to define Shakespeare's faculty, I should say superiority of Intellect, and think I had included all in that." As between the two statements about Shakespeare's mental processes, I give my suffrage to Carlyle's as representing a more intelligible and a more available notion of intellect than Mr. Eliot's, but I think I understand what Mr. Eliot is trying to do with his—he is trying to rescue poetry from the kind of misinterpretation of Carlyle's view which was once more common than it is now; he is trying to save for poetry what is peculiar to it, and for systematic thought what is peculiar to it.

As for Mr. Eliot's statement about James and ideas, it is useful to us because it gives us a clue to what might be called the sociology of our question. "Henry James had a mind so fine that no idea could violate it." In the context "violate" is a strong word, yet we can grant that the mind of the poet is a sort of Clarissa Harlowe and that an idea is a sort of Colonel Lovelace, for it is a truism of contemporary thought that the whole nature of man stands in danger of being brutalized by the intellect, or at least by some one of its apparently accredited surrogates. A specter haunts our culture—it is that people will eventually be unable to say, "They fell in love and married," let alone understand the language of *Romeo and Juliet,* but will as a matter of course say, "Their libidinal impulses being reciprocal, they activated their individual erotic drives and integrated them within the same frame of reference."

Now this is not the language of abstract thought or of any kind of thought. It is the language of non-thought. But it is the language which is developing from the peculiar status which we in our culture have given to abstract thought. There can be no doubt whatever that it constitutes a threat to the emotions and thus to life itself.

The specter of what this sort of language suggests has haunted us since the end of the eighteenth century. When he speaks of the mind being violated by an idea, Mr. Eliot, like the Romantics, is simply voicing his horror at the prospect of life being intellectualized out of all spontaneity and reality.

We are the people of the idea, and we rightly fear that the intellect will dry up the blood in our veins and wholly check the emotional and creative part of the mind. And although I said that the fear of the total sovereignty of the abstract intellect began in the Romantic period, we are of course touching here upon Pascal's opposition between two faculties of the mind, of which *l'esprit de finesse* has its heuristic powers no less than *l'esprit de géométrie,* powers of discovery and knowledge which have a particular value for the establishment of man in society and the universe.

But to call ourselves the people of the idea is to flatter ourselves. We are rather the people of ideology, which is a very different thing. Ideology is not the product of thought; it is the habit or the ritual of showing respect for certain formulas to which, for various reasons having to do with emotional safety, we have very strong ties of whose meaning and consequences in actuality we have no clear understanding. The nature of ideology may in part be understood from its tendency to develop the sort of language I parodied, and scarcely parodied, a moment ago.

It is therefore no wonder that any critical theory that conceives itself to be at the service of the emotions, and of life itself, should turn a very strict and jealous gaze upon an intimate relationship between literature and ideas, for in our culture ideas tend to deteriorate into ideology. And indeed it is scarcely surprising that criticism, in its zeal to protect literature and life from the tyranny of the rational intellect, should misinterpret the relationship. Mr. Eliot, if we take him literally, does indeed misinterpret the relationship when he conceives of "thinking" in such a way that it must be denied to Shakespeare and Dante. It must puzzle us to know what thinking is if Shakespeare and Dante did not do it.

And it puzzles us to know what René Wellek and Austin Warren mean when in their admirable *Theory of Literature* they say that literature can make use of ideas only when ideas "cease to be ideas in the ordinary sense of concepts and become symbols, or even myths." I am not sure that the ordinary sense of *ideas* actually is *concepts,* or at any rate concepts of such abstractness that they do not arouse in us feelings and attitudes. And I take it that when we speak of the relationship of literature and ideas, the ideas we refer to are not those of mathematics or of symbolic logic, but only such ideas as can arouse and traditionally have aroused the feelings—the ideas, for example, of men's relation to one another and to the world. A poet's simple statement of a psychological fact recalls us to a proper simplicity about the nature of ideas. "Our continued influxes of feeling," said Wordsworth, "are modified and directed by our thoughts, which are indeed the representatives of all our past feelings." The interflow between emotion and idea is a psychological fact which we do well to keep clearly in mind, together with the part that is played by desire, will, and imagination in philosophy as well as in literature. Mr. Eliot, and Mr. Wellek and Mr. Warren—and in general those critics who are zealous in the defense of the autonomy of poetry—prefer to forget the ground which is common to both emotion and thought; they presume ideas to be only the product of formal systems of philosophy, not remembering, at least on the occasion of their argument, that poets too have their effect in the world of thought. *L'esprit de finesse* is certainly not to be confused with *l'esprit de géométrie,* but neither—which is precisely the point of Pascal's having distinguished and named the two different qualities of mind —is it to be denied its powers of comprehension and formulation.

Mr. Wellek and Mr. Warren tell us that "the artist will be hampered by too much ideology[1] if it remains unassimilated." We note the tautology of the statement— for what else is "too much" ideology except ideology that *is* unassimilated?—not because we wish to take a disputatious advantage over authors to whom we have reason to be grateful, but because the tautology suggests the uneasiness of the position it defends. We are speaking of art, which is an activity which defines itself exactly by its powers of assimilation and of which the essence is the just amount of any of its qualities or elements; of course too much or unassimilated ideology will "hamper" the artist, but so will too much of anything, so will too much metaphor: Coleridge tells us that in a long poem there can be too much *poetry.* The theoretical question is simply being begged, out of an undue anxiety over the "purity" of literature, over its perfect literariness.

The authors of *Theory of Literature* are certainly right to question the "intellectualist misunderstanding of art" and the "confusions of the functions of art and philosophy" and to look for the flaws in the scholarly procedures which organize works of art according to their ideas and their affinities with philosophical systems. Yet on their own showing there has always been a conscious commerce between

---

[1] The word is used by Mr. Wellek and Mr. Warren, not in the pejorative sense in which I have earlier used it, but to mean simply a body of ideas.

the poet and the philosopher, and not every poet has been violated by the ideas that have attracted him. The sexual metaphor is forced upon us, not only explicitly by Mr. Eliot but also implicitly by Mr. Wellek and Mr. Warren, who seem to think of ideas as masculine and gross and of art as feminine and pure, and who permit a union of the two sexes only when ideas give up their masculine, effective nature and "cease to be ideas in the ordinary sense and become symbols, or even myths." We naturally ask: symbols of what, myths about what? No anxious exercise of aesthetic theory can make the ideas of, say, Blake and Lawrence other than what they are intended to be—ideas relating to action and to moral judgment.

This anxiety lest the work of art be other than totally self-contained, this fear lest the reader make reference to something beyond the work itself, has its origin, as I have previously suggested, in the reaction from the earlier impulse—it goes far back beyond the nineteenth century—to show that art is justified in comparison with the effective activity of the systematic disciplines. It arises too from the strong contemporary wish to establish, in a world of unremitting action and effectiveness, the legitimacy of contemplation, which it is now no longer convenient to associate with the exercises of religion but which may be associated with the experiences of art. We will all do well to advance the cause of contemplation, to insist on the right to a haven from perpetual action and effectiveness. But we must not enforce our insistence by dealing with art as if it were a unitary thing, and by making reference only to its "purely" aesthetic element, requiring that every work of art serve our contemplation by being wholly self-contained and without relation to action. No doubt there is a large body of literature to which ideas, with their tendency to refer to action and effectiveness, are alien and inappropriate. But also much of literature wishes to give the sensations and to win the responses that are given and won by ideas, and it makes use of ideas to gain its effects, considering ideas—like people, sentiments, things, and scenes—to be indispensable elements of human life. Nor is the intention of this part of literature always an aesthetic one in the strict sense that Mr. Wellek and Mr. Warren have in mind; there is abundant evidence that the aesthetic upon which the critic sets primary store is to the poet himself frequently of only secondary importance.

We can grant that the province of poetry is one thing and the province of intellection another. But keeping the difference well in mind, we must yet see that systems of ideas have a particular quality which is much coveted as their chief effect —let us even say as their chief aesthetic effect—by at least certain kinds of literary works. Say what we will as critics and teachers trying to defend the province of art from the dogged tendency of our time to ideologize all things into grayness, say what we will about the "purely" literary, the purely aesthetic values, we as readers know that we demand of our literature some of the virtues which define a successful work of systematic thought. We want it to have—at least when it is appropriate for it to have, which is by no means infrequently—the authority, the cogency, the completeness, the brilliance, the *hardness* of systematic thought.[2]

[2] Mr. Wellek and Mr. Warren say something of the same sort, but only, as it were, in a concessive way: "Philosophy, ideological content, in its proper context, seems to enhance artistic value because it corroborates several important artistic values: those of complexity and coherence. . . . But it need not be so. The artist will be hampered by too much ideology if it remains unassimilated." Earlier they say: "Serious art implies a view of life which can be stated in philosophical terms, even in terms of systems. Between artistic coherence . . . and philosophic coherence there is some kind of correlation." They then hasten to distinguish between emotion and thinking, sensibility and intellection, etc., and to tell us that art is more complex than "propaganda."

Of late years criticism has been much concerned to insist on the indirection and the symbolism of the language of poetry. I do not doubt that the language of poetry is very largely that of indirection and symbolism. But it is not only that. Poetry is closer to rhetoric than we today are willing to admit; syntax plays a greater part in it than our current theory grants, and syntax connects poetry with rational thought, for, as Hegel says, "grammar, in its extended and consistent form"—by which he means syntax—"is the work of thought, which makes its categories distinctly visible therein." And those poets of our time who make the greatest impress upon us are those who are most aware of rhetoric, which is to say, of the intellectual content of their work. Nor is the intellectual content of their work simply the inevitable effect produced by good intelligence turned to poetry; many of these poets—Yeats and Eliot himself come most immediately to mind—have been at great pains to develop consistent intellectual positions along with, and consonant with, their work in poetry.

The aesthetic effect of intellectual cogency, I am convinced, is not to be slighted. Let me give an example for what it is worth. Of recent weeks my mind has been much engaged by two statements, disparate in length and in genre, although as it happens they have related themes. One is a couplet of Yeats:

> We had fed the heart on fantasies,
> The heart's grown brutal from the fare.

I am hard put to account for the force of the statement. It certainly does not lie in any metaphor, for only the dimmest sort of metaphor is to be detected. Nor does it lie in any special power of the verse. The statement has for me the pleasure of relevance and cogency, in part conveyed to me by the content, in part by the rhetoric. The other statement is Freud's short book, his last, *An Outline of Psychoanalysis,* which gives me a pleasure which is no doubt different from that given by Yeats's couplet, but which is also similar; it is the pleasure of listening to a strong, decisive, self-limiting voice uttering statements to which I can give assent. The pleasure I have in responding to Freud I find very difficult to distinguish from the pleasure which is involved in responding to a satisfactory work of art.

Intellectual assent in literature is not quite the same thing as agreement. We can take pleasure in literature where we do not agree, responding to the power or grace of a mind without admitting the rightness of its intention or conclusion—we can take our pleasure from an intellect's *cogency,* without making a final judgment on the correctness or adaptability of what it says.

II. And now I leave these general theoretical matters for a more particular concern—the relation of contemporary American literature to ideas. In order to come at this as directly as possible we might compare modern American prose literature—for American poetry is a different thing—with modern European literature. European literature of, say, the last thirty or forty years seems to me to be, in the sense in which I shall use the word, essentially an active literature. It does not, at its best, consent to be merely comprehended. It refuses to be understood as a "symptom" of its society, although of course it may be that, among other things. It does not submit to being taped. We as scholars and critics try to discover the source of its effective energy and of course we succeed in some degree. But inevitably we become aware that it happily exists beyond our powers of explanation, although not, certainly, beyond our powers of response. Proust, Joyce, Lawrence, Kafka, Yeats and Eliot himself do not allow us to finish with them; and the refusal is repeated by a great many European writers less large than these. With exceptions that I shall note, the same thing cannot be said of modern American literature. American literature seems to me essentially passive: our minds tend always to be made up about this or that American author, and we incline to speak of him, not merely incidentally but conclusively, in terms of his moment in history, of the conditions of the culture that "produced" him. Thus American literature as an academic subject is not so much a *subject* as an *object* of study: it does not, as a literature should, put the scrutinizer of it under scrutiny but, instead, leaves its students with a too comfortable sense of complete comprehension.

When we try to discover the root of this difference between European and American literature, we are led to the conclusion that it is the difference between the number and weight or force of the ideas which the two literatures embody or suggest. I do not mean that European literature makes use of, as American literature does not, the ideas of philosophy or theology or science. Kafka does not exemplify Kierkegaard, Proust does not dramatize Bergson. One way of putting the relationship of this literature to ideas is to say that the literature of contemporary Europe is in competition with philosophy, theology, and science, that it seeks to match them in comprehensiveness and power and seriousness.

This is not to say that the best of contemporary European literature makes upon us the effect of a rational system of thought. Quite the contrary, indeed; it is precisely its artistic power that we respond to, which I take in part to be its power of absorbing and disturbing us in secret ways. But this power it surely derives from its commerce, according to its own rules, with systematic ideas.

For in the great issues with which the mind has traditionally been concerned there is, I would submit, something *primitive* which is of the highest value to the literary artist. I know that it must seem a strange thing to say, for we are in the habit of thinking of systematic ideas as being of the very essence of the not-primitive, of the highly developed. No doubt they are: but they are at the same time the means by which a complex civilization keeps the primitive in mind and refers to it. Whence and whither, birth and death, fate, free will, and immortality—these are never far from systematic thought; and Freud's belief that the child's first inquiry—beyond which, really, the adult does not go in kind—is in effect a sexual one seems to me to have an empirical support from literature. The ultimate questions of conscious and rational thought about the nature of man and his destiny match easily in the literary mind with the dark *un*conscious and with the most primitive human relationships. Love, parenthood, incest, patricide: these are what the great ideas suggest to literature, these are the means by which they express themselves. I need but mention three great works of different ages to suggest how true this is: *Oedipus, Hamlet, The Brothers Karamazov.*

Ideas, if they are large enough and of a certain kind, are not only not hostile to the creative process, as some think, but are virtually inevitable to it. Intellectual power and emotional power go together. And if we can say, as I think we can, that contemporary American prose literature in general lacks emotional power, it is possible to explain the deficiency by reference to the intellectual weakness of American prose literature.

The situation in verse is different. Perhaps this is to be accounted for by the fact that the best of our poets are, as good poets usually are, scholars of their tradition. There is present to their minds the degree of intellectual power which poetry is traditionally expected to exert. Questions of form and questions of language seem of themselves to demand, or to create, an adequate subject matter; and a highly developed aesthetic implies a matter strong enough to support its energy.

We have not a few poets who are subjects and not objects, who are active and not passive. One does not finish quickly, if at all, with the best work of, say, Cummings, Stevens, and Marianne Moore. This work is not exempt from our judgment, even from adverse judgment, but it is able to stay with a mature reader as a continuing element of his spiritual life. Of how many writers of prose fiction can we say anything like the same thing?

The topic which was originally proposed to me for this occasion and which I have taken the liberty of generalizing was the debt of four American writers to Freud and Spengler. The four writers were O'Neill, Dos Passos, Wolfe, and Faulkner. Of the first three how many can be continuing effective elements of our mental lives? I hope I shall never read Mr. Dos Passos without interest nor ever lose the warm though qualified respect that I feel for his work. But it is impossible for me to feel of this work that it is autonomous, that it goes on existing beyond our powers of explanation. As for Eugene O'Neill and Thomas Wolfe, I can respect the earnestness of their dedication, but I cannot think of having a living, reciprocal relation with what they have written. And I believe that is because these men, without intellectual capital of their own, don't owe a sufficient debt of ideas to anyone. Spengler is certainly not a great mind; at best he is but a considerable dramatist of the idea of world history and of, as it were, the natural history of cultures; and we can find him useful as a critic who summarizes the adverse views of our urban, naturalistic culture which many have held. Freud is a very great mind indeed. Without stopping to specify what actual influence of ideas was exerted by Spengler and Freud on O'Neill, Dos Passos, or Wolfe, or even to consider whether there was any influence at all, we can fairly assume that all are in something of the same ambiance. But if, in that ambiance, we want the sense of the actuality of doom—actuality being one of the qualities we expect of literature—surely we do better to seek it in Spengler himself than in any of the three literary artists, just as, if we want the sense of the human mystery, of tragedy truly conceived in the great terms of free will, necessity, and hope, surely we do far better to seek it directly in Freud himself than in these three literary men.

In any extended work of literature, the aesthetic effect, as I have said, depends in large degree upon intellectual power, upon the amount and recalcitrance of the material the mind works on, and upon the mind's success in mastering the large material. And it is exactly the lack of intellectual power that makes our three writers, after our first response of interest, so inadequate aesthetically. We have only to compare, say, Dos Passos's *USA* to a work of similar kind and intention, Flaubert's *L'Education Sentimentale,* to see that in Dos Passos's novel the matter encompassed is both less in amount and less in resistance than in Flaubert's; the energy of the encompassing mind is also less. Or we consider O'Neill's crude, dull notion of the unconscious and his merely elementary grasp of Freud's ideas about sex and we recognize the lamentable signs of a general inadequacy of mind. Or we ask what it is about Thomas Wolfe that always makes us uncomfortable with his talent, so that even his admirers deal with him not as a subject but as an object—an object which must be explained and accounted for—and we are forced to answer that it is the disproportion between the energy of his utterance and his power of mind. It is customary to say of Thomas Wolfe that he is an emotional writer. Perhaps: although it is probably not the most accurate way to describe a writer who could deal with but one single emotion; and we feel that it is a function of his unrelenting, tortured egoism that he could not submit his mind to the ideas that might have brought the variety and interest of order to the single, dull chaos of his powerful self-regard, for it is true that the intellect makes many emotions out of the primary egoistic one.

At this point it may be well to recall what our subject is. It is not merely the part that is played in literature by those ideas which may be derived from the study of systematic, theoretical works; it is the part that is played in literature by ideas in general. To be sure, the extreme and most difficult instance of the general relation of literature to ideas is the relation of literature to highly developed and formulated ideas; and because this is indeed so difficult a matter, and one so often misconceived, I have put a special emphasis upon it. But we do not present our subject adequately—we do not, indeed, represent the mind adequately—if we think of ideas only as being highly formulated. It will bring us back to the proper generality of our subject if I say that the two contemporary writers who hold out to me the possibility of a living reciprocal relationship with their work are Ernest Hemingway and William Faulkner—it will bring us back the more dramatically because Hemingway and Faulkner have insisted on their indifference to the conscious intellectual tradition of our time and have acquired the reputation of achieving their effects by means that have the least possible connection with any sort of intellectuality or even with intelligence.

In trying to explain a certain commendable quality which is to be found in the work of Hemingway and Faulkner—and a certain quality only, not a total and unquestionable literary virtue—we are not called upon by our subject to show that particular recognizable ideas of a certain force or weight are "used" in the work. Nor are we called upon to show that new ideas of a certain force and weight are "produced" by the work. All that we need to do is account for a certain aesthetic effect as being in some important part achieved by a mental process which is not different from the process by which discursive ideas are conceived, and which is to be judged by some of the criteria by which an idea is judged.

The aesthetic effect which I have in mind can be suggested by a word that I have used before—activity. We feel that Hemingway and Faulkner are intensely at work upon the recalcitrant stuff of life; when they are at their best they give us the sense that the amount and intensity of their activity are in a satisfying proportion to the recalcitrance of the material. And our pleasure in their activity is made the more secure because we have the distinct impression that the two novelists are not under any illusion that they have conquered the material upon which they direct their activity. The opposite is true of Dos Passos, O'Neill, and Wolfe; at each point of conclusion in their work we feel that *they* feel that they have said the last word, and we feel this even when they represent themselves, as O'Neill and Wolfe so often do, as puzzled and baffled by life. But of Hemingway and Faulkner we seldom have the sense that they have deceived themselves, that they have misrepresented to themselves the nature and the difficulty of the matter they work on. And we go on to make another intellectual judgment: we say that the matter they present, together with the degree of difficulty which they assume it to have, seems to be very cogent. This, we say, is to the point; this really has something to do with life as we live it; we cannot ignore it.

There is a traditional and aggressive rationalism that can understand thought only in its conscious, developed form and believes that the phrase "unconscious mind" is a meaningless contradiction in terms. Such a view, wrong as I think it is, has at least the usefulness of warning us that we must not call by the name of thought or idea all responses of the human organism whatever. But the extreme rationalist position ignores the simple fact that the life of reason, at least in its most extensive part, begins in the emotions. What comes into being when two contradictory emotions are made to confront each other and are required to have a relationship with each other is, as I have said, quite properly called an idea. Ideas may also be said to be generated in the opposition of ideals, and in the felt awareness of the impact of new circumstances upon old forms of feeling and estimation, in the response to the conflict between new exigencies and old pieties. And it can be said that a work will have what I have been calling cogency in the degree that the confronting emotions go deep, or in the degree that the old pieties are firmly held and the new exigencies strongly apprehended. In Hemingway's stories[3] a strongly charged piety toward the ideals and attachments of boyhood and the lusts of maturity is in conflict not only with the imagination of death but also with that imagination as it is peculiarly modified by the dark negation of the modern world. Faulkner as a Southerner of today, a man deeply implicated in the pieties of his tradition, is of course at the very heart of an exigent historical event which thrusts upon him the awareness of the inadequacy and wrongness of the very tradition he loves. In the work of both men the cogency is a function not of their conscious but of their unconscious minds. We can, if we admire Tolstoi and Dostoevski, regret the deficiency of consciousness, blaming it for the inadequacy in both our American writers of the talent for generalization.[4] Yet it is to be remarked that the unconscious minds of

[3] It is in the stories rather than in the novels that Hemingway is characteristic and at his best.

[4] Although there is more impulse to generalization than is usually supposed. This is especially true of Faulkner, who has never subscribed to the contemporary belief that only concrete words have power and that only the representation of things and actions is dramatic.

both men have wisdom and humility about themselves. They seldom make the attempt at formulated solution, they rest content with the "negative capability." And this negative capability, this willingness to remain in uncertainties, mysteries, and doubts, is not, as one tendency of modern feeling would suppose, an abdication of intellectual activity. Quite to the contrary, it is precisely an aspect of their intelligence, of their seeing the full force and complexity of their subject matter. And this we can understand the better when we observe how the unconscious minds of Dos Passos, O'Neill, and Wolfe do not possess humility and wisdom; nor are they fully active, as the intellectual histories of all three men show. A passivity on the part of Dos Passos before the idea of the total corruption of American civilization has issued in his later denial of the possibility of economic and social reform and in his virtually unqualified acceptance of the American status quo. A passivity on the part of O'Neill before the clichés of economic and metaphysical materialism issued in his later simplistic Catholicism. The passivity of Thomas Wolfe before all his experience led him to that characteristic *malice* toward the objects or partners of his experience which no admirer of his ever takes account of, and eventually to that simple affirmation, recorded in *You Can't Go Home Again,* that literature must become the agent of the immediate solution of all social problems and undertake the prompt eradication of human pain; and because his closest friend did not agree that this was a possible thing for literature to do, Wolfe terminated the friendship. These are men of whom it is proper to speak of their having been violated by ideas; but we must observe that it was an excess of intellectual passivity that invited the violence.

In speaking of Hemingway and Faulkner I have used the word "piety." It is a word that I have chosen with some care and despite the pejorative meanings that nowadays adhere to it, for I wished to avoid the word "religion," and piety is not religion, yet I wished too to have religion come to mind as it inevitably must when piety is mentioned. Carlyle says of Shakespeare that he was the product of medieval Catholicism, and implies that Catholicism *at the distance at which Shakespeare stood from it* had much to do with the power of Shakespeare's intellect. Allen Tate has developed in a more particular way an idea that has much in common with what Carlyle here implies. Loosely put, the idea is that religion in its decline leaves a detritus of pieties, of strong assumptions, which afford a particularly fortunate condition for certain kinds of literature; these pieties carry a strong charge of intellect, or perhaps it would be more accurate to say that they tend to stimulate the mind in a powerful way.

Religious emotions are singularly absent from Shakespeare and it does not seem possible to say of him that he was a religious man. Nor does it seem possible to say of the men of the great period of American literature in the nineteenth century that they were religious men. Hawthorne and Melville, for example, lived at a time when religion was in decline and they were not drawn to support it. But from religion they inherited a body of pieties, a body of issues, if you will, which engaged their hearts and their minds to the very bottom. Henry James was not a religious man and there is not the least point in the world in trying to make him out one. But you need not accept all the implications of Quentin Anderson's thesis that James allegorized his father's religious system to see that Mr. Anderson is right when he says that James was dealing, in his own way, with the questions that his father's system propounded. This will indicate something of why James so catches our imagination today, and why we turn so eagerly again to Hawthorne and Melville.

The piety which descends from religion is not the only possible piety, as the case of Faulkner reminds us, and perhaps also the case of Hemingway. But we naturally mention first that piety which does descend from religion because it is most likely to have in it the quality of transcendence which, whether we admit it or no, we expect literature at its best to have.

The subject is extremely delicate and complex and I do no more than state it barely and crudely. But no matter how I state it, I am sure that you will see that what I am talking about leads us to the crucial issue of our literary culture.

I know that I will not be wrong if I assume that most of us here are in our social and political beliefs consciously liberal and democratic. And I know that I will not be wrong if I say that most of us, and in the degree of our commitment to literature and our familiarity with it, find that the contemporary authors we most wish to read and most wish to admire for their literary qualities demand of us a great agility and ingenuity in coping with their antagonism to our social and political ideals. For it is in general true that the modern European literature to which we can have an active, reciprocal relationship, which is the right relationship to have, has been written by men who are indifferent to, or even hostile to, the tradition of democratic liberalism as we know it. Yeats and Eliot, Proust and Joyce, Lawrence and Gide—these men do not seem to confirm us in the social and political ideals which we hold.

If we now turn and consider the contemporary literature of America, we see that wherever we can describe it as patently liberal and democratic, we must say that it is not of lasting interest. I do not say that the work which is written to conform to the liberal democratic tradition is of no value but only that we do not incline to return to it, we do not establish it in our minds and affections. Very likely we learn from it as citizens; and as citizen-scholars and citizen-critics we understand and explain it. But we do not live in an active reciprocal relation with it. The sense of largeness, of cogency, of the transcendence which largeness and cogency can give, the sense of being reached in our secret and primitive minds—this we virtually never get from the writers of the liberal democratic tradition at the present time.

And since liberal democracy inevitably generates a body of ideas, it must necessarily occur to us to ask why it is that these particular ideas have not infused with force and cogency the literature that embodies them. This question is the most important, the most fully challenging question in culture that at this moment we can ask.

The answer to it cannot of course even be begun here, and I shall be more than content if now it is merely accepted as a legitimate question. But there are one or two things that may be said about the answer, about the direction we must take to reach it in its proper form. We will not find it if we come to facile conclusions about the absence from our culture of the impressive ideas of traditional religion. I have myself referred to the historical fact that religion has been an effective means of transmitting or of generating ideas of a sort which I feel are necessary for the literary qualities we want, and to some this will no doubt mean that I believe religion to be a necessary condition of great literature. I do not believe that; and what is more, I consider it from many points of view an impropriety to try to guarantee literature by religious belief.

Nor will we find our answer if we look for it in the weakness of the liberal democratic ideas in themselves. It is by no means true that the inadequacy of the literature that connects itself with a body of ideas is the sign of the inadequacy of those ideas, although it is no doubt true that some ideas have less affinity with literature than others.

Our answer, I believe, will rather be found in a cultural fact—in the kind of relationship which we, or the writers who represent us, maintain toward the ideas we claim as ours, and in our habit of conceiving the nature of ideas in general. If we find that it is true of ourselves that we conceive ideas to be pellets of intellection or crystallizations of thought, precise and completed, and defined by their coherence and their procedural recommendations, then we shall have accounted for the kind of prose literature we have. And if we find that we do indeed have this habit, and if we continue in it, we can predict that our literature will continue much as it is. But if we are drawn to revise our habit of conceiving ideas in this way and learn instead to think of ideas as living things, inescapably connected with our wills and desires, as susceptible of growth and development by their very nature, as showing their life by their tendency to change, as being liable, by this very tendency, to deteriorate and become corrupt and to work harm, then we shall stand in a relation to ideas which makes an active literature possible.

GILBERT HIGHET • 1906–

What Use Is Poetry?

CHILDREN ask lots of questions, about religion, about sex, about the stars. But there are some questions which they never ask: they leave grown-ups to ask them and to answer them. Often this means that the questions are silly: that they are questions about nonexistent problems, or questions to which the answer is obvious. Sometimes it means that the questions *should* be asked, but that the answer is difficult or multiplex.

So, children never ask what is the good of music. They just like singing and dancing, and even drumming on a low note of the piano. In the same way, they never ask what is the use of poetry. They all enjoy poems and songs, and very often come to like them before they can even talk properly; but it never occurs to them that they ought to find reasons for their enjoyment. But grown-ups do inquire about the justification of poetry: they ask what is the point of putting words in a special order and extracting special sound effects from them, instead of speaking plainly and directly. And often—because they get no adequate answer, either from the poets or from the professors—they conclude that poetry is only a set of tricks like conjuring, or a complicated game like chess; and they turn away from it in discouragement . . . until, perhaps, a poetic film like *Henry V* shocks them into realizing something of its power; or, as they grow older, they find that a poem learned in childhood sticks in their mind and becomes clearer and more beautiful with age.

What is the use of poetry?

There must be a number of different answers to the question. Just as a picture can be meant to give pleasure, or to carry a puzzle, or to convey information, so poems are meant for many different things. We can begin to get some of the answers if we look at the poetry that children themselves naturally enjoy, and then see how it is connected with the most famous grown-up poems.

The first pleasure of poetry is the simplest. It is the same pleasure that we have in music—the pleasure of following a pattern of sound. Everyone loves talking, and most people like what might be called doodling in sound. So, if you look through the *Oxford Dictionary of Nursery Rhymes,* you will find several tongue-twisters, like this:

Peter Piper picked a peck of pickled pepper;
A peck of pickled pepper Peter Piper picked;
If Peter Piper picked a peck of pickled pepper,
Where's the peck of pickled pepper Peter Piper picked?

On a grown-up level, many a famous poem is little more than a pattern of sound: for instance, Shakespeare's love song:

It was a lover and his lass,
  With a hey and a ho and a hey nonino,
That o'er the green cornfield did pass,
  In the spring time, the only pretty ring time,
    When birds do sing, hey ding a ding ding;
  Sweet lovers love the spring.

Much of the best poetry of Swinburne is pattern-making in sound, with a very light core of meaning. Here are four exquisite lines which really mean very little more than the sound of spring showers:

> When the hounds of spring are on winter's traces,
> The mother of months in meadow or plain
> Fills the shadows and windy places
> With lisp of leaves and ripple of rain.

Small meaning, but lovely rhythm and melody.

Now, there is a second pleasure in poetry. This is that it is sometimes better than prose for telling a story. It even gives authority to a story which is illogical or incredible, or even gruesome. That is one reason children love the poem that tells of the tragic fate of Jack and Jill. There is an interesting variant to it: the cumulative story, in which one detail is piled up on another until the whole story has been set forth with the simple exactitude of a primitive painting: for instance, 'The House That Jack Built,' and the funeral elegy, 'Who Killed Cock Robin?' and the famous old Jewish rhyme, 'Had Gadyo,' about the kid bought for two pieces of money—which is said to symbolize a vast stretch of the history of the Jewish people. Another variant is the limerick, which is simply a funny story in verse. Many a man who would protest that he knew no poetry, and cared nothing for it, could recite eight or ten limericks in the right company.

In serious adult poetry there are many superb stories, including the two oldest books in Western literature, the *Iliad* and the *Odyssey*. Every good collection of poems will include some of the most dramatic tales ever told, the English and Scottish ballads, which are still occasionally sung in our own southern states. One of the strangest things about the stories told as ballads is their terrible abruptness and directness. They leave out a great deal. They give only a few details, a name or two; they draw the outlines, harsh and black or blood-red, and they concentrate on the actions and the passions. Such is the ballad about an ambush in which a knight was killed by his own wife's brother. It is called 'The Dowie Houms of Yarrow' (that means the sad fields beside the river Yarrow, in the Scottish borders), and it opens immediately with the quarrel, almost with the clash of swords:

> Late at een, drinkin' the wine,
>   And ere they paid the lawin',
> They set a combat them between,
>   To fight it in the dawin'.

Within only a few verses, the knight has been surrounded, and treacherously murdered, fighting against heavy odds; and when his widow goes out to find his body, her anguish is described in one of the most terrible stanzas in all poetry:

> She kissed his cheek, she kamed his hair,
>   As oft she did before, O;
> She drank the red blood frae him ran,
>   On the dowie houms o' Yarrow.

That story in poetry and a few others like 'Edward, Edward'—in which a mother persuades her son to kill his own father, and drives him mad—are absolutely unforgettable.

But besides storytelling, poetry has another use, known all over the world. This is mnemonic. Put words into a pattern, and they are easier to remember. I should never have known the lengths of the months if I had not learned:

> Thirty days hath September,
> April, June, and November;
> All the rest have thirty-one,
> Excepting February alone,
> And that has twenty-eight days clear
> And twenty-nine in each leap year.

This is certainly four hundred years old, for it occurs in an English manuscript dated about 1555, and there is a French poem, with the same rhyme scheme, written three hundred years earlier. (It might be easier to change the calendar, but mankind is by nature conservative.) On a simpler level there are many nursery rhymes in every language which are designed to teach children the very simplest things; for instance, counting and performing easy actions:

> One, two,
> Buckle my shoe,
> Three, four,
> Shut the door.

And even earlier, before the child can speak, he is lucky if his mother can recite the poem that goes over his five toes or fingers, one after another:

> This little pig went to market,
> This little pig stayed at home,

up to the comical climax when the child is meant to squeak too, and to enjoy staying at home.

Adults also remember facts better if they are put into verse. Nearly every morning I repeat to myself:

Early to bed and early to rise
Makes a man healthy and wealthy and wise.

And nearly every evening I change it to Thurber's parody:

Early to rise and early to bed
Make a male healthy and wealthy and dead;

or occasionally to George Ade's variant:

Early to bed and early to rise
Will make you miss all the regular guys.

This is the source of what they call didactic poetry, poetry meant to teach. The best-known example of it is the Book of Proverbs in the Bible, which ought to be translated into rhythmical prose, or even verse. The third oldest book in Greek literature, not much younger than Homer, is a farmer's handbook all set out in poetry, so that it could be learned off by heart and remembered: it is the *Works and Days* by Hesiod. To teach has long been one of the highest functions of the poet: great poetry can be written in order to carry a message of philosophical or practical truth—or sometimes an ironical counsel, as in this strange poem by Sir Walter Scott:

> Look not thou on beauty's charming;
> Sit thou still when kings are arming;
> Taste not when the winecup glistens;
> Speak not when the people listens;
> Stop thine ear against the singer;
> From the red gold keep thy finger;
> Vacant heart and hand and eye,
> Easy live and quiet die.

There is one peculiar variation on the poem that conveys information. This is the riddle poem, which tells you something—but only if you are smart enough to see through its disguise. There are some riddles in the Bible: Samson created a good one, about the dead lion with a hive of wild bees inside it. Legend has it that Homer died of chagrin because he could not solve a rather sordid poetic puzzle. The nursery rhyme 'Humpty Dumpty' was really a riddle to begin with (before Lewis Carroll and his illustrator gave it away). We are supposed to guess what was the mysterious person or thing which fell down, and then could not possibly be put together again, not even by all the king's horses and all the king's men, and nowadays by all the republic's scientific experts: the answer is an egg. There is a beautiful folk song made up of three such riddles: the cherry without a stone, the chicken without a bone, and the baby that does not cry. It is at least five hundred years old, and yet for four hundred years it was passed on from one singer to another, without ever being printed.

Again, there are some famous and splendid poems that deal with mystical experience in riddling terms, phrases which have two meanings, or three, or one concealed: these are also didactic, informative, and yet riddles. One such poem, by an American poet, deals with the paradox of God—the complete God, who includes all the appearances of the universe, both the appearance of good and the appearance of evil. This is Emerson's 'Brahma.'

If the red slayer think he slays,
  Or if the slain think he is slain,
They know not well the subtle ways
  I keep, and pass, and turn again.

Far or forgot to me is near;
  Shadow and sunlight are the same;
The vanished gods to me appear;
  And one to me are shame and fame.

They reckon ill who leave me out;
  When me they fly, I am the wings;
I am the doubter and the doubt,
  And I the hymn the Brahmin sings.

The strong gods pine for my abode,
  And pine in vain the sacred Seven;
But thou, meek lover of the good!
  Find me, and turn thy back on heaven.

This is a riddle which is meant not for children but for adults. There are similar riddles in the Bible, sometimes equally beautiful. Such is the meditation on old age at the end of that mysterious and rather unorthodox book called *Koheleth*, or *Ecclesiastes:*

Remember now thy Creator in the days of thy youth,
  while the evil days come not,
    nor the years draw nigh, when thou shalt say, I have no pleasure in them;
while the sun or the light or the moon or the stars be
  not darkened, nor the clouds return after the rain;
in the day when the keepers of the house shall tremble,
  and the strong men shall bow themselves,
  and the grinders cease because they are few,
  and those that look out of the windows be darkened,
and the doors shall be shut in the streets,
  when the sound of the grinding is low,
and he shall rise up at the voice of the bird,
  and all the daughters of music shall be brought low,
also when they shall be afraid of that which is high,
  and fears shall be in the way,
  and the almond tree shall flourish,
  and the grasshopper shall be a burden,
  and desire shall fail:
    because man goeth to his long home
    and the mourners go about the streets;

or ever the silver cord be loosed,
  or the golden bowl be broken,
  or the pitcher be broken at the fountain
  or the wheel broken at the cistern.

Then shall the dust return to the earth as it was;
  and the spirit shall return unto God who gave it.

All these enigmatic and memorable phrases are descriptions of the symptoms of the last and almost the bitterest fact in life, old age. They show that it is pathetic, and yet they make it beautiful.

Such poetry is unusual. Or rather, its manner is unusual and its subject is a fact of common experience. It is possible for poets to speak plainly and frankly about everyday life; and that is one more of the uses of poetry—one of the best known. Poetry can express general experience: can say what many men and women have thought and felt. The benefit of this is that it actually helps ordinary people, by giving them words. Most of us are not eloquent. Most of us—especially in times of intense emotion—cannot say what we feel; often we hardly know what we feel. There, in our heart, there is turmoil, be it love or protest or exultation or despair: it stirs us, but all our gestures and words are inadequate. As the emotion departs, we know that an opportunity was somehow missed, an opportunity of realizing a great moment to the full. It is in this field that poetry comes close to religion. Religion is one of the experiences which the ordinary man finds most difficult to compass in words. Therefore he nearly always falls back on phrases which have been composed for him by someone more gifted. Many, many thousands of times, in battles and concentration camps and hospitals, beside death beds, and even on death beds, men and women have repeated a very ancient poem only six verses long, and have found comfort in it, such as no words of their own would have brought them. It begins, 'The Lord is my shepherd; I shall not want.'

If we look at poetry or any of the arts from this point of view, we shall gain a much greater respect for them. They are not amusements or decorations; they are aids to life. Ordinary men and women find living rather difficult. One of their chief difficulties is to apprehend their own thoughts and feelings, and to respond to them by doing the right things and saying the right sentences. It is the poets who supply the words and sentences. They too have felt as we do, but they have been able to speak, while we are dumb.

Not only that. By expressing common emotions clearly and eloquently, the poets help us to understand them in other people. It is difficult to understand—for any grown-up it is difficult to understand —what goes on in the mind of a boy or girl. Parents are often so anxious and serious that they have forgotten what it was like to be young, and vague, and romantic. It is a huge effort, rather an unpleasantly arduous effort to think oneself back into boyhood. Yet there are several poems which will allow us to understand it, and even to enjoy the experience. One of them is a fine lyric by Longfellow, called 'My Lost Youth':

> I remember the gleams and glooms that dart
>   Across the schoolboy's brain;
> The song and the silence in the heart,
> That in part are prophecies, and in part
>   Are longings wild and vain.
> And the voice of that fitful song
> Sings on, and is never still:
>   'A boy's will is the wind's will,
> And the thoughts of youth are long, long thoughts.'

> There are things of which I may not speak;
>   There are dreams that cannot die;
> There are thoughts that make the strong heart weak,
> And bring a pallor into the cheek,
>   And a mist before the eye.
>   And the words of that fatal song
>   Come over me like a chill:
>   'A boy's will is the wind's will,
> And the thoughts of youth are long, long thoughts.'

If you have a young son who seems to be woolgathering half the time, and who sometimes does not even answer when he is spoken to, you should read and reflect on that poem of Longfellow.

This function of poetry is not the only one, but it is one of the most vital: to give adequate expression to important general experiences. In 1897, when Queen Victoria celebrated her Diamond Jubilee, the Poet Laureate was that completely inadequate little fellow, Alfred Austin; but the man who wrote the poem summing up the emotions most deeply felt during the Jubilee was Rudyard Kipling. It is called 'Recessional.' It is a splendid poem, almost a hymn—Biblical in its phrasing and deeply prophetic in its thought:

> The tumult and the shouting dies—
>   The captains and the kings depart—
> Still stands Thine ancient sacrifice,
>   An humble and a contrite heart.
> Lord God of Hosts, be with us yet,
> Lest we forget, lest we forget!

However, as you think over the poems you know, you will realize that many of them seem to be quite different from this. They are not even trying to do the same thing. They do not express important general experiences in universally acceptable words. On the contrary, they express strange and individual experiences in abstruse and sometimes unintelligible words. We enjoy them not because they say what we have often thought but because they say what we should never have dreamed of thinking. If a poem like Kipling's 'Recessional' or Longfellow's 'Lost Youth' is close to religion, then this other kind of poetry is close to magic: its words sound like spells; its subjects are often dreams, visions, and myths.

Such are the two famous poems by Coleridge: 'The Ancient Mariner' and 'Kubla Khan.' They are scarcely understandable. They are unbelievable. Beautiful, yes, and haunting, yes, but utterly illogical; crazy. Coleridge himself scarcely knew their sources, deep in his memory and his subconscious—sources on which a modern scholar has written a superb book. Both of them end with a mythical experience that none of us has ever had: 'The Ancient Mariner' telling how, like the Wandering Jew, he must travel forever from country to country, telling his story with 'strange power of speech'; and 'Kubla Khan' with the poet himself creating a magical palace:

I would build that dome in air,
That sunny dome! those caves of ice!
And all who heard should see them there,
And all should cry, Beware! Beware!
His flashing eyes, his floating hair!
Weave a circle round him thrice,
    And close your eyes with holy dread,
    For he on honey-dew hath fed,
And drunk the milk of Paradise.

Not long after those fantastic verses were written, young Keats was composing a lyric, almost equally weird, which is now considered one of the finest odes in the English language. It ends with the famous words which we all know, and which few of us believe:

Beauty is truth, truth beauty,—that is all
    Ye know on earth, and all ye need to know.

It is the 'Ode on a Grecian Urn'; but how many of us have ever stood like Keats, meditating on the paintings that surround a Greek vase? and, even if we have, how many of us have thought that

Heard melodies are sweet, but those unheard
    Are sweeter?

It is a paradox. The entire ode is a paradox: not an expression of ordinary life, but an extreme extension of it, almost a direct contradiction of usual experience.

Most modern poetry is like this. It tells of things almost unknown to ordinary men and women, even to children. If it has power over them at all, it is because it enchants them by its strangeness. Such is the poetry of Verlaine, and Mallarmé, and Rimbaud; of the difficult and sensitive Austrian poet Rilke; in our own language, such is most of Auden's poetry, and Ezra Pound's; and what could be more unusual than most of T. S. Eliot—although he is the most famous poet writing today? Suppose we test this. Let us take something simple. Spring. What have the poets said about the first month of spring, about April? Most of them say it is charming and frail:

    April, April,
    Laugh thy girlish laughter;
    Then, the moment after,
    Weep thy girlish tears!

That is Sir William Watson: turn back, and see Shakespeare talking of

    The uncertain glory of an April day;

turn forward, and hear Browning cry

    O to be in England
    Now that April's there!

and then hundreds of years earlier, see Chaucer beginning his *Canterbury Tales* with a handshake of welcome to 'Aprille, with his shoures soote.' Indeed, that is what most of us feel about April: it is sweet and delicate and youthful and hopeful. But T. S. Eliot begins *The Waste Land* with a grim statement which is far outside ordinary feelings:

> April is the cruellest month, breeding
> Lilacs out of the dead land, mixing
> Memory and desire, stirring
> Dull roots with spring rain.

And the entire poem, the best known of our generation, is a description of several agonizing experiences which most of us not only have never had but have not even conceived as possible. Yet there is no doubt that it is good poetry, and that it has taken a permanent place in our literature, together with other eccentric and individual visions.

But some of us do not admit it to be poetry—or rather claim that, if it is so extreme and unusual, poetry is useless. This is a mistake. The universe is so vast, the universe is so various, that we owe it to ourselves to try to understand every kind of experience—both the usual and the remote, both the intelligible and the mystical. Logic is not enough. Not all the truth about the world, or about our own lives, can be set down in straightforward prose, or even in straightforward poetry. Some important truths are too subtle even to be uttered in words. A Japanese, by arranging a few flowers in a vase, or Rembrandt, by drawing a dark room with an old man sitting in it can convey meanings which no one could ever utter in speech. So also, however extravagant a romantic poem may seem, it can tell us something about our world which we ought to know.

It is easier for us to appreciate this nowadays than it would have been for our grandfathers in the nineteenth century, or for their great-grandfathers in the eighteenth century. Our lives are far less predictable; and it is far less possible to use logic alone in organizing and understanding them. Therefore there are justifications, and good ones, for reading and memorizing not only what we might call universal poetry but also strange and visionary poetry. We ourselves, at some time within the mysterious future, may well have to endure and to try to understand some experience absolutely outside our present scope: suffering of some unforeseen kind, a magnificent and somber duty, a splendid triumph, the development of some new power within us. We shall be better able to do so if we know what the poets (yes, and the musicians) have said about such enhancements and extensions of life. Many a man has lived happily until something came upon him which made him, for the first time, think of committing suicide. Such a man will be better able to understand himself and to rise above the thought if he knows the music that Rachmaninoff wrote when he, too, had such thoughts and conquered them, or if he reads the play of *Hamlet,* or if he travels through Dante's *Comedy,* which begins in utter despair and ends in the vision of

love, that moves the sun and the other stars.

And even if we ourselves are not called upon to endure such extremes, there may be those around us, perhaps very close to us, who are faced with situations the ordinary mind cannot assimilate: sudden wealth, the temptations of great beauty, the gift of creation, profound sorrow, unmerited guilt. The knowledge of what the poets have said about experiences beyond the frontiers of logic will help us at least to sympathize with them in these experiences. Such understanding is one of the most difficult and necessary efforts of the soul. Shelley compared the skylark, lost in the radiance of the sun, to

> a Poet hidden
> In the light of thought
> Singing hymns unbidden,
> Till the world is wrought
> To sympathy with hopes and fears it heeded not.

To create such sympathy is one of the deepest functions of poetry, and one of the most bitterly needed.

Index of Authors and Titles

After the Last Bulletins (Wilbur), 458
All but Death can be Adjusted (Dickinson), 393
America (McKay), 428
Amoretti, Sonnets from (Spenser), 284
ANONYMOUS POETRY, 273
ARNOLD, MATTHEW, 387
Arrival of the Bee Box, The (Plath), 463
as freedom is a breakfastfood (Cummings), 431
Astrophel and Stella, Sonnets from (Sidney), 288
At the round earth's imagined corners (Donne), 298
AUDEN, W. H., 443
Aureng-Zebe, Prologue to (Dryden), 318

Babylon Revisited (Fitzgerald), 178
BALDWIN, JAMES, 252
Barn Burning (Faulkner), 191
Batter my heart, three personed God (Donne), 299
BEDDOES, THOMAS LOVELL, 363
Bell Speech (Wilbur), 457
Belle Dame sans Merci, La (Keats), 357
Bereft (Frost), 419
Birches (Frost), 416
Bird, The (Vaughan), 315
BLAKE, WILLIAM, 338
Blind Man, The (Lawrence), 161
Blow, Blow, Thou Winter Wind (Shakespeare), 291
Break, Break, Break (Tennyson), 370
Bride Comes to Yellow Sky, The (Crane), 84
BRIDGES, ROBERT, 402
Bright Star! Would I Were Steadfast as Thou Art (Keats), 356
BRONTE, EMILY, 384
BROOKS, GWENDOLYN, 454
Brown Girl, The (Anonymous), 273
BROWNE, WILLIAM, 300
BROWNING, ROBERT, 375
BYRON, GEORGE GORDON, LORD, 349

CALDWELL, ERSKINE, 214
CAMPION, THOMAS, 294
Candle Indoors, The (Hopkins), 402
Captive, The (Pirandello), 73
CARGILL, OSCAR, 667
Chambered Nautilus, The (Holmes), 365
Chanson Innocente: in Just- spring (Cummings), 430
CHAUCER, GEOFFREY, 278
Chicago Picasso, The (Brooks), 455
"*Childe Roland to the Dark Tower Came*" (Browning), 378
children of the poor, the (Brooks), 454
City in the Sea, The (Poe), 364
COLERIDGE, SAMUEL TAYLOR, 346
Collar, The (Herbert), 302
Come Away, Death (Shakespeare), 291
Come In (Frost), 419
Compleint of Chaucer to His Empty Purse, The (Chaucer), 278

Composed a Few Miles Above Tintern Abbey, Lines: (Wordsworth), 340
Composed upon Westminster Bridge (Wordsworth), 345
CONRAD, JOSEPH, 54
Contretemps, The (Hardy), 398
CRANE, STEPHEN, 84
Crossing the Bar (Tennyson), 374
CULLEN, COUNTEE, 441
CUMMINGS, E. E., 430
Cymbeline, from (Shakespeare), 292

Darkling Thrush, The (Hardy), 398
Daughter (Caldwell), 214
DAVIS, ARTHUR P., 674
Dawn (Williams), 422
Day of Judgement, The (Swift), 320
DE QUINCEY, THOMAS, 651
Dead, The (Joyce), 130
Death, be not proud (Donne), 298
Delight in Disorder (Herrick), 301
Description of Spring (Surrey), 280
Description of the Morning, A (Swift), 319
DICKINSON, EMILY, 392
Disorder and Early Sorrow (Mann), 110
Divers Doth Use (Wyatt), 279
Do People moulder equally (Dickinson), 393
Doll's House, The (Mansfield), 173
DONNE, JOHN, 297
Dover Beach (Arnold), 388
DOWSON, ERNEST, 409
DRYDEN, JOHN, 317
DUGAN, ALAN, 459
DYER, SIR EDWARD, 281

Eagle, The (Tennyson), 373
Ecstasy, The (Donne), 299
Edward (Anonymous), 273
1887 (Housman), 405
Elegy (Bridges), 402
ELIOT, T. S., 424
Emperor of Ice-Cream, The (Stevens), 420
Experience is the Angled Road (Dickinson), 395

Fall of the House of Usher, The (Poe), 15
Fallow Deer at the Lonely House, The (Hardy), 400
FAULKNER, WILLIAM, 191
Fern Hill (Thomas), 452
First fight. Then fiddle (Brooks), 454
FITZGERALD, EDWARD, 366
FITZGERALD, F. SCOTT, 178
Flame-Heart (McKay), 429
Flight (Updike), 261
Flying Below Sea Level (Lieberman), 465
Flying on the Surface (Lieberman), 466
For the Sake of Argument (Hughes), 207
Four Epitaphs (Cullen), 441
FROST, ROBERT, 416
Frost at Midnight (Coleridge), 346

Full Fathom Five (Shakespeare), 292
GALSWORTHY, JOHN, 655
GASCOIGNE, GEORGE, 282
Gascoigne's Good-Night (Gascoigne), 282
Glass of Water, The (Stevens), 421
Go and catch a falling star (Donne), 297
Go, Lovely Rose (Waller), 304
God's Grandeur (Hopkins), 400

HANSBERRY, LORRAINE, 598
Hap (Hardy), 397
HARDY, THOMAS, 397
Hark! Hark! the Lark (Shakespeare), 292
Harlem Dancer (McKay), 427
HAWTHORNE, NATHANIEL, 3
Haystack in the Floods, The (Morris), 395
Hedda Gabler (Ibsen), 537
HEMINGWAY, ERNEST, 203
HERBERT, GEORGE, 302
Here She Was Wont to Go (Jonson), 297
HERRICK, ROBERT, 301
High-Toned Old Christian Woman, A (Stevens), 420
HIGHET, GILBERT, 692
His Return to London (Herrick), 301
HOLMES, OLIVER WENDELL, 365
Holy Sonnets (Donne), 298
Home-Thoughts, from Abroad (Browning), 375
Home-Thoughts, from the Sea (Browning), 376
HOPKINS, GERARD MANLEY, 400
HOUSMAN, A. E., 404
How Should One Read a Book? (Woolf), 660
HUGHES, LANGSTON, 207, 432
Hunger Artist, A (Kafka), 155

I Did Not Lose My Heart in Summer's Even (Housman), 406
I Knew a Woman (Roethke), 447
I Know a place where Summer strives (Dickinson), 392
I stepped from Plank to Plank (Dickinson), 394
I taste a liquor never brewed (Dickinson), 392
I Travelled Among Unknown Men (Wordsworth), 344
I Wandered Lonely As a Cloud (Wordsworth), 346
IBSEN, HENRIK, 537
Il Penseroso (Milton), 311
In a Dark Time (Roethke), 448
In Another Country (Hemingway), 203
Incarnate Devil (Thomas), 451
Insatiableness (Traherne), 319
Into My Heart an Air That Kills (Housman), 404
It was not Death, for I stood up (Dickinson), 393

JAMES, HENRY, 27
Jazz, Jive, and Jam (Hughes), 211
Johnny, I Hardly Knew Ye (Anonymous), 276
JONSON, BEN, 294

Jordan: I (Herbert), 303
JOYCE, JAMES, 130
Juggler (Wilbur), 459

KAFKA, FRANZ, 155
KEATS, JOHN, 355
Kraken, The (Tennyson), 370
Kubla Khan (Coleridge), 348

L'Allegro (Milton), 309
Lamb, The (Blake), 338
LAWRENCE, D. H., 161
Leda and the Swan (Yeats), 407
Leg, The (Shapiro), 449
Let me not to the marriage of true minds (Shakespeare), 293
LIEBERMAN, LAURENCE, 465
Life and Death of the Cantata System, The (Dugan), 459
Lines: Composed a Few Miles Above Tintern Abbey (Wordsworth), 340
Lines: When the Lamp Is Shattered (Shelley), 354
Lines on the Mermaid Tavern (Keats), 356
Literature of Knowledge and the Literature of Power, The (de Quincey), 651
Little Black Boy, The (Blake), 339
Little Fugue (Plath), 464
London (Blake), 340
London, 1802 (Wordsworth), 345
London Snow (Bridges), 403
Long Love, The (Wyatt), 279
Love Song of J. Alfred Prufrock, The (Eliot), 424
Love That Doth Reign (Surrey), 281
Lover Tells of the Rose in His Heart, The (Yeats), 406
Love's Labour's Lost, from (Shakespeare), 290
Loving in truth (Sidney), 288
LOWELL, ROBERT, 583
Lycidas (Milton), 304
Lyke as a huntsman (Spenser), 286
Lyke as a ship (Spenser), 285

MCKAY, CLAUDE, 427
Magna Est Veritas (Patmore), 390
Man Against the Sky, The (Robinson), 409
MANN, THOMAS, 110
MANSFIELD, KATHERINE, 173
MARLOWE, CHRISTOPHER, 290
Marriage à la Mode, Song from (Dryden), 317
MARVELL, ANDREW, 314
MAUGHAM, W. SOMERSET, 91
Meaning of a Literary Idea, The (Trilling), 680
Meeting at Night (Browning), 375
Merchant of Venice, from *The* (Shakespeare), 291
Merry Cuckow, The (Spenser), 285
Midsummer-Night's Dream, A (Shakespeare), 500
MILTON, JOHN, 304
Miss Muriel (Petry), 225
Montage of a Dream Deferred, from (Hughes), 432
Morning Song (Plath), 462

INDEX OF AUTHORS AND TITLES

MORRIS, WILLIAM, 395
Moss-Gathering (Roethke), 446
Most she touched me by her muteness (Dickinson), 394
Mower Against Gardens, The (Marvell), 314
Musée des Beaux Arts (Auden), 443
My Heart Leaps Up When I Behold (Wordsworth), 345
My Kinsman, Major Molineux (Hawthorne), 3
My Kinsman, Major Molineux (Lowell), 583
My Life had stood—a Loaded Gun (Dickinson), 393
My Mind to Me a Kingdom Is (Dyer), 281
My True Love Hath My Heart (Sidney), 289

NEWMAN, JOHN HENRY, CARDINAL, 363
Night Is Freezing Fast, The (Housman), 405
Night-Piece, to Julia, The (Herrick), 301
No longer mourn for me (Shakespeare), 292
No Second Troy (Yeats), 406
Non Sum Qualis Eram Bonae sub Regno Cynarae (Dowson), 409
Nostalgia (Shapiro), 448
Now Sleeps the Crimson Petal (Tennyson), 373
Now the Leaves Are Falling Fast, Song: (Auden), 443
Nymph's Reply to the Shepherd, The (Ralegh), 286

Ode on a Grecian Urn (Keats), 357
Ode on Melancholy (Keats), 359
Ode to a Nightingale (Keats), 360
Ode to the West Wind (Shelley), 351
Oedipus Rex (Sophocles), 471
On a Snake (Dugan), 461
On First Looking into Chapman's Homer (Keats), 355
On the Countess Dowager of Pembroke (Browne), 300
On the Grasshopper and the Cricket (Keats), 355
One day I wrote her name (Spenser), 286
One Waking in a Northern Fall (Dugan), 460
Onset, The (Frost), 418
Orchids (Roethke), 446
Outcast (McKay), 429
Outstation, The (Maugham), 91
Ozymandias (Shelley), 351

Parting, from (Arnold), 387
Parting at Morning (Browning), 375
Passionate Man's Pilgrimage, The (Ralegh), 287
Passionate Shepherd to His Love, The (Marlowe), 290
PATMORE, COVENTRY, 389
People who have no children (Brooks), 454
PETRY, ANN, 225
Philomela (Arnold), 387
Pied Beauty (Hopkins), 402
Pillar of the Cloud, The (Newman), 363

PIRANDELLO, LUIGI, 73
PLATH, SYLVIA, 462
POE, EDGAR ALLAN, 15, 364
Poor, The (Williams), 423
POPE, ALEXANDER, 320
Postcard from the Volcano, A (Stevens), 421
Presentiment—is that long Shadow (Dickinson), 394
Previous Condition (Baldwin), 252
Princess, Songs from *The* (Tennyson), 372
Progress of Faust, The (Shapiro), 450
Props assist the House, The (Dickinson), 395
Pupil, The (James), 27

Raisin in the Sun, A (Hansberry), 598
RALEGH, SIR WALTER, 286
Rape of the Lock, The (Pope), 320
Refusal to Mourn the Death, by Fire, of a Child in London, A (Thomas), 453
Remembrance (Bronte), 384
Requiescat (Arnold), 388
ROBINSON, EDWIN ARLINGTON, 409
ROETHKE, THEODORE, 446
Romance (Poe), 364
ROSSETTI, DANTE GABRIEL, 390
Rubáiyát of Omar Khayyám of Naishápúr, from *The* (FitzGerald), 366

Sailing to Byzantium (Yeats), 408
Sailing to Jerusalem (Dugan), 461
Scottsboro, Too, Is Worth Its Song (Cullen), 442
Sea-Limits, The (Rossetti), 390
Second Coming, The (Yeats), 407
SHAKESPEARE, WILLIAM, 290, 500
Shall I compare thee (Shakespeare), 292
SHAPIRO, KARL, 448
She Dwelt Among the Untrodden Ways (Wordsworth), 344
She Walks in Beauty (Byron), 349
SHELLEY, PERCY BYSSHE, 351
Shield of Achilles, The (Auden), 444
Sick Rose, The (Blake), 340
SIDNEY, SIR PHILIP, 288
Sir Patrick Spens (Anonymous), 275
Slow, Slow, Fresh Fount (Jonson), 294
Snow Man, The (Stevens), 419
So We'll Go No More A-Roving (Byron), 350
Solitary Reaper, The (Wordsworth), 345
Some Platitudes Concerning Drama (Galsworthy), 655
Song (Donne), 297
Song (Waller), 304
Song: Now the Leaves Are Falling Fast (Auden), 443
Songs from the Plays (Shakespeare), 290
Songs of Innocence, Introduction to (Blake), 338
Sonnet: a wind has blown the rain away (Cummings), 431
Sonnet on Chillon (Byron), 350
Sonnets, from *The* (Shakespeare), 292
SOPHOCLES, 471
SPENSER, EDMUND, 284
Splendour Falls on Castle Walls, The (Tennyson), 372

Split the Lark—and you'll find the Music (Dickinson), 394
Spring (Hopkins), 401
Spring (Shakespeare), 290
Spring and All (Williams), 423
Stanzas for Music (Byron), 350
Stanzas from the Ivory Gate (Beddoes), 363
Starlight Night, The (Hopkins), 400
Stay, Phoebus, stay! (Waller), 304
Steel Glass, from *The* (Gascoigne), 283
STEVENS, WALLACE, 419
Still to Be Neat (Jonson), 295
Stopping by Woods on a Snowy Evening (Frost), 418
Sudden Light (Rossetti), 391
Sumer Is Icumen In (Anonymous), 273
Surgeons must be very careful (Dickinson), 392
SURREY, HENRY HOWARD, EARL OF, 280
Sweet and Low (Tennyson), 372
SWIFT, JONATHAN, 319

Tell all the Truth but tell it slant (Dickinson), 395
Tell Me Where Is Fancy Bred (Shakespeare), 291
Tempest, from *The* (Shakespeare), 292
TENNYSON, ALFRED, LORD, 370
That time of year (Shakespeare), 293
That Word Black (Hughes), 210
There be none of Beauty's daughters (Byron), 350
There Is a Garden in Her Face (Campion), 294
There Was a Child Went Forth (Whitman), 385
They Flee from Me (Wyatt), 280
This holy season (Spenser), 285
THOMAS, DYLAN, 451
Three Years She Grew in Sun and Shower (Wordsworth), 344
To———: Music, when soft voices die (Shelley), 354
To———: One word is too often profaned (Shelley), 354
To Autumn (Keates), 362
To His Coy Mistress (Marvell), 315
To His Mother (Herbert), 303
To Imagination (Bronte), 385
To Marguerite (Arnold), 387
To Night (Shelley), 353
To Rosemounde (Chaucer), 278
To the Memory of My Beloved, the Author Master William Shakespeare (Jonson), 295
To the Virgins to Make Much of Time (Herrick), 301
Toward a Pluralistic Criticism (Cargill), 667
Toys, The (Patmore), 389
Tract (Williams), 422
TRAHERNE, THOMAS, 319
Trends in American Negro Literature (Davis), 674
TRILLING, LIONEL, 680
Tropics in New York, The (McKay), 429
Twelfth Night, from (Shakespeare), 291
Two Dedications (Brooks), 455
Tyger, The (Blake), 339

Ubi Sunt Qui ante Nos Fuerunt? (Anonymous), 273
Ulysses (Tennyson), 370
Up at a Villa—Down in the City (Browning), 376
UPDIKE, JOHN, 261
Upon Julia's Clothes (Herrick), 301

Valediction: Forbidding Mourning, A (Donne), 297
VAUGHAN, HENRY, 315

Waking, The (Roethke), 446
Wall, The (Brooks), 456
WALLER, EDMUND, 304
Waterfall, The (Vaughan), 316
We dream—it is good we are dreaming (Dickinson), 393
We grow accustomed to the Dark (Dickinson), 392
We Real Cool (Brooks), 455
We shall find the Cube of the Rainbow (Dickinson), 395
WEBSTER, JOHN, 300
WELTY, EUDORA, 217
What Is Our Life? (Ralegh), 288
What Use Is Poetry? (Highet), 692
When I Have Fears That I May Cease to Be (Keats), 356
When I Was One-and-Twenty (Housman), 405
When the Lamp Is Shattered, Lines: (Shelley), 354
When to Her Lute Corinna Sings (Campion), 294
White City, The (McKay), 428
White Devil, from *The* (Webster), 300
WHITMAN, WALT, 385
Why I Live at the P.O. (Welty), 217
WILBUR, RICHARD, 457
WILLIAMS, WILLIAM CARLOS, 422
wind has blown the rain away, Sonnet: a (Cummings), 431
Windhover, The (Hopkins), 401
Windows, The (Herbert), 303
Winter (Shakespeare), 291
Winter: For an Untenable Situation (Dugan), 460
With how sad steps (Sidney), 289
With Rue My Heart Is Laden (Housman), 404
wood is bare, The (Bridges), 402
Woodspurge, The (Rossetti), 391
WOOLF, VIRGINIA, 660
WORDSWORTH, WILLIAM, 340
WYATT, SIR THOMAS, 279

Ye tradefull Merchants (Spenser), 284
YEATS, WILLIAM BUTLER, 406
Yet Do I Marvel (Cullen), 441
You that do search (Sidney), 288
You that with allegory's curious frame (Sidney), 289
Youth (Conrad), 54